PART SIX Writing Across the Curriculum—and Beyond 723

PART SEVEN Writing When English Is a Second Language 805

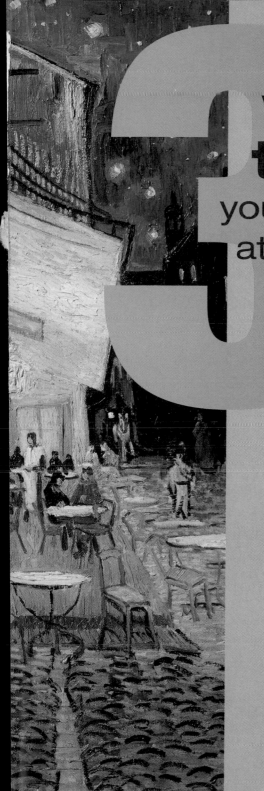

What are **three reasons** you should take a closer look at the new Seventh Edition**?**

1. A new co-author, **Douglas Hesse,** lends his voice and insight to this revision.

2. A new **"Me, Myself, and I" Book** offers you and your students instant access to the entire handbook, anytime and anywhere.

3. A new series of **Pocket Readers** that will save your students money.

Lynn Quitman Troyka

Lynn Quitman Troyka earned her Ph.D. at New York University and taught for many years at the City University of New York (CUNY), including Queensborough Community College; the Center for Advanced Studies in Education at the Graduate School; and in the graduate program in Language and Literacy at City College; and, as a Senior Research Associate in the Instructional Resource Center (CUNY).

Former Editor of the *Journal of Basic Writing* (1985-1988), Dr. Troyka has published in journals such as *College Composition and Communication, College English, Journal of Basic Writing,* and *Writing Program Administration,* and in books from Southern Illinois University Press, Random House, the National Council of Teachers of English (NCTE), and Heinemann.

Dr. Troyka is a past chair of the Two-Year College English Association (TYCA) of NCTE, the Conference on College Composition and Communication (CCCC), the College Section of NCTE, and of the Writing Division of the Modern Language Association (MLA). She was named Rhetorician of the Year in 1993; earned the Nell Ann Pickett Award for Service in 1995; and received the 2001 CCCC Exemplar Award, the highest CCCC award given for scholarship, teaching, and service. She serves on the NCTE Leadership Committee for Preparing Future Faculty (PFF), a project of the Council of Graduate School and the American Association of Colleges and Universities. *"All this information,"* says Dr. Troyka, *"tells what I've done, not who I am. I am a teacher. Teaching is my life's work, and I love it."*

Lynn Troyka can be reached via e-mail at *LQTBook@aol.com.*

Douglas Hesse

Douglas Hesse earned his Ph.D. at the University of Iowa. He is the current Director of the Center for the Advancement of Teaching and professor of English at Illinois State University, where he teaches courses in rhetorical theory, writing, creative nonfiction, narrative theory, and writing program administration. He has received awards and recognition as an outstanding researcher for both his university and college, as well as a distinguished Humanities teacher.

Former Editor of *WPA: Writing Program Administration* (1994-1998), Dr. Hesse has published in journals such as *College English, Composition Studies, Composition Chronicle, Rhetoric Review, Journal of Teaching Writing, College Composition and Communication, Journal of Advanced Composition, The New England Journal of Medicine,* and in books from Southern Illinois University Press, Boynton-Cook/Heinemann, Longman, NCTE, Routledge, University of Georgia Press, Louisiana State Press, Open University Press, Lawrence Erlbaum, and the Modern Language Association.

He is the immediate past president of the National Council of Writing Program Administrators, the Program Chair of the Conference on College Composition and Communication (2004) and Chair (2005).

Douglas Hesse can be reached via e-mail at *ddhesse@ilstu.edu.*

It's **more** than just an E-book.

Every page of this handbook is on the Web—and it's fully searchable and customizable.

What's in it for you:

■ **Progress Tracker** enables you to view students' progress as they complete online exercises and activities.

■ **Syllabus Tools** let you upload and make changes to your syllabus in students' *My Course* section so that your syllabus is only a click away.

■ **Communication Tools** allow you to post class messages on your students' homepage; e-mail class bulletins; and insert and highlight your comments in students' handbooks.

It's a "Me, Myself, and I" Book.

What's in it for your students:

■ **The E-book contains the complete handbook on the Web**

for students to
—Search every page
of the handbook
right from the Web
—Add notes, highlight,
and read your
personal comments,
all imbedded
in their E-book

Continued on next page—

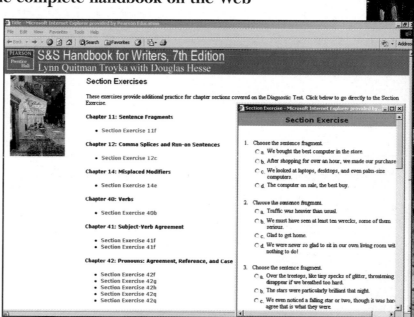

www.prenhall.com/troyka

The "Me, Myself, and I" Book with

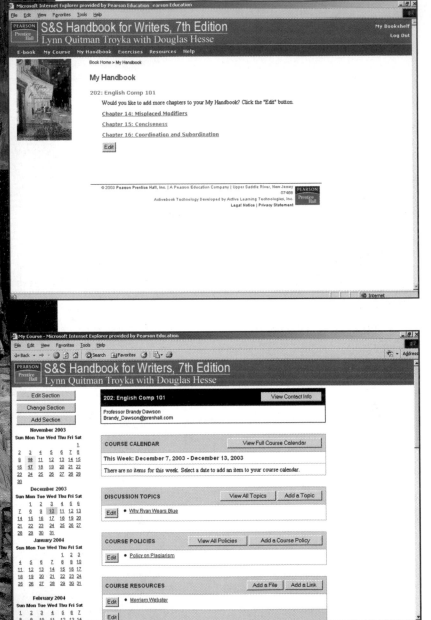

My Handbook feature enables students to
—Individually create and personalize their E-book
—Identify areas for improvement with the *Diagnostic Test* provided

Activities offer students
—Chapter exercises
—Blue Pencil editing exercises
—Self-assessment tests

My Course feature allows students to
—View the course syllabus
—E-mail the instructor
—Check progress

Resources for students
—the *Understanding Plagiarism* tutorial
—Writing workshops
—Links to discipline-specific Web sites

Research Navigator™, the one-stop research solution, gives students three exclusive databases
—a broad Academic Journal database, powered by EBSCO, with over 25,000 articles
—The *New York Times* Search-by-Subject Archive
—*Best of the Web* Link Library

www.prenhall.com/troyka

What's in your pocket?

The editors of the Prentice Hall Pocket Readers have carefully selected a collection of readings that have withstood the test of time and teaching. A Prentice Hall Pocket Reader is the perfect way to bring additional readings to your writing classes at no additional cost to your students when packaged with this text.

Pocket Readers can be packaged FREE with any of our English texts or are available stand alone to your students for only $15 suggested retail price (limit one free reader per package).

Visit *www.prenhall.com/english* for complete tables of contents and ordering information. This year's collection includes:

ARGUMENT: A Prentice Hall Pocket Reader
Edited by Christy Desmet, Deborah Church Miller, and Alexis Hart, *all of The University of Georgia,*
© *2005, 225 pp.* ISBN 0-13-189525-7

LITERATURE: A Prentice Hall Pocket Reader
Edited by Mary Balkun, *Seton Hall University,*
© *2005, 225 pp.* ISBN 0-13-144354-2

THEMES: A Prentice Hall Pocket Reader
Edited by Clyde Moneyhun, *University of Delaware,*
© *2005, 225 pp.* ISBN 0-13-144355-0

PATTERNS: A Prentice Hall Pocket Reader
Edited by Dorothy Minor, *Tulsa Community College,*
© *2005, 225 pp.* ISBN 0-13-144352-6

Simon & Schuster HANDBOOK for WRITERS

SEVENTH EDITION

Lynn Quitman Troyka
with Douglas Hesse

PEARSON
Prentice
Hall

Upper Saddle River, NJ 07458

Editor in Chief: Leah Jewell
Senior Acquisitions Editor: Stacy Best
VP/Director of Production and Manufacturing: Barbara Kittle
Executive Marketing Manager: Brandy Dawson
Marketing Manager: Emily Cleary
Director of Marketing: Beth Mejia
Marketing Assistant: Allison Peck
Senior Production Editors: Shelly Kupperman/ Barbara DeVries
Production Assistant: Marlene Gassler
Permissions Coordinator: Ronald Fox
Manufacturing Manager: Nick Sklitsis
Prepress and Manufacturing Buyer: Mary Ann Gloriande

Creative Design Director: Leslie Osher
Interior and Cover Designer: Kathryn Foot
Photo Researcher: Elaine Soares
Director, Image Resource Center: Melinda Reo
Manager, Rights and Permissions: Zina Arabia
Cover Image Specialist: Karen Sanatar
Image Permission Coordinator: Cynthia Vincenti
Manager Art Production: Guy Ruggiero
Artist: Maria Piper
Assistant Editor: Karen Schultz
Editorial Assistant: Steven Kyritz
Developmental Editor: Elaine Silverstein
Web/Media Production Manager: Lynn Pearlman
Senior Media Manager: Christy Schaack

Cover Art: *Cafe Terrace, Place du Forum, Arles,* 1888 (oil on canvas) by Vincent van Gogh (1853–90) © Rijksmuseum Kroller-Muller, Otterlo, Netherlands/Bridgeman Art Library.

This book was set in 10/11 New Caledonia by Pine Tree Composition, Inc., and was printed and bound by Quebecor Printing. Covers were printed by Phoenix Color Corp.

For permission to use copyrighted material, grateful acknowledgment is made to the copyright holders on pages xi–xiv, which are considered an extension of this copyright page.

Pearson Education LTD.
Pearson Education Singapore, Pte. Ltd
Pearson Education, Canada, Ltd
Pearson Education–Japan
Pearson Education Australia PTY, Limited

Pearson Education North Asia Ltd
Pearson Educación de Mexico, S.A. de C.V.
Pearson Education Malaysia, Pte. Ltd
Pearson Education, Upper Saddle River, NJ

10 9 8 7 6 5 4 3 2 1
ISBN 0-13-144350-X (student edition)
ISBN 0-13-144364-X (annotated instructor's edition)

Contents

*The complete student edition appears next. Annotations, which do not
appear in the student edition, include exercise answers, teaching tips,
quotations about writing, and a rich variety of other resources.*

Brief Contents of the Student Edition

PREFACE: ANNOTATED INSTRUCTOR'S EDITION

In this *Annotated Instructor's Edition (AIE)* to accompany the *Simon & Schuster Handbook for Writers,* Seventh Edition, annotations in the margins provide instructors and teaching assistants with teaching tips, annotated bibliographic citations from major journals in composition (designed especially for instructors with little time to read professional literature), thought-provoking quotations about writing, and answers to the exercises, which cite the related subsections in the chapter so that teachers can instantly diagnose each student's exact strengths and weaknesses. The annotations run alongside each page of the student edition.

This *AIE* is tailored for those who know that the teaching of writing isn't a grab bag of "what works on Monday morning." Rather, these instructors and TAs prefer a comprehensive handbook that consistently applies up-to-date theory in rhetoric, linguistics, and learning; respects and encourages students' journeys to become increasingly comfortable and skillful writers; and recognizes the benefits of rigor undergirded by time-tested, clearly presented information and a supportive, user-friendly tone.

With this edition, I'm pleased to introduce a new collaborator who shares my high esteem for students and my research-based approach to teaching: Doug Hesse, Director, Center for the Advancement of Teaching (CAT) and Professor of English at Illinois State University. His scholarship is widely published and admired. He has served as president of Writing Program Administrators (WPA) and, as we go to press, he is incoming Chair of the Conference on College Composition and Communication (CCCC). He brings extraordinary expertise to the seventh edition's assumptions that most students today write on computers; that research sources reside heavily online alongside those in libraries; and that the research process is more complex and exciting than ever. Further, his scholarship enhances and extends the annotations for teachers in this edition of the *AIE.*

To further set forth the theoretical grounding of the *Simon & Schuster Handbook for Writers,* Seventh Edition, the *AIE* starts with five bibliographic essays written specifically for it. These essays supply the underlying theoretical roots of the *AIE* concerning the long, respected intellectual tradition upon which modern teaching of composition relies; the best of current research about writing, language, and learning; and judicious applications of technological advances as they affect the teaching of writing.

Changes in the *Simon & Schuster Handbook for Writers,* Seventh Edition, are listed in the Preface of this *AIE* and on the front endpapers of the book. Of course, I retain the ever-popular core features and navigation aids of former editions of the *Simon & Schuster Handbook for Writers.* And the seven Parts of the book consider the same subjects in the same sequence. The changes include twenty percent new content for the exercises. Most important, Doug Hesse, my new collaborator, helped me considerably with the updates in Parts One, Five, and Six. We've made changes in response to commissioned reviews as well as suggestions from instructors and students who actively corresponded with me at <LQTBook@aol.com>. I invite all, teachers and students alike, to use my e-mail address to participate in the ongoing conversation with me in cyberspace.

At Prentice Hall, a dedicated professional team oversaw this *AIE:* Karen Schultz, Assistant Editor, helped coordinate the cross-references to supplements; Stacy Best, Senior Acquisitions Editor, and Leah Jewell, Editor in Chief for English, shepherded this edition through the creative process; Shelly Kupperman, Senior Project Manager, along with Barbara DeVries, Consulting Production Editor, expertly transformed the manuscript from draft to bound book. I also thank Brandy Dawson, Executive Marketing Manager, Emily Cleary, Marketing Manager, and Yolanda de Rooy, President of Prentice Hall's Humanities and Social Sciences division.

Lynn Quitman Troyka

For the most current updates on these essays, consult the Troyka Web site <www.prenhall.com/troyka>.

Annotated Instructor's Edition

TEACHING AT THE CROSSROADS: CHOICES AND CHALLENGES IN COLLEGE COMPOSITION

Barbara Gleason

When we walk into a writing class for the first time, most of us, whether we're new or experienced teachers, feel at least some apprehension. Why? In part because teaching involves performance: Both our successes and failures will be largely public. And as teachers of writing we want to be successful, not just for our own satisfaction or advancement, but because of the substantial responsibilities and challenges that we've undertaken.

Nowhere in a college curriculum are the responsibilities greater or more complex than in first-year writing courses, whether they be remedial, college-level, or mainstreamed. This is the curricular space where newly admitted students are introduced to college but also where institutional gate-keeping is expected of instructors. Moreover, despite their widespread presence in colleges and universities, the aims of first-year writing courses are frequently controversial, both within college communities and within our profession.

In a well-attended presentation at the 1991 Conference on College Composition and Communication (CCCC) in Boston, David Bartholomae and Peter Elbow offered alternative views of first-year writing course goals in speeches that were later published in *CCC* (Feb. 1995). The question that Bartholomae and Elbow disagree on is this: *Should first-year college writing courses immerse students in academic writing, or should these courses encourage students to become writers?* In support of academic writing as the goal, Bartholomae [item 2 in Works Cited] contends that students are embedded in a "linguistic present" that they should know about and work within as writers. Bartholomae argues for classes that entail critical reading, writing, and "struggling with the problems of quotation, citation, and paraphrase" (66). Taking issue with this initial emphasis on academic reading and writing, Elbow [13] argues that becoming an academic is different from becoming a writer, that is, many "academics" are not confident or effective writers and many "writers" are not academics at all. Elbow explains, "I see specific conflicts in how to design and teach my first-year writing course. And since I feel forced to choose—I choose the goal of writer over that of academic" (73).

When we construct our writing class curricula, we make decisions that will impact our students as developing writers: What sorts of writing will we assign? Which textbooks will we choose? What specific tasks should our students practice? How often? And in what order? Even when our syllabi and textbooks are determined by others, we can still slant our writing classes in one direction or another. Underlying these decisions are our assumptions/beliefs about the goals of our writing classes. The Bartholomae–Elbow debate has received widespread attention because this is an issue that is central to the experience of college writing instructors and to the development of college-wide writing programs. As professional writing instructors, we must each reflect on the issues, make choices, and act accordingly.

Choices We Make as Professional Writing Instructors

As we consider the aims of the courses we are teaching, we must also reflect on the expertise and the knowledge we need as professional writing instructors. What forms of expertise should we have as writers? If we teach academic reading and writing, should we be practicing academic readers and writers ourselves? Equally important are the knowledge bases that can inform our teaching, for example, composition theory/research, writing pedagogy, rhetorical theory, computer technologies, literacy, sociolinguistics, second-language learning and teaching, literature and literary theory. As professionals, we make our own decisions about whether or not to avail ourselves of these areas of knowledge. Although there are differing views of the

Barbara Gleason *is an Associate Professor at the City College of New York, CUNY, where she teaches in the English Department and at the Center for Worker Education. She holds a doctorate in rhetoric and composition from the University of Southern California and has taught composition for over twenty years. Gleason has coedited two books:* Composition in Four Keys: Inquiring into the Field Through Nature, Art, Science and Politics, *with Mark Wiley and Louise Wetherbee Phelps, and* Cultural Tapestry: Readings for a Pluralistic Society, *with Faun Bernbach Evans and Mark Wiley. She has been a contributing author to several edited books and has published essays on basic writing and college composition in* College Composition and Communication, Journal of Basic Writing, *and* College English.

expertise and knowledge that professional writing instructors should have, most writing teachers today acknowledge the value of teaching writing as a process.

Origins of the Writing Process Movement

Published histories of writing instruction tell us that process pedagogies did not originate in the past three or four decades. A few writing teachers included "writing process" instruction in their curricula well before process teaching became common in U.S. college writing programs. Theodore Baird of Amherst College, for example, included revision in a two-semester writing course that he developed and supervised from 1938 to 1966 [47]. However, writing process teaching was relatively rare prior to the 1970s. Two comprehensive histories of U.S. writing instruction make almost no mention of process pedagogies [23; 5]. These histories indicate that from 1850 to 1925, writing students in U.S. colleges listened to lectures, analyzed literary texts, learned rules of grammar or rhetoric, did workbook exercises, and practiced writing sentences, paragraphs, or daily themes. Instructors read their students' writing with an eye toward correct language use, a product-focused approach often mentioned as a central feature of "current-traditional" writing instruction [3] (58–76). It comes as no surprise, then, that studies of students' written products dominated the first survey of empirical research on written composition, which appeared in 1963 [4].

The importance of this landmark publication has led Stephen North [26] to identify 1963 as the year in which composition emerged as a professional field (15). In *Research in Written Composition,* Richard Braddock et al. [4] analyzed 504 empirical studies of writing instruction and of student writing; in so doing, these authors made evident to 1960s readers the prevailing emphasis on students' written products. Composing process pedagogies of the 1960s and 1970s arose in part as a reaction against product-focused pedagogies and research [29] (134). A second motivation for the emerging interest in process pedagogies was the growing presence of "nontraditional" students in writing classes. In "Where Did Composition Studies Come From? An Intellectual History" Nystrand et al. [27] argue that open admissions policies such as the one at the City University of New York (1970) created a perceived literacy crisis that then spurred the formation of composition. A third influence was the 1960s federal funding for education that resulted from Sputnik and a related math and science "crisis"; new support for seminars on teaching writing and for research fueled the creative energies that were needed to form a new professional field [26] (12). Seeded in the 1960s and established in the 1970s, the writing process movement is now widely acknowledged as the intellectual springboard for our modern field of composition.

Composing Process Pedagogies

Early versions of the writing process introduced a linear stage model, or a straight-ahead view, of composing. This later gave way to a recursive theory that sees writing as a two-steps-forward, one-step-back process in which writers can "discover" new meanings at any point along the way.

A Linear Stage Model of Composing: In a 1964 study, D. Gordon Rohman and Albert O. Wlecke [33] presented a stage model of composing comprised of prewriting, writing, rewriting, and editing. Rohman then published "Prewriting: The Stage of Discovery in the Writing Process" [32], which helped establish a view of prewriting as the most important phase of the composing process. This emphasis on prewriting prevailed in the 1970s but then gave way to increasing interests in teaching revision, in students' focusing on final written products (e.g., in portfolios), and in teachers' assessment of student writing.

Emphasis on Prewriting: In a 1972 essay entitled "Teach Writing as Process, Not Product," Donald Murray [25] described prewriting as "everything that takes place before the first draft" and as the phase of writing that "takes about 85% of a writer's time" (90). Peter Elbow, Ken McCrorie, James Britton, James Moffett, Janice Lauer, and Ann Berthoff were also well-known 1970s advocates of process pedagogies that had a special focus on teaching prewriting, or "invention." This initial emphasis on invention provided teachers with a fresh new perspective on teaching writing but also led to the criticism that too little attention was being paid to the quality of students' final drafts.

Contributions from Rhetoric: A revival of classical rhetoric during the 1960s and 1970s introduced to the discussions about writing instruction renewed emphasis on the five parts of classical rhetoric (invention, arrangement, style, memory, and delivery), among which invention enjoyed a special status with teachers. Rhetoricians such as Edward P. J. Corbett, Frank D'Angelo, Richard Larson, and W. Ross Winterowd argued that invention strategies could be taught and learned as useful tools for probing and analyzing writing topics. In a 1975 bibliographic essay, Richard Young [48] describes a wide range of invention strategies, for example, the *topoi* from classical rhetoric, Kenneth Burke's pentad, and tagmemics. In his essay, Young anticipates an upcoming challenge to linear stage models of composing by asserting, "The act of writing itself can be seen as a heuristic for discovering content" (35).

From Linear Models to Recursive Models: In 1980, the linear stage model of composing was challenged by Nancy Sommers [42] and by Sondra Perl [28]. In "Revision Strategies of Student Writers and Experienced Adult Writers," Sommers used the results of an empirical study to demonstrate that experienced writers continually "invent" new ideas as they revise. This view of "writing as discovery" suggests that revising involves writers in attending to multiple goals, for example, discovering new ideas and editing. Similarly, Perl described composing as a recursive process that entails rereading of small units of text midway through writing, with rewriting of short passages serving to move writers forward. Both Sommers and Perl argued that composing involves backward and forward movements that allow writers to generate new meanings as they write and rewrite.

Collaborative Learning and Writing

A second major shift in thinking about the writing process occurred when writing came to be viewed as a social act and as a practice that is embedded in social contexts [30; 22]. The term "collaborative learning" best captured this newly emerging view of writing and writing instruction. Among composition professionals, collaborative learning was highlighted when peer tutoring was introduced [6], when workshopping and peer groups were acknowledged as valid approaches to teaching and learning [8; 17], and when co-authoring/collaborative writing became a focus of research [12].

During the 1970s and 1980s, college writing instructors increasingly incorporated writing groups and peer response into their pedagogies. These teachers viewed writing groups as occasions for student authors to gain greater appreciation of audience, reader-writer relationships, and the communicative function of written language. Some teachers found the immediacy of oral response to be particularly advantageous to student writers [18].

However, many teachers' early attempts to use collaborative learning in their writing classes were disappointing. Writing instructors quickly learned that successful collaborative learning pedagogies require careful planning and explicit instructions. Even more to the point, the problems some teachers experienced were not merely a matter of logistics or planning: Collaborative learning pedagogies required teachers to reconsider their assumptions about knowledge. This highly social approach to learning, knowing, and writing conflicted with (A) as Kenneth Bruffee described [7], a traditional Cartesian view of knowledge as "information impressed on the individual mind by some outside source" (646), and (B) New Critical views of text as having its own "objective authority" according to John Trimbur [45], (95). In his highly influential essay entitled "Collaborative Learning and the 'Conversation of Mankind,'" Bruffee [7] importantly argued that students' collaborative learning experiences enact the process by which knowledge is "socially constructed."

Bruffee maintained that as students converse about their writing, they do not merely benefit as individual writers: Rather, they learn "to think well collectively," to "converse well," and to "establish and maintain . . . the sorts of conversation members of the community value" [7] (640). Using the terminology of Stanley Fish, Bruffee described writing groups as "interpretive communities," that is, as interactive groups of readers who form communal judgments about texts and meanings through the use of "symbolic structures, chiefly language" (640). In short, Bruffee encouraged teachers to reject the view that learning is "reflecting and synthesizing information about the objective world" (651) and to embrace the idea that learning is a social process which entails "joining larger, more experienced communities of knowledgeable peers" by accepting the group's "interests, values, language, and paradigms of perception and thought" (646). Like the writing process advocates who preceded him, Bruffee proposed innovations in teaching that were supported by a new stance toward learning and writing.

The full impact of Bruffee's argument can be seen in the many published responses to his work. In "Consensus and Difference in Collaborative Learning," for example, Trimbur [46] identifies two major criticisms of Bruffee's ideas: (A) a view that his emphasis on consensus "stifles individual voice and creativity, suppresses differences, and enforces conformity" (602); and (B) the criticism that Bruffee's ideas on social constructionism do not go far enough, that is, they are too limited to what goes on inside classrooms and are thus in danger of reproducing the unequal, unjust social structures that exist outside schools [24].

Computer Technologies and Collaborative Writing

Despite criticisms of Bruffee's views on collaborative learning, the social perspective on writing that he and others successfully promoted has played an increasingly central role in composition pedagogy and research. The intersection of collaborative writing and computer technologies offers one important example. While computer-linked classrooms and writing centers were becoming a more common feature of colleges, computer software packages were being developed for interdependent groups writing at school and at work. These uses of technology have become a focus of research that can be found in books, mainstream composition journals, and in a specialized journal, *Computers and Composition*. Of the many composition professionals who have spoken and written about computer technologies and composition, Cynthia Selfe has been most prominently at the forefront.

The use of computer technologies for collaborative writing and learning has been the subject of many research studies. In "Computing and Collaborative Writing," for example, Forman [14] argues that composition professionals should become more involved in designing computer software products for interdependent group writing ("groupware"). Three years later, Forman published a study of college students' responses to groupware products and their learning experiences while working in writing groups [15]. Her finding in "Literacy, Collaboration, and Technology" was that individual students varied in their reactions to computer-linked writing-group situations and to specific groupware products. Students' individual responses to computer-linked writing groups, Forman suggests, are likely to be affected by their prior experiences with technology, writing, and group work [15]. Forman's research (and that of many others) suggests that computer technologies will offer many choices for writing students and challenges for teachers and researchers.

One challenge is to learn more about computer technologies and their applications for writers and teachers. Cynthia Selfe [37] points out that the composition profession as a whole has been reluctant to address computer technologies systematically and aggressively, preferring instead a piecemeal approach that is "dangerously shortsighted" (413). By ignoring computer technology developments, composition specialists remain too uninvolved in designing technologies that will be used in schools and too distant from public policy decisions about education and technology. Selfe argues further that computer technologies are closely associated with the same educational and social inequities that literacy educators such as Mike Rose [34, 35], Brian Street [43], and Elspeth Stuckey [44] have described in their scholarship. Sophisticated computers, Internet access, CD-ROM equipment, and videodisc technologies are all less likely to be found in schools that primarily enroll students of color and students who are poor than students who are middle-class or affluent and white. It is therefore incumbent on literacy educators to pay close atten-

tion to these new technologies, to their uses and distribution in schools, and to the relevant social and political issues.

Multiculturalism and the Teaching of Writing

As collaborative learning pedagogies became more firmly ensconced in writing classrooms, students' learning experiences, communication styles, and political leanings became more apparent to their teachers. Now writing instructors were doing more listening and interacting in small groups and less talking to whole classes from the front of the classroom. The "authority" of teachers was placed under question as student-centered classrooms became an important goal; and while teachers were listening more, they were also learning who their students were.

One important reason for the greater attention teachers were paying to students' views and cultural identities was the changing nature of U.S. college student populations. During the 1970s and 1980s, more students entering college came from working-class communities, from previously underrepresented ethnic groups, and from other countries. Many of these students were older adults returning to the classroom. The rise in community colleges and the open admissions policies in some senior colleges created opportunities for these "new" students but also presented challenges for their teachers. The changing demographics of students entering college provided the impetus for a rising interest in multicultural perspectives on literacy and learning. This increasingly important focus on students' cultural diversity was supported by ethnographic studies of community literacies and by post-structuralist theories of interpreting literature.

Teachers who were interested in their students' cultural diversity responded by designing new forms of writing-course curricula [38]. Some teachers encouraged students to reflect on their own culturally influenced ways of thinking and to learn about others' cultural perspectives. This approach suggested a need for multicultural readers—anthologies of stories, poems, and essays written by authors representing a variety of cultures and ethnicities. This new textbook genre appeared initially in the late 1980s and became a standard offering by most composition textbook publishers by the mid-1990s. One of the earliest and best-known of the multicultural readers is *Rereading America: Cultural Contexts for Critical Thinking and Writing* [9], now in its fifth edition. This book is advertised as presenting "diverse political and cultural perspectives as grist for critical thinking" and a set of readings that "encourage students to recognize and critically examine the cultural myths that shape their own thinking and values" [10].

A second key approach to creating multicultural writing-course curricula was inspired by Shirley Brice Heath's ethnographic study of community literacies [21]. Heath proposed that teachers become ethnographers in order to learn about their students' home literacies and that students become ethnographers in order to bring their communities into the classroom. In "Multicultural Classrooms, Monocultural Teachers," Terry Dean [11] argues that students bring their own diversity into the classroom by writing about their communities, cultures, and languages and then sharing their writing to build multicultural communities of writers. This approach is further supported by Paulo Freire's theory of critical literacy, which joins becoming literate to gaining awareness of the political and social realities that affect both perceptions and conditions of living and being in the world [16]. In *Freire for the Classroom: A Sourcebook for Liberatory Teaching* [40], Ira Shor offers a collection of essays by teachers who invite students to write about their lives and cultures as a way of becoming personally and politically empowered.

Basic Writing, Mainstreaming, and the Politics of Remediation

Many of the "new" students admitted to college in recent decades were tested and found to be lacking in "basic writing skills" when they entered college. The initial response was to provide support for these students in the form of remedial writing courses and peer tutoring. Mina Shaughnessy [39] is widely acknowledged as having inspired a newly enlightened perspective on "basic writers." However, the remedial programs that Shaughnessy and many other progressive educators helped build created new difficulties for students and teachers. Mike Rose [34, 35] was the first composition scholar to point out the problems posed by placing college students in remedial writing classes: diluted writing course curricula, lowered expectations on the part of both teachers and students, inappropriate and invalid evaluations of students' literacies, and negative self-images for many students who were enrolled in these classes.

One response to these critiques has been to incorporate remedial-placed students directly in college-level composition courses. This decision to "mainstream" remedial writing students has taken two forms: (A) "directed self-placement," whereby students make their own decisions about whether to enroll in remedial or college-level writing courses [36]; and (B) direct admittance to college-level composition courses, sometimes with special adjunct tutoring/workshops for students who initially tested as "remedial" writers [20; 31; 41].

Meanwhile, conservative politicians, university officials, and educators began questioning the practice of admitting "remedial" students at all to senior colleges. Funding for remedial programs in colleges and universities has been scaled back in several states, including Florida, Georgia, California, Illinois, and New York. In the City University of New York, a "remediation phase-out" policy for senior colleges was recently approved by a vote of the CUNY Board of Trustees and is being implemented. Now students who fail entry-level skills tests (in reading, writing, and math) will not be admitted to CUNY's senior colleges, regardless of high school class rank or grade point average. Many applicants who would previously have gained admission to a senior college will now be diverted to CUNY's community colleges. This will place an unprecedented burden on these community colleges where fewer full-time faculty carry heavier teaching loads and a high proportion of classes are taught by adjunct faculty.

Many colleges and universities nationwide are restricting admissions policies and reducing funding for remediation. Those who will be hardest hit are students who have not acquired the languages and literacies associated with U.S. higher education and students from poor and working-class backgrounds. Today's college writing instructors will therefore benefit from understanding how literacy learning intersects with possible disjunctions between the discourses of home, neighborhood, work, and school. Moreover, college writing teachers may well want to consider becoming involved in decisionmaking processes that will influence students' experiences across the curriculum and that will determine their initial access to U.S. colleges and universities.

Works Cited and Suggested Readings

1. Bartholomae, David. "Inventing the University." *Journal of Basic Writing* 5 (1986): 4–23.
2. ———. "Writing with Teachers: A Conversation with Peter Elbow." *College Composition and Communication* 46 (1995): 62–71.
3. Berlin, James A. *Writing Instruction in Nineteenth-Century American Colleges.* Carbondale: Southern Illinois UP, 1984.
4. Braddock, Richard, Richard Lloyd-Jones, and Lowell Schoer. *Research in Written Composition.* Champaign: NCTE, 1963.
5. Brereton, John C., ed. *The Origins of Composition Studies in the American College, 1875–1925: A Documentary History.* Pittsburgh, PA: U of Pittsburgh P, 1995.
6. Bruffee, Kenneth. "The Brooklyn Plan: Attaining Intellectual Growth through Peer Group Tutoring." *Liberal Education* 64 (1978): 447–68.
7. ———. "Collaborative Learning and 'The Conversation of Mankind.'" *College English* 46 (1984): 635–52.

8. ———. *A Short Course in Writing*. 3rd ed. Boston: Little, 1985.

9. Colombo, Gary, Robert Cullen, and Bonnie Lisle. *Rereading America: Cultural Contexts for Critical Thinking and Writing*, 5th ed. New York: Bedford/St. Martin's, 2001.

10. *Composition Readers*. Catalog, 2001. New York: Bedford/St. Martin's.

11. Dean, Terry. "Multicultural Classrooms, Monocultural Teachers." *College Composition and Communication* 40 (1989): 23–37.

12. Ede, Lisa, and Andrea Lunsford. *Singular Texts/Plural Authors: Perspectives on Collaborative Writing*. Carbondale: Southern Illinois UP, 1990.

13. Elbow, Peter. "Being a Writer vs. Being an Academic: A Conflict in Goals." *College Composition and Communication* 46 (1995): 72–83.

14. Forman, Janis. "Computing and Collaborative Writing." *Evolving Perspectives on Computers and Composition Studies: Questions for the 1990s*. Ed. Gail E. Hawisher and Cynthia L. Selfe. Urbana, IL: NCTE, 1991.

15. ———. "Literacy, Collaboration, and Technology: New Connections and Challenges." *The Complications of Teaching and Learning with Technology*. Ed. Cynthia L. Selfe and Susan Hilligoss. New York: Modern Language Association of America, 1994.

16. Freire, Paulo. *Pedagogy of the Oppressed*. New York: Seabury, 1968.

17. Gere, Anne Ruggles. *Writing Groups: History, Theory, and Implications*. Carbondale: Southern Illinois UP, 1987.

18. Gere, Anne Ruggles, and Ralph Stevens. "The Language of Writing Groups: How Oral Response Shapes Revision." *The Acquisition of Written Language: Response and Revision*. Ed. Sarah Warshauer Freedman. Norwood, NJ: Ablex, 1985. 85–105.

19. Gleason, Barbara. "Returning Adults to the Mainstream: Towards a Curriculum for Diverse Student Writers." *Mainstreaming Basic Writers: Politics and Pedagogies of Access*. Ed. Geraldine McNenny and Sallyanne Fitzgerald. Mahwah, NJ: Erlbaum, 2001.

20. Grego, Rhonda, and Nancy Thompson. "Repositioning Remediation: Renegotiating Composition's Work in the Academy." *College Composition and Communication* 47 (1996): 62–84.

21. Heath, Shirley Brice. *Ways with Words: Language, Life and Work in Communities and Classrooms*. Cambridge: Cambridge UP, 1983.

22. Holzman, Michael. "The Social Context of Literacy Education." *College English* 48 (1986): 27–33.

23. Kitzhaber, Albert R. *Rhetoric in American Colleges, 1850–1990*. Dallas: Southern University UP, 1990.

24. Myers, Greg. "Reality, Consensus, and Reform in the Rhetoric of Composition Teaching." *College English* 48 (1986): 154–74.

25. Murray, Donald M. "Teach Writing as Process, Not Product." *Rhetoric and Composition: A Sourcebook for Teachers and Writers*. Ed. Richard L. Graves. Upper Montclair, NJ: Boynton/Cook, 1984. 89–92.

26. North, Stephen M. *The Making of Knowledge in Composition: Portrait of an Emerging Field*. Upper Montclair, NJ: Boynton/Cook, 1987.

27. Nystrand, Martin, Stuart Greene, and Jeffrey Wiemelt. "Where Did Composition Come From?: An Intellectual History." *Written Communication* 10 (1993): 267–333.

28. Perl, Sondra. "Understanding Composing." *College Composition and Communication* 31 (1980): 363–69.

29. Phelps, Louise Wetherbee. *Composition as Human Science: Contributions to the Self-Understanding of a Discipline*. New York: Oxford UP, 1988.

30. Reither, James A., and Douglas Vipond. "Writing Collaboration." *College English* 51 (1989): 855–67.

31. Rodby, Judith, and Tom Fox. "Basic Work and Material Acts: The Ironies, Discrepancies, and Disjunctures of Basic Writing and Mainstreaming." *Journal of Basic Writing* 19 (1): 84–99.

32. Rohman, D. Gordon. "Prewriting: The Stage of Discovery in the Writing Process." *College Composition and Communication* 16 (1965): 106–12.

33. Rohman, D. Gordon, and Albert O. Wlecke. *Pre-Writing: The Construction and Applications of Models for Concept Formation in Writing*. USOE: Cooperative Research Project (1964): No. 2174.

34. Rose, Mike. "Remedial Writing Courses: A Critique and a Proposal." *College English* 45 (1983): 109–28.

35. ———. "The Language of Exclusion: Writing Instruction at the University." *College English* 47 (1985): 341–59.

36. Royer, Daniel J., and Roger Gilles. "Directed Self-Placement: An Attitude of Orientation." *College Composition and Communication* 49 (1998): 54–70.

37. Selfe, Cynthia. "Technology and Literacy: A Story About the Perils of Not Paying Attention." *College Composition and Communication* 50 (1999): 411–36.

38. Severino, Carol, Juan C. Guerra, and Johnnella E. Butler. *Writing in Multicultural Settings*. New York: Modern Language Arts of America, 1997.

39. Shaughnessy, Mina. *Errors and Expectations: A Guide for the Teaching of Basic Writing*. New York: Oxford UP, 1977.

40. Shor, Ira. *Freire for the Classroom: A Sourcebook for Liberatory Teaching*. Portsmouth, NH: Heinemann/Boynton/Cook, 1987.

41. Soliday, Mary, and Barbara Gleason. "From Remediation to Enrichment: Evaluating a Mainstreaming Project." *Journal of Basic Writing* 16 (1997): 64–78.

42. Sommers, Nancy. "Revision Strategies of Student Writers and Experienced Adult Writers." *College Composition and Communication* 31 (1980): 378–88.

43. Street, Brian V. *Literacy in Theory and Practice*. Cambridge: Cambridge UP, 1984.

44. Stuckey, J. Elspeth. *The Violence of Literacy*. Portsmouth, NH: Heinemann/Boynton/Cook, 1991.

45. Trimbur, John. "Collaborative Learning and Teaching Writing." *Perspectives on Research and Scholarship in Composition*. Ed. Ben W. McClelland and Timothy R. Donovan. New York: Modern Language Association of America, 1985.

46. ———. "Consensus and Difference in Collaborative Learning." *College English* 51 (1989): 602–16.

47. Varnum, Robin. *Fencing with Words: A History of Writing Instruction at Amherst College During the Era of Theodore Baird, 1938–1966*. Urbana, IL: NCTE, 1996.

48. Young, Richard. "Invention: A Topographical Survey." *Teaching Composition: 10 Bibliographic Essays*. Ed. Gary Tate. Fort Worth: Texas Christian UP, 1976.

THE HISTORY OF RHETORIC: AN OVERVIEW

William F. Woods
Revised and updated
by Catherine L. Hobbs

From its beginnings in Sicily early in the fifth century B.C., rhetoric has been known as the art or "science" of persuasive discourse, the theory and practice of how to use available means of persuasion to affect the opinions of an audience. The earliest known treatises on rhetoric, by Corax and Tisias, responded to citizens' need to speak well before judges and large popular juries in litigations over land rights. However, as Barilli notes, a rhetoric of public decision making also must have emerged quite early [item 1 in the Annotated Bibliography at the end of this essay].

A little more than a century later, Aristotle wrote his famous *Rhetoric* [item 15], a work based on a systematic description of public persuasive oratory as it was practiced in the law courts, the deliberative assembly, and the ceremonial gatherings of Athens. Thus from the start, rhetoric served to help a general audience interpret and react to practical affairs in the everyday world. Aristotle, especially in dialogue with his teacher Plato and his rival Isocrates, still serves as a rich and provocative starting point for the study of rhetoric [19, 18].

The key to Aristotle's approach to persuasion is *probability*. Philosophical logic can formally demonstrate a truth, but

William F. Woods is Professor of English at Wichita State University, where he teaches medieval literature and the history of rhetoric. His published articles include "The Reform Tradition in Nineteenth-Century Composition Teaching," Written Communication 2 (1985): 377–90; "The Cultural Tradition of Nineteenth-Century Traditional Grammar Teaching," Rhetoric Society Quarterly 15 (1985): 3–12; and "Nineteenth-Century Psychology and the Teaching of Writing," College Composition and Communication 36 (1985): 20–41. Catherine Hobbs is Associate Professor of rhetoric and cultural studies in English at the University of Oklahoma, where she writes historical studies of eighteenth- and nineteenth-century rhetoric. She edited Nineteenth-Century Women Learn to Write (Charlottesville: University Press of Virginia, 1995).

rhetoric can show that a position is worthy of belief—that it has a high probability of being true. Thus, while logical proofs are to be preferred in philosophical or scientific works, the persuasiveness of rhetoric is more effective in speaking or writing about practical affairs for a general audience.

Aristotle's *Rhetoric* discusses three modes of appeal that can be used to reach an audience: the appeal to logical arguments (*logos*, in the Greek), the appeal to emotions, attitudes and values (*pathos*), and the appeal based on the moral or ethical character (*ethos*). In themselves, these modes are only guidelines—ways of orienting the speaker to the task. However, each of the modes was also associated with certain kinds of discourse, as well as with the rhetorical devices proper to that sort of appeal. Perhaps the easiest way to give the flavor of Aristotle's rhetoric is to describe some of the devices he suggests for appealing to the mind, heart, and moral character of an audience.

As Aristotle saw it, the appeal based on reasoned argument (*logos*) involved the use of certain basic concepts—fundamental, generally recognized strategies for thinking and expressing thought. Aristotle calls them the "common topics," because they are the commonplaces of thought. *Definition*, for example, is the classification of a subject, which in practice means identifying it by placing it in a class (e.g., *Rhetoric* is an ability or power) and then further defining it by pointing out characteristics (*differentiae*) that distinguish it from the other things in that class (e.g., *Rhetoric* is the ability to see in each particular case the available means of persuasion) [13]. The other topics that belong to the appeal to reason are as familiar and essential to us as definition. *Comparison* brings out the similarity, the difference, and the degree of difference between two subjects. *Relationship* refers to patterns such as cause and effect, antecedent and consequence, contraries, and contradictions. *Circumstance* refers to the process we go through in deciding whether something is or was possible or impossible, given the particular circumstances; here we are defining the subject in relation to its occasion, or context.

These common topics were not originated by Aristotle, of course. He merely gave them names, grouped them, and showed how they function in persuasive discourse. In the history of rhetoric since Aristotle, however, the topics have been one of the most useful and enduring parts of classical rhetorical theory. Aristotle primarily identifies the topics as aids to *invention*, or the *discovery* of arguments for or against a position. As with the other arts from classical rhetoric, contradictory interpretations exist. Are topics merely forms or a system of pigeonholes or categories for discourse, or are they strategies that can help a speaker or writer arrive at a judgment about a matter? Contemporary scholars believe inventional arts were more than devices to organize or manage language, that topics served as a basis for rhetorical thought leading to probable judgments [see 13; also Enos and Lauer chapter in 49]. Aristotle also described the *enthymeme*—a type of syllogism, or a statement with its supporting reason(s) or corollary—as a center of rhetorical logic. He presented reasoning drawn from examples as another slightly less valuable form of rhetorical invention.

The second mode of appeal Aristotle talks about (*pathos*) is the appeal to the emotions, attitudes and values—to the heart. Aristotle recognized that the most powerful appeals are those that harness the primal human emotions, our tendencies to feel protectiveness, anger, envy, pride, fear, desire. Aristotle and the rhetoricians who came after him devoted considerable thought to what we would call "audience psychology"—the types of emotions and the types of people who experience them—but they also tried to identify the kinds of subjects that would evoke such an emotional response. What are the types of description, they asked, that powerfully involve an audience by helping them to place themselves within an imagined experience? What are the phrases and the words associated with deeply felt issues? And then there were the stylistic effects associated with emotional states. The periodic or suspended sentence, for instance, was thought to create tension and a feeling of building to climax. The "rhetorical" question had its place here, as did the use of exaggeration (hyperbole), metaphor, and various other figures of speech. The study of style has always been closely connected with the appeal to the emotions. That is why both the first and later Sophists—the earliest rhetors before Plato and Aristotle as well as later professional orators who flourished about the second century A.D.—were both praised and condemned. The orators of the "Second Sophistic" were known for their panegyrics (elaborate eulogies and other ceremonial speeches) which appealed to the emotions but were not always calculated to inspire sound judgments.

The third mode of appeal (*ethos*) is best described as a perceived relationship between the character of the speaker or writer and the social and ethical beliefs of the audience. It is an appeal to ethical values, perhaps, but it also has much to do with the ability of the audience to *identify* with the speaker, to accept him or her as someone who speaks for *them*. This appeal often derives as much from the personal qualities of a speaker or writer as it does from the overt content of the discourse. "Is this a person like us, who shares our values, and whose opinion can be trusted?" These are the sorts of questions addressed by the ethical appeal, which has a

great deal to do with the *tone* of a piece of writing, and therefore with its syntax and choice of words. Tone also depends on the purpose of the discourse (to explain, persuade, entertain, etc.), and on the level of style adopted by the writer or speaker. Classical rhetoricians after Aristotle liked to identify three levels of style: (A) the high, or grand style (appropriate for epics and for the sublime, high-flown passages of persuasive oratory): (B) the middle ("pleasing," ornate) style associated with literary works and with ceremonial oratory; and (C) the low or plain style associated with the language of instruction and everyday affairs. The New Rhetoric of the 1970s and 1980s focused attention once more on studies of style.

It is worth noting that the three modes of appeal—*logos, pathos,* and *ethos*—reflect a basic way in which Western culture has conceived or "pictured" the mind ever since the days of Plato. We say *mind, body,* and *spirit*—or *reason, memory, imagination*—as if thought and substance were somehow united by a perceptive consciousness, our bond with the world outside us and the source of our state of being. Somewhat paralleling this trinity, composition as classical rhetoricians described it also had three essential phases: invention, arrangement (organization), and style. Two other phases, or "departments," of rhetoric comprised the arts of memory and techniques of delivery, the final stages of producing a speech. These last two have not been directly involved in what we in our industrial age call the "process" of writing until quite recently. However, with the advent of computer technology and new electronic media, a resurgence of thought about memory, both human and artificial, and delivery, including medium of publishing, has reinvigorated these old arts [55; 65].

As oratory gave way to written rhetoric in the seventeenth and eighteenth centuries (a recurrent trend in the history of rhetoric), it became common to characterize discourse by its literary form rather than by its situation in which it occurred or appeal to an audience. Whereas ancient oratory had been divided into deliberative (legislative), judicial (courtroom), and epideictic (ceremonial) oratory, the rhetorical spectrum by the 1700s had shifted to focus on formal letters (epistles), history, argument, narration, description, persuasion, and poetry. Since written discourse was now much more prevalent, it became customary to describe this as the art of "rhetoric and *belles lettres*" (borrowing a term from French literary criticism, which was then enjoying a period of authority) [22; 23]. With the successes of the new scientific method and theory, the method and theory of rhetoric was also changing. Rhetoricians appropriated theories of empiricist philosophers such as Locke in assuming that language and thought reflected sense impressions, especially those received through sight. Eighteenth-century writers such as Scottish rhetorician George Campbell investigated how different forms of discourse engaged the four "faculties" of the mind: the memory, imagination, intellect or understanding, and the will [23].

Later thinkers came to assume that the forms of discourse must derive from the different patterns of language we use to record our perceptions, to form a "point of view," and to influence the opinions (views) of others. For example, we record our perceptions of things (thus, *descriptive* writing); we record our perceptions of events, or "things in action" (*narrative* writing); we interpret the pattern, or "logic" of relationships in the things and events perceived (*expository*, or explanatory writing); finally, we arrange our perceptions as proof in support of our point of view (*argumentative* writing; "persuasion" generally meant oral discourse). Authors of nineteenth century textbooks on written rhetoric ("composition") found in these four terms, and in the kinds of writing they implied, a comprehensive schema for describing the teaching of writing. These four "modes of discourse" [6] (which had little or nothing to do with Aristotle's modes of appeal) were a typical feature of composition textbooks after 1850; they continued to shape teachers' approaches to English composition for at least the next hundred years. Rightly or wrongly, the four modes are now associated with the more conservative side of nineteenth-century composition teaching, which borrowed much from traditional methods of teaching English (and before that, Latin) grammar. There were other emphases, other theories at work in nineteenth-century composition teaching, but that period is remembered mainly for its drills, for the practice of having students memorize principles of grammar and style, for its increasing tendency to stress exposition (essay writing), and for giving first priority to a building-block structuring of words, sentences, paragraphs, and essays. This was also a pedagogy associated with the rigorous methods and the sometimes endearing eccentricities of writing masters and textbooks writers like Alexander Bain, George Quackenbos, and A. S. (Adams Sherman) Hill [3].

But while the main thrust of nineteenth-century rhetoric and composition teaching was on style and structure, the *character* of the speaker or writer was beginning to receive a new emphasis. In a time when political, religious, and artistic individualism was much respected, the mental nature of the individual think er, writer, and student became a serious subject of inquiry. This strand of thought had begun in the eighteenth century, culminating in Rousseau and theorists of pedagogy, language learning, and child development such as Pestalozzi. The ultimate results of this spirit of romantic individualism, along with the studies of child nature that accompanied it, can be seen in the contemporary work of James Britton [35], a British educator who specialized in research on student writing. Britton's central insight, which owes much to his studies of the early twentieth-century linguist Roman Jakobson, was that written discourse can be described in terms of "function categories" (see Figure 1) which represent what the writer is doing, in each case, in the act of writing. Writing is no longer seen as reflecting structures of the mind; rather, writing is assumed to represent three basic types of observed language behavior in a school setting (which may, of course, reflect three types of mental activity).

In Britton's first function category, the *transactional*, students participate in a problem, discussion, or other event: they get things done with words. The language relates closely to the needs of the audience and to the features of the task at hand. Language here is seen as a means to an end. In the second category, the *expressive*, students express their responses to an outside situation in language that relates closely to their own points of view or inner experiences of the situation. Here the language is less a way of getting things done than it is a way of putting feelings into intelligible form; thus, expressive discourse probably serves the writer's needs more than it does the needs of the audience or the demands of the task at hand. In the third category, the *poetic*, the writer is a spectator to the problem or situation at hand and uses language that relates closely to the overall concept or "global context" of what is being done, created, or argued. Here the writer is more a disinterested analyst than a participator in an interactive task or someone trying to verbalize an inner experience.

One striking difference between Britton's system and traditional rhetorics is the centrality of the expressive, or

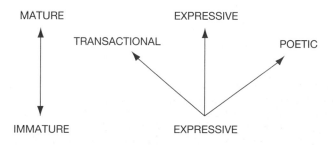

Figure 1

personal, aspect of writing in emergent literacy. Britton assumes that child language *begins* as expressive discourse and diversifies as the child grows older; the transactional and poetic modes are gradually acquired, and the resources of the expressive mode are further developed. So while Aristotle's modes of appeal were intended as ways of describing the impact of discourse on an audience, Britton's function categories are ways of identifying the kinds of discourse that emerge from three kinds of writing behavior and purpose. To put it another way, while Aristotle's modes are reader-oriented, Britton's categories are writer-oriented, since they describe discourse as the reflection of mental processes associated with certain adaptive social behaviors. Because of this emphasis on behavior, Britton's discussions were to help teachers trying to figure out "where students are coming from" in each of the various assignments that they write. Britton's work also served as a corrective influence on those who viewed expressive discourse as a sloppy aberration from expository writing or believed it should surface only in creative writing courses. This played a role in the valorization of expressive writing in the classroom. In the eighties, expressivism became a vital approach to composition, although our recent histories show it was early on a part of U.S. writing studies [2].

Despite some real differences in theoretical orientation, however, Aristotle and Britton or later expressivists are not mutually exclusive. Teachers who have studied Aristotle's account of the appeals to the reason and the emotions will probably arrive at a better appreciation of Britton's transactional and poetic functions than those who come to Britton with no preparation in rhetoric. In fact, even though social and historical conditions are vastly different now than they were in ancient Greece, Aristotle's *Rhetoric* continues to stimulate and provoke scholars [much of Section VI; 56–68], for the truth is that there have been no modern Aristotles, and no modern rhetoric has made the impact on rhetorical tradition that Aristotle and Cicero did. In the sixties, James Kinneavy [42] came as close to that goal as anyone, perhaps, in his attempt to write a comprehensive modern theory of rhetoric, or "discourse," as he calls it, to allow for the enlarged role of writing in modern communication [see also 47].

Influenced by Jakobson and linguistics, Kinneavy distinguished basic aims of discourse and described the processes and characteristics essential to each of them. He derived four aims of discourse from both ancient rhetorical and modern theory of communication, plotted on the familiar "communication triangle" (see Figure 2). The three points of the triangle refer to (A) the *writer,* (B) the *audience,* and (C) the *subject* of

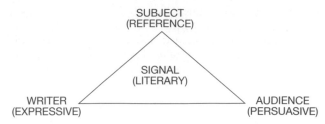

Figure 2   (adapted from Kinneavy)

discourse, while the body of the triangle refers to (D) the *signal,* in this case, the written language of the message. Each of these four terms is the point of origin for one of the four *aims,* the purposes for which we produce discourse: (A) Discourse that derives from the point of view or "inner experience" of the writer attempting to give it form is *expressive* (as in Britton's function theory). (B) Discourse that is oriented more toward channeling or intensifying an audience's concerns, ideas, and feelings is called *persuasive* (as in Aristotle's theory of rhetoric). (C) Discourse that is meant to represent accurately a subject of investigation is called *reference* discourse—this aim includes the nonpersuasive aspects of most academic and scientific writing, as well as what we call *expository* prose. (D) Discourse that is self-referential or mimetic in purpose and that aims to be used or enjoyed for its own sake is called *literary* discourse or literature (similar to Britton's *poetic* function category but not synonymous with it).

Unlike Britton, Kinneavy was not concerned mainly with the development of students' discourse toward maturity. Rather, his emphasis was on taxonomizing and describing the aims and forms of discourse and their use. We can generalize by calling Kinneavy's work a comprehensive, painstaking description of the ways prose writing is used or understood in the twentieth century. In this sense his work is reminiscent of Aristotle's systematic, analytical description of persuasive oratory in fourth-century Athens. A basic understanding of Kinneavy's four aims lends a structural perspective on written communication; moreover, his situating of English Departments and composition within a linguistic pragmatic framework lent a new and influential way of thinking about the entire profession of teaching writing. For those who wish to backtrack Kinneavy's research and pursue their own investigations in one direction or another, full bibliographies are appended to each chapter of his book [42].

At the far end of our history lies rhetoric's growing edge, the gradual assimilation of modern theory and contemporary research into the body of the discipline. Slowly, the ideas of major theorists like I. A. Richards [48], Kenneth Burke [36], Richard McKeon (whose work is just now being republished), Chaim Perelman and Lucie Olbrechts-Tyteca [47], and Stephen Toulmin [49], have entered our shared assumptions about written rhetoric. In the mid-eighties and nineties, post-structuralist and postmodern theories from Europe filtered into composition, and their implications for pedagogy are still being worked out in practice. Literary and cultural theorists such as Derrida, Foucault, Barthes, Bakhtin, and Habermas became fixtures in rhetorical theory. Research findings derived from multiple methodologies also shaped our teaching methods from the mid-eighties. But the central concerns, and thus the distinguishing traits of today's rhetoric, have more to do with our students: a varied lot, they reflect, in their challenging array of needs and abilities, the fragmentation that characterizes not only our own profession, but academia at large and the arenas of national and international politics.

Responding to social changes beginning with immigration and urbanization early in the century, rhetoric teaching has recurrently transformed itself, deepening its resources and broadening its scope to provide effective instruction for non-traditional students. The crisis-related efforts that produced, for example, Sterling A. Leonard's *English Composition as a Social Problem* (1917), or William Labov's *The Study of Non-Standard English* (1970), or Mina Shaughnessy's *Errors and Expectations* (1977), have enabled significant pedagogical advances, and they remind us that divergence and difference can also mean growth. With the turn to political and educational conservatism in the 1980s and 1990s, the focus once more turned to language difference with controversies over Ebonics rekindling values long held by the CCCC, as stated in its position paper on students' right to their own language [46]. The emphasis on writing across the curriculum, with its implied sensitivity to differences in the situations of discourse and audiences, was early on a broader, organizational response to this century-long groundswell of diversity, and the debates over "discourse communities" has been one response at the level of theory.

What is a discourse community? It has been a useful phrase, a serviceable metaphor, because it gives form to our ambivalent thoughts about rhetoric's fractured audience. If doctors (or sociologists, literary critics, street people) share a specialized body of knowledge, a common jargon, and a rhetoric that specifies the kinds of arguments acceptable within that group, then they belong to a community of shared discourse features. These communities are, in effect, political en-

tities which tend to overflow social, economic and geographical boundaries. They are "city–states of language," and as such Aristotle would have understood them well, even though his rhetoric served a smaller, more unified world, and ours must speak to so many, once again both orally and in print, where text and graphics more and more frequently work together and "interanimate" each other. Refinements of this concept of "community" and the turn to real community service have also resulted from theories of discourse that broadened into the world of work or civic involvement. Another trend enhancing this has been the growth of cultural studies and the impinging global rhetorical situation, brought about by and further complicated by the continuing transformations of electronic communication technology. In its wake, rhetoric and composition began to adopt an anthropological perspective on writing and culture [e.g., 34; 38; 41]. This means researchers of rhetoric, composition, and literacy today study how writing emerged, emerges, or functions in diverse groups and cultures with their interacting ethnicities, classes, genders, and so on, in our local classrooms and communities, nation, ever-more-present countries of northern and southern Americas, and around the globe. Studies of electronic technology and writing became central to rhetoric and composition at the dawn of the twenty-first century, just as the second generation of those trained in rhetoric and composition in its disciplinary guise reached maturity. The new millennium opened with a surge of interest in teaching verbal and visual arts in tandem, reflecting the new material realities of written communication. Inquiries into new hybrids of the oral and the literate were also spawned by changing writing technologies. The "process" generation must of necessity be protean, as our only certainty is that we must continually retool.

If there is a moral to be drawn from this lightning sketch of a few exemplary works on rhetoric, composition, and literacy, it is that a little knowledge is not a dangerous thing, but our only salvation. Not one of us has the time or dedication to absorb over two thousand years of rhetorical treatises, debates, and biases; even to desire such a thing is to miss the point badly. Our goal as teachers of writing is rather, by knowing something of the needs, ideas, and practices of former times, to understand more deeply and truly what we are engaged in doing and where we are tending. Neither Aristotle nor Kinneavy, Corbett nor Crowley, Elbow nor Trimbur should be adopted as manuals of rigidly prescribed methods for teachers. These books, as well as the others that we have mentioned or that are listed in the bibliography, are parts of the history of our profession and should be sampled, experimented with, and pondered as we proceed with our own teaching, in our own places and times, in our own reflective ways. To do so is to use history well; in so doing, we become rhetoricians—and enter history.

Annotated Bibliography and Suggested Readings

I. HISTORIES OF RHETORIC AND WRITING INSTRUCTION

1. Barilli, Renato. *Rhetoric*. Trans. Giuliana Menozzi. Theory and History of Literature 63. Minneapolis: U of Minnesota P, 1989.
2. Berlin, James A. *Writing Instruction in Nineteenth-Century American Colleges*. Carbondale: Southern Illinois UP, 1984.

   Brief and helpful overview of the century's writing instruction. Along with Berlin's *Rhetoric and Reality: Writing Instruction in American Colleges 1900–1985* (Carbondale: Southern Illinois UP, 1987), still an important introduction to the history of U.S. writing instruction.
3. Bizzell, Patricia, and Bruce Herzberg, eds. *The Rhetorical Tradition: Readings from Classical Times to the Present*. New York: St. Martin's, 1990.

   A superb anthology; the introductions and headnotes are in effect a substantial history of rhetoric.
4. Brereton, John C., ed. *The Origins of Composition Studies in the American Colleges, 1875–1925: A Documentary History*. Pittsburgh: U of Pittsburgh P, 1995.
5. Clark, Gregory, and S. Michael Halloran. *Oratorical Culture in Nineteenth-Century America: Transformations in the Theory and Practice of Rhetoric*. Carbondale: Southern Illinois UP, 1993.
6. Corbett, Edward J. P. *Classical Rhetoric for the Modern Student*. (1965) 3rd ed. New York: Oxford UP, 1990.

   The first of the modern textbooks that make classical rhetorical theory and pedagogy available to teachers and upper-level students of English composition.
7. Crowley, Sharon. *The Methodical Memory: Invention in Current-Traditional Rhetoric*. Carbondale: Southern Illinois UP, 1991.

   See also her *Ancient Rhetorics for Contemporary Students*. New York: Macmillan, 1994.
8. Eagleton, Terry. "A Small History of Rhetoric." *Walter Benjamin or Toward a Revolutionary Criticism*. London: Verso and NLB, 1981. 101–13.
9. Glenn, Cheryl. *Rhetoric Retold: Regendering the Tradition from Antiquity Through the Renaissance*. Carbondale: Southern Illinois UP, 1998.
10. Howell, Wilbur Samuel. *Eighteenth-Century British Logic and Rhetoric*. Princeton: Princeton UP, 1971.

    This classic study and *Logic and Rhetoric in England, 1500–1700* (Princeton: Princeton UP, 1956) catalog the changes rhetoric went through in response to the birth of empirical science and the resurgence of classical learning in the period between the early English Renaissance and the end of the seventeenth century.

11. Johnson, Nan. *Nineteenth-Century Rhetoric in North America*. Carbondale: Southern Illinois UP, 1991.
12. Kennedy, George A. *A New History of Classical Rhetoric*. Princeton: Princeton UP, 1994.

    Kennedy reliably overviews rhetoric in its cultural tradition in this and in his *Classical Rhetoric and Its Christian and Secular Tradition from Ancient to Modern Times* (1980). For those interested in Greek, Roman, or early Christian rhetoric, Kennedy's specialized works in those areas are standard sources.
13. Murphy, James J., and Richard A. Katula et al. *A Synoptic History of Classical Rhetoric*. Mahwah, NJ: Lawrence Erlbaum, 1994.

    Murphy's *Rhetoric in the Middle Ages*. Berkeley: California UP 1974, is still the best survey of medieval rhetoric now available. Also see his *Renaissance Eloquence* (1983) and edited collection *A Short History of Writing Instruction*, new edition forthcoming (Erlbaum).
14. Poulakis, John. *Sophistical Rhetoric in Classical Greece*. U of South Carolina P, 1995.

II. CLASSICAL AND MEDIEVAL THEORIES OF RHETORIC

15. *Aristotle on Rhetoric: A Theory of Civic Discourse*. Trans. George A. Kennedy. New York: Oxford UP, 1991.

    An invaluable resource making the knowledge of a classical scholar accessible to nonspecialists; with helpful introduction, notes and appendices by Kennedy.
16. Augustine of Hippo. *De Doctrina Christiana*, trans. D. W. Robertson Jr. Indianapolis: Bobbs Merrill, 1958.

    Books I–III of this treatise are a guide to the reading and interpretation of the scriptures. Book IV (on preaching) is probably the most important statement of rhetorical theory in the Middle Ages.
17. Cicero. *De Oratore*. Trans. E. W. Sutton and H. Rackham. 2 vols. Loeb Classical Library. Cambridge, MA: Harvard UP, 1976.

    The comprehensive treatise that represents Cicero's mature rhetorical theory.
18. Isocrates. *Isocrates in Three Volumes*. Vols. 1 & 2 trans. George Norlin. Vol. 3 trans. Larue Van Hook. Cambridge: Harvard UP, 1930, 1932, 1945.
19. Plato. *Gorgias*. Trans. W. C. Helmhold. New York: Macmillan, 1952. This and the *Phaedrus* (1956) are key dialogues on rhetoric.
20. Quintilian. *Institutio Oratoria*. Trans. H. E. Butler. 4 vols. Loeb Classical Library. Cambridge: Harvard UP, 1980.

    See also Murphy's edition of Books 1, 2 and 10: *Quintilian on the Art of Speaking and Writing* (Carbondale: Southern Illinois UP, 1987). Quintilian was a teacher of rhetoric in Rome, under the Empire. His "Institute" of rhetoric is a thoroughgoing description of the art as it was practiced and taught during his times.
21. *Rhetorica ad Herennium*. Trans. Harry Caplan. 2 vols. Loeb Classical Library. Cambridge, MA: Harvard UP, 1981.

    This relatively brief manual, and Cicero's early work *De Inventione* (On Rhetorical Invention), were the classical treatises that most influenced medieval rhetoric.

III. EARLY MODERN RHETORIC

22. Fénelon, François. *Fénelon's Dialogues on Eloquence.* Trans. W. S. Howell. Princeton: Princeton UP, 1951.

    "The greatest work on classical rhetoric written in French and the finest statement of the philosophical strand of the tradition since antiquity" (Kennedy).

23. Golden, James, and Edward P. J. Corbett, eds. *The Rhetoric of Blair, Campbell, and Whately.* Carbondale: Southern Illinois UP, 1990.

    Blair, Campbell, and Whately—sometimes called the "Scottish rhetoricians"—reflect the influence of empirical philosophy (e.g., Hume, Locke) on rhetorical theory; they also foreshadow the nineteenth-century shift in emphasis from spoken to written rhetoric (or "composition").

24. Harwood, John T. *The Rhetorics of Thomas Hobbes and Bernard Lamy.* Carbondale: Southern Illinois UP, 1986.

25. Miller, Thomas P. *The Formation of College English: Rhetoric and Belles Lettres in the British Cultural Provinces.* Pittsburgh: U of Pittsburgh P, 1997.

26. Smith, Adam. *Lectures on Rhetoric and Belles Lettres.* Ed. J. C. Bryce. Indianapolis: Liberty P, 1985.

IV. NINETEENTH-CENTURY RHETORICS

27. Adams, John Quincey. *Lectures on Rhetoric and Oratory, Delivered to the Classes of Senior and Junior Sophisters in Harvard University.* 2 vols. 1810. New York: Russell and Russell, 1962.

28. Channing, Edward T. *Lectures Read to the Seniors at Harvard College.* 1856. Carbondale: Southern Illinois UP, 1968.

29. Connors, Robert J. *Composition-Rhetoric: Backgrounds, Theory, and Pedagogy.* U of Pittsburgh P, 1997.

30. Logan, Shirley Wilson. *"We Are Coming": The Persuasive Discourse of Nineteenth-Century Black Women.* Carbondale: Southern Illinois UP, 1999.

31. Miller, Susan. *Assuming the Positions: Cultural Pedagogy and the Politics of Commonplace Writing.* Pittsburgh: U of Pittsburgh P, 1998.

32. Royster, Jacqueline Jones. *Traces of a Stream: Literacy and Social Change Among African American Women.* U of Pittsburgh P, 2000.

V. MODERN THEORIES OF RHETORIC, COMPOSITION, AND LITERACY

33. Bazerman, Charles. *Shaping Written Knowledge: The Genre and Activity of the Experimental Article in Science.* Madison: U of Wisconsin P, 1988.

34. Berlin, James A. *Rhetorics, Poetics, and Culture.* Urbana, IL: NCTE, 1996.

35. Britton, James, et al. *The Development of Writing Abilities (11–18).* London: Macmillan Education, 1975.

    Considered the best of the early studies of how writing skills develop in young students; introduces a taxonomy and vocabulary that still inform the field.

36. Burke, Kenneth. *A Grammar of Motives.* 1945. Berkeley: U of California P, 1969.

    Burke's original, syncretic thought drew on philosophical language study and a social view of traditional rhetorics. See also especially *A Rhetoric of Motives* (1950) and *Language as Symbolic Action* (1966).

37. Crowley, Sharon. *Composition in the University: Historical and Polemical Essays.* Pittsburgh: U of Pittsburgh P, 1999.

    Winner of the 1999 MLA Mina P. Shaughnessy Prize, Crowley here examines problems with the founding assumptions of the required first-year composition course.

38. Faigley, Lester. *Fragments of Rationality: Postmodernity and the Subject of Composition.* Pittsburgh: U Pittsburgh P, 1992.

39. Flower, Linda. *The Construction of Negotiated Meaning: A Social Cognitive Theory of Writing.* Carbondale: Southern Illinois UP, 1994.

40. Halesek, Kay. *A Pedagogy of Possibility: Bakhtinian Perspectives on Composition Studies.* Carbondale: Southern Illinois UP, 1999.

41. Kennedy, George. *Comparative Rhetorics.* Oxford UP, 1998.

    A cultural approach to studying rhetorics from different historical periods and places that challenges universal statements made on behalf of rhetoric based on an exclusively male, Western evidence.

42. Kinneavy, James. *A Theory of Discourse.* 1971. New York: Norton, 1980.

    Classifies the kinds of discourse according to purpose rather than form and describes the features associated with each of these purposes, or "aims." Grounded in the scholarship of linguistics, literature, communications, and philosophy.

43. Lunsford, Andrea, and Lisa Ede. *Singular Text/Plural Authors.* Carbondale: Southern Illinois UP, 1990.

    This groundbreaking exploration of collaborative writing remains the standard.

44. Miller, Susan. *Textual Carnivals: The Politics of Composition.* Carbondale: Southern Illinois UP, 1991.

45. Moffett, James. *Teaching the Universe of Discourse.* 1956. Rept. ed. Boynton/Cook, 1987.

    Helpful in understanding the neo-progressive or student-centered attitudes toward teaching writing that dominated the Dartmouth Conference (1966) and later produced the "open classroom."

46. Parks, Stephen. *Class Politics: The Movement for the Students' Right to Their Own Language.* Urbana, IL: NCTE, 2000.

47. Perelman, Chaim, and Lucie Olbrechts-Tyteca. *The New Rhetoric: A Treatise on Argumentation.* Notre Dame: U of Notre Dame P, 1969.

    An Aristotle-like attempt to give a comprehensive account of everyday argument.

48. Richards, I. A. *The Philosophy of Rhetoric.* New York: Oxford UP, 1936.

    See also Berthoff, Ann E., *Richards on Rhetoric: I.A. Richards, Selected Essays, 1929–1974* (New York: Oxford UP, 1991).

49. Toulmin, Stephen E. *The Uses of Argument.* Cambridge: Cambridge UP, 1958.

VI. STUDIES IN WRITING AND TECHNOLOGY

50. Haas, Christina. *Writing Technology: Studies on the Materiality of Literacy.* Mahwah, NJ: Erlbaum, 1996.

51. Hawisher, Gail, and Cynthia L. Selfe. *Passions, Pedagogies, and 21st Century Technologies.* Urbana, IL: NCTE, 1999.

52. Reiss, Donna, Dickie Selfe, and Art Young, ed. *Electronic Communication Across the Curriculum.* Urbana, IL: NCTE, 1998.

53. Selfe, Cynthia. *Technology and Literacy in the Twenty-First Century: The Importance of Paying Attention.* Carbondale: Southern Illinois UP, 1999.

54. Selfe, Cynthia, and Susan Hilligoss. *Literacy and Computers: The Complications of Teaching and Learning with Technology.* New York: MLA, 1994.

55. Welch, Kathleen. *Electric Rhetoric Classical Rhetoric, Oralism, and a New Literacy.* Cambridge, MA: MIT P, 2000.

VII. HELPFUL COLLECTIONS ON RHETORIC, COMPOSITION, AND LITERACY

56. Covino, William A., and David A. Joliffe, eds. *Rhetoric: Concepts, Definitions, Boundaries.* Boston: Allyn & Bacon, 1995.

57. Enos, Theresa, ed. *Learning from the Histories of Rhetoric: Essays in Honor of Winifred Bryan Horner.* Carbondale: Southern Illinois UP, 1993.

58. Enos, Theresa, and Stuart C. Brown, eds. *Defining the New Rhetorics.* Newbury Park, CA: Sage, 1993.

59. Gilyard, Keith. *Race, Rhetoric, and Composition.* Westport, CT: Heinemann, 1999.

60. Graves, Richard L., ed. *Writing, Teaching, Learning: A Sourcebook.* Westport, CT: Heinemann, 1999.

61. Harkin, Patricia, and John Schilb, eds. *Contending with Words: Composition and Rhetoric in a Postmodern Age.* New York: MLA, 1991.

62. Jarratt, Susan, and Lynn Worsham. *Feminism and Composition Studies: In Other Words.* MLA, 1998.

63. Kintgen, Eugene R., Barry M. Kroll, and Mike Rose. *Perspectives on Literacy.* Carbondale: Southern Illinois UP, 1988.

64. Horner, Winifred Bryan, and Michael Leff, eds. *Rhetoric and Pedagogy: Its History, Philosophy, and Practice: Essays in Honor of James J. Murphy.* Mahwah, NJ: Erlbaum, 1995.

65. Lunsford, Andrea A., ed. *Reclaiming Rhetorica: Women in the Rhetorical Tradition.* Pittsburgh: U of Pittsburgh P, 1995.

66. Raforth, Ben, ed. *A Tutor's Guide: Helping Writers One to One.* Westport, CT: Heinemann, 2000.

67. Shor, Ira, and Caroline Pari, ed. *Education Is Politics: Critical Teaching Across Differences, Postsecondary: A Tribute to the Life and Work of Paolo Freire.* Westport, CT: Heinemann, 1999.

68. Witte, Stephen P., Neil Nakadate, and Roger D. Cherry, eds. *A Rhetoric of Doing: Essays on Written Discourse in Honor of James L. Kinneavy.* Carbondale: Southern Illinois UP, 1992.

VIII. REFERENCE WORKS

69. *CCCC (Conference on College Composition and Communication) Bibliography of Composition and Rhetoric.* 1992–94.

   Annual bibliography in the field soon to be taken in by MLA index. See also *Communication Index, Communication Abstracts, Modern Language Association* bibliographies.

70. *Encyclopedia of English Studies and Language Arts.* Gen. Ed. Alan C. Purves. New York: NCTE, 1994.

71. *Encyclopedia of Rhetoric.* Ed. Theresa Enos. New York: Garland, 1996.

72. Horner, Winifred, ed. *The Present State of Scholarship in Historical and Contemporary Rhetoric.* Rev. ed. Columbia: U of Missouri P, 1990.

   Still a helpful starting point for historical research. See also Horner's *Historical Rhetoric: An Annotated Bibliography of Selected Sources in English* (Boston: Hall, 1980).

73. Kennedy, Mary Lynch, ed. *Theorizing Composition: A Critical Sourcebook of Theory and Scholarship in Contemporary Composition Studies.* Westport, CT: Greenwood P, 1998.

   This is a must-have reference with sophisticated analyses and bibliography.

74. Lindemann, Erika, and Gary Tate, eds. *An Introduction to Composition Studies.* New York: Oxford UP, 1990.

75. Olson, Gary A. and Todd W. Taylor, eds. *Publishing in Rhetoric and Composition.* Albany: SUNY P, 1997.

   Helpful advice on entering the conversation in published research in rhetoric and composition.

PORTFOLIOS IN THE TEACHING AND ASSESSING OF WRITING

Irwin Weiser

Irwin Weiser is Professor of English at Purdue University, where he serves as Director of Composition. He teaches undergraduate writing courses and graduate courses in Writing Across the Curriculum and Composition Research. A longtime advocate of portfolio evaluation, his most recent publication in this area is Situating Portfolios, a collection of essays on portfolio use he coedited with Kathleen Blake Yancey.

Though portfolios have been used for the assessment of writing for over twenty years, the past decade has seen interest in portfolios of student writing increase dramatically. I want to explore some of the reasons for this interest, outline some common features of portfolios, discuss various ways portfolios are being used, and raise some issues teachers and administrators wanting to implement portfolio grading assessment programs should plan to consider. While portfolios are being used in a variety of educational settings, from elementary schools through graduate programs [items 43 and 45 in the Annotated Bibliography at the end of this essay], and for subjects other than English and composition, my primary focus will be on portfolios of student writing in postsecondary settings. My goal is to provide composition teachers and administrators with an introduction to portfolios that will enable them to make informed decisions about whether portfolios are appropriate for their individual situations. This point is particularly important, since one of the central issues in any assessment program should be its fit with specific local conditions.

Indeed, one of the reasons that portfolios have become so popular is that they are consistent with newer assessment theories and practices that emphasize contextualized, authentic, local assessment, and challenge indirect, top-down externally developed assessment of student writing. Portfolios, as Edward White and Kathleen Blake Yancey point out, are a natural extension of the movement away from indirect measures of writing ability, such as multiple-choice tests of usage and vocabulary, toward the direct evaluation of written discourse [36; 40]. The same arguments that led to the advocacy and development of essays as components of the CLEP and TSWE and the use of analytical, primary trait, and holistic scoring for student writing—namely, that writing ability should be assessed by evaluating actual written texts rather than by indirect measures, such as usage, grammar, or vocabulary tests—support the use of portfolios as providing more accurate and valid evidence of writing ability [5; 15]. Further, because portfolios often have been developed in response to local educational concerns, they are responsive to the specific needs and goals of particular contexts [17; 18; 21; 24; 33]. Teachers and writing program administrators can tailor portfolio requirements to their own classroom, program, or institutional needs.

A second reason portfolios have generated so much interest, one related to their usefulness in assessing writing ability, is their compatibility with theories of writing as a process and the pedagogical emphasis on teaching strategies of invention, drafting, revising, and editing that has become a common feature of many composition classes. Because in most approaches to classroom-based portfolio evaluation, student writing is not graded until near the end of the course, when it is submitted in the portfolio, teachers can emphasize the importance of continued improvement over the term and can encourage students to continue to rethink and revise pieces of writing begun earlier in the course. No longer are students penalized by receiving low grades on work submitted early in a writing course, before they have had the opportunity to practice and develop new strategies and skills. Nor do instructors face the dilemma of how to evaluate early work that does not reflect the writing ability students will develop during the course [33]. Instead, portfolios allow instructors and students to concentrate on improvement, uninfluenced by grades on individual papers—avoiding both the discouragement that low grades can lead to and the complacency that sometimes comes when students are satisfied with the grades they receive. Further, portfolios allow instructors to shift the focus of their responses to student writing in progress and away from summative commentary, which tends to treat a text as a completed product, highlighting its strengths and weakness and to some extent justifying the grade assigned it. Instead, portfolios support formative responses, responses that suggest, raise questions, and encourage further thinking and revision. Thus, portfolios allow for an emphasis on the accumulation of writing abilities, an emphasis consistent with our understanding that the development of writing ability occurs gradually.

Common Features of Portfolios

As I said earlier, one of the strengths of portfolios for the assessment of student writing is that they can be developed in response to local contexts and needs—as local as a single classroom, a single course, or a single institution. Hence, I begin this description of some common features of portfolios with the caveat that these features should not be interpreted as "rules" for portfolios. Nevertheless, most approaches to portfolios share these five features: collection, selection, reflection, revision, and evaluation.

Collection is a fundamental aspect of portfolio use. The fact that a portfolio includes multiple samples of writing is a major part of its appeal as an assessment instrument. Writers are not judged by a single piece of writing, so their evaluation is not limited by the various constraints that may be imposed by single writing samples: ability to write a certain genre or discourse type, prior knowledge of or interest in the subject, and so on. Thus, at its simplest, a portfolio might be defined as any collection of work, so a writing portfolio could be a folder or file in which students keep all of the notes, plans, drafts, revisions, and final papers they produce in a course. Such a portfolio might be called a working portfolio, useful, as I will discuss later, as a resource from which more specific portfolios are drawn.

However, portfolios serve teaching and learning better when they are defined not just as collections but as collections of work selected for a specific purpose. For example, the guidelines for the portfolios that students are invited to submit for placement into composition courses at Miami University stipulate that students select one piece of writing that tells a story or describes; one "explanatory, exploratory, or persuasive essay"; a "response to a written text"; and a reflective letter [13]. The intention here is for students to demonstrate their ability to write the kinds of papers that parallel writing assignments they would have at the university—papers that show their preparedness for specific courses at Miami. The selection of materials for a portfolio designed to demonstrate development or growth in writing might be quite different. Students might select, for example, early work that is not as successful as writing they have done more recently in order to demonstrate how they have learned to address particular difficulties or how they have developed more sophistication and skill. Institutions with writing across the curriculum programs might determine that they would like students to develop portfolios that demonstrate their ability to write for a variety of academic disciplines. As these examples suggest, the criteria of what should be in a portfolio will not only differ according to its purpose but may also be determined in part by someone other than the writer—by administrators developing a placement procedure, by an instructor wanting to evaluate students' development in writing, and so on.

Reflection is a third feature of most portfolios, one that many portfolio advocates argue is vital [16; 42]. Since it is certainly a goal of writing courses not only to help students become better writers but also to help them become more independent and confident writers (in the sense that they are able to assess whether or not they are doing a good job with a writing assignment), a student's ability to reflect on what he or she has accomplished in a collection of work is both relevant to the assessment of a portfolio and reflective of the student as writer. A typical kind of reflection is a letter of the kind required by Miami University. In it, students are asked to evaluate their work, perhaps in terms of the content of the portfolio itself or perhaps in terms of how the pieces in the portfolio reflect their accomplishments or growth as writers [see also descriptions of reflective writing in 17; 19; 25]. While the ability of students to assess their own work is certainly a valuable aspect of their learning, several scholars have pointed out that the reflective writing that usually introduces a portfolio may have an undue influence on those evaluating the portfolio [11; 30]. In a recent piece, I have discussed the "schmooze" factor, similar to the "glow" effect discussed by Sommers et al. [30]. "Glow" refers to the positive effect a single piece of writing in a portfolio may have on the overall rating of that portfolio, and Sommers and colleagues use as an example a reflective letter that ends like this:

> Over the past few years, I've developed new attitudes toward writing, enjoying it rather than dreading it, and viewing each piece not as one completed but as a work-in-progress. There is always a more appropriate word (most often, the one that awakens me out of a sound sleep at 4 a.m. the day after the deadline), a better phrase, room for improvement. I find this stimulating, not frustrating.

"Schmooze," as I've explained elsewhere [34], "is the often indistinguishable evil twin of 'glow,' the telling-the-teacher-what-she-wants-to-hear that students may very well write in their reflective letters to set the stage for a positive evaluation." "Glow" and "schmooze" aside, the goal of encouraging students to reflect on their writing remains, and should remain, an integral part of any portfolio system. And reflective letters or portfolio introductions are not the only way in which portfolios encourage reflection. Selecting the pieces to be included in a portfolio is a reflective act, though one that may not yield any written traces. And the decisions that underlie the next feature of portfolios I'll discuss, revision, are also reflections.

As the earlier discussion of the relationship between process pedagogy and portfolio evaluation suggests, the success with which students are able to revise their writing is often considered when portfolios are evaluated. Students may be asked to include the earlier drafts of one or more of the papers or to reflect on the changes they made as they reconsidered and revised their work. However, not all portfolios demonstrate revision; that is, not all portfolios require that earlier drafts of papers be included. Similarly, not all pieces in a portfolio need to be revisions of earlier work. Portfolios may contain unrevised pieces of writing such as journal entries or in-class writing (in fact, one piece of in-class writing is sometimes required in portfolios used as part of program or course assessments as a kind of touchstone) [17; 29]. In the case of revision, as in all aspects of developing useful, appropriate portfolios, instructors and administrators need to consider what best suits their purposes for using portfolios.

The final feature of portfolio practice is evaluation. Though I have already mentioned a number of issues related to the evaluation of portfolios, I want to emphasize that how portfolios are evaluated and by whom is once more related to the particular context in which they are being used. The criteria for evaluation and the approaches to evaluation must be local, worked out by the particular instructor, faculty, program, department, institution, or agency responsible for the use of the portfolios. Locally developed criteria help lead to evaluation that is valid—that is, evaluation that measures what it intends to—since the people most intimately involved with the evaluation determine how the writing in the portfolios is to be evaluated. This point is made again and again in the portfolio literature, with respect to both positive [17; 28; 32] and negative [8; 12; 26] experiences with portfolios.

Uses and Contexts for Portfolios

As I have suggested, portfolios may be used for a variety of purposes and in a variety of contexts. Classroom teachers may choose to use portfolios rather than to grade individual writing assignments. Such a decision is frequently based on the teacher's belief that to grade individual writing assignments or every writing assignment not only conflicts with the developmental nature of learning but is also inconsistent with a process approach to teaching writing. The teacher may also wish to de-emphasize grades and emphasize progress. Portfolios enable this because since there are no grades on individual papers, stu-

dents must be more attentive to the comments and advice they receive. Writing programs may choose to incorporate portfolio evaluation for similar reasons, as well as for some of the purposes alluded to earlier: to determine placement or proficiency [31], to assess the success of the writing program, to meet institutional assessment requirements. Portfolios are useful for institutions that wish to provide evidence of student learning over time: Students may be required to keep portfolios throughout their enrollment in high school or college. Portfolios have been used in large-scale assessment programs as well, to meet statewide assessment demands. Susan Callahan's "Portfolio Expectations: Possibilities and Limits" [9] provides an excellent overview of the range of contexts and uses for portfolios.

Although much of the preceding discussion has suggested that the major reason for using portfolios is that they provide an approach to evaluating writing that is more consistent both with current assessment theories and practices and with process-based approaches to teaching writing, it is important to mention that portfolios are being used in contexts other than composition classes or in writing across the curriculum programs. In particular, and also relevant to writing program administrators and postsecondary writing teachers, is the rich literature on teaching and teacher portfolios. In a teaching portfolio, teachers select, and reflect on materials that demonstrate their approaches to teaching. Such portfolios may include teaching philosophies, course descriptions and syllabi, original teaching materials, and teaching evaluations. Like student portfolios, teaching portfolios allow their creators to represent themselves, perhaps for the purpose of obtaining a new teaching position or in place of other kinds of evaluation [1; 14]. Equally interesting is the increased use of teacher portfolios—portfolios put together by prospective teachers to serve as both indications of what they are learning about teaching and as resources to draw from as they begin to teach. Such portfolios encourage prospective teachers to see themselves as practitioners, often prior to their initial teaching experiences. Though most of the work with teacher portfolios has focused on people preparing to teach secondary school, it has clear applications for the preparation of new teachers of college writing as well [7; 37; 39; 44].

Implementing Portfolios: Some Cautionary Words

By now it has become clear that there is no single model for portfolios. Rather, to be effective, portfolios must be developed in response to specific teaching and assessment goals. It is even possible that students (and teachers) will keep more than one type of portfolio. For example, the working portfolio mentioned earlier may be a repository of notes, drafts, and revisions, with little selection guiding what it holds. What might be called a showcase portfolio might consist of a collection of finished works selected for a specific purpose to represent specific achievements or abilities. Such a portfolio is dynamic, changing for the occasion, analogous to the portfolio an artist or architect might assemble to demonstrate either a range of abilities or a particular focus on accomplishments. Assessment portfolios used, as discussed earlier, to demonstrate development or proficiency or to determine placement are often drawn from larger working portfolios. Thus, a first consideration for people planning to use portfolios in their classes, programs, or institutions is the kinds of portfolios they want students to develop, since the purpose of the portfolio will determine what it contains.

A second consideration for classroom teachers is how to deal with gradelessness. Students and teachers alike are used to grades. Often, grades motivate students when learning doesn't, and some students may be extremely nervous about not knowing where they stand. As teachers, we find it convenient to rely on a grade to send students clear messages about the quality of their work. Several strategies may help address gradelessness. First, when students are introduced to portfolios in a classroom, it is important to stress the benefit that students are not being graded before they have had the opportunity to learn. This is particularly true in courses in which students are introduced to and practice writing strategies gradually throughout the course and is certainly one reason portfolios are especially appropriate in basic writing courses [33]. Second, it helps alleviate students' anxiety about grades to offer them opportunities to receive a tentative grade: Many instructors tell students that at any time during the course, they may request a tentative grade on one assignment, though the grade is nonbinding and not recorded. Another strategy is to confer with students midway through the course to talk about their progress so far and to tell them what their midterm grade would be, were the instructor required to give one. Such conferences also provide opportunities to talk with students about what they need to do to improve. Some instructors use dual portfolios, one that is submitted and graded at midterm and one that is graded at the end of the course. Such an approach is particularly appropriate if students do receive midterm grades or if the course material divides itself logically—for example, in a course that emphasizes personal writing for half the term and argument for the second. Third, students need very specific feedback

on their work when it is not accompanied by a grade. Comments need to point to specific strengths and weaknesses. Instructors who typically rely on positive comments to encourage students, knowing that they will be tempered by the accompanying grade, may find themselves having to find a more accurate—and perhaps more blunt—vocabulary for assessing students' work. Fourth, it is important that students know how much of their grade is determined by the portfolio and how much is determined by other factors such as examinations, attendance, participation, and assignments that do not contribute to the portfolio.

A third consideration in implementing portfolios is explaining to students—and reminding them about—what the portfolio will contain, what format requirements they must meet, and other prerequisites. Students need to know at the outset of the course that they have to collect, select, revise, and reflect according to a specific set of expectations. They also need to be reminded about the content and format of the portfolio a week or two prior to its submission.

Fourth, teachers, program administrators, and others responsible for implementing a portfolio evaluation system must consider how to best handle the evaluation of the portfolios. There is no consensus about whether portfolios add huge amounts of time to teachers' work or not, but it's fair to say that whether they do or not, a stack of portfolios to be evaluated is daunting. Often, instructors collect portfolios a week or two before the end of the term to give themselves extra time to read and evaluate them. During those last weeks, students work on a final project that is graded separately. And although it takes time to read and evaluate portfolios, it is also true that instructors typically spend less time marking and commenting on the work, since students will not have the opportunity to revise and resubmit it. The more time-consuming commenting will have taken place earlier in the term. Some different evaluation concerns come into play when portfolios are read and evaluated by people other than or in addition to the classroom instructor. Much of the literature on portfolio evaluation for program and institutional contexts raises issues that parallel those for any large-scale evaluation of writing: collecting sample portfolios, both for developing scoring guidelines and for training raters (this is especially important for establishing reliability among raters); making decisions about cutoff points for passing and for demonstrating proficiency and specific skills; and deciding how to reconcile diverse evaluations of the same portfolio and how and if the portfolio evaluation relates to grades students receive in writing courses or credit they are awarded for courses they are not required to take. Discussions of some of these issues and descriptions of implementing large-scale portfolio assessments can be found elsewhere [3; 5; 9; 10; 17; 20; 22; 26; 36; 38].

Some Concluding Thoughts

Portfolios offer teachers, writing program administrators, and others responsible for the teaching and evaluation of writing many advantages over more traditional approaches. As I've indicated in this essay, portfolio assessment meets many of the criteria for valid, reliable, authentic assessment advocated by teachers of writing and assessment specialists. In particular, portfolios allow for assessment that is more consistent with theories about how people compose and how people learn to write than indirect tests of writing or single-writing sample assessments are. They allow students to represent their abilities with multiple samples of their work and to serve, through their reflective writing, as advocates for what their writing demonstrates about them as writers and thinkers. In classroom settings, portfolios allow instructors to de-emphasize grades and emphasize improvement in writing. Portfolios may even create more student-centered classes if students make decisions about which pieces of writing to include in their portfolios and participate in developing the criteria by which their work is evaluated. But portfolios, despite their many advantages, are not appropriate for every assessment of writing, nor are they without problems of their own. Some of the latter I have mentioned: the influence of "glow" and "schmooze," the anxiety some students (and some instructors) may feel about not using grades as easy touchstones for performance, the sometimes daunting amount of work and time required to read large numbers of portfolios. In addition, when portfolio evaluation is imposed on teachers, writing programs, or institutions, portfolios lose the local, contextualized features that lend them much of their validity [9; 16; 17; 23; 26; 27]. Kathleen Yancey, among the strongest proponents of portfolios for a variety of purposes, cautions that portfolios may not be appropriate for new teachers of writing if the conditions for introducing these teachers to portfolio practices are not right [41]. Nevertheless, the value of portfolios appears to outweigh their limitations and potential problems. Fortunately, anyone planning to begin using portfolios to evaluate writing can benefit from the experience of teachers, scholars, and assessment experts who have used, studied, and written about them. The books and articles in the bibliography are but a sampling of the wealth of information available.

Annotated Bibliography and Suggested Readings

1. Anson, Chris M. "Portfolios for Teachers: Writing Our Way to Reflective Practice." *New Directions in Portfolio Assessment: Reflective Practice, Critical Theory, and Large-Scale Scoring.* Ed. Laurel Black, Donald A. Daiker, Jeffrey Sommers, and Gail Stygall. Portsmouth, NH: Boynton/Cook-Heinemann, 1994. 185–200.
   Describes teaching portfolios and discusses how they contribute to teachers' development as writers, scholars, and professionals. Anson argues that teaching portfolios must be adapted to the specific contexts of their use and offers insights into what he refers to as "the problem of assessment."

2. Belanoff, Pat, and Marcia Dickson, eds. *Portfolios: Process and Product.* Portsmouth, NH: Boynton/Cook-Heinemann, 1991.
   Twenty-three chapters, on a variety of applications of portfolios, organized into four sections: portfolios for proficiency testing, program assessment, classroom portfolios, and political issues.

3. Bishop, Wendy. "Going up the Creek Without a Canoe: Using Portfolios to Train New Teachers of College Writing." *Portfolios: Process and Product.* Ed. Pat Belanoff and Marcia Dickson. Portsmouth, NH: Boynton/Cook-Heinemann, 1991. 215–27.
   A detailed discussion of procedures followed and lessons learned in implementing a portfolio evaluation system as a response to an anticipated proficiency-testing program. Bishop explains how she and the composition director introduced portfolios to new teaching assistants and, quoting from the teaching assistants' teaching journals, provides insights into their reactions to portfolio evaluation.

4. Black, Laurel, Donald A. Daiker, Jeffrey Sommers, and Gail Stygall, eds. *New Directions in Portfolio Assessment: Reflective Practice, Critical Theory, and Large-Scale Scoring.* Portsmouth, NH: Boynton/Cook Heinemann, 1994.
   Twenty-six chapters, each based on a paper delivered at the 1992 Miami University conference "New Directions in Portfolio Assessment."

5. Black, Laurel, Edwina Helton, and Jeffrey Sommers. "Connecting Current Research on Authentic and Performance Assessment Through Portfolios." *Assessing Writing* 1 (1994): 247–66.
   Discusses three alternative approaches to traditional assessment—authentic assessment, performance assessment, and portfolio assessment—and the connections among them.

6. Borrowman, Shane. "The Trinity of Portfolio Placement: Validity, Reliability, and Curriculum Reform." *WPA: Writing Program Administration* 23.1–2 (1999): 7–19.
   Describes the portfolio placement system used at the University of Arizona, including the unique partnership between the university and high schools since both university and high school faculty score the portfolios.

7. Burch, C. Beth. "Finding Out What's in Their Heads: Using Teaching Portfolios to Assess English Education Students—and Programs." *Situating Portfolios: Four Perspectives.* Ed. Kathleen Blake Yancey and Irwin Weiser. Logan: Utah State UP, 1997. 263–77.

Describes the use of portfolios in a Teaching Secondary English methods class. Burch discusses her ethnographic study of the documents comprising the portfolios, the reflective pieces introducing them, and other documents in an attempt to learn "what my preservice students as a whole know about English and how they conceptualized the discipline" (264).

8. Callahan, Susan. "All Done with the Best of Intentions: One Kentucky High School After Six Years of State Portfolio Tests." *Assessing Writing* 6.1 (1999): 5–40.

Using the portfolios mandated by the state of Kentucky as part of a larger school reform movement as her example, points out the problems of top-down mandated portfolio assessment, particularly when the assessment program does not involve teachers from the outset. A follow-up of earlier work by Callahan.

9. _____. "Portfolio Expectations: Possibilities and Limits." *Assessing Writing* 2 (1995): 117–52.

A concise yet thorough history of writing portfolios that includes a discussion of the important differences between portfolios designed for instructional purposes and those designed for testing.

10. Condon, William, and Liz Hamp-Lyons. "Introducing a Portfolio-Based Writing Assessment: Progress Through Problems." *Portfolios: Process and Product*. Ed. Pat Belanoff and Marcia Dickson. Portsmouth, NH: Boynton/Cook-Heinemann, 1991. 231–47.

Traces the evolution at the University of Michigan from a timed, impromptu exit essay to a portfolio-based exit assessment. The authors describe the decisions underlying the change and the obstacles they encountered and reflect on the first two years of the portfolio assessment.

11. Conway, Glenda. "Portfolio Cover Letters, Students' Self-Presentation, and Teachers' Ethics." *New Directions in Portfolio Assessment: Reflective Practice, Critical Theory, and Large-Scale Scoring*. Ed. Laurel Black, Donald A. Daiker, Jeffrey Sommers, and Gail Stygall. Portsmouth, NH: Boynton/Cook-Heinemann, 1994. 83–92.

Addresses the rhetorical power of reflective cover letters that introduce portfolios. Conway acknowledges that although such letters may be written merely to fulfill an assignment, they can encourage "students to think substantively about their writing processes" (92). She cautions, however, against using the cover letter as the only reflection of the semester's work, arguing that required reflection must be an ongoing part of the course.

12. Coulter, Lauren Sewell. "Lean, Mean Grading Machines? A Bourdieuian Reading of Novice Instructors in a Portfolio-Based Writing Program." *WPA: Writing Program Administration* 23.3 (2000): 33–49.

An ethnographic study of the influence, often negative, of experienced teaching-assistant evaluators of portfolios on novice evaluators. Coulter discusses how instructors' lack of commitment to the goals of portfolio assessment can weaken the effectiveness of this approach.

13. Daiker, Donald A., Jeffrey Sommers, and Gail Stygall. "The Pedagogical Implications of a College Placement Portfolio." *Assessment of Writing: Politics, Policies, Practices*. Ed. Edward M. White, William D. Lutz, and Sandra Kamusikiri. New York: MLA, 1996. 257–70.

Covers a wide range of issues concerning portfolio use while discussing the placement portfolios used at Miami University. Among the topics covered are the effects of these portfolios on high school writing programs in Ohio, the teaching of revision, self-assessment, and gender.

14. Edgerton, Russell, Patricia Hutchings, and Kathleen Quinlan. *The Teaching Portfolio: Capturing the Scholarship in Teaching*. Washington, DC: American Association of Higher Education, 1991.

A detailed discussion of and argument for the use of teaching portfolios. The authors argue that teaching portfolios enable teachers to represent the often overlooked scholarship that underlies their teaching.

15. Elbow, Peter. Foreword. *Portfolios: Process and Product*. Ed. Pat Belanoff and Marcia Dickson. Portsmouth, NH: Boynton/Cook-Heinemann, 1991. ix–xvi.

Reflects on the increasing attractiveness of portfolios as assessment instruments, arguing that a major advantage of portfolios to other kinds of writing assessment is the increased validity achieved by using multiple writing samples. Elbow also suggests that portfolios create an inevitable and healthy tension between validity and reliability, a claim disputed by other assessment experts such as White [36].

16. _____. "Will the Virtues of Portfolios Blind Us to Their Potential Dangers?" *New Directions in Portfolio Assessment: Reflective Practice, Critical Theory, and Large-Scale Scoring*. Ed. Laurel Black, Donald A. Daiker, Jeffrey Sommers, and Gail Stygall. Portsmouth, NH: Boynton/Cook-Heinemann, 1994. 40–55.

Keynote address at the 1992 Miami University conference on portfolios; Elbow argues for the value of portfolios but also suggests some potential problems portfolios may produce, including an overemphasis on evaluation.

17. Elbow, Peter, and Pat Belanoff. "State University of New York at Stony Brook Portfolio-Based Evaluation Program." *Portfolios: Process and Product*. Ed. Pat Belanoff and Marcia Dickson. Portsmouth, NH: Boynton/Cook-Heinemann, 1991. 3–16.

Details one of the earliest portfolio evaluation systems used as a substitute for an exit examination. Description covers portfolio contents, how portfolios are evaluated, and how the system may contribute to the development of a teaching community.

18. Ford, James E., and Gregory Larkin. "The Portfolio System: An End to Backsliding Writing Standards." *College English* 39 (1978): 950–55.

One of the earliest pieces published on portfolios.

19. Gay, Pamela. "A Portfolio Approach to Teaching a Biology-Linked Basic Writing Class." *Portfolios: Process and Product*. Ed. Pat Belanoff and Marcia Dickson. Portsmouth, NH: Boynton/Cook-Heinemann, 1991. 182–93.

Describes use of portfolios in a summer EOP program for non-Anglo urban basic writers. Gay argues that portfolios support her goals of encouraging basic writers to think of themselves as developing writers.

20. Hamp-Lyons, Liz, and William Condon. *Assessing the Portfolio: Principles for Practice, Theory, and Research.* Cresskill, NJ: Hampton: 2000.

    The most recent full-length examination of portfolio practice. Hamp-Lyons and Condon not only discuss the history of portfolio-based writing assessment, but also raise questions about the kinds of research that are likely to accompany the continuing interest in portfolio in the evaluation of writing.

21. Hoger, Elizabeth A. "A Portfolio Assignment for Analyzing Business Communications." *Business Communication Quarterly* 61.3 (1998): 64–66.

    Describes how a portfolio project in a business communications class contributes to students' development of critical-thinking and writing skills.

22. Huot, Brian. "Beyond the Classroom: Using Portfolios to Assess Writing." *New Directions in Portfolio Assessment: Reflective Practice, Critical Theory, and Large-Scale Scoring.* Ed. Laurel Black, Donald A. Daiker, Jeffrey Sommers, and Gail Stygall. Portsmouth, NH: Boynton/Cook-Heinemann, 1994. 325–33.

    Calls for a systematic examination of writing portfolios as tools for writing assessment beyond the classroom; in the early 1990s, much of the support for their use was based either on classroom applications or on anecdotal reports.

23. Huot, Brian, and Michael M. Williamson. "Rethinking Portfolios for Evaluating Writing: Issues of Assessment and Power." *Situating Portfolios: Four Perspectives.* Ed. Kathleen Blake Yancey and Irwin Weiser. Logan: Utah State UP, 1997. 43–56.

    Focuses on the power relationships in assessment as they apply to portfolios, particularly in large-scale, non-classroom-based contexts.

24. Kahtani, Saad Al. "Electronic Portfolios in ESL Writing: An Alternative Approach." *Computer-Assisted Language Learning* 12.3 (1999): 261–68.

    Discusses key aspects of World Wide Web–based electronic writing portfolios used by students of English as a Second Language.

25. Mullin, Joan A. "Portfolios: Purposeful Collections of Student Work." *New Directions in Teaching and Learning* 74 (Summer 1998): 79–87.

    Discusses the rhetorical awareness students must demonstrate as they select material for inclusion in their portfolios and the importance of students and teachers mutually understanding the structure, contents, and assessment criteria for the portfolio.

26. Murphy, Sandra. "Teachers and Students: Reclaiming Assess-ment via Portfolios." *Situating Portfolios: Four Perspectives.* Ed. Kathleen Blake Yancey and Irwin Weiser. Utah State UP, 1997. 72–88.

    Referring to several portfolios projects used in California public schools, discusses alternatives to the "teacher as technician," top-down approach to evaluation that well-designed portfolio projects can offer. Emphasizes that portfolio systems that are initiated and developed by teachers and are evaluated by teachers promote teacher professionalism. Also addresses the contribution portfolios can make to students' development as independent learners.

27. Murphy, Sandra, and Barbara Grant. "Portfolio Approaches to Assessment: Breakthrough or More of the Same?" *Assessment of Writing: Politics, Policies, Practices.* Ed. Edward M. White, William D. Lutz, and Sandra Kamusikiri. New York: MLA, 1996. 284–300.

    Discusses two perspectives on assessment: positivist and constructivist. The first leads to standardized, top-down assessments, whereas the second promotes collaborative, contextualized assessment. The authors offer suggestions for developing and using portfolios in ways consistent with constructivist assessment.

28. Rosenberg, Roberta. "Using the Portfolio to Meet State-Mandated Assessment: A Case Study." *Portfolios: Process and Product.* Ed. Pat Belanoff and Marcia Dickson. Portsmouth, NH: Boynton/Cook-Heinemann, 1991. 69–79.

    Describes the portfolio system used at Christopher Newport College to meet Virginia's state mandated assessment. Rosenberg points out that portfolios can be "good alternatives to standardized tests that may not reflect the goals or curriculum" (77).

29. Smit, David, Patricia Kolonosky, and Kathryn Seltzer. "Implementing a Portfolio System." *Portfolios: Process and Product.* Ed. Pat Belanoff and Marcia Dickson. Portsmouth, NH: Boynton/Cook-Heinemann, 1991. 46–56.

    A detailed description of the implementation of a portfolio system designed to establish more uniform grading standards at Kansas State University.

30. Sommers, Jeffrey, Laurel Black, Donald A. Daiker, and Gail Stygall. "The Challenge of Rating Portfolios: What WPAs Can Expect." *WPA: Writing Program Administration* 17 (1993): 7–29.

    Focuses on the scoring of portfolios, based on the authors' experience with the Miami University placement portfolio project. They address two main issues: reliability in scoring portfolios versus single essays and challenges in redefining holistic scoring for use in rating portfolios.

31. Thaiss, Christopher, and Terri Myers Zawicki. "How Portfolios for Proficiency Help Shape A WAC Program." *Assessing Writing Across the Curriculum: Diverse Approaches and Practices.* Ed. Kathleen Blake Yancey and Brian Huot. Greenwich, CT: Ablex, 1997. 79–96.

    Discusses the dual role of WAC portfolios in providing both indirect assessment of students' writing ability and professional development for faculty in the WAC program.

32. Wauters, Joan K. "Evaluation for Empowerment: A Portfolio Proposal for Alaska." *Portfolios: Process and Product.* Ed. Pat Belanoff and Marcia Dickson. Portsmouth, NH: Boynton/ Cook-Heinemann, 1991. 57–68.

    Describes how the decision was made at the University of Alaska Southeast to develop a portfolio system to address calls for assessment and accountability. Discusses the development of the assessment goals, the pilot projects, faculty training, and future plans.

33. Weiser, Irwin. "Portfolio Practice and Assessment for Collegiate Basic Writers." *Portfolios in the Writing Classroom: An Introduction.* Ed. Kathleen Blake Yancey. Urbana, IL: NCTE, 1992. 89–101.

    Argues for the appropriateness of portfolio assessment for basic writing students and describes the approach to portfolio system implemented at Purdue University in the early 1980s. Addresses advantages to students and teachers of using portfolios as well as potential problems.

34. _____. "Revising Our Practices: How Portfolios Help Teachers Learn." *Situating Portfolios: Four Perspectives.* Ed. Kathleen Blake Yancey and Irwin Weiser. Logan: Utah State UP, 1997. 293–301.

Argues that portfolios can play an important part in the preparation of new teachers of writing. Explains how portfolios can encourage reflective practice for new teachers and can help them learn to comment effectively on student writing.

35. _____. "Self-Assessment, Reflection, and the New Teacher of Writing." *Self-Assessment and Development in Writing.* Ed. Jane Bowman Smith and Kathleen Blake Yancey. Cresskill, NJ: Hampton, 2000. 139–56.

Discusses the role of teaching portfolios in a comprehensive program to encourage new teachers of writing to become evaluators of their own growth as teachers.

36. White, Edward M. "Portfolios as an Assessment Concept." *New Directions in Portfolio Assessment: Reflective Practice, Critical Theory, and Large-Scale Scoring.* Ed. Laurel Black, Donald A. Daiker, Jeffrey Sommers, and Gail Stygall. Portsmouth, NH: Boynton/Cook-Heinemann, 1994. 25–39.

Addresses some of the benefits and problems of portfolios as assessment instruments. White makes the case for the value of portfolios as direct measures of a broad range of student writing abilities. He also discusses problems of validity and reliability in writing assessment.

37. White, Edward M., William D. Lutz, and Sandra Kamusikiri, eds. *Assessment of Writing: Politics, Policies, Practices.* New York: MLA, 1996.

Twenty-one essays on a range of issues surrounding the assessment of writing, including three chapters that focus specifically on portfolios.

38. Willard-Traub, Margaret, Emily Decker, Rebecca Reed, and Jerome Johnson. "The Development of Large-Scale Portfolio Placement Assessment at the University of Michigan: 1992–1998. *Assessing Writing* 6.1 (1999): 41–84.

Describe the development of one of the largest and most respected university portfolio placement programs, the efforts to refine and improve that program, and the institutional politics that led to the program being cancelled.

39. Yagelski, Robert P. "Portfolios as a Way to Encourage Reflective Practice Among Preservice English Teachers." *Situating Portfolios: Four Perspectives.* Ed. Kathleen Blake Yancey and Irwin Weiser. Logan: Utah State UP, 1997. 225–44.

Describes a portfolio system developed by a team of university and high school teachers of English to encourage preservice English teachers to engage in self-assessment and reflection.

40. Yancey, Kathleen Blake. "Looking Back as We Look Forward: Historicizing Writing Assessment." *College Composition and Communication* 50.3 (1999): 483–503.

In examining the modern history of writing assessment, Yancey presents portfolios as a "third wave" method of assessing writing, following objective testing and holistic scoring.

41. _____. "Make Haste Slowly: Graduate Teaching Assistants and Portfolios." *New Directions in Portfolio Assessment: Reflective Practice, Critical Theory, and Large-Scale Scoring.* Ed. Laurel Black, Donald A. Daiker, Jeffrey Sommers, and Gail Stygall. Portsmouth, NH: Boynton/Cook-Heinemann, 1994. 210–18.

Acknowledges that carefully designed portfolio systems can be beneficial to new teachers of writing but suggests that it might be beneficial to new teachers to wait until they have some experience in the classroom before they adopt a portfolio system.

42. _____. "Portfolios in the Writing Classroom: A Final Reflection." *Portfolios in the Writing Classroom: An Introduction.* Ed. Kathleen Blake Yancey. Urbana, IL: NCTE, 1992. 102–16.

Provides an overview of the state of portfolio use in 1992, including characteristics of portfolios and various contexts in which they are used. Also raises questions about the future of portfolio assessment.

43. _____, ed. *Portfolios in the Writing Classroom: An Introduction.* Urbana, IL: NCTE, 1992.

Ten essays by English educators, assessment specialists, college and university faculty, and secondary school teachers, offering an introduction to a variety of portfolio practices in a wide range of educational settings.

44. _____. "Teacher Portfolios: Lessons in Resistance, Readiness, and Reflection." *Situating Portfolios: Four Perspectives.* Ed. Kathleen Blake Yancey and Irwin Weiser. Logan: Utah State UP, 1997, 244–62.

Presents and analyzes excerpts from students' portfolios, showing how to encourage students to reflect on what it means to be a teacher through elements designed to demonstrate concepts they have learned, applications of those concepts, development, and critical self-reflection.

45. Yancey, Kathleen Blake, and Irwin Weiser, eds. *Situating Portfolios: Four Perspectives.* Logan: Utah State UP, 1997.

Twenty-four chapters by teachers from elementary schools through universities and by scholars and researchers who specialize in writing assessment. Of special interest are five essays discussing portfolios.

WRITING ACROSS THE CURRICULUM: AN OVERVIEW AND UPDATE

Margot Soven

Writing across the curriculum (WAC) has just celebrated its twenty-fifth anniversary. As an educational "happening," WAC has had remarkable staying power. Despite ominous predictions about its impending demise, in an era when educators at all levels are struggling to do more with less, when demands for accountability threaten many programs, WAC survives. In the 1970s, WAC enjoyed funding from outside sources, such as the National Endowment for the Humanities. In the 1980s, as public funding was channeled in new directions, many schools took on the challenge of paying for WAC-related activities, such as faculty workshops and peer tutoring programs. As we begin the new century, the financial demands on schools at all levels grow even greater. WAC must compete for funding with plans to implement educational technology, new programs such as service learning, and ESL.

The reason for WAC's continued survival during this time of downsizing and fiscal constraint is simple. WAC has won over the faculty. They no longer need to be convinced of the importance of writing. WAC has arrived. The principles associated with WAC are now integral to the culture of schooling. Although not all faculty in all disciplines state, as I do in my course descriptions, "Writing is as important as reading in this class," many faculty recognize the importance of writing as a means for facilitating learning and agree that writing is a skill that requires practice in classes other than English if students are to become competent writers. The potential benefits of using writing as a way of learning summarized by Allan Glatthorn in 1983 have been realized in many classrooms [item 12 in the Annotated Bibliography at the end of the essay]:

1. The act of writing enhances knowing: Retrieving information, organizing it, and expressing it in writing seems to improve understanding and retention.
2. Writing is an active learning process, and active learning seems to be more effective than passive reception.
3. Writing is a way of making knowledge personal. The writer brings to bear a subjective point of view and reinterprets personally what has been learned.
4. Writing focuses attention: Students who know they are expected to write tend to be more attentive.

Margot Soven is Professor of English at La Salle University. She holds a doctorate with a specialization in the teaching of writing from the University of Pennsylvania. At La Salle, she is codirector of the Freshman Composition Program and director of the Writing Across the Curriculum Program and the Writing Fellows Program. Her essays and book reviews have appeared in such journals as College Composition and Communication, Journal of the Council of Writing Program Administrators, *and* Journal of Teaching Writing and Freshman English News. *She has written several chapters for texts on the teaching of writing and is the author of* Write to Learn: A Guide to Writing Across the Curriculum (*Southwestern Publishing, 1995) and* Teaching Writing in Middle and Secondary Schools (*Allyn & Bacon, 1999). She is coeditor of* Writing Across the Curriculum: A Guide to Developing Programs (*Sage Press, 1992) and* Writings from the Workplace (*Allyn & Bacon, 1995).*

5. Writing seems to facilitate thinking about a subject. The act of writing enables the writer to discern new relationships and make new connections.
6. Writing is a way of sharing what is known. Students can use writing to share with classmates what they have learned.
7. Writing provides immediate feedback to the learner and to the teacher about what has been learned and what has not been learned.
8. Writing is a self-paced mode of learning; the pace of writing seems to match the pace of learning better, slowing down the process of students who might be inclined to finish a learning task too quickly.
9. Each discipline has its own way of knowing and its own modes of communicating knowledge; students should have a broad knowledge of how writing is used in several disciplines. For example, a scientist reporting the results of a scientific experiment uses objective language to communicate results; a literary critic evaluating a novel writes using more subjective language to discuss reactions.

"Writing to learn" is no longer controversial on many campuses. Furthermore, whereas in the past, faculty might try to avoid the unpleasant experience of reading poorly written papers by not assigning writing, today more of them give writing assignments and help their students write better papers by reading drafts and encouraging revision. The attitudes expressed by the four professors from four disciplines (psychology, sociology, philosophy, and health and physical education) who participated in "Interchange: A Conversation Among the Disciplines" are typical of faculty in schools that have WAC programs [1]:

> Recognizing the value of personalized writing as a first stage to professional writing, enhancing communication between teacher and student, structuring the process for developing clear, organized thinking on paper, and providing a venue for self-expression, these seem to be the major reason why the four of us incorporate WAC in our classrooms.

Writing Across the Curriculum: Research and New Directions

Today, WAC faces a threefold challenge: to continue to provide faculty with the latest and best research on writing in the disciplines, to translate that research into teaching practices, and to demonstrate how writing can be used to support the goals of new programs and new curricula in the university. New directions in theory, research, and methodology will help us meet these goals. In addition, WAC must incorporate the new technologies for writing and research available to the campus community. For example, e-mail and the World Wide Web are rapidly becoming a part of the writing culture in the academy. Students are e-mailing drafts of their formal papers and daily journal entries to their classmates and instructors. Laura Mandell explains how e-mail has transformed the dynamics of her classroom [19]. "Screen conversations" seem especially liberating for students who lack confidence in their discussion and writing skills.

Writing in the Disciplines and Writing Assignments

Studies on the nature of writing in different disciplines grow more numerous. Many studies examine the relation between writing and specific disciplines [15; 16; 22]. Some studies, such as Hedley and Parker's [14], focus on the similarities of the writing assignments in various courses. Their research suggests that at four-year liberal arts colleges, the kinds of papers students write for different courses are strikingly similar. They argue that college teachers should stress generic skills such as "inquiry" rather than the discourse conventions of different disciplines. Other studies, such as Langer's [17], point out that teachers' different responses to writing in different disciplines reflect significant differences in the way they view writing. In Langer's study, the science teachers' concerns about presentation were quite different from the English teachers' concerns. Langer states: "Instead of encouraging students to formulate their own understanding and structure their explanations, [the science teacher] sees good writing (in this instance) as the ability to select relevant information from lab notes and place it in the proper category, according to his instructions."

As we develop a better understanding of the kinds of writing instructors see as valuable to their students, we are better able to devise clear guidelines for writing assignments. An assignment often fails because the instructions for the assignment are misleading. Walvoord and McCarthy's study of writing in a business course makes this point [22]. After exploring how students' difficulties with an assignment were related to the teachers' methods and students' strategies, Walvoord and McCarthy concluded that one of the most important changes the teacher could make in his strategies would be to "clarify his assignment sheet." Peer tutors in writing at my own institution report that a lot of writing problems are related to misunderstanding the assignment. After reviewing the drafts of many students in one class, they commented that most of the papers were missing at least one piece of the assignment. Their observations are not surprising in view of Langer's observation that "the overwhelming characteristic of teachers' discussions about the thinking patterns and conventions in the writing in their disciplines was their inexplicitness."

Faculty interested in improving assignment guidelines can turn to an increasing number of textbooks on writing in the disciplines. These texts include descriptions of both assignments common to many disciplines and assignments that are discipline-specific. Many of these books are designed for freshman composition courses. For example, *The Informed Writer: Using Sources in the Disciplines* has four parts: "Writing About Reading," "Writing Using Reading," "Writing in the Disciplines" and "The Craft of Writing" [3]. *Writing and Reading Across the Curriculum* introduces students to the skills necessary for all academic writing: summary, analysis, synthesis, and critique [4]. Other books are intended for courses in the disciplines [5; 6, 7]. My own text, *Write to Learn: A Guide to Writing Across the Curriculum,* provides checklists for evaluating writing and model assignments developed by La Salle University faculty in a variety of departments [20]. A list of these textbooks appears in *Writing Across the Curriculum: An Annotated Bibliography* [2].

WAC research has also focused on nontraditional assignments, appearing with increased frequency across the disciplines. In 1984, Bridgeman and Carlsen found that despite evidence of more creative and expressive forms in elementary grades in American schools, these forms were rare in college [8]. But the situation may be changing. For example, in an introductory class in psychology that included poetry and short story writing as well as more traditional assignments, the teachers concluded that poetic writing can enhance learning in classes other than English and that a mix of poetic and other kinds of writing stimulates exploration and imagination to a greater extent than traditional assignments [13]. They found that writing a poem from the point of view of a schizophrenic person helps students identify with the traumas of a patient who suffers from this mental condition, an important goal for the course.

Toby Fulwiler implemented various kinds of writing assignments to facilitate new goals for his American literature course [11]. He wanted to create a "community of learners" to make "reading and writing more fun" and "avoid training literary critics, but make the study of literature both serious and exciting at the same time." His students wrote journal entries daily "to encourage them to explore personally and react to the readings, essays to shape some of their reactions into finished pieces, and short stories to place themselves in the role of the authors." Fulwiler believes that he accomplished the goals he set for the course with the aid of writing.

At my own institution, the use of nontraditional assignments is becoming more widespread. A professor in our religion department who teaches an introductory course in the Bible uses writing to encourage his students to treat the Bible as literature rather than sacred text, a difficult task at a Catholic university. Students write personal response papers expressing their reaction to the Bible as a literary text and journalistic accounts of biblical narratives. A professor in the philosophy department finds that writing letters to their parents about the philosophers they are studying reduces students' apprehension about writing in philosophy.

Also, freshman composition programs are making room for other kinds of writing besides the expository essay. Lovitt and Young challenge the idea that teaching students how to write reports reduces the value of assignments as vehicles for learning [18]. They argue that "dismissing the teaching of reports as inimical to a liberal arts education may ironically disadvantage our students." Students will most likely be required to write reports more frequently than they will be called on to write essays, both in school and at work. Furthermore, they point out that "the teaching of the report can be as intellectually and academically challenging as teaching the essay."

Greater acceptance of nontraditional forms of writing in various disciplines should be no surprise given the findings of a study of the long-term effect of writing across the curriculum on faculty at three institutions. Barbara Walvoord and her colleagues found that the greatest effect experienced by faculty was a change in teaching philosophy, a "realization of how learners need to be involved in learning and of the many roles that writing can play in learning" [21].

WAC and Peer Tutoring Programs

Until the mid-1980s, faculty development workshops were the centerpiece of WAC programs, especially at small and medium-sized institutions. Now, peer tutoring programs not only augment faculty development but add a new and much valued student-centered dimension to WAC. At some Ivy League schools, these are often the mainstay of the WAC program. Peer tutors help teach writing in writing centers and through writing fellows programs, sometimes called curriculum-based peer tutoring programs. At schools that have such programs, the peer tutor is assigned to a specific course and helps all the students in that course with their drafts. Students in these courses learn that everyone can benefit from peer review and that revision is a natural part of the writing process. Peer tutors, to quote Ken Bruffee, "are potentially among the most powerful agents of change" in the university, because they learn the most important tool for effecting change, "the art of translation, the art of conversation at the boundaries of communities" [9]. In a presentation at a conference for peer tutors, Bruffee said, "What you do as a peer tutor, as I understand it, is to help a tutee cross the boundary between one knowledge community and another."

WAC and the Curriculum: Service Learning

Writing has become a means for achieving the objectives of curriculum initiatives such as service learning. An increasing number of schools are adding a service learning requirement, acknowledging the role of the university to create good citizens as well as knowledgeable ones. Students work at government agencies, charitable organizations, or community groups. Sometimes, this requirement is attached to specific courses. At other schools, such as Michigan State University, the service is a part of the composition program. Writing is used to help students integrate academic work with service learning. In some programs, students complete a writing project for the agency in which they are placed. They may produce a "working document" to solve a problem they identify in the agency or develop a brochure or a Web site. They often write reports reflecting about and evaluating their service learning experience.

What Might English Faculty Do?

English teachers are frequently called on to help their colleagues in other disciplines translate the latest research in composition into teaching practices related to writing. It is our task to keep abreast of this research and to use our own classrooms as laboratories for experimenting with new techniques and strategies. Writing across the curriculum is a concept that connects us to our colleagues through a shared interest: teaching our students the value of writing and helping them develop good writing skills.

Annotated Bibliography and Suggested Readings

1. Abbott, Michael M., Pearl W. Bartelt, Stephen Fishman, and Charlotte Honda. "Interchange: A Conversation Among the Disciplines." *Writing and Teaching in the Disciplines.* Ed. Anne Herrington and Charles Moran. New York: MLA, 1992.

   Answers to the question "Why do you use writing in your teaching?" by four instructors in different disciplines.

2. Anson, Chris M., John E. Schwiebert, and Michael M. Williamson. *Writing Across the Curriculum: An Annotated Bibliography.* Westport, CT: Greenwood, 1993.

   An annotated bibliography on writing across the curriculum divided into two parts, "Scholarship" and "Pedagogy."

3. Bazerman, Charles. *The Informed Writer: Using Sources in the Disciplines.* 2nd ed. Boston: Houghton, 1985.

   Introduces students to the forms and conventions of writing in the disciplines.

4. Behrens, Laurence, and Leonard J. Rosen. *Writing and Reading Across the Curriculum.* 4th ed. New York: Harper, 1991.

   Introduces to students the skills needed for writing about written texts summary, synthesis, and critique skills. Includes readings representing the perspectives of various disciplines on different topics.

5. Biddle, Arthur W., and Toby Fulwiler. *Reading, Writing, and the Study of Literature.* New York: Random, 1989.

   Addresses the conventions of literary study from the viewpoint of both reading and writing.

6. Biddle, Arthur W., and A. S. Magistrale (with Toby Fulwiler). *Writers Guide: Political Science.* Lexington, MA: Heath, 1987.

   A guide for writing papers in political science.

7. ———. *Writers Guide: Psychology.* Lexington, MA: Heath, 1987.

   A guide for writing papers in psychology.

8. Bridgeman, Brent, and Sybil Carlson. "Survey of Academic Writing Tasks." *Written Communication* 1 (1984): 247–80.

A study to determine the writing tasks faced by beginning and graduate students in 190 academic departments.

9. Bruffee, Kenneth. *Collaborative Learning: Higher Education, Interdependence, and the Authority of Knowledge.* Baltimore: Johns Hopkins UP, 1993.

   Discusses how collaborative learning activities, including peer tutoring, can transform the university.

10. Cooper, David D., and Laura Julier, eds. *Writing in the Public Interest: Service Learning and the Writing Classroom.* East Lansing: Writing Center, Michigan State U, 1995.

    Describes the Service Learning Writing Project at Michigan State University.

11. Fulwiler, Toby. "Writing and Learning in American Literature." *Writing, Teaching, and Learning in the Disciplines.* Ed. Anne Herrington and Charles Moran. New York: MLA, 1992.

    Describes a series of writing assignments in a literature class designed to encourage students to explore personal reactions to readings, to analyze readings, and to place students in the role of authors.

12. Glatthorn, Allan. "A Review of Research, Theory, and Practice." (Unpublished materials.) U of Pennsylvania P, 1983.

13. Gorman, Michael E., and Art Young. "Poetic Writing in Psychology." *Writing across the Disciplines.* Ed. Art Young and Toby Fulwiler. Portsmouth, NH: Boynton/Cook-Heinemann, 1986.

    Concludes that poetry and short story writing can enhance learning in classes other than English.

14. Hedley, Jane, and JoEllen Parker. "Writing Across the Curriculum: The Vantage of the Liberal Arts." *ADE Bulletin* 98 (1991): 22–28.

    Argues that writing assignments should emphasize general inquiry skills associated with academic thinking rather than the learning of specialized discourse conventions.

15. Herrington, Anne, and Charles Moran, eds. *Writing, Teaching, and Learning in the Disciplines.* New York: MLA, 1992.

    A collection of essays on writing in the disciplines grouped in these categories: "Historical Perspectives," "Disciplinary and Predisciplinary Theory," "Teachers' Voices: Reflections on Practice," "Studies in the Classroom," "Disciplinary Values, Discourse Practices, and Teaching," and "Writing in the Disciplines: A Prospect."

16. Jollife, David, ed. Vol. 2 of *Writing in Academic Disciplines.* Norwood, NJ: Ablex, 1988. *Advances in Writing Research.* 2 vols. 1988.

    A collection of essays on theoretical models for research related to WAC and studies on writing in different disciplines.

17. Langer, Judith. "Speaking of Knowing: Conceptions of Understanding in Academic Disciplines." *Writing, Teaching, and Learning in the Disciplines.* Ed. Anne Herrington and Charles Moran. New York: MLA, 1992.

    Explores the relationship between thinking and academic writing in various disciplines.

18. Lovitt, Carl, and Art Young. "Rethinking Genre in the First-Year Composition Course." *Profession 97.* New York: MLA, 1997. 113–26.

    Discusses the value of report writing in the freshman composition class.

19 Mandell, Laura. "Virtual Encounters: Using an Electronic Mailing List in the Literature Classroom." *Profession 97.* New York: MLA, 1997. 126–33.

Demonstrates how e-mail had a transforming effect on the dynamics of communication in a literature classroom.

20. Soven, Margot. *Write to Learn: A Guide to Writing Across the Curriculum.* Cincinnati: Southwestern, 1996.

Includes instructions and models for academic assignments.

21. Walvoord, Barbara E., Linda Lawrence Hunt, H. Fil Dowling Jr., and Joan McMahon. *In the Long Run: A Study of Faculty in Three Writing Across the Curriculum Programs.* Urbana, IL: NCTE, 1997.

Reports the long-term impact on faculty of writing across the curriculum programs.

22. Walvoord, Barbara E., and Lucille P. McCarthy. *Thinking and Writing in College: A Naturalistic Study of Students in Four Disciplines.* Urbana, IL: NCTE, 1991.

Presents the results of research on writing and thinking in four classes (in business, history, psychology and biology) taught by members of the research team. Illustrates a model of collaborative, naturalistic classroom research in a college setting.

Addendum: October 2000

These entries are representative of contributions to WAC scholarship since 1997. Most sources focus on methods of implementing WAC in the classroom. However, two entries examine the changing structure of WAC programs.

23. Dossin, Mary Mortimore. "Writing Across the Curriculum: Lessons from a Writing Teacher." *College Teaching* 45 (1997): 14–15.

Describes methods of communicating with students about error, assignment objectives, and evaluation criteria. Encourages developing writing assignments that support writing objectives.

24. Epstein, Molly Hill. "Teaching Field-Specific Writing: Results of a WAC Survey." *Business Communication Quarterly* 62 (1999): 29–40.

Discusses a faculty survey at Georgia State University College of Business Administration. Faculty reported that students demonstrated their ability to format documents but were less able to select and organize material and write with clarity. Faculty also reported that they lacked the time to teach both writing skills and course content.

25. Flynn, Elizabeth A., Kathryn Remlinger, and William Bulleit. "Interaction Across the Curriculum." *JAC: A Journal of Composition Theory* 17 (1997); 343–64.

Describes an alternative to the two-phase description (Phase I: Expressivist, Phase II: Social Constructionist) of many WAC programs. Suggests the adoption of an "interactional model" similar to the WAC program at Michigan Technical University.

26. Hilgers, Thomas L, Monica Stitt-Bergh, and Edna Lardizabal Hussey. "As You're Writing, You Have These Epiphanies: What College Students Say About Writing and Learning in Their Majors." *Written Communication* 16 (1999): 317–53.

Surveys the attitudes to writing in the disciplines of students enrolled in writing intensive classes in their majors at a large state university. Recommends an increased emphasis on a field's inquiry methods and problem-solving strategies.

27. Males, Terry. "The Dialectical Nature of Writing and Its Implications for Learning Subject Matter Courses." *English Quarterly* 29 (1997): 46–56.

Explains that the dialogical nature of writing helps students learn the subject matter of their courses.

28. McLeod, Susan H., Eric Miraglia, Margot Soven, and Christopher Thaiss. *WAC for the New Millennium: Strategies for/of Continuing WAC Programs.* Urbana, IL: NCTE (forthcoming).

Includes chapters by WAC experts on the role of WAC in the changing university. This text covers a wide range of subjects, including "WAC and Electronic Communication," "WAC and Learning Communities," "WAC and Service Learning," and "WAC and Curriculum-Based Peer Tutoring."

29. Panici, Daniel A., and Kathy B. McKee. "Writing Across the Curriculum with Mass Communication." *Journalism and Mass Communication Educator* 51 (1997): 47–53.

A survey of 2,735 American and Canadian colleges and universities. Findings indicate strong support for WAC in schools with WAC programs.

30. Sargent, Elizabeth M. "Peer Response to Low-Stakes Writing in a WAC Literature Classroom." *New Directions in Teaching and Learning* 69 (1997): 41–52.

Studied the effect of students responding to each other's writing. Findings suggest that peer response to writing improves the learning of course concepts. Guidelines for setting up peer-response groups are included.

31. Sherwood, Donna. "Writing in Chemistry: An Effective Learning Tool." *Journal of Chemical Education* 76 (1999): 1399–1403.

Suggests a systematic approach for using writing in chemistry courses and discusses the results of this approach in large general chemistry courses at the University of Tennessee-Knoxville.

32. Taylor, Katherine. "Writing in Biology: An Integration of Disciplines." *American Biology Teacher* 60 (1998): 350–53.

Applies methods of teaching writing used in composition courses to biology courses. Includes techniques such as planning activities and peer editing,

TEACHING COMPOSITION TO SPEAKERS OF OTHER LANGUAGES

Joy Reid

Even experienced teachers of composition whose students are generally native English speakers may experience discomfort and puzzlement when they find non-native speakers of English (ESL students)° in their classes—even before those ESL students submit their first writing assignment. New or less experienced composition teachers of native English speakers may face those same feelings as they first begin to teach, but *they* usually have the advantage that, at the very least, they have been native English-speaking students before they became teachers. Their experiences as students in U.S. classrooms have prepared them to understand both the expectations of their students and the nonverbal clues that native English speakers (NESs) offer in the classroom: heads nodding, notetaking, raised eyebrows, shifting in seats, shrugged shoulders, and so forth. In contrast, when teachers encounter ESL students, they may have only limited knowledge about and experience with diverse cultures.† The expected protocols for question-asking, teacher-student exchanges, indicating understanding, and even group work that seem so "normal" in a class of NESs may be foreign to ESL students.

When composition teachers encounter the writing of their ESL students, their confusion and irritation may increase. A single ESL student paper may contain word- and sentence-level errors that differ in kind (if not in number or level of severity) from NES errors. In addition, there may be differences in the writer's perceptions of the effective presentation of ideas in an academic setting [item 35 in the Annotated Bibliography at the end of the essay]. These differences between ESL and NES errors and perceptions may well make the ESL errors more visible (i.e., in the words of one

teacher, "They seem to jump off the page") and so seem even more grievous to the teacher-evaluator. This essay discusses several major areas in which the needs of ESL students differ from those of NESs; it also provides information from experienced ESL composition teachers concerning the identification of typical ESL writing problems, and suggests some solutions.

"Ear" Learners and "Eye" Learners

In much the same way that NESs differ in background knowledge, motivation, and perspective, it is important to realize that ESL students are not a homogeneous group. In addition to the clear diversity in language and cultural backgrounds, ESL students in U.S. colleges and universities can also be described in terms of the scenarios in which they acquired their second language. Specifically, most of the "international" (or "visa") students, those students who travel to the United States from their homelands to attend postsecondary institutions, differ from ESL students who have grown up in the United States, who have graduated from U.S. high schools, and/or who may be U.S. residents/citizens.

Students who have studied English as a second language outside the United States and who have entered U.S. postsecondary institutions have, for the most part, acquired English *visually:* they have read and studied about the

---

°To avoid confusion between native English speakers (NESs) and non-native speakers of English (NNSs), students for whom English is not a first language are called English as a Second Language (ESL) students in this essay, although of course, English may be their third or fourth language.

†Larry Samovar and Richard Porter [33] describe culture as the overall system of perceptions and beliefs, values and patterns of thought that direct and constrain a social group, from the way the group uses space to the meaning of widened eyes, and from the way members of the group approach relationships to the ways they view the world. Language—verbal, nonverbal, and written communication—is an integral part of culture.

Joy Reid teaches in the University of Wyoming English Department and coordinates the ESL support program. She has published a three-book ESL composition series: The Process of Composition *(Prentice Hall Regents, 3rd ed., 1998),* The Process of Paragraph Writing *(Prentice Hall Regents, 2nd ed., 1994), and* Basic Writing *(Prentice Hall Regents, 2nd ed., 1996), as well as coedited a four-level writing-grammar series,* Looking Ahead *(Heinle and Heinle, 1998). In addition, she has published teacher resource books:* Teaching ESL Writing *(Prentice Hall Regents, 1993),* Learning Styles in the ESL/EFL Classroom *(ed., Heinle and Heinle, 1995),* Grammar in the Composition Classroom *(with Pat Byrd, Heinle and Heinle, 1998), and* Understanding Learning Styles in the Second Language Classroom *(ed., Prentice Hall Regents, 1998). Her research articles and books on discourse analysis, computers and composition, learning styles, the writing-reading connection, and the change process are published in a variety of journals.*

structures of the language. However, their practice in producing written English has been limited to occasional practice in the classroom. Moreover, because cultures evolve writing styles appropriate to their own histories and the needs of their societies, many international students have assumptions about the presentation of written ideas that are appropriate for their native discourse communities. For a great majority of the students, they have neither articulated nor even considered those assumptions. As Ilona Leki [28] pointed out, not many educational systems appear to teach rhetorical patterns or the use of specific language structures for different communication purposes directly. Indeed, in most countries outside the United States there are virtually no courses in writing. Therefore, many international students have limited awareness of their writing strategies and underdeveloped (if intuitive) rhetorical skills, even in their first languages.

In contrast, U.S. residents (that is, ESL students who have lived and attended secondary schools in the United States) have acquired much of their English through their *ears*. Although they may have had ESL classes alongside their regular public school work, their English has been learned mainly through immersion in the language.° As a result of this aural basis, their spoken language may be fluent and comprehensible, and their writing may appear fluent. However, because these students have limited knowledge of the structures of English, their writing may appear more or less phonetic with limited and perhaps incorrect use of the structures of the language (e.g., correct use of verb tenses, prepositions, and word forms).

This single difference between international and U.S.–resident ESL students—whether they acquired their English principally through their eyes or their ears—bears directly on the strengths and weaknesses these students bring to their writing classes, and significantly affects the ways teachers can approach writing processes with the ESL students in each group.†

° In some cases, the acquisition of these ESL students' first languages may have been similar, particularly if they are refugees who were forced to leave their countries and may have gaps in their schooling: although they speak that language fluently, they may not read or write it fluently.

† Note that ESL students, in actuality, exist along a continuum: from immigrant families whose prior first language education was substantial (and who may have studied ESL as well) to an international student who has never studied English. Variables such as parental attitudes toward education, cultural constraints, and individual student learning styles and strategies also account for variations in student profiles.

Intercultural Communication in the Classroom

Initially, the experience of teaching ESL students may parallel the "blind-random" setting on an exercise "step" machine. At this setting, the rhythm of the stepping slows and speeds up automatically and randomly, and so the stepper is "blind": she does not control when the rhythm will change or in what direction.† Almost certainly the inexperienced teacher of ESL students encounters periods of "randomness," of surprising incidents, time frames and rhythms. Further, because of the cultural differences between the teacher and her students, and among the students themselves, the randomness is frequently not preceded by any clues—it occurs "blindly." The results: frustration and misperceptions for both teachers and students.

At the same time composition teachers are struggling to accommodate ESL student needs, their ESL students may also be struggling to adjust their perceptions to a "foreign" classroom environment; that is, "blind-random" occurs on both sides of the desk. Even ESL students who have attended U.S. public schools and have lived in the U.S. most of their lives carry many of their first-culture values, needs, and expectations into their second-language classrooms. Researchers have shown that cultural differences between (and among) ESL students and their teachers may include how students view teachers and in student attitudes toward teaching and learning [5; 20; 23]. The degree of authority invested in and expected from the teacher, as well as the degree to which the teacher directs and dominates class activities, depends to a large extent on culture. For example, many Asian cultures (both in North American populations and in Asia) have a tradition of deference: questioning a person in authority—a parent, a teacher—is disrespectful, and receptive (as opposed to proactive) learning is the key to success. In a U.S. college composition class, however, such behavior may be seen as inappropriately silent and nonparticipatory [32; 40].

In contrast, the strong cooperative values and high level of social responsibility of many Latin societies (in both North America and South America) make the highly individualized and competitive values of many U.S. students seem unpleasantly aggressive. For the newly arrived international student, the adjustment may be even more jarring: a class in the United States appears as a structureless, anarchical situation for learning. In the United States, composition students are expected to take an active part in the learning process, asking questions, challenging each other and their teachers, working (often

---

† My thanks to my English-teacher daughter, Shelley, for this analogy, gleaned during her first summer as an ESL teacher.

loudly) in small groups with peers they know only slightly. Consequently, many ESL students must identify and practice a variety of unfamiliar learning behaviors. A multicultural class can therefore result in cross-cultural tensions as students and teachers struggle to develop appropriate roles and interactions.

Contrastive Rhetoric and the Composition Teacher

Robert Kaplan first defined contrastive rhetoric when he sought to discover whether organizational patterns of written material vary from culture to culture [24]. In his investigation of 600 student expository paragraphs, written in English by native speakers of many non-English language backgrounds, Kaplan used philosophical, psychological, anthropological, and linguistic insights to describe the differences between the essentially "linear" English paragraph, which does not tolerate digression or repetition, and paragraphs that he classified generally as Semitic, Oriental, Romance, and Russian. Kaplan represented the differences graphically (Figure 3); at the same time he cautioned that "much more detailed and more accurate descriptions are required before any meaningful contrastive system can be elaborated" (12).

Since the appearance of Kaplan's article, the notion of contrastive rhetoric, along with the issues surrounding the transfer of rhetorical patterns in second language writing, has grown into an area of study. Research reported by proponents of this theory demonstrate that the style in which each culture organizes and presents written material reflects the preferences of that particular culture [10, 11; 30]. As a result, ESL writers often have problems with the identifying audience expectations and communicating effectively with different discourse communities. They may intuitively employ a rhetoric and sequence of thought that violate the expectations of the NES reader.

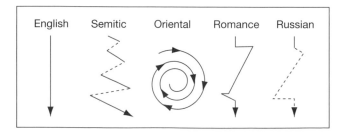

Figure 3   Kaplan's Contrastive Rhetoric Diagram

Even *within* a language, there appear to be different rhetorical rules and conventions that govern different categories of texts. John Swales [37] indicated that in U.S. academic classes, discipline-specific writing conventions differ in such diverse areas as length of sentences, choice of vocabulary, acceptability of using first person, extent of using passive voice, degree to which writers are permitted to interpret, and amount of metaphorical language accepted. The recent development of research in disciplinary differences has extended the meaning of genre from literature to rhetoric. Genre studies by Douglas Biber and his colleagues have provided theoretical background [3; 4], while pedagogical articles offer teachers of NESs as well as ESL writers insights into the rhetorics of U. S. academic disciplines [1; 9; 12; 21]. In addition, William Grabe and Robert Kaplan [17] demonstrated that the ESL writer is also likely to have a different notion of more basic rhetorical principles: what constitutes evidence, the order in which evidence should best be presented, and the amount of evidence needed in order to explain and/or persuade the reader. These substantial knowledge gaps can lead to inappropriate and unsuccessful writing [22; 32].

The Function of Background Information in the Composition Classroom

Successful communication rests on background knowledge and experience that is shared by writers and readers; that is, the prior knowledge of student writers necessarily influences what, and how, they write. Consequently, ESL students can face misunderstanding and even failure in their academic written work not just because of second language errors but also because they are often unaware of the content expectations and of the rhetorical problems in their prose.

Unfortunately, there is no reason to assume that ESL writers will acquire the conventions of written academic English without assistance. Teachers must provide necessary cultural information about the rhetorical organization of U.S. academic expository texts. For ESL writers, the composition course is much more than a skills course; it is also a *content* course in which they learn about academic audience expectations, purposes for writing, levels of content specificity, general writing strategies, and academic formats, perhaps for the first time. In addition, ESL students (and less experienced NES writers as well) need to learn repertoires of strategies to generate ideas, draft pieces of writing, and encounter feedback from peers and teachers. To assist their ESL students toward those goals, composition teachers may well need to be more didactic; certainly they must become cultural informants for their students, by

- identifying and explaining the rhetorical and contextual variables in U.S. academic writing;
- researching U.S. academic writing assignments and the expectations of the discourse communities that design, assign, and evaluate those assignments;
- investigating and discussing the writing conventions of U.S. academic discourse genres (e.g., the summary analysis of written material, the term research paper, the laboratory report, and the case study); and
- providing opportunities for students to practice and experiment with the rhetoric and language that fulfills the expectations of U.S. academic readers.

Note: While rhetorical differences between ESL and NES writers may affect communication in a U.S. academic discourse community, they should not be stigmatized as deficiencies. As Alan Purves and his colleagues reported, differences among rhetorical patterns do not represent differences in cognitive ability but rather differences in cognitive style [30]. After all, arrangement and presentation of ideas, as well as style, can all be defined, practiced, and valued in many ways. However, ESL writers (like NESs) must acquire the appropriate background knowledge necessary to identify and fulfill the expectations of the U.S. academic audience; knowledge about appropriate language use, content, and genre can empower ESL students.

Accuracy, Fluency, and the Issue of Error

Teachers of ESL writers will almost certainly face student essays with linguistic (as well as rhetorical) problems that are related to (a) the first languages of the students and/or (b) "developmental" problems that are the result of student age and writing experience and/or of limitations in students' previous education. Barbara Kroll [25] describes a useful way in which ESL writing proficiency can be broadly divided into categories: *plus-syntax* and *minus-syntax, plus-rhetoric* and *minus-rhetoric.* "One paper can provide insightful commentary on a substantive topic while replete with problems in spelling and punctuation [+ *rhetoric* and − *syntax*]. Another paper can exhibit a wide range of sentence structures, flawless syntax, adherence to mechanics, yet lack development and support of its central thesis [− *rhetoric* and + *syntax*] " (p. 40). Still another paper may be hard to read because it contains both second language errors and a lack of coherence [− *rhetoric* and

− *syntax*]. In terms of the two broad categories of ESL students described in this essay, typical international student ("eye" learner) writing will demonstrate limited coherence and particularly a limited knowledge of academic forms and audience expectations [− *rhetoric*]. In contrast, typical resident student ("ear" learner) writing will often demonstrate some knowledge of expected U.S. rhetorical forms and fluency but may also contain many language errors [− *syntax*].

The perceived dichotomy between fluency and accuracy has been discussed in language teaching for decades: Should the language teacher concentrate on one or the other? Traditionally, accuracy has been defined as the focus on discrete elements of the rules of language, while fluency has been defined as the focus on the communication of ideas without consideration of discrete language elements. This is probably a false dichotomy. A focus on fluency does not necessarily exclude consideration of the systematic properties of language; after all, it is not possible to communicate successfully without some knowledge and monitoring of the language of the message. Similarly, a focus on accuracy demands concentration on discrete points of language, but does not necessarily curb creativity and self-expression, ignore cognitive processes, or overlook personality traits of the learner.

At the basis of the accuracy-fluency controversy is the question of error. Once thought to be deviant behavior, error—in both first and second language acquisition—is now seen as a natural phenomenon. Research has demonstrated clearly that ESL errors are generally neither random nor sporadic nor deviant. Instead, they are often systematic, regular, and rule-governed, the result of intelligence, not stupidity. ESL errors come from a conscious or unconscious attempt by students to use language structures they have learned [16].

The Foundations of Error

Errors in written language can be due to inattention, memory lapse, or indifference. And in an in-class writing situation, NESs as well as ESL students will make hasty "performance errors" that they may have neither the time nor the ability to monitor. And of course, serious errors that interfere with clear communication is unacceptable in both NES and ESL writing. However, an understanding of the logical bases for second language error in writing may mediate the visceral reaction that excludes other more positive and effective components of ESL student writing [7; 16; 36].

For many ESL "ear" learners, language errors in writing can occur as a result of often unconscious rule formation that is based on their oral-aural experiences or of their misinterpretation of a rule half-learned. Some of these "rules" may be partially correct, while others may be incorrect. Following are examples of incorrect "rules" cited by U.S. resident ESL students:

- Capitalize all nouns.
- Always put a comma after *but.*
- All the verbs in one paragraph have to have the same verb tense.

In addition, these oral-aural acquirers of English often mix formal and informal language and use ear-based (phonetic) spelling that includes leaving off verb inflections. Examples, with informal language in **boldface** and incorrect spelling/word forms in *italics:*

- Young **folks** usually get a better **kick out of** trips than older people.
- which is *imparative* **to hang around** a large number of **kids**
- They will want **to take off ASAP.**
- The students are *taken* their time.
- some of the reasons *while* **guys** *getting* jobs
- students are *awared* of

In many ways, these "ear" learners are doubly disadvantaged in their writing. First, because their "eye" study of English has been limited, they may not have the necessary background knowledge to frame the structures of the language, or even to talk about and understand the structures they are using. In addition, the "rules" they have used to categorize their language experiences must be analyzed, "unlearned," then relearned and habituated, a time-consuming and often frustrating experience.

Many NESs have experienced the process of unlearning and relearning a language structure on a much smaller scale. Consider, for example, the NES child raised in a relatively standard American English atmosphere who, as an adult and an English teacher, learns that she uses one English structure incorrectly: *lay/lie.* Having habituated that error for a quarter century, she spends the next twenty-five "monitoring" for that error, thinking about the rules governing *lay/lie* before she uses those words, "unlearning," relearning, practicing, but, more often than not, avoiding that structure. Such habituated or "fossilized" language behavior, whether a single grammatical structure or an inappropriate oral response, are easy to identify but difficult to monitor, so that language behavior is nearly impossible to change permanently, at least in a short period of time. For the ESL student (and especially for the "ear" learner), with not one but rather dozens of habituated language errors, writing flawless English prose is at best an overwhelming prospect.

On the other hand, for many international students, grammatical error may come not so much from unconscious "rule" formation as from overgeneralization of rules they have learned through their eyes. That is, international ESL students may hypothesize, consciously or subconsciously, about a language form by extending the use of a rule they have learned in the second language. For instance, if the rule says that third-person singular verbs must take an *s* (i.e., "he *runs*"), ESL students may "overgeneralize" the rule to include second-person singular verbs (i.e., "you *runs*"). The hypothesis is incorrect, but it *is* a systematic application of a rule, especially when "you" refers to one person. In these cases, students who can identify or "monitor" for language errors can learn to reformulate new hypotheses and adopt new learning strategies to correct the errors.

Another way international ESL writers may err occurs when they infer rules from previous knowledge of their first language; that is, they "transfer" that knowledge into a hypothesis about the second language. For that reason, students from the same language background may well make some of the same types of errors, though their hypotheses (and therefore the resulting language) may not be exactly the same. For example, native speakers of Spanish may use adjectives that have both gender and number and that follow, rather than precede, the verb (e.g., the flowers *reds*) because those rules apply in Spanish.° Such first-language transfer occurs not only with grammatical structures but with first-language writing skills and strategies as well. ESL writers often transfer both good and weak writing skills from their first language into English, and many ESL students who have not developed good strategies for writing in their first language will not have appropriate strategies to transfer to their second language.

Next, if a language rule is particularly obscure and/or complex and/or difficult, ESL students may make errors as

°Teachers of ESL students who are interested in their students' errors may fruitfully investigate contrastive analysis studies that examine features of a native language (e.g., English) that contrast with features of another language (e.g., Spanish, Japanese) to determine what areas of second-language learning are most likely to cause difficulty for their students. For more information about contrastive analysis of grammatical differences between English and other languages, see *Thirteen Language Profiles* [39] and *Learner English* [38].

they attempt to construct the language form, or they may avoid the form altogether. For example, why is one of these sentences incorrect?

- People, who are against the English-only movement, might say that . . .
- Anne, who is against the English-only movement, might say that . . .

Level of difficulty is a complicated concept, for it is in part dependent on both first-language differences and prior student experience. For example, while English is a subject-verb-object (SVO) language, Korean is a subject-object-verb (SOV) language, and word order is relatively free. A sentence in English, translated into Korean and then retranslated, word for word, into English, shows the differences:

> *English:* Even though I told John not to take the Chemistry class, he took it.
> *Korean:* Even though I John Chemistry class not to take told John it took.

In addition to word order, many Asian languages are "tonal," that is, they have few or no inflections (such as verb tense and plural markers). Chinese, for instance, is a language that has no verb tenses and no articles; learning the complex rules for English verb tenses is an enormous task, and implementing those rules expands the task geometrically. Article use in English is often arbitrary and filled with exceptions; consequently, correct use of articles for an ESL student whose native language does not have articles is extremely difficult. For instance, try formulating the rules needed for the following examples and consider the consequent decisions Asian ESL students must make. (Correct article use is enclosed in parentheses; X indicates that no article is needed.)

> She considered him (a) genius.
> (The) only girl at (the) party was Nanan.
> (X/The) number seven is lucky.
> (A/The) funny picture on (a/the) page

And:

going to (a/the) church	versus	going to (X) church
going to (a/the) store	versus	going (X) (X) home
going on (a/the) journey	versus	going to (X) work

Some English language structures are more difficult for learners of one second language than another. For Arabic speakers, relative clauses are easier to use than auxiliary verbs in English because relative clauses in Arabic parallel use in English (though in Arabic, the relative clause requires the use of a personal pronoun, resulting in such structures as "The man who likes coffee *he* . . ."). In contrast, there are no auxiliary verbs in Arabic, so a structure like "She *taking* a class" is a common error. But native Chinese speakers may tend to avoid relative clauses in their writing because that structure does not occur in their language and is therefore difficult to use. In short, ESL students are similar to NES students of foreign languages: nativelike accuracy in nonnative language writing is a life-long struggle, so both students and their teachers must expect language errors in student writing.

Finally, because most international ("eye" learner) students have had many opportunities to practice written English at the single sentence level but only limited practice with writing English in extended discourse, they will discover that they make grammatical and sentence structure errors, even while they are following their "eye" learned rules. For example, narrative writing is often considered mere storytelling and is usually *taught* as occurring in the past tense. Yet recent work in genre studies has shown that narrative writing occurs in history textbooks, research reports, newspaper articles, and in background sections of textbooks in many fields [3]. Further, Katherine Bardovi-Harling [2] demonstrated that while the actual "story" usually occurs in simple past, the "backgrounding" in narrative (for instance, descriptions of characters and setting) is often described in past perfect and past progressive tenses.

> The boy Jody *watched* [the smoke], speculating. The fire on the kitchen hearth *was dying* down. His mother *was hanging* up pots and pans after the noon dinner. The day *was* Friday. She *would sweep* the floor with a broom of ti-ti and after that, if he *were* lucky, she *would scrub* it with the corn shucks scrub. (31)

Responding to ESL Language Errors

In light of the discussion of error above, teachers might begin their response to an ESL paper by marking, but not correcting, language errors in a draft, then query students about errors they immediately recognize (and can therefore monitor): "Why did you use past tense here? And not here?" "Why didn't you use a period there?" Then, for those errors students do not recognize, teachers can intervene and explain. Teachers should also consider the following:

- While ESL writing errors rarely approximate those of NESs either in number or in kind, their visibility should not immediately trigger negative responses in readers.

- Looking beyond the irritating errors to rhetorical and contextual successes or problems, as teachers commonly do with NES writing, is essential.
- Habituated errors are difficult for students to see and even more difficult to supplant with habituated correct forms.
- Even ESL student writers who both comprehend and are able to produce correct English grammar and sentence structures in discrete exercises often cannot manage the complexities of language use in extended English discourse without error.
- Most ESL errors are a normal, natural, and necessary part of the learning process.

Early intervention and explanation feedback can assist students to identify and solve language problems before evaluation occurs [32]. Teachers may discover that the students themselves are the best sources of error information in their writing and, importantly, that asking students to analyze (and perhaps to log) their errors may prove beneficial to their writing. Reminding students about software programs that can assist their writing processes, and/or directing them to a writing center on campus, can help ESL writers become more independent in the production of their own written work [7; 9; 20].

Finally, teachers should respond to ESL writing errors based on (A) the overall effect of an error on successful communication and (B) the students' difficulty in effectively remediating the error. An interesting area for examination is "error gravity" studies, in which researchers investigate the "irritation" or "acceptance" levels of NESs—usually university non-ESL faculty—to specific second-language errors. In order to help teachers and students prioritize language errors and edit more successfully, error gravity studies focus on what second language errors (A) interfere most with NES comprehension and/or (B) irritate the NES academic reader. Researchers Roberta Vann and her colleagues [41, 42] and Terry Santos [34] investigated the responses of faculty members to typical ESL errors. They found that most respondents did not judge all errors as equally severe; incorrect word order (as in the direct translation of the Korean sentence example above) and incorrect word use were considered the most serious, while spelling errors were among the least severe.

Teachers must therefore acquire knowledge of ESL language errors, then prioritize which ones students should focus on correcting. For example, in terms of the reactions of NESs to ESL-language errors, misuse of articles and prepositions might be most visible. However, these errors usually do not interfere with NES comprehension. Rather, they "irritate" the reader, sometimes stimulating a negative reaction ("This student can't even use articles!"). Yet the examples of article use in English above demonstrate the difficulty of correct article use for students whose first language does not contain articles. Preposition use in English is also relatively complex. English has nearly fifty prepositions, while many languages have only a few; for instance, the English prepositions *to, for,* and *by* are just one preposition in Spanish. Further, many English prepositions have little or no relevant meaning (e.g., *of*), and others have multiple meanings (e.g., *to*), so usage is particularly difficult to determine. Indeed, some NES writers use prepositions incorrectly, but because the NES reader sees and hears these misuses regularly, the errors are not so "irritating" as the ESL errors.

TYPICAL NES PREPOSITION ERRORS

bored *of* playing ball
but not *on* the norm
as a result *to* these problems
the manner *of* which it was intended

TYPICAL ESL PREPOSITION ERRORS

pay attention *on* their studies
I agree *in* some extent
brought *into* our attention
in conjunction *of* financial aid

In short, identifying and then prioritizing language errors ("Work on X first because those errors interfere with reader comprehension") can make monitoring for error easier for ESL students and can raise their self-confidence.

Evaluation of ESL Writing

Given the problems any second-language learner can have with writing, the problem of evaluation facing the composition teacher with ESL students is significant. "Lowering standards" or asking less of ESL student writers is not a viable solution, yet language errors must be seen in perspective: ESL students (and any writers in a second or foreign language) may have adequate knowledge of correct usage but find it difficult to produce accurate prose consistently. There is more, much more, to successful written communication than the use of articles. Liz Hamp-Lyons [19] notes that evaluation works best and is most fair to learners when it takes into account who the learner is, the situation in which the writer produces writing, and the overall context in which educational success is to be measured for the student writer.

Therefore, teachers must carefully develop evaluative criteria—at the same time as they develop the writing assignment and *before* they assign the writing—that are realistically grounded in the discourse communities the students will face outside the classroom. The composition teacher might then consider giving a separate grade for language, or three grades for each assignment: organization, content, and mechanics. Or teachers might even give several grades for each paper in areas of focus for that paper: coherence, use of detail, audience awareness, and so on. Such a grading scheme would allow students to identify more easily their writing strengths and weaknesses. An average of those grades, some of which might be weighted differently, might be the overall grade for the paper. *Note:* The evaluative criteria must be explicitly articulated—students have the right to know the basis for the evaluation.

Moreover, students learn to do best what teachers can demonstrate. Dana Ferris's [14, 15] seminal, large-scale studies with ESL students and revision indicate that because "a significant proportion of the comments appeared to lead to substantive student revisions" ("Influence" 315), teachers should therefore be particularly careful in

- developing their responding strategies,
- explaining their responding strategies to their students,
- helping students learn to revise,
- holding students accountable for considering feedback they receive.

Next, in any teacher intervention, marking local (i.e., discrete) errors or commenting on global alternatives must occur with consideration of the student and the writing context. The response/correction must (A) adequately describe the problem and, then, (B) suggest methods of correction. Marks that do not identify errors or rhetorical problems are ineffectual; after all, virtually no student turns in a paper for evaluation that is intentionally error-ridden and poorly written. For the same reason, asking students to "organize" when they think they already have organized is at best confusing. Further, feedback without follow-up (in the form of discussion, practice, graded revisions) will be less than effective.

Careful planning of peer-response groups and teacher intervention throughout the writing process can help ESL students to identify problems and solutions. Small group work and peer criticism may be difficult for some ESL writers. Others may believe that the time with peers is wasteful and prefer that the "teacher teach." Being aware of such potential problems can lead teachers to solutions [7; 16; 32]. Teacher-student conferencing, individually or in small groups, is another intervention technique that can prove useful for ESL students. Lynn Goldstein and Susan Conrad [18] discussed the problems and the benefits of conferencing with ESL students about specific language and rhetorical problems during the drafting process. They advise prior training of students to prepare them for the different role of a conferee, and they agree that successful conferencing can strengthen writing skills and develop independent decision making so vital in successful writing.

Finally, as Rebecca Oxford pointed out [29], ESL students (and NES students as well) must be trained in appropriate strategies for dealing with peer and teacher feedback and correcting their errors, as well as be given the necessary time to appropriately digest and then to practice corrections. Students must also acquire effective strategies that facilitate student learning of the composing, drafting, and editing processes. Knowledge of resources other than the teacher (e.g., reference books, World Wide Web, interviews and surveys, textbooks, peers, and the campus writing center) will enable students to seek help with their academic writing outside of class and even after the course has ended.

Conclusion

Identifying and studying the differences in communication styles and strategies between cultures is worthwhile, even necessary, for both ESL students and their teachers. The more understanding that exists, the better prepared teachers will be to communicate effectively with their students; the more students understand about those differences, the more easily they will fulfill their academic readers' expectations. Building background knowledge about academic writing can facilitate the student success by enabling students to learn the social processes, the appropriate use of language, and the rhetorical conventions for written communication within academic discourse communities.

How teachers focus on ESL students in their classrooms depends, at least in part, on their goals for all students, on how and for whom they want to empower those students. If, as Robert Land and Catherine Whitley [27] suggest, the objective of a composition class, particularly a class with ESL students, is "to acquire enough facility with Standard Written English (SWE) to succeed in school and in the workplace" (284), an effective pedagogy would include teaching composition not only as a skills course but also as a content course. Grabe and Kaplan [17] have indicated that, for ESL students, the content of a composition course must include such areas as composing and revision strategies, coherence systems and mechanisms, language features, rhetorical patterns, audience characteristics and expectations, and genre conventions.

Annotated Bibliography and Suggested Readings

1. Badger, R., and G. White, "A Genre Process Approach to Teaching Writing." *ELT Journal* 54 (2000): 153–60.

2. Bardovi-Harling, Katherine. Tense and Aspect in (Con)Text. *Grammar and Discourse: The Journal of TESOL France.* ed. T. Miller (1996): 19–33.

3. Biber, Douglas. *Variation Across Speech and Writing.* Cambridge: Cambridge UP, 1988.

   For this original research, Biber wrote a computer text-analysis program, then gathered a large corpus of spoken and written English. His analysis of this corpus revealed that the grammar of spoken and of written English differs in several ways, and that the grammar in each is used in "clusters." For teachers interested in language and genre, this is an essential book.

4. Biber, D., S. Conrad, and R. Reppen. *Corpus Linguistics: Investigating Language and Structure Use.* Cambridge: Cambridge UP, 1998.

5. Brislin, R. W., K. Cushner, C. Cherrie, and M. Yong. *Intercultural Interactions: A Practical Guide.* Newbury Park, CA: Sage, 1986.

   The most practical book in the Sage Series on Cross-Cultural Research and Methodology, this book contains "100 Critical Incidents." Each situation focuses on some common (and perhaps universal) characteristic of interpersonal interaction. Following are essays that integrate and interpret the points made in the critical incidents. Accessible, discussible, and eminently educational.

6. Byrd, Pat. "Grammar FROM Context." *Grammar in the Composition Classroom: Essays on Teaching ESL for College-Bound Students.* Eds. P. Byrd and J. Reid. Boston: Heinle and Heinle, 1998. 54–68.

   Insights into the paradigm that demonstrates grammar *from* context and grammar "clusters," as well as additional information about responding to and evaluating ESL writing, offer teachers both theoretical and practical ideas.

7. Campbell, C. *Teaching Second-Language Writing: Interacting with Text.* Boston: Heinle and Heinle, 1998.

   A slim volume that focuses on reflective teaching as well as on such teaching issues as creative writing, computer-based classes, and integrating language skills, the book is very reader-accessible.

8. Candlin, C., and K. Hyland. *Writing: Texts, Processes, and Practices.* London: Longman, 2000.

9. Clark, I. L., "Addressing Genre in the Writing Center." *Writing Center Journal* 20 (1999): 7–31.

10. Connor, Ulla. *Contrastive Rhetoric: Cross-Cultural Aspects of Second Language Writing.* Cambridge: Cambridge UP, 1996.

    Connor draws on a wide body of interdisciplinary literature to define and explication contrastive rhetoric. Using a variety of languages, she demonstrates how ESL writers draw on a range of cross-linguistic and cross-cultural influences. Of special interest to teachers of ESL writers are Chapter 2, "Contrastive Rhetoric in Applied Linguistics," and Chapter 8, "Genre-Specific Studies in Contrastive Rhetoric."

11. Connor, Ulla, and Robert B. Kaplan, eds. *Writing Across Languages: Analysis of L2 Text.* Reading, MA: Addison-Wesley, 1987.

    This collection of articles describes the concept of contrastive rhetoric, discusses empirical research in the contrastive rhetoric of many languages with English, and suggests applications of such research in the teaching of ESL writing.

12. Dudley-Evans, T. "Genre: How Far Can We, Should We, Go?" *World Englishes* 16 (1997): 351–58.

13. Fathman, Ann, and Elizabeth Whalley. "Teacher Response to Student Writing: Focus on Form vs. Content." *Second Language Writing: Research Insights for the Classroom.* Ed. Barbara Kroll. New York: Cambridge UP, 1990. 178–90.

14. Ferris, Dana R. "Student Reactions to Teacher Response in Multiple-Draft Composition Classrooms." *TESOL Quarterly* 29 (1995): 33–53.

15. ———. "The Influence of Teacher Commentary on Student Revisions." *TESOL Quarterly* 31 (1997): 315–39.

16. Ferris, Dana R., and J. Hedgcock. *Teaching ESL Composition: Purpose, Process, and Practices.* Mahwah, NJ: Lawrence Erlbaum, 1998.

    A comprehensive presentation of theory and practice; especially excellent are the sections that focus on teacher-response, grammar and editing, the uses of technology in the writing classroom, and writing assessment.

17. Grabe, William, and Robert B. Kaplan. "Writing in a Second Language: Contrastive Rhetoric." *Richness in Writing: Empowering ESL Students.* Ed. D. Johnson and D. Roen. New York: Longman, 263–83.

    The authors of this article (in a book that contains many valuable articles about teaching ESL writing) summarize and synthesize prior and current research in contrastive rhetoric, then detail suggestions for raising awareness and informing teachers about the fundamentals of contrastive rhetoric. In addition, Grabe and Kaplan offer specific pedagogical advice for teaching writing to ESL students from different language and cultural backgrounds.

18. Goldstein, Lynn M., and Susan M. Conrad. "Student Input and Negotiation of Meaning in ESL Writing Conferences." *TESOL Quarterly* 24 (1990): 441–60.

19. Hamp-Lyons, Liz, ed. *Assessing ESL Writing in Academic Contexts.* Norwood, NJ: Ablex, 1992.

This collection of articles, written by the growing number of researchers in ESL testing, focuses on the testing of ESL writing. It follows a clear, carefully written explanation of the issues in this research area; the assessment issues discussed range from validity questions concerning commercial writing tests to practical questions concerning classroom testing. Other issues discussed include cross-cultural assessment, academic literacy, criteria and scoring models, needs assessment, and models of feedback.

20. Harris, M. "Cultural Conflicts in the Writing Center: Expectations and Assumptions of ESL Students." *Writing in Multicultural Settings.* Ed. C. Severino, S. C. Guerra, and J. E. Butler. New York: Modern Language Association, 1997. 220–33.

21. Hyon, S. "Genre in Three Traditions: Implications for ESL." *TESOL Quarterly* 30 (1996): 693–722.

22. Johns, Ann M. *Text, Role, and Context: Developing Academic Literacies.* New York: Cambridge UP, 1997.

23. Johnson, K. *Understanding Communication in Second Language Classrooms.* Cambridge: Cambridge UP, 1995.

Using data from authentic classroom discourse, Johnson examines teacher-student interaction from both teacher and learner perspectives. By investigating classroom dynamics, teachers can recognize the patterns of culturally based classroom communication is established and the effect these patterns have on second-language learning.

24. Kaplan, Robert B. "Cultural Thought Patterns in Intercultural Education." *Language Learning* 16 (1966): 1–20.

25. Kroll, Barbara, "The Rhetoric-Syntax Split: Designing a Curriculum for ESL Students." *Journal of Basic Writing* 9 (1990): 40–55.

26. ———, ed. *Second Language Writing: Research Insights for the Classroom.* New York: Cambridge UP, 1990.

This seminal collection of thirteen articles is addressed to teachers-in-training and to experienced teachers in the field of ESL teaching as well. It is divided into two sections: the first presents "the current state of thinking on what the teaching of writing to nonnative speakers entails" (3); the second section presents a "variety of specific studies, each focused on a different aspect of writing and/or the writing classroom" (3–4).

27. Land, Robert, and Catherine Whitley. "Evaluating Second Language Essays in Regular Composition Classes: Toward a Pluralistic Society." *Richness in Writing: Empowering ESL Students.* Ed. D. Johnson and D. Roen. New York: Longman, 1989. 284–93.

28. Leki, Ilona. *Understanding ESL Writers: A Guide for Teachers.* New York: St. Martin's, 1992.

Written particularly for NES teachers of NES first-year English classes in which there are ESL students, the focus of this book is on U.S.–resident students rather than international students. Their problems with reading and writing, and the problems faced by their teachers, are discussed in clear and cogent detail, with practical suggestions offered that are based on second language acquisition research and composition theory.

29. Oxford, Rebecca L. *Language Learning Strategies: What Every Teacher Should Know.* New York: Newbury House, 1990.

Oxford bases her practical suggestions in this volume on theory and field work that she explains with clarity and simplicity. Her objective is to train teachers to train students to be more successful language learners by learning about, experimenting with, and practicing learning strategies. Chapter 3, "Applying Direct Strategies to the Four Language Skills," and Chapter 5, "Applying Indirect Strategies to the Four Language Skills," as well as the widely used Strategy Inventory for Language Learning survey (Appendix C) are especially useful for composition teachers of ESL students.

30. Purves, Alan, ed. *Writing Across Languages and Cultures: Issues in Contrastive Rhetoric.* Newbury Park, CA: Sage, 1988.

31. Rawlings, Marjorie K. *The Yearling.* New York: Scribner, 1938. As discussed in P. Byrd, "Rethinking Grammar at Various Proficiency Levels." *Grammar in the Composition Classroom.* Ed. P. Byrd and J. Reid. Boston: Heinle and Heinle. 1998. 69–97.

32. Reid, Joy. *Teaching ESL Writing.* Englewood Cliffs, NJ: Regents-Prentice Hall, 1993.

After surveying the links between first- and second-language writing, the focus of this text is on international rather than U.S.–resident ESL students. Curriculum design from more than a dozen writing programs is especially helpful.

33. Samovar, Larry A., and Richard E. Porter, eds. *Intercultural Communication: A Reader,* 9th ed. Belmont, CA: Wadsworth, 1999.

This book contains interesting and informative articles by a large number of international educators in the field of cross-cultural communication. Each chapter examines current issues in the field, ranging from the sociocultural necessity of effective communication to cultural-specific essays, from the impact of Confucianism in East Asia to Arabic concepts of effective persuasion or the cultural patterns of the Masai.

34. Santos, T. "Professors' Reactions to the Academic Writing of Nonnative-Speaking Students." *TESOL Quarterly* 22 (1988): 69–90.

35. Silva, T. "Differences in ESL and Native English-Speaking Writers: The Research and Its Implications." *Writing in Multicultural Settings.* Ed. C. Severino, S. C. Guerra, and J. E. Butler. New York: Modern Language Association, 1997. 209–19.

36. Sternglass, M. S. "Effect of Complex Social Histories on Academic Performance." *Time to Know Them: A Longitudinal Study of Writing and Learning at the College Level.* Mahwah, NJ: Erlbaum, 1997. 60–113.

37. Swales, John. *Genre Analysis: English in Academic and Research Settings.* Cambridge: Cambridge UP, 1990.

The focus of this work is the rhetorical conventions and discourse styles employed in various academic settings and how such norms are effectively taught to NES and ESL writers. The author analyses specific text types—specifically research-related genres—and addresses the pedagogic issues involved in preparing students to achieve the purposes of each for its intended audience.

38. Swan, M., and B. Smith, eds. *Learner English: A Teacher's Guide to Interference and Other Problems.* Cambridge: Cambridge UP, 1987.

39. *Thirteen Language Profiles: Practical Application of Contrastive Analysis for Teachers of English as a Second Language.* Vancouver, B.C.: Vancouver Community College English Language Training Night School, 1983.

This inexpensive, rather old, spiral-bound book, presents the basics of thirteen languages in sections that range from borrowed vocabulary and potential phonology problems for speakers of that language who are learning English to the written script and writing problems that those students might have. Very easy to understand and very worthwhile reading for teachers of ESL writers, it has applications even for those students whose languages are not included. Available directly from Vancouver Community College, King Edward Campus, Vancouver, Canada.

40. Townsend, J. S., and D. Fu. "Quiet Students Across Culture and Contexts." *English Education* 31 (1998): 4–19.

41. Vann, R., D. E. Meyer, and F. D. Lorenz. "Error Gravity: A Study of Faculty Opinion of ESL Errors." *TESOL Quarterly* 18 (1984). 427–40.

This article is one of the first empirical studies that examined the response of university faculty to ESL essay errors. The authors describe clearly their research methods, and the results have been widely used to prioritize error-monitoring in ESL writing.

42. Vann, R., F. D. Lorenz, and D. E. Meyer. "Error Gravity: Faculty Response to Errors in Written Discourse of Nonnative Speakers of English." *Assessing Second Language Writing in Academic Contexts.* Ed. L. Hamp-Lyons. Norwood, NJ: Ablex, 1991. 181–95.

Personal message to students
from Lynn Troyka and Doug Hesse

As writers, many of you have much in common with both of us. Sure, we've been at it longer, so we've had more practice, and most rules have become cemented in our heads. However, you share a common bond with us: our experiences during writing. All of us want to put ideas into words worthy of someone else's reading time.

When we write, we're often unsure of how to begin. Lynn likes to start in the middle and then work ahead and back. Doug likes to make long lists of ideas and then throw most of them away. Sometimes, we're stuck for examples sufficiently effective to get our points across, and we jump-start our ideas by talking with friends, either in person or by e-mail. Frequently, the precise expression we're looking for eludes us as we rummage through the clutter of words in our minds.

We offer this book to you as our partners in the process of writing, hoping that its pages suggest strategies that enhance your ability to give voice to your thoughts. You're always welcome to write us at <LQTBook@aol.com> to share your reactions to this book and your experiences as writers. We promise to answer.

Each of us would like to end this message with a personal story.

From Doug: I first glimpsed the power of writing in high school, when I wrote sappy—but apparently successful—love poems. Still, when I went to college, I was surprised to discover all I didn't know about writing, especially for college courses. Fortunately, I had good teachers and developed lots of patience. I needed it. I continue to learn, including from Lynn, who graciously invited me to join her in writing this edition of her handbook.

From Lynn: When I was an undergraduate, writing handbooks weren't around. Questions about writing nagged at me. One day, browsing in the library, I found an incorrectly shelved, dust-covered book whose title included the words *handbook* and *writing*. I read it hungrily and kept checking it out from the library. Back then, I could never have imagined that someday I might write such a book myself. Now that I've completed the *Simon & Schuster Handbook for Writers*, Seventh Edition, I'm amazed that I ever had the nerve to begin. This proves to me— and I hope to you—that anyone can write. Students don't always believe that. I hope you will.

With cordial regards,

Lynn Quitman Troyka   *Doug Hesse*

Preface

Welcome to the seventh edition of the *Simon & Schuster Handbook for Writers*. My purposes for writing it are three: to serve students as a classroom text, as a self-instruction manual, and as a reference book. My greatest wish is for students to succeed and fulfill their potential in writing for academic, personal, workplace, and public audiences. I hope that all my pages reflect my convictions that students are empowered by knowledge and that they deserve their instructors' unwavering respect as emerging college writers.

The *Simon & Schuster Handbook for Writers*, Seventh Edition, gives students comprehensive information about processes for writing college-level essays, source-based arguments, and research papers; thinking and reading critically; using documentation style correctly; designing documents; writing for the Web; writing about literature; writing for business; creating oral presentations; taking essay tests; and using grammar, punctuation, and mechanics correctly.

As in prior editions, I consciously include people of diverse backgrounds. You'll find no stereotyping of race, ethnicity, gender, or religion here. My language is gender neutral: *man* or *he* is never used generically to stand for the human race. In examples, I draw equally from male and female writers, both students and professionals, and from a variety of cultures.

With this edition, I'm honored to welcome my new writing associate, with whom I share a high esteem for students and a research-based orientation to the teaching of writing at all levels: Doug Hesse, Director of the Center for the Advancement of Teaching (CAT) and Professor of English at Illinois State University. Many of you know his widely admired scholarship as well as his major leadership roles in our profession. Doug has served as president of the Council of Writing Program Administrators and, when this handbook is published, he will be the new Chair of the Conference on College Composition and Communication (CCCC). He brings extraordinary expertise to the seventh edition's assumptions that most students today use computers, that research sources reside online as well as in libraries, and that the research process has become more complex and more exciting than ever. Together, we look forward to many years of cordial collaboration.

As the following material shows, the seventh edition of the *Simon & Schuster Handbook for Writers* includes extensive updates while retaining the core features of the best-selling earlier editions.

Lynn Quitman Troyka

"RAPID WAY TO LOCATE" GUIDE

RAPID WAY TO LOCATE CONTENTS

The Overview of Contents, which begins inside the front cover, gives you a brief list of contents. To find a more specific subtopic, use the Index.

RAPID WAY TO LOCATE ALL TOPICS

This handbook has seven Parts, each divided into chapters and then sections. On each Part's opening page, you'll find a detailed list of chapters. Within chapters, all sections contain uncomplicated discussions in small "chunks" of information. Each chunk carries a chapter number plus a letter in alphabetical order within the chapter. I encourage you to personalize your book by placing a sticky note, with a useful label on both sides, to overhang each page that you consult frequently.

RAPID WAY TO LOCATE EVERY PAGE'S INFORMATION

The title of each section in every chapter resembles an FAQ (Frequently Asked Question) to match the questions you might ask as you consult the *Simon & Schuster Handbook for Writers*, Seventh Edition. In a "running head" at the top of each right-hand page, look for the information repeated so that you can flip through a chapter to spot what you're looking for.

RAPID WAY TO LOCATE DOCUMENTATION STYLES

On the front of the opening page for Part Five, you'll see where to find each documentation style—MLA, APA, CM, CSE, COS. The same page lists locations for information about how to document books, articles, nonprint media, online sources, and electronic sources for each style.

RAPID WAY TO LOCATE SPECIAL ELEMENTS THROUGHOUT

Each numbered Box in this handbook provides a thumbnail sketch of key information. An icon in each box carries a message: ◎ means the box is a summary; ▦ says the box shows a pattern; and ☑ tells that the box is a checklist. Alerts ◉ announce special information about the current topic and reference additional information elsewhere in the handbook. Notes for students for whom English isn't a first language are indicated by ⊕. Also, SMALL CAPITAL LETTERS signal that a term is defined in the Terms Glossary, located immediately before the Index at the back of this handbook. This feature allows you to concentrate on the material you're reading, with the assurance that a definition you might need is always at hand.

RAPID WAY TO LOCATE GRAMMAR HELP FOR NATIVE AND MULTILINGUAL STUDENTS

In Parts Two through Four, whether English is your native language or you're multilingual, you'll find quick answers to your questions about Standard American English grammar, sentence correctness and style and punctuation. Part Seven addresses questions of special concern to multilingual students.

SUPPLEMENTS FOR THE SEVENTH EDITION

Prentice Hall now offers an *even wider choice* of student supplements and instructor supplements to help faculty augment and customize their courses.

FOR STUDENTS

NEW **"Me, Myself and I" Book**—It's more than just an e-book; it's a "me, myself and I" book! Whenever you write or do research, your handbook, as well as extra exercises, course materials, your syllabus, research help, and more, is just a click away. The Access Code Card, included with every new copy of *Simon & Schuster Handbook for Writers*, Seventh Edition, also permits access to **Research Navigator.**

NEW **Research Navigator™**—From finding the right articles and journals to citing sources, drafting and writing effective papers, and completing research assignments, **Research Navigator** is the one-stop research solution for your students. Students get a free twelve-month subscription with each copy of *Simon & Schuster Handbook for Writers*, Seventh Edition. Take a tour at <www.researchnavigator.com>.

NEW **Prentice Hall Pocket Readers**—Each essay in our pocket readers has surpassed the test of time and teaching, making them the perfect companion for any writing course. Prentice Hall Pocket Readers also offer an exceptional value: They are free when packaged with *Simon & Schuster Handbook for Writers*, Seventh Edition.

What's in your pocket?

- *Themes: A Prentice Hall Pocket Reader,* edited by Clyde Moneyhun. ISBN 0-13-144355-0
- *Patterns: A Prentice Hall Pocket Reader,* edited by Dorothy Minor. ISBN 0-13-144352-6
- *Argument: A Prentice Hall Pocket Reader,* edited by Christy Desmet. ISBN 0-13-189525-7
- *Literature: A Prentice Hall Pocket Reader,* edited by Mary Balkum. ISBN 0-13-144354-2

Understanding Plagiarism—Hailed by instructors as the best information available on understanding and avoiding plagiarism, this self-paced tutorial teaches students how to avoid committing plagiarism and how to properly quote, summarize, paraphrase, cite, and attribute information. <www.prenhall.com/understanding>

The New American Webster Handy College Dictionary— The dictionary is free to students when packaged with the text. ISBN 0-13-032870-7

The New American Roget's College Thesaurus—The thesaurus is free to students when packaged with the text. ISBN 0-13-045258-0

Simon & Schuster Workbook for Writers, Seventh Edition— This workbook contains hundreds of additional exercises and activities to help improve writing skills. ISBN 0-13-144356-9

A Writer's Guide to Research and Documentation by Kirk G. Rasmussen—This resource provides students with research and documentation guidelines in a paperback format designed for ease of use and portability, including the most recent information on MLA, APA, CM, and CSE formats. ISBN 0-13-177997-4

A Writer's Guide to Writing in the Disciplines and Oral Presentations by Christine Manion—This guide helps students write successfully in different academic disciplines, and offers advice and information on preparing oral presentations. ISBN 0-13-018931-6

A Writer's Guide to Writing About Literature by Edgar Roberts—This guide prepares students for writing about literature, with information on research and literature as well as additional sample student papers. ISBN 0-13-018932-4

Model Student Essays—This anthology features twenty-five student essays collected from around the country and organized into three broad categories: personal experience, explanatory, and persuasive writing. ISBN 0-13-645516-6

The Prentice Hall ESL Workbook—Written for students whose first language is not English, this workbook provides developmental

English language and composition practice in areas where key grammar points are proven trouble spots. ISBN 0-13-092323-0

The Prentice Hall TASP Study Guide for Writing by Robin P. Nealy and Karen Hackley—This study guide prepares students for the TASP by familiarizing them with the elements of the test, providing ample practice, and giving them strategies for success. Appropriate for students in Texas only. ISBN 0-13-041585-5

The Prentice Hall Florida Exit Test Study Guide for Writing by Patti Levine-Brown, Suzanne Hughes, and Kathleen Ciez-Volz—This self-paced study guide reinforces the skills students need to demonstrate on the Florida College Basic Skills Exit Test for Writing. ISBN 0-13-111652-5

FOR INSTRUCTORS

Annotated Instructor's Edition (AIE) for the *Simon & Schuster Handbook for Writers,* Seventh Edition—This edition offers many resources to new and experienced instructors in the composition classroom. ISBN 0-13-144364-X

Strategies and Resources for Teaching Writing with the *Simon & Schuster Handbook for Writers,* Seventh Edition— This supplement offers practical, hands-on advice for new and experienced composition instructors for organizing their syllabi, planning, and teaching. ISBN 0-13-144362-3

Answer Key to the *Simon & Schuster Workbook for Writers,* Seventh Edition—ISBN 0-13-144363-1

PH PowerPoints for Writing—Featuring exercises, examples, and suggestions for student writers, PowerPoints covers grammar, punctuation, and mechanics in paragraph form that demonstrates how sentence errors can be corrected most effectively. Available online at <www.prenhall.com/troyka>.

WebCT™, BlackBoard™, and CourseCompass adapted for the *Simon & Schuster Handbook for Writers,* Seventh Edition— These resources feature extensive content in each of these course platforms, saving instructors time in preparing online courses.

Prentice Hall Resources for Teaching Writing—Individual booklets, covering some of the most effective approaches and important concerns of today's composition instructors, are available for use with your students and teaching assistants. These include:

- *Teaching Writing Across the Curriculum* by Art Young, Clemson University. ISBN 0-13-081650-7

- *Journals* by Christopher C. Burnham, New Mexico State University. ISBN 0-13-572348-5

- *English as a Second Language* by Ruth Spack, Tufts University. ISBN 0-13-028559-5
- *Distance Education* by W. Dees Stallings, University of Maryland, University College. ISBN 0-13-088656-4
- *Collaborative Learning* by Harvey Kail and John Trimbur. ISBN 0-13-028487-4
- *Teaching English Online* by Sam Zahran. ISBN 0-13-092200-5

ACKNOWLEDGMENTS

Students, past and present, have inspired me to compose this *Simon & Schuster Handbook for Writers,* Seventh Edition. Thank you for being my audience. I hope my discussions and explanations help you excel as writers. Thank you, also, for granting me official permission to publish your fine writing and for speaking with me through e-mail or in person about your experiences with, and suggestions for, my handbooks. Please feel welcome to e-mail me directly at <LQTBook@aol.com>. I always answer personally.

Doug Hesse, Director of the Center for the Advancement of Teaching (CAT) and Professor of English at Illinois State University, becomes with this seventh edition my new collaborator and writing colleague. His vast experience as writer, teacher, and leader in our profession has greatly enriched my pages and my enjoyment of the creative process. Together, we look forward to many years of cordial collaboration. Doug warmly seconds all the thanks I extend here to students, contributors, and reviewers.

Other outstanding colleagues have contributed significantly to this *Simon & Schuster Handbook for Writers,* Seventh Edition. Esther DiMarzio of Kishwaukee College served indispensably as overall consultant. Carolyn Calhoun-Dillahunt, Director of the Writing Center and Professor of English at Yakima Valley Community College, lent her extraordinary talent to the chapter on argument; and Kip Strasma, Professor of English at Illinois Central College, enhanced the chapter on Web-based writing. Cy Strom of the Colborne Communications Centre in Toronto, Ontario, continues his critically important role as adapter of my Canadian editions and adviser to my overall work on handbooks.

My thanks to reviewers for the seventh edition, whose thoughtful comments were of great value: Mary Angelo, University of South Florida; Martha Bachman, Camden County College; Sandra Barnhill, South Plains College; Nancy Blattner, Longwood University; Brian J. Benson, A & T State University; Ken Claney, Tulsa Community College; Gary Christenson, Elgin Community College; Nita Danko, Purdue University, Calumet; David Elias, Eastern Kentucky University; Diana Grahn, Longview Community College; Jean Harmon, Chemetka Community College; Lola Harmon, Greenville Technical College; Sarah

Harrison, Tyler Junior College; Gary Hatch, Brigham Young University; Elaine Kromhout, Indian River Community College; Patrick McMahon, Tallahassee Community College; Dorothy Mino, Tulsa Community College; Catherine C. Olson, Tomball College; Lindee Owens, University of Central Florida; Michael Suwak, College of Southern Maryland; and Carolyn West, Daytona Beach Community College.

Other esteemed colleagues whose invaluable contributions I've carried over from previous editions are Kathleen Bell, University of Central Florida; Jon Bentley, Albuquerque Technical-Vocational Institute; Don Jay Coppersmith, Internet Consultant; Jo Ellen Coppersmith, Utah Valley State College, who offered outstanding material on critical thinking and research writing; Ann B. Dobie, University of Southwestern Louisiana; David Fear, Valencia Community College; Michael J. Freeman, Director of the Utah Valley State College Library; Kathryn Fitzgerald, University of Utah; Barbara Gaffney, University of New Orleans; D. J. Henry, Daytona Beach Community College; Scott Leonard, Youngstown State University, adviser on drafting and revision; Dorothy V. Lindman, Brookhaven College; Alice Maclin, DeKalb College; Darlene Malaska, Youngstown Christian University; Marilyn Middendorf, Embry Riddle University; Patricia Morgan, Louisiana State University; Mary Ruetten, University of New Orleans; Matilda Delgado Saenz; Phillip Sipiora, University of South Florida; Maggy Smith, University of Texas at El Paso; Martha Smith, Brookhaven College; Paulette Smith, Reference Librarian, Valencia Community College; Donnie Yeilding, Central Texas College; and Valerie Zimbaro, Valencia Community College.

Over the course of preparing previous editions of my handbooks, these outstanding reviewer-colleagues steered me in the right direction: Westrich Baker, Southeast Missouri State University; Marilyn Barry, Alaska Pacific University; Norman Bosley, Ocean Community College; Phyllis Brown, Santa Clara University; Judith A. Burnham, Tulsa Community College; Robert S. Caim, West Virginia University at Parkersburg; Joe R. Christopher, Tarleton State University; Marilyn M. Cleland, Purdue University, Calumet; Thomas Copeland, Youngstown State University; Janet Cutshall, Sussex Community College; Dawn Elmore-McCrary, San Antonio College; Joanne Ferreira, State University of New York at New Paltz and Fordham University; Sheryl Forste-Grupp, Villanova University; Carol L. Gabel, William Paterson College; Joe Glaser, Western Kentucky University; Michael Goodman, Fairleigh Dickinson University; Mary Multer Greene, Tidewater Community College at Virginia Beach; Jimmy Guignard, University of Nevada at Reno; Julie Hagemann, Purdue University, Calumet; John L. Hare, Montgomery College; Kimberly Harrison, Florida International University; Lory Hawkes, DeVry Institute of Technology, Irving; Janet H. Hobbs, Wake Technical Community College; Frank Hubbard, Marquette University; Rebecca Innocent, Southern Methodist University; Ursula Irwin, Mount Hood Community College; Denise Jackson, Southeast Missouri

State University; Margo K. Jang, Northern Kentucky University; Peggy Jolly, University of Alabama at Birmingham; Myra Jones, Manatee Community College; Rodney Keller, Brigham Young University, Idaho; Judith C. Kohl, Dutchess Community College; James C. McDonald, University of Southwestern Louisiana; Martha Marinara, University of Central Florida; Michael J. Martin, Illinois State University; Michael Matto, Yeshiva University; Susan J. Miller, Santa Fe Community College; Pamela Mitzelfeld, Oakland University; Rosemary G. Moffett, Elizabethtown Community College; Rhonda Morris, Lake City Community College; Roarck Mulligan, Christopher Newport University; Alyssa O'Brien, Stanford University; Jon F. Patton, University of Toledo; Pamela T. Pittman, University of Central Oklahoma; Nancy B. Porter, West Virginia Wesleyan College; Stephen Prewitt, David Lipscomb University; Kirk Rasmussen, Utah Valley State College; Edward J. Reilly, St. Joseph's College; Mary Anne Reiss, Elizabethtown Community College; Peter Burton Ross, University of the District of Columbia; Eileen Schwartz, Purdue University, Calumet; Lisa Sebti, Central Texas College; Eileen B. Seifert, DePaul University; John S. Shea, Loyola University at Chicago; Tony Silva, Purdue University; Beverly J. Slaughter, Broward Community College; Martha A. Smith, Brookhaven College; Scott R. Stankey, Anoka Ramsey Community College; Bill M. Stiffler, Harford Community College; Michael Strysick, Wake Forest University; Jack Summers, Central Piedmont Community College; Susan Swartwout, Southeast Missouri State College; Vivian A. Thomlinson, Cameron University; Michael Thro, Tidewater Community College at Virginia Beach; William P. Weiershauser, Iowa Wesleyan College; Joe Wenig, Purdue University; Carolyn West, Daytona Beach Community College; Roseanna B. Whitlow, Southeast Missouri State University; and the late and wildly admired Sally Young, University of Tennessee at Chattanooga.

At Prentice Hall, a highly professional team facilitated Doug's and my work on this new edition of the *Simon & Schuster Handbook for Writers*. Elaine Silverstein, Development Editor, expertly steered Doug and me through the complexities of updating my work; Stacy Best, Senior Acquisitions Editor for English Composition, Brandy Dawson, Executive Marketing Manager for English Composition, Emily Cleary, Marketing Manager, and Leah Jewell, Editor in Chief for English, advised us with vision and wise conviction. Shelly Kupperman, Senior Production Editor, remains our major partner not only in facilitating the conversion of our words into print but also in caring passionately about our entire team and the students who rely on our work. During large chunks of our production process, Barbara DeVries, production consultant, filled in when Shelly had to take temporary leave; we thank Barbara for her extraordinary combination of experience, grace, and leadership. In addition, we stand in awe of the talents of Vernon Nahrgang, our copyeditor, and Judy Kiviat, our amazingly skilled proofreader. Others who made major contributions to this edition include Barbara Kittle, Director of Production and Manufacturing; Ann Marie McCarthy, Executive Managing Editor; Leslie Osher, Creative Design Director; Kathryn Foot, Design Director; Nick Sklitsis, Manufacturing Manager; Mary Ann Gloriande, Prepress and Manufacturing Buyer; and Steve Kyritz, Editorial Assistant. Finally, we came through many challenges thanks to our whole team's inspired mentor, Yolanda de Rooy, President of Humanities and Social Sciences.

Doug Hesse appreciates the support of Lori Ostergaard and Beth Welch in completing this project; the professional friendships of Kathi Yancey, Jeanne Gunner, Chris Anson, and John Lovas, among many others; and the continued vitality of his students at Illinois State University. He further states, "My children, Monica, Andrew, and Paige, amaze me with their creativity, as does the very best writer I know: Becky Bradway, my wife. Finally, I value the extraordinary trust Lynn showed by inviting me to join in her amazing work. She's a generous teacher."

Lynn Quitman Troyka thanks family and friends who nourish her spirit as a writer and participant in the larger world. She says, "For ten superb years, Ida Morea, my Administrative Assistant and dear friend, has kept me organized and sane with her warmth, outstanding talents, and incredible patience. Doug Hesse, my new handbook partner, made our collaboration stimulating and grand fun. Kristen Black, beloved child of my heart if not of my womb, along with her wonderful family, Dan, Lindsey, and Ryan, sustains me with her indomitable spirit, vision, and brilliance. My treasured companions in life's journey include Susan Bartlestone; Florence Bolden; Carol Carter; Rita and Hy Cohen; Elaine Gilden Dushoff; Alan, Lynne, Adam, and Joshua Furman; Elliott Goldhush; Warren Herendeen; Edith Klausner, my sister, a true friend who generously bestows her wisdom, experience, and calming presence upon my life; my niece, Randi Klausner Friedman, and nephews Michael and Steven Klausner along with their marvelous children; Jo Ann Lavery, my much-loved 'sister' and buddy through thick and thin, and her husband, Tom Lavery; Cynthia Lester, my amazing spiritual inspiration and newest 'sister'; Edie and Alan Lipp; Brenda and John Lovas; Lois Powers; Betty Renshaw; Magdalena Rogalskaja; Avery Ryan, my cherished 'niece' and great friend, along with her delightful Jimmy, Gavin, and Ian Ryan; Shirley and Don Stearns; Ernest Sternglass and his wife, the late Marilyn Sternglass, one of my most treasured friends, generous mentors, and admired scholars; Joseph Wayne Thweatt; Douglas and Anna Young; Lisa Wallace, my other cherished 'niece' and prized friend, along with her delightful husband, Nathaniel Wallace; Muriel Wolfe; and Tzila Zwas. I'm grateful for the support of my longstanding mentors and pals at Prentice Hall, J. Phillip Miller, Publisher of Modern Languages, and Bud Therien, Publisher for Art. Above all, I thank David Troyka, my beloved husband, discerning reader, and the love of my life."

Credits

TEXT/ART

James L. Kinneavy, adapted from *Theory of Discourse*. New York: W. W. Norton & Company, 1971. Reprinted by permission of The Center for American History. (Page 4)

Ian Frazier, "Taking the F." (Pages 4–5)

Carol Grant Gould, "Out of the Mouths of Beasts" from *Science 83* (April), p. 69. (Page 5)

Sheila Tobias, *Overcoming Math Anxiety*. New York: W. W. & Norton Company, 1978. (Page 6)

Joseph D'Agnese, "Brothers with Heart" from *Discover* 22, no. 7 (July 2001). Copyright © The Walt Disney Company. (Page 7, Exercise 1-1A)

T. Berry Brazelton, "Issues for Working Parents" from *American Journal of Orthopsychiatry* 56, pp. 14–25. Used with permission. (Pages 8–9, Exercise 1-1B)

Scott Russell Sanders, "The Inheritance of Tools" from *The Paradise of Bombs*. First appeared in *The North American Review*. Copyright © 1986 by Scott Russell Sanders. Reprinted by permission of the author and the author's agents, the Virginia Kidd Agency, Inc. (Page 8, Exercise 1-1C)

Microsoft Word for Windows Screen. Copyright © Microsoft Corporation. All rights reserved. (Page 21)

FirstSearch Web Screen. Used with permission of OCLC. FirstSearch and World Cat are registered trademarks of OCLC Online Computer Library Center, Inc.; the screen capture is copyrighted by OCLC and/or its third-party database providers. (Page 22)

Google Web Screens. Copyright © Google, Inc. Used by permission of Google.com. (Pages 40 and 41)

Carol Moreno, student. (Pages 68–79)

Daniel Goleman, "Researchers Trace Empathy's Roots to Infancy" from *Working with Emotional Intelligence*. New York: Bantam Books, 1998. (Page 82)

Tara Foster, student. (Page 82)

Gerald Secor Couzens, "If Lightning Strikes" from *House Calls/How Doctors Treat Themselves and Their Own Families for Common Illnesses and Injuries: The Most Effective At-Home Remedies for Everything*. New York: Simon & Schuster, 1993. (Page 82)

Jane Goldman, "What's Bugging You?" (Page 84)

Herbert Benson, M.D., *The Relaxation Response*. New York: Morrow, 1975. Used with permission. (Page 85)

Nancy Gibbs, "Shades of Difference" from *Time* (November 18, 1991). Copyright © 1991 TIME Inc. Reprinted by permission. (Page 85)

Bradley Howard, student. (Page 86)

Remar Sutton, "Don't Get Taken Every Time" from *The Insider's Guide to Buying or Leasing Your Next Car or Truck*. New York: Penguin Books, 2001. (Page 86)

Dan Cody, "Puppet Poetry." (Page 86)

Frank T. Rhodes, "Let the Student Decide." (Page 87, Exercise 4-2A)

Anne Bryson, student. (Page 87, Exercise 4-2B)

"Horizons" from *U.S. News & World* Report. (Page 87, Exercise 4-2C)

Anastasia Toufexis, "The Dirty Seas: Threatened by Rising Pollution, the Oceans Are Sending Out an SOS" from *Time* (August 1, 1988). Copyright © 1991 TIME Inc. Reprinted by permission. (Page 88)

Tom Paradis, "A Child's Other World." (Page 91)

Michael Clugston, "Twice Struck." Oxford University Press Southern Africa. (Page 89)

Roger Rosenblatt, "What Brand of Laughter Do You Use?" from *The New York Times* (November 17, 1991), p. 86. (Page 92).

Carol Carter and Lynn Quitman Troyka, *Majoring in the Rest of Your Life*. Englewood Cliffs, NJ: Prentice Hall, 1999. (Page 92)

Credits

Margaret Mead and Rhoda Metraux, "New Superstitions for Old." (Page 93)

Claire Burke, student. (Page 94, Exercise 4-4A)

Randolph H. Manning, "Fighting Racism with Inclusion." (Page 94, Exercise 4-4B)

Tony Hillerman, *Hillerman Country*. New York: HarperCollins, 1991. (Page 94, Exercise 4-4C)

Allan Moult, "Volcanic Peaks, Tropical Rainforest, and Mangrove Swamps" adapted from *Australia the Beautiful: Wilderness*. Australia in Print, 1998. (Page 96)

Dawn Seaford, student. (Page 96)

William Knowlton Zinsser, *The Haircurl Papers and Other Searches for the Lost Individual*. New York: Harper & Row, 1964. (Page 96–97)

Danny Witt, student. (Page 97)

Patrick Regan Buckley, "Lessons in Boat-Building—and Life." (Page 97)

Adapted from Linda Weltner, "Stripping Down to Bare Happiness." (Page 98)

Edwin Bliss, *Getting Things Done: The ABC's of Time Management*. New York: Charles Scribner's Sons, 1976. Copyright © 1976. galeord@gale.com (Page 98, Exercise 4-6A)

Heather Martin, student. (Page 99, Exercise 4-6B)

Marie Hart, "Sport: Women Sit in the Back of the Bus" from *Psychology Today* (October 1971). pp. 64–66. (Page 99, Exercise 4-6C)

Deborah Harris, student. (Page 99, Exercise 4-7A)

Carol Tavris, "Old Age Isn't What It Used to Be." (Pages 99–100, Exercise 4-7B)

Jim Doherty, "The Hobby That Challenges You to Think Like a Bee." (Page 100, Exercise 4-7C)

Susan Howard, "Depth of Field" from *Newsday* (January 1, 1991). Copyright © 1991 *Newsday*. Distributed by Tribune Media Services. Reprinted with permission. (Page 101)

Gretel Ehrlich, "Other Lives" from *The Solace of Open Spaces*. New York: Penguin Books, 1986. Copyright © 1985. (Page 101)

Ruth Mehrtens Galvin, "Sybaritic to Some, Sinful to Others." Used by permission of Smith College. (Page 102)

John Warde, "Safe Lifting Techniques" from *the New York Times* (March 11, 1990). (Page 102)

Melissa Greene, "NoRms, Jungle Vu." (Page 102)

Banesh Hoffman, "My Friend, Albert Einstein," pp. 139–144. (Page 103)

John Arrend Timm, *General Chemistry*, Editions McGraw-Hill Book Company Inc., third edition, 1956. (Page 103)

Bill Siuru and John D. Busick, *Future Flight: The Next Generation of Aircraft Technology* from TAB Books, 1987. Copyright © The McGraw-Hill Companies, Inc. (Page 103)

William Ryan, *Blaming the Victim*. New York: Random House, 1976. (Page 104)

Rosanne Labonte, student. (Page 105)

Warren Bennis, "Time to Hang Up the Old Sports Clichés." (Page 105)

Alison Lurie, *The Language of Clothes* (nonfiction). New York: Random House, 1981 Copyright © 1981 by Alison Lurie. Reprinted by permission of Melanie Jackson Agency, L.L.C. (Pages 105–106)

Marie Winn, *The Plug-In Drug*. New York: Penguin Books, 2002. (Page 106)

Deborah Tannen, *You Just Don't Understand*. Copyright © 1990 by Deborah Tannen. Reprinted by permission of HarperCollins Publishers Inc./William Morrow. (Page 106, Exercise 4-9A)

Simone de Beauvoir, *Memoirs of a Dutiful Daughter*. New York: Penguin Classics, 2001. (Page 107, Exercise 4-9B)

James Gorman, "Gadgets." (Page 107, Exercise 4-9C)

June Jordan, "Waiting for a Taxi" from *Technical Difficulties: African-American Notes on the State of the Union*. New York: Pantheon 1992, pp. 161–168. (Page 107, Exercise 4-9D)

Jane Brody, "A Hoarder's Life: Filling the Cache—and Finding It" from *The New York Times* (November 19, 1991), pp. 101–102. (Pages 107–108, Exercise 4-9E)

Jean Rosenbaum, M.D., *Is Your Volkswagen a Sex Symbol?* New York: Bantam Books, Random House Inc., 1973. (Page 108).

Lisa Pratt, "A Slice of History" from *Newsday* (April 29, 1990), combined editions, p. 19. (Page 109)

John C. Sawhill, "The Collapse of Public Schools." Reprinted with permission. (Pages 109–110)

Ora Gygi, "Things Are Seldom What They Seem." (Page 117)

Annie Dillard, "Terror at Tinker Creek." (Page 122, Exercise 5-3A)

Paul De Palma, "http://www.when_is_enough_enough?.com" from *The American Scholar* 68, no. 1, (Winter 1999). Copyright 1999 by Paul De Palma. (Page 122)

Sydney J. Harris, "Sports Only Exercise Our Eyes" from *The Best of Sydney J Harris.* Copyright © 1975 by Sydney J. Harris. Reprinted by permission of Houghton Mifflin Company. All rights reserved. (Pages 125–126, Exercise 5-4)

Robert Lipsyte, "The Emasculation of Sports" from *The New York Times Sunday Magazine* (May 2, 1995). (Pages 128–129, Exercise 5-5)

Anna Lozanov, student. (Pages 130–132)

Jo Goodwin Parker, "What's Poverty?" from George Henderson, *America's Other Children,* 1998. Used by permission of the University of Oklahoma Press. (Page 134)

Carl Sagan, *Cosmos.* New York: Random House, 1980. Copyright © 1980 the Estate of Carl Sagan. (Pages 134–135)

William S. Ellis, "Brazil's Imperiled Rain Forest." (Page 136, Exercise 5-6A)

Steve Olson, "Computing Climate." (Page 136, Exercise 5-6B)

Lillian Schlissel, *Women's Diaries of the Westward Journey.* New York: Random House Inc, 1992. (Page 136, Exercise 5-6C)

Milner Library Web Screen. Used by permission of Milner Library, Illinois State University. (Page 510)

LINCC Web. Used by permission of the College Center for Library Automation. (Page 511)

Google Home Page. Copyright © Google, Inc. Reprinted by permission. (Page 513)

Milner Library Online Catalog. Used by permission of Milner Library, Illinois State University. (Page 514)

Yahoo Web Screens. Reproduced by permission of Yahoo! Inc. Copyright © 2004 by Yahoo! Inc. Yahoo and Yahoo! logo are trademarks of Yahoo Inc. (Page 518)

Library of Congress Online Web Catalog Home Page (Page 521)

Library of Congress Online Catalog Keyword Search (Page 522)

Milner Library Article Indexes Web Screen. Used by permission of Milner Library, Illinois State University. (Page 524)

PsycINFO Web Screens. Reprinted with permission of the American Psychological Association, publisher of the PsycINFO® Database. Copyright © 1872–present, APA. All rights reserved. For more information, contact PsycINFO@apa.org. (Page 526)

Matt Ridley, "What Makes You Who You Are" from *Time* 161 (June 2, 2003), pp. 54–63. Copyright © 2003 TIME Inc. Reprinted by permission. (Pages 552–553, Exercise 33-1)

Anjula Razdan, "What's Love Got to Do with It?" from *Utne* (May/June 2003) pp. 69–72. Reprinted with permission from *Utne Magazine.* To subscribe, call 800/736/UTNE or visit the Web site at www.utne.com. (Pages 553–554, Exercise 33-2)

Paul Fussell, *Uniforms: Why We Are What We Wear.* Boston: Houghton Mifflin, 2002. Copyright © 2002 by Paul Fussell. Excerpted and reprinted by permission of Houghton Mifflin Company. All rights reserved. (Page 556, Exercise 33-3)

Susan Sontag. *Regarding the Pain of Others.* New York: Farrar, Straus and Giroux, 2003. Copyright © 2003 Susan Sontag. Reprinted by permission of Farrar, Straus and Giroux, LLC. (Pages 556–557, Exercise 33-4)

Peter Wood, *Diversity: The Invention of a Concept.* San Francisco: Encounter Books, 2003. (Pages 559–560, Exercise 33-5)

Screen Shots of The Nature Club. (Pages 690, 692, 693, 709, 714)

Guthrie Theater Web Screen <http://www.guthrietheater.org>. Used by permission of the Guthrie Theater. (Page 716)

Jet Propulsion Laboratory Web Screen <http://www.jpl.nasa.gov/>. Courtesy of NASA/JPL/Caltech. (Page 717)

Valerie Cuneo, "The Sound of a Murderous Heart." (Pages 738–741, Student essay)

Peter Wong, "Gender Loyalists: A Theme in *Trifles.*" (Pages 741–746, Student essay)

Two sonnets by Claude McKay: "The White City" and "In Bondage." (Page 747)

Paule Cheek, "Words in Bondage: Claude McKay's Use of the Sonnet Form in Two Poems." (Pages 748–752, Student essay)

Adam Furman, "The Effectiveness of Common Antibiotics." (Pages 760–761, Sample student paper)

Credits

PHOTOGRAPHS

About the Authors

LYNN QUITMAN TROYKA, Professor of Writing, at the City University of New York (CUNY), has taught at Queensborough Community College and in the graduate Language and Literacy program at City College. Former editor of the *Journal of Basic Writing,* her writing and research appears in major journals and various scholarly collections. Nationally and internationally, she conducts workshops in the teaching of writing. Author of the *Simon & Schuster Quick Access Reference for Writers,* Fourth Edition, Prentice Hall (2003), and Canadian editions of her *Simon & Schuster Handbook for Writers* and *Quick Access Reference for Writers,* she is co-author of *Structured Reading,* Sixth Edition, Prentice Hall (2003), and *Steps in Composition,* Eighth Edition, Prentice Hall (2004).

Dr. Troyka received the 2001 CCCC Exemplar Award, the highest CCCC award for scholarship, teaching, and service; the Rhetorician of the Year Award; and the TYCA Pickett Award for Service. She is a past chair of the Conference on College Composition and Communication (CCCC) of the National Council of Teachers of English (NCTE); the Two-Year College Association (TYCA) of NCTE; the College Section of NCTE; and the Writing Division of the Modern Language Association.

"This information," says Dr. Troyka, "tells what I've done, not who I am. I am a teacher. Teaching is my life's work, and I love it."

DOUG HESSE is Professor of English and Director of the Center for the Advancement of Teaching at Illinois State University. There he served as director of writing programs and won both outstanding teaching and research awards. Current Chair of the Conference on College Composition and Communication and Past President of the Council of Writing Program Administrators, Dr. Hesse was editor of *WPA: Writing Program Administration.* He has published over forty articles and book chapters, mainly on writing and on creative nonfiction, and he has also taught at Findlay College, Michigan Tech University, and Miami University (Ohio). Married to a well-published essayist and fiction writer, Dr. Hesse has three children, one in high school, one in college, and one a college graduate who is herself a writer.

To David,
my husband and sweetheart

Lynn Quitman Troyka

To Coral Krukow Hesse

Doug Hesse

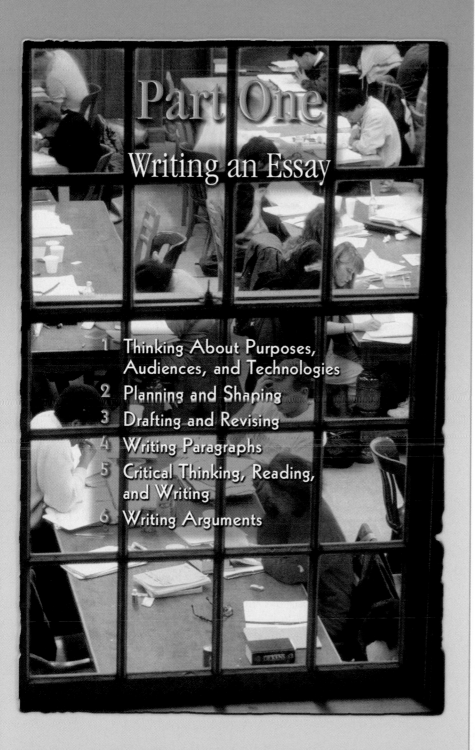

Part One

Writing an Essay

Chapter 1

Thinking About Purposes, Audiences, and Technologies

1a Why bother to write?

In this age of cellphones, video conferencing, and the Internet, why do you need the ability to write well? Surprisingly, today's fast-paced, digital world demands more, not less, writing. Whether for an entry-level job, for later advancement, or for a professional career, your success potential in workplaces of the twenty-first century relies heavily on how well you write documents. Recent surveys of people working in a variety of jobs and professional fields say that each day they spend an average of thirty percent of the time writing. They write letters, memos, product evaluations, technical manuals, business-trip reports, feasibility reports, lab reports, proposals, minutes, Web pages, newsletters, and brochures (the first four are most common).

Your success in college is another reason to have solid writing ability. Throughout your education, you need to write essays, research papers, lab reports, and other college-related assignments. The better your skills and fluency as a writer, the more smoothly your course work will go.

Yet another benefit of writing skill comes from the physical activity of writing. In the act of writing, studies show, people significantly increase their insights, understandings, and abilities to remember the subject they're writing about. Here's how this phenomenon operates.

Writing is a way of discovering and learning
The physical act of writing triggers brain processes that lead you to make new connections among ideas. Pleasant shocks of recognition occur as your mind starts from what you already know and leaps to what you did not "see" before. One of my favorite statements comes from the world-famous writer E. M. Forster: "How can I know what I mean until I've seen what I said?" Writing activates unique mental pathways that enable you to pursue knowledge, think through complex concepts, and gain solid ownership of your education.

BACKGROUND
A *Theory of Discourse* by James L. Kinneavy is a classic citation in composition and rhetoric. To this day, many theorists, researchers, and practitioners rely on Kinneavy's work. Kinneavy explores the fundamental purposes for which people use language. He explains the centrality of the concept of purpose in writing:

> Purpose in discourse is all important. The aim of a discourse determines everything else in the process of discourse. "What" is talked about, the oral or written medium which is chosen, the words and grammatical patterns used—all of these are largely determined by the purpose of the discourse. (48)

Kinneavy is enthusiastic about the potential for composition as a field of scholarship:

> It is the thesis of this work that the field of composition—or discourse as it will presently be termed—is a rich and fertile discipline with a worthy past which should be consulted before being consigned to oblivion, an exciting present, and a future that seems as limitless as either linguistics or literature. (2)

Other modern influential theorists who concentrate on writers' purposes include the highly respected James Britton, who classifies purposes as poetic, expressive, and transactional. More recently, scholars of rhetoric and composition have discussed the problems caused when teachers expect writers always to have a clear purpose in mind before writing. Writers often discover their purpose as they write, and their purpose may change from draft to draft.

Writing is a way of thinking and reflecting

Only humans can think about thinking. They can reflect on what they know and have experienced, a process greatly accelerated and enhanced during the act of writing. For you as a student, this means that writing forces you to clarify your thinking as you use words to convey your thoughts. And when you revise a draft, you push yourself further so that your writing is as close as possible to what you're thinking.

Writing is a way of owning and sharing knowledge

Few educated people remember specific classroom sessions or chapters from textbooks, but nearly everyone recalls the topics of their research papers. By writing intensively about a topic that you have thought about deeply, you become an authority on that topic. As this happens, others begin to identify you as a disciplined, educated person.

Writing is a way of participating in our democracy

Our society can thrive only when people are educated to assess information, raise important questions, evaluate the answers, and exercise their rights and responsibilities as informed citizens. The ability to write helps you influence decisions and policies, from parking issues at your college to outcomes of national elections.

1b How is "writing" defined?

Writing communicates a message for a purpose to readers. The four key terms in the prior sentence are important. **Written communication** involves sending a message to a destination. The **message** of writing is its content. The **purpose** (1c) of each writing task strongly influences decisions writers make as they put their ideas into words. **Readers,** usually referred to as the **audience** (1d), are the destination that a writer wishes to reach.

1c What are the major purposes for writing?

A writer's **purpose** for writing motivates what and how he or she writes. Some students think their purpose is to fulfill an assignment, but that's only the beginning. The concept of purpose relates to the reason that you're writing. Every writer, whether student or professional, needs to get under way by choosing which of the four major purposes of writing, listed in Box 1, they want to pursue.

BOX 1   **SUMMARY**

 ## Purposes for writing*

To express yourself
To inform a reader
To persuade a reader
To create a literary work

* Adapted from James L. Kinneavy, *A Theory of Discourse* (1971; New York: Norton, 1980).

In this handbook, I concentrate on the two major purposes you need for most **academic writing,** the writing you do for college and other scholarly endeavors: to inform a reader and to persuade a reader. I've chosen these two because they're the most practical and helpful for students. The two remaining purposes listed in Box 1 are important for contributing to human thought and culture, but they relate less to what most college writing involves.

1c.1 What is expressive writing?

Expressive writing is writing to express your personal thoughts and feelings. Much expressive writing is for the writer's eyes only, such as that in diaries, personal journals, or exploratory drafts. When expressive writing is for public reading, it usually falls into the category of literary writing. The excerpt here comes from a memoir intended for public reading.

> The smells in Brooklyn: coffee, fingernail polish, eucalyptus, the breath from laundry rooms, pot roast, Tater Tots. A woman I know who grew up here says she moved away because she could not stand the smell of cooking food in the hallway of her parents' building. I feel just the

opposite. I used to live in a converted factory above an army-navy store, and I like being in a place that smells like people live there.

—Ian Frazier, "Taking the F"

1c.2 What is informative writing?

Informative writing seeks to give information to readers and usually to explain it. Another name for this type of writing is *expository writing* because it expounds on—sets forth in detail—observations, ideas, facts, scientific data, and statistics. You can find informative writing in textbooks, encyclopedias, technical and business reports, nonfiction books, newspapers, and many magazines.

The essential goal of informative academic writing is to educate your readers about something. Like all good educators, therefore, you want to present your information clearly, accurately, completely, and fairly. In section 4i of this handbook, I show you many strategies that writers use for informative writing. These strategies can help you deliver your message, but above all, your success depends on whether your readers can verify your information as accurate. Box 2 gives you a checklist to assess your informative writing. But first, here's a paragraph written to inform.

> In 1914 in what is now Addo Park in South Africa, a hunter by the name of Pretorius was asked to exterminate a herd of 140 elephants. He killed all but 20, and those survivors became so cunning at evading him that he was forced to abandon the hunt. The area became a preserve in 1930, and the elephants have been protected ever since. Nevertheless, elephants now four generations removed from those Pretorius hunted remain shy and strangely nocturnal. Young elephants evidently learn from the adults' trumpeting alarm calls to avoid humans.
>
> —Carol Grant Gould, "Out of the Mouths of Beasts"

As informative writing, this paragraph works because it focuses clearly on its TOPIC* (elephant behavior), presents facts that can be verified (who, what, when, where), and is written in a reasonable TONE.

BOX 2   CHECKLIST

 ## Informative writing

- Is its information clear?
- Does it present facts, ideas, and observations that can be verified?
- Does its information seem complete and accurate?
- Is the writer's tone reasonable and free of distortions? (1e)

---

* Find the definition of all words in small capital letters (such as TOPIC) in the Terms Glossary at the back of this book directly before the Index.

WHAT ELSE?
Strategies and Resources is a free 400-page book written especially for instructors who adopt this handbook. Its Part One (of six) co-ordinates this handbook with many specifics of teaching writing: plans for writing courses, six complete syllabuses for integrating this handbook into writing courses, and various methods for evaluating writing (including peer evaluation).

BACKGROUND
You will find extensive practical teaching advice in *Strategies for Teaching First-Year Composition,* edited by Duane Roen, Veronica Pantoja, Lauren Yena, Susan K. Miller, and Eric Waggoner (Urbana: NCTE, 2002).

BACKGROUND
In "Up Close and Personal: A Real-World Audience Awareness Assignment" (*Teaching English in the Two-Year College,* March 1999: 286–290), Shelley M. Ellis suggests that instructors promote audience awareness by having students analyze and then respond to actual complaint letters.

BACKGROUND
The various concepts of purpose in three rhetorical traditions are explored by Arthur Walzer in "The Meanings of Purpose" (ERIC ED 303 799). He examines the subject as it is understood from the classical-poetic, romantic, and classical-rhetorical viewpoints.

1c.3 What is persuasive writing?

Persuasive writing, also called *argument writing,* seeks to convince readers about a matter of opinion. When you write to persuade, you deal with debatable topics, those that people can consider from more than one point of view. Your goal is to change your readers' minds about the topic—or at least to bring your readers' opinions closer to your point of view. To succeed, you want to evoke a reaction in your audience so that they think beyond their present position (for example, reasoning why free speech needs to be preserved) or take action (for example, register to vote). Examples of persuasive writing include newspaper editorials, letters to the editor, opinion essays in newspapers and magazines, reviews, sermons, books that argue a point of view, and business proposals that advocate certain approaches over others.

In Chapter 4 of this handbook, I show you strategies of paragraph development that effective writers use in their persuasive writing. Also, Chapter 6 of this handbook offers you a whole chapter that discusses ways to write effective arguments.

In general terms, persuasive writing means you need to move beyond merely stating your opinion. You need to give the basis for that opinion. You support your opinion by using specific, illustrative details to back up your **generalizations,** which are usually very broad statements. The first sentences of sections 1c.1, 1c.2, and 1c.3 in this chapter are examples of generalizations.

Box 3 gives you a checklist to assess your persuasive writing. But first, here's a paragraph written to persuade.

> The search for some biological basis for math ability or disability is fraught with logical and experimental difficulties. Since not all math underachievers are women, and not all women are mathematics-avoidant, poor performance in math is unlikely to be due to some genetic or hormonal difference between the sexes. Moreover, no amount of research so far has unearthed a "mathematical competency" in some tangible, measurable substance in the body. Since "masculinity" can't be injected into women to test whether or not it improves their mathematics, the theories that attribute such ability to genes or hormones must depend for their proof on circumstantial evidence. So long as about seven percent of the PhD's in mathematics are earned by women, we have to conclude either that these women have genes, hormones, and brain organization different from those of the rest of us, or that certain positive experiences in their lives have largely undone the negative fact that they're female, or both.
> —Sheila Tobias, *Overcoming Math Anxiety*

As persuasive writing, this passage works because it provides undistorted information on math ability; it expresses a point of view that resides in sound reasoning (math ability isn't based on gender); it offers evidence (a logical line of reasoning); and it tries to get the reader to agree with the point of view.

BOX 3   CHECKLIST

Persuasive writing

- Does it present a point of view about which opinions vary?
- Does it support its point of view with specifics?
- Does it base its point of view on sound reasoning and logic?
- Are the parts of its argument clear?
- Does it intend to evoke a reaction from the reader?

EXERCISE 1-1

For each paragraph, decide if the dominant purpose is informative or persuasive. Then apply the questions in Box 2 or Box 3 to the paragraph, and explain your answers.

A.   The number one challenge in tissue engineering is to get the specimen cells to grow at all. Freshly plucked from a human, a batch of cells hasn't got long to live. They need oxygen, a temperature of about 98 degrees Fahrenheit, and nutrients. So, a tissue engineer doesn't waste time. He places the cells in a petri dish with liquid nutrients—carbohydrates and amino acids do nicely—then tucks them away in an incubator. With a little luck, they multiply and in a few days produce enough cells to be considered tissue. As amazing as the process is up to this point, it's relatively useless, because clumps of tissue are of little use to a patient. The tissue engineer must convince cells to morph from a meaningless jumble of flesh into a functioning organ.

—Joseph D'Agnese, "Brothers with Heart"

B.   Efforts to involve the father in the birth process, to enhance his sense of paternity and empowerment as he adjusts to his new role, should be increased. Having the father involved in labor and delivery can significantly increase his sense of himself as a person who is important to his child and to his mate. Several investigators have shown that increased participation of fathers in the care of their babies, increased sensitivity to their baby's cues at one month, and significantly increased support of their wives can result from the rather simple maneuver of sharing the newborn baby's behavior with the new father at three days, using the Neonatal Behavioral Assessment Scale (NBAS). In light of these apparent gains, we would do well to consider a period of paid paternity leave, which might serve both symbolically and in reality as a means of stamping the father's role as critical to his family. Ensuring the father's active participation is likely to enhance his image of himself as a nurturing person

BACKGROUND

Purpose drives almost all writing. Research shows that few writers sit down and say to themselves, "I am going to write a comparison-and-contrast essay"; instead they say, "I want to give my readers some information" or "I want to convince my readers to change their minds." In the service of those purposes, writers compare and contrast, narrate, describe, draw analogies, and so forth.

Narration and description are discussed fully in Chapter 4, along with many other writing strategies for idea development, including process, definition, comparison and contrast, cause and effect, and analogy.

ANSWERS: EXERCISE 1-1

A. Dominant purpose is informative. It meets the criteria.

B. Dominant purpose is persuasive. It meets the criteria.

C. Dominant purpose is informative and/or expressive. It meets the criteria.

BACKGROUND
In "Making a Place for Music in Basic Writing" (*Journal of Basic Writing*, Fall 1995: 31–37), Sarah Coprich Johnson describes her use of music as a springboard for writing. Music helps students find topics, encourages students in their use of supporting details, and promotes their eventual understanding of the concepts of purpose and audience.

ANSWERS: EXERCISE 1-2
For each topic, the student or a group of students should write one paragraph (or more, according to how you have assigned the exercise) with an informative purpose and one paragraph with a persuasive purpose. Then the writer (or group) should also be prepared to discuss (orally or in writing, according to your assignment) the differences in the two treatments of the same topic.

and to assist him toward a more mature adjustment in his life as a whole.

—T. Berry Brazelton, "Issues for Working Parents"

C.   After proposing marriage to a neighbor girl, my grandfather used this hammer to build a house for his bride on a stretch of river bottom in northern Mississippi. The lumber for the place, like the hickory for the handle, was cut on his own land. By the day of the wedding, he had not quite finished the house, and so right after the ceremony, he took his wife home and put her to work. My grandmother had worn her Sunday dress for the wedding, with a fringe of lace tacked on around the hem in honor of the occasion. She removed this lace and folded it away before going out to help my grandfather nail siding on the house. "There she was in her good dress," he told me some fifty-odd years after that wedding day, "holding up them long pieces of clapboard while I hammered, and together we got the place covered up before dark." As the family grew to four, six, eight, and eventually thirteen, my grandfather used this hammer to enlarge his house room by room, like a chambered nautilus expanding its shell.

—Scott Russell Sanders, "The Inheritance of Tools"

EXERCISE 1-2

Using each topic listed here, work individually or with your peer-response group to think through two different essays: one informative, the second persuasive. Be ready to discuss in detail how the two essays would differ. For help, consult section 1c.

1. Fast food
2. Tastes in music
3. Required college courses
4. Road rage
5. Storms

1d What does "audience" mean for writing?

Your **audience** consists of everyone who will read your writing. After college, your audiences will be readers of your business, professional, and public writing (Chapter 42). In college, you address a mix of audience types, each of which expects to read ACADEMIC WRITING. Here's a list of categories of audiences for academic writing, each of which is detailed in the section listed in parentheses.

- Your peers (1d.1)
- A general audience (1d.2)
- A specialist audience (1d.3)
- Your instructor (who represents either general or specialized readers) (1d.4)

The more specifics you can assume about your audience for your academic writing, the better your chances of reaching it successfully. The questions in Box 4 can serve as a guide.

BOX 4   **SUMMARY**

 ## Characteristics of reading audiences

What Setting Are They Reading In?

- Academic setting?
- Workplace setting?
- Public setting?

Who Are They?

- Age, gender
- Ethnic backgrounds, political philosophies, religious beliefs
- Roles (student, parent, voter, wage earner, property owner, veteran, and others)
- Interests, hobbies

What Do They Know?

- Level of education
- Amount of general or specialized knowledge about the topic
- Probable preconceptions and prejudices brought to the topic

---

When you know or can reasonably assume who will be in your reading audience for each assignment, your chances of reaching it improve. For example, if you're writing a sales report for your supervisor,

QUOTATION: ON WRITING

I have come to feel that "the voice of the text" best describes what actually happens. We all speak one way to grandfather in the nursing home and another to an old acquaintance at a party. We have child voices and parent voices, neighborhood voices and stranger voices, a hundred varieties of work voices, voices for friends and voices for lovers.

—Donald M. Murray

TEACHING TIP

The concept of audience is meant to help writers get their message across. The concept is supposed to facilitate, not block. A writer is not expected to tell readers what they want to hear even if the writer agrees with the readers. A writer is, however, expected to choose words the readers know and to use a tone suitable to the occasion.

You might find that some students feel inhibited when they have to think about an audience for their writing. Studies show that some students misunderstand the concept of audience. They think it means that writers should act as if someone is constantly looking over their shoulders. Other students have trouble with the concept because they think that they must never say something that would be unpopular with their audience. Some students might not want to admit these or other misunderstandings of the concept of audience, so you might want to clear the matter up without asking students to give you their negative impressions. Once you start talking about the subject, you might find that students start chiming in to help you get at their concerns.

USING COLLABORATION

Although students may understand the concept of audience in a general way, many find that consciously writing for others can be intimidating. The following group exercise can help students overcome this anxiety and simultaneously explore the concrete characteristics of an audience.

Assign students to work in groups of three or four. Ask the class to envision a group of people who are time travelers from an earlier era. They now take refuge in a modern American city. Even after being shown how to operate the lights and faucets in their apartments, these people remain innocent of technologies we take for granted. For example, they have no idea how to use modern appliances, and so they wash their clothes by soaking them in the sink and then pounding them with heavy objects.

Ask each group to craft a set of instructions that would tell the time travelers how to wash and dry their clothes using a modern washer and dryer. Students will have to bear in mind that they cannot take what they would consider "common knowledge" for granted. Even simple commands like "open the lid" or "check the lint filter" will require careful explanation—perhaps even illustration.

Because this exercise requires intense focus on audience, it encourages students to articulate and practice what they know about the needs of readers. By your visiting each of the groups as they work, you can help keep students on track, ask focusing questions, and encourage peer interaction.

you can use terms such as *product life cycle, break-even quantity, competition,* and *markup.* In contrast, if general readers were the audience for the same information, you would want to avoid specialized, technical vocabulary—or if you had to use some essential specialized terms, you would define them in a nontechnical way.

🌐 **ESL NOTE:** As someone from a non-U.S. culture, you might be surprised—even offended—by the directness with which people speak and write in the United States. If so, I hope you'll read my open letter—it introduces Part Seven of this handbook—to multilingual students about honoring their cultures. You may come from a written-language tradition that expects elaborate, formal, or ceremonial language; that reserves the central point of an academic essay for the middle; that requires tactful, indirect discussions (at least in comparison to the U.S. style); and, in some cultures, that accommodates digressions that might, or might not, lead back to the main point. In contrast, U.S. writers and readers expect language and style that is very direct, straightforward, and without embellishment (as compared to the styles of many other cultures). U.S. college instructors expect essays in academic writing to contain a thesis statement (usually at the end of the introductory paragraph). They further expect your writing to contain an organized presentation of information that moves tightly from one paragraph to the next, with generalizations that you always back up with strong supporting details, and with an ending paragraph that presents a logical conclusion to your discussion. Also, for writing in the United States you need to use so-called standard English grammar. This means following the rules used by educated speakers. In reality, the United States has a rich mixture of grammar systems, but academic writing requires standard English grammar. If you want to hear these forms spoken, listen to the anchors of television and radio news programs. Your writing also needs to choose words that are accurate in meaning and spelled correctly. 🌐

1d.1 What is a peer audience?

Your *peers* are other writers like you. In some writing classes, instructors divide students into **peer-response groups.** Participating in a peer-response group makes you part of a respected tradition of colleagues helping colleagues. Professional writers often seek comments from other writers to improve their rough drafts. As a member of a peer-response group, you're not expected to be a writing expert. Rather, you're expected to offer responses as a practiced reader and as a fellow student writer who understands what writers go through.

The role of members of a peer-response group is to react and discuss, not to do the work for someone. Hearing or reading comments from your peers might be your first experience with seeing how others read your writing. This can be very informative, surprising, and helpful. Also, when peers share their writing with the group, each member gets the added advantage of learning about other students' writing for the same assignment.

Peer-response groups are set up in different ways. One arrangement calls for students to pass around and read each other's drafts silently, writing down reactions or questions in the margins or on a response form created by the instructor. In another arrangement, students read their drafts aloud, and then each peer responds either orally or in writing on a response form. Yet another arrangement asks for focused responses to only one or two features of each draft (perhaps each member's thesis statement, or topic sentences and supporting details, or use of transitional words, etc.). Still another method is for the group to BRAINSTORM a topic together before writing, to discuss various sides of a debatable topic, or to share reactions to an essay or piece of literature the class has read, and so on.

Whatever the arrangement of your group, you want to be clear about exactly what you are expected to do, both as a peer-responder and as a writer. If your instructor gives you guidelines for working in a peer-response group, follow them carefully. If you've never before participated in a peer-response group, or in the particular kind of group that your instructor forms, here are ways to get started: Consult the guidelines in Box 5 at the end of this section; watch what experienced peers do; and ask questions of your instructor (your interest shows a positive, cooperative attitude). Otherwise, just dive in knowing that you will learn as you go.

Now to the sometimes sticky issue of how to take criticism of your writing: Here's my personal advice as a writer for being able (or at least appearing able) to take constructive criticism gracefully. First, know that most students don't like to criticize their peers. They worry about being impolite, inaccurate, or losing someone's friendship. Try, therefore, to cultivate an attitude that encourages your peers to respond as freely and as helpfully as possible. Show, also, that you can listen without getting angry or feeling intruded upon.

Second, realize that most people tend to be a little (or quite a bit) defensive about even the best-intentioned and tactful criticism. Of course, if a comment is purposely mean or sarcastic, you and all others in your peer-response group have every right to say so and not tolerate it. Third, if you don't understand a comment fully, ask for clarification. Otherwise, you might misunderstand what's suggested and go off in the wrong direction.

Finally, no matter what anyone says about your writing, it remains yours alone. You retain "ownership" of your writing always, and you don't have to make every suggested change. Use only the comments that you think can move you closer to reaching your intended audience. Of course, if a comment from your instructor points out a definite problem, and you choose to ignore it, it could have an impact on your grade—though many instructors are open to an explanation of your rationale for deciding to ignore what they said.

QUOTATION: ON WRITING
The mere imparting of information is not education. Above all things, the effort must result in making a man think and do for himself.
—Carter G. Woodson, 1933

BACKGROUND
Wim Westera suggests in "Paradoxes in Open, Networked Learning Environments: Toward a Paradigm Shift" (*Education Technology*, January-February 1999: 17–23) that computer-mediated collaborative learning, along with distance learning and changing teacher-student relationships, could potentially revolutionize education.

BACKGROUND
Joseph Janangelo warns in "Intricate Inscriptions: Negotiating Conflict Between Collaborative Writers" (ERIC EJ 544 163) that collaborators don't always treat each other with reciprocal integrity and compassion. Janangelo suggests several precautions that writing instructors can take to help ensure more responsible collaboration.

ALERT: Some instructors and students use the terms *peer-response group* and *collaborative writing* to mean the same thing. In this handbook, I assign the terms to two different situations. I use peer-response group (1d.1) for students getting together in small groups to help each other write and revise, as I explain below. I use collaborative writing (3f) for students writing an essay, a research paper, or a report together in a group. 👁

BOX 5   SUMMARY

Guidelines for participating in peer-response groups

One major principle needs to guide your participation in a peer-response group: Always take an upbeat, constructive attitude, whether you're responding to someone else's writing or receiving responses from others.

As a Responder

- Think of yourself in the role of a coach, not a judge.
- Consider all writing by your peers as "works in progress."
- After hearing or reading a peer's writing, briefly summarize it to check that you and your peer are clear about what the peer said or meant to say.
- Start with what you think is well done. No one likes to hear only negative comments.
- Be honest in your suggestions for improvements.
- Base your responses on an understanding of the writing process, and remember that you're reading drafts, not finished products. All writing can be revised.
- Give concrete and specific responses. General comments such as "This is good" or "This is weak" aren't much help. Say specifically what is good or weak.
- Follow your instructor's system for putting your comments in writing so that your fellow writer can recall what you said. If one member of your group is supposed to take notes, speak clearly so that the person can be accurate. If you're the note taker, be accurate, and ask the speaker to repeat what he or she said if it went by too quickly.

As a Writer

- Adopt an attitude that encourages your peers to respond freely. Listen and try to resist any urge to interrupt during a comment or to jump in to react.

→

> ### Guidelines for participating in peer-response groups (*continued*)
>
> - Remain open-minded. Your peers' comments can help you see your writing in a fresh way, which, in turn, can help you produce a better-revised draft.
> - Ask for clarification if a comment isn't clear. If a comment is too general, ask for specifics.
> - As much as you encourage your peers to be honest, remember that the writing is yours. You "own" it, and you decide which comments to use or not use.

⊕ ESL NOTE: Students from cultures other than those in the United States or Canada might feel uncomfortable in the role of critic or questioner of other people's writing. Please know, however, that peer-response groups are fairly common in schools and at jobs because people usually think that "two heads are better than one." Sharing and questioning others' ideas—as well as how they are expressed in writing—is an honorable tradition in the United States and Canada. Peer-response groups help writers politely but firmly explore concepts and language, so please feel free to participate fully. In fact, some instructors grade you on your open participation in such activities. ⊕

1d.2 What is a general audience?

A **general audience** of readers is composed of educated, experienced readers. These are people who regularly read newspapers, magazines, and books. These readers, with general knowledge of many subjects, likely know something about your topic. However, if you get too technical, you're writing for readers who possess specialized knowledge on a particular subject (1d.3). Consequently, avoid specialized or technical terms, although you can use a few as long as you include everyday definitions.

In addition, general readers approach a piece of writing expecting to become interested in it. They hope to learn about a new topic, to add to their store of knowledge about a subject, and, often, to see a subject from a perspective other than their own. As a writer, you need to fulfill those expectations. Of course, there are also readers who are not particularly well read or open to new ideas, but in most academic writing not intended for specialized audiences, you want to target a general audience, as defined above.

BACKGROUND

In *A Sourcebook for Responding to Student Writing* (Portsmouth, NH: Boynton/Cook, 1999), Richard Straub gathers several useful articles about effective ways to respond to students, both by instructors and by peers. In "Asynchronous Electronic Peer Response in a Hybrid Basic Writing Classroom," Virginia Crank shows how basic writers can benefit from peer response (*Teaching English in the Two-Year College,* December 2002: 145–155).

BACKGROUND

The essays in *Public Works: Student Writing as Public Text,* edited by Emily J. Isaacs and Phoebe Jackson (Portsmouth, NH: Boynton/Cook-Heinemann, 2001), offer strategies for having students publish their writings, as well as several cautions.

QUOTATION: ON WRITING

[Writing is] the sense of being in contact with people who are part of a particular audience that really makes a difference to me.
—Sherley Anne Williams

TEACHING TIP
To help students understand the importance of audience, you may want to ask them to collect articles from various magazines and newspapers that are addressed to different types of readers. The articles and the diverse audiences they assume can lead to lively conversations, especially if the class is divided into groups for early discussion and later reconvenes as a whole class. Giving students a list of publications popular with varied groups of people will ensure effective contrasts in the articles they find. (The monthly magazine *Writer's Digest* lists publication sources, with a brief description of audiences for many magazines.)

EXTRA EXERCISE
Ask students to write three letters: one to a close friend, a second to their parents, and a third to the class. In each, they are to recount an experience they had at an imaginary party when someone they knew (perhaps the person they went to the party with) embarrassed them in some way. In peer groups, students can read the letters, discussing the differences in them that result from the different audiences.

TEACHING TIP
As a collaborative project, choose a single subject about which your students are likely to have some knowledge (for example, their first experiences at college). Assign each group an audience to whom they will write a letter describing the assigned situation. To get them to think about the different language choices they must use to make a favorable impression on different audiences, it is often very effective to assign groups a comparatively informal, friendly relationship—a parent, a grandparent, a good friend, a sibling, a member of the clergy, a favorite high school teacher. Even without being coached, students will notice the difference that audience makes to word choice, information selection, and tone.

1d.3   What is a specialist audience?

A **specialist audience** is composed of readers who have expert knowledge of specific subjects or who are particularly committed to those subjects. Many people are experts in their occupational fields, and some become experts in areas that simply interest them, such as astronomy or raising orchids. People from a particular group background (for example, Democrats, Republicans, Catholics, or military veterans) are knowledgeable in those areas.

Specialist readers, however, share more than knowledge: They share assumptions and beliefs. For example, suppose you're writing for an audience of immigrants to the United States who feel strongly about keeping their cultural traditions alive. You can surely assume your readers know those traditions well, so you wouldn't need to describe and explain the basics. Similarly, if you want to argue that immigrants should abandon their cultural traditions in favor of U.S. practices, you want to write respectfully about their beliefs. Additionally, whenever you introduce a concept that's likely to be new to a specialist audience, explain the new concept thoroughly rather than assume that they'll understand it right away.

1d.4   What is my instructor's role as audience?

As your audience, your instructor functions in three ways. First, your instructor assumes the role of your target audience, either as general readers (1d.2) or specialist readers (1d.3). Second, your instructor is a coach, someone committed to helping you improve your writing. Third, your instructor is the eventual evaluator of your final drafts.

Instructors know that few students are experienced writers or experts on the subjects they write about. Still, instructors expect your writing to reflect your having taken the time to learn something worthwhile about a topic and then to write about it clearly. Instructors are experienced readers who can recognize a minimal effort almost at once.

As important, instructors are people whose professional lives center on intellectual endeavors. You need, therefore, to write on topics that contain intrinsic intellectual interest (2d) and to discuss them according to the expectations for academic writing.

If you're a relatively inexperienced college writer, you don't want to assume that your instructor can mentally fill in what you leave out of your writing. Indeed, you might think that it's wrong, even insulting to your instructor, if you extend your discussion beyond simple statements. Instructors—indeed, all readers—can't be mind readers, so they expect students to write on a topic fully. If you think you might be saying too little, ask your peers to read your writing and tell you if you've developed your topic sufficiently.

1e What is "tone" in writing?

Tone is more than what you say; tone is *how* you say it. As a writer, your tone reveals your attitude toward your AUDIENCE as well as the topic. Tone in writing operates like tone of voice, except in writing you can't rely on facial expressions and voice intonations to communicate your message.

Your DICTION (choice of words), LEVEL OF FORMALITY, and writing style create your tone. While you can use SLANG and other highly INFORMAL LANGUAGE in a note to your roommate or a close friend, such a relaxed tone isn't appropriate for ACADEMIC WRITING or BUSINESS WRITING. As a rule, when you write for an audience about which you know little, use more formality in your tone. "More formality," by the way, doesn't mean dull and drab. Indeed, lively language in a serious discussion enhances your message.

Problems with tone result from combining words into certain phrases. It's the combination and location, not the words taken separately, that create a tone. For example, you want to avoid sarcastic language in an academic or business setting that calls for a reasonable tone. If you were to write "He was a regular Albert Einstein" to describe a person interviewed for a paper, those sarcastic words would say more about you than about the person interviewed. Such a tone implies that you have an overly critical or nasty streak. Conversely, you could introduce IRONY if you wrote "The chief assistant to Governor Marie Ghoti claimed that the governor could give me up-to-date information about my topic, but then the assistant turned out to know much more than the governor."

In business and professions, if you write a memo to your supervisor about a safety hazard in your workplace, you want to avoid writing a chatty message with a joke about an accident that could happen. Using such a tone directed at your supervisor would be considered "flippant" or "irresponsible." Equally important, if you include minute details of background information that your supervisor already knows, your tone would likely seem condescending and your supervisor might become annoyed with you.

Academic writing usually calls for a medium-to-formal tone (21b), which is a reasonable, even-handed tone. It's somewhat formal and serious but never pompous. Also, such a tone avoids language that attempts to manipulate your readers. Distorted facts or SLANTED LANGUAGE (21h) (for example, *the corrupt, deceitful politician*) rather than neutral words (for example, *the politician under investigation for taking bribes*) jump off the page, making your readers decide immediately that your message isn't objective or trustworthy.

Additionally, in all types of writing, GENDER-NEUTRAL LANGUAGE that represents both men and women fairly (for example, replace *policeman* with *police officer*, and replace *doctors' wives* with *doctors' spouses*)

QUOTATION: ON WRITING

I started writing because of a terrible feeling of powerlessness: I felt I was drifting and obscure, and I rebelled against that. I didn't see what I could do to change my condition. I wanted to control rather than be controlled, to ordain rather than be ordained, and to relegate rather than be relegated.

—Anita Brookner

BACKGROUND

Dictionary definitions of *tone* tend to differ slightly, but they deliver the same essential message. For example, *Webster's New World Dictionary,* Fourth Edition, reads, "[Tone] is a manner of speaking or writing that shows a certain attitude on the part of the speaker or writer, consisting of choice of words, phrasing, etc."

The American Heritage Dictionary reads, "[Tone] is a manner of expression in speech or writing (*an angry tone of voice*); a general quality, effect, or atmosphere (*the tone of the debate was antagonistic*)."

QUOTATION: ON WRITING

I write rather quickly. I've come to accept it. For a long time I was ashamed of myself for writing fast because I talked to people and I thought I wasn't taking enough pains or something. But I do write the first draft very quickly, and then I come back and work on it.

—Eilis Ni Dhuibhne

ANSWERS: EXERCISE 1-3

Answers will vary. The focus is on differences in tone for the same topic to three different audiences.

demonstrates an even-handed tone. Similarly, avoid SEXIST LANGUAGE, which involves words with sexist overtones (21g), or you'll alienate your readers because you appear to be insensitive to gender issues or crude in your understanding about the effects of language choices.

Another type of language that carries a message larger than the words themselves is pretentious language. Its use implies either that you're showing off to impress people (which always backfires) or that you're obscuring a message. Choose straightforward rather than extravagant words (use *concert,* not *orchestral event*) if you want readers to take you seriously. Also, readers usually assume that you want to conceal something unpleasant if you use EUPHEMISMS (such as *downsizing* or *rightsizing* instead of *cutting jobs*). Box 6 lists guidelines for handling tone in your writing.

BOX 6   **SUMMARY**

 How to use tone in writing

- Reserve a highly informal tone for conversational writing.
- Use a formal or medium level of formality in your academic writing and when you write for supervisors, professionals, and other people you know from a distance.
- Avoid an overly formal, ceremonial tone.
- Avoid sarcasm and other forms of nastiness.
- Choose language appropriate for your topic and your readers.
- Choose words that work with your message, not against it.
- Whatever tone you choose to use, be consistent in each document.

EXERCISE 1-3

Using the topics listed here, work individually or with your peer-response group to think through specific ways the tone of an essay would differ for the following three audiences: a college instructor, a close friend, and a supervisor at a job. Be ready to discuss in some detail how the three essays on each topic would differ for each audience. For help, consult sections 1d and 1e.

1. Suggestions for a fair way to evaluate each person's work
2. Benefits of having a more casual dress code
3. An explanation of why you were absent from class yesterday

1f What does "sources for writing" mean?

Sources for writing consist of material that contains someone else's ideas, not yours. Sources, often called *outside sources,* include credible information on the Internet, library collections, and the spoken words of experts. Sources can add authority to what you write, especially if the topic is open to debate. But be careful: Different instructors have differing policies on students' using outside sources. Some instructors want students to draw on sources only when writing a research paper (Chapters 31–37). Other instructors encourage "source-based writing" for most assignments. Still other instructors never want students to use outside sources. Find out your instructor's stand on the use of sources so you can fulfill the requirements of your course successfully.

Some students wonder whether consulting sources for their writing might suggest that they can't come up with ideas of their own. Actually, the opposite is true. When students use sources well, they demonstrate their ability to locate relevant sources, assess whether the sources are credible and worth using, integrate the material with skill, and credit the sources accurately. To achieve this, follow the guidelines in Box 7 at the end of this section.

Of course, no matter how many outside sources you refer to, you remain your own first source. Throughout your life, you've been building a fund of knowledge by reading, going to school, attending cultural and sports events, hearing speeches, watching television, and exploring the Internet. The basis for your writing is the information you have, as well as your ideas, reflections, reactions, and opinions. Sources offer support and additional information and points of view, but you're always the starting point for your writing.

When you use sources in your writing, never plagiarize. As a student, you want to become a full participant in the community of knowledge seekers and makers. The expected honorable standard for participants is always to credit thinkers who have come before you and upon whose shoulders you stand as you learn and create. You therefore never want to behave unethically by stealing someone's thinking or language.

PLAGIARISM occurs when you take ideas or words from a source without revealing that you used a source. Always reveal your source and credit it by using DOCUMENTATION to tell your readers the exact place where your thinking is influenced by a source. Adhering to the requirements of the DOCUMENTATION STYLE you're using (Chapters 34–36), state the name of the source and where anyone who wishes to consult it can find it.

If you forget to document your sources, you're plagiarizing (Chapter 33). Using quotation marks without naming your source is a form of plagiarizing. Leaving out quotation marks from a direct quotation that you take from a source, even if you name the source, is a form of plagiarizing.

QUOTATION: ON WRITING
A warm smile is the universal language of kindness.
—William Arthur Ward

QUOTATION: ON WRITING
No person is your friend who demands your silence, or denies your right to grow.
—Alice Walker

Plagiarism is a major academic offense. A student who plagiarizes can instantly fail a course or be expelled from college.

New computer technologies make plagiarism especially easy to detect today. If ethical reasons aren't enough to prevent you from plagiarizing, then the real chance of strong punishment definitely should be.

BOX 7   SUMMARY

 Guidelines for using sources in writing

- Evaluate sources critically. Not all are accurate, true, or honest (5g, especially Box 34).
- Represent your sources accurately. Be sure to quote, PARAPHRASE, and summarize well so that you avoid distorting the material (Chapter 33).
- Never plagiarize (Chapter 33).
- Know the difference between writing a SUMMARY and writing a SYNTHESIS (5e). A summary means all you do is report the source material. That is not enough. A synthesis means you make intelligent connections between the source and your ideas, or between a variety of sources, or between a variety of sources and your ideas. Synthesizing is what college writers are expected to do.
- Credit your sources with DOCUMENTATION that names them clearly and completely. Ask your instructor which DOCUMENTATION STYLE to use. Five widely used styles are presented in Chapters 34–36.

ESL NOTE: In many cultures other than those in the United States and Canada, original thinking and responses to reading aren't acceptable. Instead, instructors expect students to respect and copy the thoughts and exact language of scholars, without naming the people who wrote the scholarship. This practice is not acceptable in the United States and most British-based educational systems. You always need to use documentation to credit your source. Otherwise, you are plagiarizing—that is, "stealing" the ideas of others, which is a major offense.

1g   What resources can help me with writing?

Your **personal bookshelf** needs to contain three essential volumes: a dictionary, a thesaurus, and a handbook for writers. A **dictionary** is indispensable. Most college bookstores offer a variety of hardback "college dictionaries." Before buying one, browse through a few to read some definitions you want to learn or to understand more clearly.

Choose the book you like best. Also, a lightweight paperback abridged dictionary in your book pack can be very handy for checking unknown words on the spot. Unabridged dictionaries list all recognized words in standard use in English. Being comprehensive, they're usually heavy and oversized, so the reference section of every library usually stocks one for all students to consult (21e.1).

Another valuable resource for writers is a **thesaurus,** which is a collection of synonyms. The alphabetically arranged ones are the easiest to use. Check for this feature, as it is not an automatic arrangement for a thesaurus. *Roget's 21st Century Thesaurus* (Dell, 1999) is an excellent volume arranged alphabetically.

A **handbook for writers** is also vital for you to own. A handbook—such as the one you're holding as you read this—gives you detailed information about rules of grammar, punctuation, and other writing conventions. It also offers extensive advice about how to write successfully, whether for college, business, or the public. It shows you step by step how to write and document research papers. Some handbooks, including this one, contain guidance on how to write for a variety of courses other than English. You need all this information to write successfully in courses other than English and in your career after college.

Finally, **college libraries,** sometimes called *learning resource centers,* are essential for writers. Libraries are fully stocked with all manner of reference books, circulating books, resources for online access, and more. Some of the books listed above are available online through computers, although you'll likely need to be connected by going through the library's Web site. Before you actually use the library, spend some time getting to know what's available. Then you can dive right in when you need to get information. Chapter 32 provides extensive advice on using the library.

1h How do writers use technology?

For centuries, new technologies have changed how writers write. Consider, for example, the difference between writing with a quill pen, a pencil, and a manual typewriter. Today, of course, when you think of technology and writing, computers and everything associated with them usually come to mind: printers, scanners, the Internet, e-mail and instant messaging, the World Wide Web, digital still and video cameras, and thousands of software programs.

Writing for most jobs now requires at least some use of computers. Similarly, more and more college writing assignments need to be done on computers. Some professors make allowances for students for whom this is impossible, but the clear trend is toward word-processed final drafts. If you own a computer or live with someone who does, you enjoy some obvious conveniences. If you do not, however, you can take advantage of computer labs on most campuses, often in libraries or student centers; public

QUOTATION: ON WRITING
Writing is the hardest work in the world not involving heavy lifting.

—Pete Hamill

libraries; Internet cafes; and printing shops (although these last two will cost you money). Computers are important tools for writers in four ways.

1h.1 Word processing tools

A computer's word processing software (Microsoft Word or WordPerfect) offers invaluable help at various stages of the WRITING PROCESS. Word processing allows you easily to add, delete, revise, or move around material, including from one document to another. You can always have a clean copy. Some writers prefer to print their drafts to revise or edit them by hand and then enter the changes in the computer; other writers do almost all their revising and editing on the screen. As you gain more experience in writing, you'll likely develop strategies that best suit your process.

Word processing also allows you to make quick format changes. You can easily shift between single-spacing and double-spacing or put a WORKS CITED page or bibliography into the correct DOCUMENTATION STYLE. In addition, word processing allows you to create clean-looking tables or graphs. The toolbar at the top of the word processing window contains numerous formatting options, and spending some time exploring how they work can save you time in the long run.

Formatting toolbar

Title bar   Menu bar   Standard toolbar   Ruler

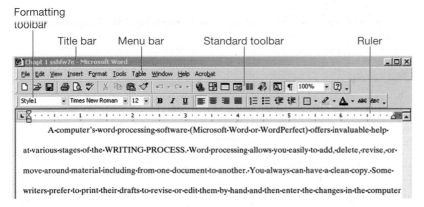

A·computer's·word·processing·software·(Microsoft·Word·or·WordPerfect)·offers·invaluable·help·

at·various·stages·of·the·WRITING·PROCESS.·Word·processing·allows·you·easily·to·add,·delete,·revise,·or·

move·around·material·including·from·one·document·to·another.·You·always·can·have·a·clean·copy.·Some·

writers·prefer·to·print·their·drafts·to·revise·or·edit·them·by·hand·and·then·enter·the·changes·in·the·computer

Microsoft Word for Windows toolbar and document

Word processing programs also have special aids for writers built into their software. They offer some advantages, but they also have severe limitations. In no case are such tools substitutes for your own careful editing and proofreading. Software, after all, can't "think" and make distinctions between *form* and *from* in spelling, between the way you use or misuse *deep* and *profound,* or between an unwarranted and a warranted use of a passive construction (8p).

- **Spell-check programs** show you words that don't match the dictionary in the software. These programs are a big help for spotting a misspelling or mistyping (called *typos*), but they won't call your attention to your having typed *west* when you intended to type *rest.*
- **Thesaurus programs** give you SYNONYMS for words. They can't, however, tell you which ones fit well into your particular sentences. Whenever a synonym is unfamiliar or hazy, look it up in your dictionary. You don't want to use words that strike you as attractive options, but then turn out to distort your communication. For example, a synonym for *friend* is *acquaintance,* but these words have different senses.
- **Grammar- or style-check programs** check your writing against the software's strict interpretations of rules of grammar, word use, punctuation, and other conventions. They signal you about elements of your writing that differ from the program's standards. Can you always rely on those standards? No. While most signals are useful for getting you to rethink the way you've said something, the final decision about how to deliver your message is yours. You might decide to use a semicolon even when the program suggests a period, to keep the spelling of a HOMONYM (such as *it's* versus *its*), to retain a phrase even when the program says you aren't being concise, or to accept a long sentence when it follows or is followed by a few very short sentences. Consult this handbook when you're not sure what a program is suggesting or whether you're justified in deviating from the program's rules.

QUOTATION: ON WRITING
Character—the willingness to accept responsibility for one's own life—is the source from which self-respect springs.
—Joan Didion

21

1h.2 Computers as research tools

In addition to helping you produce and revise writing, computers help you find sources. Most library catalogs and databases are now searchable with computers. Catalogs and databases are large collections of references that experts have gathered and organized in several ways, most

Location is
Humanities
Index

Options for searches
on FirstSearch

Extended URL
for this page

URL for FirstSearch is
<http://firstsearch.oclc.org>

Navigation bar in
FirstSearch

List continues

Sources found
in this search

Results of a FirstSearch of the *Humanities Index*

importantly by topic. You can search them from computers in the library itself or, often, remotely online. Chapter 32 provides extensive explanations of such catalogs and databases and how best to use them.

Computers also help you find sources on the World Wide Web (the Web), a vast collection of Web sites and pages that are accessible through the Internet. Chapter 32 explains how to use the Web—and how to avoid misusing it. As you find information on the Web, keep in mind that anyone can post anything on the Web. Some of what you find is just plain wrong, although much is accurate and useful. To help you evaluate the quality of a Web site, see Boxes 141 and 142 in Chapter 32. The following example shows results from a search for sources on "animal rights" in an online database. This database, the *Humanities Index,* is a high-quality site compiled by professional bibliographers.

1h.3 Computers as tools for managing your work

Computers allow you to save different drafts of your papers as they evolve or to organize your work into various folders. For example, you might create a folder for each paper you write and also keep all notes, drafts, and ideas related to that project in the folder. Many people now take notes from sources directly into computer files. Below you can see how one student has started a folder for all the projects in her Writing 001 course. In the sub-folder for project 2 she has ideas, notes, peer comments, and drafts. She created this folder in the "My Documents" directory in Microsoft Word.

Name of student's work folder (in My Documents)

URL (in My Documents)

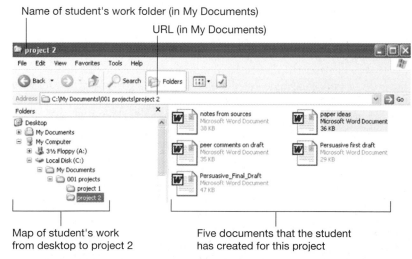

Map of student's work from desktop to project 2

Five documents that the student has created for this project

Student's directory for her writing projects

QUOTATION: ON WRITING
I can say now that one of the big reasons [for writing] was this: I instinctively recognized an opportunity to transcend some of my personal failings—things about myself I didn't particularly like and wanted to change but didn't know how.

—John Steinbeck

BACKGROUND
In his essay "Field Trips to Virtual Public Squares? Purposes, Audiences, Teachers, and Student-Written Web Pages," in *Public Works: Student Writing as Public Text*, edited by Emily J. Isaacs and Phoebe Jackson (Portsmouth, NH: Boynton/Cook-Heinemann, 2001, 61–68), Jonathan Benda explores issues that students confront when they write for the Internet.

1h.4 Computers as communication tools

You're probably familiar with e-mail and instant messaging as ways to communicate with friends and others. These and similar technologies can sometimes also help you with formal writing projects. Discussing a TOPIC online with classmates can help generate ideas for writing, and some instructors organize such discussions in Web-based programs like WebCT, Blackboard, and WebBoard.

Computers also allow you to share drafts of your work with others without physically meeting them. You can send a draft as an e-mail attachment to classmates for peer response—or even to your instructors for comments, if they invite you to do so. Some instructors post student papers on class Web pages so that other students can read and respond to the writing. Obviously, if you're working on a collaborative project, the ability to share drafts and to discuss revisions online has many advantages.

1h.5 Computers and new forms of writing

For decades, student writing in college has been essays and reports consisting only of words, with occasional tables and figures. These forms will always remain essential, and you need to master them. However, computers enable new kinds of writing. Instead of traditional diaries, writers can keep Web logs (or Blogs), which are online journals that anyone can read through the Internet. In addition, writers can now copy and paste photographs or illustrations into documents, and they can use different fonts and graphical elements such as ruler lines or textboxes. Interestingly, certain documents today can exist only in digital form on computers because they contain audio or video files, or they connect to other documents and Web sites. Yet another development is that some instructors may ask students to develop a Web page rather than write a traditional paper.

If you, like most students, have a limited knowledge of how to produce these emerging types of documents, don't worry. Instructors who require such projects know that many of you need help to get started. On the other hand, even if you're technologically skilled, always check with your instructors before you use graphical and other elements in your papers because instructors may have important reasons for assigning traditional papers—they may want you to focus more on crafting ideas and arguments through words than on designing and manipulating images.

Chapter 2

Planning and Shaping

2a What is the writing process?

Many people think that professional writers can sit down at their computers, think of ideas, and magically produce a finished draft, word by perfect word. Experienced writers know better. They know that writing is a process, a series of activities that starts the moment they begin thinking about a subject and ends with proofreading the final draft. Experienced writers also know that good writing is rewriting, again and yet again. Their drafts are filled with additions, deletions, rewordings, and rearrangements.

For example, see below how I revised the paragraph you just read. I didn't make all the changes at the same time, even though it looks that way on the example. I went through the paragraph four times before I

~~Chapter One discusses what writing is. This chapter explains how writing happens.~~ Many people think that professional writers can sit down at their computers, think of ideas, and *magically* produce a finished draft, word by perfect word. Experienced writers know better. They know that writing is a process. ~~The writing process is~~ a series of activities that starts the moment *they begin* thinking about a subject ~~begins~~ and ends with *proofreading* the final draft. Experienced writers also know that good writing is rewriting, again and yet again. *Their drafts are filled with additions, deletions, rewordings, and rearrangements.*

Draft and revision of Lynn Troyka's first paragraph in Chapter 2

was satisfied with it. Notice that I deleted one sentence, combined two sentences, added a sentence at the end, and changed wording throughout.

Writing is an ongoing process of considering alternatives and making choices. The better you understand the writing process, the better you'll write; and the more you feel in control of your writing, the more you'll enjoy it.

In this chapter, I discuss each part of the writing process separately. In real life, the steps overlap. They loop back and forth, which is why writing is called a recursive process. Box 8 lists the steps.

BOX 8   SUMMARY

 Steps in the writing process

Planning means discovering and compiling ideas for your writing.

Shaping means organizing your material.

Drafting means writing your material into sentences and paragraphs.

Revising means evaluating your draft and then rewriting it by adding, deleting, rewording, and rearranging.

Editing means checking for correct grammar, spelling, punctuation, and mechanics.

Proofreading means reading your final copy to eliminate typing or handwriting errors.

Do you like, as I do, to visualize a process? If so, see the drawing here. The arrows show movement. You might move back before going ahead (perhaps as you revise, you realize you need to plan some more); or you might skip a step and come back to it later (perhaps in the middle of revising, you jump into editing for a few minutes because a punctuation or grammar rule affects how you express your point); and so on.

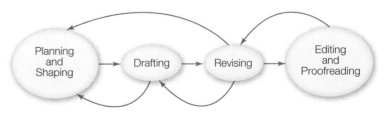

Visualizing the writing process

As you work with the writing process, allow yourself to move freely through each step to see what's involved. Notice what works best for you. As you develop a sense of your preferred writing methods, adapt the process to fit each writing situation. No single way exists for applying the writing process.

My personal advice from one writer to another is this: Most writers struggle some of the time with ideas that are difficult to express, sentences that won't take shape, and words that aren't precise. Be patient with yourself. Don't get discouraged. Writing takes time. The more you write, the easier it will become—though writing never happens magically.

2b What terms describe different kinds of writing?

Terms that describe different types of writing are often used interchangeably. Most instructors attach specific meanings to each one. Listen closely so you can sort out what terms your instructor uses. If your instructor's use of terms isn't clear, ask for clarification. For example, the words *essay, theme,* and *composition* usually—but not always—refer to writing of about 500 to 1,000 words. In this handbook, I use *essay.* Similarly, the word *paper* can mean anything from a few paragraphs to a complex research project. In this handbook, I use *paper* for longer writing projects, such as research papers. Also, I sometimes use the general term *piece of writing* to refer to all types of writing.

2c What is a "writing situation"?

The writing situation of each assignment is the place to start with thinking about your writing. Its four elements are *topic, purpose, audience,* and *special requirements.* The questions in Box 9 cover each aspect.

BOX 9   SUMMARY

 Analyzing each writing situation

Topic: What topic will you be writing about?
Purpose: What is your purpose for writing? (1c)
Audience: Who is your audience? (1d)
Special requirements: How much time do you have to complete the assignment? What is the length requirement?

QUOTATION: ON WRITING
The number one reason why any professional writer writes is to pay the bills. This isn't the Lawn Tennis Association where you play just for the thrill of it.
—Jimmy Breslin

BACKGROUND
In his article "Publishing Group Projects: Decentering the Writing Classroom" (*Teaching English in the Two-Year College,* March 1999: 262–268), Kevin Alexander Boon describes a book production assignment that encourages students to examine the differing purposes of many different forms of communication.

TEACHING TIP
The concept of a writing situation may be new to many students. It is an inclusive term for the combination of topic, purpose, audience, and special requirements such as word or time limits. Each of these variables influences every decision a writer makes. These variables are especially important in narrowing a topic, as demonstrated by the inclusion of writing situation in the examples for narrowing a topic I give in 2d.3.

BACKGROUND
Much of what we believe about the composing processes of students comes from the
work of three researchers and their colleagues. Although their work was done years
ago, the influence of their ideas remains
strong. James Britton, in Britain's School
Council Project *The Development of Writing
Abilities*, 11–18 (London: Macmillan Education, 1975), observed that "writing is a deliberate act; one has to make up one's mind to
do it." Once we decide to write, he points
out, we begin the process by prewriting,
which involves trying to understand and solve
a particular writing problem. Also fundamental to our current understanding of the writing process is the work of Janet Emig,
reported in *The Composing Processes of
Twelfth Graders*, NCTE Research Report
No. 13 (Urbana: NCTE, 1971). As the title
suggests, she followed in detail the methods
of high school seniors as they made their way
through writing tasks. Finally, John R. Hayes
and Linda S. Flower provided a model for
other researchers with their "thinking aloud"
protocols, verbal descriptions of what writers
report they think and do while they compose
("Identifying the Organization of Writing
Processes" and "The Dynamics of Composing: Making Plans and Juggling Constraints,"
in *Cognitive Processes in Writing*, ed. Lee W.
Gregg and Erwin R. Steinberg. Hillsdale, NJ:
Erlbaum, 1980, 3–50). Although the methods
and terminology of these investigators vary,
they arrived at a fundamental agreement
about the writing process.

A **topic** is the foundation of every writing situation. As you think through a topic, you want to remain within the constraints of academic writing. Whatever your topic, stick to it, and resist any temptation to bend it in another direction.

The PURPOSE of most college writing is to inform or persuade (1c.2 and 1c.3). Some assignments state the writing purpose, while some only imply it. For example, if you were asked to "Describe government re-strictions on cigarette advertising," your purpose would be informative. In contrast, if you were asked to respond to the statement "Smoking should (or should not) be banned in all public places," your purpose would be persuasive.

But suppose your assignment doesn't indicate a writing purpose: for example, "Write an essay on smoking." Here, you're expected to choose a purpose and think about what you intend to write on the topic. As you plan how to develop the topic, you'll begin to see whether your purpose is informative or persuasive. It's normal to find yourself deciding to switch purposes midstream to better suit what you are saying.

Your reading AUDIENCE (1d) consists of everyone who will read what you write. According to your assignment and the procedures in your class, your audience includes your PEER-RESPONSE GROUP (1d.1), friends, readers who have specialized knowledge (1d.3) about your topic, and your instructor (1d.4). Think through the characteristics and expecta-tions of your audience so that your writing will successfully deliver its intended meaning.

Special requirements are practical matters such as how much time you're given to complete the assignment and how long your writing should be. For example, for an assignment due in one week, your read-ing audience expects more than one day's work. However, if an assign-ment is due overnight, your reading audience realizes you had to write in relative haste, though they never expect sloppy or careless work. Per-haps the highest expectations in a reading audience are applied to an as-signment that calls for reading or other research, so be sure to build time for that early in your schedule.

Some instructors put each assignment in writing, either on the board or in a handout. But other instructors give assignments orally during class, expecting you to write them down. Try to record every word. Don't hesitate to ask questions if you don't catch all the words or if something isn't clear—and be sure to write down the answers because they often tend to slip from memory. Listen, too, to questions other stu-dents ask, and write down the answers. Such notes can serve as useful springboards when you start writing. In the rest of this chapter, I pre-sent the writing processes of two college students, Carol Moreno and Lacie Juris, as they plan and shape their material. Then, in Chapter 3, you'll see Moreno's essay evolving through three separate, complete drafts. Later, in Chapter 6, you'll see how Juris's essay developed. To start, here are the written assignments each student received.

BACKGROUND
In "Say It, Don't Write It: Oral Structures as Framework for Teaching Writing" (*Journal of Basic Writing*, Spring 1994: 41–49), Pamela D. Dykstra explains how students benefit from becoming aware that speaking and writing are "two valid but different forms of communication."

Carol Moreno received this assignment:

Write an essay of 700 to 800 words discussing a challenge you faced and tried to meet. Your writing purpose can be informative or persuasive. Expect to write three drafts. (1) Your first draft, typed double-spaced, is due two classes from today. (2) Your clean second draft, typed double-spaced, without notes or comments, is due two classes later. Clip to it your first draft showing all notes you made to yourself or from comments your peer-response group made; you can handwrite notes and comments. I'll read your second draft as an "essay in progress" and will make comments to help you toward a third (and final) draft. (3) The third draft, typed double-spaced, is due one week after I return your second draft with my comments.

Lacie Juris was given this assignment:

Write an essay of 900 to 1,000 words that argues for a particular action on an issue that interests you. Your final draft is due in two weeks.

Moreno's first step was to analyze her writing situation (Box 9). She looked at the *topic*—a challenge she faced and tried to meet—and she saw that she needed to narrow it. She tentatively decided her *purpose* would be informative, though she thought she might have to switch to a persuasive purpose as she went along. She knew that she would share her first draft with her peer-response group to help her toward her second draft. She also understood that her instructor would be her final *audience*. She was aware of the *requirements* for time and length.

Juris also read her assignment and analyzed her writing situation. Because the *topic* was very broad, she knew she would have to spend a good deal of time deciding what she wanted to write about. On the other hand, she understood that her assigned *purpose* was persuasive. The *audience* was not specified; she knew that her instructor would be the main audience, but she also decided to write in such a way that would address a broader public audience. She kept in mind the *requirements* for time and length.

EXERCISE 2-1

For each assignment below, work individually or with a peer-response group to list the elements in the writing situation. Consult section 2c for help.

1. *Family and Consumer Science:* Write a 500- to 700-word essay that explains important safety procedures to daycare providers. This assignment is due in one week.

2. *Journalism:* Write a 300-word editorial for the student newspaper (to be published next week) supporting or attacking your college's plan to replace the food court with bookstore space for selling software and CDs. Draw on your personal experience or that of students you know.

3. *Art:* You have twenty minutes in class to discuss the differences between a photograph and painting of the same scene, using a specific example from the textbook or class discussions.

4. *Politics:* Write a one-paragraph description of what is meant by "freedom of the press."

5. *Computer Science:* Write a 1,000-word paper that argues that computers will/will not simulate most aspects of human intelligence in the next ten years. Read and draw on sources to support your argument. Be sure to document your sources. This assignment is due in two weeks.

2d How can I think through a writing topic?

Situations vary. Some assignments are very specific. For example, here's an assignment that leaves no room for choice: "Explain how oxygen is absorbed in the lungs." Students need to do precisely what's asked, taking care not to wander off the topic. Only rarely, however, are writing-class assignments as specific as that one. Often, you'll be expected to select your own topic (2d.1), broaden a narrow topic (2d.2), or narrow a broad topic (2d.3). Regardless of the situation, keep in mind that **what separates most good writing from bad is the writer's ability to move back and forth between general statements and specific details.**

2d.1 Selecting your own topic

If you have to choose a topic, don't rush. Take time to think through your ideas. Avoid getting so deeply involved in one topic that you cannot change to a more suitable topic in the time allotted.

Not all topics are suitable for ACADEMIC WRITING. Your topic needs to have inherent intellectual interest: ideas and issues meaty enough to demonstrate your thinking and writing abilities. Think through potential topics by breaking each into its logical subsections. Then, make sure you can supply sufficiently specific details to back up each general statement. Conversely, make sure you aren't bogged down in so many details you can't figure out what GENERALIZATIONS they support.

Work toward balance by finding a middle ground. Beware of topics so broad they lead to well-meaning but vague generalizations (for example, "Education is necessary for success"). Also, beware of topics so narrow that they lead nowhere after a few sentences (for example, "Jessica Max attends Tower College").

2d.2 Broadening a narrow topic

You know a topic is too narrow when you realize there's little to say after a few sentences. When faced with a too-narrow topic, think about underlying concepts. For example, suppose you want to write about Oprah Winfrey. If you chose "Oprah Winfrey's television show debuted in 1986," you'd be working with a single fact rather than a topic. To expand beyond such a narrow thought, you could think about the general area that your fact fits into—say, the impact of television shows on American culture. Although that is too broad to be a useful topic, you're headed in the right direction. Next, you might think of a topic that relates to Oprah's influence, such as "What impact has Oprah Winfrey's television show had on American culture since she began broadcasting in 1986?" Depending on your writing situation (2c), you might need to narrow your idea further by focusing on Oprah's impact in a single area, such as how her book club influenced publishing and reading habits, how her guests and topics brought certain issues to national visibility, or how the style of her show affected other talk shows.

2d.3 Narrowing a broad topic

Narrowing a broad topic calls for you to break the topic down into subtopics. Most broad subjects can be broken down in hundreds of ways, but you need not think of all of them. Settle on a topic that interests you, one narrowed enough—but not too much—from a broad topic. For example, if you're assigned "marriage" as the topic for a 1,000-word essay, you'd be too broad if you chose "What makes a successful marriage?" You'd be too narrow if you came up with "Alexandra and Gavin were married by a justice of the peace." You'd likely be on target with a subtopic such as "In successful marriages, husbands and wives learn to accept each other's faults." You could use 1,000 words to explain and give concrete examples of typical faults and discuss why accepting them is important. Here are two more examples:

SUBJECT	*music*
WRITING SITUATION	freshman composition class
	informative purpose
	instructor as audience
	500 words; one week
POSSIBLE TOPICS	"How music affects moods"
	"The main characteristics of country music"
	"The relationships between plots of Puccini's operas"

BACKGROUND
In his classic, often-cited essay "Writing as Process: How Writing Finds Its Own Meaning," in *Eight Approaches to Teaching Composition,* edited by Timothy Donovan and Ben McClelland (Urbana: NCTE, 1980, 3–20), Donald Murray discusses four forces that interact as the writer goes through the stages of rehearsing, drafting, and revising, moving in a recursive manner from exploration to clarification. They are the forces of collecting and connecting, writing and reading. Although writing may be ignited by any one of these forces in conjunction with any other, says Murray, once writing has begun, all of them begin to interact. The writer is often unaware of this interaction, as innate curiosity leads naturally to the act of collecting information, which at some point calls for control and order that make the act of connecting necessary. Connections, in turn, make the writer see information in a new way, generating more collected data. The acts of writing and reading proceed in a similar fashion. The writer sets down what is heard mentally, then reads the product, checking it against what was heard, and then rewrites it. Murray asserts that although each writing act is a complex, instantaneous interaction, the scale tips rapidly from one force to the other in response to the various needs of the writer dealing with rehearsing, drafting, or revising.

BACKGROUND
In *Composition-Rhetoric: Backgrounds, Theory, and Pedagogy* (Pittsburgh: University of Pittsburgh Press, 1997), Robert J. Connors recounts various notions of invention that have been studied and taught in American colleges since the early nineteenth century.

QUOTATION: ON WRITING
I don't wait to be struck by lightning and don't need certain slants of light in order to write.

—Toni Morrison

BACKGROUND
Many instructors today accept the system
defined by Richard Young that classifies
the theoretical bases for teaching invention
(planning) into four main categories: classical
invention, romantic invention, dramatism,
and tagmemic invention. *Classical invention*
refers to various systems based on the theories of ancient Greek and Roman rhetoricians
such as Aristotle and Cicero. *Romantic invention,* associated with D. Gordon Rohman,
tries to tap into the mysterious nonconscious
and nonrational creative powers of the mind
and often eschews formal methods of invention. *Dramatism* or *dramatistic invention* is
based on Kenneth Burke's pentad of agent,
scene, act, agency, and purpose, first described in *A Grammar of Motives* (1945).
Tagmemic invention is derived from Kenneth
Pike's tagmemic linguistic theory, but it has
its fullest realization in Richard Young, Alton
Becker, and Kenneth Pike's *Rhetoric: Discovery and Change* (1950).

TEACHING TIP
Students may be surprised to learn that all
writers find the blank sheet of paper (or blank
computer screen) a source of anxiety. The experienced writer knows that the most effective way to move past that feeling is to write
something, regardless of its value. Once the
clean surface has words on it, other words follow more easily. Unrelated ideas, notes, questions, examples—all help relieve the writer's
discomfort with getting started. A good habit
for students to cultivate is to jot down responses and reactions to writing tasks as soon
as they're given. These jottings can sometimes
be effective, lively catalysts for writing.

SUBJECT	*cities*
WRITING SITUATION	sociology course
	persuasive purpose
	peers and then instructor as audience
	950 to 1,000 words; ten days
POSSIBLE TOPICS	"Comforts of city living"
	"Discomforts of city living"
	"Importance of city planning for open spaces"

Carol Moreno knew her assigned topic—"a challenge you faced and
tried to meet" (2c)—was too broad. To narrow it, she used the following
structured techniques for discovering and compiling ideas: browsing her
journal (2f), FREEWRITING (2g), and MAPPING (2j). They helped her decide to write about the challenge of increasing her strength.

Lacie Juris also needed to narrow her topic. To explore several possible topics, she used BRAINSTORMING (2h). Once she had chosen a topic
(whether wild animals should be kept as pets), she used the "journalist's
questions" (2i) to compile more ideas and then a subject tree (2p) to
check whether she was ready to begin drafting.

2e What can I do if no ideas occur to me?

If you've ever felt you'll never think of anything to write about, don't
despair. Instead, use structured techniques, sometimes called *prewriting strategies* or *invention techniques,* for discovering and compiling
ideas. Professional writers use them to uncover hidden resources in
their minds. For a list of the techniques, see Box 10 (the parentheses

---

BOX 10   SUMMARY

 Ways to discover and compile ideas for writing

- Keep an idea log and a journal (2f).
- Freewrite (2g).
- Brainstorm (2h).
- Ask the "journalist's questions" (2i).
- Map (2j).
- Talk it over (2k).
- Do an Internet search (2l).
- Incubate (2m).

after each technique tell you where to find more explanation and an example).

Try out each one. Experiment to find out which techniques suit your style of thinking. Even if one technique produces good ideas, try another to see what additional possibilities might turn up.

Save all of the ideas you generate as you explore possible topics. You never know when something you have initially rejected might become useful from another point of view. Computers make it easy to keep a folder labeled, for example, "explorations," in which you can store your ideas.

ESL NOTE: The structured techniques discussed here aim to let your ideas flow out of you without judging them right away. If such ways of using language are unfamiliar to you or seem difficult to implement, consider doing them first in your native language and then translating them into English when one idea seems to have potential for your writing.

2f How do I use an idea log and a journal?

As you develop the habits of mind and behavior of a writer, your ease with writing will grow. One such habit is keeping an idea log. Professional writers are always on the lookout for ideas to write about and details to develop their ideas. They listen, watch, talk with people, and generally keep an open mind. Because they know that good ideas can evaporate as quickly as they spring to mind, they're always ready to jot down their thoughts and observations. Some carry a pocket-size notepad, while others use a PDA (personal digital assistant, such as a Palm Pilot) or a laptop. If you use an idea log throughout your college years, you'll see your powers of observation increase dramatically.

Additionally, many professional writers keep a daily writing **journal.** This allows you to have a conversation in writing with yourself. Your audience is you, so the content and tone can be as personal and informal as you wish. Even fifteen minutes a day can be enough. If you don't have that chunk of time, write in your journal before you go to bed, between classes, on a bus. Some people find that the feel of pen on paper, perhaps in a bound blank journal, is important to this kind of writing. Others keep journals in computer files. Several people even put their journals online as Blogs (short for Web logs). For examples of Blogs (or to start one of your own), go to <http://www.blogger.com/>.

Unlike a diary, a journal isn't a record of what you do each day. A journal is for your thoughts from your reading, your observations, even your dreams. You can respond to quotations, react to movies or plays, or reflect on your opinions, beliefs, and tastes. Keeping a journal can help you in three ways. First, writing every day gives you the habit of productivity so

TEACHING TIP: ESL
An activity that both ESL students and native speakers enjoy is the exchange journal. ESL students exchange entries on cultural matters with native speakers in a different class. In the first entry, students introduce themselves to their partners, perhaps including information like age, sex, marital status, place of birth, college major, and hobbies or interests. They then list some topics they're interested in learning about. In each subsequent weekly or biweekly entry, students explain an aspect of their culture: dating, courtship, family structure, food, school, manners, holidays, language, sports, entertainment, and so on. Entries are as long as students want to make them. Instructors rarely necessarily read the journals—and certainly never correct them—but instructors may require a report about the experience at the end of the term (and perhaps interim reports). The two instructors pass the journals back and forth to each other to distribute in classes; they should also arrange for the students to meet and interview each other near the end of the term, if possible. The assignment helps break down stereotypes and develops students' fluency in writing; indeed, some students write considerably better in journals than in compositions.

Note: Using two journals—one from ESL student to native speaker and one from native speaker to ESL student—makes it more convenient for students to write their reports. Bluebooks may be used for easy portability; when one is filled, the student can staple another to the back of the previous one.

that the more you write, the more you feel words pouring out of you onto paper, the more easily you'll write in all situations. Second, a journal instills the practice of close observation and discovery, two habits of mind that good writers cultivate. Third, a journal is an excellent source of ideas for assignments.

Here's an excerpt of a journal entry Carol Moreno had made before she got the assignment to write about having faced a challenge (see page 29). Even though she hadn't thought of her entry as a potential subject for a later essay, when she read through her journal for ideas, she realized that improving her physical preparedness for nursing school was indeed a challenge she had faced.

September 30 I got to add 5 more reps today and it's only the sixth weight lifting class. I wasn't really surprised— I can tell I'm stronger. I wonder if I'm strong enough yet to lift Gran into the wheelchair alone. I was so scared last summer when I almost dropped her. Besides being terrified of hurting her, I thought that somehow the admissions committee would find out and tell me I was too weak to be accepted into nursing school. What if I hadn't noticed the weight lifting course for P.E. credit!?! Weight lifting is the best exercise I've ever done and I'm not getting beefy looking either.

Excerpt from Carol Moreno's journal

2g What is freewriting?

Freewriting is writing nonstop. You write down whatever comes into your mind without stopping to wonder whether the ideas are good or the spelling is correct. When you freewrite, don't do anything to interrupt the flow. Don't censor any thoughts or flashes of insight. Don't go back and review. Don't delete.

Freewriting helps get you used to the "feel" of your fingers rapidly hitting computer keys or your pen moving across paper. Freewriting works best if you set a goal—perhaps writing for fifteen minutes or filling one or two pages. Keep going until you reach that goal, even if you have to write one one word repeatedly until a new word comes to mind. Some days when you read over your freewriting, it might seem mindless, but other days your interesting ideas may startle you.

In **focused freewriting,** you write from a specific starting point—a sentence from your general freewriting, an idea, a quotation, or anything else you choose. Except for this initial focal point, focused freewriting is the same as regular freewriting. Write until you meet your time or page limit, and don't censor yourself. If you go off the topic, that's fine: See where your thoughts take you. Just keep moving forward.

Like a journal, freewriting is a good source of ideas and details. When Carol Moreno thought her weight-training course might qualify for her assignment (see page 29), she explored the topic through focused freewriting on "pumping iron."

BACKGROUND
Peter Elbow, among the first theorists to discuss why freewriting is fundamental, explains in *Writing Without Teachers* (New York: Oxford University Press, 1973) how this process allows students to record their perceptions and feelings without the constraints of logic or structure. Elbow claims that this process allows student writers to generate a "center of gravity" that can later be revised more formally.

BACKGROUND
In "Mediated Texts: A Heuristic for Academic Writing" (*Journal of Basic Writing,* September 1998: 56–72), Eileen Biser, Linda Rubel, and Rose Marie Toscano offer an innovative invention technique that may be particularly valuable for ESL and basic writers.

Pumping iron—what the steroid jocks call it and exactly what I DO NOT want to be—a muscle cube. Great that Prof. Moore told us women's muscles don't bulk up much unless a weight lifting program is really intense—they just get longer. No bulk for me PLEASE. Just want upper body strength—oh and the aerobic stuff from swimming which makes me fell great. Lift sweat swim, lift sweat swim, lift sweat swim.

Excerpt from Carol Moreno's freewriting

2h   What is brainstorming?

Brainstorming means listing everything you can think of about a topic. Let your mind range freely, generating quantities of ideas. Write words, phrases, or sentence fragments—whatever comes to you. If you run out of ideas, ask yourself exploratory questions, such as *What is it? What is*

USING COLLABORATION
Recent research on small group dynamics suggests that the quality and number of ideas generated by invention can be enhanced by having group members first engage individually in such planning activities as mapping, clustering, and focused freewriting before coming together for group brainstorming.

Sometimes, the group will decide to narrow its focus to one of the ideas suggested during a brainstorming session. Before the group pursues its topic any further, you might repeat the individual-first, group-second planning process on the new, narrower idea.

it the same as? How is it different? Why or how does it happen? How is it done? What causes it or results from it? What does it look, smell, sound, feel, or taste like?

After you've compiled a list, go to step two: Look for patterns, ways to group the ideas into categories. You'll probably find several categories. Set aside any items that don't fit into a group. If a category interests you but has only a few items, brainstorm that category alone.

You can brainstorm in one concentrated session or over several days, depending on how much time you have for an assignment. Brainstorming in a PEER-RESPONSE GROUP can be especially fruitful: One person's ideas bounce off the next person's, and collectively more ideas come to mind.

When brainstorming or FREEWRITING on a computer, try "invisible writing." Temporarily turn off your computer monitor. A blank screen can help you focus on getting the words out without the temptation to stop and criticize, but the computer will still be recording your words. When you can write no more, turn on the monitor to see what you have.

Brainstorming was a technique Lacie Juris used to find her topic about keeping wild animals as pets (6b). Brainstorming helped her think through several topics and generate some ideas about the one that most appealed to her.

— women on TV commercials: realistic?
— health care for poor people—don't know much on that
— holidays are too commercial
— parking situation at this college—solutions?
— protecting wild animals
— wild animals as pets—that bothers me; why?
— is it healthy for the animals? for people? is it fair?
— famous people and their pets nope
— laws about pets and pet owners

Lacie Juris's brainstorming

EXERCISE 2-2

Here's a list brainstormed for a writing assignment. The topic was "Ways to promote a new movie." Working individually or in a peer-response group, look over the list and group the ideas. You'll find that some ideas don't fit into a group. Then, add any other ideas you have to the list.

coming attractions	suspense
TV ads	book the movie was based on
provocative	locations
movie reviews	rating
how movie was made	adventure
sneak previews	newspaper ads
word of mouth	stars
director	dialogue
topical subject	excitement
special effects	photography

2i What are the "journalist's questions"?

When journalists report a story, they gather and write about information by asking who did what, where it happened, when it happened, and why and how it happened. The same questions come in handy for writers exploring a topic. The **journalist's questions** are *Who? What? When? Where? Why?* and *How?*

Lacie Juris used the journalist's questions to expand her thinking on the problems of keeping wild animals as pets. Her answers, listed below, showed her that she had enough material for a good essay.

WHO?   **Who** benefits from keeping wild animals as pets?

WHAT?   **What** kinds of pets do people keep?

WHEN?   **When** did the practice of owning wild animals begin?

WHERE?   **Where** can I find evidence that wild animals make dangerous pets?

WHY?   **Why** do some people think they have a right to do this?

HOW?   **How** exactly would we stop this process?

2j What is mapping?

Mapping, also called *clustering,* is a visual form of brainstorming. When some writers actually see ways that their ideas connect, they begin to think more creatively. Other writers like mapping to help them check the logical relationships between ideas.

To map, write your topic in the middle of a sheet of paper, and draw a circle around it. Now, moving out from the center, use lines and circles to show ideas that are subtopics of the topic in the center circle. Continue to subdivide and add details, as the example below shows. At any time, you can move to a blank space on your map and start a new subtopic. Try to keep going without censoring yourself.

Carol Moreno used mapping to prompt herself to discover ideas about women and weight training. When she finished, she was satisfied that she'd have enough to say in her essay.

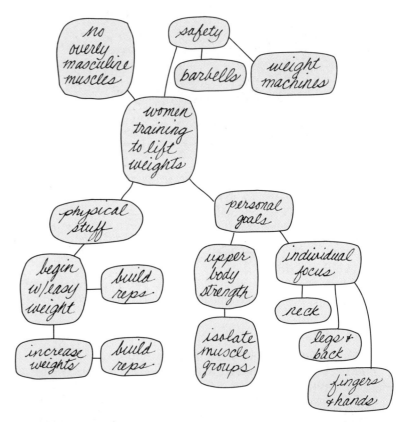

Carol Moreno's mapping

2k How can "talking it over" help?

Talking it over is based on the notion that two heads are better than one. The expression "bouncing ideas off each other" captures this idea. When you discuss a topic with someone interested in listening and making suggestions, you often think of new ideas. You can collaborate with others while brainstorming, asking the journalist's questions, or mapping. Ways of approaching a point of discussion include debating, questioning, analyzing (5b), evaluating (5c), synthesizing (5e), and assessing reasoning (5i).

People you trust can serve as "sounding boards" and tell you if your ideas are complete and reasonable. If your instructor sets up PEER-RESPONSE GROUPS in your class, you might ask the other members to serve as sounding boards. Otherwise, talk with a good friend or another adult.

2l How can an Internet search help?

Internet searches help you find topics to write about; understand your subject's categories from the most general to the most specific; and locate specific information. Internet searches scan the WORLD WIDE WEB using **search engines,** which are software programs that rapidly search and find online information sources. Some instructors want students to think of ideas on their own, without searching the Web. If that's the case, don't.

Chapter 33 provides extensive guidelines for searching the Internet. Briefly, however, try <http://www.google.com>. When you get there, click the "Directory" button to see a screen that lists broad subject areas.

Next, click on "Society" to see a number of slightly more specific topics. Note that each of them would be much too broad to write about. However, if you keep clicking on topic headings, you'll move to more and more specific subjects. Browsing through the layers of topics can help you think of several ideas for your writing. If you know a general topic area, you can type it in the search window of the program, then click on more specific subcategories.

EXERCISE 2-3

On a computer connected to the Internet, go to <http://www.google.com>. Click on "Directory" and then choose one of the headings. Continue to click on topics under that heading to create a "path" to a specific possible topic. Be ready to explain the sequence (or path) you used, what you found, and what you think the strengths and weaknesses of the topics you identified would be. Finally, go back to the opening "Directory" page and repeat the process with a different heading.

TEACHING TIP
Still fresh today are the ideas of Jeanne H. Simpson in *The Elements of Invention* (New York: Macmillan, 1990). Simpson suggests six guidelines for students using planning techniques.

1. *Try to do all the steps in an invention system.* If you don't, the world won't end; but you might miss a good opportunity to explore an idea.

2. *Ignore redundancies.* Most invention systems will have you repeating yourself a bit. It's all right to do that. In fact, you may get a better grip on a slippery idea the second time you write about it.

3. *Write as much as you can in response to any step in a system.* Don't worry about the beauty of your writing; the main thing is to get your ideas down on paper where you can see them and work with them.

4. *Forget about grammar, punctuation, and spelling for now.* Just dump the ideas down however you can. You can clean them up later.

5. *Keep going, even if you are drawing a blank.* Make the pen, pencil, or cursor move no matter what. Eventually, something will occur to you.

6. *Reward yourself when you've finished a good workout with an invention system.* Take a break or perhaps have a snack. A mental "cool-down" period is often as important as a physical one; use it to help you gain some perspective on what you have written so far.

"Doing invention the right way," Simpson writes, "just means doing it consistently and with commitment. The only wrong answer in invention is a blank page" (3).

ANSWERS: EXERCISE 2-3
Answers will vary according to topic chosen. This is an Internet-based activity. The point is that each topic should be explored for sequences with sections 2f to 2k in mind.

QUOTATION: ON WRITING
Genius begins great works; labor alone finishes them.

—Joseph Joubert

QUOTATION: ON WRITING
Writing is just having a sheet of paper, a pen and not a shadow of an idea of what you're going to say.

—Françoise Sagan

ANSWERS: EXERCISE 2-4
Answers will vary.

URL for Google
<http://www.google.com>

Choices within Google

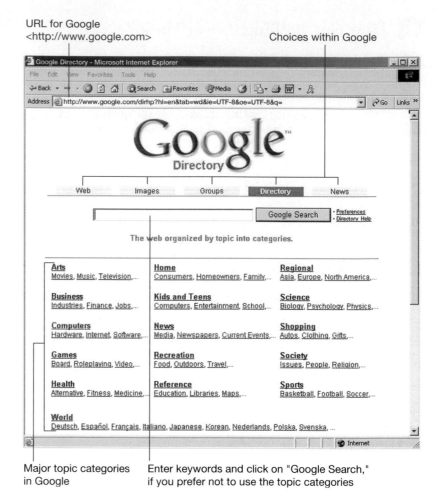

Major topic categories in Google

Enter keywords and click on "Google Search," if you prefer not to use the topic categories

Google subject directory

EXERCISE 2-4

Explore some of the following topics by typing them into the search window of a search engine. You can use Google, as for Exercise 2-3, or you can try a different search engine. Be ready to explain the sequence of topics you discover.

1. global warming
2. intelligence
3. plagiarism
4. memory
5. disability

URL for major topic category "Society"

Enter keywords and click "Google Search" if you prefer not to use the "Society" topic categories

Topic categories within major topic "Society"

Google "Society" directory

2m How can incubation help me?

Incubation refers to giving your ideas time to grow and develop. This technique works especially well when you need to step back and evaluate what you've discovered and compiled for your writing. For example, you might not see how your material can be pulled together at first, but if you let it incubate, you might discover connections you didn't see originally. Conversely, if some parts of your essay seem too thin in content, incubation gives you distance from your material so that you can decide what works. Ideally, incubate your ideas overnight or for a couple of days; but even a few hours can help.

BACKGROUND
In "Habits of Mind: Historical Configurations
of Textual Ownership in Peer Writing
Groups" (*College Composition and Communication,* May 1998: 234–255), Candace
Spigelman argues that students' attitudes
about authorship and intellectual property
rights are evidence of cultural "habits of
mind." She examines Western historical ideas
that have influenced current concepts of textual ownership.

ANSWERS: EXERCISE 2-5
Answers will vary.

If you don't have the luxury of a lengthy incubation period, some
strategies may help you jump-start it. One method is to turn your attention to something entirely unrelated to your writing. Concentrate hard
on that other matter so that you give your conscious mind over to it totally. After a while, relax and guide your mind back to your writing.
Often, you'll see what you've discovered and compiled for writing in a
different way. Another strategy for incubation is to allow your mind to
wander without thinking about anything in particular. Relax and open
your mind to random thoughts, but don't dwell on any one thought very
long. After a while, guide your mind back to your writing. Often, you'll
see solutions that hadn't occurred to you before.

EXERCISE 2-5

Try each structured technique for discovering and compiling ideas discussed in 2e through 2m. Use your own topics or select from the suggestions below.

1. A dream trip
2. An important personal decision
3. Professional sports
4. Advertisements on television
5. What you want in a life partner

2n   How can shaping help me?

Shaping writing means organizing your material. Like a story, an essay
needs a beginning, a middle, and an end. The essay's introduction sets
the stage; the essay's body paragraphs provide the substance of your
message in a sequence that makes sense; the conclusion ends the essay
logically. The major elements in an informative essay are listed in Box
11. (For the major elements in a persuasive essay using classical argument, see Box 39 in 6f.)

BOX 11   SUMMARY

 Elements in an informative essay

1. **Introductory paragraph:** Leads into the topic of the essay and tries
   to capture the reader's interest.
2. **Thesis statement:** States the central message of the writing. The
   thesis statement (2q) usually appears at the end of the introductory
   paragraph.
3. **Background information:** Provides a context for understanding
   the points a writer wants to make. You can integrate background

→

> ## Elements in an informative essay (*continued*)
>
> information into the introductory paragraph. More complex information may require a separate paragraph of information (as in the second paragraph in Carol Moreno's essay, in section 3g).
>
> 4. **Points of discussion:** Support the essay's thesis statement. They're the essential content of the body paragraphs in an essay. Each point of discussion consists of a general statement backed up by specific details.
> 5. **Concluding paragraph:** Ends the essay smoothly, flowing logically from the rest of the essay (4k).

Each paragraph's length in an informative essay needs to be in proportion to its function. Introductory and concluding paragraphs are usually shorter than body paragraphs. Body paragraphs need to be somewhat approximate to each other in length. If one body paragraph becomes overly long in relation to the others, consider breaking it into two paragraphs. (I discuss paragraph writing extensively in Chapter 4.)

2o How can looking for "levels of generality" help me?

Generality is a relative term. Concepts exist in the context of—in relationship with—other concepts. More general concepts belong together (can be grouped), while less general concepts belong grouped. When you look for **levels of generality,** you're figuring out which ideas or concepts can be grouped. Levels of generality start with the most general and work down to the most specific. Conversely, **levels of specificity** start with the most specific and work up to the most general. Being aware of levels, particularly when writing body paragraphs, gives you a sensible sequence for presenting your material. Use whichever pattern works for you because each sequence is merely the reverse of the other. Here's an example.

LEVELS OF GENERALITY (BIG TO SMALL) ▽

MOST GENERAL: LEVEL 1	a bank
LESS GENERAL: LEVEL 2	money in the bank
LESS GENERAL: LEVEL 3	bank account
LESS GENERAL: LEVEL 4	checking account
LEAST GENERAL: LEVEL 5	account #123456 at Bank EZCome, EZGo

BACKGROUND

Writers, both amateurs and professionals, tend to devise rituals that help them begin and carry out a piece of writing. Some of them are elaborate; some are relatively simple. They're identifiable by the fact that they're repeated actions that seem to be irrelevant to the task at hand but that are in some way helpful to the writer looking for ideas and ways to express them. Some are silly, such as using the same coffee mug each time one writes, or illogical, such as sweeping the front walk before getting started, but the fact is that they're effective in helping a writer make the transition from some other activity to that of composition. In "Writing Rituals" (ERIC ED 295 172), Ann B. Dobie shares the results of her study of students' and professional writers' composing habits. Dobie suggests that an understanding of these rituals can help improve student writing.

Writers who are in the process of devising writing rituals can make their individual habits more productive by being aware of which steps are helpful and which are not. They can begin by asking themselves questions about where, when, and with what they write. Where do they get the most work done? Does it afford them access to materials they need? Is it free from interruptions? Does it make them comfortable but not too relaxed? Can they see well? Do they have room to spread out notes and books? What time of day or night do they usually do their writing? Are they alert and energetic at that time? Does it give them a block of time in which to work? Do they use a typewriter? a legal pad? a word processor? a spiral notebook? What objects, environments, or activities that aren't directly connected with writing provide a sense of well-being during the process?

The answers will vary from one writer to another, but for best results, the process should remain fairly constant with the individual. Rituals are habits that provide structure—reassurance that the writer has done a task this way once before. With each repetition, they become more comfortable, making the writer feel more competent, more at home with the act of writing.

LEVELS OF SPECIFICITY (SMALL TO BIG) △

MOST SPECIFIC: LEVEL 5	account #123456 at Bank EZCome, EZGo
LESS SPECIFIC: LEVEL 4	checking account
LESS SPECIFIC: LEVEL 3	bank account
LESS SPECIFIC: LEVEL 2	money in the bank
LEAST SPECIFIC: LEVEL 1	a bank

2p How can a subject tree help me?

A **subject tree** shows you visually whether you have sufficient content, at varying levels of generality or specificity, to start a first draft of your writing. A subject tree also visually demonstrates whether you have a good balance of general ideas and specific details. If what you have are mostly general ideas—or, the other way around, mostly specific details—go back to techniques for discovering and compiling ideas (2e through 2m) so that you can come up with the sorts of materials that are missing.

Lacie Juris used a subject tree, created using tools available in Microsoft Word, to help her shape the fifth paragraph in her essay (6m).

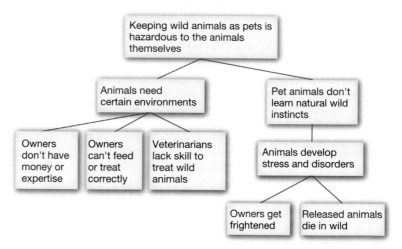

Lacie Juris's subject tree for her essay

2q What is a thesis statement?

A **thesis statement** is the central message of an essay. It's the essay's main idea. As a writer, you want to write a thesis statement with great care so that it prepares your readers for what follows in the essay. This means your thesis statement has to reflect with some accuracy the content of your essay. Box 12 lists the basic requirements for a thesis statement.

BOX 12   SUMMARY

 Basic requirements for a thesis statement

- It states the essay's subject—the topic that you discuss.
- It conveys the essay's purpose—either informative or persuasive.
- It indicates your focus—the assertion that presents your point of view.
- It uses specific language, not vague words.
- It may briefly state the major subdivisions of the essay's topic.

Some instructors add to these basic requirements for a thesis statement. You might, for example, be asked to put your thesis statement at the end of your introductory paragraph (as in the final draft of Carol Moreno's essay, in section 3g.3). Some instructors require that the thesis statement be contained in one sentence; other instructors permit two sentences if the topic is complex. All requirements, basic and additional, are designed to help you develop a thesis statement that will guide the writing of your essay and help you communicate clearly with your reader. By the way, never confuse the role of a thesis statement with the role of an essay's title (3c.3).

ESL NOTE: A thesis statement, especially in the introductory paragraph, is commonly found in the ACADEMIC WRITING of North American and some other cultures. If your culture would consider such an early, blunt, and straightforward statement to be rude or crude, respect your tradition but nevertheless write one for classes at North American colleges.

Most writers find that their thesis statement changes somewhat with each successive draft of an essay. Still, when you revise its language, be sure to stick to the essential idea you want to communicate. A thesis statement is a guide; it helps you stay on the topic and develop your ideas in an essay. To start, make an **assertion**—a sentence stating your topic and the point you want to make about it. This assertion focuses your thinking as you develop a preliminary thesis statement. Next, move toward a final thesis statement that most accurately reflects the content of your essay.

Following is the evolution of Carol Moreno's thesis statement as she moved from a simple assertion to her final version for her essay on weight training. The final version fulfills all the requirements described in Box 12.

Write thesis statements for persuasive papers on the following topics, making sure that they have the five characteristics of a good thesis statement listed in the basic requirements summary box (Box 12).

1. Rap music
2. Financial aid
3. Current movies
4. A holiday ritual
5. Mothers and daughters

NO I think women can pump iron like men. [This assertion is a start.]

NO If she is trained well, any woman can "pump iron" well, just like a man. [This can be considered a preliminary thesis because it's more specific (it mentions training), but the word *any* is vague and inaccurate, and the word *well* appears twice.]

NO In spite of most people thinking only men can "pump iron," women can also do it successfully with the right training. [This draft is better because it's more specific, but "most people thinking only men" goes off Moreno's intended topic. Also, this draft doesn't mention Moreno's central concept of building strength.]

YES With the right training, women can also "pump iron" to build strength. [This is a good thesis statement.]

Thesis statements for information essays

For essays with an informative purpose (1c.2), here are more examples of thesis statements for 500- to 700-word essays. The NO versions are assertions or preliminary thesis statements. The YES versions are good because they fulfill the requirements in Box 12.

TOPIC *suing for malpractice*

NO There are many kinds of malpractice suits.

YES Many people know about medical malpractice suits, and increasingly people are becoming aware of suits against lawyers, teachers, and even parents.

TOPIC *women artists*

NO Paintings by women are getting more attention.

YES During the past ten years, the works of the artists Mary Cassatt and Rosa Bonheur have finally gained widespread critical acclaim.

Thesis statements for persuasive essays

For essays written with a persuasive purpose (1c.3), here are examples of thesis statements written for 500- to 700-word essays. Again, the NO versions are assertions or preliminary thesis statements. The YES versions fulfill the requirements in Box 12.

TOPIC *discomforts of city living*

NO The discomforts of living in a modern city are many.

YES Rising crime rates, increasingly overcrowded conditions, and rising taxes make living comfortably in a modern city difficult.

TOPIC   *deceptive advertising*

NO   Deceptive advertising can cause many problems for consumers.

YES   Deceptive advertising costs consumers not only money but also their health.

EXERCISE 2-6

Each set of sentences below offers several versions of a thesis statement. Within each set, the thesis statements progress from weak to strong. The fourth thesis statement in each set is the best. Based on the requirements listed in Box 12, work individually or with a peer-response group to explain why the first three choices in each set are weak and the last is best.

A. 1. Advertising is complex.
   2. Magazine advertisements appeal to readers.
   3. Magazine advertisements must be creative and appealing to all readers.
   4. To appeal to readers, magazine advertisements must skillfully use language, color, and design.
B. 1. Tennis is excellent exercise.
   2. Playing tennis is fun.
   3. Tennis requires various skills.
   4. Playing tennis for fun and exercise requires agility, stamina, and strategy.
C. 1. *Hamlet* is a play about revenge.
   2. Hamlet must avenge his father's murder.
   3. Some characters in the play *Hamlet* want revenge.
   4. In the play *Hamlet,* Hamlet, Fortinbras, and Laertes all seek revenge.
D. 1. We should pay attention to the environment.
   2. We should worry about air pollution.
   3. Automobile emissions cause air pollution.
   4. Congress should raise emissions standards for passenger cars and SUVs.
E. 1. Many people aren't interested in politics.
   2. Adults have become increasingly dissatisfied with the political process.
   3. Fewer adults than ever vote in local elections.
   4. Fewer college students participated in state primaries and voted in state elections this year than in either of the last two elections.

ANSWERS: EXERCISE 2-6

A. The fourth thesis statement succeeds because it states a main idea (about magazine advertisements' appeal to readers); it reflects a purpose (to persuade); it has a focus (that magazine advertisements must be skillfully done); and it briefly presents subdivisions (language, color, and design). The first and second thesis statements are too general, showing neither a purpose nor a focus. The third thesis statement shows a persuasive purpose but is still too general and has no focus ("must" isn't explained).

B. The fourth thesis statement succeeds because it states a main idea (about playing tennis for fun and exercise); it reflects a purpose (to inform); it has a focus (what is required for playing tennis for fun and exercise); and it briefly presents subdivisions (agility, stamina, and strategy). The first statement is too general ("excellent" is a very broad term) and shows no purpose or focus. The second statement is also too vague ("fun" is a very broad term when used without a context) and shows no purpose or focus. The third statement reflects an informative purpose but lacks a focus ("various skills" is too vague).

C. The fourth thesis statement succeeds because it states a main idea (characters in *Hamlet* seek revenge); it reflects a purpose (to inform); it has a focus (all three characters seek revenge); and it briefly states the major subdivisions (Hamlet, Fortinbras, and Laertes). The first statement is much too general, and though it suggests an informative intent, the statement lacks a focus. The second and third statements reflect an informative purpose but lack a focus ("must" and "want" are vague words here).

D. The fourth thesis statement succeeds because it states a main idea (about car emission standards); it reflects a purpose (to persuade); and it has a focus (the specific action that Congress should take). The first statement uses vague language ("pay attention" and "environment"), and it suggests neither a persuasive nor an informative intent. The

Answers: Exercise 2-6 (continued)

second statement reflects a persuasive purpose, but "worry" is vague. The third statement reflects either an informative or persuasive purpose, but the broad claim is so obvious that it will not lead to an effective paper.

E. The fourth thesis statement succeeds because it states a main idea (about college students' voting); it reflects a purpose (to inform); and it has a focus (how these students voted in state primaries and state elections this year compared with the last two years). The first statement relies on too much vague language ("many," "people," "aren't interested") and lacks a purpose or focus. The second statement suggests an informative purpose, but it relies on vague language ("dissatisfied" and "political process") and lacks a focus. The third statement suggests an informative purpose but lacks a focus.

ANSWERS: EXERCISE 2-7

1. The thesis is good because it reflects the purpose (to persuade), states a main idea, and focuses specifically on logical subdivisions of the topic.

2. The thesis suggests that the theater review will do what such reviews should do: evaluate in an attempt to persuade a reader. The words "was very interesting," however, are too vague; they need to be revised to be more specific. A brief indication of subdivisions might help the thesis communicate its message.

3. The thesis, though specific and focused, doesn't reflect a careful response to the assignment: the assignment requires an informative report, but this thesis reflects a persuasive purpose.

4. This thesis is good because it states a main idea, reflects a purpose (to inform), and includes a focus.

5. This thesis doesn't address the assignment adequately because it reflects an informative rather than a persuasive purpose, as was required by the assignment.

EXERCISE 2-7

Here are writing assignments, narrowed topics, and tentative thesis statements. Alone or with a peer-response group, evaluate each thesis statement according to the basic requirements in Box 12.

1. *Marketing assignment:* 700- to 800-word persuasive report on the cafeteria. *Audience:* the instructor and the cafeteria's manager. *Topic:* cafeteria conditions. *Thesis:* The college cafeteria could attract more students if it improved the quality of its food, its appearance, and the friendliness of its staff.

2. *Theater assignment:* 300- to 500-word review of a performance. *Audience:* the instructor and other students in the class. *Topic:* a touring production of the musical *Rent*. *Thesis:* The recent performance of *Rent* was very interesting.

3. *Chemistry assignment:* 800- to 1,000-word informative report about the ozone layer. *Audience:* the instructor and visiting students and instructors attending a seminar at the state college. *Topic:* recent research on the ozone layer. *Thesis:* The United States should increase efforts to slow the destruction of the ozone layer.

4. *Journalism assignment:* 200- to 300-word article about campus crime. *Audience:* the instructor, the student body, and the college administration. *Topic:* recent robberies. *Thesis:* During the fall term, campus robberies at the college equaled the number of robberies that took place in the prior five years combined.

5. *Nursing assignment:* 400- to 500-word persuasive report about technology changes in nursing. *Audience:* nursing students and professionals. *Topic:* using hand-held computers to track patient information. *Thesis:* More hospitals are requiring nurses to use hand-held computers to enter patient data instead of using traditional charts.

2r What is outlining?

An **outline** lays out the relationships among ideas in a piece of writing. Outlines can lead writers to see how well their writing is organized. Many instructors require that outlines be handed in either before or with an essay.

Some writers like to outline; others don't. If you don't, but you're required to write one, tackle the job with an open mind. You may be pleasantly surprised at what the rigor of outline writing does to your perception of your essay.

An outline can be *informal* or *formal*. Try outlining at various steps of the WRITING PROCESS: before drafting, to arrange ideas; while you draft, to keep track of your material; while you revise, to check the logical flow of thought or to reveal what information is missing, repeated, or off the topic; or in whatever other ways you find helpful.

Informal outlines

An **informal outline** is a working plan that lays out the major points of an essay. Because it's informal, it doesn't need to use the numbering and lettering conventions of a formal outline. Complete sentences aren't required; words and phrases are acceptable. Carol Moreno used an informal outline for planning her essay (3g). Here's how she roughed out her third paragraph.

CAROL MORENO'S INFORMAL OUTLINE

Thesis statement: With the right training, women can also "pump iron" to build strength.

> how to use weights
>> safety is vital
>> free weights
>>> don't bend at waist
>>> align neck and back
>>> look straight ahead
>> weight machines—safety

Formal outlines

A **formal outline** requires you to use the conventions that dictate how to display relationships among ideas. You need to adhere strictly to the numbering and lettering conventions required, as shown below. A formal outline can be either a topic outline or a sentence outline. In a topic outline, each entry is a word or phrase. In a sentence outline, each entry is a complete sentence. Never mix the two types.

Writers who use formal outlines say that a sentence outline brings them closer to drafting than a topic outline does. This makes sense because topic outlines carry less information. But you have to find out which type works better for you.

Here's a topic outline of the final draft of Carol Moreno's essay on weight lifting for women (3g.3). A sentence outline follows it so that you can compare the two types of outlines.

TOPIC OUTLINE

Thesis statement: With the right training, women can "pump iron" to build strength.

I. Avoidance of massive muscle development
    A. Role of women's biology
        1. Not much muscle-bulking hormone
        2. Muscles get longer, not bulkier

TEACHING TIP
TEACHING TIP
Writers use outlines in a variety of ways. They turn to them, for example, at different stages of the composing process. Some writers find it productive to move from mapping or freewriting directly into a listing of ideas in a particular order, using the outline to plan the drafting process; others use outlines to check the organization of a draft after it is written, testing to see if the paper has order and balance. Some writers find topic outlines helpful; some prefer a sentence outline. Each writer has to find the shaping strategies that prove to be most effective in his or her case.

QUOTATION: ON WRITING
A work has form insofar as one part of it leads a reader to anticipate another part, to be gratified by the sequence.
—Kenneth Burke

QUOTATION: ON WRITING
I had to make my own living and my own opportunity. . . . Don't sit down and wait for the opportunities to come; you have to get up and make them.
—Madame C. J. Walker

QUOTATION: ON WRITING
Opportunity follows struggle. It follows effort. It follows hard work. It doesn't come before.
—Shelby Steele

BACKGROUND
In "Ethical Issues Raised by Students' Personal Writing" (*College English,* March 1998: 318–325), Dan Morgan explores teachers' responsibility to respond to student writing that is "confessional." He suggests assignment topics that circumvent this problem.

    B. Role of combining exercise types
       1. Anaerobic (weight lifting)
       2. Aerobic (swimming)
II. Safe use of weights
    A. Free weights
       1. Unsafe lifting techniques
       2. Safe lifting techniques
          a. Head alignment
          b. Neck and back alignment
    B. Weight machines
III. Individualized program based on physical condition
    A. Role of resistance and reps
    B. Characteristics for personalizing the program
       1. Weight
       2. Age
       3. Physical condition
IV. Individualized weight-training program
    A. Upper body strength
    B. Individual objectives
       1. Mine
       2. Car crash victim's
       3. Physical therapist's

SENTENCE OUTLINE
Thesis statement: With the right training, women can also "pump iron" to build strength.
  I. The right training lets women who lift weights avoid developing massive muscles.
    A. Women's biology plays a role.
       1. Women don't produce much of a specific muscle-bulking hormone.
       2. Women's muscles tend to grow longer rather than bulkier.
    B. Combining different kinds of exercise also plays a role.
       1. Anaerobic exercise, like weight lifting, builds muscle.
       2. Aerobic exercise, like swimming, builds endurance and stamina.
  II. The right training shows women how to use weights safely to prevent injury.
    A. Free weights require special precautions.
       1. Bending at the waist and jerking a barbell up are unsafe.
       2. Squatting and using leg and back muscles to straighten up are safe.
          a. The head is held erect and faces forward.
          b. The neck and back are aligned and held straight.
    B. Weight machines make it easier to lift safely because they force proper body alignment.

III. The right training includes individualized programs based on a woman's physical condition.
  A. Progress comes from resistance and from repetitions tailored to individual capabilities.
  B. Programs consider a woman's physical characteristics.
    1. Her weight is a factor.
    2. Her age is a factor.
    3. Her physical conditioning is a factor.
IV. The right training includes individualized programs based on a woman's personal goals.
  A. Certain muscle groups are targeted to increase women's upper body strength.
  B. Other muscle groups are targeted based on individual objectives.
    1. I wanted to strengthen muscles needed for lifting patients.
    2. An accident victim wanted to strengthen her neck muscles.
    3. A physical therapist wanted to strengthen her fingers and hands.

EXERCISE 2-8

Here is a sentence outline. Individually or with your peer-response group, revise it into a topic outline. Then, be ready to explain why you prefer using a topic outline or a sentence outline as a guide to writing. For help, consult 2r.

Thesis statement: Common noise pollution, although it causes many problems in our society, can be reduced.

I. Noise pollution comes from many sources.
  A. Noise pollution occurs in many large cities.
    1. Traffic rumbles and screeches.
    2. Construction work blasts.
    3. Airplanes roar overhead.
  B. Noise pollution occurs in the workplace.
    1. Machines in factories boom.
    2. Machines used for outdoor construction thunder.
  C. Noise pollution occurs during leisure-time activities.
    1. Stereo headphones blare directly into eardrums.
    2. Film soundtracks bombard the ears.
    3. Music in discos assaults the ears.
II. Noise pollution causes many problems.
  A. Excessive noise damages hearing.
  B. Excessive noise alters moods.
  C. Constant exposure to noise limits learning ability.

TEACHING TIP: COLLABORATION
In both workplace and college settings, writers often team up to develop a single document. When two or three students write a paper together, they usually see the need to articulate the how and why of every dimension of the writing task, from topic selection to word choice. This ongoing discussion within collaborative groups about their writing encourages students to view effective writing as a process under each individual's conscious control.

ANSWERS: EXERCISE 2-8
Answers may vary.

I. Sources of noise pollution
  A. Large cities
    1. Traffic
    2. Construction work
    3. Airplanes
  B. Workplace
    1. Factory machines
    2. Outdoor construction machines
  C. Leisure-time activities
    1. Stereo headphones
    2. Film soundtracks
    3. Disco music
II. Problems from noise pollution
  A. Damage to hearing
  B. Mood alteration
  C. Limits to learning ability
III. Ways to reduce noise pollution
  A. Pressure from community groups
  B. Traffic regulations
  C. Pressure on management by workers
  D. Earplugs
  E. Reasonable sound levels

TEACHING TIP: COLLABORATION

You might want to start a course with a collaborative component. The concept underlying collaboration is that the whole is greater than the sum of its parts. Providing opportunities for students to work together allows them to see other points of view, to capitalize on each other's strengths, to develop concepts more extensively than they could on their own, and to learn from each other. When you assign groups, allow students a little time to introduce themselves and get to know one another. Personalizing learning can be an important part of collaboration.

Collaborative groups work best when they comprise two or three students whose schedules allow them to work together outside class, if practical. When groups meet in class only, students can work toward the group's goals by completing individual responsibilities outside class and then work to merge all their work during class time. Collaborative papers, like single-authored texts, go through a series of drafts. But unlike single-authored texts, collaborative papers will actively integrate concepts of audience, tone, planning, and purpose into the writing process because at every step students must articulate to one another what they think the paper needs and why.

BACKGROUND

In "Preparing Students for Teamwork Through Collaborative Writing and Peer Review Techniques" (*Teaching English in the Two-Year College*, May 1996: 127–136), Vidya Singh-Gupta and Eileen Troutt-Ervin argue that students who learn the techniques of effective collaboration are far better prepared for today's workplace.

BACKGROUND

Mark Mabrito suggests in "From Workplace to Classroom: Teaching Professional Writing" (*Business Communication Quarterly*, September 1999: 101–104) that instructors can add the dimension of workplace reality to their classrooms by focusing on collaborative writing and audience analysis.

III. Reduction in noise pollution is possible.

   A. Pressure from community groups can support efforts to control excessive noise.

   B. Traffic regulations can help alleviate congestion and noise.

   C. Pressure from workers can force management to reduce noise.

   D. People can wear earplugs to avoid excessive noise.

   E. Reasonable sound levels for headphones, soundtracks, and discos can be required.

Chapter 3

Drafting and Revising

In the WRITING PROCESS, drafting and revising come after PLANNING and SHAPING (Chapter 2). **Drafting** means you get ideas onto paper or into a computer file in sentences and paragraphs. In everyday conversation, people use the word *writing* to talk about drafting, but writing is too broad a term here. The word *drafting* more accurately describes what you do when you write your first attempt—your first *draft*—to generate words. **Revising** means you look over your first draft, analyze and evaluate it for yourself, and then rewrite it by composing a number of subsequent versions, or drafts, to get closer to what you want to say. Revising involves adding, cutting, moving material, and after that, EDITING and PROOFREADING.

3a What can help me write a first draft?

A **first draft** is the initial version of a piece of writing. Before you begin a first draft, seek out places and times of the day that encourage you to write. You might write best in a quiet corner of the library, or at 4:30 a.m. at the kitchen table before anyone else is awake, or outside alone with nature, or with a steady flow of people walking by. Most experienced writers, myself among them, find they concentrate best when they're alone and writing where they won't be interrupted. But individuals differ, and you may prefer background noise—a crowded cafeteria, with the low hum of conversation at the next table or in the next room, for example.

A caution: Don't mislead yourself. You can't produce a useful first draft while talking to friends and stopping only now and then to jot down a sentence. You won't draft smoothly while watching television or being constantly interrupted.

Some writers do all their planning, shaping, drafting, revising, and editing on the computer. Other writers create first drafts by hand and reserve the computer for revising and editing. Experiment to see which steps are easier for you to do by hand, and which by computer.

QUOTATION: ON WRITING
Writing is a deliberate act; one has to make up one's mind to do it.
—James Britton

WHAT ELSE?
In *Strategies and Resources,* a free 400-page book written especially for instructors who adopt this handbook, Part Three offers detailed ideas to writing instructors who want to use portfolios to enhance learning as well as to assess student writing. Also, for a discussion of portfolios in this *Annotated Instructor's Edition,* see the annotations in Part Five.

BACKGROUND
In her classic article, "Hand, Eye, Brain: Some 'Basics' in the Writing Process," in *Research on Composing: Points of Departure,* edited by Charles Cooper and Lee Odell (Urbana: NCTE, 1978, 61), Janet Emig suggests that the reason many experienced writers prefer to write in longhand is that it gives them more time to think. The slower pace of handwriting, as opposed to typing at a computer, allows ideas to develop and surface.

BACKGROUND
In "The Effects of Computer Skills and Feedback on the Gains in Students' Overall Writing Quality in College Freshman Composition Courses" (ERIC ED 435 097), Wes Davis and Kelley Mahoney explain that commentary from instructors during computer-aided planning and composing is more effective than written responses on students' handwritten products.

BACKGROUND
In *Passions, Pedagogies, and 21st Century Technologies* (Logan: Utah State University Press and NCTE, 1999), Gail E. Hawisher and Cynthia L. Selfe offer a considerable collection of essays that address the technologies and the technocultural contests that writing instructors are grappling with.

TEACHING TIP
You might want to ask your students to keep a writing log that works this way: At the end of each piece of writing, they note where, when, and how they have worked. The more detailed their notations, the more what they say will help students draw conclusions about how their best writing takes place. After a series of such notations, the students can write a paragraph evaluating the approaches they used, summarizing the information, reflecting on it, and planning for future writing.

QUOTATION: ON WRITING
There is always a point in the writing of a piece when I sit in a room literally papered with false starts and cannot put one word after another and imagine that I have suffered a small stroke, leaving me apparently undamaged but actually aphasic.

—Joan Didion

BACKGROUND
In "Revision and Process: 'Round Robin' Group Writing" (*Teaching English in the Two-Year College,* March 2000: 342), Judith Platz describes a group drafting assignment that encourages students to thoughtfully consider organization, structure, and content.

Finally, resist delaying tactics. While you certainly need a computer or a pad of paper and a pen or pencil, you don't need fifteen perfectly sharpened pencils neatly lined up on your desk.

Box 13 offers suggestions for ways to transition from PLANNING and SHAPING into drafting. Experiment to see what works best for you. And be ready to adjust what works according to each WRITING SITUATION.

BOX 13 **SUMMARY**

Ways to start drafting

- **Write a discovery draft.** Put aside all your notes from planning and shaping, and write a discovery draft. This means using FOCUSED FREEWRITING to get ideas on paper or onto your computer screen so that you can make connections that spring to mind as you write. Your discovery draft can serve as a first draft or as one more part of your notes when you write a more structured first draft.

- **Work from your notes.** Sort your notes from planning and shaping into groups of subtopics. When you start writing, you can systematically concentrate on each subtopic without having to search repeatedly through your pile of notes. Arrange the subtopics in what seems to be a sensible sequence, knowing you can always go back later and re-sequence the subtopics. Now write a first draft by working through your notes on each subtopic. Draft either the entire essay or chunks of a few paragraphs at one time.

- **Use a combination of approaches.** When you know the shape of your material, write according to that structure. When you feel "stuck" and don't know what to say next, switch to writing as you would for a discovery draft.

Now, dive in. Based on the planning and shaping you've done (Chapter 2), start writing. The direction of drafting is forward: Keep pressing ahead. If you wonder about the spelling of a word or a point in grammar, don't stop. Use a symbol or other signal to alert you to revisit later. Use whatever you like: boldface, underlining, a question mark before and after, an asterisk, or all capital letters. If the exact word you want escapes you while you're drafting, substitute an easy synonym and mark it to go back to later. If you question your sentence style or the order in which you present supporting details, boldface or underline it, or insert a symbol or the word *Style?* or *Order?* nearby so that you can return to it later. If you begin to run out of ideas, reread what you have written—not to start revising prematurely, but only to propel yourself to keep moving ahead with your first draft. Once you finish your draft, you search for the boldfaces, underlines, symbols, or words that you've used to alert you to reconsider something. If it's a word, you can use the "Edit>Find" function on your word processing program toolbar.

When drafting on the computer, use your "Save" function often to protect your work, at least every ten minutes. This prevents your losing what you've written. Also, print your work regularly—very definitely at the end of each work session—so that you always have a hard copy in case your computer develops problems (a not unusual occurrence).

A first draft is a preliminary or rough draft. Its purpose is to get your ideas onto disk or into computer memory or on paper. Never are first drafts meant to be perfect.

3b How can I overcome writer's block?

If you're afraid or otherwise feel unable to start writing, perhaps you're being stopped by **writer's block.** You want to get started but somehow can't. Often, writer's block occurs because the writer harbors a fear of being wrong. To overcome that fear, or any other cause of your block, first admit it to yourself. Face it honestly so that you can understand whatever is holding you back. Writer's block can strike professional as well as student writers, and a variety of techniques to overcome it have become popular.

The most common cause of writer's block involves a writer's belief in myths about writing.

MYTH	Writers are born, not made.
TRUTH	Everyone can write. Writers don't expect to "get it right" the first time. Being a good writer means being a patient rewriter.
MYTH	Writers have to be "in the mood" to write.
TRUTH	If writers always waited for "the mood" to occur, few would write at all. News reporters and other professional writers have deadlines to meet, whether or not they're in the mood to write.
MYTH	Writers have to be really good at grammar and spelling.
TRUTH	Writers don't let spelling and grammar block them. They write, and when they hear that quiet inner voice saying that a word or sentence isn't quite right, they mark the spot with a symbol or word in all capitals. After they're finished drafting, they return to those spots and work on them, perhaps using this handbook or a dictionary or thesaurus to check themselves.

BACKGROUND

Erica E. Goode cites tips for people who tend to procrastinate. They include the following helpful suggestions.

- Break your work into small, clearly defined steps. Instead of vowing vaguely to "catch up on paperwork," resolve to spend one hour sorting out the papers on your desk.
- Reward yourself for progress toward your goal. Ice cream is nice; so is a walk in the park.
- The hardest step to take is the first, so pick something easy. A task that can be polished off in fifteen minutes is a good one for a starter.
- Set a series of small but realistic interim deadlines rather than a final date.
- Enlist support. Other people may be able to tell you if you're setting up expectations that are impossible to meet.

TEACHING TIP

Getting started seems hardest for writers at the point when they have to move from planning and shaping to actual writing. Dealing with writer's block is no small matter for writers, instructors of writing, and students. You might take some class time to discuss myths about writing. I am interested in gathering more myths. If you or your students think of any, please e-mail me the MYTH/TRUTH information for publication—with a byline—in the next edition of this *Annotated Instructor's Edition:* <LQTBOOK@aol.com>.

TEACHING TIP
Students may be skeptical of the value of picturing themselves working. Share with them these examples of successful people who use visualization.

John Ueless, a champion pole-vaulter, used visualization before each meet. He would see himself winning by clearing the bar at a particular height. In his mind, he rehearsed every movement, as well as seeing the crowd and even smelling the grass when pole-vaulting out of doors.

Jack Nicklaus, a champion golfer, says visualization gives him a "winning feeling": "This gives me a line to the cup just as clearly as if it's been tattooed on my brain. With that feeling, all I have to do is swing the club and let nature take its course."

You might want to give students time to visualize in class prior to writing. Ask them to close their eyes and sit comfortably. Tell them to imagine themselves reading a question and knowing how they want to respond. Tell them to imagine themselves making a list of notes, rearranging their material, or writing. At each stage, remind them to imagine themselves feeling confident and successful. Then, have them write. Later, discuss how they felt when writing this time in contrast to their past experiences. Often this technique does little for people at first, so try to give your students a series of opportunities to employ visualization techniques.

QUOTATION: ON WRITING
To write is to write is to write is to write is to write is to write is to write.
—Gertrude Stein

BACKGROUND
In "What Works for Me: A Grocery List and Audience Analysis" (*Teaching English in the Two-Year College*, May 1999: 431–432), Lawrence Barkley describes a writing assignment that demonstrates how readers influence a text and why considering readers is important.

MYTH	Writers don't have to revise.
TRUTH	Writers expect to revise—several times. Once words are on paper, writers can see what readers will see. This "re-vision" helps writers revise.
MYTH	Writing can be done at the last minute.
TRUTH	Drafting and revising take time. Ideas don't leap onto paper in final, polished form.

Box 14 lists reliable strategies writers have developed to overcome writer's block. If you feel blocked, experiment to discover which works best for you. Also, add your own ideas about how to get started. As you use the list in Box 14, suspend judgment of your writing. Let things flow. Don't find fault with what you're keyboarding or writing. Your goal is to get yourself under way. You can evaluate and improve your writing when you're revising it. According to research, premature revision stops many writers cold—and leads to writer's block. Your reward for waiting to revise until after you finish your first draft is the comfort of having a springboard for your revising in front of you.

BOX 14 **SUMMARY**

 Ways to overcome writer's block

- **Check that one of the myths about writing listed above, or one of your own, isn't stopping you.**
- **Avoid staring at a blank page.** Relax and move your hand across the keyboard or page. Write words, scribble, or draw while you think about your topic. The physical act of getting anything on paper can stir up ideas and lead you to begin drafting.
- **Visualize yourself writing.** Many professional writers say that they write more easily if they first picture themselves doing it. Before getting out of bed in the morning or while waiting for a bus or walking to classes, mentally construct a visual image of yourself in the place where you usually write, with the materials you need, busy at work.
- **Picture an image or a scene, or imagine a sound that relates to your topic.** Start writing by describing what you see or hear.
- **Write about your topic in a letter or e-mail to a friend.** This technique helps you relax and makes drafting nothing more than a chat on paper with someone you feel comfortable with.
- **Try writing your material as if you were someone else.** When they take on a role, many writers feel less inhibited about writing.

→

Ways to overcome writer's block (*continued*)

- **Start by writing the middle of your essay.** Skip the introduction and begin with a body paragraph, and write from the center of your essay out, instead of from beginning to end.
- **Use FREEWRITING or FOCUSED FREEWRITING.**
- **Change your method of writing.** If you usually use a computer, try writing by hand. When you write by hand, switch between pencil and pen or ink colors and treat yourself to good-quality paper so that you can enjoy the pleasure of writing on smooth, strong paper. Often that pleasure propels you to keep going.
- **Switch temporarily to writing about a topic that you care about passionately.** Write freely about that topic. Once writing starts to pour out of you, you can often use the momentum to switch back to the topic of your assignment.

3c How do I revise?

Revising is rewriting. When you see the word *revision*, break it down to *re-vision*, which means "to see again with fresh eyes." To revise, evaluate, change, and reevaluate your draft to figure out ways to improve it. To do this, you need to read your writing honestly, without losing confidence or becoming defensive. After all, what's on the page is ink, not ego. As you work, look at whatever you change and evaluate the revision first on its own and then in the context of the surrounding material. Continue until you're satisfied that your essay is the best you can make it, in light of your specific WRITING SITUATION.

Whenever possible within your time frame, distance yourself from each draft. The best way is to leave a chunk of time between finishing a first draft and starting to revise. Doing so helps you develop an objective sense of your work. Student writers often want to hold on to their every word, especially if they had trouble getting started on a first draft. Resist such a feeling vigorously. Put away your draft, and allow the rosy glow of authorial pride to dim a bit. The classical writer Horace recommended waiting nine years before revising! You might try to wait a few hours or even thirty minutes. Better yet, take a day or two before going back to look at your work with fresh eyes.

Also, as you're revising, don't start EDITING too soon. Editing comes after revising. Research shows that premature editing distracts writers from dealing with the larger issues that revision involves.

QUOTATION: ON WRITING

An ox at the roadside, when it is dying of hunger and thirst, does not lie down; it walks up and down—up and down, seeking it knows not what—but it does not lie down.

—Olive Schreiner,
From Man to Man

TEACHING TIP

Revising is a process just as composing is a process. Students may find it helpful to examine and make conscious the steps they go through when revising, editing, and proofreading. Here are some questions they can use:

1. What helped you make the mental shift from suspending judgment to making judgment?

2. Did you use the questions in material supplied by your instructor or the revision checklists in Box 17?

3. If you had peer readers, did you use their suggestions? Did you use all of them? If some of them, which ones?

4. Did you need to make any changes in your introduction or conclusion because of other changes in your text? Explain.

5. Was your title still appropriate?

6. Where did you add new words, sentences, or paragraphs?

7. Where did you cut out words, sentences, or paragraphs?

8. Did you change the sequence of paragraphs?

9. Did you edit your paper in a single reading, or look for possible errors in a series of readings?

10. Did you use a checklist, either the one in this chapter or one supplied by your instructor, to examine your writing for grammar, spelling, punctuation, and capitalization problems?

BACKGROUND
In their article "Writing Across Culture: Using Distanced Collaboration to Break Intellectual Barriers in Composition Courses" (*Teaching English in the Two-Year College,* May 1998: 107–114), Kathy Mosdal O'Brien and Chuck Denny explain how writing students at different colleges can use technology to collaborate. The authors suggest that this approach to revision can help writing students escape cultural, ideological, and intellectual isolation.

BACKGROUND
In "Finding Grand's Works: A Case Study in the Art of Revising" (*Journal of Basic Writing,* Summer 1996: 3–22), Rebecca Williams Mlynarczyk suggests how teacher responses can help students become revisers who move beyond surface-level features to content-based analysis.

3c.1 Goals and activities during revision

Your goal during revision is to improve your draft at two levels: the *global level,* which involves the whole essay and paragraphs, and the *local level,* which involves sentences and words.

To revise successfully, you need first to expect to revise. The myth that good writers never have to revise is nonsense. Only the opposite is true: Writing is revising. Final drafts evolve from first drafts. Here's how to prepare your mind for revising:

- Shift mentally from suspending judgment (during idea gathering and drafting) to making judgments. Read your draft objectively with "a cold eye" to evaluate it.
- Decide whether to write an entirely new draft or to revise the one you have. Be critical as you evaluate your first draft, but don't be overly harsh. Many early drafts provide sufficient raw material for revision to get under way.
- Be systematic. Don't evaluate at random. Most writers work best when they concentrate on each element sequentially. Start with your draft's overall organization; next, move to its paragraphs, then to its sentences, and finally to its word choice. If you need practice in being systematic, try using a revision checklist, either one supplied by your instructor or the ones in this handbook in Box 17 on pages 61–62.

You can engage in the activities of revision, listed in Box 15, by using a computer or revising by hand. Computers have relieved much of the tedious work of copying and recopying material, allowing you to make both large and small changes easily. For example, "Move," a major revision activity, is easy on a computer. First, print a copy of your original

---

BOX 15   SUMMARY

 Major activities during revision

Add: Insert needed words, sentences, and paragraphs. If your additions require new content, return to the structured techniques shown in Chapter 2.

Cut: Get rid of whatever goes off the topic or repeats what has already been said.

Replace: As needed, substitute new words, sentences, and paragraphs for what you have cut.

Move: Change the sequence of paragraphs if the material isn't presented in logical order. Move sentences within paragraphs or to other paragraphs when your PARAGRAPH ARRANGEMENT does not allow the material to flow.

draft to have at hand in case you later decide that you prefer your original version of a sentence or a section. Then "Cut" and "Paste" to reorder sentences or rearrange paragraphs. You might, for example, split up a paragraph, join two paragraphs, or otherwise shuffle them. Similarly, you might reorder the sequence of some sentences or interchange sentences between paragraphs. Sometimes, these experiments won't yield anything useful, but they might reveal a few surprises that help you "re-vision" your work.

Beware of two temptations when writing with the computer. Because you can rearrange and otherwise revise endlessly, you may need to set limits, or you'll never finish the assignment. The opposite seduction is also possible: A neatly printed page may look like a final draft, but it definitely isn't one.

3c.2 The role of a thesis statement in revision

The THESIS STATEMENT of your essay has great organizing power because it controls and limits what your essay can cover. The thesis statement presents the TOPIC of your essay, your particular focus on that topic, and your PURPOSE for writing about that topic. Your first draft of a thesis statement is usually only an estimate of what you plan to cover in your essay. Therefore, as you revise, keep checking the accuracy of your thesis statement. Use the thesis statement's controlling power to bring it and your essay into line with each other. When your essay is finished, the thesis statement and what you say in your essay should match. If they don't, you need to revise either the thesis statement or the essay—or sometimes both.

Every writer's experience with revising a thesis statement varies from essay to essay. Carol Moreno, the student you met in Chapter 2 as she did her planning and shaping, wrote several versions of her thesis statement (shown in 2q) before she started to draft. After writing her first draft, she checked her last draft of her thesis statement, "With the right training, women can also 'pump iron' to build strength," and decided that it communicated what she wanted to say. But that wasn't the end of it: Moreno had to change parts of her essay to conform more closely to her thesis statement. You can read Moreno's three complete drafts, along with comments, at the end of this chapter (3g).

3c.3 The role of an essay title in revision

Your essay **title** can also show you what needs revising because it clarifies the overall point of the essay. An effective title sets you on your course and tells your readers what to expect. Some writers like to begin their first drafts with a title at the top of the page to focus their thinking. Then, as they revise drafts, they revise the title. If, however, no title springs to mind, don't be concerned. Often, a good title doesn't surface

TEACHING TIP
Many students think that revisers are poor writers. Indeed, I have been scolded more than once by people who have seen me writing in waiting rooms, on the bus, or on a park bench: "Don't you know not to make a mess when you write?" The tone is always well meaning, as if the person is trying to help me out of a deep difficulty I seem to be having. I have always been amazed at how forward strangers can be after watching me write while they supposedly stare straight ahead. Some people start to squirm, and the wise ones simply move away. But a few hardy folks want to let me know that I could suddenly become "a writer" if only I would stop crossing out and drawing arrows on my paper. For a while, the confrontations inhibited me about writing outside my home, but I soon became so interested in the reactions that I got caught up in the "research" of the situations. (Try it sometime—a doctor's office or a barber or beauty shop would be prime territory.) Students are always similarly surprised when they see how messy real writing can be.

QUOTATION: ON TITLES
Were it inquired of an ingenius writer what page of his work had occasioned his most perplexity, he would often point to the title-page. The curiosity which we there would excite, is, however, most fastidious to gratify.

It is too often with the Title of Books, as with those painted representations exhibited by the keepers of wild beasts; where, in general, the picture itself is made more striking and inviting to the eye, than the enclosed animal is always found to be.

—Isaac Disraeli,
Curiosities of Literature

until after drafting, revising, and even editing. It can take that long to come up with one. Whatever you do, never tack on a title as an afterthought right before handing in your essay. A suitable title is essential for readers to think about as they begin focusing on your essay.

Titles can be direct or indirect. A **direct title** tells exactly what your essay is about. A direct title contains key words under which the essay could be cataloged in a library or an online database.

A direct title shouldn't be too broad. For example, Moreno's first and second drafts of a title were "Pumping Iron" (3g.1 and 3g.2). By her final draft (3g.3), Moreno realized her early title was too broad, so she revised it to "Women Can Pump Iron, Too." Conversely, a direct title should not be too narrow. "Avoiding Injury When Pumping Iron" is too narrow a title for Moreno's essay, given what she discusses in it.

An **indirect title** only hints at the essay's topic. It tries to catch the reader's interest by presenting a puzzle that can be solved by reading the essay. When writing an indirect title, you don't want to be overly obscure or too cute. For example, a satisfactory indirect title for Moreno's final draft might be "On Goals." In contrast, the indirect title "Equal Play" wouldn't work because it's only remotely related to the point of the essay. Also, "Thanks, Granny!" would likely be seen as overly cute for ACADEMIC WRITING.

ALERT: When you write the title at the top of the page or on a title page, never enclose it in quotation marks or underline it. Let your title stand on its own, without decoration, on your title page or at the top center of the first page of your essay. 👁

BOX 16   **SUMMARY**

Guidelines for writing essay titles

- Don't wait until the last minute to tack a title on your essay. Try writing a title before you begin drafting or while you're revising. Then double-check as you prepare your final draft to confirm that the title clearly relates to your essay's content.

- For a direct title, use key words that relate to your topic, but don't get overly specific and try to reveal your entire essay.

- For an indirect title, be sure that its meaning will become very clear when your readers have finished your essay. Be sure, also, that it isn't too cute.

- Don't use quotation marks with the title or underline it (unless your title includes another title; see section 28d).

- Don't consider your essay title as the first sentence of your essay.

Whether direct or indirect, your essay title stands on its own. It's never the opening sentence of your essay. For example, Moreno's essay, titled "Women Can Pump Iron, Too," would suffer a major blow if the first sentence were "Women certainly can" or "I am the proof." Similarly, never does the first sentence of an essay refer to the essay's title. Rather, the first sentence starts the flow of the essay's content. Box 16 on the facing page offers you guidelines for writing effective essay titles.

3c.4 The role of unity and coherence in an essay

Chapter 4 in this handbook shows you many techniques for achieving unity and coherence in an essay, but here I need to preview the concepts because they're central concerns as you revise.

An essay has **unity** (4d) when all of its parts relate to the THESIS STATEMENT and to each other. You want to use two criteria to judge this. First, does the thesis statement clearly tie in to all TOPIC SENTENCES? Second, does each paragraph—especially the body paragraphs—contain examples, reasons, facts, and details that relate directly to its topic sentence and, in turn, to the thesis statement? In a nutshell, as you revise make sure that nothing in the essay is off the topic.

An essay achieves **coherence** (4g) through closely built relationships among ideas and details that are built on word choice, use of TRANSITIONAL EXPRESSIONS, clear use of PRONOUNS, and effective PARALLELISM.

3c.5 Using a revision checklist

A revision checklist can focus your attention as you evaluate and revise your writing. Use such a checklist, either one provided by your instructor or one that you compile on your own, based on Box 17.

BOX 17   CHECKLIST

 Revision

Your goal is to answer yes to each question. If you answer no, you need to revise. The section numbers in parentheses tell you where to look in this handbook for help.

The Global View: Whole Essay and Paragraphs

1. Is your essay topic suitable and sufficiently narrow? (Chapter 2)

2. Does your thesis statement communicate your topic, focus, and purpose? (2q, Box 12)

→

TEACHING TIP

At the other end of the spectrum from non-revisers are overrevisers. Some students are never satisfied with their work and so never hand it in. This phenomenon is a form of writer's block. Students who suffer from this sort of inhibition often need a little special treatment at first. For example, you might help such students by telling them that for the first few assignments, you will consider their work to be "in progress," even its final version. You might also share with them the words of Eudora Welty:

> I know I can never get it perfect. You just have to know when you've done it the best way. A friend of mine who is a writer said he kept thirteen drafts of a story and put them all in a drawer. Years later he went back, and it was number 7 that was the right one. That taught me a real, true lesson.

QUOTATION: ON WRITING

I praise loudly; I blame softly.
—Catherine II

BACKGROUND

In "Revising Beyond the Sentence Level: One Adolescent Writer and the Pregnant Pause" (*English Journal,* May 1999: 81–86), Elizabeth Blackburn Brockman provides an extensive case study to analyze recursivity in the revision process.

BACKGROUND

In "'Fare from the Madding Crowd': The Lighter Side of Error in Student Writing" (*Teaching English in the Two-Year College,* March 1999: 291–298), Gary Vaughn and Barbara Wenner use Michel Foucault's and Roland Barthes's theories to explain mistakes in student writing. They suggest in-class activities and essay assignments that use these perspectives to assist students in developing an enhanced understanding of error.

Revision (*continued*)

3. Does your essay show that you are aware of your audience? (Box 4)

4. Is your essay arranged effectively? (4i)

5. Have you checked for material that strays off the topic? (4d)

6. Does your introduction prepare your reader for the rest of the essay? (4b)

7. Do your body paragraphs express main ideas in topic sentences as needed? (4c) Are your main ideas clearly related to your thesis statement? (4d)

8. Do your body paragraphs provide specific, concrete support for each main idea? (4c, 4f)

9. Do you use transitions and other techniques to connect ideas within and between paragraphs? (4j)

10. Does your conclusion give your essay a sense of completion? (4k)

The Local View: Sentences and Words

1. Are your sentences concise? (Chapter 16)

2. Do your sentences show clear relationships among ideas? (Chapter 17)

3. Do you use parallelism, variety, and emphasis correctly and to increase the impact of your writing? (Chapters 18 and 19)

4. Have you eliminated sentence fragments? (Chapter 12) Have you eliminated comma splices and fused sentences? (Chapter 13)

5. Have you eliminated confusing shifts? (Chapter 15)

6. Have you eliminated disjointed sentences? (Chapter 15)

7. Have you eliminated misplaced and dangling modifiers? (Chapter 14)

8. Have you used exact words? (21e, 21f)

9. Is your usage correct and your language appropriate? (Chapter 21)

10. Have you avoided sexist language? (21g)

⊕ ESL NOTE: If you'd like information about issues of English grammar that often affect ESL students, consult Part Seven in this handbook. Topics covered include ARTICLES (Chapter 46); word order (Chapter 47); VERB-PREPOSITION combinations (Chapter 48); VERBALS (Chapter 49); and MODAL AUXILIARIES (Chapter 50). ⊕

3d How do I edit?

Editing means checking the technical correctness of your writing. You carefully examine your writing for correct grammar, spelling, punctuation, capitalization, and use of numbers, italics, and abbreviations. Some people use the terms *editing* and *revising* interchangeably, but they're very different steps in the writing process. In contrast to revising, editing means looking at each word for its technical correctness. By editing, you fine-tune the surface features of your writing.

Editing is crucial in writing. No matter how much attention you've paid to planning, shaping, drafting, and revising, you need to edit carefully. Slapdash editing distracts and annoys your reader; lowers that reader's opinion of you and what you say in your essay; and, if on a college assignment, usually earns a lower grade.

My best advice to you about editing is this: Don't rush. Editing takes time. Inexperienced writers sometimes rush editing, eager to "get it over with." Resist any impulse to hurry. Be systematic and patient. Checking grammar and punctuation takes your full concentration, along with time to look up and apply the rules in this handbook.

When do you know you've finished revising and are ready to edit? Ask yourself, "Is there anything else I can do to improve the content, organization, development, and sentence structure of this draft?" If the answer is no, you're ready to edit.

Many word processing programs include editing tools such as a spell-checker, style-checker, thesaurus, readability analyzer. As I explained in Chapter 1, each tool has shortcomings serious enough to create new errors. Yet, if you use the tools intelligently with their shortcomings in mind, they can be useful.

Whenever possible, edit on a paper copy of your writing. It's much easier to spot editing errors on a printed page than on a computer screen. Double-space your paper before printing it for revising or editing. The extra space gives you room to write in your changes clearly so that you can read them easily later. After you finish editing, you can transfer your corrections to the computer. If you must edit onscreen, highlight every two or three sentences, and read each slowly. By working in small segments, you reduce the tendency to read too quickly and miss errors.

An editing checklist helps you find errors. Using an editing checklist, either one provided by your instructor or one based on Box 18 (at the end of this section) that you tailor to your particular needs, can help you move through editing systematically.

A timesaving method for editing is to create a personal file of editing errors you tend to make repeatedly. For example, if the difference between *its* and *it's* always escapes you, or if you tend to misuse the colon, your personal file of editing errors can remind you to look over your draft for those problems.

QUOTATION: ON WRITING

After making a start, children sometimes decide that it won't do and begin again. The strength of their conviction that a new start must be made, even though the teacher may have no complaints about what has been written, is sometimes remarkable. They are not easily persuaded to reconsider a decision to reject what they have done. Some seem to make a habit of rejecting their beginning, and rarely complete anything. These may be timid children for whom committing themselves to paper at all—"finding a tone to talk with" and "being oneself in talking"—imposes a severe strain.

—James Britton, writing about young writers

QUOTATION: ON WRITING

I set myself 600 words a day as a minimum output, regardless of the weather, my state of mind or if I'm sick or well. There must be 600 finished words—not almost right words. Before you ask, I'll tell you that yes, I do write 600 at the top of my pad every day, and I keep track of the word count to insure I reach my quota daily—without fail.

—Arthur Hailey

QUOTATION: ON WRITING

I love spending an hour or two with a dictionary and a thesaurus looking for a more nearly perfect word. Or taking my pen and ruthlessly pruning all the unnecessary adjectives, or fooling around with the rhythm of a sentence or a paragraph by changing a verb into a participle or making any number of little changes that a magazine editor I work with calls "mouse milking."

—Marie Winn

BOX 18 CHECKLIST

 Editing

Your goal is to answer yes to each question below. If you answer no, you need to edit. The numbers in parentheses tell you which chapters in this handbook to go to for more information.

1. Is your grammar correct? (Chapters 7–15)
2. Is your spelling, including hyphenation, correct? (Chapter 22)
3. Have you used commas correctly? (Chapter 24)
4. Have you used all other punctuation correctly? (Chapters 23 and 25–29)
5. Have you used capital letters, italics, abbreviations, and numbers correctly? (Chapter 30)

3e How do I proofread?

To **proofread,** check your final draft for accuracy and neatness before handing it in. In contrast to editing, which is a check for technical correctness, proofreading is typographical. This is your last chance to catch typing (or handwriting) errors and to make sure what you hand in is a clean transcription of your final draft. No matter how hard you worked on earlier parts of the writing process, your final copy needs to be free of proofreading oversights. Shoddy proofreading distracts and annoys your reader; lowers that reader's opinion of you and what you say in your essay; and, if you're writing for college, usually earns a lower grade.

When proofreading, read your work carefully line by line, looking for typing errors, such as letters or words accidentally omitted, words typed twice in a row, wrong indents to start each paragraph, and similar typos or slips. Whenever a page has more than one error, consider printing (or rewriting) a new page. Never expect your instructor to make allowances for crude typing (or handwriting). If you can't type well (or write legibly), arrange to have your paper typed properly.

Unless your instructor gives different directions, proofreading calls also for you to type, at the top right of each page, your last name and the page number. At the left margin, and below this information, type your full name, your professor's name (initial for first name, only if needed), your course title, your class and section number, and the date (for an example, see 3g.3).

Some techniques for proofreading include (1) using a ruler under each line as you read it to prevent yourself from looking beyond that line; (2) reading backwards, sentence by sentence, to prevent yourself from being distracted by the content of the paper; and (3) proofreading your final draft aloud, to yourself or to a friend, so that you can hear errors that have slipped past your eyes. As with revising and editing, whenever possible print and proofread a double-spaced paper copy of your writing. Again, it's much easier to spot errors on a printed page than onscreen.

 ALERT: If you can't type and your instructor permits you to handwrite your essay, check that every word can be read easily. Make sure that your *e*'s are open and your *i*'s are not; that each sentence starts with a clearly written capital letter (avoid making your handwritten capitals and small letters look alike); and that you've attended to other matters of legibility.

3f What is collaborative writing?

Some instructors use the term **collaborative writing** interchangeably with the term *peer-group writing*. In this handbook, I use the term *collaborate* to mean "students working together to write a paper." The underlying idea is that two (or more) heads are better than one.

Writing collaboratively enhances confidence, as writers support one another. Also important, the benefits of acquiring experience in collaborative writing extend beyond your college years. Many professions require participation in writing committees; members of the group must reach general agreement on how to proceed and contribute equally to a written report. Marketing managers, for example, head up teams who conduct consumer research, and then—as a group—write up their findings. Box 19 provides guidelines for collaborative writing.

BOX 19   SUMMARY

Guidelines for collaborative writing

Starting

1. Learn each other's names. If the group wishes, exchange e-mail addresses and/or phone numbers so that you can be in touch outside of class.

2. Participate actively in the group process. During discussions, help set a tone that encourages everyone to participate, including people who don't like to interrupt, who want time to think before they talk, or who are shy. Conversely, help the group set limits if someone dominates the discussions or makes all the decisions. If you lack experience contributing in a group setting, plan personal ways you'll take an active role.

→

BACKGROUND
In "Using the Collage for Collaborative Writing" (*Composition Studies,* Spring 1999: 7–14), Peter Elbow cites the acknowledged problems with collaborative writing and describes a collage writing assignment that helps solo writers begin to feel comfortable collaborating with other writers.

Guidelines for collaborative writing (*continued*)

3. As a group, assign work to be done between meetings. Distribute the responsibilities as fairly as possible. Also, decide whether to choose one discussion leader or to rotate leadership, unless your instructor assigns a particular procedure.

4. Make decisions regarding the technology you'll use. If everyone can use the same word processing program, for example, that will make sharing drafts or parts of drafts much easier. If not, you can use the "Save As" function in major word processing programs like Microsoft Word to save in a common format. Decide if you'll share materials via a floppy disk or as an e-mail attachment. If any group members are unfamiliar with these processes, others need to help them learn. (Different areas and levels of expertise are an advantage of working in groups.)

5. Set a timeline and deadlines for the project. Agree on what to do in the event that someone misses a deadline.

Planning the Writing

6. After discussing the project, BRAINSTORM as a group or use structured techniques for discovering and compiling ideas.

7. Together agree on the ideas that seem best and allow for a period of INCUBATION, if time permits. Then, discuss your group choices again.

8. As a group, divide the project into parts and distribute assignments fairly. For example, if the project requires research, decide who will do it and how they'll share findings with others. If one person is going to be responsible for preparing drafts from pieces that others have written, make sure his or her other responsibilities are balanced.

9. As you work on your part of the project, take notes in preparation for giving your group a progress report.

10. As a group, OUTLINE or otherwise sketch an overview of the paper to get a preliminary idea of how best to use material contributed by individuals.

Drafting the Writing

11. Draft a THESIS STATEMENT. The thesis statement sets the direction for the rest of the paper. Each member of the group can draft a thesis statement and the group can discuss the advantages of each, but the group needs to agree on one version before getting too far into the rest of the draft. Your group might revise the thesis statement after the whole paper has been drafted, but using a preliminary version gets everyone started in the same direction.

→

Guidelines for collaborative writing (*continued*)

12. Draft the rest of the paper. Decide whether each member of the group should write a complete draft or one part of the whole. For example, each group member might take one main idea and be responsible for drafting that section. Share draft materials among the group members using disks or e-mail attachments (see step 4). If this is impossible, make photocopies. For most group meetings it will be important to have a paper copy of group materials, so print (or photocopy) copies for everyone.

Revising the Writing

13. Read over the drafts. Are all the important points included?
14. Use the revision checklist (Box 17 in 3c.5), and work either as a group or by assigning portions to subgroups. If different people have drafted different sections, COHERENCE and UNITY should receive special attention in revision, as should your introduction and conclusion.
15. Agree on a final version. Assign someone to prepare the final draft and make sure every group member has a copy.

Editing and Proofreading the Writing

16. As a group, review printouts or photocopies of the final draft. Don't leave the last stages to a subgroup. Draw on everyone's knowledge of grammar, spelling, and punctuation. Use everyone's eyes for proofreading.
17. Use the editing checklist (Box 18 in 3d) to double-check for errors. If you find more than one or two errors per page, correct and print out the page again. No matter how well the group has worked collaboratively, or how well the group has written the paper, a sloppy final version reflects negatively on the entire group.
18. If your instructor asks, be prepared to describe your personal contribution to the project and/or to describe or evaluate the contributions of others.

3g A student essay in three drafts

The following sections observe Carol Moreno, a student, planning to write on the topic of weight lifting for women. In Chapter 2, you'll find her writing assignment (2c), how she used an entry in her journal (2f), mapped her ideas (see 2j), wrote her THESIS STATEMENT (2q), and outlined (2r). During these activities, Moreno chose an informative writing purpose (1c.2).

3g.1 The first draft of a student essay

Here's Moreno's first draft showing her own notes to herself about revisions to make in the second draft. The notes resulted from comments of her PEER-RESPONSE GROUP and from her personal rereading of her draft.

Carol Moreno's first draft, with notes

Pumping Iron

What do I mean here?

It all began when my grandmother broke her hip. I

I should say why she needed lifting

She does not weigh much, but she was too much for me.

couldn't lift her alone when I was helping take care of her. I

I have to check when I revise whether this thesis statement fits the rest of my essay

needed strength, and I'm planning to be a nurse. Then I

I need to clarify the connection

found out I could satisfy a physical ed requirement in

college with a weight lifting course for women. I thought

Lots of I's — is this only about me?

only big, macho men lift weights. But if she is trained well,

any woman can "pump iron" well, just like a man.

Hoping for strength and endurance

~~The first day of class we did not exercise. We talked~~

~~about who we are and why we wanted to take the course.~~

MOVE. This should be my third ¶. My second ¶ should give background

can lead to   *unless lifters*

~~We heard about how to avoid~~ injury by learning the safe

and weight machines. Free weights are barbells.

use of free weights ~~(barbells).~~ To be safe, no matter how

little the weight, lifters must never raise a barbell by

grasp

bending at the waist. Instead, they should squat, ~~grab~~ the

barbell, and then straighten up into a standing position.

To avoid a   that   serious

Twists can lead to injury so lifters must keep head erect,

I need to go into more detail here

facing forward, back and neck aligned. Lifters use weight

machines sitting down, which is a big advantage of the

Nautilus and Universal.

→

BACKGROUND
In his article "10:00 and 2:00: A Ten-Paragraph Defense of the Five-Paragraph Theme" (*Teaching English in the Two-Year College*, March 2000: 312–314), Robert Perrin defends the five-paragraph essay, arguing that the maligned form may actually foster creativity.

happy
~~I was~~ relieved that I won't develop overly masculine

move up to be #2 (background)

muscle mass. We learned that we can rely on women's

I have to bring in more than myself to say who we are

biology. Our bodies produce only very small amounts of

With normal training,

the hormones that enlarge muscles in men. ~~Normally,~~

I need to tie these together (check 4d)

muscles
women's ~~grow~~ longer rather than bulkier. Weight lifting is a

form of anareobic *(SP)* exercise. It does not make people breathe

harder or their hearts beat faster. Arobic *(SP)* exercise like

Am I too informal here?

running, walking, and
swimming builds endurance, so I took up swimming.

My topic sentence needs work

After safety comes our needs for physical strength. A

It
well-planned, progressive weight training program. ~~You~~

a person
begin with whatever weight ~~you~~ can lift comfortably and

to the base weight as she gets stronger.
~~then gradually add.~~ What builds muscle strength is the

the lifter does;
number of "reps" ~~we do~~, not necessarily an increase in the

resistance from adding
amount of ~~added~~ weight. In my class, we ranged from 18 to

pudgy couch potato
43, scrawny to ~~fat~~, and ~~lazy~~ to superstar, and we each

I'm not trying here

developed a program that was OK for us. Some women

try
didn't listen to our instructor who urged us not to ~~do~~ more

Start sentence here? Not sure

our first workouts
reps or weight than our programs called for, even if ~~it~~

seemed too easy. This turned out to be good advice because

the next morning
those of us who didn't listen woke up feeling as though our

bodies had been twisted by evil forces.

→

TEACHING TIP

Certainly, all of us sometimes feel that we are drowning in student writing. The battle rages constantly: Do I spend twenty minutes on each essay, or do I spend five minutes, thereby responding to more students?

Given the few minutes that we have for each essay, decisions about what and how to write are important. Codes (abbreviations, such as *sp* and *agr*, or references to text, such as *15a*, or proofreader's symbols, such as # for space) are a clear, fast way to refer to unambiguous matters in grammar, punctuation, and mechanics. Of course, be sure students know what the messages mean—you might review the codes and symbols you ordinarily use as part of the follow-up to their receiving their first piece of writing back from you, or you can refer students to the chart of correction symbols in this handbook. Along with citing errors, symbols send a secondary message: "This matter is important but relatively uninspiring. Fix it quickly (and learn the information) and move on to the more interesting aspects of your essay."

Many issues of substance are impossible to respond to exclusively by code. Besides, students like to feel that a real human being is reading their work—and real people ask questions when they are puzzled. Therefore, whenever possible, phrase your reactions as questions. Instead of writing "unclear," ask "How does this relate to your thesis?" If you do not have time to write many questions, try at least one or two per paper. Psychologically, people can't help but answer questions—at least in their own minds. So, to ask a question is to guarantee an answer. And with the answer in mind, a student can revise. Whenever time permits, a good description deserves more than "nice" scribbled in the margin; you might say, "You really made me see the lake at sundown." If a student tells you about a cooking disaster, you might say, "You had me laughing in sympathy. The same thing happened to me." Such comments validate students' experiences and also demonstrate compassionate reading.

→

In addition to ~~fitting to~~

~~After meeting her~~ physical capabilities, a weight lifter needs to design her personal goals. Most students in

I need specific examples of students

my group wanted to improve their upper body strength. Each student learned to use specific exercises to isolate certain muscle groups, for example we might work on our

sp?

arms and abdomen one day and our shoulders and chest the next day. ~~My goal is nursing, which I want to pursue. I want to help others, but I'm also very interested in the science I'll learn. I hear there is a lot of memorization, which I'm pretty good at. I also will have "clinical" assignments to give us hands on experience in hospitals.~~

I'm off the topic

Because I had had such trouble lifting my grandmother, I added exercises to strengthen my legs and back. Another student added neck strengthening exercises. Someone else added finger and hand exercises.

I forget to talk about my swimming

At the end of the course, we had to evaluate our progress. When I started, I could lift 10 pounds, *over my head for 3 reps.* but by the

over my head

end, I could lift 10 pounds for 20 reps and 18 pounds for 3

still

reps. I am so proud of my accomplishments that I work out

I need a stronger ending

three or four times a week. I am proof that any woman can become stronger and have more stamina.

3g.2 The second draft of a student essay

For her second draft, Moreno revised by working systematically through the notes she had written on the draft. The notes came from her own thinking as well as from the comments of the PEER-RESPONSE GROUP with which she had shared her paper.

From the assignment (2c), Moreno knew that her instructor would consider this second draft an "essay in progress." Her instructor's responses would help her write a final draft. She expected two types of comments: questions to help her clarify and expand on some of her ideas, and references to some of this handbook's section codes (number-letter combinations) to point out errors. Here is her second draft.

Carol Moreno's second draft, with her instructor's responses

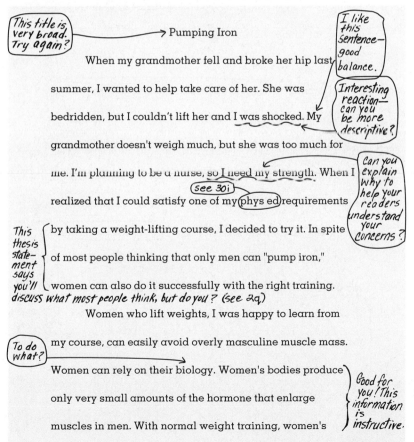

Teaching Tip (continued)
Reaction comments are most useful in the final response to an essay. Many students turn to the end of their final draft essay returned by the instructor before reading marginal comments. After the grade, the ending response is most crucial to students. The final comment is our total impression; the margins are a kind of running commentary. To be useful, a closing comment needs to clarify, not duplicate, the grade: A student whose grade has jumped from D to B knows his or her work is "better," so try to be specific about what has made it better.

A useful end comment has several sentences at least. A serviceable pattern consists of a personal response, a sentence about the content and organization of the piece (positive as well as negative observations—see the end comment to Moreno's third draft), and, where pertinent, a sentence about a recurring mechanical or grammatical issue (for example, "Try to hear and pronounce the ends of words. You frequently omit -*s* and -*ed* endings.")

QUOTATION: ON WRITING
No one can make you feel inferior without your consent.

—Eleanor Roosevelt

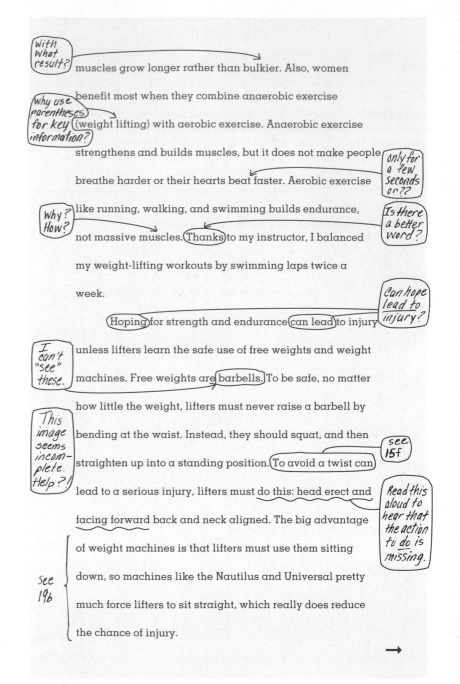

With what result? muscles grow longer rather than bulkier. Also, women

benefit most when they combine anaerobic exercise

Why use parentheses for key information? (weight lifting) with aerobic exercise. Anaerobic exercise

strengthens and builds muscles, but it does not make people *only for a few seconds or??*

breathe harder or their hearts beat faster. Aerobic exercise

Why? How? like running, walking, and swimming builds endurance, *Is there a better word?*

not massive muscles. Thanks to my instructor, I balanced

my weight-lifting workouts by swimming laps twice a

week.

Hoping for strength and endurance can lead to injury *Can hope lead to injury?*

I can't "see" these. unless lifters learn the safe use of free weights and weight

machines. Free weights are barbells. To be safe, no matter

how little the weight, lifters must never raise a barbell by

This image seems incomplete. Help?! bending at the waist. Instead, they should squat, and then

straighten up into a standing position. To avoid a twist can *see 15f*

lead to a serious injury, lifters must do this: head erect and *Read this aloud to hear that the action to do is missing.*

facing forward back and neck aligned. The big advantage

see 19b of weight machines is that lifters must use them sitting

down, so machines like the Nautilus and Universal pretty

much force lifters to sit straight, which really does reduce

the chance of injury.

→

*Do you
want to
use one
word so
much?*

Once a weight lifter understands how to lift safely,
she needs to meet her personal needs No one needs to

be strong to get started. A well-planned progressive

See 12b.2

weight training program. It begins with whatever weight

a person can lift comfortably and gradually adds to the

base weight as she gets stronger. What builds strength

is the number of "reps" the lifter does, not necessarily an

meaning?

increase in the amount of resistance from adding weight.

Our instructor helped the women in our class, who rang-

*These
adjectives
are fun.*

ed from 18 to 43, scrawny to pudgy, couch potato to

superstar, to develop a program that suited us. Our

instructor urged us not to try more reps or weight than our

programs called for, even if our first workouts seemed too

easy. This turned out to be good advice because those

*Fun again.
Your voice
(personality)
comes
through.*

of us who did not listen woke up the next morning

feeling as though our bodies had been twisted by evil

forces.

In addition to fitting a program to her physical

*Does
one
design
a goal?*

capabilities, a weight lifter needs to design her personal

goals. Most students in my group wanted to improve their

upper body strength, so we focused on exercises to

→

73

QUOTATION: ON WRITING
It takes me six months to do a story. I think it out and then write it sentence by sentence—no first draft. I can't write five words but that I change seven.

—Dorothy Parker

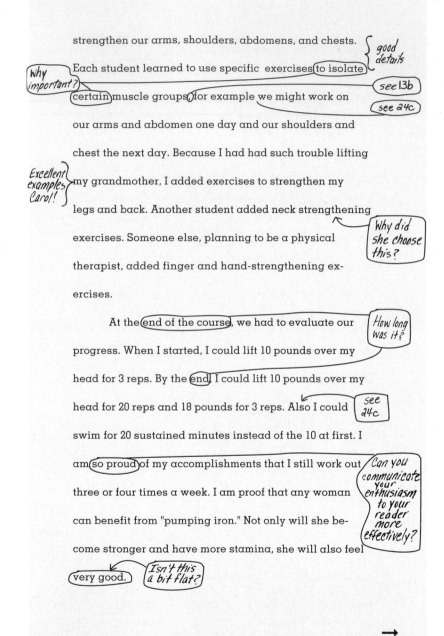

strengthen our arms, shoulders, abdomens, and chests. { *good details*

Why important? Each student learned to use specific exercises (to isolate

certain) muscle groups, for example we might work on *see 13b*

see 24c

our arms and abdomen one day and our shoulders and

chest the next day. Because I had had such trouble lifting

Excellent examples Carol! my grandmother, I added exercises to strengthen my

legs and back. Another student added neck strengthening

exercises. Someone else, planning to be a physical *Why did she choose this?*

therapist, added finger and hand-strengthening ex-

ercises.

At the (end of the course), we had to evaluate our *How long was it?*

progress. When I started, I could lift 10 pounds over my

head for 3 reps. By the (end), I could lift 10 pounds over my

head for 20 reps and 18 pounds for 3 reps. Also I could *see 24c*

swim for 20 sustained minutes instead of the 10 at first. I

am (so proud) of my accomplishments that I still work out *Can you communicate your enthusiasm to your reader more effectively?*

three or four times a week. I am proof that any woman

can benefit from "pumping iron." Not only will she be-

come stronger and have more stamina, she will also feel

(very good.) *Isn't this a bit flat?*

→

Dear Carol,
You have truly earned the right to feel proud of yourself. You've also inspired me to consider weight training myself!
As you revise for your final draft, I'd urge you to get more <u>voice</u> (your personality) into the essay. To do this, you don't have to become too informal; instead, think about how you <u>felt</u> about what you were doing and try to put that into words. Also, think about my questions and the codes that refer you to sections of the Troyka handbook.
I will enjoy reading your final draft, I'm sure.

3g.3 A student's final draft

For her final draft, Moreno worked systematically through her second draft with an eye on her instructor's responses. Also, she revised in

places where her instructor hadn't commented. As another check, Moreno referred to the revision checklist (Box 17 in 3c.5).

Next, to edit her final draft, Moreno looked up the handbook codes (number-letter combinations) her instructor wrote on her second draft. She also consulted the editing checklist (Box 18 in 3d). Then, before she started to proofread, she took a break from writing so she could refresh her ability to see typing errors. Distance from her work, she knew, would also help her see it more objectively.

Moreno's final draft appears on the following pages with notes in the margins to point out elements that help the essay succeed. These notes are for you only; don't write any notes on your final drafts.

QUOTATION: ON WRITING
Let your literary compositions be kept from the public eye for nine years at least.
—Horace

Carol Moreno's final draft

Moreno 1

Carol Moreno

Professor K. Norris

Freshman Composition 101, Section LR

4 December 2003

TITLE   Women Can Pump Iron, Too

INTRODUCTION: When my grandmother fell and broke her hip last summer,
Gets reader's
attention   I wanted to help take care of her. Because she was bedridden,
with personal
anecdote   she needed to be lifted at times, but I was shocked to discover

that I could not lift her without my mother's or brother's help. My

grandmother does not weigh much, but she was too much for me.

My pride was hurt, and even more important, I began to worry

Question to   about my plans to be a nurse specializing in the care of elderly
add sentence
variety   people. What if I were too weak to help my patients get around?

When I realized that I could satisfy one of my Physical Education

requirements by taking a weight-lifting course for women, I

decided to try it. Many people picture only big, macho men

THESIS   wanting to lift weights, but times have changed. With the right
STATEMENT:
Focus of essay   training, women can also "pump iron" to build strength.

BODY   Women who lift weights, I was happy to learn from my
PARAGRAPH
ONE: Gives   course, can easily avoid developing overly masculine muscle
background
information   mass. Women can rely on their biology to protect them. Women's

bodies produce only very small amounts of the hormones that

Refutes   enlarge muscles in men. With normal weight training, women's
possible
objection   muscles grow longer rather than bulkier. The result is smoother,

Transition   firmer muscles, not massive bulges. Also, women benefit most
to signal
additional point   when they combine weight lifting, which is a form of anaerobic

exercise, with aerobic exercise. Anaerobic exercise strengthens

→

(Proportions shown in this paper are adjusted to fit space limitations of this book. Follow actual dimensions discussed in this book and your instructor's directions.)

Moreno 2

and builds muscles, but it does not make people breathe harder

Specific details of two types of conditioning

or their hearts beat faster for sustained periods. In contrast, aerobic exercises like running, walking, and swimming build endurance, but not massive muscles, because they force a person to take in more oxygen, which increases lung capacity, improves circulatory health, and tones the entire body. Encouraged by my instructor, I balanced my weight-lifting workouts by swimming laps twice a week.

BODY PARAGRAPH TWO: Describes safe use of equipment and lifting techniques

Striving for strength can end in injury unless weight lifters learn the safe use of free weights and weight machines. Free weights are barbells, the metal bars that round metal weights can be attached to at each end. To be safe, no matter how little the weight, lifters must never raise a barbell by bending at the waist, grabbing the barbell, and then

Transition to show contrast

straightening up. Instead, they should squat, grasp the barbell, and then use their leg muscles to straighten into a standing position. To avoid a twist that can lead to serious injury, lifters must use this posture: head erect and facing forward, back and neck aligned. The big advantage of weight machines, which use weighted handles and bars hooked to wires and pulleys, is that lifters must use them sitting down. Therefore, machines like the Nautilus and Universal actually force lifters to keep their bodies properly aligned, which drastically reduces the chance of injury.

BODY PARAGRAPH THREE: Describes and explains the design and purpose of weight-training programs

Once a weight lifter understands how to lift safely, she needs a weight-lifting regimen personalized to her specific physical needs. Because benefits come from "resistance," which is the stress that lifting any amount of weight puts on a muscle, no one has to be strong to get started. A well-planned,

→

QUOTATION: ON WRITING
When you say something, make sure you have said it. The chances of your having said it are only fair.

—E. B. White

progressive weight-training program begins with whatever weight a person can lift comfortably and gradually adds to the base weight as she gets stronger. What builds muscle strength is the number of repetitions, or "reps," the lifter does, not necessarily an increase for resistance from adding weight. Our

Specific details for reader to visualize a class

instructor helped the women in the class, who ranged from 18 to 43, scrawny to pudgy, and couch potato to superstar, to develop a program that was right for our individual weight, age, and overall level of conditioning. Everyone's program differed in how much weight to start out with and how many reps to do for each exercise. Our instructor urged us not to try more weight or reps than our programs called for, even if our first workouts seemed too easy. This turned out to be good advice because those of us who did not listen woke up the next day feeling as though evil forces had twisted our bodies.

BODY PARAGRAPH FOUR: Explains the need for developing a program to fit individual needs

In addition to fitting a program to her physical capabilities, a weight lifter needs to design an individual routine to fit her personal goals. Most students in my group wanted to improve their upper body strength, so we focused on exercises to strengthen arms, shoulders, abdomens, and chests. Each student learned to use specific exercises to isolate certain muscle groups. Because muscles strengthen and grow when they're rested after a workout, our instructor taught us to work alternate muscle groups on different days. For example, a

Specific examples to add interest

woman might work on her arms and abdomen one day and then her shoulders and chest the next day. Because I had had such trouble lifting my grandmother, I added exercises to strengthen my legs and back. Another student, who had hurt her neck in a car crash, added neck-strengthening exercises. Someone

→

Moreno 4

else, planning to be a physical therapist, added finger- and hand-strengthening exercises.

CONCLUSION: Reports writer's personal progress

At the end of our 10 weeks of weight training, we had to evaluate our progress. Was I impressed! I felt ready to lift the world. When I started, I could lift only 10 pounds over my head for 3 reps. By the end of the course, I could lift 10 pounds over my head for 20 reps, and I could lift 18 pounds for 3 reps. Also, I could swim laps for 20 sustained minutes instead of the 10 I had barely managed at first. I am so proud of my weight-training accomplishments that I still work out three or four times a week. I am proof that any woman can benefit from "pumping iron." Not only will she become stronger and have more stamina, but she will also feel energetic and confident. After all, there isn't a thing to lose--except maybe some flab.

QUOTATION: ON WRITING
To be a writer is to throw away a great deal, not to be satisfied, to type again, and then again and once more, and over and over.
—John Hersey

Chapter 4

Writing Paragraphs

4a What is a paragraph?

A **paragraph** is a group of sentences that work together to develop a unit of thought. Paragraphing permits writers to divide material into manageable parts. When a group of paragraphs works together in logical sequence, the result is a complete essay or other whole piece of writing.

To signal the start of a new paragraph, indent the first line about one-half inch. Skip no extra lines between paragraphs. business writing (Chapter 42) is an exception: It calls for *block format* for paragraphs, which means you do not indent the first line but rather leave a double space between paragraphs. If you're already double-spacing, then leave two double lines for a total of four lines.

I explain later in this chapter the rich variety of paragraph arrangements (4h) and rhetorical strategies (4i) at your disposal for writing paragraphs. Types of arrangements and rhetorical strategies reflect patterns of thought in Western cultures. But first, let's look at characteristics of paragraphs in general. I start by discussing introductory paragraphs (4b); then, body paragraphs (4c through 4j); and last, concluding paragraphs (4k).

4b How can I write effective introductory paragraphs?

An **introductory paragraph** leads the reader to sense what's ahead. It sets the stage. It also, if possible, attempts to arouse a reader's interest in the topic.

A THESIS STATEMENT can be an important component in an introduction. Many instructors require students to place their thesis statement at the end of the opening paragraph. Doing so disciplines students to state early the central point of the essay. If an introduction points in one direction, and the rest of the essay goes off in another, the essay isn't communicating a clear message. Professional writers don't necessarily include a thesis statement in their introductory paragraphs. Most have the skill to maintain a line of thought without overtly stating a main idea. Introductory paragraphs, as well as concluding paragraphs (4k), are usually shorter than body paragraphs (4c).

Be careful not to tack on a sloppy introduction at the last minute. The introductory paragraph plays too important a role to be tossed off with merely a few shallow lines. While many writers prefer to write only a thesis statement as an introduction in an early draft, they always return to write a complete introductory paragraph after the body—the main part—of the writing is finished. For a list of specific strategies to use—and pitfalls to avoid for introductory paragraphs—see Box 20.

BOX 20 **SUMMARY**

 ## Introductory paragraphs

Strategies to Use

- Providing relevant background information
- Relating briefly an interesting story or anecdote
- Giving one or more pertinent—perhaps surprising—statistics
- Asking one or more provocative questions
- Using an appropriate quotation
- Defining a KEY TERM (6e)
- Presenting one or more brief examples (4i)
- Drawing an ANALOGY (4i)

Strategies to Avoid

- Don't write statements about your purpose, such as "I am going to discuss the causes of falling oil prices."
- Don't apologize, as in "I am not sure this is right, but this is my opinion."
- Don't use overworked expressions, such as "Haste makes waste, as I recently discovered" or "Love is grand."

Always integrate an introductory device into the paragraph so that it leads smoothly into the thesis statement. Some examples follow. In this chapter, each example paragraph has a number to its left for your easy reference. Here's an introductory paragraph that uses two brief examples to lead into the thesis statement at the end of the paragraph.

On seeing another child fall and hurt himself, Hope, just nine months old, stared, tears welling up in her eyes, and crawled to her

Teaching Tip (continued)

and expose them to new vocabulary used in complete sentences, but such reading alone is not likely to help them form subconscious ideas about paragraph structure that can be usefully applied to academic writing. To learn to write essays, the student must—at least part of the time—read essays.

One way to show your students the difference between essay paragraphing and newspaper paragraphing is to give them copies of pieces dealing with the same experience: a newspaper account of a fire and an essay (such as an editorial) written in response to the event; a newspaper account of a trial and a magazine essay discussing the case. Ask students to list the differences. At minimum, they will mention differences in length and number of paragraphs and in the presence or absence of personal opinion. They may also notice the lack of a thesis statement and a conclusion in the newspaper article and the presence of both in the essay.

You might also ask students how satisfied they would be if they were given only the first paragraph of the newspaper article and of the essay. The article's introduction will probably be far more satisfying in terms of information but less satisfying in terms of graceful presentation, background, pacing, and the like.

Another way to underscore the difference between the genres is to give students (or assign them to find) a meaty newspaper article—the kind that runs for two pages. Have them rewrite the article as an essay. Before the students write, you might discuss with them the kinds of changes they anticipate making.

QUOTATION: ON WRITING
To write an interesting introduction is almost always to write in concrete language and specific detail. If your prose limps along the reader's interest will wane.
—Charles W. Dawe

mother to be comforted—as though she had been hurt, not her friend. When 15-month-old Michael saw his friend Paul crying, Michael fetched his own teddy bear and offered it to Paul; when that didn't stop Paul's tears, Michael brought Paul's security blanket from another room. Such small acts of sympathy and caring, observed in scientific studies, are leading researchers to trace the roots of empathy—the ability to share another's emotions—to infancy, contradicting a long-standing assumption that infants and toddlers were incapable of these feelings.
—Daniel Goleman, "Researchers Trace Empathy's Roots to Infancy"

In paragraph 2, the opening quotation sets up a dramatic contrast with the thesis statement.

2   "Alone one is never lonely," says May Sarton in her essay "The Rewards of Living a Solitary Life." Most people, however, don't share Sarton's opinion: They're terrified of living alone. They're used to living with others—children with parents, roommates with roommates, friends with friends, spouses with spouses. When the statistics catch up with them, therefore, they're rarely prepared. Chances are high that most adult men and women will need to know how to live alone, briefly or longer, at some time in their lives.
—Tara Foster, student

In paragraph 3, the writer asks a direct question, and next puts the reader in a dramatic situation to arouse interest in the topic.

3   What should you do? You're out riding your bike, playing golf, or in the middle of a long run when you look up and suddenly see a jagged streak of light shoot across the sky, followed by a deafening clap of thunder. Unfortunately, most outdoor exercisers don't know whether to stay put or make a dash for shelter when a thunderstorm approaches, and sometimes the consequences are tragic.
—Gerald Secor Couzens, "If Lightning Strikes"

EXERCISE 4-1

Write an introduction for the three essays informally outlined on the facing page. Then, for more practice, write one alternative introduction for each. If you have a peer-response group, share the various written introductions and decide which are most effective. For help, see 4b.

1. Reading for fun
   Thesis statement: People read many kinds of books for pleasure.
   Body paragraph 1: murder mysteries and thrillers
   Body paragraph 2: romances and westerns
   Body paragraph 3: science fiction
2. Cellphones
   Thesis statement: Cellphones have changed how some people behave in public.
   Body paragraph 1: driving
   Body paragraph 2: restaurants
   Body paragraph 3: movies and concerts
   Body paragraph 4: sidewalks, parks, and other casual spaces
3. Using credit cards
   Thesis statement: Although credit cards can help people manage their finances wisely, they also offer too much temptation.
   Body paragraph 1: convenience and safety
   Body paragraph 2: tracking of purchases
   Body paragraph 3: overspending dangers

4c What are body paragraphs?

Each **body paragraph,** which belongs between an introductory paragraph (4b) and a concluding paragraph (4k), consists of a main idea and support for that idea. To be effective, a body paragraph needs three characteristics: unity (4d and 4e), development (4f), and coherence (4g). The sections shown in parentheses explain how you can achieve each characteristic. Box 21 gives an overview of all three characteristics.

BOX 21   SUMMARY

Characteristics of effective body paragraphs

Unity: Have you made a clear connection between the main idea of the paragraph and the sentences that support the main idea (4d and 4e)?

Development: Have you included detailed and sufficient support for the main idea of the paragraph (4f)?

Coherence: Have you progressed from one sentence to the next in the paragraph smoothly and logically (4g)?

ANSWERS: EXERCISE 4-1
Answers will vary.

TEACHING TIP: ESL
Some ESL students may attempt to weave every fact included in the body of the paper into their introductions. Unfortunately, this "tapestry" technique usually strikes native speakers as repetitive, even though it demonstrates considerable skill. Instructors might explain that introductions in English are less all-encompassing and more subtle. See Joy Reid's essay for teachers in this book. Also see Part Seven in the student edition.

QUOTATION: ON WRITING
One of the most difficult things is the first paragraph. I have spent many months on a first paragraph, and once I get it, the rest just comes out very easily.
—Gabriel García Márquez

QUOTATION: ON WRITING
I have two methods of working. One of them involves tapping the sources of creativity. . . . I might be anywhere when it comes and I could end up writing all over the floor or up the walls and not knowing what is going on. It is like having a fit. . . .

The second method is following a trail made by my words themselves—by sitting down and writing . . . writing anything, fast. The words include the vision. That rush—that vision or high or whatever it is—doesn't last very long. A lot of writing gets done in a very short time, but it's not very good writing. Often it turns out to be just a reminder about how something felt. It has to be reworked.
—Maxine Hong Kingston

BACKGROUND

The concept of the paragraph as a self-contained or organic unit of language first appeared in *English Composition and Rhetoric* (1866), a textbook by Alexander Bain, professor of rhetoric at the University of Aberdeen in Scotland. Bain defined the paragraph as "a collection of sentences with unity of purpose" and declared unity, coherence, and emphasis to be the characteristics of an effective paragraph, a proclamation that has had a vast influence on textbooks ever since. He gave students seven guidelines for achieving these effects:

1. **Distribution into sentences:** The paragraph is composed of individual sentences, each with its own unity, working together to form the whole.

2. **Explicit reference:** The connection of each sentence to the ones preceding it must be clear.

3. **Parallel construction:** Consecutive sentences that carry the same meaning or idea should be formed alike.

4. **Indication of the theme:** The first sentence in the paragraph should indicate its scope.

5. **Unity:** Unity derives from a sustained purpose and admits neither digressions nor irrelevancies.

6. **Consecutive arrangement:** Related topics should be placed close together.

7. **Marking of subordination:** The principal and subordinate statements should have their relative importance clearly indicated, as such elements in a sentence do.

Later textbooks influenced by Bain treated the paragraph as an "essay in miniature" and encouraged a meristic, or parts-to-whole, approach to teaching the essay, first teaching students how to write sentences and paragraphs and then teaching them to put these parts together to build essays. Other researchers and theorists have disputed the idea of the paragraph as an "essay in miniature." Instead of a "bottom up" approach, they say that experienced writers work "top down," from ideas and purpose to sentences and paragraphs.

Paragraph 4 is an example of an effective body paragraph. It's from an essay called "What's Bugging You?"

4   The cockroach lore that has been daunting us for years is mostly true. Roaches can live for twenty days without food, fourteen days without water; they can flatten their bodies and crawl through a crack thinner than a dime; they can eat huge doses of carcinogens and still die of old age. They can even survive "as much radiation as an oak tree can," says William Bell, the University of Kansas entomologist whose cockroaches appeared in the movie *The Day After.* They will eat almost anything—regular food, leather, glue, hair, paper, even the starch in book bindings. (The New York Public Library has quite a cockroach problem.) They sense the slightest breeze, and they can react and start running in .05 second; they can also remain motionless for days. And if all this isn't creepy enough, they can fly too.

—Jane Goldman, "What's Bugging You?"

Paragraph 4 has UNITY (4d) in that the main idea (stories we've heard about cockroaches are true), stated in the TOPIC SENTENCE (4e), which is also the first sentence, is supported by detailed examples. It has COHERENCE (4g) in that the content of every sentence ties into the content of the other sentences. Also, the paragraph *coheres*—sticks together—by word choices (repeating *they can* each time to put the emphasis on the interesting facts) and with consistent grammar (a different ACTIVE VERB [see VOICE, 8n through 8p] for each example). It has PARAGRAPH DEVELOPMENT (4c and 4i) in that the details provide support for the main idea.

4d How can I create unity in paragraphs?

A paragraph has **unity** when the connection between the main idea and its supporting sentences is clear. Paragraph 4 in section 4c is a good example.

Unity is ruined when any sentence in a paragraph "goes off the topic," which means its content doesn't relate to the main idea or to the other sentences in the paragraph. To show you broken unity, in paragraph 5 I've deliberately inserted two sentences (the fourth and the next to last) that go off the topic and ruin a perfectly good paragraph, shown as paragraph 6. (Neither a personal complaint about stress nor hormones produced by men and women during exercise belong in a paragraph defining different kinds of stress.)

NO   Stress has long been the subject of psychological and physiological speculation. In fact, more often than not, the word itself is ill defined and overused, meaning different things to different people. Emotional stress, for example, can come about as the

84

result of a family argument or the death of a loved one. Everyone says, "don't get stressed," but I have no idea how to do that. Environmental stress, such as exposure to excessive heat or cold, is an entirely different phenomenon. Physiologic stress has been described as the outpouring of the steroid hormones from the adrenal glands. During exercise, such as weightlifting, males and females produce different hormones. Whatever its guise, a lack of a firm definition has seriously impeded past research.

5

YES Stress has long been the subject of psychological and physiological speculation. In fact, more often than not, the word itself is ill defined and overused, meaning different things to different people. Emotional stress, for example, can come about as the result of a family argument or the death of a loved one. Environmental stress, such as exposure to excessive heat or cold, is an entirely different phenomenon. Physiologic stress has been described as the outpouring of the steroid hormones from the adrenal glands. Whatever its guise, a lack of a firm definition has seriously impeded past research.

6

—Herbert Benson, M.D., *The Relaxation Response*

4e How can topic sentences create paragraph unity?

A **topic sentence** contains the main idea of a paragraph and controls its content. Often, the topic sentence comes at the beginning of a paragraph, though not always. Professional essay writers, because they have the skill to carry the reader along without explicit signposts, sometimes decide not to use topic sentences. However, instructors often require students to use topic sentences. As apprentice writers, students might have more difficulty writing unified paragraphs.

Topic sentence starting a paragraph

In ACADEMIC WRITING, most paragraphs begin with a topic sentence (shown here in italics) so that readers know immediately what to expect. Paragraph 7 is an example.

To travel the streets of Los Angeles is to glimpse America's ethnic future. At the bustling playground at McDonald's in Koreatown, a dozen shades of kids squirt down the slides and burrow through tunnels and race down the catwalks, not much minding that no two of them speak the same language. Parents of grade-school children say they rarely know the color of their youngsters' best friends until they meet them; it never seems to occur to the children to say, since they have not yet been taught to care.

7

—Nancy Gibbs, "Shades of Difference"

BACKGROUND

u-ni-ty (yōō' nə tē) n. *pl.* -ties (1) The state, property, or product of being united physically, socially, or morally; oneness; opposed to *division, plurality.*

—*Britannica World Language Dictionary*

TEACHING TIP

You may want to encourage students to look for topic sentences in the newspapers and magazines they read. They may be surprised to discover that in materials published for a nonacademic setting, topic sentences occur at beginnings and endings of paragraphs, just as they do in textbook examples. In some cases, they will probably find that paragraphs manage to make a unified statement without the presence of a stated topic sentence. The examples they find can provide a basis for class discussion.

BACKGROUND

The use of topic sentences by published writers has been the subject of a great deal of research and study over the past two decades. Richard Braddock's groundbreaking research in the 1970s revealed that in the essays he examined, he found topic sentences in paragraphs only 13 percent of the time. The percentage has varied in other studies, but most have found that under half of the paragraphs in published writing begin with topic sentences.

Braddock felt that the essays he studied would have been improved if the paragraphs had used more explicit topic sentences. Recent research shows that people are able to read faster and remember and comprehend more when a paragraph begins with a sentence that states the main idea and indicates the organization of the material to follow.

A helpful review of early theories of paragraphing is Rochelle Smith's "Paragraphing for Coherence: Writing as Implied Dialogue," in *College English* 46.1 (1984): 8–21.

TEACHING TIP
Regardless of students' interests, virtually any topic, if well written, can capture their imaginations. You can choose to invite students to bring in feature articles of events that intrigue them or case studies of industries that capture their attention. Ideally, ask for writing samples on topics that initially don't seem interesting but which prompt them to dive in and read because of the writing style and delivery. Ask students to pinpoint a paragraph or even a sentence that they especially like.

Sometimes, a topic sentence both starts a paragraph and, in different wording, ends the paragraph. Paragraph 8 is an example.

8   *Burnout is a potential problem for hardworking and persevering students to fight.* A preliminary step for preventing student burnout is for students to work in moderation. Students can concentrate on school every day, if they don't overtax themselves. One method students can use is to avoid concentrating on a single project for an extended period. For example, if students have to read two books for a midterm history test, they should do other assignments at intervals so that the two books will not get boring. Another means to moderate a workload is to regulate how many extracurricular projects to take on. When a workload is manageable, a student's immunity to burnout is strengthened.

—Bradley Howard, student

Topic sentence ending a paragraph

Some paragraphs give supporting details first and wait to state the topic sentence at the paragraph's end. This approach is particularly effective for building suspense or for creating a bit of drama. Paragraph 9 is an example.

9   Most people don't lose ten dollars or one hundred dollars when they trade cars. They lose many hundreds or even a thousand. They buy used cars that will not provide them service through the first payment. They overbuy new cars and jeopardize their credit, only to find themselves "hung," unable even to sell their shiny new toys. The car business is one of the last roundups in America, the great slaughterhouse of wheeling and dealing, where millions of people each year willingly submit to being taken.

—Remar Sutton, *Don't Get Taken Every Time*

Topic sentence implied, not stated

Some paragraphs are a unified whole even without a single sentence that readers can point to as the topic sentence. Yet, most readers can catch the main idea anyway. Paragraph 10 is an example. What do you think might be a straightforward topic sentence for it?

10   The Romans were entertained by puppets, as were the rulers of the Ottoman Empire with their favorite shadow puppet, Karaghoiz, teller of a thousand tales. In the Middle Ages, puppets were cast as devil and angel in religious mystery and morality plays until cast out entirely by the church. For centuries, a rich puppetry heritage in India has matched that country's multilayered culture. The grace of Bali is reflected in its stylized, ceremonial rod and shadow puppets. The Bunraku puppets of Japan, unequaled for technique anywhere in the world, require a puppet master and two assistants to create one dramatic character on stage.

—Dan Cody, "Puppet Poetry"

EXERCISE 4-2

Working individually or with a peer-response group, identify the topic sentences in the following paragraphs. If the topic sentence is implied, write the point the paragraph conveys. For help, consult section 4e.

A.   A good college program should stress the development of high-level reading, writing, and mathematical skills and should provide you with a broad historical, social, and cultural perspective, no matter what subject you choose as your major. The program should teach you not only the most current knowledge in your field but also—just as important— prepare you to keep learning throughout your life. After all, you'll probably change jobs, and possibly even careers, at least six times, and you'll have other responsibilities, too—perhaps as a spouse and as a parent and certainly as a member of a community whose bounds extend beyond the workplace.

11

                         —Frank T. Rhodes, "Let the Student Decide"

B.   The once majestic oak tree crashes to the ground amid the destructive flames, as its panic-stricken inhabitants attempt to flee the fiery tomb. Undergrowth that formerly flourished smolders in ashes. A family of deer darts furiously from one wall of flame to the other, without an emergency exit. On the outskirts of the inferno, firefighters try desperately to stop the destruction. Somewhere at the source of this chaos lies a former campsite containing the cause of this destruction—an untended campfire. This scene is one of many that illustrate how human apathy and carelessness destroy nature.

12

                         —Anne Bryson, student

C.   Rudeness isn't a distinctive quality of our own time. People today would be shocked by how rudely our ancestors behaved. In the colonial period, a French traveler marveled that "Virginians don't use napkins, but they wear silk cravats, and instead of carrying white handkerchiefs, they blow their noses either with their fingers or with a silk handkerchief that also serves as a cravat, a napkin, and so on." In the 19th century, up to about the 1830s, even very distinguished people routinely put their knives in their mouths. And when people went to the theater, they would not just applaud politely—they would chant, jeer, and shout. So, the notion that there's been a downhill slide in manners ever since time began is just not so.

13

                       —"Horizons," *U.S. News & World Report*

4f   How can I develop my body paragraphs?

You develop a **body paragraph** by supplying detailed support for the main idea of the paragraph communicated by your TOPIC SENTENCE (4e), whether stated or implied. **Paragraph development** is not merely a rep-

---

ANSWERS: EXERCISE 4-2

A (paragraph 11). The topic sentence is the first sentence.

B (paragraph 12). The topic sentence is the last sentence.

C (paragraph 13). The topic sentence is the first sentence; the second sentence is a limiting sentence.

BACKGROUND

In "What Works for Me: Letting Students Critique Textbooks" (*Teaching English in the Two-Year College*, December 1996: 313), Charles Kovach reports that when students challenge the rhetorical categories in their readers (textbooks), they improve their skills in critical reading and analysis.

BACKGROUND

In "The Ill Effects of the Five Paragraph Theme" (*English Journal* 90, September 2000: 57–60), Kimberly Wesley argues that adhering too rigidly to the five-paragraph theme format hinders the development of critical thinking. In contrast, Robert Perrin still sees some value in emphasizing this format ("10:00 and 2:00: A Ten-Paragraph Defense of the Five-Paragraph Theme," *Teaching English in the Two-Year College*, March 2000: 312–314).

QUOTATION: ON WRITING

That's the purpose of paragraphing: to give the reader a breather by sensibly breaking up the prose. A paragraph is to a writer what a quick intake of breath is to a singer—a little interruption that makes possible refreshed continuation.

                —William Safire

etition, using other words, of the main idea. When this happens, you're merely going around in circles. I've deliberately created paragraph 14 to show you a bad example of development. It goes nowhere because all that happens is that one idea is restated three times in different words. Compare it with the well-developed paragraph 4 that appears in section 4c.

> **NO**
> **14** The cockroach lore that has been daunting us for years is mostly true. Almost every tale we have heard about cockroaches is correct. The stories about cockroaches have frightened people for generations.

What separates most good writing from bad is the writer's ability to move back and forth between main ideas and specific details. To check whether you are providing sufficient detail in a body paragraph, use the RENNS Test. Each letter in the made-up word RENNS cues you to remember a different kind of supporting detail at your disposal, as listed in Box 22.

BOX 22 SUMMARY

The RENNS Test: Checking for supporting details

R = **Reasons** provide support.
E = **Examples** provide support.
N = **Names** provide support.
N = **Numbers** provide support.
S = **Senses**—sight, sound, smell, taste, touch—provide support.

Use the RENNS Test to check the quality of your paragraph development. Of course, not every paragraph needs all five kinds of RENNS details, nor do the supporting details need to occur in the order of the letters in RENNS. Paragraph 15 contains three of the five types of RENNS details. Identify the topic sentence and as many RENNS as you can before reading the analysis that follows the paragraph.

> **15** U.S. shores are also being inundated by waves of plastic debris. On the sands of the Texas Gulf Coast one day last September, volunteers collected 307 tons of litter, two-thirds of which was plastic, including 31,733 bags, 30,295 bottles, and 15,631 six-pack yokes. Plastic trash is being found far out to sea. On a four-day trip from Maryland to Florida that ranged 100 miles offshore, John Hardy, an Oregon State University marine biologist, spotted "Styrofoam and other plastic on the surface, most of the whole cruise."
>
> —"The Dirty Seas," *Time*

In paragraph 15, the first sentence serves as the topic sentence. Supporting details for that main idea include examples, names, and numbers. The writer provides examples of the kinds of litter found washed up on the beach and floating offshore. The writer names many specific things: Texas Gulf Coast, September, bags, bottles, six-pack yokes, Maryland, Florida, John Hardy, Oregon State University, marine biologist, and Styrofoam. And the writer uses specific numbers to describe the volume of litter collected (307 tons), to give counts of specific items (such as 31,733 bags), and to tell how far from shore (100 miles) the litter had traveled.

Paragraph 16 contains four of the five types of RENNS. Identify the topic sentence and as many RENNS as you can before you read the analysis that follows the paragraph.

16   Tennyson called it a "flying flame," Benjamin Franklin termed it a "sudden and terrible mischief." In Roman mythology, the god Jupiter used spiky thunderbolts as letters to the editor when he chose to show displeasure to the poor mortals below. By whatever name, lightning is a spectacular natural event. Captured in photographs, its grandeur and beauty are safely petrified in static portraits of primal energy. In reality, at 24,000 to 28,000 degrees C., it is four times hotter than the surface of the sun. It can vaporize steel, plough up fields, shatter giant trees, and scatter live incendiary sparks over vast forests. Each day it kills 20 people.
—Michael Clugston, "Twice Struck"

In paragraph 16, the third sentence is the topic sentence. Supporting details for the main idea include examples (vaporize steel, plough up fields, shatter giant trees); the writer also uses names (Tennyson, Franklin) and numbers (24,000 to 28,000 degrees C., 20 people). Sensory details, given in images, provide more support (flying flame, sudden and terrible mischief).

EXERCISE 4-3

Working individually or with a peer-response group, look again at the paragraphs in Exercise 4-2. Identify the RENNS in each paragraph. For help, consult 4f.

4g How can I write coherent paragraphs?

A paragraph has **coherence** when its sentences relate to each other, not only in content but also in choice of words and grammatical structures. A coherent paragraph conveys continuity because the sentences follow naturally from one to the next. Techniques for achieving coherence are listed in Box 23 on the next page, with the section that offers a complete explanation shown in parentheses.

ANSWERS: EXERCISE 4-3

A (paragraph 11). Reasons include learning current knowledge, keeping you learning through life, having a job, and being a spouse, a parent, and a member of the community. Examples include job, spouse, parent, and member of the community. Number named is six.

B (paragraph 12). Names include oak, deer, firefighters. Senses are invoked by sound of crashing oak, sight of flames, "fiery tomb," smoldering in ashes, deer family darting furiously, and the smell (implied) of burning trees.

C (paragraph 13). Examples include colonial Virginians using their cravats as handkerchiefs and people putting their knives in their mouths. Names include the French traveler, distinguished people, people in the theater. Numbers include the dates the 1830s and the 19th century. Senses include the noise—chants, jeers, and shouts—made by the audience in the theater.

EXTRA EXERCISE A

Mark all of the transitional expressions used in the following paragraph. (Answers appear in italics.)

Edith Newbold Jones was the descendant of wealthy, socially prominent New York families. *As a result,* she made her formal debut before she married Edward Wharton of Boston in 1885. *Soon after* her marriage, she began writing as a therapeutic measure. She *also* used her writing as a means of occupying her free time when her husband was suffering from a mental illness. *Naturally,* much of her writing was concerned with the closed, wealthy New York society she had known as a child. In the 1890s, *as a result* of her "hobby," she published her first short stories in *Scribner's* magazine, using her married name, Edith Wharton. *Subsequently,* she was recognized as one of America's best popular writers. *For example,* in 1924 she became the first woman ever to receive an honorary degree from Yale University. *Equally* important, she was awarded the Pulitzer Prize in 1921 for *The Age of Innocence,* a novel about the unbreakable moral code of Victorian society. Her most famous work, *however,* is *Ethan Frome,* a tragic love story. *Although* she continued to write about American subjects and characters, she spent much of her later life in France, where she had a home. She died there in 1937.

QUOTATION: ON WRITING

You must once and for all give up being worried about successes and failures. Don't let that concern you. It's your duty to go on working steadily day by day, quite steadily, to be prepared for mistakes, which are inevitable, and for failures.

—Anton Chekhov

BOX 23   SUMMARY

Techniques for achieving coherence

- Using appropriate transitional expressions (4g.1)
- Using pronouns when possible (4g.2)
- Using deliberate repetition of a key word (4g.3)
- Using parallel structures (4g.4)
- Using coherence techniques to create connections between paragraphs (4g.5)

4g.1 Using transitional expressions for coherence

Transitional expressions are words and phrases that signal connections among ideas. **Transitions** are bridges that lead your reader along your line of thought. They offer cues about what follows. Commonly used transitional expressions are listed in Box 24.

BOX 24   SUMMARY

Transitional expressions and the relationships they signal

ADDITION	also, in addition, too, moreover, and, besides, furthermore, equally important, then, finally
EXAMPLE	for example, for instance, thus, as an illustration, namely, specifically
CONTRAST	but, yet, however, nevertheless, nonetheless, conversely, in contrast, still, at the same time, on the one hand, on the other hand
COMPARISON	similarly, likewise, in the same way
CONCESSION	of course, to be sure, certainly, granted
RESULT	therefore, thus, as a result, so, accordingly
SUMMARY	hence, in short, in brief, in summary, in conclusion, finally
TIME	first, second, third, next, then, finally, afterward, before, soon, later, meanwhile, subsequently, immediately, eventually, currently
PLACE	in the front, in the foreground, in the back, in the background, at the side, adjacent, nearby, in the distance, here, there

👁 **ALERT:** In ACADEMIC WRITING, set off a transitional expression with a comma, unless the expression is one short word (24g). 👁

Vary your choices of transitional words. For example, instead of always using *for example,* try *for instance.* Also, when choosing a transitional word, make sure it correctly says what you mean. For example, don't use *however* in the sense of *on the other hand* if you mean *therefore* in the sense of *as a result.* The three brief examples below demonstrate how to use transitional expressions for each context.

COHERENCE BY ADDITION
Woodpeckers use their beaks to find food and to chisel out nests. In addition, they claim their territory and signal their desire to mate by using their beaks to drum on trees.

COHERENCE BY CONTRAST
Most birds communicate by singing. Woodpeckers, however, communicate by the duration and rhythm of the drumming of their beaks.

COHERENCE BY RESULT
The woodpecker's strong beak enables it to communicate by drumming on dry branches and tree trunks. As a result, woodpeckers can communicate across greater distances than songbirds can.

Paragraph 17 demonstrates how transitional expressions (shown in bold) enhance a paragraph's COHERENCE. The TOPIC SENTENCE is the final sentence.

17   Before the days of television, people were entertained by exciting radio shows such as *Superman, Batman,* and "War of the Worlds." **Of course,** the listener was required to pay careful attention to the story if all details were to be comprehended. **Better yet,** while listening to the stories, listeners would form their own images of the actions taking place. When the broadcaster would give brief descriptions of the Martian space ships invading earth, **for example,** every member of the audience would imagine a different space ship. **In contrast,** television's version of "War of the Worlds" will not stir the imagination at all, for everyone can clearly see the actions taking place. All viewers see the same space ship with the same features. Each aspect is clearly defined, and **therefore,** no one will imagine anything different from what is seen. **Thus,** television can't be considered an effective tool for stimulating the imagination.
—Tom Paradis, "A Child's Other World"

4g.2 Using pronouns for coherence

Pronouns—words that refer to nouns or other pronouns—allow readers to follow your train of thought from one sentence to the next without boring repetition. Without pronouns, you would have to repeat nouns over and over. For example, this sentence uses no pronouns and therefore has needless repetition: *The woodpecker scratched the woodpecker's head with the woodpecker's foot.* In contrast, with pronouns the sentence can be: *The woodpecker scratched **its** head with **its** foot.* Paragraph 18 illustrates how pronouns (shown in bold) contribute to COHERENCE.

18   The funniest people I know are often unaware of just how ticked off **they** are about things until **they** start to kid around about **them.** Nature did not build **these** people to sputter or preach; instead, in response to the world's irritations, **they** create little plays in **their** minds—parodies, cartoons, fantasies. When **they** see how funny **their** creations are, **they** also understand how really sore **they** were at **their** sources. **Their** anger is a revelation, one that works backward in the minds of an audience: the audience starts out laughing and winds up fuming.
            —Roger Rosenblatt, "What Brand of Laughter Do You Use?"

4g.3 Using deliberate repetition for coherence

A key word is a strong word that's central to the main idea of the paragraph. **Repetition** of a key word is a useful way to achieve COHERENCE in a paragraph. The word usually appears first in the paragraph's TOPIC SENTENCE (4e) and then again throughout the paragraph. The idea of key-word repetition is to keep a concept in front of the reader.

Use this technique sparingly to avoid being monotonous. Also, limit your selection of a key word to one or at the most two words. The shorter a paragraph, the more likely a repeated key word will seem repetitious, and the less likely it'll be effective. In a longer paragraph, however, the repetition of a key word can be effective. Paragraph 19 contains repeated words (shown in bold) closely tied to the concept of emotions, making the paragraph more coherent.

19   **Emotions** are, technically speaking, chemical impulses to act. The root of the word *emotion* is *motere*, the Latin verb meaning "to move," plus the prefix *e* which means "away," suggesting a tendency to act is implicit in every **emotion.** One of the primary functions of **emotion** is to warn us of danger. Goleman refers to this warning process as an "**emotional** alarm." When you experience an **emotional** alarm, like an unexpectedly loud noise, the **emotional** part of your brain takes over the analytical part of your brain, and you react.
            —Carol Carter and Lynn Quitman Troyka,
            Majoring in the Rest of Your Life

4g.4 Using parallel structures for coherence

Parallel structures are created when grammatically equivalent forms are used in series, usually of three or more items, but sometimes only two (see PARALLELISM, Chapter 18). Using parallel structures helps to give a paragraph coherence. The repeated parallel structures reinforce connections among ideas, and they add both tempo and sound to the sentence.

In paragraph 20, the authors use several parallel structures (shown in bold): a parallel series of words (*the sacred, the secular, the scientific*); parallel phrases (*sometimes smiled at, sometimes frowned upon*); and six parallel clauses (the first being *banish danger with a gesture*).

20 Superstitions are **sometimes smiled at** and **sometimes frowned upon** as observances characteristic of **the old-fashioned, the unenlightened,** children, peasants, servants, immigrants, foreigners, or backwoods people. Nevertheless, they give all of us ways of moving back and forth among the different worlds in which we live—**the sacred, the secular,** and **the scientific.** They allow us to keep a private world also, where, smiling a little, we can **banish danger with a gesture** and **summon luck with a rhyme, make the sun shine in spite of storm clouds, force the stranger to do our bidding, keep an enemy at bay,** and **straighten the paths of those we love.**
—Margaret Mead and Rhoda Metraux, "New Superstitions for Old"

4g.5 Creating coherence among paragraphs

The same techniques for achieving COHERENCE in a paragraph apply to showing connections among paragraphs in a piece of writing. All four techniques help: transitional expressions (4g.1), pronouns (4g.2), deliberate repetition (4g.3), and parallel structures (4g.4). To see them in action, look over this handbook's student essays (one in 3g, two in 40g), research papers (6m, 34e.2, and 35h.2), and a science report (41h.1).

Example 21 shows two short paragraphs and the start of a third. The writer achieves coherence among the paragraphs by repeating the key word *gratitude* and the related words *grateful, thankful,* and *thank* and by using them as a transition into the next paragraph. The writer also uses PARALLELISM within the paragraphs in this example.

21 To me, gratitude and inner peace go hand in hand. The more genuinely grateful I feel for the gift of my life, the more peaceful I feel. Gratitude, then, is worthy of a little practice.

If you're anything like me, you probably have many people to be thankful for: friends, family members, people from your past, teachers, gurus, people from work, someone who gave you a break, as well as countless others. You may want to thank a higher power for the gift of life itself, or for the beauty of nature.

As you think of people to be grateful for, remember that it can be anyone—someone who held a door open for you, or a physician who saved your life. . . .

ANOTHER EXAMPLE OF PARALLEL STRUCTURES
I am not complaining that the brewing and baking were taken over by the men. If they can brew and bake as well as women or better, then by all means let them do it. But they cannot have it both ways. If they are going to adopt the very sound principle that the job should be done by the person who does it best, then that rule must be applied universally. If the women make better office-workers than men, then they must have the office work. If any individual woman is able to make a first-class lawyer, doctor, architect or engineer, then she must be allowed to try her hand at it.
—Dorothy L. Sayers, "Are Women Human?"

QUOTATION: ON WRITING
Composing is like an organic process, not an assembly line on which some prefabricated parts are fitted together. . . . The task of the computer is to find the forms that find forms; the structures that guide and encourage growth; the limits by means of which development can be shaped. [Composing] is a way of making meanings by using the forms provided by language to re-present the relationships we see.
—Ann E. Berthoff

QUOTATION: ON WRITING
As writing teachers, we find ourselves under enormous pressure to master a broader range of communication technologies, which places even greater stress on the already demanding responsibility of teaching writing. Of course, some of that pressure has been felt by everyone in our culture with the growth of the Internet and the proliferation of email and electronic commerce.
—David Blakesley

ANSWERS: EXERCISE 4-4

A (paragraph 22). *Pronouns:* her, she. *Deliberate repetition:* Kathy, arms, hands opened, closed. *Parallel structures:* Many parallel clauses, starting with "Her shoulders raised"; open hands reaching out and closed hands bringing back.

B (paragraph 23). *Pronouns:* we, whom, this. *Deliberate repetition:* we, world. *Parallel structures:* Once set in motion, will remain in motion; we must.

C (paragraph 24). *Pronouns:* them, they. *Transitional expressions:* first, but, then. *Deliberate repetition:* cloud, always, line, layer, white. *Parallel structures:* always shifting, but always orderly; line after line; layer above layer.

QUOTATION: ON WRITING

The secret to a clear and readable style is in the first five or six words of every sentence.
—Joseph M. Williams,
Style: Toward Clarity and Grace

ANSWERS: EXERCISE 4-5

Each paragraph will obviously differ in content, but this exercise should help students see that they need to support general statements with graphic details (developed through RENNS, discussed in 4f) that are smoothly linked by the techniques of coherence discussed in 4g: transitional expressions, pronouns, repetition, and parallel structures.

EXERCISE 4-4

Working individually or with a peer-response group, locate the coherence techniques in each paragraph. Look for transitional expressions, pronouns, deliberate repetition, and parallel structures. For help, consult 4g.

A. Kathy sat with her legs dangling over the edge of the side of the hood. The band of her earphones held back strands of straight copper hair that had come loose from two thick braids that hung down her back. She swayed with the music that only she could hear. Her shoulders raised, making circles in the warm air. Her arms reached out to her side; her open hands reached for the air; her closed hands brought the air back to her. Her arms reached over her head; her opened hands reached for a cloud; her closed hands brought the cloud back to her. Her head moved from side to side; her eyes opened and closed to the tempo of the tunes. Kathy was motion.
    —Claire Burke, student

B. Newton's law may have wider application than just the physical world. In the social world, racism, once set into motion, will remain in motion unless acted upon by an outside force. The collective "we" must be the outside force. We must fight racism through education. We must make sure every school has the resources to do its job. We must present to our children a culturally diverse curriculum that reflects our pluralistic society. This can help students understand that prejudice is learned through contact with prejudiced people, rather than with the people toward whom the prejudice is directed.
    —Randolph H. Manning, "Fighting Racism with Inclusion"

C. The snow geese are first, rising off the ponds to breakfast in the sorghum fields up the river. Twenty thousand of them, perhaps more, great white birds with black wing tips rising out of the darkness into the rosy reflected light of dawn. They make a sweeping turn, a cloud of wings rising above the cottonwoods. But cloud is the wrong word. They don't form a disorderly blackbird rabble but a kaleidoscope of goose formations, always shifting, but always orderly. The light catches them—white against the tan velvet of the hills. Then they're overhead, line after line, layer above layer of formations, and the sky is filled with the clamor of an infinity of geese.
    —Tony Hillerman, *Hillerman Country*

EXERCISE 4-5

Working individually or with a peer-response group, use RENNS (4f) and techniques for achieving coherence (4g) to develop three of the following topic sentences into paragraphs. When finished, list the RENNS and the coherence techniques you used in each paragraph.

1. Newspaper comic strips reflect current concerns in our culture.
2. The contents of trash in the United States says a great deal about U.S. culture.
3. Dramas on television tend to have several common elements.
4. Part-time jobs can be very unappealing.
5. Time management is a lifesaver for college students.

4h How can I arrange a paragraph?

When you choose a **paragraph arrangement** during DRAFTING, you order its sentences to communicate the paragraph's message most clearly and effectively. Later, during REVISION, experiment with other arrangements to see how else your sentences might be arranged for greatest impact. You may find sometimes that only one possible arrangement can work. For example, if you're explaining how to bake a cake, you want to give the directions in a particular order. At other times, you may find that more than one arrangement is possible. For example, if you're writing about solving a problem and therefore using the problem-to-solution arrangement, you might also use the technique of ordering from least to most important—or its reverse. Box 25 lists the most common ways to arrange a paragraph. More about each arrangement appears below in this section.

BOX 25   SUMMARY

 Ways to arrange sentences in a paragraph

- By time
- By location
- From general to specific
- From specific to general
- From least to most important
- From problem to solution

Arranging by time

In a paragraph arranged according to time, or **chronological order,** events are presented in whatever order they took place. For example, when you tell a story, you write what happened first, then second, then third, and so on. Using a time sequence is a very natural and easy way to organize a paragraph. Paragraph 25 on the next page is an example.

EXAMPLE OF SPATIAL SEQUENCE

The wash [low land that is sometimes flooded and at other times nearly dry] looked perfectly dry in my headlights. I drove down, across, up the other side and on into the night. Glimpses of weird humps of pale rock on either side, like petrified elephants, dinosaurs, stone-age hobgoblins. Now and then something alive scurried across the road: kangaroo mice, a jackrabbit, an animal that looked like a cross between a raccoon and a squirrel—the ringtail cat. Farther on a pair of mule deer started from the brush and bounded obliquely through the beams of my lights, raising puffs of dust which the wind, moving faster than my pickup truck, caught and carried ahead of me out of sight into the dark. The road, narrow and rocky, twisted sharply left and right, dipped in and out of tight ravines, climbing by degrees toward a summit which I would see only in the light of the coming day.

—Edward Abbey,
"The Most Beautiful Place on Earth"

TEACHING TIP

When they learn new subjects, students may differ in the way they organize the material in their minds. Some students may prefer to consider the broad "big picture" objectives first, with the details following behind. By contrast, other students might like to know the details first so they can fit them into the larger context. Interestingly, students' preferences for how they receive a new assignment may reveal the way they are inclined to write. Some students may like to arrange their paragraphs from general to specific, whereas other students would choose a specific-to-general approach. You might invite students to explain their preferred ways of learning new material and then ask them to think about whether different learning patterns affect how they arrange their paragraphs.

Other visitors include schools of dolphin swimming with synchronized precision and the occasional humpback whale. Before 1950, these 14-meter marine mammals were a common sight in the waters of the Great Barrier Reef as they passed on their annual migration between Antarctic waters and the tropics, where their calves were born. Then in the 1950s, whaling stations were set up on the New South Wales and Queensland coasts, and together with the long-established Antarctic hunts by the Soviet Union and America, whales were slaughtered in the thousands. By the time the whaling stations on the eastern Australian coast closed in the early 1960s, it was estimated that only two hundred remained in these waters. Today, their numbers are slowly increasing, but sightings are still rare.

25

—Allan Moult, "Volcanic Peaks, Tropical Rainforest, and Mangrove Swamps"

Arranging by location

A paragraph arranged according to location, or **spatial order,** leads the reader's attention from one place to another. The movement can be in any direction—from top to bottom, left to right, inside to outside, and so on. Paragraph 26 traces natural disasters across the United States from west to east.

26
In the United States, most natural disasters are confined to specific geographical areas. For example, the West Coast can be hit by damaging earthquakes at any time. Most Southern and Midwestern states can be swept by devastating tornadoes, especially in the spring, summer, and early fall. The Gulf of Mexico and the Atlantic Ocean can experience violent hurricanes in late summer and fall. These different natural disasters, and others as dangerous, teach people one common lesson—advance preparation can mean survival.

—Dawn Seaford, student

Arranging from general to specific

The most common pattern for arranging information is from **general to specific.** Typically, the general statement is the TOPIC SENTENCE, and the supporting details (see RENNS, 4f) explain the specifics. Paragraph 27 is an example.

Unwanted music is privacy's constant enemy. There is hardly an American restaurant, store, railroad station or bus terminal that doesn't gurgle with melody from morning to night, nor is it possible any longer to flee by boarding the train or bus itself, or even by taking a walk in the park. Transistor radios have changed all that. Men, women and children

carry them everywhere, hugging them with the desperate attachment that a baby has for its blanket, fearful that they might have to generate an idea of their own or contemplate a blade of grass. Thoughtless themselves, they have no thought for the sufferers within earshot of their portentous news broadcasts and raucous jazz. It's hardly surprising that
27 RCA announced a plan that would pipe canned music and pharmaceutical commercials to 25,000 doctors' offices in eighteen big cities—one place where a decent quietude might be expected. This raises a whole new criterion for choosing a family physician. Better to have a second-rate healer content with the sounds of his stethoscope than an eminent specialist poking to the rhythms of Gershwin.

—William Zinsser, *The Haircurl Papers*

Arranging from specific to general

A less common paragraph arrangement moves from **specific to general.** Paragraph 28 is an example. To achieve greatest impact, the paragraph starts with details that support the topic sentence, which ends the paragraph.

Replacing the spark plugs is probably the first thing most home auto mechanics do. But too often, the problem lies elsewhere. In the ignition system, the plug wires, distributor unit, coil, and ignition control unit play just as vital a role as the spark plugs. Moreover, performance prob-
28 lems are by no means limited to the ignition system. The fuel system and emissions control system also contain several components that equal the spark plug in importance. The do-it-yourself mechanic who wants to provide basic care for a car must be able to do more than change the spark plugs.

—Danny Witt, student

Arranging from least to most important

A paragraph arranged from **least to most important** uses **climactic order,** which means that the high point—the climax—comes at the end. For a paragraph to be arranged from least to most important, it has to have at least three items: least, better, best. And remember that the last item always packs the greatest impact and is the most memorable. Paragraph 29 is an example.

For a year, Hal and I worked diligently on that boat. At times, it was a real struggle for me to stay on course: as an 11-year-old, my attentions often wandered and the work was not always exciting. But Hal's dedica-
29 tion profoundly influenced me. By his own example, he taught me important lessons about how to be organized, how to set priorities, and how to be responsible. He also, through working with me on the design of the boat's electronics, played a pivotal role in developing my passion for science.

—Patrick Regan Buckley, "Lessons in Boat-Building—and Life"

EXAMPLE: FROM GENERAL TO SPECIFIC
We all listen to music according to our separate capacities. But, for the sake of analysis, the whole listening process may become clearer if we break it up into its component parts, so to speak. In a certain sense we all listen to music on three separate planes. For lack of a better terminology, one might name these: (1) the sensuous plane, (2) the expressive plane, (3) the sheerly musical plane.

—Aaron Copland

TEACHING TIP
One function that paragraphs serve is to cue readers about shifts in ideas. Paragraphs, then, have an aspect of design to them, however modest. Consider, for example, how pages would look different without the white space breaks provided by paragraphing. Web pages cue readers in other fashions. In pages that were designed specifically for the Web (as opposed to being first written for traditional print, then copied onto the Web), the screen functions in ways parallel to the paragraph. In other words, writers and designers think in terms of what readers and viewers will grasp in one screen, without scrolling down. You might have students look at several documents that are designed to be read online and compare the relationship between paragraphs and screens full of information in those documents.

BACKGROUND

In the mid-1960s, A. L. Becker wrote a now classic article on paragraph structures: "A Tagamemic Approach to Paragraph Analysis" (*College Composition and Communication*, December 1965: 237–242). He noted that paragraphs for exposition often follow two basic patterns: topic-restriction-illustration (TRI) and problem-solution (PS).

The TRI pattern has three "slots"—topic, restriction, and illustration. It begins with a topic sentence or proposition in the **T** slot. The **R** slot defines, restates, or explains the proposition at a lower level of generality. The **I** slot often provides one or more examples, an extended analogy, or a series of comparisons that describe or exemplify the topic at a still lower level of generality.

The problem-solution (PS) pattern states a problem or effect in the opening **P** slot, sometimes in question form, and follows by stating the solution or cause in the **S** slot. If the explanation of the solution or cause is extended, it may follow the TRI pattern.

Becker illustrates both the TRI and PS patterns with a paragraph from Frank Gibney's *Five Gentlemen of Japan:*

> **(P)** How obsolete is Hearn's judgment? **(S1) (T)** On the surface the five gentlemen of Japan do not themselves seem to be throttled by this rigid society of their ancestors. **(R)** Their world is in fact far looser in its demands upon them than it once was. **(I)** Industrialization and the influence of the West have progressively softened the texture of the web. Defeat in war badly strained it. A military occupation, committed to producing a democratic Japan, pulled and tore at it. **(S2) (T)** But it has not disappeared. **(R)** It is still the invisible adhesive that seals the nationhood of the Japanese. **(I)** Shimizu, Sanada, Yamazaki, Kisfi and Hirohito were all born within its bonds. Despite their individual work, surroundings and opinions, they have lived most of their lives as cogs geared into a group society. Literally as well as figuratively speaking, none of them has a lock on his house door.

Arranging from problem to solution

In some cases, an effective arrangement for a paragraph is **problem to solution.** Usually, the topic sentence presents the problem. The very next sentence presents the main idea of the solution. Then, the rest of the paragraph covers the specifics of the solution. Paragraph 30 is an example.

> 30   When I first met them, Sara and Michael were a two-career couple with a home of their own, and a large boat bought with a large loan. What interested them in a concept called voluntary simplicity was the birth of their daughter and a powerful desire to raise her themselves. Neither one of them, it turned out, was willing to restrict what they considered their "real life" into the brief time before work and the tired hours afterward. "A lot of people think that as they have children and things get more expensive, the only answer is to work harder in order to earn more money. It's not the only answer," insists Michael. The couple's decision was to trade two full-time careers for two half-time careers, and to curtail consumption. They decided to spend their money only on things that contributed to their major goal, the construction of a world where family and friendship, work and play, were all of a piece, a world, moreover, which did not make wasteful use of the earth's resources.
>
> —Linda Weltner, "Stripping Down to Bare Happiness"

EXERCISE 4-6

Working individually or with a peer-response group, rearrange the sentences in each paragraph below so that it flows logically. To begin, identify the topic sentence, use it as the paragraph's first sentence, and continue from there. For help, consult 4h.

PARAGRAPH A

1. Remember, many people who worry about offending others wind up living according to other people's priorities.
2. Learn to decline, tactfully but firmly, every request that doesn't contribute to your goals.
3. Of all the timesaving techniques ever developed, perhaps the most effective is the frequent use of the word *no.*
4. If you point out that your motivation isn't to get out of work but to save your time to do a better job on the really important things, you'll have a good chance of avoiding unproductive tasks.
   —Edwin Bliss, "Getting Things Done: The ABC's of Time Management"

PARAGRAPH B

1. After a busy day, lens wearers often don't feel like taking time out to clean and disinfect their lenses, and many wearers skip the chore.
2. When buying a pair of glasses, a person deals with just the expense of the glasses themselves.

3. Although contact lenses make the wearer more attractive, glasses are easier and less expensive to care for.

4. However, in addition to the cost of the lenses themselves, contact lens wearers must shoulder the extra expense of cleaning supplies.

5. This inattention creates a danger of infection.

6. In contrast, contact lenses require daily cleaning and weekly enzyming that inconvenience lens wearers.

7. Glasses can be cleaned quickly with water and tissue at the wearer's convenience.

—Heather Martin, student

PARAGRAPH C

1. The researchers found that the participation of women in sport was a significant indicator of the health and living standards of a country.

2. Today, gradually, women have begun to enter sport with more social acceptance and individual pride.

3. In 1952, researchers from the Finnish Institute of Occupational Health who conducted an intensive study of the athletes participating in the Olympics in Helsinki predicted, "Women are able to shake off civil disabilities which millennia of prejudice and ignorance have imposed upon them."

4. Myths die hard, but they do die.
—Marie Hart, "Sport: Women Sit In the Back of the Bus"

EXERCISE 4-7

Working individually or with a peer-response group, determine the arrangements in these paragraphs. Choose from time, location, general to specific, specific to general, least to most important, and problem to solution. For help, consult 4h.

A.   A combination of cries from exotic animals and laughter and gasps from children fills the air along with the aroma of popcorn and peanuts. A hungry lion bellows for dinner, his roar breaking through the confusing chatter of other animals. Birds of all kinds chirp endlessly at curious children. Monkeys swing from limb to limb,
31 performing gymnastics for gawking onlookers. A comedy routine by orangutans employing old shoes and garments incites squeals of amusement. Reptiles sleep peacefully behind glass windows, yet they send shivers down the spines of those who remember the quick death many of these reptiles can induce. The sights and sounds and smells of the zoo inform and entertain children of all ages.
—Deborah Harris, student

B.   No one even agrees anymore on what "old" is. Not long ago, 30 was middle-aged and 60 was old. Now, more and more people are

QUOTATION: ON WRITING
Writing is a lot like sewing. You bring pieces together and make a quilt.
—Rosario Ferre

QUOTATION: ON WRITING
Sometimes you get a line, a phrase, sometimes you're crying, or it's the curve of a chair that hurts you and you don't know why, or sometimes you just want to write a poem, and you don't know what it's about. I will fool around on the typewriter. It might take me ten pages of nothing, of terrible writing, and then I'll get a line, and I'll think, "That's what I mean!" What you're doing is hunting for what you mean, what you're trying to say. You don't know when you start.
—Anne Sexton

ANSWERS: EXERCISE 4-8
Answers will vary according to how each student conceives of each subject. Comparisons of the methods of arrangement can reveal the multiplicity of available choices.

BACKGROUND
Richard M. Coe, in *Process, Form, and Substance: A Rhetoric for Advanced Writers*, 2nd ed. (Englewood Cliffs, NJ: Prentice Hall, 1990), groups patterns of development into report and explanatory patterns and into analytical and progressive patterns. Description and narration are report patterns that depend on observation and "compose our perceptions" (261). Explanatory patterns (comparison and contrast, classification and division, definition, analogy, process analysis, causal explanation, and logical progression), by contrast, are "abstracted" from description and narration to explain and make distinctions (301). Analytical patterns (description, comparison and contrast, classification and division, definition, and analogy) report and explain in static and spatial terms. Progressive patterns (narration, process, cause and effect, and logical progression), conversely, are organized by time, and they report and explain process and change.

BACKGROUND
The theory that paragraph structures often resemble sentence structures was presented in the mid-1960s by the widely respected rhetorician Francis Christensen. In "A Generative Rhetoric of the Paragraph," in *Notes Toward a New Rhetoric* (New York: Harper & Row, 1967), he points out that the topic sentence is parallel to the base clause of a sentence, and the supporting sentences are parallel to the added sentence modifiers.

Given such a structure, the paragraph, like the sentence, develops with addition that has direction of modification or direction of movement. When sentences are added to develop a topic, they are usually at a lower level of generality, and the more sentences the writer adds, the denser the texture. To use

➡

32 living into their 70s, 80s and beyond—and many of them are living well, without any incapacitating mental or physical decline. Today, old age is defined not simply by chronological years, but by degree of health and well-being.

—Carol Tavris, "Old Age Isn't What It Used to Be"

C. Lately, bee researchers have been distracted by a new challenge from abroad. It's, of course, the so-called "killer bee" that was imported into Brazil from Africa in the mid-1950s and has been heading our way ever since. The Africanized bee looks like the Italian bee but is more defensive and more inclined to attack in force. It consumes much of the honey that it produces, leaving relatively little for anyone who attempts to work with it. It travels fast, competes with local bees and, worse, mates with them. It has ruined the honey industry in Venezuela and now the big question is: Will the same thing happen here?

—Jim Doherty, "The Hobby That Challenges You to Think Like a Bee"

EXERCISE 4-8

Working individually or with a peer-response group, decide what would be the best arrangement for a paragraph on each topic listed here. Choose from one or a combination of time, location, general to specific, specific to general, least to most important, and problem to solution. For help, consult 4h.

1. ways to make friends
2. automobile accidents
3. how to combine work and college
4. teaching children table manners

4i How can rhetorical strategies help me write paragraphs?

Rhetorical strategies are techniques for presenting ideas clearly and effectively. Rhetorical strategies reflect patterns of thought long in use in our Western culture. You choose a specific rhetorical strategy according to what you want to accomplish. Box 26 lists the common rhetorical strategies at your disposal.

Often, your TOPIC SENTENCE will steer you toward a particular pattern. For example, if a topic sentence is "Grilling a great hot dog is easy," the implied pattern—or rhetorical strategy—is to explain the process of how to grill a hot dog. Or if a topic sentence is "To see many different styles of architecture in one U.S. city, visit Chicago," the implied pattern—or rhetorical strategy—is to give examples.

Sometimes, you need to use a combination of rhetorical strategies. For example, in a paragraph on types of color blindness, you might use a

Common rhetorical strategies (patterns of thought) for paragraphs

- Narrative
- Description
- Process
- Examples
- Definition

- Analysis
- Classification
- Comparison and contrast
- Analogy
- Cause-and-effect analysis

combination of definition and classification. A paragraph explaining why one brand of house paint is superior to another might call for comparison and contrast combined with description—and, perhaps, also definition and examples.

Writing a narrative

Narrative writing is a rhetorical strategy that tells a story. A *narration* relates what is happening or what has happened. Paragraph 34 is an example.

34 Gordon Parks speculates that he might have spent his life as a waiter on the North Coast Limited train if he hadn't strolled into one particular movie house during a stopover in Chicago. It was shortly before World War II began, and on the screen was a hair-raising newsreel of Japanese planes attacking a gunboat. When it was over the camera operator came out on stage and the audience cheered. From that moment on Parks was determined to become a photographer. During his next stopover, in Seattle, he went into a pawnshop and purchased his first camera for $7.50. With that small sum, Parks later proclaimed, "I had bought what was to become my weapon against poverty and racism." Eleven years later, he became the first black photographer at *Life* magazine.
　　　　　　　　　　　　　　　　　　—Susan Howard, "Depth of Field"

Writing a description

Writing a **description** is a rhetorical strategy that appeals to a reader's senses—sight, sound, smell, taste, and touch. *Descriptive writing* paints a picture in words. Paragraph 35 is an example.

35 Walking to the ranch house from the shed, we saw the Northern Lights. They looked like talcum powder fallen from a woman's face. Rouge and blue eye shadow streaked the spires of a white light which exploded, then pulsated, shaking the colors down—like lives—until they faded from sight.
　　　　　　　　　　　　　　　　　　—Gretel Ehrlich, "Other Lives"

Background (continued)
this structural analysis of the paragraph to generate paragraphs, Christensen proposes nine principles that can be applied and taught. Your students need not regard these principles as laws but should regard them rather as rules of thumb that can help them generate certain kinds of paragraphs.

1. The paragraph may be defined as a sequence of sentences that are related by coordination and subordination.

2. Often the most general sentence of the sequence is the topic sentence, the sentence on which the others depend.

3. The topic sentence is typically the first sentence of the sequence. Topics may be established explicitly or may be only suggested.

4. Simple sequences consist of two sorts— coordinate and subordinate. In a coordinate sequence, the repetition of structure—parallelism—is necessary; in a subordinate sequence, repetition must be avoided, each added sentence taking a different form.

5. The two sorts of sequence combine to produce the commonest sort—the mixed sequence. The opportunity to generate the paragraph lies here with the addition of subordinate sentences to clarify and of the coordinate sentences to emphasize or enumerate.

6. Some paragraphs have no topic sentence; in these cases, the topic can usually be inferred from the preceding paragraph, where it may be implied or stated.

7. Some paragraphs have sentences at the beginning or at the end that do not belong to the sequence. They furnish a transition either to the new paragraph (at the beginning) or from the current paragraph (at the end), or they may provide a conclusion or coda at the end.

8. Some paragraphing is illogical.

9. Punctuation should be by the paragraph, not by the sentence. Paragraph punctuation involves choosing whether to make compound sentences or not.

Writing about a process

Writing about a **process** is a rhetorical strategy that reports a sequence of actions by which something is done or made. A process usually proceeds chronologically—first do this, then do that. A process's complexity dictates the level of detail in the writing. For example, paragraph 36 provides an overview of a complicated process. Paragraph 37, on the other hand, gives explicit step-by-step directions.

36   Making chocolate isn't as simple as grinding a bag of beans. The machinery in a chocolate factory towers over you, rumbling and whirring. A huge cleaner first blows the beans away from their accompanying debris—sticks and stones, coins and even bullets can fall among cocoa beans being bagged. Then they go into another machine for roasting. Next comes separation in a winnower, shells sliding out one side, beans falling from the other. Grinding follows, resulting in chocolate liquor. Fermentation, roasting, and "conching" all influence the flavor of chocolate. Chocolate is "conched"—rolled over and over against itself like pebbles in the sea—in enormous circular machines named conches for the shells they once resembled. Climbing a flight of steps to peer into this huge, slow-moving glacier, I was expecting something like molten mud but found myself forced to conclude it resembled nothing so much as chocolate.
    —Ruth Mehrtens Galvin, "Sybaritic to Some, Sinful to Others"

37   Carrying loads of equal weight like paint cans and toolboxes is easier if you carry one in each hand. Keep your shoulders back and down so that the weight is balanced on each side of your body, not suspended in front. With this method, you'll be able to lift heavier loads and also to walk and stand erect. Your back will not be strained by being pulled to one side.
    —John Warde, "Safe Lifting Techniques"

Writing using examples

A paragraph developed by **examples** presents particular instances of a larger category. For instance, examples of the category "endangered animals" could include the black rhinoceros, South China tiger, Bulmer's fruit bat, and silvery gibbon. Paragraph 38 is an example of this strategy. On the other hand, sometimes one **extended example,** often called an *illustration,* is useful. Paragraph 39 is an example of this technique.

38   The current revolution in zoo design—the landscape revolution—is driven by three kinds of change that have occurred during this century. First are great leaps in animal ecology, veterinary medicine, landscape design, and exhibit technology, making possible unprecedented realism in zoo exhibits. Second is the progressive disappearance of wilderness— the very subject of zoos—from the earth. Third is knowledge derived from market research and from environmental psychology, making possible a sophisticated focus on the zoo-goer.
    —Melissa Greene, "No Rms, Jungle Vu"

He was one of the greatest scientists the world has ever known, yet if I had to convey the essence of Albert Einstein in a single word, I would choose *simplicity*. Perhaps an anecdote will help. Once, caught in a downpour, he took off his hat and held it under his coat. Asked why, he explained, with admirable logic, that the rain would damage the hat, but his hair would be none the worse for its wetting. This knack of going instinctively to the heart of the matter was the secret of his major scientific discoveries—this and his extraordinary feeling for beauty.

—Banesh Hoffman, "My Friend, Albert Einstein"

39

Writing using definition

When you define something, you give its meaning. **Definition** is often used together with other rhetorical strategies. If, for example, you were explaining how to organize a seashell collection, you'd probably want to define the two main types of shells: bivalve and univalve. You can also develop an entire paragraph by definition, called an **extended definition.** An extended definition discusses the meaning of a word or concept in more detail than a dictionary definition. If the topic is very abstract, the writer tries to put the definition in concrete terms. Sometimes a definition tells what something is not, as well as what it is, as in paragraph 40.

Chemistry is that branch of science that has the task of investigating the materials out of which the universe is made. It is not concerned with the forms into which they may be fashioned. Such objects as chairs, tables, vases, bottles, or wires are of no significance in chemistry; but such substances as glass, wool, iron, sulfur, and clay, as the materials out of which they are made, are what it studies. Chemistry is concerned not only with the composition of such substances, but also with their inner structure.

—John Arrend Timm, *General Chemistry*

40 appears at left margin of this paragraph.

Writing using analysis

Analysis, sometimes called *division,* divides things up into their parts. It usually starts, often in its topic sentence, by identifying one subject and continues by explaining the subject's distinct parts. Paragraph 41 discusses the parts of the wing of a supersonic aircraft.

A wing design is a compromise. For example, if a designer wants a wing for an aircraft that will cruise at supersonic speeds, he must also design the wing to fly at subsonic speeds as well as for takeoffs and landings. Thus, the optimum cruise configuration is compromised to gain other necessary characteristics. Granted, devices such as ailerons, flaps, spoilers, and slats can partially compensate for deficiencies, but these still do not give the optimum performance of a wing designed for a particular flight regime.

—Bill Siuru and John D. Busick,
The Next Generation of Aircraft Technology

41 appears at left margin of this paragraph.

EXTRA EXERCISE E

To practice the principles of classification, arrange the following terms into three groups based on their similarities. Give each group a heading.

1. violin
2. helmet
3. bulb
4. conductor
5. perennial
6. referee
7. concerto
8. touchdown
9. blossom
10. baton
11. Mozart
12. quarterback
13. leaves and stems
14. spectators
15. nursery

Answers to Extra Exercise E

Symphony Orchestra: violin, conductor, concerto, baton, Mozart

Football: helmet, referee, touchdown, quarterback, spectators

Flowers: bulb, perennial, blossom, leaves and stems, nursery

QUOTATION: ON WRITING

Purpose and craftsmanship—ends and means—these are the keys to your judgment.
—Marya Mannes

Writing using classification

Classification groups items according to an underlying, shared characteristic. Paragraph 42 groups—classifies—interior violations of building-safety codes.

42   A public health student, Marian Glaser, did a detailed analysis of 180 cases of building code violation. Each case represented a single building, almost all of which were multiple-unit dwellings. In these 180 buildings, there were an incredible total of 1,244 different recorded violations—about seven per building. What did the violations consist of? First of all, over one-third of the violations were exterior defects: broken doors and stairways, holes in the walls, sagging roofs, broken chimneys, damaged porches, and so on. Another one-third were interior violations that could scarcely be attributed to the most ingeniously destructive rural southern migrant in America. There were, for example, a total of 160 instances of defective wiring or other electrical hazards, a very common cause of the excessive number of fires and needless tragic deaths in the slums. There were 125 instances of inadequate, defective, or inoperable plumbing or heating. There were 34 instances of serious infestation by rats and roaches.
—William Ryan, "Blaming the Victim"

Writing using comparison and contrast

A paragraph developed by *comparison* deals with similarities; a paragraph developed by *contrast* deals with differences. **Comparison and contrast** writing is usually organized one of two ways: You can use *point-by-point organization,* which moves back and forth between the items being compared; or you can use *block organization,* which discusses one item completely before discussing the other. Box 27 lays out the two patterns visually.

BOX 27   **PATTERN**

   Comparison and contrast

Point-by-Point Structure

Student body: college A, college B
Curriculum: college A, college B
Location: college A, college B

Block Structure

College A: student body, curriculum, location
College B: student body, curriculum, location

Paragraph 43 is structured point by point, going back and forth between the two children (whose names are in boldface) being compared.

43
> My husband and I constantly marvel at the fact that our two sons, born of the same parents and only two years apart in age, are such completely different human beings. The most obvious differences became apparent at their births. Our firstborn, **Mark,** was big and bold—his intense, already wise eyes, broad shoulders, huge and heavy hands, and powerful, chunky legs gave us the impression he could have walked out of the delivery room on his own. Our second son, **Wayne,** was delightfully different. Rather than having the football physique that **Mark** was born with, **Wayne** came into the world with a long, slim, wiry body more suited to running, jumping, and contorting. **Wayne's** eyes, rather than being intense like **Mark's,** were impish and innocent. When **Mark** was delivered, he cried only momentarily, and then seemed to settle into a state of intense concentration, as if trying to absorb everything he could about the strange, new environment he found himself in. Conversely, **Wayne** screamed from the moment he first appeared. There was nothing helpless or pathetic about his cry either—he was darn angry!
> —Rosanne Labonte, student

Paragraph 44 uses the block pattern for comparison and contrast. The writer first discusses games and then business (each key word is in boldface).

44
> **Games** are of limited duration, take place on or in fixed and finite sites, and are governed by openly promulgated rules that are enforced on the spot by neutral professionals. Moreover, they're performed by relatively evenly matched teams that are counseled and led through every move by seasoned hands. Scores are kept, and at the end of the game, a winner is declared. **Business** is usually a little different. In fact, if there is anyone out there who can say that the business is of limited duration, takes place on a fixed site, is governed by openly promulgated rules that are enforced on the spot by neutral professionals, competes only on relatively even terms, and performs in a way that can be measured in runs or points, then that person is either extraordinarily lucky or seriously deluded.
> —Warren Bennis, "Time to Hang Up the Old Sports Clichés"

Writing using analogy

An **analogy** is an extended comparison between objects or ideas from different classes—things not normally associated. Analogy is particularly effective in explaining unfamiliar or abstract concepts because a comparison can be drawn between what is familiar and what is not. An analogy often begins with a SIMILE or METAPHOR (21d), as in paragraph 45.

> Casual dress, like casual speech, tends to be loose, relaxed, and colorful. It often contains what might be called "slang words": blue jeans, sneakers, baseball caps, aprons, flowered cotton housedresses, and the

EXAMPLE OF CAUSE AND EFFECT

It is warm down here on Earth because the Sun shines. If the Sun were somehow turned off, the Earth would rapidly cool. The oceans would freeze, eventually the atmosphere itself would condense out and our planet would be covered everywhere by snowbanks of solid oxygen and nitrogen 10 meters (about 30 feet) high. Only the tiny trickle of heat from the Earth's interior and the faint starlight would save our world from a temperature of absolute zero.

—Carl Sagan

QUOTATION: ON WRITING

Philosophers sometimes talk about cause-and-effect thinking as "the billiard ball model of the universe." In cause-and-effect reasoning, events are explained in much the same way as a motion on the billiard table.... One billiard ball ("the cause") strikes another, which moves ("the effect"). But if the second ball also strikes something, it becomes a cause and the reaction of that something becomes an effect.

—Richard M. Coe

ANSWERS: EXERCISE 4-9

Some paragraphs can be interpreted to illustrate more than one pattern. This is a basic list only.

A (paragraph 47). extended definition (or illustration)

B (paragraph 48). description, narrative, analysis, examples

C (paragraph 49). cause and effect, definition, analogy

D (paragraph 50). narration, description

E (paragraph 51). classification, example

like. These garments could not be worn on a formal occasion without causing disapproval, but in ordinary circumstances, they pass without remark. "Vulgar words" in dress, on the other hand, give emphasis and get immediate attention in almost any circumstances, just as they do in speech. Only the skillful can employ them without some loss of face, and even then, they must be used in the right way. A torn, unbuttoned shirt or wildly uncombed hair can signify strong emotions: passion, grief, rage, despair. They're most effective if people already think of you as being neatly dressed, just as the curses of well-spoken persons count for more than those of the customarily foul-mouthed do.

45

—Alison Lurie, *The Language of Clothes*

Writing using cause-and-effect analysis

Cause-and-effect analysis examines outcomes and the reasons for those outcomes. Causes lead to an event or an effect, and effects result from causes. (For a discussion of correct logic for assessing CAUSE AND EFFECT, see 5h.) Paragraph 46 discusses how television (the cause) becomes indispensable (the effect) to parents of young children.

Because television is so wonderfully available as child amuser and child defuser, capable of rendering a volatile three-year-old harmless at the flick of a switch, parents grow to depend upon it in the course of their daily lives. And as they continue to utilize television day after day, its importance in their children's lives increases. From a simple source of entertainment provided by parents when they need a break from childcare, television gradually changes into a powerful and disruptive presence in family life. But despite their increasing resentment of television's intrusions into their family life, and despite their considerable guilt at not being able to control their children's viewing, parents don't take steps to extricate themselves from television's domination. They can no longer cope without it.

46

—Marie Winn, *The Plug-In Drug*

EXERCISE 4-9

Working individually or with a peer-response group, decide what rhetorical strategies are used in each paragraph. Choose from any one or combination of narrative, description, process, examples, definition, analysis, classification, comparison and contrast, analogy, and cause and effect. For help, consult 4i.

A.   Another way to think about metamessages is that they frame a conversation, much as a picture frame provides a context for the images in the picture. Metamessages let you know how to interpret what someone is saying by identifying the activity that is going on. Is this an argument or a chat? Is it helping, advising, or scolding? At the same time, they let you know what position the speaker is assuming in the activity, and what position you are being assigned.

47

—Deborah Tannen, *You Just Don't Understand*

B.   I retain only one confused impression from my earliest years: it's all red, and black, and warm. Our apartment was red: the upholstery was of red moquette, the Renaissance dining-room was red, the figured silk hangings over the stained-glass doors were red, and the velvet curtains in Papa's study were red too. The furniture in this awful sanctum was made of black pear wood; I used to creep into the kneehole under the desk and envelop myself in its dusty glooms; it was dark and warm, and the red of the carpet rejoiced my eyes. That is how I seem to have passed the early days of infancy. Safely ensconced, I watched, I touched, I took stock of the world.

48

—Simone de Beauvoir, *Memoirs of a Dutiful Daughter*

C.   In the case of wool, very hot water can actually cause some structural changes within the fiber, but the resulting shrinkage is minor. The fundamental cause of shrinkage in wool is felting, in which the fibers scrunch together in a tighter bunch, and the yarn, fabric, and garment follow suit. Wool fibers are curly and rough-surfaced, and when squished together under the lubricating influence of water, the fibers wind around each other, like two springs interlocking. Because of their rough surfaces, they stick together and can't be pulled apart.

49

—James Gorman, "Gadgets"

D.   After our lunch, we drove to the Liverpool public library, where I was scheduled to read. By then, we were forty-five minutes late, and on arrival we saw five middle-aged white women heading away toward an old car across the street. When they recognized me, the women came over and apologized: They were really sorry, they said, but they had to leave or they'd get in trouble on the job. I looked at them. Every one of them was wearing an inexpensive, faded housedress and, over that, a cheap and shapeless cardigan sweater. I felt honored by their open-mindedness in having wanted to come and listen to my poetry. I thought and I said that it was I who should apologize: I was late. It was I who felt, moreover, unprepared: What in my work, to date, deserves the open-minded attention of blue-collar white women terrified by the prospect of overstaying a union-guaranteed hour for lunch?

50

—June Jordan, "Waiting for a Taxi"

E.   Lacking access to a year-round supermarket, the many species—from ants to wolves—that in the course of evolution have learned the advantages of hoarding must devote a lot of energy and ingenuity to protecting their stashes from marauders. Creatures like beavers and honeybees, for example, hoard food to get them through cold winters. Others, like desert rodents that face food scarcities throughout the year, must take advantage of the short-lived harvests that follow occasional rains. For animals like burying beetles that dine on mice hundreds of times their size, a habit of biting off more than they can chew at the moment forces them to store their leftovers. Still others, like the male MacGregor's bowerbird,

51

EXAMPLE OF CAUSE AND EFFECT
Considering the whole span of earthly time, the opposite effect, in which life actually modifies its surroundings, has been relatively slight. Only within the moment of time represented by the present century has one species—[humans]—acquired significant power to alter the nature of this world.

—Rachel Carson,
The Obligation to Endure

USING COLLABORATION
With full class participation, establish a shared text by having students retell a traditional children's story such as *Jack and the Beanstalk* or *Little Red Riding Hood*. Divide the class into groups, assigning each group one pattern for developing a paragraph. Ask each group to choose any element in the story and write a paragraph according to the assigned pattern of development. One group might write a detailed *description* of the hen that lays golden eggs. Another might explain the *process* by which Jack climbs the beanstalk. Another might *analyze* the root cause of Jack and his mother's poverty. Have one member of each group read its paragraph aloud, providing you and the class with an opportunity for comment and response. Such entertaining activities can also make the writing process seem less onerous to resistant students.

A (paragraph 31). description, example

B (paragraph 32). definition

C (paragraph 33). definition, cause and effect, process, examples

QUOTATION: ON WRITING

You must *write*, not just think you're going to. . . . And you must widen your vocabulary, enjoy words. You just read widely, not in order to copy, but to find your own voice. It's a matter of going through life with all one's senses alive, to be responsive to experience, to other people.

—P. D. James

QUOTATION: ON WRITING

Whatever the method used, the conclusion must exist, in spirit or in fact, in order to save the end of your essay from creating an unpleasant sense of abruptness. Yet it should not be unnecessarily long . . . but should be designed to make a lasting impression on the reader.

—Esther DiMarzio,
"The Preliminaries"

stockpile goodies during mating season so they can concentrate on wooing females and defending their arena d'amour.

—Jane Brody, "A Hoarder's Life: Filling the Cache—and Finding It"

EXERCISE 4-10

Working individually or with a peer-response group, reread the paragraphs in Exercise 4-7 and determine the rhetorical strategy (or strategies) being used in each.

4j   What is a transitional paragraph?

Transitional paragraphs are found in long essays. These paragraphs form a bridge between one long discussion on a single topic that requires a number of paragraphs and another discussion, usually lengthy, of another topic. Paragraph 52 is an example of a transitional paragraph that allows the writer to move from a long discussion of people's gestures to a long discussion of people's eating habits.

52   Like gestures, eating habits are personality indicators, and even food preferences and attitudes toward food reveal the inner self. Food plays an important role in the lives of most people beyond its obvious one as a necessity.

—Jean Rosenbaum, M.D.,
Is Your Volkswagen a Sex Symbol?

4k   What are effective concluding paragraphs?

A **concluding paragraph** ends the discussion smoothly by following logically from the essay's introductory paragraph (4b) and the essay's body paragraphs (4c). Always integrate a concluding device into the final paragraph so that the discussion does not end abruptly. A conclusion that is hurriedly tacked on is a missed opportunity to provide a sense of completion and a finishing touch that adds to the whole essay. Box 28 on the facing page lists strategies for concluding your essay as well as strategies to avoid.

The same writers who wait to write their introductory paragraph until they've drafted their body paragraphs often also wait to write their concluding paragraph until they've drafted their introduction. They do this to coordinate the beginning and end so that they can make sure they don't repeat the same strategy in both places.

Paragraph 53 is a concluding paragraph from an essay on the history of pizza and its modern appeal. It summarizes the main points of the essay.

53 For a food that is traced to Neolithic beginnings, like Mexico's tortillas, Armenia's lahmejoun, Scottish oatcakes, and even matzos, pizza has remained fresh and vibrant. Whether it's galettes, the latest thin-crusted invasion from France with bacon and onion toppings, or a plain slice of a cheese pie, the varieties of pizza are clearly limited only by one's imagination.

—Lisa Pratt, "A Slice of History"

BOX 28 SUMMARY

 ### Strategies for concluding paragraphs

Strategies to Try

- A strategy adapted from those used for introductory paragraphs (4b)—but be careful to choose a different strategy for your introduction and conclusion:
  - Relating a brief concluding interesting story or anecdote
  - Giving one or more pertinent—perhaps surprising—concluding statistics
  - Asking one or more provocative questions for further thought
  - Using an appropriate quotation to sum up the THESIS STATEMENT
  - Redefining a key term for emphasis
- An ANALOGY that summarizes the thesis statement
- A SUMMARY of the main points, but only if the piece of writing is longer than three to four pages
- A statement that urges awareness by the readers
- A statement that looks ahead to the future
- A call to readers

Strategies to Avoid

- Introducing new ideas or facts that belong in the body of the essay
- Rewording your introduction
- Announcing what you've discussed, as in "In this paper, I have explained why oil prices have dropped."
- Making absolute claims, as in "I have proved that oil prices don't always affect gasoline prices."
- Apologizing, as in "Even though I'm not an expert, I feel my position is correct."

Paragraph 54 is a concluding paragraph from an essay on the potential collapse of public schools. It looks ahead to the future and calls for action that involves taking control of them.

BACKGROUND
Many of the conventions followed by contemporary writers did not exist in the ancient world. For example, words were not divided from each other until sometime in the seventh century AD, and word division was not systematically practiced until the eleventh century. Some marks of punctuation, such as the question mark and the exclamation point, evolved during the Middle Ages. Paragraphs had been indicated since pre-Christian days, first by short horizontal strokes or wedge-shaped signs. Later, they were noted in Latin manuscripts by a new line. At the same time, it became the practice to indicate the beginning of a new paragraph with enlarged letters, sometimes extending the length of the page. Such elaborate figures became the ancestors of our capital letters. The paragraph as it is known today took shape late in the seventeenth century but was not systematically described until the nineteenth century, when Alexander Bain published his *English Composition and Rhetoric* (1866).

QUOTATION: ON WRITING
The perfect ending should take the reader slightly by surprise and yet seem exactly right.

—William Zinsser

QUOTATION: ON WRITING
In the end is my beginning.

—T. S. Eliot

ANSWERS: EXERCISE 4-11
Answers will vary.

TEACHING TIP
One way to help students succeed with Exercise 4-11 is to talk them through these imaginary essays before they think about the endings and how they might relate to the beginnings they wrote in Exercise 4-1. A class discussion about what details might support the topics of each paragraph can strengthen students' understanding of the importance of evidence. At the same time, it can give students a fuller concept of the essays on which they based their introductory and now their concluding paragraphs. When the students write their conclusions, you can alert them to the lists of useful devices and of what to avoid, explained in Box 28 in section 4k.

54 Our schools provide a key to the future of society. We must take control of them, watch over them, and nurture them if they are to be set right again. To do less is to invite disaster upon ourselves, our children, and our nation.

—John C. Sawhill, "The Collapse of Public Schools"

EXERCISE 4-11

Working individually or in a peer-response group, return to Exercise 4-1, in which you wrote introductory paragraphs for three informally outlined essays. Now, write a concluding paragraph for each.

Chapter 5

Critical Thinking, Reading, and Writing

Getting a college education and living a reflective life mean participating in a world of ideas and opinions. Your success with these activities depends largely on your level of comfort with critical thinking as a concept (5a) and as an activity (5b); critical reading as a concept (5c) and as an activity (5d and 5e); critical writing (5f); and critical reasoning (5g through 5j). The word *critical* here has a neutral meaning. It doesn't mean taking a negative view or finding fault, as when someone criticizes another person for doing something wrong. Rather, *critical* here applies to a mental stance of examining ideas thoroughly and deeply, refusing to accept ideas merely because they seem sensible at first thought, and tolerating questions that often lack definitive answers.

5a What is critical thinking?

Thinking isn't something you choose to do, any more than a fish chooses to live in water. To be human is to think. But while thinking may come naturally, awareness of how you think doesn't. Thinking about thinking is the key to critical thinking.

Critical thinking means taking control of your conscious thought processes. If you don't take control of those processes, you risk being controlled by the ideas of others. In fact, critical thinking is an attitude as much as an activity. If you face life with curiosity and a desire to dig beneath the surface, you're a critical thinker. The essence of critical thinking is thinking beyond the obvious—beyond the flash of visual images on a television screen, the alluring promises of glossy advertisements, the evasive statements by some people in the news, the half-truths of propaganda, the manipulations of SLANTED LANGUAGE, and faulty reasoning. As an example of why critical thinking is crucial, consider how the various elements of the picture at the top of the next page shape our response to the image.

A look at the obvious, surface content of the photograph tells us that students have to pass through metal detectors to enter many of today's

BACKGROUND

In recent years, visual literacy has become increasingly important in composition courses. Diana George, in "From Analysis to Design: Visual Communication in the Teaching of Writing (*College Composition and Communication* 54, September 2002: 11–39), provides an extensive review of historical and current theories, research, and pedagogy on visual literacy. Already in the 1940s, composition textbooks pointed out the significance of being able to read pictures as well as words. Calling contemporary culture "aggressively visual," George notes that students today need to be skilled not only as analysts but also as producers of visual rhetoric. Two emphases that have increased the importance of the visual are the cultural studies movement of the 1980s and the way that computers have enabled, even demanded, that writers consider design elements, not just writing elements. For additional background on this topic, see John Berger's *Ways of Seeing* (London: BBC and Penguin, 1977); Lester Faigley's "Material Literacy and Visual Design," in *Rhetorical Bodies: Toward a Material Rhetoric*, edited by Jack Selzer and Sharon Crowley (Madison: University of Wisconsin Press, 1999: 171–201); and Bill Cope and Mary Kalantzi's *Multiliteracies: Literacy Learning and the Design of Social Futures* (London: Routledge, 2000).

BACKGROUND

In "Advertising and Interpretive Analysis: Developing Reading, Thinking, and Writing Skills in the Composition Course" (*Teaching English in the Two-Year College*, May 2002: 355–366), Matthew Henry explains how teaching students to analyze advertisements develops broad critical thinking, reading, and writing skills.

schools. A closer look shows us the deeper message that the photographer seeks to convey. The details in the photograph combine to lead viewers to a negative "close reading" of the everyday security screening process at schools.

Several elements of the photograph convey the idea that going to school has become something sinister or oppressive. Notice that the boy stands in the center of a group of three men, with one of them directly blocking his entry to the building. All of them are obviously larger than he is, all have stern looks on their face, and the man on the right is reaching out as if to restrain the boy further. The man facing the camera is staring sternly at him. The entire grouping is set against a dark background, while the other parts of the photograph are light.

Furthermore, the boy is gazing downward, as if intimidated. We do not see his face, so he becomes anonymous. The boy is isolated from his friends, who stare at him along with the adults. Also looking on are shadowy dark figures inside the school, the one on the right appearing to grin at the boy. This fellow student may either be sympathizing with the boy or enjoying his discomfort. The boy's backpack is spread open on the table, as if to increase his humiliation by revealing its supposedly private contents.

The photographer has placed the figure of the security guard in the very center of the picture. Dressed in a dark uniform, in contrast to the white t-shirt and colorful clothing of the boy and his friends, the guard commands not only this situation but also the photograph itself. The guard holds what is probably a metal detecting device. However, at a quick glance, the object appears to be a club, which, as an extension of his muscular arm, adds to the imbalance of power between him and the boy.

Other details contribute to a sense of foreboding. Notice that a chain hangs from the door, which is propped open by some kind of metal bar. Only one of the two doors is open, yet another way of restricting entrance to the building. The building is hardly an inviting place. In contrast to the bright outdoors (we can see sun shining on the backs of two of the onlooking boys), the interior of the school is dark.

The total effect of these visual elements makes going to school seem less like pursuing the joy of learning than like serving a prison term. The photographer could have chosen many ways to shoot this scene, and some of them would have made going to school seem less threatening. However, he or she chose instead to call our attention to many disturbing elements and make us feel some sympathy for the boy at center.

EXERCISE 5-1

Alone or in a group, use critical thinking to consider one or both of the photographs that follow. Write either informal notes or a mini-essay, according to what your instructor requires. "Read" each photograph in two ways: first, what you see at first glance; second, what you see beneath the surface in a "close reading" of the photograph to understand the message that the photographer wants to deliver. As I did in discussing the photograph of the screening process at a school, support your "close reading" by describing and explaining specific details in the photo.

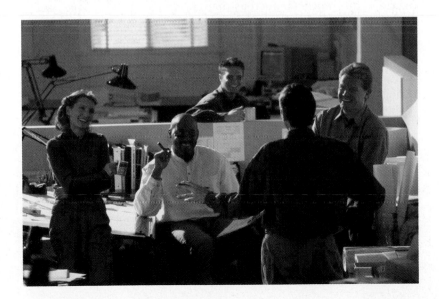

QUOTATION: ON WRITING
If any man wishes to write in a clear style, let him first be clear in his thoughts.
—Goethe

QUOTATION: ON THINKING
A man is not idle because he is absorbed in thought. There is a visible labor and there is an invisible labor.
—Victor Hugo

QUOTATION: ON THINKING
Where there is an open mind, there will always be a frontier.
—Charles F. Kettering

5b How do I engage in critical thinking?

To engage in CRITICAL THINKING, you become fully aware of an idea or an action, reflect on it, and ultimately react to it. Actually, you already engage in this process numerous times every day. For example, you're thinking critically when you meet someone new and decide whether you like the person; when you read a book and form an opinion of it based on reasonable analysis; or when you interview for a job and then evaluate its requirements and your ability to fulfill them.

Box 29 describes the general process of critical thinking in academic settings. This same process applies as well to reading critically (5c and 5d) and writing critically (5f).

BOX 29   SUMMARY

 Steps in the critical thinking process

1. **Summarize.** Extract and restate the material's main message or central point. Use only what you see on the page. Add nothing.
2. **Analyze.** Examine the material by breaking it into its component parts. By seeing each part of the whole as a distinct unit, you

→

Steps in the critical thinking process (*continued*)

discover how the parts interrelate. Consider the line of reasoning as shown by the EVIDENCE offered (5g) and logic used (5j). Read "between the lines" to draw INFERENCES (5c.2), gaining information that's implied but not stated. 0When reading or listening, notice how the reading or speaking style and the choice of words work together to create a TONE (1e).

3. **Synthesize.** Pull together what you've summarized and analyzed by connecting it to your own experiences, such as reading, talking with others, watching television and films, using the Internet, and so on. In this way, you create a new whole that reflects your newly acquired knowledge and insights combined with your prior knowledge.

4. **Evaluate.** Judge the quality of the material now that you've become informed through the activities of SUMMARY, ANALYSIS, and SYNTHESIS. Resist the very common urge to evaluate before you summarize, analyze, and synthesize.

The steps in the critical thinking process are somewhat fluid, just as are the steps in the WRITING PROCESS. Expect sometimes to combine steps, reverse their order, and return to parts of the process you thought you had completed. As you do so, remember that synthesis and evaluation are two different mental activities: *Synthesis* calls for making connections; *evaluation* calls for making judgments.

5c What is the reading process?

Reading is an active process—a dynamic, meaning-making interaction between the page and your brain. Understanding the **reading process** helps people become critical thinkers.

Making **predictions** is a major activity in the reading process. Your mind is constantly guessing what's coming next. When it sees what comes next, it either confirms or revises its prediction and moves on. For example, suppose you're glancing through a magazine and come upon the title "The Heartbeat." Your mind begins guessing: Is this a love story? Is this about how the heart pumps blood? Maybe, you say to yourself, it's a story about someone who had a heart attack. Then, as you read the first few sentences, your mind confirms which guess was correct. If you see words like *electrical impulse, muscle fibers,* and *contraction,* you know instantly that you're in the realm of physiology. In a few more

QUOTATION: ON READING
A room without books is like a body without a soul.
—Cicero

BACKGROUND
Two pioneers in research about reading as a process are Robert J. Tierney and P. David Pearson. They have drawn many parallels between the processes of writing and reading. They have found that, like writers, readers plan by determining their purposes for reading a text, assessing what they know about the topic, focusing their goals and topics, and questioning themselves. Each reader's goals and knowledge influence how he or she reads and understands the text. Like writers, when they begin, readers approach the text with particular goals and review what they know about a subject and then discover, revise, and delete goals and call up other knowledge as they read.

Like writers, readers draft, at first trying to discover a lead or hypothesis that will help them make sense of the rest of the text, refining and developing that lead as they read, making connections and filling in gaps in the text with their own inferences and knowledge, and trying to fit all the pieces of the text together into a coherent whole. Readers and writers also both engage in aligning. Readers take a stance (passive, critical, sympathetic, challenging) in relation to the author to help them construct meaning from the text, just as writers take a stance toward their audiences.

Readers and writers both need to revise. Readers need to reflect on and evaluate the meanings they have constructed from the text, rereading the text and questioning and revising their interpretations. Finally, readers and writers need to monitor themselves as they compose, distancing themselves from the meaning they compose and examining their composing activities. Readers and writers should both be in dialogue with their "other self," to determine how well they are accomplishing their purposes.

TEACHING TIP
You might want to discuss with your students the research finding that most students believe the mark of a competent reader is the ability to read a text once quickly and remember much of what was read. Students seldom see a need to reread a text, to reflect on what they read, or to question their interpretation. To get used to critical reading practices, students need support and encouragement from teachers, in the same way they learn and use planning and revising strategies when they write.

sentences, you narrow your prediction to either "the heart as pump" or "the heart suffering an attack."

To make predictions efficiently, consciously decide your purpose for reading the material. People generally read for two reasons—for relaxation or for learning. Reading a popular novel helps you relax. Reading for college courses calls for you to understand material and remember it. When you read to learn, you usually have to reread. One encounter with new material is rarely enough to understand it fully.

The speed at which you read depends on your purpose for reading. When you're hunting for a particular fact, you can skim the page until you come to what you want. When you read about a subject you know well, you might read somewhat rapidly, slowing down when you come to new material. When you're unfamiliar with the subject, you need to work slowly because your mind needs time to absorb the new material.

The reading process involves your thinking on three levels, which is another reason why college work calls for much rereading, as described in Box 30.

BOX 30   SUMMARY

 Steps in the reading process

1. **Reading for literal meaning:** Read "on the lines" to see what's stated (5c.1).
2. **Reading to draw inferences:** Read "between the lines" to see what's not stated but implied (5c.2).
3. **Reading to evaluate:** Read "beyond the lines" to form your own opinion about the material (5c.3).

5c.1 Reading for literal meaning

Reading for **literal meaning** is reading for comprehension. Your goal is to discover the main ideas, the supporting details, or, in a work of fiction, the central details of plot and character.

Reading for literal meaning is not as easy as it might sound. When you come across a new concept, think it through. Rushing through material to "cover" it rather than to understand it takes more time in the end. If the author's writing style is complex, "unpack" the sentences: Break them into smaller units or reword them in a simpler style. Also, see Box 31 for specific suggestions about ways to improve your reading comprehension.

BOX 31   SUMMARY

Ways to help your reading comprehension

- **Make associations.** Link new material to what you already know, especially when you're reading about an unfamiliar subject. You may even find it helpful to read an easier book on the subject first in order to build your knowledge base.
- **Make it easy for you to focus.** If your mind wanders, be fiercely determined to concentrate. Do whatever it takes: Arrange for silence or music, for being alone or in the library with others who are studying. Try to read at your best time of day (some people concentrate better in the morning, others in the evening).
- **Allot the time you need.** To comprehend new material, you must allow sufficient time to read, reflect, reread, and study. Discipline yourself to balance classes, working, socializing, and family activities. Reading and studying take time. Nothing prevents success in college as much as poor time management.
- **Master the vocabulary.** If you don't understand the key terms in your reading, you can't fully understand the concepts. As you encounter new words, first try to figure out their meanings from context clues (21e). Also, many textbooks list key terms and their definitions (called a *glossary*) at the end of each chapter or the book. Of course, nothing replaces having a good dictionary at hand.

5c.2 Reading to draw inferences

When you read for **inferences,** you're reading to understand what's suggested or implied but not stated. This is similar to the kind of critical thinking discussed in 5b. Often, you need to infer the author's PURPOSE. Here's an example.

> How to tell the difference between modern art and junk puzzles many people, although few are willing to admit it. The owner of an art gallery in Chicago had a prospective buyer for two sculptures made of discarded metal and put them outside his warehouse to clean them up. Unfortunately, some junk dealers, who apparently didn't recognize abstract expressionism when they saw it, hauled the two 300-pound pieces away.
> —Ora Gygi, "Things Are Seldom What They Seem"

The literal meaning of the Gygi paragraph is that some people can't tell the difference between art and junk. A good summary would say that two abstract metal sculptures were carted away as junk when an art dealer set them outside a warehouse to clean them. However, looking at

QUOTATION: ON READING
We always read for some purpose—unless some sad, bad, mad schoolteacher has got hold of us. There is no such thing as merely reading words; always through the words we are trafficking or trying to traffic with things—things gone by, present, to come or eternal.
—I. A. Richards

BACKGROUND
In the highly respected *Elements of Critical Reading* (New York: Macmillan, 1991), John Peters explains several useful reading habits.

1. Examine organizational features. "When you first encounter a text of any kind, you should pause to examine its outward features. Depending on the kind of text, those may include cover, title page, table of contents, chapter or section divisions, glossary, notes, bibliography, and other accessories" (13). They will provide a useful first impression of the text.

2. Know when the text was written.

3. Determine apparent aims. "Spot reading" selected passages (also known as "pre-reading" and "X-raying") "allows you to inspect parts which can give you an idea of the text's aims and audience level" (15). Generally, begin with the preface or the opening paragraphs and, with nonfiction texts, then skip to the conclusion because it often summarizes the main points and purposes of the text. You should also drift a little back and forth through the center of the text, "eyeing those spots where expository writing often focuses its aims" (15–16), such as the first and last paragraphs of a section, the first sentence of each body paragraph, and any visual aids and illustrations.

4. Adapt to the genre. "From nonfiction you should usually expect an orderly discussion such as you might hear at a lecture or business meeting. In general, your relation to nonfiction is that of a student, colleague, or general reader who wants information upon which to base opinions, decisions, or future

Background (continued)

activity related to the subject—but it's a good idea to be slightly skeptical, aware that a text may have misinformation or raise more questions than it answers" (16–17).

5. Listen to the language. Reading only for the message of the text, ignoring its emotions, tone, and rhythms, can cause a reader to miss much of what the text offers as well as much of the pleasure in reading.

6. Become aware of contrasts. "It is said that there are two sides to everything. As a reader you should become aware of the contrasts within a text. The inner structure is bound to reveal a play of opposites that close reading uncovers" (21).

7. Get to the heart of the matter. "For some readers, the heart of a text may be a passage or series of passages that seem to tie everything together and coordinate the flow of ideas throughout the entire work" (23). "The 'heart' can also be viewed as a sort of overall personality that characterizes the text. . . . But on the best occasions and as a result of our patient attentiveness, the heart of a text may reveal itself in the fullness of its meaning, both logical and emotional, and make us feel that we truly know what we've read" (25).

8. Sense what may be missing. "Of the many responses that reading can inspire, a few may be strong while plenty of others remain inactive. The intensity of your feelings is important, but so is the absence of those emotions which a text might have brought you but did not. . . . Knowing what a text means to you depends on your sense of what is present or missing in the relationship you've just concluded" (26).

the inferential meaning reveals that the paragraph explains that few people will admit it when they don't know the difference between art and junk. Further, the paragraph implies that people often don't want to appear uneducated or show themselves lacking in good taste because something called "art" looks like "junk" to them. The word *apparently*—a good word for writing inferences—uses IRONY (21d) to seem tactful but is just the opposite. Therefore, the art dealer doesn't end up feeling embarrassed because he left the sculp-

tures outdoors unattended. If we are laughing, it is at the junk dealers— although the ultimate laugh is on the whole art world.

Drawing inferences takes practice. Box 32 lists questions to help you read "between the lines." A discussion of each point follows the box.

Drawing inferences during reading

- Is the **tone** of the material appropriate?
- Can I detect **prejudice** or **bias** in the material?
- Is the separation of **fact** and **opinion** clear or muddy?
- What is the writer's **position,** even if he or she doesn't come out and state it?

Tone

Tone in writing emerges from many aspects of what you write, but mostly from your word choice. Tone in writing is like tone in speaking: it can be formal, informal, pompous, sarcastic, and so on. If you read exclusively for literal meaning (5c.1), you'll likely miss the tone and possibly the point of the whole piece.

For example, as a critical reader, be suspicious of a highly emotional tone in writing. If you find it, chances are the writer is trying to manipulate the audience. Resist this. Also as a writer, if you find your tone growing emotional, step back and rethink the situation. No matter what point you want to make, your chance of communicating successfully to an audience depends on your using a moderate, reasonable tone. For instance, the exaggerations below in the NO example (*robbing treasures, politicians are murderers*) might hint at the truth of a few cases, but they're too extreme to be taken seriously. The language of the YES version is far more likely to deliver its intended message.

> NO Urban renewal must be stopped. Urban redevelopment is ruining this country, and money-hungry capitalists are robbing treasures from law-abiding citizens. Corrupt politicians are murderers, caring nothing about people being thrown out of their homes into the streets.

> YES Urban renewal is revitalizing our cities, but it has caused some serious problems. While investors are trying to replace slums with decent housing, they must also remember that they're displacing people who don't want to leave their familiar neighborhoods. Surely, a cooperative effort between government and the private sector can lead to creative solutions.

Prejudice or bias

For inferential reading, you want to detect **prejudice** or **bias.** These concepts go further than the idea that most writers try to influence readers to accept their points of view. When writing is distorted by hatred or dislike of individuals, groups of people, or ideas, you as a critical reader want to suspect the accuracy and fairness of the material. Prejudice and bias can be worded in positive language, but critical readers aren't deceived by such tactics. Similarly, writers can merely imply their prejudices and bias rather than state them outright. For example, suppose you read, "Poor people like living in crowded conditions because they're used to such surroundings" or "Women are so wonderfully nurturing that they can't succeed in business." As a critical reader, you will immediately detect the prejudice and bias. Always, therefore, question material that rests on a weak foundation of discrimination and narrow-mindedness.

Fact versus opinion

Another skill in reading inferentially is the ability to differentiate **fact** from **opinion.** *Facts* are statements that can be verified. *Opinions* are statements of personal beliefs. Facts can be verified by observation, research, or experimentation, but opinions are open to debate. A problem arises when a writer intentionally blurs the distinction between fact and opinion. Critical readers will know the difference.

EXTRA EXERCISE A
Determine which sentences state facts and which state opinions.

1. Nuclear fusion releases energy.

2. Nuclear fusion is a possible solution to our energy problems.

3. Solar energy has attracted a great deal of public attention over the past decade.

4. Many people hope that it will produce a clean, nonpolluting means of heating our homes and offices.

5. Oil and gas production in the United States has been falling for over a decade.

6. The petroleum industry is shrinking yearly.

7. In the interest of national security, the petroleum industry should be encouraged by government legislation.

8. The early pioneers generated energy from the wind on the frontier.

9. Such nonpolluting means of creating energy should immediately replace those produced by fossil fuels.

10. Because natural gas, methane, is a clean fuel, the government should encourage its use.

Answers to Extra Exercise A

1. fact	**6.** fact
2. opinion	**7.** opinion
3. fact	**8.** fact
4. fact	**9.** opinion
5. fact	**10.** opinion

ANSWERS: EXERCISE 5-2

1. opinion	**6.** fact
2. fact	**7.** fact
3. opinion	**8.** opinion
4. opinion	**9.** opinion
5. fact	**10.** opinion

For example, here are two statements, one a fact and one an opinion.

1. Women can never make good mathematicians.
2. Although fear of math isn't purely a female phenomenon, girls tend to drop out of math classes sooner than boys, and some adult women have an aversion to math and math-related activity that is akin to anxiety.

Reading inferentially, you can see that statement 1 is clearly an opinion. Is it worthy of consideration? Perhaps it could be open to debate, but the word *never* implies that the writer is unwilling to allow for even one exception. Conversely, statement 2 at least seems to be factual, though research would be necessary to confirm or deny the position.

As a reader, when you can "consider the source"—that is, find out who exactly made a statement—you hold an advantage in trying to distinguish between fact and opinion. For example, you would probably read an essay for or against capital punishment differently if you knew the writer was an inmate on death row rather than a non-inmate who wished to express an opinion. To illustrate, statement 1 above is from a male Russian mathematician, as reported by David K. Shipler, a well-respected veteran reporter on Russian affairs for the *New York Times.* Statement 2 is from the book *Overcoming Math Anxiety* by Sheila Tobias, a university professor who has extensively studied why many people dislike math. Her credentials can help readers accept her statement as true. If, however, someone known for belittling women had made statement 2, a critical reader's reaction would be quite different.

To differentiate between fact and opinion, reflect on the material and think beyond the obvious. For example, is the statement "Strenuous exercise is good for your health" a fact? It has the ring of truth, but it definitely isn't a fact. Some people with severe arthritis or heart trouble should avoid some forms of exercise. Also, what does *strenuous* mean—a dozen push-ups, jogging two miles, aerobics for an hour?

EXERCISE 5-2

Working individually or with a peer-response group, decide which statements are facts and which are opinions. When the author and source are provided, explain how that information influenced your judgment. For help, consult 5c.2.

1. The life of people on earth is better now than it has ever been—certainly much better than it was 500 years ago.
   —Peggy Noonan, "Why Are We So Unhappy When We Have It So Good?"

2. The fast food industry pays the minimum wage to a higher proportion of its workers than any other American industry.
   —Eric Schlosser, *Fast Food Nation*

3. Every journey into the past is complicated by delusions, false memories, false naming of real events.
   —Adrienne Rich, poet, *Of Woman Born*

4. A mind is a terrible thing to waste.
   —United Negro College Fund

5. History is the branch of knowledge that deals systematically with the past.
   —*Webster's New World College Dictionary,* Fourth Edition

6. In 1927, F. E. Tylcote, an English physician, reported in the medical journal *Lancet* that in almost every case of lung cancer he had seen or known about, the patient smoked.
   —William Ecenbarger, "The Strange History of Tobacco"

7. At present, carbon emissions are about 6.5 billion metric tons each year worldwide—that works out to 22 billion tons of CO_2, which is created when carbon is burned. . . . Now, with climate worries on the rise, many scientists believe these emissions are doing damage to the planet.
   —"Surviving the Greenhouse,"
   <http://www.msnbc.com/news/291336.asp>

8. You can, Honest Abe notwithstanding, fool most of the people all of the time.
   —Stephen Jay Gould, "The Creation Myths of Cooperstown"

9. You change laws by changing lawmakers.
   —Sissy Farenthold, political activist, *Bakersfield Californian*

10. A critical task for all of the world's religions and spiritual traditions is to enrich the vision—and the reality—of the sense of community among us.
    —Joel D. Beversluis,
    A Sourcebook for Earth's Community of Religions

EXERCISE 5-3

Read the following passages, then (1) list all literal information, (2) list all implied information, and (3) list the opinions stated. Refer to sections 5c.1 and 5c.2 for help.

EXAMPLE   The study found many complaints against the lawyers were not investigated, seemingly out of a "desire to avoid difficult cases."
—Norman F. Dacey

ANSWERS: EXERCISE 5-3
Answers may vary somewhat, but here is a fairly complete list of possibilities.

A. *Literal information*

1. It is the first of February.
2. "Everyone" (see "implied information") is talking about starlings.
3. Starlings came to this country on a passenger liner from Europe.
4. "This country" is the United States. (Central Park and New York are mentioned.)
5. One hundred starlings were deliberately released in Central Park.
6. From these hundred are descended the countless millions of starlings today.
7. Edwin Way Teale said, "Their . . . Shakespeare."
8. Eugene Schieffelin was a wealthy New York drug manufacturer.
9. Schieffelin's hobby was introducing into America all the birds mentioned in Shakespeare.
10. The starlings adapted to their new country.

Implied information

1. "Everyone" is used for effect; the author does not mean each and every person.
2. By saying that the birds came "on a passenger liner" (rather than, for example, "in the cargo hold of a ship"), the author begins to alert the reader to expect the unexpected (in this case, that someone wanted to introduce to America all the birds in Shakespeare).
3. Central Park is in New York City. (This is information the author assumes the reader has.)
4. "One man's fancy" are words that suggest that the man had somewhat unusual tastes.
5. The drugs that Schieffelin manufactured were legitimate, not illegal.
6. See item 2 in "Opinions."

Answers: Exercise 5-3 (continued)
Opinions
1. (In Teale's opinion) Schieffelin's hobby was somewhat strange ("curious").
2. (In Dillard's opinion) the starlings adapted too well ("splendidly"); here, Dillard assumes that the reader knows that flocks of starlings can be a nuisance and even a danger (if they get into airplane engines).

B. *Literal information*
1. Roger Schank was interviewed on National Public Radio.
2. Schank was a computer science professor at Yale.
3. Schank was well known in computer science circles.
4. Schank insisted that most people do not need to own computers.

Implied information
1. The Schank interview took place several years ago, probably before 1990.
2. De Palma did not work in the field of artificial intelligence.
3. De Palma owns a personal computer himself.

Opinions
1. The phrase "information superhighway" is now a cliché.
2. People who own computers fret about upgrades.
3. People who don't own computers fret that when they buy one it will soon become obsolete.
4. There are worse ways to spend money than on computers.
5. Computers are fiendishly clever machines.

Literal information: Few complaints against lawyers are investigated.
Implied information: The words *difficult cases* imply a cover-up: Lawyers, or others in power, hesitate to criticize lawyers for fear of being sued or for fear of a public outcry if the truth about abuses and errors were revealed.
Opinions: No opinions. It reports on a study.

A. It is the first of February, and everyone is talking about starlings. Starlings came to this country on a passenger liner from Europe. One hundred of them were deliberately released in Central Park, and from those hundred descended all of our countless millions of starlings today. According to Edwin Way Teale, "Their coming was the result of one man's fancy. That man was Eugene Schieffelin, a wealthy New York drug manufacturer. His curious hobby was the introduction into America of all the birds mentioned in William Shakespeare." The birds adapted to their new country splendidly.

—Annie Dillard, "Terror at Tinker Creek"

B. In the misty past, before Bill Gates joined the company of the world's richest men, before the mass-marketed personal computer, before the metaphor of an information superhighway had been worn down to a cliché, I heard Roger Schank interviewed on National Public Radio. Then a computer science professor at Yale, Schank was already well known in artificial intelligence circles. Because those circles did not include me, a new programmer at Sperry Univac, I hadn't heard of him. Though I've forgotten the details of the conversation, I have never forgotten Schank's insistence that most people do not need to own computers.

That view, of course, has not prevailed. Either we own a personal computer and fret about upgrades, or we are scheming to own one and fret about the technical marvel yet to come that will render our purchase obsolete. Well, there are worse ways to spend money, I suppose. For all I know, even Schank owns a personal computer. They're fiendishly clever machines, after all, and they've helped keep the wolf from my door for a long time.

—Paul De Palma, <http://www.when_is_enough_enough?.com>

5c.3 Reading to evaluate

When you read to evaluate, you're judging the writer's work. **Evaluative reading** comes after you've summarized, analyzed, and synthesized the material (Box 29). Reading "between the lines" is usually concerned with recognizing tone, detecting prejudice, and differentiating fact from opinion. Reading to evaluate, "beyond the lines," requires an overall assessment of the soundness of the writer's reasoning, evidence, or observations and the fairness and perceptiveness the writer shows, from accuracy of word choice and tone to the writer's respect for the reader.

5d How do I engage in critical reading?

Critical reading is a process parallel to CRITICAL THINKING (5a and 5b). To read critically is to think about what you're reading while you're reading it. This means that words don't merely drift by as your eyes scan the lines. To prevent that from happening, use approaches such as reading systematically (5d.1) and reading closely and actively (5d.2).

5d.1 Reading systematically

To **read systematically** is to use a structured plan: **P**review, **R**ead, and **R**eview. Reading systematically closely parallels the writing process. Like PLANNING in writing, *previewing* gets you ready and keeps you from reading inefficiently. Like DRAFTING in writing, *reading* means moving through the material so that you come to understand and remember it. Like REVISION in writing, *reviewing* takes you back over the material to clarify, fine-tune, and make it thoroughly your own. Here are techniques for reading systematically.

1. **Preview:** Before you begin reading, look ahead. Glance at the pages you intend to read so that your mind can start making predictions (5c). As you look over the material, ask yourself questions. Don't expect to answer all the questions at this point; their purpose is to focus your thoughts.

   - To preview a chapter in a textbook, first look at the table of contents. How does this chapter fit into the whole book? What topics come before? Which come after? Now turn to the chapter you're assigned and read all the headings, large and small. Note the boldfaced words (in darker print), and all visuals and their captions, including photographs, drawings, figures, tables, and boxes. If there's a glossary at the end of the chapter, scan it for words you do and do not know.

   - To preview a book or material in a book that has few or no headings, again, begin with the table of contents and ask questions about the chapter titles. If the book has a preface or introduction, skim it. Check for introductory notes about the author and head notes, which often precede individual works in collections of essays or short stories. Read pivotal paragraphs, such as the opening paragraphs and (unless you're reading for suspense) the last few paragraphs.

2. **Read:** Read the material closely and actively (5d.2). Seek the full meaning at all three levels of reading: *literal, inferential,* and *evaluative* (5c). Most of all, expect to reread. Rarely can anyone fully understand and

BACKGROUND
In her article "Remembering Writing, Remembering Reading" (*College Composition and Communication*, December 1994: 459–479), Deborah Brandt discusses reading-writing relationships from a cultural perspective. She focuses mainly on literacy practices within families.

QUOTATION: ON READING
As soon as I open it, I *occupy* the book, I stomp around in it. I underline passages, scribble in the margins, leave my mark—in effect I write my own book, a counterversion. I've come to understand that there are two dramas in reading: the drama of the book's internal relations and the drama of its relation to me.

—Anatole Broyard

BACKGROUND
In *Society and Solitude,* Ralph Waldo Emerson suggests three practical rules for reading.

1. Never read any book that is not a year old.
2. Never read any but the famed books.
3. Never read any but what you like.

QUOTATION: ON READING
I took a course in speed reading and was able to read *War and Peace* in twenty minutes. It's about Russia.

—Woody Allen

absorb college-level material in one reading. When you read, always set aside time to allow for more than one rereading.

3. **Review:** Go back to the spots you looked at when you previewed the material. Also, go back to other important places you discovered as you were reading. Ask yourself the same sorts of questions as when you previewed, this time answering as fully as possible. If you can't come up with answers, reread. For best success, review in *chunks*—small sections that you can capture comfortably. Don't try to cover too much material at one time.

- To help you concentrate as you read, keep in mind that you intend to review—and then do it: Review immediately after you read. Review again the next day and again about a week later. Each time you review, add new knowledge to refine your understanding of the material. As much as time permits, review at intervals during a course. The more reinforcement, the better.

- Collaborative learning can reinforce what you learn from reading. Ask a friend or classmate to discuss the material with you and quiz you. Conversely, offer to teach the material to someone; you'll quickly discover whether you've mastered it well enough to communicate it.

5d.2 Reading closely and actively

The secret to **reading closely** and **actively** is to annotate as you read. Annotating means writing notes to yourself in a book's margins and using asterisks and other codes to alert you to special material. Some readers start annotating right away, while others wait to annotate after they've previewed the material and read it once. Experiment to find what works best for you. I recommend your using two different ink colors, one for close reading (blue in the example on the facing page) and one for active reading (black in the example below).

Close reading means annotating for content. You might, for example, number and briefly list the steps in a process or summarize major points in the margin. When you review, your marginal notes help you glance over the material and quickly recall what it's about.

Active reading means annotating to make connections between the material and what you already know or have experienced. This is your chance to converse on paper with the writer. Consider yourself a partner in the making of meaning, a full participant in the exchange of ideas that characterizes a college education.

If you feel uncomfortable writing in a book—even though the practice of annotating texts dates back to the Middle Ages—create a *double-entry notebook.* Draw a line down the center of your notebook page. On one side, write content notes (close reading). On the other, write synthesis notes (active reading). Be sure to write down exactly where in the reading you're referring to. Illustrated on page 126 is a short example from a double-entry notebook (the symbol ¶ stands for "paragraph").

Although I like to play, and sometimes like to watch, I cannot see what possible difference it makes which team beats which. The tactics are sometimes interesting, and certainly the prowess of the players deserves applause—but most men seem to use commercial sports as a kind of narcotic, shutting out reality, rather than heightening it.

There is nothing more boring, in my view, than a prolonged discussion by laymen of yesterday's game. These dreary conversations are a form of social alcoholism, enabling them to achieve a dubious rapport without ever once having to come to grips with a subject worthy of a grown man's concern.

It is easy to see the opiate quality of sports in our society when tens of millions of men will spend a splendid Saturday or Sunday fall afternoon sitting stupefied in front of the TV, watching a "big game," when they might be out exercising their own flaccid muscles and stimulating their lethargic corpuscles.

Handwritten annotations (blue — content):
Doesn't matter who wins, but tactics and prowess can be admired.

When my son and husband watch together, the rapport is very real.

Handwritten annotations (black — synthesis):
Sports talk is boring.

Other examples include soap operas and sitcoms.

Instead of watching men should exercise.

Annotations of an excerpt from the essay shown in Exercise 5-4, using blue for content (close reading) and black for synthesis (active reading).

EXERCISE 5-4

The following essay was published as a newspaper column. Annotate the entire essay, using one color of ink for your notes about content and another for your notes that synthesize as you connect the material to your knowledge and experience. Use the annotated excerpt above as a model.

Sports Only Exercise Our Eyes

By Sydney J. Harris

Before I proceed a line further, let me make it clear that I enjoy physical exercise and sport as much as any man. I like to bat a baseball,

WHAT ELSE?

A free supplement for instructors, *The Prentice Hall Critical Thinking Audio Tape*, provides additional guidelines on active reading in sections 1A and 1B.

QUOTATION: ON READING

Literature is no one's private ground, literature is common ground; let us trespass freely and fearlessly and find our own way for ourselves.

—Virginia Woolf

ANSWERS: EXERCISE 5-4

Answers will vary.

QUOTATION: ON WRITING
Good writing uses every technique and tool available in order to make its effect.
—Gloria Anzaldua

QUOTATION: ON READING
Some books are to be tasted, others to be swallowed, and some few to be chewed and digested. . . .
—Francis Bacon

QUOTATION: ON READING
I think of life as a good book. The further you get into it, the more it begins to make sense.
—Harold S. Kushner

S. Harris essay, "Sports Only"

content	connections I make
#1 H. likes sports and exercise. He even built a tennis court for his summer home.	H. isn't "everyman." It takes big bucks to build one's own tennis court.
#2 H. thinks the average American male is obsessed with sports.	That "average" (if there is such a thing) male sounds a lot like my husband.
#3 Athletics/Sports are one strand, not the web, of society.	It's worth thinking why sports have such a major hold on men. And why not women, on "average"? (This might be a topic for a paper someday.)

Double-entry notebook excerpt, based on the first three paragraphs of the essay in Exercise 5-4. The left column deals with content (close reading), and the right covers synthesis (active reading).

dribble a basketball, kick a soccer ball and, most of all, swat a tennis ball. A man who scorned physical activity would hardly build a tennis court on his summerhouse grounds, or it every day.

Having made this obeisance, let me now confess that I am puzzled and upset—and have been for many years—by the almost obsessive interest in sports taken by the average American male.

Athletics is one strand in life, and even the ancient Greek philosophers recognized its importance. But it is by no means the whole web, as it seems to be in our society. If American men are not talking business, they're talking sports, or they're not talking at all.

This strikes me as an enormously adolescent, not to say retarded, attitude on the part of presumed adults. Especially when most of the passion and enthusiasm center on professional teams, which bear no indigenous relation to the city they play for, and consist of mercenaries who will wear any town's insignia if the price is right.

Although I like to play, and sometimes like to watch, I cannot see what possible difference it makes which team beats which. The tactics are sometimes interesting, and certainly the prowess of the players deserves applause—but most men seem to use commercial sports as a kind of narcotic, shutting out reality, rather than heightening it.

There is nothing more boring, in my view, than a prolonged discussion by laymen of yesterday's game. These dreary conversations are a form of social alcoholism, enabling them to achieve a dubious rapport without ever once having to come to grips with a subject worthy of a grown man's concern.

It is easy to see the opiate quality of sports in our society when tens of millions of men will spend a splendid Saturday or Sunday fall afternoon sitting stupefied in front of the TV, watching a "big game," when they might be out exercising their own flaccid muscles and stimulating their lethargic corpuscles.

Ironically, our obsession with professional athletics not only makes us mentally limited and conversationally dull, it also keeps us physically inert—thus violating the very reason men began engaging in athletic competitions. Isn't it tempting to call this national malaise of "spectatoritis" childish? Except children have more sense, and would rather run out and play themselves.

5e How do I tell the difference between summary and synthesis?

Distinguishing between summary and synthesis is crucial in critical thinking, critical reading, and critical writing. **Summary** comes before synthesis (Box 29 in 5b) in the critical thinking process. To summarize is to extract the main message or central point and restate it in a sentence or two. A summary doesn't include supporting evidence or details. It is the gist, the hub, the seed of what the author is saying. Also, it isn't your personal reaction to what the author says. (For help in writing a summary, see Box 131, section 31i.)

Synthesis comes after summary in the critical thinking process (Box 29 in 5b). To *synthesize* is to weave together material from several sources, including your personal prior knowledge, to create a new whole. Unsynthesized ideas and information are like separate spools of thread, neatly lined up, possibly coordinated but not integrated. Synthesized ideas and information are threads woven into a tapestry—a new whole that shows relationships.

People synthesize unconsciously all the time—interpreting and combining ideas from various sources to create new patterns. These thought processes are mirrored in the RHETORICAL STRATEGIES used in writing (4i). To synthesize, consciously apply those strategies. For instance, compare ideas in sources, contrast ideas in sources, create definitions that combine and extend definitions in individual sources, apply examples or descriptions from one source to illustrate ideas in another, and find causes and effects described in one source that explain another.

QUOTATION: ON READING
My education was the liberty I had to read indiscriminately and all the time, with my eyes hanging out.

—Dylan Thomas

QUOTATION: ON READING
A book is meant not only to be read, but to haunt you, to importune you like a lover or a parent, to stick in your teeth like a piece of gristle.

—Anatole Broyard

QUOTATION: ON READING
No entertainment is so cheap as reading; nor any pleasure so lasting.
—Lady Mary Wortley Montagu

QUOTATION: ON READING
No book is really worth reading at the age of ten which is not equally (and often far more) worth reading at the age of fifty and beyond.
—C. S. Lewis

QUOTATION: ON WRITING
I've always disliked words like *inspiration*. Writing is probably like a scientist thinking about some scientific problem, or an engineer about an engineering problem.
—Doris Lessing

QUOTATION: ON READING
There is no frigate like a book
  To take us lands away
—Emily Dickinson

QUOTATION: ON WRITING
We have read your manuscript with boundless delight. If we were to publish your paper, it would be impossible for us to publish any work of lower standard. And as it is unthinkable that in the next thousand years we shall see its equal, we are, to our regret, compelled to return your divine composition, and to beg you a thousand times to overlook our short sight and timidity.
—Rejection slip from a Chinese economic journal, quoted in the *Financial Times*

Now, let's examine two different examples of synthesis. Their sources are the essay by Sydney J. Harris in Exercise 5-4 on pages 126–127 and the following excerpt from a long essay by Robert Lipsyte. (Lipsyte, a sports columnist for the *New York Times*, is writing in the spring of 1995, at the end of a nine-month U.S. baseball strike. Lipsyte argues that commercial interests have invaded sports and, therefore, that sports no longer inspire loyalty, teach good sportsmanship, or provide young people with admirable role models.)

> Baseball has done us a favor. It's about time we understood that staged competitive sports events—and baseball can stand for all the games—are no longer the testing ground of our country's manhood and the theater of its once seemingly limitless energy and power.
> As a mirror of our culture, sports now show us spoiled fools as role models, cities and colleges held hostage and games that exist only to hawk products.
> The pathetic posturing of in-your-face macho has replaced a once self-confident masculinity.
> —Robert Lipsyte, "The Emasculation of Sports"

SYNTHESIS BY COMPARISON AND CONTRAST

Both Harris and Lipsyte criticize professional sports, but for different reasons. In part, Harris thinks that people who passively watch sports on TV and rarely exercise are ruining their health. Lipsyte sees a less obvious but potentially more sinister effect of sports: the destruction of traditional values by athletes who are puppets of "big business."

SYNTHESIS BY DEFINITION

The omission of women from each writer's discussion seems a very loud silence. Considered together, these essays define sports only in terms of males. Harris criticizes men for their inability to think and talk beyond sports and business, an insulting and exaggerated description made even less valid by the absence of women. Lipsyte, despite the numbers of women excelling both in team and individual sports, claims that sports have lost a "once self-confident masculinity." An extended definition would include women, even though they might prefer to avoid the negative portraits of Harris and Lipsyte.

Each synthesis belongs to the person who made the connections. Another person might make entirely different connections.

Here are techniques to help you recall prior knowledge and synthesize several sources. (The CRITICAL RESPONSE essay by a student, Anna Lozanov, in section 5f, is an excellent example of making connections between reading and personal experience.)

■ Use MAPPING to discover relationships between sources and your prior knowledge.

■ Use your powers of play. Mentally toss ideas around, even if you make connections that seem outrageous. Try opposites (for example, read about athletes and think about the most non-athletic person you know). Try turning an idea upside down (for example, list the benefits of being a bad sport). Try visualizing what you're reading about, and then tinker with the mental picture (for example, picture two people playing tennis and substitute dogs playing Frisbee or seals playing table tennis). The possibilities are endless—make word associations, think up song lyrics, draft a TV advertisement. The goal is to jump-start your thinking so that you can see ideas in new ways.

■ Discuss your reading with someone else. Summarize its content, and elicit the other person's opinions and ideas. Deliberately debate that opinion or challenge those ideas. Discussions and debates are good ways to get your mind moving.

EXERCISE 5-5

Here is another excerpt from the essay by Robert Lipsyte quoted earlier. First, summarize the excerpt. Then, annotate it for its content and for the connections you make between Lipsyte's ideas and your prior knowledge. Finally, write a synthesis of this excerpt and the Sydney J. Harris essay in Exercise 5-4. Words in brackets supply background information some readers might need.

> We have come to see that [basketball star] Michael Jordan, [football star] Troy Aikman and [baseball star] Ken Griffey have nothing to offer us beyond the gorgeous, breathtaking mechanics of what they do. And it's not enough, now that there's no longer a dependable emotional return beyond the sensation of the moment itself. The changes in sports—the moving of franchises, free agency—have made it impossible to count on a player, a team, and an entire league still being around for next year's comeback. The connection between player and fan has been irrevocably destabilized, for love and loyalty demand a future. Along the way, those many virtues of self-discipline, responsibility, altruism, and dedication seem to have been deleted from the athletic contract with America.
> —Robert Lipsyte, "The Emasculation of Sports"

5f   How do I write a critical response?

A **critical response** essay has two missions: to SUMMARIZE a source's main idea and to respond to the main idea based on your SYNTHESIS (5b and 5e).

A well-written critical response accomplishes these two missions with style and grace. That is, it doesn't say, "My summary is . . ." or "Now, here's what I think. . . ." Instead, you want the two missions to blend together as seamlessly as possible. A critical response essay may be short or somewhat long, depending on whether you're asked to

**QUOTATION: ON READING
AND WRITING**

For me, philosophically, existentially, the fundamental task of human beings should be reading the world, writing the world; reading the words, writing the words. If we did that consciously, with a critical consciousness, of course we would be active, willing, choosing subjects of history. Then we could speak freely about our presence in the world.

—Paulo Freire

**QUOTATION: ON WRITING
AND READING**

Read, read, read. Read everything—trash, classics, good and bad, and see how they do it. Just like a carpenter who works as an apprentice and studies the master. Read! You'll absorb it. Then write. If it is good, you'll find out. If it's not, throw it out the window.

—William Faulkner

respond to a single passage or to an entire work. Box 33 gives general guidelines for writing a critical response.

BOX 33   SUMMARY

 Guidelines for writing a critical response

1. Write a SUMMARY of the main idea or central point of the material you're responding to.
2. Write a smooth TRANSITION between that summary and what comes next: your response. This transitional statement, which bridges the two parts, need not be a formal THESIS STATEMENT (2q), but it needs to signal clearly the beginning of your response.
3. Respond to the source based on your prior knowledge and experience.
4. Fulfill all DOCUMENTATION requirements. See Chapters 34–36 for coverage of five DOCUMENTATION STYLES (MLA, APA, CM, CSE, and COS). Ask your instructor which to use.

Here's a student essay written as a critical response. The assignment was to read and respond to "Sports Only Exercise Our Eyes" by Sydney J. Harris, shown in Exercise 5-4. Anna Lozanov's transition from summary to response comes at the beginning of her third paragraph.

Lozanov 1

Anna Lozanov

Professor Dawson

English 102

24 September 2003

Critical Response to "Sports Only Exercise

Our Eyes" by Sydney J. Harris

Except for a brief period in high school when I was wild

about a certain basketball player, I never gave sports much

thought. I went to games because my friends went, not because

→

Lozanov 2

I cared about football or baseball or track. I certainly never expected to defend sports, and when I first read Sydney Harris's essay "Sports Only Exercise Our Eyes," I thoroughly agreed with him. Like Harris, I believed that men who live and breathe sports are "mentally limited and conversationally dull" (111).

For the entire thirteen years of my marriage, I have complained about the amount of time my husband, John, spends watching televised sports. Of course, I've tried to get him to take an interest in something else. There was the time as a newlywed when I flamboyantly interrupted the sixth game of the World Series--wearing only a transparent nightie. Then, one year, I had the further audacity to go into labor with our first child--right in the middle of the Super Bowl.

Even the child tried to help me cure my husband of what Harris calls an "obsession" (111). Some months after the fateful Super Bowl, the kid thoroughly soaked his father, who was concentrating so intently on the struggle for the American League pennant that he didn't even notice! Only a commercial brought the dazed sports fan back into the living room from the baseball Stadium.

Just this weekend, however, I had an occasion to reconsider the value of sports. Having just read the Harris essay, I found myself paying closer attention to my husband and sons' weekend afternoon television routine. I was surprised to discover that they didn't just "vegetate" in front of the TV; during the course of the afternoon, they actually discussed ethics, priorities, commitments, and the consequences of abusing one's body. When one of the commentators raised issues like point shaving and using steroids, John and the kids talked about cheating and using steroids. When another commentator

→

QUOTATION: ON WRITING
Writing has laws of perspective, of light and shade, just as painting does, or music. If you are born knowing them, fine. If not, learn them. Then rearrange the rules to suit yourself.
—Truman Capote

QUOTATION: ON WRITING
There is only one trait that marks the writer. He is always watching. It's a kind of trick of the mind and he is born with it.
—Morley Callaghan

Lozanov 3

brought up the issue of skipping one's senior year to go straight to the pros, John explained the importance of a college education and discussed the short career of most professional football players.

Then, I started to think about all the times I've gone to the basement and found my husband and sons performing exercise routines as they watched a game on TV. Even our seven-year-old, who loathes exercise, pedals vigorously on the exercise bike while the others do sit-ups and curls. Believe it or not, there are times when they're all exercising more than just their eyes.

I still agree with Harris that many people spend too much time watching televised sports, but after this weekend, I certainly can't say that all of that time is wasted--at least not at my house. Anything that can turn my couch potatoes into thinking, talking, active human beings can't be all bad. Next weekend, instead of putting on a nightie, I think I'll join my family on the couch.

Lozanov 4

Work Cited

Harris, Sydney J. "Sports Only Exercise Our Eyes." The Best of Sydney J. Harris. Boston: Houghton, 1975. 111-12.

5g How do I assess evidence critically?

The cornerstone of all reasoning is evidence. **Evidence** consists of facts, statistical information, examples, and opinions of experts. As a reader, you expect writers to provide solid evidence for any claim made or conclusion reached. As a writer, you want to use evidence well to support your claims and conclusions. To assess evidence, you want to know how to evaluate it (5g.1) and how to tell the differences between primary and secondary sources (5g.2).

5g.1 Evaluating evidence

You can evaluate evidence by asking the following questions to guide your judgment.

- **Is the evidence sufficient?** To be sufficient, evidence can't be skimpy. As a rule, the more evidence, the better. Readers have more confidence in the results of a survey that draws on a hundred respondents rather than on ten. As a writer, you may convince your reader that violence is a serious problem in high schools based on only two examples, but you'll be more convincing with additional examples.
- **Is the evidence representative?** Evidence is representative if it is typical. As a reader, assess the objectivity and fairness of evidence. Don't trust a claim or conclusion about a group based on only a few members rather than on a truly typical sample. A pollster surveying national political views would not get representative evidence by interviewing people only in Austin, Texas, because that group doesn't represent the regional, racial, political, and ethnic makeup of the entire U.S. electorate. As a writer, the evidence you offer should represent your claim fairly; don't base your point on an exception.
- **Is the evidence relevant?** Relevant evidence is directly related to the conclusion you're drawing. Determining relevance often demands subtle thinking. Suppose you read that one hundred students who had watched television for more than two hours a day throughout high school earned significantly lower scores on a college entrance exam than one hundred students who had not. Can you conclude that students who watch less television perform better on college entrance exams? Not necessarily. Other differences between the two groups could account for the different scores: geographical region, family background, socioeconomic group, or the quality of schools attended.
- **Is the evidence accurate?** Accurate evidence is correct and complete. Inaccurate evidence is useless. Evidence must come from a reliable source, whether it is primary or secondary (5g.2). Equally important, evidence must be presented honestly, not misrepresented or distorted.
- **Is the evidence qualified?** Reasonable evidence doesn't make extreme claims. Claims that use words such as *all, always, never,* and *certainly* are disqualified if even one exception is found. Conclusions are more sensible and believable when qualified with words such as *some, many, may, possibly, often,* and *usually.* Remember that today's "facts" may be revised as time passes and knowledge grows.

BACKGROUND

In a *New York Times* article, "Voters Assailed by Unfair Persuasion" (October 27, 1992), Daniel Goleman cites research about the effect of political propaganda on the human psyche. Studies indicate that near election time candidates may use propaganda techniques to sway voters. Sometimes these tactics work, but they can also backfire. As Golemen notes, "In one study, attack ads were found to discourage voters from voting at all."

According to Goleman and other psychologists, the best "inoculation" for falling prey to manipulation lies in the voter's own mind. In a sidebar titled "Persuasion: A Consumer's Guide," Dr. Anthony Pratkanis, a psychologist who studies persuasion at the University of California, outlines several propaganda methods used by politicians, including "Appeal to Fear." When voters are aware of these techniques, they're less likely to believe distorted appeals and more likely to think for themselves.

QUOTATION: ON THINKING
Man can believe the impossible but can never believe the improbable.
—Oscar Wilde

BACKGROUND
A 1998 study in the *Journal of Consumer Research* reports: "Individuals who were in the market for compact disc players were influenced more by magazine ads that presented relevant facts and allowed readers to draw their own conclusions than by ads that presented the same facts and then stated the conclusions."

QUOTATION: ON TEACHING
We have this kind of understanding when students are taught to interpret texts, including the texts other students create, or the texts that hang in the air as talk, or those that emerge within us from our experiences and feelings. This is the kind of work that encourages critical thinking.
—Anthony Petrosky

QUOTATION: ON LANGUAGE
The difference between the right word and the almost right word is the difference between lightning and lightning bug.
—Mark Twain

5g.2 Recognizing primary versus secondary sources as evidence

Primary sources are firsthand evidence. They're based on your own or someone else's original work or direct observation. Because there's no one to distort the meaning of the original work, firsthand evidence has the greatest impact on a reader. For example, here's an eyewitness account that is a solid example of a primary source.

> Poverty is dirt. . . . Let me explain about housekeeping with no money. For breakfast, I give my children grits with no oleo or cornbread without eggs and oleo. This doesn't use up many dishes. What dishes there are, I wash in cold water and with no soap. Even the cheapest soap has to be saved for the baby's diapers. Look at my hands, so cracked and red. Once I saved for two months to buy a jar of Vaseline for my hands and the baby's diaper rash. When I had saved enough, I went to buy it and the price had gone up two cents. The baby and I suffered on.
> —Jo Goodwin Parker, "What's Poverty?"

What in Parker's account makes the reader trust what she says? She is specific, and she is authoritative. She is therefore reliable.

Of course, not all eyewitnesses are reliable, so you must judge which ones to believe. Few people will ever see the top of Mount Everest. People rely, therefore, on the firsthand observation of mountain climbers who've been there. Indeed, much of what we learn of history depends on letters, diaries, and journals—the reports of eyewitnesses who have seen events unfold.

Surveys, polls, and experiments—if the data are carefully controlled and measured—extend everyone's powers of observation. The outcomes of such work are considered primary sources. What can one individual know about the attitude of the U.S. public toward marriage, or a presidential candidate, or inflation? For evidence on such matters, polls or surveys constitute primary evidence.

Secondary sources report, describe, comment on, or analyze the experiences or work of others. As evidence, a secondary source is at least once removed from the primary source. It reports on the original work, the direct observation, or the firsthand experience. Still, secondary evidence can have great value and impact if it meets the evaluation criteria listed in 5g.1. Here's a secondhand report of an observation:

> The immediate causes of death from nuclear attack are the blast wave, which can flatten heavily reinforced buildings many kilometers away, the firestorm, the gamma rays, and the neutrons, which effectively fry the insides of passersby. A schoolgirl who survived the American nuclear attack on Hiroshima, the event that ended the Second World War, wrote this firsthand account:

> > Through a darkness like the bottom of hell, I could hear the voices of the other students calling for their mothers. And at the base of

the bridge, inside a big cistern that had been dug out there, was a mother weeping, holding above her head a naked baby that was burned bright red all over its body. . . . But every single person who passed was wounded, all of them, and there was no one, there was no one to turn to for help. And the singed hair on the heads of the people was frizzled and whitish and covered with dust. They did not appear to be human, not creatures of this world.

—Carl Sagan, *Cosmos*

The value of a secondhand account hinges on the reliability of the reporter. And that reliability comes from how specific, accurate, and authoritative the observations are. An expert's reputation comes from some special experience (the parents of children) or special training (an accountant could be an expert on taxes). Carl Sagan, the author of the sample paragraph above, was a respected scientist, scholar, and writer; therefore, readers can be quite confident that he has fully and fairly represented what the schoolgirl said. Still, of course, no one can be sure of that without seeing her original account. Box 34 gives guidelines for evaluating a secondary source.

BOX 34   CHECKLIST

 Evaluating a secondary source

- **Is the source authoritative?** Did an expert or a person you can expect to write credibly on the subject write it?
- **Is the source reliable?** Does the material appear in a reputable publication—a book published by an established publisher, a respected journal or magazine—or on a reliable Internet site?
- **Is the source well known?** Is the source cited elsewhere as you read about the subject? (If so, the authority of the source is probably widely accepted.)
- **Is the information well supported?** Is the source based on primary evidence? If the source is based on secondary evidence, is the evidence authoritative and reliable?
- **Is the tone balanced?** Is the language relatively objective (and therefore more likely reliable), or is it slanted (probably not reliable)?
- **Is the source current?** Is the material up to date and therefore more likely reliable, or has later authoritative and reliable research made it outdated? ("Old" isn't necessarily unreliable. In many fields, classic works of research remain authoritative for decades or even centuries.)

QUOTATION: ON THINKING
Experimental studies have shown that juries believe more readily in the closing arguments of prosecuting attorneys when they begin by arguing against their own position.

—Daniel Goleman

QUOTATION: ON WRITING
Writing stops the more chaotic and undisciplined breadth of my often random thought and makes me frame and focus on fewer possibilities.

—Toby Fulwiler

QUOTATION: ON READING
The one thing I regret is that I will never have time to read all the books I want to read.

—Françoise Sagan

QUOTATION: ON WRITING
Don't expect readers to believe you merely because you say something is the cause: proof is the writer's job.

—Sheena Gillespie

ANSWERS: EXERCISE 5-6

A. (1) Primary evidence. The author is describing his own experiences in a first-person narrative. (2) It seems to be balanced and objective, but a reader cannot know whether the information is reliable from the paragraph.

B. (1) Secondary evidence. (2) The assertions are carefully qualified and seem well substantiated by evidence. Students cannot know whether the information is reliable from this paragraph.

C. (1) Both secondary and primary evidence. The opening paragraph presents secondary evidence, but the second paragraph presents primary evidence—a firsthand account from a diary by Mrs. John Kirkwood. (2) The quoted material makes Schlissel's observations reliable.

QUOTATION: ON READING

Reading is a basic tool in the living of a good life.

—Mortimer J. Adler

ANSWERS: EXERCISE 5-7

Answers will vary.

EXERCISE 5-6

Indicate for each passage whether it constitutes primary or secondary evidence. Then, decide whether the evidence is reliable or not, and explain why or why not. Refer to section 5g for help.

A.   I went one morning to a place along the banks of the Madeira River where the railroad ran, alongside rapids impassable to river traffic, and I searched for any marks it may have left on the land. But there was nothing except a clearing where swarms of insects hovered over the dead black hen and other items spread out on a red cloth as an offering to the gods of macumba, or black magic. This strain of African origins in Brazil's ethnic character is strong in the Northwest Region.
—William S. Ellis, "Brazil's Imperiled Rain Forest"

B.   Most climatologists believe that the world will eventually slip back into an ice age in 10,000 to 20,000 years. The Earth has been unusually cold for the last two to three million years, and we are just lucky to be living during one of the warm spells. But the concern of most weather watchers looking at the next century is with fire rather than ice. By burning fossil fuels and chopping down forests, humans have measurably increased the amount of carbon dioxide in the atmosphere. From somewhere around 300 parts per million at the turn of the century, this level has risen to 340 parts per million today. If the use of fossil fuels continues to increase, carbon dioxide could reach 600 parts per million during the next century.
—Steve Olson, "Computing Climate"

C.   Marriages on the frontier were often made before a girl was half through her adolescent years, and some diaries record casualness in the manner such decisions were reached. Mrs. John Kirkwood recounts:

> The night before Christmas, John Kirkwood . . . the pathfinder, stayed at our house over night. I had met him before and when he heard the discussion about my brother Jasper's wedding, he suggested that he and I also get married. I was nearly fifteen years old and I thought it was high time that I got married so I consented.
> —Lillian Schlissel, *Women's Diaries of the Westward Journey*

EXERCISE 5-7

Individually or with a peer-response group, choose one of the following thesis statements and list the kinds of primary and secondary sources you might consult to support the thesis (you can guess intelligently, rather than being sure that the sources exist). Then, decide which sources in your list would be primary and which secondary.

Thesis statement 1: Public schools in this area receive adequate funding.

Thesis statement 2: Public schools in this area do not receive adequate funding.

5h How do I assess cause and effect critically?

Some evidence has to rely on the accuracy of a cause-and-effect relationship. **Cause and effect** describes the relationship between one event (cause) and another event that happens as a result (effect). The relationship also works in reverse: One event (effect) results from another event (cause). Whether you begin with a cause or with an effect, you're using the same basic pattern.

Cause A ——→ produces ——→ effect B

You may seek to understand the effects of a known cause:

More studying ——→ produces ——→ ?

Or you may seek to determine the cause or causes of a known effect:

? ——→ produces ——→ recurrent headaches

Be careful not to take cause-and-effect statements at face value. Think through the relationship between cause A and effect B. Sometimes, the relationship is exactly the opposite of what's being claimed. Consult the guidelines in Box 35.

BOX 35 CHECKLIST

 Assessing cause and effect

■ **Is there a clear relationship between events?** Related causes and effects happen in sequence: A cause occurs before an effect. First the wind blows; then a door slams; then a pane of glass in the door breaks. But CHRONOLOGICAL ORDER merely implies a cause-and-effect relationship. Perhaps someone slammed the door shut. Perhaps someone threw a baseball through the glass pane. A cause-and-effect relationship must be linked by more than chronological sequence. The fact that B happens after A doesn't prove that A causes B.

■ **Is there a pattern of repetition?** Scientific proof depends on a pattern of repetition. To establish that A causes B, every time A is

→

TEACHING TIP
You may want to ask your students to think about their own experiences, analyzing them for their causes and effects. You might ask your students to diagram these causes and effects and to write some of these diagrams on the board for discussion. The questions that follow can help stimulate students' thinking.

1. How did you get your first job?

2. What did you learn from that job?

3. Whose advice is particularly important to you?

4. How do you reach a decision?

5. What difference do you expect college to make in your life?

6. Why do you have a particular way of doing something?

7. How do you make friends?

8. Who is the most important person in your life? Why?

9. When did you learn to drive a car?

10. What will you be doing in ten years?

EXTRA EXERCISE B

Supply answers for the blanks in the sentences that follow, checking each choice by the guidelines for evaluating cause and effect to be sure that it is accurate.

1. Frequently eating food with high sodium content can cause _____.

2. _____ can lead to a traffic violation.

3. Regular exercise produces _____.

4. _____ is a leading cause of _____.

5. Because she _____, she is expected to be named Gourmet of the Year.

6. Her mother refuses to intervene so that _____.

7. If you don't quit _____, you are likely to end up in a lawsuit.

8. She decided to stay in college when she learned that _____.

9. More funding for preschool education is needed in order to _____.

10. _____ has resulted in increased numbers of homeless people in our major cities.

Answers to Extra Exercise B

Answers will vary, but here are possible responses:

1. high blood pressure

2. Ignoring a stop sign

3. better health

4. Inattention in class, low grades

5. led a revolt against the school cafeteria

6. the daughter would become more independent

7. telling lies about your neighbor

8. employers in her profession usually hire people with college degrees

9. prepare all children adequately for school

10. Slashing the budget for public housing

Assessing cause and effect (*continued*)

present, B must occur. Or, put another way, B never occurs unless A is present. The need for repetition explains why the U.S. Food and Drug Administration (FDA) runs thousands of clinical trials before approving a new medicine.

- **Are there multiple causes and/or effects?** Avoid oversimplification. The basic pattern of cause and effect—single cause, single effect (A causes B)—rarely represents the full picture. Multiple causes and/or effects are more typical of real life. For example, it would be oversimplification to assume that a lower crime rate is strictly due to high employment rates. Similarly, one cause can produce multiple effects. For example, advertisements for a liquid diet drink focus on the drink's most appealing effect, rapid weight loss, ignoring less desirable effects such as lost nutrients and a tendency to regain the weight.

5i How do I assess reasoning processes critically?

To think, read, and write critically, you need to distinguish *sound reasoning* from *faulty reasoning*. **Induction** and **deduction** are the two basic reasoning processes. They're natural thought patterns people use every day to help them think through ideas and make decisions. The two processes are summarized in Box 36.

BOX 36   SUMMARY

Comparison of inductive and deductive reasoning

	Inductive Reasoning	Deductive Reasoning
Argument begins	with specific evidence	with a general claim
Argument concludes	with a general statement	with a specific statement
Conclusion is	reliable or unreliable	true or false
Purpose is	to discover something new	to apply what's known

Recognizing and using inductive reasoning

Inductive reasoning moves from particular facts or instances to general principles. Suppose you go to the Registry of Motor Vehicles to renew your driver's license and have to stand in line for two hours. A few months later you return to get new license plates, and once again you have to stand in line for two hours. You mention your annoyance to a couple of friends who say they had exactly the same experience. You conclude that the registry is inefficient and indifferent to the needs of its patrons. You've arrived at this conclusion by means of induction. Box 37 shows the features of inductive reasoning.

BOX 37   SUMMARY

 Inductive reasoning

- **Inductive reasoning moves from the specific to the general.** It begins with specific evidence—facts, observations, or experiences—and moves to a general conclusion.

- **Inductive conclusions are considered reliable or unreliable, not true or false.** Because inductive thinking is based on a sampling of facts, an inductive conclusion indicates probability—the degree to which the conclusion is likely to be true—not certainty.

- **An inductive conclusion is held to be reliable or unreliable in relation to the quantity and quality of the evidence** (5g) on which it's based.

- **Induction leads to new "truths."** It can support statements about the unknown based on what's known.

Recognizing and using deductive reasoning

Deductive reasoning is the process of reasoning from general claims to a specific instance. Suppose you know that students who don't study for Professor Sanchez's history tests tend to do poorly. If your friend tells you she didn't study, you can make a reasonable conclusion about her grade. Your reasoning might go something like this:

PREMISE 1   Students who don't study do poorly on Professor Sanchez's exams.
PREMISE 2   My friend didn't study.
CONCLUSION   Therefore, my friend probably did poorly on the exam.

Deductive arguments have three parts: two **premises** and a conclusion. This three-part structure is known as a **syllogism.** The first and second premises of a deductive argument may be statements of fact or

TEACHING TIP
Using analogy is a way to think inductively. An analogy compares two dissimilar objects, ideas, or experiences by focusing on what they have in common. For example, some people make an analogy between the role of a teacher and that of a coach. Like coaches, teachers train people in fundamentals through repetition and practice, recommend changes in technique, and try to inspire excellence. However, despite points of similarity, two dissimilar items remain dissimilar.

First, coaches work primarily with the body rather than the mind, developing physical rather than mental skills. Second, team coaches praise the team player, whereas good teachers reward independence and originality. Thus, the analogy between teachers and coaches breaks down at some point.

In the absence of other evidence, an analogy will not prove anything. Nevertheless, although an analogy can always be shown as flawed under close scrutiny, it can still help explain a point and thus help persuade an audience.

QUOTATION: ON WRITING
The Latin roots of the word *induction* give us a clue as to how this method of arguing works: *in* = intro + *ducere* = to lead—literally, "to lead into." After noting a series of similar phenomena, we draw some conclusion, we make some generalization about all phenomena of that kind. In other words, after observing a number of similar examples of something, we are "led into" a conclusion about all examples of that kind.
—Edward P. J. Corbett

QUOTATION: ON THINKING
Logic is in the eye of the logician.
—Gloria Steinem

OTHER EXAMPLES OF SYLLOGISMS

INVALID

Some round things are bubbles.

Some human heads are round things.

Therefore, some human heads are bubbles.

VALID

All mammals are animals.

All whales are mammals.

Therefore, all whales are animals.

TEACHING TIP
You may want to ask students to consider a controversial issue such as whether violent juvenile offenders are promising candidates for rehabilitation. You might choose to engage the class in a discussion on the topic and compile lists of the different factors to consider on the blackboard. Questions could include: What sources would students need to cite or consult to support a position (e.g., child psychologists, probation officers, rehabilitation counselors)? What factors would students weigh in their decision? A partial list might include: age of the offender, degree of remorse, and severity of crime.

assumptions. They lead to a conclusion, which is the point at which you want to think as precisely as possible because you're into the realm of *validity*.

Whether or not an argument is **valid** has to do with its form or structure. Here the word *valid* isn't the general term people use in conversation to mean "acceptable" or "well grounded." In the context of reading and writing logical arguments, the word *valid* has a very specific meaning. A deductive argument is *valid* when the conclusion logically follows from the premises; a deductive argument is *invalid* when the conclusion doesn't logically follow from the premises. For example:

VALID DEDUCTIVE ARGUMENT

PREMISE 1	When it snows, the streets get wet. [fact]
PREMISE 2	It is snowing. [fact]
CONCLUSION	Therefore, the streets are getting wet.

INVALID DEDUCTIVE ARGUMENT

PREMISE 1	When it snows, the streets get wet. [fact]
PREMISE 2	The streets are getting wet. [fact]
CONCLUSION	Therefore, it is snowing.

Here's the problem with the invalid deductive argument: It has acceptable premises because they are facts. However, the argument's conclusion is wrong because it ignores other reasons why the streets might be wet. For example, the street could be wet from rain, from street-cleaning trucks that spray water, or from people washing their cars. Therefore, because the conclusion doesn't follow logically from the premises, the argument is invalid.

Another problem in a deductive argument can occur when the premises are implied but not stated—called **unstated assumptions.** Remember that an argument can be logically valid even though it is based on wrong assumptions. To show that such an argument is invalid, you need to attack the assumptions, not the conclusion, as wrong. For example, suppose a corporation argues that it can't install pollution-control devices because the cost would cut deeply into its profits. This argument rests on the unstated assumption that no corporation should do something that would lower its profits. That assumption is wrong, and so is the argument. To show that both are wrong, you need to challenge the assumptions.

Similarly, if a person says that certain information is correct because it's written in the newspaper, that person's deductive reasoning is flawed. The unstated assumption is that everything in a newspaper is correct—which isn't true. Whenever there's an unstated assumption, you need to state it outright and then check that it's true. Box 38 summarizes deductive reasoning.

BOX 38   SUMMARY

Deductive reasoning

- **Deductive reasoning moves from the general to the specific.** The three-part structure that makes up a deductive argument, or SYLLOGISM, includes two premises and a conclusion drawn from them.
- **A deductive argument is valid if the conclusion logically follows from the premises.**
- **A deductive conclusion may be judged true or false.** If both premises are true, the conclusion is true. If the argument contains an assumption, the writer must prove the truth of the assumption to establish the truth of the argument.
- **Deductive reasoning applies what the writer already knows.** Though it doesn't yield new information, it builds stronger arguments than inductive reasoning because it offers the certainty that a conclusion is either true or false.

EXERCISE 5-8

Working individually or with a peer-response group, determine whether each conclusion here is valid or invalid. Be ready to explain your answers. For help, consult 5i.

1. Faddish clothes are expensive.
   This shirt is expensive.
   This shirt must be part of a fad.
2. When a storm is threatening, small-craft warnings are issued.
   A storm is threatening.
   Small-craft warnings will be issued.
3. The Pulitzer Prize is awarded to outstanding literary works.
   The Great Gatsby never won a Pulitzer Prize.
   The Great Gatsby isn't an outstanding literary work.
4. All states send representatives to the United States Congress.
   Puerto Rico sends a representative to the United States Congress.
   Puerto Rico is a state.
5. Finding a good job requires patience.
   Sherrill is patient.
   Sherrill will find a good job.

ANSWERS: EXERCISE 5-8

1. *Invalid.* The shirt's being expensive does not mean that it shares other characteristics of faddish clothing.
2. *Valid.* The conclusion follows logically from the premises.
3. *Invalid.* Some outstanding literary works have not received a Pulitzer Prize.
4. *Invalid.* All states do send representatives, but that does not mean that all representatives come from a state.
5. *Invalid.* The first premise does not say that patience alone is sufficient to find a good job.

TEACHING TIP

Many students enjoy finding and correcting logical fallacies in newspaper editorials and opinion columns, as well as in the work of their peers. You might distribute copies of works containing fallacies, as a spur to class discussion or for revision. A less adept class might benefit from a preliminary lesson based on a list of logical fallacies you can cull from assorted sources (newspapers, political literature, advertisements, student papers); tell the students all the passages are illogical and have them explain why, as a prelude to revision (oral or written, as time allows).

Your analytically minded students may be interested in additional logical fallacies:

A *question-begging phrase* (sometimes called *alleged certainty*) presents something as certain that is open to debate: "Everyone knows" and "It is obvious that" are typical phrases that beg the question. This statement is flawed: "It is common knowledge that jobs in Texas pay more than jobs in Idaho"; whereas this statement is logical: "A recent government survey revealed that, on the average, workers in the oil fields of Texas are paid more than loggers in the timber industries of Idaho." To correct: Drop the question-begging phrase and substitute evidence that supports your claim.

A *complex question* (also known as a *loaded question*) contains one or more unproven assumptions: "Are you still spending

→

Teaching Tip (continued)
time with known criminals?" Notice what happens when you try to answer such a question. If you say yes, you are guilty. If you say no, you are still guilty, because you are admitting that you used to spend time with criminals. To correct: Split the question into its parts ("Are you still spending time with those people?" "Are those people criminals?") and deal with each separately.

Appeal to fear uses scare tactics instead of legitimate evidence. Such an argument implies danger: "Anyone who stages a protest against the government is a communist, so we must outlaw all protests."

Appeal to the people (also known as an *ad populum* appeal) draws on whatever the people hold dear—for example, country, religion, family. This approach tries to sway people by using a favorable label instead of providing reasons: "A vote for Joe Smith is a vote for the flag."

Name-calling attaches an unpleasant label to something or someone. Consider how a label can stop people from thinking: "Jane Jones was once an alcoholic, so she cannot possibly say anything of value about politics."

Appeal to pity attempts to arouse sympathy: "He embezzled $1,500 of company money, but after all, his wife recently died and his child needs surgery."

The *genetic fallacy,* a special form of hasty generalization, predicts something about a person based on that person's origins: "Joe Smith is from New York City, so he knows how to deal with street crime." Often, this fallacy involves a person's religion, sex, race, or economic status.

EXTRA EXERCISE C
Each analogy here can be defended. Like all analogies, each can also be attacked. First, defend each one—give one or more arguments to show that the two parts of the analogy are similar and are relevant to the claim being made. Second, attack each one by pointing out how they are not similar. Finally,

→

5j   How can I recognize and avoid logical fallacies?

Logical fallacies are flaws in reasoning that lead to illogical statements. Though logical fallacies tend to occur when ideas are argued, they can be found in all types of writing. Interestingly, most logical fallacies masquerade as reasonable statements, but in fact, they're attempts to manipulate readers by appealing to their emotions instead of their intellects, their hearts rather than their heads. The name for each logical fallacy indicates the way that thinking has gone wrong.

Hasty generalization

A hasty generalization draws conclusions from inadequate evidence. Suppose someone says, "My hometown is the best place in the state to live," and gives only two examples to support the opinion. That's not enough. And others might not feel the same way, perhaps for many reasons. Therefore, the person who makes such a statement is indulging in a hasty generalization. **Stereotyping** is another kind of hasty generalization. It happens, for example, when someone says, "Everyone from country X is dishonest." Such a sweeping claim about all members of a particular ethnic, religious, racial, or political group is stereotyping. Yet another kind of stereotyping is **sexism,** which occurs when someone discriminates against another person based on GENDER. For example, when an observer of a minor traffic accident involving women makes negative comments about all "women drivers," the person is guilty of a combination of stereotyping and sexism—both components of hasty generalization.

False analogy

A false analogy draws a comparison in which the differences outweigh the similarities or the similarities are irrelevant. For example, "Old Joe Smith would never make a good president because an old dog can't learn new tricks" is a false analogy. Joe Smith isn't a dog. Also, learning the role of a president bears no comparison to a dog's learning tricks. Homespun analogies like this have an air of wisdom about them, but they tend to fall apart when examined closely.

Begging the question

Begging the question, also called *circular reasoning*, tries to offer proof by simply using another version of the argument itself. For example, the statement "Wrestling is a dangerous sport because it is unsafe" begs the question. Because *unsafe* is a synonym for *dangerous,* the statement goes around in a circle, getting nowhere. Here's another example of circular reasoning but with a different twist: "Wrestling is a dangerous sport because wrestlers get injured." Here, the support for the second part of the statement "wrestlers get injured" is the argument made in the first part of the statement. Obviously, since wrestling is a popular sport, it can be safe when undertaken with proper training and practice.

Irrelevant argument

An irrelevant argument reaches a conclusion that doesn't follow from the premises. Irrelevant argument is also called *non sequitur* (Latin for "it does not follow"). An argument is irrelevant when a conclusion doesn't follow from the premises. Here's an example: "Jane Jones is a forceful speaker, so she'll make a good mayor." You'd be on target if you asked, "What does speaking ability have to do with being a good mayor?"

False cause

A false cause assumes that because two events are related in time, the first caused the second. False cause is also known as *post hoc, ergo propter hoc* (Latin for "after this, therefore because of this"). For example, if someone claims that a new weather satellite launched last week has caused the rain that's been falling ever since, that person is connecting two events that, while related in time, have no causal relationship to each other. The launching didn't cause the rain.

Self-contradiction

Self-contradiction uses two premises that can't both be true at the same time. Here's an example: "Only when nuclear weapons have finally destroyed us will we be convinced of the need to control them." This is self-contradictory because no one would be around to be convinced if everyone has been destroyed.

Red herring

A red herring, also called *ignoring the question*, tries to distract attention from one issue by introducing a second that's unrelated to the first. Here's an example: "Why worry about pandas becoming extinct when we haven't solved the plight of the homeless?" You'd be on target if you asked, "What do homeless people have to do with pandas?" If the argument were to focus on proposing that the money spent to prevent the extinction of pandas should go instead to the homeless, the argument would be logical; however, the original statement is a fallacy. By using an irrelevant issue, a person hopes to distract the audience, just as putting a herring in the path of a bloodhound would distract it from the scent it's been following.

Argument to the person

An argument to the person means attacking the person making the argument rather than the argument itself. It's also known as the *ad hominem* (Latin for "to the man") attack. When someone criticizes a

EXTRA EXERCISE D
Identify the kind of fallacy in each item, then explain why it's a fallacy. If there's no logical flaw in a statement, explain why it isn't a fallacy.

1. Joanna Hayes should write a book about the Central Intelligence Agency. She has starred in three films that show the inner workings of the agency.

2. It is ridiculous to have spent thousands of dollars to rescue those two whales trapped in the Arctic ice. Why, look at all of the people trapped in jobs that they don't like.

3. Every time my roommate has a math test, she becomes extremely nervous. Clearly, she isn't good at math.

4. Plagiarism is deceitful because it is dishonest.

5. The local political coalition to protect the environment would get my support if its leaders did not drive cars that are such gas hogs.

6. UFOs must exist because no reputable studies have proved conclusively that they don't.

7. Water fluoridation affects the brain. Citywide, students' test scores began to drop five months after fluoridation began.

8. Learning to manage a corporation is exactly like learning to ride a bicycle: Once you learn the skills, you never forget how, and you never fall.

9. Medicare is free; the government pays for it from taxes.

10. Reading good literature is the one way to appreciate culture.

person's appearance, habits, or character instead of the merits of that person's argument, the attack is a fallacy. Here's an example: "We'd take her position on child abuse seriously if she were not so nasty to her husband." You'd be on target if you were to ask, "What does nastiness to an adult, though not at all nice, have to do with child abuse?"

Guilt by association

Guilt by association means that a person's arguments, ideas, or opinions lack merit because of that person's activities, interests, or companions. Here's an example: "Jack belongs to the International Hill Climbers Association, which declared bankruptcy last month. This makes him unfit to be mayor of our city." That Jack is a member of a group that declared bankruptcy has nothing to do with Jack's ability to be mayor.

Jumping on the bandwagon

Jumping on the bandwagon means something is right or permissible because "everyone does it." It's also called *ad populum* (Latin for "to the people"). This fallacy operates in a statement such as "How could bungee jumping be unhealthy if thousands of people have done it?" Following the crowd doesn't work because research shows that many people who bungee jump suffer serious sight impairments later in life.

False or irrelevant authority

Using false or irrelevant authority means citing the opinion of someone who has no expertise in the subject at hand. This fallacy attempts to transfer prestige from one area to another. Many television commercials rely on this tactic—a famous golf player praising a brand of motor oil or a popular movie star lauding a brand of cheese.

Card-stacking

Card-stacking, also known as *special pleading*, ignores evidence on the other side of a question. From all available facts, people choose only those facts that show the best (or worst) possible case. Many television commercials use this strategy. When three slim, happy consumers praise a diet plan, only at the very end of the ad does the announcer say—in a very low and speedy voice—that results vary. Indeed, even that statement is vague and uninformative.

The either-or fallacy

The either-or fallacy, also called *false dilemma*, offers only two alternatives when more exist. Such fallacies tend to touch on emotional issues, so many people accept them until they analyze the statement. Here's an example: "Either go to college or forget about getting a job." Obviously, this rigid, two-sided statement ignores the truth that many jobs don't require a college education.

Taking something out of context

Taking something out of context deliberately distorts an idea or a fact by removing it from its previously surrounding material. Here's an example: Suppose that a newspaper movie critic writes, "The plot was predictable and boring, but the music was sparkling." The next day, an advertisement for the movie claims "critics call it 'sparkling.'" Clearly, the ad has taken the critic's words out of context (only the music was called "sparkling") and thereby distorts the original.

Appeal to ignorance

Appeal to ignorance tries to make an incorrect argument based on something never having been shown to be false—or, the reverse, never having been shown to be true. Here's an example: "Because it hasn't been proven that eating food X doesn't cause cancer, we can assume that it does." The statement is a fallacy because the absence of opposing evidence proves nothing. Such appeals can be very persuasive because they prey on people's superstitions or lack of knowledge. Often, they're stated in the fuzzy language of DOUBLE NEGATIVES.

Ambiguity and equivocation

Ambiguity and equivocation are statements open to more than one interpretation, thus concealing the truth. Here's an example: Suppose a person is asked, "Is she doing a good job?" and the person answers, "She's performing as expected." The answer is a fallacy because it's open to positive or negative interpretation.

EXERCISE 5-9

Following are letters to the editor of a newspaper. Working alone or with a group, do a critical analysis of each, paying special attention to logical fallacies.

1. To the Editor:

I am writing to oppose the plan to convert the abandoned railroad tracks into a bicycle trail. Everyone knows that the only reason the mayor wants to do this is so that she and her wealthy friends can have a new place to play. No one I know likes this plan, and if they did, it would probably be because they're part of the wine and cheese set, too. The next thing you know, the mayor will be proposing that we turn the schools into art museums or the park into a golf course. If you're working hard to support a family, you don't have time for this bike trail nonsense. And if you're not working hard, I don't have time for you.

Russell Shields

2. To the Editor:

I encourage everyone to support the bicycle trail project. Good recreation facilities are the key to the success of any community. Since the

Answers to Extra Exercise D

1. *False authority.* An actor is not an authority on the CIA.

2. *Red herring.* The social issue is introduced to divert attention from the real issue—whether or not money should have been spent to rescue the whales.

3. *Irrelevant argument,* or *non sequitur.* A person can be nervous about something and still be good at it.

4. *Begging the question,* or *circular argument.* "Dishonest" is merely a slightly different term for "deceitful."

5. *Argument to the person,* or *ad hominem.* These people are being attacked for materialism, but they are perhaps serious environmentalists whose cars and shoes are irrelevant to their environmental stance.

6. *Appeal to ignorance.* Just because no evidence exists for one side of the argument does not mean that the other side of the argument is valid.

7. *False cause,* or *post hoc, ergo propter hoc.* The sequence of events does not prove any connection between them.

8. *False analogy.* Analogies are dangerous in argument because they equate things that are not the same. Riding a bicycle is much different from learning to run a company, and although the skills for riding a bicycle remain the same, those of running a company may change with the economy and other pressures so that one could "fall" if he or she did not adopt those skills.

9. *Self-contradiction.* Medicare cannot be free if it is paid for.

10. *Either-or fallacy.* Reading good literature is not the only way to appreciate culture.

ANSWERS: EXERCISE 5-9

Answers will vary. Following are possible analyses.

1. The letter writer relies heavily on *ad hominem* argument. He attacks the mayor for being wealthy (yet provides no evidence that she is) rather than providing arguments ➡

Answers: Exercise 5-9 (continued)

against the proposal. He also uses hasty generalizations by claiming that "everyone knows" the mayor's motives; that "no one I know likes this plan"; and that "if you're working hard" you won't have time for the trail. He provides no evidence for any of these claims, which are also a form of jumping on the bandwagon. He makes an extreme assertion that the mayor would "turn schools into art museums or the park into a golf course," which is a form of false analogy. Finally, the tone of the letter tends to be biased. He characterizes the mayor as wanting a "place to play" and as being part of "the wine and cheese set," and he calls the plan "nonsense." His final statement is confrontational, which implies he is not someone who has examined this issue openly.

2. The letter writer begs the question. The claim that "Good recreation facilities are the key to the success of any community" comes without any evidence, and the assertion that building the trail will guarantee success is just that: an assertion, which is debatable. She also uses a false cause argument. Just because the town of Springfield went into an economic decline after it failed to build a new park does not mean that the absence of the park caused the town's decline. Calling opponents "narrow-minded, selfish, and almost unpatriotic" is an *ad hominem* argument. Quoting John Paul Jones has nothing to do with the issue at hand.

3. The letter writer relies on hasty generalizations. He cites some cold days in the winter and summer as evidence that there is no global warming, but this evidence is not nearly comprehensive enough. He cites a false authority when he quotes his dentist, who is hardly an expert on global warming. His assertion that "you can't trust numbers" comes with no evidence; instead, he questions the integrity of "liberal scientists" and goes on to add a further unsubstantiated claim about their motives (making us feel guilty). The letter concludes with a red herring by turning attention to the unrelated issue of finding a cure for cancer.

bike trail will add more recreation opportunities, it will guarantee the success of our town. Remember that several years ago our neighbors over in Springfield decided not to build a new park, and look what happened to their economy, especially that city's high unemployment rate. We can't afford to let the same thing happen to us. People who oppose this plan are narrow-minded, selfish, and almost unpatriotic. As that great patriot John Paul Jones said, "I have not yet begun to fight."
Susan Thompson

3. To the Editor:

I'm tired of all this nonsense about pollution and global warming. We had plenty of cold days last winter, and as my dentist said, "If this is global warming, then I'd sure hate to see global cooling." Plus, there were lots of days this summer when I haven't had to turn on my air conditioner. I know there are statistics that some people say show the climate is changing, but you can't trust numbers, especially when they come from liberal scientists. These people just aren't happy unless they're giving us something to feel guilty about, whether it's smoking, drinking, or driving SUVs. Maybe if they stopped wasting their time worrying about pollution they could do something useful, like find a cure for cancer.

Marcus Johnson

Chapter 6

Writing Arguments

6a What is a written argument?

When you write an **argument,** you attempt to convince a reader to agree with you on a topic open to debate. You support your position, proposal, or interpretation with evidence, reasons, and examples—factual, logical data, not opinions. Some people use the terms *argument writing* and *persuasive writing* interchangeably. When people distinguish between them, *persuasive writing* is the broader term. It includes advertisements, letters to editors, emotionally charged speeches and writing, and formal written arguments. This chapter focuses on the kind of formal written argument usually assigned in college courses.

Taking and defending a position in a written argument is an engaging intellectual process, especially when it involves a topic of substance. For ACADEMIC WRITING, arguments are ways of demonstrating CRITICAL THINKING. In fact, before you choose a position and convincingly defend it, you want to examine all sides of the issue critically. This means considering your intended audience's likely feelings and beliefs about your topic. Your audience's viewpoints and values need to influence your decisions about content, organization, and style.

Written arguments are completely different from the arguing people do in everyday life. Verbal arguments often originate in anger and involve bursts of temper or unpleasant emotional confrontations. Written argument, in contrast, is constructive, setting forth a debatable position calmly and respectfully. The passion that underlies a writer's position comes not from angry words but from the force of a balanced, well-developed, clearly written presentation.

The ability to argue reasonably and effectively is an important skill not only in college but also throughout life—in family relationships, with friends, and in the business world. And as you become experienced with written arguments, you can apply the same techniques to oral arguments.

In this chapter, you'll examine three approaches to writing about argument: the classical pattern, the Toulmin model, and the Rogerian approach. In addition, you'll find information about how to analyze and

QUOTATION: ON WRITING
Mere knowledge of the truth will not give you the art of persuasion.
—Plato

BACKGROUND
Karen Quinn and Ann Matsuhashi's article "Stalking Ideas: The Generation and Elaboration of Arguments" (ERIC ED 257 043) reports on specific college students who used reading to generate argumentative writing.

QUOTATION: ON WRITING
A writer needs three things, experience, observation and imagination, any two of which, at times any one of which, can supply the lack of the others.
—William Faulkner

REFERENCE TO SUPPLEMENTS
You may find that ESL students sometimes need help adapting to argumentation style in the U.S. classroom. If so, see the article by C. Myers, "ESL Writers in the Composition Class," in *Strategies and Resources*.

BACKGROUND
In "Moments of Argument: Agonistic Inquiry and Confrontational Cooperation" (*College Composition and Communication*, February 1997: 61–85), Dennis A. Lynch, Diana George, and Marilyn M. Cooper argue that we need to stimulate students to debate, challenge, and oppose in writing arguments. They explain that the approach of cooperation and collaboration in finding common ground does not prepare students for a "bureaucratic world that resists change."

BACKGROUND
Chapter 2 of this handbook lists four aspects of writing situations that affect the decisions that the writer makes. They are (1) the topic, (2) the purpose, (3) the audience that will read or hear it, and (4) the special requirements that influence every writing situation, such as deadlines and length. For explanations of each aspect, see section 2c.

EXTRA EXERCISE A
Which of the following topics are concerned with fact, and which state a position open to debate?

1. The term *journalism* refers to the business of publishing a regularly recurring text.

2. Television news programs are more influential than they should be.

3. Journalists in the United States operate under the protection of the First Amendment to the Constitution.

4. Most reporters are biased in their descriptions of political figures.

5. The government should not let journalists have access to information dealing with national security.

6. Journalism involves both reporting the news and forming public opinion.

7. Reporters should verify a controversial story with two sources before running it.

8. Weekly newspapers are becoming increasingly popular in large cities.

9. Cartoons are one of the most entertaining features of newspapers.

10. Television commentators should not give their own opinions about political and social matters.

refute opposing arguments. As you read this chapter, I suggest that you keep your eye on what I discuss in Chapters 1 through 5 of this handbook. I need to assume you're familiar with them. If you take a few minutes to review those chapters, you'll have a richer context for understanding this chapter.

6b How do I choose a topic for an argument?

When you choose a topic for written argument, be sure that it's open to debate. Don't confuse matters of information (facts) with matters of debate. An essay becomes an argument when it makes a claim—that is, *takes a position*—about a debatable topic. An effective way to develop a position is to ask two (or more) opposing questions about a topic, each of which takes a position that differs from, or entirely opposes, the other(s).

FACT	Students at Calhoon College must study a foreign language.
DEBATABLE	Should Calhoon College require students to study a foreign language?
ONE SIDE	Calhoon College should not require students to study a foreign language.
OTHER SIDE	Calhoon College should require students to study a foreign language.

For your essay, you select only one side of a debatable question to defend, always keeping the opposing side(s) in mind. The bulk of your essay systematically presents and discusses the position you're defending, but some space remains for you to state and counter the opposing viewpoint. If multiple alternative viewpoints exist, choose the major opposing one, unless otherwise directed by your instructor. If you neglect to mention opposing views, your readers could justifiably assume you're not well informed, fair-minded, or disciplined as a thinker.

Instructors sometimes assign students the argument topic and the position to take about it. In such cases, you need to fulfill the assignment even if you disagree with the point of view. Readers expect you to reason logically about the assigned position.

If you choose your own topic and position, think of one that has sufficient substance for college writing. Readers expect you to take an intelligent, defensible position on your chosen topic and to support it reasonably and convincingly. For example, "book censorship in public libraries" is worthy of a college-level essay; "the best way to eat apples" is not.

If you think that all sides of a debatable topic have merit, you need to choose one of them anyway. Don't become paralyzed from indecision. You're not making a lifetime commitment. Beware, also, of switching sides at the last minute; you'll be wasting valuable time. Concentrate on the merits of one position and argue that position as effectively as possible. Once you decide on the assertion you want to argue, don't stop there. The more thoroughly you think through all sides of the topic, the broader the perspective you'll bring to your writing, and the more likely it will be effective.

6c How do I develop an assertion and a thesis statement for my argument?

An **assertion** is a statement that expresses a point of view on a debatable topic. It can be supported by evidence, reasons, and examples (including facts, statistics, names, experiences, and experts). The exact wording of the assertion rarely finds its way into the essay, but the assertion serves as a focus for your thinking. Later, it serves as the basis for developing your thesis statement.

TOPIC	Wild animals as domestic pets.
ASSERTION	People should not be allowed to own wild animals.
ASSERTION	People should be allowed to own wild animals.

Before you decide on an assertion—the position you want to argue—explore the topic. Don't rush. Consider all sides. **Remember that what mainly separates most good writing from bad is the writer's ability to move back and forth between general statements and specific details.** Therefore, before you start drafting, use the RENNS formula (4f) to check whether you can marshal sufficient details to support your generalizations.

To stimulate your thinking about the topic and the assertion of your position, work with the PLANNING techniques discussed in Chapter 2. Another well-favored strategy is to create a two-column list, labeling one column *pro* or *for*, the other *con* or *against*. If there are more than two opposing sides, label the columns accordingly. The columned list displays the quantity and quality of your material so that you can decide whether you're ready to start DRAFTING.

6d How does source-based writing work for arguments?

Source-based writing, also called *research writing*, means that writers conduct research about a topic and draw on their findings to support their position. If your instructor assigns such writing, use the library and the Internet to research your topic so that your essay has additional depth. Chapters 31 through 38 in this handbook guide you in writing research.

Answers to Extra Exercise A

1.	fact	**6.**	fact
2.	opinion	**7.**	opinion
3.	fact	**8.**	fact
4.	opinion	**9.**	opinion
5.	opinion	**10.**	opinion

QUOTATION: ON WRITING
Rhetoric may be defined as the faculty of observing in any given case the available means of persuasion.

—Aristotle

QUOTATION: ON WRITING
Had I been blessed with even a limited access to my own mind there would have been no reason to write. I write entirely to find out what I'm thinking, what I'm looking at, what I see and what it means.

—Joan Didion

BACKGROUND
Many techniques for discovering means of developing a subject have been devised in recent years. It is helpful to be reminded, however, that the ancient Greeks devised a set of topics—*topoi*, meaning "places or regions"—that can be used to generate "arguments" to persuade an audience. They suggest material for the writer who does not have a ready opinion on a subject or an effective way to present it. They cover the topics of definition (including genus and division), comparison (similarity, difference, and degree), relationship (cause and effect, antecedent and consequence, contraries, and contradictions), circumstance (the possible and impossible, past and future fact), and testimony (authority, testimonial, statistics, maxims, law, and examples). They remain the basis for many arguments of a general nature presented today. Particular kinds of argument were (and are) drawn from special topics devised to suit the type of discourse chosen by the writer. For example, the writer, or speaker, engaged in judicial discourse is concerned with justice and injustice, making it necessary to establish whether something happened (evidence), what it is (definition), and what kind of thing it is (cause and effect).

EXTRA EXERCISE B

Practice devising assertions and thesis statements by working with the following topics. (Answers will vary.)

1. Safety on interstate highways

2. The value of knowing a second language

3. Making purchases on the Internet

4. The use of television commercials in elementary schools

5. Paperless offices

6. Should everyone who wants to go to college be admitted?

7. Violence in the movies

8. Smoking restrictions in public places

9. Computer literacy as a requirement for high school graduation

10. Installing metal detectors in public schools

BACKGROUND

Although rhetoric, as defined by Aristotle, appears in the speeches and debates of the epics and plays of ancient Greece, its principles were not systematically formulated until the fifth century BC. Corax of Syracuse, recognizing the need for a system by which citizens of Sicily could argue in the courts to recover property that they had lost during the reign of Thrasybulus, began to set down the principles of argumentation. Lacking documents to prove their claims, ordinary citizens had to argue their cases by relying on inferential reasoning and probability. Tisias, the student of Corax, extended the study of rhetoric from the courtroom and wrote speeches for other people to deliver. Others who quickly followed to develop the art of rhetoric, or persuasion, include Gorgias of Leotini (fl. 420 BC), known principally for his ornate style characterized by the extensive use of figures of speech, and Isocrates (436–338 BC), one of the leading Athenian teachers of rhetoric and an author of influential books on rhetorical theory.

ANSWERS: EXERCISE 6-1

Assertions and thesis statements will vary.

Lacie Juris, the student who wrote the argument essay that appears in section 6m, was permitted to choose her own topic for her essay assignment. Juris was thinking about a career as a zookeeper, which in turn led her to become interested in issues concerning wild animals. In her career research, especially when she looked for the latest information on the Web, she discovered a major controversy: the problem of private ownership of wild animals. Her curiosity aroused, Juris read a number of sources and discovered a topic appropriate for her assignment. She worked on developing a position about that topic and then extended it into the thesis statement for her essay. Here's how Juris progressed from the topic to the first draft of her thesis statement and then its final draft.

TOPIC	Private ownership of wild animals
MY POSITION	I think private ownership of wild animals should not be allowed.
THESIS STATEMENT (FIRST DRAFT)	It is bad for private citizens to own wild animals as pets. [This is a preliminary thesis statement. It clearly states the writer's position, but the word *bad* is vague, and the writer doesn't address how to stop private ownership of wild animals.]
THESIS STATEMENT (SECOND DRAFT)	To eliminate what few people realize are increasingly dangerous situations for people and animals alike, ownership of wild animals as pets by ordinary people needs to be made completely illegal. [This revised thesis statement is better, but it suffers from lack of conciseness and from the unnecessary passive construction *needs to be made*.]
THESIS STATEMENT (FINAL DRAFT)	To eliminate dangerous situations for both people and animals, policymakers need to ban private ownership of wild animals as pets. [This final version works well because it states the writer's claim clearly and its language is concise, with verbs all in the active voice. The writer now has a thesis statement suitable for the time and length given in her assignment. Also, it meets the requirements for a thesis statement given in Box 12 in 2q.]

EXERCISE 6-1

Working individually or with a peer-response group, develop an assertion and a thesis statement for each of the topics listed at the end of the exercise. You may choose any defensible position. For help, consult 6a through 6d.

EXAMPLE **Topic:** Book censorship in high school
Assertion: Books should not be censored in high school.
Thesis statement: When books are taken off high school library shelves or are dropped from high school curricula, students are denied an open exchange of ideas.

1. Watching television many hours each day
2. The commercialization of holidays
3. Taking body-building supplements
4. Grading on a pass/fail system

6e Why might I need to define key terms?

Key terms in an essay are the words central to its topic and message. While the meaning of some key terms might be readily evident in your writing, others may be open to interpretation. For example, abstract words such as *love, freedom,* and *democracy* have different meanings in different contexts. Therefore, if you want to argue that "Justice demands capital punishment in the case of murder," the definition of *justice* would be crucial to your argument.

Many students ask whether they can use dictionary definitions in their college writing. While you always want to look up words in a dictionary to understand their precise meanings, you want to avoid quoting directly from a dictionary, which is often seen as lacking in grace or SYNTHESIS. Avoid also the unappealing, inexact expression "according to Webster's" to introduce a definition. However, if the meaning of a word is complex, highly unfamiliar to most readers, or easily misinterpreted, you can indeed decide that a quoted dictionary definition would serve well. If you do, include the complete title of the dictionary you're citing: for example, *Webster's New World College Dictionary*, Fourth Edition.

6f What is the structure of a classical argument?

No single method is best for organizing all arguments, but a frequently used structure is the **classical argument.** The ancient Greeks and Romans developed this six-part structure which is described in Box 39 on the next page.

BACKGROUND

Classical persuasion consisted of six parts that represented six basic functions. Although the writer or orator was granted some flexibility in how and in what order the parts were presented, they provided effective guidelines for presenting an argument. Often used today, the six parts of an argument, according to the classical precept, are as follows:

1. *Exordium*, meaning "beginning a web." As an introduction, the purpose of the exordium is to attract the attention of the audience, indicate the subject, and favorably dispose the audience to what will follow.

2. *Narratio*. In this section, now usually referred to as "statement of fact," the issue is defined by stating pertinent facts about the subject. It is, therefore, basically expository.

3. *Partitio*. If the thesis has not yet been identified, it will be presented here, along with an indication of how the rest of the argument will be organized. The purpose of *partitio* is to prepare the reader or listener for what will follow.

4. *Confirmatio*. Arguments to support the thesis, forming the bulk of the piece, are developed at this point. The question of the order of presentation of arguments is critical to the effectiveness of the confirmation.

5. *Refutatio*. Opposing arguments are considered and rendered ineffective in the refutation section. To ignore them is to risk letting them appear to be more attractive than one's own thesis. The refutation may be placed at various points in the piece, depending on where it will be most effective.

6. *Peroratio*. The classical rhetoricians used a number of terms to indicate the conclusion of a piece; it usually furnished a summary of proofs and refutations, a restatement of the major points, and a re-creation of emotional and ethical appeals.

BOX 39   SUMMARY

The structure of a classical argument

1. **Introductory paragraph:** Sets the stage for the position argued in the essay. It gains the reader's interest and respect (4b).

2. **Thesis statement:** States the topic and position you want to argue (2q).

3. **Background information:** Gives readers the basic information they need for understanding your thesis and its support. As appropriate, you might include definitions of key terms (6e), historical or social context, prior scholarship, and other related material. You can include this as part of your introductory paragraph, or it can appear in its own paragraph placed immediately after the introduction.

4. **Evidence and reasons:** Supports the position you are arguing on the topic. This is the core of the essay. Each reason or piece of evidence usually consists of a general statement backed up with specific details, including examples and other RENNS (4f). Evidence needs to meet the standards for critical thinking (5g) and reasoning (5h through 5j) to be logical. Depending on the length of the essay, you might devote one or two paragraphs to each reason or type of evidence. For organization, you might choose to present the most familiar reasons and evidence first, saving the most unfamiliar for last. Alternatively, you might proceed from least important to most important point so that your essay builds to a climax, leaving the most powerful impact for the end. (For alternative ways to arrange paragraphs, consult 4h and 4i.)

5. **Response to opposing position:** Sometimes referred to as the *rebuttal* or *refutation*. This material mentions and defends against an opposite point of view. Often this refutation, which can be lengthy or brief according to the overall length of the essay, appears in its own paragraph or paragraphs, usually immediately before the concluding paragraph or immediately following the introductory paragraph, as a bridge to the rest of the essay. If you use the latter structure, you can choose to place your thesis statement either at the end of the introductory paragraph or at the end of the rebuttal paragraph. Yet another choice for structure consists of each paragraph's presenting one type of evidence or reason and then immediately stating and responding to the opposing position. (See 6k for advice on handling opposing arguments.)

6. **Concluding paragraph:** Ends the essay logically and gracefully— never abruptly. It often summarizes the argument, elaborates its significance, or calls readers to action (4k).

6g What is the Toulmin model for argument?

One powerful method of analyzing arguments is the **Toulmin model.**
This model defines three essential elements in an effective argument:
the claim, the support, and the warrants. They describe concepts that
you've encountered before, as Box 40 explains.

BOX 40   SUMMARY

 ### The Toulmin model of argument

Toulmin's Term	More Familiar Terms
claim	the main point or central message, usually expressed in the thesis statement
support	data or other evidence, from broad reasons to specific details
warrants	underlying assumptions, usually not stated but clearly implied; readers infer assumptions

---

Analyzed in Toulmin's terms, here's the argument in the student essay
written by Lacie Juris, the final draft of which appears in section 6m.

- **Claim:** Policymakers need to ban private ownership of wild animals as pets.
- **Support:** (1) Wild animals are dangerous to humans. (2) Domestication
  is hazardous to the animals themselves.
- **Warrants:** (1) We should outlaw situations that are dangerous to people.
  (2) We should outlaw situations that are dangerous to animals.

   The concept of *warrant* is similar to the concept of *inferences*, a key
component of reading critically (5d). Inferences are not stated outright but
are implied "between the lines" of the writing. Similarly, warrants are unspoken underlying assumptions in an argument. Consider the following
simple argument: "Johnson should not be elected mayor. She was recently
divorced." The claim is that Johnson shouldn't be elected. The support is
that Johnson has been divorced. The unstated warrant is "divorced people
are not qualified to be mayor." Before they can accept the claim that Johnson shouldn't be elected, readers have to accept this warrant. Of course, a
majority of readers would reject the warrant. Thus, this argument is weak.
To identify the warrants in an argument, ask "What do I need to assume so
that the support is sufficient for establishing each claim?"
   The concepts in the Toulmin model can help you write arguments
with a critical eye. They can be quite useful on their own as well as
applied to the CLASSICAL ARGUMENT structure (Box 39 in 6f). As you

TEACHING TIP
Persuasive writing has much in common with
argumentation. Both aim to lead the audience to agreement with the opinions of the
writer. Persuasion additionally attempts to induce the reader to commit to a particular
action. Advertising is probably the form of
persuasive writing we encounter most often
in the course of our daily lives. Because students enjoy looking at familiar advertisements in an analytical way, you may want to
ask them to bring their favorites to class,
or perhaps you will prefer to provide some.
Helpful background information is available
in such publications as *Advertising Age*.

QUOTATION: ON WRITING
For Toulmin, argument evaluation is field-
dependent. That is, arguments are not
judged good or bad on the basis of universal
and timeless criteria, but are determined to
be solid or defective on the basis of accepted
standards of the field in which they are used.
—Richard Fulkerson,
Teaching the Argument in Writing

BACKGROUND
According to Aristotle's *Rhetoric*, the conclusion of an argument can have as many as
four functions. It should create a favorable
impression toward the speaker and an un-
favorable impression toward the speaker's
opponents. It should emphasize the points
of the speaker while minimizing the points
of the opposition. It should appeal strongly to
the audience's emotions. And it should summarize the chief points of the argument.

ANSWERS: EXERCISE 6-2

1. *Claim:* The college should raise tuition.

Support: The football stadium is in such poor repair that the coach is having trouble recruiting players.

Warrants: Tuition and fees should go toward repairing the football stadium.

A football team is important to the college.

Repairing the stadium will improve recruiting.

2. *Claim:* People should vote against raising taxes.

Support: In the past two years, we have already had a 2 percent tax increase.

Warrants: Taxes are too high.

A 2 percent increase in the past two years is a good reason for not increasing taxes again.

3. *Claim:* The college should require all students to own laptop computers.

Support: Most students will have to use computers in their jobs after graduation.

Warrants: Students have to own computers in order to use them.

Owning a computer will help students get and keep a job.

read and revise your own arguments, identify the claim, support, and warrants. If you don't have a clear claim or support, you will likely have to assume that your argument is weak. Furthermore, make sure that each of your warrants will be convincing to readers. If they aren't, you need to provide backing, or reasons why the warrant is reasonable. For example, consider the following argument: "People should not receive a driver's license until the age of 25 because the accident rate for younger drivers is much higher than for older ones." One of the warrants here is that reducing the number of accidents should have highest priority. Obviously, many readers will not find that warrant convincing.

EXERCISE 6-2

Individually or with a peer-response group, discuss these simple arguments. Identify the claim, support, and warrants for each.

EXAMPLE   The college should establish an honor code. Last semester over fifty students were caught cheating on exams.

> **Claim:** The college should establish an honor code.
>
> **Support:** Last semester, over fifty students were caught cheating on exams.
>
> **Warrants:** Enough students cheat on exams that the college should address the problem.
>
> Cheating should be prevented.
>
> Students would not have cheated if there had been an honor code.

1. The college should raise student tuition and fees. The football stadium is in such poor repair that the coach is having trouble recruiting players.

2. Vote against raising our taxes. In the past two years, we have already had a 2 percent tax increase.

3. The college should require all students to own laptop computers. Most students will have to use computers in their jobs after graduation.

6h What part does audience play in my argument?

The PURPOSE of written argument is to convince your readers—your AUDIENCE—either to agree with you or to be open to your position. In writing an argument, you want to consider the degree of agreement you can expect from your readers. Will the audience be hostile or open-minded to your position? Will it resist or adopt your point of view?

The more emotionally charged a topic, the greater the chance that any position argued will elicit either strong agreement or strong disagreement. For example, abortion, school prayer, and gun control are emotionally loaded topics because they touch on matters of personal belief, including individual rights and religion. Topics such as the best responses to air pollution or bans on loud radios in recreation areas are usually less emotionally loaded. Even less emotionally loaded, yet still open to debate, would be whether computer X is better than computer Y. The degree to which you can expect your readers to be friendly or firmly opposed will influence your choice of strategies.

Rogerian argument, an approach that seeks common ground between points of view, might be an effective context for reaching readers when you're quite certain they'll disagree with you. The Rogerian approach is based on the principles of communication developed by the psychologist Carl Rogers. According to Rogers, communication is eased when people find common ground in their points of view. For example, the common ground in a debate over capital punishment might be that serious crimes are increasing in numbers and viciousness. Once both sides agree that this is the problem, they might be more willing to consider opposing opinions. Box 41 explains the structure of a Rogerian argument.

BOX 41   SUMMARY

The structure of a Rogerian argument

1. **Introduction:** Sets the stage for the position that is argued in the essay. It gains the reader's interest and respect (4b).
2. **Thesis statement:** States the topic and position you want to argue (2q and 6c).
3. **Common ground:** Explains the issue, acknowledging that your readers likely don't agree with you. Speculates and respectfully gives attention to the points of agreement you and your readers likely share concerning the underlying problem or issue about your topic. As appropriate, you might include definitions of key terms (6e), historical or social context, prior scholarship, and other related material. This may take one paragraph or several, depending on the complexity of the issue.
4. **Discussion of your position:** Gives evidence and reasons for your stand on the topic, elaborated similarly to the parallel material in classical argument (Box 39 in 6f).
5. **Concluding paragraph:** Summarizes why your position is preferable to your opponent's (4k).

BACKGROUND
The ideal format of a Rogerian argument, according to experts, is as follows:

Introduction. State the subject as a problem rather than as an issue to interest your audience in reading about something with which they disagree.

Fair statement of the opposing position. In this section, the writer states the reader's position in a manner that seems fair and accurate to the reader.

Statement of contexts in which that position may be valid. The writer tries to show readers that he or she understands their position by asserting that it is valid in some contexts.

Fair statement of the writer's position. The goal of this section is to get readers to understand the writer's position as fairly and thoroughly as the writer has understood theirs.

Statement of contexts in which the writer's position is valid. The writer tries to get readers to look at the problem from new perspectives and in new contexts.

Statement of how readers would benefit by adopting at least some elements of the writer's position. The writer appeals to readers' self-interest. In this section, the writer's position turns from a threat to a promise.

Aristotle believed that the most important element of persuasion wasn't the logical appeal, or the emotional appeal, but the ethical appeal—by which he meant both the force of the speaker's reputation and the qualities such as fair-mindedness and common sense—reflected in the argument itself.

—Sally DeWitt Spurgin

**OTHER EXAMPLES
OF APPEALS TO REASON**

Emotional Appeal

A child's world is fresh and new and beautiful, full of wonder and excitement. It is our misfortune that for most of us that clear-eyed vision, that true instinct for what is beautiful and awe-inspiring, is dimmed and even lost before we reach adulthood. If I had influence with the good fairy who is supposed to preside over the christening of all children I should ask that her gift to each child in the world be a sense of wonder so indestructible that it would last throughout life, as an unfailing antidote against the boredom and disenchantments of later years, the sterile preoccupation with things that are artificial, the alienation from the sources of our strength.

I sincerely believe that . . . it is not half so important to *know* as to *feel*. If facts are the seeds that later produce knowledge and wisdom, then the emotions and the impressions of the senses are the fertile soil in which the seeds must grow. The years of early childhood are the time to prepare the soil. Once the emotions have been aroused—a sense of the beautiful, the excitement of the new and the unknown, a feeling of sympathy, pity, admiration or love—then we wish for knowledge about the object of our emotional response.

—Rachel Carson,
The Sense of Wonder Ethical Appeal

→

In many instances, of course, you can't expect to change your reader's mind, though you can seek to convince your reader that your point of view has merit. People often "agree to disagree" in the best spirit of intellectual exchange. As you write a Rogerian argument, remember that your audience wants to see how effectively you've reasoned and presented your position. This stance approaches that of a formal oral debate in which all sides are explored with similar intellectual rigor.

6i How do I appeal to my audience by reasoning effectively in an argument?

A sound argument relies on three types of appeals to reason: logical, emotional, and ethical. Box 42 summarizes how to use the three appeals.

BOX 42 **SUMMARY**

 Guidelines for reasoning effectively in written argument

- **Be logical**: Use sound reasoning.
- **Enlist the emotions of the reader**: Appeal to the values and beliefs of the reader by arousing the reader's "better self."
- **Establish credibility**: Show that you as the writer can be relied on as a knowledgeable person with good sense.

The **logical appeal,** called *logos* by the ancient Greeks, is the most widely used appeal in arguments. The logic relies on evidence provided for claims and on sound reasoning (5g). When Lacie Juris argues that owning pets is dangerous, for example, she provides facts about deaths, injuries, and property damage. Logical writers analyze CAUSE AND EFFECT correctly. Also, they use appropriate patterns of INDUCTIVE REASONING and DEDUCTIVE REASONING, and they distinguish clearly between fact and opinion. Finally, sound reasoning means avoiding LOGICAL FALLACIES.

Emotional appeals, called *pathos* by the ancient Greeks, can be effective when used in conjunction with logical appeals. The word *emotional* has a specific meaning in this context: "arousing and enlisting the emotions of the reader." Used honestly and with restraint, emotional appeals arouse the audience's "better self" by eliciting sympathy, civic pride, or similar feelings based on values and beliefs. Effective emotional appeals use description and examples to stir emotions; they do not rely on sentimentality or biased, SLANTED LANGUAGE designed to exploit human feelings and thereby manipulate them.

In her essay, Juris uses an emotional appeal well in her sixth paragraph. By referring to baby wild animals whose "capture robs [them] of the chance to learn skills necessary for survival," Juris invokes the image of young and helpless creatures. At one point she writes, "Sadly, these animals never learned how to survive on their own." But she doesn't overdo it in her choice of language. Suppose she had written instead, "Picture these poor, innocent, forlorn animal babies racked with life-threatening hunger and viciously stalked by cruel beasts of the wild." Such words would be excessively dramatic, and the audience would resent being manipulated.

Ethical appeals, called *ethos* by the ancient Greeks, establish the credibility of the writer. Audiences don't trust a writer who states opinions as fact, distorts evidence, or makes claims that can't be supported. They do trust a writer who comes across as honest, knowledgeable, and fair. Ethical appeals can't take the place of logical appeals, but the two work well together. One effective way to make an ethical appeal is to draw on your personal experience. (Some college instructors don't want students to write in the first person, so check with your instructor before you try this technique.) For example, suppose you wanted to argue that prisoners should have access to education in jail. If you yourself had been the victim of a crime, you would have strong personal credibility for your position. Just be sure that any personal experience relates directly to the generalization you're supporting.

6j What is a reasonable tone in an argument?

A reasonable TONE tells your audience that you're being fair-minded. When you anticipate opposing positions and refute them with balanced language and emphasis, you demonstrate that you respect the other side. No matter how strongly you disagree with opposing arguments, never insult the other side. Name-calling reflects poor judgment and a lack of self-control. The saying "It's not what you say but how you say it" needs to be on your mind at all times as you write an argument. Avoid exaggerating, and never show anger. The more emotionally loaded a topic (for example, abortion or capital punishment), the more tempted you might be to use careless, harsh words. For instance, calling the opposing position "stupid" would say more about you as the writer than it would about the issue.

Other Examples of Appeals to Reason (continued)

Our tragedy today is a general and universal physical fear so long sustained by now that we can even bear it. There are no longer problems of the spirit. There is only the question: When will I be blown up? Because of this, the young man or woman writing today has forgotten the problems of the human heart in conflict with itself which alone can make good writing because only this is worth writing about, worth the agony and the sweat.

He must learn them again. He must teach himself that the basest of all things is to be afraid; and, teaching himself that, forget it forever, leaving no room in his workshop for anything but the old verities and truths of the heart, the old universal truths lacking which any story is ephemeral and doomed—love and honor and pity and pride and compassion and sacrifice. Until he does so, he labors under a curse. He writes not of love but of lust, of defeats in which nobody loses anything of value, of victories without hope and, worst of all, without pity or compassion. His griefs grieve on no universal bones, leaving no scars. He writes not of the heart but of the glands.

—William Faulkner,
Nobel Prize acceptance speech

QUOTATION: ON WRITING
Real communication occurs . . . when we listen with understanding. What does this mean? It means to see the expressed idea and attitude from the other person's point of view, to sense how it feels to him, to achieve his frame of reference in regard to the thing he is talking about.

—Carl Rogers

ANSWERS: EXERCISE 6-3

The e-mail is rich with emotional and ethical appeals. A few examples follow.

Ethical appeals:

Author claims she is humble.

Author appears to be sensitive to the reader's concerns, noting possible apprehensions and offering assurances.

Author asserts that she is a Christian and expresses trust in the reader.

Author says "Thank you and God bless."

Emotional appeals:

Author claims her father was killed by rebels.

Author portrays herself as unknowledgeable and uncertain (for example, she doesn't know where to invest the money; she needs the help of a "trusted" foreigner).

EXTRA EXERCISE D

Analyze the following paragraphs to discover the dominant appeal of each.

1. We observe today not a victory of party but a celebration of freedom—symbolizing an end as well as a beginning—signifying renewal as well as change. For I have sworn before you and Almighty God the same solemn oath our forebears prescribed nearly a century and three quarters ago.

The world is very different now. For man holds in his mortal hands the power to abolish all forms of human poverty and all forms of human life. And yet the same revolutionary beliefs for which our forebears fought are still at issue around the globe—the belief that the rights of man come not from the generosity of the state but from the hand of God.

We dare not forget today that we are the heirs of that first revolution. Let the word go forth from this time and place, to friend and foe alike, that the torch has been passed to a new generation of Americans—born in this century, tempered by war; disciplined by a hard and bitter peace, proud of our ancient heritage—and unwilling to witness or permit the slow undoing of those human rights to which this nation has always been committed,

→

EXERCISE 6-3

Here is the text of a notorious e-mail fraud that has been sent to many people. Hundreds of variations of this e-mail exist, but usually the writer claims to have a large amount of money that he or she wants to transfer to an American bank. The writer wants the recipient's help in making the transfer. This is a complete lie. The writer has no money and is trying to trick people into revealing their bank account numbers and then steal their money.

Either alone or in a small group, examine the ways this writer tries to establish emotional and ethical appeals. *Note*: I have reproduced the e-mail with the often incorrect original wording, grammar, and punctuation.

Good day,

It is my humble pleasure to write this letter irrespective of the fact that you do not know me. However, I came to know of you in my private search for a reliable and trustworthy person that can handle a confidential transaction of this nature in respect of this, I got your contact through an uprooted search on the internet. Though I know that a transaction of this magnitude will make any one apprehensive and worried, but I am assuring you that all will be well at the end of the day.

I am Ruth Malcasa, daughter of late Mr James Malcasa of Somalia, who was killed by the Somalian rebel forces on the 24th of December,1999 in my country Somalia. When he was still alive, he deposited one trunk box containing the sum of USD$10 million dollars in cash (Ten Million dollars). with a private security and safe deposit company here in Lagos Nigeria. This money was made from the sell of Gold and Diamond by my mother and she has already decided to use this money for future investment of the family.

My father instructed me that in the case of his death, that I should look for a trusted foreigner who can assist me to move out this money from Nigeria immediately for investment. Based on this, I solicit for your assistance to transfer this fund into your Account, but I will demand for the following requirement: (1) Could you provide for me a safe Bank Account where this fund will be transferred to in your country after retrieving the box containing the money from the custody of the security company. (2) Could you be able to introduce me to a profitable business venture that would not require much technical expertise in your country where part of this fund will be invested?

I am a Christian and I want you to handle this transaction based on the trust I have established on you. For your assistance in this transaction, I have decided to compensate you with 10 percent of the total amount at the end of this business. The security of this business is very important to me and as such, I would like you to keep this business very confidential. I shall expect an early response from you. Thank you and God bless. Yours sincerely, Ruth Malcasa.

6k How do I handle opposing arguments?

Dealing with opposing positions is crucial to writing an effective argument. If you don't acknowledge arguments that your opponents might raise and explain why they are faulty or inferior, you create doubts that you have thoroughly explored the issue. You risk looking narrow-minded.

The next to last paragraph in Juris's paper (6m), which summarizes opposing arguments, strengthens both her ethos and her logic. She is so confident in her own position that she can state the possible opponents' argument that owners will be able to control their wild pets. Then she provides reasons why that argument is wrong. Juris had encountered this counterargument while doing her research. While you do research for your own arguments, you need to look for essays, articles, and opinions that oppose your position, not only ones that agree with yours.

If your research doesn't generate opposing arguments, you need to develop them yourself. Imagine that you're debating someone who disagrees with you; what positions would they take and why? Note that you can ask a classmate or friend to perform this role. Another strategy is to take the opposite side of the argument and try to develop the best reasons you can for that position. (In some formal debating situations, people are expected to prepare both sides of an issue and only learn immediately before the debate which position they are to argue.)

Once you have generated opposing arguments, you need to refute them, which means to show why they are weak or undesirable. Imagine that you're writing about national security and individual rights. You believe that the government should not be allowed to monitor a private citizen's e-mail without a court order, and you have developed a number of reasons for your position. To strengthen your paper, you also generate some opposing arguments, including "People will be safer from terrorism if police can monitor e-mail," "Only people who have something to hide have anything to fear," and "It is unpatriotic to oppose the government's plans." How might you refute these claims? Following are some suggestions.

- **Examine the evidence for each opposing argument** (5g). Look especially for missing or contradictory facts (5j). In the given example, you might question the evidence that people would be safer from terrorism if police could monitor e-mail.
- **Use the Toulmin model to analyze the opposing argument** (6g). What are the claims, support, and warrants? Often it's possible to show that the warrants are questionable or weak. For example, a warrant in the counterarguments above is that the promise of increased safety is worth the price of privacy or individual rights. You might show why this warrant is undesirable.
- **Demonstrate that an opposing argument depends on emotion rather than reasoning.** The assertion that it is unpatriotic to oppose the government is primarily an emotional one.

Sample Answers to Extra Exercise D

1. In his Inaugural Address, John F. Kennedy makes extensive use of ethical appeal. By referring to the "solemn oath" he has just taken before God and the American people, he calls attention to his commitment to work for what is good and right. When, in reference to the complexity of the modern world, he again invokes the name of God as the source of "the rights of man," he underscores the high moral calling of his office. In the final paragraph, he appeals to the ethical sense of the audience by exhorting citizens to join him in the struggle to make a better world. By using the pronoun *we*, he repledges himself to work with all Americans for the spread and preservation of the beliefs on which this country was founded.

2. James Baldwin's comments about Riverton seethe with anger, bitterness, and even hatred. The strong emotions that the reader hears and feels emanate not only from words such as "violent bitterness of spirit," "hated it," "hating it," and "despised them" but also from the images of destruction that he provides: "smashing windows, defacing walls, urinating in the elevators, and fornicating in the playgrounds." Any positive term that Baldwin uses, such as "improvement," he puts in quotation marks, suggesting its unreality.

ANSWERS: EXERCISE 6-4
Answers will vary.

- **Redefine key terms.** The term "patriotism" can be defined in various ways. You might point out, for example, that at the time of the American Revolution, "patriots" were the people who were opposing the British government then in power.

- **Explain the negative consequences of the opposing position.** Imagine that the opposing position actually won out, and explain how the results would be damaging. For example, if everyone knew that government officials might monitor their computer use, consider how this might affect free speech. Would people hesitate to order a book about Islam?

- **Concede an opposing point, but explain that doing so doesn't destroy your own argument.** For example, you might decide to concede that governmental monitoring of e-mails could reduce terrorism. However, you might argue that the increase in safety is not worth the threat to privacy and personal freedom.

- **Explain that the costs of the other position are not worth the benefits.**

EXERCISE 6-4

Individually or with a peer-response group, practice developing objections to specific arguments and responses to those objections. To do this, choose a debatable topic and brainstorm a list of points on that topic, some on one side of the topic, some on another. Following are some arguments to get you started. If you're part of a group, work together to assign the different positions for each topic to different sets of students. Then, conduct a brief debate on which side has more merit, with each side taking turns. At the end, your group can vote for the side that is more convincing.

1. It should be legal/illegal to ride motorcycles without a helmet.
2. Women should/should not expect pay equal to men's for the same work.
3. Students should/should not be required to take certain courses in order to graduate.

6l How did one student draft and revise her argument essay?

Lacie Juris chose the topic of the essay shown in section 6m because of her career interest in being a zookeeper. Her preliminary reading on the Internet about keeping wild animals as pets led her to develop a thesis statement (see 6d). In a discovery draft, Juris focused on why it was unfair to wild animals to be kept as pets, but she realized that she would need to be more precise. That led to her argument that being kept as a pet could be harmful to the animal. In a second draft, she realized that harm to animals might not by itself be convincing to members of her audience. She then developed a second main point, that pet wild animals could be dangerous to people. Knowing that this claim required evidence, Juris did further research in databases and on the Internet to find the support she needed.

In a third draft, Juris considered some opposing arguments to her position. She also looked carefully at her use of pathos and ethos. At one point she realized that she was relying on excessively emotional language, which she knew could turn off some readers, so she revised several sentences. Also, she consulted the revision checklist (Box 17 in 3c). Finally, she referred to the special checklist for revising written arguments in Box 43.

TEACHING TIP
Most newspapers, including campus newspapers, carry numerous pieces of persuasive discourse in the letters to the editor, daily columns, and editorials. You may want to ask students to bring examples to class that can be analyzed in terms of assertions and thesis, as well as the order and means of development.

A different kind of experience, but an equally interesting one, can come from analysis of a longer, more sustained argument, such as Thoreau's essay "Civil Disobedience" or Martin Luther King Jr.'s "Letter from Birmingham Jail."

ANSWERS: EXERCISE 6-5
Answers will vary.

BOX 43   CHECKLIST

Revising written arguments

- Is the thesis statement about a debatable topic? (6b and 6c)
- Do the reasons or evidence support the thesis statement? Are the generalizations supported by specific details? (6f)
- Does the argument deal with reader needs and concerns? (6h)
- Does the argument appeal chiefly to reason? Is it supported by an ethical appeal? If it uses an emotional appeal, is the appeal restrained? (6i)
- Is the tone reasonable? (6j)
- Is the opposing position stated and refuted? (6k)

EXERCISE 6-5

Working individually or with a peer-response group, choose a topic from this list. Then plan an essay that argues a debatable position on the topic. Apply all the principles you've learned in this chapter.

1. Animal experimentation
2. Luxury taxes for sports utility vehicles
3. Cloning of human beings
4. Celebrity endorsements
5. Value of space exploration
6. Laws requiring seat belt use

QUOTATION: ON WRITING

To persuade, there are two things which must be carefully studied by the orator. The first is to excite some desire or passion in the hearers; the second is to satisfy their judgment that there is a connection between the action to which he would persuade them and the gratification of the desire or passion he excites.

—George Campbell

QUOTATION: ON WRITING

We seldom defend a view that we do not favor and we often assume that any view we favor is true. Hence, when we are constructing arguments in support of our views, it often happens that we simply assume the view we should be proving.

—Alex. C. Michalos

QUOTATION: ON WRITING

Many suffer from the incurable disease of writing, and it becomes chronic in their sick minds.

—Juvenal

BACKGROUND

In "Teaching Critical Thinking in First-Year Composition: Sometimes More is More" (*Teaching English in the Two-Year College*, December 2001: 162–171), Ruth Stewart advocates teaching argument by having students analyze primary source materials. In order to make sure that students focus on critical thinking, she provides materials and asks them to argue positions from them. Stewart details her approach by explaining how her students used documents from the 1763 Conestoga Massacre.

| 6m | **Final draft of a student's argument essay in MLA style** |

Juris 1

HEADING Lacie Juris

Professor Calhoon-Dillahunt

English 101

16 June 2003

TITLE   Lions, Tigers, and Bears, Oh My!

INTRODUCTION: Captures reader's attention   Fuzzy, orange, and white tiger cubs playfully fight over a chew toy while baby chimps hang precariously in front of the nursery window, looking almost human with their big ears and adorable expressions. They look so cute at the zoo. Wouldn't it be exciting to have one for your very own, to play with in your living room and show off to your neighbors? It would be a childhood fantasy come true--and for many people living in the United States, it is. Tigers, for example, cost the same as purebred puppies. Animal-rights advocates estimate that as many tigers are kept as pets in the United States as exist in the wild worldwide (Boehm). Unfortunately, these exotic dreams come true can turn deadly at any moment. Because regulation of wild animal ownership varies from county to county in the United States, laws are difficult to enforce ("Wild Animals Are

THESIS STATEMENT Not"). To eliminate dangerous situations for both people and animals alike, policymakers need to ban private ownership of wild animals as pets.

BODY: Logical appeal—first main point   Wild animals are dangerous to humans, both owners and nearby residents. Wild animals have inborn behavior patterns and instincts, such as stalking prey, attacking when threatened, and defending themselves. Such patterns remain no matter where or how the animals grow up, no matter how well the

Juris 2

owners train them for domesticated living. This is what makes

the animals truly wild. Humans cannot influence, change, or

even predict the wild behaviors of animals. An attack can occur

at any time when their wild instincts take over without warning

("Wild Animals Are Not"). In fact, in the past three years,

authorities blame pet tigers for at least seven deaths and thirty-

one injuries (Davenport). In addition, wild pets can cause

tremendous property damage, as illustrated by the case of Stoli,

a tiger who caused $20,000 worth of damage to his owner's

Mercedes in less than five minutes ("Stoli and Lil").

Anecdote to support thesis and bolster logical appeal

Many animal owners teach their young exotic pets little

games and tricks. Owners don't realize, however, that when the

wild animals have grown to three or four times the strength of

most people, the "pets" still expect to take part in the same

games and tricks. Take, for example, the story of a pet African

Serval named Kenya. Servals are known as "leaping cats," with

the capacity to jump twelve feet straight up and run forty-five

miles an hour. Kenya belonged to a woman who purchased him

at a pet store. Because Kenya was small, he seemed like the

perfect "exotic pet." However, no one told the woman about

Servals' amazing jumping abilities--or about their becoming

extremely territorial as adults. At home, the woman taught the

baby Kenya to leap onto her shoulder, without realizing that she

was actually teaching him to leap onto people in general. In

addition, as he grew, he became so territorial that he attacked

anyone who would come to her house ("Kenya").

Additional logical appeal

Another little-realized fact is that wild animals greatly

endanger owners and people in the surrounding areas by

transmitting diseases. When people purchase exotic animals,

→

QUOTATION: ON WRITING
I find the process of writing very difficult, and often painful, but I love to revise. For me, this involves polishing, listening to the rhythm of sentences and making sure I've heard them right, cutting out excess words, varying sentence structure, eliminating repetition.

—Susan Allen Toth

QUOTATION: ON WRITING
I write double-spaced to leave plenty of room for the inevitable revisions and I never write on both sides of the paper. I write on a right-hand page, leaving the facing page blank for insertions and revisions. Then I leave the following double-page blank.

—Len Deighton

QUOTATION: ON WRITING
The art of writing has for backbone some fierce attachment to an idea.

—Virginia Woolf

Juris 3

no one tells them if the animals are carrying diseases. Wild animals can host internal parasites, such as ascarid worms, tapeworms, flukes, and protozoa, all of which can be debilitating or even fatal to their human caretakers--especially their small children. The animals can also carry the external parasites that cause spotted fever and bubonic plague ("Questions" 3). In addition, no known vaccination can protect wild animals from rabies ("Rabies").

Transition to second main point While the risk to humans of exotic pet ownership is very high, domestication is hazardous to the animals themselves. After all, wild animals need specific and natural environments to survive. Such settings do not include humans, houses, or backyard kennels. Owners of wild animals usually lack the knowledge and funds to re-create the animal's environment or to provide proper nutrition, let alone care for the animals if they were to become sick or injured (Boehm). Very few, if any, professional veterinarians are trained or willing to work on wild animals.

Emotional appeal Usually, infant wild animals are stolen from their parents at only a few weeks, or even days, of life. Their capture robs the babies of the chance to learn skills necessary for survival if they are ever abandoned or re-released into the wild. These animals often develop stress and behavior disorders because they have never experienced social interaction with their own species ("Wild Animals Are Not"). Eventually, many owners become frightened or confused by sudden behavior problems with their "little babies," and they decide to leave the animals in remote places to fend for themselves. Sadly, these animals never learned how to survive on their own. As a result, they starve to death, or they seek out human

→

Juris 4

habitation for food, which frequently ends in their death at the hands of frightened people ("Wild Animals Do Not").

Summary of opposing arguments   Some people may argue for the benefits of personal ownership of wild animals. It allows ordinary people to enjoy exotic pets in their own homes. These people insist that they can safety restrict their wild animals' movements to their own property. Further, defenders of the private possession of wild animals argue that owners can help preserve endangered species. Increasingly, however, exotic pet owners' fantasies turn into nightmares as the wild animals become adults increasingly controlled by their basic instincts and inbred behaviors. Owners often expect local animal control agencies or animal sanctuaries to deal with their problems, even though such facilities are already over capacity or are staffed by people unequipped to deal with undomesticated animals (Milloy).

CONCLUSION   Keeping wild animals as pets must be outlawed. Though exotic creatures may look like Simba or Tigger, they are still completely wild, and it is in the wild that they belong. As pointed out in "Wild Animals Are Not Pets," "The only ones who benefit from the practice of sales of exotic animals as pets are the breeders and sellers. These people make an enormous amount of money by exploiting these animals once they are sold." Poachers also profit when they capture baby wild animals from their native habitats and sell them as pets to the highest bidder. The best way for humans to see and experience wild animals in safe environments is to visit and support zoos and wildlife parks that specialize in providing professionally constructed natural habitats for animals. In such settings, people can enjoy twild animals without putting humans and the animals at risk.

→

QUOTATION: ON WRITING
I think of my first draft as a beautiful piece of marble. That is what is given; it is the gift that is given. But the hard work—how I earn the gift—is what I make out of it.

—Julia Alvarez

QUOTATION: ON WRITING
Dr. King prepared a text for the march on Washington address during the early morning hours of August 28, 1963. Several of his close advisers worked with him for many hours, passing revisions back and forth.

—D. Louise Cook

QUOTATION: ON WRITING
The exigence of the situation provides the motivation to write about the issue in the first place. Issues often emerge from real-life events that signal something is wrong.
—Nancy V. Wood

BACKGROUND
Andrea Greenbaum's book *Emancipatory Movements in Composition: The Rhetoric of Possibility* (Albany: SUNY Press, 2002) argues that first-year writing teachers should help students develop abilities to think and argue clearly as citizens in a democracy. Greenbaum synthesizes recent developments in rhetorical theory.

Juris 5

Works Cited

Boehm, Ted. "A New Local Worry: Exotic Cats—Lion and Tiger Prices Fall, and Once Rare Pets Become a Costly Menace." Wall Street Journal 30 June 2000: B1.

Davenport, Christian. "Fighting the Lure of the Wild: Danger of Exotic Animals as Pets Spurs Quest for Regulation." Washington Post 11 Mar. 2002: B1.

"Kenya." 1999. Cat Tales Zoological Park. 19 May 2003 <http://cattales.org/kenya.html>.

Milloy, Ross E. "Banning Lions and Other Large Pets." New York Times 10 Dec. 2001: A19.

"Questions and Answers about Captive Exotic and Wild Animals as Pets." 2002. 3 pp. Humane Society of the United States. 11 June 2003 <http://www.hsus.org/ace/12055>.

"Rabies and Animal Bites." York County Virginia. 6 June 2003 <http://www.yorkcounty.gov/fls/ac/rabies.htm>.

"Stoli and Lil." 1999. Cat Tales Zoological Park. 19 May 2003 <http://cattales.org/stolilil.html>.

"Wild Animals Are Not Pets." 2001. The Wild Animal Orphanage. 19 May 2003 <http://www.wildanimalorphanage.org/wild.html>.

"Wild Animals Do Not Make Good Pets." 1999. Cat Tales Zoological Park. 19 May 2003 <http://cattales.org/notapet.html>.

Part Two

Understanding Grammar and Writing Correct Sentences

BACKGROUND
Grammar is one of the oldest fields of study in Western education. Greek and Roman boys were enrolled in grammar schools to study language and literature in preparation for the study of rhetoric in their adolescence. The *praelectio* was the central exercise of these schools. After reading a model of good or bad writing, the teacher dissected it meticulously and systematically, one word and sometimes one syllable at a time. The *praelectio* identified parts of speech, inflections, gender, meter, figures of speech, and other grammatical and stylistic concerns in the model; provided background about the work; discussed its meaning; noted errors and ineffective passages; and praised eloquent passages. As students advanced, they analyzed the works themselves, answering the teacher's questions. In turn, each student's composition was also subject to the same microanalysis.

Chapter 7

Parts of Speech and Sentence Structures

PARTS OF SPEECH

7a Why learn the parts of speech?

Knowing the names and definitions of parts of speech gives you a vocabulary for identifying words and understanding how language works to create meaning. No part of speech exists in a vacuum. To identify a word's part of speech correctly, you need to see how the word functions in a sentence. Sometimes the same word functions differently in different sentences, so check the part of speech used in each instance.

> We ate **fish.** [*Fish* is a noun. It names a thing.]
> We **fish** on weekends. [*Fish* is a verb. It names an action.]

7b What is a noun?

A **noun** names a person, place, thing, or idea: *student, college, textbook, education.* Box 44 on the facing page lists different kinds of nouns.

🌐 **ESL NOTES:** Here are some useful tips for working with nouns.

- Nouns often appear with words that tell how much or how many, whose, which one, and similar information. These words include ARTICLES* (a, an, the) and other determiners or limiting adjectives; see 7f and Chapter 46.

- Nouns sometimes serve as ADJECTIVES. For example, in the term *police officer*, the word *police* serves as an adjective to describe *officer.*

* Find the definition of all words in small capital letters (such as ARTICLES) in the Terms Glossary at the back of this book directly before the Index.

```
┌──────────── BOX 44    SUMMARY ┐
```

⟳ Nouns

PROPER	names specific people, places, or things (first letter is always capitalized)	*Garth Brooks, Paris, Buick*
COMMON	names general groups, places, people, or things	*singer, city, automobile*
CONCRETE	names things experienced through the senses: sight, hearing, taste, smell, and touch	*landscape, pizza, thunder*
ABSTRACT	names things not knowable through the senses	*freedom, shyness*
COLLECTIVE	names groups	*family, team*
NONCOUNT OR MASS	names "uncountable" things	*water, time*
COUNT	names countable items	*lake, minute*

- Nouns in many languages other than English are inflected. This means they change form, usually with a special ending, to communicate gender (male, female, neuter); number (singular, plural); and case (see 9a through 9k).
- Words with these suffixes (word endings) are usually nouns: *-ness, -ence, -ance, -ty,* and *-ment.* ⊕

7c What is a pronoun?

A **pronoun** takes the place of a NOUN. The words or word that a pronoun replaces is called the pronoun's ANTECEDENT. See Box 45 on the next page for a list of different kinds of pronouns. For information on how to use pronouns correctly, see Chapters 9 and 10.

David is an accountant. [noun]
He is an accountant. [pronoun]
The finance committee needs to consult **him.** [The pronoun *him* refers to its antecedent *David.*]

TEACHING TIP: ESL

ESL students may have questions about the difference in usage between indefinite *a* or *an* and definite *the*. In sentence 3 in Exercise 7-1, the article *a* is used because the nouns *lobster* and *mask* are mentioned for the first time. (The "first mention" rule applies only to singular countable nouns, not to plurals like *humans, scientists, experiments,* and *treadmills.*) In sentence 5, *a* and *an* mean "one," reflecting their historical origin; the indefinite articles developed from the Anglo-Saxon word for *one.*

The refers to a noun that is definite, often because it has already been mentioned ("the lobster," "the mask," "the crustacean," which is a synonym for *lobster*) or because the context makes it specific, usually with a phrase ("of the crustacean") or clause ("that they are studying") following the noun. See Chapter 46.

ANSWERS: EXERCISE 7-1

1. Not only humans^N use them.^{P}

2. Scientists^N conduct experiments^N by placing lobsters^N on treadmills.^{N}

3. Scientists^N can study a lobster^N when it^P is fitted with a small mask.^{N}

4. The mask^N allows researchers^N to monitor the crustacean's^N heartbeat.^{N}

5. The lobster^N may reach speeds^N of a half-mile^N or more an hour.^{N}

BOX 45   SUMMARY

🌀 Pronouns

PERSONAL *I, you, its, her, they, ours,* and others	refers to people or things	*I saw **her** take a book to **them.***
RELATIVE *who, which, that*	introduces certain NOUN CLAUSES and ADJECTIVE CLAUSES	*The book **that** I lost was valuable.*
INTERROGATIVE *which, who, whose,* and others	introduces a question	***Who** called?*
DEMONSTRATIVE *this, that, these, those*	points out the ANTECEDENT	*Whose books are **these?***
REFLEXIVE OR INTENSIVE *myself, themselves,* and other *-self* or *-selves* words	reflects back to the antecedent; intensifies the antecedent	*They claim to support **themselves. I myself** doubt it.*
RECIPROCAL *each other, one another*	refers to individual parts of a plural antecedent	*We respect **each other.***
INDEFINITE *all, anyone, each,* and others	refers to nonspecific persons or things	***Everyone** is welcome here.*

EXERCISE 7-1

Underline and label all nouns (N) and pronouns (P). Refer to 7a through 7c for help.

EXAMPLE $\overset{N}{\underline{Treadmills}}$ help $\overset{N}{\underline{people}}$ achieve $\overset{N}{\underline{fitness}}$ and $\overset{N}{\underline{rehabilitation}}$.

1. Not only humans use them.
2. Scientists conduct experiments by placing lobsters on treadmills.
3. Scientists can study a lobster when it is fitted with a small mask.
4. The mask allows researchers to monitor the crustacean's heartbeat.
5. The lobster may reach speeds of a half-mile or more an hour.

7d What is a verb?

Main verbs express action, occurrence, or state of being. For information on how to use verbs correctly, see Chapter 8.

> I **dance.** [action]
> The audience **became** silent. [occurrence]
> Your dancing **was** excellent. [state of being]

👁 **ALERT:** If you're not sure whether a word is a verb, try substituting a different TENSE for the word. If the sentence still makes sense, the word is a verb.

> **NO** He is a **changed** man. He is a **will change** man. [*Changed* isn't a verb because the sentence doesn't make sense when *change* is substituted.]
>
> **YES** The man **changed** his profession. The man **will change** his profession. [*Changed* is a verb because the sentence makes sense when the verb *will change* is substituted.] 👁

EXERCISE 7-2

Underline all verbs. Refer to 7d for help.

> **EXAMPLE** The history of eyeglasses <u>reveals</u> a long road to a simple design.

1. People used a magnifying lens as a reading glass about AD 1000.
2. An Italian invented the first eyeglasses in 1284.
3. For centuries, people held eyeglasses to their eyes with their hands or nose.
4. In the 1700s, a French optician added three-inch wires on both sides of the glasses.
5. Finally, in the eighteenth century, an English optician lengthened the wires to the ears.

7e What is a verbal?

Verbals are verb parts functioning as NOUNS, ADJECTIVES, or ADVERBS. Box 46 on the next page lists the three different kinds of verbals.

🌐 **ESL NOTE:** For information about correctly using the verbals called infinitives and gerunds as objects, see Chapter 49. 🌐

TEACHING TIP

Using the most appropriate verb can make the difference between a vague sentence and a meaningful one. You might stimulate a lively discussion if you ask students to explain the differences in meanings (and to compose a sentence for each meaning) of these verbs that deal with the same subjects.

1. stride, march, glide, strut
2. gobble, nibble, devour, eat
3. giggle, guffaw, chuckle, snicker

QUOTATION: ON WRITING

Just as verbs and actions go together, so do subjects and characters. There are different kinds of characters. Usually—but not always—the most important characters are the agents of actions, the source of action, or the condition that the writer is describing.

—Joseph M. Williams,
Style: Toward Clarity and Grace

ANSWERS: EXERCISE 7-2

1. People <u>used</u> a magnifying lens as a reading glass about AD 1000.
2. An Italian <u>invented</u> the first eyeglasses in 1284.
3. For centuries, people <u>held</u> eyeglasses to their eyes with their hands or nose.
4. In the 1700s, a French optician <u>added</u> three-inch wires on both sides of the glasses.
5. Finally, in the eighteenth century, an English optician <u>lengthened</u> the wires to the ears.

TEACHING TIP

To give students a sense of the range of uses for -*ing* words, you might hand out a list of -*ing* words and ask your students to use each word in three different sentences: in one as a noun, in another as an adjective, and in a third as part of a verb phrase. As another step, you can collect the sentences and select twenty-five to thirty to reproduce and distribute. Then, for an exercise or quiz, ask the students to identify each -*ing* word as a noun, an adjective, or part of a verb phrase. Often, the author of a sentence is eager for others to get the identification correct and is therefore quite willing to explain the answer.

TEACHING TIP: ESL

An inductive way to help students discover and thus remember the differences among -*ing* forms is to have them circle the forms in a piece of writing and discuss which type is used: participles (adjectives), gerunds (nouns), or parts of verb phrases. For example, they could exchange papers with other students and then analyze and discuss all the -*ing* forms. See Chapter 49.

BACKGROUND

Knowing whether to use the article *a* or *an* before words that start with the consonant *h* can be a vexing problem for writers. In "Jericho, Trumpets, Walls, Etc.," William Safire solves this dilemma by using the words *history*, *historian*, and *historic* as examples. He proposes that article discrimination depends on which syllable, the first or the second, is emphasized. For instance, phonetic emphasis of the noun *history* falls on the first syllable, so we write "*a* history." By contrast, when pronouncing the adjective *historic*, emphasis falls on the second syllable, "turning the initial *h* into a wimp, requiring a consonant to firm it up: *an historian* covering *an historic* event." (This contradicts the more modern view presented in 7f.)

	BOX 46 SUMMARY

Verbals and their functions

INFINITIVE	1. noun	***To eat*** *now is inconvenient.*
to + verb	2. adjective or adverb	*Still, we have far* ***to go.***
PAST PARTICIPLE -*ed* form of REGULAR VERB or equivalent in IRREGULAR VERB	adjective	***Boiled, filtered*** *water is safe.*
PRESENT PARTICIPLE -*ing* form of verb	1. noun (called a GERUND) 2. adjective	***Eating*** *in diners on the road is an adventure.* ***Running*** *water may not be safe.*

7f What is an adjective?

Adjectives modify—that is, they describe or limit—NOUNS, PRONOUNS, and word groups that function as nouns. For information on how to use adjectives correctly, see Chapter 11.

> I saw a **green** tree. [*Green* modifies the noun *tree*.]
> It was **leafy**. [*Leafy* modifies the pronoun *it*.]
> The flowering trees were **beautiful**. [*Beautiful* modifies the noun phrase *the flowering trees*.]

ESL NOTE: You can identify some kinds of adjectives by looking at their endings. Usually, words with the SUFFIXES -*ful*, -*ish*, -*less*, and -*like* are adjectives.

Determiners, frequently called **limiting adjectives,** tell whether a noun is general (*a* tree) or specific (*the* tree). Determiners also tell which one (*this* tree), how many (*twelve* trees), whose (*our* tree), and similar information.

The determiners *a*, *an*, and *the* are almost always called **articles.** *The* is a **definite article.** Before a noun, *the* conveys that the noun refers to a specific item (*the* plan). *A* and *an* are **indefinite articles.** They convey that a noun refers to an item in a nonspecific or general way (*a* plan).

👁 **ALERT:** Use *a* when the word following it starts with a consonant: *a carrot, a broken egg, a hip.* Also, use *a* when the word following starts with an *h* that is sounded: *a historical event, a home.* Use *an* when the word following starts with a vowel sound: *an honor, an old bag, an egg.* 👁

🌐 **ESL NOTE:** For information about using articles with COUNT and NONCOUNT NOUNS, and about articles with PROPER NOUNS and GERUNDS, see Chapter 46. 🌐

Box 47 lists kinds of determiners. Notice, however, that some words in Box 47 function also as PRONOUNS. To identify a word's part of speech, always check to see how it functions in each particular sentence.

That car belongs to Harold. [*That* is a demonstrative adjective.]
That is Harold's car. [*That* is a demonstrative pronoun.]

BOX 47   SUMMARY

 Determiners (or limiting adjectives)

ARTICLES
a, an, the

*The news reporter used **a** cellphone to report **an** assignment.*

DEMONSTRATIVE
this, these, that, those

***Those** students rent **that** house.*

INDEFINITE
any, each, few, other, some, and others

***Few** films today have complex plots.*

INTERROGATIVE
what, which, whose

***What** answer did you give?*

NUMERICAL
one, first, two, second, and others

*The **fifth** question was tricky.*

POSSESSIVE
my, your, their, and others

***My** violin is older than **your** cello.*

RELATIVE
what, which, whose, whatever, and others

*We do not know **which** road to take.*

TEACHING TIP
To help students become aware of adverbs and how they function, you may want to provide a series of sentences that have blanks to be filled in with appropriate adverbs. Here is an example:

The cat sat _____ under the kitchen table, _____ watching the mouse scampering _____ly, _____ly, almost _____ly.

BACKGROUND
In "Grammar for Writers: How Much Is Enough?" in *The Place of Grammar in Writing Instruction: Past, Present, Future,* edited by Susan Hunter and Ray Wallace (Portsmouth, NH: Boynton-Cook, 1995), R. Baird Shuman addresses the ongoing debate about the value of grammar instruction and provides exercises designed to help students both understand the vocabulary of grammar and develop a repertoire of strategies related to recognizing options of style.

QUOTATION ON WRITING
Grammar is more a way of thinking, a style of inquiry, than a way of being right.
—Mina P. Shaughnessy,
Errors and Expectations

7g What is an adverb?

Adverbs modify—that is, adverbs describe or limit—VERBS, ADJECTIVES, other adverbs, and CLAUSES. For information on how to use adverbs correctly, see Chapter 11.

Chefs plan meals **carefully**. [*Carefully* modifies the verb *plan*.]
Vegetables provide **very** important vitamins. [*Very* modifies the adjective *important*.]
Those potato chips are **too** heavily salted. [*Too* modifies the adverb *heavily*.]
Fortunately, people are learning that overuse of salt is harmful. [*Fortunately* modifies the rest of the sentence, an independent clause.]

Descriptive adverbs show levels of intensity, usually by adding *more* (or *less*) and *most* (or *least*): *more* happily, *least* clearly (see section 11e). Many descriptive adverbs are formed by adding *-ly* to adjectives: *sadly, loudly, normally*. But many adverbs do not end in *-ly: very, always, not, yesterday,* and *well* are a few. Some adjectives look like adverbs but are not: *brotherly, lonely, lovely*.

Relative adverbs are words such as *where, why,* and *when*. They are used to introduce ADJECTIVE CLAUSES.

Conjunctive adverbs modify—that is, conjunctive adverbs describe or limit—by creating logical connections to give words meaning. Conjunctive adverbs can appear anywhere in a sentence: at the start, in the middle, or at the end.

However, we consider Isaac Newton an even more important scientist.
We consider Isaac Newton, **however,** an even more important scientist.
We consider Isaac Newton an even more important scientist, **however.**

Box 48 lists the kinds of relationships that conjunctive adverbs can show.

BOX 48 SUMMARY

Conjunctive adverbs and relationships they express

Relationship	Words
ADDITION	*also, furthermore, moreover, besides*
CONTRAST	*however, still, nevertheless, conversely, nonetheless, instead, otherwise*
COMPARISON	*similarly, likewise*
RESULT OR SUMMARY	*therefore, thus, consequently, accordingly, hence, then*
TIME	*next, then, meanwhile, finally, subsequently,*
EMPHASIS	*indeed, certainly*

EXERCISE 7-3

Underline and label all adjectives (ADJ) and adverbs (ADV). For help, consult 7e through 7g.

EXAMPLE
ADJ ADJ
Scientific evidence shows that massage therapy can
ADV ADJ
dramatically improve people's health.

1. Premature babies who are massaged gently gain 47 percent more weight than babies who do not receive touch treatment.
2. Frequently, massaged premature babies go home from the hospital sooner, saving an average of $10,000 per baby.
3. Also, daily massage helps many people with stomach problems digest their food easily because important hormones are released during the rubdown.
4. People with the HIV virus find their weakened immune system significantly improved by targeted massage.
5. In addition, massage treatments have helped people with asthma breathe more freely.

7h What is a preposition?

Prepositions are words that convey relationships, usually in time or space. Common prepositions include *in, under, by, after, to, on, over,* and *since.* A PREPOSITIONAL PHRASE consists of a preposition and the words it modifies. For information about prepositions and commas, see 24k.2.

> **In the fall,** we will hear a concert **by our favorite tenor.**
> **After the concert,** he will fly **to San Francisco.**

🌐 **ESL NOTE:** For a list of prepositions and the IDIOMS they create, see Chapter 48. 🌐

7i What is a conjunction?

A **conjunction** connects words, PHRASES, or CLAUSES. **Coordinating conjunctions** join two or more grammatically equal words, phrases, or clauses. Box 49 on the next page lists the coordinating conjunctions and the relationships they express.

> We hike **and** camp every summer. [*And* joins two words.]
> We hike along scenic trails **or** in the wilderness. [*Or* joins two phrases.]
> I love the outdoors, **but** my family does not. [*But* joins two independent clauses.]

To help students become aware of what conjunctions do, you might want to distribute the following passage by Langston Hughes. Omit all conjunctions and ask students to supply them. When the passage is complete, ask students to discuss the function and the effect of each word they supplied. Then distribute the original, complete passage.

I was saved from sin *when* I was going on thirteen. *But* not really saved. It happened like this. There was a big revival at my Auntie Reed's church. Every night for weeks there had been much preaching, singing, praying *and* shouting, *and* some very hardened sinners had been brought to Christ, *and* the membership of the church had grown by leaps *and* bounds. Then just *before* the revival ended, they held a special meeting for children, "to bring the young lambs to the fold." My aunt spoke of it for days ahead. That night I was escorted to the front *and* placed on the mourners' bench with the other young sinners, who had not yet been brought to Jesus. . . . Then I was left all alone on the mourners' bench. My aunt came *and* knelt at my knees *and* cried, *while* prayers *and* songs swirled all around me in the little church. The whole congregation prayed for me alone, in a mighty wail of moans *and* vices. *And* I kept waiting serenely for Jesus, waiting, waiting—*but* he didn't come. I wanted to see him, *but* nothing happened to me. Nothing! I wanted something to happen to me, *but* nothing happened.
　　　　　　　　—Langston Hughes, "Salvation"

BACKGROUND
In his article "Weather Report: Yucky," William Safire defines the word *yuck* as an "onomatopoeic" interjection: He says *yuck* means what it sounds like.

BOX 49   SUMMARY

Coordinating conjunctions and relationships they express

Relationship	Words
ADDITION	*and*
CONTRAST	*but, yet*
RESULT OR EFFECT	*so*
REASON OR CAUSE	*for*
CHOICE	*or*
NEGATIVE CHOICE	*nor*

Correlative conjunctions are two conjunctions that work as a pair: *both . . . and; either . . . or; neither . . . nor; not only . . . but (also); whether . . . or;* and *not . . . so much as.*

Both English **and** Spanish are spoken in many homes in the United States.
Not only students **but also** businesspeople should study a second language.

Subordinating conjunctions introduce DEPENDENT CLAUSES. Subordinating conjunctions express relationships making the dependent clause in a sentence grammatically less important than the INDEPENDENT CLAUSE in the sentence. Box 50 lists the most common subordinating conjunctions. For information about how to use them correctly, see 17e through 17h.

Because it snowed, school was canceled.
Many people were happy **after** they heard the news.

BOX 50   SUMMARY

Subordinating conjunctions and relationships they express

Relationship	Words
TIME	*after, before, once, since, until, when, whenever, while*
REASON OR CAUSE	*as, because, since*

→

Subordinating conjunctions and relationships they express (*continued*)

RESULT OR EFFECT	*in order that, so, so that, that*
CONDITION	*if, even if, provided that, unless*
CONTRAST	*although, even though, though, whereas*
LOCATION	*where, wherever*
CHOICE	*than, whether*

7j What is an interjection?

An **interjection** is a word or expression that conveys surprise or a strong emotion. Alone, an interjection is usually punctuated with an exclamation point (!). As part of a sentence, an interjection is usually set off by one or more commas.

> **Hooray!** I won the race.
> **Oh,** my friends missed seeing the finish.

EXERCISE 7-4

Identify the part of speech of each numbered and underlined word. Choose from noun, pronoun, verb, adjective, adverb, preposition, coordinating conjunction, correlative conjunction, and subordinating conjunction. For help, consult 7b through 7i.

1
The geneticist Barbara McClintock was a <u>nonconformist</u>. She

2   3   4
<u>preferred</u> the company <u>of</u> the corn plants that <u>she</u> eagerly studied

5
to the <u>companionship</u> of many of the people she knew. When she won

6
the Nobel Prize in 1983, she learned of it over the radio <u>because</u> she

had no telephone.

7
McClintock worked <u>alone</u> throughout her fifty-year career at the

ANSWERS EXERCISE 7-4

Instructors can require students to identify the part of speech of any word in this paragraph, in addition to those with number labels.

1. noun (7b)
2. verb (7d)
3. preposition (7h)
4. pronoun (7c)
5. noun (7b)
6. subordinating conjunction (7i)
7. adverb (7g)
8. preposition (7h)
9. coordinating conjunction (7i)
10. verb (7d)
11. verb (7d)
12. adjective (7f)
13. adjective (7f)
14. subordinating conjunction (7i)
15. preposition (7h)
16. noun (7b)
17. subordinating conjunction (7i)
18. verb (7d)
19. coordinating conjunction (7i)
20. verb (7d)
21. adjective (7f)
22. adverb (7g)
23. adverb (7g)
24. verb (7d)
25. noun (7b)

                                         8   9
Cold Spring Harbor Laboratory in New York. In the 1940s and
                                   10
1950s, McClintock discovered that parts of chromosomes break off
           11   12   13
and recombine with neighboring chromosomes to create unique genetic
                                        14
combinations. This process, known as crossing over, amazed scientists

and demonstrated that chromosomes formed the basis of genetics.

Still, scientists resisted McClintock's findings and did not recognize the
                  15   16   17   18
importance of her research for many years. Only after geneticists found
                          19
crossing over genes in both plants and animals was the great value of

McClintock's discovery acknowledged. Thirty to forty years later, she
20
won the 1983 Nobel Prize for her groundbreaking achievement.
                                            21   22
     Overall, McClintock's life was lonely, but her career was very

productive. By the time of her death in 1992, her colleagues had
     23   24   25
finally come to realize that Barbara McClintock was one of the

towering giants of genetics.

SENTENCE STRUCTURES

7k How is a sentence defined?

A **sentence** is defined in several ways: On a strictly mechanical level, a sentence starts with a capital letter and finishes with a period, question mark, or exclamation point. Grammatically, a sentence consists of an INDEPENDENT CLAUSE: *Skydiving is dangerous.* You might hear a sentence described as a "complete thought," but that definition is too vague to help much. From the perspective of its purpose, a sentence is defined as listed in Box 51.

Sentences and their purposes

- A **declarative sentence**
  makes a statement: Skydiving is dangerous.

- An **interrogative sentence**
  asks a question: Is skydiving dangerous?

- An **imperative sentence**
  gives a command: Be careful when you skydive.

- An **exclamatory sentence**
  expresses strong feeling: How I love skydiving!

71 What is a subject and a predicate in a sentence?

The **subject** and **predicate** of a sentence are its two essential parts. Without both, a group of words isn't a sentence. Box 52 shows the sentence pattern with both. Terms used in the box are defined after it.

Sentence pattern I: Subjects and predicates

- Complete Subject   +   Complete Predicate
  The red telephone   rang loudly.
        ↑   ↑
  SIMPLE SUBJECT   SIMPLE PREDICATE (VERB)

- Complete Subject   +   Complete Predicate
  The telephone and the doorbell   rang loudly.
         ↖   ↗
     COMPOUND SUBJECT

- Complete Subject   +   Complete Predicate
  The red telephone   rang and startled everyone in the room.
                           ↖   ↗
                       COMPOUND PREDICATE

QUOTATION: ON WRITING

Language, like the body, is so comfortable and familiar that we hardly notice its presence or complexity. Yet once examined closely, the accomplishment of any ordinary speaker is rather astonishing. He can produce and understand an indefinite number of new sentences—sentences he has never encountered previously.

—Richard Ohmann

QUOTATION: ON WRITING

In a significant way, a predicate is more intensely a word than a subject of a sentence is. . . . A word is an event; it is a happening.

—Walter J. Ong

BACKGROUND

A continuum of techniques for building good sentences is demonstrated at the Web site <http://www.csc.calpoly.edu/~ebrunner/ GrammatiCat/Style/Sentences.html>. For example: "Rain fell. Maybe the rain has only minimal importance in your story. Clean the prose down to the most basic *subject + verb.*"

—Elizabeth Brunner, at <http:// www.csc.calpoly.edu/~ebrunner/ GrammatiCat/CatIndex.html>

BACKGROUND
In "Some New Approaches Toward Teaching" (reprinted in *Journal of Basic Writing*, Spring 1994: 103–116), Mina P. Shaughnessy says, "There is a kind of carpentry in sentence making, various ways of joining or hooking up modifying units to the base sentence. Suffixes added to make adjectives or adverbs, prepositions, *wh-* words like *where*, *when*, *who*, *which*, etc., the double commas used in appositional constructions—all of these can be seen as hooking devices that preserve us from the tedium of Dick-and-Jane sentences."

QUOTATION: ON WRITING
A story can be wrecked by a faulty rhythm in a sentence—especially if it occurs toward the end—or a mistake in paragraphing, even punctuation.

—Truman Capote

The **simple subject** is the word or group of words that acts, is described, or is acted upon.

> The **telephone** rang. [Simple subject, *telephone*, acts.]
> The **telephone** is red. [Simple subject, *telephone*, is described.]
> The **telephone** was being connected. [Simple subject, *telephone*, is acted upon.]

The **complete subject** is the simple subject and its MODIFIERS.

> **The red telephone** rang.

A **compound subject** consists of two or more NOUNS or PRONOUNS and their modifiers.

> **The telephone and the doorbell** rang.

The **predicate** contains the VERB in the sentence. The predicate tells what the subject is doing or experiencing or what is being done to the subject.

> The telephone **rang.** [*Rang* tells what the subject, *telephone*, did.]
> The telephone **is** red. [*Is* tells what the subject, *telephone*, experiences.]
> The telephone **was being connected.** [*Was being connected* tells what was being done to the subject, *telephone*.]

A **simple predicate** contains only the verb.

> The lawyer **listened.**

A **complete predicate** contains the verb and its modifiers.

> The lawyer **listened carefully.**

A **compound predicate** contains two or more verbs.

> The lawyer **listened and waited.**

⊕ ESL NOTES: (1) The subject of a declarative sentence usually comes before the predicate, but there are exceptions (19e). In sentences that ask a question, part of the predicate usually comes before the subject. For more information about word order in English sentences, see Chapter 47. (2) In English, don't add a PERSONAL PRONOUN to repeat the stated noun.

> NO My **grandfather he** lived to be eighty-seven. [The personal pronoun, *he*, repeats the stated noun, *grandfather*.]
>
> YES My **grandfather** lived to be eighty-seven.
>
> NO **Winter storms** that bring ice, sleet, and snow **they** can cause traffic problems. [The personal pronoun, *they*, repeats the stated noun, *winter storms*.]
>
> YES **Winter storms** that bring ice, sleet, and snow can cause traffic problems. ⊕

EXERCISE 7-5

Use a slash to separate the complete subject from the complete predicate. For help, consult 7l.

EXAMPLE   The Panama Canal in Central America / provides a water route between the Atlantic and Pacific Oceans.

1. Ships sailed an extra 3,000 to 5,000 miles around South America before the construction of the Panama Canal.
2. Over 800,000 ships have traveled the 50 miles of the Panama Canal.
3. The United States built the canal and then operated it for 86 years at a cost of $3 billion.
4. The United States has collected about $2 billion from Panama Canal operations.
5. Panama was awarded total ownership of the Panama Canal by the United States on December 31, 1999.

7m   What are direct and indirect objects?

A **direct object** is a noun, pronoun, or group of words acting as a noun that receives the action of a TRANSITIVE VERB. To check for a direct object, make up a *whom?* or *what?* question about the verb.

An **indirect object** is a noun, pronoun, or group of words acting as a noun that tells *to whom* or *for whom* the action expressed by a transitive verb was done. To check for an indirect object, make up a *to whom? for whom? to what?* or *for what?* question about the verb.

Direct objects and indirect objects always fall in the PREDICATE of a sentence. Box 53 shows how direct and indirect objects function in sentences.

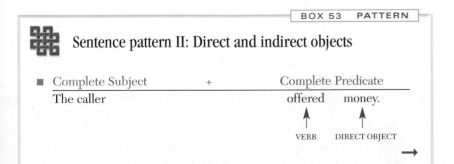

BOX 53   PATTERN

Sentence pattern II: Direct and indirect objects

- Complete Subject   +   Complete Predicate
  The caller   offered   money.
                                          ↑   ↑
                                        VERB   DIRECT OBJECT

ANSWERS: EXERCISE 7-5

1. Ships / sailed an extra 3,000 to 5,000 miles before the construction of the Panama Canal.

2. Over 800,000 ships / have traveled the 50 miles of the Panama Canal.

3. The United States / built the canal and then operated it for 86 years at a cost of $3 billion.

4. The United States / has collected about $2 billion from canal operations.

5. Panama / was awarded total ownership of the Panama Canal by the United States on December 31, 1999.

QUOTATION: ON WRITING

Incidentally, the word *me* is not always an indirect object; it can also serve as a direct object. Bless *me!* Contact *me* if you have questions.

—<http://cctc2.commnet.edu/grammar/definitions.htm>

BACKGROUND
According to the helpful Web site <http://www.grammarlady.com>, inquiries are fielded each day by the Grammar Hotline. Here is one question that was received:

> **Dear Grammar Lady:** If we have the word "elsewhere," as in "We'll have to look elsewhere for the answer," why don't we have words such as "elsewhen" or "elsewhy"?
>
> **Response:** If we look in a dictionary that has historical records of words, such as the multivolume *Oxford English Dictionary* (OED), available in most libraries, we find that at one time these were viable parts of the English language. We can't know exactly why "elsewhere" survived when the others did not, but it is a good lesson in language change—a living language changes over time in ways we cannot predict.
>
> —Mary Newton Bruder,
> <http://www.grammarlady.com>

Sentence pattern II: Direct and indirect objects (*continued*)

■ Complete Subject   +   Complete Predicate

The caller   offered the lawyer money.

    VERB   INDIRECT OBJECT   DIRECT OBJECT

■ Complete Subject   +   Complete Predicate

The client   sent the lawyer a retainer.

    VERB   INDIRECT OBJECT   DIRECT OBJECT

ESL NOTES: (1) In sentences with indirect objects that follow the word *to* or *for,* always put the direct object before the indirect object.

NO   Will you please give **to John** this letter?
YES   Will you please give this letter **to John?**

(2) When a PRONOUN is used as an indirect object, some verbs require *to* or *for* before the pronoun, and others do not. Consult the *Dictionary of American English* (Heinle and Heinle) about each verb when you're unsure.

NO   Please explain **me** the rule. [*Explain* requires *to* before an indirect object.]
YES   Please explain the rule **to me.**
YES   Please give **me** that book. Please give that book **to me.** [*Give* uses both patterns.]

(3) When both the direct object and the indirect object are pronouns, put the direct object first and use *to* with the indirect object.

NO   He gave **me it.**
YES   He gave **it to me.**
YES   Please give **me the letter.** [*Give* does not require *to* before an indirect object.]

(4) Even if a verb does not require *to* before an indirect object, you may use *to* if you prefer. If you do use *to,* be sure to put the direct object before the indirect object.

YES   Our daughter helped **our son write** his name.
YES   Our daughter helped **our son to write** his name.

EXERCISE 7-6

Draw a single line under all direct objects and a double line under all indirect objects. For help, consult 7m.

EXAMPLE   Toni Morrison's award-winning novels give <u>readers</u> the <u>gifts</u> of wisdom, inspiration, and pleasure.

1. Literary critics gave high praise to Toni Morrison for her first novel, *The Bluest Eye,* but the general public showed little interest.
2. *Song of Solomon* won Morrison the National Book Critics Circle Award in 1977, and *Beloved* won her the Pulitzer Prize in 1988.
3. A literary panel awarded Toni Morrison the 1993 Nobel Prize in Literature, the highest honor a writer can receive.
4. Her 1998 novel, *Paradise,* traces for readers the tragic lives of a rejected group of former slaves.
5. Twenty-five years after *The Bluest Eye* was published, Oprah Winfrey selected it for her reader's list, and it immediately became a bestseller.

7n   What are complements, modifiers, and appositives?

Complements

A **complement** renames or describes a SUBJECT or an OBJECT. It appears in the PREDICATE of a sentence.

A **subject complement** is a NOUN, PRONOUN, or ADJECTIVE that follows a LINKING VERB. **Predicate nominative** is another term for a noun used as a subject complement, and **predicate adjective** is another term for an adjective used as a subject complement.

An **object complement** follows a DIRECT OBJECT and either describes or renames the direct object. Box 54 shows how subject and object complements function in a sentence.

BOX 54   PATTERN

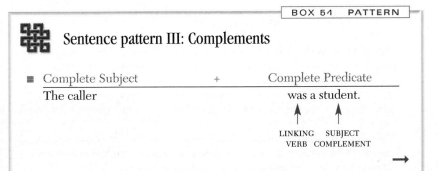

Sentence pattern III: Complements

■ Complete Subject   +   Complete Predicate
The caller   was a student.
                                        ↑   ↑
                                     LINKING SUBJECT
                                      VERB   COMPLEMENT

→

QUOTATION: ON WRITING

[Dangling modifiers] most frequently occur at the beginning of sentences but can also appear at the end. Example: The experiment was a failure, having not studied the lab manual carefully. (The experiment—the subject of the main clause—did not study the lab manual.)

—<http://owl.english.purdue.edu>

TEACHING TIP

Combining sentences by using modifiers and appositives can not only reduce repetition but also create more graceful statements. Students are sometimes surprised by what they produce when they are asked to combine several choppy sentences into a single effective one.

ANSWERS: EXERCISE 7-7

1. native (SUB)
2. inhabitants (SUB)
3. plant (SUB)
4. invasives (OB)
5. threats (OB)

A HUMOROUS NOTE

Dangling participial phrases can produce some unintended meanings, such as these:

- Plunging 1,000 feet into the gorge, we saw Yosemite Falls.

- He rode his horse across Highway 12 and up and down the sidewalk in front of the saloon a good half hour before deputies arrived, shouting obscenities and being obnoxious.

- Locked in a vault for 50 years, the owner of the jewels has decided to sell them.

—Richard Lederer,
Anguished English

Sentence pattern III: Complements *(continued)*

Complete Subject	+	Complete Predicate
The student		called himself a victim.

VERB · DIRECT OBJECT · OBJECT COMPLEMENT

EXERCISE 7-7

Underline all complements and identify each as a subject complement (SUB) or an object complement (OB).

EXAMPLE   Many of the most familiar North American wildflowers are actually
                                       SUB
nonnative plants.

1. The dainty Queen Anne's lace is a native of Europe.
2. The daisies and cornflowers that decorate our roadsides all summer were originally inhabitants of Europe as well.
3. The common purple loosestrife, originally from Asia, came to the North American continent as a garden plant.
4. Many scientists call these plants "alien invasives."
5. Many ecologists consider them to be threats to the forests, meadows, and wetlands of North America.

Modifiers

A **modifier** is a word or group of words that describes or limits other words. Modifiers appear in the SUBJECT or the PREDICATE of a sentence.

The **large red** telephone rang. [The adjectives *large* and *red* modify the noun *telephone*.]

The lawyer answered **quickly.** [The adverb *quickly* modifies the verb *answered*.]

The person **on the telephone** was **extremely** upset. [The prepositional phrase *on the telephone* modifies the noun *person*; the adverb *extremely* modifies the adjective *upset*.]

Therefore, the lawyer spoke **gently.** [The adverb *therefore* modifies the independent clause *the lawyer spoke gently*; the adverb *gently* modifies the verb *spoke*.]

Because the lawyer's voice was calm, the caller felt reassured. [The adverb clause *because the lawyer's voice was calm* modifies the independent clause *the caller felt reassured*.]

Appositives

An **appositive** is a word or group of words that renames the NOUN or PRONOUN preceding it.

> The student's story, **a tale of broken promises,** was complicated. [The appositive *a tale of broken promises* renames the noun *story.*]
>
> The lawyer consulted an expert, **her law professor.** [The appositive *her law professor* renames the noun *expert.*]
>
> The student, **Joe Jones,** asked to speak to his lawyer. [The appositive *Joe Jones* renames the noun *student.*]

👁 **ALERT:** When an appositive is not essential for identifying what it renames (that is, when it is NONRESTRICTIVE), use a comma or commas to set off the appositive from the rest of the sentence; see section 24g). 👁

70 What is a phrase?

A **phrase** is a group of words that does not contain both a SUBJECT and a PREDICATE and therefore cannot stand alone as an independent unit.

Noun phrase
A **noun phrase** functions as a NOUN in a sentence.

> **The modern census** dates back to the seventeenth century.

Verb phrase
A **verb phrase** functions as a VERB in a sentence.

> Two military censuses **are mentioned** in the Bible.

Prepositional phrase
A **prepositional phrase** always starts with a PREPOSITION and functions as a MODIFIER.

> William the Conqueror conducted a census **of landowners in newly conquered England in 1086.** [three prepositional phrases in a row, beginning with *of, in, in*]

Absolute phrase
An **absolute phrase** usually contains a noun or PRONOUN and a PRESENT or PAST PARTICIPLE. An absolute phrase modifies the entire sentence that it's in.

> **Censuses being the fashion,** Quebec and Nova Scotia took sixteen counts between 1665 and 1754.
>
> Eighteenth-century Sweden and Denmark had complete records of their populations, **each adult and child having been counted.**

TEACHING TIP
Because students sometimes feel that phrases are peculiar constructions of grammar books, you might find it useful to reproduce and distribute copies of a newspaper article on a popular subject. Ask students to identify any noun phrases, verb phrases, and prepositional phrases. Students will be amazed at how often phrases appear in "real" writing. Class discussion might next cover the functions of the noun phrases and prepositional phrases (subject, object, complement, adjective, adverb).

BACKGROUND
At <http://owl.english.purdue.edu/>, the Online Writing Lab (OWL) of Purdue University, accessed at:provides a wealth of information on grammar. Here is a sampling of facts on gerunds:

A. A gerund is a verbal used as a noun. Therefore, it may be used in any place that a noun would fit: subject, object, indirect object, subject complement, or object of the preposition.
B. The gerund always ends in -ing.
C. The gerund may be written as a phrase with its own modifiers, complements, and prepositional phrases.
D. The gerund usually does not require any punctuation.

ANSWERS: EXERCISE 7-8
Answers will vary. Here is one set of possibile responses.

1. Independent stores develop creative marketing strategies *and figure out ways to offer* special features to compete with chain stores. (verb phrase)
2. One independent children's bookstore attracted new customers *by bringing live animals into the store.* (prepositional phrases)
3. *Animals being popular with children,* the store purchased two pet chickens, plus tarantulas, rats, cats, and fish. (absolute phrase)

→

Verbal phrase

A **verbal phrase** contains a verb part that functions not as a verb, but as a noun or an ADJECTIVE. Such cases are INFINITIVES, present participles, and past participles.

> In 1624, Virginia began **to count its citizens** in a census. [*To count its citizens* is an infinitive phrase.]
>
> **Going from door to door,** census takers interview millions of people. [*Going from door to door* is a present participial phrase.]
>
> **Amazed by some people's answers,** census takers always listen carefully. [*Amazed by some people's answers* is a past participial phrase.]

Gerund phrase

A **gerund phrase** functions as a noun. Telling the difference between a gerund phrase and a present participial phrase can be tricky because both use the *-ing* verb form. The key is to determine how the phrase functions in the sentence: A gerund phrase functions only as a noun, and a participial phrase functions only as a modifier.

> **Including each person in the census** was important. [This is a gerund phrase because it functions as a noun, which is the subject of the sentence.]
>
> **Including each person in the census,** Abby spent many hours on the crowded city block. [This is a present participial phrase because it functions as a modifier, namely, an adjective describing Abby.]

EXERCISE 7-8

Combine each set of sentences into a single sentence by converting one sentence into a phrase—either a noun phrase, verb phrase, prepositional phrase, absolute phrase, verbal phrase, or gerund phrase. You can omit, add, or change words. Identify which type of phrase you created.

You can combine most sets in several correct ways, but make sure the meaning of your finished sentence is clear. For help, consult 7o.

EXAMPLE Large chain stores often pose threats to local independent retailers. Smaller store owners must find innovative ways to stay in business.

With large chains posing threats to local independent retailers, smaller store owners must find innovative ways to stay in business. (prepositional phrase)

1. Independent stores develop creative marketing strategies to compete with chain stores. Independent stores figure out ways to offer special features.

2. One independent children's bookstore attracted new customers. It did that by bringing live animals into the store.

3. Animals are popular with children. The store purchased two pet chickens, plus tarantulas, rats, cats, and fish.

4. This children's bookstore did not need to lower prices to draw customers. The store could survive by owning animals that appeal to youngsters.

5. Other sorts of independent stores sometimes take a slightly different approach. They compete by offering better service than the large chain stores can.

6. For example, independent hardware and housewares stores can be service-oriented and customer friendly. They sometimes can thrive financially doing this.

7. Many independent hardware and housewares store owners have begun to offer home-repair and decorating advice as well as to recommend house calls from staff members. They do this to attract and hold customers.

8. These store owners also feature high-end items that chains do not carry. They feature in-store displays and advertise heavily about their high-end items.

9. Independent hardware and housewares stores often stock fine items such as expensive lawn ornaments, costly brand-name paints, and rare Italian tiles. These stores tend to attract wealthier customers.

10. Some independent stores struggle for survival. They cannot always compete with the lower prices at impersonal chain stores.

7p What is a clause?

A **clause** is a group of words with both a SUBJECT and a PREDICATE. Clauses can be either *independent clauses*, also called *main clauses*, or *dependent clauses*, also called *subordinate clauses*.

Independent clauses

An **independent clause** contains a subject and a predicate and can stand alone as a sentence. Box 55 shows the basic pattern.

BOX 55   PATTERN

Sentence pattern IV: Independent clauses

Independent Clause

■ Complete Subject   +   Complete Predicate

The telephone   rang.

Answers: Exercise 7-8 (continued)

4. *To draw customers without lowering prices,* this children's bookstore store could survive by owning animals that appeal to youngsters. (verbal [infinitive] phrase)

5. *In a slightly different approach,* other independent stores compete by offering better service than the large chain stores can. (prepositional phrase)

6. *Independent service-oriented and customer-friendly hardware and housewares stores,* for example, sometimes can thrive financially. (noun phrase)

7. *To attract and hold customers,* many independent hardware and housewares store owners have begun to offer home-repair and decorating advice as well as to recommend house calls from staff members. (verbal [infinitive] phrase)

8. These store owners also *feature in-store displays and advertise heavily* about their high-end items that chains do not carry. (verb phrase)

9. *Stocking fine items such as expensive lawn ornaments, costly brand-name paints, and rare Italian tiles,* independent hardware and housewares stores tend to attract wealthier customers. (verbal [participial] phrase)

10. *Some independent stores struggling for survival* cannot always compete with the lower prices at impersonal chain stores. (gerund phrase as subject)

TEACHING TIP
To determine whether a clause is independent or dependent, students can make up a yes-or-no question about the clause's statement. An independent clause leads to a sensible question; a dependent clause does not.

The knave stole the tarts.
Did the knave steal the tarts?
[a sensible question]

Because he was very hungry.
Because was he very hungry?
[not a sensible question]

TEACHING TIP
To improve students' recognition of adjective and adverb clauses, as well as to increase their powers of concentration, you may want to read aloud the following passage by Katherine Anne Porter. Ask students to note every use of an adverb or adjective clause by listening for key words such as relative pronouns and subordinating conjunctions. After you read the passage, you may want to distribute and discuss it.

In my grandmother's day, in Texas, everybody seemed to remember that man *who* had a way of showing up with a dozen grains of real coffee in his hand, *which* he exchanged for a month's supply of corn meal. My grandmother parched a mixture of sweet potato and dried corn *until* it was black, ground it up and boiled it, *because* her family couldn't get over its yearning for a dark hot drink in the mornings, but she would never allow them to call it coffee. It was known as That Brew. . . . The woman *who* made That Brew and the soldier *who* ate the bacon rind had been bride and groom in a Kentucky wedding somewhere around 1850. Only a few years ago a cousin of mine showed me a letter from a lady then rising ninety-five *who* remembered that wedding as if it had been only yesterday.

—Katherine Anne Porter, "Memories of the Old South"

Dependent clauses

A **dependent clause** contains a subject and a predicate but cannot stand alone as a sentence. To be part of a complete sentence, a dependent clause must be joined to an independent clause. Dependent clauses are either *adverb clauses* or *adjective clauses*.

Adverb clauses

An **adverb clause,** also called a *subordinate clause*, starts with a SUBORDINATING CONJUNCTION, such as *although, because, when,* or *until.* A subordinating conjunction expresses a relationship between a dependent clause and an independent clause; see Box 50 in section 7i. Adverb clauses usually answer some question about the independent clause: *How? Why? When? Under what circumstances?*

> **If the bond issue passes,** the city will install sewers. [The adverb clause modifies the verb *install;* it explains under what circumstances.]
> They are drawing up plans **as quickly as they can.** [The adverb clause modifies the verb *drawing up;* it explains how.]
> The homeowners feel happier **because they know the flooding will soon be better controlled.** [The adverb clause modifies the entire independent clause; it explains why.]

👁 **ALERT:** When you write an adverb clause before an independent clause, separate the clauses with a comma; see section 24b. 👁

Adjective clauses

An **adjective clause,** also called a *relative clause*, starts with a RELATIVE PRONOUN, such as *who, which,* or *that.* Or an adjective clause can start with a RELATIVE ADVERB, such as *when* or *where.* An adjective clause modifies the NOUN or PRONOUN that it follows. Box 56 shows how adverb and adjective clauses function in sentences. See also Box 71 in section 9s.

> The car **that Jack bought** is practical. [The adjective clause describes the noun *car; that* is a relative pronoun referring to *car.*]
> The day **when I can buy my own car** is getting closer. [The adjective clause modifies the noun *day; when* is a relative adverb referring to *day.*]

Use *who, whom, whoever, whomever,* and *whose* when an adjective clause refers to a person or to an animal with a name.

> The Smythes, **who collect cars,** are wealthy.
> Their dog Bowser, **who is large and loud,** has been spoiled.

Use *which* or *that* when an adjective clause refers to a thing or to an animal that isn't a pet. Sometimes, writers omit *that* from an adjective clause. For grammatical analysis, however, consider the omitted *that* to be implied and, therefore, present.

BOX 56   PATTERN

Sentence pattern V: Dependent clauses

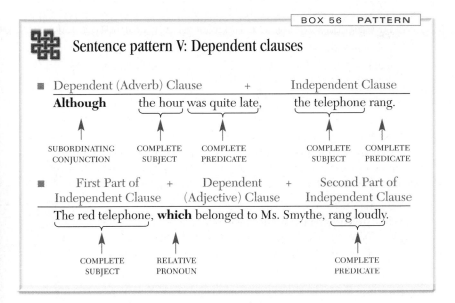

- Dependent (Adverb) Clause   +   Independent Clause

  Although   the hour was quite late,   the telephone rang.

  SUBORDINATING   COMPLETE   COMPLETE   COMPLETE   COMPLETE
  CONJUNCTION   SUBJECT   PREDICATE   SUBJECT   PREDICATE

- First Part of   +   Dependent   +   Second Part of
  Independent Clause   (Adjective) Clause   Independent Clause

  The red telephone, **which** belonged to Ms. Smythe, rang loudly.

  COMPLETE   RELATIVE   COMPLETE
  SUBJECT   PRONOUN   PREDICATE

For help in deciding whether to use *that* or *which*, see Box 71 in section 9s.

👁 **ALERT:** When an adjective clause is NONRESTRICTIVE, use *which* and set it off from the independent clause with commas. Don't use commas with *that* in a RESTRICTIVE CLAUSE.

My car, **which** I bought used, needs major repairs. [The adjective clause is nonrestrictive, so it begins with *which* and is set off with commas.]

The car **that** I want to buy has a CD player. [The adjective clause uses *that* and is restrictive, so it is not set off with commas.] 👁

EXERCISE 7-9

Underline the dependent clause in each sentence, and label it an ADJ or an ADV clause. For help, consult 7p.

                        ADV
EXAMPLE   When umbrellas were invented, people used them for sun
               protection.

1. Eighteenth-century ladies carried fancy umbrellas as a fashion statement while strolling down the street.
2. Although umbrellas are mostly used today in the rain, they have many other uses.

ANSWERS: EXERCISE 7-9

1. Eighteenth-century ladies carried fancy umbrellas as a fashion statement <u>while strolling down the street</u> (ADV).

2. <u>Although umbrellas are mostly used today in the rain</u> (ADV), they have many other uses.

3. Gentlemen in England carry sturdy umbrellas, <u>which make convenient walking sticks</u> (ADJ).

4. One company makes a "sporting umbrella" <u>that unfolds into a seat</u> (ADJ).

5. Marketing consultants, who receive requests for moveable advertising, suggest umbrellas can be mini-billboards <u>when they are decorated with a company's name and logo</u> (ADV).

BACKGROUND
At the Web site <http://www.protrainco.com/essays/grammarterms.htm>, students can find published articles on grammar usage, including examples of noun clauses.

TEACHING TIP
Elliptical clauses: To enhance students' appreciation of their options, you might ask them whether they prefer the elliptical or full forms of the text's sentences—and why. Here are alternate examples to use.

- Living in Spain was one of the best experiences [that] Carol had during college. When [she was] living with a family in Spain, Carol started to feel like a native.

- James Naismith, [who was] a Presbyterian minister, believed that through athletics he could teach lessons in Christian ideals. After [he had graduated from] divinity school, Naismith enrolled in the School for Christian Workers, [which] later [became] known as the International YMCA Training School. Naismith, [who was] a young man full of ideas, was given the job of devising a game that had less running and tackling than other ball games [had]. Limited indoor space and the hard surface of a wooden floor were two of the biggest problems [that] he faced. The game [that] he devised is known today as basketball.

3. Gentlemen in England carry sturdy umbrellas, which make convenient walking sticks.
4. One company makes a "sporting umbrella" that unfolds into a seat.
5. Marketing consultants, who receive requests for moveable advertising, suggest umbrellas can be mini-billboards when they are decorated with a company's name and logo.

Noun clauses

Noun clauses function as nouns. Noun clauses can begin with many of the same words that begin adjective clauses: *that, who, which,* and their derivatives, as well as *when, where, whether, why,* and *how.*

> **Promises** are not always dependable. [noun]
> **What politicians promise** is not always dependable. [noun clause]
> The electorate often cannot figure out the **truth.** [noun]
> The electorate often cannot know **that the truth is being manipulated.** [noun clause]

Because they start with similar words, noun clauses and adjective clauses are sometimes confused with each other. The way to tell them apart is that the word starting an adjective clause has an ANTECEDENT, while the word starting a noun clause doesn't.

> Good politicians understand **whom they must please.** [Noun clause; *whom* does not have an antecedent.]
> Good politicians **who make promises** know all cannot be kept. [Adjective clause modifies *politicians*, which is the antecedent of *who*.]

ESL NOTE: Noun clauses in INDIRECT QUESTIONS are phrased as statements, not questions: *Kara asked why we needed the purple dye.* Don't phrase a noun clause this way: *Kara asked why **did** [or **do**] we need the purple dye?* If you prefer to change to a DIRECT QUESTION, usually VERB TENSE, PRONOUN, and other changes are necessary; see section 15e.

Elliptical clauses

In an **elliptical clause,** one or more words are deliberately left out for CONCISENESS. For an elliptical clause to be correct, the one or more words you leave out need to be identical to those already appearing in the clause.

> Engineering is one of the majors [**that**] **she considered.** [*that*, functioning as a relative pronoun, omitted from adjective clause]
> She decided [**that**] **she would rather major in management.** [*that*, functioning as a conjunction, omitted between clauses]

After [he takes] a refresher course, he will be eligible for a raise.
[subject and verb omitted from adverb clause]
Broiled fish tastes better **than boiled fish [tastes].** [second half of the comparison omitted]

EXERCISE 7-10

Use subordinate conjunctions and relative pronouns from the list below to combine each pair of sentences. You may use words more than once, but try to use as many different ones as possible. Some sentence pairs may be combined in several ways. Create at least one elliptical construction.

since   which   if   after   when   as   that   although   so that   unless

EXAMPLE   Reports of flying snakes have been around for hundreds of years. Scientists have never believed them.

Even though reports of flying snakes have been around for hundreds of years, scientists have never believed them.

1. The idea that snakes can fly or even glide from treetops seems impossible. They lack wings, feathers, or any kind of flying or gliding apparatus.
2. Yet, what seems impossible is not so for the paradise tree snake. This snake possesses many adaptations to allow it to soar long distances through the air.
3. The paradise tree snake has evolved into an animal of amazing agility. This allows it both to escape from predators and to catch its prey.
4. The paradise tree snake can land as far as sixty-nine feet from its launch point. People who visit the jungles of Southeast Asia can see this.
5. The snake jumps by dangling like the letter J from a tree branch. Then it throws itself upward and away from the branch, giving the impression of leaping in midair.
6. Immediately, it begins to fall at a steep angle. It then takes on an S-shape, ripples through the air, and appears to be crawling.
7. The snake changes to an S-shape. Its fall becomes much less steep. The snake then soars outward from its launch point.
8. A special characteristic permits the snake to change its shape and begin to glide. This characteristic permits the snake to flatten its body.
9. Most snakes cannot glide through the air. The paradise tree snake most certainly can.
10. The paradise tree snake must maintain its ability to glide effortlessly through the treetops. Otherwise, birds and mammals may eat it into extinction.

ANSWERS: EXERCISE 7-10

1. It seems impossible for snakes to fly, or even to glide from treetops, ***because*** *they lack wings, feathers, or any kind of flying or gliding apparatus.*

2. Yet, what seems impossible is not so for the paradise tree snake, ***which*** *possesses many adaptations to allow it to soar long distances through the air.*

3. ***So that*** *it can both escape from predators and catch its prey,* the paradise tree snake has evolved into an animal of amazing agility.

4. ***If*** *people visit the jungles of Southeast Asia,* they can see the paradise tree snake land as far as sixty-nine feet from its launch point.

5. ***After*** *the snake throws itself upward and away from the branch, giving the impression of leaping in midair,* it jumps by dangling like the letter J from a tree branch.

6. ***As*** it immediately begins to fall at a steep angle, *it takes on an S-shape, ripples through the air, and appears to be crawling.*

7. ***When*** *the snake changes to an S-shape,* its fall becomes much less steep, and it then soars outward from its launch point.

8. A special characteristic ***that*** *permits the snake to flatten its body* allows the snake to change its shape and begin to glide.

9. ***Although*** *most snakes cannot glide through the air,* the paradise tree snake most certainly can.

10. ***Unless*** *the paradise tree snake maintains its ability to glide effortlessly through the treetops,* birds and mammals may eat it into extinction.

7q What are the four sentence types?

English uses four **sentence types:** simple, compound, complex, and compound-complex. A **simple sentence** is composed of a single INDEPENDENT CLAUSE and no DEPENDENT CLAUSES.

> Charlie Chaplin was born in London on April 16, 1889.

A **compound sentence** is composed of two or more independent clauses. These clauses may be connected by a COORDINATING CONJUNCTION (*and, but, for, or, nor, yet, so*), a semicolon alone, or a semicolon and a CONJUNCTIVE ADVERB.

> His father died early, **and** his mother, with whom he was very close, spent time in mental hospitals.
> Many people enjoy Chaplin films; others do not.
> Many people enjoy Chaplin films; **however,** others do not.

A **complex sentence** is composed of one independent clause and one or more dependent clauses.

> **When times were bad,** Chaplin lived in the streets. [dependent clause starting *when;* independent clause starting *Chaplin*]
> **When Chaplin was performing with a troupe that was touring the United States,** he was hired by Mack Sennett, **who owned the Keystone Company.** [dependent clause starting *when;* dependent clause starting *that;* independent clause starting *he;* dependent clause starting *who*]

A **compound-complex sentence** integrates a compound sentence and a complex sentence. It contains two or more independent clauses and one or more dependent clauses.

> Chaplin's comedies were immediately successful, and he became rich **because he was enormously popular for playing the Little Tramp, who was loved for his tiny mustache, baggy trousers, big shoes, and trick derby** [independent clause starting *Chaplin's;* independent clause starting *he;* dependent clause starting *because;* dependent clause starting *who*]

When studios could no longer afford him, Chaplin cofounded United Artists, **and** then he produced and distributed his own films. [dependent clause starting *when*; independent clause starting *Chaplin*; independent clause starting *then*]

👁 **ALERTS:** (1) Use a comma before a coordinating conjunction connecting two independent clauses; see 24b. (2) When independent clauses are long or contain commas, use a subordinating conjunction— or use a semicolon to connect the sentences; see 25d. 👁

EXERCISE 7-11

Decide whether each of the following sentences is simple, compound, complex, or compound-complex. For help, consult 7q.

EXAMPLE   Many people would love to eat a healthy meal at a fast-food restaurant or a food concession at the movies. (*simple*)

1. Fast-food restaurants and healthy meals rarely go together.
2. A fried-chicken sandwich packs an enormous number of calories and fat, and a fried-fish sandwich is no better.
3. A double cheeseburger with bacon at a fast-food restaurant can contain over 1,000 calories and 80 grams of fat, but a plain burger reduces the unhealthy overload considerably.
4. You can purchase other relatively healthy meals at a fast-food restaurant, if you first get to know the chart of nutritional values provided for customers.
5. Even though U.S. government regulations require that nutritional charts be posted on the wall in the public areas of every fast-food restaurant, consumers often ignore the information, and they choose main meals and side dishes with the most flavor, calories, and fat.
6. A healthy meal available at many fast-food restaurants is a salad with low-fat dressing, along with bottled water.
7. The temptations of high fat and calories also entice people at the food concessions in movie theaters.
8. Because calories from sugar have zero nutritional value, health experts use the expression "empty calories" for all sugar products, yet sales of sugar-laden colossal sodas at the movies continue to increase yearly.
9. The silent ingredient in a serving of chips with melted cheese, or nachos, is artery-clogging fat, and the culprits in extra-large candy bars are not only fat but also "empty calories."
10. In truth, many people need to stay away from fast-food restaurants and food concessions at the movies and thereby avoid the tasty temptations of high-calorie foods.

Chapter 8

Verbs

8a What do verbs do?

A **verb** expresses an action, an occurrence, or a state of being. Verbs also reveal when something occurs—in the present, the past, or the future. Verbs convey other information as well; see Box 57. For types of verbs, see Box 58 on the next page.

> Many people **overeat** on Thanksgiving. [action]
> Mother's Day **fell** early this year. [occurrence]
> Memorial Day **is** tomorrow. [state of being]

BOX 57   SUMMARY

 Information that verbs convey

PERSON	First person (the speaker: *I dance*), second person (the one spoken to: *you dance*), or third person (the one spoken about: *the dog dances*).
NUMBER	Singular (one) or plural (more than one).
TENSE	Past (*we danced*), present (*we dance*), or future (*we will dance*); see 8g through 8k.
MOOD	Moods are indicative (*we dance*), imperative (commands and polite requests: *Dance*), or conditional (speculation, wishes: *if we were dancing . . .*); see 8l and 8m.
VOICE	Active voice or passive voice; see 8n through 8p.

> BOX 58 SUMMARY

Types of verbs

MAIN VERB	The word in a PREDICATE that says something about the SUBJECT: *She **danced** for the group.*
AUXILIARY VERB	A verb that combines with a main verb to convey information about TENSE, MOOD, or VOICE (8e). The verbs *be, do,* and *have* can be auxiliary verbs or main verbs. The verbs *can, could, may, might, should, would, must,* and others are MODAL AUXILIARY VERBS. They add shades of meaning such as ability or possibility to verbs: *She **might dance** again.*
LINKING VERB	The verb that links a subject to a COMPLEMENT, a word or words that rename or describe the subject: *She **was** happy dancing. Be* is the most common linking verb; sometimes sense verbs (*smell, taste*) or verbs of perception (*seem, feel*) function as linking verbs. See also Box 59.
TRANSITIVE VERB	The verb followed by a DIRECT OBJECT that completes the verb's message: *They **sent** her a fan letter.*
INTRANSITIVE VERB	A verb that does not require a direct object: *Yesterday she **danced.***

Linking verbs

Linking verbs are main verbs that indicate a state of being or a condition. They link a SUBJECT with one or more words that rename or describe the subject, which is called a SUBJECT COMPLEMENT. A linking verb works like an equal sign between a subject and its complement. Box 59 shows how linking verbs function in sentences.

> BOX 59 SUMMARY

Linking verbs

■ Linking verbs may be forms of the verb *be* (*am, is, was, were;* see 8e for a complete list).

George Washington **was** president.
⎣_____⎦ ⎣___⎦ ⎣_____⎦
   SUBJECT   LINKING   COMPLEMENT (PREDICATE
             VERB   NOMINATIVE: RENAMES SUBJECT) →

TEACHING TIP

Some of your students may speak a non-standard English dialect. Black English is perhaps the most discussed of these, but non-black rural and inner-city students and students from former British colonies and U.S. protectorates may also speak nonstandard dialects.

Two-dialect students can pick up changes in vocabulary comparatively easily. Their verbs, however, might need to be monitored with care. You might consider reviewing the following chart with such students:

NONSTANDARD ENGLISH	STANDARD ENGLISH
	Present Tense
I you we they } *loves*	I you we they } *love*
he, she, it *love*	he, she, it *loves*
	Past Tense
I you we they } *love*	I you we they } *loved*
he, she, it *love*	he, she, it *loved*

Linking verbs (*continued*)

■ Linking verbs may deal with the senses (*look, smell, taste, sound, feel*).

George Washington   **sounded**   confident.
SUBJECT   LINKING VERB   COMPLEMENT (PREDICATE ADJECTIVE: DESCRIBES SUBJECT)

■ Linking verbs can be verbs that convey a sense of existing or becoming—*appear, seem, become, get, grow, turn, remain, stay,* and *prove,* for example.

George Washington   **grew**   old.
SUBJECT   LINKING VERB   COMPLEMENT (PREDICATE ADJECTIVE DESCRIBES SUBJECT)

■ To test whether a verb other than a form of *be* is functioning as a linking verb, substitute *was* (for a singular subject) or *were* (for a plural subject) for the original verb. If the sentence makes sense, the original verb is functioning as a linking verb.

NO   George Washington **grew** a beard ⟶ George Washington **was** a beard. [*Grew* is not functioning as a linking verb.]

YES   George Washington **grew** old ⟶ George Washington **was** old. [*Grew* is functioning as a linking verb.]

VERB FORMS

8b What are the forms of main verbs?

A **main verb** names an action (*People **dance***), an occurrence (*Christmas **comes** once a year*), or a state of being (*It **will be** warm tomorrow*). Every main verb has five forms.

■ The **simple form** conveys an action, occurrence, or state of being taking place in the present (*I **laugh***) or, with an AUXILIARY VERB, in the future (*I **will laugh***).

■ The **past-tense form** conveys an action, occurrence, or state completed in the past (*I **laughed***). REGULAR VERBS add *-ed* or *-d* to the simple form. IRREGULAR VERBS vary (see Box 60 on pages 199–202).

■ The **past participle form** in regular verbs uses the same form as the past tense. Irregular verbs vary; see Box 60. To function as a verb, a past participle must combine with a SUBJECT and one or more auxiliary verbs (*I **have laughed***). Otherwise, past participles function as ADJECTIVES (***crumbled** cookies*).

■ The **present participle form** adds -*ing* to the simple form (***laughing***). To function as a verb, a present participle combines with a subject and one or more auxiliary verbs (*I **was laughing***). Otherwise, present participles function as adjectives (*my **laughing** friends*) or as NOUNS (***Laughing** is healthy*).

■ The **infinitive** usually consists of *to* and the simple form following *to* (*I started **to laugh** at his joke*); see 9i. The infinitive functions as a noun or an adjective, not a verb.

🌐 **ESL NOTE:** When verbs function as other parts of speech, they're called VERBALS: INFINITIVES, PRESENT PARTICIPLES, PAST PARTICIPLES. When present participles function as nouns, they're called GERUNDS. For information about using gerunds and infinitives as OBJECTS after certain verbs, see Chapter 49. 🌐

8c What is the -*s* form of a verb?

The **-*s* form of a verb** is the third-person singular in the PRESENT TENSE. The ending -*s* (or -*es*) is added to the verb's SIMPLE FORM (*smell* becomes *smells*, as in *The bread **smells** delicious*).

Be and *have* are irregular verbs. For the third-person singular, present tense, *be* uses *is* and *have* uses *has*.

The cheesecake **is** popular.
The éclair **has** chocolate icing.

If you tend to drop the -*s* or -*es* ending when you speak, always use it when you write. Proofread carefully to make sure you've not omitted any -*s* forms.

👁 **ALERT:** In informal speech, the LINKING, or *copula*, VERB *to be* sometimes doesn't change forms in the present tense. However, ACADEMIC WRITING requires you to use standard third-person singular forms in the present tense.

He **is** [not *be*] hungry.
The bakery **has** [not *have*] fresh bread. 👁

EXERCISE 8-1

Rewrite each sentence, changing the subjects to the word or words given in parentheses. Change the form of the verbs shown in italics to match the new subject. Keep all sentences in the present tense. For help, consult 8c.

EXAMPLE   The Oregon giant earthworm *escapes* all attempts at
           detection. (Oregon giant earthworms)
           Oregon giant earthworms escape all attempts at detection.

WORD HISTORY

Infinitive comes from the Latin *infinitivus*, meaning "unlimited" or "indefinite." This is appropriate, since the infinitive shows no person or number. Coming from the same Latin verb, *finire* ("to limit"), the term *finite verb* refers to a verb that is limited by person and number. In contrast, a *nonfinite verb* (also known as a *verbal*) is not limited in these ways.

TEACHING TIP

Leaving the -*s* off verbs is a common error, even among students who can quote the rule for its use. Many of these students speak or have studied second languages that have more complex systems of verb endings than English does. A discussion of the English -*s* in the context of other languages the students know may reduce the number of carelessly omitted -*s* endings.

Here is a comparison of the verb *speak* (present tense) in four languages, with endings shown in boldface. When no pronouns appear, the pronoun is communicated by the verb's ending.

Singular	Plural
English	
I speak	we speak
you speak	you speak
he, she, it speak**s**	they speak
Spanish	
habl**o**	habl**amos**
habl**as**	habl**áis**
habl**a**	habl**an**
Italian	
parl**o**	parl**iamo**
parl**i**	parl**ate**
parl**a**	parl**ano**
French	
je parl**e**	nous parl**ons**
tu parl**es**	vous parl**ez**
il, elle, on parl**e**	ils, elles parl**ent**

1. Before declaring the Oregon giant earthworm a protected species, a U.S. government agency *requires* concrete proof that they *are* not extinct.

2. Scientists who *find* one alive will demonstrate that the Oregon giant earthworm *does* still exist, in spite of no one's having seen any for over twenty years.

3. Last seen in the Willamette Valley near Portland, Oregon, the earthworm *is* white, and it *smells* like lilies.

4. The Oregon giant earthworm *grows* up to three feet long.

5. Clumps of soil with a strange shape *indicate* that the giant creature *continues* to live, but to demonstrate that it *is* not extinct, only a real specimen will do.

QUOTATION: ON WRITING

You don't know what it is to stay a whole day with your head in your hands trying to squeeze your unfortunate brain so as to find a word. Ah! I know the agonies of style.
—Gustave Flaubert

WORD HISTORY

The word *conjugation* has been used since the early sixteenth century to refer to all the forms of a particular verb. *Conjugation* and *conjugate* both come from the Latin *conjugare,* basically meaning "to join together." In Latin, a list of the forms of a verb was called a *conjugatio,* and *conjugata verba* (literally "joined words") referred to words that were etymologically related.

BACKGROUND

At the site <http:www.discoverwriting.com/jan99.html>, Barry Lane offers teaching activities on verbs. One of his suggestions is for students to create a personal thesaurus to help them avoid using the same verbs repeatedly in their papers.

1. Before declaring the Oregon giant earthworm a protected species, U.S. government agencies *require* concrete proof that it *is* not extinct. (a government agency) (they)

2. A scientist who *finds* one alive will demonstrate that Oregon giant earthworms *do* still exist, in spite of no one's having seen any for over twenty years. (Scientists) (the Oregon giant earthworm)

3. Last seen in the Willamette Valley near Portland, Oregon, the earthworms *are* white, and they *smell* like lilies. (the earthworm) (it)

4. Oregon giant earthworms *grow* up to three feet long. (The Oregon giant earthworm)

5. A clump of soil with a strange shape *indicates* that the giant creatures *continue* to live, but to demonstrate that they *are* not extinct, only a real specimen will do. (clumps of soil) (creature) (it)

8d What is the difference between regular and irregular verbs?

A **regular verb** forms its PAST TENSE and PAST PARTICIPLE by adding *-ed* or *-d* to the SIMPLE FORM: *type, typed; cook, cooked; work, worked.* Most verbs in English are regular.

In informal speech, some people skip over the *-ed* sound, pronouncing it softly or not at all. In ACADEMIC WRITING, however, you're required to use it. If you're not used to hearing or pronouncing this sound, proofread carefully to see that you have all the needed *-ed* endings in your writing.

NO   The cake was **suppose** to be tasty.
YES   The cake was **supposed** to be tasty.

Irregular verbs, in contrast, don't consistently add *-ed* or *-d* to form the past tense and past participle. Some irregular verbs change an internal vowel to make past tense and past participle: *sing, sang, sung.* Some change an internal vowel and add an ending other than *-ed* or *-d: grow, grew, grown.* Some use the simple form throughout: *cost, cost, cost.* Unfortunately, a verb's simple form doesn't provide a clue about whether the verb is irregular or regular.

Although you can always look up the principal parts of any verb, memorizing any you don't know solidly is much more efficient in the long run. About two hundred verbs in English are irregular. Box 60 lists the most frequently used irregular verbs.

👁 **ALERT:** For information about changing *y* to *i*, or doubling a final consonant before adding the *-ed* ending, see 22d. 👁

BOX 60 SUMMARY

 Common irregular verbs

SIMPLE FORM	PAST TENSE	PAST PARTICIPLE
arise	arose	arisen
awake	awoke *or* awaked	awaked *or* awoken
be (is, am, are)	was, were	been
bear	bore	borne *or* born
beat	beat	beaten
become	became	become
begin	began	begun
bend	bent	bent
bet	bet	bet
bid ("to offer")	bid	bid
bid ("to command")	bade	bidden
bind	bound	bound
bite	bit	bitten *or* bit
blow	blew	blown
break	broke	broken
bring	brought	brought
build	built	built
burst	burst	burst
buy	bought	bought
cast	cast	cast
catch	caught	caught
choose	chose	chosen
cling	clung	clung
come	came	come
cost	cost	cost
creep	crept	crept
cut	cut	cut
deal	dealt	dealt
dig	dug	dug
dive	dived *or* dove	dived
do	did	done
draw	drew	drawn
drink	drank	drunk
drive	drove	driven
eat	ate	eaten
fall	fell	fallen
feed	fed	fed
feel	felt	felt
fight	fought	fought

→

BACKGROUND
Old English, ancestor of our language as we know it today, used only two tenses, present and past. All other information, such as number, person, mood, and voice, was indicated by inflectional endings. All that remains of the personal endings is the -*es* or -*s* of the third-person singular, which comes from the Middle English and Early Modern English -*eth* used by Chaucer, translators of the King James Bible, and Shakespeare. English verbs, like all their Germanic cognates, are distinguished by their division into weak and strong classes. In Old English, the strong classes indicated tense by changing the medial vowels; the weak ones did so by changing their endings. After the Norman Invasion, when French and Latin became the languages of power (the court and the church), many strong English verbs became weak, adopting the -*ed* ending to indicate tense changes. New verbs admitted to the language were all placed in the weak category. Today, the mixture of strong and weak forms makes it necessary for English speakers to memorize the principal parts of irregular verbs.

QUOTATION: ON WRITING

I started off with the desire to use language experimentally. Then I saw that the right way was the way of simplicity. Straight sentences, no involutions, no ambiguities. Not much description, description isn't my line. Get on with the story. Present the outside world economically and exactly.

—Graham Greene

QUOTATION: ON WRITING

True ease in writing comes from art, not chance,
As those move easiest who have learned to dance.
'Tis not enough no harshness gives offense,
The sound must seem an echo to the sense.

—Alexander Pope

Common irregular verbs (*continued*)

SIMPLE FORM	PAST TENSE	PAST PARTICIPLE
find	found	found
flee	fled	fled
fling	flung	flung
fly	flew	flown
forbid	forbade *or* forbad	forbidden
forget	forgot	forgotten *or* forgot
forgive	forgave	forgiven
forsake	forsook	forsaken
freeze	froze	frozen
get	got	got *or* gotten
give	gave	given
go	went	gone
grow	grew	grown
hang ("to suspend")*	hung	hung
have	had	had
hear	heard	heard
hide	hid	hidden
hit	hit	hit
hurt	hurt	hurt
keep	kept	kept
know	knew	known
lay	laid	laid
lead	led	led
leave	left	left
lend	lent	lent
let	let	let
lie	lay	lain
light	lighted *or* lit	lighted *or* lit
lose	lost	lost
make	made	made
mean	meant	meant
pay	paid	paid
prove	proved	proved *or* proven
quit	quit	quit
read	read	read
rid	rid	rid
ride	rode	ridden
ring	rang	rung

* When it means "to execute by hanging," *hang* is a regular verb: *In wartime, some armies routinely **hanged** deserters.*

→

Common irregular verbs (continued)

SIMPLE FORM	PAST TENSE	PAST PARTICIPLE
rise	rose	risen
run	ran	run
say	said	said
see	saw	seen
seek	sought	sought
send	sent	sent
set	set	set
shake	shook	shaken
shine ("to glow")*	shone	shone
shoot	shot	shot
show	showed	shown *or* showed
shrink	shrank	shrunk
sing	sang	sung
sink	sank *or* sunk	sunk
sit	sat	sat
slay	slew	slain
sleep	slept	slept
sling	slung	slung
speak	spoke	spoken
spend	spent	spent
spin	spun	spun
spring	sprang *or* sprung	sprung
stand	stood	stood
steal	stole	stolen
sting	stung	stung
stink	stank *or* stunk	stunk
stride	strode	stridden
strike	struck	struck
strive	strove	striven
swear	swore	sworn
sweep	swept	swept
swim	swam	swum
swing	swung	swung
take	took	taken
teach	taught	taught
tear	tore	torn
tell	told	told
think	thought	thought

* When it means "to polish," *shine* is a regular verb: We **shined** our shoes.

→

BACKGROUND

The site <http://www.chompchomp.com> features interactive exercises on a variety of writing topics. The following is a sample exercise on irregular verbs: "Rachel *would have wrote* a better essay for Mr. Parker, but she *drank* a double espresso and found that she had too much energy to sit still at a computer. Response: The first verb, *would have wrote,* is incorrect. This verb requires the past participle *written* because of the auxiliary verbs *would* and *have. Write* is an irregular verb."
—Robin L. Simmons, at <http://www.chompchomp.com>

BACKGROUND

The site <http://ccc.commnet.edu/cgi-shl/par2_quiz.pl/irregular_quiz.htm> features an interactive quiz on irregular verbs. The quiz takes only a few minutes and students can receive immediate feedback on their answers.

BACKGROUND

In late antiquity and the Middle Ages, grammar, rhetoric, and logic were organized into the *trivium,* the three language arts of education. The trivium and *quadrivium* (geometry, arithmetic, astronomy, and music) together formed the seven liberal arts. Grammar meant the study of Latin until the eighteenth and nineteenth centuries, when English and other vernacular languages began to displace Latin as the language of education.

ANSWERS: EXERCISE 8-2

1. needed
2. dumped; lacked; caused
3. developed; cooled
4. placed; increased
5. resulted; flowed; reduced

ANSWERS: EXERCISE 8-3

1. became
2. grew
3. got
4. taught
5. wrote
6. was
7. came
8. began, won, made, beat
9. broke, cut
10. came, was, drew
11. kept
12. ran, spent
13. knew
14. swore

Common irregular verbs (*continued*)

SIMPLE FORM	PAST TENSE	PAST PARTICIPLE
throw	threw	thrown
understand	understood	understood
wake	woke *or* waked	waked *or* woken
wear	wore	worn
wring	wrung	wrung
write	wrote	written

EXERCISE 8-2

Write the correct past-tense form of the regular verbs given in parentheses.
For help, consult 8d.

EXAMPLE   The Stanford University football team (uses) used an innovative system to cool down after workouts.

(1) Many athletes (need) _____ a way to lower their body
temperatures quickly. (2) They normally just (dump) _____ ice on
themselves, but this method (lack) _____ efficiency and sometimes
even (cause) _____ collapse. (3) To solve the problem, scientists
(develop) _____ the Rapid Thermal Exchange system, which (cools)
_____ an athlete from inside. (4) To test the new device, a football
player (places) _____ his hand on a cool metal plate inside an airtight
chamber, where a mild vacuum pressure (increases) _____ blood flow.
(5) This (results) _____ in lowered body temperature as the cooled-down
blood (flows) _____ throughout the body and (reduces) _____ the
discomfort of being overly hot.

EXERCISE 8-3

Write the correct past-tense form of the irregular verbs given in parentheses. For help, consult Box 60 in 8d.

EXAMPLE   Ben Johnson (think) thought as he (speak) spoke to prison
inmates that his story might help them.

(1) At age 33, Ben Johnson (become) _____ the youngest chief of
pediatric neurosurgery in the United States at one of the top hospitals,

Baltimore's Johns Hopkins. (2) This accomplishment seemed impossible for a young African American youth who (grow) _____ up in run-down apartments in Boston and Detroit. (3) In fifth grade, he (get) _____ Fs and Ds on his report card. (4) His mother, with only a third-grade education herself, (teach) _____ Ben to care about his education. (5) Ben and his older brother, Curtis, (write) _____ two book reports each week and watched no more than three TV shows a week. (6) By seventh grade, Ben (be) _____ at the top of his class at Wilson Junior High. (7) However, excelling in an interracial sports center (come) _____ with problems. (8) His most humiliating experience (begin) _____ when Ben (win) _____ the Outstanding Athlete award, and his white coach (make) _____ insulting comments to Ben's white teammates because they had let a black athlete (beat) _____ them. (9) Also, Ben had a terrible temper and (break) _____ a classmate's nose with a rock and (cut) _____ another with a padlock. (10) The turning point for Ben (come) _____ when he (be) _____ fourteen and (draw) _____ a knife on a friend. (11) Fortunately, the friend's belt buckle (keep) _____ the knife from entering his stomach. (12) Ben (run) _____ home horrified and (spend) _____ several hours alone thinking. (13) This experience changed him because he now (know) _____ that if people could make him angry they could control him. (14) He (swear) _____ never to give anyone else power over his life.

8e What are auxiliary verbs?

Auxiliary verbs, also called *helping verbs*, combine with MAIN VERBS to make VERB PHRASES. Box 61 shows how auxiliary verbs work.

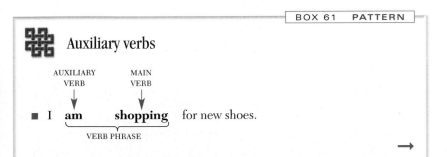

BOX 61   PATTERN

Auxiliary verbs

AUXILIARY VERB   MAIN VERB

■ I **am** **shopping** for new shoes.

VERB PHRASE

→

EXTRA EXERCISE A
Identify all modal auxiliaries in the following passage. (Answers appear in italics.)

Most professionals in the field of medicine agree that the public *ought to* be better informed about recent developments in medical science. One of the tools that patients frequently experience but *may* know little about is the X-ray. Its discoverer, Professor Wilhelm Roentgen, thought he *might* have a powerful new means of examining the body when, in 1895, he saw the glimmer of a fluorescent screen. His discovery meant that medical professionals *could* peer into the innermost recesses of the body without surgery. For example, Dr. William B. Cannon realized that fluoroscopy *could* be used to examine the alimentary canal or digestive system. Today X-ray means that doctors *can* carry diagnostic methods to previously inaccessible areas of the human body by painless techniques. A list of all of the diagnostic uses of X-ray films *would* be too lengthy to include here, but it is safe to say that they *can* be used on all parts of the body. Of course, because improper use of X-rays *may* be harmful, technologists *should* have adequate training. They *must* complete a rigorous course of study before being allowed to operate X-ray machines.

—Emily Gordon

QUOTATION: ON WRITING
In the lexicon of *iffiness, may* and *might* mark ranges of possibility from the probable to the unlikely.

—William Safire

Auxiliary verbs (*continued*)

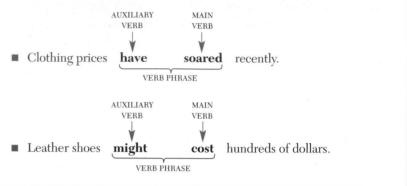

- Clothing prices **have** **soared** recently.

  AUXILIARY VERB · MAIN VERB · VERB PHRASE

- Leather shoes **might** **cost** hundreds of dollars.

  AUXILIARY VERB · MAIN VERB · VERB PHRASE

Using be, do, have

The three most common auxiliary verbs are *be, do,* and *have.* These three verbs can also be main verbs. Their forms vary more than most irregular verbs, as Boxes 62 and 63 show.

BOX 62 SUMMARY

Forms of the verb *be*

SIMPLE FORM	be
-S FORM	is
PAST TENSE	was, were
PRESENT PARTICIPLE	being
PAST PARTICIPLE	been

Person	Present Tense	Past Tense
I	am	was
you (singular)	are	were
he, she, it	is	was
we	are	were
you (plural)	are	were
they	are	were

BOX 63   SUMMARY

 Forms of the verbs *do* and *have*

SIMPLE FORM	do	have
-S FORM	does	has
PAST TENSE	did	had
PRESENT PARTICIPLE	doing	having
PAST PARTICIPLE	done	had

👁 **ALERT:** In ACADEMIC WRITING, always use the standard forms for *be*, *do*, and *have*, as shown in Boxes 62 and 63.

The gym **is** [not *be*] a busy place.

The gym **is** [not *be*] filling with spectators. 👁

🌐 **ESL NOTE:** When *be, do,* and *have* function as auxiliary verbs, change their form to agree with a third-person singular subject—and don't add *-s* to the main verb.

NO   **Does** the library **closes** at 6:00?

YES   **Does** the library **close** at 6:00? 🌐

Modal auxiliary verbs

Can, could, shall, should, will, would, may, might, and *must* are the nine modal auxiliary verbs. **Modal auxiliary verbs** communicate ability, permission, obligation, advisability, necessity, or possibility. They never change form.

Exercise **can lengthen** lives. [possibility]

She **can jog** for five miles. [ability]

The exercise **must occur** regularly. [necessity, obligation]

People **should protect** their bodies. [advisability]

May I **exercise?** [permission]

🌐 **ESL NOTE:** For more about modal auxiliary verbs and the meanings they communicate, see Chapter 50. 🌐

EXERCISE 8-4

Using the auxiliary verbs in the list below, fill in the blanks in the following passage. Use each auxiliary word only once, even if a listed word can fit into more than one blank. For help, consult section 8e.

are   have   may   will   might   can   has

EXTRA EXERCISE B
Circle all transitive verbs and underline all intransitive verbs in the following sentences.

1. Yellowstone National Park is the oldest and largest park in the national system.
2. It lies in the northwestern corner of Wyoming, slightly overlapping the boundaries of Montana on the north and Idaho on the west and south.
3. The planners originally designed the park to run 62 miles from east to west and 54 miles from north to south.
4. Yellowstone has several lofty plateaus, and the Continental Divide crosses it.
5. The Yellowstone River flows north into Yellowstone Lake and then through its canyon across Montana to join the Missouri.
6. The most famous sights in Yellowstone Park are the geysers.
7. The park has more than three thousand springs, pools, and geysers.
8. Old Faithful is the most famous of the geysers, but in the same basin with it are a number of other impressive water jets.
9. Wildlife in the park, which includes bear, deer, elk, antelope, and mountain sheep, is protected.

Answers to Extra Exercise B

1. is (intransitive)
2. lies (intransitive)
3. designed (transitive)
4. has (transitive); crosses (transitive)
5. flows (intransitive)
6. are (intransitive)
7. has (transitive)
8. is (intransitive); are (intransitive)
9. includes (transitive); is (intransitive)

EXAMPLE   Psychologists <u>have</u> discovered that most personal memories focus on recent events.

(1) Most adults _____ recall recent events more readily than distant ones when they _____ presented with a standard test of memory. (2) However, an important exception _____ been found among older adults, those age 50 and above. (3) People in this older age group _____ most readily recall events that happened in their late teens and early adulthood. (4) Researchers _____ concluded that because many significant life events, such as getting married and choosing a career, occur during this period, older adults _____ prefer to look back on this highly memorable period. (5) Similarly, younger adults _____ tend to focus on those same memorable events, which means that they summon more recent memories.

8f What are intransitive and transitive verbs?

A verb is **intransitive** when an OBJECT isn't required to complete the verb's meaning: *I sing.* A verb is **transitive** when an object is necessary to complete the verb's meaning: *I need a guitar.* Many verbs have both transitive and intransitive meanings. Some verbs are only transitive: *need, have, like, owe, remember.* Only transitive verbs function in the PASSIVE VOICE. Dictionaries label verbs as transitive (*vt*) or intransitive (*vi*). Box 64 shows how transitive and intransitive verbs operate in sentences.

BOX 64   SUMMARY

 Comparing intransitive and transitive verbs

INTRANSITIVE (OBJECT NOT NEEDED)

They **sat** together quietly. [*Together* and *quietly* are not direct objects; they are modifiers.]
The cat **sees** in the dark. [*In the dark* is not a direct object; it is a modifier.]
I can **hear** well. [*Well* is not a direct object; it is a modifier.]

TRANSITIVE (OBJECT NEEDED)

They **sent** a birthday card to me. [*Birthday card* is a direct object.]
The cat **sees** the dog. [*Dog* is a direct object.]
I can **hear** you. [*You* is a direct object.]

The verbs *lie* and *lay* are particularly confusing. *Lie* means "to recline, to place oneself down, or to remain." *Lie* is intransitive (it cannot be followed by an object). *Lay* means "to put something down." *Lay* is transitive (it must be followed by an object). As you can see in Box 65, the word *lay* is both the past tense of *lie* and the present-tense simple form of *lay*. That makes things difficult. My best advice is memorize them. Yet truthfully, each time I use *lie* and *lay*, I need to pause, think, and recite the list to myself.

BOX 65   SUMMARY

Using *lie* and *lay*

	lie	lay
SIMPLE FORM	lie	lay
-S FORM	lies	lays
PAST TENSE	lay	laid
PRESENT PARTICIPLE	lying	laying
PAST PARTICIPLE	lain	laid

Intransitive Forms

PRESENT TENSE	The hikers **lie** down to rest.
PAST TENSE	The hikers **lay** down to rest.

Transitive Forms

PRESENT TENSE	The hikers **lay** their backpacks on a rock. [*Backpacks* is a direct object.]
PAST TENSE	The hikers **laid** their backpacks on a rock. [*Backpacks* is a direct object.]

Two other verb pairs tend to confuse people because of their intransitive and transitive forms: *raise* and *rise* and *set* and *sit*.

Raise and *set* are transitive (they must be followed by an object). *Rise* and *sit* are intransitive (they cannot be followed by an object). Fortunately, although each word has a meaning different from the other words, they don't share forms: *raise, raised, raised; rise, rose, risen;* and *set, set, set; sit, sat, sat.*

EXERCISE 8-5

Underline the correct word of each pair in parentheses. For help, consult 8f.

EXAMPLE   Whenever I come home, I always check to see where my cat is (laying, <u>lying</u>).

ANSWERS AND COVERAGE: EXERCISE 8-5

1. laid [first-person singular past of *lay*]; lying [present participle of *lie*]

2. sat; rose; lay [third-person singular past of *lie*]

3. Sitting [present participle of *sit*]

4. raised; lay [third-person plural past of *lie*]

5. lay [third-person plural past of *lie*]; lie [third-person singular present of *lie*]

EXTRA EXERCISE C
For practice in identifying verbs and forming past-tense verbs, rewrite the following paragraph, changing the present-tense verbs to past tense. (Answers appear in italics within parentheses.)

Recuperation is (*was*) like spring: dormancy and vitality collide (*collided*). In any year I'm (*I was*) like a bear, a partial hibernator. During January thaws I stick (*stuck*) my nose out and peruse (*perused*) the frozen desolation as if reading a book whose language I don't (*didn't*) know. In March I'm (*I was*) ramshackle, weak in the knees, giddy, dazzled by broken-backed clouds, the passing of Halley's comet, the on-and-off strobe of sun. Like a sheepherder I X (*Xed*) out each calendar day as if time were (*no change, subjunctive voice*) a forest through which I could clear-cut (*no change, subjunctive voice*) a way to the future. My physicist friend straightens (*straightened*) me out on this point too. The notion of "time passing," like a train through a landscape, is (*was*) an illusion, he says (*said*). I hold (*held*) the Big Ben clock taken from a dead sheepherder's wagon and look (*looked*) at it. The clock measures (*measured*) intervals of time, not the speed of time, and the calendar is (*was*) a scaffolding we hang (*hung*) as if time were (*no change, subjunctive voice*) rushing water we could harness (*no change, subjunctive voice*). Time-bound, I hinge (*hinged*) myself to a linear bias—cause and effect all laid out in a neat row—and in this we learn (*learned*) two things: blame and shame.

—Gretel Ehrlich, "Spring"

(1) Coming home from jogging one morning, I (laid, lay) my keys on the counter and saw my cat, Andy, (laying, lying) in a patch of sunlight on the living room floor. (2) When I (sat, set) down beside him, he (raised, rose) up on his toes, stretched, and then (laid, lay) down a few feet away. (3) (Sitting, Setting) there, I reached out to Andy, and my contrary cat jumped up onto the couch. As he landed, I heard a clinking noise. (4) I (raised, rose) the bottom of the slipcover, and there (laid, lay) my favorite earrings, the ones I thought I had lost last week. Deciding he had earned a special privilege, Andy curled up on a red silk pillow in the corner of the couch. (5) Since the earrings now (laid, lay) safely in my pocket, I let him (lay, lie) there undisturbed.

VERB TENSE

8g What is verb tense?

Verb tense conveys time. Verbs show tense (time) by changing form. English has six verb tenses, divided into simple and perfect groups. The three **simple tenses** divide time into present, past, and future. The simple **present tense** describes what happens regularly, what takes place in the present, and what is consistently or generally true. The simple **past tense** tells of an action completed or a condition ended. The simple **future tense** indicates action yet to be taken or a condition not yet experienced.

Rick **wants** to speak Spanish fluently. [simple present tense]
Rick **wanted** to improve rapidly. [simple past tense]
Rick **will want** to progress even further next year. [simple future tense]

The three **perfect tenses** also divide time into present, past, and future. They show more complex time relationships than the simple tenses. For information on using the perfect tenses, see section 8i.

The three simple tenses and the three perfect tenses also have **progressive forms.** These forms indicate that the verb describes what is ongoing or continuing. For information on using progressive forms, see section 8j. Box 66 on the facing page summarizes verb tenses and progressive forms.

ESL NOTE: Box 66 shows that most verb tenses are formed by combining one or more AUXILIARY VERBS with the SIMPLE FORM, the PRESENT PARTICIPLE, or the PAST PARTICIPLE of a MAIN VERB. Auxiliary verbs are necessary in the formation of most tenses, so never omit them.

NO   I **talking** to you.
YES   I **am talking** to you. ⊕

BOX 66   SUMMARY

Simple, perfect, and progressive tenses

Simple Tenses

	REGULAR VERB	IRREGULAR VERB	PROGRESSIVE FORM
PRESENT	I talk	I eat	I am talking; I am eating
PAST	I talked	I ate	I was talking; I was eating
FUTURE	I will talk	I will eat	I will be talking; I will be eating

Perfect Tenses

	REGULAR VERB	IRREGULAR VERB	PROGRESSIVE FORM
PRESENT PERFECT	I have talked	I have eaten	I have been talking; I have been eating
PAST PERFECT	I had talked	I had eaten	I had been talking; I had been eating
FUTURE PERFECT	I will have talked	I will have eaten	I will have been talking; I will have been eating

---

TEACHING TIP: ESL
The term *present* can be confusing for ESL students because in English, the simple present tense does not describe the present moment. Rather, our simple present is "timeless" (The sun *rises* in the east and *sets* in the west) or general (*Democracy* means "rule by the people"). In English, the present moment is expressed in the present progressive. ESL students might need many examples and much practice to grasp the confusing labels. For example: *I work in an office.* [simple present tense] *I am working on a report.* [present progressive]

8h How do I use the simple present tense?

The **simple present tense** uses the SIMPLE FORM of the verb (see 8b). It describes what happens regularly, what takes place in the present, and what is generally or consistently true. Also, it can convey a future occurrence with verbs like *start, stop, begin, end, arrive,* and *depart.*

> Calculus class **meets** every morning. [regularly occurring action]
> Mastering calculus **takes** time. [general truth]
> The course **ends** in eight weeks. [specific future event]

👁 **ALERT:** For a work of literature, always describe or discuss the action in the present tense. This holds true no matter how old the work.

> In Shakespeare's *Romeo and Juliet,* Juliet's father **wants** her to marry Paris, but Juliet **loves** Romeo. 👁

8i How do I form and use the perfect tenses?

The **perfect tenses** generally describe actions or occurrences that are still having an effect at the present time or are having an effect until a specified time. The perfect tenses are composed of an AUXILIARY VERB and a main verb's PAST PARTICIPLE (see 8b).

For the **present perfect tense** (see Box 66), use *has* only for the THIRD-PERSON SINGULAR subjects and *have* for all other subjects. For the **past perfect,** use *had* with the past participle. For the **future perfect,** use *will have* with the past participle.

PRESENT PERFECT	Our government **has offered** to help. [having effect now]
PRESENT PERFECT	The drought **has created** terrible hardship. [having effect until a specified time—when the rains come]
PAST PERFECT	As soon as the tornado **had passed,** the heavy rain started. [Both events occurred in the past; the tornado occurred before the rain, so the earlier event uses *had*.]
FUTURE PERFECT	Our chickens' egg production **will have reached** five hundred per day by next year. [The event will occur before a specified time.]

8j How do I form and use progressive forms?

Progressive forms describe an ongoing action or condition. They also express habitual or recurring actions or conditions. The **present progressive** uses the present-tense form of *be* that agrees with the subject in PERSON and NUMBER, plus the *-ing* form (PRESENT PARTICIPLE) of the main verb. The **past progressive** uses *was* or *were* to agree with the subject in person and number, and it uses the present participle of the main verb. The **future progressive** uses *will be* and the present participle. The **present perfect progressive** uses *have been* or *has been* to agree with the subject, plus the *-ing* form of the main verb. The **past perfect progressive** uses *had been* and the *-ing* form of the main verb. The **future perfect progressive** uses *will have been* plus the PRESENT PARTICIPLE.

PRESENT PROGRESSIVE	The smog **is stinging** everyone's eyes. [event taking place now]
PAST PROGRESSIVE	Eye drops **were selling** well last week. [event ongoing in the past within stated limits]
FUTURE PROGRESSIVE	We **will be ordering** more eye drops than usual this month. [recurring event that will take place in the future]

PRESENT PERFECT PROGRESSIVE	Scientists **have been warning** us about air pollution for years. [recurring event that took place in the past and may still take place]
PAST PERFECT PROGRESSIVE	We **had been ordering** three cases of eye drops a month until the smog worsened. [recurring past event that has now ended]
FUTURE PERFECT PROGRESSIVE	By May, we **will have been selling** eye drops for eight months. [ongoing condition to be completed at a specific time in the future]

EXERCISE 8-6

Underline the correct verb in each pair of parentheses. If more than one answer is possible, be prepared to explain the differences in meaning between the choices. For help, consult 8g through 8j.

EXAMPLE Planet Earth (<u>experiences</u>, will be experiencing) a dramatic attack every eleven years.

1. A huge magnetic force, called a "solar maximum," (is racing, races) every eleven years from the sun toward the earth at two million miles per hour.
2. The magnetic force (is, was) 30 times more concentrated than the normal force that (will reach, reaches) the earth.
3. A less violent "solar wind," of one million miles per hour, (hits, will have hit) the earth now and then between the solar maximums.
4. While these occurrences (had, were having) little effect in previous years, advances in technology today (had made, have made) us vulnerable to the sun's shifting winds.
5. Since 1996, solar winds occasionally (had been wiping, have wiped) out cellphones, pagers, and pay-at-the-pump gasoline services.
6. A solar maximum suddenly (knocked, was knocking) out electrical power to six million people in the U.S. Northeast in 1989.
7. Such communication disruptions (cost, have been costing) over $100 million a year in repairs and lost business, which (affects, has affected) government offices, companies, and individual citizens.
8. Fortunately, no astronaut (has been orbiting, orbited) the earth when a solar wind (will be occurring, has occurred).
9. Currently, government space scientists (are collecting, will be collecting) data and soon (are evaluating, will evaluate) the effects of solar maximums on satellites, airplanes, power lines, oil and gas pipelines, and spacecraft.
10. Space experts at NASA, the National Aeronautics and Space Administration, (hope, were hoping) the new "Living with a Star" program (will be telling, will tell) them how the next solar maximum in 2011 (will affect, was affecting) us.

ANSWERS AND COVERAGE: EXERCISE 8-6

1. races [8h, simple present for regularly occurring action]

2. is [8h, simple present for general truth]; reaches [8h, simple present for recurring action]

3. hits [8h, simple present for recurring action]

4. had [8g, past tense for completed action]; have made [8i, present perfect for condition still prevailing]

5. have wiped [8i, present perfect for condition still prevailing]

6. knocked [8g, past tense for completed action]

7. have been costing [8j, present perfect progressive for action begun in the past and still occurring]; has affected [8i, present perfect for action still in effect and condition still prevailing]

8. has been orbiting [8j, present perfect progressive for recurring event that took place in the past and may still take place]; has occurred [8i, present perfect for action still in effect]

9. are collecting [8j, present progressive for ongoing event]; will evaluate [8g, future tense for action yet to be taken]

10. hope [8h, simple present for general truth]; will tell [8g, future tense for action yet to be taken]; will affect [8g, future tense for condition not yet experienced]

EXTRA EXERCISE E

Circle the verbs in the following sentences; then name their tenses and explain what meaning is expressed.

1. Dolphins, porpoises, and whales belong to the order Cetacea, which means that they are not fish but mammals.

2. They give birth to their young, nourish them with milk, and have warm blood.

3. Once whales probably lived on the land and walked on four legs, but now they are completely aquatic.

4. Once they had left the land and moved to the water, their body structure changed radically.

5. Because they are land mammals that have become adapted to an aquatic existence, if water enters their lungs, they will die.

6. Consequently, when a whale is diving beneath the surface, it literally holds its breath by closing its nostrils.

7. Whales dive for different periods of time to various depths.

8. The humpback whale has been known to remain submerged for twenty minutes and the blue whale for fifty, though both could probably remain longer if necessary.

9. For years, scientists have been researching the depths to which the various types of whale can dive.

10. The sperm whale has been known to dive to a depth of over 3,000 feet, subjecting it to a pressure of around 1,400 pounds per square inch.

Answers to Extra Exercise E

1. belong; means; are [all present tense; express general truths]

2. give; nourish; have [all present tense; express general truths]

3. lived; walked [both past tense; express past events]; are [present tense; expresses current fact]

4. had left [past perfect tense; expresses an act completed in the past before another one took place]; moved; changed [past tense; both express an act completed in the past]

⟶

8k How do I use tense sequences accurately?

Verb **tense sequences** communicate time relationships. They help deliver messages about actions, occurrences, or states that take place at different times. Box 67 shows how tenses in the same sentence can vary depending on when actions (or occurrences or states) occur.

BOX 67   SUMMARY

Tense sequences

■ If your independent clause contains a simple-present-tense verb, then in your dependent clause you can

- Use PRESENT TENSE to show same-time action:
  I **avoid** shellfish because I **am** allergic to it.

- Use PAST TENSE to show earlier action:
  I **am** sure that I **deposited** the check.

- Use the PRESENT PERFECT TENSE to show (1) a period of time extending from some point in the past to the present or (2) an indefinite past time:
  They **claim** that they **have visited** the planet Venus.
  I **believe** that I **have seen** that movie before.

- Use the FUTURE TENSE for action to come:
  The book **is** open because I **will be reading** it later.

■ If your independent clause contains a past-tense verb, then in your dependent clause you can

- Use the past tense to show another completed past action:
  I **closed** the door because you **told** me to.

- Use the PAST PERFECT TENSE to show earlier action:
  The sprinter **knew** that she **had broken** the record.

- Use the present tense to state a general truth:
  Christopher Columbus **determined** that the world is round.

■ If your independent clause contains a present-perfect-tense or past-perfect-tense verb, then in your dependent clause you can

- Use the past tense:
  The bread **has become** moldy since I **purchased** it.
  Sugar prices **had** already **declined** when artificial sweeteners first **appeared.**

⟶

Tense sequences (*continued*)

- If your independent clause contains a future-tense verb, then in your dependent clause you can
  - Use the present tense to show action happening at the same time:

    You **will be** rich if you **win** the prize.
  - Use the past tense to show earlier action:

    You **will** surely **win** the prize if you **remembered** to mail the entry form.
  - Use the present perfect tense to show future action earlier than the action of the independent-clause verb:

    The river **will flood** again next year unless we **have built** a better dam by then.

- If your independent clause contains a future-perfect-tense verb, then in your dependent clause you can
  - Use either the present tense or the present perfect tense:

    Dr. Chang **will have delivered** five thousand babies by the time she **retires.**

    Dr. Chang **will have delivered** five thousand babies by the time she **has retired.**

👁 **ALERT:** Never use a future-tense verb in a dependent clause when the verb in the independent clause is in the future tense. Instead, use a present-tense verb in the independent clause.

   NO   The river **will flood** us unless we **will prepare** our defense.

   YES   The river **will flood** us unless we **prepare** our defense.
       [*Prepare* is a present-tense verb.]

   YES   The river **will flood** us unless we **have prepared** our defense.
       [*Have prepared* is a present perfect verb.] 👁

Tense sequences may include INFINITIVES and PARTICIPLES. To name or describe an activity or occurrence coming either at the same time or after the time expressed in the MAIN VERB, use the **present infinitive.**

I **hope to buy** a used car. [*To buy* comes at a future time. *Hope* is the main verb, and its action is now.]

I **hoped to buy** a used car. [*Hoped* is the main verb, and its action is over.]

Answers to Extra Exercise E (continued)

5. are [present tense; expresses current truth]; have become adapted [present perfect tense; act begun and completed in the past but continuing into the present]; enters [present tense; expresses general truth]; will die [future tense; expresses future action]

6. is diving [present progressive tense; expresses an action taking place at the moment]; holds [present tense; expresses regularly occurring action]

7. dive [present tense; expresses habitual action]

8. has been known [present perfect tense; expresses action in the past that continues into the present]; could remain [present tense with modal auxiliary; expresses possible action]

9. have been researching [present perfect progressive; expresses action ongoing in the past and likely to continue into the future]; can dive [present tense with modal auxiliary; expresses possible action]

10. has been known [present perfect tense; expresses action in the past that continues into the present]

EXTRA EXERCISE F
Identify the tenses of the verbs in the following sentences.

1. My neighbor walks to work every morning.

2. Jill is studying for her math test.

3. I will take my lunch with me to the park.

4. The secretary has been typing the manuscript for days.

5. Her mother will be speaking with the supervisor in the morning.

6. Ms. Conrad had been planning to change jobs when her company was sold.

7. I closed my bank account yesterday.

8. We will have discussed the topic by the time you get to the meeting.

9. The program has generated little interest among the attendees.

10. The babies in the nursery were crying when I went in.

                      →

1. present
2. present progressive
3. future
4. present perfect progressive
5. future progressive
6. past perfect progressive; past
7. past
8. future perfect; present
9. present perfect
10. past progressive; past

QUOTATION: ON WRITING

Grammar is the prism through which all writing is refracted.

—Patricia Robertson

ANSWERS AND COVERAGE: EXERCISE 8-7

1. was born [dependent clause in past tense for completed action]; lives [independent clause in present tense for current action]; tours [present tense for regularly occurring action]

2. will treasure [independent clause in future tense for situation continuing beyond action of dependent clause]

3. began [dependent clause in past tense]

4. became [dependent clause in simple past for a completed action]; plays [independent clause in simple present for regularly occurring action]

5. continues [independent clause in simple present]; take [dependent clause in simple present for same-time action]

6. know [dependent clause in simple present for general truth]; has made [independent clause in present perfect for action completed but condition still in effect]

7. was traveling [dependent clause in past progressive for ongoing action completed in the past]; filmed [independent clause in simple past for action completed in the past]

8. became; studied [independent and dependent clauses in simple past for actions completed in the past]

9. fell asleep; was [dependent clauses in simple past for completed past action]

10. failed [dependent clause in simple past for completed past action]

I **had hoped to buy** a used car. [*Had hoped* is the main verb, and its action is over.]

The PRESENT PARTICIPLE (a verb's *-ing* form) can describe action happening at the same time.

Driving his new car, the man **smiled.** [The driving and the smiling happened at the same time.]

To describe an action that occurs before the action in the main verb, use the **perfect infinitive** (*to have gone, to have smiled*), the PAST PARTICIPLE, or the **present perfect participle** (*having gone, having smiled*).

Candida **claimed to have written** fifty short stories in college. [*Claimed* is the main verb, and *to have written* happened first.]

Pleased with the short story, Candida **mailed** it to several magazines. [*Mailed* is the main verb, and *pleased* happened first.]

Having sold one short story, Candida **invested** in a computer. [*Invested* is the main verb, and *having sold* happened first.]

EXERCISE 8-7

Underline the correct verb in each pair of parentheses that best suits the sequence of tenses. Be ready to explain your choices. For help, consult 8k.

EXAMPLE   When he (is, was) seven years old, Yo-Yo Ma, possibly the world's greatest living cellist, (moves, moved) to the United States with his family.

1. Yo-Yo Ma, who (had been born, was born) in France to Chinese parents, (lived, lives) in Boston, Massachusetts, today and (toured, tours) as one of the world's greatest cellists.

2. Years from now, after Mr. Ma has given his last concert, music lovers still (treasure, will treasure) his many fine recordings.

3. Mr. Ma's older sister, Dr. Yeou-Cheng Ma, was nearly the person with the concert career. She had been training to become a concert violinist until her brother's musical genius (began, had begun) to be noticed.

4. Even though Dr. Ma eventually (becomes, became) a physician, she still (had been playing, plays) the violin.

5. The family interest in music (continues, was continuing), for Mr. Ma's children (take, had taken) piano lessons.

6. Although most people today (knew, know) Mr. Ma as a brilliant cellist, he (was making, has made) films as well.

7. One year, while he (had been traveling, was traveling) in the Kalahari Desert, he (films, filmed) dances of southern Africa's Bush people.

8. Mr. Ma first (becomes, became) interested in the Kalahari people when he (had studied, studied) anthropology as an undergraduate at Harvard University.

9. When he shows visitors around Boston now, Mr. Ma has been known to point out the Harvard University library where, he claims, he (fell asleep, was falling asleep) in the stacks when he (had been, was) a student.

10. Indicating another building, Mr. Ma admits that in one of its classrooms he almost (failed, had failed) German.

MOOD

8l What is "mood" in verbs?

Mood in verbs conveys an attitude toward the action in a sentence. English has three moods: *indicative, imperative,* and *subjunctive.* Use the **indicative mood** to make statements about real things, about highly likely things, and for questions about fact.

INDICATIVE	The door to the tutoring center opened. [real]
	She seemed to be looking for someone. [highly likely]
	Do you want to see a tutor? [question about a fact]

The **imperative mood** expresses commands and direct requests. Often the subject is omitted in an imperative sentence, but nevertheless the subject is implied to be either *you* or one of the indefinite pronouns such as *anybody, somebody,* or *everybody.*

👁 **ALERT:** Use an exclamation point after a strong command; use a period after a mild command or a request (23e, 23a).

| IMPERATIVE | Please shut the door. |
| | Watch out! That screw is loose. 👁 |

The **subjunctive mood** expresses speculation, other unreal conditions, conjectures, wishes, recommendations, indirect requests, and demands. Often, the words that signal the subjunctive mood are *if, as if, as though,* and *unless.* In speaking, subjunctive verb forms were once used frequently in English, but they're heard far less today. Nevertheless, in ACADEMIC WRITING, you need to use the subjunctive mood.

| SUBJUNCTIVE | If I **were** you, I would ask for a tutor. |

8m What are subjunctive forms?

For the **present subjunctive,** always use the SIMPLE FORM of the verb for all PERSONS and NUMBERS.

BACKGROUND
Mood in verb inflection is the form of a verb that indicates its manner of doing or being. In English, the forms are called *indicative* (for direct statement or question, or to express an uncertain condition), *imperative* (for commands), and *subjunctive* (for sentences suggesting doubt, condition, or a situation contrary to fact). The infinitive is sometimes considered an example of mood, as are phrases formed with *may, might, can, could, should, would, must,* and *ought.*
—<http://www.Encyclopedia.com>

QUOTATION: ON WRITING
If it were not for the subjunctive, we would be less able to express desire, supposition, doubt; more important, we would find it hard to set up a situation contrary to fact—a shocker, something ridiculous—to see how we would deal with it.
—William Safire

OTHER EXAMPLES
OF SUBJUNCTIVE MOOD

People find it interesting to speculate about how the future *could be* affected if a single aspect of our world *were* different today. For example, if the average yearly temperature *were* only a few degrees higher, the oceans *would* rise due to the melting of the polar icecaps. If serious worldwide droughts *were* to occur in several successive summers, the food supply *would* dwindle. Unless science *were* able to divert the swelling oceans or grow crops without the use of water, civilization as we know it *would be* radically changed. It is, consequently, important that everyone *recognize* the importance of environmental decisions. The world *should* not act as though the future *were* inevitably bad. If, in the early part of this century, the industrialized world *had considered* the effects of water and air pollution, our world *would* be a healthier one today.

TEACHING TIP: ESL

For ESL students, conditions and wishes are often difficult to master because to indicate hypothetical or unreal states requires changes in verb forms that usually indicate *time* shifts. For example, the form for a wish or an unreal condition in the present (*I wish I had a car* or *If I were you . . .*) uses the *past* form of the verb. Similarly, unreality in the past calls for the *past perfect* form (*I wish he had told me his problem*). Students can better understand these tricky structures when they can be seen and analyzed, preferably in essays the class is reading.

The prosecutor asks that she **testify** [not *testifies*] again.
It is important that they **be** [not *are*] allowed to testify.

For the **past subjunctive,** use the simple past tense: *I wish that I had a car.* The one exception is for the past subjunctive of *be:* Use *were* for all forms.

I wish that I **were** [not *was*] leaving on vacation today.
They asked if she **were** [not *was*] leaving on vacation today.

Using the subjunctive in *if,* as if, as though, *and* unless *clauses*

In dependent clauses introduced by *if* and sometimes by *unless,* the subjunctive describes speculations or conditions contrary to fact.

If it **were** [not *was*] to rain, attendance at the race would be disappointing. [speculation]
The runner looked as if he **were** [not *was*] winded, but he said he wasn't. [a condition contrary to fact]

In an *unless* clause, the subjunctive signals that what the clause says is highly unlikely.

Unless rain **were** [not *was*] to create floods, the race will be held this Sunday. [Floods are highly unlikely.]

Not every clause introduced by *if, unless, as if,* or *as though* requires the subjunctive. Use the subjunctive only when the dependent clause describes speculation or a condition contrary to fact.

INDICATIVE	If she **is** going to leave late, I will drive her to the race. [Her leaving late is highly likely.]
SUBJUNCTIVE	If she **were** going to leave late, I would drive her to the race. [Her leaving late is a speculation.]

Using the subjunctive in *that clauses*

When *that* clauses describe wishes, requests, demands, or recommendations, the subjunctive can convey the message.

I wish that this race **were** [not *was*] over. [a wish about something happening now]
He wishes that he **had seen** [not *saw*] the race. [a wish about something that is past]
The judges are demanding that the doctor **examine** [not *examines*] the runners. [a demand for something to happen in the future]

Also, MODAL AUXILIARY VERBS *would, could, might,* and *should* can convey speculations and conditions contrary to fact.

If the runner **were** [not *was*] faster, we **would** see a better race. [*Would* is a modal auxiliary verb.]

The issue here is that when an INDEPENDENT CLAUSE expresses a conditional statement using a modal auxiliary verb, you want to be sure that in the DEPENDENT CLAUSE you don't use another modal auxiliary verb.

> **NO** If I **would have trained** for the race, I **might have** won.
> **YES** If I **had trained** for the race, I **might have** won.

EXERCISE 8-8

Fill in each blank with the correct form of the verb given in parentheses. For help, consult 8l and 8m.

> EXAMPLE Imagining the possibility of brain transplants requires that we (to be) <u>be</u> open-minded.

(1) If almost any organ other than the brain (to be) _____ the candidate for a swap, we would probably give our consent. (2) If the brain (to be) _____ to hold whatever impulses form our personalities, few people would want to risk a transplant. (3) Many popular movies have asked that we (to suspend) _____ disbelief and imagine the consequences should a personality actually (to be) _____ transferred to another body. (4) In real life, however, the complexities of a successful brain transplant require that not-yet-developed surgical techniques (to be) _____ used. (5) For example, it would be essential that during the actual transplant each one of the 500 trillion nerve connections within the brain (to continue) _____ to function as though the brain (to be) _____ lying undisturbed in a living human body.

VOICE

8n What is "voice" in verbs?

Voice in a verb tells whether a SUBJECT acts or is acted upon. English has two voices, *active* and *passive*. A subject in the **active voice** performs the action.

Most clams **live** in salt water. [The subject *clams* does the acting: Clams *live*.]

They **burrow** into the sandy bottoms of shallow waters. [The subject *they* does the acting: They *burrow*.]

A subject in the **passive voice** is acted upon. The person or thing doing the acting often appears in a PHRASE that starts with *by*. Verbs in

**ANOTHER EXAMPLE:
NECESSARY PASSIVE VOICE**
In the days of Aristotle, air was believed to be one of four fundamental substances that could not be further subdivided into constituent components.
—Frederick K. Lutgens
and Edward J. Tarbuck,
The Atmosphere

ANSWERS: EXERCISE 8-8
1. were
2. were
3. suspend; be
4. be
5. continue; were

the passive voice use forms of *be, have,* and *will* as AUXILIARY VERBS with the PAST PARTICIPLE of the MAIN VERB.

> Clams **are considered** a delicacy by many people. [The subject *clams* is acted upon *by many people.*]
> Some types of clams **are** highly **valued** by seashell collectors. [The subject *types* is acted upon *by seashell collectors.*]

8o How do I write in the active, not passive, voice?

Because the ACTIVE VOICE emphasizes the doer of an action, active constructions are more direct and dramatic. Active constructions usually require fewer words than passive constructions, which makes for greater conciseness (see 16c). Most sentences in the PASSIVE VOICE can be converted to active voice.

> PASSIVE African tribal masks are often imitated by Western sculptors.
> ACTIVE Western sculptors often imitate African tribal masks.

8p What are proper uses of the passive voice?

Although the active voice is usually best, in special circumstances you need to use the passive voice.

When no one knows who or what did something or when the doer of an action isn't important, writers use the passive voice.

> The lock **was broken** sometime after four o'clock. [Who broke the lock is unknown.]
> In 1899, the year I was born, a peace conference **was held** at The Hague. [The doers of the action—holders of the conference—aren't important.]
> —E. B. White, "Unity"

Sometimes the action in the sentence is more important than the doer of the action. For example, if you want to focus on historical discoveries in a narrative, use the passive voice. Conversely, if you want to emphasize the people making the discoveries, use the active voice.

> ACTIVE **Joseph Priestley discovered** oxygen in 1774. [*Joseph Priestley* is the subject.]
> PASSIVE **Oxygen was discovered** in 1774 by Joseph Priestley. [*Oxygen* is the subject.]
> ACTIVE **The postal clerk sent** the unsigned letter before I could retrieve it from the mailroom. [The emphasis is on the person, *the postal clerk,* rather than the action, *sent.*]

PASSIVE The unsigned letter **was sent** before it **could be retrieved** from the postal clerk. [The emphasis is on the events, *was sent* and *could be retrieved*, not on the doer of the action, the unknown sender and *the postal clerk*.]

In former years, the social sciences and natural sciences preferred the passive voice. Recently, style manuals for these disciplines have been advising writers to use the active voice whenever possible. "Verbs are vigorous, direct communicators," point out the editors of the *Publication Manual of the American Psychological Association.* "Use the active rather than the passive voice," they say.*

EXERCISE 8-9

First, determine which sentences are in the active voice and which the passive voice. Second, rewrite the sentence in the other voice, and then decide which voice better suits the meaning. Be ready to explain your choice. For help, consult 8n through 8p.

EXAMPLE In the West African country of Ghana, a few woodcarvers are creating coffins that reflect their occupants' special interests. (*active; change to passive*)

In the West African country of Ghana, *coffins that reflect their occupants' special interests are being created by a few woodcarvers.*

1. A coffin in the shape of a green onion was chosen by a farmer.
2. A hunter's family buried him in a wooden coffin shaped like a leopard.
3. A dead chief was carried through his fishing village by friends and relatives bearing his body in a large pink wooden replica of a fish.
4. The family of a wealthy man who greatly admired cars buried him in a coffin shaped like a Mercedes car.
5. Although a few of these fantasy coffins have been displayed in museums, most of them end up buried in the ground.

*American Psychological Association, *Publication Manual of the American Psychological Association,* 5th ed. (Washington: APA, 2001) 41.

ANSWERS AND COVERAGE: EXERCISE 8-9

Rewrites may vary somewhat from the possibilities shown here. Coverage is three passive to active sentences; two active to passive sentences.

1. *Passive, change to active:* A farmer chose a coffin in the shape of a green onion.

2. *Active, change to passive:* A hunter was buried by his family in a wooden coffin shaped like a leopard.

3. *Passive, change to active:* The friends and relatives of a dead chief carried his body through his fishing village in a large pink wooden replica of a fish.

4. *Active, change to passive:* A wealthy man who greatly admired cars was buried by his family in a coffin shaped like a Mercedes car.

5. *Passive, change to active:* Museums have displayed a few of these fantasy coffins, although most of them end up buried in the ground.

BACKGROUND

Using passive verbs does not usually create sharp prose. *Nominalization,* the grammatical process of transforming verbs and adjectives into nouns, is another dulling grammatical choice. In *Style: Toward Clarity and Grace,* Joseph Williams warns writers to avoid nominalizing verbs. Here are a few examples: *Dull:* We conducted an investigation of the accident. *Sharper:* We investigated the accident. *Dull:* The class held a discussion about crime prevention. *Sharper:* The class discussed crime prevention. *Dull:* The college students have no expectation of getting great coffee from the school cafeteria. *Sharper:* The college students don't expect to get great coffee from the school cafeteria.

Chapter 9

Pronouns: Case and Reference

PRONOUN CASE

9a What does "case" mean?

Case applies in different ways to PRONOUNS and to NOUNS. For pronouns, case refers to three pronoun forms: the **subjective** (pronoun as a SUBJECT), the **objective** (pronoun as an OBJECT), and the **possessive** (pronouns used in possessive constructions). For nouns, case refers to only one noun form: the possessive. (For help in using apostrophes in the possessive case, see Chapter 27.)

9b What are personal pronouns?

Personal pronouns refer to persons or things. Box 68 shows the case forms of personal pronouns (subjective, objective, and possessive), in both the singular and the plural.

Many of the most difficult questions about pronoun case concern *who/whom* and *whoever/whomever.* For a full discussion of how to choose between them, see 9g.

BOX 68   SUMMARY

 Case forms of personal pronouns

	SUBJECTIVE	OBJECTIVE	POSSESSIVE
SINGULAR	I, you, he, she, it	me, you, him, her, it	mine, yours, his, hers, its
PLURAL	we, you, they	us, you, them	ours, yours, their

9c How do pronouns work in case?

In the subjective case, pronouns function as SUBJECTS.

> **We** were going to get married. [*We* is the subject.]
> John and **I** wanted an inexpensive band for our wedding. [*I* is part of the compound subject *John and I.*]
> **He and I** found an affordable one-person band. [*He and I* is the compound subject.]

In the objective case, pronouns function as OBJECTS.

> We saw **him** perform in a public park. [*Him* is the direct object.]
> We showed **him** our budget. [*Him* is the indirect object.]
> He wrote down what we wanted and shook hands with **us**. [*Us* is the object of the preposition *with*.]

In the possessive case, nouns and pronouns usually indicate ownership or imply a relationship.

> The **musician's contract** was very fair. [The possessive noun *musician's* implies a type of ownership.]
> **His contract** was very fair. [The possessive pronoun *his* implies a type of ownership.]
> The **musicians' problems** stem from playing cheap instruments. [The possessive noun *musicians'* implies a type of relationship.]
> **Their problems** stem from playing with cheap instruments. [The possessive pronoun *their* implies a type of relationship.]

Sometimes, however, the notion of ownership or relationship calls for a major stretch of the imagination in possessive constructions. In such cases, look for the following pattern: noun + the *s* sound + noun. This means that two nouns work together, one of which does the possessing and the other of which is possessed.

> The **musician's arrival** was eagerly anticipated. [The musician neither owns the arrival nor has a relationship with the arrival. Instead, the pattern noun + the *s* sound + noun is operating.]

👁 **ALERT:** Never use an apostrophe in personal pronouns: *ours, yours, its, his, hers, theirs* (27c). 👁

9d Which case is correct when *and* connects pronouns?

When *and* connects pronouns, or nouns and pronouns, the result is a **compound construction.** Compounding, which means "putting parts together in a whole," has no effect on case. Always use pronouns in the

---

TEACHING TIP
English once distinguished between the personal and impersonal relationships in the second-person pronoun *you*. Some modern languages continue to do so. French, for example, makes a distinction between *tu* and *vous*; Spanish does so between *tu* (singular), *vosotros* (plural), informally, and *usted* (singular), *ustedes* (plural), formally. You might wish to have your bilingual students explain the difference in such forms.

LANGUAGE HISTORY
Changes in the second-person singular pronouns (subjective and objective cases) are rooted in the Roman Empire of the fourth century AD. At that time, there were two emperors, one in Rome and one in Constantinople. People speaking to either emperor were required to use the plural form of address. The practice of using the plural as a sign of respect slowly spread to France, where *tu* is the second-person singular pronoun (*toi* in the objective case) and *vous* the plural. During the thirteenth century, in imitation of the French nobles who occupied their country, the English began using *thou* (*thee* in the objective case) and *you* the same way. *You* became a mark of mutual respect in conversations among the elite and a sign of deference when a person spoke to a social superior. In contrast, *thou* became a sign of intimacy among members of the same family or among those who believed in the same things.

QUOTATION: ON WRITING
Form the possessive singular of nouns with *'s*. Follow this rule whatever the final consonant. Thus write, Charles's friend; Burns's poems; the witch's malice.

—William Strunk Jr.,
The Elements of Style

subjective case when they serve as the subjects of a sentence; also, always use pronouns in the objective case when they serve as objects in a
sentence. Never mix cases.

COMPOUND PRONOUN SUBJECT	**He and I** saw the solar eclipse. [*He and I* is a compound subject.]
COMPOUND PRONOUN OBJECT	That eclipse astonished **him and me.** [*Him and me* is a compound object.]

When you're unsure of the case of a pronoun, use the "Troyka test
for case" in Box 69. In this four-step test, you drop some of the words
from your sentence so that you can tell which case sounds correct.

When pronouns are in a PREPOSITIONAL PHRASE, they are always in
the objective case. (That is, a pronoun is always the OBJECT of the preposition.) This rule holds whether the pronouns are singular or plural. You
can also use the test in Box 69 to check what is correct.

BOX 69   SUMMARY

Troyka test for case

Subjective Case

STEP 1: Write the sentence twice, once using the subjective case, and
once using the objective case.

STEP 2: Cross out enough words to isolate the element you are
questioning.

~~Janet and~~ **me**

~~Janet and~~ **I**

> learned about the moon.

STEP 3: Omit the crossed-out words and read each sentence aloud to
determine which one sounds right.

NO   **Me** learned about the moon. [This doesn't sound right.]

YES   **I** learned about the moon. [This sounds right, so the
subjective case is correct.]

STEP 4: Select the correct version and restore the words you crossed out.

Janet and I learned about the moon.

→

Troyka test for case (*continued*)

Objective Case

STEP 1: Write the sentence twice, once using the subjective case, and once using the objective case.

STEP 2: Cross out enough words to isolate the element you are questioning.

> The astronomer taught ~~Janet and~~ **I**
>
> about the moon.
>
> The astronomer taught ~~Janet and~~ **me**

STEP 3: Omit the crossed-out words and read each sentence aloud to determine which one sounds right.

> **NO** The astronomer taught **I** about the moon. [This doesn't sound right.]
>
> **YES** The astronomer taught **me** about the moon. [This sounds right, so the objective case is correct.]

STEP 4: Select the correct version and restore the words you crossed out.

> The astronomer taught **Janet and me** about the moon.

NO Ms. Lester gave an assignment *to* **Sam and I.** [The prepositional phrase, which starts with the preposition *to*, cannot use the subjective-case pronoun *I*.]

YES Ms. Lester gave an assignment *to* **Sam and me.** [The prepositional phrase, which starts with the preposition *to*, calls for the objective-case pronoun *me*.]

Be especially careful when one or more pronouns follow the preposition *between*.

NO The dispute is *between* **Thomas and I.** [The prepositional phrase, which starts with the preposition *between*, cannot use the subjective-case pronoun *I*.]

YES The dispute is *between* **Thomas and me.** [The prepositional phrase, which starts with the preposition *between*, calls for the objective-case pronoun *me*.]

QUOTATION: ON WRITING
The discipline of the writer is to learn to be still and listen to what his subject has to tell him.
— Rachel Carson

QUOTATION: ON LANGUAGE
A writer lives in awe of words for they can be cruel or kind, and they can change their meanings right in front of you. They pick up flavors and odors like butter in a refrigerator.
— John Steinbeck

BACKGROUND
The *Guide to Grammar and Writing* site at <http://cctc2.commnet.edu/grammar/cases.htm>, by Capital Community College, makes the following distinction between nouns and pronouns: "Except for the possessive forms (usually formed by the addition of an apostrophe and the letter *s*), nouns do not change form in English. (This is one of the few ways in which English is easier than other languages.) Pronouns, however, do change form when they change case."

ANSWERS AND COVERAGE: EXERCISE 9-1

1. me [9d, objective case after preposition *at*]

2. they [9c, subjective case]

3. me [9d, objective case, compound direct object]

4. me [9d, objective case after preposition *between*]; we [9c, subjective case]

5. He and I [9c and 9d, subjective case, compound subject]

6. I [9c, subjective case]

7. We [9c, subjective case]

8. they [9c, subjective case]

9. I [9c, subjective case]

10. him and me [9d, objective case after preposition *at*, compound object]; us [9d, objective case after preposition *of*]

QUOTATION: ON WRITING
You can be a little ungrammatical if you come from the right part of the country.
—Robert Frost

QUOTATION: ON WRITING
It's not wise to violate the rules until you know how to observe them.
—T. S. Eliot

QUOTATION: ON LANGUAGE
I say *her*, but the pronoun is one of the most terrifying masks [ever] invented; what came to Charles was not a pronoun, but eyes, looks, the line of the hair over a temple, a nimble step, a sleeping face.
—John Fowles

EXERCISE 9-1

Underline the correct pronoun from each pair in parentheses. For help, consult 9c and 9d.

EXAMPLE Bill and (I, me) noticed two young swimmers being pulled out to sea.

(1) The two teenagers caught in the rip current waved and hollered at Bill and (I, me). (2) The harder (they, them) both swam toward shore, the further away the undercurrent pulled them from the beach. (3) The yellow banners had warned Bill and (I, me) that a dangerous rip current ran beneath the water. (4) I yelled at Bill, "Between you and (I, me), (we, us) have to save them!" (5) (He and I, Him and me) both ran and dove into the crashing waves. (6) As former lifeguards, Bill and (I, me) knew what to do. (7) (We, Us) two remembered the rule for surviving a rip current is to swim across the current. (8) Only when swimmers are safely away from the current should (they, them) swim toward shore. (9) I reached the teenage girl, who cried, "My boyfriend and (I, me) are drowning." (10) Bill rescued the frightened teenage boy, and when they were safely on shore, the boy looked at (he and I, him and me) and gasped, "Thanks. The two of (we, us) know you saved our lives."

9e How do I match cases with appositives?

You can match cases with APPOSITIVES by putting pronouns and nouns in the same case as the word or words the appositive is renaming. Whenever you're unsure about whether to use the subjective or objective case, use the "Troyka test for case" in Box 69 to get the answer.

■ **We** (not *Us*) tennis players practice hard. [Here, the subjective-case pronoun *we* matches the noun *tennis players,* which is the subject of this sentence.]

■ The winners, **she and I** (not *her and me*), advanced to the finals. [The subjective-case pronouns *she and I* match the noun *winners,* which is the subject of this sentence.]

■ The coach tells **us** (not *we*) tennis players to practice hard. [The objective-case pronoun *us* matches the noun *tennis players,* which is the object in this sentence.]

■ The crowd cheered the winners, **her and me** (not *she and I*). [The objective-case pronouns *her and me* match the noun *winners,* which is the object in this sentence.]

9f How does case work after linking verbs?

A pronoun that comes after a LINKING VERB either renames the SUBJECT or shows possession. In both constructions, always use a pronoun in the subjective case. If you're unsure about how to identify a pronoun's case, use the "Troyka test for case" in Box 69.

■ The contest winner was **I** (not *me*). [*Was* is a linking verb. *I* renames the subject, which is the noun *contest winner,* so the subjective-case pronoun *I* is correct.]

■ The prize is **mine.** [*Is* is a linking verb. *Mine* shows possession, so the possessive-case pronoun *mine* is correct.]

EXERCISE 9-2

Underline the correct pronoun of each pair in parentheses. For help, consult 9c through 9f.

EXAMPLE   Dad, because your wedding anniversary is next week, (we, us) sisters decided to get you and Mother a memorable gift.

(1) Anne and (me, I) have given this a great deal of thought, especially in light of the conversations you and Mom have had with us about stress at work. (2) You and Mom have always insisted that (we, us) children save money for special occasions, and Anne asked (me, I) if she and I could use our savings for a weekend getaway for you as the perfect anniversary gift. (3) It is (she and I, she and me) who most worry about how (you and her, you and she) are doing, so Anne and (I, me) think this trip will benefit everyone. (4) In fact, Dad, Mom mentioned to Anne last week how much she'd love for you and (she, her) to spend more time together. (5) It would make Anne and (me, I) feel great to do something nice for you two. (6) So, Dad, you and Mom start packing for a weekend at your favorite bed and breakfast, a time you and (her, she) desperately need and deserve. (7) Anne and (I, me) will be waiting when you two come home rested and free of stress.

9g When should I use *who, whoever, whom,* and *whomever*?

The pronouns *who* and *whoever* are in the SUBJECTIVE CASE. The pronouns *whom* and *whomever* are in the OBJECTIVE CASE.

Informal spoken English tends to blur distinctions between *who* and *whom,* so with these words some people can't rely entirely on what "sounds right." Whenever you're unsure of whether to use *who* or

QUOTATION: ON WRITING

For your born writer, nothing is so healing as the realization that he has come upon the right word.

—Catherine Drinker Bowen

QUOTATION: ON LANGUAGE

Let us resolve to follow Safire's Rule on *Who-Whom:* whenever *whom* sounds correct recast the sentence.

—William Safire

TEACHING TIP

If your students have trouble choosing the appropriate relative pronoun in dependent clauses, they can do the "Troyka test for case" using these additional sentences.

Subjective Case

1. I enjoy playing volleyball with anyone (who, whom) has time to play. [*who*]

2. (Whoever, whomever) wins is obligated to buy lunch for the rest. [*Whoever*]

3. I wonder (who, whom) will show up for today's game. [*who*]

Objective Case

1. The volleyball players (who, whom) I met yesterday were too skillful for me. [*whom*]

2. I reserve the right to play with (whoever, whomever) I choose. [*whomever*]

3. The opponent (who, whom) I want is honest as well as skillful. [*whom*]

---

whoever or to use *whom* or *whomever,* apply the "Troyka test for case." If you see *who* or *whoever,* test by temporarily substituting *he, she,* or *they.* If you see *whom* or *whomever,* test by temporarily substituting *him, her,* or *them.*

- My father tells the same story to **whoever/whomever** he meets.
- My father tells the same story to ~~she/her.~~ [*Note:* When substituting, stop at *she/her.* The objective case *whomever* is correct because the sentence works when you substitute *her* for *whoever/whomever.* In contrast, the subjective case *whoever* is wrong because the sentence doesn't work when you substitute *she* for *whoever/whomever.*]
- My father tells the same story to **whomever** he meets.

The most reliable variation of the test for *who, whom, whoever, whomever* calls for you to add a word before the substituted word set. In this example, the word *if* is added:

- I wondered **who/whom** would vote for Ms. Wallace.
- I wondered ***if he/if him*** would vote for Ms. Wallace. [The subjective case *who* is correct because the sentence works when you substitute *if he* for *who/whom.* In contrast, the objective case *whom* is wrong because the sentence doesn't work when you substitute *if him* for *who/whom.*]
- I wondered **who** would vote for Ms. Wallace.

Another variation of the test for *who, whom, whoever, whomever* calls for you to invert the word order in the test sentence.

- Babies **who/whom** mothers cuddle grow faster and feel happier.
- Mothers cuddle ~~they/them.~~ [*Note:* When substituting, stop at *she/her.* By inverting the word order in the sentence—that is, by temporarily using *mothers* as the subject of the sentence—and substituting *they/them* for *who/whom,* you see that *them* is correct. Therefore, the objective case *whom* is correct.]
- Babies **whom** mothers cuddle grow faster and feel happier.

At the beginning or end of a question, use *who* if the question is about the subject and *whom* if the question is about the object. To determine which case to use, recast the question into a statement, substituting *he* or *him* (or *she* or *her*).

- **Who** watched the space shuttle liftoff? [*He* (not *Him*) *watched the space shuttle liftoff* uses the subjective case, so *who* is correct.]
- Ted admires **whom?** [*Ted admires him* (not *he*) uses the objective case, so *whom* is correct.]
- **Whom** does Ted admire? [*Ted admires him* (not *he*) uses the objective case, so *whom* is correct.]
- To **whom** does Ted speak about becoming an astronaut? [*Ted speaks to them* (not *they*) uses the objective case, so *whom* is correct.]

EXERCISE 9-3

Underline the correct pronoun of each pair in parentheses. For help, consult 9g.

EXAMPLE   Women (<u>who</u>, whom) both hold jobs outside the home and are mothers serve a "double shift."

(1) Women (who, whom) raise a family do as much work at home as at their jobs. (2) In North American society, it is still women (who, whom) cook dinner, clean the house, check the children's homework, read to them, and put them to bed. (3) Nevertheless, self-esteem runs high, some researchers have found, in many women on (who, whom) a family depends for both wage earning and child rearing. (4) Compared with women (who, whom) pursue careers but have no children, those (who, whom) handle a double shift experience less anxiety and depression, according to the research. (5) Perhaps the reason for this finding is that those for (who, whom) the extra paycheck helps pay the bills feel pride and accomplishment when they rise to the challenge. (6) However, other studies note that women (who, whom) have both jobs and children experience tremendous stress. (7) Those (who, whom) feel unable both to support and to nurture their children despite their maximum efforts are the women for (who, whom) the dual responsibility is an almost unbearable burden.

9h   What pronoun case comes after *than* or *as*?

When *than* or *as* is part of a sentence of comparison, the sentence sometimes doesn't include words to complete the comparison outright. Rather, by omitting certain words, the sentence implies the comparison. For example, *My two-month-old Saint Bernard is larger **than** most full-grown dogs [are]* doesn't need the final word *are*.

When a pronoun follows *than* or *as*, the meaning of the sentence depends entirely on whether the pronoun is in the subjective case or the objective case. Here are two sentences that convey two very different messages, depending on whether the subjective case (*I*) or the objective case (*me*) is used.

1. My sister loved that dog more ***than* I.**
2. My sister loved that dog more ***than* me.**

In sentence 1, because *I* is in the subjective case, the sentence means *My sister loved that dog more than **I** [loved it]*. In sentence 2, because *me* is in the objective case, the sentence means *My sister loved that dog more than [she loved] **me.*** In both situations, you can check whether you're using the correct case by supplying the implied words to see if they make sense.

9i How do pronouns work before infinitives?

Most INFINITIVES consist of the SIMPLE FORMS of verbs that follow *to:* for example, *to laugh, to sing, to jump, to dance.* (A few exceptions occur when the *to* is optional: *My aunt helped the elderly man [to] cross the street;* and when the *to* is awkward: *My aunt watched the elderly man [to] get on the bus.*) For both the SUBJECTS of infinitives and the OBJECTS of infinitives, use the objective case.

> Our tennis coach expects **me *to serve.*** [Because the word *me* is the subject of the infinitive *to serve,* the objective-case pronoun is correct.]
> Our tennis coach expects **him *to beat*** me. [Because the word *him* is the subject of the infinitive *to beat,* and *me* is the object of the infinitive, the objective-case pronoun is correct.]

9j How do pronouns work with *-ing* words?

When a verb's *-ing* form functions as a NOUN, it's called a GERUND: *Brisk **walking** is excellent exercise.* When a noun or PRONOUN comes before a gerund, the POSSESSIVE CASE is required: ***His* brisk *walking** built up his stamina.* In contrast, when a verb's *-ing* form functions as a MODIFIER, it requires the subjective case for the pronoun, not the possessive case: ***He, walking*** *briskly, caught up to me.*

Here are two sentences that convey different messages, depending entirely on whether a possessive comes before the *-ing* word.

1. The detective noticed the **man *staggering.***
2. The detective noticed the **man's *staggering.***

Sentence 1 means that the detective noticed the *man;* sentence 2 means that the detective noticed the *staggering.* The same distinction applies to pronouns: When *the man* is replaced by either *him* or *his,* the meaning is the same as in sentences 1 and 2.

1. The detective noticed **him *staggering.***
2. The detective noticed **his *staggering.***

In conversation, such distinctions are often ignored, but use them in ACADEMIC WRITING.

EXERCISE 9-4

Underline the correct pronoun of each pair in parentheses. For help, consult 9h through 9j.

EXAMPLE   Few contemporaries of the most famous novelist of the Victorian era had careers as productive as (<u>he</u>, him).

(1) The reading public wanted (him, his) to continue spinning new tales for their enjoyment, and he managed to write forty-seven novels over a thirty-year career. (2) In his *Autobiography,* published near the end of his life, Anthony Trollope boasted that few people had led so full a life as (he, him). (3) His story begins with (him, his) landing a low-level civil service job that took him from his native England to Ireland and allowed (him, he) to view first-hand the terrible hardships facing the Irish people in the 1850s. (4) He absorbed what he saw so well that few people could depict Ireland better than (he, him). (5) Trollope's keen observations inspired (him, he) to write a series of novels about the Irish poor, each of which made him more popular as a writer. (6) After receiving a promotion and a transfer to London, Trollope became a keen observer of the English upper class and commented satirically in his novels on (their, them) hunting, shooting, and gambling. (7) Later in his life, his growing fame led to (him, his) mixing with the same rich and famous people he had earlier satirized in what some consider his greatest works, the massive six-novel Palliser series. (8) Indeed, no group of people is more realistically depicted than (they, them), although Trollope never lost his early fascination with the lives of the poor.

9k   What case should I use for -*self* pronouns?

Two types of pronouns end in -*self:* reflexive pronouns and intensive pronouns.

A **reflexive pronoun** reflects back on the subject, so it needs a subject in the sentence to be reflected back on. Without a subject, the reflexive pronoun cannot operate correctly.

The **detective** disguised **himself.** [The reflexive pronoun *himself* reflects back on the subject *detective.*]

Never use a reflexive pronoun to replace a personal pronoun in the subjective case.

NO   My teammates and **myself** will vote for a team captain.
YES   My teammates and **I** will vote for a team captain.

ANSWERS AND COVERAGE: EXERCISE 9-4

1. him [9i, objective case before infinitive]

2. he [9h, subjective case in elliptical *so full a life as he had*]

3. his [9j, possessive case before gerund]; him [9i, objective case before infinitive]

4. he [9h, subjective case in elliptical *depict Ireland better than he could*]

5. him [9i, objective case before infinitive]

6. their [9j, possessive case before gerund]

7. his [9j, possessive case before gerund]

8. they [9h, subjective case in elliptical *so realistically depicted as they are*]

EXTRA EXERCISE C

From each group of pronouns in parentheses, select the correct word and underline it.

EXAMPLE   My softball teammates and (myself, me, I) are confident we will make the finals this year. [*I*]

1. I am so certain of our success that I have already bought (me, myself) a new glove to celebrate. [*myself*]

2. Every practice session, the coach tells the others and (me, myself) that we are getting better and better. [*me*]

3. The sponsor (himself, hisself), Big Al of Big Al's Used Cars, even comes to games now. [*himself*]

4. The other women and (I, myself) are glad that our hard work has paid off. [*I*]

5. We had an exhibition game against our husbands, who tired (theirselves, themselves) out and lost by four runs. [*themselves*]

From the pronouns in parentheses, select the correct one and underline it.

1. My girlfriend and (I, me) agreed long ago that we would someday take a romantic ocean cruise together. [*I*]

2. (We, Us) and a few friends would sail the legendary seas and dock at exotic ports. [*We*]

3. Together, (we, us) and (they, them) would shop in the mysterious bazaars of ancient cultures and eat the spicy foods of distant lands. [*we, they*]

4. Unfortunately, an unexpected misfortune was visited on (she, her) and (I, me). [*her, me*]

5. The day we were to leave, (she, her) and (I, me) both discovered that we had chickenpox! [*she, I*]

6. Instead of visiting romantic places, the romantic places visited (she, her) and (I, me). [*her, me*]

7. Our friend Tom gave (we, us) travel books with pictures of the many places we longed to see. [*us*]

8. They were the same books someone had given (he, him) when he missed a trip to Mexico. [*him*]

9. I guess (we, us) will have to give them to (whoever, whomever) can't make the next scheduled vacation trip. [*we, whoever*]

WORD HISTORY

Antecedent comes from the Latin *ante,* meaning "before," and *cedere,* meaning "to go." Thus, the antecedent is the word that "goes before" the pronoun.

Also, never use a reflexive pronoun to replace a personal pronoun in the objective case. The only exception is when the object restates the subject.

NO   That decision is up to my teammates and **myself.**

YES   That decision is up to my teammates and **me.**

Intensive pronouns, which reflect back in the same way as reflexive pronouns, provide emphasis by making the message of the sentence more intense in meaning.

The detective felt that **his career** *itself* was at risk. [*Itself* intensifies the idea that the detective's career was at risk.]

PRONOUN REFERENCE

9l   What is pronoun reference?

The word or group of words that a pronoun replaces is called its **antecedent.** In order for your writing to communicate its message clearly, each pronoun must relate precisely to an antecedent.

I knew a **woman,** lovely in **her** bones / When small **birds** sighed, **she** would sigh back at **them.**

—Theodore Roethke, "I Knew a Woman"

9m   What makes pronoun reference clear?

Pronoun reference is clear when your readers know immediately to whom or what each pronoun refers. Box 70 lists guidelines for using pronouns clearly, and the section in parentheses is where each is explained.

BOX 70   SUMMARY

 Guidelines for clear pronoun reference

- Place pronouns close to their ANTECEDENTS (9n).
- Make a pronoun refer to a specific antecedent (9n).
- Do not overuse *it* (see 9q).
- Reserve *you* only for DIRECT ADDRESS (9r).
- Use *that, which,* and *who* correctly (9s).

9n How can I avoid unclear pronoun reference?

Every pronoun needs to refer to a specific, nearby ANTECEDENT. If the same pronoun in your writing has to refer to more than one antecedent, replace some pronouns with nouns.

NO In 1911, **Roald Amundsen** reached the South Pole just thirty-five days before **Robert F. Scott** arrived. **He** [who? Amundsen or Scott?] had told people that **he** [who? Amundsen or Scott?] was going to sail for the Arctic, but **he** [who? Amundsen or Scott?] was concealing **his** [whose? Amundsen's or Scott's?] plan. Soon, **he** [who? Amundsen or Scott?] turned south for the Antarctic. On the journey home, **he** [who? Amundsen or Scott?] and **his** [whose? Amundsen's or Scott's?] party froze to death just a few miles from safety.

YES In 1911, **Roald Amundsen** reached the South Pole just thirty-five days before **Robert F. Scott** arrived. **Amundsen** had told people that **he** was going to sail for the Arctic, but **he** was concealing **his** plan. Soon, **Amundsen** turned south for the Antarctic. Meanwhile, on **their** journey home, **Scott** and **his party** froze to death just a few miles from safety.

👁 **ALERT:** Be careful with the VERBS *said* and *told* in sentences that contain pronoun reference. To maintain clarity, use quotation marks and slightly reword each sentence to make the meaning clear.

NO **Her** mother told **her she** was going to visit **her** grandmother.
YES **Her** mother told **her,** "**You** are going to visit **your** grandmother."
YES **Her** mother told **her,** "**I** am going to visit **your** grandmother." 👁

Further, if too much material comes between a pronoun and its antecedent, readers can lose track of the meaning.

Alfred Wegener, a German meteorologist and professor of geophysics

at the University of Graz in Austria, was the first to suggest that all

the continents on earth were originally part of one large landmass.

According to this theory, the supercontinent broke up long ago and

Wegener
the fragments drifted apart. ~~He~~ named this supercontinent Pangaea.

[*He* can refer only to Wegener, but material about Wegener's theory intervenes, so using *Wegener* again instead of *he* jogs the reader's memory and makes reading easier.]

ANSWERS: EXERCISE 9-5

Answers may vary somewhat. Some students may think that some of the pronouns replaced here are acceptable, but clarity is the issue—avoiding intervening information that distracts the reader, ambiguous references, and so on. Here is one possible answer.

Most companies used to frown on employees who became involved in office romances. Companies often considered these employees to be using company time for their own enjoyment. Now, however, managers realize that happy employees are productive employees. With more women than ever before in the workforce and with people working longer hours, managers have begun to see that male and female employees want and need to socialize. Managers are also dropping their opposition to having married couples on the payroll, because managers no longer automatically believe that such couples will bring family matters into the workplace or stick up for one another at the company's expense.

One departmental manager had doubts when a systems analyst for research named Laura announced that she had become engaged to Peter, who worked as a technician in the same department. The departmental manager told Laura, "Either Peter or you might have to transfer out of the research department." After listening to Laura's plea that the couple be allowed to work together on a trial basis, the manager reconsidered. She decided to give Laura and Peter a chance to prove that their relationship would not affect their work. The decision paid off. Laura and Peter demonstrated that they could work as an effective research team, right through their engagement and subsequent marriage. Two years later, when Laura was promoted to assistant manager for product development and after Peter asked to move also, the research manager enthusiastically recommended that Peter follow Laura to her new department.

When you start a new paragraph, be cautious about beginning it with a pronoun whose antecedent is in a prior paragraph. You're better off repeating the word.

⊕ **ESL NOTE:** Many languages omit a pronoun as a subject because the verb delivers the needed information. English requires the use of the pronoun as a subject. For example, never omit *it* in the following: *Political science is an important academic subject. **It** is studied all over the world.* ⊕

EXERCISE 9-5

Revise so that each pronoun refers clearly to its antecedent. Either replace pronouns with nouns or restructure the material to clarify pronoun reference. For help, consult 9n.

EXAMPLE   People who return to work after years away from the corporate world often discover that business practices have changed. They may find fiercer competition in the workplace, but they may also discover that they are more flexible than before.

Here is one possible revision: *People who return to work after years away from the corporate world often discover that business practices have changed. Those people may find fiercer competition in the workplace, but they may also discover that business practices are more flexible than before.*

Most companies used to frown on employees who became involved in office romances. They often considered them to be using company time for their own enjoyment. Now, however, managers realize that happy employees are productive employees. With more women than ever before in the workforce and with people working longer hours, they have begun to see that male and female employees want and need to socialize. They are also dropping their opposition to having married couples on the payroll. They no longer automatically believe that they will bring family matters into the workplace or stick up for one another at the company's expense.

One departmental manager had doubts when a systems analyst for research named Laura announced that she had become engaged to Peter, who worked as a technician in the same department. She told her that either one or the other might have to transfer out of the research department. After listening to her plea that they be allowed to work together on a trial basis, the manager reconsidered. She decided to give Laura and Peter a chance to prove that their relationship would not affect their work. The decision paid off. They demonstrated that they could work as an effective research team, right through their engagement and subsequent marriage. Two years later, when Laura was promoted to assistant manager of a different department and after he asked to move also, she enthusiastically recommended that Peter follow Laura to her new department.

9o How do pronouns work with *it, that, this,* and *which*?

When you use *it, that, this,* and *which,* be sure that your readers can easily understand what each word refers to.

> **NO** Comets usually fly by the earth at 100,000 mph, whereas asteroids sometimes collide with the earth. **This** interests scientists. [Does *this* refer to the speed of the comets, to comets flying by the earth, or to asteroids colliding with the earth?]

> **YES** Comets usually fly by the earth at 100,000 mph, whereas asteroids sometimes collide with the earth. **This difference** interests scientists. [Adding a noun after *this* or *that* clarifies the meaning.]

> **NO** I told my friends that I was going to major in geology, **which made my parents happy.** [Does *which* refer to telling your friends or to majoring in geology?]

> **YES** My parents were happy **because I discussed my major with my friends.**

> **YES** My parents were happy **because I chose to major in geology.**

Also, the title of any piece of writing stands on its own. Therefore, in your introductory paragraph, never refer to your title with *this* or *that.* For example, if an essay's title is "Geophysics as a Major," the following holds for the first sentence:

> **NO** **This subject** unites the sciences of physics, biology, and paleontology.

> **YES** **Geophysics** unites the sciences of physics, biology, and paleontology.

9p How do I use *they* and *it* precisely?

The expression *they say* can't take the place of stating precisely who is doing the saying. Your credibility as a writer depends on your mentioning a source precisely.

A HUMOROUS NOTE

Carelessly placed pronouns can result in some unintentionally funny statements, as Richard Lederer demonstrates in *Anguished English.* Consider the difference between what the writers of the following sentences meant to say and what they really said.

- Anti-nuclear protestors released live cockroaches inside the White House Friday, and these were arrested when they left and blocked a security gate.
- My mother wants to have the dog's tail operated on again, and if it doesn't heal this time, she'll have to be put away.
- About two years ago, a wart appeared on my left hand, which I wanted removed.
- Guilt, vengeance, and bitterness can be emotionally destructive to you and your children. You must get rid of them.

BACKGROUND

Pronoun reference errors can have several causes. Sometimes, the errors occur when students try to improve a sentence in revision without paying attention to how the changes affect the relationship between a pronoun and its referent. Sometimes, as Mina P. Shaughnessy writes in *Errors and Expectations* (New York: Oxford UP, 1977, 114), errors in pronoun reference and agreement are signs of problems a student has with perception, with keeping track of what he or she has written in previous sentences and clauses. Shaughnessy also points out that the impersonal conventions of much academic writing compared to other kinds of writing also make pronoun reference errors more likely. Analytical style often "pushes writers out of reportage (description and narration), where experience grounds their generalizations, into vaguer statements about a *person* or *they* or *one,* which are more difficult to control, or even care about."

NO **They say** that earthquakes are becoming more frequent. [*They* doesn't identify the authority who made the statement.]

YES **Seismologists** say that earthquakes are becoming more frequent.

The expressions *it said* and *it is said that* reflect imprecise thinking. Also, they're wordy. Revising such expressions improves your writing.

NO **It said** in the newspaper that California has minor earthquakes almost daily. [*It said in the newspaper that* is wordy.]

YES **The newspaper reported** that California has minor earthquakes almost daily.

9q How do I use *it* to suit the situation?

The word *it* has three different uses in English. Here are examples of correct uses of *it*.

1. PERSONAL PRONOUN: Ryan wants to visit the 18-inch Schmidt telescope, but **it** is on Mount Palomar.
2. EXPLETIVE (sometimes called a *subject filler*, it delays the subject): **It** is interesting to observe the stars.
3. IDIOMATIC EXPRESSION (words that depart from normal use, such as using *it* as the sentence subject when writing about weather, time, distance, and environmental conditions): **It** is sunny. **It** is midnight. **It** is not far to the hotel. **It** is very hilly.

All three uses listed above are correct, but avoid combining them in the same sentence. The result can be an unclear and confusing sentence.

NO Because our car was overheating, **it** came as no surprise that **it** broke down just as **it** began to rain. [*It* is overused here, even though all three uses—2, 1, and 3 on the above list, respectively—are acceptable.]

YES **It** came as no surprise that our overheating car broke down just as the rain began. [The word order is revised so that *it* is used once.]

ESL NOTE: In some languages, *it* in an expletive is not used. In English, it is.

NO Is a lovely day.
YES **It** is a lovely day.

9r When should I use *you* for direct address?

Reserve *you* for **direct address,** writing that addresses the reader directly. For example, I use *you* in this handbook to address you, the student. *You* is not a suitable substitute for specific words that refer to people, situations, or occurrences.

NO   Prison uprisings often happen **when you allow** overcrowding. [The reader, *you,* did not allow the overcrowding.]

YES   Prison uprisings often happen **when prisons are** overcrowded.

NO   In Russia, **you** usually have to stand in long lines to buy groceries. [Are *you,* the reader, planning to do your grocery shopping in Russia?]

YES   **Russian consumers** usually have to stand in long lines to buy groceries.

EXERCISE 9-6

Revise these sentences so that all pronoun references are clear. If a sentence is correct, circle its number. For help, consult 9q and 9r.

EXAMPLE   By collecting data on animal species around the world, you gain insight into the ways animals communicate.

By collecting data on animal species around the world, researchers gain insight into the ways animals communicate. [Revision changes person from *you* not used for direct address to third person, the noun *researchers.*]

1. Researchers find that animal communication is more complex and more varied than you might expect.
2. Throughout the animal kingdom, they use low-pitched noises to convey aggression and high-pitched noises to convey fear.
3. They say that dogs bark for many reasons: to ask for food, to alert a family to danger, to convey excitement.
4. Elephants send messages to herds three miles away using sounds too low for you to hear.
5. In the water, damselfish emit squeaks and dolphins send out clicks and whistles. This interests marine biologists.
6. Elk males have rutting contests to prove which male is stronger, with the one that ruts louder and longer proving his dominance.
7. They do not communicate only by using sounds: lobsters use chemical signals, lizards use head bobs, fireflies use light signals.
8. You can teach chimps to use sign language to communicate in simple sentences, such as "Give JoJo banana."

ANSWERS AND COVERAGE: EXERCISE 9-6

Answers will vary somewhat. Here is one set of possibilities.

1. Researchers find that animal communication is more complex and more varied than the public/people might expect. [9r, revision changes person from *you* not used for direct address to third person]

2. Throughout the animal kingdom, creatures use low-pitched noises to convey aggression and high-pitched noises to convey fear. [9p, revision eliminates *they* used as a pronoun for adjective *animal*]

3. Dog trainers say that dogs bark for many reasons: to ask for food, to alert a family to danger, to convey excitement. [9p, revision removes imprecise use of *they*]

4. Elephants send messages to herds three miles away using sounds too low for humans to hear. [9r, revision changes person from *you* not used for direct address to third person]

5. In the water, damselfish emit squeaks and dolphins send out clicks and whistles. The variety of animal sounds interests marine biologists. [9o, revision eliminates imprecise use of *this*]

6. Correct sentence

7. Animals do not communicate only by using sounds: lobsters use chemical signals, lizards use head bobs, fireflies use light signals. [9p, revision eliminates imprecise use of *they*]

8. Animal trainers can teach chimps to use sign language to communicate in simple sentences, such as "Give JoJo banana." [9r, revision changes person from *you* not used for direct address to third person]

9s **When should I use *that*, *which*, and *who*?**

To use the pronouns *that* and *which* correctly, you want to check the context of the sentence you're writing. *Which* and *that* refer to animals and things. Only sometimes do they refer to anonymous or collective groups of people. Box 71 shows how to choose between *that* and *which*. For information about the role of commas with *that* and *which*, see 24f.

BOX 71   SUMMARY

 Choosing between *that* and *which*

Choice: Some instructors and style guides use either *that* or *which* to introduce a RESTRICTIVE CLAUSE (a DEPENDENT CLAUSE that is essential to the meaning of the sentence or part of the sentence). Others may advise you to use only *that* so that your writing distinguishes clearly between restrictive and NONRESTRICTIVE CLAUSES. Whichever style you use, be consistent in each piece of writing:

■ The zoos **that** (or **which**) **most children like** display newborn and baby animals. [The point in this sentence concerns children's preferences. Therefore, the words *most children like* are essential for delivering the meaning and make up a restrictive clause.]

No choice: You are required to use *which* to introduce a nonrestrictive clause (a dependent clause that isn't essential to the meaning of the sentence or part of the sentence).

■ Zoos, **which most children like,** attract more visitors if they display newborn and baby animals. [The point in this sentence concerns attracting more visitors to zoos. Therefore, the words *most children like* are not essential to the meaning of the sentence and make up a nonrestrictive clause.]

Who refers to people and to animals mentioned by name.

John Polanyi, who was awarded the Nobel Prize in chemistry, speaks passionately in favor of nuclear disarmament. [*John Polanyi* is a person.]
Lassie, who was known for her intelligence and courage, was actually played by a series of male collies. [*Lassie* is the name of an animal.]

Many professional writers reserve *which* for nonrestrictive clauses and *that* for restrictive clauses. Other writers have begun to use *that* and *which* interchangeably. Current practice allows the use of either as long as you're consistent in each piece of writing. However, for ACADEMIC WRITING, your instructor might expect you to maintain the distinction.

👁 **ALERT:** Use commas before and after a nonrestrictive clause. Don't use commas before and after a restrictive clause; see 24k.4. 👁

EXERCISE 9-7

Fill in the blanks with *that, which,* or *who*. For help, consult 9s.

EXAMPLE   For years, consumers who want the very latest electronic gadgets have had to travel to Japan to buy them.

1. In Japan, consumers can buy a set of tiny clip-on headphones _____ have enough memory for an hour's worth of music.
2. These headphones, _____ are a popular item in Japan, are unlikely to reach foreign markets, because manufacturers don't export them.
3. People from outside Japan _____ crave innovative Japanese products now have an alternative way of buying them _____ is less expensive than traveling to Japan.
4. Web-based businesses, _____ are springing up every day, now specialize in exporting products _____ are trend-setting in Japan.
5. These companies, _____ offer extra advantages such as English-language warranties and manuals, are finding a ready market among English-speaking technophiles.

Chapter 10

Agreement

10a What is agreement?

In everyday speech, agreement indicates that people hold the same ideas. Grammatical **agreement** is also based on sameness. Specifically, you need to match SUBJECTS and VERBS; see 10b through 10n. You also need to match PRONOUNS and ANTECEDENTS; see 10o through 10t.

SUBJECT-VERB AGREEMENT

10b What is subject-verb agreement?

Subject-verb agreement means that a SUBJECT and its VERB match in NUMBER (singular or plural) and PERSON (first, second, or third person). Box 72 presents these major concepts in grammatical agreement.

BOX 72   SUMMARY

 Major concepts in grammatical agreement

- **Number,** as a concept in grammar, refers to *singular* (one) and *plural* (more than one).
- The **first person** is the speaker or writer. *I* (singular) and *we* (plural) are the only subjects that occur in the first person.

SINGULAR	**I see** a field of fireflies.
PLURAL	**We see** a field of fireflies.

→

Major concepts in grammatical agreement (*continued*)

■ The **second person** is the person spoken or written to. *You* (for both singular and plural) is the only subject that occurs in the second person.

SINGULAR   **You see** a shower of sparks.

PLURAL   **You see** a shower of sparks.

■ The **third person** is the person or thing being spoken or written about. *He, she, it* (singular) and *they* (plural) are the third-person subject forms. Most rules for subject-verb agreement involve the third person.

SINGULAR   The **scientist sees** a cloud of cosmic dust.

PLURAL   The **scientists see** a cloud of cosmic dust.

The **firefly glows.** [*Firefly* is a singular subject in the third person; *glows* is a singular verb in the third person.]

Fireflies glow. [*Fireflies* is a plural subject in the third person; *glow* is a plural verb in the third person.]

10c Why is a final -*s* or -*es* in a subject or verb so important?

SUBJECT-VERB AGREEMENT often involves one letter: *s* (or *es*) for words that end in -*s*. For verbs in the present tense, you form the SIMPLE FORM of third-person singular by adding -*s* or -*es*: *laugh, laugh**s***; *kiss*, *kiss**es.*** Major exceptions are the verbs *be (is), have (has)* and *do (does)*; see 8c.

That **student agrees** that **young teenagers watch** too much television.

Those **young teenagers are** taking valuable time away from studying.

That **student has** a part-time job for ten or twenty hours a week.

Still, that **student does** well in college.

For a subject to become plural, you add -*s* or -*es* to its end: *lip, lip**s**; princess, princess**es.*** Major exceptions include most pronouns (*they, it*) and a few nouns that for singular and plural either don't change (*deer, deer*) or change internally (*mouse, mice*). Box 73 shows you how to visualize the basic pattern for agreement using -*s* or -*es*.

BACKGROUND

Although English requires agreement between subject and verb, it is unlike some other modern languages in that it does not extend agreement to the gender and number of adjectives. Mario Pei, in *The Story of English* (New York: Fawcett, 1952), says that although the diminished number of endings used to indicate number and gender is thought to represent a great economy of time, space, and thought, it is probably as natural for a Spanish speaker to indicate that information by the article, adjective, and noun—for example, *las muchachas bonitas*—as it is for the English speaker not to do so. Another situation is found in the Chinese languages, which use word order instead of agreement to establish relationships among words.

TEACHING TIP

Controlled composition exercises are easy to construct and are often useful for helping students with subject-verb agreement and other grammatical and stylistic concerns. A controlled composition exercise asks the student to copy a passage several sentences long—but to make one change in the passage that addresses an area in which the student needs to improve. For example, to work on subject-verb agreement, a student might rewrite a passage changing the verbs from past tense to present tense. For help with past-tense verb forms, a student might rewrite a different passage, converting the verbs from present tense to past tense. Although the exercise focuses the efforts of the student on one particular area—copying passages—it, like other imitation exercises, helps students develop syntactic fluency in other ways at the same time.

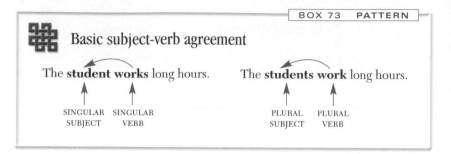

Here's a device for remembering how agreement works for most subject-verb agreement. Note that the final *-s* or *-es* can take only one path at a time—to the end of the verb or to the end of the subject.

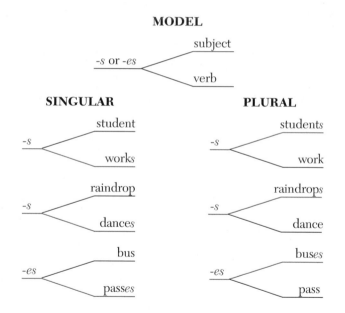

👁 **ALERT:** When you use an AUXILIARY VERB with a main verb, never add *-s* or *-es* to the main verb: *The coach **can walk*** [not *can walks*] *to campus. The coach **does like*** [not *does likes*] *his job.* 👁

EXERCISE 10-1

Use the subject and verb in each set to write two complete sentences—one with a singular subject and one with a plural subject. Keep all verbs in the present tense. For help, consult 10c.

EXAMPLE   climber, increase

>   **Singular subject:** Without proper equipment, a mountain *climber increases* the risk of falling.

>   **Plural subject:** Without proper equipment, mountain *climbers increase* the risk of falling.

1. dog, bark
2. flower, bloom
3. team, compete
4. planet, rotate
5. author, write
6. tornado, demolish
7. jet, depart
8. professor, might quiz

10d Can I ignore words between a subject and its verb?

You can ignore all words between a subject and its verb. Focus strictly on the subject and its verb. Box 74 shows you this pattern.

>   **NO** **Winners** of the state contest **goes** to the national finals.
>   [*Winners* is the subject; the verb must agree with it. Ignore the words *of the state contest.*]

>   **YES** **Winners** of the state contest **go** to the national finals.

The words *one of the* . . . often require a second look. Use a singular verb to agree with the word *one*. Don't be distracted by the plural noun

BOX 74   PATTERN

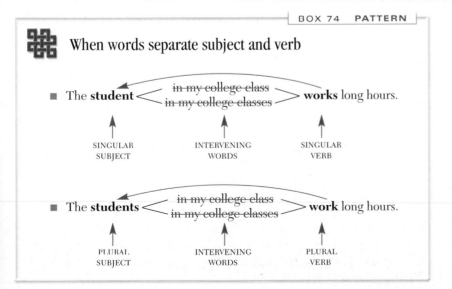

When words separate subject and verb

ANSWERS: EXERCISE 10-1
Answers will vary. Each set of sentences must use the subject once as a singular and once as a plural, and the verbs must agree accordingly.

EXTRA EXERCISE A
Fill in the blank with the correct present-tense form of the verb in parentheses.

EXAMPLE
Psychologists often (to use) _____ projective tests to investigate clients' unconscious memories and drives. [*use*]

1. Psychologists sometimes (to present) _____ their clients with questions to which there are no correct answers.
2. The client then (to tell) _____ what he or she (to see) _____, thus showing the psychologist some of his or her inner self.
3. The popular Rorschach Psycho-diagnostic Inkblot Test (to require) _____ that the client examine ten cards containing symmetrical inkblots and say what he or she (to think) _____ each means.
4. Next, the client (to point) _____ out where in the blot he or she (to find) _____ each image or idea.
5. Several scoring systems (to exist) _____ to guide psychologists in interpreting clients' responses.

Answers to Extra Exercise A

1. present
2. tells; sees
3. requires; thinks
4. points; finds
5. exist

EXTRA EXERCISE B

Fill in the blank with the correct present-tense form of the verb in parentheses.

EXAMPLE

In the eyes of many people, the Rorschach inkblots (to be) _____ the psychologists' standard tool for getting at clients' hidden thoughts and feelings.

[*are*]

1. Either the Holtzman Inkblot Technique or the Thematic Apperception Test (TAT) (to be) _____ given by psychologists who feel the Rorschach is unreliable.

2. Not only does the Holtzman series have more inkblots than the Rorschach, but the Holtzman also (to have) _____ a more standardized system of administration.

3. The TAT (to use) _____ a series of pictures showing people engaged in a wide range of activities.

4. Although the pictures show people in realistic situations, there (to be) _____ many possible acceptable answers.

5. It (to be) _____ the task of the person interpreting the picture to make up a story, deciding what has occurred and what the characters are thinking and feeling.

Answers to Extra Exercise B

1. is
2. has
3. uses
4. are
5. is

QUOTATION: ON WRITING

I have rewritten—often several times—every word I have ever published. My pencils outlast their erasers.

—Vladimir Nabokov

that comes after *of the.* (For information on the phrase *one of the . . . who,* see 10l.)

> **NO**   **One** of the problems **are** the funds needed for traveling to the national finals.
>
> **YES**   **One** of the problems **is** the funds needed for traveling to the national finals.

Similarly, eliminate all word groups between the subject and the verb, starting with *including, together with, along with, accompanied by, in addition to, except,* and *as well as.*

> **NO**   The **moon,** *as well as* the planet Venus, **are** visible in the night sky. [*Moon* is the subject. The verb must agree with it. Ignore the words *as well as Venus.*]
>
> **YES**   The **moon,** as well as the planet Venus, **is** visible in the night sky.

10e   How do verbs work when subjects are connected by *and*?

When two SUBJECTS are connected by *and*, they create a single COMPOUND SUBJECT. A compound subject calls for a plural verb. Box 75 shows you this pattern. (For related material on PRONOUNS and ANTECEDENTS, see 10p.)

> **The Cascade Diner *and* the Wayside Diner *have*** [not *has*] fried catfish today. [These are two different diners.]

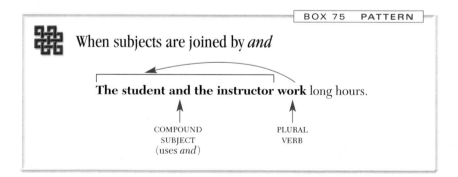

BOX 75   PATTERN

When subjects are joined by *and*

The student and the instructor work long hours.

COMPOUND SUBJECT (uses *and*)   PLURAL VERB

One exception occurs when *and* joins subjects that refer to a single thing or person.

My friend *and* neighbor *makes* [not *make*] excellent chili. [In this sentence, the friend is the same person as the neighbor. If they were two different people, *makes* would become *make*.]

Macaroni *and* cheese *contains* [not *contain*] carbohydrates, protein, and many calories. [*Macaroni and cheese* is one dish, not two separate dishes, so it requires a singular verb.]

10f How do verbs work with *each* and *every*?

The words *each* and *every* are singular even if they refer to a compound subject. Therefore, they take a singular verb.

> ***Each* human hand and foot *makes*** [not *make*] a distinctive print. To identify lawbreakers, ***every* police chief, sheriff, and federal marshal *depends*** [not *depend*] on such prints.

👁 **ALERT:** Use one word, either *each* or *every*, not both at the same time: ***Each*** (not *Each and every*) *robber has been caught.* (For more information about pronoun agreement for *each* and *every*, see 10i, 10p, and 10r.) 👁

10g How do verbs work when subjects are connected by *or*?

As Box 76 shows, when SUBJECTS are joined by *or*, or the sets *either . . . or, neither . . . nor, not only . . . but (also)*, the verb agrees with the subject closest to it. Ignore everything before the last-mentioned noun or

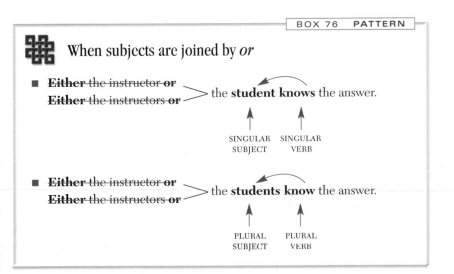

BOX 76 PATTERN

When subjects are joined by *or*

- ~~**Either** the instructor **or**~~
  ~~**Either** the instructors **or**~~ the **student knows** the answer.

  SINGULAR SUBJECT SINGULAR VERB

- ~~**Either** the instructor **or**~~
  ~~**Either** the instructors **or**~~ the **students know** the answer.

  PLURAL SUBJECT PLURAL VERB

good book, is a true book. All too often, that's
more than Mummy and Daddy know; for, in
denying . . . childhood, an adult has denied
half his or her knowledge, and is left with the
sad, sterile little fact: "A unicorn isn't real."
And that fact is one that never got anybody
anywhere (except in the story "The Unicorn
in the Garden," by another great fantasist, in
which it is shown that a devotion to the unreality of a unicorn may get you straight into
the loony bin). It is by such statements as,
"Once upon a time there were dragons," or
"In a hole in the ground there lived a hob-
bit"—it is by such beautiful non-facts that we
fantastic human beings may arrive, in our peculiar fashion, at the truth.

BACKGROUND
In "Oh Fudge," William Safire pledges allegiance to the *Rule of Proximity* for subject-
verb agreement. However, he also recognizes
that grammatical ambiguity can still occur, as
in the following example: "Neither Mr. Baker
nor I am young." In such cases, Safire offers
sage advice passed down from other grammarians: "When it looks funny, don't argue
the grammar; recast the sentence: Mr. Baker
is no spring chicken, nor am I."

QUOTATION: ON WRITING
After college, I sat all day in a captain's chair
up on 84th Street trying to write plays for live
television. Each morning I would thread my
bathrobe sash through the spokes of the chair
and tie myself in.

—John McPhee

pronoun. The box shows this pattern with *either . . . or.* (For related material on pronouns and antecedents, see 10q.)

> ~~Neither~~ spiders ~~nor~~ **flies upset** me.
> ~~Not only~~ spiders *but also* ~~all other~~ **arachnids have** four pairs of legs.
> ~~A dinner of six clam fritters, four blue crabs, or one steamed~~ **lobster sounds** good.

10h How do verbs work with inverted word order?

In English sentences, the SUBJECT normally comes before its VERB:
Astronomy is *interesting.* **Inverted word order** reverses the typical
subject-verb pattern by putting the verb first. Most questions use inverted word order: ***Is astronomy*** *interesting?* In inverted word order,
find the subject first and then check whether the verb agrees with it.

> Into deep space **shoot** probing **satellites.** [The plural verb *shoot* agrees
> with the inverted plural subject *satellites.*]
> On the television screen **appears** an **image** of Saturn. [The singular verb
> *appears* agrees with the inverted singular subject *image.*]

👁 **ALERT:** When you start a sentence with *there,* check whether the
subject is singular or plural, and then choose the right form of *be* to agree
with the subject. If your sentence begins with *it,* always use the singular
form of *be* (*is, was*) no matter whether the subject is singular or plural.

> **There *are*** nine **planets** in our solar system. [The verb *are* agrees with
> the subject *planets.*]
> **There *is*** probably no **life** on eight of them. [The verb *is* agrees with the
> subject *life.*]
> **It *is*** the property owners who are seeking changes in the tax laws.
> [The verb *is* agrees with *it,* not with *property owners.*] 👁

EXERCISE 10-2

Supply the correct present-tense form of the verb in parentheses. For help,
consult 10c through 10h.

> EXAMPLE   Detectives and teachers (to know) <u>know</u> experienced liars can
> fool almost anybody, but a new computer can tell who is telling
> the truth.

1. Police officers and teachers often (to wish) _____ they could "read"
   people's facial expressions.

2. Trained police officers or a smart teacher (to know) _____ facial tics and nervous mannerisms (to show) _____ someone is lying.

3. However, a truly gifted liar, along with well-coached eyewitnesses, (to reveal) _____ very little through expressions or behavior.

4. There (to be) _____ forty-six muscle movements in the human face which create all facial expressions.

5. Neuroscientist Terrence Seinowski, accompanied by a team of researchers, (to be) _____ developing a computer program to recognize even slight facial movements made by the most expert liars.

10i How do verbs work with indefinite pronouns?

Indefinite pronouns usually refer to nonspecific persons, things, quantities, or ideas. The nonspecific aspect is why these pronouns are labeled "indefinite." As part of a sentence, however, the indefinite pronoun is usually clear from the meaning.

Most indefinite pronouns are singular and require a singular verb for agreement. Yet, others are always plural, and a few can be singular *or* plural. Box 77 clarifies this situation by listing indefinite pronouns according to what verb form they require. (For related material on pronouns and antecedents, see 10r.)

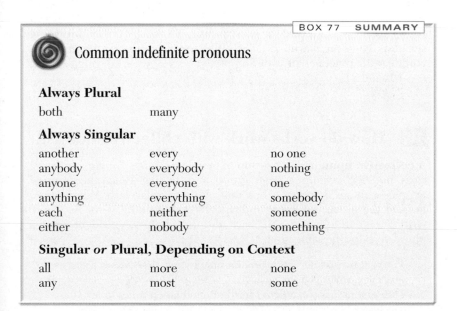

BOX 77   SUMMARY

Common indefinite pronouns

Always Plural

both   many

Always Singular

another	every	no one
anybody	everybody	nothing
anyone	everyone	one
anything	everything	somebody
each	neither	someone
either	nobody	something

Singular *or* Plural, Depending on Context

| all | more | none |
| any | most | some |

BACKGROUND

At the site <http://www.wisc.edu/writing/Handbook/GramPunct.html>, the Online Writing Center of the University of Wisconsin at Madison features an extensive, well-organized collection of material on grammar. The following is a sample from one of its Web pages: "Other words such as *none, any, all, more, most,* and *some* may take either singular or plural verbs, depending on the context. *Some of the dollar was spent. Some of the dollars were spent.* Note: Here, the prepositional phrase does affect the subject. It tells you whether you are talking about a part of one thing (singular) or of a number of things (plural)."

BACKGROUND

In "Breaking the Rules," Patricia T. O'Conner addresses the following myth: *None is always singular.* "Not so," she says. "Many people seem to have been taught (mistakenly) that *none* always means *not one.*" However, "*none* is closer in meaning to *not any.* Though it can be singular, *none* is more likely to be plural, as Fowler and others have pointed out. For example: *None of the windows are broken.*"

BACKGROUND

In "O Solecism Mio," William Safire says that intention dictates whether to use a singular or plural verb form with the pronoun *one*, as in the following example: "Ms. Mitchell is *one* of the reporters who *were*—not *was*—denied permission to stay. . . . In this case, the reporter is not seeking to separate herself from the crowd to assert her singularity; on the contrary, she is expressing solidarity with her fellow female journalists, stressing the collective."

QUOTATION: ON WRITING

When regarded as a unit, collective nouns, as well as noun phrases denoting quantity, take singular verbs. *The whole family is active.* (*Family* is a collective noun regarded as a unit.)

—<http://www.wisc.edu/writing/Handbook/SubjectVerb.html#collective>

EXTRA EXERCISE D

In writing groups, students can work together to edit the following sentences for subject-verb agreement.

1. The couple who move into a new apartment face many decisions.

2. One of the biggest choices have to do with how to decorate it.

3. Probably the most important decision of all are the color choices.

4. Green is one of the colors that looks good in any room.

Answers to Extra Exercise D

1. The couple who *moves* into a new apartment *faces* many decisions.

2. One of the biggest choices *has* to do with how to decorate it.

3. Probably the most important decision of all *is* the color choices.

4. Green is one of the colors that *look* good in any room.

Here are sample sentences:

SINGULAR INDEFINITE PRONOUNS

Everything about that intersection **is** dangerous.

But whenever **anyone says** anything, **nothing is** done.

Each of us **has** [not *have*] to shovel snow; **each is** [not *are*] expected to help.

Every snowstorm of the past two years **has** [not *have*] been severe.

Every one of them **has** [not *have*] caused massive traffic jams.

SINGULAR OR PLURAL INDEFINITE PRONOUNS (DEPENDING ON MEANING)

Some of our streams **are** polluted. [*Some* refers to the plural noun *streams*, so the plural verb *are* is correct.]

Some pollution **is** reversible, but **all** pollution **threatens** the balance of nature. [*Some* and *all* refer to the singular noun *pollution*, so the singular verbs *is* and *threatens* are correct.]

All that environmentalists ask **is** to give nature a chance. [*All* has the meaning here of "everything" or "the only thing," so the singular verb *is* is correct.]

Winter has driven the birds south; **all have** left. [*All* refers to the plural noun *birds*, so the plural verb *have* is correct.]

👁 **ALERTS:** (1) Don't mix singular and plural with *this, that, these,* and *those* used with *kind* and *type. This* and *that* are singular, as are *kind* and *type; these* and *those* are plural, as are *kinds* and *types:* **This** [not *These*] **kind** of rainwear is waterproof. **These** [not *This*] **kinds** of sweaters keep me warm. (2) The rules for indefinite pronouns often collide with practices of avoiding SEXIST LANGUAGE. For suggestions, see 10s and 21g. 👁

10j How do verbs work with collective nouns?

A **collective noun** names a group of people or things: *family, audience, class, number, committee, team, group,* and the like. When the group of people or things is acting as one unit, use a singular verb. When members of the group are acting individually, use a plural verb. As you're writing, be careful not to shift back and forth between a singular and a plural verb for the same noun.

The senior **class** nervously *awaits* final exams. [The *class* is acting as a single unit, so the verb is singular.]

The senior **class** *were fitted* for their graduation robes today. [The members (of the class) were fitted as individuals, so the verb is plural.]

10k Why does the linking verb agree with the subject, not the subject complement?

Even though a LINKING VERB connects a sentence's SUBJECT to its SUBJECT COMPLEMENT, the linking verb agrees with the subject. It does not agree with the subject complement.

> **NO** The worst **part** of owning a car *are* the bills. [The subject is the singular *part,* so the plural verb *are* is wrong. The subject complement is the plural *bills* and doesn't affect agreement.]

> **YES** The worst **part** of owning a car *is* the bills. [The singular subject *part* agrees with the singular verb *is.* The subject complement doesn't affect agreement.]

10l What verbs agree with *who, which,* and *that?*

If the ANTECEDENT of *who, which,* or *that* is singular, use a singular verb. If the antecedent is plural, use a plural verb.

> The scientist will share the prize with the **researchers *who* work** with her. [*Who* refers to *researchers,* so the plural verb *work* is used.]
> George Jones is the **student *who* works** in the science lab. [*Who* refers to *student,* so the singular verb *works* is used.]

If you use phrases including *one of the* or *the only one of the* immediately before *who, which,* or *that* in a sentence, be careful about the verb you use. *Who, which,* or *that* always refers to the plural word immediately following *one of the,* so the verb must be plural. Although *the only one of* is also always followed by a plural word, *who, which,* or *that* must be singular to agree with the singular *one.*

> Tracy is ***one of the*** students ***who*** talk in class. [*Who* refers to *students,* so the verb *talk* is plural. *Tracy* is pointed out, but the talking is still done by all the students.]
> Jim is ***the only one of the*** students ***who*** talks in class. [*Who* refers to *one,* so the verb *talks* is singular. *Jim* is the single person who is talking.]

EXERCISE 10-3

Supply the correct present-tense form of the verb in parentheses. For help, consult 10i through 10l.

> **EXAMPLE** Everybody on a class trip to the coastal waters of the Pacific Ocean (to enjoy) <u>enjoys</u> an opportunity to study dolphins in their natural habitat.

QUOTATION: ON WRITING
Linking verbs in subjective completions agree with the subject, not the completion: My favorite thing to buy *is* compact discs. But compare: Compact discs *are* my favorite thing to buy.
—<http://web.uvic.ca/wguide/Pages/SentSVAgr.html>

QUOTATION: ON WRITING
When a student makes a particular type of error in mechanics, it may be part of a larger set of related errors. For example, one error in verb agreement is generally accompanied by other errors in verb agreement.
—Arthur N. Applebee

QUOTATION: ON WRITING
I began to write because I was too shy to talk, and too lonely not to send messages.
—Heather McHugh

QUOTATION: ON WRITING
I had to develop an ear for the music of English.
—Elizabeth White

1. A class of college students in marine biology (to take) _____ notes individually while watching dolphins feed off the California coast.
2. Everyone in the class (to listen) _____ as a team of dolphin experts (to explain) _____ some of the mammals' characteristics.
3. A group of dolphins, called a pod, usually (to consist) _____ of 10,000 to 30,000 members.
4. One unique characteristic of dolphins' brains (to be) _____ the sleep patterns that (to keep) _____ one-half of the brain awake at all times.
5. All (to need) _____ to stay awake to breathe or else they would drown.

10m How do verbs work with amounts, fields of study, and other special nouns?

Amounts

SUBJECTS that refer to time, sums of money, distance, or measurement are singular. They take singular verbs.

> **Two hours *is*** not enough time to finish. [time]
> **Three hundred dollars *is*** what we must pay. [sum of money]
> **Two miles *is*** a short sprint for some serious joggers. [distance]
> **Three-quarters of an inch *is*** needed for a perfect fit. [measurement]

Fields of study

When you refer to a field of study, it's singular even though it appears to be plural: *economics, mathematics, physics,* and *statistics.*

> ***Statistics* is required** of science majors. [*Statistics* is a course of study, so the singular verb *is* is correct.]
> ***Statistics* show** that a teacher shortage is coming. [*Statistics* isn't used here as a field of study, so the plural verb *show* is correct.]

Special nouns

Athletics, news, ethics, and *measles* are singular despite their plural appearance. Also, *United States of America* is singular: It is one nation. However, *politics* and *sports* take singular or plural verbs, depending on the meaning of the sentence.

> The ***news* gets** better each day. [*News* is a singular noun, so the singular verb *gets* is correct.]
> ***Sports* is** a good way to build physical stamina. [*Sports* is one general activity, so the singular verb *is* is correct.]
> Three ***sports* are offered** at the recreation center. [*Sports* are separate activities, so the plural verb *are offered* is correct.]

Jeans, pants, scissors, clippers, tweezers, eyeglasses, thanks, and *riches* are some of the words that require a plural verb, even though they refer to one thing. However, if you use *pair* with *jeans, pants, scissors, clippers, tweezers,* or *eyeglasses,* use a singular verb for agreement.

Those **slacks need** pressing. [plural]
That **pair** of slacks **needs** pressing. [singular]

Series and *means* can be singular or plural, according to the meaning you intend.

Two new TV **series are** big hits. [*Series* refers to individual items (two different series), so the plural verb *are* is correct.]
A **series** of disasters **is** plaguing our production. [*Series* refers to a whole group (the whole series of disasters), so the singular verb *is* is correct.]

10n How do verbs work with titles, company names, and words as themselves?

Titles
A title itself refers to one work or entity (even when plural and compound NOUNS are in the title), so a singular verb is correct.

Breathing Lessons by Anne Tyler **is** a prize-winning novel.

Company Names
Many companies have plural words in their names. However, a company should always be treated as a singular unit, requiring a singular verb.

Cohn Brothers boxes and **delivers** fine art.

Words as Themselves
Whenever you write about words as themselves to call attention to those words, use a singular verb, even if more than one word is involved.

We implies that everyone is included.
During the Vietnam War, **protective reaction strikes was** a euphemism for *bombing.*

EXERCISE 10-4

Supply the correct present-tense form of the verb in parentheses. For help, consult 10j through 10n.

EXAMPLE   In a fast-growing trend, some of the people who (to live) live on college campuses and (to participate) participate in campus life today are not students but retired persons.

EXTRA EXERCISE E
Complete the following sentences by supplying an appropriate verb.

1. Physics _____ a demanding subject.
2. Do you think physics or economics _____ harder?
3. Sports _____ the favorite pastime.
4. Three-quarters of an hour of exercise several times a week _____ enough to keep a person in reasonably good shape.
5. Statistics _____ that exercise of the body as well as the mind _____ important for good health.

Answers to Extra Exercise E

1. is
2. is
3. is
4. is
5. show (indicate); is

QUOTATION: ON WRITING
I work all day, morning and afternoon, just about every day. If I sit there like that for two or three years, at the end I have a book.
—Philip Roth

QUOTATION: ON WRITING
You never have to change anything you got up in the middle of the night to write.
—Saul Bellow

ANSWERS AND COVERAGE: EXERCISE 10-4

1. is [10n, singular verb with term or words as themselves; also 10k, a subject/complement construction]

2. gratify [10l, *which* refers to the plural *communities*]

3. require [10i, *many* is always plural]; open [10i, *some* is plural in this case because it refers to *communities*]

4. is [10k, verb agrees with the singular subject *advantage,* not the plural complement *opportunities*]

5. benefits [10j, singular verb with collective noun *student body*]

BACKGROUND

At the site <http://webster.commnet.edu/sensen/part2/thirteen/pronouns_fun.html>, exercises on pronoun agreement are available.

ANSWERS AND COVERAGE: EXERCISE 10-5

1. invites [10f, singular verb with subject modified by *each*]

2. are [10h, words in inverted order]; remain [10c, plural subject *roses*]

3. symbolizes [10f, singular verb with *each*]

4. are [10h, words in inverted order]; flourish [10c, plural subject *thirty-five*]

5. was [10b, singular subject *rose*]

6. suggests [10d, singular verb with *one*]

7. says [10d, ignoring intervening words]

8. explain [10c, plural subject *theories*]

9. demonstrates [10j, singular-context collective noun]

10. remains [10k, agreeing with subject *best seller*]

1. *College-linked retirement communities* (to be) _____ the general term for retirement homes based on or near colleges and universities.

2. These communities, which (to gratify) _____ a retiree's desire for an active life and lifelong learning, are springing up on many campuses.

3. Many college-linked communities (to require) _____ their residents to have been formerly linked to the affiliated university, in a role such as a faculty or staff member, but some (to open) _____ their doors to all interested retirees.

4. To the residents of such retirement communities, the major advantage (to be) _____ opportunities for ongoing cultural, intellectual, and social growth.

5. However, the younger student body often (to benefit) _____ when retirees take part in courses and activities and thereby bring decades of wisdom and experience to their studies.

EXERCISE 10-5

This is an exercise covering all of subject-verb agreement (10b through 10n). Supply the correct form of the verb in parentheses.

> **EXAMPLE** Of the thirty thousand plant species on earth, the rose (to be) <u>is</u> the most universally known.

1. Each plant species (to invite) _____ much discussion about origins and meanings, and when talk turns to flowers, the rose is usually the first mentioned.

2. More fragrant and colorful (to be) _____ other types of flowers, yet roses (to remain) _____ the most popular worldwide.

3. Each of the types of roses (to symbolize) _____ beauty, love, romance, and secrecy.

4. There (to be) _____ over two hundred pure species of roses and thousands of mixed species, thirty-five of which (to flourish) _____ in the soil of North America.

5. It's impossible to determine exactly where or when the first rose (to be) _____ domesticated, because roses have existed for so many centuries; one of the earliest references dates back to 3000 BC.

6. One myth from Greek mythology (to suggest) _____ that the rose first appeared with the birth of the goddess Aphrodite.

7. Another myth, which focuses on the rose's thorns, (to say) _____ that an angry god shot arrows into the stem to curse the rose forever with arrow-shaped thorns.

8. While theories of this kind (to explain) _____ the significance and evolution of the rose, few people can explain the flower's enduring popularity.

9. Even today, a couple (to demonstrate) _____ love by exchanging red roses.
10. Of all flowers, the best seller (to remain) _____ the rose.

PRONOUN-ANTECEDENT AGREEMENT

10o What is pronoun-antecedent agreement?

Pronoun-antecedent agreement means that a PRONOUN matches its ANTECEDENT in NUMBER (singular or plural) and PERSON (first, second, or third person). Box 78 shows you how to visualize this pattern of grammatical agreement. You might also want to consult Box 72 in 10b for explanations and examples of the concepts *number* and *person*.

> The **firefly** glows when **it** emerges from **its** nest at night. [The singular pronouns *it* and *its* match their singular antecedent, *firefly*.]
> **Fireflies** glow when **they** emerge from **their** nests at night. [The plural pronouns *they* and *their* match their plural antecedent, *fireflies*.]

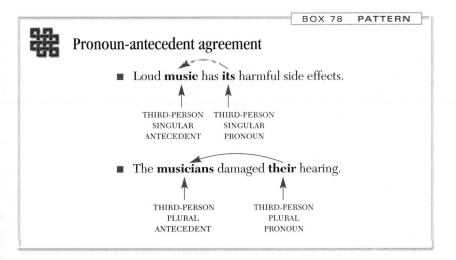

BOX 78 PATTERN

Pronoun-antecedent agreement

- Loud **music** has **its** harmful side effects.

  THIRD-PERSON SINGULAR ANTECEDENT — THIRD-PERSON SINGULAR PRONOUN

- The **musicians** damaged **their** hearing.

  THIRD-PERSON PLURAL ANTECEDENT — THIRD-PERSON PLURAL PRONOUN

10p How do pronouns work when *and* connects antecedents?

When *and* connects two or more ANTECEDENTS, they require a plural pronoun. This rule applies even if each separate antecedent is singular. (For related material on subjects and verbs, see 10e.)

251

QUOTATION: ON WRITING

When used as a grammatical term *antecedent* means the word or group of words referred to by a pronoun. It does not necessarily come before the pronoun and it may not be mentioned at all.

—Cornelia Evans and Bergen Evans

EXTRA EXERCISE F

In writing groups, students can work together to edit the inaccurate agreement of pronouns and antecedents in the following paragraph.

Plaids have been a favorite fabric design for many centuries. It consists of bars of color crossing each other at right angles. Scotland is the home of the plaid, where they are called a tartan, or, in song, story, and legend, *plaidies*. The tartan, which distinguish the clan of their wearers, is ancient, but their origin is unknown. In its earliest forms they were pieces of cloth about two yards broad and four yards long, which was drawn round the waist in folds that was tightly buckled with a belt. The lower part came down to the knees, and the upper part fell over the left shoulder so that they left the right arm free. Early in the eighteenth century, the "belted plaid" disappeared. They were replaced by the kilt. The particular pattern of tartans which distinguish each clan must have been fixed before 1645, probably before 1600. Later, in 1746, trying to end the clan system, the British Parliament prohibited the Scots from wearing tartans. The action against it was taken following the Battle of Culloden where Prince Charles Edward Stuart, grandson of James II, was defeated by the Duke of Cumberland. To be caught wearing them carried a penalty of six months' imprisonment. The kilt is worn today so that when the wearer is standing erect, their edges should reach the center of the kneecap. They should be made of a tartan associated with the name of the wearer. In the absence of a family claim to wear them, the Scots allow the wearing of the Royal Stuart tartan.

—Emily Gordon

Answers to Extra Exercise F

Plaids have been favorite fabric *designs* for many centuries. *They consist* of bars of color crossing each other at right angles. Scotland is the home of the plaid, where *it is* called a tartan, or, in song, story, and legend, *a plaidie*. The tartan, which *distinguishes* the clan of *its wearer*, is ancient, but *its* origin is unknown. In its earliest *form it was a piece* of cloth about two yards broad and four yards long, which was drawn round the waist in folds that *were* tightly buckled with a belt. The lower part came down to the knees, and the upper part fell over the left shoulder so that *it* left the right arm free. Early in the eighteenth century, the "belted plaid" disappeared. *It was* replaced by the kilt. The particular pattern of *tartan* which *distinguishes* each clan must have been fixed before 1645, probably before 1600. Later, in 1746, trying to end the clan system, the British Parliament prohibited the Scots from wearing *the tartan.* The action against it was taken following the Battle of Culloden where Prince Charles Edward Stuart, grandson of James II, was defeated by the Duke of Cumberland. To be caught wearing *it* carried a penalty of six months' imprisonment. The kilt is worn today so that when the wearer is standing erect, *its* edges should reach the center of the kneecap. *It* should be made of a tartan associated with the name of the wearer. In the absence of a family claim to wear *one*, the Scots allow the wearing of the Royal Stuart tartan.

The Cascade Diner *and* the Wayside Diner closed for New Year's Eve to give **their** [not *its*] employees the night off. [Two separate diners require a plural pronoun.]

When *and* joins singular nouns that nevertheless refer to a single person or thing, use a singular pronoun.

My friend *and* neighbor makes **his** [not *their*] excellent chili every Saturday. [The friend is the same person as the neighbor, so the singular *his* (or *her*) is correct. If two different people were involved, the correct pronoun would be *their,* and *make* would be the correct verb.]

each, every

The words *each* and *every* are singular, even when they refer to two or more antecedents joined by *and.* The same rule applies when *each* or *every* is used alone (10i). (For related material on subjects and verbs, see 10f.)

Each human hand *and* foot leaves **its** [not *their*] distinctive print.

The rule still applies when the construction *one of the* follows *each* or *every.*

Each one of the robbers left **his** [not *their*] fingerprints at the scene.

10q   How do pronouns work when *or* connects antecedents?

When ANTECEDENTS are joined by *or* or by CORRELATIVE CONJUNCTIONS such as *either . . . or, neither . . . nor,* or *not only . . . but (also),* the antecedents might mix singulars and plurals. For the purposes of agreement, ignore everything before the final antecedent. Box 79 shows you how to visualize this pattern. (For related material on subjects and verbs see 10g.)

BOX 79   PATTERN

When antecedents are joined by *or*

- ~~Either the loudspeakers~~ **or the microphone** needs **its** electric cord repaired.

  SINGULAR   SINGULAR
  ANTECEDENT   PRONOUN

When antecedents are joined by *or* (*continued*)

- ~~Either the microphone~~ **or the loudspeakers** need **their** electric cords repaired.

  PLURAL ANTECEDENT · PLURAL PRONOUN

~~After the restaurant closes, *either* the resident mice *or* the owner's~~ **cat** gets **itself** a meal.

~~After the restaurant closes, *either* the owner's cat *or* the resident~~ **mice** get **themselves** a meal.

10r How do pronouns work when antecedents are indefinite pronouns?

INDEFINITE PRONOUNS usually refer to unknown persons, things, quantities, or ideas. The unknown aspect is why these pronouns are labeled "indefinite." But in a sentence, context gives an indefinite pronoun a clear meaning, even if the pronoun doesn't have a specific antecedent. Most indefinite pronouns are singular. Two indefinite pronouns, *both* and *many*, are plural. A few indefinite pronouns can be singular or plural, depending on the meaning of the sentence.

For a list of indefinite pronouns, grouped as singular or plural, see Box 77 in 10i. For more information about avoiding sexist language, especially when using indefinite pronouns, see 10s and 21g. (For related material on subjects and verbs, see 10i.)

SINGULAR INDEFINITE PRONOUNS

Everyone taking this course hopes to get **his or her** [not *their*] college degree within a year.

Anybody wanting to wear a cap and gown at graduation must have **his or her** [not *their*] measurements taken.

Each of the students handed in **his or her** [not *their*] final term paper.

SINGULAR *OR* PLURAL INDEFINITE PRONOUNS

When winter break arrives for students, **most** leave **their** dormitories for home. [*Most* refers to *students*, so the plural pronoun *their* is correct.]

As for the luggage, **most** is already on **its** way to the airport. [*Most* refers to *luggage*, so the singular pronoun *its* is correct.]

BACKGROUND ON LANGUAGE

According to Martha Kolln of Pennsylvania State University, a major theorist in language studies, we shouldn't be too concerned about the usage *everyone . . . their* or *anybody . . . their*. She notes in "Everyone's Right to Their Own Language" (*College Composition and Communication* 37, 1986: 100–102) that *everybody* has been treated as a plural for over four hundred years and *everyone* for over two hundred, appearing this way in the works of Cardinal Newman, Shakespeare, and Swift. Despite this evidence (available since 1957), the rule stands—at least on the record.

Kolln argues for treating indefinite pronouns as we treat collective nouns. A collective noun such as *crowd* takes a singular verb but takes a plural pronoun when it clearly refers to more than one person. She gives as an example:

> At first *the crowd* was singing; then *they* began to laugh.

Kolln gives this useful example for indefinite pronouns:

> At first *everyone* in the room was singing; then *they* began to laugh.

In fact, any singular pronoun other than *everyone* or *someone* would be out of place in the second clause. She demonstrates that the same applies when the indefinite pronoun appears as the direct object or as the subject of a tag question.

Kolln ends by calling for the acceptance of the plural possessive pronoun (*their*) after collective indefinite pronouns:

> These dicta that designate all indefinite pronouns as singular have no basis either in actual usage or in the rules of logic. Yet the current handbooks apply the same rule to all of the indefinite pronouns, whether they are collective or not, whether singular or not. (102)

Whether you agree or disagree with Kolln, the issue is certainly worth discussion.

EXTRA EXERCISE G
Rewrite this paragraph so that pronoun-antecedent agreement in person and number is maintained. It may also be necessary to change verbs or other words.

Buying stock involves many steps. Once a stockbroker receives an order, they call their firm's telephone clerk, who is located near the edge of the trading area. The telephone clerk summons his firm's floor broker by flashing their code number on a large electronic board posted in the trading area. Seeing their number, the floor broker goes to the telephone clerk and picks up the buy order. You then go to the small area set aside for trading in that company's stock. An employee of the Stock Exchange keeps track of all bids to buy and sell that particular stock. The floor broker makes an offer. If they are accepted by the selling broker, the stock is his. If you have bid too low, he must make another bid before someone else gets the stock. Then a reporter enters the deal into the Exchange computer, and they become part of the official record in seconds. After all this, the floor broker returns to the telephone clerk, who reports the deal to the original stockbroker, who bills the client.

—Emily Gordon

Answers to Extra Exercise G
Buying stock involves many steps. Once a stockbroker receives an order, *he calls his* firm's telephone clerk, who is located near the edge of the trading area. The telephone clerk summons his firm's floor broker by flashing *his* code number on a large electronic board posted in the trading area. Seeing *his* number, the floor broker goes to the telephone clerk and picks up the buy order. *The floor broker* then *goes* to the small area set aside for trading in that company's stock. An employee of the Stock Exchange keeps track of all bids to buy and sell that particular stock. The floor broker makes an offer. If *it is*

→

None thinks that **he or she** will miss graduation. [*None* is singular as used in this sentence, so the singular pronoun *he or she* is correct.]
None of the students has paid **his or her** [not *their*] graduation fee yet. [*None* is singular as used in this sentence, so the singular pronoun *his or her* is correct.]
None are so proud as **they** who graduate. [*None* is plural as used in this sentence, so the plural pronoun *they* is correct.]

10s How do I use nonsexist pronouns?

A word is **nonsexist** when it carries neither male nor female gender. Each PRONOUN in English carries one of three genders: male (*he, him, his*); female (*she, her, hers*); or neutral (*you, your, yours, we, our, ours, them, they, their, theirs, it, its*). Usage today favors nonsexist terms in all word choices. You therefore want to use gender-free pronouns whenever possible. In the past, it was grammatically correct to use only masculine pronouns to refer to INDEFINITE PRONOUNS: "*Everyone* open **his** book.*" Today, however, people know that the pronouns *he, his, him,* and *himself* exclude women, who make up over half the population. Box 80 shows three ways to avoid using masculine pronouns when referring to males and females together. For more information on gender-neutral language, see 21g.

BOX 80 SUMMARY

 Avoiding the masculine pronoun when referring to males and females together

■ **Solution 1:** Use a pair of pronouns—*he or she.* However, avoid using a pair more than once in a sentence or in many sentences in a row. A *he or she* construction acts as a singular pronoun.

Everyone hopes that **he or she** will win a scholarship.

A **doctor** usually has time to keep up to date only in **his or her** specialty.

■ **Solution 2:** Revise into the plural.

Many students hope that **they** will win a scholarship.

Most doctors have time to keep up to date only in **their** specialties.

■ **Solution 3:** Recast the sentence.

Everyone hopes to win a scholarship.

Few specialists have time for general reading.

Questions often arise concerning the use of *he or she* and *his or her*. In general, writers find these gender-free pronoun constructions awkward. To avoid them, many writers make the antecedents plural. Doing this becomes problematic when the subject is a SINGULAR INDEFINITE PRONOUN (Box 77 in section 10i). In the popular press (such as newspapers and magazines), the use of the plural pronoun *they* or *them* with a singular antecedent has been gaining favor. Indeed, some experts find that the history of English supports this use. In ACADEMIC WRITING, however, it is better for you not to follow the practice of the popular press. Language practice changes, however, so what I say here is my best advice as I write this book.

10t How do pronouns work when antecedents are collective nouns?

A COLLECTIVE NOUN names a group of people or things, such as *family, group, audience, class, number, committee,* and *team.* When the group acts as one unit, use a singular pronoun to refer to it. When the members of the group act individually, use a plural pronoun. In the latter case, if the sentence is awkward, substitute a plural noun for the collective noun. (For related material on subjects and verbs, see 10j.)

The **audience** was cheering as **it** stood to applaud the performers. [The audience was acting as one unit, so the singular pronoun *it* is correct.]

The **audience** put on **their** coats and walked out. [The members of the audience were acting as individuals, so all actions become plural; therefore, the plural pronoun *their* is correct.]

The **family** is spending **its** vacation in Rockport, Maine. [All the family members went to one place together.]

The parallel sentence to the last example above would be *The **family** are spending **their** vacations in Maine, Hawaii, and Rome,* which might mean that each family member is going to a different place. But such a sentence is awkward. Therefore, revise the sentence.

The **family members** are spending **their** vacations in Maine, Hawaii, and Rome. [Substituting a plural noun *family members* for the collective noun *family* sounds more natural.]

EXERCISE 10-6

Underline the correct pronoun in parentheses. For help, consult 10o through 10t.

EXAMPLE   Many people wonder what gives certain leaders (his or her, their) spark and magnetic personal appeal.

---

1. its [10o]

2. himself or herself [10s]

3. they [10p]

4. his or her [10s]

5. He or she [10s]; their [10o]

6. their [10o]

7. their [10o]

8. their [10t]

9. their [10o]; he or she is [10s]

10. their [10o]; his or her [10r and 10s]; their [10o]

QUOTATION: ON WRITING
They ask me if I were on a desert island and knew nobody would ever see what I wrote, would I go on writing. My answer is most emphatically yes, I would go on writing for company. Because I'm creating an imaginary—it's always imaginary—world in which I would like to live.
—William Burroughs

QUOTATION: ON WRITING
Observing correctness in writing is like observing the speed limit while driving: Following the "rules" may have the negative virtue of keeping you out of trouble, but, in and of itself, it cannot produce the positive virtue of good writing.
—Marshall W. Gregory and Wayne C. Booth

1. The cluster of personal traits that produces star quality is called *charisma,* a state that bestows special power on (its, their) bearers.

2. Charisma is the quality that allows an individual to empower (himself, herself, himself or herself, themselves) and others.

3. Power and authority alone don't guarantee charisma; (it, they) must be combined with passion and strong purpose.

4. A charismatic leader has the ability to draw other people into (his, her, his or her, their) dream or vision.

5. (He, She, He or she, They) can inspire followers to believe that the leader's goals are the same as (his, her, his or her, their) own.

6. Not all leaders who possess charisma enjoy having this ability to attract and influence (his, his or her, their) followers.

7. Charismatic leaders are often creative, especially in (his, her, his or her, their) capacity for solving problems in original ways.

8. Today, a number of major corporations offer (its, their) employees charisma-training courses to enhance leadership qualities.

9. Usually, it's not the quiet, low-profile manager but rather the charismatic manager with strong leadership qualities who convinces others that (his, her, his or her, their) best interests are served by the course of action (he, she, he or she, they) is/are proposing.

10. Charisma trainers advise would-be leaders to start by bringing order to (his, her, his or her, their) activities; in stressful times, anyone who appears to have some part of (his, her, his or her, their) life under control makes others relax and perform (his, her, his or her, their) responsibilities better.

Chapter 11

Adjectives and Adverbs

11a What are the differences between adjectives and adverbs?

The differences between adjectives and adverbs relate to how they function. **Adjectives** modify NOUNS and PRONOUNS. **Adverbs** modify VERBS, adjectives, and other adverbs. What's the same about adjective and adverbs is that they are both MODIFIERS—that is, words or groups of words that describe other words. Box 81 compares adjectives and adverbs in action.

ADJECTIVE	The **brisk** *wind* blew. [Adjective *brisk* modifies noun *wind*.]
ADVERB	The wind *blew* **briskly.** [Adverb *briskly* modifies verb *blew*.]

 BOX 81 SUMMARY

Differences between adjectives and adverbs

WHAT ADJECTIVES MODIFY	EXAMPLES
nouns	The **busy** *lawyer* took a **quick** *look* at her schedule.
pronouns	*She* felt **triumphant,** for *they* were **attentive.**

WHAT ADVERBS MODIFY	EXAMPLES
verbs	The lawyer *spoke* **quickly** and **well.**
adverbs	The lawyer spoke **very** *quickly.*
adjectives	The lawyer was **extremely** *busy.*
independent clauses	**Therefore,** *the lawyer rested.*

WORD DERIVATION
Adjective comes from the Latin *adjectivus,* meaning "that is added," and *adverb* comes from the Latin *adverbum,* meaning "to a word." Both etymologies reflect the use of adjectives and adverbs as enhancers of other words' meanings.

QUOTATION: ON WRITING
The adjective is the enemy of the noun.
—Voltaire

QUOTATION: ON WRITING
What you say is found not in the noun but in what you add to qualify the noun. . . . The noun, the verb, and the main clause serve merely as the base on which meaning will rise. . . . The modifier is the essential part of any sentence.
—John Erskine

QUOTATION: ON WRITING
I don't think in any language. I think in images. I don't believe that people think in languages.
—Vladimir Nabokov

QUOTATION: ON WRITING
I don't like too many adjectives or adverbs—I say if a noun or a verb is worth describing, do it properly, take a sentence to do it.
—Fay Weldon

BACKGROUND
The Web site <http://webster.commnet.edu/grammar/quizzes/adjectives_quiz2.htm> provides multiple-choice quizzes on adjectives and adverbs, with answer keys.

ANSWERS: EXERCISE 11-1

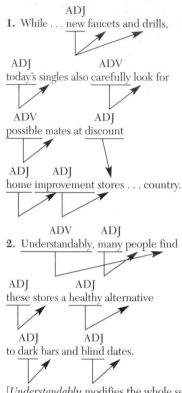

ADJ
1. While . . . new faucets and drills,

ADJ   ADV
today's singles also carefully look for

ADV   ADJ
possible mates at discount

ADJ   ADJ
home improvement stores . . . country.

ADV   ADJ
2. Understandably, many people find

ADJ   ADJ
these stores a healthy alternative

ADJ   ADJ
to dark bars and blind dates.

[*Understandably* modifies the whole sentence as well as the verb *find.*]

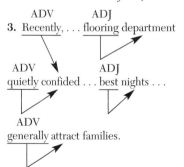

ADV   ADJ
3. Recently, . . . flooring department

ADV   ADJ
quietly confided . . . best nights . . .

ADV
generally attract families.

[*Recently* modifies the whole sentence as well as the verb *confided.*]   →

Some people think that all adverbs end in *-ly*. But this isn't correct. While many adverbs do end in *-ly* (eat *swiftly*, eat *frequently*, eat *hungrily*), some do not (eat *fast*, eat *often*, eat *seldom*). To complicate matters further, some adjectives end in *-ly* (*lovely* flower, *friendly* dog). Use meaning, not an *-ly* ending, to identify adverbs.

⊕ **ESL NOTES:** (1) In English, the adjective is always singular, even if its noun is plural: *The **hot** [not *hots*] drinks warmed us up.* (2) Word order in English calls for special attention to the placement of adjective and adverbs. Here is an example using the adverb *carefully: Thomas closed* [don't place *carefully* here] *the window **carefully*** (see 47b and 47c). ⊕

EXERCISE 11-1

Underline and label all adjectives (ADJ) and adverbs (ADV). Then, draw an arrow from each adjective and adverb to the word or words it modifies. For help, consult 11a.

EXAMPLE   Leaky faucets are unexpectedly leading to genuine romance in super-sized hardware stores.

1. While shopping for new faucets and drills, today's singles also carefully look for possible mates at discount home improvement stores across the country.

2. Understandably, many people find these stores a healthy alternative to dark bars and blind dates.

3. Recently, an employee in the flooring department quietly confided that the best nights for singles are Wednesdays and Thursdays, while weekends generally attract families.

4. A young single mom returns home excitedly because a quick trip to the lumber department for a new door resulted in a date for Saturday night.

5. A lonely widower in his fifties jokingly says he wishes he had developed earlier an interest in wallpapering and gardening.

11b When should I use adverbs—not adjectives—as modifiers?

Adverbs MODIFY verbs, adjectives, and other adverbs. Don't use adjectives as adverbs.

NO	The candidate inspired us **great.** [Adjective *great* cannot modify verb *inspired.*]
YES	The candidate inspired us **greatly.** [Adverb *greatly* can modify verb *inspired.*]
NO	The candidate felt **unusual** energetic. [Adjective *unusual* cannot modify adjective *energetic.*]
YES	The candidate felt **unusually** energetic. [Adverb *unusually* can modify adjective *energetic.*]
NO	The candidate spoke **exceptional** forcefully. [Adjective *exceptional* cannot modify adverb *forcefully.*]
YES	The candidate spoke **exceptionally** forcefully. [Adverb *exceptionally* modifies adverb *forcefully.*]

11c What is wrong with double negatives?

A **double negative** is a nonstandard form. It is a statement with two negative MODIFIERS, the second of which repeats the message of the first. Negative modifiers include *no, never, not, none, nothing, hardly, scarcely,* and *barely.*

NO	The factory workers will **never** vote for **no** strike.
YES	The factory workers will **never** vote for **a** strike.
NO	The union members did **not** have **no** money in reserve.
YES	The union members did **not** have **any** money in reserve.
YES	The union members had **no** money in reserve.

Take special care to avoid double negatives with contractions of *not: isn't, don't, didn't, haven't,* and the like (27d). The contraction containing *not* serves as the only negative in a sentence. Don't add a second negative.

NO	He **didn't** hear **nothing.**
YES	He **didn't** hear **anything.**
NO	They **haven't** had **no** meetings.
YES	They **haven't** had **any** meetings.

Similarly, be careful to avoid double negatives when you use *nor.* The word *nor* is correct only after *neither* (7i). Use the word *or* after any other negative.

NO	Stewart **didn't** eat dinner **nor** watch television last night.
YES	Stewart **didn't** eat dinner **or** watch television last night.
YES	Stewart **neither** ate dinner **nor** watched television last night.

LANGUAGE HISTORY
The rule banning double negatives in English is a relatively new one. Double, triple, and even quadruple negatives were acceptable in Old English and Middle English. They are also acceptable in many modern languages. The first attempts to regularize English were made in the eighteenth century. It was then that the first English dictionaries and usage books were written. One of these was Robert Lowth's *Short Introduction to English Grammar,* in which he stated that "two Negatives in English destroy one another, or are equivalent to an affirmative." The new rich of the merchant class, eager to fit in by speaking and writing correctly, accepted Lowth's rule, and it became the standard.

11d Do adjectives or adverbs come after linking verbs?

LINKING VERBS connect a SUBJECT to a COMPLEMENT. Always use an adjective, not an adverb, as the complement.

> The *guests looked* **happy.** [Verb *looked* links subject *guests* to adjective *happy*.]

The words *look, feel, smell, taste, sound,* and *grow* are usually linking verbs, but sometimes they're simply verbs. Check how any of these verbs is functioning in a sentence.

> Zora *looks* **happy.** [*Looks* functions as a linking verb, so the adjective *happy* is correct.]
> Zora *looks* **happily** at the sunset. [*Looks* doesn't function as a linking verb, so the adverb *happily* is correct.]

bad, badly

The words *bad* (adjective) and *badly* (adverb) are particularly prone to misuse with linking verbs.

> **NO** The students felt **badly.** [This means the students used their fingers badly.]
>
> **YES** The student felt **bad.** [This means the student had a bad feeling about something.]
>
> **NO** The food smelled **badly.** [This means the food had a bad ability to smell.]
>
> **YES** The food smelled **bad.** [This means the food had a bad smell to it.]

good, well

When the word *well* refers to health, it is an adjective; at all other times, *well* is an adverb. The word *good* is always an adjective.

> Evander looks **well.** [This means that Evander seems to be in good health, so the adjective *well* is correct.]
> Evander writes **well.** [This means that Evander writes skillfully, so the adverb *well* is correct.]

Use *good* as an adjective, except when you refer to health.

> **NO** She sings **good.** [*Sings* isn't a linking verb, so it calls for an adverb, not the adjective *good*.]
>
> **YES** She sings **well.** [*Sings* isn't a linking verb, so the adverb *well* is correct.]

EXERCISE 11-2

Underline the correct uses of negatives, adjectives, and adverbs by selecting between the choices in parentheses. For help, consult 11a through 11d.

EXAMPLE   Because she was only five when her father died, Bernice King, Martin Luther King's youngest child, (barely, bare) remembers the details of her father's (solemnly, solemn) funeral, yet her father's image lives (strong, strongly) within her.

1. Although she did feel (badly, bad) about her father's death when she was younger, King's daughter has managed to put his influence on her to good use by speaking (passionately, passionate) about issues her father first introduced.

2. In her (widely, wide) acclaimed book of sermons and speeches, titled *Hard Questions, Hard Answers,* Bernice King strives to deal with the (intensely, intense) topic of race relations.

3. Bernice King believes, as did her father, that all people must connect (genuinely, genuine), or they won't (never, ever) manage to coexist.

4. Bernice King decided to enter the ministry after she heard a (deeply, deep) voice within her directing her to this (extremely, extreme) (spiritually, spiritual) profession.

5. Bernice King entered the public eye in 1993, when she gave a (locally, local) televised Martin Luther King Day sermon at her father's church, and since then she has lived (happily, happy) in her home in Atlanta with memories of her father that are (peacefully, peaceful) recollections.

11e What are comparative and superlative forms?

When you write about comparisons, ADJECTIVES and ADVERBS often carry the message. The adjectives and adverbs also communicate degrees of intensity. When a comparison is made between two things, a **comparative** form is used. When a comparison is made about three or more things, a **superlative** form is used.

Regular forms of comparison

Most adjectives and adverbs are regular. They communicate degrees of intensity in one of two ways: either by adding *-er* and *-est* endings or by adding the words *more, most, less,* and *least* (see Box 82 on the next page).

ANSWERS AND COVERAGE: EXERCISE 11-2

1. bad [11d, adjective modifies noun *feel*]; passionately [11b, adverb modifies verb *speaking*]

2. widely [11b, adverb modifies verb *acclaimed*]; intense [11a, adjective modifies noun *topic*]

3. genuinely [11b, adverb modifies verb *connect*]; ever [11c, avoid double negative with *won't*]

4. deep [11a, adjective modifies noun *voice*]; extremely [11b, adverb modifies adjective *spiritual*]; spiritual [11a, adjective modifies noun *profession*]

5. locally [11b, adverb modifies adjective *televised*]; happily [11b, adverb modifies verb *lived*]; peaceful [11a, adjective modifies noun *recollections*]

LANGUAGE HISTORY
Adverbs in Old English and Middle English were formed differently than they are today. To make an adverb, an *-e* was simply added to an adjective. The modern *-ly* ending for adverbs comes from an adjective ending, *-lice* (meaning "like"), which became softened to *-ly* and was reinterpreted as an adverb signal. Some modern adjectives ending in *-ly* (such as *friendly* and *heavenly*) are descendants of those old *-lice* adjectives.

BACKGROUND

An adjective can be made from a noun by adding a different ending that can color the meaning of the word. For example, the *-ish* ending and the *-y* ending mean "similar to" or "characteristic of." A *yellowish substance* suggests a substance that is not exactly yellow, but close, and a *flowery paragraph* is so ornate and beautiful that it is reminiscent of a flower. Words often take an *-en* ending when they turn from nouns into adjectives (as in *wooden* and *silken*), and adjectives that had a Latin origin frequently end in *-al*, *-ar*, or *-ory* (as in *beneficial*, *oracular*, and *promissory*).

BACKGROUND

Students can find examples and interactive exercises on correct adjective and adverb use at the site <http://www.grammarbook.com/>.

BACKGROUND

The Web site <http:www.edunet.com/english/ grammar/toc.cfm> hosts a comprehensive menu on adjectives and adverbs, including a section on using comparative and superlative forms.

QUOTATION: ON LANGUAGE

Adjectives are used so freely these days that we feel almost naked, robbed, if we don't get at least a couple.

—Paul Stevens

> BOX 82   SUMMARY
>
> ### Regular forms of comparison for adjectives and adverbs
>
> **POSITIVE**   Use when nothing is being compared.
> **COMPARATIVE**   Use when two things are being compared. Add the ending *-er* or the word *more* or *less*.
> **SUPERLATIVE**   Use to compare three or more things. Add the ending *-est* or the word *most* or *least*.
>
> | POSITIVE [1] | COMPARATIVE [2] | SUPERLATIVE [3+] |
> |---|---|---|
> | green | greener | greenest |
> | happy | happier | happiest |
> | selfish | less selfish | least selfish |
> | beautiful | more beautiful | most beautiful |
>
> That tree is **green.**
> That tree is **greener** than this tree.
> That tree is the **greenest** tree on the block.

   The number of syllables in the adjective or adverb usually determines whether to use *-er*, *-est* or *more*, *most* and *less*, *least*.

- **One-syllable words** usually take *-er* and *-est* endings: *large, larger, largest* (adjectives); *far, farther, farthest* (adverbs).
- **Adjectives of two syllables** vary. If the word ends in *-y*, change the *y* to *i* and add *-er*, *-est* endings: *pretty, prettier, prettiest*. Otherwise, some two-syllable adjectives take *-er*, *-est* endings: *yellow, yellower, yellowest*. Others take *more*, *most* and *less*, *least*: *tangled, more tangled, most tangled; less tangled, least tangled*.
- **Adverbs of two syllables** take *more*, *most* and *less*, *least*: *easily, more easily, most easily; less easily, least easily*.
- **Three-syllable words** take *more*, *most* and *less*, *least*: *dignified, more/most dignified, less/least dignified* (adjective); *carefully, more/most carefully, less/least carefully* (adverb).

   👁 **ALERT:** Be careful not to use a double comparative or double superlative. Use either the *-er* and *-est* endings or *more*, *most* or *less*, *least*.

   He was **younger** [not *more younger*] than his brother.
   Her music was the **loudest** [not *most loudest*] on the stereo.
   Children are **more easily** [not *more easier*] influenced than adults. 👁

Irregular forms of comparison

A few comparative and superlative forms are irregular. Box 83 gives you the list. I suggest that you memorize them so they come to mind easily.

BOX 83	SUMMARY

Irregular forms of comparison for adjectives and adverbs

POSITIVE [1]	COMPARATIVE [2]	SUPERLATIVE [3+]
good (*adjective*)	better	best
well (*adjective* and *adverb*)	better	best
bad (*adjective*)	worse	worst
badly (*adverb*)	worse	worst
many	more	most
much	more	most
some	more	most
little*	less	least

The Wallaces saw a **good** movie.
The Wallaces saw a **better** movie than the Pascals did.
The Wallaces saw the **best** movie they had ever seen.
The Millers had **little** trouble finding jobs.
The Millers had **less** trouble finding jobs than the Smiths did.
The Millers had the **least** trouble finding jobs of everyone.

*When you're using *little* for items that can be counted (e.g., pickles), use the regular forms *little, littler, littlest.*

👁 **ALERTS:** (1) Be aware of the difference between *less* and *fewer*. They aren't interchangeable. Use *less* with NONCOUNT NOUNS, either items or values: *The sugar substitute has less **aftertaste.*** Use *fewer* with numbers or COUNT NOUNS: *The sugar substitute has fewer **calories.*** (2) Don't use *more, most* or *less, least* with **absolute adjectives,** that is, adjectives that communicate a noncomparable quality or state, such as *unique* or *perfect*. Something either *is*, or *is not*, one of a kind. No degrees of intensity are involved: *This teapot is **unique*** [not the most unique]; *The artisanship is **perfect*** [not the most perfect]. 👁

EXERCISE 11-3

Complete the chart on the next page. Then, write a sentence for each word in the completed chart. For help, consult 11e.

Positive	Comparative	Superlative
small	smaller	smallest
greedy	greedier	greediest
complete	more complete	most complete
gladly	more gladly	most gladly
few	fewer	fewest
thick	thicker	thickest
some	more	most

WORD HISTORIES

Common irregular adjectives (and adverbs) can be confusing to students because the comparative and superlative forms seem unconnected to the positive form. The realization that these irregularities are only accidents of history rather than the product of difficult rules can make them less intimidating to students.

For example, *good* comes from the Old English *god*, related to the German *gut*, both of which come from the Indo-European word meaning "to be suitable." *Better* and *best* come from the Old English *betera* and *betst*, respectively, based on the Indo-European word meaning "good."

Another example is *worse* and *worst*, which come from their Old English synonyms, *wiersa* and *wyrsta*. However, *bad* does not come from *yfel*, the Old English word for "bad" or "evil," but from the Old English *baeddel*, meaning "hermaphrodite."

QUOTATION: ON WRITING

As to the adjective: when in doubt, strike it out.

—Mark Twain

QUOTATION: ON WRITING

I love writing. I love the swirl and swing of words as they tangle with human emotions.

—James Michener

EXAMPLE   *funny, funnier, funniest:* My brother has a *funny* laugh; he thinks Mom has a *funnier* laugh; the person who has the *funniest* laugh in our family is Uncle Dominic.

POSITIVE	COMPARATIVE	SUPERLATIVE
small	_____	_____
_____	greedier	_____
_____	_____	most complete
gladly	_____	_____
_____	_____	fewest
_____	thicker	_____
some	_____	_____

11f Why avoid a long string of nouns as modifiers?

NOUNS sometimes MODIFY other nouns: *truck driver, train track, security system.* Usually, these terms create no problems. However, avoid using several nouns in a row as modifiers. A string of too many nouns makes it difficult for your reader to figure out which nouns are being modified and which nouns are doing the modifying. You can revise such sentences in several ways.

REWRITE THE SENTENCE

NO   I asked my adviser to write **two college recommendation letters** for me.

YES   I asked my adviser to write ***letters of recommendation to two colleges*** for me.

CHANGE ONE NOUN TO A POSSESSIVE AND ANOTHER TO AN ADJECTIVE

NO   He will take the **United States Navy examination** for **navy engineer training.**

YES   He will take the *United States **Navy's** examination* for ***naval engineer training.***

CHANGE ONE NOUN TO A PREPOSITIONAL PHRASE

NO   Our **student adviser training program** has won many awards.

YES   Our *training program **for student advisers*** has won many awards. [This change requires a change from the singular *adviser* to the plural *advisers*.]

EXERCISE 11-4

Underline the better choice in parentheses. For help, consult this entire chapter.

EXAMPLE Alexis, a huge and powerful six-year-old Siberian tiger, (curious, <u>curiously</u>) explores her new zoo home together with five other tigers.

1. The new tiger home at the world-famous Bronx Zoo is a (special, specially) designed habitat, planted with (dense, denser) undergrowth so that it (close, closely) imitates the tigers' natural wilderness.

2. Like tigers in the wild, the six tigers in this habitat, which (more, many) experts consider the (more authentic, most authentic) of all artificial tiger environments in the world, will face some of the physical challenges and sensory experiences that keep them happy and (healthy, healthier).

3. Research shows that tigers feel (bad, badly) and fail to thrive in zoos without enrichment features placed in (good, well) locations to inspire tigers to stalk (stealthy, stealthily) through underbrush, loll (lazy, lazily) on heated rocks, or tug (vigorous, vigorously) on massive pull toys.

4. Wildlife zoologists think that the new Tiger Mountain exhibit will also serve zoo visitors (good, well) by allowing them to observe and admire the amazing strength, agility, and intelligence of a (rapid, rapidly) dwindling species.

5. Today, (fewer, less) than 5,000 Siberian tigers remain in the wild, which makes it imperative for zoos to raise people's awareness of the (great, greatest) need to prevent the extinction of these big cats that are considered among the (more, most) powerful, beautiful animals in the world.

ANSWERS AND COVERAGE: EXERCISE 11-4

1. specially [11b, adverb modifies adjective *designed*]; dense [11e, positive form—nothing is being compared]; closely [11b, adverb modifies verb *imitates*]

2. many [11e, positive form—nothing is being compared]; most authentic [11e, superlative form]; healthy [11e, positive form—nothing is being compared]

3. bad [11d, adjective with the linking verb *feel*]; good [11d, adjective modifies noun *locations*]; stealthily, lazily, vigorously [11b, adverbs modify verbs *stalk, loll,* and *tug*]

4. well [11d, adverb modifies verb *serve*]; rapidly [11b, adverb modifies adjective *dwindling*]

5. fewer [11e, countable items use *fewer*]; great [11e, positive form—nothing is being compared]; most [11e, superlative form]

BACKGROUND

In *Errors and Expectations* (New York: Oxford UP, 1977), Mina P. Shaughnessy describes the use of modifiers by three groups of first-year college writers. The few adverbs used by *basic* writers, she notes, usually come from the most overworked ones in the language, such as *too, very, quite,* and *hardly.* Similarly, basic writers modify their nouns and verbs with what she calls "the common adjectives": *a lot, many, good, easy, big, certain,* familiar words that slip into place without mental effort, thereby making it impossible for the writer to achieve the precision needed for complex consideration of the topic. *Intermediate* writers, moving closer to precise diction, use *-ly* adverbs and more specific adjectives. Although they are likely to use multiple adjectives, doing so does not usually increase the precision of the statement. *Advanced* first-year writers, working with more confidence, lean on adverbial conjunctions for paragraph cohesion—*furthermore, however, consequently*—and include figurative language, which is more descriptive.

BACKGROUND
In "The Patterns of Language: Perspective on Teaching Writing" (*Teaching English in the Two-Year College*, May 1997: 136–144), Pamela Dykstra argues that when students examine syntactic units, they come to understand the concept of *sentence boundaries*. She offers three detailed ways of teaching the concept.

BACKGROUND
The site <http://www.as.ysu.edu/~english/fragments.html> offered by Youngstown State University includes suggestions for identifying and correcting sentence fragments.

QUOTATION: ON WRITING
Fragments, or incomplete sentences, occur quite frequently when we speak, so it's no wonder sentence fragments are often found in formal writing.
— <http://writing2.richmond.edu/writing/wweb/fragment.html>

Chapter 12

Sentence Fragments

12a What is a sentence fragment?

A **sentence fragment** looks like a sentence, but it's actually only part of a sentence. That is, even though a sentence fragment begins with a capital letter and ends with a period (or question mark or exclamation point), it doesn't contain an INDEPENDENT CLAUSE. Fragments are merely unattached PHRASES or DEPENDENT CLAUSES.

FRAGMENT	The telephone with redial capacity. [no verb]
CORRECT	The telephone has redial capacity.
FRAGMENT	Rang loudly for ten minutes. [no subject]
CORRECT	The telephone rang loudly for ten minutes.
FRAGMENT	At midnight. [a phrase without a verb or subject]
CORRECT	The telephone rang at midnight.
FRAGMENT	Because the telephone rang loudly. [dependent clause starting with subordinating conjunction *because*]
CORRECT	Because the telephone rang loudly, the family was awakened in the middle of the night.
FRAGMENT	Which really annoyed me. [dependent clause with relative pronoun *which*]
CORRECT	The telephone call was a wrong number, which really annoyed me.

Sentence fragments can ruin the clarity of your writing. Moreover, in ACADEMIC WRITING and BUSINESS WRITING, sentence fragments imply that you don't know basic sentence structure or that you're a careless proofreader.

NO	The lawyer was angry. When she returned from court. She found the key witness waiting in her office. [Was the lawyer angry when she returned from court, or when she found the witness in her office?]
YES	The lawyer was angry when she returned from court. She found the key witness waiting in her office.
YES	The lawyer was angry. When she returned from court, she found the key witness waiting in her office.

Let's go beyond the grammatical terms to a more practical approach to recognizing SENTENCE FRAGMENTS, so that you avoid them in your writing. (Remember that any words in small capital letters in this handbook are defined, usually with examples, in the Terms Glossary at the back of this book.) To learn to recognize sentence fragments, see 12b; to learn several ways to correct sentence fragments, see 12c and 12d.

Many writers wait until the REVISING and EDITING stages of the WRITING PROCESS to check for sentence fragments. During DRAFTING, the goal is to get ideas down on paper or disk. As you draft, if you suspect that you've written a sentence fragment, simply underline or highlight it in boldface or italics and move on. Later, you can easily find it to check and correct.

12b How can I recognize a sentence fragment?

If you tend to write SENTENCE FRAGMENTS, you want a system for recognizing them. Box 84 shows you a Sentence Test for checking that you haven't written a sentence fragment. Following Box 84, I discuss each question in more detail in 12b.1 through 12b.3.

BOX 84   SUMMARY

 Sentence Test to identify sentence fragments

Question 1: Is the word group a dependent clause?

A DEPENDENT CLAUSE is a word group that has a subject and a verb but starts with a word that creates dependence—either a SUBORDINATING CONJUNCTION or a RELATIVE PRONOUN.

FRAGMENT	**When** winter comes early. [starts with *when*, a word that creates dependence]
CORRECT	**When** winter comes early, **ships often rescue the stranded whales.** [adds an independent clause to create a sentence]

→

BACKGROUND

In *Under the Grammar Hammer: The 25 Most Important Grammar Mistakes and How to Avoid Them* (Los Angeles: Lowell House, 1992), Doug Cazort claims that the third most frequently made mistake in English is using sentence fragments instead of complete sentences.

QUOTATION: ON WRITING

With sixty staring me in the face, I have developed inflammation of the sentence structure and a definite hardening of the paragraphs.

—James Thurber

You might find it useful to have students work in groups to identify and correct fragments found in paragraphs taken from their own writing or those that occur in the following paragraph. Each group can present to the class a revision of a paragraph, pointing out the merits of the new version. In the paragraph shown here, fragments are often signaled by the words *just, only, for example, also, mainly,* and *such as.*

In their early history, the people of Asia followed the seasons through the valleys until they found no more land. Only the sea and sky and a sheet of ice stretching across the Bering Strait. They did not think about the past. Just the present. For example, making weapons. Such as tree limbs used for bows. Also knives made from sharpened stones. Just like their forefathers. Moving south, they eventually reached the Rio Grande. Mainly known today as the river that separates Mexico and the United States.

The Internet TESL Journal: For Teachers of English as a Second Language, a monthly Web journal, provides articles and other teaching resources at <http://iteslj.org>. The link at <http://a4esl.org/q/j> offers a large collection of interactive quizzes on grammar, including sentence fragments, for ESL students.

Sentence Test to identify sentence fragments (*continued*)

FRAGMENT	**Which** can happen quickly. [starts with *which,* a word that creates dependence]
CORRECT	**Whales cannot breathe through the ice and will drown, which** can happen quickly. [adds an independent clause to create a sentence]

Question 2: Is there a verb?

FRAGMENT	Thousands of whales in the Arctic Ocean. [Because a verb is missing, it's a phrase, not a sentence.]
CORRECT	Thousands of whales **live** in the Arctic Ocean. [adds a verb to create a sentence]

Question 3: Is there a subject?

FRAGMENT	Stranded in the Arctic Ocean. [Because a subject is missing, this is a phrase, not a sentence.]
CORRECT	**Many whales *were*** stranded in the Arctic Ocean [adds a subject (and the verb *were* to *stranded*) to create a sentence]

12b.1 Question 1: Is the word group a dependent clause?

If you answer yes to question 1, you're looking at a sentence fragment. A DEPENDENT CLAUSE is a word group that has a subject and a verb but starts with a word that creates dependence. The only words that create dependence are SUBORDINATING CONJUNCTIONS and RELATIVE PRONOUNS. Such a word before an INDEPENDENT CLAUSE creates a dependent clause, which can't stand alone as a sentence and is therefore a sentence fragment. To become a complete sentence, the fragment needs either to be joined to an independent clause or to be rewritten.

Fragments with subordinating conjunctions

A complete list of subordinating conjunctions appears in Box 50 in 7i. Some frequently used ones are *after, although, because, before, if, unless,* and *when.*

FRAGMENT	**Because** she returned my books. [*Because,* a subordinating conjunction, creates a dependent clause.]

CORRECT **Because** she returned my books, *I can study.* [A comma and the independent clause *I can study* are added, and the sentence becomes complete.]

FRAGMENT **Unless** I study. [*Unless,* a subordinating conjunction, creates a dependent clause.]

CORRECT *I won't pass the test* **unless** I study. [The independent clause *I won't pass the test* is added, and the sentence becomes complete.]

👁 **ALERT:** When a dependent clause starts with a subordinating conjunction and comes before its independent clause, use a comma to separate the clauses (24c). 👁

Fragments with relative pronouns

Relative pronouns are *that, which, who, whom,* and *whose.*

FRAGMENT **That** we had studied for all week. [*That,* a relative pronoun, creates a dependent clause here.]

CORRECT *We passed our midterm exam* **that** we had studied for all week. [The independent clause *We passed our midterm exam* is added, and the sentence becomes complete.]

When *which, who,* and *whose* begin questions, they function as INTERROGATIVE PRONOUNS, not relative pronouns. Questions are complete sentences, not fragments: *Which* class are you taking? *Who* is your professor? *Whose* book is that?

12b.2 Question 2: Is there a verb?

If you answer no to question 2, you're looking at a sentence fragment. When a VERB is missing from a word group, the result is a PHRASE, not a sentence. You can figure out if a word is a verb by seeing if it can change in TENSE. Verbs have tenses to tell what *is* happening, what *has* happened, or what *will* happen.

Now the telephone **rings.** [present tense]
Yesterday, the telephone **rang.** [past tense]

When you check for verbs, remember that VERBALS are not verbs. Verbals might look like verbs, but they don't function as verbs (see 7e).

FRAGMENT Yesterday, the students **registering** for classes. [*Registering* is a verbal called a present participle, which isn't a verb.]

CORRECT Yesterday, the students **were registering** for classes. [Adding the auxiliary verb *were* to the present participle *registering* creates a verb.]

BACKGROUND
Purdue University's Online Writing Lab (OWL) features several informative Web pages on sentence fragments. Also, the page at <http://owl.english.purdue.edu/handouts/grammar/g_frag.html> contains links to its fragment exercises for editing practice.

TEACHING TIP
Students sometimes create fragments as they attempt to write longer or more complicated sentences and experiment with their style. Without a range of syntactic structures available to them, students may try to vary the rhythm of their sentences, suggest pauses for emphasis, and establish sentence variety with the placement of periods. Fragments often appear because students begin using dependent clauses, participial phrases, elliptical constructions, and absolute phrases in their writing before they have enough knowledge and control of these structures.

Students benefit when they learn new sentence patterns that also help them avoid fragments. Students who use periods to suggest a long pause may benefit from instruction on the dash (Chapter 29). Students creating fragments from dependent clauses, absolute phrases, and participial phrases may benefit from studying coordination and subordination (Chapter 17), parallelism (Chapter 18), and techniques for achieving sentence variety and emphasis (Chapter 19).

FRAGMENT	They **informed** that the course was not being offered. [*Informed* is a verbal called a past participle, which isn't a verb.]
CORRECT	They **had been informed** that the course was not being offered. [Adding the auxiliary verbs *had been* to the past participle *informed* creates a verb.]
FRAGMENT	Now the students **to register** for classes. [*To register* is a verbal called an infinitive, which isn't a verb.]
CORRECT	Now the students **want to register** for classes. [Adding the verb *want* to the infinitive *to register* creates a verb.]

12b.3 Question 3: Is there a subject?

If you answer no to question 3, you're looking at a sentence fragment. When a SUBJECT is missing from a word group, the result is a PHRASE, not a sentence. To see if a word is a subject, ask, "Who (or "What) performs the action?"

FRAGMENT	Studied hard for class. [*Who* studied hard for class? unknown]
CORRECT	The students studied hard for class. [*Who* studied hard for class? *The students* is the answer, so a subject makes the sentence complete.]
FRAGMENT	Contained some difficult questions. [*What* contained some difficult questions? unknown]
CORRECT	The test contained some difficult questions. [*What* contained some difficult questions? *The test* is the answer, so a subject makes the sentence complete.]

Be especially careful with COMPOUND PREDICATES—for example, *We took the bus to the movie **and walked** home.* If you were to place a period after *movie*, the second part of the compound predicate would be a sentence fragment. Every sentence needs its own subject. To check for this kind of sentence fragment, ask the question "Who?" or "What?" of each verb.

| NO | A few students organized a study group to prepare for midterm exams. **Decided to study together for the rest of the course.** [*Who* decided to study together? The answer is *The students* (who formed the group), but this subject is missing.] |
| YES | A few students organized a study group to prepare for midterm exams. ***The students* decided to study together for the rest of the course.** |

IMPERATIVE SENTENCES—commands and some requests—may appear at first glance to be fragments caused by missing subjects. They're not fragments, however. Imperative sentences are complete sentences because their subjects are implied. An implied subject can be *you, anybody, somebody,* or *everybody,* and other INDEFINITE PRONOUNS.

Run! [This sentence implies the pronoun *you*. The complete sentence would be *You run!*]

Return all library books to the front desk. [This sentence implies the indefinite pronoun *everyone*. The complete sentence would be *Everyone (should) return all library books to the front desk.*]

EXERCISE 12-1

Identify each word group as either a complete sentence or a fragment. If the word group is a sentence, circle its number. If it's a fragment, tell why it's incomplete. For help, see Box 84 in 12b and sections 12b.1 through 12b.3.

EXAMPLE   Because gold is shiny, flexible, and scarce. [Starts with a subordinating conjunction (*because*), creating dependence, and lacks an independent clause to complete the thought; see Box 84 and section 12c.1]

1. Making gold ideal for a variety of uses.
2. Since gold does not easily tarnish, corrode, or rust.
3. Provides brilliance to coins, jewelry, and artwork.
4. Because gold combines easily to strengthen copper, silver, or nickel.
5. Weighs twice as much as a square inch of lead.
6. One ounce of gold can be rolled out to a 300-square-foot sheet.
7. Or can be pulled into a 40-mile-long wire.
8. The melting point of gold is 1,945 degrees Fahrenheit.
9. Although tons of gold lie under the oceans.
10. The value of gold being less than the cost of mining gold from ocean floors.

12c What are major ways of correcting fragments?

Once you've identified a SENTENCE FRAGMENT (12b), you're ready to correct it. You can do this in one of two ways: by joining it to an independent clause (12c.1) or by rewriting it (12c.2).

BACKGROUND
In a survey of eighty-four professionals representing sixty-three different occupations reported by Maxine Hairston ("Not All Errors Are Created Equal: Nonacademic Readers in the Profession Respond to Lapses in Usage," *College English*, 1981: 794–806), respondents ranked sentence fragments among the most serious errors, below only "status markers" such as nonstandard verbs ("brung"), double negatives, and beginning a sentence with an objective pronoun.

ANSWERS AND COVERAGE: EXERCISE 12-1

Two pieces of information are given for each item: the reason for the sentence fragment (as explained in sections 12b.1 through 12b.3) and the number of the question in Box 84 (in 12b) that explains what has caused each sentence fragment. (Exercise 12-3 asks students to correct the sentence fragments in this exercise.)

1. No verb; *making* is a verbal. [2]
2. Starts with a subordinating conjunction (*since*), which creates dependence, and lacks an independent clause to complete the thought. [1]
3. No subject [3]
4. Starts with a subordinating conjunction (*because*), which creates dependence, and lacks an independent clause to complete the thought [1]; *to strengthen* is a verbal [2].
5. No subject [3]
6. Complete sentence
7. No subject [3]
8. Complete sentence
9. Starts with a subordinating conjunction (*although*), which creates dependence, and lacks an independent clause to complete the thought. [1]
10. No verb; *being* is a verbal. [2]

TEACHING TIP
In *Grammar and the Teaching of Writing: Limits and Possibilities* (Urbana: NCTE, 1991), Rei R. Noguchi proposes that students can identify declarative sentences and fragments if they attempt to transform the construction into tag questions and yes-no questions. For example, "Doing math problems isn't one of Billy's favorite activities" can be transformed into the tag question "Doing math problems isn't one of Billy's favorite activities, is it?" and the yes-no question "Isn't doing math problems one of Billy's favorite activities?" With fragments such as "Enjoyed the baseball game on Saturday" or "Whatever you could do to help my sister," students will find it impossible to create such questions unless they add words to the fragment, revealing that the construction was an incomplete sentence. You might ask students to try this method with Exercise 12-1.

ANOTHER EXAMPLE
If your students have trouble recognizing dependent clauses as fragments, you may want to give them practice. Ask them to identify the fragments in the following mixture of complete and incomplete sentences. You might also ask them to combine the sentences so that each one is complete, being careful to separate with a comma each opening dependent clause from the independent one that follows.

Many elderly people have pets as companions. Because the elderly are often lonely. Nevertheless, pets make demands on their energy. For example, if a cat is sick, and when a dog must be bathed. Unless the owner has the strength and funds to care for the pet's needs. Then the pet is better off with a younger owner. Since the pet deserves a good home too. Before getting a cat or dog, people should be certain that they can provide adequate care.

12c.1 Correcting a sentence fragment by joining it to an independent clause

One way that a sentence fragment can be corrected is by joining it to an INDEPENDENT CLAUSE—that is, a complete sentence. The first two examples below deal with dependent-clause fragments; the examples following the ALERT examine fragments with missing subjects and/or verbs.

FRAGMENT **Because** the ice was thick. [Although this word group has a subject (*ice*) and verb (*was*), it starts with the subordinating conjunction *because*.]

CORRECT **Because** the ice was thick, *icebreakers were required to serve as rescue ships.* [By adding a comma and joining the fragment to the independent clause *icebreakers were required to serve as rescue ships*, a complete sentence is created.]

CORRECT *Icebreakers were required to serve as rescue ships* **because** the ice was thick. [By joining the fragment to the independent clause *Icebreakers were required to serve as rescue ships*, a complete sentence is created.]

FRAGMENT **Who** feared the whales would panic. [This fragment starts with the relative pronoun *who*.]

CORRECT *The noisy motors of the ships worried the crews,* **who** feared the whales would panic. [By joining the fragment to the independent clause *The noisy motors of the ships worried the crews*, a complete sentence is created.]

👁 **ALERT:** Be careful with all words that indicate time, such as *after, before, since,* and *until.* They aren't always subordinating conjunctions. Sometimes they function as ADVERBS—especially if they begin a complete sentence. At other times, they function as PREPOSITIONS. When you see one of these words that indicate time, realize that you aren't necessarily looking at a dependent-clause fragment.

Before, the whales had responded to classical music. [This is a complete sentence in which *Before* is an adverb that modifies the independent clause *the whales had responded to classical music*.]

Before the whales had responded to classical music, some crewmembers tried rock and roll music. [If the word group before the comma stood on its own, it would be a sentence fragment because it starts with *Before* functioning as a subordinating conjunction.] 👁

FRAGMENT **To announce new programs for crime prevention.** [*To announce* starts an infinitive phrase, not a sentence.]

CORRECT | *The mayor called a news conference last week* **to announce** new programs for crime prevention. [The infinitive phrase starting with *to announce* is joined with an independent clause.]

FRAGMENT | **Hoping for strong public support.** [*Hoping* starts a present-participle phrase, not a sentence.]

CORRECT | **Hoping** for strong public support, *she gave examples of problems throughout the city.* [The present-participle phrase starting with *Hoping* is joined with an independent clause.]

FRAGMENT | **Introduced by her assistant.** [*Introduced* starts a past-participle phrase, not a sentence.]

CORRECT | **Introduced** by her assistant, *the mayor began with an opening statement.* [The past-participle phrase starting with *Introduced* is joined with an independent clause.]

FRAGMENT | **During the long news conference.** [*During* functions as a preposition—starting a prepositional phrase, not a sentence.]

CORRECT | *Cigarette smoke made the conference room seem airless* **during** the long news conference. [The prepositional phrase starting with *during* is joined with an independent clause.]

FRAGMENT | **A politician with fresh ideas.** [*A politician* starts an appositive phrase, not a sentence.]

CORRECT | *Most people respected the mayor,* **a politician** with fresh ideas. [The appositive phrase starting with *a politician* is joined with an independent clause.]

EXERCISE 12-2

Find and correct any sentence fragments. If a sentence is correct, circle its number. For help, consult 12a through 12c.

EXAMPLE   Many communities prohibit the building of cellphone transmission towers. Which they consider to be unsightly.

Many communities prohibit the building of cellphone transmission towers, which they consider to be unsightly.

1. Although telephone companies always need to build more towers to fulfill the increasing demand for cellphone service.
2. The companies are hard-pressed to find suitable locations, especially on the densely populated east and west coasts of the United States.
3. Because cellphone use is expanding rapidly. One telecommunications analyst predicts that the number of cellphone towers, which now is around 100,000, will triple over five years.

ANSWERS AND COVERAGE: EXERCISE 12-2

Answers will vary. Here is one set of possible responses.

1. Telephone companies always need to build many more towers to fulfill the increasing demand for cellphone service. [subordinating conjunction dropped from dependent (adverb) clause]

2. Correct complete sentence

3. Because cellphone use is expanding rapidly, one telecommunications analyst predicts that the number of cellphone towers, which is now around 100,000, will triple over five years. [dependent (subordinate) clause attached to independent clause]

4. Companies have built the cellphone towers inside tall structures such as flagpoles, silos, water towers, even smokestacks to disguise the ugly structures. [infinitive phrase joined to independent clause]

5. The best hiding places of all are church steeples, which are often the tallest structures in a community. [dependent (relative) clause attached to independent clause]

6. While the equipment that runs the towers usually fits out of sight in the church basement, the tall antenna is concealed inside the steeple. [dependent (subordinate) clause attached to independent clause]

7. Strapped for funds, churches are often eager to rent space to telecommunications companies. [past-participle phrase attached to independent clause]

8. Correct complete sentence

9. The steeple is a historic structure that appears on the town's seal. [subordinating conjunction dropped from dependent (adverb) clause]

10. The reconstruction preserved the historic architecture, hid the tower, and even left room for the bats and pigeons that traditionally inhabited the picturesque original steeple. [dependent (relative) clause attached to independent clause]

BACKGROUND
The Lynchburg College Web site at <http://www.lynchburg.edu/writcntr/guide/grammar/sentfrag.htm> suggests likely causes of sentence fragments.

TEACHING TIP
To demonstrate how phrases can be turned into complete sentences, you might ask two students to read the following dialogue aloud in class and then improvise each comment as a sentence.

A: When are you coming?

B: In a minute.

A: Really?

B: Really.

A: Hurry up!

B: OK, OK. Just a second. How about Mother?

A: Who?

B: Mother.

A: Sure. Ready hours ago.

4. Companies have built the towers inside tall structures such as flagpoles, silos, water towers, even smokestacks. To disguise the ugly structures.

5. The best hiding places of all are church steeples. Which are often the tallest structures in a community.

6. While the equipment that runs the towers usually fits out of sight in the church basement. The tall antenna is concealed inside the steeple.

7. Strapped for funds. Churches are often eager to rent space to telecommunications companies.

8. In one case, a church whose steeple had burned down was unable to rebuild it without payments provided by a cellular company.

9. Even though the steeple is a historic structure that appears on the town's seal.

10. The reconstruction preserved the historic architecture, hid the tower, and even left room for the bats and pigeons. That traditionally inhabited the original steeple.

12c.2 Correcting a sentence fragment by rewriting it

A second way that a sentence fragment can be corrected is by rewriting it as an INDEPENDENT CLAUSE—that is, a complete sentence. The first two examples below deal with dependent-clause fragments; the others examine fragments with missing subjects and/or verbs.

FRAGMENT **Because** the ice was thick. [Although this word group has a subject (*ice*) and verb (*was*), it starts with the subordinating conjunction *because*.]

CORRECT The ice was thick. [The fragment starting with *Because* is rewritten to become a complete sentence.]

FRAGMENT **Who** feared the whales would panic. [This fragment starts with the relative pronoun *who*.]

CORRECT ***The crew*** feared the whales would panic. [The fragment starting with *Who* is rewritten to become a complete sentence.]

FRAGMENT **To announce** new programs for crime prevention. [*To announce* starts an infinitive phrase, not a sentence.]

CORRECT ***The mayor called a news conference last week because she wanted*** to announce new programs for crime prevention. [The infinitive phrase starting with *To announce* is rewritten to become a complete sentence.]

FRAGMENT **Hoping** for strong public support. [*Hoping* starts a present-participle phrase, not a sentence.]

CORRECT **She was hoping** for strong public support. [The present-participle phrase starting with *Hoping* is rewritten to become a complete sentence.]

FRAGMENT **Introduced** by her assistant. [*Introduced* starts a past-participle phrase, not a sentence.]

CORRECT **Introduced** by her assistant, *the mayor began with an opening statement.* [The past-participle phrase starting with *Introduced* is rewritten to become a complete sentence.]

FRAGMENT **During** the long news conference. [*During* functions as a preposition that starts a prepositional phrase, not a sentence.]

CORRECT *It was hard to breathe* **during** the long news conference. [The prepositional phrase starting with *During* is rewritten to become a complete sentence.]

FRAGMENT **A politician** with fresh ideas. [*A politician* starts an appositive phrase, not a sentence.]

CORRECT *She seemed to be* **a politician** with fresh ideas. [The appositive phrase is rewritten to become a complete sentence.]

12d How can I fix a fragment that is part of a compound predicate?

A COMPOUND PREDICATE contains two or more VERBS. When the second half of a compound predicate is punctuated as a separate sentence, it becomes a sentence fragment.

FRAGMENT The reporters asked the mayor many questions about the new program. **And then discussed her answers among themselves.** [*And then discussed* starts a compound predicate fragment, not a sentence.]

CORRECT The reporters asked the mayor many questions about the new program and then discussed her answers among themselves. [The compound predicate fragment starting with *and then discussed* is joined to the independent clause.]

CORRECT The reporters asked the mayor many questions about the new program. *Then the reporters* **discussed** her answers among themselves. [The compound predicate fragment starting with *And then discussed* is rewritten as a complete sentence.]

EXERCISE 12-3

Go back to Exercise 12-1 and revise the sentence fragments into complete sentences. In some cases, you may be able to combine two fragments into one complete sentence.

12e What are the two special fragment problems?

Two special fragment problems sometimes involve lists and examples. Lists and examples must be part of a complete sentence, unless they are formatted as a column.

You can connect a list fragment by attaching it to the preceding independent clause using a colon or a dash. You can correct an example fragment by attaching it to an independent clause (with or without punctuation, depending on the meaning) or by rewriting it as a complete sentence.

FRAGMENT   You have a choice of desserts. **Carrot cake, chocolate silk pie, apple pie, or peppermint ice cream.** [The list cannot stand on its own as a sentence.]

CORRECT   You have a choice of desserts: carrot cake, chocolate silk pie, apple pie, or peppermint ice cream. [A colon joins the sentence and the list.]

CORRECT   You have a choice of desserts—carrot cake, chocolate silk pie, apple pie, or peppermint ice cream. [A dash joins the sentence and the list.]

FRAGMENT   Several good places offer brunch. **For example, the restaurants Sign of the Dove and Blue Yonder.** [Examples can't stand on their own as a sentence.]

CORRECT   Several good places offer brunch— **for example,** the restaurants Sign of the Dove and Blue Yonder.

CORRECT   Several good places offer brunch. **For example,** *there are* the restaurants Sign of the Dove and Blue Yonder.

12f How can I recognize intentional fragments?

Professional writers sometimes intentionally use fragments for emphasis and effect.

But in the main, I feel like a brown bag of miscellany propped against a wall. Pour out the contents, and there is discovered a jumble of small things priceless and worthless. **A first-water diamond, an empty spool, bits of broken glass, lengths of string, a key to a door long since crumbled away, a rusty knife-blade, old shoes saved for a road that never was and never will be, a nail bent under the weight of things too heavy for any nail, a dried flower or two still a little fragrant.**

—Zora Neale Hurston, *How It Feels to Be Colored Me*

Being able to judge the difference between an acceptable and unacceptable sentence fragment comes from years of reading the work of skilled writers. For ACADEMIC WRITING, most instructors don't accept sentence fragments in student writing until a student demonstrates a consistent ability to write well-constructed, complete sentences. As a rule, avoid sentence fragments in academic writing.

EXERCISE 12-4

Revise this paragraph to eliminate all sentence fragments. In some cases, you can combine word groups to create complete sentences; in other cases, you must supply missing elements to rewrite. Some sentences may not require revision. In your final version, check not only the individual sentences but also the clarity of the whole paragraph. For help, consult 12a through 12d.

EXAMPLE   Although many people considered him crazy. George Ferris decided to build a "Great Wheel" in 1892.

Although many people considered him *crazy, George* Ferris decided to build a "Great Wheel" in 1892.

(1) The 1893 World's Columbian Exposition Committee contacted George Ferris. Because the members knew he was a creative designer. (2) The World's Columbian Exposition received its name from Christopher Columbus. Who had discovered what he called the "New World" 400 years earlier. (3) The Chicago exposition committee wanted a more dramatic structure than the Eiffel Tower. Which the French had built for the Paris Exposition of 1889. (4) George Ferris, who was an architect and bridge-builder with a vision, proposed a gigantic rotating wheel that people could ride on safely. (5) Since he designed a wheel that was 250 feet in diameter and held 36 cars, each 27 feet long and 13 feet wide. (6) Many people, including the exposition director Daniel Burnham, doubted that Ferris could build a large steel structure. That could carry 2,160 passengers each ride. (7) Ferris built his giant wheel, and people paid fifty cents for a twenty-minute ride. Even though most other rides only cost five cents. (8) At night, 3,000 incandescent bulbs lit the rotating wheel. Which fascinated the people who stared in amazement. (9) William Sullivan, who was also a bridge-builder, later designed a smaller, more practical wheel. Sullivan's company has made over 1,300 Ferris Wheels since 1906. (10) George Ferris, the "crackpot" with wheels in his head, built an extraordinarily creative moving structure. That remains today a sentimental favorite at carnivals and amusement parks.

ANSWERS AND COVERAGE:
EXERCISE 12-4
Answers will vary. One set of possibilities is shown here.

(1) The 1893 World's Columbian Exposition Committee contacted George Ferris because the members knew he was a creative designer. [*because* dependent clause with subordinating conjunction, attached to independent clause] (2) The World's Columbian Exposition received its name from Christopher Columbus, who had discovered what he called the "New World" 400 years earlier. [*who* dependent clause with relative pronoun, attached to independent clause] (3) The Chicago exposition committee wanted a more dramatic structure than the Eiffel Tower, which the French had built for the Paris Exposition of 1889. [*which* dependent clause with relative pronoun, attached to independent clause] (4) Correct complete sentence. (5) He designed a wheel that was 250 feet in diameter and held 36 cars, each 27 feet long and 13 feet wide. [*since,* which starts a dependent clause with subordinating conjunction, is dropped] (6) Many people, including the exposition director Daniel Burnham, doubted that Ferris could build a large steel structure that could carry 2,160 passengers each ride. [*that* dependent clause with relative pronoun, attached to independent clause] (7) Ferris built his giant wheel, and people paid fifty cents for a twenty-minute ride even though most other rides only cost five cents. [*even though* dependent clause with subordinating conjunction, attached to independent clause] (8) At night, 3,000 incandescent bulbs lit the rotating wheel, which fascinated the people who stared in amazement. [*which* dependent clause with relative pronoun, attached to independent clause] (9) Correct complete sentences. (10) George Ferris, the "crackpot" with wheels in his head, built an extraordinarily creative moving structure that remains today a sentimental favorite at carnivals and amusement parks. [*that* dependent clause with relative pronoun, attached to independent clause]

ANSWERS: EXERCISE 12-5

Answers will vary. Here is one set of possibilities.

Some teenagers and young adults are continually on instant messaging almost every moment that they are using their computers, which are rarely turned off. According to America Online (AOL), the most popular instant-messaging company, 195 million people use its instant-messaging service, creating more than 1.6 billion messages per day. Becoming an integral part of the social fabric of our world, instant messaging has replaced the telephone and even e-mail for millions of young adults. As a result, AOL and its main rivals, Microsoft and Yahoo, continue to add new features, such as tiny video images embedded in messages or interface between messaging and cellphones, to their instant-messaging services. All these companies acknowledge, however, that instant messaging, while a wildly popular communications tool, does not make money for them. While provided as a free service, instant messaging may eventually become a way for these companies to increase their income. Perhaps the companies could sell the software that manages multitudes of instant messages that are sent within large corporations for the business-related use of their employees.

EXERCISE 12-5

Revise this paragraph to eliminate all sentence fragments. In some cases, you can combine word groups to create complete sentences; in other cases, you must supply missing elements to revise word groups. Some sentences may not require revision. In your final version, check not only the individual sentences but also the clarity of the whole paragraph. Refer to sections 12a through 12e for help.

(1) Some teenagers and young adults. (2) Are continually on instant messaging almost every moment that they are using their computers. (3) Which are rarely turned off. (4) According to America Online (AOL), the most popular instant-messaging service. (5) 195 million people use its instant-messaging service. (6) Creating more than 1.6 billion messages per day. (7) Becoming an integral part of the social fabric of our world. (8) Instant messaging has replaced the telephone, and even some e-mail. (9) For millions of young adults. (10) As a result, AOL and its main rivals, Microsoft and Yahoo. (11) Continue to add new features to their instant-messaging services. (12) Such as tiny video images embedded in messages or interface between messaging and cellphones. (13) All these companies acknowledge, however. (14) That instant messaging, while a wildly popular communications tool, does not make money for them. (15) Now provided as a free service. (16) Instant messaging may eventually become a way for these companies to increase their income. (17) Perhaps the companies could sell the software that manages multitudes of instant messages. (18) That are sent within large corporations for the business-related use of their employees.

Chapter 13

Comma Splices and Run-on Sentences

13a What are comma splices and run-on sentences?

Comma splices and run-on sentences are somewhat similar errors: One has a comma by itself between two complete sentences, and one has no punctuation at all between two complete sentences.

A **comma splice,** also called a *comma fault,* occurs when a comma, rather than a period, is used incorrectly between complete sentences. The word *splice* means "to fasten ends together," which is a handy procedure, except when splicing has anything to do with sentences.

A **run-on sentence,** also called a *fused sentence* and a *run-together sentence,* occurs when two complete sentences run into each other without any punctuation. Comma splices and run-on sentences create confusion because readers can't tell where one thought ends and another begins.

COMMA SPLICE	The icebergs broke off from the **glacier, they** drifted into the sea.
RUN-ON SENTENCE	The icebergs broke off from the **glacier they** drifted into the sea.
CORRECT	The icebergs broke off from the **glacier. They** drifted into the sea.

There is one exception. You can use a comma between two independent clauses, but only if the comma is followed by one of the seven coordinating conjunctions: *and, but, for, or, nor, yet, so.* A comma in such a construction is correct; see Chapter 24.

CORRECT	The icebergs broke off from the glacier, **and** they drifted into the sea.

QUOTATION: ON WRITING
We write comma splices and run-on sentences because we sense that the sentences involved are closely related—a full-stop period just doesn't seem right.
—<http://www.io.com/~hcexres/tcm1603/acchtml/gram1.html#commasplice>

BACKGROUND
In the second chapter of *Errors and Expectations,* titled "Handwriting and Punctuation" (Oxford: Oxford University Press, 1977), Mina P. Shaughnessy observes that the urge to string sentences together reflects a need on the part of the writer for other ways of making links between sentences. Comma splices, for example, reflect a writer's effort to control a sentence, to simplify it by breaking it up into smaller segments by the use of a comma as a conjunction. She argues that punctuation should not be studied apart from other aspects of writing; instead, it should be integrated with work in composition, for "the process whereby writers *mark* sentences is related to the process whereby they *make* them." She suggests that punctuation skills will improve as novice writers study first to recognize and create simple subject and predicate phrases; second, to embed sentences in sentences (using *who, which, that, when,* and *if*); third, to embed appositional forms; and fourth, to embed *-ing* phrases.

279

Students who write comma splices or run-on sentences have a better chance of finding and correcting their errors if they can find a pattern in them. To help students detect patterns, set aside one class or conference session to have students review all the paragraphs and essays they have written for the course. First, if they have not already done so, they should correct all comma splices and run-on sentences. Then, they should tally the *types* of sentences involved, using Box 85 in section 13b for reference. Encourage students to create additional categories, if needed, for errors that do not fit the four basic patterns shown. Make yourself available to answer questions, and encourage students to ask advice of their peers.

At the end of the exercise, have students submit a review statement. Here is one student's response:

> Of the twelve comma splices and run-together sentences I have written this semester, seven involved a second independent clause starting with a pronoun, four involved conjunctive adverbs, and one involved an explanation. I need to be careful, when I use a pronoun as the subject of an independent clause, to punctuate that clause as a sentence.

An explicit statement of results will force students to do the analysis, and the "I need to be careful . . ." sentence will force them to verbalize a plan of attack. Both steps work to overcome students' perceptions of punctuation errors as being random and uncontrollable.

You can then keep the statements on file (1) to help you determine who needs to work on a particular kind of comma splice or run-on sentence, and (2) as a contract between you and each student, acknowledging that he or she knows what to do and will do it.

👁 **ALERT:** Occasionally, when your meaning allows it, you can use a colon or a dash to join two independent clauses. 👁

Many writers wait until the REVISING and EDITING stages of the WRITING PROCESS to check for comma splices and/or run-on sentences. During DRAFTING, the goal is to put ideas down on paper or disk. As you draft, if you suspect that you've written a comma splice or a run-on sentence, simply underline or highlight it in boldface or italics, and move on. Later, you can easily find it to check and correct.

13b How can I recognize comma splices and run-on sentences?

When you know how to recognize an INDEPENDENT CLAUSE, you'll know how to recognize COMMA SPLICES and RUN-ON SENTENCES. An independent clause can stand alone as a complete sentence. An independent clause contains a SUBJECT and a PREDICATE. Also, an independent clause doesn't begin with a word that creates dependence—that is, it doesn't begin with a SUBORDINATING CONJUNCTION or a RELATIVE PRONOUN.

Interestingly, almost all comma splices and run-on sentences are caused by only four patterns. If you become familiar with these four patterns, listed in Box 85, you'll more easily locate them in your writing.

BOX 85   PATTERN

Detecting comma splices and run-on sentences

- Watch out for a PRONOUN starting the second independent clause.

  NO   The physicist Marie Curie discovered **radium, she** won two Nobel Prizes.

  YES   The physicist Marie Curie discovered **radium. She** won two Nobel Prizes.

- Watch out for a CONJUNCTIVE ADVERB (such as *furthermore, however, similarly, therefore,* and *then;* see Box 48, section 7g, for a complete list) starting the second independent clause.

  NO   Marie Curie and her husband, Pierre, worked together at **first, however,** he died tragically at age forty-seven.

  YES   Marie Curie and her husband, Pierre, worked together at **first. However,** he died tragically at age forty-seven.

  →

Detecting comma splices and run-on sentences (*continued*)

■ Watch out for a TRANSITIONAL EXPRESSION (such as *in addition, for example, in contrast, of course,* and *meanwhile;* see Box 24, section 4g.1, for a reference list) starting the second independent clause.

NO   Marie Curie and her husband won a Nobel Prize for the discovery of **radium, in addition, Marie** herself won another Nobel Prize for her work on the atomic weight of radium.

YES   Marie Curie and her husband won a Nobel Prize for the discovery of **radium; in addition, Marie** herself won another Nobel Prize for her work on the atomic weight of radium.

■ Watch out for a second independent clause that explains, says more about, contrasts with, or gives an example of what's said in the first independent clause.

NO   Marie Curie died of leukemia in **1934, exposure** to radioactivity killed her.

YES   Marie Curie died of leukemia in **1934. Exposure** to radioactivity killed her.

👁 **ALERT:** To proofread for comma splices, cover all words on one side of the comma and see if the words remaining form an independent clause. If they do, next cover all words you left uncovered, on the other side of the comma. If the second side of the comma is also an independent clause, you're looking at a comma splice. (This technique doesn't work for run-on sentences because a comma isn't present.) 👁

Experienced writers sometimes use a comma to join very short independent clauses, especially if one independent clause is negative and the other is positive: *Mosquitoes don't **bite, they** stab.* In ACADEMIC WRITING, however, many instructors consider this an error, so you'll be safe if you use a period. (Another option is a semicolon, if the two independent clauses are closely related in meaning: *Mosquitoes don't **bite; they** stab.*

13c How can I correct comma splices and run-on sentences?

Once you have identified a COMMA SPLICE or a RUN-ON SENTENCE, you're ready to correct it. You can do this in one of four ways, as shown in Box 86 on the next page and discussed further in the sections given in parentheses.

BACKGROUND
The Web site <http://webster.commnet.edu/grammar/quizzes/nova/nova4.htm> provides excellent exercises for repairing comma splices and run-on sentences.

TEACHING TIP
Students can use a simple test to determine whether a word is a conjunction or a conjunctive adverb. Conjunctive adverbs can be shifted from the beginning of a clause to another position in the middle of the clause; conjunctions cannot be shifted.

Comma splices and run-on sentences sometimes occur when students begin a sentence with *not only* but omit *but also* at the start of the second clause. Students should remember that *but* is functioning as a conjunction in this construction and that they need to separate the clauses with a period or semicolon when they omit *but.*

BACKGROUND
The Web site <http://owl.english.purdue.edu/handouts/grammar/g_sentpr.html> provides rules for punctuating compound sentences correctly, as well as suggestions for fixing run-on sentences.

BACKGROUND
Professional writers often intentionally separate two independent clauses with just a comma. The clauses in these comma splices never have internal commas and are normally short, balanced, and closely related in meaning. The teacher, of course, should decide whether to allow students to experiment with this form in their writing.

BACKGROUND
The Web site <http://webster.commnet.edu/sensen/part2/nine/index.html> provides suggestions on how to spot and correct run-on sentences.

BACKGROUND
The Web site <http://cctc.commnet.edu/grammar/indep_clauses.htm> shows how to punctuate between two independent clauses and offers links to related sites.

| BOX 86 | SUMMARY |

Ways to correct comma splices and run-on sentences

- Use a period between the INDEPENDENT CLAUSES (13c.1).
- Use a semicolon between the independent clauses (13c.2).
- Use a comma together with a COORDINATING CONJUNCTION (13c.3).
- Revise one independent clause into a DEPENDENT CLAUSE (13c.4).

13c.1 Using a period to correct comma splices and run-on sentences

You can use a period to correct comma splices and run-on sentences by placing the period between the two sentences. For the sake of sentence variety and emphasis (see Chapter 19), however, you want to choose other options as well, such as those shown in 13c.3 and 13c.4. Strings of short sentences rarely establish relationships and levels of importance among ideas.

COMMA SPLICE	A shark is all **cartilage, it** doesn't have a bone in its body.
RUN-ON SENTENCE	A shark is all **cartilage it** doesn't have a bone in its body.
CORRECT	A shark is all **cartilage. It** doesn't have a bone in its body. [A period separates the independent clauses.]
COMMA SPLICE	Sharks can smell blood from a quarter mile **away, they** then swim toward the source like a guided missile.
RUN-ON SENTENCE	Sharks can smell blood from a quarter mile **away they** then swim toward the source like a guided missile.
CORRECT	Sharks can smell blood from a quarter mile **away. They** then swim toward the source like a guided missile. [A period separates the independent clauses.]

13c.2 Using a semicolon to correct comma splices and run-on sentences

You can use a semicolon to correct comma splices and run-on sentences by placing the semicolon between the two sentences. Use a semicolon only when the separate sentences are closely related in meaning. For the sake of sentence variety and emphasis, however, you'll want to choose other options, such as those shown in 13c.1, 13c.3, and 13c.4; for correct semicolon use, see Chapter 25.

COMMA SPLICE	The great white shark supposedly eats **humans, research** shows that most white sharks spit them out after the first bite.
RUN-ON SENTENCE	The great white shark supposedly eats **humans research** shows that most white sharks spit them out after the first bite.
CORRECT	The great white shark supposedly eats **humans; research** shows that most white sharks spit them out after the first bite. [A semicolon separates two independent clauses that are close in meaning.]

13c.3 Using a comma together with a coordinating conjunction to correct comma splices and run-on sentences

You can connect independent clauses with a comma together with a coordinating conjunction (*and, but, for, or, nor, yet, so*) to correct a comma splice. You can also correct a run-on sentence by inserting a comma followed by a coordinating conjunction.

👁 **ALERT:** Use a comma before a coordinating conjunction that links independent clauses (24b). 👁

When you use a coordinating conjunction, be sure that your choice fits the meaning of the material. *And* signals addition; *but* and *yet* signal contrast; *for* and *so* signal cause; and *or* and *nor* signal alternatives.

COMMA SPLICE	Every living creature gives off a weak electrical charge in the **water, special** pores on a shark's skin can detect these signals.
RUN-ON SENTENCE	Every living creature gives off a weak electrical charge in the **water special** pores on a shark's skin can detect these signals.
CORRECT	Every living creature gives off a weak electrical charge in the **water, *and* special** pores on a shark's skin can detect these signals.

EXERCISE 13-1

Revise the comma splices and run-on sentences by using a period, a semicolon, or a comma and coordinating conjunction. For help, consult 13c.1 through 13c.3.

**ANSWERS AND COVERAGE:
EXERCISE 13-1**

The correction strategies will vary. Here is one set of possibilities.

1. Every summer, Santa Fe holds the country's oldest and largest open market for traditional Hispanic work; [13c.2, comma splice corrected by using a semicolon] however, few people know how respected and valuable the artistry is.

2. Some artists sell small items such as silver jewelry and prayer books covered in buffalo hide; [13c.2, run-on sentence corrected by using a semicolon] other artists offer detailed altarpieces and Spanish colonial furniture.

3. Members of the Lopez family never use commercial dyes, so [13c.3, run-on sentence corrected by using a comma and coordinating conjunction] they go to nearby caves to gather plants for brewing into natural colors.

4. Teenagers of the Rodriguez family create straw appliqué crucifixes. [13c.1, comma splice corrected by using a period] They take tiny pieces of flattened straw, rub them until shiny, and lay them delicately into wood.

5. Market visitors admire the colorful blankets Mr. Irwin Trujillo weaves to his own designs, but [13c.3, comma splice corrected by using a comma and coordinating conjunction] he rarely mentions that one of his blankets was purchased by the famous Smithsonian Institution, a museum in Washington, D.C.

QUOTATION: ON WRITING

Word-carpentry is like any other kind of carpentry: you must join your sentences smoothly.

—Anatole France

EXAMPLE Artists in Santa Fe, New Mexico, are proudly reviving interest in ancient Hispanic crafts the artists display their handmade items during the annual Traditional Spanish Market in July.

Artists in Santa Fe, New Mexico, are proudly reviving interest in ancient Hispanic *crafts. The* artists display their handmade items during the annual Traditional Spanish Market in July.

1. Every summer, Santa Fe holds the country's oldest and largest open market for traditional Hispanic work, however, few people know how respected and valuable the artistry is.

2. Some artists sell small items such as silver jewelry and prayer books covered in buffalo hide other artists offer detailed altarpieces and Spanish colonial furniture.

3. Members of the Lopez family never use commercial dyes they go to nearby caves to gather plants for brewing into natural colors.

4. Teenagers of the Rodriguez family create straw appliqué crucifixes, they take tiny pieces of flattened straw, rub them until shiny, and lay them delicately into wood.

5. Market visitors admire the colorful blankets Mr. Irwin Trujillo weaves to his own designs he rarely mentions that one of his blankets was purchased by the famous Smithsonian Institution, a museum in Washington, D.C.

13c.4 Revising one independent clause into a dependent clause to correct comma splices and run-on sentences

You can revise a comma splice or run-on sentence by revising one of the two independent clauses into a dependent clause. This method is suitable only when one idea can logically be subordinated (17e) to the other. Also, be careful never to end the dependent clause with a period or semicolon. If you do, you've created the error of a SENTENCE FRAGMENT.

Create dependent clauses with subordinating conjunctions

One way to create a dependent clause is to insert a SUBORDINATING CONJUNCTION (such as *because, although, when,* and *if*—see Box 50, section 7i, for a complete list). Always choose a subordinating conjunction that fits the meaning of each particular sentence: *because* and *since* signal cause; *although* signals contrast; *when* signals time; and *if* signals condition. Dependent clauses that begin with a subordinating conjunction are called ADVERB CLAUSES.

COMMA SPLICE	Homer and Langley Collyer had packed their house from top to bottom with **junk, police** could not open the front door to investigate a reported smell.
RUN-ON SENTENCE	Homer and Langley Collyer had packed their house from top to bottom with **junk police** could not open the front door to investigate a reported smell.
CORRECT	**Because** Homer and Langley Collyer had packed their house from top to bottom with **junk, police** could not open the front door to investigate a reported smell. [*Because* starts a dependent clause that is joined by a comma with the independent clause starting with *police*.]
COMMA SPLICE	Old newspapers and car parts filled every room to the **ceiling, enough** space remained for fourteen pianos.
RUN-ON SENTENCE	Old newspapers and car parts filled every room to the **ceiling enough** space remained for fourteen pianos.
CORRECT	**Although** old newspapers and car parts filled every room to the **ceiling, enough** space remained for fourteen pianos. [The subordinating conjunction *although* starts a dependent clause that is joined by a comma with the independent clause starting with *enough*.]

👁 **ALERT:** Place a comma between an introductory dependent clause and the independent clause that follows (24c). 👁

Create dependent clauses with relative pronouns

You can create a dependent clause with a RELATIVE PRONOUN (*who, whom, whose, which, that*). Dependent clauses with a relative pronoun are called ADJECTIVE CLAUSES.

COMMA SPLICE	The Collyers had been crushed under a pile of **newspapers, the newspapers** had toppled onto the brothers.
RUN-ON SENTENCE	The Collyers had been crushed under a pile of **newspapers the newspapers** had toppled onto the brothers.
CORRECT	The Collyers had been crushed under a pile of **newspapers** *that* **had toppled** onto the brothers. [The relative pronoun *that* starts a dependent clause and is joined with the independent clause starting with *The Collyers* after deletion of *the newspapers*.]

👁 **ALERT:** Sometimes you need commas to set off an adjective clause from the rest of the sentence. This happens only when the adjective is NONRESTRICTIVE (nonessential), so check carefully (see 24f). 👁

ANSWERS AND COVERAGE: EXERCISE 13-2

1. Drug dealers sentenced to Rikers Island Detention Center in New York City listen carefully. They like the thought of making $200,000 a year legally. [comma splice caused by a pronoun, corrected by adding a period]

2. Speaking to them is a 33-year-old self-made millionaire who knows firsthand about gangs and drugs. [run-on sentence caused by a pronoun, corrected by adding the relative pronoun *who* to make final clause dependent]

3. Fernando Mateo dropped out of school in the tenth grade; however, he learned how to be a carpet layer. [comma splice caused by a conjunctive adverb, corrected by adding a semi-colon before conjunctive adverb]

4. Mateo's bosses showed him no respect; therefore, he started his own business with a $2,000 loan from his father. [run-on sentence caused by a conjunctive adverb, corrected by adding a semicolon before conjunctive adverb]

5. Thirteen years later, he owns two big stores, and his business brings in $3 million per year. [comma splice caused by second clause that amplifies first independent clause, corrected by adding coordinating conjunction *and*]

6. Mateo now pays for and supervises a program that trains young prison inmates to lay carpet. [comma splice caused by a pronoun, corrected by adding the relative pronoun *that* to make final clause dependent]

7. The young men usually install carpet in office buildings. They are grateful that Mateo's clients fully support this project. [run-on sentence caused by a pronoun, corrected by adding a period]

8. Correct complete sentence

9. Mateo knows many young men serve their time and walk out unprepared to hold an honest job; instead, his trainees leave the Detention Center with a trade. [comma splice caused by a conjunctive adverb, corrected by adding a semicolon before conjunctive adverb]

10. Correct complete sentence

EXERCISE 13-2

Identify and then revise the comma splices and run-on sentences. Circle the numbers of correct sentences. For help, consult 13b through 13c.4.

(1) Drug dealers sentenced to Rikers Island Detention Center in New York City listen carefully, they like the thought of making $200,000 a year legally. (2) Speaking to them is a 33-year-old self-made millionaire he knows firsthand about gangs and drugs. (3) Fernando Mateo dropped out of school in the tenth grade, however, he learned how to be a carpet layer. (4) Mateo's bosses showed him no respect therefore, he started his own business with a $2,000 loan from his father. (5) Thirteen years later, he owns two big stores, his business brings in $3 million per year. (6) Mateo now pays for and supervises a program, it trains young prison inmates to lay carpet. (7) The young men usually install carpet in office buildings they are grateful that Mateo's clients fully support this project. (8) Business people see the value in helping these inmates. (9) Mateo knows many young men serve their time and walk out unprepared to hold an honest job instead, his trainees leave the Detention Center with a trade. (10) One former drug peddler said, "I don't have to worry about watching my back or getting shot, and my mom knows I won't end up dead or in jail."

13d How can I correctly use a conjunctive adverb or other transitional expression between independent clauses?

CONJUNCTIVE ADVERBS and other TRANSITIONAL EXPRESSIONS link ideas between sentences. When these words fall between sentences, a period or semicolon must immediately precede them—and a comma usually immediately follows them.

Conjunctive adverbs include such words as *however, therefore, also, next, then, thus, furthermore,* and *nevertheless* (see Box 48, section 7g, for a complete list). Be careful to remember that conjunctive adverbs are not COORDINATING CONJUNCTIONS (*and, but,* and so on; see 13c.3).

COMMA SPLICE	Buying or leasing a car is a matter of individual preference, **however,** it's wise to consider several points before making a decision.
RUN-ON SENTENCE	Buying or leasing a car is a matter of individual preference **however** it's wise to consider several points before making a decision.

CORRECT   Buying or leasing a car is a matter of individual preference. **However,** it's wise to consider several points before making a decision.

CORRECT   Buying or leasing a car is a matter of individual preference**; however,** it's wise to consider several points before making a decision.

Transitional expressions include *for example, for instance, in addition, in fact, of course,* and *on the one hand/on the other hand* (see Box 24, section 4g.1, for a complete list).

COMMA SPLICE   Car leasing requires a smaller down payment**, for example,** in many cases, you need only $1,000 or $2,000 and the first monthly payment.

RUN-ON SENTENCE   Car leasing requires a smaller down payment **for example** in many cases, you need only $1,000 or $2,000 and the first monthly payment.

CORRECT   Car leasing requires a smaller down payment. **For example,** in many cases, you need only $1,000 or $2,000 and the first monthly payment.

CORRECT   Car leasing requires a smaller down payment**; for example,** in many cases, you need only $1,000 or $2,000 and the first monthly payment.

⊙ **ALERT:** A conjunctive adverb or a transitional expression is usually followed by a comma when it starts a sentence (24g). ⊙

EXERCISE 13-3

Revise comma splices or run-on sentences caused by incorrectly punctuated conjunctive adverbs or other transitional expressions. If a sentence is correct, circle its number. For help, consult 13d.

EXAMPLE   African American cowboys in the 1800s made up 25 percent of the cowboy population unfortunately, their contributions were not included in old history books and early western movies.

African American cowboys in the 1800s made up 25 percent of the cowboy *population. Unfortunately,* their contributions were not included in old history books and early western movies.

1. During the nineteenth century, over 2,500 black cowboys and cowgirls herded cattle in the West however, few people are familiar with their accomplishments.

BACKGROUND
The site <http://www.english.uiuc.edu/cws/wworkshop/index.htm> offered by the University of Illinois at Champaign-Urbana suggests how to distinguish between conjunctive adverbs and coordinating conjunctions.

QUOTATION: ON WRITING
What's so hard about the first sentence is that you're stuck with it. Everything else is going to flow out of that sentence. And by the time you've laid down the first two sentences, your options are all gone.

—Joan Didion

ANSWERS AND COVERAGE: EXERCISE 13-3

1. During the nineteenth century, over 2,500 black cowboys and cowgirls herded cattle in the West; however, few people are familiar with their accomplishments. [comma splice: conjunctive adverb]

2. Many former Texas slaves had become expert riders and cattle handlers; therefore, ranchers hired them to round up five to six million loose cattle after the Civil War. [comma splice: conjunctive adverb]

3. Black cowboys often guarded the railroad boss and his cash payroll. For example, the black cowhand Bose Ikard often guarded up to $20,000 and "never lost a dime." [run-on sentence: transitional expression]

4. Stagecoach Mary battled blizzards, rain, and heat as she delivered the U.S. mail to isolated cabins in Montana. In addition, this elderly black woman managed to fight off thieves and wolves along the way. [comma splice: transitional expression]

5. Paul W. Stewart spent eleven years collecting information and artifacts about African Americans and the westward movement. As a result, everyone can see the displays at the Black American West Museum in Denver, Colorado. [run-on sentence: conjunctive adverb]

ANSWERS: EXERCISE 13-4

Answers will vary. The following is one possible revision.

(1) For many years, the women of a village in northwestern India have walked five miles to do their laundry. They do this once a week. (2) Their destination is the edge of a small canal, where they can spread their wash and beat it rhythmically. (3) When they're done, they bind up the sheets and clothes, and then they walk the five miles back to their homes. (4) Foreign aid workers who came to help the villagers believed that five miles was too far to walk with all that laundry, so they built a place for washing nearer the village. (5) The women praised the washing place, which was designed for them to do their laundry in the traditional way; still, they refused to use it. (6) The women's refusal to use the new washing place was a mystery, so the aid workers asked an anthropologist to visit the village to study the problem. (7) When she gained the women's confidence, she learned that the village women are seldom allowed to go outside their homes. (8) Because they spend most of their lives inside their families' mud castles, they look forward to their weekly excursion to the canal five miles away. (9) Laundry day got them out of the village; therefore, it was their one opportunity to see their friends, to laugh, and to share stories.

2. Many former Texas slaves had become expert riders and cattle handlers, therefore, ranchers hired them to round up five to six million loose cattle after the Civil War.

3. Black cowboys often guarded the railroad boss and his cash payroll for example, the black cowhand Bose Ikard often guarded up to $20,000 and "never lost a dime."

4. Stagecoach Mary battled blizzards, rain, and heat as she delivered the U.S. mail to isolated cabins in Montana, in addition, this elderly black woman managed to fight off thieves and wolves along the way.

5. Paul W. Stewart spent eleven years collecting information and artifacts about African Americans in the West as a result, everyone can see the displays at the Black American West Museum in Denver, Colorado.

EXERCISE 13-4

Revise all comma splices and run-on sentences, using as many different methods of correction as you can.

(1) For many years, the women of a village in northwestern India have walked five miles to do their laundry they do this once a week. (2) Their destination is the edge of a small canal, they can spread their wash and beat it rhythmically. (3) When they're done, they bind up the sheets and clothes then they walk the five miles back to their homes. (4) Foreign aid workers who came to help the villagers believed that five miles was too far to walk with all that laundry they built a place for washing nearer the village. (5) The women praised the washing place, which was designed for them to do their laundry in the traditional way still, they refused to use it. (6) The women's refusal to use the new washing place was a mystery the aid workers asked an anthropologist to visit the village to study the problem. (7) She gained the women's confidence she learned that the village women are seldom allowed to go outside their homes. (8) They spend most of their lives inside their families' mud castles they look forward to their weekly excursion to the canal five miles away. (9) Laundry day got them out of the village therefore, it was their one opportunity to see their friends, to laugh, and to share stories.

Chapter 14

Misplaced and Dangling Modifiers

MISPLACED MODIFIERS

14a What is a misplaced modifier?

A **modifier** is a word or group of words that describes or limits another word or group of words. A **misplaced modifier** is positioned incorrectly in a sentence, which means, therefore, that it describes the wrong word and changes the writer's meaning. Always place a modifier as close as possible to what it describes.

Avoiding squinting modifiers

A **squinting modifier** is misplaced because it modifies both the word that comes before it and the word that follows it. Check that your modifiers are placed so that they communicate the meaning you intend.

> **NO** The football player being recruited **eagerly** believed each successive offer would be better. [What was *eager*? The recruitment or the player's belief?]
>
> **YES** The football player being recruited believed **eagerly** that each successive offer would be better.
>
> **YES** The football player being **eagerly** recruited believed that each successive offer would be better.

Placing limiting words carefully

Words such as *only, not only, just, not just, almost, hardly, nearly, even, exactly, merely, scarcely,* and *simply* serve to limit the meaning of a word according to where they are placed. When you use such words, position them precisely. Consider how moving the placement of the word *only* changes the meaning of this sentence: *Professional coaches say that high salaries motivate players.*

QUOTATION: ON WRITING
It is not sufficient to know what one ought to say, but one must also know how to say it.
—Aristotle

BACKGROUND
The Web site <http://webster.commnet.edu/grammar/modifiers.htm> offers examples, suggestions, and quizzes on misplaced modifiers.

QUOTATION: ON WRITING
Any one who wishes to become a good writer should endeavor, before he allows himself to be tempted by the more showy qualities, to be direct, simple, brief, vigorous, and lucid.
—H. W. Fowler

BACKGROUND
The Web site <http://leo.stcloudstate.edu/grammar/modifiers.html> offered by St. Cloud State University includes examples of dangling and misplaced modifiers, with possible revisions for each, and explanations of why the revisions are necessary.

TEACHING TIP
If your students feel that modifier placement is a slapdash business, you might ask them to look at some ludicrous sentences and have them try to draw what is written. Here are a few.

1. When people first saw whales, they were still wearing animal skins and had stone axes.

2. The man kissed the baby with a beard.

3. Walking down the street, the Eiffel Tower came into view.

4. The wildlife specialist said that most bears are dangerous on television.

5. Poison ivy is common in the forest, which gives many people an itchy rash.

Only professional coaches say that high salaries motivate players. [No one else says this.]

Professional coaches **only** say that high salaries motivate players. [The coaches probably do not mean what they say.]

Professional coaches say **only** that high salaries motivate players. [The coaches say nothing else.]

Professional coaches say that **only** high salaries motivate players. [Nothing except high salaries motivates players.]

Professional coaches say that high salaries **only** motivate players. [High salaries do nothing other than motivate players.]

Professional coaches say that high salaries motivate **only** players. [High salaries do motivate the players but not the coaches and managers.]

14b How can I avoid split infinitives?

An INFINITIVE is a VERB form that starts with *to*: *to motivate*, *to convince*, *to create* are examples (see 7e). A **split infinitive** occurs when words are placed between the word *to* and its verb. The effect is awkward.

> **NO** Orson Welles's radio drama "War of the Worlds" managed ***to, in October 1938, convince*** listeners that they were hearing an invasion by Martians. [*In October 1938* is misplaced because the words come between *to* and *convince*.]

> **YES** **In October 1938,** Orson Welles's radio drama "War of the Worlds" managed ***to convince*** listeners that they were hearing an invasion by Martians.

Often, the word that splits an infinitive is an ADVERB ending in *-ly*. In general, place adverbs either before or after the infinitive.

> **NO** People feared that they would no longer be able **to *happily* live** in peace.

> **YES** People feared that they would no longer be able **to live *happily*** in peace.

The rule about split infinitives has changed recently. Current usage says that when the best placement for a single adverb is actually between *to* and the verb, use that structure freely.

> Welles wanted **to *realistically* portray** a Martian invasion for the radio audience.

If you want to avoid splitting infinitives in your ACADEMIC WRITING, revise to avoid the split:

> Welles wanted his "Martian invasion" **to sound *realistic*** for the radio audience. [The adverb *realistically* was changed to the adjective *realistic*.]

14c How can I avoid other splits in my sentences?

When too many words split—that is, come between—a SUBJECT and its VERB or between a verb and its OBJECT, the result is a sentence that lurches rather than flows from beginning to end.

NO The **announcer,** because the script, which Welles himself wrote, called for perfect imitations of emergency announcements, **opened** with a warning that included a description of the "invasion." [The subject *announcer* is placed too far away from the verb *opened,* so this split is too large.]

YES Because the script, which Welles himself wrote, called for perfect imitations of emergency announcements, the **announcer opened** with a warning that included a description of the "invasion." [The subject and verb, *announcer opened,* aren't split.]

NO Many churches **held** for their frightened communities **"end of the world" prayer services.** [The verb *held* is placed too far away from the object *"end of the world" prayer services,* so this split is too large.]

YES Many churches **held "end of the world" prayer services** for their frightened communities. [The verb and object, *held "end of the world" prayer services,* aren't split.]

EXERCISE 14-1

Revise these ten sentences to correct misplaced modifiers, split infinitives, and other splits. If a sentence is correct, circle its number. For help, consult 14a through 14c.

EXAMPLE Barrow, Alaska, is closer to the North Pole located on the Arctic Ocean than any other U.S. city.

Located on the Arctic Ocean, Barrow, Alaska, is closer to the North Pole than any other U.S. city.

1. The 4,400 residents of Barrow, Alaska, in a region where wind chills can go down to 100 degrees below zero Fahrenheit not only survive but thrive.

2. These hardy residents adjust their lives to 24-hour nights in winter and 24-hour days in summer, 64 percent of whom are original natives.

3. The mayor of Barrow rides over the hard-packed snow his bike to work every day.

4. Businesses provide electric plug-in stations so customers while they shop can keep their cars running and heated.

5. Fran Tate runs Pepe's North of the Border, the Mexican restaurant closest to the North Pole, and she asks customers to every time they visit sign her guest book.

ANSWERS AND COVERAGE:
EXERCISE 14-1
Answers may vary somewhat. The final result must avoid all incorrect placements.

1. The 4,400 residents of Barrow, Alaska, *not only survive but thrive* in a region where wind chills can go down to 100 degrees below zero Fahrenheit.[14c, awkward placement]

2. These hardy residents, *64 percent of whom are original natives,* adjust their lives to 24-hour nights in winter and 24-hour days in summer.[14c, awkward placement]

3. *The mayor of Barrow rides his bike to work every day* over the hard-packed snow. [14c, awkward interruption]

4. Businesses provide electric plug-in stations so *customers can keep their cars running and heated* while they shop. [14c, interruption of subject and verb]

5. Fran Tate runs Pepe's North of the Border, the Mexican restaurant closest to the North Pole, and she asks customers *to sign her guest book every time they visit.* [14b, split infinitive]

6. Fran sends Christmas cards and a personal note to the *nearly* 7,000 people on her list, including psychologist Dr. Joyce Brothers and basketball legend Karl Malone. [14a, ambiguous placement]

7. At Ipalook Elementary School's enormous indoor playground, students who are playing go outside *happily* whenever the weather is above 20 degrees below zero Fahrenheit. [14a, squinting modifier]

8. Correct sentence

9. *The airport is essential* for one of Alaska's largest corporations, which is a fuel and construction business owned by the Inupiat natives. [14c, interruption of subject and verb]

10. Because they have no mall or movie theater, *residents read, talk with friends in town, chat on the Internet, and enjoy the peace and quiet of the open tundra.* [14c, interruption of subject and verb]

ANSWERS: EXERCISE 14-2

1. (a) Chicken soup, / according to folklore, / helps / cure colds.

(b) According to folklore, / chicken soup / helps / cure colds.

(c) Chicken soup / helps / cure colds, / according to folklore.

2. (a) Instinctively, / tadpoles / swim / toward / their genetic relatives.

(b) Tadpoles / instinctively / swim / toward / their genetic relatives.

(c) Tadpoles / swim / toward / their genetic relatives / instinctively.

(d) Tadpoles / swim / instinctively / toward / their genetic relatives.

3. (a) While driving / carelessly, / the young driver / skidded / in the snow.

(b) The young driver / carelessly / skidded / in the snow / while driving.

(c) While driving, / the young driver / skidded / carelessly / in the snow.

(d) While driving / in the snow, / the young driver / skidded / carelessly.

(e) In the snow, / the young driver / skidded / carelessly / while driving.

(f) Carelessly, / the young driver / skidded / while driving / in the snow.

4. (a) The limber teenager / quickly / climbed / a tall palm tree / to pick a ripe coconut.

(b) The limber teenager / climbed / a tall palm tree / quickly / to pick a ripe coconut.

(c) To pick a ripe coconut, / the limber teenager / quickly / climbed / a tall palm tree.

(d) Quickly, / the limber teenager / climbed / a tall palm tree / to pick a ripe coconut.

5. (a) To prevent big avalanches, / ski patrollers / often / set explosives / and cause mini-avalanches.

(b) Ski patrollers / often / set explosives / and cause mini-avalanches / to prevent big avalanches.

6. Fran nearly sends Christmas Cards and a personal note to the 7,000 people on her list, including psychologist Dr. Joyce Brothers and basketball legend Karl Malone.

7. At Ipalook Elementary School's enormous indoor playground, students who are playing happily go outside whenever the weather is above 20 degrees below zero Fahrenheit.

8. Barrow has no roads connecting it with the outside world, which means the residents rely on airplanes for supplies and mail.

9. The airport for one of Alaska's largest corporations, which is a fuel and construction business owned by the Inupiat natives, is essential.

10. Residents, because they have no mail or movie theater, read, talk with friends in town, chat on the Internet, and enjoy the peace and quiet of the open tundra.

EXERCISE 14-2

Using each list of words and phrases, create all the possible logical sentences. Insert commas as needed. Explain differences in meaning among the alternatives you create. For help, consult 14a through 14c.

EXAMPLE   exchange students
learned to speak French
while in Paris
last summer

A. Last summer, / exchange students / learned to speak French / while in Paris.

B. While in Paris, / exchange students / learned to speak French / last summer.

C. Exchange students / learned to speak French / while in Paris / last summer.

D. Exchange students / learned to speak French / last summer / while in Paris.

1. chicken soup according to folklore helps cure colds	2. tadpoles instinctively swim toward their genetic relatives
3. the young driver while driving in the snow skidded carelessly	4. climbed the limber teenager a tall palm tree to pick a ripe coconut quickly

→

5. and cause mini-avalanches
    ski patrollers
    set explosives
    often
    to prevent big avalanches

DANGLING MODIFIERS

14d How can I avoid dangling modifiers?

A **dangling modifier** describes or limits a word or words that never actually appear in the sentence. Aware of the intended meaning, the writer unconsciously supplies the missing words, but the reader gets confused. To correct a dangling modifier, state clearly your intended SUBJECT in the sentence.

NO   **Having read Faulkner's short story "A Rose for Emily,"** ***the ending*** surprised us. [This sentence says *the ending* was *reading the story,* which is impossible.]

YES   Having read Faulkner's short story "A Rose for Emily," **we were surprised by the ending.** [Second half of sentence is rewritten to include the subject *we.*]

YES   **We** read Faulkner's short story "A Rose for Emily" **and were surprised by the ending.** [Sentence is rewritten to include the subject *We.*]

NO   **When courting Emily,** ***the townspeople*** gossiped about her. [This sentence says *the townspeople* were *courting Emily,* which isn't true.]

YES   **When Emily was being courted** ***by Homer Barron,*** the townspeople gossiped about her. [First half of sentence is rewritten to include the name of the person doing the courting: *Homer Barron.*]

A major cause of dangling modifiers is the unnecessary use of the PASSIVE VOICE. Whenever possible, use the ACTIVE VOICE.

NO   **To earn money, china-painting lessons** were offered by Emily to wealthy young women. [*China-painting lessons* cannot *earn money. Were offered by Emily* is in the passive voice.]

YES   **To earn money, Emily** offered china-painting lessons to wealthy young women. [Change to the active voice; *Emily offered* corrects the problem.]

**ANSWERS AND COVERAGE:
EXERCISE 14-3**

Answers may differ somewhat. Here is one set of possibilities.

1. Women won few high-status science awards in the past, a situation that failed to give many outstanding women scientists the recognition they deserve. [unnecessary passive]

2. Having entered many fields of science in large numbers since the 1970s, women now hold numerous low-level and mid-level jobs. [dangling participle]

3. Correct sentence

4. When the announcement of the newly elected members of the prestigious National Academy of Sciences was made in 2003, women suddenly realized that they had made a major advance. [unnecessary passive]

5. Choosing seventy-two new members in 2003, the National Academy of Sciences selected seventeen women, a larger number than ever before. [unexpressed subject]

6. When selecting new members, the Academy uses important scientific discoveries as the major decisive factor. [unexpressed subject]

7. Having discovered the relationship between telomeres (the tips of chromosomes) and aging, Dr. Carol Grieder of Johns Hopkins School of Medicine was an obvious choice for membership. [dangling participle]

8. Correct sentence

9. The Academy recognized Dr. Jeanne Altmann for having made the study of primates less subjective and more scientifically organized. [dangling participle]

10. Rising from 12 percent in the mid-1980s to 20 percent today, memberships for women in the National Academy of Sciences are expected to increase still further. [dangling participle]

EXERCISE 14-3

Identify and correct any dangling modifiers in these sentences. If a sentence is correct, circle its number. For help, consult 14d.

EXAMPLE To succeed as scientists, obstacles must be overcome by women.
To succeed as scientists, women must overcome obstacles.

1. In the past, few high-status science awards were won by women, a situation that failed to give many outstanding women scientists the recognition they deserve.

2. Having entered many fields of science in large numbers since the 1970s, numerous low-level and mid-level jobs are now held by women.

3. Attaining the highest achievements and awards has been beyond the grasp of even the most gifted women scientists.

4. When the announcement of the newly elected members of the prestigious National Academy of Sciences was made in 2003, a major advance by women was suddenly realized.

5. Having chosen seventy-two new members in 2003, seventeen were women, a larger number than ever before.

6. When selecting new members, important scientific discoveries are the major decisive factor.

7. Having discovered the relationship between telomeres (the tips of chromosomes) and aging, an obvious choice for membership was Dr. Carol Grieder of Johns Hopkins School of Medicine.

8. By discovering that a surprisingly large number of human genes control the sense of smell, Dr. Linda Buck earned her Academy membership.

9. To make the study of primates less subjective and more scientifically organized, the Academy recognized Dr. Jeanne Altmann.

10. Rising from 12 percent in the mid-1980s to 20 percent today, an increasingly greater membership for women in the National Academy of Sciences is expected.

14e **How can I proofread successfully for misplaced and dangling modifiers?**

Sentence errors like MISPLACED MODIFIERS and DANGLING MODIFIERS are hard to spot because of the way the human brain works. Writers know what they mean to say when they write. When they PROOFREAD, however, they often misread what they've written for what they intended to write. The mind unconsciously adjusts for the error. In contrast, readers see only what's on the paper or screen. I suggest that you, or someone else while you're listening, read your writing aloud to proofread it for these kinds of problems.

Chapter 15

Shifting and Mixed Sentences

SHIFTING SENTENCES

15a What is a shifting sentence?

A **shift** within a sentence is an unnecessary abrupt change in PERSON, NUMBER, SUBJECT, VOICE, TENSE, MOOD, or DIRECT or INDIRECT DISCOURSE. These shifts blur meaning. Sometimes a shift occurs between two or more sentences in a paragraph. If you set out on one track (writing in FIRST PERSON, for example), your readers expect you to stay on that same track (don't unnecessarily shift to THIRD PERSON, for example). When you go off track, you have written a shifting sentence or paragraph.

15b How can I avoid shifts in person and number?

Who or what performs or receives an action is defined by the term *person*. FIRST PERSON (*I, we*) is the speaker or writer; SECOND PERSON (*you*) is the one being spoken or written *to;* and THIRD PERSON (*he, she, it, they*) is the person or thing being spoken or written *about*.

The essential point is that SHIFTS are incorrect unless the meaning in a particular context makes them necessary.

> NO   I enjoy reading financial forecasts of the future, but **you** wonder which will turn out to be correct. [The first person *I* shifts to the second person *you.*]
>
> YES   I enjoy reading financial forecasts of the future, but **I** wonder which will turn out to be correct.

NUMBER refers to whether words are *singular* (one) or *plural* (more than one) in meaning. Do not start to write in one number and then shift for no reason to the other number.

BACKGROUND
When using the generalized *you,* writers must guard against inappropriate shifts to third-person nouns and pronouns (*person, one, he, they*). Students who use the generalized *you* of adages like "You can fool some of the people some of the time . . ." may not sense the dissonance of a shift from *you* to *he* or from *you* to *they* in their writing.

ANOTHER EXAMPLE
To improve students' skills in recognizing person and number, you might ask them to read the following passage by Susan Allen Toth. Then, ask students to work in groups to label the subject of each clause by person and number. (The subjects here appear in italics.)

> When *Pete and I* [third, first, plural] go to the movies, *we* [first, plural] take turns driving so *no one* [third, singular] owes anyone else anything. *We* [first, plural] leave the car far from the theater so *we* [first, plural] don't have to pay for a parking space. If *it's* [third, singular] raining or snowing, *Pete* [third, singular] offers to let me off at the door, but *I* [first, singular] can tell *he'll* [third, singular] feel better if *I* [first, singular] go with him while *he* [third, singular] finds a spot, so *we* [first, plural] share the walk too. Inside the theater *Pete* [third, singular] will hold my hand when *I* [first, singular] get scared if *I* [first, singular] ask him. *He* [third, singular] puts my hand firmly on his knee and covers it completely with his own hand. His *knee* [third, singular] never twitches. After a while, when the scary *part* [third, singular] is past, *he* [third, singular] loosens his hand slightly and *I* [first, singular] know *that* [third, singular] is a signal to take mine away. *He* [third, singular] sits companionably close, letting his *jacket* [third, singular] just touch my sweater, but *he* [third, singular] does not infringe. *He* [third, singular] thinks *I* [first, singular] ought to know *he* [third, singular] is there if *I* [first, singular] need him.
>
> —Susan Allen Toth, "Cinematypes"

NO   Because **people** are living longer, **an employee** now retires later. [The plural *people* shifts to the singular *employee*.]

YES   Because **people** are living longer, **employees** now retire later.

In ACADEMIC WRITING, reserve *you* for addressing the reader directly. Use the third person for general statements.

NO   **I** like my job in customer service because **you** get to solve people's problems. [*I* is in the first person, so a shift to the second person *you* is incorrect.]

YES   **I** like my job in customer service because **I** get to solve people's problems.

NO   **People** enjoy feeling productive, so when a job is unsatisfying, **you** usually become depressed. [*People* is in the third person, so a shift to the second person *you* is incorrect.]

YES   **People** enjoy feeling productive, so when a job is unsatisfying, **they** usually become depressed.

Be careful with words in the singular (usually NOUNS) used in a general sense, such as *employee, student, consumer, neighbor,* and *someone.* These words are always third-person singular. The only ANTECEDENTS in the third-person singular are *he, she,* and *it.* Remember that *they* is plural, so the word *they* can't be used with singular nouns.

NO   When **an employee** is treated with respect, **they** are more motivated to do a good job. [*Employee* is third-person singular, so the shift to the third-person plural *they* is incorrect.]

YES   When **an employee** is treated with respect, **he or she** is more motivated to do a good job.

YES   When **employees** are treated with respect, **they** are more motivated to do a good job.

YES   **An employee** who is treated with respect is more motivated to do a good job.

YES   **Employees** who are treated with respect are more motivated to do a good job.

👁 **ALERT:** When you use INDEFINITE PRONOUNS (such as *someone, everyone,* or *anyone*), you want to use GENDER-NEUTRAL LANGUAGE. For advice, see 10s and 21g. 👁

EXERCISE 15-1

Eliminate shifts in person and number between, as well as within, sentences. Some sentences may not need revision. For help, consult 15b.

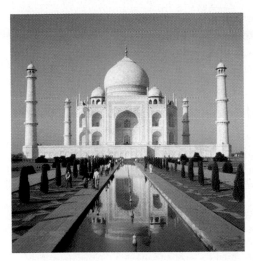

(1) In Agra, India, millions of visitors to the Taj Mahal see a glorious white-marble building that serves as a tribute to undying love, but you also see pollution and serious deterioration of the property. (2) The tourist arrives in horse-drawn carts or electric cars because they may not travel in vehicles that burn fossil fuel in the vicinity of the monument. (3) Government officials have closed down polluting factories in the immediate area, but it allows a petrochemical plant owned by people who have political connections to remain open, darkening the air and the monument. (4) Huge crowds arrive daily to see the gorgeous Taj Mahal, which is perfect in its architectural proportions and is topped with beautiful minarets. (5) But he or she also sees terrible neglect, such as huge beehives hanging from archways, litter on the lawns and in the gardens, and canals choked with trash. (6) The whole place smells of pigeon droppings, decorative panels are faded and destroyed, and many sections are off limits to sightseers. (7) However, recently a large Indian corporation has begun managing the monument, and they are starting to make improvements. (8) Soon visitors will enter through a new, clean tourist center, complete with a cafe and computerized ticketing, and you will find a tour of the cleansed, restored monument to eternal love a very pleasant experience.

15c How can I avoid shifts in subject and voice?

A SHIFT in SUBJECT is rarely justified when it is accompanied by a shift in VOICE. The voice of a sentence is either *active* (*People expect changes*) or *passive* (*Changes are expected*). Some subject shifts, however, are justified by the meaning of a passage: for example, *People look forward to the future, but the future holds many secrets.*

> NO   Most **people expect** major improvements in the future, but some **hardships are** also **anticipated.** [The subject shifts from *people* to *hardships,* and the voice shifts from active to passive.]

ANSWERS AND COVERAGE: EXERCISE 15-1

Answers may vary somewhat because of the various ways to eliminate shifts in person and number.

(1) Millions of visitors to the Taj Mahal, in Agra, India, see a glorious white-marble building that serves as a tribute to undying love, but *they* also see pollution and serious deterioration of the property. [reserve *you* for direct address and avoid shift in person and number] (2) *Tourists arrive* in horse-drawn carts or electric cars because they may not travel in vehicles that burn fossil fuel in the vicinity of the monument. [shift in person and number] (3) Government officials have closed down polluting factories in the immediate area, but *they* allow a petrochemical plant owned by people who have political connections to remain open, darkening the air and the monument. [shift in person and number] (4) Sentence correct (5) But *they* also see terrible neglect, such as huge beehives hanging from archways, litter on the lawns and in the gardens, and canals choked with trash. [shift in person and number from the last sentence] (6) Sentence correct (7) However, recently a large Indian corporation has begun managing the monument, and *it is* starting to make improvements. [shift in person] (8) Soon visitors will enter through a new, clean tourist center, complete with a cafe and computerized ticketing, and *they* will find a tour of the cleansed, restored monument to eternal love a very pleasant experience. [reserve *you* for direct address and avoid shift in person and number]

WORD HISTORY

According to the *Oxford English Dictionary,* the word *voice* comes from the Latin word *vox,* meaning "voice" or "sound." The earliest recorded statement in English using *voice* as a grammatical term is from 1382 by John Wyclif: "A participle of a present tens, either preterit, or actif vois, eithir passif."

ANOTHER EXAMPLE

To improve your students' skill in identifying subject and voice, you might ask them to work in groups to locate the subject and name the voice in each of the clauses in the following passage by Jack London. (The subjects and verbs appear in italics.)

The *earthquake* [subject] *shook* [active] down in San Francisco hundreds of thousands of dollars' worth of walls and chimneys. But the *conflagration* [subject] *that* [subject] *followed* [active] *burned* [active] up hundreds of millions of dollars' worth of property. *There* ["dummy" subject] *is* [active] no estimating within hundreds of millions the actual *damage* [subject] *that* [subject] *was wrought* [passive].

Not in history *has* a modern imperial *city* [subject] *been* so completely *destroyed* [passive]. *San Francisco* [subject] *is* [active] gone. *Nothing* [subject] *remains* [active] of it but memories and a fringe of dwelling houses on its outskirts. Its industrial *section* [subject] *is* [active] wiped out. Its social and residential *section* [subject] *is* [active] wiped out. The *factories* [subject] and *warehouses* [subject], the great *stores* [subject] and newspaper *buildings* [subject], the *hotels* [subject] and *palaces* [subject] of the nabobs, *all* [subject] *are* [active] gone. *There* ["dummy" subject] *remains* [active] only the *fringe* [subject] of dwelling houses on the outskirts of *what* [subject] *was* [active] once San Francisco.

—Jack London

YES Most **people expect** major improvements in the future, but **they** also **anticipate** some hardships.

YES Most **people expect** major improvements in the future but also **anticipate** some hardships.

15d How can I avoid shifts in tense and mood?

TENSE refers to the time in which the action of a VERB takes place—past, present, or future: *We **will go** to the movies after we **finish** dinner.* An unnecessary tense SHIFT within or between sentences can make the statement confusing or illogical.

NO A campaign to clean up movies in the United States **began** in the 1920s as civic and religious groups **try** to ban sex and violence from the screen. [The tense incorrectly shifts from the past *began* to the present *try*.]

YES A campaign to clean up movies in the United States **began** in the 1920s as civic and religious groups **tried** to ban sex and violence from the screen.

NO Film producers and distributors **created** the Production Code in the 1930s. At first, violating its guidelines **carried** no penalty. Eventually, however, films that **fail** to get the board's seal of approval **do not receive** wide distribution. [This shift occurs between sentences—the past tense *created* and *carried* shift to the present tense *fail* and *do not receive*.]

YES Film producers and distributors **created** the Production Code in the 1930s. At first, violating its guidelines **carried** no penalty. Eventually, however, films that **failed** to get the board's seal of approval **did not receive** wide distribution.

MOOD indicates whether a sentence is a statement or a question (INDICATIVE MOOD), a command or request (IMPERATIVE MOOD), or a conditional or other-than-real statement (SUBJUNCTIVE MOOD). A shift in mood creates an awkward construction and can cause confusion.

NO The Production Code included two guidelines on violence: **Do not show** the details of brutal killings, and movies **should not be** explicit about how to commit crimes. [The verbs shift from the imperative mood *do not show* to the indicative mood *movies should not be*.]

YES The Production Code included two guidelines on violence: **Do not show** the details of brutal killings, and **do not show** explicitly how to commit crimes. [This revision uses the imperative mood for both guidelines.]

YES   The Production Code included two guidelines on violence: Movies **were not to show** the details of brutal killings or explicit ways to commit crimes.

NO   The code's writers worried that **if a crime were to be** accurately **depicted** in a movie, **copycat crimes will follow.** [The sentence shifts from the subjunctive mood *if a crime were to be depicted* to the indicative mood *copycat crimes will follow.*]

YES   The code's writers worried that **if a crime were to be** accurately **depicted** in a movie, **copycat crimes would follow.**

15e   How can I avoid shifts between indirect and direct discourse?

Indirect discourse is not enclosed in quotation marks because it reports, rather than quotes, something that someone said. In contrast, **direct discourse** is enclosed in quotation marks because it quotes exactly the words that someone said. It's incorrect to write direct discourse and omit the quotation marks. Also, it's incorrect to write sentences that mix indirect and direct discourse. Such SHIFT errors confuse readers who can't tell what was said and what is being merely reported.

NO   A critic said that board members were acting as censors and **what you are doing is unconstitutional.** [*Said that* sets up indirect discourse, but *what you are doing is unconstitutional* is direct discourse; it also lacks quotation marks and the changes in language that distinguish spoken words from reported words.]

YES   A critic said that board members were acting as censors and **that what they were doing was unconstitutional.** [This revision uses indirect discourse consistently.]

YES   A critic, in stating that board members were acting as censors, added, **"What you are doing is unconstitutional."** [This revision uses discourse correctly, with quotation marks and other changes in language to distinguish spoken words from reported words.]

Whenever you change your writing from direct discourse to indirect discourse (when you decide to paraphrase rather than quote someone directly, for example), you need to make changes in VERB TENSE and other grammatical features for your writing to make sense. Simply removing the quotation marks is not enough.

NO   He asked **did we enjoy the movie?** [This version has the verb form needed for direct discourse, but the pronoun *we* is wrong and quotation punctuation is missing.]

WORD HISTORY

According to the *Oxford English Dictionary,* the term *mood* has been used since the sixteenth century to refer to verb forms that indicate commands or wishes. The earliest recorded use of the word in this way dates back to 1573, when a scholar named Golding asked a question that still concerns our students: "How shall men directly fynde the Coniugation, Nomber, Person, Tence and Moode of Verbes togither in their Kynde?"

When we speak of the *mood* of a verb, we are not discussing its emotional state. *Mood* when it refers to a mental state is related to the Latin *mos,* meaning "custom." In contrast, *mood* used to discuss verbs is an alteration of *mode,* which comes from the Latin *modus,* meaning "measure," "moderation," or (most relevant here) "manner." The earliest use of *mode* to refer to verbs dates back to 1520: "Sometyme of the infinytyve mode folowynge." Other early references make it clear that *mood/mode* was originally used for discussions of Greek and Latin rather than of English.

ANOTHER EXAMPLE

To improve your students' skill in identifying direct and indirect discourse, you might ask them to work in groups to identify the types of discourse found in the following passage by Russell Baker.

In the country, I am told, the trick is to let the weather roam free through the house. [indirect] "You're spoofing me, aren't you?" [direct] I asked the real-estate man. He wasn't.

In the country, he explained, you're supposed to wear long underwear all winter. [indirect] "It can get itchy if you don't have freezing wind coming between the logs," [direct] he said.

In the summer, you're expected to hang flypaper in the kitchen. "If your logs are chinked tightly they'll keep out the varmints that give your flypaper a businesslike appearance," [direct] he explained.

—Russell Baker, "Country Living"

ANSWERS AND COVERAGE: EXERCISE 15-2

Answers will vary. Here is one set of possible answers.

1. Congress needed money to pay for U.S. participation in World War II, *so members proposed a new tax system.* [15c, shift in subject and voice]

2. Tax payments were due on March 15, not April 15 as *they are* today. [15b, shift in number]

3. For the first time, Congress taxed millions of lower-income citizens. Most people *had not saved* enough to pay the amount of taxes due. [15d, shift in tense]

4. When a scientific poll showed lawmakers that only one in seven Americans had saved enough money, *they* became worried. [15b, shift in person]

ANSWERS AND COVERAGE: EXERCISE 15-3

Answers may vary. Here is one set of possibilities.

(1) According to sociologists, people experience role conflict when *they* find *themselves* trying to juggle too many different social roles. [15b, person and number] (2) When people reach overload, *they* may decide to cut back somewhere. [15b, person and number; 15d, tense; 15e, indirect/direct discourse] (3) For example, a well-known politician might decide not to run for reelection because *the demands of the campaign would interfere with* family life. [15c, voice] (4) In other cases, *people might* delay having children so they can achieve early career success. [15b, reserve *you* for direct address and avoid shift in person and number] (5) *People* might say to themselves, *"I can't start a family right now,"* and focus instead on career goals. [15b, number; 15e, indirect/direct discourse] (6) In yet another example, a plant manager might enjoy social interaction with employees but consequently find *himself* (or *herself,* or *himself or herself*) unable to evaluate *them* objectively. [15b, person and

→

| YES | He asked **whether we enjoyed the movie.** [This version is entirely indirect discourse, and the verb has changed from *enjoy* to *enjoyed.*] |

| YES | He asked, **"Did you enjoy the movie?"** [This version is direct discourse. It repeats the original speech exactly, with correct quotation punctuation.] |

EXERCISE 15-2

Revise these sentences to eliminate incorrect shifts within sentences. Some sentences can be revised in several ways. For help, consult 15b through 15e.

EXAMPLE   In 1942, the United States government is faced with arresting five million people for not paying their federal income taxes.

In 1942, the United States government *was faced* with arresting five million people for not paying their federal income taxes.

1. Congress needed money to pay for U.S. participation in World War II, so a new tax system was proposed.

2. Tax payments were due on March 15, not April 15 as it is today.

3. For the first time, Congress taxed millions of lower-income citizens. Most people do not save enough to pay the amount of taxes due.

4. When a scientific poll showed lawmakers that only one in seven Americans had saved enough money, he became worried.

EXERCISE 15-3

Revise this paragraph to eliminate incorrect shifts between sentences and within sentences. For help, consult 15b through 15e.

(1) According to sociologists, people experience role conflict when we find ourselves trying to juggle too many different social roles. (2) When people reach overload, he or she decided, "to cut back somewhere." (3) For example, a well-known politician might decide not to run for reelection because family life would be interfered with by the demands of the campaign. (4) In other cases, you may delay having children so they can achieve early career success. (5) A person might say to themselves that I can't do this right now and focus instead on career goals. (6) In yet another example, a plant manager might enjoy social interaction with employees but consequently find themselves unable to evaluate him or her objectively. (7) In short, sociologists find that although not all role conflicts cause problems, great hardships are suffered by some individuals faced with handling difficult balancing acts. (8) People can minimize role conflicts, however, if we learn to compartmentalize our lives. (9) A good example of this is

people saying that I'm going to stop thinking about my job before I head home to my family.

MIXED SENTENCES

15f What is a mixed sentence?

A mixed sentence has two or more parts, with the first part starting in one direction and the rest of the parts going off in another. This mixing of sentence parts leads to unclear meaning. To avoid this error, as you write each sentence, remember how you started it and make sure that whatever comes next in the sentence relates grammatically and logically to that beginning.

NO Because our side lost the contest eventually motivated us to do better. [*Because our side lost the contest* starts the sentence in one direction, but *eventually motivated us to do better* goes off in another direction.]

YES Because our side lost the contest, **we** eventually became motivated to do better.

YES Our side lost the contest, **which** eventually motivated us to do better.

NO Because television's first transmissions in the 1920s included news programs quickly became popular with the public. [The opening dependent clause starts off on one track (and is not correctly punctuated), but the independent clause goes off in another direction. What does the writer want to emphasize, the first transmissions or the popularity of news programs?]

YES Because television's first transmissions in the 1920s included news, programs became popular with the public. [The revision helps but is partial: the dependent clause talks about the news, but the independent clause goes off in another direction by talking about the popularity of the programs in general.]

YES Television's first transmissions in the 1920s included news programs, **which were** popular with the public. [Dropping *because* and adding *which were* solves the problem by keeping the focus on news programs throughout.]

NO By increasing the time for network news to thirty minutes increased the prestige of network news programs. [A prepositional phrase, such as *by increasing,* can't be the subject of a sentence.]

YES Increasing the time for network news to thirty minutes increased the prestige of network news programs. [Dropping the preposition *by* clears up the problem.]

Answers and Coverage:
Exercise 15-3 (continued)

number—twice] (7) In short, sociologists find that although not all role conflicts cause problems, *some individuals faced with handling difficult balancing acts suffer great hardships.* [15c, subject and voice] (8) People can minimize role conflicts, however, if *they* learn to compartmentalize *their* lives. [15b, person and number] (9) A good example of this is people saying, *"I'm going to stop thinking about my job before I head home to my family."* [15e, indirect/direct discourse].

BACKGROUND
In "Teaching the Grammar of Vernacular English," in *Language Variation in North American English: Research and Teaching,* edited by A. Wayne Glowka and Donald M. Lance (New York: MLA, 1993), Walt Wolfram provides a basic guide as well as a useful bibliography for instructors who teach students whose original English is not what is commonly termed "standard."

BACKGROUND
The quizzes at <http://a4esl.org/q/h> give ESL students practice with arranging words in correct sequence to form a sentence.

TEACHING TIP
Students frequently become aware of problem sentences when they hear their papers read aloud. Particularly with long sentences, students sometimes compose chunk by chunk and fail to notice how the sections are connected. Reading aloud forces students to read the entire sentence, and hearing themselves stumble may signal a poorly constructed sentence. At home, students can read their papers into a tape recorder and then play back the tape to identify problem sentences. In class, student groups can listen for sentences that need revision as students read their papers aloud. Because some students make verbal corrections in their problem sentences when they read aloud without noticing a problem on the page, it is often useful to ask students in pairs to exchange papers and listen to their partners read the papers aloud.

MORE EXAMPLES
What is inconsistent in the following mixed constructions? You might want to ask students to work in groups to revise these four sentences so that the parts make sense together.

1. Because you want to visit the great art museums of the world is why you should go to the Louvre in Paris.

2. Paris, the capital of France, one of the great museums of the world is located there.

3. Tourists from all over the world, the Louvre draws them.

4. The collection is composed of works of art from many cultures is what distinguishes the Louvre.

YES By increasing the time for network news to thirty minutes, **the network executives** increased the prestige of network news programs. [Inserting a logical subject, *the network executives,* clears up the problem.]

The phrase *the fact that* lacks CONCISENESS, and it also tends to cause a mixed sentence.

NO The fact that quiz show scandals in the 1950s prompted the networks to produce even more news shows.

YES The fact **is** that quiz show scandals in the 1950s prompted the networks to produce even more news shows. [Adding *is* clarifies the meaning.]

YES Quiz show scandals in the 1950s prompted the networks to produce even more news shows. [Dropping *the fact that* clarifies the meaning.]

15g How can I correct a mixed sentence due to faulty predication?

Faulty predication, sometimes called *illogical predication,* occurs when a SUBJECT and its PREDICATE don't make sense together.

NO The purpose of television was invented to entertain people. [A *purpose* cannot be *invented.*]

YES The purpose of television was to entertain people.

YES Television was invented to entertain people.

Faulty predication often results from a lost connection between a subject and its SUBJECT COMPLEMENT.

NO Walter Cronkite's outstanding **characteristic** as a newscaster **was credible.** [The subject complement *credible* could logically describe *Walter Cronkite,* but *Walter Cronkite* is not the sentence's subject. Rather, the sentence's subject is his *characteristic.* Therefore, the sentence lacks a subject complement that would name a *characteristic* of *Walter Cronkite as a newscaster.*]

YES Walter Cronkite's outstanding **characteristic** as a newscaster **was credibility.** [When *credibility* is substituted for *credible,* the sentence is correct.]

YES Walter Cronkite was credible as a newscaster. [When *Walter Cronkite* becomes the sentence's subject, *credible* is correct.]

In ACADEMIC WRITING, avoid nonstandard constructions such as *is when* and *is where*. They should be avoided not only because they are nonstandard, but also because they usually lead to faulty predication.

> **NO** A disaster **is when** TV news shows get some of their highest ratings.
>
> **YES** TV news shows get some of their highest ratings during a disaster.

In academic writing, avoid constructions such as *the reason . . . is because*. By using both *reason* and *because*, the construction is redundant (it says the same thing twice). Instead, use either *the reason . . . is that* or *because* alone.

> **NO** One **reason** that TV news captured national attention in the 1960s **is because** it covered the Vietnam War thoroughly.
>
> **YES** One **reason** TV news captured national attention in the 1960s **is that** it covered the Vietnam War thoroughly.
>
> **YES** TV news captured national attention in the 1960s **because** it covered the Vietnam War thoroughly.

EXERCISE 15-4

Revise the mixed sentences so that the beginning of each sentence fits logically with its end. If a sentence is correct, circle its number. For help, consult 15f and 15g.

> **EXAMPLE** The reason women and men sometimes behave differently is because their brains operate differently.
>
> *Women and men sometimes behave differently* because their brains operate differently.

1. By studying brain scans has provided researchers with pictures of neuron activity in the human brain.
2. The reason that a man's brain is 10 to 15 percent larger than a woman's brain is because men's bodies are generally 10 to 15 percent larger than women's.
3. The fact that women use both sides of the brain and more readily see relationships among objects or ideas.
4. One theory focuses on whether women have more brain neurons that control difficult intellectual functions such as language is being studied.
5. Whether walking or doing complicated math, women activate neurons in several areas of the brain at the same time.

BACKGROUND
At the site <http://web.uccs.edu/wrtgcntr/>, you will find a practice exercise on correcting predication problems.

ANSWERS AND COVERAGE: EXERCISE 15-4

1. Studying brain scans has provided researchers with pictures of neuron activity in the human brain. [15f, mixed sentence]

2. The reason that a man's brain is 10 to 15 percent larger than a woman's brain is that men's bodies are generally 10 to 15 percent larger than women's. [15g, faulty predication with *the reason . . . is because*]

3. Women use both sides of the brain and more readily see relationships among objects or ideas. [15f, mixed sentence with *the fact that*]

4. One theory being studied focuses on whether women have more brain neurons that control difficult intellectual functions such as language. [15f, mixed sentence]

5. Correct sentence

6. Most men are able to focus more intently on an activity because their neural action stays only in one area of the brain. [15g, faulty predication with *the reason . . . is because*]

7. A woman's ability to think simultaneously about a variety of topics enables her to read or sew while watching television. [15f, mixed sentence]

8. While reading a map, people's differences in brain activity show up on the scans. [15g, faulty predication with *is when*]

9. Correct sentence

10. Even though women perform better on a memory test, they are three times as likely as men to develop Alzheimer's disease. [15g, faulty predication because tests cannot develop Alzheimer's]

6. The reason most men are able to focus more intently on an activity is because their neural action stays only in one area of the brain.
7. Because of a woman's ability to think simultaneously about a variety of topics enables her to read or sew while watching television.
8. While reading a map is usually when differences in brain activity show up on the scans.
9. Neurologists are interested in men's ability to look at maps and mentally rotate positions on them.
10. Even though women perform better on a memory test are three times as likely as men to develop Alzheimer's disease.

15h   What are correct elliptical constructions?

An **elliptical construction** deliberately leaves out one or more words in a sentence for CONCISENESS.

> Victor has his book and Joan's. [This means *Victor has his book and Joan's book*. The second *book* is left out deliberately.]

For an elliptical construction to be correct, the one or more words you leave out need to be identical to those already appearing in the sentence. For instance, the sample sentence above about Victor and Joan would have an incorrect elliptical construction if the writer's intended meaning were *Victor has his book and Joan has her own book.*

> NO   During the 1920s in Chicago, the cornetist Manuel Perez **was leading** one outstanding jazz group, and Tommy and Jimmy Dorsey another. [The words *was leading* cannot take the place of *were leading*, which is required after *Tommy and Jimmy Dorsey*.]

> YES   During the 1920s in Chicago, the cornetist Manuel Perez **was leading** one outstanding jazz group, and Tommy and Jimmy Dorsey **were leading** another.

> YES   During the 1920s in Chicago, the cornetist Manuel Perez **led** one outstanding jazz group, and Tommy and Jimmy Dorsey another. [*Led* is correct with both *Manuel Perez* and *Tommy and Jimmy Dorsey*, so *led* can be omitted after *Dorsey*.]

15i   What are correct comparisons?

When you write a sentence in which you want to compare two or more things, make sure that no important words are omitted.

> NO   Individuals driven to achieve make **better** business executives. [*Better* is a word of comparison (11e), but no comparison is stated.]

YES Individuals driven to achieve make **better** business executives **than do people not interested in personal accomplishments.**

NO Most personnel officers value high achievers **more than risk takers.** [*More* is a word of comparison, but it's unclear whether the sentence says *personnel officers value high achievers over risk takers* or *personnel officers value high achievers more than risk takers value them.*]

YES Most personnel officers value high achievers **more than they value** risk takers.

YES Most personnel officers value high achievers **more than** risk takers **do.**

15j How can I proofread successfully for little words I forget to use?

If you're rushing or distracted as you write, you might unintentionally omit little words, such as ARTICLES, PRONOUNS, CONJUNCTIONS, and PREPOSITIONS. I do, unfortunately. I solve this by reading my writing aloud, word by word; or, better still, I ask someone else to read it aloud because I tend to fill in any missing words in my own work.

NO On May 2, 1808, citizens Madrid rioted against French soldiers and were shot.

YES On May 2, 1808, citizens **of** Madrid rioted against French soldiers and were shot.

NO The Spanish painter Francisco Goya recorded both the riot the execution in a pair of pictures painted 1814.

YES The Spanish painter Francisco Goya recorded both the riot **and** the execution in a pair of pictures painted **in** 1814.

EXERCISE 15-5

Revise this paragraph to create correct elliptical constructions, to complete comparisons, and to insert any missing words. For help, see 15h through 15j.

(1) A giant tsunami is as destructive and even larger than a tidal wave. (2) The word *tsunami* is Japanese for "harbor wave," for this kind wave appears suddenly in harbor or bay. (3) A tsunami begins with rapid shift in ocean floor caused by an undersea earthquake or volcano. (4) The wave this produces in the open sea is less than three

---

TEACHING TIP
Because conversation frequently includes incomplete comparisons, you might want to ask students to turn the following spoken dialogue into a paragraph written in the third person.

A: I'm so glad we came here. This restaurant is so much better.
B: You're right. A place that has fresh flowers on the tables is more appealing.
A: I always think linen napkins are nicer.
B: This place has a fine reputation for good service, but it's a shame that it's so much less spacious.

ANSWERS: EXERCISE 15-5
Answers may vary somewhat. One set of possibilities is shown here.

(1) A giant tsunami is as destructive *as* [15i, incomplete comparison] and even larger than a tidal wave. (2) The word *tsunami* is Japanese for "harbor wave," for this kind *of* wave appears suddenly in *a* [15j, small words omitted] harbor or bay. (3) A tsunami begins with *a* rapid shift in *the* [15j, small words omitted] ocean floor caused by an undersea earthquake or volcano. (4) The wave this produces in the open sea is less than three feet high, but it can grow to a height of a hundred feet as it rushes *toward* [15h, incorrect elliptical] and strikes against the shore. (5) For this reason, tsunamis are much more dangerous to seaside towns than *they are to* [15i, ambiguous comparison] ships on the open sea. (6) In 1960, a huge tsunami that struck *the* coasts of Chile, Hawaii, and Japan killed *a* [15j, small words omitted] total of 590 people.

QUOTATION: ON WRITING

There are days when the result is so bad that no fewer than five revisions are required. In contrast, when I'm greatly inspired, only four revisions are needed.

—John Kenneth Galbraith

feet high, but it can grow to a height of a hundred feet as it rushes and strikes against the shore. (5) For this reason, tsunamis are much more dangerous to seaside towns than ships on the open sea. (6) In 1960, a huge tsunami that struck coasts of Chile, Hawaii, and Japan killed total of 590 people.

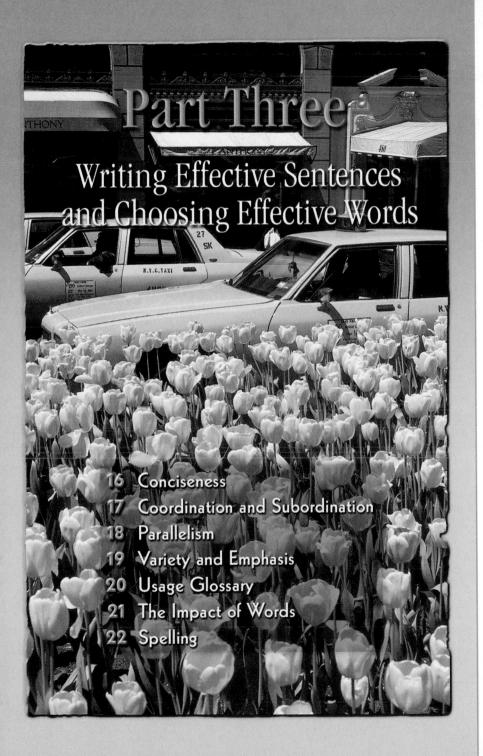

Part Three

Writing Effective Sentences and Choosing Effective Words

Chapter 16

Conciseness

16a What is conciseness?

Conciseness requires you to craft sentences that are direct and to the
point. Its opposite, **wordiness,** means you are filling sentences with
empty words and phrases that increase the word count but contribute
nothing to meaning. Wordy writing is padded with deadwood, forcing
readers to clear away the branches and overgrowth—an annoying waste
of time that implies the writer isn't skilled. Usually, the best time to
work on making your writing more concise is while you're REVISING.*

WORDY As a matter of fact, the ^ television station which is situated
in the local area wins a great many awards in the final
analysis because of its type of coverage of all kinds of
controversial issues.

CONCISE The local television station wins many awards for its
coverage of controversial issues.

16b What common expressions are not concise?

Many common expressions we use in informal speech are not concise.
Box 87 lists some and shows you how to eliminate them.

* Find the definition of all words in small capital letters (such as REVISING) in the Terms
Glossary at the back of this book directly before the Index.

BOX 87   **SUMMARY**

 ## Cutting unnecessary words and phrases

EMPTY WORD OR PHRASE	WORDY EXAMPLE REVISED
as a matter of fact	Many marriages, ~~as a matter of fact,~~ end in divorce.
at the present time	The revised proposal for outdoor lighting angers many villagers ∧*now*. ~~at the present time.~~
because of the fact that, in light of the fact that, due to the fact that	Because ~~of the fact that~~ the museum has a special exhibit, it stays open late.
by means of	We traveled by ~~means of a~~ car.
factor	The project's final cost was the essential factor∧ ~~to consider.~~
for the purpose of	Work crews arrived ~~for the purpose of~~ ∧*to* fixing the potholes.
have a tendency to	The team ~~has a tendency~~ ∧*tends* to lose home games.
in a very real sense	~~In a very real sense,~~ ∧all firefighters are heroes.
in the case of	~~In the case of~~ *The* the election, ~~it~~ will be close.
in the event that	~~In the event that~~ ∧*If* you're late, I will buy our tickets.
in the final analysis	~~In the final analysis,~~ *N* ~~n~~o two eyewitnesses agreed on what they saw.
in the process of	We are ~~in the process of~~ reviewing the proposal.
it seems that	~~It seems that~~ *T* ~~t~~he union went on strike over health benefits.

→

The language must be careful and must appear effortless. It must not sweat. It must suggest and be provocative at the same time.

—Toni Morrison

TEACHING TIP

Truman Capote, known for a prose style marked by clarity and lucidity, never relented in his efforts to delete everything that marred the lean simplicity of his work. In a book of essays published toward the end of his life, he included a description of an experience he had in a Moscow subway. To Capote's surprise, he recognized a man who had lived in Capote's apartment building in New York ten years earlier. Blind, crippled, and dignified, Mr. Jones never left his apartment but received a steady stream of visitors and telephone calls. Suddenly, he disappeared. Using the following excerpt from Capote's remembrance, you might ask students if they can delete any words, reduce any phrases, or otherwise revise the passage to be more concise.

> Ten years pass.
> Now it is a zero-cold December afternoon, and I am in Moscow. I am riding in a subway car. There are only a few other passengers. One of them is a man sitting opposite me, a man wearing boots, a thick long coat and a Russian-style fur cap. He has bright eyes, blue as a peacock's.
> After a doubtful instant, I simply stared, for even without the black glasses, there was no mistaking that lean distinctive face, those high cheekbones with a single scarlet star-shaped birthmark.
> I was just about to cross the aisle and speak to him when the train pulled into a station, and Mr. Jones, on a pair of fine sturdy legs, stood up and strode out of the car. Swiftly, the train door closed behind him.

—Truman Capote,
Music for Chameleons

What is written without effort is in general read without pleasure.

—Samuel Johnson

ANSWERS: EXERCISE 16-1

First, students underline wordy material. Second, they revise each sentence (these answers will vary somewhat).

1. ~~As a matter of fact~~, in the popular imagination, motor scooters are the ~~very~~ essence of European style.

2. Today, over one million scooters ~~are purchased by~~ people in Europe each year, compared with ~~a number that amounts to~~ only 70,000 buyers in the United States.

3. ~~In fact~~, Europeans have long used fuel-efficient, clean-running scooters for ~~the purpose of~~ getting around ~~in a manner that is~~ relatively easy in congested cities.

4. The use of ~~these~~ brightly colored, maneuverable scooters allows city dwellers to zip through traffic jams and thereby to save time as well as ~~to save gas~~.

5. However, sales of scooters, ~~it might interest you to know~~, are ~~in the process of~~ increasing in North America.

6. ~~What I am trying to say is that~~ motor scooters use much less gasoline than cars, and ~~that as a matter of fact~~ the cost ~~factor~~ is about one-fourth that of an inexpensive new car.

7. In addition, some motor scooters, ~~it is pleasing to note~~, now run on electricity, which ~~in fact~~ makes them noise and emission free.

8. A scooter running ~~by means of~~ electrical power ~~amounts to a cost~~ ~~in the neighborhood of~~ 25 cents to travel 50 miles at 30 miles per hour.

9. ~~Members of many different population groups~~, from college students to retired persons, ~~have begun to be~~ finding this type of vehicle ~~to be of a~~ useful ~~nature in a very real sense~~.

10. ~~Traveling by means of~~ an agile, snappy scooter makes getting around a college campus or doing errands in a city neighborhood quick and easy.

→

Cutting unnecessary words and phrases (*continued*)

EMPTY WORD OR PHRASE	WORDY EXAMPLE REVISED
manner	The child spoke _reluctantly._ ~~in a reluctant manner.~~
nature	The movie review was ~~of a~~ sarcastic _∧_~~nature~~.
that exists	The crime rate ~~that exists~~ is unacceptable.
the point I am trying to make	~~The point I am trying to make is~~ _T_elevision reporters invade our privacy.
type of, kind of	Gordon took a relaxing ~~type of~~ vacation.
What I mean to say is	~~What I mean to say is~~ I love you.

EXERCISE 16-1

Working individually or with a group, revise this paragraph in two steps. First, underline all words that interfere with conciseness. Second, revise each sentence to make it more concise. (You'll need to drop words and replace or rearrange others.)

EXAMPLE   It seems that most North Americans think of motor scooters as vehicles that exist only in European countries.

It seems that most North Americans think of motor scooters as vehicles that exist only in European countries.

Most North Americans think of motor scooters as only European vehicles.

1. As a matter of fact, in the popular imagination, motor scooters are the very essence of European style.

2. Today, over one million scooters are purchased by people in Europe each year, compared with a number that amounts to only 70,000 buyers in the United States.

3. In fact, Europeans have long used fuel-efficient, clean-running scooters for the purpose of getting around in a manner that is relatively easy in congested cities.

4. The use of these brightly colored, maneuverable scooters allows city dwellers to zip through traffic jams and thereby to save time as well as to save gas.

5. However, sales of scooters, it might interest you to know, are in the process of increasing in North America.

6. What I am trying to say is that motor scooters use much less gasoline than cars, and that as a matter of fact the cost factor is about one-fourth that of an inexpensive new car.

7. In addition, some motor scooters, it is pleasing to note, now run on electricity, which in fact makes them noise and emission free.

8. A scooter running by means of electrical power amounts to a cost in the neighborhood of 25 cents to travel 50 miles at 30 miles per hour.

9. Members of many different population groups, from college students to retired persons, have begun to be finding this type of vehicle to be of a useful nature in a very real sense.

10. Traveling by means of an agile, snappy scooter makes getting around a college campus or doing errands in a city neighborhood quick and easy.

16c What sentence structures usually work against conciseness?

Two sentence structures, although appropriate in some contexts, often work against CONCISENESS because they can lead to WORDINESS: writing EXPLETIVE constructions and writing in the PASSIVE VOICE.

Avoiding expletive constructions

An expletive construction starts with *it* or *there* followed by a form of the VERB *be*. When you cut the expletive construction and revise, the sentence becomes more direct.

~~It is necessary for~~ *S*tudents ~~to~~ ^must^ fill in both questionnaires.

~~There are~~ *E*ight instructors ~~who~~ teach in the Computer Science Department.

🌐 **ESL NOTES:** (1) *It* in an expletive construction is not a PRONOUN referring to a specific ANTECEDENT. *It* is an "empty" word that fills the SUBJECT position in the sentence but does not function as the subject. The actual subject appears after the expletive construction: ***It was the teacher*** *who answered the question.* If concise, the sentence would be *The teacher answered the question.* (2) *There* in an expletive construction does not indicate a place. Rather, *there* is an "empty" word that fills the subject position in the sentence but does not function as the subject. The actual subject appears after the expletive construction: ***There are many teachers*** *who can answer the question.* If concise, the sentence would be *Many teachers can answer the question.* 🌐

Answers: Exercise 16-1 (continued)

1. In the popular imagination, motor scooters are the essence of European style.

2. Over one million scooters are purchased each year in Europe, compared with only 70,000 in the United States. [The use of the passive voice is justified here because the focus is on the scooters being purchased.]

3. Europeans have long used fuel-efficient, clean-running scooters for getting around relatively easily in congested cities.

4. The use of brightly colored, maneuverable scooters allows city dwellers to zip through traffic jams and thereby save time and gas.

5. However, sales of scooters are increasing in North America.

6. Motor scooters use much less gasoline than cars, and the cost is about one-fourth that of an inexpensive new car.

7. In addition, some motor scooters now run on electricity, which makes them noise and emission free.

8. A scooter running by electrical power costs about 25 cents to travel 50 miles at 30 miles per hour.

9. Many different population groups, from college students to retired persons, are finding this type of vehicle useful.

10. An agile, snappy scooter makes getting around a college campus or doing errands in a city neighborhood quick and easy.

QUOTATION: ON WRITING
There is no artifice as good and desirable as simplicity.
—Francis de Sales

QUOTATION: ON WRITING
We stand now, in linguistic awe, before the mysterious word *there*. It can be an adverb ("*There* you go again"), a noun ("Let Newt take it from *there*"), an interjection ("*There, there* our day will come"), and a pronoun replacing a name ("Hi, *there*").
—William Safire

QUOTATION: ON WRITING
What I like in a good author is not what he says, but what he whispers.
—Logan Pearsall Smith

TEACHING TIP
You might find it effective to take a passage of good prose (professional or student writing) and clutter it with wordy language. Distribute copies and ask students to delete all unnecessary words, phrases, and clauses. Discuss their cuts. End by distributing copies of the original for students to compare with their versions. The discussion can become particularly lively if students question the conciseness of the original or champion the value of your padding.

BACKGROUND
At <http://www.wisc.edu/writing/Handbook/ClearConciseSentences.html>, the Web site offered by the University of Wisconsin-Madison Writing Center, students can learn ways of shifting from the passive to the active voice.

TEACHING TIP
In *Style: Ten Lessons in Clarity and Grace,* 7th ed. (Boston: Longman, 2002), Joseph M. Williams writes that "the first principle of clear writing" can be stated in two parts:

1. In the subjects of your sentences, name your cast of characters.

2. In the verbs of your sentences, name the crucial actions in which you involve those characters. (9)

TEACHING TIP
Mel Silberman in *Active Learning: 101 Strategies to Teach Any Subject* offers a variety of writing activities. One invites students to write a television commercial "that advertises the subject of the class." You might choose to divide the class into pairs or teams and ask students to write a commercial about their school for a free local cable-access channel. A partial list of selling points could be: collaborative exercises, friendly students, and the writing lab. You may want to end the activity with a discussion about the value of pithy writing for modern communication mediums. The premise is that people are being bombarded by so many messages that they need writers to present information as concisely as possible.

Avoiding the passive voice

In general, the passive voice is less concise—as well as less lively—than the ACTIVE VOICE. In the active voice, the subject of a sentence does the action named by the verb.

ACTIVE Professor Higgins teaches public speaking. [*Professor Higgins* is the subject, and he does the action: He *teaches.*]

In the passive voice, the subject of a sentence receives the action named by the verb.

PASSIVE Public speaking is taught by Professor Higgins. [*Public speaking* is the subject, and it receives the action *taught.*]

Unless your meaning justifies using the passive voice, choose the active voice. (For more information, see 8n through 8p.)

PASSIVE Volunteer work was done by students for credit in sociology. [The passive phrase *was done by students* is unnecessary for the intended meaning. *Students,* not *volunteer work,* are doing the action and should get the action of the verb.]

ACTIVE **The students did** volunteer work for credit in sociology.

ACTIVE **Volunteer work earned** students credit in sociology. [Since the verb has changed to *earned, volunteer work* performs the action of the verb.]

In mistakenly believing the passive voice sounds "mature" or "academic," student writers sometimes deliberately use it. The result is wordy, overblown sentences that suggest a writer's lack of careful revision.

NO One very important quality developed by individuals during their first job is self-reliance. This strength was gained by me when I was allowed by my supervisor to set up and conduct a survey project on my own.

YES Many individuals develop the important quality of self-reliance during their first job. I gained this strength when my supervisor allowed me to set up and conduct my own survey project.

YES During their first job, many people develop self-reliance, as I did when my supervisor let me set up and conduct my own survey project.

16d **How else can I revise for conciseness?**

Four other techniques can help you achieve CONCISENESS: eliminating unplanned repetition (16d.1); combining sentences (16d.2); shortening CLAUSES (16d.3); and shortening PHRASES and cutting words (16d.4). These techniques involve matters of judgment.

16d.1 Eliminating unplanned repetition

Unplanned repetition lacks conciseness because it delivers the same message more than once, usually in slightly different words. Unplanned repetition, or redundancy, implies that the writer lacks focus and judgment. The opposite, planned repetition, reflects both focus and judgment, as it creates a powerful rhythmic effect; see 19f. As you revise, check that every word is necessary for delivering your message.

NO	Bringing **the project** to **final completion** three weeks early, the supervisor of **the project** earned our **respectful regard.** [*Completion* implies *bringing to final; project* is used twice in one sentence; and *regard* implies *respect.*]
YES	Completing the project three weeks early, the supervisor earned our respect. [eighteen words reduced to eleven by cutting all redundancies]
NO	The package, **rectangular in shape,** lay on the counter. [*Rectangular* is a shape, so *shape* is redundant.]
YES	The **rectangular** package lay on the counter.
NO	**Astonished,** the architect **circled around** the building **in amazement.**
YES	**Astonished,** the architect **circled** the building.
YES	The architect **circled** the building **in amazement.**

ESL NOTE: In all languages, words often carry an unspoken message. This implied meaning is assumed by native speakers of the language. In English, some implied meanings can cause redundancy in writing. For example, *I sent an e-mail by computer* is redundant. In American English, *to send an e-mail* implies *by computer.* As you become more familiar with American English, you'll begin to notice such redundancies.

16d.2 Combining sentences

Look at sets of sentences in your writing to see if you can fit information contained in one sentence into another sentence. (For more about combining sentences, see Chapter 17, particularly section 17i.)

TWO SENTENCES	The *Titanic* hit an iceberg and sank. Seventy-three years later, a team of French and American scientists located the ship's resting site.
SENTENCES COMBINED	Seventy-three years after the *Titanic* hit an iceberg and sank, a team of French and American scientists located the ship's resting site.

TEACHING TIP

You might demonstrate conciseness by showing students how you as a writer work toward it in your own work. Simply telling a student "I always revise to eliminate wordiness" rarely works. Instead, you might try one of two approaches:

1. Distribute copies of a first, messy draft and a final version of one of your current projects. Invite students to trace the changes you made as you took out unnecessary words and passages, wavered between synonyms, adjusted verb tenses, and so forth. If you are using an anthology of essays that includes facsimile pages from writers' early drafts, students can also look for changes there. Students are likely to take the process more seriously, however, if they see your work. A page from Keats or Faulkner is not as immediate as one from their own teacher's current project.

2. Distribute three or four versions of a piece (each successively more concise) without noting their order of composition. Ask the students to guess which came earlier or later and explain how they know. This activity helps prove that revising for conciseness produces noticeable results.

TEACHING TIP

In class, you might ask the students to exchange papers and look for unnecessary words. As a courtesy, you should notify students ahead of time that their classmates are going to read their work. This lesson can be structured in several ways:

1. Have pairs of students write directly on one another's papers. You can then collect the paragraphs, add your own comments, and return the material at the next class.

2. Have pairs or trios of students confer on papers one at a time and arrive at a consensus. You can circulate around the room, answering questions, and give credit for each paragraph completed.

3. Have authors number each of their lines in the margin. Ask students to pass their assignments to the left. The students write

→

TWO SENTENCES	Cameras revealed that the stern of the ship was missing and showed external damage to the ship's hull. Otherwise, the *Titanic* was in excellent condition.
SENTENCES COMBINED	Aside from a missing stern and external damage to the ship's hull, the *Titanic* was in excellent condition.

16d.3 Shortening clauses

Look at clauses in your writing to see if you can more concisely convey the same information. For example, sometimes you can cut a RELATIVE PRONOUN and its verb:

WORDY	The *Titanic*, **which was** a huge ocean liner, sank in 1912.
CONCISE	The Titanic, a huge ocean liner, sank in 1912.

Sometimes you can reduce a clause to a word.

WORDY	The scientists held a memorial service for the passengers and crew **who had drowned.**
CONCISE	The scientists held a memorial service for the **drowned** passengers and crew.

Sometimes a ELLIPTICAL CONSTRUCTION (7p and 15h) can shorten a clause. If you use this technique, be sure that any omitted word is implied clearly.

WORDY	**When they were** confronted with disaster, some passengers behaved heroically, **while** others **behaved** selfishly.
CONCISE	Confronted with disaster, some passengers behaved heroically, others selfishly.

16d.4 Shortening phrases and cutting words

Sometimes you can reduce a phrase or redundant word pair to a single word. Redundant word pairs include *each and every, one and only, forever and ever, final and conclusive, perfectly clear, few* (or *many*) *in number, consensus of opinion,* and *reason . . . is because.*

NO	**Each and every** person was hungry after the movie.
YES	**Every** person was hungry after the movie.
YES	**Each** person was hungry after the movie.

NO	The **consensus of opinion** was that the movie was disappointing.
YES	The **consensus** was that the movie was disappointing.
YES	**Everyone agreed** that the movie was disappointing.

WORDY	More than fifteen hundred **travelers on that voyage** died in the shipwreck.
CONCISE	More than fifteen hundred **passengers** died in the shipwreck.

Sometimes you can rearrange words so that others can be deleted.

WORDY	**Objects** found inside the ship included **unbroken** bottles of wine and expensive **undamaged** china.
CONCISE	Found **undamaged** inside the ship were bottles of wine and expensive china.

16e How do verbs affect conciseness?

ACTION VERBS are strong verbs. *Be* and *have* are weak verbs that often lead to wordy sentences. When you revise weak verbs to strong ones, you can both increase the impact of your writing and reduce the number of words in your sentences. Strong verbs come into play when you revise your writing to reduce PHRASES and to change NOUNS to verbs.

WEAK VERB	The plan before the city council **has to do with** tax rebates.
STRONG VERB	The plan before the city council **proposes** tax rebates.

WEAK VERB	The board members **were of the opinion** that the changes in the rules **were changes they would not accept.**
STRONG VERB	The board members **said** that **they would not accept** the changes in the rules.

Replacing a phrase with a verb

Phrases such as *be aware of, be capable of, be supportive of* can often be replaced with one-word verbs.

I **envy** [not *am envious of*] your mathematical ability.
I **appreciate** [not *am appreciative of*] your modesty.
Your skill **illustrates** [not *is illustrative of*] how hard you studied.

Revising nouns into verbs

Many nouns are derived from verbs. Such nouns usually end with *-ance*, *-ment*, and *-tion* (*tolerance*, *enforcement*, *narration*). When you turn such wordy nouns back into verbs, your writing is more concise.

NO	The **accumulation of** paper lasted thirty years.
YES	The paper **accumulated** for thirty years.

Teaching Tip (continued)
comments on a separate sheet of paper, keying each comment to a line number. After five minutes, students sign their comments and pass the paragraphs and comment sheets to the left again. Repeat as time and class interest allow. At the end of the class, give the comment sheets to the authors. For homework, students can review the responses to their work and incorporate whichever comments they feel are valid. At the next class, collect the revised paragraphs attached to the comment sheets.

TEACHING TIP
In *Style: Ten Lessons in Clarity and Grace*, 7th ed. (Boston: Longman, 2002), Joseph M. Williams describes several sources of wordiness that students can look for in their writing. These sources include redundant pairs ("each and every," "hopes and desires"), redundant modifiers ("completely finish," "terrible tragedy"), irrelevant detail, and unnecessary negatives ("not many" instead of "few," "did not remember" instead of "forgot").

ANSWERS AND COVERAGE: EXERCISE 16-2
Answers will vary considerably. Here is one set of possibilities, containing only a selection of conciseness techniques. All answers demonstrate revision by combining sentences (16d.2).

1. Each new attempt of ranchers to raise exotic animals like emu, ostrich, and bison for the commercial value of their meat follows a similar pattern that begins when a few people make the claim that some exotic animal tastes better than beef and is more nutritious. [16c, avoiding expletives; 16d.1, eliminating unplanned repetition; 16d.4, cutting words]

2. Ranchers discovered that emus, birds with undeveloped wings that look like small ostriches, quickly became unprofitable to raise because few consumers found the meat tasty. [16c, unnecessary passive; 16d.1, unplanned repetition; 16d.4 cutting words]

→

Answers and Coverage:
Exercise 16-2 (continued)

3. Although ranchers found an early, strong demand for the meat of ostriches, consumers' interest soon fizzled out. [16c, avoiding expletive and passive constructions; 16d.1, unplanned repetition; 16d.4, cutting words]

4. The American Ostrich Association once had 3,000 members, but today 500 people belong to it. [16c, avoiding expletive constructions; 16d.4, shortening phrases and cutting words]

5. Bison, also known as buffalo, were a longer-lasting craze because ranchers had a strong desire to own the mighty animals; however, demand made the price of bison increase greatly, and ranchers found that purchasing young animals became uneconomical. [16c, avoiding expletive constructions and the passive voice; 16d.4, cutting words; 16e, replacing weak verb with strong verb]

6. Also, bison are difficult to raise because they need strong fences to hold them in and they cannot find enough food by grazing on poor pasture land or in mountainous terrain. [16d.3, shortening clauses]

7. Ranchers recently discovered the yak, an animal from Central Asia that thrives in rugged mountainous areas and has supported the people of the Himalayan region for centuries. [16c, eliminating passive voice; 16e, choosing strong verbs]

8. Compared with bison or cows, yaks can forage more efficiently, are easier to care for, and resist many diseases better. [16d.1, unplanned repetition; 16d.2, combining sentences; 16e, choosing strong verbs, replacing nouns with verbs and phrases with verbs]

9. Chefs in gourmet restaurants have begun to devise fancy recipes for yak meat and to feature the low-fat, mild-tasting, succulent meat on their menus. [16d.1, eliminating repetition; 16d.2, combining sentences; 16d.4, cutting words]

10. Even though yaks are easy to raise and environmentally friendly, ranchers must overcome consumers' lack of familiarity with and reluctance to try yak meat. [16c, avoiding expletives; 16d.4, shortening phrases; 16e, replacing phrase with verb]

NO	We **arranged for the establishment of** a student advisory committee.
YES	We **established** a student advisory committee.
NO	The building **had the appearance of** having been neglected.
YES	The building **appeared** to have been neglected.

EXERCISE 16-2

Working individually or with a group, combine each set of sentences to eliminate wordy constructions. For help, consult 16c through 16e.

EXAMPLE In recent years, ranchers have tried to raise and market many exotic meats. These meats have included emu, ostrich, and bison. These attempts have failed.

In recent years, ranchers have tried and failed to raise and market many exotic meats, such as emu, ostrich, and bison.

1. Each new attempt of ranchers to raise exotic animals like emu, ostrich, and bison for the commercial value of their meat follows a pattern. There is a similar pattern to each new attempt. Each new attempt begins when a few people make the claim that some exotic animal tastes better than beef and is more nutritious.

2. Emus were discovered by ranchers. Emus are birds with undeveloped wings that look like small ostriches. Emus quickly became unprofitable to raise. Only a few consumers found emu meat tasty.

3. It was found by ostrich ranchers that there was an early, strong demand for the meat of ostriches. That strong demand soon fizzled out quite a bit, the ranchers found.

4. There is the American Ostrich Association. The membership of the American Ostrich Association once used to be 3,000. Today, the membership of the American Ostrich Association now has only 500 people belonging to it.

5. Bison, also known as buffalo, was a longer-lasting craze. Ranchers had a strong desire to own the mighty animals; however, the price of bison was increased greatly by the demand. It became uneconomical for ranchers to purchase young animals.

6. Also, bison are difficult to raise. They tend to need strong fences to hold them in. They cannot find enough food to eat. They eat by grazing. The land of some buffalo ranches consists of poor pasture land or is in mountainous terrain.

7. Recently, the yak has been discovered by ranchers. The yak is an animal from Central Asia. It is from rugged mountainous areas. For centuries, the yak has supported the people of the Himalayan region.

8. Yaks have the ability to forage more efficiently compared to bison or cows. Yaks are easier to care for than bison or cows. Yaks possess a better resistance to many diseases.

9. Chefs in a few gourmet restaurants are beginning to serve yak meat. They are devising fancy recipes for it. They are featuring it on their menus. The meat is mild-tasting and succulent. The meat is also low in fat.

10. Even though yaks are easy to raise and even are environmentally friendly, there is a problem. The ranchers must overcome that problem before they can raise yaks profitably. That problem is the fact that consumers lack familiarity with yaks. Consumers have a reluctance to try yak meat.

EXERCISE 16-3

Working individually or with a group, revise this paragraph in two steps. First, underline all words that interfere with conciseness. Second, revise the paragraph to make it more concise. (You'll need to drop words and re-place or rearrange others.)

EXAMPLE   Within a matter of minutes after the completion of a champion-ship game, the winning team's players are enabled to put on caps that have been embroidered with their team's name, the year, as well as the word "champions."

Within a matter of minutes after the completion of a champion-ship game, the winning team's players are enabled to put on caps that have been embroidered with their team's name, the year, as well as the word "champions."

Minutes after the completion of a championship game, the winning team's players receive caps embroidered with their team's name, the year, and the word "champions."

(1) At the present time, caps for sports teams are manufactured in factories located primarily in Asian countries such as China, Korea, and Taiwan. (2) Championship caps are quickly produced and shipped by factories wherever they are needed for both of the two teams playing in a final game or series. (3) The very moment the game ends, a trucking company delivers the caps to the winning team's locker room, and it then immediately and instantly burns the losing team's caps so as to prevent embarrassing anyone. (4) Companies that produce all types of sports apparel know that in most cases there is only a short period of time available for making and earning high profits from merchandise connected to a winning team. (5) Within barely a day or two, they flood the market with all sorts of every kind of t-shirts, jackets, caps, coffee mugs, in addition to banners showing and presenting the winning team's championship information.

ANSWERS: EXERCISE 16-3

First, students underline wordy material. Second, they revise each sentence (these answers will vary somewhat).

(1) At the present time, caps for sports teams are manufactured in factories located primarily in Asian countries such as China, Korea, and Taiwan. (2) Championship caps are quickly produced and shipped by factories wherever they are needed for both of the two teams playing in a final game or series. (3) The very moment the game ends, a trucking company delivers the caps to the winning team's locker room, and it then immediately and instantly burns the losing team's caps so as to prevent embarrassing anyone. (4) Companies that produce all types of sports apparel know that in most cases there is only a short period of time available for making and earning high profits from merchandise connected to a winning team. (5) Within barely a day or two, they flood the market with all sorts of every kind of t-shirts; jackets, caps, coffee mugs, in addition to banners showing and presenting the winning team's championship information.

(1) Manufacturers of caps for sports teams are located primarily in China, Korea, and Taiwan. (2) The factories quickly ship championship caps wherever needed for the two teams playing in a final game. (3) The moment the game ends, a trucking company delivers the caps to the winning team's locker room, and it then immediately burns the losing team's caps to prevent embarrassing anyone. (4) Companies that produce sports apparel know that only a short time is available for making high profits from merchandise connected to a winning team. (5) Within a day or two, they flood the market with t-shirts, jackets, caps, coffee mugs, and banners showing the winning team's championship.

QUOTATION: ON WRITING

In composing, as a general rule, run your pen through every other word you have written; you have no idea what vigor it will give your style.

—Sydney Smith

Chapter 17

Coordination and Subordination

Used well, **coordination** and **subordination** in sentences enhance writing style. These structuring methods reflect the relationships between ideas that a writer seeks to express. Some writers enlist coordination and subordination while they DRAFT, but often writers wait until they REVISE to check for good opportunities to use these two techniques.

TWO SENTENCES	The sky turned dark gray. The wind died down.
USING COORDINATION	The sky turned dark gray, **and** the wind died down.
USING SUBORDINATION 1	**As** the sky turned dark gray, the wind died down. [Here, the wind is the focus.]
USING SUBORDINATION 2	**As** the wind died down, the sky turned dark gray. [Here, the sky is the focus.]

COORDINATION

17a What is coordination of sentences?

Coordination of sentences is a grammatical strategy to communicate that the ideas in two or more INDEPENDENT CLAUSES are equivalent or balanced. Coordination can produce harmony by bringing related elements together. Whenever you use the technique of coordination of sentences, make sure that it works well with the meaning you want to communicate.

The sky turned **brighter, and** people emerged happily from buildings.
The sky turned **brighter;** people emerged happily from buildings.

318

17b What is the structure of a coordinate sentence?

A **coordinate sentence,** also known as a *compound sentence,* consists of two or more INDEPENDENT CLAUSES joined either by a semicolon or by a comma working in concert with a COORDINATING CONJUNCTION (*and, but, for, or, nor, yet, so*). Box 88 shows the pattern for coordination of sentences.

BOX 88   PATTERN

Coordinate (compound) sentences

Independent clause
$\left\{\begin{array}{l}\text{, and}\\ \text{, but}\\ \text{, for}\\ \text{, or}\\ \text{, nor}\\ \text{, yet}\\ \text{, so}\\ \text{;}\end{array}\right\}$
independent clause.

17c What meaning does each coordinating conjunction convey?

Each COORDINATING CONJUNCTION has its own meaning. When you choose one, be sure that its meaning accurately expresses the relationship between the equivalent ideas that you want to convey.

- **and** means addition
- **but** and **yet** mean contrast
- **for** means reason or choice
- **or** means choice
- **nor** means negative choice
- **so** means result or effect

👁 **ALERT:** Always use a comma before a coordinating conjunction that joins two INDEPENDENT CLAUSES (24b). 👁

QUOTATION: ON WRITING
Blot out, correct, insert, refine,
Enlarge, diminish, interline;
Be mindful, when invention fails,
To scratch your head, and bite your nails.
—Jonathan Swift

QUOTATION: ON WRITING
Anything is better than not to write clearly.
—W. Somerset Maugham

BACKGROUND
In "Breaking the Rules," Patricia T. O'Conner rejects popular opinion that the conjunctions *and* and *but* "should only be used to join elements." She asserts that they also should be used to begin sentences: "But it has been common practice to begin sentences this way at least as far back as the 10th century. And don't let anyone tell you otherwise."

TEACHING TIP
You might try using a box containing miscellaneous items, such as a teapot, a flower, an old photograph, and so on. Each student picks an object from the box and has ten or fifteen minutes to write a descriptive essay about the object. When the time is up, students can share their writing. A variation calls for each student to write about different items in one category such as flowers or photographs. Students then guess which description matches which item.

Here is an example that illustrates the contrast between coordination and subordination.

> When we toss a handful of good-luck rice at newlyweds, we're gracing them with one of the world's most important and versatile foods.
> —Jack Denton Scott,
> "Rice: A Food for All Reasons"

This sentence mentions (1) the idea of tossing rice at a wedding and (2) the fact that rice is an essential grain with many uses. Scott wants to stress the importance of rice as a food because he puts that information in the independent clause. Rice as a ceremonial custom gives an ironic context to the main idea, but according to the way the sentence is written, it is a less important idea.

If Scott had been writing on marriage customs, he could have used subordination to provide a different emphasis:

> Although rice is one of the world's most important and versatile foods, many Americans value it most as a good-luck symbol for newlyweds.

Here, the independent clause stresses the connection of rice with weddings, and the food value of rice is mentioned as a less central point.

QUOTATION: ON WRITING
In stating as fully as I could how things really were, it was often very difficult and I wrote awkwardly and the awkwardness is what they called my style. All mistakes and awkwardness are easy to see, and they called it style.
—Ernest Hemingway

17d How can I avoid misusing coordination?

One major misuse of COORDINATION occurs when unrelated or nonequivalent ideas, each in its own INDEPENDENT CLAUSE, are coordinated. The result looks like a coordinated sentence, but the ideas are unrelated.

> **NO** Computers came into common use in the 1970s, and they sometimes make costly errors. [The statement in each independent clause is true, but the ideas are not related or equivalent.]

> **YES** Computers came into common use in the 1970s, and now they are indispensable business tools.

A second major misuse of coordination occurs when it's overused. Simply stringing sentences together with COORDINATING CONJUNCTIONS makes relationships among ideas unclear—and it lacks style.

> **NO** Dinosaurs could have disappeared for many reasons, **and** one theory holds that a sudden shower of meteors and asteroids hit the earth, **so** the impact created a huge dust cloud that caused a false winter. The winter lasted for years, **and** the dinosaurs died.

> **YES** Dinosaurs could have disappeared for many reasons. One theory holds that a sudden shower of meteors and asteroids hit the earth. The impact created a huge dust cloud that caused a false winter. The winter lasted for years, killing the dinosaurs.

EXERCISE 17-1

Working individually or with a group, revise these sentences to eliminate illogical or overused coordination. If you think a sentence needs no revision, explain why. For help, consult 17a through 17d.

EXAMPLE Fencing, once a form of combat, has become a competitive sport worldwide, and today's fencers disapprove of those who identify fencing with fighting.

Fencing, once a form of combat, has become a competitive sport worldwide, <u>but</u>

today's fencers disapprove of those who identify fencing with fighting.

1. As depicted in movies, fencing sometimes appears to be reckless swordplay, and fencing requires precision, coordination, and strategy.
2. In the 1800s, fencing became very popular, and it was one of the few sports included in the first modern Olympic Games in 1896, and fencing has been part of the Olympics ever since.
3. Fencing equipment includes a mask, a padded jacket, a glove, and one of three weapons—a foil, épée, or saber—and a fencer's technique and targets differ depending on the weapon used and the fencer's experience.
4. Generally, a fencer specializes in one of the three weapons, but some competitors are equally skilled with all three.
5. The object of fencing is to be the first to touch the opponent five times, and a "president," who is sometimes assisted by a number of judges, officiates at competitions.

SUBORDINATION

17e **What is subordination in sentences?**

Subordination is a grammatical strategy to communicate that one idea in a sentence is more important than another idea in the same sentence. To use subordination, you place the more important idea in an INDE-PENDENT CLAUSE and the less important—the subordinate—idea in a DEPENDENT CLAUSE. The information you choose to subordinate depends on the meaning you want to deliver.

INDEPENDENT CLAUSE	DEPENDENT

Two cowboys fought a dangerous Colorado snowstorm **while they**

CLAUSE	DEPENDENT CLAUSE

were looking for cattle. When they came to a canyon,

INDEPENDENT CLAUSE

they saw outlines of buildings through the blizzard.

To illustrate the difference in writing style when you use subordination, here's a passage with the same message as the example above, but without subordination.

ANSWERS AND COVERAGE: EXERCISE 17-1

Answers will vary somewhat. Here is one set of possibilities.

1. As depicted in movies, fencing sometimes appears to be reckless swordplay, but fencing requires precision, coordination, and strategy. [17c, incorrect coordinating conjunction]

2. In the 1800s, fencing became very popular, and it was one of the few sports included in the first modern Olympic Games in 1896. Fencing has been part of the Olympics ever since. [17d, misuse]

3. Fencing equipment includes a mask, a padded jacket, a glove, and one of three weapons—a foil, épée, or saber. A fencer's technique and targets differ depending on the weapon used and the fencer's experience. [17d, misuse]

4. Correct

5. The object of fencing is to be the first to touch the opponent five times. A "president," who is sometimes assisted by a number of judges, officiates at competitions. [17d, misuse]

QUOTATION: ON WRITING

1. Never use a metaphor, simile or other figure of speech which you are used to seeing in print.

2. Never use a long word where a short one will do.

3. If it is possible to cut a word out, always cut it out.

4. Never use the passive where you can use the active.

5. Never use a foreign phrase, a scientific word or jargon word if you can think of an everyday English equivalent.

6. Break any of these rules sooner than say anything barbarous.

—George Orwell

TEACHING TIP
You might want to ask your students to read these two versions of the same passage from the opening of the twenty-second chapter of Genesis. Then, mark the instances of coordination and subordination with them and consider the differences in style and meaning that result. The first, from the King James translation of 1611, uses coordination heavily; the second, from the Revised Standard Version of 1971, uses much less.

King James Version

And it came to pass after these things, that God did tempt Abraham, and said unto him, Abraham: and he said, Behold, here I am. And he said, Take now thy son, thine only son Isaac, whom thou lovest, and get thee into the land of Moriah; and offer him there for a burnt offering upon one of the mountains which I will tell thee of. And Abraham rose up early in the morning, and saddled his ass, and took two of his young men with him, and Isaac his son, and clave the wood for the burnt offering, and rose up, and went unto the place of which God had told him. Then on the third day Abraham lifted up his eyes, and saw the place afar off. And Abraham said unto his young men, Abide ye here with the ass; and I and the lad will go yonder and worship, and come again to you. And Abraham took the wood for the burnt offering, and laid it upon Isaac his son; and he took the fire in his hand, and a knife; and they went both of them together.

Revised Standard Version

After these things God tested Abraham, and said to him, "Abraham!" And he said, "Here am I." He said, "Take your son, your only son Isaac, whom you love, and go to the land of Moriah, and offer him there as a burnt offering upon one of the mountains of which I shall tell you." So Abraham rose early in the morning, saddled his ass, and took two of his young men with him, and his son Isaac; and he cut the wood for the burnt offering, and

Two cowboys fought a dangerous Colorado snowstorm. They were looking for cattle. They came to a canyon. They saw outlines of buildings through the blizzard.

17f What is the structure of a subordinate sentence?

A subordinate sentence starts the DEPENDENT CLAUSE with either a SUB-ORDINATING CONJUNCTION (see Box 90 in 17g) or a RELATIVE PRONOUN.

If they are very lucky, the passengers may glimpse dolphins breaking water playfully near the ship.

—Elizabeth Gray, student

Pandas are solitary animals, **which** means they are difficult to protect from extinction.

—Jose Santos, student

For patterns of subordination with dependent clauses, see Box 89. Dependent clauses are of two types: ADVERB CLAUSES and ADJECTIVE CLAUSES. An adverb clause starts with a subordinating conjunction. An adjective clause starts with a relative pronoun.

BOX 89   **PATTERN**

Subordination

Sentences with Adverb Clauses

- **Adverb clause,** independent clause.
  - **After the sky grew dark,** the wind died suddenly.
- Independent clause, **adverb clause.**
  - Birds stopped singing, **as they do during an eclipse.**
- Independent clause, **adverb clause.**
  - The stores closed **before the storm began.**

Sentences with Adjective Clauses

- Independent clause, **restrictive (essential)* adjective clause.**
  - Weather forecasts warned of a storm **that might bring a thirty-inch snowfall.**
- Independent clause, **nonrestrictive (nonessential)* adjective clause.**
  - Spring is the season for tornadoes, **which may have wind speeds over 220 miles an hour.**

→

Subordination (*continued*)

- Beginning of independent clause, **restrictive (essential)*** **adjective clause,** end of independent clause.
  - Anyone **who lives through a tornado** remembers its power.
- Beginning of independent clause, **nonrestrictive (nonessential)*** **adjective clause,** end of independent clause.
  - The sky, **which had been clear,** turned greenish black.

*For an explanation of RESTRICTIVE and NONRESTRICTIVE ELEMENTS, see 24f.

17g What meaning does each subordinating conjunction convey?

Each SUBORDINATING CONJUNCTION has its own meaning. When you choose one, be sure that its meaning accurately expresses the relationship between the ideas that you want to convey. Box 90 lists subordinating conjunctions according to their different meanings.

BOX 90   SUMMARY

 Subordinating conjunctions and their meanings

Time

after, before, once, since, until, when, whenever, while

- **After** you have handed in your report, you cannot revise it.

Reason or Cause

as, because, since

- **Because** you have handed in your report, you cannot revise it.

Purpose or Result

in order that, so that, that

- I want to read your report **so that** I can evaluate it.

Condition

if even, if, provided that, unless

- **Unless** you have handed in your report, you can revise it.

➞

---

arose and went to the place of which God had told him. On the third day Abraham lifted up his eyes, and saw the place afar off. Then Abraham said to his young men, "Stay here with the ass; I and the lad will go yonder and worship, and come again to you." And Abraham took the wood of the burnt offering, and laid it on Isaac his son; and he took in his hand the fire and the knife. So they went both of them together.

TEACHING TIP

You might choose to have students read the following examples to see how sentences that seem disconnected can be improved through subordination.

NO	We went shopping for new winter boots. We ate ice cream despite the cold.
YES	After we went shopping for new winter boots, we ate ice cream despite the cold.
NO	Good writers can earn huge sums of money. They like to write mysteries, thrillers, and science fiction.
YES	Because good writers can earn huge sums of money, they like to write mysteries, thrillers, and science fiction.
NO	I must budget carefully. I hope to buy a new car next year.
YES	Since I hope to buy a new car next year, I must budget carefully.

ANSWERS: EXERCISE 17-2
Students' answers will vary. Here is one set of possibilities.

1. a. Although the U.S. Mint can produce more than 50 million coins a day, the U.S. Bureau of Engraving and Printing can produce only 20 million notes a day.

b. Although the U.S. Bureau of Engraving and Printing can produce 20 million notes a day, the U.S. Mint can produce more than 50 million coins a day.

2. a. Even though the Federal Reserve Banks are responsible for both destroying old money and ordering new coins and notes, they must keep the right amount of money in circulation.

b. Since the Federal Reserve Banks must keep the right amount of money in circulation, they are responsible for both destroying old money and ordering new coins and notes.

3. a. Coins can stay in circulation for decades unless people let them accumulate in jars and drawers in their homes.

b. While coins can stay in circulation for decades, people sometimes let them accumulate in jars and drawers in their homes.

4. a. Whenever a $1 bill lasts fifteen to eighteen months, it reaches its average life span.

b. If it reaches its average life span, a $1 bill lasts about fifteen to eighteen months.

5. a. When the U.S. Federal Reserve Banks destroy dirty, worn, and torn bills, they are destroying more than $40 billion worth of money a year.

b. When they destroy more than $40 billion worth of money a year, the U.S. Federal Reserve Banks are destroying dirty, worn, and torn bills.

Subordinating conjunctions and their meanings (*continued*)

Contrast
although, even though, though, whereas, while

■ **Although** you have handed in your report, you can ask to revise it.

Choice
than, whether

■ You took more time to revise **than** I did before the lab report deadline.

Place or Location
where, wherever

■ **Wherever** you say, I'll come to hand in my report.

EXERCISE 17-2

Working individually or with a group, combine each pair of sentences, using an adverb clause to subordinate one idea. Then, revise each sentence so that the adverb clause becomes the independent clause. For help, see 17e through 17g, especially Box 89.

EXAMPLE   The U.S. Mint produces new coins. The U.S. Bureau of Engraving and Printing makes $1, $5, $10, $20, $50, and $100 bills.

a. While the U.S. Mint produces new coins, the U.S. Bureau of Engraving and Printing makes $1, $5, $10, $20, $50, and $100 bills.

b. While the U.S. Bureau of Engraving and Printing makes $1, $5, $10, $20, $50, and $100 bills, the U.S. Mint produces new coins.

1. The U.S. Mint can produce more than 50 million coins a day. The U.S. Bureau of Engraving and Printing can produce 20 million notes a day.

2. The Federal Reserve Banks are responsible for both destroying old money and ordering new coins and notes. They must keep the right amount of money in circulation.

3. Coins can stay in circulation for decades. People let them accumulate in jars and drawers in their homes.

4. A $1 bill lasts about fifteen to eighteen months. It reaches its average life span.

5. The U.S. Federal Reserve Banks destroy dirty, worn, and torn bills. The Federal Reserve Banks are destroying more than $40 billion worth of money a year.

EXERCISE 17-3

Working individually or with a group, combine each pair of sentences, using an adjective clause to subordinate one idea to the other. Then, revise each sentence so that the adjective clause becomes the independent clause. Use the relative pronoun given in parentheses. For help, consult 17e through 17g, especially Box 89.

EXAMPLE   Aristides was an ancient Greek politician famous for his honesty and judgment. He was known as Aristides the Just. (who)

    a. Aristides, <u>who</u> was an ancient Greek politician famous for his honesty and judgment, was known as Aristides the Just.

    b. Aristides, <u>who</u> was known as Aristides the Just, was an ancient Greek politician famous for his honesty and judgment.

1. An ancient Greek law allowed voters to banish politicians from their city. It asked citizens to write the name of an unpopular politician on their ballots. (that)
2. A voter was filling out a ballot when Aristides the Just walked by. The voter needed help in spelling *Aristides*. (who)
3. Aristides knew the voter did not recognize him. He asked why the voter wanted to banish that particular politician. (who)
4. The voter said he resented hearing someone called "the Just" all the time. He handed Aristides his ballot. (who)
5. Aristides' reaction demonstrated that the nickname "the Just" was well deserved. His reaction was to write his own name on the voter's ballot even though that person's vote helped banish Aristides. (which)

17h How can I avoid misusing subordination?

One major misuse of SUBORDINATION occurs when a SUBORDINATING CONJUNCTION doesn't communicate a sensible relationship between the INDEPENDENT CLAUSE and the DEPENDENT CLAUSE. See Box 90 in 17g for a list of subordinating conjunctions and their different meanings.

  NO   Because Beethoven was deaf when he wrote them, his final symphonies were masterpieces. [*Because* is illogical here; it says the masterpieces resulted from the deafness.]

  YES   Although Beethoven was deaf when he wrote them, his final symphonies were masterpieces. [*Although* is logical here; it says Beethoven wrote masterpieces in spite of his being deaf.]

ANSWERS: EXERCISE 17-3

Having students compare and discuss the differences in emphasis between the answers to each item may help them clarify their understanding of these differences.

1. a. An ancient Greek law *that* allowed voters to banish politicians from their city asked citizens to write the name of an unpopular politician on their ballots.

  b. An ancient Greek law *that* asked citizens to write the name of an unpopular politician on their ballots allowed voters to banish politicians from their city.

2. a. A voter *who* was filling out a ballot when Aristides the Just walked by needed help in spelling *Aristides*.

  b. A voter *who* needed help in spelling *Aristides* was filling out a ballot when Aristides the Just walked by.

3. a. Aristides, *who* knew the voter did not recognize him, asked why the voter wanted to banish that particular politician.

  b. Aristides, *who* asked why the voter wanted to banish that particular politician, knew the voter did not recognize him.

4. a. The voter, *who* said he resented hearing someone called "the Just" all the time, handed Aristides his ballot.

  b. The voter, *who* handed Aristides his ballot, said he resented hearing someone called "the Just" all the time.

5. a. Aristides' reaction, *which* demonstrated that the nickname "the Just" was well deserved, was to write his own name on the voter's ballot even though that person's vote helped banish Aristides.

  b. Aristides' reaction, *which* was to write his own name on the voter's ballot even though that person's vote helped banish Aristides, demonstrated that the nickname "the Just" was well deserved.

ANSWERS: EXERCISE 17-4

Each sentence contains misused subordination. Answers will vary considerably. Here is one possibility.

Although people in the United States think of hot dogs as their traditional food, this American favorite originated in Germany in 1852. Butchers in Frankfurt, Germany, stuffed meat into a long casing, and in honor of the town they called their creation a "frankfurter." Because one butcher noticed that the frankfurter resembled the shape of his dog, a dachshund, he decided to name the meat roll a "dachshund sausage." Soon, the new name caught on in Germany. Germans brought dachshund sausages to the United States, and peddlers sold them on the street. The dachshund sausages were so hot that people often burned their fingers and had trouble holding the meat. When one clever peddler put the sausage in a bun, a *New York Times* cartoonist decided to draw a picture of hot dachshund sausages in buns. He didn't know how to spell *dachshund*, so he called them "hot dogs."

QUOTATION: ON WRITING

I revise the manuscript till I can't read it any longer, then I get somebody to type it. Then I revise the typing. Then it's retyped again. Then there's a third typing, which is the final one. Nothing should then remain that offends the eye.

—Robert Graves

A second major misuse of subordination occurs when it's overused, resulting in too many images or ideas crowded together in one sentence. This causes readers to lose track of the message. Whenever you write a sentence with two or more dependent clauses, check that your message is clear. If it isn't, you've likely overused subordination.

NO   A new technique for eye surgery, **which is supposed to correct nearsightedness, which previously could be corrected only by glasses,** has been developed, **although many eye doctors do not approve of the new technique because it can create unstable vision, which includes intense glare from headlights on cars and many other light sources.** [The base sentence *A new technique for eye surgery has been developed* is crowded with five dependent clauses attached to it.]

YES   A new technique for eye surgery, **which is supposed to correct nearsightedness,** has been developed. Previously, only glasses could correct nearsightedness. Many doctors do not approve of the new technique **because it can create unstable vision.** The problems include intense glare from car headlights and many other sources of light. [In this revision, one long sentence has been broken into four sentences, making the material easier to read and the relationships among ideas clearer. Two dependent clauses remain, which balance well with the other sentence constructions. Some words have been moved to new positions.]

ESL NOTE: If you're told that your sentences are too long and complex, limit the number of words in each sentence. The advice of many ESL teachers is to revise any sentence you write that contains more than three independent and dependent clauses in any combination.

EXERCISE 17-4

Working individually or with a group, correct illogical or excessive subordination in this paragraph. As you revise according to the message you want to deliver, use some dependent clauses as well as some short sentences. (Also, if you wish, apply the principles of coordination discussed in sections 17a through 17d.) For help, consult 17h.

Although people in the United States think of hot dogs as their traditional food, this American favorite originated in Germany in 1852 when butchers in Frankfurt, Germany, stuffed meat into a long casing, which in honor of the town, they called their creation a "frankfurter." Because one butcher noticed that the frankfurter resembled the shape of his dog, a dachshund, he decided to name the meat roll a "dachshund sausage," a name which caught on in Germany. When Germans brought dachshund sausages to the United States, peddlers sold them on the street, although the dachshund sausages were so hot that people often burned their fingers because they had trouble holding the meat. When one clever peddler put the sausage in a bun, a *New York Times* cartoonist decided to draw a picture of hot dachshund sausages in buns, although he called them "hot dogs" because he didn't know how to spell *dachshund*.

17i How can I effectively use coordination and subordination together?

Your writing style improves when you use a logical and pleasing variety of SENTENCE TYPES, utilizing COORDINATION and SUBORDINATION to improve the flow of ideas. Here's a paragraph that demonstrates a good balance in the use of coordination and subordination.

> When I was growing up, I lived on a farm just across the field from my grandmother. My parents were busy trying to raise six children and to establish their struggling dairy farm. It was nice to have Grandma so close. While my parents were providing the necessities of life, my patient grandmother gave her time to her shy, young granddaughter. I always enjoyed going with Grandma and collecting the eggs that her chickens had just laid. Usually, she knew which chickens would peck, and she was careful to let me gather the eggs from the less hostile ones.
> —Patricia Mapes, student

When you use both coordination and subordination, never use both a COORDINATE CONJUNCTION and a SUBORDINATE CONJUNCTION to express one relationship in one sentence.

NO	**Although** the story was well written, **but** it was too illogical.
	[The subordinating conjunction *although* expresses the contrast, so also using *but* is incorrect.]
YES	**Although** the story was well written, it was too illogical.
YES	The story was well written, **but** it was too illogical.

EXERCISE 17-5

Working individually or in a group, use subordination and coordination to combine these sets of short, choppy sentences. For help, consult all sections of this chapter.

EXAMPLE   Owls cannot digest the bones and fur of the mice and birds they eat. They cough up a furry pellet every day.

Because owls cannot digest the bones and fur of the mice and birds they eat, they cough up a furry pellet every day.

ANSWERS: EXERCISE 17-5
Students' answers will vary. Here is one set of possibilities.

1. Owl pellets are the latest teaching tool in biology classrooms around the country *because they* provide an alternative to dissecting frogs and other animals.

2. Inside the pellets are the remains of the owl's nightly meal, *which* include beautifully cleaned hummingbird skulls, rat skeletons, and lots of bird feathers.

3. The owl-pellet market has been cornered by companies in New York, California, and Washington *that* distribute pellets to thousands of biology classrooms all over the world.

4. Company workers scour barns and the ground under trees where owls nest to pick up the pellets, *which* sell for $1 each.

5. The owl-pellet business may have a short future *because* the rural areas of the United States are vanishing. Old barns are being bulldozed. *When* all the barns are torn down, the owls will be gone, too.

ANSWERS: EXERCISE 17-6
Answers will vary. Here's one possibility.

Thirst is the body's way of surviving. Because every cell in the body needs water, people can die by losing as little as 15 to 20 percent of their water requirements. Blood, which contains 83 percent water, provides indispensable nutrients for the cells. Blood carries water to the cells, and blood carries waste away from the cells. Insufficient water means cells cannot be fueled or cleaned, so the body becomes sluggish. Although the body can survive eleven days without water, bodily functions are seriously disrupted by a lack of water for more than one day. When the body loses water, the blood thickens. The heart must pump harder, for thickened blood is harder to pump through the heart. Some drinks replace the body's need for fluids, but alcohol or caffeine in drinks leads to dehydration. Unless people know they should drink water often, they can become moderately dehydrated before they even begin to develop a thirst.

1. Owl pellets are the latest teaching tool in biology classrooms around the country. The pellets provide an alternative to dissecting frogs and other animals.
2. Inside the pellet are the remains of the owl's nightly meal. They include beautifully cleaned hummingbird skulls, rat skeletons, and lots of bird feathers.
3. The owl-pellet market has been cornered by companies in New York, California, and Washington. These companies distribute pellets to thousands of biology classrooms all over the world.
4. Company workers scour barns and the ground under trees where owls nest to pick up the pellets. The pellets sell for $1 each.
5. The owl-pellet business may have a short future. The rural areas of the United States are vanishing. Old barns are being bulldozed. All the barns are torn down. The owls will be gone, too.

EXERCISE 17-6

Working individually or with a group, revise this paragraph to make it more effective by using coordination and subordination. For help, consult all sections of this chapter.

Thirst is the body's way of surviving. Every cell in the body needs water. People can die by losing as little as 15 to 20 percent of their water requirements. Blood contains 83 percent water. Blood provides indispensable nutrients for the cells. Blood carries water to the cells. Blood carries waste away from the cells. Insufficient water means cells cannot be fueled or cleaned. The body becomes sluggish. The body can survive eleven days without water. Bodily functions are seriously disrupted by a lack of water for more than one day. The body loses water. The blood thickens. The heart must pump harder. Thickened blood is harder to pump through the heart. Some drinks replace the body's need for fluids. Alcohol or caffeine in drinks leads to dehydration. People know they should drink water often. They can become moderately dehydrated before they even begin to develop a thirst.

Chapter 18

Parallelism

18a What is parallelism?

When you write words, PHRASES, or CLAUSES within a sentence to match
in their grammatical forms, the result is **parallelism.** Parallelism serves
to emphasize information or ideas in writing. The technique relates to
the concept of parallel lines in geometry, lines that run alongside each
other and never meet. Parallelism delivers grace, rhythm, and impact.

> The deer often come to eat their grain, the wolves to destroy their
> sheep, the bears to kill their hogs, and the foxes to catch their poultry.
> [The message of the multiple, accumulating assaults is echoed by the parallel
> structures.]

> —J. Hector St. Jean de Crèvecoeur,
> *Letters from an American Farmer*

You gain several advantages in using parallel structures:

- You can express ideas of equal weight in your writing.
- You can emphasize important information or ideas.
- You can add rhythm and grace to your writing style.

Many writers attend to parallelism when they are REVISING. If you think
while you're DRAFTING that your parallelism is faulty or that you can enhance your writing style by using parallelism, underline or highlight the
material and keep moving forward. When you revise, you can return to
the places you've marked.

18b What is a balanced sentence?

A **balanced sentence** is a type of parallelism in which contrasting content is delivered. The two parallel structures are usually, but not always,
INDEPENDENT CLAUSES. A balanced sentence uses COORDINATION. The

BACKGROUND
Although parallelism is the best known of the
balanced sentence patterns, some others are
also available. *Antithesis*, for one, juxtaposes
contrasting ideas, often in parallel structure.
Neil Armstrong was using antithesis when he
made his famous comment as he stepped on
the moon in 1969: "That's one small step for a
man, one giant leap for mankind." *Chiasmus,*
sometimes called "the criss-cross," reverses
grammatical structures in successive phrases
or clauses. One of John Kennedy's well-
known statements in his inaugural address,
for example, uses chiasmus: "Ask not what
your country can do for you; ask what you can
do for your country."

TEACHING TIP
In *Style: Ten Lessons in Clarity and Grace,*
7th ed. (Boston: Longman, 2002), Joseph M.
Williams suggests two simple ways to "enhance the rhythm and grace of coordination."
First, a series of parallel clauses or phrases
"will move more gracefully if each . . . is
longer than the one before it." Second, writers can enhance parallel elements if they
"consciously balance parts of phrases and
clauses against one another."

BACKGROUND
The site <http://owl.english.purdue.edu/
handouts/grammar/g_parallel.html> offered
by Purdue University gives examples of faulty
parallel structures, including proofreading
strategies for recognizing parallelism errors.

QUOTATION: ON WRITING
It doesn't matter how you write the first draft
or even the second draft, but it makes all the
difference in the world how you write the
final draft.

—Elizabeth White

two coordinate structures are characterized by opposites in meaning, sometimes with one structure cast in the negative.

> By night, the litter and desperation disappeared as the city's glittering lights came on; by day, the filth and despair reappeared as the sun rose.

—Jennifer Kirk, student

👁 **ALERT:** Authorities differ about using a comma, a semicolon, or nothing between the parts of a short balanced sentence. In ACADEMIC WRITING, to avoid appearing to make the error of a COMMA SPLICE, use a semicolon (or revise in some other way), as in the following sentence.

> Mosquitoes don't bite; they stab. 👁

18c How do words, phrases, and clauses work in parallel form?

When you put words, PHRASES, and CLAUSES into parallel form, you enhance your writing style with balance and grace.

PARALLEL WORDS Recommended exercise includes running, swimming, and cycling.

PARALLEL PHRASES Exercise helps people maintain healthy bodies and handle mental pressures.

PARALLEL CLAUSES Many people exercise because they want to look healthy, because they need to increase stamina, and because they hope to live longer.

18d How does parallelism deliver impact?

Parallel structures serve to emphasize the meaning that sentences deliver. Deliberate, rhythmic repetition of parallel forms creates an effect of balance, reinforcing the impact of a message.

> Go back to Mississippi, go back to Alabama, go back to South Carolina, go back to Georgia, go back to Louisiana, go back to the slums and

ghettos of our northern cities, knowing that somehow this situation can and will be changed.

—Martin Luther King Jr., "I Have a Dream"

If King had not used PARALLELISM, his message would have made less of an impact on his listeners. His structures reinforce the power of his message. A sentence without parallelism could have carried his message, but with far less effect: *Return to your homes in Mississippi, Alabama, South Carolina, Georgia, Louisiana, or the northern cities, and know that the situation will be changed.*

Here's a longer passage in which parallel structures, concepts, and rhythms operate. Together, they echo the intensity of the writer's message.

You ask me what is **poverty?** Listen to me. Here I am, dirty, **smelly,** and with no "proper" underwear on and with the stench of my rotting teeth near you. I will tell you. Listen to me. Listen without pity. I cannot use your pity. Listen with understanding. Put yourself in my dirty, worn-out, ill-fitting shoes, and hear me.

Poverty is getting up every morning from a dirt- and illness-stained mattress. The sheets have long since been used for diapers. **Poverty** is living in a **smell** that never leaves. This is a **smell** of urine, sour milk, and spoiling food sometimes joined with the strong **smell** of long-cooked onions. Onions are cheap. If you have **smelled** this **smell,** you did not know how it came. It is **the smell** of the outdoor privy. It is **the smell** of young children who cannot walk the long dark way in the night. It is **the smell** of the mattresses where years of "accidents" have happened. It is **the smell** of the milk that has gone sour because the refrigerator long has not worked, and it costs money to get it fixed. It is **the smell** of rotting garbage. I could bury it, but where is the shovel? Shovels cost money.

—Jo Goodwin Parker, "What Is Poverty?"

EXERCISE 18-1

Working individually or with a group, highlight all parallel elements of the Jo Goodwin Parker passage above in addition to those shown in boldface.

18e How can I avoid faulty parallelism?

Faulty parallelism usually results when you join nonmatching grammatical forms.

Teaching Tip (continued)
5. Students should copy patiently and with care. Too much speed can make the exercise meaningless. One way of controlling speed is to require that work be legible.

A second kind of imitation exercise uses sentences as patterns. The students duplicate the *kind, number,* and *order* of clauses and phrases in the model. The aim of this exercise is not to achieve a word-for-word correspondence with the model but rather to achieve an awareness of the variety of sentence structures of which the English language is capable.

Parody can be an enjoyable imitation exercise for students. Writing a "restaurant review" of the cafeteria or a literary analysis of a comic book not only engages students in wordplay but also requires that they notice the stylistic and structural conventions of the model they are parodying.

ANSWERS: EXERCISE 18-1
Elements of parallelism in Parker's passage not shown in boldface include: *Repetitions:* you, me, I, dirty (dirt), pity, onions, mattress(es), cost(s) money, this, urine (privy, "accidents"), long, it is, sour, rotting, shovel(s). *Paired words:* with / and with. *Imperatives* (mild commands): Listen, Put, hear. *Contrasts:* pity / understanding, without / with. *Words in a series:* my dirty, worn-out, ill-fitting shoes; smell of urine, sour milk, and spoiling food.

BACKGROUND

Martin Luther King Jr. (1929–1968) was a powerful and eloquent speaker and writer for the civil rights movement in the United States. His works include *Stride Toward Freedom* (1958), *Strength to Love* (1963), *Why We Can't Wait* (1964), and *Where Do We Go from Here: Chaos or Community* (1967), as well as his famous "I Have a Dream" speech, which he delivered to a crowd of over 250,000 people in 1963 at a massive civil rights demonstration in Washington, D.C.

Among his best-known writings is his "Letter from Birmingham Jail," which he wrote from prison in 1963 in response to a published statement by eight Alabama clergymen who called his activities "unwise and untimely." In "The *Other* Beauty of Martin Luther King, Jr.'s 'Letter from Birmingham Jail'" (*College Composition and Communication,* February 1981: 30–37), Mia Klein Anderson describes the musical, rhythmical effect of parallelism in King's powerful letter. King parallels clauses, nouns, verbs, adverbs, adjectives, and adjective-noun pairs throughout the letter. Using antithesis and parallelism, he juxtaposes contrasting ideas with an engaging rhythm. King often combines parallelism with deliberate repetition of a word or group of words at the start of successive clauses, a rhetorical figure called *anaphora.* "Martin Luther King, Jr., knew that his effectiveness in reaching his wider audience would come both from what he said and from how he said it," Anderson writes. "The words can reach the mind, but the music and imagination can reach the heart and soul" (36).

Parallelism with coordinating conjunctions

The coordinating conjunctions are *and, but, for, or, nor, yet,* and *so.* To avoid faulty parallelism, write the words that accompany coordinating conjunctions in matching grammatical forms.

> NO   **Love *and* being married** go together.
> YES   **Love *and* marriage** go together.
> YES   **Being in love *and* being married** go together.

Parallelism with correlative conjunctions

Correlative conjunctions are paired words such as *not only . . . but (also), either . . . or,* and *both . . . and.* To avoid faulty parallelism, write the words joined by correlative conjunctions in matching grammatical forms.

> NO   Differing expectations for marriage ***not only* can lead to disappointment *but also* makes the couple angry.**
> YES   Differing expectations for marriage ***not only* can lead to disappointment *but also* can make the couple angry.**

Parallelism with than and as

To avoid faulty parallelism when you use *than* and *as* for comparisons, write the elements of comparison in matching grammatical forms.

> NO   **Having a solid marriage** can be more satisfying ***than* the acquisition of wealth.**
> YES   **Having a solid marriage** can be more satisfying ***than* acquiring wealth.**
> YES   **A solid marriage** can be more satisfying ***than* wealth.**

Parallelism with function words

Function words include ARTICLES (*the, a, an*); the *to* of the INFINITIVE (*to* love); PREPOSITIONS (for example, *of, in, about*); and sometimes RELATIVE PRONOUNS. When you write a series of parallel structures, be consistent in the second and successive structures about either repeating or omitting a function word. Generally, repeat function words only if you think that the repetition clarifies your meaning or highlights the parallelism that you intend.

> NO   **To assign** unanswered letters their proper weight, **free** us from the expectations of others, **to give** us back to ourselves—here lies the great, singular power of self-respect.

YES **To assign** unanswered letters their proper weight, **to free** us from the expectations of others, **to give** us back to ourselves— here lies **the great, the singular** power of self-respect.
—Joan Didion, "On Self-Respect"

I have in my own life a precious friend, a woman of 65 **who has** lived very hard, **who is** wise, **who listens** well, **who has been** where I am and can help me understand it, and **who represents** not only an ultimate ideal mother to me but also the person I'd like to be when I grow up.
—Judith Viorst, "Friends, Good Friends— and Such Good Friends"

We looked into the bus, which **was** painted blue with orange daisies, **had** picnic benches instead of seats, and **showed** yellow curtains billowing out its windows.
—Kerrie Falk, student

EXERCISE 18-2

Working individually or with a group, revise these sentences by putting appropriate information in parallel structures. For help, consult 18a through 18e.

EXAMPLE Difficult bosses affect not only their employees' performances but their private lives are affected as well.

Difficult bosses affect not only their employees' performances *but their private lives as well.*

1. According to the psychologist Harry Levinson, the five main types of bad boss are the workaholic, the kind of person you would describe as bullying, a person who communicates badly, the jellyfish type, and someone who insists on perfection.
2. As a way of getting ahead, to keep their self-respect, and for simple survival, wise employees handle problem bosses with a variety of strategies.
3. To cope with a bad-tempered employer, workers can both stand up for themselves and reasoning with a bullying boss.
4. Often, bad bosses communicate poorly or fail to calculate the impact of their personality on others; being a careful listener and sensitivity to others' responses are qualities that good bosses possess.
5. Employees who take the trouble to understand what makes their boss tick, engage in some self-analysis, and staying flexible are better prepared to cope with a difficult job environment than suffering in silence like some employees.

ANSWERS AND COVERAGE: EXERCISE 18-3

Answers may vary. Here is one set of possible answers.

1. A married couple *who* met at Juniata College in Huntingdon, Pennsylvania, and *who* are both left-handed have set up a scholarship for needy left-handed students attending Juniata. [18e, repeating parallel function words]

2. Writers who specialize in humor bankroll a student humor writer at the University of Southern California in Los Angeles; a horse-racing association sponsors a student sportswriter at Vanderbilt University in Nashville, Tennessee. [18b, balanced sentence]

3. The Rochester Institute of Technology in New York State is choosing 150 students born on June 12, 1979. *It is granting each one $1,500 per year. It is awarding these grants to select students to honor the school's 150th anniversary,* which it celebrated on June 12, 1979. [18d, parallelism among sentences]

4. The College of Wooster in Ohio grants generous scholarships to students if they *play the Scottish bagpipes, play the traditional Scottish drums,* or *excel in Scottish folk dancing.* [18c, parallel phrases]

5. In return for their scholarships, Wooster's *bagpipers must pipe for the school's football team,* the *drummers must drum for the team,* and the *dancers must cheer the athletes from the sidelines.* [18c, parallelism among clauses]

ANSWERS: EXERCISE 18-4

The answers here list the examples' parallel elements.

A. The description "a planet *unvexed* by war, *untroubled* by hunger or fear, *undivided* by senseless distinctions of race, color, or theory" has parallel structure based on parallel words (in italics). [Some students may also list the parallel words *race, color, theory.*]

B. The clauses beginning with the word *Some* are parallel.

C. The two clauses *I am lonely* are parallel, as are all the clauses beginning with *when.*

EXERCISE 18-3

Working individually or with a group, combine the sentences in each numbered item, using techniques of parallelism. For help, consult 18a through 18e.

EXAMPLE   College scholarships are awarded not only for academic and athletic ability, but there are also scholarships that recognize unusual talents. Other scholarships even award accidents of birth, like left-handedness.

College scholarships are awarded not only for academic and athletic ability *but also for unusual talents and even for accidents of birth, like left-handedness.*

1. A married couple met at Juniata College in Huntingdon, Pennsylvania. They are both left-handed, and they have set up a scholarship for needy left-handed students attending Juniata.

2. Writers who specialize in humor bankroll a student humor writer at the University of Southern California in Los Angeles. A horse-racing association sponsors a student sportswriter. The student must attend Vanderbilt University in Nashville, Tennessee.

3. The Rochester Institute of Technology in New York State is choosing 150 students born on June 12, 1979. Each one is to receive a grant of $1,500 per year. These awards are to be given to select students to honor the school's 150th anniversary, which was celebrated on June 12, 1979.

4. The College of Wooster in Ohio grants generous scholarships to students if they play the bagpipes, a musical instrument native to Scotland. Students playing the traditional Scottish drums and those who excel in Scottish folk dancing also qualify.

5. In return for their scholarships, Wooster's bagpipers must pipe for the school's football team. The terms of the scholarships also require the drummers to drum for the team. The dancers have to cheer the athletes from the sidelines.

EXERCISE 18-4

Working individually or with a group, find the parallel elements in these three passages. Next, imitate the parallelism in the examples, using a different topic of your choice for each.

A.   Our earth is but a small star in a great universe. Yet of it we can make, if we choose, a planet unvexed by war, untroubled by hunger or fear, undivided by senseless distinctions of race, color, or theory.

—Stephen Vincent Benét

B.   Some would recover [from polio] almost entirely. Some would die. Some would come through unable to move their legs, or unable to move arms and legs; some could move nothing but an arm, or nothing but a few fingers and their eyes. Some would leave the hospital with a cane, some with crutches, crutches and steel leg braces, or in wheelchairs—white-faced, shrunken, with frightened eyes, light blankets over their legs. Some would remain in an iron lung—a great, eighteen-hundred-pound, casket-like contraption, like the one in which the woman in the magic show (her head and feet sticking out of either end) is sawed in half.
—Charles L. Mee Jr., "The Summer Before Salk"

C.   I am lonely only when I am overtired, when I have worked too long without a break, when for the time being I feel empty and need filling up. And I am lonely sometimes when I come back home after a lecture trip, when I have seen a lot of people and talked a lot, and am full to the brim with experience that needs to be sorted out.
—May Sarton, "The Rewards of a Solitary Life"

18f How does parallelism work in outlines and lists?

All items in formal OUTLINES and lists must be parallel in grammar and structure. (For more about outline format and outline development, see 2r.)

Outlines

NO

Reducing Traffic Fatalities
I. Stricter laws
  A. Top speed should be 55 mph on highways.
  B. Higher fines
  C. Requiring jail sentences for repeat offenders
II. The use of safety devices should be mandated by law.

YES

Reducing Traffic Fatalities
I. Passing stricter speed laws'
  A. Making 55 mph the top speed on highways
  B. Raising fines for speeding
  C. Requiring jail sentences for repeat offenders
II. Mandating by law the use of safety devices

Lists

NO Workaholics share these characteristics:
  1. They are intense and driven.
  2. Strong self-doubters
  3. Labor is preferred to leisure by workaholics.

ANSWERS: EXERCISE 18-5

Answers will vary. Here is one possibility.

Reducing Traffic Fatalities

I.   Stricter laws are needed.
  A. The top highway speed should be 55 mph.
  B. Fines for speeding should be higher.
  C. Repeat offenders should be sentenced to jail.
II. Use of safety devices should be legislated.
  A. All passengers, front and back, should be required to have safety belts.
  B. Drivers must be held responsible when passengers are not wearing seat belts.
  C. Car manufacturers must be required to offer side and front airbags in all cars.

 YES   Workaholics share these characteristics:
  1. They are intense and driven.
  2. They have strong self-doubts.
  3. They prefer labor to leisure.

EXERCISE 18-5

Working individually or with a group, revise this outline so that all lines are complete sentences in parallel form. For help, consult 2r and 18f.

Reducing Traffic Fatalities

I.   Stricter laws needed
  A. Legislating top speed of 55 mph for highways
  B. Higher fines
  C. Repeat offenders sentenced to jail
II. Legislating uses of safety devices
  A. All passengers, back and front, should be required to have safety belts.
  B. Drivers must be held responsible when passengers are not wearing seat belts.
  C. Forcing car manufacturers to offer side and front airbags in all cars.

Chapter 19

Variety and Emphasis

19a What are variety and emphasis in writing?

When you write sentences of various lengths and structures within a paragraph or longer piece of writing, you create **sentence variety**. Working in concert with sentence variety, **emphasis** allows you to add weight to ideas of special importance.

Using techniques of variety and emphasis adds style and clarity to your writing. Usually, the best time to apply the principles of variety and emphasis is while you are REVISING.

19b How do different sentence lengths create variety and emphasis?

To emphasize one idea among many others, you can express it in a sentence noticeably different in length from the sentences surrounding it. In the following example, a four-word sentence between two longer sentences carries the key message of the passage.

> Today is one of those excellent January partly cloudies in which light chooses an unexpected landscape to trick out in gilt, and then shadow sweeps it away. **You know you're alive.** You take huge steps, trying to feel the planet's roundness arc between your feet.
> —Annie Dillard, *Pilgrim at Tinker Creek*

Sometimes a string of short sentences creates impact and emphasis. Yet, at other times, a string of short sentences can be dull to read.

NO   There is a problem. It is widely known as sick-building syndrome. It comes from indoor air pollution. It causes office

337

ANSWERS: EXERCISE 19-1
In this exercise, the first item has too many short sentences and the second has long and complicated sentences. Students will revise in various ways. Here is one set of possible answers.

1. Biometeorology, the science that studies weather's unseen power over living things, concentrates on the effects of weather patterns on human behavior and health. One researcher, William Ferdinand Peterson, who has spent the past twenty years collecting statistics and anecdotes, wrote the book *The Patient and the Weather.* His research focuses on the invisible elements of air, including passing fronts, falling barometric pressure, and shifting wind directions.

2. Feared winds and all their variations—from katabatic to chinook to Santa Ana—are frequently considered to be the cause of every illness that can be imagined. In Russia, high winds and the frequency of strokes seem related; in Italy, southern winds and heart attacks seem connected; and in Japan, changes in wind direction seem to bring an increase in asthma attacks.

workers to suffer. They have trouble breathing. They have painful rashes. Their heads ache. Their eyes burn.

YES   Widely known as sick-building syndrome, indoor air pollution causes office workers to suffer. They have trouble breathing. They have painful rashes. Their heads ache. Their eyes burn. [Many revisions are possible. This uses a long sentence to mention indoor air pollution and its victims; next, this retains the series of short sentences to emphasize each problem. Also, the conciseness of the revised version reduces 37 words to 27.]

Similarly, a string of COMPOUND SENTENCES can be monotonous to read and may fail to communicate relationships among ideas.

NO   Science fiction writers are often thinkers, **and** they are often dreamers, **and** they let their imaginations wander. Jules Verne was such a writer, **and** he predicted spaceships, **and** he forecast atomic submarines, **but** most people did not believe airplanes were possible.

YES   Science fiction writers are often thinkers and dreamers who let their imaginations wander. Jules Verne was one such writer. He predicted spaceships and atomic submarines before most people believed airplanes were possible.

EXERCISE 19-1

Working individually or with a group, revise these sets of sentences to vary the sentence lengths effectively. For help, consult 19a and 19b.

1.   Biometeorology is a science. It examines the study of weather's unseen power over living things. The science concentrates on the effects of weather patterns on human behavior and health. Many researchers study these effects. One researcher is William Ferdinand Peterson. He has spent the past twenty years collecting statistics and anecdotes. He wrote the book *The Patient and the Weather.* His research focuses on the invisible elements of air. These elements include passing fronts. These elements include falling barometric pressure. The elements include shifting wind directions.

2.   Feared winds and all their variations—from katabatic to chinook to Santa Ana—are frequently considered the cause of every illness that can be imagined by many people in every country. In Russia, high winds and the frequency of strokes seem related, and in Italy, southern winds and heart attacks seem connected, and in Japan, researchers have noticed an increase in asthma attacks whenever the wind changes direction.

19c How do occasional questions, commands, or exclamations create variety and emphasis?

The majority of sentences in English are DECLARATIVE—they declare something by making a statement. Declarative sentences offer an almost infinite variety of structures and patterns. For variety and emphasis, you might want to use three alternative types of sentences occasionally.

A sentence that asks a question is called INTERROGATIVE. Occasional questions, placed appropriately, tend to involve readers. A sentence that issues a mild or strong command is called IMPERATIVE. Occasional mild commands, appropriately used, gently urge a reader to think along with you. A sentence that makes an exclamation is called EXCLAMATORY. An occasional exclamatory sentence, appropriate to the context, can enliven writing, but you should use this sentence type only rarely in ACADEMIC WRITING.

👁 **ALERT:** A declarative statement ends with a period (Chapter 23)—or semicolon (Chapter 25) or colon (Chapter 26). A mild command ends with a period. A strong command and an exclamation end with an exclamation point (Chapter 23). 👁

Here's a paragraph with declarative, interrogative, and imperative sentences.

> Imagine what people ate during the winter as little as seventy-five years ago. They ate food that was local, long-lasting, and dull, like acorn squash, turnips, and cabbage. Walk into an American supermarket in February and the world lies before you: grapes, melons, artichokes, fennel, lettuce, peppers, pistachios, dates, even strawberries, to say nothing of ice cream. Have you ever considered what a triumph of civilization it is to be able to buy a pound of chicken livers? If you lived on a farm and had to kill a chicken when you wanted to eat one, you wouldn't ever accumulate a pound of chicken livers.
> —Phyllis Rose, "Shopping and Other Spiritual Adventures in America Today"

EXERCISE 19-2

Working individually or with a group, write an imitation of the following paragraph. This paragraph varies sentence lengths and uses a question and a command effectively. The result emphasizes the key points. Choose your own topic, but follow the style of the paragraph closely. For help, consult 19c.

BACKGROUND

Adding modifiers to basic sentences is the central feature of the "generative rhetoric" developed by Francis Christensen in his classic work *Notes Toward a New Rhetoric*. The Christensen program teaches students various ways to expand a sentence by showing them model sentences, giving students a basic sentence and having them expand it following the pattern of the models, and then having students compose their own sentences according to that pattern. These exercises not only develop the writing style of students but also teach them ways of elaborating their ideas.

QUOTATION: ON WRITING

Bain saw a hierarchical structural relationship between words, sentences, paragraphs, and entire compositions.

—Ned A. Shearer,
"Alexander Bain and the Genesis
of Paragraph Theory"

ANSWERS AND COVERAGE: EXERCISE 19-3

Students are to expand each sentence by adding (a) an adjective, (b) an adverb, (c) a prepositional phrase, (d) a participial phrase, (e) an absolute phrase, (f) an adverb clause, and (g) an adjective clause. They can refer for guidance to the expansion techniques listed in section 19d. Here is a possible set of answers for item 1:

a. We bought a two-story house.

b. Recently, we bought a house.

c. We bought a house near the train station.

d. Excited by low interest rates, we bought a house costing more than we could afford.

e. Space being too cramped in the apartment, we bought a house.

f. Because we saved enough for a down payment, we bought a house.

g. We bought a house, which overlooks the river.

Why are some animal species easily pushed to the verge of extinction while others thrive in almost every type of environment? Consider the humble cottontail rabbit. Equally at home in city parks, suburban backyards, or wilderness areas, this species thrives everywhere it can find a little greenery. It is not choosy about diet, either. It survives by eating woody stems in winter and gorging on the lush growth of summer. And what about shelter? The cottontail rabbit builds a nest and raises its young wherever it locates bits of dried grass to hide its babies. Other small mammals, such as possums, woodchucks, weasels, and beaver, have more exacting needs for food or shelter that limit their adaptability. The cottontail survives by remaining flexible, refusing to specialize.

19d How can modifiers create variety and emphasis?

MODIFIERS can expand sentences to add richness to your writing and create a pleasing mixture of variety and emphasis. Your choice of where to place modifiers to expand your sentences depends on the focus you want each sentence to communicate, either on its own or in concert with its surrounding sentences. Be careful where you place modifiers because you don't want to introduce the error known as a MISPLACED MODIFIER.

BASIC SENTENCE	The river rose.
ADJECTIVE	The **swollen** river rose.
ADVERB	The river rose **dangerously.**
PREPOSITIONAL PHRASE	The river rose **above its banks.**
PARTICIPIAL PHRASE	**Swelled by melting snow,** the river rose.
ABSOLUTE PHRASE	**Uprooted trees swirling away in the current,** the river rose.
ADVERB CLAUSE	**Because the snows had been heavy that winter,** the river rose.
ADJECTIVE CLAUSE	The river, **which runs through vital farmland,** rose.

EXERCISE 19-3

Working individually or with a group, expand each sentence by adding each kind of modifier illustrated in 19d.

1. We bought a house.
2. The roof leaked.
3. I remodeled the kitchen.
4. Neighbors brought food.
5. Everyone enjoyed the barbeque.

19e How does repetition affect variety and emphasis?

You can repeat one or more words that express a main idea when your message is suitable. This technique creates a rhythm that focuses attention on the main idea. Here's an example that uses deliberate repetition along with a variety of sentence lengths to deliver its meaning.

> Coal is **black** and it warms your house and cooks your food. The night is **black,** which has a moon, and a million stars, and is beautiful. Sleep is **black,** which gives you rest, so you wake up feeling **good.** I am **black.** I feel very **good** this evening.
>
> —Langston Hughes, "That Word *Black*"

At the same time, don't confuse deliberate repetition with a lack of vocabulary variety.

NO An insurance agent can be an excellent adviser when you want to buy a car. An insurance agent has complete records on most cars. An insurance agent knows which car models are prone to have accidents. An insurance agent can tell you which car models are the most expensive to repair if they are in a collision. An insurance agent can tell you which models are most likely to be stolen. [Although only a few synonyms exist for *insurance agent, car,* and *model,* some do and should be used. Also, the sentence structure here lacks variety.]

YES If you are thinking of buying a new car, an insurance agent, who usually has complete records on most cars, can be an excellent adviser. Any professional insurance broker knows which automobile models are prone to have accidents. Did you know that some cars suffer more damage than others in a collision? If you want to know which vehicles crumple more than others and which are least expensive to repair, ask an insurance agent. Similarly, some car models are more likely to be stolen, so find out from the person who specializes in dealing with car insurance claims.

BACKGROUND
The balanced sentence presents two equally weighted pieces of meaning. Usually, a punctuation mark or a coordinating conjunction (or both) acts as a centerpoint on which the meaning balances, much like a seesaw on its base, as in this example:

> Freedom is the right to be wrong, not the right to do wrong.
>
> —John Diefenbaker

EXTRA EXERCISE
Apply techniques of variety and emphasis to revise the following paragraph. Use different kinds of modifiers (19d). You can reduce or increase the number of words and of sentences. Try to include at least one question or exclamation. Also, try to vary the word order.

Huge caves known collectively as the Carlsbad Caverns are hidden beneath the sands of New Mexico. The caverns contain a mysterious underground world. More than 20 miles of caves have been discovered. Miles more are found each year. Some of the caves contain mysterious underground lakes. Others are huge chambers, and their ceilings rise 200 feet. Electric lights illuminate the caves for visitors. The lights create an effect that is dramatic. The lights reveal unusual rock formations. Spikes of rock hang from the ceiling. Tall, pointy rocks rise from the floor. Delicate sheets of thin rock are hanging like drapery. The slow drip of minerals through the caves' limestone roof formed them all. The caves echo with watery noises and glimmer with reflected light. The desert is above. In the desert, the sun shines, and winds blow, and birds sing, and coyotes howl. Below in the caverns, no daylight penetrates. The air is cold and still. There are no winds or animal sounds. Such sounds do not disturb the silence. It is amazing to see the contrast between the desert and the caves. Not many people would have guessed that these caves beneath the desert originated as a coral reef in an ancient sea. →

Hidden beneath the sands of New Mexico, [19d, modifiers] the huge caves known as the Carlsbad Caverns contain a mysterious underground world. [19b, sentence lengths] More than 20 miles of caves have been discovered, and miles more are found each year. [19b, revise for suitable mix by combining two sentences] Some of the caves, which echo with watery noises and glimmer with reflected light, contain mysterious underground lakes. [19f, periodic sentence] Others are huge chambers whose ceilings rise 200 feet. [19d, modifiers] Electric lights, which illuminate the caves for visitors, are placed for dramatic effect [19f, word order] to reveal unusual rock formations. Spikes of rock hang from the ceiling, and tall, pointy rocks rise from the floor. [19b, sentence lengths] Hanging like drapery are delicate sheets of thin rock. [19f, word order] All were formed by the slow drip of minerals through the caves' limestone roof. [19f, word order] In the desert above, the sun shines, winds blow, birds sing, and coyotes howl. [19b, sentence lengths] Below in the caverns, where no daylight penetrates, [19d, modifiers] the air is cold and still. No winds or animal sounds disturb the silence. [19b, sentence lengths] How amazing the contrast is between the desert and the caves! [19c, exclamation for variety] Who would have guessed that these caves beneath the desert originated as a coral reef in an ancient sea? [19c, question for variety]

19f   How else can I create variety and emphasis?

Changing word order

Standard word order in English places the SUBJECT before the VERB.

> The **mayor** *walked* into the room. [*Mayor* is the subject, which comes before the verb *walked*.]

Any variation from standard word order creates emphasis. For example, **inverted word order** places the verb before the subject.

> Into the room *walked* the **mayor.** [*Mayor* is the subject, which comes after the verb *walked*.]

Changing a sentence's subject

The subject of a sentence establishes the focus for that sentence. To create the emphasis you want, you can vary each sentence's subject. All the sample sentences below express the same information, but the focus changes in each according to the subject (and its corresponding verb).

> **Our study** *showed* that 25 percent of college students' time is spent eating or sleeping. [Focus is on the study.]
> **College students** *eat or sleep* 25 percent of the time, according to our study. [Focus is on the students.]
> **Eating or sleeping** *occupies* 25 percent of college students' time, according to our study. [Focus is on eating and sleeping.]
> **Twenty-five percent of college students' time** *is spent* eating or sleeping, according to our study. [Focus is on the percentage of time.]

Using a periodic sentence among cumulative sentences

The **cumulative sentence** is the most common sentence structure in English. Its name reflects the way information accumulates in the sentence until it reaches a period. Its structure starts with a SUBJECT and VERB and continues with modifiers. Another term for a cumulative sentence is *loose sentence* because it lacks a tightly planned structure.

For greater impact, you might occasionally use a **periodic sentence,** also called a *climactic sentence,* which reserves the main idea for the end of the sentence. This structure tends to draw in the reader as it moves toward the period. If overused, however, periodic sentences lose their punch.

CUMULATIVE	A car hit a shoulder and turned over at midnight last night on the road from Las Vegas to Death Valley Junction.
PERIODIC	At midnight last night, on the road from Las Vegas to Death Valley Junction, a car hit a shoulder and turned over.

—Joan Didion, "On Morality"

Chapter 20

Usage Glossary

A usage glossary presents the customary manner of using particular words and phrases. "Customary manner," however, is not as firm in practice as the term implies. Usage standards change. If you think a word's usage might differ from what you read here, consult a dictionary published more recently than the current edition of this handbook.

The meaning of *informal* or *colloquial* in the definition of a word or phrase is that it's found in everyday or conversational speech, but it needs to be avoided in ACADEMIC WRITING. Another term, *nonstandard*, indicates that the word or phrase, although widely understood in speech and dialect writing, isn't suitable in standard spoken or written English.

All terms of grammar and writing in this Usage Glossary are defined in the Terms Glossary, which begins directly before the Index.

a, an   Use *a* before words that begin with a consonant (***a** dog*, ***a** grade*, ***a** hole*) or a consonant sound (***a** one-day sale*, ***a** European*). Use *an* before words or acronyms that begin with a vowel sound or a silent *h* (***an** owl*; ***an** hour*; ***an** MRI*, because the *M* is sounded *em*). American English uses *a*, not *an*, before words starting with a pronounced *h*: ***a*** (not *an*) *historical event.*

accept, except   The verb *accept* means "agree to; receive." As a preposition, *except* means "leaving out." As a verb, *except* means "exclude; leave out."

- The workers wanted to **accept** [verb] management's offer **except** [preposition] for one detail: They wanted the limit on overtime **excepted** [verb] from the contract.

advice, advise   *Advice,* a noun, means "recommendation." *Advise,* a verb, means "recommend; give advice."

- I **advise** [verb] you to follow your car mechanic's **advice** [noun].

affect, effect   As a verb, *affect* means "cause a change in; influence." (*Affect* is a noun in psychology.) As a noun, *effect* means "result or conclusion"; as a verb, *effect* means "bring about."

- Loud music **affects** people's hearing for life, so some bands have **effected** changes to lower the volume. Many fans, however, don't care about the harmful **effects** of high-decibel levels.

aggravate, irritate   *Aggravate* is used colloquially to mean "irritate." In academic writing, use *aggravate* only to mean "intensify; make worse." Use *irritate* to mean "annoy; make impatient."

- The coach was **irritated** by reduced time for practice, which **aggravated** the team's difficulties with concentration.

ain't   *Ain't* is a nonstandard contraction. Use *am not, is not,* or *are not* for standard spoken and written English.

all ready, already   *All ready* means "completely prepared." *Already* means "before; by this time."

- The team was **all ready** to play, but the coach was **already** in a bad mood.

all right   *All right* is always written as two words, never one (never *alright*).

all together, altogether   *All together* means "in a group; in unison." *Altogether* means "entirely; thoroughly."

- The twelve jurors told the judge that it was **altogether** absurd for them to stay **all together** in a single hotel room.

allude, elude   *Allude* means "refer to indirectly." *Elude* means "escape notice."

- The detectives **alluded** to budget cuts by saying that "conditions beyond their control allowed the suspect to **elude** us."

allusion, illusion   An *allusion* is an indirect reference to something. An *illusion* is a false impression or idea.

- The couple's casual **allusions** to European tourist sites created the **illusion** that they had visited them.

a lot   *A lot* is informal for *a great deal* or *a great many.* Avoid using it in academic writing. If you must use it, write it as two words (never *alot*).

a.m., p.m.   Use these abbreviations only with numbers, not as substitutes for the words *morning, afternoon,* and *evening.* Some editors consider capital letters wrong for these abbreviations, yet many editors and dictionaries allow both. Whichever you choose, be consistent in each piece of writing.

- We will arrive in the **evening** [not *p.m.*], and we must leave by **8:00 a.m.**

among, amongst, between   Use *among* for three or more items. Use *between* for two items. American English prefers *among* to *amongst*.

- My three housemates discussed **among** [not *between* or *amongst*] themselves the choice **between** staying in college and getting full-time jobs.

amoral, immoral   *Amoral* means "neither moral (conforming to standards of rightness) nor immoral (the opposite of *moral*)." *Amoral* also means "without any sense of what's moral or immoral." *Immoral* means "morally wrong."

- Although many people consider birth control an **amoral** issue, the Catholic Church considers it **immoral.**

amount, number   Use *amount* for noncountable things (wealth, work, happiness). Use *number* for countable items.

- The **amount** of rice to cook depends on the **number** of guests.

an   See *a, an.*

and/or   This term is appropriate in business and legal writing when either or both of the two items can apply: *Sending messages is quicker by e-mail and/or fax.* In the humanities, writers usually express the alternatives in words: *Sending messages is quicker by e-mail, fax, or both.*

anymore   Use *anymore* with the meaning "now, any longer" only in negations or questions. In positive statements, instead of *anymore*, use an adverb such as *now.*

- No one wants to live without air conditioning **anymore.** Summers are so hot **now** [not *anymore*] that more people than ever suffer from heatstroke.

anyone, any one   *Anyone* is a singular indefinite pronoun meaning "any person at all." *Any one* (two words), an adjective that modifies a pronoun, means "a member of a group."

- **Anyone** could test-drive **any one** of the display vehicles.

anyplace   *Anyplace* is informal. Use *any place* or *anywhere* instead.

anyways, anywheres   *Anyways* and *anywheres* are nonstandard for *anyway* and *anywhere.*

apt, likely, liable   *Apt* and *likely* are used interchangeably. Strictly, *apt* indicates a tendency or inclination. *Likely* indicates a reasonable expectation or greater certainty than *apt* does. *Liable* usually denotes legal responsibility or implies unpleasant consequences but usage today allows it to mean *likely*.

- Evander is **apt** to run stop signs, so he'll **likely** get a ticket. That means he's **liable** for any consequences.

as, as if, as though, like   Use *as*, *as if*, or *as though*, but not *like*, when the words coming after include a verb.

- This hamburger tastes good, **as** [not *like*] a hamburger should. It tastes **as if** [or *as though*, not *like*] it were barbequed over charcoal, not gas.

Both *as* and *like* can function as prepositions in comparisons. However, use *as* to indicate equivalence between two nouns or pronouns, and use *like* to indicate similarity but not equivalence.

- My friend Roger served **as** [not *like*] mediator in a dispute about my neighbor's tree that dripped sap on my driveway **like** [not *as*] a leaky water faucet.

assure, ensure, insure   *Assure* means "promise; convince." *Ensure* and *insure* both mean "make certain or secure," but *insure* is reserved for financial or legal matters.

- The insurance agent **assured** me that he could **insure** my car, but only I could **ensure** that I would drive safely.

as to   *As to* is nonstandard for *about*.

awful, awfully   *Awful* is an adjective meaning "inspiring awe" and "creating fear." *Awfully* is an adverb meaning "in a way to inspire awe" and "terrifying." Only colloquially are *awful* and *awfully* used to mean "very" or "extremely."

- I was **extremely** [not *awfully*] tired yesterday.

a while, awhile   As two words, *a while* (an article and a noun) can function as a subject or object. As one word, *awhile* is an adverb. In a prepositional phrase, the correct form is *for a while, in a while,* or *after a while.*

- It took **a while** [article and noun] to drive to the zoo, where we saw the seals bask **awhile** [adverb modifying verb *bask*] in the sun after romping **for a while** [prepositional phrase] in the water.

backup, back up   As a noun, *backup* means "a replacement, fill-in, surrogate; a copy of computer files." As an adjective, *backup* means "alternate; alternative." As a verb, *back up* (two words) means "to serve as a substitute or support"; "to accumulate, as from a stoppage"; and "to make a backup copy of a computer disk or hard drive."

- I'll need a **backup** [noun] of your hard drive if I'm going to serve as your **backup** [adjective] computer consultant. I **back up** [verb] all computer disks and drives when I work with them.

bad, badly   *Bad* is an adjective only after linking verbs (*look, feel, smell, taste, sound;* these verbs can function as either linking verbs or action verbs depending on the context). *Badly* is an adverb; it's non-standard after linking verbs.

- Farmers feel **bad** [*feel* is a linking verb, so *bad* is the adjective] because a **bad** [adjective] drought is **badly** [adverb] damaging their crops.

been, being   *Been* and *being* cannot stand alone as main verbs. They work only with auxiliary verbs.

- You **are being** [not *being*] honest to admit that you **have been** [not *been*] tempted to eat the whole pie.

being as, being that   *Being as* and *being that* are nonstandard for *because* or *since.*

- We had to forfeit the game **because** [not *being as* or *being that*] our goalie was badly injured.

beside, besides   As prepositions, *beside* means "next to, by the side of," and *besides* means "other than, in addition to." As an adverb, *besides* means "also, moreover."

- She stood **beside** the new car, insisting that she would drive. No one **besides** her had a driver's license. **Besides,** she owned the car.

better, had better   *Better* is informal for *had better.*

- We **had better** [not *better* alone] be careful of the ice.

between   See *among, amongst, between.*

bias, biased   As a noun, *bias* means "a mental leaning for or against something or someone." As an adjective, *biased* means "prejudiced."As a verb, *bias* means "to be prejudiced." The past tense of this verb is *biased.*

- Horace's **bias** [noun] against federal-level politicians grew from his disapproval of their **biased** [adjective] attitudes toward certain foreign countries. Beverly was **biased** [verb] against all politicians, no matter their level.

breath, breathe   *Breath* is a noun; *breathe* is a verb.

- Take a deep **breath** [noun] before you start so that you can **breathe** [verb] normally afterward.

bring, take   *Bring* indicates movement from a distant place to a near place. *Take* indicates movement from a near to a distant place.

- If you **bring** over sandwiches, we'll have time to **take** [not *bring*] the dog to the vet.

but, however, yet   Use *but, however,* or *yet* alone, not in combination with each other.

- The economy is strong, **but** [not *but yet* or *but however*] unemployment is high.

calculate, figure   These are colloquial terms for *estimate, imagine, expect, think,* and the like.

can, may   *Can* signifies ability or capacity. *May* requests or grants permission. In negative expressions, *can* is acceptable for *may.*

- When you **can** [not *may*] get here on time, you **may** [not *can*] be excused early. However, if you are ***not*** on time, you **cannot** [or *may not*] expect privileges.

can't hardly, can't scarcely   These double negatives are nonstandard for *can hardly* and *can scarcely.*

capitol, capital   *Capitol* means "a building in which legislators meet." *Capital* means a city (Denver, the *capital* of Colorado), wealth, or "most important" (a *capital* offense).

- If the governor can find enough **capital,** the state legislature will agree to build a new **capitol** for our state.

censor, censure   The verb *censor* means "delete objectionable material; judge." The verb *censure* means "condemn or reprimand officially."

- The town council **censured** the mayor for trying to **censor** a report.

chairman, chairperson, chair   Many writers and speakers prefer the gender-neutral terms *chairperson* and *chair* to *chairman.* In general, *chair* is used more than *chairperson.*

choose, chose   *Choose* is the simple form of the verb. *Chose* is the past-tense form of the verb.

- I **chose** a movie last week, so you **choose** one tonight.

cite, site   The verb *cite* means "quote by way of example, authority, or proof." The noun *site* means "a particular place or location."

- The private investigator **cited** evidence from the crime **site** and the defendant's Web **site.**

cloth, clothe *Cloth* is a noun meaning "fabric." *Clothe* is a verb meaning "dress with garments or fabric."

■ "**Clothe** me in red velvet," proclaimed the king, and the royal tailors ran to gather samples of **cloth** to show him.

complement, compliment As a noun, *complement* means "something that goes well with or completes." As a noun, *compliment* means "praise, flattery." As a verb, *complement* means "brings to perfection; goes well with, completes." As a verb, *compliment* means "praise, flatter."

■ The dean's **compliment** was a perfect **complement** to the thrill of my graduating. My parents felt proud when she **complimented** me publicly, an honor that **complemented** their joy.

comprise, include See *include, comprise.*

conscience, conscious The noun *conscience* means "a sense of right and wrong." The adjective *conscious* means "being aware or awake."

■ Always be **conscious** of what your **conscience** is telling you.

consensus of opinion This phrase is redundant; use *consensus* only.

■ The legislature reached **consensus** on the issue of campaign reform.

continual(ly), continuous(ly) *Continual* means "occurring repeatedly." *Continuous* means "going on without interruption."

■ Larry needed intravenous fluids **continuously** for days, so the nurses **continually** monitored him.

could care less *Could care less* is nonstandard for *could not care less.*

could of *Could of* is nonstandard for *could have.*

couple, a couple of These terms are nonstandard for *a few* or *several.*

■ Rest here for **a few** [not *a couple* or *a couple of*] minutes.

criteria, criterion A *criterion* is "a standard of judgment." *Criteria* is the plural of *criterion.*

■ A sense of history is an important **criterion** for judging political candidates, but voters must consider other **criteria** as well.

data *Data* is the plural of *datum,* a word rarely used today. Informally, *data* is used as a singular noun that takes a singular verb. In academic or professional writing, *data* is considered plural and takes a plural verb (although this usage is currently viewed as overly formal by some).

■ The **data** suggest [not *suggests*] some people are addicted to e-mail.

different from, different than   In academic and professional writing, use *different from* even though *different than* is common in informal speech.

- Please advise us if your research yields data **different from** past results.

disinterested, uninterested   The preferred use of *disinterested* means "impartial, unbiased." Colloquially, *disinterested* can mean "not interested, indifferent," but in more formal contexts, *uninterested* is preferred for "not interested, indifferent."

- Jurors need to be **disinterested** in hearing evidence, but never **uninterested.**

don't   *Don't* is a contraction for *do not,* never for *does not* (its contraction is *doesn't*).

- She **doesn't** [not *don't*] like crowds.

effect   See *affect, effect.*

elicit, illicit   The verb *elicit* means "draw forth or bring out." The adjective *illicit* means "illegal."

- The senator's **illicit** conduct **elicited** a mass outcry from her constituents.

elude   See *allude, elude.*

emigrate (from), immigrate (to)   *Emigrate* means "leave one country to live in another." *Immigrate* means "enter a country to live there."

- My great-grandmother **emigrated** from Kiev, Russia, to London, England, in 1890. Then, she **immigrated** to Toronto, Canada, in 1892.

enclose, inclose; enclosure, inclosure   In American English, *enclose* and *enclosure* are the preferred spellings.

ensure   See *assure, ensure, insure.*

enthused   *Enthused* is nonstandard for *enthusiastic.*

- Adam was **enthusiastic** [not *enthused*] about the college he chose.

etc.   *Etc.* is the abbreviation for the Latin *et cetera,* meaning "and the rest." For writing in the humanities, avoid using *etc.* Acceptable substitutes are *and the like, and so on,* or *and so forth.*

everyday, every day   The adjective *everyday* means "daily." *Every day* (two words) is an adjective with a noun that can function as a subject or an object.

- Being late for work has become an **everyday** [adjective] occurrence for me. **Every day** [subject] brings me closer to being fired. I worry about it **every day** [object].

everyone, every one   *Everyone* is a singular, indefinite pronoun. *Every one* (two words) is an adjective and a pronoun, meaning "each member in a group."

- **Everyone** enjoyed **every one** of the comedy skits.

everywheres   *Everywheres* is nonstandard for *everywhere*.

except   See *accept, except.*

explicit, implicit   *Explicit* means "directly stated or expressed." *Implicit* means "implied, suggested."

- The warning on cigarette packs is **explicit:** "Smoking is dangerous to health." The **implicit** message is, "Don't smoke."

farther, further   Although many writers reserve *farther* for geographical distances and *further* for all other cases, current usage treats them as interchangeable.

fewer, less   Use *fewer* for anything that can be counted (that is, with count nouns): *fewer* dollars, *fewer* fleas, *fewer* haircuts. Use *less* with collective (or other noncount nouns): *less* money, *less* scratching, *less* hair.

firstly, secondly, thirdly   These are from British English. In American English, use *first, second,* and *third.*

former, latter   When two items are referred to, *former* signifies the first item and *latter* signifies the second item. Never use *former* and *latter* when referring to more than two items.

- Brazil and Ecuador are South American countries. Portuguese is the official language in the **former,** Spanish in the **latter.**

go, say   All forms of *go* are nonstandard when used in place of all forms of *say.*

- While stepping on my hand, Frank **says** [not *goes*], "Your hand is in my way."

gone, went   *Gone* is the past participle of *go; went* is the past tense of *go.*

■ They **went** [not *gone*] to the concert after Ira **had gone** [not *had went*] home.

good, well   *Good* is an adjective. As an adverb, *good* is nonstandard. Instead, use *well.*

■ **Good** [adjective] maintenance helps cars run **well** [adverb; not *good*].

good and   *Good and* is a nonstandard intensifier. Instead, use more precise words.

■ They were **exhausted** [not *good and tired*].

got, have   *Got* is nonstandard for *have.*

■ What do we **have** [not *got*] for supper?

hardly   Use *hardly* with *can,* never with *can't.*

have, of   Use *have,* not *of,* after such verbs as *could, should, would, might,* and *must.*

■ You ***should* have** [not *should of*] called first.

have got, have to, have got to   Avoid using *have got* when *have* alone delivers your meaning. Also, avoid using *have to* or *have got to* for *must.*

■ I **have** [not *have got*] several more sources to read. I **must** [not *have got to*] finish my reading today.

he/she, s/he, his/her   When using gender-neutral language, write out *he or she* or *his or her* instead of using and/or constructions. To be more concise, switch to plural pronouns and antecedents. (For more about gender-neutral language, see 21g.)

■ **Everyone** bowed ***his or her*** head. [***Everyone*** bowed **his** head is considered sexist language if women were present when the heads were bowed.]
■ The **people** bowed **their** heads.

historic, historical   The adjective *historic* means "important in history" or "highly memorable." The adjective *historical* means "relating to history." Use *a,* not *an,* before these words because they start with the consonant *h.*

hopefully   *Hopefully* is an adverb meaning "with hope, in a hopeful manner," so as an adverb, It can modify a verb, an adjective, or another adverb. However, *hopefully* is nonstandard as a sentence modifier meaning "we hope"; therefore, in academic writing, avoid this usage.

- They waited **hopefully** [adverb] for the crippled airplane to land. **We hope** [not *Hopefully,*] it will land safely.

humanity, humankind, humans, mankind   To use gender-neutral language, choose *humanity, humankind,* or *humans* instead of *mankind.*

- Some think that the computer has helped **humanity** more than any other twentieth-century invention.

i.e.   This abbreviation refers to the Latin term *id est.* In academic writing, use the English translation, *that is.*

if, whether   At the start of a noun clause that expresses speculation or unknown conditions, you can use either *if* or *whether.* However, in such conditional clauses use only *whether* (or *whether or not*) when alternatives are expressed or implied. In a conditional clause that does not express or imply alternatives, use only *if.*

- **If** [not *whether*] you promise not to step on my feet, I might dance with you. Still, I'm not sure **if** [or *whether*] I want to dance with you. Once I decide, I'll dance with you **whether** [not *If*] I like the music or **whether** [not *if*] the next song is fast or slow.

illicit   See *elicit, illicit.*

illusion   See *allusion, illusion.*

immigrate   See *emigrate, immigrate.*

immoral   See *amoral, immoral.*

imply, infer   *Imply* means "hint at or suggest." *Infer* means "draw a conclusion." A writer or speaker *implies;* a reader or listener *infers.*

- When the governor **implied** that she wouldn't seek reelection, reporters **inferred** that she was planning to run for vice president.

include, comprise   The verb *include* means "contain or regard as part of a whole." The verb *comprise* means "consist of or be composed of."

incredible, incredulous   *Incredible* means "extraordinary; not believable." *Incredulous* means "unable or unwilling to believe."

■ Listeners were **incredulous** as the freed hostages described the **incredible** hardships they had experienced.

in regard to, with regard to, as regards, regarding   Use *about, concerning,* and *for* in place of these wordy phrases. Also, avoid the nonstandard *as regards to.*

■ **Concerning** [not *in regard to, with regard to, as regards,* or *regarding*] your question, we can now confirm that your payment was received.

inside of, outside of   These phrases are nonstandard when used to mean *inside* or *outside.* When writing about time, never use *inside of* to mean "in less than."

■ She waited **outside** [not *outside of*] the apartment house. He changed to clothes that were more informal in **less than** [not *inside of*] ten minutes.

insure   See *assure, ensure, insure.*

irregardless   *Irregardless* is nonstandard for *regardless.*

is when, is where   Never use these constructions when you define something. Instead, use active verbs.

■ Defensive driving **involves staying** [not *is when you stay*] alert.

its, it's   *Its* is a personal pronoun in the possessive case. *It's* is a contraction of *it is.*

■ The dog buried **its** bone today. **It's** hot today, which makes the dog restless.

kind, sort   Combine *kind* and *sort* with *this* or *that* when referring to singular nouns. Combine *kinds* and *sorts* with *these* or *those* when referring to plural nouns. Also, never use *a* or *an* after *kind of* or *sort of.*

■ To stay cool, drink **these kinds** of fluids [not *this kind*] for **this sort of** day [not *this sort of a*].

kind of, sort of   These phrases are colloquial adverbs. In academic writing, use *somewhat.*

■ The campers were **somewhat** [not *kind of*] dehydrated after the hike.

later, latter   *Later* means "after some time; subsequently." *Latter* refers to the second of two items.

■ The college library stays open **later** than the town library; also, the **latter** is closed on weekends.

lay, lie   The verb *lay* (**lay,** *laid, laid, laying*) means "place or put some-thing, usually on something else" and needs a direct object. The verb *lie* (**lie,** *lay, lain, lying*), meaning "recline," doesn't need a direct object. Substituting *lay* for *lie,* or the opposite, is nonstandard.

- ■   **Lay** [not *lie*] down the blanket [direct object], and then place the baby to **lie** [not *lay*] in the shade.

leave, let   *Leave* means "depart." *Leave* is nonstandard for *let. Let* means "allow, permit."

- ■   Could you **let** [not *leave*] me use your car tonight?

less   See *fewer, less.*

lie   See *lay, lie.*

like   See *as, as if, as though, like.*

likely   See *apt, likely, liable.*

lots, lots of, a lot of   These are colloquial constructions. Instead, use *many, much,* or *a great deal.*

mankind   See *humanity, humankind, humans, mankind.*

may   See *can, may.*

maybe, may be   *Maybe* is an adverb; *may be* (two words) is a verb phrase.

- ■   **Maybe** [adverb] we can win, but our team **may be** [verb phrase] too tired.

may of, might of   *May of* and *might of* are nonstandard for *may have* and *might have.*

media   *Media* is the plural of *medium,* yet colloquial usage now pairs it with a singular verb: *The media saturates us with information about every fire.*

morale, moral   *Morale* is a noun meaning "a mental state relating to courage, confidence, or enthusiasm." As a noun, *moral* means an "ethi-cal lesson implied or taught by a story or event." As an adjective, *moral* means "ethical."

- ■   One **moral** [noun] of the story is that many people who suffer from low **morale** [noun] still abide by high **moral** [adjective] standards.

most   *Most* is nonstandard for *almost.* Also, *most* is the superlative form of an adjective (*some* words, *more* words, ***most*** words) and of adverbs (*most* suddenly).

- **Almost** [not *Most*] all writers agree that Shakespeare penned the **most** [adjective] brilliant plays ever written.

Ms.   *Ms.* is a woman's title free of reference to marital status, equivalent to *Mr.* for men. Generally, use *Ms.* unless a woman requests *Miss* or *Mrs.*

must of   *Must of* is nonstandard for *must have.*

nowheres   *Nowheres* is nonstandard for *nowhere.*

number   See *amount, number.*

of   Use *have,* not *of,* after modal auxiliary verbs (*could, may, might, must, should, would*). See also *could of; may of, might of; must of; should of; would of.*

off of   *Off of* is nonstandard for *off.*

- Don't fall **off** [not *off of*] the stage.

OK, O.K., okay   These three forms are informal. In academic writing, choose words that express more specific meanings. If you must use the term, choose the full word *okay.*

- The weather was **suitable** [not *okay*] for a picnic.

on account of, owing to the fact that   Use *because* or *because of* in place of these wordy phrases.

- **Because of the rain** [not *On account of the rain* or *Owing to the fact that it rained*], the picnic was cancelled.

oral, verbal   The adjective *oral* means "spoken or being done by the mouth." The adjective *verbal* means "relating to language" (*verbal* skill) or to words rather than actions, facts, or ideas.

outside of   See *inside of, outside of.*

percent, percentage   Use *percent* with specific numbers: two *percent,* 95 *percent.* Use *percentage* to refer to portions of a whole in general terms.

- Of the eligible U.S. population, **35 percent** votes regularly in national elections. In local elections, **the percentage** [not *the percent*] is much lower.

pixel, pixelation, pixilated   *Pixel,* a relatively new word created from "picture/pix" and "element," is the name for a small dot on a video screen. *Pixelation* (with an *e*, as in *pixel*) is a noun meaning "a film technique that makes people appear to move faster than they are." *Pixilated* (with an *i*), a verb unrelated to *pixels*, derives from *pixie*, meaning "a mischievous elf," and now describes someone who is slightly drunk.

plus   *Plus* is nonstandard for *and, also, in addition*, and *moreover.*
- The band booked three concerts in Hungary, **and** [not *plus*] it will tour Poland for a month. **In addition,** [not *Plus,*] it may perform once in Austria.

precede, proceed   *Precede* is a verb that means "go before." *Proceed* is a verb that means "to advance, go on, undertake, carry on."
- **Preceded** by elephants and music, the ringmaster **proceeded** into the main tent.

pretty   *Pretty* is informal for *rather, quite, somewhat*, or *very*.
- The flu epidemic was **quite** [not *pretty*] severe.

principal, principle   As a noun, *principal* means "chief person; main or original amount." As an adjective, *principal* means "most important." *Principle* is a noun that means "a basic truth or rule."
- During the assembly, the **principal** [noun] said, "A **principal** [adjective] value in our democracy is the **principle** [noun] of free speech."

proceed   See *precede, proceed*.

quotation, quote   *Quotation* is a noun, and *quote* is a verb. Don't use *quote* as a noun.
- One newspaper reporter **quoted** [verb] the U.S. President, and soon the **quotations** [noun—not *quotes,* which is a verb] were widely broadcast.

raise, rise   *Raise* is a verb (***raise,** raised, raising*) that means "lift" or "construct" and needs a direct object. *Rise* (***rise,** rose, risen, rising*) means "go upward" and doesn't need a direct object. Substituting *rise* for *raise*, or the opposite, is nonstandard.
- When the soldiers **rise** [not *raise*] early, they **raise** [not *rise* or *rise up*] the flag of liberty.

real, really   These words are nonstandard for *very* and *extremely*.

reason is because   This phrase is redundant. To be concise and correct, use *reason is that*.
- One **reason** we moved **is that** [not *is because*] our factory was relocated.

reason why This phrase is redundant. To be concise and correct, use *reason* or *why*.

- I don't know **why** [not *the reason why*] they left home.

regarding See *in regard to, with regard to, as regards, regarding*.

regardless See *irregardless*.

respectful, respectfully As an adjective, *respectful* means "marked by, shows regard for, or gives honor to." *Respectfully* is the adverb form of *respectful*. Be careful not to confuse these words with *respective* and *respectively* (see next entry).

- The child listened **respectfully** [adverb] to the lecture about **respectful** [adjective] behavior.

respective, respectively *Respective,* a noun, refers to two or more individual persons or things. *Respectively,* an adverb, refers back to two or more individuals or things in the same sequence that they were originally mentioned.

- After the fire drill, Dr. Daniel Eagle and Dr. Jessica Chess returned to their **respective** offices [that is, he returned to his office, and she returned to her office] on the second and third floors, **respectively** [his office is on the second floor, and her office is on the third floor].

right *Right* is sometimes used colloquially for *quite, very, extremely,* or similar intensifiers.

- You did **very** [not *right*] well on the quiz.

rise See *raise, rise*.

scarcely Use *scarcely* with *can*, never with *can't*.

secondly See *firstly, secondly, thirdly*.

seen *Seen* is the past participle of the verb *see* (*see, saw,* **seen,** *seeing*). *Seen* is nonstandard for *saw,* a verb in the past tense. Always use *seen* with an auxiliary verb.

- Last night, I **saw** [not *seen*] the movie that you **had** seen [not *seen*] last week.

set, sit The verb *set* (**set,** *setting*) means "put in place, position, put down" and needs a direct object. The verb *sit* (**sit,** *sat, sitting*) means "be seated" and doesn't need a direct object. Substituting *set* for *sit*, and the opposite, is nonstandard.

- Susan **set** [not *sat*] the sandwiches beside the salad, made Spot **sit** [not *set*] down, and then **sat** [not *set*] on the sofa.

shall, will, should   *Shall* was once used with *I* and *we* for future-tense verbs, and *will* was used for all other persons. Today, *shall* is considered highly formal, and *will* is more widely used. Similarly, distinctions were once made between *shall* and *should*, but today *should* is preferred. However, in questions, *should* is used about as often as *shall*.

- We **will** [or *shall*] depart on Monday, but he **will** [never *shall*] wait until Thursday to depart. **Should** [or *Shall*] I telephone ahead to reserve a suite at the hotel?

should of   *Should of* is nonstandard for *should have*.

sit   See *set, sit*.

site   See *cite, site*.

sometime, sometimes, some time   The adverb *sometime* means "at an unspecified time." The adverb *sometimes* means "now and then." *Some time* (two words) is an adjective with a noun that means "an amount or span of time."

- **Sometime** [adverb for "at an unspecified time"] next year, I must take my qualifying exams. I **sometimes** [adverb for "now and then"] worry whether I'll find **some time** [adjective with a noun] to study for them.

sort of   See *kind of, sort of*.

stationary, stationery   *Stationary* means "not moving; unchanging." *Stationery* refers to paper and related writing products.

- Using our firm's **stationery**, I wrote to city officials about a **stationary** light pole that had been knocked over in a car accident.

such   *Such* is informal for intensifiers such as *very* and *extremely*. However, *such* is acceptable to mean "of the same or similar kind."

- The play got **very** [not *such*] bad reviews. The playwright was embarrassed by **such** strong criticism.

supposed to, used to   The final *-d* is essential in both phrases.

- We were **supposed** to [not *suppose to*] leave early. I **used to** [not *use to*] wake up before the alarm rang.

sure   *Sure* is nonstandard for *surely* or *certainly*.

- I was **certainly** [not *sure*] surprised at the results.

sure and, try and   Both phrases are nonstandard for *sure to* and *try to*.

- Please **try to** [not *try and*] reach my doctor.

than, then   *Than* indicates comparison; *then* relates to time.

- Please put on your gloves, and **then** your hat. It's colder outside **than** you think.

that, which   Use *that* with restrictive (essential) clauses only. You can use *which* with both restrictive and nonrestrictive (nonessential) clauses; however, many people reserve *which* to use only with nonrestrictive clauses.

- The house **that** [or *which*] Jack built is on Beanstalk Street, **which** [not *that*] runs past the reservoir.

that there, them there, this here, these here   These phrases are nonstandard for *that, them, this, these,* respectively.

their, there, they're   *Their* is a possessive pronoun. *There* means "in that place" or is part of an expletive construction. *They're* is a contraction of *they are*.

- **They're** going to **their** accounting class in the building over **there** near the library. Do you know that **there** are twelve sections of Accounting 101?

theirself, theirselves, themself   These words are nonstandard for *themselves*.

them   Use *them* as an object pronoun only. Do not use *them* in place of the adjectives *these* and *those*.

- Let's buy **those** [not *them*] delicious looking strawberries.

then   See *than, then*.

thirdly   See *firstly, secondly, thirdly*.

thusly   *Thusly* is nonstandard for *thus*.

till, until   Both are acceptable, although *until* is preferred for academic writing.

to, too, two   *To* is a preposition. *Too* is an adverb meaning "also; more than enough." *Two* is a number.

- When you go **to** Chicago, visit the Art Institute. Try **to** visit Harry Caray's for dinner, **too.** It won't be **too** expensive because **two** people can share a meal.

toward, towards   Although both are acceptable, writers of American English generally prefer *toward*.

try and, sure and   See *sure and, try and*.

type   *Type* is nonstandard when used to mean *type of*.
- I recommend that you use only that **type of** [not *type*] glue on plastic.

unique   Never combine *unique* with *more, most,* or other qualifiers.
- Solar heating is **unique** [not *somewhat unique*] in the Northeast. One **unique** [not *very unique*] heating system in a Vermont house uses hydrogen for fuel.

uninterested   See *disinterested, uninterested*.

used to   See *supposed to, used to*.

utilize   *Utilize* is considered an overblown word for *use* in academic writing.
- The team **used** [not *utilized*] all its players to win the game.

verbal, oral   See *oral, verbal*.

wait on   *Wait on* is an informal substitute for *wait for. Wait on* is appropriate only when people give service to others.
- I had to **wait for** [not *wait on*] half an hour for the hotel desk clerk to **wait on** me.

way, ways   When referring to distance, use *way* rather than *ways*.
- He is a long **way** [not *ways*] from home.

Web site, website   Usage at the time of this book's publication calls for two words and a capital *W*. Increasingly, the informal *website* is being used.

well   See *good, well*.

where   *Where* is nonstandard for *that* when *where* is used as a subordinating conjunction.
- I read **that** [not *where*] salt raises blood pressure.

where . . . at   This phrase is redundant; use only *where*.
- **Where** is your house? [not *Where is your house at?*]

whether   See *if, whether*.

which See *that, which*.

who, whom Use *who* as a subject or a subject complement; use *whom* as an object (see 9g).

who's, whose *Who's* is the contraction of *who is*. *Whose* is a possessive pronoun.
- **Who's** willing to drive? **Whose** truck should we take?

will See *shall, will*.

-wise The suffix *-wise* means "in a manner, direction, or position." Never attach *-wise* indiscriminately to create new words. Instead, choose words that already exist; when in doubt, consult a dictionary to see if the *-wise* word you have in mind is acceptable.

World Wide Web Written out, the three words start with a capital *W*. Its abbreviation only in URLs is *www*. When you use only the word *Web*, start it with a capital *W*.

would of *Would of* is nonstandard for *would have*.

your, you're *Your* is a possessive. *You're* is the contraction of *you are*.
- **You're** kind to volunteer **your** time at the senior center.

Chapter 21

The Impact of Words

21a What is American English?

Evolving over centuries into a rich language, **American English** is the variation of English spoken in the United States. It demonstrates that many cultures have created the U.S. "melting pot" society. Food names, for example, reflect that Africans brought the words *okra, gumbo,* and *goober* (peanut); Spanish and Latin American peoples contributed *tortilla, taco, burrito,* and *enchilada.* Greek speakers gave us *pita,* Cantonese speakers *chow,* and Japanese speakers *sushi.*

In all languages, the meanings of some words change with time. For example, W. Nelson Francis points out in *The English Language* (New York: Norton, 1965) that the word *nice* "has been used at one time or another in its 700-year history to mean: *foolish, wanton, strange, lazy, coy, modest, fastidious, refined, precise, subtle, slender, critical, attentive, minutely accurate, dainty, appetizing, agreeable.*"

21b What are levels of formality in language?

Levels of formality in DICTION and SENTENCE VARIETY can be divided into three levels: highly informal (an e-mail or a letter to a friend); highly formal (the language of ceremony, written and often spoken); and medium or semiformal (ACADEMIC WRITING). A medium or semiformal level is expected in academic writing because its TONE is reasonable and evenhanded, its writing style clear and efficient, and its word choice appropriate for an academic audience.

INFORMAL	Stars? Wow! They're, like, made of gas!
MEDIUM OR SEMIFORMAL	Gas clouds slowly transformed into stars.
FORMAL	The condensations of gas spun their slow gravitational pirouettes, slowly transmogrifying gas cloud into star.

—Carl Sagan, "Starfolk: A Fable"

363

After analyzing the sentences that follow, decide if they are in formal, medium, or informal language. Which words are particularly effective in establishing the level of usage in the sentence?

1. Weather forecasting is a pretty good field to be in.

2. My old man watches the TV weather news every morning.

3. It takes a whole lot of work to put a forecast together.

4. The Weather Bureau collects data from reporting stations that, after analysis, are reported to the public as forecasts, weather maps, and storm warnings.

5. The bureau conducts research on a variety of topics, from solar radiation and the ozone layer to snowfall patterns.

6. My father just wants to know if it's going to rain.

7. I can't get into all that stuff either.

8. You gotta admit that the bureau has done plenty of good things.

9. In 1942, Dr. F. W. Reichelderfer was the recipient of a prestigious award for his pioneering work in advancing the practice of meteorology as it is applied to aeronautics.

Answers to Extra Exercise A

1. Informal: *pretty good, be in*

2. Informal: *old man, TV*

3. Informal: *a whole lot of*

4. Formal: *collects data*

5. Medium: familiar words, but no slang, throughout

6. Medium: *just wants to know, it's, going to*

7. Informal: *get into, all that stuff*

8. Informal: *gotta, plenty, good things*

9. Formal: *recipient, prestigious award, practice of meteorology, applied to aeronautics*

In the informal example, the writer's attitude toward the subject is playful and humorous, so it's appropriate when writing to a close friend or in a journal. In the medium or semiformal example, the writer's attitude toward the subject is straightforward, so it's appropriate for most academic and professional situations. In the formal example, the writer's words are appropriate for readers who know about scientific phenomena and understand FIGURATIVE LANGUAGE.

21c   What is edited American English?

Edited American English, also known as STANDARD ENGLISH, reflects the standards of the written language expected of a textbook; these standards apply in magazines such as *U.S. News and World Report* and *National Geographic;* in newspapers such as the *Washington Post* and the *Wall Street Journal;* and in most nonfiction books. With edited American English, you can achieve the medium or semiformal language level required in ACADEMIC WRITING.

Edited American English isn't a special or fancy dialect for elite groups. Rather, it's a form of the language used by educated people to standardize communication in the larger world. Edited American English conforms to widely established rules of grammar, sentence structure, punctuation, and spelling—as covered in this handbook.

Nonstandard English is legitimately spoken by some groups in our society. With its own grammar and usage customs, it communicates clearly to other speakers of nonstandard English. Yet, one thing is certain: Speakers of nonstandard English often benefit when they can switch, either temporarily or permanently, to the medium or semiformal level of language (21b) required in academic writing. This means that speakers of nonstandard English never need to reject their preferred or home language. Indeed, it's the right of all individuals to decide what works for them in various situations in their lives, and the ability to "code switch" gives them options.

Also, advertising language and other writing intended for a large, diverse audience might ignore the conventions of edited American English. Such published, nonstandard departures from edited American English are not appropriate in academic writing.

21d   What is figurative language?

Figurative language uses words for more than their literal meanings. Such words aren't merely decorative or pretentious (21h). Figurative language greatly enhances meaning. It makes comparisons and connections that draw on one idea or image to explain another. Box 91 explains the different types of figurative language and describes one type you should avoid, the **mixed metaphor**.

BOX 91   SUMMARY

 Types of figurative language

- **Analogy:** Comparing similar traits shared by dissimilar things or ideas. Its length can vary from one sentence (which often takes the form of a simile or metaphor) to a paragraph.

  A **cheetah sprinting across the dry plains** after its prey, the **base runner dashed** for home plate, cleats kicking up dust.

- **Irony:** Using words to suggest the opposite of their usual sense.

  Told that a minor repair on her home would cost $2,000 and take two weeks, she said, **"Oh, how nice!"**

- **Metaphor:** Comparing otherwise dissimilar things. A metaphor doesn't use the word *like* or *as* to make a comparison.

  Rush-hour **traffic** in the city **bled out through major arteries** to the suburbs.

- **Personification:** Assigning a human trait to something not human. (See below about not using mixed metaphors.)

  The **book begged** to be read.

- **Overstatement** (also called *hyperbole*): Exaggerating deliberately for emphasis.

  If this paper is late, the professor will **kill** me.

- **Simile:** Comparing dissimilar things. A simile uses the word *like* or *as*.

  Langston Hughes observes that a deferred **dream dries up "like a raisin in the sun."**

- **Understatement:** Emphasizing by using deliberate restraint.

  It feels **warm** when the temperature reaches **105 degrees.**

- **Mixed metaphor:** Combining two or more inconsistent images in one sentence or expression. Never use a mixed metaphor.

  NO   The violence of the hurricane reminded me of a train ride.
  [A train ride is not violent, stormy, or destructive.]

  YES   The violence of the hurricane reminded me of a train's crashing into a huge tractor trailer.

TEACHING TIP

TEACHING TIP

Sports has been a fertile field for metaphor in America. You might remind your students of these common metaphors. What does each mean within its sport? What does each mean in a general context? You might want to ask students if they can add to the lists or start lists for other sports or interests. Many metaphors listed here are discussed in Tim Considine's "Starting from Scratch" (*New York Times,* June 8, 1985).

> *Soccer:* kick off, get the ball rolling
> *Baseball:* right off the bat, off base, touch base with, go to bat for, out of left field, drop the ball
> *Football:* huddle, chalk talk, a flag on the play, all-American
> *Boxing:* answer the bell, a low blow, hitting below the belt, on the ropes

ANSWERS: EXERCISE 21-1

1. mixed metaphor; We stand with one foot in the twentieth century and one in the twenty-first. [Answers to the correction will vary.]

2. simile

3. overstatement

4. irony

5. personification

6. simile

7. analogy

8. irony

9. overstatement

10. metaphor

WORD DERIVATION

The etymology of *Rhode Island* is a mystery. There are two theories. According to one, Italian explorer Giovanni da Verrazano saw a resemblance between the island on which the city of Newport is now located and the Greek island of Rhodes. According to the second, Dutch explorers named the area *Roode Eylandt* ("red island") because of its red clay soil.

EXERCISE 21-1

Working individually or with a group, identify each figure of speech. Also, revise any mixed metaphors. For help, consult 21d.

1. In the year 2000, we stood with one foot in the twentieth century while we set sail on the sea of a new era in the twenty-first.
2. Having spent the whole day on the beach, he came home as red as a lobster.
3. If I eat one more bite of that chocolate cake, I'll explode.
4. What I love best about you is that you use all the hot water every time you take a shower.
5. The daisies nodded their heads in the hot sun.
6. Beginning to testify in the courtroom, the defendant was as nervous as a long-tailed cat in a roomful of rocking chairs.
7. Think of the environment as a human body, where small problems in one part do not much affect other parts, any more than a paper cut causes most of us more than an instant's pain and a heartfelt "Ouch!" Problems throughout a system like the air or the oceans, however—say, pollution building up beyond the system's ability to cleanse itself—can kill the entire organism just as surely as cholesterol building up in arteries can kill you or me.
8. The actor displayed the entire range of human emotions from A to B.
9. My heart stopped when I opened the gift my parents gave me.
10. Our supervisor said that reorganizing the department according to our recommendations would be trading a headache for an upset stomach.

21e How can using exact diction enhance my writing?

Diction, the term for choice of words, affects the clarity and impact of any writing you do. Your best chance of delivering your intended message to your readers is to choose words that fit exactly with each piece of writing. To choose words correctly—that is, to have good diction—you need to understand the concepts of *denotation* and *connotation* in words.

21e.1 What is denotation in words?

The **denotation** of a word is its exact, literal meaning. It's the meaning you find when you look up the word in a dictionary. Readers expect you to use words according to their established meanings for their established functions.

Using dictionaries

A dictionary is your ultimate authority for a word's denotation—that is, its definition. The reference section in most college libraries includes one or more kinds of dictionaries for general use and for specialized areas.

■ An **unabridged dictionary** contains the most extensive, complete, and scholarly entries. *Unabridged* means "not shortened." Such dictionaries include all infrequently used words that abridged dictionaries often omit. The most comprehensive, authoritative unabridged dictionary of English is the *Oxford English Dictionary* (OED), which traces each word's history and gives quotations to illustrate changes in meaning and spelling over the life of the word.

■ An **abridged dictionary** contains most commonly used words. *Abridged* means "shortened." When an abridged dictionary serves the needs of most college students, the dictionaries are referred to as "college editions." Typical of these is *Merriam-Webster's Collegiate Dictionary* (at <http://www.m-w.com/netdict.htm> online and also in print) and *The New American Webster Handy College Dictionary.*

■ A **specialized dictionary** focuses on a single area of language. You can find dictionaries of slang (for example, *Dictionary of Slang and Unconventional English*, ed. Eric Partridge); word origins (for example, *Dictionary of Word and Phrase Origins*, ed. William Morris and Mary Morris); synonyms (for example, *Roget's 21st Century Thesaurus*), usage (for example, *Modern American Usage: A Guide,* ed. Jacques Barzun); idioms (for example, *A Dictionary of American Idioms*, by Adam Makkai); regionalisms (for example, *Dictionary of American Regional English*, ed. Frederic Cassidy); and many others.

ESL NOTE: *The Dictionary of American English* (Boston: Heinle & Heinle, distributed by Berlitz, 2000) is particularly useful for students who speak English as a second (or third, etc.) language.

21e.2 What is connotation in words?

Connotation refers to ideas implied by a word. Connotations are never completely fixed, for they can vary in differing contexts. Connotations involve associations and emotional overtones that go beyond a word's definition. For example, *home* usually evokes more emotion than its denotation "a dwelling place" or its synonym *house. Home* carries the connotation, for some, of the pleasures of warmth, security, and love of family. For others, however, *home* may carry unpleasant connotations, such as abusive experiences or the impersonal atmosphere of an institution to house the elderly.

EXTRA EXERCISE C

List two synonyms for each of the following words. On the basis of information that you can find about them in a dictionary, explain the differences between the pairs of synonyms. (Answers will vary.)

1. indulge
2. egotism
3. lazy
4. fame
5. friendly
6. frugal
7. red
8. good
9. govern
10. industry

ANSWERS: EXERCISE 21-2

The response to this exercise is likely to elicit much debate, given that shades of connotative meaning are often fairly personal. The following are some possible answers.

1. *Positive:* harmony, melody; *Neutral:* sound, music, pitch, voice; *Negative:* racket, shriek, noise

2. *Positive:* articulate, eloquent, fluent; *Neutral:* vocal, talkative, verbose; *Negative:* chattering, gossipy, gabby

3. *Positive:* beautiful, dazzling, elegant, sparkling; *Neutral:* decorative, modern, ornate; *Negative:* overelaborate, flashy

4. *Positive:* enduring, unbreakable; *Neutral:* long, continued, stretched; *Negative:* lingering, drawn-out, never-ending, incessant

5. *Positive:* ingenious, keen, sensible; *Neutral:* shrewd, crafty, smooth; *Negative:* calculating, sly, underhanded

Using a thesaurus

Sometimes a good college dictionary explains the small differences among synonyms, but a thesaurus is devoted entirely to providing synonyms for words. In distinguishing among **synonyms**—the other words close in meaning to a word—a thesaurus demonstrates connotation in operation. As you use a thesaurus, remain very alert to the subtle shades of meaning that create distinctions among words. For instance, using *notorious* to describe a person famous for praiseworthy achievements in public life is wrong. Although *notorious* means "well-known" and "publicly discussed"—which is true of famous people—the connotation of the word is "unfavorably known or talked about." George Washington is famous, not notorious. Al Capone, by contrast, is notorious.

Here's another example with the word *obdurate*, which means "not easily moved to pity or sympathy." Its synonyms include *inflexible, obstinate, stubborn,* and *hardened.*

NO	Footprints showed in the **obdurate** concrete.
YES	The supervisor remained **obdurate** in refusing to accept excuses.
YES	My **obdurate** roommates won't let my pet boa constrictor live in the bathtub.

👁 **ALERT:** Most word processing programs include a thesaurus. But be cautious in using it. Unless you know the exact meaning of an offered synonym, as well as its part of speech, you may choose a wrong word or introduce a grammatical error into your writing. For example, one word processing program's thesaurus offers these synonyms for *deep* in the sense of "low (down, inside)": *low, below, beneath,* and *subterranean.* None of these words could replace *deep* in a sentence such as *The crater is too deep* [not *too low, too below, too beneath,* or *too subterranean*] *to be filled with sand or rocks.* 👁

EXERCISE 21-2

Working individually or with a group, look at each list of words, and divide the words among three headings: "Positive" (good connotations); "Negative" (bad connotations); and "Neutral" (no connotations). If you think that a word belongs under more than one heading, you can assign it more than once, but be ready to explain your thinking. For help, consult a good dictionary and 21e.2.

EXAMPLE   grand, big, bulky, significant, oversized

Positive: grand, significant; *Negative:* bulky, oversized; *Neutral:* big

1. harmony, sound, racket, shriek, melody, music, noise, pitch, voice
2. talkative, articulate, chattering, eloquent, vocal, verbose, gossipy, fluent, gabby
3. decorative, beautiful, modern, ornate, overelaborate, dazzling, flashy, elegant, sparkling
4. long, lingering, enduring, continued, drawn-out, stretched, never-ending, unbreakable, incessant
5. calculating, shrewd, crafty, ingenious, keen, sensible, sly, smooth, underhanded

21f How can using specific words enhance my writing?

Specific words identify individual items in a group (*Buick, Honda*). **General words** relate to an overall group (*car*). **Concrete words** identify what can be perceived by the senses, by being seen, heard, tasted, felt, smelled (*black padded leather dashboard*), and convey specific images and details. **Abstract words** denote qualities (*kind*), concepts (*speed*), relationships (*friends*), acts (*cooking*), conditions (*bad weather*), and ideas (*transportation*) and are more general.

Usually, specific and concrete words bring life to general and abstract words. Therefore, whenever you use general and abstract words, try to supply enough specific, concrete details and examples to illustrate them. Here are sentences with general words that come to life when revised with specific words.

GENERAL	His car gets good gas mileage.
SPECIFIC	His Slurpo gets about 35 mpg on the highway and 30 mpg in the city.
GENERAL	Her car is comfortable and easy to drive.
SPECIFIC	When she drives her new Cushia on a five-hour trip, she arrives refreshed and does not need a long nap to recover, as she did when she drove her ten-year-old Upushme.

What separates most good writing from bad is the writer's ability to move back and forth between the general and abstract and the specific and concrete. Consider these sentences that effectively use a combination of general and specific words to compare cars:

GENERAL   CONCRETE   ┌──── SPECIFIC ────┐   ABSTRACT
My car, a midnight black Corvette LS1 convertible, has a powerful

---

TEACHING TIP

A host of new words has been added to the English language in the past few decades. Modern science and technology, in particular, have been responsible for enriching our vocabularies both by creating new terms and by making many old words new by using them in surprising ways. The names of various experiments in space, for example, were drawn from classical mythology. Students can become aware of the evolving history of the language by collecting terms and phrases in current usage that their parents would not have known when they were children or terms that would have carried a different meaning back then.

QUOTATION: ON WRITING

I hear things in a kinesthetic way. I tap into a rhythm of language to portray what I feel.
—Mary Gordon

TEACHING TIP

To underscore the importance of subtle shades of meaning and connotation, you might ask your students how they would react to each of the following statements. Once their egos are involved, students quickly see that not all synonyms are equivalent.

You are wrong.
You are incorrect.
What you say is false.
You are inaccurate.
You are imprecise.
You are evil.
You are improper.
You are unethical.
You are unrighteous.
You are bad.
You are willfully misleading.

ANSWERS: EXERCISE 21-3

Because of the many possibilities for rewording posed by this exercise, answers are likely to vary widely. Students may enjoy comparing the different choices they have made. The important principle for revision is that the new versions should have a high degree of specificity and concreteness. Here is an example of an acceptable response.

I hope to get a job as an administrative assistant in the textbook division of a major publishing company. At the interview, the supervisor of my position was easy to relate to and supportive. We seemed to be able to talk to each other easily, and she even laughed at my jokes. The other assistants in the division appeared to be friendly, interesting people. My college courses in writing, Web design, and communications have clearly prepared me to perform the tasks required for the position, such as composing memos, designing brochures, and working with authors. I think the job would teach me a great deal about the process of book publishing. The salary is $100 per month less than I had hoped for, but the Human Resources interviewer promised me moderate raises every six months if my work is well liked by my boss. Also, my daily drive to work would take about 20 minutes, which is quite reasonable for me. If my interviewer calls to offer me the job, I will happily accept it without hesitation.

```
┌──SPECIFIC──┐   GENERAL   SPECIFIC   GENERAL
```
5.7 liter, V8 engine with ride controls, the Tour for regular driving and
```
SPECIFIC     ┌──CONCRETE──┐                GENERAL
```
the Sport for a close-to-the-road feel. In contrast, Harvey's automobile,
```
CONCRETE ┌──────SPECIFIC──────┐        ABSTRACT
```
a bright red Dodge Viper SRT-10 convertible, has a mighty
```
┌──────────────SPECIFIC──────────────┐
```
8.3 liter, V10 engine with 6-speed manual transmission.

EXERCISE 21-3

Revise this paragraph by providing specific and concrete words and phrases to explain and enliven the ideas presented here in general and abstract language. You may revise the sentences to accommodate your changes in language. For help, consult 21f.

I hope to get a job as an administrative assistant in the company. At the interview, the person who would be my supervisor was pleasant. We seemed to get along well. The other assistants in the division appeared to be nice. My college courses clearly have prepared me for the position. I think the job would teach me a great deal more. The salary is a bit less than I had hoped for, but the Human Resources representative promised me raises at regular intervals if my work is good. Also, my trip to work would not take too much time for me. If my interviewer calls to offer me the job, I will accept it.

21g What is gender-neutral language?

Gender-neutral language, also referred to as gender-free or *nonsexist language*, relies on terms that don't communicate whether the person is male or female (for example, in replacing *policeman* with *police officer* or *doctors' wives* with *doctors' spouses*).

Sexist language assigns roles or characteristics to people based on their sex and gender. Most women and men today feel that sexist language unfairly discriminates against both sexes. It inaccurately assumes that every nurse and homemaker is female (and therefore referred to as "she"), and that every physician and stockbroker is male (and therefore referred to as "he"). One common instance of sexist language occurs when the pronoun *he* is used to refer to someone whose sex is unknown or irrelevant. Although tradition holds that *he* is correct in such situations, many men and women find it offensive. Using only masculine pronouns to represent all humans excludes women and thereby distorts reality.

Gender-neutral language rejects demeaning STEREOTYPES or outdated assumptions, such as "women are bad drivers," "men can't cook," and "all children have two parents." In your writing, never describe women's looks, clothes, or age unless you do the same for men. Never use a title for one spouse and the first name for the other spouse: *Phil Miller* (not *Mr. Miller*) and *his wife, Jeannette,* travel on separate planes; or *Jeannette and Phil Miller* live in Idaho. Box 92 gives you guidelines for using gender-neutral language.

 ### How to avoid sexist language

- Avoid using only the masculine pronoun to refer to males and females together. The *he or she* and *his or hers* constructions act as SINGULAR PRONOUNS, and they therefore call for SINGULAR VERBS. Try to avoid using *he or she* constructions, especially more than once in a sentence or in consecutive sentences. A better solution is revising to the plural. You can also revise to omit the gender-specific pronoun.

    NO   A **doctor** has little time to read outside **his** specialty.

    YES   A **doctor** has little time to read outside **his or her** specialty.

    NO   A successful **stockbroker** knows **he** has to work long hours.

    YES   Successful **stockbrokers** know **they** have to work long hours.

    NO   **Everyone** hopes that **he or she** will win the scholarship.

    YES   **Everyone** hopes to win the scholarship.

- Avoid using *man* when referring to both men and women.

    NO   **Man** is a social animal.

    YES   **People** are social animals.

    NO   The history of **mankind** is predominately violent.

    YES   **Human** history is predominately violent.

    NO   Dogs are **men's** best friends.

    YES   Dogs are **people's** best friends.

- Avoid stereotyping jobs and roles by gender when referring to both men and women.

NO	**YES**
chairman	chair, chairperson
policeman	police officer
businessman	businessperson, business executive
statesman	statesperson, diplomat
teacher . . . she	teachers . . . they
principal . . . he	principals . . . they

    →

BACKGROUND
In "A Brief Writing Assignment for Introducing Non-Sexist Pronoun Usage" (*Teaching English in the Two-Year College*, September 2000: 74–77), Christopher G. Hayes describes how he convinces students of "the connection between language and constructions of reality" from their own writing. Hayes follows this assignment with a lively—and sometimes "warmly heated"—discussion.

TEACHING TIP
In addition to the techniques given in Box 92, here are a few more tactics for avoiding sexist language.

1. When appropriate, use the first person or the second person.

NO   *A person should always keep an eye on his luggage in airports.*

YES   *I should always keep my eye on my luggage in airports.*

YES   *We should always keep an eye on our luggage in airports.*

YES   *Keep an eye on your luggage in airports.*

2. Repeat a noun or use a synonym in place of the troublesome pronoun.

NO   *A preoccupied traveler is an easy target for thieves, who can pick his pocket in a second.*

YES   *A preoccupied traveler is an easy target for thieves, who can pick a traveler's pocket in a second.*

YES   *A preoccupied traveler is an easy target for thieves, who can pick a tourist's pocket in a second.*

3. Use *who.*

NO   *A traveler has little to worry about, if he stays alert.*

YES   *A traveler who stays alert has little to worry about.*

BACKGROUND

The Web site <http://cctc2.commnet.edu/ grammar/quizzes/nova/nova6.htm> offered by Capital Community College features an interactive quiz on gender-neutral language.

ANSWERS: EXERCISE 21-4

Answers will vary. Here are some possible gender-neutral versions.

1. Many of humanity's most important inventions are found not in scientific laboratories but in the home.

2. Among these inventions are the many home appliances that were designed in the early 1900s to simplify housework.

3. Every homemaker should be grateful to the inventors of labor-saving appliances such as vacuum cleaners, washing machines, and water heaters.

4. Before such appliances became available, a family was fortunate if it could afford to hire somebody to help with the housework.

5. Otherwise, family members had tasks to do that could include washing their clothes by hand or carrying hot water for bathing up or down the stairs.

6. Once family members were freed from these difficult duties early in the twentieth century, parents had more time to spend with their children.

7. Also, now everyone in the household had more time for favorite pastimes and hobbies.

8. None of the inventors of modern home appliances could have guessed what far-reaching effects their inventions would have on our society.

9. Every worker, from laborer to business executive, could return each day to a house where there was not nearly as much heavy housework waiting to be done.

10. Even more important, with less housework to do, women could now leave the home to take jobs as office workers, doctors, and lawyers.

How to avoid sexist language (*continued*)

■ Avoid expressions that seem to exclude one sex.

NO	YES
mankind	humanity
the common man	the average person
man-sized sandwich	huge sandwich
old wives' tale	superstition

■ Avoid using demeaning and patronizing labels.

NO	YES
male nurse	nurse
gal Friday	assistant
coed	student
My girl can help.	My secretary can help (or better still, Ida Morea can help).

EXERCISE 21-4

Working individually or with a group, revise these sentences by changing sexist language to gender-neutral language. For help, consult 21g.

1. Many of man's most important inventions are found not in scientific laboratories but in the home.

2. Among these inventions are the many home appliances that were designed in the early 1900s to simplify women's housework.

3. Every housewife should be grateful to the inventors of labor-saving appliances such as vacuum cleaners, washing machines, and water heaters.

4. Before such appliances became available, a family was fortunate if the husband could afford to hire a cleaning lady or a maid to help with the housework.

5. Otherwise, each family member had tasks to do that could include washing his clothes by hand or carrying hot water for bathing up or down the stairs.

6. Once family members were freed from these difficult duties early in the twentieth century, women had more time to spend with their children.

7. Also, now everyone in the household had more time for his favorite pastimes and hobbies.

8. None of the inventors of modern home appliances could have guessed what far-reaching effects his inventions would have on our society.

9. Every worker, from laborer to businessman, could return each day to a house where there was not nearly as much heavy housework waiting to be done.

10. Even more important, with less housework to do, women could now leave the home to take jobs as office girls and sometimes even lady doctors and lawyers.

21h What other types of language do I want to avoid?

Language that distorts or tries to manipulate a reader needs to be avoided in ACADEMIC WRITING. These and other types of language to avoid in an academic LEVEL OF FORMALITY are listed, with examples, in Box 93.

BOX 93   SUMMARY

Language to avoid in academic writing

- Never use **slanted language,** also called *loaded language;* readers feel manipulated by the overly emotional TONE and DICTION.

    NO   Our senator is a deceitful, crooked thug.
    YES Our senator lies to the public and demands bribes.

    NO   Why do labs employ Frankensteins to maim helpless kittens and puppies?
    YES Why do labs employ uncaring technicians who harm kittens and puppies?

- Never use **pretentious language;** readers realize you're showing off.

    NO   As I alighted from my vehicle, my clothing became besmirched with filth.
    YES My coat got muddy as I got out of my car.

    NO   He has a penchant for ostentatiously flaunting recently acquired haberdashery accoutrements.
    YES He tends to show off his new clothes shamelessly.

    →

TEACHING TIP

If you have any doubts about whether encouraging nonsexist language is worth the effort, consider this passage from the introduction to "Guidelines for Nonsexist Use of Language" in NCTE (National Council of Teachers of English) Publications:

"Sexism" may be defined as words or actions that arbitrarily assign roles or characteristics to people on the basis of sex. Originally used to refer to practices that discriminated against women, the term now includes any usage that unfairly delimits the aspirations or attributes of either sex. Neither men nor women can reach their full potential when men are conditioned to be only aggressive, analytical, and active and women are conditioned to be only submissive, emotional, and passive. The man who cannot cry and the woman who cannot command are equally victims of their socialization.

Language plays a central role in socialization, for it helps teach children the roles that are expected of them. Through language, children conceptualize their ideas and feelings about themselves and their world. Thought and action are reflected in words, and words in turn condition how a person thinks and acts. Eliminating sexist language will not eliminate sexist conduct, but as the language is liberated from sexist usages and assumptions, women and men will begin to share more equal, active, caring roles.

TEACHING TIP

Discussions about slanted language make students more aware of biased writing. A logical follow-up assignment is to ask them to be alert to loaded diction in news articles and television broadcasts. Examples are particularly abundant during an election year. The words and phrases students collect can be the basis of another lesson, this one specific and close to home.

TEACHING TIP

You may want to ask students to work in groups to research the origins of a slang expression, a commonly used phrase, or a regional expression of their own choice. The results can take the form of an oral report to the rest of the class.

WORD DERIVATION

Florida was named by the explorer Ponce de León. *Florida* is Spanish for "abounding in flowers."

QUOTATION: ON WRITING

Why shouldn't we quarrel about a word? What is the good of words if they aren't important enough to quarrel over? Why do we choose one word more than another if there isn't any difference between them?

—G. K. Chesterton

WORD DERIVATION

Kentucky comes from the Iroquoian words for "level land."

Language to avoid in academic writing (*continued*)

- Never use **sarcastic language;** readers realize you're being nasty.

  NO   He was a regular Albert Einstein with my questions. [This is sarcastic if you mean the opposite.]

  YES   He had trouble understanding many of my questions.

- Never use **colloquial language;** readers sense you're being overly casual and conversational.

  NO   Christina flunked chemistry.

  YES   Christina failed chemistry.

- Never use **euphemisms,** also called *doublespeak;* readers realize you're hiding the truth (more in 21l).

  NO   Our company will **downsize** to meet efficiency standards.

  YES   Our company has to cut jobs to maintain our profits.

  NO   We consider our hostages as **foreign guests** being guarded by **hosts.**

  YES   We consider our hostages as enemies to be guarded closely.

- Never use NONSTANDARD ENGLISH (more in 21c).
- Never use MIXED METAPHORS (more in 21d).
- Never use SEXIST LANGUAGE or STEREOTYPES (more in 21g and 5j).
- Never use regional language (more in 21i).
- Never use CLICHÉS (more in 21j).
- Never use unnecessary JARGON (more in 21k).
- Never use BUREAUCRATIC LANGUAGE (more in 21m).

21i   What is regional language?

Regional language, also called *dialectal language,* is specific to certain geographical areas. For example, a *dragonfly* is a *snake feeder* in parts of Delaware, a *darning needle* in parts of Michigan, and a *snake doctor* or an *ear sewer* in parts of the southern United States. Using a dialect in writing for the general reading public tends to shut some people out of the communication. Except when dialect is the topic of the writing, ACADEMIC WRITING rarely accommodates dialect well. Avoid it in academic assignments.

21j What are clichés?

A **cliché** is a worn-out expression that has lost its capacity to communicate effectively because of overuse. Many clichés are SIMILES or METAPHORS, once clever but now flat. For example, these are clichés: *dead as a doornail, gentle as a lamb,* and *straight as an arrow.*

If you've heard certain expressions repeatedly, so has your reader. Instead of a cliché, use descriptive language that isn't worn out. If you can't think of a way to rephrase a cliché, drop the words entirely.

Interestingly, however, English is full of frequently used word groups that aren't clichés: for example, *up and down* and *from place to place.* These common word groups aren't considered clichés, so you can use them freely. If you're not sure of how to tell the difference between a cliché and a common word group, remember that a cliché often—but not always—contains an image (*busy as a bee* and *strong as an ox*).

EXERCISE 21-5

Working individually or with a group, revise these clichés. Use the idea in each cliché to write a sentence of your own in plain, clear English. For help, consult 21j.

1. The bottom line is that Carl either raises his grade point average or finds himself in hot water.
2. Carl's grandfather says, "When the going gets tough, the tough get going."
3. Carl may not be the most brilliant engineering major who ever came down the pike, but he has plenty of get-up-and-go.
4. When they were handing out persistence, Carl was first in line.
5. The $64,000 question is, Will Carl make it safe and sound, or will the college drop him like a hot potato?

21k When is jargon unnecessary?

Jargon is the specialized vocabulary of a particular group. Jargon uses words that people outside that group might not understand. Specialized language exists in every field: professions, academic disciplines, business, various industries, government departments, hobbies, and so on.

Reserve jargon for a specialist AUDIENCE. As you write, keep your audience in mind as you decide whether a word is jargon in the context of your material. For example, a football fan easily understands a sportswriter's use of words such as *punt* and *safety,* but they are jargon words

QUOTATION: ON WRITING
Those of us who enjoy living in synonymy know that an *adage* is not quite as graven in collective wisdom as a *proverb* or a *maxim;* it is not as legalistic as a *dictum* or as scientific as an *axiom* or as sentimental as a *homily* or as corny as a *saw,* nor as formalized as a *motto,* but it is more rooted in tradition than an *observation.*

—William Safire

BACKGROUND
In English, we say we "didn't sleep a wink." The equivalent phrase in the African language Xhosa translates: "When dawn broke, we were looking through yesterday's eyes."

—Programmed Language Courses, Johannesburg, South Africa

BACKGROUND
The site <http://owl.english.purdue.edu/internet/resources/genre.html> offers suggestions and links to specialized fields of writing, including English for scientific research.

TEACHING TIP
Because every professional discipline has its own jargon, your students may find it interesting to investigate the language used by people in a particular field of work. They can do so by interviewing individuals active in that profession, talking to those who teach courses preparing people to enter a field, reading professional literature, or observing someone at work.

QUOTATION: ON WRITING
I write from my knowledge not my lack, from my strength not my weakness. I am not interested if anyone knows whether or not I am familiar with big words, I am interested in trying to render big ideas in a simple way. I am interested in being understood, not admired. I wish to celebrate and not be celebrated.

—Lucille Clifton

to people unfamiliar with American-style football. Avoid using jargon unnecessarily. When you must use jargon for a nonspecialist audience, be sure to explain any special meanings.

The example below shows specialized language used appropriately; it's taken from a college textbook. The authors can assume that students know the meaning of *eutrophicates, terrestrial,* and *eutrophic.*

> As the lake eutrophicates, it gradually fills until the entire lake will be converted into a terrestrial community. Eutrophic changes (or eutrophication) are the nutritional enrichment of the water, promoting the growth of aquatic plants.
>
> —Davis and Solomon, *The World of Biology*

21l What are euphemisms?

Euphemisms attempt to avoid the harsh reality of truth by using more pleasant, "tactful" words. Good manners dictate that euphemisms sometimes be used in social situations: For example, in U.S. culture, *passed away* is, in some situations, thought to be gentler than *died.* Such uses of euphemisms are acceptable.

In other situations, however, euphemisms drain meaning from truthful writing. Unnecessary euphemisms might describe socially unacceptable behavior (for example, *Johnny has a wonderfully vivid imagination* instead of *Johnny lies*). They also might try to hide unpleasant facts (for example, *She is between assignments* instead of *She's lost her job*). Avoid unnecessary euphemisms.

21m What is bureaucratic language?

Bureaucratic language uses words that are stuffy and overblown. Bureaucratic language (or *bureaucratese,* a word created to describe the style) is marked by unnecessary complexity. This kind of language can take on a formality that complicates the message and makes readers feel left out.

> NO In reference to the above captioned, you can include a page that additionally contains an Include instruction under the herein stated circumstances. The page including the Include instruction is included when you paginate the document, but the included text referred to in its Include instruction is not included. [This message is meaningless, but the writer seems to understand the message. Anyone who doesn't is clearly uninformed or unable to read intelligently.]
>
> —From instructions for compiling a user's manual

In response to earlier editions of this handbook, I've been asked to give a YES alternative for this example. I regret that I can't understand enough of the NO example to do that. If you, gentle reader, can, please contact me at <LQTBook@aol.com>.

EXERCISE 21-6

Working individually or with a group, revise these examples of pretentious language, jargon, euphemism, and bureaucratic language. For help, consult 21h and 21k through 21m.

1. In-house employee interaction of a nonbusiness nature is disallowed.
2. Shortly after Mrs. Harriman went to her reward, Mr. Harriman moved to Florida to be near his son and daughter-in-law and their bundle of joy.
3. Your dearest, closest acquaintance, it has been circulated through rumor, is entering into matrimony with her current beloved.
4. My male sibling concocted a tale that was entirely fallacious.
5. An individual's cognitive and affective domains are at the center of his or her personality.
6. When the finalization of this negotiation comes through, it will clarify our position in a positive manner.
7. The refuse has accumulated because the sanitation engineers were on strike last month.
8. Employees who are employed by the company for no less than five years in a full-time capacity fulfill the eligibility requirements for participation in the company's savings program.

ANSWERS AND COVERAGE: EXERCISE 21-6

Answers will vary. Following is one set of possibilities.

1. Socializing on the job is not allowed. [bureaucratic language]

2. Shortly after Mrs. Harriman died, Mr. Harriman moved to Florida to be near his son and daughter-in-law and their new baby. [euphemism, cliché]

3. Your best friend, I've heard, is going to marry her boyfriend. [pretentious language]

4. My brother told a lie. [pretentious language, euphemism]

5. An individual's systems of thinking and feeling are at the center of his or her personality. [jargon]

6. When the negotiation is finished, we will be in a better position. [jargon, pretentious language]

7. The trash has piled up because the trash collectors were on strike last month. [pretentious language, euphemism]

8. Full-time employees who have worked at the company for five years can participate in the savings program. [bureaucratic language]

QUOTATION: ON WRITING

Words and words and words, how they gallop—how they lash their long manes and tails.

—Virginia Woolf

WORD DERIVATION

The state name *Louisiana* comes from *La Louisianne*. The French, who controlled the Mississippi Valley before selling the area to the United States in 1803, had named the territory after their king, Louis XIV.

BACKGROUND
The earliest writing systems were developed not much more than six thousand years ago to meet the needs of increasingly complex cultures. In particular, the Egyptians and Babylonians contrived ways of recording their sacred records, commercial transactions, and royal decrees in pictographs—drawings that attempted to convey a general idea by visually reproducing the major elements in it. Writing can be said to have begun when a method for making a linguistic statement of the facts was devised. The earliest systems did not make use of the *phonology,* or sounds of language. Instead, they used signs to represent *morphemes* (roots and affixes). Chinese is the only language that continues to use this system exclusively. The Egyptians and other ancient Middle Eastern cultures based their writing systems on the sounds of the syllables that made up words. Alphabetic writing was invented by the peoples of the Eastern Mediterranean. At first, they used only consonants, depending on readers to fill in the vowels as well as to supply such information as intonation and stress. When the Greeks adopted a Semitic alphabet, they used the characters for consonant sounds that did not exist in Greek to represent vowels. That tradition is the basis of all modern alphabets used in the West today.

BACKGROUND
The Web site <http://www.sentex.net/~mmcadams/spelling.html> features an interactive spelling test of fifty of the most commonly misspelled words in American English, including links to spelling tips.

Chapter 22

Spelling

22a What makes a good speller?

You might be surprised to hear that good spellers don't know how to spell and hyphenate every word they write. What they do know, however, is to check if they're not sure of a word's spelling. If your inner voice questions a spelling, do what good spellers do—consult a dictionary.

What do you do if even the first few letters of a word seem mysterious? This is a common dilemma among writers. My best advice is that you think of an easy-to-spell SYNONYM for the word you need; look up that synonym in a thesaurus; and among the synonyms, find the word you need to spell.

Many people, surveys show, incorrectly believe that only naturally skilled spellers can write well. The truth is that correct spelling matters a great deal in final drafts, but not in earlier drafts. The best time to check spellings you doubt is when you're EDITING.

The various origins and ways that English-speaking people around the world pronounce words make it almost impossible to rely solely on pronunciation to spell a word. What you can rely on, however, are the proofreading hints and spelling rules explained in this chapter.

👁 **ALERT:** Word processing software usually includes a spell-check program, which claims to spot spelling errors because the words typed in don't match the spellings in the software's dictionary. Such programs have one major drawback. The programs can't detect that you've spelled a wrong word if what you've typed is a legitimate spelling of a legitimate word. For example, if you mean *top* but type *too,* or if you mean *from* and type *form,* no spell-check program "sees" a mistake. In these and other similar cases, only the human eye (that is, a reader) can discover the errors. 👁

22b How can I proofread for errors in spelling and hyphen use?

Many spelling errors are the result of illegible handwriting, slips of the pen, or typographical mistakes. Catching these "typos" requires especially careful proofreading, using the techniques in Box 94.

BOX 94   SUMMARY

 Proofreading for errors in spelling

- Slow down your reading speed to allow yourself to concentrate on the individual letters of words rather than on the meaning of the words.
- Stay within your "visual span," the number of letters you can identify with a single glance (for most people, about six letters).
- Put a ruler or large index card under each line as you proofread, to focus your vision and concentration.
- Read each paragraph in reverse, from the last sentence to the first. This method can keep you from being distracted by the meaning of the material.

22c How are plurals spelled?

In American English, plurals take many forms. The most common form adds an *s* or *es* at the end of the word. The list below covers all variations of creating plurals.

- **Adding -s or -es:** Plurals of most words are formed by adding an *s*, including words that end in "hard" *-ch* (sounding like *k*): *leg, legs; shoe, shoes; stomach, stomachs.* Words ending in *-s, -sh, -x, -z,* or "soft" *-ch* (as in *beach*) are formed by adding *-es* to the singular: *lens, lenses; tax, taxes; beach, beaches.*

- **Words ending in -o:** Add *-s* if the *-o* is preceded by a vowel: *radio, radios; cameo, cameos.* Add *-es* if the *-o* is preceded by a consonant: *potato, potatoes.* With a few words, you can choose the *-s* or *-es* plural form, but current practice generally supports adding *-es: cargo, cargoes; tornado, tornadoes; zero, zeros* or *zeroes.*

- **Words ending in -f or -fe:** Some final *f* and *fe* words are made plural by adding an *s: belief, beliefs.* Others require changing *-f* or *-fe* to *-ves: life, lives; leaf, leaves.* Words ending in *-ff* or *-ffe* simply add *-s: staff, staffs; giraffe, giraffes.*

WORDS OFTEN MISSPELLED
Throughout this chapter, we present lists of commonly misspelled words, organized in the following categories: double consonants, word endings (suffixes), unstressed syllables, *ie/ei*, silent letters and blended sounds, and other commonly misspelled words. It's a good idea to assign words for study in groups of twenty-five at a time.

LANGUAGE HISTORY
During the period of colonization, English continued to expand. From Native American words we took *tomahawk, wigwam, squash, homing,* among many other familiar terms, and place names, such as *Nebraska, Allegheny, Kentucky, Seattle,* and *Dakota.* From spoken Spanish in the New World we have *mustang, ranch, patio, bonanza, rodeo, vigilante, sombrero,* and others. From words arrived from India, we have *thug, loot, pajamas, bandana.* From German words we have *kindergarten, semester, delicatessen, frankfurter, hamburger.*

Borrowing continues unabated. Recent borrowings have come from Italian (*casino, malaria, studio*); Spanish (*cigar, canyon, cafeteria*); German (*pumpernickel, iceberg, protein*); Slavic (*pogrom, soviet, robot*); Arabic (*genie, candy, safari*); Hebrew (*hallelujah, kosher*); Persian (*spinach, lilac, bazaar*); Tibeto-Chinese (*tea, ketchup*); and Japanese (*zen, karate*).

Over the centuries, the Anglo-Saxons' vocabulary of 50,000 words has expanded to more than 600,000 words. Irregular spellings are the price we pay for this acquired richness and flexibility.

BACKGROUND
In "Can't Spell? Yur Not Dumm" (*Newsweek,* June 6, 1988: 52), Melinda Beck asserts that poor spelling "has little to do with basic intelligence." For example, "F. Scott Fitzgerald was a notoriously bad speller. The first printing of *This Side of Paradise* contained approximately 100 misspellings."

ANSWERS: EXERCISE 22-1

1. yourselves
2. sheep
3. photos
4. women
5. appendixes (or appendices)
6. millennia
7. lamps
8. runners-up
9. criteria
10. lunches
11. echoes
12. syllabi
13. wives
14. get-togethers
15. crises

WORDS OFTEN MISSPELLED

ie/ei

achievement	conceive	niece
apiece	conscientious	receive
atheist	eighth	relief
belief	foreign	relieve
believed	forfeit	review
ceiling	height	seize
chief	leisure	view
conceited	lenient	weird

Unstressed Syllables (including syllables frequently not pronounced)

adolescent	category
alcohol	cemetery
amateur	census
analysis	certain
angel	challenge
apology	channel
article	children
aspirin	chocolate
average	chosen
bargain	coarsely
boundary	concentrate
cafeteria	controversial
calendar	curious

➡

- **Compound words:** For most compound words, add an *s* or *es* at the end of the last word: *checkbooks, player-coaches.* In a few cases, the first word is made plural: *sister-in-law, sisters-in-law; miles per hour.* (For information about hyphens in compound words, see 22g.)

- **Internal changes and endings other than -s:** A few words change internally or add endings other than an *s* to become plural: *foot, feet; man, men; crisis, crises; child, children.*

- **Foreign words:** The best advice is to check your dictionary. In general, many Latin words ending in *-um* form the plural by changing *-um* to *-a: curriculum, curricula; datum, data; medium, media.* Also, Latin words that end in *-us* usually form the plural by changing *-us* to *-i: alumnus, alumni; syllabus, syllabi.* Additionally, Greek words that end in *-on* usually form the plural by changing *-on* to *-a: criterion, criteria; phenomenon, phenomena.*

- **One-form words:** Some words have the same form in both the singular and the plural: *deer, elk, fish.* You need to use modifiers, as necessary, to indicate which form you mean: **one** *deer,* **nine** *deer.*

EXERCISE 22-1

Write the correct plural form of these words. For help, consult 22c.

1. yourself
2. sheep
3. photo
4. woman
5. appendix
6. millennium
7. lamp
8. runner-up
9. criterion
10. lunch
11. echo
12. syllabus
13. wife
14. get-together
15. crisis

22d How are suffixes spelled?

A **suffix** is an ending added to a word that changes the word's meaning or its grammatical function. For example, adding the suffix *-able* to the VERB *depend* creates the ADJECTIVE *dependable.*

- **-y words:** If the letter before a final *y* is a consonant, change the *y* to *i* and add the suffix: *try, tries, tried.* In the case of *trying* and similar words, the following rule applies: Keep the *y* when the suffix begins with *i* (*apply, applying*). If the letter before the final *y* is a vowel, keep the final *y: employ, employed, employing.* These rules don't apply to IRREGULAR VERBS (see Box 60 in section 8d).

- **-e words:** Drop a final *e* when the suffix begins with a vowel, unless doing this would cause confusion: for example, *be + ing* can't be written *bing,* but *require* does become *requiring; like* does become *liking.* Keep the final *e* when the suffix begins with a consonant: *require, requirement; like, likely.* Exceptions include *argue, argument; judge, judgment; true, truly.*

■ **Words that double a final letter:** If the final letter is a consonant, double it *only* if it passes three tests: (1) its last two letters are a vowel followed by a consonant; (2) it has one syllable or is accented on the last syllable; (3) the suffix begins with a vowel: *drop, dropped; begin, beginning; forget, forgettable.*

■ **-cede, -ceed, -sede words:** Only one word in the English language ends in *-sede: supersede.* Only three words end in *-ceed: exceed, proceed, succeed.* All other words with endings that sound like "seed" end in *-cede: concede, intercede, precede.*

■ **-ally and -ly words:** The suffixes *-ally* and *-ly* turn words into adverbs. For words ending in *-ic,* add *-ally: logically, statistically.* Otherwise, add *-ly: quickly, sharply.*

■ **-ance, -ence, and -ible, -able:** No consistent rules govern words with these suffixes. When in doubt, look up the word.

22e What is the *ie, ei* rule?

The famous three-line, rhymed rule for using *ie* and *ei* is usually true:

I before *e* [bel**ie**ve, f**ie**ld, gr**ie**f],
Except after *c* [c**ei**ling, conc**ei**t],
Or when sounded like "ay"—
As in n**ei**ghbor and w**ei**gh [**ei**ght, v**ei**n].

There are major exceptions (sorry!) to the *ie, ei* rule, listed here. My best advice is that you memorize them.

■ *ie:* consc**ie**nce, financ**ie**r, sc**ie**nce, spec**ie**s

■ *ei:* **ei**ther, n**ei**ther, l**ei**sure, s**ei**ze, counterf**ei**t, for**ei**gn, forf**ei**t, sl**ei**gh, sl**ei**ght (as in *sleight of hand*), w**ei**rd

EXERCISE 22-2

Follow the directions for each group of words. For help, consult 22d and 22e.

1. Add *-able* or *-ible:* (a) profit; (b) reproduce; (c) control; (d) coerce; (e) recognize.
2. Add *-ance* or *-ence:* (a) luxuri_____; (b) prud_____; (c) devi_____; (d) resist_____; (e) independ_____.

Words Often Misspelled (continued)	
decorate	poison
delicate	practical
despair	prepare
destroy	privilege
develop	propaganda
disease	pumpkin
dispel	purpose
divide	pursue
divine	pursuit
ecstasy	quandary
embarrass	rebel
enemy	recognize
escape	regular
everything	remember
exercise	reproduce
family	resources
favorite	restaurant
grammar	sacrifice
heroes	saxophone
holiday	sentence
hundred	separate
imagine	several
imitate	sheriff
integrate	similar
interest	sophomore
introduce	specimen
laboratory	sponsor
liable	statistics
luxury	strategy
magazine	surprise
manual	temperature
mathematics	therefore
medicine	thorough
miniature	tobacco
participle	together
perhaps	tomorrow
persuade	typical
physical	vitamins
pigeon	Wednesday
pitiful	woman
pleasant	women

1. **a.** profitable
   b. reproducible
   c. controllable
   d. coercible
   e. recognizable
2. **a.** luxuriance
   b. prudence
   c. deviance
   d. resistance
   e. independence
3. **a.** truly
   b. joking
   c. fortunately
   d. appeasing
   e. appeasement
4. **a.** happiness
   b. pried
   c. prying
   d. dryly
   e. beautifying
5. **a.** committed
   b. commitment
   c. dropped
   d. occurred
   e. regretful
6. **a.** relief
   b. achieve
   c. weird
   d. niece
   e. deceive

BACKGROUND

A survey of problems found in student writing at the University of Michigan reports the following most frequent spelling errors: "Words that contain unstressed vowels: Is it *seperate* or *separate*, *indispensible* or *indispensable*? Metathesis, the name we give that wrong ordering of cart and horse that makes us write *calvary* for *cavalry*. Problems in handling an unstressed *i*, as in *efficient*."

3. Drop the final *e* as needed: (a) true + ly; (b) joke + ing; (c) fortunate + ly; (d) appease + ing; (e) appease + ment.
4. Change the final *y* to *i* as needed: (a) happy + ness; (b) pry + ed; (c) pry + ing; (d) dry + ly; (e) beautify + ing.
5. Double the final consonant as needed: (a) commit + ed; (b) commit + ment; (c) drop + ed; (d) occur + ed; (e) regret + ful.
6. Insert *ie* or *ei* correctly: (a) rel____f; (b) ach____ve; (c) w____rd; (d) n____ce; (e) dec____ve.

22f **How are homonyms and other frequently confused words spelled?**

Homonyms are words that sound exactly like other words: *to, too, two; no, know*. The different spellings of homonyms tend to confuse many writers. The same holds for words that sound almost alike (*accept, except; conscience, conscious*).

Another reason for spelling problems is so-called swallowed pronunciation, which means one or more letters at the end of a word aren't pronounced clearly. For example, the *-d* ending in *used to* or *prejudiced* or the *-ten* ending in *written* are often swallowed rather than pronounced. When writers spell as they mispronounce, spelling errors result.

For more information about word usage that affects spelling, see Chapter 20, "Usage Glossary." Box 95 lists homonyms and other words that can be confused and lead to misspellings.

BOX 95 SUMMARY

Homonyms and other frequently confused words

■	ACCEPT	to receive
	EXCEPT	with the exclusion of
■	ADVICE	recommendation
	ADVISE	to recommend
■	AFFECT	to influence [verb]; emotion [noun]
	EFFECT	result [noun]; to bring about or cause [verb]
■	AISLE	space between rows
	ISLE	island
■	ALLUDE	to make indirect reference to
	ELUDE	to avoid

→

Homonyms and other frequently confused words
(*continued*)

- ALLUSION — indirect reference
  ILLUSION — false idea, misleading appearance

- ALREADY — by this time
  ALL READY — fully prepared

- ALTAR — sacred platform or place
  ALTER — to change

- ALTOGETHER — thoroughly
  ALL TOGETHER — everyone or everything in one place

- ARE — PLURAL form of *to be*
  HOUR — sixty minutes
  OUR — plural form of *my*

- ASCENT — the act of rising or climbing
  ASSENT — consent [noun]; to consent [verb]

- ASSISTANCE — help
  ASSISTANTS — helpers

- BARE — nude, unadorned
  BEAR — to carry; an animal

- BOARD — piece of wood
  BORED — uninterested

- BRAKE — device for stopping
  BREAK — to destroy, make into pieces

- BREATH — air taken in
  BREATHE — to take in air

- BUY — to purchase
  BY — next to, through the agency of

- CAPITAL — major city; money
  CAPITOL — government building

- CHOOSE — to pick
  CHOSE — PAST TENSE of *choose*

- CITE — to point out
  SIGHT — vision
  SITE — a place

- CLOTHES — garments
  CLOTHS — pieces of fabric

- COARSE — rough
  COURSE — path; series of lectures

→

WORDS OFTEN MISSPELLED

Double Consonants

accommodate	committee	missile
accompanied	controlled	occasion
accomplish	different	occurred
accordion	disappear	parallel
accustomed	disappoint	processes
address	disapprove	quizzes
annihilate	efficient	satellite
appoint	equipped	stepped
appreciate	fulfill	succeed
appropriate	happened	suppose
arrest	harass	surround
bulletin	interrupt	tyranny
commercial	mirror	villain

Word Ending (Suffixes)

acceptable	calculator
accessible	carrying
accidentally	changeable
accuracy	changing
acreage	characteristic
actually	Christianity
admission	commitment
affectionately	competent
aggression	competition
announcement	completely
apparent	confident
appearance	consistent
approximately	continuous
arguing	convenient
argument	coolly
assassination	criticism
attendance	criticize
barbarous	cruelty
basically	curiosity
beautiful	decision
beginning	definitely
beneficial	description
biggest	desirable
bureaucracy	desperate
business	despicable

→

Words Often Misspelled (continued)

disastrous	innocuous
discussion	insurance
dormitory	intelligent
easily	interference
elaborately	irrelevant
entirely	irresistible
environment	irritated
equipment	likelihood
especially	listening
evidently	liveliest
existence	livelihood
experiment	lying
explanation	magnificent
extremely	maintenance
finally	manageable
financially	management
generally	marriage
government	meanness
governor	mischievous
guidance	mysterious
happily	narrative
hindrance	naturally
hoping	necessary
humorous	noticeable
hungry	noticing
hurriedly	nuisance
hypocrisy	numerous
ideally	occasionally
idiosyncrasy	occurrence
ignorant	occurring
illogical	official
imaginary	omission
immediately	omitting
immensely	opponent
incalculable	opportunity
incidentally	opposite
incredible	oppression
independent	optimism
indispensable	ordinarily
individually	originally
influential	particularly

→

Homonyms and other frequently confused words (*continued*)

- **COMPLEMENT** something that completes
  COMPLIMENT praise, flattery
- **CONSCIENCE** sense of morality
  CONSCIOUS awake, aware
- **COUNCIL** governing body
  COUNSEL advice [noun]; to advise [verb]
- **DAIRY** place associated with milk production
  DIARY personal journal
- **DESCENT** downward movement
  DISSENT disagreement
- **DESERT** to abandon [verb]; dry, usually sandy area [noun]
  DESSERT final, sweet course in a meal
- **DEVICE** a plan; an implement
  DEVISE to create
- **DIE** to lose life (dying) [verb]; one of a pair of dice [noun]
  DYE to change the color of something (dyeing)
- **DOMINANT** commanding, controlling
  DOMINATE to control
- **ELICIT** to draw out
  ILLICIT illegal
- **EMINENT** prominent
  IMMANENT living within; inherent
  IMMINENT about to happen
- **ENVELOP** to surround
  ENVELOPE container for a letter or other papers
- **FAIR** light-skinned; just, honest
  FARE money for transportation; food
- **FORMALLY** conventionally, with ceremony
  FORMERLY previously
- **FORTH** forward
  FOURTH number four in a series
- **GORILLA** animal in ape family
  GUERRILLA soldier conducting surprise attacks
- **HEAR** to sense sound by ear
  HERE in this place

→

Homonyms and other frequently confused words
(*continued*)

■	HOLE	opening
	WHOLE	complete; an entire thing
■	HUMAN	relating to the species *Homo sapiens*
	HUMANE	compassionate
■	INSURE	buy or give insurance
	ENSURE	guarantee, protect
■	ITS	POSSESSIVE form of *it*
	IT'S	CONTRACTION for *it is*
■	KNOW	to comprehend
	NO	negative
■	LATER	after a time
	LATTER	second one of two things
■	LEAD	heavy metal substance [noun]; to guide [verb]
	LED	past tense of *lead*
■	LIGHTNING	storm-related electricity
	LIGHTENING	making lighter
■	LOOSE	unbound, not tightly fastened
	LOSE	to misplace
■	MAYBE	perhaps [adverb]
	MAY BE	might be [verb]
■	MEAT	animal flesh
	MEET	to encounter
■	MINER	a person who works in a mine
	MINOR	underage
■	MORAL	distinguishing right from wrong; the lesson of a fable, story, or event
	MORALE	attitude or outlook, usually of a group
■	OF	PREPOSITION indicating origin
	OFF	away from; not on
■	PASSED	past tense of *pass*
	PAST	at a previous time
■	PATIENCE	forbearance
	PATIENTS	people under medical care
■	PEACE	absence of fighting
	PIECE	part of a whole; musical arrangement

→

Words Often Misspelled (*continued*)

peaceable	shrubbery
peculiar	significant
performance	simply
permanence	sincerely
permissible	skiing
politician	strenuous
possession	stubbornness
practicality	studying
predominant	suburban
preparation	succession
prevalent	sufficient
prisoner	summary
probably	superintendent
professor	supersede
prominent	suppress
pronunciation	surely
publicly	susceptible
pursuing	suspicious
questionnaire	swimming
rarity	technical
reality	temporary
realize	tendency
really	tragedy
recession	tremendous
recommend	truce
referring	unanimous
regulate	unconscious
rehearsal	undoubtedly
religious	usage
remembrance	using
repetition	usually
representative	valuable
resemblance	various
ridiculous	vegetable
scarcity	vengeance
scenery	violence
secretary	visible
senseless	writing
shining	written

TEACHING TIP

Much of the recent research on spelling improvements stresses the importance of using as many of the senses as possible during word study. You may want to suggest to students that they try to improve their visual memory by writing a word in the air, using a finger to make the troublesome letters especially large. Ask them to try to imagine a word as if it were on an outdoor movie screen. Then they can try to write the word mentally in "longhand." The auditory sense can be invoked by making exaggerated pronunciations. That is, the speaker emphasizes the problem portion of a word when saying it. For example, the person who habitually leaves off the final -d of used should practice pronouncing the word as "you said." The kinesthetic and tactile senses are combined when a writer records a problem word on paper using a different kind of medium to write the difficult spots, changing from a ballpoint pen, for instance, to a crayon. This technique can include a visual element if the student puts the problem letters in red or some other bright color.

QUOTATION: ON WRITING

English orthography satisfies all the requirements of the canons of reputability under the law of conspicuous waste. It is archaic, cumbrous, and ineffective; its acquisition consumes much time and effort; failure to acquire it is easy of detection.

—Thorstein Veblen

Homonyms and other frequently confused words (*continued*)

- PERSONAL — intimate
  PERSONNEL — employees
- PLAIN — simple, unadorned
  PLANE — to shave wood; aircraft
- PRECEDE — to come before
  PROCEED — to continue
- PRESENCE — being at hand; attendance at a place or in something
  PRESENTS — gifts
- PRINCIPAL — foremost [ADJECTIVE]; school head [noun]
  PRINCIPLE — moral conviction, basic truth
- QUIET — silent, calm
  QUITE — very
- RAIN — water that falls to earth [noun]; to fall like rain [verb]
  REIGN — to rule
  REIN — strap to guide or control an animal [noun]; to guide or control [verb]
- RAISE — to lift up
  RAZE — to tear down
- RESPECTFULLY — with respect
  RESPECTIVELY — in that order
- RIGHT — correct; opposite of *left*
  RITE — ritual
  WRITE — to put words on paper
- ROAD — path
  RODE — past tense of *ride*
- SCENE — place of an action; segment of a play
  SEEN — viewed
- SENSE — perception, understanding
  SINCE — measurement of past time; because
- STATIONARY — standing still
  STATIONERY — writing paper
- THAN — in comparison with; besides
  THEN — at that time; next; therefore
- THEIR — possessive form of *they*
  THERE — in that place
  THEY'RE — contraction of *they are*

→

Homonyms and other frequently confused words
(*continued*)

- THROUGH   finished; into and out of
  THREW   past tense of *throw*
  THOROUGH   complete

- TO   toward
  TOO   also; indicates degree (*too much*)
  TWO   number following *one*

- WAIST   midsection of the body
  WASTE   discarded material [noun]; to squander, to fail to use up [verb]

- WEAK   not strong
  WEEK   seven days

- WEATHER   climatic condition
  WHETHER   if, when alternatives are expressed or implied

- WHERE   in which place
  WERE   past tense of *be*

- WHICH   one of a group
  WITCH   female sorcerer

- WHOSE   possessive form of *who*
  WHO'S   contraction for *who is*

- YOUR   possessive form of *you*
  YOU'RE   contraction for *you are*
  YORE   long past

EXERCISE 22-3

Circle the correct homonym or commonly confused word of each group in parentheses.

Imagine that you (are, our) standing in the middle of a busy sidewalk, with a worried look on (your, you're, yore) face. In your hand (your, you're, yore) holding a map, (which, witch) you are puzzling over. If that happened in (real, reel) life, (its, it's) almost certain that within (to, too, two) or three minutes a passerby would ask if you (where, were) lost and would offer you (assistance, assistants). That helpful passerby, (buy, by) taking a (personal, personnel) interest in your problem, is displaying a quality known as empathy—the ability (to, too, two) put oneself in another person's place. Some researchers claim that empathy is an instinct that (human, humane)

ANSWERS: EXERCISE 22-3

Imagine that you *are* standing in the middle of a busy sidewalk, with a worried look on *your* face. In your hand *you're* holding a map, *which* you are puzzling over. If that happened in *real* life, *it's* almost certain that within *two* or three minutes a passerby would ask if you *were* lost and would offer you *assistance*. That helpful passerby, *by* taking a *personal* interest in your problem, is displaying a quality known as empathy—the ability *to* put oneself in another person's place. Some researchers claim that empathy is an instinct that *human* beings share with many other animals. Other scientists wonder *whether* empathy is instead a *conscious moral* choice that people make. Whatever explanation for the origin *of* empathy is *right*, such empathy generally has a positive *effect*—especially if *you're* a person who *may be too* lost to *know where to* turn.

TEACHING TIP

A sophisticated relative of the spelling test is the dictation exercise. Passages can be created to test students' ability to spell, punctuate, or capitalize. Here is a sample dictation passage aimed at testing whether students can distinguish among homonyms and commonly confused words. The context gives students clues about which word is intended (much as the sentences normally given as part of a spelling test do); at the same time, the paragraph format is more interesting than random illustrative sentences.

The institution of marriage has received its share of public attention over the past few years. Rising divorce rates, seen as a symptom of a troubled society, have led people to question why some marriages break up and others succeed. One reason may be that the effect of courtship is to cause the bride and groom to lose sight of reality. Researchers cite evidence that some couples are too unrealistic. They proceed to the altar carrying romantic illusions about themselves, each other, and marriage itself. Having grown accustomed to compliments and presents, they find themselves walking down the aisle expecting a lifetime of romantic bliss to follow. The groom may assume that his bride is an angel, and she may choose to think of him as a knight on a white horse. They may fail to realize that one expects to dominate rather than complement the other or that he lacks patience and she is not as quiet as she seems. They're reluctant to look at the whole situation until later, when they are called on to accept the serious responsibilities of marriage. The best advice, of course, is for husbands and wives to live by principles that lead them to treat each other respectfully, lightening each other's troubles and acknowledging each other's rights.

beings share with many other animals. Other scientists wonder (weather, whether) empathy is instead a (conscience, conscious) (moral, morale) choice that people make. Whatever explanation for the origin (of, off) empathy is (right, rite, write), such empathy generally has a positive (affect, effect)—especially if (your, you're, yore) a person who (maybe, may be) (to, too, two) lost to (know, no) (where, were) (to, too, two) turn.

22g What are compound words?

A **compound word** puts together two or more words to express one concept.

Open compound words remain as separate words, such as *decision making, problem solving,* and *editor in chief.*

Hyphenated compound words use a hyphen between the words, such as *trade-in, fuel-efficient,* and *tax-sheltered.* For punctuation advice about hyphens, see 29i.

Closed compound words appear as one word, such as *proofread, citywide,* and *workweek.*

The history of compound terms that end up as single words usually starts with the compound as two words, and then moves to a hyphenated compound. To check whether a compound term consists of closed, hyphenated, or open words, consult an up-to-date dictionary.

Part Four

Using Punctuation and Mechanics

Chapter 23

Periods, Question Marks, and Exclamation Points

Periods, question marks, and **exclamation points** are collectively called *end punctuation* because they occur at the ends of sentences.

I love you. Do you love me? I love you!

PERIODS

23a When does a period end a sentence?

A **period** ends a statement, a mild command, or an INDIRECT QUESTION.* Never use a period to end a DIRECT QUESTION, a strong command, or an emphatic declaration.

END OF A STATEMENT

A journey of a thousand miles must begin with a single step.

—Lao-tsu, *The Way of Lao-tsu*

MILD COMMAND

Put a gram of boldness into everything you do.

—Baltasar Gracian

INDIRECT QUESTION

I asked if they wanted to climb Mt. Everest. [As an indirect question, this sentence reports that a question was asked. If it were a direct question, it would end with a question mark: *I asked, "Do you want to climb Mt. Everest?"*]

*Find the definition of all words in small capital letters (such as INDIRECT QUESTION) in the Terms Glossary at the back of this book directly before the Index.

23b How do I use periods with abbreviations?

Most **abbreviations,** though not all, call for periods. Typical abbreviations with periods include *Mt., St., Dr., Mr., Ms., Mrs., Fri., Feb., R.N., a.m.,* and *p.m.* (For more about *a.m.* and *p.m.,* see Chapter 20, "Usage Glossary" and section 30j; for more about abbreviations in general, see 30i through 30l.

👁 **ALERT:** Spell out the word *professor* in ACADEMIC WRITING; never abbreviate it. 👁

Abbreviations without periods include the names of states (for example, IL, CO) and some organizations and government agencies (for example, CBS and NASA).

Ms. Yuan, who works at **NASA,** lectured to **Dr.** Garcia's physics class at 9:30 **a.m.**

👁 **ALERT:** When the period of an abbreviation falls at the end of a sentence that calls for a period, the period of the abbreviation serves also to end the sentence. If, however, your sentence ends in a question mark or an exclamation point, put it after the period of the abbreviation.

The phone rang at 4:00 **a.m.**
It's upsetting to answer a wrong-number call at 4:00 **a.m.!**
Who would call at 4:00 **a.m.?** 👁

QUESTION MARKS

23c When do I use a question mark?

A **question mark** ends a **direct question,** one that quotes the exact words the speaker used. (In contrast, an **indirect question** reports a question and ends with a period.)

How many attempts have been made to climb Mt. Everest? [An indirect question would end with a period: *She wants to know how many attempts have been made to climb Mt. Everest.*]

👁 **ALERT:** Never use a question mark with any other punctuation.

NO　She asked, "How are you**?.**"
YES　She asked, "How are you**?**" 👁

Questions in a series are each followed by a question mark, whether or not each question is a complete sentence.

After the fierce storm, the mountain climbers debated what to do next. Turn back? Move on? Rest for a while?

👁 **ALERT:** When questions in a series are not complete sentences (as in the above example), you can choose whether to capitalize the first letter, but be consistent within each piece of writing. 👁

Sometimes a statement or mild command is phrased as a question to be polite. In such cases, a question mark is optional, but be consistent in each piece of writing.

Would you please send me a copy.

23d When can I use a question mark in parentheses?

The only time to use a question mark in parentheses (?) is if a date or other number is unknown or doubtful. Never use (?) to communicate that you're unsure of information.

Mary Astell, a British writer of pamphlets on women's rights, was born in 1666 **(?)** and died in 1731.

The word *about* is often a more graceful substitute for (?): *Mary Astell was born* **about** *1666.*

Also, never use (?) to communicate IRONY or sarcasm. Choose words to deliver your message.

NO	Having altitude sickness is a pleasant **(?)** experience.
YES	Having altitude sickness is **as** pleasant **as having a bad case of the flu.**

EXCLAMATION POINTS

23e When do I use an exclamation point?

An **exclamation point** ends a strong command or an emphatic declaration. A strong command is a firm and direct order: *Look out behind you!* An emphatic declaration is a shocking or surprising statement: *There's been an accident!*

👁 **ALERT:** Never combine an exclamation point with other punctuation.

NO	"There's been an accident**!,**" she shouted.
YES	"There's been an accident**!**" she shouted.
YES	"There's been an accident," she shouted. [Use this form if you prefer not to use an exclamation point.] 👁

23f What is considered overuse of exclamation points?

In ACADEMIC WRITING, words, not exclamation points, need to communicate the intensity of your message. Reserve exclamation points for an emphatic declaration within a longer passage.

> When we were in Nepal, we tried each day to see Mt. Everest. But each day we failed. **Clouds defeated us!** The summit never emerged from a heavy overcast.

Also, using exclamation points too frequently suggests an exaggerated sense of urgency.

NO   Mountain climbing can be dangerous. You must know correct procedures**!** You must have the proper equipment**!** Otherwise, you could die**!**

YES   Mountain climbing can be dangerous. You must know correct procedures**.** You must have the proper equipment**.** Otherwise, you could die**.**

Never use (!) to communicate amazement or sarcasm. Choose words to deliver your message.

NO   At 29,035 feet **(!)**, Mt. Everest is the world's highest mountain. Yet, Chris **(!)** wants to climb it.

YES   At **a majestic** 29,035 feet, Mt. Everest is the world's highest mountain. Yet, Chris, **amazingly,** wants to climb it.

EXERCISE 23-1

Insert any needed periods, question marks, and exclamation points and delete any unneeded ones. For help, consult all sections of this chapter.

EXAMPLE   Dr Madan Kataria, who calls himself the Giggling Guru (!), established the world's first laughter club in 1995.

Dr**.** Madan Kataria, who calls himself the Giggling Guru**,** established the world's first laughter club in 1995.

1. More than 1,000 (?) laughter clubs exist throughout the world, each seeking to promote health by reducing stress and strengthening the immune system!

2. Dr Madan Kataria, a physician in Bombay, India, developed a yoga-like (!) strategy based on group (!) laughter and then set up laughter clubs.

3. Laughter clubs say, "Yes!" when asked, "Is laughter the best medicine."

ANSWERS: EXERCISE 23-2

In May 2003, the fiftieth anniversary of the first successful ascent of Mt. Everest drew 500 climbers to the icy, treacherous peak. A 15-year-old became the youngest person to scale Everest and a 70-year-old became the oldest. Can you imagine that some people broke speed records as well, several records on the same day? One man climbed Everest for the thirteenth time! When Edmund Hillary and Tenzing Norgay were the first people to reach the summit, on May 29, 1953, they did not have the advantage of oxygen tanks, thousands of yards of fixed rope, or 60 aluminum ladders set up across a perilous ice fall. Today's climbers benefit from all these technological advances, plus ultralight equipment and thousands of local people organized to carry supplies and set up camp. If the climb is no longer as difficult as it was for Hillary and Norgay, what is the reason for Everest's continuing fascination? Other Himalayan peaks are harder to climb, but none, of course, is taller. Perhaps that is the reason for Everest's special lure: nowhere else can a climber actually sit on top of the world!

4. The clubs' activities include breathing and stretching exercises and playful (?) behaviors, such as performing the opera laugh (!), the chicken laugh (!), and the "Ho-Ho, Ha-Ha" (?) exercise.
5. According to the German psychologist Dr Michael Titze, "In the 1950s people used to laugh eighteen minutes a day (!), but today we laugh not more than six (?) minutes per day, despite huge rises in the standard of living."

EXERCISE 23-2

Insert needed periods, question marks, and exclamation points. For help, consult all sections of this chapter.

In May 2003, the fiftieth anniversary of the first successful ascent of Mt Everest drew 500 climbers to the icy, treacherous peak A 15-year-old became the youngest person to scale Everest and a 70-year-old became the oldest Can you imagine that some people broke speed records as well, several records on the same day One man climbed Everest for the thirteenth time When Edmund Hillary and Tenzing Norgay became the first people to reach the summit, on May 29, 1953, they did not have the advantage of oxygen tanks, thousands of yards of fixed rope, or 60 aluminum ladders set up across a perilous ice fall Today's climbers benefit from all these technological advances, plus ultralight equipment and thousands of local people organized to carry supplies and set up camp If the climb is no longer as difficult as it was for Hillary and Norgay, what is the reason for Everest's continuing fascination Other Himalayan peaks are harder to climb, but none, of course, is taller Perhaps that is the reason for Everest's special lure: nowhere else can a climber actually sit on top of the world

Chapter 24

Commas

24a What is the role of the comma?

Commas are the most frequently used marks of punctuation, occurring twice as often as all other punctuation marks combined. A comma must be used in certain places, it must not be used in other places, and it's optional in still other places. This chapter helps you sort through the various rules.

For quick access to most answers when you have a comma question, consult Box 96. The sections in parentheses indicate where you can find fuller explanations.

BOX 96   SUMMARY

 Key uses of commas

Commas with Coordinating Conjunctions Linking Independent Clauses (24b)

- Postcards are ideal for brief greetings, **and** they can also be miniature works of art. [*and* is a coordinating conjunction]

Commas after Introductory Elements (24c)

- **Although most postcards cost only a dime,** one recently sold for thousands of dollars. [clause]
- **On postcard racks,** several designs are usually available. [phrase]
- **For example,** animals are timeless favorites. [transitional expression]
- **However,** most cards show local landmarks. [word]

Commas with Items in Series (24d)

- **Places, paintings, and people** appear on postcards. [*and* between last two items]   →

QUOTATION: ON WRITING
All morning I worked on the proof of one of my poems, and I took out a comma; in the afternoon I put it back.

—Oscar Wilde

EXTRA EXERCISE A
Insert commas before coordinating conjunctions that link independent clauses. Some sentences may be correct.

1. England, Scotland, and Wales are located on the same island.

2. Wales is located on the western peninsula of the island and England and Scotland occupy the rest of it.

3. It is bounded on the east by the North Sea and on the south by the English Channel.

4. The Teutonic invaders of the fifth century had to struggle with native Britons for possession of the island for the Romans had virtually abandoned the island by that time.

5. Britain is the proper name of the whole island but England is the political name of the part conquered by the Angles.

6. Neither the Jutes nor the Saxons moved north for they chose to settle in what is today Kent or moved on to Sussex, Wessex, and Essex.

7. The Scots were actually the people of Ireland yet a small colony they established in the northern part of the island eventually gave it its name.

8. The Norman Conquest of Britain was begun under William the Conqueror and was continued by his sons.

9. With few exceptions, all the existing shires of England had been established at the time of the Norman Conquest but the boundaries were not always exactly the same as they are now.

10. Since the eleventh century, the map of Britain has remained little changed yet the reins of power have shifted many times.

Key uses of commas (*continued*)

- **Places, paintings, people, animals** occupy dozens of display racks. [no *and* between last two items]

Commas with Coordinate Adjectives (24e)

- Some postcards feature **appealing, dramatic** scenes.

NO COMMAS WITH CUMULATIVE ADJECTIVES (24e)

- Other postcards feature **famous historical** scenes.

Commas with Nonrestrictive Elements (24f)

- **Four years after the first postcard appeared,** the U.S. government began to issue prestamped postcards. [nonrestrictive element introduces independent clause]

- The Golden Age of postcards, **which lasted from about 1900 to 1929,** yielded many especially valuable cards. [nonrestrictive element interrupts independent clause]

- Collectors attend postcard shows, **which are similar to baseball-card shows.** [nonrestrictive element ends independent clause]

No Commas with Restrictive Elements (24f)

- Collectors **who attend these shows** may specialize in a particular kind of postcard. [restrictive clause]

Commas with Quoted Works (24h)

- One collector told me, "Attending a show is like digging for buried treasure." [quoted words at end of sentence]

- "I always expect to find a priceless postcard," he said. [quoted words at start of sentence]

- "Everyone there," he joked, "believes a million-dollar card is hidden in the next stack." [quoted words interrupted mid-sentence]

24b How do commas work with coordinating conjunctions?

Never use a comma when a coordinating conjunction links only two words, two PHRASES, or two DEPENDENT CLAUSES.

NO Habitat for Humanity depends on volunteers for **labor, and donations** to help with its construction projects. [*Labor* and *donations* are two words; the conjunction explains their relationship. No comma is needed.]

YES   Habitat for Humanity depends on volunteers for **labor and donations** to help with its construction projects.

NO   Each language has **a beauty of its own, and forms of expression** that are duplicated nowhere else. [*A beauty of its own* and *forms of expression* are only two phrases.]

YES   Each language has **a beauty of its own and forms of expression** that are duplicated nowhere else.

—Margaret Mead, "Unispeak"

Do use a comma when a coordinating conjunction links two or more INDEPENDENT CLAUSES. Place the comma before the coordinating conjunction. Box 97 shows this pattern.

BOX 97   PATTERN

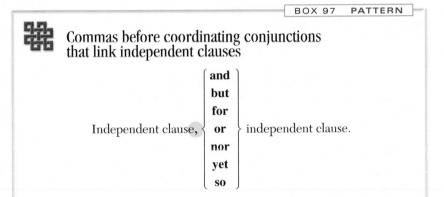

Commas before coordinating conjunctions that link independent clauses

Independent clause, { and / but / for / or / nor / yet / so } independent clause.

The sky turned dark gray, **and** the wind died suddenly.
The November morning had just begun, **but** it looked like dusk.
Shopkeepers closed their stores early, **for** they wanted to get home.
Soon high winds would start, **or** thick snow would begin silently.
Farmers could not continue harvesting, **nor** could they round up their animals in distant fields.
People on the road tried to reach safety, **yet** a few unlucky ones were stranded.
The firehouse whistle blew four times, **so** everyone knew a blizzard was closing in.

Exceptions

■ When two independent clauses are very short, and they contrast with each other, you can link them with a comma without using a coordinating conjunction: *Mosquitoes don't bite, they stab.* Some instructors consider this an error, so in ACADEMIC WRITING, you'll never be wrong if you use a period or semicolon (Chapter 25) instead of a comma.

BACKGROUND

We use *of course* in two ways, one with the comma and one without, according to Bill Walsh, Copy Desk Chief, the *Washington Post*, in his book *Lapsing into a Comma*. With the comma, *of course* means "by the way": *I can attend your meeting on Friday.* **Of course,** *that will postpone by a few hours my finishing the report.* Without the comma, *of course* emphasizes a point: *Will I be there?* **Of course** *I will.*

ANSWERS: EXERCISE 24-1

1. California's 6,000 almond growers produce over 70 percent of the world's almonds, and this crop is worth nearly $800 million a year.

2. Central California provides ideal growing conditions for almonds, for the flat land is rich in nutrients.

3. Almonds and peaches are genetically related, so a small almond cutting can be spliced to a peach pit root to make the almond tree sturdier.

4. Almond trees cannot self-pollinate, so growers depend on bees from over one million beehives to pollinate the pale pink blossoms.

5. Bees will not fly when the temperature is below 54 degrees, nor will bees fly when it rains.

6. Picking almonds from the trees takes too long, but shaking the trees makes most nuts fall to the ground.

7. Workers used to shake the branches with long poles, but mechanical shaking machines make harvesting the nuts much easier today.

8. Machines blow and rake the nuts to areas between the trees, and another machine lifts the almonds into a wagon.

9. The nuts are hulled and shelled by machine, yet many nuts remain flawless and demand a high price.

10. Chipped nuts are bought by companies that make candy bars, or the nuts are purchased to package for baking.

■ When one or both independent clauses linked by a coordinating conjunction happen to contain other commas, drop the coordinating conjunction and use a semicolon instead of the comma. This can help clarify meaning.

With temperatures below freezing, the snow did not melt; ~~and~~ **people** wondered, gazing at the white landscape, when they would see grass again.

ALERTS: (1) Never put a comma *after* a coordinating conjunction that joins independent clauses.

NO	A house is renovated in two weeks **but,** an apartment takes a week.
YES	A house is renovated in two weeks**, but** an apartment takes a week.

(2) Never use a comma alone between independent clauses, or you'll create the error known as a COMMA SPLICE.

NO	Five inches of snow fell in two hours, driving was hazardous.
YES	Five inches of snow fell in two hours, **and** driving was hazardous. ◉

EXERCISE 24-1

Combine each pair of sentences using the coordinating conjunction shown in parentheses. Rearrange words when necessary. For help, consult 24b.

EXAMPLE   Almonds originated in China. They are now the top export crop from the United States. (but)

Almonds originated in China, *but* they are now the top export crop from the United States.

1. California's 6,000 almond growers produce over 70 percent of the world's almonds. This crop is worth nearly $800 million a year. (and)

2. Central California provides ideal growing conditions for almonds. The flat land is rich in nutrients. (for)

3. Almonds and peaches are genetically related. A small almond cutting can be spliced to a peach pit root to make the almond tree sturdier. (so)

4. Almond trees cannot self-pollinate. Growers depend on bees from over one million beehives to pollinate the pale pink blossoms. (so)

5. Bees will not fly when the temperature is below 54 degrees. Bees will not fly when it rains. (nor)

6. Picking almonds from the trees takes too long. Shaking the trees makes most nuts fall to the ground. (but)

7. Workers used to shake the branches with long poles. Mechanical shaking machines make harvesting the nuts much easier today. (but)
8. Machines blow and rake the nuts to areas between the trees. Another machine lifts the almonds into a wagon. (and)
9. The nuts are hulled and shelled by machine. Many nuts remain flawless and demand a high price. (yet)
10. Chipped nuts are bought by companies that make candy bars. The nuts are purchased to package for baking. (or)

24c How do commas work with introductory clauses, phrases, and words?

A comma follows any introductory element that comes before an INDEPENDENT CLAUSE. An introductory element can be a CLAUSE, PHRASE, or words. Because these elements are not sentences by themselves, you need to join them to independent clauses. Box 98 shows this pattern.

BOX 98   PATTERN

Commas with introductory clauses, phrases, and words

- Introductory clause,
- Introductory phrase,
- Introductory word,

independent clause.

When the topic is dieting, many people say sugar craving is their worst problem. [introductory dependent clause]

Between 1544 and 1689, sugar refineries appeared in London and New York. [introductory prepositional phrase]

Beginning in infancy, we develop lifelong tastes for sweet foods. [introductory participial phrase]

Sweets being a temptation for many adults, most parents avoid commercial baby foods that contain sugar. [introductory absolute phrase]

For example, fructose comes from fruit, but it's still sugar. [introductory transitional expression]

Nevertheless, many people think fructose isn't harmful. [introductory conjunctive adverb]

To satisfy a craving for ice cream, even timid people sometimes brave midnight streets. [introductory infinitive phrase]

BACKGROUND
The site <http://www.wisc.edu/writing> offered by the University of Wisconsin at Madison features an interactive quiz on comma use under the heading "The Writer's Handbook" in the section titled "Grammar and Punctuation."

QUOTATION: ON WRITING
Anyone who can improve a sentence of mine by the omission or placing of a comma is looked upon as my dearest friend.
—George Moore

TEACHING TIP
A surprising number of students, especially those inexperienced with academic writing, tend to equate writing ability with knowledge of spelling and rules for the comma. (Not all students who have these ideas admit them freely, but often such notions emerge on anonymous questionnaires or in teacher-student conferences.) You might deal with this misperception about comma rules in two ways. First, you can put commas in their place by referring to the writing process, especially the different concerns that occupy a writer during drafting, revision, and editing—students can reread Chapters 2 and 3 to refresh their memories about these activities. Second, you can invite students to circle any comma in their writing about which they have a question—or any spot where they have not written a comma and have a question—and to jot the question in the margin. This helps students avoid getting snagged on commas while at the same time allowing them to get answers to their questions when you return their work. You will likely find that students have used most commas correctly (a fact that when pointed out enhances students' confidence) and that you can categorize the areas of confusion and thus clarify them for the students. Finally, after students have studied topics such as coordination, subordination, parallelism, and variety and emphasis, you can offer a tutorial review of commas—and students will be happy to discover how much they already know.

BACKGROUND
In a letter to the editors of *Time* magazine (July 4, 1988: 6), Grover A. Reynolds writes about his method for teaching punctuation. Note the examples he uses. Before punctuation: "Woman without her man has no reason for living." After punctuation: "Woman: without her, man has no reason for living." Another: "Call me fool if you wish" and "Call me, fool, if you wish."

TEACHING TIP
Unless they are set off by commas, some adverbs that double as prepositions are likely to cause confusion when placed before the subject of a sentence. You can advise students to apply common sense to avoid confusion.

NO Below the submarine checked the water for mines. [What is below the submarine?]

YES Below, the submarine checked the water for mines.

NO After the crew expected to escort the president's ship. [Then what?]

YES After, the crew expected to escort the president's ship.

Exception

When an introductory element is short, and the sentence can be understood easily, some writers omit the comma. However, in ACADEMIC WRITING, you'll never be wrong if you use the comma.

> YES   In 1992, the Americans with Disabilities Act was passed. [preferred]

> YES   In 1992 the Americans with Disabilities Act was passed.

An **interjection** is an introductory word that conveys surprise or other emotions. Use a comma after an interjection at the beginning of a sentence: ***Oh,*** *we didn't realize that you're allergic to cats.* ***Yes,*** *your sneezing worries me.*

👁 **ALERT:** Use a comma before and after a transitional expression that falls in the middle of a sentence. When the transitional expression starts a sentence, follow it with a comma. When the transitional expression ends a sentence, put a comma before it.

> **By the way,** the parade begins at noon. [introductory transitional expression with comma after it]
>
> The parade, **by the way,** begins at noon. [transitional expression with comma before and after it, in middle of sentence]
>
> The parade begins at noon, **by the way.** [transitional expression with comma before it, at end of sentence]
>
> **However,** our float isn't finished. [introductory conjunctive adverb with comma after it]
>
> Our float, **however,** isn't finished. [conjunctive adverb with comma before and after it, in middle of sentence]
>
> Our float isn't finished, **however.** [conjunctive adverb with comma before it, at end of sentence] 👁

EXERCISE 24-2

Using a comma after the introductory element, combine each set of sentences into one sentence according to the directions in parentheses. You can add, delete, and rearrange words as needed. For help, consult 24c.

EXAMPLE   Several magicians have revealed their secrets. They have revealed their secrets recently. (begin with *recently*)

Recently, several magicians have revealed their secrets.

1. One famous trick involves sawing a woman in half. This trick actually uses two women. (begin with *for example*)

2. The magician opens the lid to a large rectangular box. The magician shows the audience it's empty. (begin with *first*)

3. The brave female assistant lies down in the box. The opened box lid faces away from the audience. (begin with *when*)

4. The assistant puts her head outside one end of the box. She seems to put her wiggling feet out the other end. (begin with *locked inside*)

5. Observers watch in astonishment. The magician pushes a saw through the middle of the box. (begin with *in astonishment*)

6. This illusion seems impossible. This illusion is safely performed with two women participating. (begin with *although*)

7. The first assistant walks behind the box. This assistant lies down in the box and pulls her knees up to her chest. (begin with *walking*)

8. The first woman now occupies only one side. And the other woman hidden under the box's false bottom emerges to get into position on the second side. (begin with *in the closed box*)

9. The second woman folds her body by bending forward at the waist. She puts her feet out the holes at her end of the box (begin with *to create the illusion*)

10. Each woman is positioned in different ends of the box. The magician can safely make a grand show of sawing a woman in half. (begin with *because*)

24d How do commas work with items in a series?

A **series** is a group of three or more elements—words, PHRASES, or CLAUSES—that match in grammatical form and are of equal importance in a sentence. Box 99 shows this pattern.

BOX 99   PATTERN

 Commas in a series

- word, word, **and** word
- phrase, phrase, **and** phrase
- clause, clause, **and** clause

- word, word, word
- phrase, phrase, phrase
- clause, clause, clause

Marriage requires **sexual, financial, and emotional** discipline.
—Anne Roiphe, "Why Marriages Fail"

Culture is a way of **thinking, feeling, believing.**
—Clyde Kluckhohn, *Mirror for Man*

ANSWERS AND COVERAGE: EXERCISE 24-2

1. For example, the famous trick of sawing a woman in half actually uses two women. [introductory words—transitional expression]

2. First, the magician opens the lid to a large rectangular box to show the audience it is empty. [introductory word—transitional expression]

3. When the brave female assistant lies down in the box, the opened lid faces away from the audience. [introductory adverb clause]

4. Locked inside, the assistant seems to put her head out one end of the box and her wiggling feet out the other end. [introductory past participial phrase]

5. In astonishment, observers watch the magician push a saw through the middle of the box. [introductory prepositional phrase]

6. Although this illusion seems impossible, it is safely performed with two women participating. [introductory adverb clause]

7. Walking behind the box, the first assistant lies down in the box and pulls her knees up to her chest. [introductory present-participial phrase]

8. In the closed box, the first woman now occupies only one side, and the other woman hidden under the box's false bottom emerges to get into position on the second side. [introductory prepositional phrase]

9. To create the illusion, the second woman folds her body by bending forward at the waist and putting her feet out the holes at her end of the box. [introductory infinitive phrase]

10. Because each woman is positioned in different ends of the box, the magician can safely make a grand show of sawing a woman in half. [introductory adverb clause]

BACKGROUND

In a letter to the editors of *Time* magazine (July 4, 1988: 6–7), Michael Priestley writes about the magazine's policy of omitting the final comma before the conjunction in a series of words or phrases. "The omission," he writes, "reminds me of my fifth grade teacher's lesson on the subject. A father's will stipulated that his estate be shared equally by his three sons: 'Tom, Dick and Harry.' Tom took the matter to grammar court and won the case: he inherited half the estate, and Dick and Harry split the other half."

QUOTATION: ON WRITING

[Punctuation] scores the music in our minds, gets our thoughts moving to the rhythm of our hearts. Punctuation is the notation in the sheet music of our words, telling us when to rest, or when to raise our voices; it acknowledges that the meaning of our discourse, as of any symphonic composition, lies not in the units but in the pauses, the pacing and the phrasing.

—Pico Iyer

BACKGROUND

The placement of a comma can have important consequences. Consider these examples:

1. A comma once saved a man's life. Czar Alexander III had signed a death warrant reading: "Pardon impossible, to be sent to Siberia." Being sent to Siberia inevitably led to death. However, Czarina Maria Fyodorovna saved the man by altering the message to read: "Pardon, impossible to be sent to Siberia."

2. Elizabeth Langmore (Letters, *Time*, July 4, 1988) points out how very different it is to ask, "Have you seen the elephant eating Tom?" and "Have you seen the elephant eating, Tom?"

3. In another letter to *Time*, Leslie Bryant asks readers to decipher "That that is is that that is not is not is that it it is." With commas and periods, it reads: "That that is, is. That that is not, is not. Is that it? It is."

My love of flying goes back to those early days **of roller skates, of swings, and of bicycles.**

—Tresa Wiggins, student

We have been taught **that children develop by ages and stages, that the steps are pretty much the same for everybody, and that to grow out of the limited behavior of childhood, we must climb them all.**

—Gail Sheehy, *Passages*

Many general publications omit the comma between the next to last item of a series and the coordinating conjunction. Recently, practice is changing even in ACADEMIC WRITING, which means that some instructors require the use of a comma here and others consider it an error. Check with your instructor.

NO The sweater comes in **blue, green, pink and black.** [Do the sweaters come in three or four colors?]

YES The sweater comes in **blue, green, pink, and black.** [The comma before *and* clarifies that the sweaters come in four colors.]

At all times, however, follow the "toast, juice, and ham and eggs rule." That is, when one of the items in a series contains *and*, don't use a comma in that item.

When items in a series contain commas or other punctuation, separate them with SEMICOLONS instead of commas (25e).

If it's a bakery, they have to sell cake; if it's a photography shop, they have to develop film; and if it's a dry-goods store, they have to sell warm underwear.

—Art Buchwald, "Birth Control for Banks"

Numbered or lettered lists within a sentence are considered items in a series. With three or more items, use commas (or semicolons if the items themselves contain commas) to separate them.

To file your insurance claim, please enclose (1) a letter requesting payment, (2) a police report about the robbery, **and** (3) proof of purchase of the items you say are missing.

👁 **ALERT:** In a series, never use a comma before the first item or after the last item, unless a different rule makes it necessary.

NO Many **artists, writers, and composers, have indulged** in daydreaming.

YES Many artists, writers, and composers have indulged in daydreaming.

NO Such dreamers include, Miró, Debussy, Dostoevsky, and Dickinson.

YES Such dreamers include, Miró, Debussy, Dostoevsky, and Dickinson.

YES Such dreamers include, **of course,** Miró, Debussy, Dostoevsky, and Dickinson. [As a transitional expression, *of course* is set off from the rest of the sentence by commas before and after it (24c).] 👁

EXERCISE 24-3

Insert commas to separate the items in a series. If a sentence needs no commas, explain why. For help, consult 24d.

EXAMPLE Families from New York New Jersey and Pennsylvania raise the puppies that become Seeing Eye dogs.

Families from *New York, New Jersey, and Pennsylvania* raise the puppies that become Seeing Eye dogs

1. To socialize future Seeing Eye dogs, families with children age 9 to 14 care for specially bred German shepherds retrievers and mixed-breed puppies for up to 16 months.

2. One youngster in each family becomes the pup's primary caretaker and is responsible for feeding training and grooming the future Seeing Eye dog.

3. While living with their families, the pups learn basic obedience commands, such as sit stay come and down.

4. Groups of families get together frequently to take their Seeing Eye dogs-in-training on outings, so that the puppies become familiar with things that frighten some dogs, such as riding in cars being in crowds walking on slippery floors and hearing loud noises.

5. When the puppies grow up, the families have the pain of giving them up but the satisfaction of knowing that their dogs will lead happy and productive lives while improving the quality of life for their future owners.

24e How do commas work with coordinate adjectives?

Coordinate adjectives are two or more ADJECTIVES of equal weight that describe—that is, modify—a NOUN. In contrast, **cumulative adjectives** build meaning from word to word, as they move toward the noun. Box 100 on the next page shows the pattern for coordinate adjectives. The key to applying this rule is recognizing when adjectives are coordinate and when they aren't. Box 101 on the next page tells you how.

ANSWERS: EXERCISE 24-3

1. To socialize future Seeing Eye dogs, families with children age 9 to 14 care for specially bred German shepherds, retrievers, and mixed-breed puppies for up to 16 months.

2. One youngster in each family becomes the pup's primary caretaker and is responsible for feeding, training, and grooming the future Seeing Eye dog.

3. While living with their families, the pups learn basic obedience commands, such as sit, stay, come, and down.

4. Groups of families get together frequently to take their Seeing Eye dogs-in-training on outings, so that the puppies become familiar with things that frighten some dogs, such as riding in cars, being in crowds, walking on slippery floors, and hearing loud noises.

5. Correct; no series of items.

QUOTATION: ON WRITING

In music, the punctuation is absolutely strict; the bars and rests are absolutely defined. But our prose cannot be quite strict, because we have to relate it to the audience. In other words, we are continually changing the score.

—Sir Ralph Richardson

QUOTATION: ON WRITING

A world that has only periods is a world without inflections. It is a world without shade. It has a music without sharps and flats. It is a martial music. It has a jackboot rhythm. Words cannot bend and curve. A comma, by comparison, catches the gentle drift of the mind in thought, turning in on itself and back on itself, reversing, re-doubling and returning along the course of its own sweet river music; while the semicolon brings clauses and thoughts together with all the silent discretion of a hostess arranging guests around her dinner table.

—Pico Iyer

BOX 100   PATTERN

Commas with coordinate adjectives

coordinate adjective, coordinate adjective noun

BOX 101   SUMMARY

 ### Tests for coordinate and cumulative adjectives

If either one of these tests works, the adjectives are coordinate and require a comma between them.

■ Can the order of the adjectives be reversed without changing the meaning or creating nonsense? If yes, use a comma.

> **NO** The concert featured **new several** bands. [*New several* makes no sense.]

> **YES** The **huge, restless** crowd waited for the concert to begin. [*Restless, huge* still carries the same meaning so these are coordinate adjectives.]

■ Can *and* be sensibly inserted between the adjectives? If yes, use a comma.

> **NO** The concert featured **several and new** bands. [*Several and new* makes no sense.]

> **YES** The **huge and restless** crowd waited. [Modifier *huge and restless* makes sense, so these are coordinate adjectives.]

The audience cheered when the **pulsating, rhythmic** music filled the stadium. [*Pulsating* and *rhythmic* are coordinate adjectives.]

Each band had a **distinctive musical** style. [*Distinctive* and *musical* aren't coordinate adjectives.]

👁 **ALERT:** Don't put a comma between a final coordinate adjective and the noun it modifies.

> **NO** Hundreds of **roaring, cheering, yelling, fans** filled the stadium.

> **YES** Hundreds of **roaring, cheering, yelling fans** filled the stadium. 👁

EXERCISE 24-4

Insert commas to separate coordinate adjectives. If a sentence needs no commas, explain why. For help, consult 24e.

EXAMPLE   Only corn grown for popcorn pops consistently because all other kinds of corn lack tough enamel-like shells.

Only corn grown for popcorn pops consistently because all other kinds of corn lack *tough,* *enamel-like* shells.

1. The outside of an unpopped popcorn kernel is a hard plastic-like coating.
2. Inside an unpopped kernel is a soft starchy substance combined with water.
3. Applying heat causes the water molecules to expand until the pressure pops the dark yellow kernel.
4. The popped kernel turns itself inside out and absorbs air into its white pulpy matter.
5. The thinner softer shells of nonpopcorn corn don't allow water to heat to the high popping temperature.

24f How do commas work with nonrestrictive elements?

A **restrictive element** contains information (a descriptive word, clause, or phrase) that's essential for a sentence to deliver its message; thus, it is often called an *essential element.* A **nonrestrictive element** contains information that's not essential for a sentence to deliver its meaning, and therefore, it is often called a *nonessential element.* The key is in recognizing what's essential (restrictive) and what's nonessential (nonrestrictive) in a sentence. Box 102 defines and explains the differences in the meanings of these terms.

BOX 102   SUMMARY

 Restrictive and nonrestrictive defined

Restrictive

   A restrictive element contains information essential for the sentence to deliver its message. By being essential, the words in the element limit—that is, "restrict"—the meaning in some way. Don't use commas with restrictive elements.

   Many U.S. states retest drivers **who are over sixty-five** to check their driving competency.   ➞

EXTRA EXERCISE B

Circle unnecessary commas and add needed commas where restrictive and nonrestrictive phrases, clauses, and appositives appear in the following sentences.

1. Elizabeth II, who is queen of the United Kingdom, was born in London in 1926.

2. She is the elder daughter of King George VI and Queen Consort Elizabeth who was known as the Queen Mother.

3. Her education administered at home by private tutors included many subjects.

4. She was married, at Westminster Abbey to Philip Mountbatten, who was formerly Prince Philip of Greece.

5. He was created Duke of Edinburgh, with all the rights and privileges of the title, on the eve of the marriage.

6. Prince Charles Elizabeth's first child was born on November 14, 1948.

7. Princess Anne the second child was born on August 15, 1950.

8. Elizabeth's father George VI died in 1952.

9. Elizabeth was crowned, queen of England, in Westminster Abbey a historic site on June 2, 1953.

10. Prince Charles, now himself a parent, thus became, the heir apparent.

Answers to Extra Exercise B

1. Correct

2. Elizabeth, who

3. education, administered . . . tutors, included

4. married at

5. Correct

6. Charles, Elizabeth's first child, was

7. Anne, the second child, was

8. father, George VI, died

9. crowned queen of England in Westminster Abbey, a historic site, on

10. became the

Restrictive and nonrestrictive defined (*continued*)

The information *who are over sixty-five* is essential to understanding the sentence because it limits or restricts the meaning of *drivers* to only those over the age of sixty-five. Drivers *under* sixty-five are not included. To check whether an element is essential, drop it and read the sentence. If the meaning of the sentence changes, then the information element is essential in delivering the message intended in the sentence. This means the element is restrictive (essential), and <u>commas are not used</u>.

Nonrestrictive

A nonrestrictive element contains information that's *not* essential for the sentence to deliver its message. By being nonessential, the words in the element don't limit—or "restrict"—the meaning in some way. Use commas with nonrestrictive (nonessential) elements.

My parents**, who are both over sixty-five,** took a defensive driving course.

The information *who are both over sixty-five* is not essential because the words *my parents* carry the sentence's message so that we know who took a defensive driving course. (Information about their age is "extra" to this message, so <u>commas are required</u>.)

Box 103 shows the pattern for comma use with nonrestrictive elements. The pattern for restrictive elements calls for no commas.

BOX 103   PATTERN

Commas with nonrestrictive elements

- **Nonrestrictive element,** independent clause.
- Beginning of independent clause**, nonrestrictive element,** end of independent clause.
- Independent clause**, nonrestrictive element.**

Restrictive and nonrestrictive elements can fall at the beginning, in the middle, or at the end of a sentence. To test whether an element is nonrestrictive, read the sentence without the element. If the meaning of the sentence does not change, the element is nonrestrictive.

MORE EXAMPLES OF RESTRICTIVE ELEMENTS

Some people **in my neighborhood** enjoy jogging. [The reader needs the information *in my neighborhood* to know which people enjoy jogging. The information is essential, so no commas are used.]

Some people **who are in excellent physical condition** enjoy jogging. [The reader needs the information *who are in excellent physical condition* to know which people enjoy jogging. The information is essential, so no commas are used.]

The agricultural scientist **Wendy Singh** has developed a new fertilization technique. [*Wendy Singh* is essential to identify exactly which agricultural scientist developed the new technique, so no commas are used.]

MORE EXAMPLES OF NONRESTRICTIVE ELEMENTS

An energetic person, Anna Hom enjoys jogging. [Without knowing that Anna Hom is *an energetic person,* the reader can understand that she enjoys jogging. The information is nonessential, so commas are used.]

Anna Hom, **who is in excellent physical condition,** enjoys jogging. [Without knowing Anna Hom's *physical condition,* the reader can understand that Anna Hom enjoys jogging. The information is nonessential, so commas are used.]

Anna Hom enjoys jogging, **which is also Adam's favorite pastime.** [Without knowing about *Adam's favorite pastime,* the reader can understand that Anna Hom enjoys jogging. The information is nonessential, so commas are used.]

The agricultural scientist, **a new breed of farmer,** explains how to control a farming environment. [Without knowing that the scientist is *a new breed of farmer,* the reader can understand that the agricultural scientist explains how to control a farming environment. The information is nonessential, so commas are used.]

EXERCISE 24-5

Using your knowledge of restrictive and nonrestrictive elements, insert commas as needed. If a sentence is correct, explain why. For help, consult 24f.

EXAMPLE   During the 1990s when Internet start-ups were proliferating computer science majors often received many job offers even before they graduated.

During the 1990s, *when Internet start-ups were proliferating,* computer science majors often received many job offers even before they graduated.

1. In the fall of 2000 at the height of the Internet boom over 700 students packed a lecture hall for an introductory computer science course at the University of California at Berkeley.

ADDITIONAL EXAMPLES

Restrictive Clauses and Phrases

1. People *who travel abroad* should be willing to alter their eating habits.

2. Tours *that make dining decisions for travelers* sometimes provide surprises.

3. Diners *with conservative tastes* are sometimes offended.

4. For example, the evening meal *in Spain* is usually served after 9 p.m.

5. The restaurant *where I often had dinner in Madrid* was never filled until after 10.

Nonrestrictive Clauses and Phrases

1. My aunt, *who often travels abroad,* enjoys experimenting with unusual foods.

2. Holiday Tours, *which makes all the dining decisions for its travelers,* provides too few surprises for her.

3. Her tastes, *after her many excursions to exotic places,* are still adventuresome.

4. For example, eating in Spain, *which is always a late-evening affair,* is one of her favorite excursions.

5. Las Tres Encinas, *where she often dines when she is in Madrid,* is never filled until after 10 p.m.

ANSWERS AND COVERAGE: EXERCISE 24-5

1. In the fall of 2000, at the height of the Internet boom, over 700 students packed a lecture hall for an introductory computer science course at the University of California at Berkeley. [nonrestrictive prepositional phrase]

2. Correct: no commas with restrictive relative clause.

3. A few years later, when the boom began to turn to bust, only 350 students registered for the introductory course. [nonrestrictive dependent clause]

4. Something similar occurred at Carnegie Mellon University, where the number of students applying to the School of Computer Science fell by 36 percent. [nonrestrictive relative clause]

Answers and Coverage:
Exercise 24-5 (continued)

5. These students, who understood the U.S. economic cycle, switched to less-specialized majors. [nonrestrictive relative clause]

6. A typical student might change his or her major from computer science to business information technology, which offers a wider variety of commercial skills. [nonrestrictive relative clause]

7. Other business-related majors, such as communications and advertising, are becoming more popular. [nonrestrictive adjectival phrase]

8. Because educators and computer scientists know that the decrease in the number of computer-science majors is only temporary, they are not worried about the future. [nonrestrictive dependent clause, and no comma with the restrictive relative clause]

9. Each time the U.S. economy gathers steam again, leading to demands for advances in computer technology, companies suddenly need programmers and systems analysts again. [nonrestrictive participial phrase]

10. Then students whose strongest interest is computer science will flock back to the courses that once more promise lucrative and interesting job possibilities. [no commas with restrictive relative clauses]

2. Students who arrived late for class had to stand around the sides and back of the room.

3. A few years later when the boom began to turn to bust only 350 students registered for the introductory course.

4. Something similar occurred at Carnegie Mellon University where the number of students applying to the School of Computer Science fell by 36 percent.

5. These students who understood the U.S. economic cycle switched to less-specialized majors.

6. A typical student might change his or her major from computer science to business information technology which offers a wider variety of commercial skills.

7. Other business-related majors such as communications and advertising are becoming more popular.

8. Because educators and computer scientists know that the decrease in the number of computer-science majors is only temporary they are not worried about the future.

9. Each time the U.S economy gathers steam again leading to demands for advances in computer technology companies suddenly need programmers and systems analysts again.

10. Then students whose strongest interest is computer science will flock back to the courses that once more promise lucrative and interesting job possibilities.

24g How do commas set off parenthetical expressions, contrasts, words of direct address, and tag sentences?

Parenthetical expressions are "asides." They add information but aren't necessary for understanding the message of a sentence. Set them off with parentheses or commas.

American farmers **(according to U.S. government figures)** export more wheat than they sell at home.
A major drought, **sad to say,** wiped out this year's wheat crop.

Expressions of **contrast** state what is *not* the case. Set them off with commas.

Feeding the world's population is **a serious, though not impossible,** problem.
We must work against world hunger continuously, **not only when famines strike.**

Words of **direct address** name the person or group being spoken to (addressed). Set them off with commas.

> Join me, **brothers and sisters,** to end hunger.
> Your contribution to the Relief Fund, **Steve,** will help us greatly.

A **tag sentence** is a normal sentence that ends with a "tag," an attached phrase or question. Set off a tag with a comma. When the tag is a question, the sentence ends with a question mark. This holds whether or not the **tag question** is formed with a CONTRACTION.

> People will give blood regularly, **I hope.**
> The response to the blood drive was impressive, **wasn't it?**

EXERCISE 24-6

Add commas to set off any parenthetical or contrasting elements, words of direct address, and tag sentences. Adjust end punctuation as necessary. For help, consult 24g.

EXAMPLE   Writer's block it seems to me is a misunderstood phenomenon.

              Writer's block, *it seems to me,* is a misunderstood phenomenon.

1. An inability to write some say stems from lack of discipline and a tendency to procrastinate.
2. In other words the only way to overcome writer's block is to exert more willpower.
3. But writer's block is a complex psychological event that happens to conscientious people not just procrastinators.
4. Strange as it may seem such people are often unconsciously rebelling against their own self-tyranny and rigid standards of perfection.
5. If I told you my fellow writer that all it takes to start writing again is to quit punishing yourself, you would think I was crazy wouldn't you?

24h How do commas work with quoted words?

Explanatory words are words such as *said, stated, declared,* and others that introduce DIRECT DISCOURSE. When they fall in the same sentence, quoted words are set off from explanatory words. Box 104 on the next page shows this pattern.

> Speaking of ideal love, the poet William Blake wrote, "Love seeketh not itself to please."
> "My love is a fever," said William Shakespeare about love's passion.
> "I love no love," proclaimed poet Mary Coleridge, "but thee."

ANSWERS AND COVERAGE: EXERCISE 24-6
Answers may vary slightly. Here is one set of possibilities.

1. An inability to write, some say, [parenthetical expression] stems from lack of discipline and a tendency to procrastinate.

2. In other words, [parenthetical expression] the only way to overcome writer's block is to exert more willpower.

3. But writer's block is a complex psychological event that happens to conscientious people, not just procrastinators. [expression of contrast]

4. Strange as it may seem, [parenthetical phrase] such people are often unconsciously rebelling against their own self-tyranny and rigid standards of perfection.

5. If I told you, my fellow writer, [direct address] that all it takes to start writing again is to quit punishing yourself, you would think I was crazy, wouldn't you? [tag sentence]

BACKGROUND

Here is the complete poem by William Blake quoted in section 24h.

The Clod and the Pebble

"Love seeketh not itself to please,
Nor for itself hath any care,
But for another gives its ease,
And builds a Heaven in Hell's despair."

So sung a little Clod of Clay
Trodden with the cattle's feet,
But a Pebble of the brook
Warbled out these metres meet:

"Love seeketh only self to please,
To bind another to its delight,
Joys in another's loss of ease,
And builds a Hell in Heaven's despite."

BACKGROUND

Here is the complete poem by Mary Coleridge quoted in section 24h.

My True Love Hath My Heart
and I Have His

None ever was in love with me but grief.
  She wooed me from the day that I was
    born;
She stole my playthings first, the jealous
  thief,
  And left me there forlorn.

The birds that in my garden would have
  sung,
  She scared away with her unending
    moan;
  She slew my lovers too when I was
    young,
  And left me there alone.

Grief, I have cursed thee often—now at
  last
  To hate thy name I am no longer free;
Caught in thy bony arms and prisoned
  fast,
  I love no love but thee.

BOX 104   PATTERN

Commas with quoted words

- Explanatory words, "Quoted words."
- "Quoted words," explanatory words.
- "Quoted words begin," explanatory words, "quoted words continue."

Exception

When the quoted words are blended into the grammatical structure of your sentence, don't use commas to set them off. These are instances of INDIRECT DISCOURSE, usually occurring with *as* and *that*.

> The duke describes the duchess **as** "too soon made glad."
> The duchess insists **that** "appearing glad often is but a deception."

⊚ **ALERT:** When the quoted words end with an exclamation point or a question mark, retain that original punctuation, even if explanatory words follow.

QUOTED WORDS	*"O Romeo! Romeo!"*
NO	"O Romeo! Romeo**!,**" whispered Juliet from her window.
NO	"O Romeo! Romeo**,**" whispered Juliet from her window.
YES	"O Romeo! Romeo**!**" whispered Juliet from her window.

QUOTED WORDS	*"Wherefore art thou Romeo?"*
NO	"Wherefore art thou Romeo**?,**" Juliet urgently said.
NO	"Wherefore art thou Romeo**,**" Juliet urgently said.
YES	"Wherefore art thou Romeo**?**" Juliet urgently said. ⊚

EXERCISE 24-7

Punctuate the following dialogue correctly. If a sentence is correct, explain why. For help, consult 24h.

EXAMPLE   "Can you tell me just one thing?," asked the tourist.

"Can you tell me just one thing**?**" asked the tourist.

1. "I'm happy to answer any questions you have" said the rancher to the tourist.

2. "Well, then" said the tourist "I'd like to know how you make ends meet on such a tiny ranch."

3. "Do you see that man leaning against the shed over there?" asked the rancher.

4. The rancher continued "He works for me, but I don't pay him any money. Instead, I have promised him that after two years of work, he will own the ranch."

5. "Then, I'll work for him, and in two more years, the ranch will be mine again!," said the rancher with a smile.

24i How do commas work in dates, names, addresses, correspondence, and numbers?

When you write dates, names, addresses, correspondence, and numbers, use commas according to accepted practice. Boxes 105 through 108 explain.

BOX 105   SUMMARY

Commas with dates

- Use a comma between the date and the year: *July 20, 1969.*
- Use a comma between the day and the date: *Sunday, July 20.*
- Within a sentence, use a comma on both sides of the year in a full date: *Everyone planned to be near a TV set on July 20, 1969, to watch the lunar landing.*
- Never use a comma when only the month and year, or the month and day, are given. Also, never use a comma between the season and year.

  YES People knew that one day in **July 1969** would change the world.

  YES News coverage was especially heavy on **July 21.**

  YES In **summer 1969** a man walked on the moon.

- Never use a comma in an inverted date, a form used in the U.S. military and throughout the world except in the United States.

  YES People stayed near their televisions on **20 July 1969** to watch the moon landing.

ANSWERS AND COVERAGE: EXERCISE 24-7

1. "I'm happy to answer any questions you have," said the rancher to the tourist. [explanatory words at the end of a quotation]

2. "Well, then," said the tourist, "I'd like to know how you make ends meet on such a tiny ranch." [explanatory words in the middle of a quotation]

3. Correct; no comma should follow a question mark.

4. The rancher continued, "He works for me, but I don't pay him any money. Instead, I have promised him that after two years of work, he will own the ranch." [explanatory words at the beginning of a quotation]

5. "Then, I'll work for him, and in two more years, the ranch will be mine again!" said the rancher with a smile. [no comma should follow an exclamation point]

QUOTATION: ON WRITING
The earliest grammar books defined punctuation marks as cues for oral reading. From the Middle Ages to the twentieth century, however, grammarians in Europe and England slowly dissociated punctuation from speech, defining language as a spatial *structure* rather than a spoken linear stream. As stated in the classic grammar book *The King's English*, 1906 [H. W. Fowler and F. G. Fowler]: "The old stopping was frankly to guide the voice in reading aloud, while the modern is mainly to guide the mind in *seeing* through the construction."

—*Period Styles:*
A History of Punctuation, catalog,
The Cooper Union for the
Advancement of Science and Art

QUOTATION: ON WRITING
The comma tells the reader to pause, just as the blinking yellow light tells a driver to slow down and proceed with caution.

—Gary A. Olson

QUOTATION: ON WRITING
By clearing up any errors you may be making in using commas, you will probably clear up a high percentage of your total mistakes in punctuation.

—Charles W. Dawe

QUOTATION: ON WRITING
I can't turn out slews of stuff each day. I wish I could. I seem to have some neurotic need to perfect each paragraph—each sentence, even—as I go along.

—William Styron

QUOTATION: ON WRITING
During the rise of printing, punctuation was left to the compositor's discretion: in English, as in other vernacular languages, there were not yet any strict conventions to follow. The *Mechanick Exercises of the Whole Art of Printing*, 1683 [Joseph Moxon], outlines the haphazard method of an English shop:

> *As he Sets on, he considers how to* Point *his* Work, *viz. when to Set, where; where, where to make ( ) where [ ] and when to make a Break . . . When he meets with proper Names of Persons or Places he Sets them in* Italick *. . . and Sets the first* Letter *with a* Capital. . . .

—*Period Styles:*
A History of Punctuation, catalog,
The Cooper Union for the
Advancement of Science and Art

BOX 106   SUMMARY

Commas with names, places, and addresses

- When an abbreviated academic degree (*M.D.*, *Ph.D.*) comes after a person's name, use a comma between the name and the title (*Angie Eng, M.D.*), and also after the title if other words follow in the sentence: *The jury listened closely to the expert testimony of **Angie Eng, M.D., last week.***

- When an indicator of birth order or succession (*Jr.*, *Sr.*, *III*, *IV*) follows a name, never use a comma: *Martin Luther **King Jr.*** or *Henry **Ford II***

- When you invert a person's name, use a comma to separate the last name from the first: ***Troyka, David***

- When city and state names are written together, use a comma to separate them: ***Philadelphia, Pennsylvania.*** If the city and state fall within a sentence, use a comma after the state as well: *My family settled in **Philadelphia, Pennsylvania,** before I was born.*

- When a complete address is part of a sentence, use a comma to separate all the items, except the state and zip code: *I wrote to **Shelly Kupperman, 1001 Rule Road, Upper Saddle River, NJ 07458,** for more information about the comma.*

BOX 107   SUMMARY

Commas in correspondence

- For the opening of an informal letter, use a comma: **Dear Betty,**
- For the opening of a business or formal letter, use a colon: **Dear Ms. Kiviat:**
- For the close of a letter, use a comma:
  Sincerely yours,   Best regards,   Love,

BOX 108   SUMMARY

Commas with numbers

- Counting from right to left, put a comma after every three digits in numbers with more than four digits.

  72,867   156,567,066

  →

Commas with numbers (*continued*)

■ A comma is optional in most four-digit numbers. Be consistent within each piece of writing.

$1776	$1,776
1776 miles	1,776 miles
1776 potatoes	1,776 potatoes

■ Never use a comma in a four-digit year: **1990** (*Note:* If the year has five digits or more, do use a comma: **25,000 BC.**)

■ Never use a comma in an address of four digits or more: **12161 Dean Drive**

■ Never use a comma in a page number of four digits or more: *see page 1338*

■ Use a comma to separate related measurements written as words: *five feet, four inches*

■ Use a comma to separate a scene from an act in a play: *act II, scene iv* (or *act 2, scene 4*)

■ Use a comma to separate references to a page and a line: *page 10, line 6*

EXERCISE 24-8

Insert commas where they are needed. For help, consult 24i.

EXAMPLE   On June 1 1984 the small German-French production company released a feature film called *Paris Texas*.

On June 1, 1984, the small German-French production company released a feature film called *Paris, Texas*.

1. Made by the noted German director Wim Wenders, *Paris Texas* was set in an actual town in Lamar County Texas with a population of 24699.

2. The movie's title was clearly intended to play off the slightly more famous Paris in France.

3. The custom of naming little towns in the United States after cosmopolitan urban centers in the Old World has resulted in such places as Athens Georgia and St. Petersburg Florida.

4. As of June 1 2003 the American St. Petersburg had 248232 citizens and the American Athens had 100266.

5. By comparison, St. Petersburg Russia and Athens Greece have populations of approximately 4 million and 1 million, respectively.

ANSWERS AND COVERAGE:
EXERCISE 24-8

1. Made by the noted German director Wim Wenders, *Paris, Texas* [comma after city in title] was set in an actual town in Lamar County, Texas, [commas after county and state] with a population of 24,699. [comma with numbers]

2. Correct

3. The custom of naming little towns in the United States after cosmopolitan urban centers in the Old World has resulted in such places as Athens, Georgia, and St. Petersburg, Florida. [commas after cities and after state within sentence]

4. As of June 1, 2003, [commas with dates] the American St. Petersburg had 248,232 [comma with numbers] citizens and the American Athens had 100,266. [comma with numbers]

5. By comparison, St. Petersburg, Russia, and Athens, Greece, [commas after cities and countries within sentences] have populations of approximately 4 million and 1 million, respectively.

ANSWERS: EXERCISE 24-9

1. Flying at night, owls consult a mental "map" of their surroundings.
2. During the daylight hours, healthy owls who can, fly over their territories and create a map using their eyes and ears.
3. Correct
4. The bespectacled owl, scientists found, wears its glasses as contentedly as humans.
5. In a short time, after they have produced a new mental map using their glasses, the owls once again can spot and chase small rodents across the ground.

24j How do commas clarify meaning?

A comma is sometimes needed to clarify the meaning of a sentence, even though no rule calls for one. The best solution is to revise the sentence.

NO Of the gymnastic team's twenty five were injured.
YES Of the gymnastic team's **twenty, five** were injured.
YES Of **twenty on** the gymnastic team, five were injured. [preferred]

NO Those who can practice many hours a day.
YES **Those who can,** practice many hours a day.
YES **They** practice many hours a day **when they can.** [preferred]

NO George dressed and performed for the sellout crowd.
YES **George dressed,** and performed for the sellout crowd.
YES **After** George dressed, **he** performed for the sellout crowd. [preferred]

EXERCISE 24-9

Insert commas to prevent misreading. For help, consult, 24j.

EXAMPLE When hunting owls use both vision and hearing.
When hunting, owls use both vision and hearing.

1. Flying at night owls consult a mental "map" of their surroundings.
2. During the daylight hours, healthy owls who can fly over their territories and create a map using their eyes and ears.
3. A team of scientists gave owls distorting eyeglasses to make the birds relearn their mental maps.
4. The bespectacled owl scientists found wears its glasses as contentedly as humans.
5. In a short time after they have produced a new mental map using their glasses the owls once again can spot and chase small rodents across the ground.

24k How can I avoid misusing commas?

Throughout this chapter, Alert notes remind you about comma misuses, as they relate to each comma rule. Most of these misuses are overuses—inserting a comma where one is unnecessary. This section summarizes the Alert notes and lists other frequent misuses of the comma.

When advice against overusing a comma clashes with a rule requiring one, follow the rule that requires the comma.

The town of Kitty Hawk, North Carolina, attracts thousands of tourists each year. [Even though the comma after *North Carolina* separates the subject and its verb (which it normally shouldn't), the comma is required here because of the rule that calls for a comma when the name of a state follows the name of a city within a sentence (24i).]

24k.1 Commas with coordinating conjunctions

Never use a comma after a COORDINATING CONJUNCTION that joins two INDEPENDENT CLAUSES, unless another rule makes it necessary (24b). Also, don't use a comma to separate two items joined with a coordinating conjunction—there must be at least three (see 24d).

NO   The sky was dark gray **and,** it looked like dusk.
YES   The sky was dark gray, **and** it looked like dusk.

NO   **The moon, and the stars** were shining last night.
YES   **The moon and the stars** were shining last night.

24k.2 Commas with subordinating conjunctions and prepositions

Never put a comma after a SUBORDINATING CONJUNCTION or a PREPOSITION unless another rule makes it necessary.

NO   **Although,** the storm brought high winds, it did no damage.
YES   **Although the storm brought high winds,** it did no damage. [comma follows full subordinated dependent clause, not the subordinate conjunction that begins it]

NO   The storm did no damage **although,** it brought high winds.
YES   The storm did no damage **although it brought high winds.** [no comma when subordinate clause follows the independent clause]

NO   People expected worse **between,** the high winds and the heavy downpour.
YES   People expected worse **between the high winds and the heavy downpour.** [preposition begins sentence element that needs no comma before or after]

24k.3 Commas in a series

Never use a comma before the first, or after the last, item in a series, unless another rule makes it necessary (24d).

QUOTATION: ON WRITING
Unlike the period, question mark, exclamation [point], colon, dash, and parentheses, the comma has no clear special quality. . . . It is not a terminal marking like the period, a specialized coordinating mark like the semicolon, or an anticipatory mark like the colon. Even the dash, which comes nearest the comma in variety of uses, has a characteristic quality, and all the points except the dash have a much more limited number of uses. The comma may be used alone or in pairs; it may stand between coordinate expressions or may separate expressions of different grammatical rank; it may set off a group for emphasis or clearness even when the grammatical relation is close.
—George Summey Jr.

QUOTATION: ON WRITING
I have performed the necessary butchery. Here is the bleeding corpse.
—Henry James, comment following a request to cut three lines from a 5,000-word article

QUOTATION: ON WRITING
Avoid commas, that are not necessary.
—William Safire, *Fumblerules*

QUOTATION: ON WRITING
The most important fact about a comma is that there are places where it must not be used. That is, there are places where a comma alters the meaning of a statement. Max Beerbohm was being witty when he used a comma in writing about *Frank Harris, and many good writers.* There are also a few places where a comma must be used in order to protect the meaning.
—Bergen Evans and Cornelia Evans

BACKGROUND
The power of the comma was demonstrated a few years ago at a Republican National Convention. An item proposed for the party platform read, "The Convention opposes any form of tax increase which would hurt the economy." Someone called for the addition of a comma, so that the item would read, "The Convention opposes any form of tax increase, which would hurt the economy."

That comma was a reflection of the conservative economic position of its proposer. In the first version of the sentence, *which* begins a restrictive clause. The author of the proposal was talking only of harmful tax increases and implying that nonharmful increases would be acceptable. In the second version, *which* begins a nonrestrictive clause. This author saw all tax increases as harmful.

QUOTATION: ON WRITING
Commas separate adjectives in a series [a]. When the noun and the adjective directly preceding it are a conceptual unit, do not separate them [b].

> [a] Jane is a little, radiant, polite girl.
> [b] Jane is a radiant, polite little girl.
> —*Period Styles:*
> *A History of Punctuation,* catalog,
> The Cooper Union for the
> Advancement of Science and Art

BACKGROUND
Period Styles: A History of Punctuation, a catalog from The Cooper Union for the Advancement of Science and Art, offers these examples of when commas are and are not needed with appositives: *Dick, a boy, chased Jane, a girl* [commas needed; nonrestrictive]; *The boy Dick chased the girl Jane* [no commas needed; restrictive].

NO   The gymnasium was decorated **with, red, white, and blue** ribbons for the Fourth of July.

NO   The gymnasium was decorated with **red, white, and blue, ribbons** for the Fourth of July.

YES   The gymnasium was decorated with **red, white, and blue** ribbons for the Fourth of July.

Never put a comma between a final COORDINATE ADJECTIVE and the NOUN that the adjectives modify. Also, don't use a comma between adjectives that are not coordinate (24e).

NO   He wore an **old, baggy, sweater.**

YES   He wore an **old, baggy sweater.** [coordinate adjectives]

NO   He has **several, new sweaters.**

YES   He has **several new sweaters.** [noncoordinate or cumulative adjectives]

24k.4 Commas with restrictive elements

Never use a comma to set off a RESTRICTIVE (essential) element from the rest of a sentence (24f).

NO   **Vegetables, stir-fried in a wok,** are crisp and flavorful. [The words *stir-fried in a wok* are essential, so they are not set off with commas.]

YES   **Vegetables stir-fried in a wok** are crisp and flavorful.

24k.5 Commas with quotations

Never use a comma to set off INDIRECT DISCOURSE; use a comma only with DIRECT DISCOURSE (24h).

NO   Jon said **that, he likes** stir-fried vegetables.

YES   Jon said **that he likes** stir-fried vegetables.

YES   **Jon said, "I like** stir-fried vegetables."

24k.6 Commas that separate a subject from its verb, a verb from its object, or a preposition from its object

A comma does not make sense between these elements, though in some cases another comma rule might supersede this guideline (as in the first example in section 24k).

NO	**The brothers Wright, made** their first successful airplane flights on December 17, 1903. [As a rule, a comma doesn't separate a subject from its verb.]
YES	**The brothers Wright made** their first successful airplane flights on December 17, 1903.

NO	These inventors enthusiastically **tackled, the problems** of powered flight and aerodynamics. [As a rule, a comma doesn't separate a verb from its OBJECT.]
YES	These inventors enthusiastically **tackled the problems** of powered flight and aerodynamics.

NO	Airplane hobbyists visit Kitty Hawk's flight museum **from, all over the world.** [As a rule, a comma doesn't separate a preposition from its object.]
YES	Airplane hobbyists visit Kitty Hawk's flight museum **from all over the world.**

EXERCISE 24-10

Some commas have been deliberately misused in these sentences. Delete misused commas. If a sentence is correct, explain why. For help, consult all parts of this chapter, especially 24j and 24k.

EXAMPLE   People who live in earthquake-prone regions, have long looked forward to reliable means of forecasting tremblers.

          People who live in earthquake-prone *regions have* long looked forward to reliable means of forecasting tremblers.

1. Since the 1970s, scientists have attempted to provide accurate predictions of, earthquake size and intensity.
2. The task has turned out to be harder than expected, for research geologists have yet to develop a clear understanding of the many complex forces, that cause earthquakes.
3. The earth's crust is made up of large, rigid, plates that slide over a semiliquid mantle, and stress builds up when two plates meet.
4. Scientists need to understand, exactly when the stress will become so great that a quake results, but that has proved difficult.
5. Although, geologists can accurately predict the local aftershocks that result from a large earthquake, they cannot precisely determine when a big quake will hit or, when distant aftershocks will occur.
6. Scientists use information about tensions, along major cracks in rock layers, to understand the general process of predicting, where a large tremor will hit.

ANSWERS AND COVERAGE: EXERCISE 24-10

1. Since the 1970s, [keep: introductory phrase, 24c] scientists have attempted to provide accurate predictions of [omit: no comma between preposition and its object, 24k.6] earthquake size and intensity.

2. The task has turned out to be harder than expected, [keep: comma before coordinating conjunction that separates two independent clauses, 24b] for research geologists have yet to develop a clear understanding of the many complex forces [omit: restrictive clause, 24k.4] that cause earthquakes.

3. The earth's crust is made up of large, rigid [omit: no comma between final of two coordinate adjectives and noun, 24k.3] plates that slide over a semiliquid mantle, [keep: comma before coordinating conjunction that separates two independent clauses, 24b] and stress builds up when two plates meet.

4. Scientists need to understand [omit: no comma between verb and its object, 24k.6] exactly when the stress will become so great that a quake results, [keep: comma before coordinating conjunction that separates two independent clauses, 24b] but that has proved difficult.

5. Although [omit: no comma after subordinating conjunction, 24k.2] geologists can accurately predict the local aftershocks that result from a large earthquake, [keep: comma after introductory dependent clause, 24c] they cannot precisely determine when a big quake will hit or [omit: no comma with coordinating conjunction between two items, 24k.1] when distant aftershocks will occur.

6. Scientists use information about tensions [omit: no commas for restrictive prepositional phrase, 24k.4] along major cracks in rock layers [omit: no commas for restrictive prepositional phrase, 24k.4] to understand the general process of predicting [omit: no comma with restrictive element, 24k.4] where a large tremor will hit.

7. For example, [keep: comma after introductory element (a transitional expression), 24c] geologists have predicted that the next major →

earthquake along [omit: no comma between preposition and its object, 24k.6] the North Anatolian fault in Turkey [omit: no comma between subject and verb, 24k.6] will strike near the city of Istanbul.

8. Unfortunately, [keep: comma after introductory element (conjunctive adverb), 24c] scientists cannot save thousands of lives by determining [omit: no comma between verb and its object, 24k.6] even the approximate date of the expected large quake.

9. Interestingly, [keep: comma after introductory element (transitional expression), 24c] scientists once had amazing success in predicting a 1975 earthquake in Haicheng, China, [keep: comma between city and country and after country within sentence, 24i] after [omit: no comma between preposition and its object, 24k.6] a sequence of small earthquakes, [keep: items in series, 24d] changes in groundwater level, [keep: items in series, 24d] and strange behavior by animals.

10. However, [keep: comma after introductory element (conjunctive adverb), 24c] geologists say that [omit: no comma before indirect discourse, 24k.5] even these clues did not successfully reveal the magnitude [omit: no comma with coordinating conjunction between two words, 24k.1] and timing of any other major earthquake.

QUOTATION: ON WRITING
The commas are the most useful and usable of all the stops. It is highly important to put them in place as you go along. If you try to come back after doing a paragraph and stick them in the various spots that tempt you you will discover that they tend to swarm like minnows into all sorts of crevices whose existence you hadn't realized and before you know it the whole long sentence becomes immobilized and lashed up squirming in commas. Better to use them sparingly, and with affection, precisely when the need for each one arises, nicely, by itself.
—Lewis Thomas

7. For example, geologists have predicted that the next major earthquake along, the North Anatolian fault in Turkey, will strike near the city of Istanbul.

8. Unfortunately, scientists cannot save thousands of lives by determining, even the approximate date of the expected large quake.

9. Interestingly, scientists once had amazing success in predicting a 1975 earthquake in Haicheng, China, after, a sequence of small earthquakes, changes in groundwater level, and strange behavior by animals.

10. However, geologists say that, even these clues did not successfully reveal the magnitude, and timing of any other major earthquake.

24l How can I avoid comma errors?

You can avoid most comma errors with these two bits of advice:

■ As you write or reread what you've written, never insert a comma simply because you happen to pause to think or take a breath before moving on. Pausing isn't a reliable guide for writers, although that myth continues to thrive. Throughout the United States, and indeed the world, people's breathing rhythms, accents, and thinking patterns vary greatly.

■ As you're writing, if you're unsure about a comma, insert it and circle the spot. Later, when you're EDITING, check this handbook for the rule that applies.

Chapter 25

Semicolons

25a What are the uses of a semicolon?

While a period signals the complete separation of INDEPENDENT CLAUSES, a **semicolon** indicates only a partial ("semi") separation. Use a semicolon in only two situations. A semicolon can replace a period between sentences that are closely related in meaning (25b and 25c). Also, a semicolon belongs between sentence structures that already contain one or more commas (25d) and with certain lists (25e).

25b When can I use a semicolon, instead of a period, between independent clauses?

The choice between a period and a semicolon for separating independent clauses depends on whether your meaning is better communicated by a complete separation (period) or a partial separation (semicolon). Box 109 shows this pattern for using semicolons.

BOX 109   PATTERN

Semicolon I

■ Independent clause; independent clause.

The desert known as Death Valley became a U.S. National Park in 1994; it used to be a U.S. National Monument.
This is my husband's second marriage; it's the first for me.
—Ruth Sidel, "Marion Deluca"

QUOTATION: ON WRITING
For what is Punctuation, and what its aim? It is the art of dividing a literary composition into sentences, and parts of sentences, by means of points, for the purpose of exhibiting the various combinations, connections, and dependencies of words. And what is this process but a means of facilitating that analysis and combination which must be made, consciously or unconsciously, before we can penetrate to the very core of an author's thoughts, and appropriate them as food for the life and growth of our own minds?
—John Wilson

QUOTATION: ON WRITING
I have grown fond of semicolons in recent years. The semicolon tells you that there is still some question about the preceding full sentence; something needs to be added; it reminds you sometimes of the Greek usage. It is almost always a greater pleasure to come across a semicolon than a period. The period tells you that is that; if you didn't get all the meaning you wanted or expected, anyway you got all the writer intended to parcel out and now you have to move along. But with a semicolon there you get a pleasant little feeling of expectancy; there is more to come; to read on; it will get clearer.
—Lewis Thomas

BACKGROUND
Students will find a practice exercise on the use of commas and semicolons at the Web site <http://owl.english.purdue.edu/handouts/grammar/g_commacompEX1.html>. The Web site also links to the answers.

ADDITIONAL EXAMPLES OF SEMICOLON PATTERNS

1. Each year, people from all over the world visit the Tower of London; for centuries, it served as a prison for famous persons who were deemed to be enemies of the crown.

2. The tower is located in the borough of Stepney; it covers about eighteen acres.

3. The central portion, called the White Tower, was begun in 1078; it was modernized by the architect Christopher Wren.

4. The Beauchamp Tower has ninety-one inscriptions of prisoners in it; the Bloody Tower served as the prison of Sir Walter Raleigh, who wrote an incomplete history of the world during his stay there in 1614.

5. The place of execution within the walls was Tower Green; Anne Boleyn was beheaded there in 1536.

6. Black varieties of the leopard are common in humid parts of India; however, they are rare in Africa.

7. Leopards prey on monkeys, birds, and reptiles; consequently, they must hunt both in trees and on the ground.

8. A leopard begins its meal by tearing at the forequarters of its prey; in contrast, the tiger starts with the hindquarters of its victim.

9. One Indian leopard was alleged to have killed two hundred human beings in two years before it was shot; similarly, a leopard in Ceylon used to lie in wait for passersby on a main road.

10. The leopard's roar of belligerence is different from its mating call; nevertheless, both sound fierce to the human ear.

👁 **ALERT:** Never use a comma alone between independent clauses—this rule will prevent you from creating the error known as a COMMA SPLICE. 👁

25c When else can I use a semicolon between independent clauses?

When the second of a set of independent clauses closely related in meaning starts with a CONJUNCTIVE ADVERB or with a TRANSITIONAL EXPRESSION, you can choose to separate the clauses with a semicolon instead of a period. Also, insert a comma following a conjunctive adverb or transitional expression that starts an independent clause. Although some professional writers today omit the comma after short words (*then, next, soon*), the rule remains for most ACADEMIC WRITING. Box 110 shows this pattern for using semicolons.

BOX 110   PATTERN

Semicolon II

- Independent clause; conjunctive adverb, independent clause.
- Independent clause; transitional expression, independent clause.

The average annual rainfall in Death Valley is about two inches; **nevertheless,** hundreds of plant and animal species survive and even thrive there. [conjunctive adverb]

Photographers have spent years recording desert life cycles; **as a result,** we can watch bare sand flower after a spring storm. [transitional expression]

👁 **ALERT:** Never use only a comma between independent clauses that are connected by a conjunctive adverb or word of transition—this rule will prevent you from creating the error known as a COMMA SPLICE. 👁

25d How do semicolons work with coordinating conjunctions?

As a general rule, when INDEPENDENT CLAUSES are linked by a COORDINATING CONJUNCTION, good practice calls for a comma, not a period or semicolon, before the coordinating conjunction (24b). However, when one or more of the independent clauses already contain a comma, link the independent clauses by substituting a semicolon for the period. This can help your reader see the relationship between the ideas more clearly. Box 111 shows the various combinations of this pattern.

BOX 111 PATTERN

 Semicolon III

- Independent clause, one that contains a comma; coordinating conjunction followed by independent clause.
- Independent clause; coordinating conjunction followed by independent clause, one that contains a comma.
- Independent clause, one that contains a comma; coordinating conjunction followed by independent clause, one that contains a comma.

When the peacock has presented his back, the spectator will usually begin to walk around him to get a front view; **but** the peacock will continue to turn so that no front view is possible.

> —Flannery O'Connor, "The King of the Birds"

Our Constitution is in actual operation; everything appears to promise that it will last; **but** in this world, nothing is certain but death and taxes.

> —Benjamin Franklin, in a 1789 letter

For anything worth having, one must pay the price; **and** the price is always work, patience, love, self-sacrifice.

> —John Burroughs

25e When should I use semicolons between items in a series?

When a sentence contains a series of items that are long or that already contain one or more commas, separate the items with semicolons. Punctuating this way groups the elements so that your reader can see where one item ends and the next begins. Box 112 shows this pattern.

BOX 112 PATTERN

 Semicolon IV

- Independent clause containing a series of items, any of which contain a comma; another item in the series; and another item in the series.

ANSWERS AND COVERAGE: EXERCISE 25-1

1. The Tour de France is the world's best-known bicycle race; the 94-year-old Giro d'Italia runs a close second. [25b, closely related independent clauses]

2. Both are grueling, three-week-long events that require cyclists to cover over 2,000 miles of difficult, mountainous terrain; and both are eagerly anticipated, draw enormous crowds along their routes, and receive extensive media coverage. [25d, two closely related independent clauses connected by a coordinating conjunction]

3. That media attention leads to marketing opportunities for the events' sponsors, which place ads along the race's route, in the nearby towns, and on the cyclists themselves. [25f, no semicolon with dependent clause]

4. Martin Hvastija, a participant in the 2003 Giro d'Italia, had no chance of winning the race; nevertheless, he drew extensive media attention for his sponsors. [25c, second closely related independent clause starts with conjunctive adverb]

5. Correct sentence; semicolon separates closely related independent clauses.

6. Although he had no chance of winning the race, newscasters beamed his image around the world during the short time he was a front-runner, during the same period showing the world the brightly colored advertising logos on his jersey. [25f, no semicolon after dependent clause; also, 25f, no semicolon after introductory phrase]

7. In addition to sponsoring individual athletes, corporations plaster ads all over the towns that the race goes through; they toss samples, coupons, and gadgets to spectators from promotional vehicles that ride the route an hour ahead of the cyclists; and they run ads during TV and radio coverage of the race. [25e, items in a series that contain commas; also, 25b, closely related independent clauses]

→

The assistant chefs chopped onions, green peppers, and parsley; sliced chicken and duck breasts into strips; started a broth simmering; **and** filled a large, shallow copper pan with oil.

25f How do I avoid misusing the semicolon?

Not using a semicolon after an introductory phrase

If you use a semicolon after an introductory PHRASE, you create the error known as a SENTENCE FRAGMENT.

NO	**Open until midnight;** the computer lab is well used. [Using a semicolon turns an introductory phrase into a sentence fragment.]
YES	Open until midnight, the computer lab is well used.

Not using a semicolon after a dependent clause

If you use a semicolon after a DEPENDENT CLAUSE, you create the error known as a sentence fragment.

NO	**Although the new dorms have computer facilities;** many students still prefer to go to the computer lab. [Using a semicolon turns a dependent clause into a sentence fragment.]
YES	Although the new dorms have computer facilities, many students still prefer to go to the computer lab.

Not using a semicolon to introduce a list

When the words that introduce a list form an independent clause, use a colon, never a semicolon (26b).

NO	**The newscast featured three major stories;** the latest pictures of Uranus, a speech by the president, and dangerous brush fires in Nevada. [*The newscast featured three major stories* is an independent clause, so the punctuation before the list should be a colon, not a semicolon.]
YES	The newscast featured three major stories: the latest pictures of Uranus, a speech by the president, and dangerous brush fires in Nevada.

EXERCISE 25-1

Insert semicolons as needed in these items. Also, fix any incorrectly used semicolons. If a sentence is correct, explain why. For help, consult all sections of this chapter.

EXAMPLE   Bicycle racing is as popular in Europe as baseball or basketball is in the United States, it is even more heavily commercialized.

Bicycle racing is as popular in Europe as baseball or basketball is in the United States; it is even more heavily commercialized.

1. The Tour de France is the world's best-known bicycle race, the 94-year-old Giro d'Italia runs a close second.

2. Both are grueling, three-week-long events that require cyclists to cover over 2,000 miles of difficult, mountainous terrain, and both are eagerly anticipated, draw enormous crowds along their routes, and receive extensive media coverage.

3. That media attention leads to marketing opportunities for the events' sponsors; which place ads along the race's route, in the nearby towns, and on the cyclists themselves.

4. Martin Hvastija, a participant in the 2003 Giro d'Italia, had no chance of winning the race, nevertheless, he drew extensive media attention for his sponsors.

5. His method was simple; he managed to ride out in front of the field for a few brief miles.

6. Although he had no chance of winning the race; newscasters beamed his image around the world during the short time he was a front-runner, during the same period; showing the world the brightly colored advertising logos on his jersey.

7. In addition to sponsoring individual athletes, corporations plaster ads all over the towns that the race goes through, they toss samples, coupons, and gadgets to spectators from promotional vehicles that ride the route an hour ahead of the cyclists, and they run ads during TV and radio coverage of the race.

8. In 2003, the organizers of the Giro took in over $8 million in fees from advertisers and $12 million in broadcast rights from the Italian state-owned TV network, RAI, however, these figures were down a bit from the previous year.

9. An additional source of revenues for race organizers is fees from the towns where the race starts and ends each day, as a result, organizers determine the actual course according to which cities are willing to pay the $120,000 charge.

**ANSWERS AND COVERAGE:
EXERCISE 25-2**

Answers will vary. One set of possibilities follows here.

1. This defiant stand against bigotry by a single African American woman made Parks one of the most respected civil rights leaders of the 1950s; now in her eighties, she has not lost her pep. [25b, closely related independent clauses]

2. Parks remains active in the quest for improved race relations; in fact, she frequently travels to advocate equality, devotes much of her time to an organization that she helped found, and has written two autobiographical books. [25c, second closely related independent clause starts with transitional expression]

3. Parks neither sought nor expected the attention that her act of defiance brought her; nevertheless, she is pleased that people consider her the "mother of the civil rights movement." [25c, second closely related independent clause starts with conjunctive adverb]

4. Parks continues to spread her message to the people of the world, as she did when she embarked on a 381-day tour throughout the United States and many foreign countries in 1996; she advises her audiences to coexist peacefully and to live as one. [25d, semicolons between independent clauses already containing commas]

5. The message from 1955 reverberates strongly today because of one enthusiastic, honored, and respected woman; moreover, the message Rosa Parks has brought to the world is sure to outlast each generation that hears it. [25c, second closely related independent clause starts with transitional expression]

10. Media watchers think the Giro d'Italia could become even more profitable and popular, especially among young adults, but only if it took a cue from the Tour de France by encouraging; more international press coverage, more star riders, and even heavier corporate sponsorship.

EXERCISE 25-2

Combine each set of sentences into one sentence so that it contains two independent clauses. Use a semicolon correctly between the two clauses. You may add, omit, revise, and rearrange words. Try to use all the patterns in this chapter and explain the reasoning behind your decisions. More than one revision may be correct. For help, consult all sections of this chapter.

EXAMPLE   Rosa Parks's refusal to move to the back of a bus in Montgomery, Alabama, in 1955 sparked the modern civil rights movement. Her action led to the greatest social revolution in U.S. history.

Rosa Parks's refusal to move to the back of a bus in Montgomery, Alabama, in 1955 sparked the modern civil rights movement; *her* action led to the greatest social revolution in U.S. history.

1. This defiant stand against bigotry by a single African American woman made Parks one of the most respected civil rights leaders of the 1950s. Now in her eighties, she has not lost her pep.

2. Parks remains active in the quest for improved race relations. She frequently travels to advocate equality. She devotes much of her time to an organization that she helped found. And she has written two autobiographical books.

3. Parks neither sought nor expected the attention that her act of defiance brought her. Nevertheless, she is pleased that people consider her the "mother of the civil rights movement."

4. Parks continues to spread her message to the people of the world, as she did when she embarked on a 381-day tour throughout the United States and many foreign countries in 1996. She advises her audiences to coexist peacefully. She tells them to live as one.

5. The message from 1955 reverberates strongly today because of one enthusiastic, honored, and respected woman. The message Rosa Parks has brought to the world is sure to outlast each generation that hears it.

Chapter 26

Colons

26a What are the uses of a colon?

A **colon** is a full stop that draws attention to the words that follow. It can be placed only at the end of an INDEPENDENT CLAUSE. A colon introduces a list, an APPOSITIVE, or a QUOTATION.

26b When can a colon introduce a list, an appositive, or a quotation?

When a complete sentence—that is, an INDEPENDENT CLAUSE—introduces a list, an APPOSITIVE, or a QUOTATION, place a colon before the words being introduced. These words don't have to form an independent clause themselves, but a complete sentence before the colon is essential. Box 113 shows this pattern for using a colon.

BOX 113   PATTERN

Colon sentence I

- Independent clause: list.
- Independent clause: appositive.
- Independent clause: "Quoted words."

Introducing listed items

When a complete sentence introduces a list, a colon is required, as demonstrated in the example at the top of the next page.

425

BACKGROUND
A colon (in Greek, *kōlon*) was originally a person's or an animal's limb. As such, it came to be used to refer to a portion of a strophe in choral dancing, then to a division in prosody, and later to a principal clause in a sentence. Finally, it became the sign marking the breathing space at the end of a clause.

Historically, the colon as a mark of punctuation was preceded by the semicolon; but in English, the colon had more use than the semicolon until the nineteenth century, when it began to be employed almost solely as a mark of anticipation. It regained prestige with the publication of H. W. Fowler's *Dictionary of Modern English Usage* in 1926 and has experienced increased usage since that time.

BACKGROUND
Emoticons are clusters of punctuation used in electronic messages, such as :-) for a smile, and :-(for a frown, that are used to set the tone for the sentence that precedes them. The knack for interpreting them starts with tilting your head sideways to the left and looking for a facial expression or symbol. Here are a few other examples:

:-D	a laughing smile
*<:-)	a birthday smile
;-)	a wink
@–>–>-	a long-stemmed rose

QUOTATION: ON WRITING
The colon is usually a mark of addition or expectation, with emphasis on a following explanation, list, table, or quotation. With formal words (*as follows* or the like) it raps for attention; with easy wording it is little more formal than the somewhat lighter semicolon. It is not a series or balancing point like the semicolon; it seems to say "Watch carefully what comes next."

—George Summey Jr.

Remember that colons—perhaps the mark we exploit least—generally mean that what is to come will explain what has just gone by. They imply identity, whereas semicolons imply "separate but equal" status. "I have just learned three facts: that St. Paul is the capital of Minnesota; that Helena is the capital of Montana; and that Lincoln is the capital of Nebraska." Everything after the colon adds up to "three facts"—whereas the three statements of fact, though they have much in common, are not identical.

Colons can also save words and create special effects. Compare:

- I admire her poetry. Its imagery is magnificent.
- I admire her poetry for its magnificent imagery.
- I admire her poetry: its imagery is magnificent.

All three versions are "correct." The first is emphatic and probably clear—or clear enough: Probably your reader will realize that the second sentence explains the first. The second version is clearer, and it flows along smoothly. The third is clearer than the first and just as clear as the second, and it gives us a unique kind of silence—not just a break (the period did that) but mild suspense. Your job is to decide which way of punctuating best expresses what you want to express.

—Robert M. Pierson

QUOTATION: ON WRITING
Punctuation is like an engine: it pulls the sentence along.

—Anonymous

If you really want to lose weight, you must do three things: eat smaller portions, exercise, and drink lots of water. [The required independent clause comes before the listed items, so a colon is correct.]

When the lead-in words at the end of an independent clause are *such as, including, like,* or *consists of,* never use a colon. In contrast, if the lead-in words at the end of an independent clause are *the following* or *as follows,* do use a colon.

The students demanded improvements *such as* an expanded menu in the cafeteria, improved janitorial services, and more up-to-date textbooks.

The students demanded *the following*: an expanded menu in the cafeteria, improved janitorial services, and more up-to-date textbooks.

Introducing appositives

An APPOSITIVE is a word or words that rename a NOUN or PRONOUN. When an appositive is introduced by an independent clause, use a colon.

Only cats would likely approve of one old-fashioned remedy for cuts: a lotion of catnip, butter, and sugar. [The required independent clause comes before the appositive: *a lotion of catnip, butter, and sugar* renames *old-fashioned remedy.*]

Introducing quotations

When an independent clause introduces a quotation, use a colon after it. (If the words introducing a quotation don't form an independent clause, use a comma.)

The little boy in E.T. did say something neat: "How do you explain school to a higher intelligence?" [The required independent clause comes before the quotation.]

—George F. Will, "Well, I Don't Love You, E.T."

26c When can I use a colon between two independent clauses?

When a second INDEPENDENT CLAUSE explains or summarizes a first independent clause, you can use a colon to separate them. Box 114 on the facing page shows this pattern for using a colon.

👁 **ALERT:** You can choose to use a capital letter or a lowercase letter for the first word of an independent clause that follows a colon. Whichever you choose, be consistent within a piece of writing. I use a capital letter in this handbook.

We will never forget the first time we made dinner together: **He** got stomach poisoning and was too sick to go to work for four days.

—Lisa Baladendrum, student 👁

BOX 114   PATTERN

 Colon sentence II

■ Independent clause: Independent clause that explains or summarizes the prior independent clause.

26d What standard formats require a colon?

A variety of standard formats in American English require a colon. Also, colons are used in many DOCUMENTATION STYLES, as shown in Chapters 34, 35, and 36.

TITLE AND SUBTITLE

A Brief History of Time: From the Big Bang to Black Holes

HOURS, MINUTES, AND SECONDS

The plane took off at 7:15 p.m.
The track star passed the halfway point at 1:23.02.

👁 **ALERT:** In the military, hours and minutes are written without colons and with four digits on a 24-hour clock: *The staff meeting originally scheduled for Tuesday at **0930** will be held Tuesday at **1430** instead.* 👁

REFERENCES TO BIBLE CHAPTERS AND VERSES

Psalms 23:1–3
Luke 3:13

MEMOS

To: Dean Kristen Olivero
From: Professor Daniel Black
Re: Student Work-Study Program

SALUTATION IN A BUSINESS LETTER

Dear Dr. Jewell:

QUOTATION: ON WRITING

When we are very young, we tend to regard the ability to use a colon much as a budding pianist regards the ability to play with crossed hands: many of us, when we are older, regard it as a proof of literary skill, maturity, even of sophistication: and many, whether young, not so young, or old, employ it gauchely, haphazardly, or at best inconsistently.

—Eric Partridge

ADDITIONAL EXAMPLES

To introduce quotations, summaries, and lists:

1. Alice Roosevelt Longworth's colorful reputation is exemplified by this remark: "I have a simple philosophy. Fill what's empty. Empty what's full. And scratch where it itches."

2. Greek mythology comprises the description of the gods and the various stories told about them: It is a series of narratives depicting their personalities, functions, and relationships.

3. Zeus, the supreme god of the Greeks, served in a number of capacities: weather god, sender of rain and lightning, and ruler over the other gods.

To separate material:

1. Eric Partridge is the author of *You Have a Point There: A Guide to Punctuation and Its Allies* as well as *Usage and Abusage: A Guide to Good English.*

2. I will cite the work in the bibliography as follows:

O'Connor, Flannery. "The Life You Save May Be Your Own." *The Realm of Fiction: Seventy-Four Stories.* Ed. James B. Hall and Elizabeth Hall. 3rd ed. New York: McGraw, 1977. 479–88.

3. To: Professor Jill Alexander
From: Professor Max Gregorian
Re: Selection of textbooks

1. The institution of marriage is generally divided by sociologists into four main types: monogamy, polygamy, polyandry, and group marriage.

2. An early reference to group marriage was made by Julius Caesar concerning the early Britons: "Ten and even twelve have wives common to them, and particularly brothers among brothers, and parents among their children."

3. Monogamy, the marriage of one man with one woman, is the most widely approved form in contemporary society: It is the basis of the modern family.

4. Polygamy is practiced by some religious sects: It is acceptable, for example, in some Arab countries.

5. Most Modern women do not generally favor such an arrangement: They have no desire to be one of several wives.

QUOTATION: ON WRITING
An unnecessary [punctuation] mark is worse than useless. It is an interruption.
—George Summey Jr.

26e When is a colon wrong?

Independent clauses

A colon can introduce a list, an APPOSITIVE, or a QUOTATION, but only when an INDEPENDENT CLAUSE does the introducing. Similarly, a colon can be used between two independent clauses when the second summarizes or explains the first. In following these rules, be sure that you're dealing with independent clauses, not other word groups.

NO   The cook bought**:** eggs, milk, cheese, and bread. [*The cook bought* isn't an independent clause.]

YES   The cook bought eggs, milk, cheese, and bread.

Never use a colon to separate a PHRASE or DEPENDENT CLAUSE from an independent clause. Otherwise, you'll create the error known as a SENTENCE FRAGMENT.

NO   Day after day**:** the drought dragged on. [*Day after day* is a phrase, not an independent clause.]

YES   Day after day**,** the drought dragged on.

NO   After the drought ended**:** the farmers celebrated. [*After the drought ended* is a dependent clause, not an independent clause.]

YES   After the drought ended**,** the farmers celebrated.

Lead-in words

Never use a colon after the lead-in words *such as, including, like,* and *consists of.*

NO   The health board discussed many problems **such as:** poor water quality, aging sewage treatment systems, and the lack of alternate water supplies. [A colon is incorrect after *such as.*]

YES   The health board discussed poor water quality, aging sewage treatment systems, and the lack of alternate water supplies. [*Such as* is dropped and the sentence slightly revised.]

YES   The health board discussed many problems**,** **such as** poor water quality, an aging sewage treatment system, and the lack of alternate water supplies. [Comma before *such as* tells the reader that the list coming up is nonrestrictive (nonessential)—it illustrates *problems.*]

YES   The health board discussed many problems**:** poor water quality, aging sewage treatment systems, and the lack of alternate water supplies. [If *such as* is dropped, a colon after the independent clause is correct.]

EXERCISE 26-1

Insert colons where needed and delete any not needed. If a sentence is correct, explain why. For help, consult all sections of this chapter.

EXAMPLE   The twentieth century saw a flowering of Irish literature, W. B. Yeats, G. B. Shaw, Samuel Beckett, and Seamus Heaney all won the Nobel Prize in Literature.

The twentieth century saw a flowering of Irish literature: W. B. Yeats, G. B. Shaw, Samuel Beckett, and Seamus Heaney all won the Nobel Prize in Literature.

1. People who work the night shift are typically deprived of essential sleep, an average of nine hours a week.

2. The Iroquois of the Great Lakes region lived in fortified villages and cultivated: corn, beans, and squash.

3. Five nations originally formed the Iroquois Confederacy: the Mohawk, the Oneida, the Onondaga, the Cayuga, and the Seneca.

4. Later, these five Iroquois nations were joined by: the Tuscarora.

5. Shouting: "Come back!" Adam watched the vehicle speed down the highway.

6. When a runner breaks through that unavoidable wall of exhaustion, a very different feeling sets in; an intense sense of well-being known as the "runner's high."

7. However: the "runner's high" soon disappears.

8. Two new nations were born on the same day in 1947, India and Pakistan achieved their independence from Britain at midnight on August 15.

9. To   English 101 Instructors
   From   Dean of Instruction
   Re   Classroom Assignments

10. Only a hurricane could have kept Lisa from meeting Nathaniel at 800 p.m.; unfortunately, that night a hurricane hit.

11. George's interests were typical of a sixteen-year-old, cars, music videos, and dating.

12. Like many people who have never learned to read or write, the woman who told her life story in *Aman; The Story of a Somali Girl* was able to remember an astonishing number of events in precise detail.

13. The Greek philosopher Socrates took these words as his motto, "The unexamined life is not worth living."

14. Socrates was executed after being found guilty of: teaching young people new ideas.

15. The voice coming from the radio could belong to only one person; the great jazz singer Ella Fitzgerald.

ANSWERS AND COVERAGE: EXERCISE 26-1

1. (insert colon) essential sleep: an [26b, introducing appositives]

2. (delete colon) cultivated corn, beans, and squash [26e, no colon when listed items are not introduced by an independent clause]

3. Correct; colon introduces listed items after an independent clause

4. (delete colon) joined by the Tuscarora [26e, no colon to separate a phrase from the rest of its independent clause]

5. (delete colon) Shouting, "Come [26b, no colon when introduction to quotation is not an independent clause]

6. (insert colon) sets in: an intense [26b, introducing appositives]

7. (delete colon) However, the [26e, no colon to separate an introductory word from the rest of its independent clause]

8. (insert colon) in 1947: India and Pakistan [26c, separating two complete independent clauses]

9. (insert colons)
   To: English
   From: Dean
   Re: Classroom [26d, memos]

10. (insert colon) 8:00 p.m. [26d, hours, minutes, and seconds]

11. (insert colon) sixteen-year-old: cars [26b, introducing listed items]

12. (insert colon) *Aman: The Story* [26d, title and subtitle]

13. (insert colon) motto: "The [26b, introducing quotations]

14. (delete colon) of teaching [26e, no colon to separate a phrase from the rest of its independent clause]

15. (insert colon) person: the great [26b, introducing appositives]

Chapter 27

Apostrophes

27a What is the role of the apostrophe?

The **apostrophe** plays four roles in writing: It creates the POSSESSIVE CASE of NOUNS, forms the possessive case of INDEFINITE PRONOUNS, stands for one or more omitted letters in a word (a CONTRACTION), and can help form plurals of letters and numerals.

In contrast, here are two roles the apostrophe doesn't play: It doesn't belong with plurals of nouns, and it doesn't form the plural of PERSONAL PRONOUNS in the possessive case.

27b How do I use an apostrophe to show a possessive noun?

An apostrophe works with a NOUN to form the POSSESSIVE CASE, which shows ownership or a close relationship.

OWNERSHIP	The **writer's** pen ran out of ink.
CLOSE RELATIONSHIP	The **novel's** plot is complicated.

Possession in nouns can be communicated in two ways: by a PHRASE starting with *of* (*comments **of** the instructor; comments **of** Professor Furman*) or by an apostrophe and the letter *s* (*the instructor**'s** comments; Professor Furman**'s** comments*). Here's a list of specific rules governing usage of *'s*.

■ **Add 's to nouns not ending in s:**

She felt a **parent's** joy. [*Parent* is a singular noun not ending in *s*.]
They care about their **children's** education. [*Children* is a plural noun not ending in *s*.]

430

■ **Add 's to singular nouns ending in s:**

You can add 's or the apostrophe alone to show possession when a singular noun ends in *s*. In this handbook, I use 's to clearly mark singular-noun possessives, no matter what letter ends the noun. Whichever rule variation you choose, be consistent within each piece of writing.

The **bus's** (or **bus'**) air conditioning is out of order.
Chris's (or **Chris'**) ordeal ended.

If you encounter a tongue-twisting pronunciation (*Charles* **Dickens's** *novel*), you may decide not to add the additional *s* (*Charles* **Dickens'** *novel*). You must, however, be consistent in each piece of writing.

■ **Add only an apostrophe to a plural noun ending in s:**

The **boys'** statements were taken seriously.
Three **months'** maternity leave is in the **workers'** contract.

■ **Add 's to the last word in compound words and phrases:**

His **mother-in-law's** corporation has bought out a competitor.
The **tennis player's** strategy was brilliant.
We want to hear the **caseworker's** recommendation.

■ **Add 's to each noun in individual possession:**

Shirley's and **Kayla's** houses are next to each other. [Shirley and Kayla each own a house; they don't own the houses jointly.]

■ **Add 's to only the last noun in joint or group possession:**

Kareem and Brina's house has a screened porch. [Kareem and Brina own one house.]
Avram and Justin's houses always have nice lawns. [Avram and Justin jointly own more than one house.]

27c How do I use an apostrophe with possessive pronouns?

When a POSSESSIVE PRONOUN ends with the letter *s* (*hers, his, its, ours, yours,* and *theirs*), never add an apostrophe. Below and continued on the next page is a list of PERSONAL PRONOUNS and their possessive forms.

PERSONAL PRONOUNS	POSSESSIVE FORMS
I	my, mine
you	your, yours
he	his
she	her, hers

The questions that follow this brief paragraph are designed to point out how much information about the situation has been provided by the apostrophes. You may want to use the questions in a class discussion of apostrophe usage.

The jury's deliberations were over. Charles's lawsuit had at last come to an end. The defendants' lawyers seemed calm as they waited, but the prosecuting attorney's hands twitched with nervousness. Charles's and Robert's businesses would be either ruined or saved by the verdict of the court. Charles and his family's holdings would be seriously affected. The judge's face was impassive as he addressed the jury about its verdict. The jury foreman's voice trembled as he began to speak.

1. Does the writer think of the jury as a single body or as individuals?
2. Is there one defendant, or are there several?
3. Is there one prosecuting attorney, or are there several?
4. Do Charles and Robert own businesses together or separately?
5. Does Charles have a share in his family's holdings?
6. Why is there no apostrophe in *its verdict* (next to last sentence)?
7. Why do the words *jury's* (first sentence), *judge's* (next to last sentence), and *foreman's* (last sentence) end in 's?

Answers to Extra Exercise A

1. as a single body
2. several
3. one
4. separately
5. yes
6. The personal pronoun *its* is possessive without an apostrophe.
7. Each word is a singular noun that does not end in *s*.

PERSONAL PRONOUNS	POSSESSIVE FORMS
it	its
we	our, ours
they	their, theirs
who	whose

27d How do I use an apostrophe with contractions?

In a **contraction,** an apostrophe takes the place of one or more omitted letters. Be careful not to confuse a contraction with a POSSESSIVE PRONOUN. Doing so is a common spelling error, one that many people—including employers—consider evidence of a poor education. Whether or not that's fair, it's usually true.

it's (contraction for *it is*)	**its** (possessive pronoun)
they're (contraction for *they are*)	**their** (possessive pronoun)
who's (contraction for *who is*)	**whose** (possessive form of *who*)
you're (contraction for *you are*)	**your** (possessive pronoun)

> **NO** The government has to balance **it's** budget.
> **YES** The government has to balance **its** budget.
>
> **NO** The professor **who's** class was canceled is ill.
> **YES** The professor **whose** class was canceled is ill.

In choosing whether or not to use a contraction or a full form, consider that many instructors think contractions aren't appropriate in ACADEMIC WRITING. Nevertheless, the *MLA Handbook* accepts contractions, including *'90s* for *the 1990s.* In this handbook, I use contractions because I'm addressing you, the student. I suggest, however, that before you use contractions in your academic writing, check with your instructor. Here's a list of common contractions.

COMMON CONTRACTIONS

aren't = *are not*	it's = *it is*
can't = *cannot*	let's = *let us*
didn't = *did not*	she's = *she is*
don't = *do not*	there's = *there is*
he's = *he is*	they're = *they are*
I'd = *I would, I had*	wasn't = *was not*
I'm = *I am*	we're = *we are*
isn't = *is not*	weren't = *were not*

→

QUOTATION: ON WRITING
Such forms as *Achilles' heel, Moses' laws, Isis' temple* are commonly replaced by *the heel of Achilles, the laws of Moses, the temple of Isis.*
—William Strunk Jr.,
Elements of Style

QUOTATION: ON WRITING
It is perhaps appropriate that the plural possessive *s',* which struggled so long to attain acceptance, should be among the primary victims of confusion regarding the apostrophe. One of the commonest errors in student writing is the treatment of the genitive [possessive] plural as if it were a genitive singular construction: "These player's money demands are going to kill pro basketball."
—Elizabeth S. Sklar

BACKGROUND
In *Rhetorical Grammar,* 3rd ed. (Needham Heights, MA: Allyn & Bacon, 1999), Martha Kolln concludes that despite warnings against using contractions in formal writing, most formal writing does include them. In negative questions, Kolln asserts, "the contracted form is essentially required."

TEACHING TIP
Some instructors despair of ever having students remember the differences between certain common contractions and their homonyms (*their, they're; its, it's*). You might find it helpful to let students know how experienced writers recognize the differences. Many writers pronounce the two-word form of each possibility. If the two-word form makes no sense in that context, then the other word (usually a possessive pronoun) is needed. If the two-word form makes sense, experienced writers ask themselves if the informal contraction is appropriate. Of course, experienced writers do this in a microsecond, but some of our students need to do it slowly, consciously, and methodically.

I need to know if *their/they're* home. [I need to know if *they are* home.]

I need to know if *their/they're* gas meter is working. [I need to know if *they are* gas meter is working = nonsense; therefore, *their* is correct.]

we've = *we have*   won't = *will not*
who's = *who is*   you're = *you are*

👁 **ALERT:** One contraction required in all writing is *o'clock* (which stands for *of the clock,* an expression used long ago). 👁

27e How do I use an apostrophe with possessive indefinite pronouns?

An apostrophe works with an INDEFINITE PRONOUN (see list in Box 77 in 10i) to form the POSSESSIVE CASE, which shows ownership or a close relationship.

OWNERSHIP	**Everyone's** dinner is ready.
CLOSE RELATIONSHIP	**Something's** aroma is appealing.

Possession in indefinite pronouns can be communicated in two ways: by a PHRASE starting with *of* (*comments of everyone*) or by an apostrophe and the letter *s* (*everyone's comments*).

27f How do I form the plural of miscellaneous elements?

Until recently, the plural of elements such as letters meant as letters, words meant as words, numerals, and symbols could be formed by adding either *'s* or *s.* The most current MLA guidelines endorse the use of *s* only, with the exception of adding *'s* to letters meant as letters. MLA requires underlining—never italics—for two elements only: (1) letters meant as letters and (2) words meant as words. Don't underline the *s* or *'s* that creates the plural for any of the elements discussed in this section. (For published books, any underlined words in a manuscript are printed in italics, as is done in this handbook.) The examples below reflect MLA practices.

PLURAL OF LETTERS MEANT AS LETTERS	Printing **M's** and **N's** confuses young children.
	Printing **m's** and **n's** confuses young children.
PLURAL OF LETTERS MEANT AS WORDS	He was surprised to get all **Bs** in his courses.
PLURAL OF WORDS MEANT AS WORDS	Too many **ifs** in a contract make me suspicious.
PLURAL OF NUMBERS	Her e-mail address contains many **7s**.
PLURAL OF YEARS	I remember the **1990s** well.
PLURAL OF SYMBOLS	What do those **&s** mean?

BACKGROUND

In "What Works for Me: Picture's of Mistakes' with Apostrophe's" [sic] (*Teaching English in the Two-Year College* October 1995: 218), George J. Searles uses his file of color slides (he keeps an inexpensive camera in his glove compartment) to illustrate errors and confusions surrounding apostrophes in the everyday world.

QUOTATION: ON WRITING

Have some sort of a private place to work in. Put up a sign to keep from being interrupted. Mine says: "PLEASE, do *not* knock, do *not* say hello or goodbye, do *not* ask what's for dinner, do *not* disturb me unless the police or firemen have to be called."

—Judith Krantz

ANSWERS: EXERCISE 27-1

1. product's; consumers'

2. people's; product's

3. box's; product user's; shopper's

4. Arm & Hammer's; Tide's

5. Heinz's; Coca-Cola's

6. company's; adult female's; adult males'; children's; teenagers'

7. marketing business's; consumers'; companies'

8. test takers'; Gross's; Sylvester Stallone's; Oprah Winfrey's; someone else's

9. companies'; Gross's; image makers'

10. Sports teams'; teams'

27g When is an apostrophe wrong?

If you're a writer who makes the same apostrophe errors repeatedly, memorize the rules you need (some you likely know almost without thought). Then, you won't be annoyed by "that crooked little mark," a nickname popular with students who wish the apostrophe would go away. Box 115 lists the major apostrophe errors.

BOX 115   SUMMARY

Leading causes of apostrophe errors

■ Never use an apostrophe with the PRESENT-TENSE VERB.
  Cholesterol **plays** [not **play's**] an important role in how long we live.

■ Always use an apostrophe after the *s* in a POSSESSIVE plural of a noun.
  Patients' [not **Patients**] questions seek detailed answers.

■ Never add an apostrophe at the end of a nonpossessive noun ending in *s*.
  Medical **studies** [not **studies'** or **study's**] show this to be true.

■ Never use an apostrophe to form a nonpossessive plural.
  Teams [not **Team's**] of doctors have studied the effects of cholesterol.

EXERCISE 27-1

Rewrite these sentences to insert *'s* or an apostrophe alone to make the words in parentheses show possession. (Delete the parentheses.) For help, consult 27b and 27e.

EXAMPLE   All boxes, cans, and bottles on a (supermarket) shelves are designed to appeal to (people) emotions.

All boxes, cans, and bottles on a *supermarket's* shelves are designed to appeal to *people's* emotions.

1. A (product) manufacturer designs packaging to appeal to (consumers) emotions through color and design.

2. Marketing specialists know that (people) beliefs about a (product) quality are influenced by their emotional response to the design of its package.

3. Circles and ovals appearing on a (box) design supposedly increase a (product user) feelings of comfort, while bold patterns and colors attract a (shopper) attention.

4. Using both circles and bold designs in (Arm & Hammer) and (Tide) packaging produces both effects in consumers.

5. (Heinz) ketchup bottle and (Coca-Cola) famous logo achieve the same effects by combining a bright color with an old-fashioned, "comfortable" design.

6. Often, a (company) marketing consultants will custom-design products to appeal to the supposedly "typical" (adult female) emotions or to (adult males), (children), or (teenagers) feelings.

7. One of the (marketing business) leading consultants, Stan Gross, tests (consumers) emotional reactions to (companies) products and their packages by asking consumers to associate products with well-known personalities.

8. Thus, (test takers) responses to (Gross) questions might reveal that a particular brand of laundry detergent has (Sylvester Stallone) toughness, (Oprah Winfrey) determination, or (someone else) sparkling personality.

9. Manufacturing (companies) products are not the only ones relying on (Gross) and other corporate (image makers) advice.

10. (Sports teams) owners also use marketing specialists to design their (teams) images, as anyone who has seen the angry bull logo of the Chicago Bulls basketball team will agree.

EXERCISE 27-2

Rewrite these sentences so that each contains a possessive noun. For help, consult 27b and 27e.

EXAMPLE   Strangely, the weight of the kilogram seems to be decreasing.

Strangely, the *kilogram's weight* seems to be decreasing.

1. The weight of a kilogram depends on precise measurements so that scientists of the world can assume international consistency of the mass of a kilogram in scientific reports.

2. For all measurement units except the kilogram, international standards that refer to natural phenomena such as the speed of light and electrical currents of magnetic fields are used.

3. A platinum-iridium bar created in 1889 in England became the standard of the world for the weight of a kilogram.

**ANSWERS AND COVERAGE:
EXERCISE 27-2**

If students revise this material to include all possible uses of the apostrophe, you might point out that good style usually calls for a balance of possessive and nonpossessive structures in a single passage. Then you might ask them to restore some nonpossessive structures to achieve a suitable balance in the material.

1. The *kilogram's weight* depends on precise measurements so that the *world's scientists* can assume international consistency of a *kilogram's mass* in scientific reports. [27b]

2. For all measurement units except the kilogram, international standards that refer to natural phenomena such as *light's speed* and *magnetic field's electrical currents* are used. [27b]

3. A platinum-iridium bar created in 1889 in England became the *world's standard* for a *kilogram's weight*. [27b]

4. Because even the *platinum-iridium bar's relatively stable metal* has been decaying slowly over time, the *bar's decrease in weight* raises the possibility of imprecise results in *scientists' current research*. [27b]

5. The *National Institute of Standards and Technology's* efforts have captured *everyone's interest* as it works to equate *a kilogram's weight* to *an electrical unit's mass*. [27b; 27e]

EXTRA EXERCISE B

You may want to see if students can identify all the unnecessary and misplaced apostrophes in the following paragraph.

(1) A good cook stay's busy doing many tasks that make cooking possible. (2) The oven's interior must be cleaned, the pots' and pans' scrubbed, and the knives sharpened. (3) Once the kitchen is tidy, the grocery list's have to be made and menu's planned. (4) Then comes the shopping so that the pantry's shelves will be full. (5) When the chopping and stirring start, most cook's pleasure begins.

Answers and Coverage:
Extra Exercise B

1. stay's [error for *stays*: present-tense verb]

2. oven's [correct: possessive singular noun]; pots', pans' [errors for *pots, pans*: nonpossessive plural nouns]

3. list's, menu's [errors for *lists, menus*: nonpossessive plural nouns]

4. pantry's [correct: possessive singular noun]

5. cook's [error for *cooks'*: possessive plural noun]

4. Because even the relatively stable metal of a platinum-iridium bar has been decaying slowly over time, the decrease in weight of the bar raises the possibility of imprecise results in the current research of scientists.

5. The efforts of the National Institute of Standards and Technology have captured the interest of everyone as it works to equate the weight of a kilogram to the mass of an electrical unit.

Chapter 28

Quotation Marks

28a What is the role of quotation marks?

Quotation marks are used most often to enclose **direct quotations**—the exact spoken or written words of a speaker or writer. Quotation marks also set off some titles, and quotation marks can call attention to words used in a special sense.

Double quotation marks (" ") are standard. In most computer fonts, the opening marks differ slightly in appearance from the closing marks. The opening marks look like tiny 6s, the closing marks like tiny 9s. In some computer fonts, the opening and closing marks look the same (" "). Single quotation marks (' ' or ' ') are used for quotations within quotations: *Gregory said, "I heard the man shout 'help me' but could not reach him in time."* Quotation marks operate only in pairs: to open and to close. When you proofread your writing, check carefully that you've inserted the closing mark.

Please note, before you continue reading this chapter, that I use MLA STYLE to format the examples here and in other chapters. This affects the documentation features and the lengths of "short" and "long" quotations. These factors vary with different documentation styles. For MLA style, used in most English courses, see Chapter 34. For APA STYLE, see Chapter 35.

28b How do I use quotation marks with short direct quotations?

A DIRECT QUOTATION is any exact words from a print or nonprint source. In MLA STYLE, a quotation is considered *short* if it occupies no more than four typed lines. Use double quotation marks at the start and finish of a short quotation. Give DOCUMENTATION information after a short quotation, before the sentence's ending period.

SHORT QUOTATIONS

Gardner has suggested the possibility of a ninth intelligence: existential, "the proclivity to pose (and ponder) questions about life, death, and ultimate realities" (72).

Susana Urbina, who surveyed many studies about intelligence, found that intelligence "is such a multifaceted concept that no single quality can define it . . ." (1130).

28c Are quotation marks used with long quotations?

No. With a long DIRECT QUOTATION, don't use quotation marks. In MLA STYLE, a quotation is *long* if it occupies more than four typed lines. Instead of using quotation marks with a long quotation, indent all its lines as a block (that is, the quotation is "set off" or "displayed"). This format makes quotation marks unnecessary. Give DOCUMENTATION information after the long quotation and after the period that ends the quotation.

LONG QUOTATIONS

Gardner uses criteria by which to judge whether an ability deserves to be categorized as an "intelligence." Each must confer

> a set of skills of problem solving--enabling the individual to resolve genuine problems or difficulties [author's emphasis] that he or she encounters and laying th e groundwork for the acquisition of new knowledge. (Frames 60-61)

In the Gardner example above, note that a capital letter is *not* used to start the quotation. The lead-in words (*Each must confer*) are an incomplete sentence, so they need the quotation to complete the sentence.

Goleman also emphasizes a close interaction of the emotional and rational states with the other intelligences that Gardner has identified:

> These two minds, the emotional and the rational, operate in tight harmony for the most part, intertwining their very different ways of knowing to guide us through the world. Ordinarily there is a balance between emotional and rational minds, with emotion feeding into and informing the operations of the rational mind, and the rational mind refining and sometimes vetoing the inputs of the emotions. (9)

In the Goleman example above, note that a capital letter starts the quotation because the lead-in words are a complete sentence. (A colon can—but isn't required to—end the lead-in sentence because it's an independent clause; see 26b.)

👁 **ALERT:** Whether a quotation is one word or occupies many lines, always DOCUMENT its SOURCE. Also, when you quote material, be very careful to record the words exactly as they appear in the original. 👁

28d How do I use quotation marks for quotations within quotations?

In MLA STYLE, practice varies between short and long quotations when a quotation contains internal quotation marks. In short quotations of poetry, use single quotation marks for any internal quotation marks, and use double quotation marks for the entire quotation. Give DOCUMENTATION information after the entire quotation, before the sentence's ending period. For other documentation styles, check each style's manual.

In long quotations of poetry—those that are displayed (set off in a block) and not enclosed in quotation marks—keep the double quotation marks as they appear in the original. Give DOCUMENTATION information after the long quotation following any closing punctuation; and before the period that ends a short quotation (see 28e).

Short quotations: Use single within double quotation marks (MLA style)

With short quotations, the double quotation marks show the beginning and end of words taken from the source; the single quotation marks replace double marks used in the source.

ORIGINAL SOURCE

Most scientists concede that they don't really know what "intelligence" is. Whatever it might be, paper and pencil tests aren't the tenth of it.
—Brent Staples, "The IQ Cult," p. 293

STUDENT'S USE OF THE SOURCE

Brent Staples argues in his essay about IQ as object of reverence: "Most scientists concede that they don't really know what 'intelligence' is. Whatever it might be, paper and pencil tests aren't the tenth of it" (293).

Long quotations: Use quotation marks as in source

All long quotations must be set off (displayed) without being enclosed in quotation marks. Therefore, show any double and single quotation marks exactly as the source does.

28e How do I use quotation marks for quotations of poetry and dialogue?

Poetry (MLA Style)

A quotation of poetry is *short* if it includes three lines or fewer of the poem. As with prose quotations (28d), use double quotation marks to enclose the material. If the poetry lines have internal double quotation marks, change them to single quotation marks. To show when a line of poetry breaks to the next line, use a slash (/) with one space on each side. Give DOCUMENTATION information after a short poetry quotation, before the period that ends the sentence (see also 29e).

> As Auden wittily defined personal space, "some thirty inches from my nose / The frontier of my person goes" (*Complete,* 205).

A quotation of poetry is *long* if it includes more than three lines of the poem. As with prose quotations (28d), indent all lines as a block, without quotation marks to enclose the material. Start new lines exactly as they appear in your source. Give documentation information after the long quotation and after the period that ends the quotation.

👁 **ALERT:** When you quote lines of poetry, follow the capitalization of your source. 👁

Dialogue (MLA and APA Styles)

Dialogue, also called DIRECT DISCOURSE, presents a speaker's exact words. Enclose direct discourse in quotation marks. In contrast, INDIRECT DISCOURSE reports what a speaker said. Don't enclose indirect discourse in quotation marks. In addition to these differences in punctuation, PRONOUN use and VERB TENSES also differ for these two types of discourse.

DIRECT DISCOURSE	The mayor said**, "I intend** to veto that bill.**"**
INDIRECT DISCOURSE	The mayor said **that he intended** to veto that bill.

Whether you're reporting the words of a real speaker or making up dialogue in a short story, use double quotation marks at the beginning and end of a speaker's words. This tells your reader which words are the speaker's. Also, start a new paragraph each time the speaker changes.

> "I don't know how you can see to drive," she said.
> "Maybe you should put on your glasses."
> "Putting on my glasses would help you to see?"
> "Not me; you," Macon said. "You're focused on the windshield instead of the road."
>
> —Anne Tyler, *The Accidental Tourist*

In American English, if two or more paragraphs present a single speaker's words, use double opening quotation marks at the start of each paragraph, but save the closing double quotation marks until the end of the last quoted paragraph.

EXERCISE 28-1

Decide whether each sentence below is direct or indirect discourse and then rewrite each sentence in the other form. Make any changes needed for grammatical correctness. With direct discourse, put the speaker's words wherever you think they belong in the sentence. For help, consult 28b through 28e.

EXAMPLE   A medical doctor told some newspaper reporters that he was called into a television studio one day to treat a sick actor.

A medical doctor told some newspaper *reporters, "I* was called into a television studio one day to treat a sick actor."

1. The doctor was told that he would find his patient on the set of *Side Effects,* a new television series that takes place in a hospital.
2. On his arrival at the television studio, the doctor announced, "I'm Dr. Gatley, and I'm looking for *Side Effects.*"
3. The studio security guard asked him if he meant to say that he was auditioning for the part of Dr. Gatley in *Side Effects*.
4. The visitor insisted that he really was Dr. Gatley.
5. The security guard whispered, "I like your attitude. With such self-confidence, you're sure to go far in television."

28f | How do I use quotation marks with titles of short works?

When you refer to certain short works by their titles, enclose the titles in quotation marks (other works, usually longer, need to be in italics or underlined; see 30g). Short works include short stories, essays, poems, articles from periodicals, pamphlets, brochures, songs, and individual episodes of a series on television or radio.

What is the rhyme scheme of Andrew Marvell's "Delight in Disorder"? [poem]

Have you read "The Lottery"? [short story]

The best source I found is "The Myth of Political Consultants." [magazine article]

"Shooting an Elephant" describes George Orwell's experiences in Burma. [essay]

BACKGROUND
The Web site <http://webster.commnet.edu/grammar/quizzes/quotes_quiz.htm> features an interactive quiz on using quotation marks.

ANSWERS AND COVERAGE: EXERCISE 28-1

1. The doctor was told, "You'll find your patient on the set of *Side Effects.* It's a new television series that takes place in a hospital." [from indirect to direct discourse]

2. On his arrival at the television studio, the doctor announced that he was Dr. Gatley and that he was looking for *Side Effects.* [from direct to indirect discourse]

3. The studio security guard asked, "Don't you mean to say that you're auditioning for the part of Dr. Gatley in *Side Effects*?" [from indirect to direct discourse]

4. The visitor insisted, "I really am Dr. Gatley." [from indirect to direct discourse]

5. The security guard whispered that he liked the man's attitude and that with such self-confidence, the man was sure to go far in television. [from direct to indirect discourse]

ANSWERS AND COVERAGE:
EXERCISE 28-2

1. In her short story "The Lady from Lucknow," Bharati Mukherjee describes a visitor from India who resents being treated as an exotic object. [title of short story]

2. Although his poem "The Red Wheelbarrow" contains only sixteen words, William Carlos Williams creates in it both a strong visual image and a sense of mystery. [title of poem]

3. With her soulful singing and relaxed gestures, Billie Holiday gave a bare television studio the atmosphere of a smoky jazz club in "The Sound of Jazz." The program was broadcast in 1957 as part of the television series *The Seven Lively Arts*. [title of television episode]

4. Woody Guthrie wrote "This Land Is Your Land" as both a hymn to a vast continent and a song of protest against the selfish misuse of its resources. [title of song]

5. In her essay "The Imagination of Disaster," Susan Sontag writes that viewers of disaster movies like to see how these movies succeed in "making a mess"—especially if the mess includes the make-believe destruction of a big city. [title of essay; closing quotation marks needed]

QUOTATION: ON WRITING
If we had to say what writing is, we would have to define it essentially as an act of courage.

—Cynthia Ozick

Titles of some other works are neither enclosed in quotation marks nor written in italics or underlined. For guidelines, see Box 119 in 30e and Box 120 in 30g.

👁 **ALERT:** When placing the title of your own piece of writing on a title page or at the top of a page, never use quotation marks. 👁

EXERCISE 28-2

Correct any misuses of quotation marks. If you think a sentence is correct, explain why. For help, consult 28f.

1. In her short story The Lady from Lucknow, Bharati Mukherjee describes a visitor from India who resents being treated as an exotic object.

2. Although his poem The Red Wheelbarrow contains only sixteen words, William Carlos Williams creates in it both a strong visual image and a sense of mystery.

3. With her soulful singing and relaxed gestures, Billie Holiday gave a bare television studio the atmosphere of a smoky jazz club in The Sound of Jazz. The program was broadcast in 1957 as part of the television series *The Seven Lively Arts*.

4. Woody Guthrie wrote This Land Is Your Land as both a hymn to a vast continent and a song of protest against the selfish misuse of its resources.

5. In her essay "The Imagination of Disaster, Susan Sontag writes that viewers of disaster movies like to see how these movies succeed in "making a mess"—especially if the mess includes the make-believe destruction of a big city.

28g How do I use quotation marks for words used as words?

When you refer to a word as a word, you can choose to either enclose it in quotation marks or put it in italics (or use underlining). Whichever you choose, be consistent throughout each piece of writing.

NO Many people confuse affect and effect.
YES Many people confuse "affect" and "effect."
YES Many people confuse *affect* and *effect*.

Always put quotation marks around the English translation of a word or PHRASE. Also, use italics (or underlining) for the word or phrase in the other language.

My grandfather usually ended arguments with *de gustibus non disputandum est* ("there is no disputing about tastes").

Many writers use quotation marks around words or phrases meant ironically or in other nonliteral ways.

The proposed tax "reform" is actually a tax increase.

Some writers put technical terms in quotation marks and define them—but only the first time they appear. Never reuse quotation marks after a term has been introduced and defined.

"Plagiarism"—the undocumented use of another person's words or ideas—can result in expulsion. Plagiarism is a serious offense.

Some student writers put quotation marks around words that they sense might be inappropriate for ACADEMIC WRITING, such as a SLANG term or a CLICHÉ used intentionally to make a point. However, when possible, use different language—not quotation marks. Take time to think of accurate, appropriate, and fresh words instead. If you prefer to stick with the slang or cliché, use quotation marks.

They "eat like birds" in public, but they "stuff their faces" in private.
They **eat almost nothing** in public, but they **eat hefty heaps of food** in private.

A nickname doesn't call for quotation marks, unless you use the nickname along with the full name. When a person's nickname is widely known, you don't have to give both the nickname and the full name. For example, use *Senator Ted Kennedy* or *Senator Edward Kennedy,* whichever is appropriate in context. Because he's well known, don't use *Senator Edward "Ted" Kennedy.*

EXERCISE 28-3

Correct any misuses of quotation marks. If you think a sentence is correct, explain why. For help, consult 28g.

EXAMPLE   *Bossa nova,* Portuguese for new wave, is the name of both a dance and a musical style originating in Brazil.

Bossa nova, Portuguese for "new wave," is the name of both a dance and a musical style originating in Brazil.

1. To Freud, the "superego" is the part of the personality that makes moral demands on a person. The "superego" is the third of Freud's three elements of personality.

2. Although many people believe the old adage "Where there's a will, there's a way," psychologists say that to get results, willingness must be combined with ability and effort.

BACKGROUND
Classical Greek and Latin manuscripts usually had no word separation, but in both inscriptions and nonliterary works, dots or apostrophes were often used to set off individual words. The custom of separating words by spacing was used off and on, beginning in the seventh century, becoming systematic only in the eleventh.

ANSWERS AND COVERAGE: EXERCISE 28-3

1. To Freud, the "superego" is the part of the personality that makes moral demands on a person. The superego is the third of Freud's three elements of personality. [no quotation marks for the second use of a technical term]

2. Correct; quotation marks used for cliché

3. Observation and empathy are two of the chief qualities that mark the work of the Dutch painter Rembrandt. [misuse of quotation marks to call attention to words]

4. *Casbah,* an Arabic word meaning "fortress," is the name given to the oldest part of many North African cities. [translation of a term]

5. *Flammable* and *inflammable* [or "Flammable" and "inflammable"] are a curious pair of words that once had the same meaning but today are often considered opposites. [consistent treatment needed]

ADDITIONAL EXAMPLES

1. Virginia Woolf was a member of the "Bloomsbury group," the name taken from the district of London in which she and her sister lived after the death of their father.

2. She was the author of many short stories, essays, and sketches, such as "The Mark on the Wall."

3. She was an early user of "stream of consciousness" writing.

4. Have you read her long essay called "A Room of One's Own"?

QUOTATION: ON WRITING

How to read writers on writing: With respect, amusement, and skepticism. They will contradict one another—as they should—for each writer brings an individual history to the writing task. There is no single theology here.
—Donald M. Murray

3. "Observation" and "empathy" are two of the chief qualities that mark the work of the Dutch painter Rembrandt.

4. *Casbah,* an Arabic word meaning fortress, is the name given to the oldest part of many North African cities.

5. "Flammable" and *inflammable* are a curious pair of words that once had the same meaning but today are often considered opposites.

28h How do I use quotation marks with other punctuation?

Commas and periods with quotation marks

A comma or period that is grammatically necessary is always placed inside the closing quotation mark.

> Jessica enjoyed F. Scott Fitzgerald's story "The Freshest Boy," so she was eager to read his novels. [comma before closing quotation mark]
> Max said, "Don't stand so far away from me." [comma before opening quotation mark (24k.5); period before closing quotation mark]
> Edward T. Hall coined the word "proxemia." [period before closing quotation mark]

Semicolons and colons with quotation marks

A semicolon or colon is placed outside the closing quotation mark, unless it is part of the quotation.

> Computers offer businesses "opportunities that never existed before"; some workers disagree. [semicolon after closing quotation mark]
> We have to know each culture's standard for "how close is close": No one wants to offend. [colon after closing quotation mark]

Question marks, exclamation points, and dashes with quotation marks

If the punctuation marks belong to the words enclosed in quotation marks, put them inside the quotation marks.

> "Did I Hear You Call My Name?" was the winning song.
> "I've won the lottery!" Arielle shouted.
> "Who's there? Why don't you ans—"

If a question mark, an exclamation point, or a dash doesn't belong to the material being quoted, put the punctuation outside the quotation marks.

> Have you read Nikki Giovanni's poem "Knoxville, Tennessee"?
> If only I could write a story like David Wallace's "Girl with Curious Hair"!
> Weak excuses—a classic is "I have to visit my grandparents"—change little.

When you use quotation marks and want to know how they work with capital letters, see 30d; with brackets, 29c; with ellipsis points, 29d; and with the slash, 29e.

28i When are quotation marks wrong?

Never enclose a word in quotation marks to call attention to it, to intensify it, or to be sarcastic.

NO I'm "very" happy about the news.
YES I'm very happy about the news.

Never enclose the title of your paper in quotation marks (or underline it). However, if the title of your paper contains another title that requires quotation marks, use those marks only for the included title.

NO "The Elderly in Nursing Homes: A Case Study"
YES The Elderly in Nursing Homes: A Case Study

NO Character Development in Shirley Jackson's Story The Lottery
YES Character Development in Shirley Jackson's Story "The Lottery"

EXERCISE 28-4

Correct any errors in the use of quotation marks and other punctuation with quotation marks. If you think a sentence is correct, explain why. For help, consult 28e through 28i.

1. Dying in a shabby hotel room, the witty writer Oscar Wilde supposedly said, "Either that wallpaper goes, or I do".

2. Was it the Russian novelist Tolstoy who wrote, "All happy families resemble one another, but each unhappy family is unhappy in its own way?"

3. In his poem A Supermarket in California, Allen Ginsberg addresses the dead poet Walt Whitman, asking, Where are we going, Walt Whitman? The doors close / in an hour. Which way does your beard point tonight?

4. Toni Morrison made this reply to the claim that "art that has a political message cannot be good art:" She said that "the best art is political" and that her aim was to create art that was "unquestionably political" and beautiful at the same time.

5. Benjamin Franklin's strange question—"What is the use of a newborn child?—" was his response to someone who doubted the usefulness of new inventions.

ANSWERS AND COVERAGE: EXERCISE 28-4

1. Dying in a shabby hotel room, the witty writer Oscar Wilde supposedly said, "Either that wallpaper goes, or I do." [28h, period always placed inside closing quotation mark]

2. Was it the Russian novelist Tolstoy who wrote, "All happy families resemble one another, but each unhappy family is unhappy in its own way"? [28h, question mark not part of the quotation]

3. In his poem "A Supermarket in California," Allen Ginsberg addresses the dead poet Walt Whitman, asking, "Where are we going, Walt Whitman? The doors close / in an hour. Which way does your beard point tonight?" [28f, title of poem; 28e, direct quotation; 28h, question mark part of the quotation]

4. Toni Morrison made this reply to the claim that "art that has a political message cannot be good art": She said that "the best art is political" and that her aim was to create art that was "unquestionably political" and beautiful at the same time. [28h, colon always placed outside closing quotation mark]

5. Benjamin Franklin's strange question— "What is the use of a newborn child?"—was his response to someone who doubted the usefulness of new inventions. [28h, dash not part of the quotation]

Chapter 29

Other Punctuation Marks

This chapter explains the uses of the **dash, parentheses, brackets, ellipsis points,** the **slash,** and the **hyphen.** These punctuation marks aren't used often, but each serves a purpose and gives you options with your writing style.

DASH

29a When can I use a dash in my writing?

The **dash,** or a pair of dashes, lets you interrupt a sentence to add information. Such interruptions can fall in the middle or at the end of a sentence. To make a dash, hit the hyphen key twice (--). Do not put a space before, between, or after the hyphens. Some word processing programs automatically convert two hyphens into a dash; either form is correct. In print, the dash appears as an unbroken line approximately the length of two hyphens joined together (—). If you handwrite, make the dash at least twice as long as a hyphen.

Using dashes for special emphasis

If you want to emphasize an example, a definition, an APPOSITIVE, or a contrast, you can use a dash or dashes. Some call a dash "a pregnant pause"—that is, take note, something special is coming. Use dashes sparingly so that you don't dilute their impact.

EXAMPLE

The care-takers—those who are helpers, nurturers, teachers, mothers—are still systematically devalued.

—Ellen Goodman, "Just Woman's Work?"

DEFINITION

Although the emphasis at the school was mainly language—speaking, reading, writing—the lessons always began with an exercise in politeness.

—Elizabeth Wong, *Fifth Chinese Daughter*

APPOSITIVE

Two of the strongest animals in the jungle are vegetarians—the elephant and the gorilla.

—Dick Gregory, *The Shadow That Scares Me*

CONTRAST

Fire cooks food—and burns down forests.

—Smokey the Bear

Place what you emphasize with dashes next to or nearby the material it refers to so that what you want to accomplish with your emphasis is not lost.

NO   The current **argument is**—one that faculty, students, and coaches debate fiercely—whether to hold athletes to the same academic standards as others face.

YES   The current **argument**—one that faculty, students, and coaches debate fiercely—**is** whether to hold athletes to the same academic standards as others face.

Using dashes to emphasize an aside

An **aside** is a writer's comment, often the writer's personal views, on what's been written. Generally, this technique isn't appropriate for ACADEMIC WRITING, so before you insert an aside, carefully consider your writing PURPOSE and your AUDIENCE.

Television showed us the war. It showed us the war in a way that was—if you chose to watch television, at least—unavoidable.

—Nora Ephron, *Scribble Scribble*

👁 **ALERTS:** (1) If the words within a pair of dashes require a question mark or an exclamation point, place it before the second dash.

A first date—do you remember?—stays in the memory forever.

(2) Never use commas, semicolons, or periods next to dashes. If such a need arises, revise your writing.

(3) Never enclose quotation marks in dashes except when the meaning requires them. These two examples show that, when required, the dash stops before or after the quotation marks; the two punctuation marks do not overlap. See examples at the top of the next page.

ADDITIONAL EXAMPLES: DASH

Appositive

Elizabeth Barrett Browning—the wife of Robert Browning—was probably a more popular poet than her husband in the nineteenth century.

Example

Many students—elementary school, high school, and college students—find themselves taking required courses that they would not choose for themselves.

Definition

A meaningful relationship—one that is satisfying to those involved and promises to last—is sought by most single people.

Futuristic novels with a bleak vision of the prospects for the free individual characteristically portray a society in which history—knowledge of the past—has been systematically eliminated.

—Diane Ravitch

Dinner at the Huntercombes possessed only two dramatic features—the wine was a farce and the food a tragedy.

—Anthony Powell

Contrast

It's not right or wrong—it's just fattening.

An Aside

If you choose to vote for that candidate—and I don't care whether you do or not—then you have put yourself in the conservative camp.

Broken-off Speech

"It's not that I don't love you, Tom, it's just that—"

QUOTATION: ON WRITING

The dash has been described as the interruption, the mark of abruptness, the sob, the stammer, and the mark of ignorance. The last name—which might be equally well applied to the comma as crude writers use it—records the fact that the uninformed mistake the dash for an all-purpose mark for every possible occasion.

—George Summey Jr.

**ANSWERS AND COVERAGE:
EXERCISES 29-1**
Answers will vary. When checking them, make sure the dashes are used according to the instructions.

Many of George Orwell's essays—"A Hanging," for example—draw on his experiences as a civil servant.
"Shooting an Elephant"—another Orwell essay—appears in many anthologies. ◉

EXERCISE 29-1

Write a sentence about each topic, shown in italics. Use dashes to set off what is asked for, shown in roman, in each sentence, For help, consult 29a.

EXAMPLE   *science,* a definition

Ecology—the study of the interactions among animals, plants, and the physical environment—is closely related to both biology and geology.

1. *movie,* a contrast
2. *singer,* an appositive
3. *hobby,* an example
4. *a fact,* an aside
5. *career,* a definition
6. *social science,* a contrast
7. *writing,* an example
8. *teacher,* an appositive
9. *business,* a definition
10. *technology,* an aside

PARENTHESES

29b When can I use parentheses in my writing?

Parentheses let you interrupt a sentence to add various kinds of information. Parentheses are like dashes (29a) in that they set off extra or interrupting words—but unlike dashes, which emphasize material, parentheses de-emphasize what they enclose. Use parentheses sparingly because overusing them can make your writing lurch, not flow.

Using parentheses to enclose interrupting words

EXPLANATION
After they've finished with the pantry, the medicine cabinet, and the attic, they will throw out the red geranium (too many leaves), sell the dog (too many fleas), and send the children off to boarding school (too many scuffmarks on the hardwood floors).
—Suzanne Britt, "Neat People vs. Sloppy People"

EXAMPLE
Though other cities (Dresden, for instance) had been utterly destroyed in World War II, never before had a single weapon been responsible for such destruction.
—Laurence Behrens and Leonard J. Rosen, *Writing and Reading Across the Curriculum*

ASIDE

The older girls (non-graduates, of course) were assigned the task of making refreshments for the night's festivities.

—Maya Angelou, *I Know Why the Caged Bird Sings*

The sheer decibel level of the noise around us is not enough to make us cranky, irritable, or aggressive. (It can, however, affect our mental and physical health, which is another matter.)

—Carol Tavris, *Anger: The Misunderstood Emotion*

Using parentheses for listed items and alternative numbers

When you number listed items within a sentence, enclose the numbers (or letters) in parentheses. Never use closing parentheses to set off numbers in a displayed list; use periods.

Four items are on the agenda for tonight's meeting: (1) current treasury figures, (2) current membership figures, (3) the budget for renovations, and (4) the campaign for soliciting additional public contributions.

👁 **ALERTS:** For listed items that fall within a sentence, (1) use a colon before a list only if an INDEPENDENT CLAUSE comes before the list, and (2) Use commas or semicolons to separate the items, but be consistent within a piece of writing. If, however, any item contains punctuation itself, use a semicolon to separate the items. 👁

In legal writing and in some BUSINESS WRITING, you can use parentheses to enclose a numeral that repeats a spelled-out number.

The monthly rent is three hundred fifty dollars ($350).
Your order of fifteen (15) gross was shipped today.

In ACADEMIC WRITING, especially in subjects in which the use of figures or measurements is frequent, enclose alternative or comparative forms of the same number in parentheses: *2 mi (3.2 km).*

Using other punctuation with parentheses

When a complete sentence enclosed in parentheses stands alone, start it with a capital letter and end it with a period. When a sentence in parentheses falls within another sentence, never start with a capital or end with a period.

NO Looking for his car keys (He had left them at my sister's house.) wasted an entire hour.

YES Looking for his car keys (he had left them at my sister's house) wasted an entire hour.

YES Looking for his car keys wasted an entire hour. (He had left them at my sister's house.)

ADDITIONAL EXAMPLES: PARENTHESES

Explanations
Most Americans try to be honest about filing their income tax returns (no matter how much it hurts to pay).

Examples
Many modern zoos (such as the Santa Barbara Zoo) try to present the animals so that young children can easily see them.

Asides
House plants are subject to bug infestations (at least mine are) that require special treatment if the attack is to be repelled.

Numbers and Letters
There are five basic ingredients in a good gumbo: (1) a roux, (2) a variety of chopped vegetables, (3) water, (4) seafood or chicken, and (5) seasonings.

Numerical Repetition
A freshman is required to take twelve (12) hours of course work to be in regular status.

Expression of Doubt
She was born in 1463 (?) in Rome.

QUOTATION: ON WRITING
Writing is my vacation from living.
—Eugene O'Neill

BACKGROUND
In "#@\/()! = Hash, At, Slash, Backslash, Open, Close, Bang," William Safire reflects on the changes in nomenclature for computer keyboard symbols. Safire writes, "What we old-timers know as 'parentheses' are now just *open* and *close,* or more descriptively, *left banana* and *right banana.*"

When eating at a formal restaurant (such as Chez Marcelle), a man is expected to wear a coat and tie.

Although the rain kept falling (and the river rising!), we decided to wait for the rescue boat instead of striking out on our own.

Casablanca has become a favorite film of many people too young to have seen it when it was originally released (or to have seen Bogart and Bergman in their other films).

BACKGROUND

Literally, *parenthesis* indicates "an insertion beside" the basic meaning of the sentence. (The term applies to both the insertion itself and either of the punctuation marks used to surround it.) The Greek from which it comes (by way of Medieval Latin) is composed of *para,* "beside"; *en,* "in"; and *thesis,* "placing, position," from *tithenai,* "to place or put." Hence, a parenthesis is a thought placed beside the principal meaning.

QUOTATION: ON WRITING

The author must keep his mouth shut when his work starts to speak.

—Friedrich Nietzsche

Never put a comma before an opening parenthesis. If the material before the parenthetical material requires a comma, place that comma after the closing parenthesis.

> **NO** Although clearly different from my favorite film, **(**The Wizard of Oz**)** Gone with the Wind is also outstanding.

> **YES** Although clearly different from my favorite film **(**The Wizard of Oz**),** Gone with the Wind is also outstanding.

You can use a question mark or an exclamation point within parentheses that occur in a sentence.

> Looking for clues **(**what did we expect to find**?)** wasted four days.

Never use quotation marks around parentheses that come before or after any quoted words.

> **NO** Alberta Hunter **"(**Down Hearted Blues**)"** is known for singing jazz.

> **YES** Alberta Hunter **(**"Down Hearted Blues"**)** is known for singing jazz.

BRACKETS

29c When do I need to use brackets in my writing?

Brackets allow you to enclose words that you want to insert into quotations, but only in the specific cases discussed below.

Adjusting a quotation with brackets

When you use a quotation, you might need to change the form of a word (a verb's tense, for example), add a brief definition, or fit the quotation into the grammatical structure of your sentence. In such cases, enclose the material you have inserted into the quotation in brackets. (These examples use MLA STYLE for PARENTHETICAL REFERENCES; see 34b.)

ORIGINAL SOURCE

Current research shows that successful learning takes place in an active environment.

—Deborah Moore, "Facilities and Learning Styles," p. 22

QUOTATION WITH BRACKETS

Deborah Moore supports a student-centered curriculum and agrees with "current research **[which]** shows that successful learning takes place in an active environment" (22).

ORIGINAL SOURCE

The logic of the mind is *associative;* it takes elements that symbolize a reality, or trigger a memory of it, to be the same as that reality.
—Daniel Goleman, *Emotional Intelligence,* p. 294

QUOTATION WITH BRACKETS

The kinds of intelligence are based in the way the mind functions: "The logic of the mind is *associative* **[one idea connects with another]**; it takes elements that symbolize a reality, or trigger a memory of it, to be the same as that reality" (Goleman 294).

Using brackets to point out an error in a source or to add information within parentheses

In words you want to quote, sometimes page-makeup technicians or authors make a mistake without realizing it—a wrong date, a misspelled word, or an error of fact. You fix that mistake by putting your correction in brackets, without changing the words you want to quote. This tells your readers that the error was in the original work and not made by you.

Using [sic]

Insert *sic* (without italics), enclosed in brackets, in your MLA-style essays and research papers to show your readers that you've quoted an error accurately. *Sic* is a Latin word that means "so," or "thus," which says "It is so (or thus) in the original."

USE FOR ERROR

A journalist wrote, "The judge accepted an **[sic]** plea of not guilty.

USE FOR MISSPELLING

The building inspector wrote about the consequence of doubling the apartment's floor space: "With that much extra room per person, the tennants **[sic]** would sublet."

Using brackets within parentheses

Use brackets to insert information within parentheses.

That expression **(first used in *A Fable for Critics* [1848] by James R. Lowell)** was popularized in the early twentieth century by Ella Wheeler Wilcox.

ADDITIONAL EXAMPLES: BRACKETS

Insertion of Words
Describing the end of grief, Marjorie Waters wrote, "[It] was a homecoming, a returning to myself made sweeter by the long separation."

To be reasonably comfortable for even short walks outdoors [in Moscow during the winter] it is necessary to wear coats of natural fur.
—Leona P. Schecter, "Moscow"

Brief Parenthetical Material Inside Parentheses
The Declaration of Independence (subtitled "The Unanimous Declaration of the Thirteen United States of America" [and published by Congress in 1776]) is an eloquent assertion of human rights.

ELLIPSIS POINTS

29d How do I use ellipsis points in my writing?

The word *ellipsis* means "omission." **Ellipsis points** in writing are a series of three spaced dots (use the period key on the keyboard). You're required to use ellipsis points to indicate you've intentionally omitted words—perhaps even a sentence or more—from the source you're quoting. These rules apply to both prose and poetry.

The *MLA Handbook* no longer recommends that ellipsis points you have inserted be enclosed in brackets to make it clear to your reader that the omission is yours. See Chapter 34 for more information.

29d.1 Using ellipsis points with prose

ORIGINAL SOURCE

These two minds, the emotional and the rational, operate in tight harmony for the most part, intertwining their very different ways of knowing to guide us through the world. Ordinarily, there is a balance between emotional and rational minds, with emotion feeding into and informing the operations of the rational mind, and the rational mind refining and sometimes vetoing the inputs of the emotions. Still, the emotional and rational minds are semi-independent faculties, each, as we shall see, reflecting the operation of distinct, but interconnected, circuitry in the brain.

———Daniel Goleman, *Emotional Intelligence,* p. 9

QUOTATION OF SELECTED WORDS, NO ELLIPSIS NEEDED

Goleman explains that the "two minds, the emotional and the rational" usually provide "a balance" in our daily observations and decision making (9).

QUOTATION WITH ELLIPSIS MID-SENTENCE

Goleman emphasizes the connections between parts of the mind: "Still, the emotional and rational minds are semi-independent faculties, each . . . reflecting the operation of distinct, but interconnected, circuitry in the brain (9).

QUOTATION WITH ELLIPSIS AND PARENTHETICAL REFERENCE

Goleman emphasizes that the "two minds, the emotional and the rational, operate in tight harmony for the most part . . ." (9). [*Note:* In MLA style, place a sentence-ending period after the parenthetical reference.]

QUOTATION WITH ELLIPSIS ENDING THE SENTENCE

On page 9, Goleman states: "These two minds, the emotional and the rational, operate in tight harmony for the most part. . . ." [*Note:* In MLA style, when all needed documentation information is written into a sentence—that is, not placed in parentheses at the end of the sentence—there's no space between the sentence-ending period and an ellipsis.]

QUOTATION WITH SENTENCE OMITTED

Goleman explains: "These two minds, the emotional and the rational, operate in tight harmony for the most part, intertwining their very different ways of knowing to guide us through the world. . . . Still, the emotional and rational minds are semi-independent faculties" (9).

QUOTATION WITH WORDS OMITTED FROM THE MIDDLE OF ONE SENTENCE TO THE MIDDLE OF ANOTHER

Goleman states: "Ordinarily, there is a balance between emotional and rational minds . . . reflecting the operation of distinct, but interconnected, circuitry in the brain" (9).

QUOTATION WITH WORDS OMITTED FROM THE MIDDLE OF ONE SENTENCE TO A COMPLETE OTHER SENTENCE

Goleman explains: "Ordinarily, there is a balance between emotional and rational minds. . . . Still, the emotional and rational minds are semi-independent faculties, each, as we shall see, reflecting the operation of distinct, but interconnected, circuitry in the brain" (9).

When you omit words from a quotation, you also omit punctuation related to those words, unless it's needed for the sentence to be correct.

Goleman explains: "These two minds . . . operate in tight harmony" (9). [comma in original source omitted after *minds*]

Goleman explains that the emotional and rational minds work together while, "still, . . . each, as we shall see, [reflects] the operation of distinct, but interconnected, circuitry in the brain" (9). [comma kept after *still* because it's an introductory word; form of *reflecting* changed for sense of sentence]

29d.2 Using ellipsis points with poetry

When you omit one or more words from a line of poetry, follow the rules stated above for prose. However, when you omit a full line or more from poetry, use a full line of spaced dots.

QUOTATION: ON WRITING
In the camp, this meant committing my verse—many thousands of lines—to memory. To help me with this I improvised decimal counting beads and, in transit prisons, broke up matchsticks and used the fragments as tallies. As I approached the end of my sentence I grew more confident of my powers of memory, and began writing down and memorizing prose—dialogue at first, but then, bit by bit, whole densely written passages. My memory found room for them! It worked. But more and more of my time—in the end as much as one week every month—went into the regular repetition of all I had memorized.
—Aleksandr Solzhenitsyn

QUOTATION: ON WRITING
Speech is highly elliptical. It would scarcely be endurable otherwise. Ellipsis is indispensable to the writer or speaker who wants to be brief and pithy, but it can easily cause confusion and obscurity and must be used with skill.
—Cornelia Evans and Bergen Evans

BACKGROUND
The punctuation mark we call the *slash* is called a *stroke* in British English. Technically, a slash is a *virgule*, a noun pronounced vir-*gool* (rhymes with tool). Here is one dictionary definition of the term: "A slanting line used to indicate a choice between two alternatives, as in the phrase *and/or*" (*New International Dictionary of the English Language*, Comprehensive Edition, Funk & Wagnalls, 1994). Also, the virgule is sometimes called a *solidus*.

ORIGINAL SOURCE

Little Boy Blue

Little boy blue, come blow your horn,
The sheep's in the meadow, the cow's in the corn
Where is the little boy who looks after the sheep?
He's under the haystack, fast asleep.

QUOTATION WITH LINES OMITTED

Little Boy Blue

Little boy blue, come blow your horn,

. . . .

Where is the little boy who looks after the sheep?
He's under the haystack, fast asleep.

SLASH

29e When can I use a slash in my writing?

The **slash** (/), also called a *virgule* or *solidus*, is a diagonal line that separates or joins words in special circumstances.

Using a slash to separate quoted lines of poetry

When you quote more than three lines of a poem, no slash is involved; you merely follow the rules in 29d. When you quote three lines or fewer, enclose them in quotation marks and run them into your sentence—and use a slash to divide one line from the next. Leave a space on each side of the slash.

> One of my mottoes comes from the beginning of Anne Sexton's poem "Words": "Be careful of words, / even the miraculous ones."

Capitalize and punctuate each line of poetry as in the original—but even if the quoted line of poetry doesn't have a period, use one to end your sentence. If your quotation ends before the line of poetry ends, use ellipsis points (29d).

Using a slash for numerical fractions in manuscripts

To type numerical fractions, use a slash (with no space before or after the slash) to separate the numerator and denominator. In mixed numbers—that is, whole numbers with fractions—leave a space between the whole number and its fraction: 1 2/3, 3 7/8. Do not use a hyphen. (For information about using spelled-out and numerical forms of numbers, see 30o.)

Using a slash for and/or

When writing in the humanities, try not to use word combinations connected with a slash, such as *and/or*. In academic disciplines in which such combinations are acceptable, separate the words with a slash. Leave no space before or after the slash. In the humanities, listing both alternatives in normal sentence structure is usually better than separating choices with a slash.

NO	The best quality of reproduction comes from 35 mm slides/direct-positive films.
YES	The best quality of reproduction comes from 35 mm slides **or** direct-positive films.

EXERCISE 29-2

Supply needed dashes, parentheses, brackets, ellipsis points, and slashes. If a sentence is correct as written, circle its number. In some sentences, when you can use either dashes or parentheses, explain your choice. For help, consult all sections of this chapter.

EXAMPLE Two tiny islands in the English Channel Jersey and Guernsey have breeds of cows named after them.

Two tiny islands in the English Channel—Jersey and Guernsey—have breeds of cows named after them.

1. In *The Color Purple* a successful movie as well as a novel, Alice Walker explores the relationships between women and men in traditional African American culture.

2. W. C. Fields offered two pieces of advice on job hunting: 1 never show up for an interview in bare feet, and 2 don't read your prospective employer's mail while he is questioning you about your qualifications.

3. A series of resolutions was passed 11–0 with one council member abstaining calling on the mayor and the district attorney to improve safety conditions and step up law enforcement on city buses.

4. All the interesting desserts ice cream, chocolate fudge cake, pumpkin pie with whipped cream are fattening, unfortunately.

5. Thunder is caused when the flash of lightning heats the air around it to temperatures up to 30,000°F 16,666°C.

6. Christina Rossetti wonders if the end of a life also means the end of love in a poem that opens with these two lines: "When I am dead, my dearest, Sing no sad songs for me."

7. After the internationally famous racehorse Dan Patch died suddenly from a weak heart, his devoted owner, Will Savage, died of the same condition a mere 32 1/2 hours later.

ANSWERS AND COVERAGE:
EXERCISE 29-2

Answers may vary somewhat, especially in usage of dashes and parentheses.

1. In *The Color Purple* (a successful movie as well as a novel), Alice Walker explores the relationships between women and men in traditional African American culture. [29b, parentheses for interruptive aside; dashes too distracting]

2. W. C. Fields offered two pieces of advice on job hunting: (1) never show up for an interview in bare feet, and (2) don't read your prospective employer's mail while he is questioning you about your qualifications. [29b, parentheses around numbers for listed items in sentence]

3. A series of resolutions was passed 11–0 (with one council member abstaining) calling on the mayor and the district attorney to improve safety conditions and step up law enforcement on city buses. [29b, parentheses for interruptive explanation; dashes too distracting]

4. All the interesting desserts—ice cream, chocolate fudge cake, pumpkin pie with whipped cream—are fattening, unfortunately. [29a, dashes for interruptive example; dashes add emphasis]

5. Thunder is caused when the flash of lightning heats the air around it to temperatures up to 30,000°F (16,666°C). [29b, parentheses for alternative numbers]

6. Christina Rossetti wonders if the end of life also means the end of love in a poem that opens with these two lines: "When I am dead, my dearest, / Sing no sad songs for me." [29e, slash between lines of quoted poetry]

7. Correct

8. In his famous letter from the Birmingham jail on April 16, 1963, Martin Luther King Jr. wrote: "You [the eight clergymen who had urged him not to hold a protest] deplore the demonstrations taking place in Birmingham." [29c, brackets for words inserted into quotation]

→

Answers and Coverage:
Exercise 29-2 (continued)

9. The world's most expensive doll house (sold for $256,000 at a London auction) [29b, parentheses for interruptive explanation because dash used later in sentence] contains sixteen rooms, a working chamber organ, and a silver clothes press—but no toilet. [29a, dash for contrast]

10. The person renting this apartment agrees to pay seven hundred fifty dollars ($750) per month in rent. [29b, parentheses for repetition of a spelled-out number]

11. Railroad entrepreneur George Francis Train (his real name!) dreamed of creating a chain of great cities across the country connected by his Union Pacific Railroad. [29b, par-entheses for interruptive aside; dashes too distracting]

12. Patients who pretend to have ailments are known to doctors as "Munchausens" after Baron Karl Friedrich Hieronymus von Münchhausen. (He was a German army officer who had a reputation for wild and unbelievable tales.) [29b, parentheses for interruptive explanation because explanation is separate sentence]

ANSWERS: EXERCISE 29-3
Answers will vary greatly. When checking them, make sure that the directions were followed.

8. In his famous letter from the Birmingham jail on April 16, 1963, Martin Luther King Jr. wrote: "You the eight clergymen who had urged him not to hold a protest deplore the demonstrations taking place in Birmingham."

9. The world's most expensive doll house sold for $256,000 at a London auction contains sixteen rooms, a working chamber organ, and a silver clothes press but no toilet.

10. The person renting this apartment agrees to pay seven hundred fifty dollars $750 per month in rent.

11. Railroad entrepreneur George Francis Train his real name! dreamed of creating a chain of great cities across the United States, all connected by his Union Pacific Railroad.

12. Patients who pretend to have ailments are known to doctors as "Munchausens" after Baron Karl Friedrich Hieronymus von Münchhausen he was a German army officer who had a reputation for wild and unbelievable tales.

EXERCISE 29-3

Follow the directions for each item. For help, consult all sections of this chapter.

EXAMPLE Write a sentence about getting something right using a dash.

I tried and failed, I tried and failed again—and then I did it.

1. Write a sentence that quotes only three lines of the following sonnet by William Shakespeare:

Let me not to the marriage of true minds
Admit impediments. Love is not love
Which alters when it alteration finds,
Or bends with the remover to remove.
O, no! it is an ever-fixèd mark
That looks on tempests and is never shaken;
It is the star to every wand'ring bark,
Whose worth's unknown, although his height be taken.
Love's not Time's fool, though rosy lips and cheeks
Within his bending sickle's compass come;
Love alters not with his brief hours and weeks,
But bears it out even to the edge of doom.
  If this be error, and upon me proved,
  I never writ, nor no man ever loved.

2. Write a sentence using parentheses to enclose a brief example.

3. Write a sentence using dashes to set off a definition.

4. Write a sentence that includes four numbered items in a list.

5. Quote a few sentences from any source you choose. Omit words without losing meaning or use brackets to insert words to maintain meaning or grammatical structure. Use ellipsis points to indicate the omission, and place the parenthetical reference where it belongs.

HYPHEN

29f When do I need a hyphen in my writing?

A **hyphen** serves to divide words at the end of a line, to combine words into compounds, and to communicate numbers.

29g When do I use a hyphen at the end of a line?

Generally, try not to divide a word with a hyphen at the end of a line. It makes reading easier. (In printed books, hyphens are acceptable because of the limits on line length.) If you must divide a word, try hard not to divide the last word on the first line of a paper, the last word in a paragraph, or the last word on a page.

When you can't avoid using a hyphen at the end of a line, break the word only between syllables. If you aren't sure about the syllables in a word, consult a dictionary. Box 116 lists guidelines for end-of-line word breaks.

BOX 116   SUMMARY

Hyphens in end-of-line word breaks

- Divide words only between syllables.

  NO   ent-ertain   proc-eed
  YES   enter-tain   pro-ceed

- Never divide words that are short, of one syllable, or pronounced as one syllable.

  NO   we-alth   en-vy   scream-ed
  YES   wealth   envy   screamed

→

BACKGROUND

In *How Do You Spell*, Perry W. Buffington cites research to suggest that gifted spellers are avid readers. He also notes that "the ancient Greeks believed that a lesser god named Skripto was responsible for all errors in spelling, grammar, and diction."

QUOTATION: ON WRITING

Hooray for the hyphen! Or, rather, Hoo-ray!
—George Plimpton

BACKGROUND

In *It's Hyphen Time*, Carl Kane suggests inserting a hyphen "whenever a *re* prefix creates a word identical to another word," such as, *recreation* and *re-creation*; *resigned* and *re-signed*; *resolve* and *re-solve*.

BACKGROUND

A single missing hyphen cost U.S. citizens $18.5 million in 1962. *Mariner I*, a U.S. space exploration vehicle, went off course and had to be destroyed. The reason: a missing hyphen in its computer-run flight program.

Hyphens in end-of-line word breaks (*continued*)

- Never divide a word when only one or two letters would be left or carried over.

NO	a-live	touch-y	he-licopter	helicopt-er
YES	alive	touchy	heli-copter	helicop-ter

- Divide between two consonants according to pronunciation.

NO	ful-lness	omitt-ing	punct-ure
YES	full-ness	omit-ting	punc-ture

29h # How do I use a hyphen with prefixes and suffixes?

Prefixes are syllables in front of a **root**—a word's core, which carries the origin or meaning. Prefixes modify meanings. **Suffixes** also have modifying power, but they follow roots. Some prefixes and suffixes are attached to root words with hyphens, but others are not. Box 117 shows you how to decide.

BOX 117   SUMMARY

 ### Hyphens with prefixes and suffixes

- Use hyphens after the prefixes *all-*, *ex-*, *quasi-*, and *self-*.

YES	all-inclusive	self-reliant

- Never use a hyphen when *self* is a root word, not a prefix.

NO	self-ishness	self-less
YES	selfishness	selfless

- Use a hyphen to avoid a distracting string of letters.

NO	ant**ii**ntellectual	be**lll**ike	pr**oo**utsourcing
YES	ant**i-i**ntellectual	bel**l-l**ike	pr**o-o**utsourcing

- Use a hyphen to add a prefix or suffix to a numeral or a word that starts with a capital letter.

NO	post1950s	proAmerican	Rembrandtlike
YES	post-1950	pro-American	Rembrandt-like

Hyphens with prefixes and suffixes (*continued*)

■ Use a hyphen before the suffix -*elect*.

NO	presidentelect
YES	president-elect

■ Use a hyphen to prevent confusion in meaning or pronunciation.

YES	re-dress (means *dress again*)		redress (means *set right*)
YES	un-ionize (means *remove the ions*)		unionize (means *form a union*)

■ Use a hyphen when two or more prefixes apply to one root word.

YES	pre- and post-Renaissance

29i # How do I use hyphens with compound words?

A **compound word** puts two or more words together to express one concept. Compound words come in three forms: an *open-compound word,* as in *night shift,* hyphenated words, as in *tractor-trailer,* and a *closed-compound word,* as in *handbook.* Box 118 lists basic guidelines for positioning hyphens in compound words.

BOX 118   SUMMARY

Hyphens with compound words

■ Divide a compound word already containing a hyphen only after that hyphen, if possible. Also, divide a closed-compound word only between the two complete words, if possible.

NO	self-con-scious	sis-ter-in-law	mas-terpiece
YES	self-conscious	sister-in-law	master-piece

■ Use a hyphen between a prefix and an open-compound word.

NO	antigun control [*gun control* is an open-compound word]
YES	anti-gun control

→

QUOTATION: ON WRITING

This morning I deleted the hyphen from "hell-bound" and made it one word; this afternoon I redivided it and restored the hyphen.

—Edwin Arlington Robinson

BACKGROUND

In *Hyphenated Americans,* William Safire recalls Justice Thurgood Marshall's insistence on being called *Afro-American* to introduce the topic of hyphenated "appellations" such as *Irish-Americans* and *Italian-Americans.* Safire writes, "At the turn of the 20th century, *hyphenated American* was a term of contempt used by nativists to demean the allegiance of immigrants; now such hyphenation is sought-after."

BACKGROUND

In *Back to Front,* Chauncey Mabe reflects on the "quirky inventiveness" of palindromes: "words or phrases that spell the same frontwards and backwards." According to Mabe, "A man, a plan, a canal: Panama," is a perfect example of a palindrome: "It not only makes sense, it tells the story of the Panama Canal in miniature." Following are briefer examples: *civic, madam, pull-up, race car,* and *radar.*

Hyphens with compound words (*continued*)

- Use a hyphen for most compound words that precede a noun but not for most compound words that follow a noun.

YES	well-researched report	report is well researched
YES	two-inch clearance	clearance of two inches

- Use hyphens when a compound modifier includes a series.

YES	two-, three-, or four-year program

- Never use a hyphen when a compound modifier starts with an *-ly* adverb.

NO	happily-married couple	loosely-tied package
YES	happily married couple	loosely tied package

- Never use a hyphen with COMPARATIVE (*more, less*) and SUPERLATIVE (*most, least*) compound forms.

NO	more-appropriate idea [*more* is a comparative adverb]
YES	more appropriate idea

NO	least-significant factors [*least* is a superlative adverb]
YES	least significant factors

- Never use a hyphen when a compound modifier is a foreign phrase.

YES	*post hoc* fallacies

- Never use a hyphen with a possessive compound.

NO	a full-week's work	eight-hours' pay
YES	a full week's work	eight hours' pay

EXERCISE 29-4

Provide the correct form of the words in parentheses, according to the rules in 29f through 29i. Explain your reasoning for each.

1. The tiger is (all powerful) _____ in the cat family.

2. (Comparison and contrast) _____ studies of tigers and lions show that the tiger is the (more agile) _____ and powerful.

3. Male tigers and lions look similar except for their hair length: Tigers have (ultra short) _____ hair and male lions have (extra long) _____ hair in their manes.

4. The tiger's body is a (boldly striped) _____ yellow, with a white (under body) _____.

5. The Bengal tiger, the largest of the family, is aggressive and (self confident) _____.

6. In India, where the Bengal tiger is called a (village destroyer) _____, it goes (in to) _____ villages to hunt for food.

7. Entire villages have been temporarily abandoned by (terror stricken) _____ people who have seen a Bengal tiger nearby.

8. Villagers seek to protect their homes by destroying tigers with traps, (spring loaded) _____ guns, and (poisoned arrows) _____.

9. Bengal tigers are also called (cattle killers) _____, although they attack domestic animals only when they cannot find wild ones.

10. Many people who do not live near a zoo get to see tigers only in (animal shows) _____, although (pro animal) _____ activists try to prevent tigers from being used this way.

ANSWERS AND COVERAGE: EXERCISE 20-4

1. all-powerful [*all-* prefix hyphenated]

2. Comparison-and-contrast [hyphenate open compound preceding noun it modifies]; more agile [no hyphen with *more*]

3. ultra-short; extra-long [in both cases, hyphenate compound before the noun]

4. boldly striped [no hyphen after *-ly* adverb in a compound modifier]; underbody [*under-* prefix spelled closed]

5. self-confident [*self-* prefix hyphenated]

6. village destroyer [open compound]; into [closed compound]

7. terror-stricken [hyphenate compound before the noun]

8. spring-loaded [hyphenate compound before the noun]; poisoned arrows [not a compound]

9. cattle killers [open compound]

10. animal shows [not a compound]; pro-animal [*pro-* prefix hyphenated before vowel]

Chapter 30

Capitals, Italics, Abbreviations, and Numbers

CAPITALS

30a When do I capitalize a "first" word?

First word in a sentence

Always capitalize the first letter of the first word in a sentence.

> **F**our inches of snow fell last winter.

A series of questions

If questions in a series are complete sentences, start each with a capital letter. If, however, the questions aren't complete sentences, you can choose to capitalize or not. Whatever your choice, be consistent in each piece of writing. In this handbook, I use capitals for a series of questions.

> What facial feature would most people like to change? **E**yes? **E**ars? **N**ose?
>
> What facial feature would most people like to change? **e**yes? **e**ars? **n**ose?

Small words in titles or headings

Capitalize small words (*the, a, an,* and short PREPOSITIONS such as *with, of, to*) in a title or heading only when they begin the title or when the source capitalizes these small words.

Always capitalize *I*, no matter where it falls in a sentence or group of words: *I love you now, although I didn't used to.* The same holds for *O,* the INTERJECTION: *You are, O my fair love, a burning fever; O my gentle love, embrace me.* In contrast, never capitalize the interjection *oh,* unless it starts a sentence or is capitalized in words you're quoting.

After a colon

When a complete sentence follows a colon, you can choose to start that sentence with either a capital or a lowercase letter, but be consistent in each piece of writing. When the words after a colon are not a complete sentence, do not capitalize.

> She reacted instantly: **S**he picked up the ice cream and pushed it back into her cone.
>
> She reacted instantly: **s**he picked up the ice cream and pushed it back into her cone.
>
> She bought four pints of ice cream: **v**anilla, chocolate, strawberry, and butter pecan.

👁 **ALERT:** A colon can follow only a complete sentence (an INDEPENDENT CLAUSE; see 26a). 👁

Formal outline

In a formal outline (2r), start each item with a capital letter. Use a period only when the item is a complete sentence.

30b When do I use capitals with listed items?

A list run into a sentence

If run-in listed items are complete sentences, start each with a capital and end each with a period (or question mark or exclamation point). If the run-in listed items are incomplete sentences, start each with a lowercase letter and end each with a comma—unless the items already contain commas, in which case use semicolons. If you list three or more items that are incomplete sentences, use *and* before the last item.

YES	We found three reasons for the delay: (1) **B**ad weather held up delivery of materials. (2) **P**oor scheduling created confusion. (3) **I**mproper machine maintenance caused an equipment failure.
YES	The reasons for the delay were (1) **b**ad weather**,** (2) **p**oor scheduling**, and** (3) **e**quipment failure.
YES	The reasons for the delay were (1) **b**ad weather, which had been predicted**;** (2) **p**oor scheduling, which is the airline's responsibility**; and** (3) **e**quipment failure, which no one can predict.

A displayed list

In a displayed list, each item starts on a new line. If the items are sentences, capitalize the first letter and end with a period (or question mark or exclamation point). If the items are not sentences, you can use a

TEACHING TIP
Because capitalization practice sometimes varies from one publisher to another, and even from one instructor to another, writers must be aware of the basic rules that are in general use but should stand prepared to adjust minor matters, depending on the guidelines under which they are working at the time. Students should also be aware that capitalization (as well as research documentation and other conventions of the mechanics of writing) varies from one discipline to another, making it necessary for students to be alert to the requirements of the situation in which they are writing.

ESL students may need special attention when they are learning capitalization conventions in English, since practices are not the same in all languages. German, for instance, capitalizes all nouns, whereas English does not. Many Asian and Middle Eastern languages have no capital letters at all.

BACKGROUND
Some readers of *Time* have wondered why the magazine does not capitalize the name of the planet earth, since they do capitalize other planets, such as Venus and Pluto. Here is the magazine's editorial reply (June 12, 1989): "Following grammatical rules for capitalizing proper names, we uppercase those celestial bodies named after mythological gods. Inasmuch as the earth, the moon, and the sun have no mythical forebears, they remain lowercase."

capital letter or not. Whichever you choose, be consistent in each piece of writing. Punctuate a displayed list as you would a run-in list.

> **YES** We found three reasons for the delay:
> (1) **B**ad weather held up delivery of materials.
> (2) **P**oor scheduling created confusion.
> (3) **I**mproper machine maintenance caused an equipment failure.

> **YES** The reasons for the delay were
> (1) **b**ad weather,
> (2) **p**oor scheduling, **and**
> (3) **e**quipment failure.

ALERTS: (1) If a complete sentence leads into a displayed list, you can end the sentence with a colon. However, if an incomplete sentence leads into a displayed list, use no punctuation. (2) Use PARALLELISM for items in a list. For example, if one item is a sentence, use sentences for all the items (18f); or if one item starts with a VERB, start all items with a verb in the same TENSE; and so on.

30c When do I use capitals with sentences in parentheses?

When you write a complete sentence within parentheses that falls within another sentence, don't start with a capital or end with a period—but do use a question mark or exclamation point, if needed. When you write a sentence within parentheses that doesn't fall within another sentence, capitalize the first word and end with a period (or question mark or explanation point).

> I did not know till years later that they called it the Cuban Missile Crisis. But I remember Castro. **(W**e called him Castor Oil and were awed by his beard.**)** We might not have worried so much **(w**hat would the communists want with our small New Hampshire town**?)** except we lived 10 miles from a U.S. air base.
> —Joyce Maynard, "An 18-Year-Old Looks Back on Life"

30d When do I use capitals with quotations?

If a quotation within your sentence is itself less than a complete sentence, never capitalize the first quoted word. If the quotation you have used in your sentence is itself a complete sentence, capitalize the first word.

Mrs. Enriquez says that students who are learning a new language should visit that country and "**a**bsorb a good accent with the food."

Mrs. Enriquez likes to point out that when students live in a new country**,** "**T**hey'll absorb a good accent with the food."

When you write DIRECT DISCOURSE—which you introduce with verbs such as *said, stated, reported,* and others (see 33k) followed by a comma, capitalize the first letter of the quoted words only if it's capitalized in the original. However, never capitalize a partial quotation, and never capitalize the continuation of a one-sentence quotation within your sentence.

Mrs. Enriquez said**,** "**S**tudents who are learning a new language should visit that country. They'll absorb a good accent with the food."

Mrs. Enriquez told me that the best way to "**a**bsorb a good accent" in a language is to visit the country and eat its food.

"Of course," she continued with a smile, "**t**he accent lasts longer than the food."

30e When do I capitalize nouns and adjectives?

Capitalize PROPER NOUNS (nouns that name specific people, places, and things): *Abraham Lincoln, Mexico, World Wide Web.* Also, capitalize **proper adjectives** (adjectives formed from proper nouns): *a Mexican entrepreneur, a Web address.* Don't capitalize ARTICLES (*the, a, an*) that accompany proper nouns and proper adjectives, unless they start a sentence.

When a proper noun or adjective loses its very specific "proper" association, it also loses its capital letter: *french fries, pasteurized.* When you turn a common noun (*lake*) into a proper noun (*Lake Mead*), capitalize all words.

Expect sometimes that you'll see capitalized words that this handbook says not to capitalize. For example, a corporation's written communications usually capitalize their own entities (*our Board of Directors* or *this Company*), even though the rule calls for lowercase (*the board of directors, the company*). Similarly, the administrators of your school might write *the Faculty* and *the College* (or *the University*), even though the rule calls for a lowercase *f, c,* and *u.* How writers capitalize can depend on AUDIENCE and PURPOSE in each specific context.

Box 119 on pages 466–468 is a capitalization guide. If you don't find what you need, locate an item in it (or in Box 120 on pages 470–471) that's close to what you want, and use it as a model.

TEACHING TIP

You might find that students overcapitalize in their writing. Comparison can be a useful tool in encouraging them to distinguish between common and proper nouns. First, review the basic rule: Proper (capitalized) nouns are the official names of specific people, places, or things; common (uncapitalized) nouns refer more generally to people, places, or things. Then, give students pairs of noun phrases, one of which contains a proper noun and one a common noun. Omit all capitals. Ask students to identify and capitalize the proper noun: *president washington, the president of the country; hunter high school, the high school band; a new car, a cadillac seville; psychological testing, psychology 101.* Augment this list with pairs representing your students' most common errors.

Your students will probably find this rather easy because contrast highlights the specific nouns. The next step can be to make up or edit a paragraph to eliminate all capital letters except those that begin sentences. Ask students to capitalize the first letters of all proper nouns. Upon completion, you might have students exchange papers and discuss the correct answers. Students can correct one another's exercises, and you can collect the papers to review or record grades.

BOX 119   SUMMARY

Capitalization

	CAPITALS	LOWERCASE LETTERS
NAMES	Mother Teresa (*also*, used as names: Mother, Dad, Mom, Pa)	my mother [relationship]
	Doc Holliday	the doctor [role]
TITLES	President Truman	the president
	Democrat [party member]	democrat [believer in democracy]
	Representative Harold Ford	the congressional representative
	Senator Edward M. Kennedy	a senator
	Queen Elizabeth II	the queen
GROUPS OF PEOPLE	Caucasian [race]	white, black [*also* White, Black]
	African American, Hispanic, [ethnic group]	
	Irish, Korean, Canadian [nationality]	
	Jewish, Catholic, Protestant, Buddhist [religious affiliation]	
ORGANIZATIONS	Congress	legislative branch of the U.S. government
	the Ohio State Supreme Court	the state supreme court
	the Republican Party	the party
	National Gypsum Company	the company
	Chicago Cubs	baseball team
	American Medical Association	professional group
	Sigma Chi	fraternity
	Alcoholics Anonymous	self-help group
PLACES	Los Angeles	the city
	the South [region]	turn south [direction]
	the West Coast	the U.S. states along the western seaboard

→

Capitalization (*continued*)

	CAPITALS	LOWERCASE LETTERS
PLACES (*cont.*)	Main Street	the street
	Atlantic Ocean	the ocean
	the Black Hills	the hills
BUILDINGS	the Capitol [in Washington, DC]	the state capitol
	Ace High School	a high school
	Front Road Café	a restaurant
	Highland Hospital	a hospital
SCIENTIFIC TERMS	Earth [as one of nine planets]	the earth [otherwise]
	the Milky Way, the Galaxy [as name]	our galaxy, the moon, the sun
	Streptococcus aureus	a streptococcal infection
	Gresham's law	the theory of relativity
LANGUAGES SCHOOL COURSES	Spanish, Chinese	
	Chemistry 342	a chemistry course
	English 111	my English class
	Introduction to Photography	a photography course
NAMES OF SPECIFIC THINGS	Black Parrot tulip	climbing rose
	Purdue University	the university
	Heinz ketchup	ketchup, sauce
	a Toyota Camry	a car
	Twelfth Dynasty	the dynasty
	the *Boston Globe*	a newspaper
TIMES, SEASONS, HOLIDAYS	Monday, Fri.	today
	September, February	a month
	the Roaring Twenties	the decade
	the Christmas season	spring, summer, autumn, winter, the fall semester
	Kwanzaa, New Year's Day	feast day, the holiday
	Passover, Ramadan	religious holiday or observance

→

TEACHING TIP

To draw students' attention to standard (and perhaps nonstandard) capitalization practice, you may want to ask them to bring to class examples from advertising and newspapers that demonstrate the use of capital letters for a variety of purposes. The examples can be the basis for a class discussion on the reasons for using capital letters and their effectiveness.

QUOTATION: ON WRITING

Some readers think my writing is a capital offense. Others think it is capital fun. I hope it converts into capital.

—Diana Davis

BACKGROUND

The three basic type forms are gothic, old-style roman, and modern roman. (There are many variations of these basic ones.) Italic type is a companion form of modern roman, one that is lighter and slopes to the right. The earliest type forms were based on contemporary manuscript hands, for the printer was replacing the scribe. The old-style roman form reached its zenith in the fifteenth century, and in 1501, Aldus Manutius of Venice produced and used the first italic form in the printing of a series of Latin texts, the first volume of which was called *Aldine Virgil*. The "modern" roman form, the kind of type most used in Western publishing today, originated about 1693 with Philippe Grandjean. Benjamin Franklin was responsible for introducing a variety of roman type, designed by William Caslon, to the American colonies. The Declaration of Independence was printed using it. The early type founders were artists who were concerned about the aesthetics of their typefaces. In the nineteenth century, however, emphasis shifted from artistry to quantity, and attention to the beauty of printed letters suffered a decline.

BACKGROUND

In a column, "MAIL CALL (ALL CAPS)," William Safire comments on the postal service standards for addressing envelopes entirely in "uppercase letters." According to Safire, "the term *capital letters* comes more naturally than *uppercase letters* to native speakers, few of whom, it seems, work at the postal service."

Capitalization (*continued*)

	CAPITALS	LOWERCASE LETTERS
HISTORICAL EVENTS AND DOCUMENTS	World War II	the war
	Battle of the Bulge	the battle
	the Great Depression (of the 1930s)	the depression [any serious economic downturn]
	the Reformation	the eighteenth century
	Paleozoic	era or age, prehistory
	the Civil Rights Movement (of the 1960s)	a civil rights activist
	the Bill of Rights	fifth-century manuscripts
RELIGIOUS TERMS	Athena, God	a goddess, a god
	Islam	a religion
	the Torah, the Koran	a holy book
	the Bible, Scripture	biblical, scriptural
LETTER PARTS	Dear Ms. Schultz:	
	Sincerely,	
	Yours truly,	
PUBLISHED AND RELEASED MATERIAL	"The Lottery"	[Capitalize first letter of first word and all
	A History of the United States to 1877	other major words]
	Jazz on Ice	the show, a performance
	Nixon Papers	the archives
	Mass in B Minor	the B minor mass
ACRONYMS AND INITIALISMS	NASA, NATO,	
	UCLA, AFL-CIO, DNA	
COMPUTER TERMS	Gateway, Dell	a computer company
	Microsoft Word, WordPerfect	computer software
	Netscape Navigator	a browser
	the Internet	a computer network
	World Wide Web, the Web	www
	Web site, Web page	a home page, a link
PROPER ADJECTIVES	Victorian	southern
	Midwestern	transatlantic
	Indo-European	alpine

EXERCISE 30-1

Add capital letters as needed. See 30a through 30e for help.

1. When the philosopher Bertrand Russell was asked if he'd be willing to die for his beliefs, he replied, "of course not. After all, i may be wrong."
2. "Please hurry," pleaded Rebecca, "or we'll be late for the opening curtain of the san francisco ballet company."
3. The fine art course taught by professor Sanzio accepts only students who already have credits in fine art 101 and Renaissance studies 211.
4. *Let's go,* a series of guidebooks (they advise travelers about less touristy places), are found in thousands of backpacks and suitcases every summer.
5. Lovers of Mexican american food know there's far more to that cuisine than tacos and enchiladas.
6. At one point in the action, the script calls for the "assembled multitudes" to break into shouts of "hail, o merciful queen Tanya!"
7. How should we think of the start of the french revolution? Was it the best of times? the worst of times? a time of indecision, perhaps?
8. In the chapter "the making of a new world," among those credited with the european discovery of the americas before Columbus are (1) the vikings, (2) groups of fishers and whalers from europe, and (3) peoples who crossed the Bering strait to alaska in prehistoric times.
9. People sometimes forget that the bible was not originally written in english.
10. The organization of african unity (oau) was founded in 1962, when many african nations were winning their independence.

ITALICS

30f What are italics?

Italics is the typeface that slants to the right (*hello there*). In contrast, **roman typeface** is the most common type in print (you're looking at it right now). If your word processing program doesn't give you the option of italics, underline instead. In fact, MLA STYLE requires underlining, not italics, in all documents.

ROMAN	your writing
UNDERLINING	your writing
ITALICS	*your writing*

ANSWERS: EXERCISE 30-1

The words that need capital letters are italicized here.

1. When the philosopher Bertrand Russell was asked if he'd be willing to die for his beliefs, he replied, "*Of* course not. After all, *I* may be wrong."

2. "Please hurry," pleaded Dorothy, "or we'll be late for the opening curtain of the *San Francisco Ballet Company.*"

3. The fine art course taught by *Professor* Sanzio accepts only students who already have credits in *Fine Art* 101 and Renaissance *Studies* 211.

4. *Let's Go,* a series of guidebooks (they advise travelers about less touristy places), are found in thousands of backpacks and suitcases every summer.

5. Lovers of Mexican *American* food know there's far more to that cuisine than tacos and enchiladas.

6. At one point in the action, the script calls for the "assembled multitudes" to break into shouts of "*Hail, O* merciful *Queen* Tanya!"

7. How should we think of the start of the *French Revolution?* Was it the best of times? *The* worst of times? *A* time of indecision, perhaps? [lowercase for *the* and *a* are also acceptable]

8. In the chapter "*The Making* of a *New World,*" among those credited with the *European* discovery of the *Americas* before Columbus are (1) the *Vikings,* (2) groups of fishers and whalers from *Europe,* and (3) peoples who crossed the Bering *Strait* to *Alaska* in prehistoric times.

9. People sometimes forget that the *Bible* was not originally written in *English.*

10. The *Organization* of *African Unity* (*OAU*) was founded in 1962, when many *African* nations were winning their independence.

EXTRA EXERCISE B

What is the difference in meaning suggested by the following changes in the italicized words? (Answers will vary.)

1. a. Six *different* bodies compose the United Nations.
   b. Six different bodies compose the *United Nations.*

2. a. All members of the UN can send *five* representatives to the General Assembly.
   b. All members of the UN can send five representatives to the *General Assembly.*

3. a. The *primary* responsibility of the Security Council is to maintain international peace and security.
   b. The primary responsibility of the Security Council is to maintain *international* peace and security.

ADDITIONAL EXAMPLES: ITALICS

Can your students cite the rule governing the following italicized words?

1. *Hamlet* is still one of the world's most frequently produced plays.

2. Several magazines, such as *TV Guide* and *U.S. News & World Report*, have significantly changed their format in recent years.

3. Some people prefer to keep up with current events by watching *CBS Evening News* instead of reading *USA Today.*

4. The reruns of *Star Trek* continue to attract viewers.

5. The *Challenger* disaster will be long remembered.

6. My grandfather always told me, "Mind your *p*'s and *q*'s, young man!"

7. The literary works of the *fin de siècle* were shocking to many readers.

8. English has borrowed many words from other languages, including *chauffeur, taco,* and *moccasin.*

9. *The Red Badge of Courage* is a modern epic.

10. The *Titanic* was originally thought to be invulnerable.

30g How do I choose between using italics and quotation marks?

As a rule, use italics for titles of long works (*The Matrix*, a movie) or for works that contain subsections (*Masterpiece Theater*, a television show). Generally, use quotation marks for titles of shorter works ("I Wanna Hold Your Hand," a song) and for titles of subsections within longer works such as books (Chapter 1, "Loomings").

Box 120 is a guide for using italics, quotation marks, or nothing. If you don't find what you need, locate an item that is as much like what you want as possible and use it as a model.

BOX 120   SUMMARY

 Italics, quotation marks, or nothing

Titles and Names

ITALICS	QUOTATION MARKS OR NOTHING
Sense and Sensibility [a novel]	title of student essay
Death of a Salesman [a play]	act 2 [part of a play]
A Beautiful Mind [a film]	the Epilogue [a part of a film or book]
Collected Works of O. Henry [a book]	"The Last Leaf" [a story in a book]
Simon & Schuster Handbook for Writers [a textbook]	"Agreement" [a chapter in a book]
The Prose Reader [a collection of essays]	"Putting in a Good Word for Guilt" [an essay]
Iliad [a book-length poem]	"Nothing Gold Can Stay" [a short poem]
Scientific American [a magazine]	"The Molecules of Life" [an article in a magazine]
Symphonie Fantastique [a long musical work]	Violin Concerto No. 2 in B-flat Minor [a musical work identified by form, number, and key—neither quotation marks nor underlining]
The Best of Bob Dylan [a CD]	"Mr. Tambourine Man" [a song]
Twilight Zone [a television series]	"Terror at 30,000 Feet" [an episode of a television series]
Kids Count [a Web site title]	Excel [a software program]
the *Los Angeles Times* [a newspaper]*	

*When *The* is part of a newspaper's title, don't capitalize or italicize it in MLA-style or CM-style documentation. In APA-style, COS, and CSE-style documentation, capitalize and italicize *The.*

→

Italics, quotation marks, or nothing (*continued*)

Other Words

ITALICS	QUOTATION MARKS OR NOTHING
semper fidelis [words in a language other than English]	burrito, chutzpah [widely understood non-English words]
What does *our* imply? [a word meant as a word]	
the *abc*'s; the letter *x* [letters meant as letters]	6s and 7s; & [numerals and symbols]

30h Can I use italics for special emphasis?

Some professional writers, especially writers of nonfiction and self-help material, occasionally use italics to clarify a meaning or stress a point. In ACADEMIC WRITING, however, you're expected to convey special emphasis through your choice of words and sentence structure, not with italics (or underlining). If your message absolutely calls for it, use italics sparingly—and only after you're sure nothing else will do.

> Many people we *think* are powerful turn out on closer examination to be merely frightened and anxious.
>
> —Michael Korda, *Power!*

EXERCISE 30-2

Edit these sentences for correct use of italics (or underlining), quotation marks, and capitals. For help, consult 30a through 30h.

1. The article "the Banjo" in the Encyclopaedia Britannica calls the Banjo "America's only national instrument" because it combines the traditional mbanza (a Bantu word native to certain southern areas of africa) and some European string instruments.

2. The writer of a humor column at a newspaper called The "Globe and Mail" has described an imaginary newspaper called The mop and pail, where things are more ridiculous than in Real Life.

3. "Porgy and Bess," a Folk Opera by George and ira Gershwin and Du Bose Heyward, introduced the beautiful, haunting song *Summertime*.

4. Marlon Brando persuaded the Director of *The Godfather* to cast him as the Elderly don Corleone by auditioning with cotton-stuffed cheeks and mumbling hoarsely.

ANSWERS: EXERCISE 30-2
Corrected words appear underlined here. Corrections to capitals are in boldface.

1. The article "**T**he Banjo" in the *Encyclopaedia Britannica* calls the **b**anjo "America's only national instrument" because it combines the traditional *mbanza* (a Bantu word native to certain southern areas of **A**frica) and some European string instruments.

2. The writer of a humor column at a newspaper called **t**he *Globe and Mail* has described an imaginary newspaper called **t**he *Mop and Pail*, where things are more ridiculous than in real life.

3. *Porgy and Bess*, a **f**olk **o**pera by George and **I**ra Gershwin and Du Bose Heyward, introduced the beautiful, haunting song "Summertime."

4. Marlon Brando persuaded the **d**irector of *The Godfather* to cast him as the **e**lderly **D**on Corleone by auditioning with cotton-stuffed cheeks and mumbling hoarsely.

5. When the name of a **s**mall **b**usiness begins with the letter *a* repeated many times, as in AAAAAbc Auto Body, we know its marketing plan includes being listed first in the telephone directory.

5. When the name of a Small Business begins with the letter a repeated many times, as in AAAAAbc "Auto Body," we know its marketing plan includes being listed First in the telephone directory.

ABBREVIATIONS

30i   What are standard practices for using abbreviations?

Some abbreviations are standard in all writing circumstances (*Mr.,* not *Mister,* in a name; *St.* Louis, the city, not *Saint* Louis). In some situations, you may have a choice whether to abbreviate or spell out a word. Choose what seems suited to your PURPOSE for writing and your AUDIENCE, and be consistent within each piece of writing.

> **NO** The great painter Vincent Van Gogh was **b.** in Holland in 1853, but he lived most of his life and died in **Fr.**

> **YES** The great painter Vincent Van Gogh was **born** in Holland in 1853, but he lived most of his life and died in **France.**

> **NO** Our field hockey team left after Casey's **psych** class on **Tues., Oct.** 10, but the flight had to make an unexpected stop (in **Chi.**) before reaching **L.A.**

> **YES** Our field hockey team left after Casey's **psychology** class on **Tuesday, October** 10, but the flight had to make an unexpected stop (in **Chicago**) before reaching **Los Angeles.**

> **NO** Please confirm in writing your order for one **doz.** helmets in **lg** and **x-lg.**

> **YES** Please confirm in writing your order for one **dozen** helmets in **large** and **extra large.**

👁 **ALERTS:** (1) Many abbreviations call for periods (*Mrs., Ms., Dr.*), but practice is changing. The trend today is to drop the periods (*PS,* not *P.S.; MD,* not *M.D.; US,* not *U.S.*), yet firm rules are still evolving.

(2) **Acronyms** (pronounceable words formed from the initials of a name) generally have no periods: *NASA* (National Aeronautics and Space Administration) and *AIDS* (*a*cquired *i*mmune *d*eficiency *s*yndrome).

(3) **Initialisms** (names spoken as separate letters) usually have no periods (*IBM, ASPCA, UN*).

(4) Postal abbreviations for states have no periods (see Box 122 in 30k).

(5) When the final period of an abbreviation falls at the end of a sentence, that period serves also to end the sentence. 👁

30j How do I use abbreviations with months, time, eras, and symbols?

Months

According to MLA STYLE, abbreviations for months belong only in "Works Cited" lists, tables, charts, and the like. Write out the full spelling; never the abbreviation in your ACADEMIC WRITING. Box 121 shows month abbreviations in MLA style.

BOX 121   SUMMARY

Month abbreviations—MLA style

January	Jan.	May	(none)	September	Sept.
February	Feb.	June	(none)	October	Oct.
March	Mar.	July	(none)	November	Nov.
April	Apr.	August	Aug.	December	Dec.

Times

Use the abbreviations *a.m.* and *p.m.* only with exact times: *7:15 a.m.; 3:47 p.m.* Although some publication styles use the capitalized versions, *A.M.* and *P.M.,* MLA style calls for the use of lowercase letters.

👁 **ALERT:** Never use *a.m.* and *p.m.* in place of the words *morning, evening,* and *night.*

> **NO** My hardest final exam is in the **a.m.** tomorrow, but by early **p.m.,** I'll be ready to study for the rest of my finals.

> **YES** My hardest final exam is in the **morning** tomorrow, but by early **evening,** I'll be ready to study for the rest of my finals. 👁

Eras

In MLA style, use capital letters, without periods, in abbreviations for eras. Some writers prefer using CE ("common era") in place of AD (Latin for anno Domini, "in the year of our Lord") as the more inclusive term. In addition, many writers prefer use BCE ("before the common era") in place of BC (Latin for "before Christ").

When writing the abbreviations for eras, place AD before the year (*AD 476*) and all the others after the year (*29 BC; 165 BCE; 1100 CE*).

Symbols

In MLA style, decide whether to use symbols or spelled-out words based on your topic and the focus of your document (see also 30m). However, never use a freestanding symbol, such as *$, %,* or *¢* in your

---

TEACHING TIP

The letters *BC* follow a date, whereas the letters *AD* precede a date. William Safire reports that a plaque left on the moon by the first Americans to land there reads: "July 1969, A.D." He further reports that at the time he was a speechwriter in the White House and he approved the wording. He writes:

> In a century or so, I hope some descendant of mine will take a sharp stylus on some weekend rocket to the moon and, while awaiting a transfer rocket to Mars, will draw a little circle around the A.D. and put an arrow placing it in front of the word *July.* This will show that human beings in the early days of space were grammatically fallible; that mankind (since changed to *humankind,* but you can leave it the old way on the plaque, Junior) is forever editing, and that a little precision is a dangerous thing.
>
> —William Safire, "On Language"

BACKGROUND
During the administration of President Franklin D. Roosevelt, a number of new government agencies became known by their initials. The Tennessee Valley Authority, for example, was called the TVA, and the National Industrial Recovery Act was the NIRA. World War II strengthened the policy of using initials without periods, and since that time it has been common practice to use an abbreviation without periods in place of some proper names, such as the UN (United Nations), USC (University of Southern California), the NYPD (New York Police Department), and DDT (dichlorodiphenyl-trichloroethane).

sentences; always use it with a numeral. With many exceptions, spell out both the symbol and the numeral accompanying it (*twenty centimeters*), unless the number is more than one or two words (*345 centimeters*, not *three hundred-forty-five centimeters*).

The exceptions include *$18; 7 lbs.; 24 KB; 6:34 a.m., 5″; 32°;* and numbers in addresses, dates, page references, and decimal fractions (*8.3*). In writing about money, the form *$25 million* is an acceptable combination of symbol, numeral, and spelled-out word.

In confined spaces, such as charts and tables, use symbols with numerals (*20¢*). In documents that focus on technical matters, use numerals but spell out the unit of measurement (*2,500 pounds*)—in MLA style. In other documentation styles, such as APA, CM, and CSE, the guidelines differ somewhat, so you need to check each style's manual.

30k How do I use abbreviations for other elements?

Titles

Use either a title of address before a name (***Dr.** Daniel Klausner*) or an academic degree after a name (*Daniel Klausner, **PhD***), not both. However, because *Jr., Sr., II, III,* and so forth are part of a given name, you can use both titles of address and academic degree abbreviations: ***Dr.** Martin Luther King **Jr.;** Gavin Alexander **II, MD***

👁 **ALERTS:** (1) Insert a comma both before and after an academic degree that follows a person's name, unless it falls at the end of a sentence: *Joshua Coleman, **LLD,** is our guest speaker,* or *Our guest speaker is Joshua Coleman, **LLD*** (2) Never put a comma before an abbreviation that is part of a given name: *Steven Elliott Sr., Douglas Young III.* 👁

Names and terms

If you use a term frequently in a piece of writing, follow these guidelines: The first time you use the term, spell it out completely and then put its abbreviation in parentheses immediately after. In later references, use the abbreviation alone.

> Spain voted to continue as a member of the **North Atlantic Treaty Organization** (**NATO**), to the surprise of other **NATO** members.

> When referring to the *United States,* use the abbreviation *U.S.* as a modifier before a noun (*the **U.S.** ski team*), but spell out *United States* when you use it as a noun (*the ski team from the **United States.***)

Addresses

If you include a full address in a piece of writing, use the postal abbreviation for the state name, as listed in Box 122. For any other combination of a city and a state, or a state by itself, spell out the state name; never abbreviate it.

BOX 122   SUMMARY

Postal abbreviations

United States

AL	Alabama	**MT**	Montana
AK	Alaska	**NE**	Nebraska
AZ	Arizona	**NV**	Nevada
AR	Arkansas	**NH**	New Hampshire
CA	California	**NJ**	New Jersey
CO	Colorado	**NM**	New Mexico
CT	Connecticut	**NY**	New York
DE	Delaware	**NC**	North Carolina
DC	District of Columbia	**ND**	North Dakota
FL	Florida	**OH**	Ohio
GA	Georgia	**OK**	Oklahoma
HI	Hawaii	**OR**	Oregon
ID	Idaho	**PA**	Pennsylvania
IL	Illinois	**RI**	Rhode Island
IN	Indiana	**SC**	South Carolina
IA	Iowa	**SD**	South Dakota
KS	Kansas	**TN**	Tennessee
KY	Kentucky	**TX**	Texas
LA	Louisiana	**UT**	Utah
ME	Maine	**VT**	Vermont
MD	Maryland	**VA**	Virginia
MA	Massachusetts	**WA**	Washington [state]
MI	Michigan	**WV**	West Virginia
MN	Minnesota	**WI**	Wisconsin
MS	Mississippi	**WY**	Wyoming
MO	Missouri		

Canada

AB	Alberta	**NT**	Northwest Territories
BC	British Columbia	**NU**	Nunavut
MB	Manitoba	**ON**	Ontario
NB	New Brunswick	**PE**	Prince Edward Island
NL	Newfoundland and Labrador	**QC**	Quebec
		SK	Saskatchewan
NS	Nova Scotia	**YT**	Yukon Territory

EXTRA EXERCISE C
You may want to organize your class into competing teams, giving each in turn a postal abbreviation to which a member is to respond by naming a city in that state. For example, an acceptable answer for a player who is given the abbreviation MN would be *Minneapolis*. When a player cannot answer, the abbreviation is given to a player on the other team.

BACKGROUND
In "Linguaclip," William Safire discusses the use of abbreviations and symbols as substitutes for "the full term[s]." Safire writes: "Whether they save space or show insiderhood, initials soon gain a life, or meaning, of their own." Following is one of his examples: "The initials *F.B.I.* have connotations and resonances that the full name does not have; an arresting agent could get himself killed by shouting the full 'Federal Bureau of Investigation—*freeze!*'" [Today, FBI is always written without periods.]

👁 **ALERT:** When you write the names of a U.S. city and state within a sentence, use a comma before and after the state. If you include a zip code, however, don't use a comma after the state. Do place the comma after the zip code.

NO Portland, Oregon is much larger than Portland, Maine.

YES Portland, Oregon, is much larger than Portland, Maine. 👁

Scholarly writing (MLA style)

MLA style permits abbreviations for a selection of scholarly terms. These are listed in Box 123. Never use them in the body of your ACADEMIC WRITING. Reserve them for your "Works Cited" lists and for any Notes you might write in a separate list at the end of your research paper.

BOX 123 SUMMARY

Major scholarly abbreviations—MLA style

anon.	anonymous	**ms., mss.**	manuscript, manuscripts
b.	born	**NB**	note well (*nota bene*)
c. *or* ©	copyright	**n.d.**	no date (of publication)
c. *or* **ca.**	circa *or* about [with dates]	**p., pp.**	page, pages
cf.	compare	**par.**	paragraph
col., cols.	column, columns	**pref.**	preface, preface by
d.	died	**rept.**	report, reported by
ed., eds.	edition, edited by, editor(s)	**rev.**	review, reviewed by; revised, revised by
e.g.	for example		
esp.	especially	**sec., secs.**	section, sections
et al.	and others	**v.** *or* **vs.**	versus [*v.* in legal cases]
ff.	following pages, following lines, folios	**vol., vols.**	volume, volumes
i.e.	that is		

---

301 ## When can I use *etc.*?

The abbreviation *etc.* comes from the Latin *et cetera*, meaning "and the rest." In ACADEMIC WRITING, don't use *etc.* Accepted substitutes include *and the like, and so on, and so forth*, among others. Even better is a more concrete description. An acceptable use of *etc.* is in tables and charts.

NO We took paper plates, plastic forks, **etc.,** to the picnic.

YES We took paper plates, plastic forks, **and other disposable items** to the picnic.

👁 **ALERT:** If you do write *etc.,* always put a comma after the period if the abbreviation falls in the middle of a sentence. 👁

EXERCISE 30-3

Revise these sentences for correct use of abbreviations. For help, consult 30i through 30l.

1. A college prof. has compiled a list of bks. that she thinks every educated person in the U.S. should read.
2. Although Ian Ryan Fleming junior hoped that one day he'd live at 1 Broadway, Dallas, T.X., an even bigger dream came true when he and his fam. moved to 1600 Pennsylvania Ave., Washington D.C.
3. Police officer Adam Furman knew from Lucinda's accent that she came from S. America and couldn't possibly have been b. in SD, as she claimed.
4. Dozens of hrs. and thousands of $ later, the contractors finally finished their work at three in the P.M., having extended the driveway to the main rd., just about four ft. away.
5. In Aug., the pres. of the apt. owners' assoc. addressed a 12-p. letter to the attn. of every tenant who had a cracked window.

NUMBERS

30m When do I use spelled-out numbers?

Your decision to write a number as a word or as a figure depends on what you're referring to and how often numbers occur in your piece of writing. The guidelines I give in this handbook are for MLA STYLE, which focuses on writing in the humanities. For other disciplines, follow the guidelines in their style manuals.

When you write numbers for more than one category in a piece of writing, reserve figures for some categories of numbers and spelled-out words for other categories. Never mix spelled-out numbers and figures for a particular category.

NO In **four** days, our volunteers increased from **five** to **eight** to **17** to **233.**

YES In **four** days, our volunteers increased from **5** to **8** to **17** to **233.**
[Numbers referring to volunteers are in numerals, while *four* is spelled out because it refers to a different category: days.]

ANSWERS: EXERCISE 30-3
The corrected abbreviations are shown here in italics.

1. A college *professor* has compiled a list of *books* that she thinks every educated person in the *United States* should read.

2. Although Ian Ryan Fleming *Jr.* hoped that one day he'd live at 1 Broadway, Dallas, *TX,* an even bigger dream came true when he and his *family* moved to 1600 Pennsylvania *Avenue,* Washington *DC.*

3. Police officer Adam Furman knew from Lucinda's accent that she came from *South America* and couldn't possibly have been *born* in *South Dakota,* as she claimed.

4. Dozens of *hours* and thousands of *dollars* later, the contractors finally finished their work at three in the *afternoon,* having extended the driveway to the main *road,* just about four *feet* away.

5. In *August,* the *president* of the *apartment* owners' *association* addressed a 12-*page* letter to the *attention* of every tenant who had a cracked window.

BACKGROUND
Conventions for written numbers differ from place to place and from one institution to another. Where Americans use a decimal point to separate numbers, for example, Europeans use a comma; in Britain, an earlier practice called for a raised dot in that position. The traveler should also be aware that dates are cited in a different way in some other countries. The American who invites a British friend to a spring picnic on 6/1/04, the first day of June, will cause some confusion, because the invited person will assume the event is to take place in the snow, planned as it seems to be for January 6. The American military follows the European practice, even in letters, using as a heading, for instance, 2 July 2004 instead of July 2, 2004.

TEACHING TIP
Some writers mix suffixes with figures: *1st, 33rd*. Traditional practice calls for the spelled-out word (the *first* robin), except for days, when only the figure without a suffix is correct (November 1). When you clarify this issue for students, you might also want to point out that this is among the few cases in English in which formal spoken practice differs from formal written practice. That is, a person can say in a formal speech: "The crisis occurred on November 21st." In written form, however, the formal convention is November 21 or 21 November.

BACKGROUND
In *Head Over Googol*, Alan W. Powers examines the meanings of macronumerals. Following is a dictionary definition of the word *googol*, coined in 1938 by Milton Sirotta, an American mathematician: "the figure 1 followed by 100 zeros equal to 10^{100}" (*Merriam-Webster Online*, at <http://www.m-w.com/>).

👁 **ALERT:** When you write a two-word number, use a hyphen between the spelled-out words, starting with *twenty-one* and continuing through *ninety-nine.* 👁

If you use numbers infrequently in a document, spell out all numbers that call for no more than two words: *fifty-two cards, twelve hundred students*. If you use specific numbers often in a document (temperatures when writing about climate, percentages in an economics essay, or other specific measurements of time, distance, and other quantities), use figures: *36 inches, 11 nanoseconds.* If you give only an approximation, spell out the numbers: *About twelve inches of snow fell.*

In the humanities, the names of centuries are always spelled out: *the eighteenth century.*

When you write for courses in the humanities, never start a sentence with a figure. Spell out the number—or better still, revise the sentence so that the number doesn't need to fall at the beginning. For practices in other disciplines, consult their manuals.

NO	**\$375 dollars** for each credit is the tuition rate for nonresidents.
YES	**Three hundred seventy-five dollars** for each credit is the tuition rate for nonresidents.
YES	The tuition rate for nonresidents is **\$375** for each credit.

30n What are standard practices for writing numbers?

Box 124 shows standard practices for writing numbers. Consider it a basic guide, and rely on the manual of each documentation style for answers to other questions you may have.

BOX 124   SUMMARY

 Specific numbers in writing

DATES	August 6, 1941
	1732–1845
	from 34 BC to AD 230 (*or* 34 BCE to 230 CE)
ADDRESSES	10 Downing Street
	237 North 8th Street
	Export Falls, MN 92025

→

Specific numbers in writing (*continued*)

TIMES	8:09 a.m., 6:00 p.m.
	six o'clock (*not* 6 o'clock)
	four in the afternoon *or* 4 p.m. (*not* four p.m.)
DECIMALS AND FRACTIONS	0.01
	98.6
	3.1416
	7/8
	12 1/4
	a sixth
	three-quarters (*not* 3-quarters)
	one-half
CHAPTERS AND PAGES	Chapter 27, page 2
	p. 1023 *or* pp. 660–62 (MLA style)
SCORES AND STATISTICS	a 6–0 score
	29 percent
	a 5 to 1 ratio (*and* a ratio of 5:1)
	a one percent change (*and* at the 1 percent level)
IDENTIFICATION NUMBERS	94.4 on the FM dial
	please call (012) 345–6789
MEASUREMENTS	67.8 miles per hour
	2 level teaspoons
	a 700-word essay
	8-1/2-by 11-inch paper (MLA style)
	2 feet
	1.5 gallons
	14 liters
ACT, SCENE, AND LINE	act 2, scene 2 (*or* act II, scene ii)
	lines 75–79
TEMPERATURES	40°F *or* –5°F
	20° Celsius
MONEY	$1.2 billion
	$3.41
	25¢ (*or* twenty-five cents)
	$10,000

TEACHING TIP

William Safire, an essayist on language for the *New York Times,* says that practice varies greatly on how to write *noon* or *midnight* when the number 12 is involved. Some people use 12:00 a.m. for midnight, while others use 12:00 p.m. The same is true for noon. Safire suggests using 12 *noon* and 12 *midnight* for greater clarity.

ANSWERS: EXERCISE 30-4

The corrected numbers are in italics.

1. At *5:15 p.m.*, the nearly empty city streets filled with *thousands* of commuters.

2. A tarantula spider can survive without food for about two years and *three* months.

3. By the end of *act 1, scene 5* [or *act I, scene v*], Romeo and Juliet are in love and at the mercy of their unhappy fate.

4. Sound travels through air at a speed of 1,089 feet per second, but in water it travels *450* percent faster, at *4,859* feet per second.

5. *Twenty-one* years old and unhappily married, Cleopatra met middle-aged Julius Caesar in *48* BCE. [Or, revised start of sentence: When she was twenty-one years old and . . .]

6. An adult blue whale, which can weigh one hundred tons—the combined weight of *thirty* elephants, has gained over *seven and a half* pounds an hour since infancy. [*However, in more technical writing:* An adult blue whale, which can weigh *100* tons—the combined weight of 30 elephants—has gained over 7.5 pounds an hour since infancy.]

7. On the morning of August *13, 1930, three* huge meteorites smashed into the Amazon jungle.

8. *Two* out of every *five* people who have ever lived on earth are alive today, according to *one* estimate. [Or, revised start of sentence: Of all the people who have ever lived on earth, two out of every five are alive today . . .]

9. The house at *653* Oak Street—the *one* that children think is haunted—has been empty for *eight* years, waiting for a buyer willing to pay its price of *$6,049,000*.

10. The 1912 sinking of the *Titanic,* in which *1,503* people drowned, is widely known, but few people remember that more than *3,000* people lost their lives aboard the ferryboat *Doña Paz* when it hit an oil tanker in the Philippines in *1987*.

EXERCISE 30-4

Revise these sentences so that the numbers are in correct form, either spelled out or as figures. For help, consult 30m and 30n.

1. At five fifteen p.m., the nearly empty city streets filled with 1000's of commuters.

2. A tarantula spider can survive without food for about two years and 3 months.

3. By the end of act one, scene five, Romeo and Juliet are in love and at the mercy of their unhappy fate.

4. Sound travels through air at a speed of 1,089 feet per second, but in water it travels four hundred and fifty percent faster, at four thousand, eight hundred fifty-nine feet per second.

5. 21 years old and unhappily married, Cleopatra met middle-aged Julius Caesar in forty-eight BCE.

6. An adult blue whale, which can weigh one hundred tons—the combined weight of 30 elephants—has gained over seven-point-five pounds an hour since infancy.

7. On the morning of August thirteen, nineteen hundred thirty, 3 huge meteorites smashed into the Amazon jungle.

8. 2 out of every 5 people who have ever lived on earth are alive today, according to 1 estimate.

9. The house at six hundred and fifty-three Oak Street—the 1 that children think is haunted—has been empty for 8 years, waiting for a buyer willing to pay its price of $ six million, forty-nine thousand dollars.

10. The 1912 sinking of the *Titanic,* in which one thousand five hundred and three people drowned, is widely known, but few people remember that more than three thousand people lost their lives aboard the ferryboat *Doña Paz* when it hit an oil tanker in the Philippines in nineteen eighty-seven.

30o How do I use hyphens with spelled-out numbers?

A **spelled-out number** uses words, not figures. Box 125 on the facing page gives you guidelines.

👁 **ALERT:** Use figures rather than words for a fraction written in more than two words. If your context calls for figures, use hyphens only between the words of the numerator and only between the words of the denominator—but never between the numerator and the denominator: two one-hundredths (2/100), thirty-three ten-thousandths (*33/10,000*). 👁

BOX 125   SUMMARY

Hyphens with spelled-out numbers

- Use a hyphen between two-word numbers from twenty-one through ninety-nine, whether they stand alone or are part of a larger number.

  YES thirty-five   two hundred thirty-five

- Use a hyphen in a COMPOUND-WORD modifier formed from a number and a word, whether the number is in words or figures.

  YES fifty-minute class [*also* 50-minute class]

  YES three-to-one odds [*also* 3-to-1 odds]

- Use a hyphen between the numerator and the denominator of two-word fractions.

  YES one-half   two-fifths   seven-tenths

- Use a hyphen between compound nouns joining two units of measure.

  YES light-years   kilowatt-hours

Part Five

Writing Research

Chapter 31

Research Writing as a Process

31a What is research writing?

Research writing involves three steps: conducting research, understanding and evaluating the results of your research, and writing the research paper with accurate DOCUMENTATION.* Every research project requires these steps. Moreover, research writing, as is true of the WRITING PROCESS itself, often moves forward, loops back, and jumps ahead according to what unfolds as you work.

The writing process for a research paper resembles the writing process for all academic papers. (Indeed, you will notice an unusually large number of words in SMALL CAPITAL LETTERS, indicating terms that are introduced and defined in other sections of this book and are also listed and defined in the Terms Glossary.) Using print, electronic, and online sources adds one more level for your attention.

Some student researchers use information from **primary sources**—from direct observations, interviews, surveys, measurements, original documents and records, and so on. However, most students, especially when writing college research papers, use information from **secondary sources**—from reading, using ANALYSIS, discussing, and reviewing what people with respected credentials and authority have written. In planning the paper, you choose a suitable research TOPIC; develop that topic into a RESEARCH QUESTION; use a search strategy to locate and evaluate sources; and take notes. In DRAFTING and REVISING the paper, you present a SYNTHESIS of your findings, supported by QUOTATIONS, PARAPHRASES, and SUMMARIES of your sources.

Research is an engrossing, creative activity. By gathering information, analyzing the separate elements, and creating a synthesis of what you've learned, you come to know your subject deeply. Also, the very act of writing leads you to fresh connections and unexpected insights. All

---

* Find the definition of all words in small capital letters (such as DOCUMENTATION) in the Terms Glossary at the back of this book directly before the Index.

this adds up to the chance to sample the pleasures of being a self-reliant learner, an independent person with the discipline and intellectual resources to track down, absorb, synthesize, and write about your topic.

Nevertheless, many researchers—inexperienced and experienced—feel intimidated at the beginning of a research writing project. My personal approach is to break it into manageable chunks. Those chunks construct a series of steps, each of which is explained in this chapter.

31b   How do I choose and narrow a research topic?

Some instructors assign a specific TOPIC for research (for example, "The feasibility of making robots that act like humans"). Others assign a general subject area ("Artificial Intelligence") and expect you to narrow it to a manageable topic. Still other instructors expect you to choose a topic on your own ("Write a research paper on a topic of current importance").

A good research topic is one that your readers will perceive as significant and worthwhile. That is, the topic is important or timely, your insights are fresh, or your SYNTHESIS is clear and skillful.

On a practical level, a good research topic is narrow enough for you to research within the constraints of time and length imposed by the assignment. Also, you want to determine, before you commit too firmly to a topic, that enough print and online material exists about it to offer you a sufficient number of sources and perspectives to answer your RESEARCH QUESTION and write your paper.

The expectation that you will demonstrate CRITICAL THINKING in your research paper is another variable that needs to influence your topic decisions. You can use critical thinking in one of two broad ways, each of which is grounded in your PURPOSE for writing the paper. First, you can choose a topic on which intelligent people have differing opinions. Next, you analyze your sources to decide which position appears most reasonable. Your paper would then take the form of an ARGUMENT that shows readers you have considered the various positions and chosen a reasonable one.

Second, you can choose to write an INFORMATIVE paper in which you synthesize several sources related to a complex subject. Writing a synthesis means pulling together sometimes extensive information on a topic by finding connections within it to explain the essential points as you see them. For example, after you read a dozen articles on the topic of creating artificial intelligence, you might try to identify three or four key points and then organize information from your reading about these and closely related points. You integrate material from various sources to make each point. Your paper's goal is to clarify and create a new whole from complicated or scattered information.

HISTORY

The research paper originated when American universities adopted the research ideal and began developing a curriculum to educate students for careers in specialized disciplines. According to David R. Russell in *Writing in the Academic Disciplines, 1870–1990* (Carbondale: Southern Illinois University Press, 1991), young college instructors who had studied in research-oriented German universities began occasionally to assign a "scholarly thesis" in U.S. colleges around 1870. Ten years later, many colleges began to require seniors to write a "graduating thesis" of 1,000 to 3,000 words, and by the 1890s, these were frequently required in the new seminar courses for advanced students. At first, instructors required little formal documentation in a thesis, but by the turn of the twentieth century, the typical thesis paper provided a bibliography, extensive footnotes, and charts and diagrams. Faculty regarded students as "apprentices" in a profession, and the thesis was an opportunity for students to develop the investigative skills needed to become experts in their fields and to learn to address readers in their professions. The research paper soon moved into lower-level courses, and by 1931, high school students were often required to write a term paper in their junior or senior year.

Research paper instruction began to be offered in freshman composition courses in the 1920s. By the early 1980s, according to James E. Ford and Dennis R. Perry ("Research Paper Instruction in the Undergraduate Writing Program," *College English*, December 1982: 825–831), 84 percent of freshman writing programs and 40 percent of advanced composition programs were teaching the research paper, and the research paper was a requirement in 78 percent of the freshman programs and 42 percent of the advanced programs.

HISTORY

In 2003, Margaret Moulton and Vicki Holmes reviewed over 350 articles about the process of having students write research papers, tracing the history of these assignments since the 1870s ("The Research Paper: A Historical Perspective," *Teaching English in the Two-Year College,* May 2003: 365–373). They show that research papers have long been controversial, with critics of the practice as well as advocates. Among their findings: (1) originally, the purpose of a research paper was to create new universal knowledge, but later the emphasis shifted to teaching the process of researching; (2) teachers have tended to value relevance and interest to students when assigning research-paper topics—or allowing students to choose their own; (3) the use of primary sources—interviews, surveys, work with primary documents—creates interest and also helps lessen the possibility of plagiarism; (4) multiple media have begun to play an important role in research papers, although as early as the 1940s, media had a place in the curriculum; (5) many instructors have begun to use multiple shorter source-based papers, rather than a single long research paper, to teach text analysis and documentation skills.

Moulton and Holmes's work updates a study from a quarter century ago. In the early 1980s, James E. Ford and Dennis R. Perry ("Research Paper Instruction in the Undergraduate Writing Program," *College English,* December 1982: 825–831) reported:

> Research paper instruction is currently being offered in 84.09% of freshman composition programs and in 40.03% of advanced composition programs. In general this high level of occurrence is fairly uniform in all types and sizes of institutions and in all regions of the country. There is, however, a slight tendency for research paper instruction to decrease as the size of the school increases (down to 71.06% in the large schools). Also, occurrence is highest in the Rocky Mountain

→

Choosing a topic on your own

When you can select any topic that appeals to you, be sure to choose one that's worthy of research writing. You want a topic that allows you to demonstrate your ability to use critical thinking and to synthesize ideas.

Such freedom of choice pleases some students. For others, it leads to what can be called a "research-topic block." If this happens, rest assured you can overcome it by remaining calm and being proactive by using the suggestions in Box 126. Also, try using the suggestions in Box 14 in Chapter 3.

BOX 126   SUMMARY

 Finding ideas for research

- **Get ready.** Carry a pocket-size notebook and a pen, or use a PDA (such as a Palm Pilot). Ideas have a way of popping into your mind when you least expect them. Jot down your thoughts on the spot, no matter where you are, so that they don't slip away.

- **Overcome any block that prevents you from moving ahead.** First, look back at section 3b for practical ideas. Second, stop yourself from thinking about the "whole" of your research project at once. Instead, break it into chunks, according to the small steps in your research schedule (discussed in 31d).

- **Think actively.** Use the structured techniques for gathering ideas demonstrated in sections 2f through 2m.

- **Browse through textbooks.** Pick a field that interests you, and look over a textbook or two (in the bookstore, borrowed from a friend, or—at some colleges—on reserve in the library). Read the table of contents and major headings. Scan the text for material that catches your eye. Note the names of important books and experts, often mentioned in reference lists at the end of chapters or at the back of the book. See what catches your attention and makes you want to keep reading.

- **Browse the Internet.** Many Web search engines provide topic directories, as illustrated in section 1h.2. Click on some general categories and review subcategories until you locate specific topics that interest you. Then try further subject searches or KEYWORD SEARCHES (32c.4) to see where they lead.

- **Use the *Library of Congress Subject Headings.*** This is a multivolume reference work now in print only. In many libraries, it sits on the counter at the research librarian's station; at others, it's shelved with the other reference volumes. The *LCSH* lists every single topic (and the library call number of books on each topic)

→

Finding ideas for research (*continued*)

with many sublists, often coded to explain their purpose. Section 32d discusses specifically how the *LCSH* volumes can help you as a researcher.

- **Browse general encyclopedias.** They offer a wide-ranging survey of topics. Be aware, however, that the articles give you only a general, superficial sense of each subject. These reference works—available as books, CDs, or on the Internet (often through connections to a library database)—come in handy for identifying general topics within areas that interest you. However, the actual content of general encyclopedias is rarely suitable for research for a college-level research paper.
- **Browse specialized encyclopedias.** These volumes are considered "specialized" because each is devoted to only one specific area (for example, social science, history, philosophy, the natural sciences). Their articles and chapters treat topics in some depth, and the material is usually suitable for research for a college-level research paper. Most selections mention names of major figures in the field, information that comes in handy when evaluating your sources (32j).
- **Browse through books and periodicals.** These are available when your library has open stacks (fully accessible bookshelves). Browse books and academic journals, as well as popular magazines, in fields that interest you. Or you might spend some time in a good bookstore or at a public library.

region (91.66%) and . . . lowest on the Pacific coast (72.40%). Instruction in the research paper is required in 78.11% of freshman composition programs offering it and 42.35% of advanced writing programs where it is offered. Although 4.16% of the schools not offering instruction in the research paper at the basic level indicated their reason for omitting it as "faculty think it unnecessary," the most common reason given for not offering it came under the "other" category, checked by 12.12%. About half of these (that is, about 6% of the total respondents) said the course was already too full to allow time for such instruction. (827)

QUOTATION: ON RESEARCH
One of the skills of research is knowing when you have enough information; in considering too many side issues or too many perspectives, you may lose the main thread of your subject.

—Charles Bazerman

Narrowing a general topic into a workable one
Whether you're working with a topic of your choice or an assigned one, you want to check that it's sufficiently narrow for the time frame and other requirements of your research paper. Also, you want to be sure that the narrowed topic is worthy of a college research project. Box 127 offers guidelines.

BOX 127   SUMMARY

Deciding on a workable, worthwhile research topic

1. **Expect to consider various topics before making your final choice.** Don't rush. Give yourself time to think. Keep your mind open to flashes of insight and to alternative ideas. At the same time, be careful not to let indecision paralyze you. →

TEACHING TIP

Students might feel overwhelmed if they had to do a research paper on, say, the role of the media in shaping public attitudes toward politics or the implications of cloning mammals. The problem has more to do with students' fears than the actual complexity of such assignments. You can build students' confidence with research skills if you assign "accessible" topics—especially for preliminary exercises in research skills and note-taking. Here are a few possibilities.

1. Write a biography of someone you would like to know more about: a sports figure, a cartoonist, a movie director, a state legislator, a dictator.

2. Write an essay recommending a particular type or model of some expensive consumer item that you are interested in buying, such as a car, a computer, or a home gym.

3. Write an essay recommending and explaining an eating regimen that can help someone lose weight, train for a sport, or control a health problem (such as diabetes or high blood pressure).

4. Imagine you're a U.S. travel agent hired to plan a tour of Asia or Africa. Money is no object. You have been instructed to arrange stops in all countries with which the United States has friendly relations. For each country they'll visit, advise your clients of (1) entry requirements, such as a visa and limitations on what they may bring into each country; (2) health precautions needed, including inoculations; and (3) local laws or customs that they must not violate, such as those dealing with alcohol and drugs.

5. If you've not chosen a career or major, write an essay exploring the pros and cons of a particular career or major you're considering. If you have chosen your field, write an essay exploring a particular job in that field or arguing a position about an ethical or political problem in the field.

Deciding on a workable, worthwhile research topic (*continued*)

2. **Choose a topic that has a sufficient number of appropriate sources available.** If you can't find useful sources—ones that relate directly to your topic, and ones that are credible, not simply plentiful—drop the topic. Keep your RESEARCH QUESTION (31c) in mind as you look over your sources.

3. **Narrow the topic sufficiently.** Avoid topics that are too broad, such as "intelligence." Conversely, avoid topics that are so narrow that you can't present a suitable mix of GENERALIZATIONS and specific details. As you formulate your research question, you'll also be narrowing your topic.

4. **Choose a topic worth researching.** Avoid trivial topics that prevent you from doing what instructors and others expect of a student researcher: investigating ideas, analyzing them critically, and creating a synthesis of complex concepts.
   NO The size of different kinds of cars
   YES The effect of SUVs on the environment

5. **Select a topic that interests you.** Your topic will be a companion for a while, sometimes for most of a semester. Select a topic that arouses your interest and allows you the pleasure of satisfying your intellectual curiosity.

6. **Confer with a professor in your field of interest, if possible.** Before the meeting, read a little about your topic so that your questions and remarks show you've prepared for the conversation. Ask whether you've narrowed your topic sufficiently and productively. Also, ask for the titles of the major books and names of major authorities on your topic.

Case Study

"Computers" was the general subject area assigned to Chandra Johnson, the student whose research paper appears in Chapter 34. The paper was to be 1,800 to 2,000 words long and based on about a dozen sources. It was due in six weeks.

To get started, Johnson went to her library's online catalog and searched for books with the word "computer" in their titles. She found 188 book titles and began browsing through them. One title caught her attention: *Computers Ltd.: What They Really Can't Do.* From what she found as she browsed the book, she started to wonder if computers can really think. That idea led her into the area of artificial intelligence.

→

Case Study (*continued*)

Although this description shows each of Johnson's decisions flowing smoothly, the actual process wasn't neat and tidy. She met dead ends with a subtopic's keywords and frustration with searches for books she wanted to look over but were unavailable in her library or online searches. What looks clear-cut at the end of the research process was likely a more circuitous path of backing out of dead ends and making some sharp turns in searching for answers to a research question.

A more detailed narrative, including a flowchart, of Johnson's complete research process appears in 34e.1, and the final draft of her research paper appears in 34e.2.

31c What is a research question?

A **research question** about your topic is the controlling question that drives your research. Few research paper assignments are phrased as questions. Therefore, most research writing calls on you to figure out a thought-provoking underlying question and then to search for answers to it. By regarding research as a quest for an answer, you give your work a specific focus: You can't know whether you've found useful source material unless you know what you're looking for.

Research questions, whether stated or implied, and the strategies needed to answer them, vary widely. Your purpose might be to present and explain information: "How does penicillin destroy bacteria?" Or your purpose might be to argue one side of an issue: "Is Congress more important than the Supreme Court in setting social policy?" You can then consult various sources in an attempt to work toward an answer.

Attempt is an important word in relation to research. Some research questions lead to a final, definitive answer, but some do not. The question above about penicillin leads to a reasonably definitive answer (you describe how the antibiotic penicillin destroys the cell walls of some bacteria); this means your writing has an informative purpose. The question about social policy has no definitive answer, so you're asked to offer an informed opinion based on facts and authoritative viewpoints gathered from your research; this means your writing has a persuasive purpose.

To formulate a research question, begin by BRAINSTORMING a list of questions that comes to mind about your topic. Write your list of ideas in your research log (31e).

Suppose, for example, the topic you want to write about is "homelessness." Here are some typical questions you might ask.

- Why can't a rich country like the United States eliminate homelessness?
- Who is homeless?

TEACHING TIP

Saying something original based on several sources is an imposing challenge for most students. Many instead treat the research paper as a knowledge-telling exercise in which they restate what they have read. The research paper then becomes a string of quotations, paraphrases, and summaries that drown out the student's voice, lack purpose and focus, and often invite plagiarism. According to Margaret Kantz ("Helping Students Use Textual Sources Persuasively," *College English,* January 1990: 74–91), "Writing an original persuasive argument based on sources requires students to apply material to a problem or to use it to answer a question, rather than simply to repeat it or evaluate it" (78). But students "have learned to see texts statically, as descriptions of truths, instead of as arguments" (79). This view encourages students simply to collect facts into a research paper in the belief that the facts will settle any disagreements and reveal the truth.

Kantz recommends that teachers encourage students to regard the research paper and its sources "as existing to solve problems" (84). You can model the thinking processes (by narrating your thought process aloud), with an emphasis on curiosity, to show students that a major goal in using a source is to understand what the author of a source is trying to accomplish—and for what audience. Students can see you treat facts as claims that might need to be challenged or interpreted differently. As students begin, along with you, to experience the pleasures of inquiry, they can see that a research paper seeks to solve a problem or answer a question for a particular audience.

QUOTATION: ON RESEARCH

By asking students to stick to researching the known, we teach them to fear the unknown.
—Robert Davis and Mark Shadle

- How do people become homeless?
- Is it true that many families—not just adults—are homeless?
- Is the homeless problem getting better or worse?
- What are we doing to solve the problem of homelessness?
- What is it like to be homeless?

Some questions will interest you more than others, so begin with one of those. If a question leads to a dead end, pursue another. Only when you find yourself accumulating answers—or in the case of questions without definitive answers, accumulating viewpoints—is it likely you're dealing with a usable research question. Once you have an explicitly stated research question, you can streamline your research by taking notes only from those sources that help you answer your research question.

Stay flexible as you work. The results of your research may lead you to modify the research question slightly. Actually, such modifying is part of the "moving ahead and circling back" that characterizes research writing. When you've finished researching and notetaking based on your final research question, you have a starting place for formulating the preliminary THESIS STATEMENT for your research paper.

31d   How do I set up my schedule for research writing?

Dividing a research project into a series of steps makes the project far less intimidating. Research takes time, so plan ahead and budget your time intelligently. As soon as you get an assignment for a research paper, plan your schedule, using Box 128 as a model. Because no two research paper projects are alike, adapt this schedule to your needs. You might, for example, need only one day for some steps but two weeks for others. So, while you need to stay flexible, you also want to keep your eye on the calendar.

BOX 128   **SUMMARY**

Sample schedule for a research project

Assignment received _____

Assignment due date _____

Planning   **Finish by (Date)**

1. Start my research log (31e).   _____
2. Choose a topic suitable for research (31b).   _____

$\longrightarrow$

Sample schedule for a research project (*continued*)

Planning (*cont.*)   **Finish by (Date)**

3. Draft my research question (31c).   _____
4. Decide on my purpose and audience (31f).   _____
5. Take practical steps (31g):
   a. Gather equipment.   _____
   b. Get to know layout and resources of my college library. _____
   c. Get to know available online resources.   _____
6. Decide what documentation style I'll use (31h).   _____

Researching

7. Plan my "search strategy," but modify as necessary (32b). _____
8. Generate list of subject headings and keywords, consulting *Library of Congress Subject Headings,* databases, and directories (32c).   _____
9. Decide the kinds of research I need to do:
   a. Print sources (32d, 32e).   _____
   b. Online and/or electronic sources (32c).   _____
   c. Field research? (32i) If yes, schedule tasks.   _____
10. Locate and evaluate sources (32c, 32j).   _____
11. Take content notes from sources I find useful (31j). _____

Writing

12. Draft my preliminary thesis statement (31k).   _____
13. Outline, as required (31l).   _____
14. Draft my paper (31m).   _____
15. Use correct parenthetical citations (34b–34c; 35b–35c; 36a, 36c, 36e).   _____
16. Write my final thesis statement (31k).   _____
17. Revise my paper (31m).   _____
18. Compile my final bibliography, using the documentation style required (Chapters 34–36).   _____

Evaluation of this schedule

Have I planned realistically for my completion date?

If I haven't, what steps do I need to revise in my schedule?

31e   What is a research log?

A **research log** is your diary of your research process. Start your research log as soon as you get an assignment. Use a separate notebook for
the log or create a new folder or file on the computer. Whichever format
you rely on, make your research schedule one of the first entries. If your
instructor tells students to use Web logs, known as Blogs, see section 42h.

Although much of your research log will never find its way into your
research paper itself, what you write in it greatly increases your efficiency. A well-kept log traces your line of reasoning as your project
evolves, tells where you've ended each work session, and suggests what
your next steps might be. Since college students take several courses at
the same time, keeping this sort of record means you'll waste no time re-
tracing a research path or reconstructing a thought. In your log, always
record the date as well as the following elements:

- Your current step in your search for information; the search strategy you
  used to find that information; the name, location, and other details of exactly where you found the information; the main point of the information
  you found; and where you've placed your detailed content notes—for example, the exact file or folder name—when it's time to take them
- Your suggested next step for when you return to your research
- Your evolving overall thoughts and insights as you move through the research and writing processes

October 16: Got online to find sources for "artificial
intelligence" and was overwhelmed by the number of hits
in Yahoo. Gave up. Logged onto the college library's
Web site and searched some databases there. PsycINFO
turned up lots of promising stuff. Chose several
citations and emailed full records to myself to check
out later. Readers Guide Abstracts also had articles,
and some were available as full text. Printed out three
of the best ones. Need to start taking notes on them.
Will go to the library tomorrow to find PsycINFO sources.

Excerpt from Chandra Johnson's research log

■ Your awareness that you're becoming ready to move away from gathering material to organizing it; from organizing it to writing about it; and from drafting to revising

31f How do I determine the purpose and audience for my research paper?

To decide whether your paper will have an informative purpose or a persuasive purpose, see what your research question asks. If the answer to it involves giving facts, information, and explanation, your purpose is to inform. For example, "How have computers changed over time?" calls for INFORMATIVE WRITING. Conversely, if the answer involves offering an educated opinion based on contrasting views and supporting evidence, your purpose is to persuade. For example, "Why should people be aware of current developments in computers?" calls for PERSUASIVE WRITING.

You may find that your purpose shifts during your research process, as Chandra Johnson's did (see 34e). As you work, balance the need to remain open-minded with the need to decide on your purpose before you get too far along.

AUDIENCES for research papers vary. In some situations, only your instructor will read your paper (1d.4). More often, your audience starts with your peers, the other students in your class. Next, it moves on to a general public audience or to specialists on your topic, with your instructor as one among many readers. Your sense of these other readers' expertise in your topic can guide your decisions about content, level of detail, and DICTION.

31g What practical steps can help me work efficiently?

To conduct your research with greatest efficiency, you need to do some footwork before you start researching. First, gather the "equipment" listed in Box 129 on the next page so that it's organized and ready for use at a moment's notice. Second, become familiar with your college library's layout and resources (32c). Third, be sure to become skilled and comfortable with searching topics online, if you're not already (32c).

Gathering supplies for research
Box 129 on the next page offers a list of supplies that many students use. Adapt the list to your needs.

TEACHING TIP
You may find it helpful to ask students to bring to class research assignments made in other classes. Working in groups, they can analyze the assignments in terms of audience, purpose, and scope of topic. Also, they might discuss a search strategy for carrying out the assignment, something that the student charged with doing the work would find quite helpful.

BACKGROUND
In "'Building a Mystery': Alternative Research Writing and the Academic Act of Seeking" (*College Composition and Communication,* February 2000: 417–446), Robert Davis and Mark Shadle suggest that "the research paper as we now teach it, like many things modern, scarcely lives up to" its promise as a means of constructing knowledge within the academy. Davis and Shadle offer "alternative research writing strategies" that ask students to move past the habit of reporting sources and toward more personal, academic, and social purposes for research. These authors discuss one research model currently endorsed in composition classes, the research argument, but they add three additional models for research paper assignments: "the personal research paper," "the research essay," and "the multi-genre/media/ disciplinary/cultural research paper."

HISTORY

During the Middle Ages, the libraries of Western Europe were affiliated with religious houses and cathedrals. The few private libraries belonged to bishops. The clergy were the only people who could read, and the church maintained the tradition of schools and libraries. These religious libraries were quite small by twentieth-century standards. The largest (at Canterbury and Bury St. Edmunds) had two thousand volumes each, but libraries of only a few hundred volumes were the rule. The libraries contained theological and biblical works, law books, classical texts, and medical and historical works. Contemporary histories, written in monasteries, remain the best records of what happened during the period. In the thirteenth and fourteenth centuries, the rise of the new universities, the rediscovery of Aristotle (from Arabic), and the position of the friars as university teachers undermined the dominance of the monastic libraries. Although the university libraries were not open to undergraduates, the Franciscan friars opened their own libraries (some still survive in England). They printed small, portable books that contrasted with the bulky illuminated manuscripts of the monasteries. The monastic libraries of England were destroyed in the period from 1536 to 1540 (during Henry VIII's reign), and their books were dispersed. In 1550, university libraries, schools, and churches were purged. Many treasures saved during the thousand years of the Dark Ages were lost.

Medieval libraries were apparently noisier than libraries today. Silent reading was not a common practice until the Renaissance. Until then, most people mumbled as they read. Small private enclosures called *carrels* were invented so that readers would not disturb other people in the library with their noise.

BOX 129   SUMMARY

Equipment needed for research

1. A copy of your assignment.
2. This handbook, especially Part Five, or access to the Internet so that you can read the book online. With its guidelines at hand, work efficiently as you evaluate sources, document your sources, and correctly handle other tasks that come up.
3. Your research log (31e).
4. Index cards for taking notes (unless you use a laptop). If you use different colors of index cards, you might color code the different categories of information you find. Also, you might use one size for bibliography cards and the other for content note cards. Another coding strategy is to use pens of different ink colors or self-sticking dots of various colors.
5. Coins (or cash or a debit card) for copy machines or printers.
6. Empty floppy disks for downloading material—but make sure your library allows downloading to disk.
7. If you use index cards and other paper, a small stapler, paper clips, and rubber bands.
8. A separate book bag to carry research-project books you check out from the library. (Librarians joke about researchers with wheelbarrows. You might need a backpack.)

Learning how the library is organized

When you learn how your college library is organized, your research efficiency increases. Though almost all libraries in the United States and Canada are organized around the same principles for grouping information, layouts of library buildings differ considerably. Your time is well spent if you visit your college library for the sole purpose of figuring out what's located where, so that you'll feel comfortable and confident when you work there.

Some college libraries provide class tours for English courses; some offer individual training sessions; and most offer informative, free fliers to help students learn the library layout and the resources available to students. Box 130 provides a checklist for familiarizing yourself with your library.

BOX 130 CHECKLIST

 Touring a library

1. Where is the general reference collection? (You can't check out reference books, so when you need to use them, build extra time into your schedule to spend at the library.)
2. Where is the special reference collection? (Same rules apply as for general reference books.)
3. How does the library's catalog work?
4. What periodical indexes or databases does your library have? (These are lists of articles in journals and magazines, grouped by subject areas.)
5. How and where are the library's collections of journals and magazines stored? Most libraries place periodicals published in the past year in open areas, while older periodicals are on microfiche, CDs, or online. Become adept at using whatever system is in place at your library.
6. Are the book and journal stacks open (fully accessible shelves) or closed (request each item by filling out a form to hand to library personnel)? If the latter, become familiar with the required procedures not only for asking for a book or journal but also for picking it up when it's ready.
7. What, if anything, is stored on microfilm or microfiche? If you think you'll use that material, take the time to learn how to use the machines. (I find that each library's machines work differently enough to stump me at first.)
8. Does the library have special collections, such as local historical works or the writings of persons worthy of such an exclusive honor?
9. Does the library give you access to the Internet? If not, find out if this service is available elsewhere on campus—for example, in a student center or computer lab. When at home or in a residence hall, can you access the library's computerized systems with your computer?

BACKGROUND
Before it was burnt down in the third century AD, the famous library at Alexandria, Egypt, contained as many as 700,000 scrolls. Under the Ptolemies (third century BC on), the library became a repository for copies of all important texts. Books were edited to a standard format, and systems of punctuation and accents were introduced. Textual scholarship, revisions of books to incorporate new knowledge, and the writing of new books went on constantly. Most of the books have been lost. Only works that were widely copied and distributed have managed to survive. For example, evidence indicates that Aeschylus, Sophocles, Euripides, and Aristophanes wrote about 330 plays in total; only 43 remain.

HISTORY
The Swiss naturalist Konrad von Gesner (1516–1565) wrote the *Universal Library,* a summary of *all* books known in Hebrew, Greek, and Latin.

Deciding how to use the computer

Today, computers allow you to carry out research quite differently than students did only a few years ago. How you use the computer is largely a matter of personal preference. Some students use a computer only for finding sources and for DRAFTING the paper itself. These students do the

TEACHING TIP
The entire process of writing a research paper can be facilitated by computers for students who have access to a laptop. They can use it to take notes by saving information in separate files for each section, as well as for drafting, organizing, and revising. The latter steps will be easier because sources will be readily accessible in the computer's memory.

BACKGROUND
An innovative approach to research paper assignments is suggested by Jennie C. Cooper in "Writing for Real People: A Client-Centered Approach" (*College Composition and Communication,* October 1993: 386–388). Cooper describes the process she used in contacting local journalists, government officials, faculty members, and business leaders (among others) and asking them whether they had any research projects they would like her students to pursue. Evaluations of these projects, by both those who suggested research projects and the initially reluctant students, were overwhelmingly positive.

rest of their research steps "by hand" on index cards and sheets of paper: keeping their research log (31e), compiling their WORKING BIBLIOGRAPHY (31i), taking content notes (31j), and so forth.

Other students carry out their entire research process on computer. They set up folders for every phase of their project. To accumulate print sources for their working bibliography, these students download them onto a disk or a laptop computer—always carefully recording the origin of the source in the documentation style they've selected (31h). They type their research log, working bibliography, and content notes directly into computer files. Finally, they draft and revise their papers on computer, often using the "Track Changes" feature, or its equivalent, on their word processing program to keep track of their revisions.

Experiment to find which method works best for you in each research situation. No right or wrong way to use the new technologies exists. Do what feels most comfortable to you.

Arranging field research, if appropriate and necessary

Field research is primary research that involves going into real-life situations to observe, survey, or interview. The majority of college research projects don't require field research. However, if your project does, you need to organize that experience well in advance (32i).

31h What documentation style should I use?

Ask your instructor which DOCUMENTATION STYLE you're required to use for your research paper: MLA (Chapter 34)? APA (Chapter 35)? Another (Chapter 36)? As you compile your WORKING BIBLIOGRAPHY (31i), be sure to record all the documentation elements the required style demands. Documentation styles vary in their details, and you don't want to have to track down a source again merely to get documentation facts you didn't write down on your first pass.

31i What is a working bibliography?

A **working bibliography** emerges from your search for and evaluation of sources. It's your preliminary list of potentially useful sources for each research project. This list, which is an essential part of your research process, remains fluid in the early stage of your search for sources.

Think of compiling a working bibliography as a survey process. You want to find out what is available on a particular subject before you commit to extensive reading and notetaking. To do this, set aside more than one span of hours to search on a given subject.

As you compile a working bibliography, you want to evaluate the sources you are considering using. Never waste your time looking at unsound or irrelevant sources. First, your sources need to pertain to your topic and RESEARCH QUESTION. Second and more important, they need to be authoritative and reliable. Unfortunately, a tremendous amount of bad information exists in print and, especially, online. Expect to add and drop sources as you refine your research question and locate other sources. Be sure to consult the guidelines in 32j for evaluating sources.

Box 131 lists some of the information you need to include in your working bibliography. You can record your working bibliography on

---

BOX 131   SUMMARY

Formatting bibliography information on each source

- For a library source, write the *call number* in the upper left corner, being careful to copy it exactly. If you conduct research at more than one library, also note the library where you found that source.

- For magazines and journals, write the exact title of the periodical and article, the date of the issue, the volume and issue numbers, and the page numbers on which the article appears.

- For an online source, write the URL (uniform resource locator) address in the upper left corner of the card, being careful to copy it exactly. Also, record any date related to the source: most recent update, date originally made available, and so forth. Most important, write down the date on which you are accessing the material and the date you are downloading the material. If you take notes directly from the screen, use the date you are taking notes. This information is required in *all* documentation styles.

- If you actually look at the source, write two key messages to yourself on the back of the card: (a) the reason the source seems useful at the moment, and (b) the results of your evaluation of the source (32j). Here are typical content notes students have written on their working bibliography cards:
  - "One of the most credible authors about my subject."
  - "Book is old, but has useful background information and definitions."
  - "Article published only two months ago in scholarly journal and answers my research question perfectly!"
  - "This Web page has pertinent information, but I must check whether the author is really an authority on the subject."

USING COLLABORATION

Working together, students can undertake more extensive primary research than students working alone. A group of students can draw up a list of interview questions to ask in individually conducted interviews. The identical question set ensures that students can compare the information from each interview. Conversely, some projects may benefit from having members of the group ask different questions so that each gathers information on a different aspect of the topic. Indeed, you could decide to tell students that the person they interview might sometimes mention new and intriguing subjects. In such cases, even though questions about these new areas don't appear on the prepared list, students can choose to explore the new subjects during the interview. Interviewer flexibility usually pays off in such situations.

TEACHING TIP

To make an interview valuable, the interviewer must approach the expert with questions that will produce answers that supply the information needed for the project at hand. Simply holding an open-ended conversation with a knowledgeable person may be interesting, but it won't necessarily be helpful for the researcher. You may want to ask students to work in groups to formulate a series of "ice-breaker" questions to use as they begin an interview, some general questions that can be applied to any topic. Then ask the students to list specific questions designed especially for the person being interviewed.

3-by-5-inch note cards or on a computer. Note cards have the advantage of being easy to sift through when you're adding and discarding sources. Also, you can carry them with you to the library when you do library research. Their best use is at the end of your writing process, when you can easily sort and alphabetize cards for the final list of sources you used. Keeping your working bibliography on the computer has the advantage of allowing you to alphabetize and organize it, which can save you time as you complete your WORKS CITED (MLA style) or REFERENCES (APA style) final list of sources at the end of your paper. The computer also allows you to delete or rearrange sources easily. Whichever method you choose, write only one source per card or clearly separate one entry from another in your computer document.

When you come across a source that seems to have potential for your project, write a bibliography card for it immediately, while the source is in front of you. Doing this serves as an excellent cross-check to help you evaluate the sources by seeing if expert names, book title, or article title reoccur, thus suggesting that you've found a good source. Include all the information you would eventually need to fulfill the requirements of the DOCUMENTATION STYLE your instructor specifies. Record it exactly as it would appear in your finished paper. Spending a few extra moments at this stage can save endless hours of work and frustration later on. If you find that a source is not useful, keep your working bibliography card anyway, and jot on it the reason you rejected it. What seems useless now may become useful when you revise.

The two working bibliography cards shown here, one of which has a content note on the back, are for two sources Chandra Johnson found when she was doing the research for her paper (shown in 34e.2).

BF 311 .D33 1999

Damasio, Antonio.
The Feeling of What Happens: Body and Emotion in the Making of Consciousness

New York: Harcourt Brace, 1999.

Bibliography card: Book

http://www-formal.stanford.edu/jmc/whatisai/whatisai.html

McCarthy, John
"What Is Artificial Intelligence?"

Access date: 10/14/2003
Date published on Web: 3/29/2003

Bibliography card: Online source

McCarthy's a computer science prof at Stanford U. An expert source. Web site has lots of basic info.

Content note on the back of the McCarthy bibliography card.

As a rough estimate, your working bibliography needs to be about twice as long as the list of sources you end up using. (If your assignment asks for ten to twelve sources as a minimum, you want your set of working bibliography cards to have no fewer than twenty to twenty-five items.)

Don't be discouraged if your search goes slowly at first. As your knowledge of the topic grows, and your searching skills improve, you'll find yourself narrowing your search and becoming increasingly productive.

31j   How do I take content notes?

When you write **content notes,** you record information and ideas from your sources that relate specifically to your topic. You start taking content notes when you think your preliminary search has produced enough sources in your WORKING BIBLIOGRAPHY that relate to your RESEARCH QUESTION. Always try to sort major information from minor information about the topic. This will help you when you organize ideas for DRAFTING. Also, write down whatever understanding you've gained from your reading of the source as it directly relates to your paper.

You can make content notes either in a computer file or on index cards. If you're using the computer, leave plenty of space between notes, and keep careful track of what ideas came from each source. One strategy is to open a new file for each source. Later, after you've taken notes on many of your sources, you can determine what subtopics are important for your paper. You can then open a new file for each topic and use the "Cut" and "Paste" functions to gather notes from all of your sources under each topic.

If you're making content notes on index cards, put a heading on each card that gives a precise link to one of your bibliography items. As with bibliography cards, always include in your content notes the source's title, the page numbers from which you're taking notes, and whatever other information ties your notes to a specific source. Never put notes from more than one source on the same index card. If your notes on a source require more than one index card, number the cards sequentially (that is, when you need two cards, write "1 of 2" on the first card and "2 of 2" on the second card). If you take notes about more than one idea or topic from the same source, start a new card for each.

Keeping track of the kind of note you are taking will help you avoid PLAGIARISM. You might use the code Q for quotation, P for paraphrase, and S for summary. Or you might use a different font (on computer) or ink color (on index cards) for QUOTATIONS, PARAPHRASES, and SUMMARIES. (Every precaution you take by coding your content notes helps you avoid the risk of plagiarism; see Chapter 33.) Also, you'll progress more quickly if, on the spot, you compose your SYNTHESIS of the

EXTRA EXERCISE C
To practice methods of preventing unconscious plagiarism, paraphrase or summarize the following paragraphs. (Answers will vary.)

1. Jane Austen, an English novelist, was born in 1775, the daughter of the Reverend George Austen, rector of Steventon and Deane, and Cassandra Leigh Austen. She was the youngest of seven children. Her childhood at Steventon was quiet, domestic, and moderately studious. Much of her spare time was spent in writing, mostly for her own amusement. In 1801, the family moved to Bath. After the death of her father in 1805, she settled in Chawton, where she remained until shortly before her death.

2. Jane Austen began writing stories at an early age and by the time she was twenty-two had completed one of her best-known novels, *Pride and Prejudice*. Other works for which she is remembered include *Sense and Sensibility* and *Northanger Abbey*, which was published by her family after her death. The novels were not especially popular in Austen's lifetime, but today they are regarded as among the best novels in the English language. Although her people are neither intellectual nor heroic and her plots are not elaborate, her skill at telling stories and drawing characters continues to please her readers.

3. On the map, Mexico resembles a great funnel, or rather, a cornucopia, with its widest part towards the north and its smallest end twisting to the south and east, meeting there the sudden expansion of the Maya area. There are few regions in the world with such a diverse geography as we find within this area—Mexico is not one, but many countries. All the climatic extremes of our globe are found, from arctic cold near the summits of the highest volcanoes to the Turkish-bath atmosphere of the coastal jungle. Merely to pass from one valley to another is to enter a markedly different ecological zone.

—Michael D. Coe, *Mexico*, p. 12

➡

Extra Exercise C (continued)
4. In 1773 we know that [Francisco] Goya was in Madrid, where he married Josefa Bayeau, the sister of the painter who had introduced him into Madrid society. His first important chance was a commission for a series of cartoons for tapestries, which Mengs (possibly advised by Bayeau, who had acquired a certain reputation and had become part of a group of young academic painters, which included his brothers) commissioned for the Royal Tapestry Factory at Santa Barbara. It was an important opportunity because it meant that Goya was admitted to court circles; in addition this kind of work allowed him great freedom in his choice of subject matter and of technique. Perhaps most important of all, the sketchy nature of the cartoon medium spared Goya the necessity of "finishing" his work. His style was slow to mature; until now he had displayed a dextrous hand but had shown no signs of genius.

—Margherita Abbaruzzese,
Goya, p. 5

material—that is, if you write down connections between the new source and other sources you have found or your personal knowledge of a subject.

Shown below are two content notes written by Chandra Johnson, the student whose research and writing process comprise the case study in this chapter and the narrative and commentary in Chapter 34. The full title of the book by Antonio Damasio is *The Feeling of What Happens: Body and Emotion in the Making of Consciousness.* Johnson put full information about this source in her working bibliography. She kept her notes on index cards. With each note, she used a shortened form of the title, listed the related page numbers, and recorded whether the information was a quotation, paraphrase, or summary.

Some instructors require students to submit photocopies of all sources they consult for research. Photocopying an article or downloading an online source can also save you time as you draft your research paper. Having a copy of articles, book chapters, or Web pages in your research file gives you access to each item in full. Also, photocopies allow you to check for accuracy and prevent your misquoting or plagiarizing from the source. If you use photocopies, always be sure to write the same bibliography information and content notes as you would if you did not have the photocopies. Remember to label each photocopied or downloaded source with the author's name, the source, and other identifying information. (It's easy, but wrong, to think that if you have a photocopy, you don't need all crucial bibliographic and content information.) It's also a good idea to underline (on your own copy) the section that caught your attention and to write alongside it why it looks useful. The

> Damasio. The Feeling
> p. 39
>
> Summary:
> Many scientists and philosophers think emotion interferes
> with intelligence (Damasio disagrees)

Summary note card

> Damasio. The Feeling
> p.41
>
> Quotation:
> "emotion is integral to the process of reasoning and decision
> making"

Quotation note card

more detailed you are, the more helpful your comments will be as you narrow your working bibliography and as you draft your paper.

31k How do I draft a thesis statement for a research paper?

Drafting a THESIS STATEMENT for a research paper marks the transition from the research process to the writing process. A thesis statement in a research paper is like the thesis statement in any essay: It sets out the central theme, which you need to sustain throughout the paper (see section 2q, especially Box 12). As with any piece of writing, your research paper must fulfill the promise of its thesis statement.

You might begin thinking of the preliminary thesis statement for your paper at some middle point in the research process, although it's perfectly acceptable to wait until you've completely finished researching. To start your thesis statement, you might try to convert your RESEARCH QUESTION into a preliminary thesis statement. Of course, because a question is not an assertion, you want to state your thesis as a DECLARATIVE SENTENCE, not as a question. Remember that a good thesis statement makes an assertion that conveys your point of view about your topic and foreshadows the content of your paper (again, see Box 12 in 2q). And not least, remember that your research paper needs to support your thesis statement. Ask yourself whether the material you've gathered from sources can effectively give support. If not, revise your thesis statement, conduct further research, or do both.

As you revise your thesis statement, keep your eye on the research question that guided your research process so that you can point, in gen-

Case Study

Chandra Johnson (whose research paper appears in Chapter 34) revised her preliminary thesis statement twice before she felt that it expressed the point she wanted to make. Johnson also took the key step of checking that she would be able to support it sufficiently with sources throughout her paper.

FIRST PRELIMINARY THESIS STATEMENT

Artificial intelligence is a complicated problem. [Johnson realized that this draft was much too general for her paper and didn't prepare readers for her specific focus on computers.] ➡

QUOTATION: ON RESEARCH
Research is formalized curiosity. It is poking and prying with a purpose.
—Zora Neale Hurston

EXTRA EXERCISE D
For each of the following subjects, devise a narrowed topic, then a research question, followed by a thesis statement, noting its purpose.

1. Fishing
2. Large families
3. Retirement communities
4. Competitive swimming
5. Study habits
6. Current clothing styles
7. Contemporary American novels
8. Olympics
9. Professional football
10. Diets

Case Study (*continued*)

NEXT PRELIMINARY THESIS STATEMENT

Determining whether a computer is "intelligent" is an unsolved problem. [Johnson liked this thesis better but rejected it because it still described a very broad topic, and she wanted to concentrate specifically on the role of emotion in intelligence.]

FINAL THESIS STATEMENT

An unsolved problem is whether computers need emotion for scientists to consider them intelligent. [Johnson felt this got closer to her message; she then checked it to make sure it also satisfied the criteria for a thesis statement listed in Box 12 in 2q.]

eral terms, to the question's answer. Here are examples of subjects narrowed to topics, focused into research questions, and then cast as thesis statements.

SUBJECT	*rain forests*
TOPIC	The importance of rain forests
RESEARCH QUESTION	What is the importance of rain forests?
INFORMATIVE THESIS STATEMENT	Rain forests provide the human race with many irreplaceable resources.
PERSUASIVE THESIS STATEMENT	Rain forests must be preserved because they offer the human race many irreplaceable resources.
SUBJECT	*nonverbal communication*
TOPIC	Personal space
RESEARCH QUESTION	How do standards for personal space differ among cultures?
INFORMATIVE THESIS STATEMENT	Everyone has expectations concerning the use of personal space, but accepted distances for that space are determined by each person's culture.
PERSUASIVE THESIS STATEMENT	To prevent intercultural misunderstandings, people must be aware of cultural differences in standards for personal space.
SUBJECT	*smoking*
TOPIC	Curing nicotine addiction
RESEARCH QUESTION	What are new approaches to curing nicotine addiction?

| INFORMATIVE THESIS STATEMENT | Some approaches to curing nicotine addiction are themselves addictive. |
| PERSUASIVE THESIS STATEMENT | Because some methods of curing addiction are themselves addictive, doctors should prescribe them with caution. |

31l How do I outline a research paper?

Some instructors require an OUTLINE of your research paper, either before you hand in the paper or along with the paper. In such cases, your instructor is probably expecting you to be working from an outline as you write your drafts. Your research log often comes in handy when you group your ideas, especially for a first draft of your paper—and as you make an *informal outline* for it. An outline can serve as a guide as you plan and write your paper. For directions on composing a *formal outline,* see section 2r. The material in 2r shows you how to head your outline with the paper's thesis statement, and it explains your choices in using either a *topic outline* (a format that requires words or phrases for each item) or a *sentence outline* (a format that requires full sentences for each item). Whatever your choice, never mix the two types. To see a topic outline of Chandra Johnson's research paper, turn to section 34e.2.

31m How do I draft and revise a research paper?

The processes of DRAFTING and REVISING a research paper are much like those of drafting and revising any other piece of writing (Chapters 2 and 3), but more is demanded. You need to demonstrate that you've followed the research steps discussed in this chapter; you've used SOURCES correctly, employing QUOTATIONS, PARAPHRASES, and SUMMARIES without PLAGIARISM (Chapter 33); you've moved beyond summary to SYNTHESIS of your various sources; and you've used DOCUMENTATION correctly (Chapters 34 through 36). To fulfill these special demands, allow ample time for drafting, thinking, revising, reflecting, and completing your paper.

Expect to write a number of drafts of your research paper. Successive drafts help you master the information you've learned and add it authoritatively to the knowledge you already had about the topic. In the first draft, organize the broad categories of your paper. Many research writers move material around within a category or from one category to another. That happens because the act of writing gives you new insights and helps you make fresh connections. A *first draft* is a rough draft. It is a prelude to revising and polishing. Box 132 on the next page suggests some ways to write your first draft.

BACKGROUND
In "Students as Ethnographers: Guiding Alternative Research Projects" (*English Journal,* September 1999: 82–90), Richard Beach and Margaret J. Finders argue that micro-ethnographic research projects provide students with interesting alternatives to the traditional research paper. The authors provide a detailed course plan for incorporating alternative research projects in the writing classroom.

TEACHING TIP
Composing a formal outline of an article read by the entire class can be either a small-group or whole-class activity. It will not only provide practice for students in following formal outline form but will also help them, through discussion, improve their ability to distinguish between major ideas, subordinate ideas, and supporting details. You must of course use care in selecting the article, as many professionally written pieces do not lend themselves to outline form. (This is one reason that outlines are not universally used in schools.)

TEACHING TIP
TEACHING TIP
Since the processes of drafting and revising vary from one writer to another, students may gain insight into their own processes by interviewing one another about how they approach these stages of writing a research paper. Students can base their interviews on the following questions.

1. Do you organize your note cards in piles?

2. Do you work with your notes in front of you?

3. Do you write the first draft without referring to your note cards?

4. Is your first draft a complete draft?

5. When do you insert the parenthetical citations?

6. Is your first draft composed slowly and carefully or quickly and sketchily?

7. Do you proceed immediately to a second draft, or do you let some time elapse between drafting and revising?

8. Do you show your work to other people for responses and suggestions?

BOX 132   SUMMARY

 Suggestions for drafting a research paper

■ Some researchers work with their notes in front of them. They use the organized piles they've made to group material into categories. They spread out each pile and work according to the subcategories of information that have emerged in the course of their research, proceeding deliberately from one pile to the next. They expect this process to take time, but they are assured of a first draft that includes much of the results of their research.

■ Some researchers review all their information and then set it aside to write a *partial first draft*. This involves a quickly written first attempt at getting the material under control. This method can help you get a broad view of the material. The second step is to go back and write a *complete first draft*, with research notes at hand. When you combine the two drafts, the pieces begin to fall into place as you move material, add what's been left out, correct information, and insert in-text references.

■ Some researchers write their first draft almost as if FREEWRITING (2g), writing without stopping, just getting the words down on paper. Afterward, or whenever they get a sense of how to proceed, they slow down and use their notes.

■ Some researchers, when working on computer, use the "Cut" and "Paste" functions to move around the parts of their paper. (If you do this, be sure to save a copy of each draft and partial draft—even random pages—you've written so that you can refer to earlier versions later. You never know when something you've discarded can become useful again.)

■ Some researchers like the physical act of working with a printout (or photocopy) of their first draft. They literally cut up the paper to move paragraphs and sentences, a kind of "unpacking" of their thinking. If a new and more readable order suggests itself, these researchers tape the paper together in its new form.

Second drafts (and subsequent versions) emerge from reading your first (or a later) draft critically and then revising. If possible, distance yourself from your material by taking a break for a few days (or at least for a few hours, if you're pressed for time). Then, reread your draft, looking for ways to improve it—something that's hard to do unless you've taken time off between readings. You might ask friends or classmates to read the draft and react. Also, now is the time to begin thinking about the DOCUMENT DESIGN you want for your paper (see Chapter 37).

One key to revising any research paper is to carefully examine the **evidence** you have included. Evidence consists of facts, statistics, expert studies and opinions, examples, and stories. As a reader, you expect writers to provide solid evidence to back up their claims and conclusions. Similarly, when you write, your readers expect evidence that clearly supports your claims and conclusions. Identify each of the points you have made in your paper; these will include your thesis and all of your subpoints. Then ask the following questions:

- **Is the evidence sufficient?** To be sufficient, evidence isn't thin or trivial. As a rule, the more evidence, the more convincing the argument is to readers.

- **Is the evidence representative?** To be representative, evidence is customary and normal, not based on exceptions. When evidence is representative, it provides a view of the issue that reflects usual circumstances, not rare ones.

- **Is the evidence relevant?** To be relevant, evidence relates directly to your claim. It illustrates your reasons straightforwardly and never introduces unrelated material. Only if the evidence is important and central to what you're claiming will readers accept your claim.

- **Is the evidence accurate?** To be accurate, evidence is correct, complete, and up-to-date. It comes from a reliable SOURCE (32a, 32j). Equally important, you present it honestly, without distorting or misrepresenting the issue.

- **Is the evidence reasonable?** To be reasonable, evidence never makes extreme claims by using words like *all, never,* and *certainly.* Reasonable evidence is logically sound and avoids logical fallacies (5j).

As you work, pay attention to any uneasy feelings you have that hint at the need to rethink or rework your material. Experienced writers know that writing is really *rewriting.* Research papers are among the most demanding composing assignments, and most writers revise several times. Once you've produced a *final draft,* you're ready to EDIT (3d), format (Chapter 37), and PROOFREAD (3e) your work. Check for correct grammar, punctuation, capitalization, and spelling. (No amount of careful research and good writing can make up for an incorrectly presented, sloppy, error-laden document.)

Consult Box 17 in section 3c to remind yourself of the general principles of revising, and consult the revision checklist in Box 133 on the next page to verify that you've remained aware of all aspects of research writing.

To see one example of the research writing process in action, turn to Chandra Johnson's MLA-style research paper in section 34e. There you'll see the final draft of an MLA-style research paper; a narrative of decisions that the student made during her research process; and

QUOTATION: ON WRITING
Writing is a process of dealing with not-knowing. . . . At best there's a slender intuition, not much greater than an itch.
—Donald Barthelme

BOX 133   CHECKLIST

 Revision checklist for a research paper

If the answer to a question is no, you need to revise. The section numbers in parentheses tell you where to find useful information.

1. Does your introductory paragraph lead effectively into the material?
   (4b)

2. Have you met the basic requirements for a written thesis
   statement? (2q and 31k)

3. Does your thesis statement allude to, or directly address, the research
   question upon which you based your research? (31c and 31k)

4. Does the content of your paper address your research question(s)?
   (31c and 31e)

5. Have you discussed the topic of each paragraph fully, using
   RENNS? (4f)

6. Do you stay on the topic of each paragraph? (4f)

7. Have you included appropriate and effective evidence? (4f and
   31m)

8. Have you deleted irrelevant or insignificant information from your
   material? (4d)

9. Do your ideas follow sensibly and logically within each paragraph
   and from one paragraph to the next? (4g)

10. Have you used quotations, paraphrases, and summaries well? (31j)

11. Have you integrated your source material well without plagiarizing?
    (Chapter 33)

12. Are the formats for your parenthetical citations correct? (Chapters
    34–36) Does each tie into an item in your WORKS CITED (MLA
    style) list of sources at the end of your paper?

13. Does the concluding paragraph end your paper effectively? (4k)

14. Does the paper exactly match the format you've been assigned to
    follow in terms of margins, spacing, title, name-and-page number
    headings, and so on? (Chapter 37)

commentary (on the text page facing each page of Johnson's paper) that
gives you insight into specific aspects of her paper.

For an APA-style research paper, turn to Carlos Velez's APA-style research paper in section 35h. There you'll see the final draft of the paper
and a narrative of the decisions that the student made during his research process. For an APA-style science report, see section 41h.1.

Chapter 32

Finding and Evaluating Sources

32a What is a source?

A **source** is any form of information that provides ideas, examples, information, or evidence. For a research paper, sources can be books, articles, Web pages, Internet files, CD-ROMs, videos, lectures, and other types of communication. Sources can also be interviews, surveys, or direct observations, such as when you attend a performance or visit a museum. Sources differ greatly in terms of how accurate and reliable they are. To be able to use sources responsibly for your research, you need to judge each source's trustworthiness and quality. This chapter explains how to locate and then evaluate sources.

A source is either *primary* or *secondary*. A **primary source** is original work such as firsthand reports of experiments, observations, or other research projects; field research you carry out yourself; and documents like letters, diaries, novels, poems, short stories, autobiographies, and journals. When you use a primary source, no one comes between you and the material.

A **secondary source** reports, describes, comments on, or analyzes someone else's work. This information comes to you secondhand. That is, someone other than the primary source relays the information, adding a layer between you and the original material. This does not mean secondary sources are inferior to primary sources. Indeed, scholars and other experts are excellent secondary sources. However, you need to evaluate secondary sources carefully to make sure that what's being relayed to you isn't distorted or biased in the process." Turn to 32j for detailed guidelines for evaluating sources.

32b What is a search strategy?

A **search strategy** is an organized procedure for locating and assembling information for your research. You find this information in two places: on the Internet and in the library. Developing a strategy for your

HISTORY

Benjamin Franklin organized the Library Company of Philadelphia in 1731, the first American subscription library. Its original purpose was to provide ready access to books for members of the Junto Club, a public service group to which Franklin belonged. Franklin himself said that he spent time at the library almost daily, learning foreign languages or reading for general knowledge.

Until the founding of the Library Company, there were few public libraries in the American colonies. The earliest one was the library of Harvard College, which was founded in 1638 with nearly four hundred volumes bequeathed by John Harvard. Libraries were established at Yale and at William and Mary around 1700. In the Southern colonies, the Reverend Thomas Bray (1656–1730), working by appointment of the Bishop of London as commissary of the Anglican Church, established parochial libraries. In 1876, a report titled *Public Libraries in the United States* read: "So far as is known, there were, in 1776, twenty-nine public libraries in the thirteen American colonies, and they numbered altogether 45,623 volumes; in the year 1800 the number of libraries had increased to forty-nine, and the number of volumes to about 80,000." The Library of Congress, which contains over 72 million pieces of material (among them 16.5 million books and 31 million manuscripts), was begun by Congress in 1800 with a budget of $5,000.

search is crucial. An effective, successful search strategy results from your working systematically and thoroughly to find material that helps to answer your RESEARCH QUESTION. A good search strategy helps you structure your research work so that you don't mistake activity for productivity.

No two research processes are exactly alike. Be guided by your personal needs as you adapt the search strategies I explain. Most of all, know that no search strategy is as tidy as I describe here. Following are three frequently used designs.

The **expert method** is useful when you know your specific topic. Begin by reading articles or books by an expert in the field. Of course, this means that you have to know who the experts are, and sometimes that's difficult. Talk with people who are generally knowledgeable about your topic, learn what you can from them, and ask them to refer you to work by experts on the topic. (For example, if you're interested in researching artificial intelligence, a computer science instructor may be able to tell you who are the leading experts on that topic.) Alternatively or in addition, INTERVIEW an expert, either in person, on the phone, or through e-mail. Turn to 32i for detailed advice about conducting effective interviews.

The **chaining method** is useful when you know your general topic and need to narrow it to a more specific, manageable topic. Start with reference books and bibliographies from current articles or Web sites. These references will lead you to additional sources. Keep up the chain, watching closely for sources that are mentioned frequently. The frequency is usually evidence that the sources are probably expert and well respected. As you work, your general topic usually begins to group and divide itself into subtopics, one of which might serve as the topic of your research paper. If such division and grouping doesn't emerge for you, take a break of a few hours so that you can reconsider the material with fresh eyes.

The **layering method** is useful when you need to find your own topic. You layer information by first consulting general sources and then finding ones that are more specific. You try to relate the information you gather to other scholarly sources in the same subject area. Chandra Johnson, the student whose research paper appears in 34e, started with the layering method and soon combined it with chaining.

You, too, may find yourself switching or combining methods. This is perfectly acceptable. "Flexibility with focus" is the guiding principle for experienced researchers. Complete your search as soon as possible after you get the assignment. Discovering early in the process what sources are available allows you time to find those that are harder to locate; to use interlibrary loan if an item isn't available in your library or online; to wait for someone to return checked-out books you need; or to schedule interviews, arrange visits, or conduct surveys.

32c How do I find sources?

You want to start your search strategy by consulting library and online sources on your topic. To do this, you need to figure out the keywords (32c.4) and subject categories that can lead you to useful material.

The **library** building is where generations of college students have traditionally gone to find sources. Today, the **Internet,** which includes the World Wide Web and additional files, greatly expands the ways you can access information. At the library, you find books, periodicals, and lists of sources in catalogs, indexes, and databases. While many college libraries offer home pages to give you remote access to their holdings via Internet connections, the library building itself continues to be a vital place for all research. One key advantage of going to the library is your chance to consult with librarians. They trained for their profession by learning how to advise students and other researchers about using library resources to greatest advantage. Never hesitate to ask questions about how to proceed or where to find a resource.

Catalogs list sources—usually books—that the library owns (see 32d). **Indexes** list articles in periodicals; each index covers a specific topic area (see 32e). Catalogs and indexes exist mainly in electronic format; less commonly, some catalogs and indexes are still in print format. **Databases** always exist electronically (see 32c.1). They consist of one or more indexes and contain extensive lists of articles, reports, and books. You can access and search electronic catalogs, indexes, and databases from computers in the library or by connecting to the library online. You can also subscribe to databases, but this can be expensive. At most colleges, your tuition pays for access to online library resources, so take advantage of them.

If you're accessing a database by connecting to the library online, you need to use a **browser,** a software program that gives you access to the Web and the search engines located there. Netscape Navigator™ and Microsoft Internet Explorer™ are the two most frequently used browsers.

32c.1 Using databases

Each entry in a database contains bibliographic information, including a title, author, date of publication, and publisher (in the case of books or reports) or periodical (in the case of articles). The entry might also provide an abstract, or summary, of the material. Once you locate an entry that seems promising, you might need to read a print copy of the source. Some databases provide the full texts of the articles they cite. Other databases allow you to purchase full copies of the sources you find. If you're on a tight budget, try to purchase only what looks truly useful. You can request materials that are not in your library through interlibrary loan (32g).

BACKGROUND
According to Curtis and Bernhardt, computers and the information explosion are changing the nature of indexing ("Keywords, Titles, Abstracts, and Online Searches: Implications for Indexing," *The Technical Writing Teacher,* 18(2): 142–161). Books and articles increasingly are indexed by title and search keywords instead of by subject. Subject indexing requires readers to scan and classify each item for the index and is a slower, more expensive process than indexing by title and keywords, which can be done by computers. The process of having readers scan and classify makes it difficult and more expensive for indexes to adjust to the present rapid increase in journals and the development of new subject areas. Curtis and Bernhardt argue that the new emphasis on titles and keywords in indexes and computer searches means that writing teachers and students need to give more attention to composing titles.

USING COLLABORATION
Group members may divide by subject matter areas or source materials. For example, in an essay on automobile exhaust pollution, dividing by subject matter might send one student to look up "regulation," another to investigate "industry response," and another to search for "testing results." Dividing by source might send one student to a business database, another to periodical indexes, and another to a library's catalog. By dividing the work and pooling information, students can gain a broader perspective on their topics and compose more balanced papers.

Sources that you identify through scholarly databases are almost always more reliable and appropriate than sources you find through simply browsing the World Wide Web. Some scholarly research is available from World Wide Web sites, while others reside at Internet sites not necessarily part of the Web. The reliability of scholarly databases stems from their origins: Only experts and professionals who recognize works of merit compile them.

The best way to access a database at your library is to go to your college library's Web site, whether you're online in the library, at home, or in a dormitory. Below and on the facing page you can see typical home pages of two college libraries. (Of course, your library's home page will undoubtedly look quite different.) Each home page of a library shows the resources available through that Web site. More might be available at the library building itself. Sections 32d and 32e explain how to use the catalog to find books and periodicals (newspapers, magazines, and journals). Most college libraries subscribe to one or more database services, such as EBSCO, FirstSearch, and IBIS. Because the college pays for these services, you don't have to, but you'll need an ID or password to use them. Commonly, your student number serves as your ID, but check with a librarian to see what's required at your college.

Resources available through this Web site

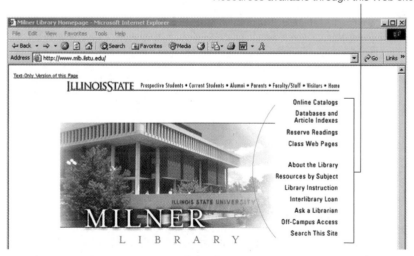

Home page of Illinois State University Library

Resources available through this Web site

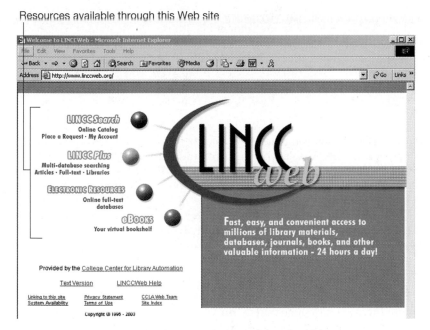

Home page of the Community Colleges of Florida library interface

EXERCISE 32-1

Working either individually or as part of a group, access your library's Web site. You may do this either by going to the library itself or by connecting to the library online. List all of the types of information available. In particular, list the indexes and databases you can search and the subject areas each one covers. Note whether any of the databases have full-text versions of articles. Note if the library's Web site has any online "help" or "search suggestions."

32c.2 Searching the World Wide Web

The **World Wide Web** is organized around pages (called *Web pages*) that are linked together electronically. A group of pages that an individual or organization has created and linked together is called a **Web site.** The main page in a Web site (called the *home page*) acts as a table of contents. Although the Web contains billions of pages, including a great many books and periodical articles, only a fraction of these sources are available on the Web without subscribing or paying a fee. Therefore, searching library databases remains your most important method of

BACKGROUND

Some very famous people have been librarians. A few of them may even have helped students with research papers.

- The German diplomat and philosopher-mathematician Gottfried von Leibniz (1646–1716) served two terms as a university librarian.

- The British philosopher, economist, and historian David Hume (1711–1776) spent five years as a librarian at the Library of the Faculty of the Advocates at Edinburgh while writing his *History of England.*

- The infamous Casanova (1725–1798) served as a private librarian to royalty for thirteen years at the end of his life.

- Pope Pius XI (1857–1939) spent nineteen years at the Ambrosian Library in Milan, where he then served as chief librarian. In 1911, he began updating and reorganizing the Vatican Library and four years later was named its prefect. He became pope in 1922.

- Archibald MacLeish (1892–1982), poet, playwright, assistant secretary of state, and three-time winner of the Pulitzer Prize, served as Librarian of Congress under Franklin D. Roosevelt.

- Mao Zedong (1893–1976) was at one time assistant to the chief librarian of the University of Beijing.

- The longtime Federal Bureau of Investigation chief J. Edgar Hoover (1895–1972) was a messenger and cataloger at the Library of Congress as a young man.

finding many scholarly sources. However, the principles for searching the World Wide Web are much like those for searching databases (32c.1). You start with a broad subject and narrow it to arrive at a suitable topic for an academic research paper.

Once you use a browser to get on the Web, you can search for sites by using a SEARCH ENGINE (32c.3) or by typing an address (called a **URL,** for Universal Resource Locator) into the search box.

ALERT: When you read, write, or type a URL, the Modern Language Association (MLA) tells you to surround it with angle brackets. For example, <www.prenhall.com/troyka> is the URL for my publisher's Web site about my books, including this handbook. The brackets separate a URL from sentence punctuation so that no one mistakes it as part of the URL. However, never use angle brackets when you type a URL in the locator box at the top of your computer screen. ☜

32c.3 Using search engines

Search engines are programs designed to hunt the World Wide Web and Internet files for sources on specific topics that you identify by using keywords (32c.4). When you use a search engine, you generally can access materials in one of two ways: through keyword searches (32c.4) and through subject directories (32c.5). Box 134 lists some commonly used search engines. Shown on the facing page is the opening page of Google.com, a search engine.

BOX 134   SUMMARY

 Addresses for some search engines

AltaVista	<http://altavista.com>
Excite	<http://www.excite.com>
Lycos	<http://www.lycos.com>
Yahoo!	<http://www.yahoo.com>
Ask Jeeves	<http://www.ask.com>
Google	<http://www.google.com>
Metacrawler	<http://www.metacrawler.com>
Dogpile	<http://www.dogpile.com>
HotBot	<http://www.hotbot.com>
AlltheWeb	<http://www.alltheweb.com>

Directory page of Google.com, showing search categories

BACKGROUND
The Nuremberg Chronicle (1493) was the world's first encyclopedia. Its three volumes were written by one man, Hartmann Schedel, who used his extensive personal library for most of the research such a work requires.

ANSWERS: EXERCISE 32-2
Answers will vary.

EXERCISE 32-2

Use at least three different search engines to search online for the same topic. List the different results for each search engine, and also note the strengths and weaknesses of each. (Pay attention to usefulness, ease of use, and so on.) Write a brief report on your findings. You may wish to try this exercise with a second topic before drawing your conclusions.

32c.4 Using keywords

When searching for sources online or in library databases, **keywords,** also called *descriptors* or *identifiers,* are your lifeline to success. Keywords are the main words in a source's title or the words that the author or editor has identified as central to that source. Without keywords, you'd have no way to access sources listed in online or electronic database book catalogs and periodical indexes. Similarly, to find information on the World Wide Web or on the Internet, keywords are essential. Because Web search engines, such as Yahoo, often look for any occurrence

QUOTATION: ON RESEARCH

Research is the ability to investigate systematically and truly all that comes under your observation in life.

—Marcus Aurelius

QUOTATION: ON WRITING

The presence of humans, in a system containing high-speed electronic computers and high-speed, accurate communications, is quite inhibiting.

—Stuart Luman Seaton

of a word in the title or body of a page, you need to take particular care with keyword searches on the Web.

When you use keywords to search for Web sources, chances are you'll come up with a large or even overwhelming number of sources. Much of what turns up won't be relevant to your topic. As a result, you need to figure out which items on the list might be useful. Whenever possible, narrow your list of keywords by using BOOLEAN EXPRESSIONS. Your other alternative is to use a "try and see" approach. Whichever approach you use, always keep a record of poor and good keywords for your TOPIC in your research log so that you'll remember which keywords do and do not work well for you on each topic. This process might seem tedious at times, but don't get discouraged. If you're stumped, try asking a friend who's experienced with online searches or a research librarian for help.

Advice for using this Guided Search feature

Guided keyword search

As you become more adept at using keywords, your searches will become more directed and less time-consuming. The two main ways to make keyword searches more efficient are using guided searches and using Boolean expressions.

Using guided searches

Using **guided searches** means that you search a database or search engine by answering prompts provided, usually by filling in a form on the screen. Guided searches often allow you to select a range of dates of publication (for example, after 2002 or between 1990 and 1995) and to specify only a certain language (such as English) or a certain format (such as books). Shown on the facing page is an example of a search for sources that have *artificial intelligence* in their titles, that use *computers* as another keyword, but that are not about *robots*.

Using Boolean expressions

Using **Boolean expressions** means that you search a database or search engine by using keyword combinations that narrow and refine your search. To combine keywords, you use the words *AND, OR, NOT,* and *NEAR* or the symbols that represent those words. Boolean expressions, generally placed between keywords, instruct the search engine to list only those Web sites in which your keywords appear in certain combinations and to ignore others. Other commands similarly help you go directly to the sources you most need.

Box 135 explains ways to search with keywords more effectively, using the subject of artificial intelligence as an example. Simply typing

HISTORY

Denis Diderot spent over twenty years writing and editing his *Encyclopédie*. In twenty-eight volumes, he and famous contributors, such as Rousseau and Voltaire, collected all the scientific thinking of the Age of Reason. The project began as a commission from a French publisher to translate a one-volume British encyclopedia into French. Diderot earned about $12 a week while working on the encyclopedia. When the project was completed, he was forced to sell his library to provide his daughter with a dowry. Catherine II, Empress of Russia, paid him $5,000—and also allowed him access to the books for the rest of his life.

BOX 135   SUMMARY

 Refining keyword searches

AND or the + ("plus") symbol: Narrows the focus of your search because both keywords must be found. If you want to find information on the role of emotions in artificial intelligence, try the expression *artificial AND intelligence AND emotions*. While some search engines, such as Google.com, don't require the word *AND* between terms because they assume that two or more terms are always connected by *AND*, most require it. When in doubt, definitely use *AND*.

NOT or the – ("minus") symbol: Narrows a search by excluding texts containing the specified word or phrase. If you want to eliminate robots from your search, type *artificial AND intelligence AND emotions NOT robots*.

→

BACKGROUND
In "Re-envisioning Research" (*English Journal*, September 1999: 45–50), Gregory Shafer laments how little has changed in the "traditional, rule-laden procedure" of teaching students to write research papers. He supports the recent trend to allow students to conduct primary research in sites of their own choosing. As a suggestion, he describes his experiences in teaching students how to engage in anthropological research.

Refining keyword searches (*continued*)

OR: Expands a search's boundaries by including more than one keyword. If you want to expand your search to include sources about artificial intelligence in either computers or robots, try the expression *artificial AND intelligence AND emotions AND computers OR robots.* You'll get pages mentioning artificial intelligence and emotions only if they mention computers or robots.

NEAR: Indicates that the keywords may be found close to each other or on either side of each other. However, depending on the search engine, *NEAR* produces hits that are found only in the same sentence or on the same Web site. For example, entering *intelligence NEAR emotions* will yield only pages in which the words "intelligence" and "emotions" are very close to one another.

( ): These are parentheses that group two or more expressions together. For example, *(artificial intelligence AND emotions) AND (Turing Test OR Chinese Room)* would find documents about artificial intelligence and emotions along with either the Turing Test or the Chinese Room Test. (Chandra Johnson's research paper in section 34e.2 explains that these are two tests for judging whether people can regard a computer as "intelligent.")

" ": These are quotation marks that direct a search engine to match your exact word order on a Web page. For example, a search for *"robots that think"* will find pages that contain the exact phrase *robots that think.* However, it won't return pages with the phrase *thinking robots.* Also, if you search for *James Joyce* without using quotation marks, most engines will return all pages containing the words *James* and *Joyce* anywhere in the document; however, a search using *"James Joyce"* brings you closer to finding Web sites about the Irish writer.

*: The asterisk functions as a wildcard in some search engines. It allows you to look for sites by listing only the first few letters of a keyword. This approach, known as a *truncated search,* is helpful when a term comes in varying forms. For example, a Yahoo search for *cogni** would turn up directory entries for both *cognitive* and *cognition.* You can also direct the search engine to look for variants of a keyword by using the wildcard symbol * in place of either the word ending or some of the letters in the word. For example, a truncated search for *wom*n* would return hits for *woman* and *women.* Please note that not all search engines allow wildcarding; Google.com, for example, does not. A few search engines use specialized symbols such as *?* or *:* instead of the * for wildcarding.

the words *intelligence computers emotions* would yield pages that include any of these words—and not necessarily in that order. Imagine the staggeringly long list of pages you'd get for the word *computers* alone, and then almost triple that number when you include the two other seemingly unrelated words in your list. In contrast, note the huge amount of weeding out that the Boolean expressions allow.

The examples in Box 135 are not all-inclusive. Always review the database's or search engine's own search tips, as engines differ in how they handle expressions and formats. For example, some search engines are "case sensitive," which means that they look for keywords exactly as you type them, including capitals and lowercase letters. To be sure, check the "Help" box or the "Search Tips" feature of any database or search engine you use. For virtually all search engines (including ask.com, altavista.com, lycos.com, google.com, and yahoo.com), a "Help" button or link appears on the search engine's home page.

To conduct a keyword search, type a word or group of words in the search box on the opening page of the search engine, and click on the "Search" or "Enter" button. The engine scans for your word(s) in Web pages, and then lists sites that contain them. Because the Web has billions of pages, a search on even a moderately common topic may produce thousands of **hits**—sites listed or visited in a search. Not every hit will be what you are looking for. Very general terms may appear on thousands of Web sites. If a search engine finds thousands of hits for your keyword, do not give up. Instead, try more specific keywords, use a guided or "advanced" search feature, or use the strategies listed in Box 135 for refining a keyword search.

EXERCISE 32-3

Use a search engine of your choice to search for sources on "artificial intelligence." For each option below, record how many hits occur.

1. Enter the word *artificial*.
2. Enter the word *intelligence*.
3. Enter the phrase *artificial AND intelligence*.
4. Enter the phrase *"artificial intelligence"* (in quotation marks).
5. Enter the search phrase *"artificial intelligence" computers emotions*.
6. Explore adding other words to your search phrase or using Boolean expressions (Box 135).
7. Repeat this exercise by searching for another topic that interests you.

32c.5 Using subject directories

Subject directories included on most search engines' home pages provide a good alternative to keyword searches. These directories are lists of topics (Education, Computing, Entertainment, and so on) or resources

Click on
"Computer
Science"

Click on
"Artificial
Intelligence"

Sources on "Artificial Intelligence"

Subject directory search for "artificial intelligence"

and services (Shopping, Travel, and so on), with links to Web sites on
those topics and resources. Most search engines' home pages have one
or more subject directories.

Clicking on a general category within a subject directory will take
you to lists of increasingly specific categories. Eventually, you will get a
list of Web pages on the most specific subtopic you select. These search
engines also allow you to click on a category and enter keywords for a
search. For example, suppose that you are using yahoo.com to search for
information on *artificial intelligence*. As the figure above shows, you
would first go to Yahoo's general category of *science*. Under *science* you
would find the category of *computer science*, and within *computer science* you would find a link to *artificial intelligence*, a page that lists nineteen additional categories and dozens of sources.

Several subject directories exist independently of search engines
(see Box 134 in 32c). Box 136 lists the Internet addresses of some directories. One useful directory is the *Librarians' Index to the Internet*

BOX 136   SUMMARY

Addresses for subject directories

Educator's Reference Desk (contains ERIC)	<http://www.eduref.org>
Infomine	<http://infomine.ucr.edu>
Internet Public Library	<http://www.ipl.org>
Librarians' Index to the Internet	<http://lii.org>
Library of Congress	<http://lcweb.loc.gov>
Refdesk.com	<http://www.refdesk.com>

(LII). To use the *Librarians' Index,* type its URL, <http://lii.org>, in the browser's search box. The first screen you see is the lii.org home page. You'll see a number of broad topic areas, and when you click on one of them, you'll see a number of subtopics. As you refine your search, you'll eventually come to specific pages. One advantage of the *Librarians' Index* is that professional librarians have gathered the pages.

Box 137 summarizes the information in this section by providing some general guidelines for using search engines and directories with keywords.

BOX 137   SUMMARY

Tips on using search engines and directories

- Use keyword searches only when you have a very specific, narrow topic with unique keywords. If you enter a general topic in most search engines, you will be overwhelmed with thousands of returns. If this happens, switch to a subject directory or see if using additional keywords or Boolean expressions sufficiently restricts the number of hits.

- Most search engines attempt to search as much of the Web as possible. But because the World Wide Web is vast and unorganized, different search engines will give different results for the same search. Try using more than one search engine, or use a **metasearch engine,** one that searches several search engines at once. (Google.com and Dogpile.com are metasearch engines.)

- Always check the "Help" screen for the search engine you use. As with the rest of the Web, search engines add or change features frequently.

- Specify that the search engine list results by "ranking." If you do not, the search results will be returned in random order, and the most important source may be last.

→

TEACHING TIP
Most browsers allow an additional search within a Web page; this is useful in pinpointing a concept or name in a lengthy document. For example, in Netscape, for some versions, click on "Find" at the top of the screen; in other versions of Netscape, click on "Edit" in the menu bar, choose "Find in page," and click. A window will open. Type a word or a phrase, and each occurrence on the page will be highlighted.

HISTORY

Melvil Dewey (1851–1931) is famous for devising the Dewey decimal system of book classification (1876). He was also a founder and editor of the *Library Journal* and of the American Library Association. In 1883, he became librarian at Columbia University, New York City, and founded its school of library economy, the first program to train and certify librarians. Dewey and the school moved to Albany, New York, where it became the state library school. Dewey served as director of the New York State library (1899–1906), secretary of the University of the State of New York (1899–1900), and state director of libraries (1904–1906). He remade the state library into one of the most efficient in the country, and he set up traveling libraries and picture collections. His innovations were widely copied throughout the United States and abroad.

Tips on using search engines and directories (*continued*)

- If possible, limit the date range. For example, you can often ask to see only pages that were updated in the past six months or one year.
- When you find a useful site, go to the toolbar at the top of the screen and click on "Bookmark" (or "Favorites") and then click on "Add." Doing so allows you to return to a good source easily by opening "Bookmarks" or "Favorites" and double-clicking on the address.
- Use the "History" or "Go" function to track the sites you visit, in case you want to revisit one you previously thought was not helpful. You can also move a site from "History" to "Bookmark."

32d How do I find books?

A library's **book catalog,** which lists its holdings (its entire collection), exists as a computer database in almost every modern library. You can find a book by searching by **author,** by **title,** by **subject,** and by KEYWORD. The Library of Congress in Washington, DC, is the largest library in the world and, as you might expect, it has the largest catalog. The figure on the facing page shows the home page for the Library of Congress online catalog. Note that it allows you to search by title, author, subject, call number, or keyword; to search particular indexes; or to search using BOOLEAN EXPRESSIONS.

Suppose a source recommends that you find a book by the **author** Antonio Damasio, but you don't know its title. You can search the catalog for books by this author. A screen on your library's computer will have a place for you to type "Damasio, Antonio" in a space for "author." (Usually, you enter last name, then first name, but check which system your library uses.) If your library owns any books by Antonio Damasio, the computer will display their titles and other bibliographic information, such as the library call number. Then you can use the call number to request the book or to find it yourself.

Among the books you might find when searching for "Damasio, Antonio" is *The Feeling of What Happens: Body and Emotion in the Making of Consciousness* (New York: Harcourt Brace, 1999). Suppose you know that book's **title,** but not its author, and want to see if your library owns a copy. A screen on your library's computer will have a place for you to type in the title; in some systems, you usually do not type words like "the" or "a," so that in this case, you would type in only "Feeling of What Happens."

Suppose, however, you don't know an author's name or a book title. You only have a research topic, and you need to find sources. In this

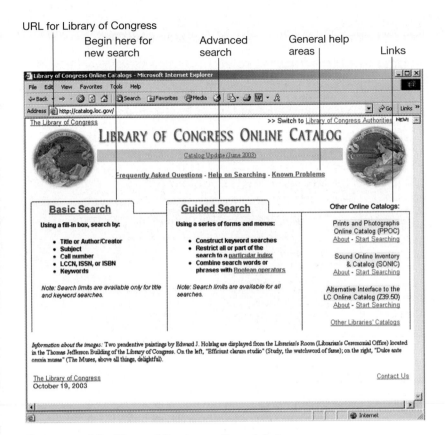

URL for Library of Congress

Begin here for new search

Advanced search

General help areas

Links

Home page of the Library of Congress online catalog

HISTORY

Under the strong influence of the Renaissance, Italy became the center of book collecting in the Western world. Florence was one of the major trading cities because of the support of the princes, who served as patrons to scholars who searched for lost treasures of Greek and Latin literature. The scholars' efforts were in large measure responsible for transmitting classical learning to a new age through the works they found, translated, recopied, and sold. Among the princes of that time, Cosimo de Medici (1389–1464) is especially notable for building the Medici Library, the first public library in Europe to have been opened since the Romans. The Medicis invested $15 million from 1434 to 1469, collecting and commissioning copies of manuscripts. The collection acquired under their patronage, especially that of Cosimo and his successor, Lorenzo the Magnificent (1449–1492), are now housed in the Laurentian and National Libraries of Florence.

case, you need to search by **subject,** using the terms listed in the *Library of Congress Subject Headings (LCSH)*. The *LCSH* is a multivolume catalog available, as of this handbook's publication, only in book form, and it's located in the reference section of every library. The *LCSH* lists only **subject headings,** which are organized from most general to most narrow. Suppose you're researching the topic of "consciousness." If you enter that term into a space for subject searches in your own library's "Search" screen, *The Feeling of What Happens: Body and Emotion in the Making of Consciousness* by Antonio Damasio will be listed, whether available in your library or through interlibrary loan.

Finally, you may wish to search by KEYWORD in your library's holdings. You could find Damasio's book using the keywords "feeling," "body," "emotion," "consciousness," "intelligence," "mind," and so on. A sample book catalog keyword search is shown on the next page.

BACKGROUND

The Guinness Book of Records was founded as a result of the curiosity of Sir Hugh Beaver, the managing director of the Arthur Guinness, Son and Co. brewery. One day in 1954, Sir Hugh went bird hunting. He shot at some plovers—and missed. He started wondering if plovers were the fastest game birds, and he tried to satisfy his curiosity in an encyclopedia. Neither it nor any other reference work had the answer.

As a result, Sir Hugh decided that people needed a book that would accurately list record sizes, speeds, and durations. His plan was to have a copy of the book in every pub that sold Guinness stout, as an aid in settling bets. He set about finding someone to compile such a book, and one of his executives recommended the McWhirter brothers. Trivia history was made.

Norris and Ross McWhirter, identical twin sons of a newspaper writer, had grown up around newspapers, magazines, and reference books. Their childhood hobby had been to collect information of the very type Sir Hugh was seeking. They had frequently found contradictions in their sources, so as adults they had founded a company to verify these statistics and to "supply facts and figures to newspapers, yearbooks, encyclopedias, and advertisers."

Four months after Sir Hugh interviewed them, the McWhirters published the first book in the series. The 198-page "bet-settler" became England's all-time nonfiction bestseller in only four months. Immediately, readers began submitting their own fantastic facts. The McWhirters collected and checked these submissions, and soon an updated volume was on the way. Norris and Ross McWhirter served as coeditors until 1975.

QUOTATION: ON WRITING

It's not a bad idea to get in the habit of writing down one's thoughts. It saves one having to bother anyone else with them.

—Isabel Colegate

List of titles about artificial intelligence

Information about one book from the list of titles

Options for saving this page

Example of a Library of Congress book catalog keyword search

An entry in the library's book catalog contains a great deal of useful information: a book's title, author, publisher, date and place of publication, and length, along with its location in the library. A full record catalog entry (a complete set of information about the source rather than a brief listing that may have only author, title, and call number) lists additional subjects covered in that book. The list of additional subjects can provide valuable clues for further searching.

Some libraries allow you to print out this information, send it to your e-mail account, or download it to a disk. Whether you choose one of these options or copy the information yourself directly into your WORKING BIBLIOGRAPHY, it is crucial to record the **call number** exactly as it appears, with all numbers, letters, and decimal points. The call number tells where the book is located in the library's stacks (storage shelves). If you're researching in a library with *open stacks* (that is, you can go where books are shelved), the call number leads you to the area in the library where all books on the same subject can be found. Simply looking at what's on the shelves may yield useful sources. Keep in mind that in physically browsing the stacks, however, you're missing sources that other students likely have checked out or that are "on hold" at the library's reserve desk. The book catalog generally will contain information about whether a book is checked out or on reserve.

A call number is especially crucial in a library or special collection with *closed stacks* (that is, a library where you fill in a call slip, hand it in at the call desk, and wait for the book to arrive). Such libraries don't permit you to browse the stacks, so you have to rely entirely on the book catalog. If you fill in the wrong number or an incomplete number, your wait will be in vain.

32e How do I find periodicals?

Periodicals are magazines and journals published at set intervals during the year. To use periodicals efficiently, consult indexes to periodicals. These indexes allow you to search by subject and author. Most exist as online databases, which are updated frequently. Some indexes are published on CD-ROMs, and a few are published only in print.

Using indexes

Your library's home page generally provides different ways to access various indexes. One example is shown in the figure on the next page. Users who select "Show Databases" under "By Subject" will see an alphabetical list of subject areas, beginning "General Indexes, Agriculture, Anthropology, Art, Biography," and so on. When you choose a subject area, you'll see a list of all the databases for that area, as shown in the same figure. It's important to choose the right index for your search, because the wrong index may miss some of the best sources for your paper. The following paragraphs and boxes describe the contents of commonly used indexes.

Most indexes exist in electronic format. However, to use them you have to subscribe, which means pay a fee to search them. Fortunately,

HISTORY

Libraries are as old as recorded history. In fact, they were the repository of the records of past civilizations. In what was ancient Mesopotamia, for example, temples and princely houses have been excavated that held thousands of clay tablets inscribed with epic poems, liturgic and magic texts, and commercial records. The palace of Ashurbanipal, who reigned 668–633 BC in Nineveh, has provided tablets bearing stamps of ownership, catchwords, and sometimes source and place indications, thereby testifying to the existence of a well-developed cataloging system. In Egypt, every temple had its library and school. Although the Egyptian collections were made on papyrus (and thus have been found mostly in graves and tombs rather than in temples), the content was similar. Much has been lost, but records often remain. In the temple at Edfu, for instance, a full catalog of all the hieratical works the library contained was incised on the walls, bearing witness to what was once there.

List of article indexes
available at this library

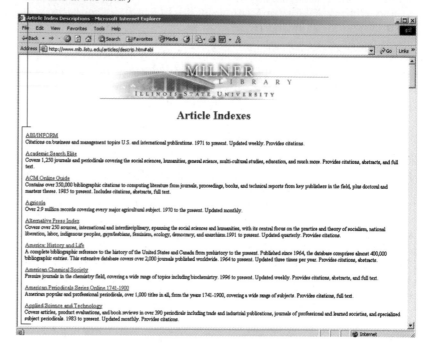

Listing of indexes that include relevant articles

your library likely subscribes to several of the indexes that you'll need, and you can access them through the library's Web site. The URL for accessing each index online will vary from college to college.

General indexes to periodicals list articles in journals, magazines, and newspapers. Large libraries have many general indexes. Find out how to log on by consulting the librarian in your college library. Among them are

- *The Readers' Guide to Periodical Literature* (online at *Readers' Guide Abstracts*) is the most well-known index, though its uses are limited for college-level research because it doesn't include scholarly journals. Some libraries still have the print volumes. This index includes over two hundred magazines and journals for general readers. Nevertheless, you can try it to find topics, get a broad overview, and narrow a subject. Chandra Johnson used this guide in the initial stages of her student research paper, shown in 34e.2.

- *Periodical Abstracts* indexes general and academic journals in business, current affairs, psychology, religion, and many other areas.

- *NewsBank* covers over four hundred U.S. newspapers. It has full-text coverage from 1993 on. NewsBank also offers reproductions of articles from 1980 to 1992, but they are stored on microfiche, not online, in some libraries.

Specialized indexes are more appropriate than general indexes for most college-level research. Specialized indexes list articles in journals published by and for expert, academic, or professional readers. Many specialized indexes include the abstract, or summary, that is printed at the beginning of each scholarly article. Box 138 provides examples of specialized indexes.

BOX 138   SUMMARY

 Examples of specialized indexes

Art Abstracts
Business Abstracts
Education Full Text
General Science Abstracts
Humanities Index
MLA International Bibliography of Books and Articles in the Modern
    Languages and Literatures
Music Index Online
PsycINFO
Social Sciences Abstracts

You search periodical indexes by using KEYWORDS. Shown on the next page are three screens from a keyword search of PsycINFO for *artificial intelligence*. Chandra Johnson, whose research paper appears in section 34e.2, consulted this source in her research.

Locating the articles themselves

Periodical indexes help you locate the titles of specific articles on your topic. Once you have the listing, though, how do you get your hands on the article itself? Sometimes you can find an online version of the article to read, copy to a disk, or print. Frequently, however, you need to find a paper copy of the periodical.

To do this, you begin by checking what periodicals your college library lists in its online catalogs. This list might be in the library's catalog, or the list might be available separately; ask how your library lists periodicals. In either case, search for the periodical name you want (for example, *American Literature* or *The Economist*), not for the article's

BACKGROUND

The retention and pass rates of underprepared writers may increase in classes where students learn and compose on computers, according to Smokey Wilson ("When Computers Come to English Class," TETYC, May 2000: 387–399). Wilson compares the retention and pass rates of two discussion-based and two computer-based classes and concludes that moving composition instruction to an online format in a workshop-style class has a measurable positive effect on student performance.

Keyword search

Partial search result

One article selected
from database

Three screens from a search of the PsycINFO database for sources on "artificial intelligence"

author or title. If your library subscribes to that periodical, you use its call number to find its location in the library. You then need to find the specific article you want by looking for the issue in which the article you're looking for is printed.

Few libraries subscribe to all the periodicals listed in specialized indexes. Although you may not be able to locate every periodical and article you find listed in the indexes, the interlibrary loan system (generally free of charge) or document delivery (generally at a small cost to the student) allows you to request that your library get it from another library (32g).

32f How do I use reference works?

Reference works include encyclopedias, almanacs, yearbooks, fact books, atlases, dictionaries, biographical reference works, and bibliographies. Some references are *general,* providing information on a vast number of subjects, but without any depth. Others are *specialized,* providing information on selected topics, often for more expert or professional audiences.

32f.1 General reference works

Reference works are the starting point for many college and other advanced researchers—but they're no more than a starting point. **General reference works** contain basic information and are therefore insufficient for academic research. Still, because they can give you an overall picture, they're one of the best places to find useful KEYWORDS for subject headings and online catalog searches. In addition, general reference works are excellent sources for finding examples and verifying facts. Most widely used reference works are available in electronic versions, either on CD-ROMs or, more commonly, online. Check your library's Web site to see if the reference work you want is available online through a subscription or license the library has purchased. Alternatively, you can search the Web by entering the work's name to see if it is available there. (For example, *Encyclopaedia Britannica* is at <http://www.britannica.com>.) Be aware that often you have to pay a fee for works you don't access through the library.

General encyclopedias

Articles in multivolume general encyclopedias, such as the *Encyclopaedia Britannica,* summarize information on a wide variety of subjects. The articles can give you helpful background information and the names of major figures and experts in the field. Best of all, many articles end with a brief bibliography of major works on the subject. General encyclopedias aren't the place to look for information on recent events or current research, although sometimes they cover a field's ongoing controversies up until the date that the reference was published.

To locate information in an encyclopedia, start with the index volume. (If you are using an online version, type the keywords into the search screen.) An index volume gives you the volume number or letter and the page numbers for your topic. The letters *bib* at the end of an index entry mean that the article contains a bibliography, which makes the entry especially worth checking for the additional sources it can lead you to. If you can't find what you are looking for, try alternative subject headings or KEYWORDS.

HISTORY

One of the most famous libraries of antiquity was the one at Alexandria, founded by Ptolemy I (c. 323–285 BC) and greatly augmented by his son and heir Ptolemy II Philadelphus (c. 285–247 BC) and his grandson Ptolemy III Euergetes (c. 247–221 BC). Manuscripts were imported from all parts of Greece and Asia, resulting in holdings that are estimated to have been as high as 700,000 papyrus rolls during the time of Julius Caesar (100–44 BC). Because of its riches, leading scholars of the Hellenistic world were drawn to it, resulting in a flurry of scholarly activity. Books were edited to a standard format, and systems of punctuation and accents were introduced. Textual scholarship, revisions of books to incorporate new knowledge, and the writing of new books went on constantly. Most of the books have been lost. Only works that were widely copied and distributed have managed to survive. As the political importance of Alexandria waned, the library suffered from neglect. Finally, in AD 270, much of it was razed, and a good part of the rest was destroyed by fire a century later.

HISTORY

Abdul Kassem Ismael (938–995), Grand Vizier of Persia, had a library of 117,000 volumes. When he traveled, he took his books along—all of them. He had four hundred camels trained to walk in order; the books they carried remained in strict alphabetical sequence. His camel drivers doubled as librarians.

Almanacs, yearbooks, fact books

Almanacs, yearbooks, and fact books are huge compilations of facts in many subject areas. They're often available both in print and online. They're excellent for verifying information from other sources and, in some cases, for finding supporting facts and figures on the subject you're investigating. Almanacs, such as *The World Almanac*, present capsule accounts of a year's events and data about government, politics, economics, science and technology, sports, and many other categories. *Facts on File*, which is indexed online by LexisNexis™, covers world events in a weekly digest and in an annual one-volume yearbook. The annual *Statistical Abstract of the United States* (accessed online through <http://www.census.gov>) contains a wealth of data on the United States. *Demographic Yearbook* and the *United Nations Statistical Yearbook* carry worldwide data.

Atlases and gazetteers

Atlases (such as *The Times Atlas of the World*) contain maps of our planet's continents, seas, and skies. Gazetteers (such as *The Columbia Gazetteer of the World,* available online for a fee at <http://www.columbiagazetteer.org>) provide comprehensive geographical information on topography, climates, populations, migrations, natural resources, crops, and so on.

Dictionaries

Dictionaries define words and terms. In addition to general dictionaries, specialized dictionaries exist in many academic disciplines to define words and phrases specific to a field.

Biographical reference works

Biographical reference books give brief factual information about famous people—their accomplishments along with pertinent events and dates in their lives. Biographical references include the *Who's Who* series, *The Dictionary of American Biography,* and many others. Specialized biographical references in various fields are also available.

Bibliographies

Bibliographies list books, articles, documents, films, and other resources and provide publication information so that you can find those sources. Some bibliographies are comprehensive and list sources on a wide range of topics. Others list only sources on a particular subject. Specialized bibliographies can be very helpful in your research process. Annotated or critical bibliographies describe and evaluate the works that they list. These resources are increasingly available online but require you either to access them through a library's paid subscription service or to pay a fee each time you use them.

32f.2 Specialized reference works

Specialized reference works provide more authoritative and specific information than do general reference works. Specialized reference works are usually appropriate for college-level research because the information is more advanced and detailed. They can be invaluable for introducing you to the controversies and KEYWORDS in a subject area. In particular, finding author's names in such books can help you begin to accumulate a list of credible authors.

Here are a few examples of specialized references:

Encyclopedia of Banking and Finance
Handbook of Modern Marketing
New Grove Dictionary of Music and Musicians
Oxford Companion to Art
Dictionary of American Biography
An Encyclopedia of World History
A Dictionary of Literary Terms
Oxford Companion to American Literature
Encyclopedia of Philosophy
Encyclopedia of Religion
Political Science Bibliographies
Encyclopedia of Chemistry
Encyclopedia of the Biological Sciences
Encyclopedia of Psychology
International Encyclopedia of Film
Oxford Companion to the Theatre

Because hundreds of one-volume works are highly specific (for example, *Encyclopedia of Divorce, Encyclopedia of Aging,* and *Encyclopedia Dictionary of Psychology*), I haven't listed them here. Check what specialized reference books your college library has available that might help you in your search.

32g What if my library doesn't have a source I need?

Almost no library owns every book on every topic or subscribes to every periodical. However, many libraries are connected electronically to other libraries' book catalogs, giving you access to additional holdings. Some states link their public and private colleges and universities into one system, and some libraries use the Internet to connect to colleges

BACKGROUND
In "Teaching About Plagiarism in the Age of the Internet" (*Teaching English in the Two-Year College,* December 1999: 209–212), Jeffrey Klausman claims that most students do not plagiarize intentionally. He offers a pedagogical approach for teaching students about plagiarism and the Internet.

and universities outside their state systems. Librarians can request materials from other libraries through interlibrary loan (generally free of charge). Alternatively, your college may have a different document delivery system (generally at a cost to you).

32h How do I find government documents?

Government publications are available in astounding variety. You can find information on laws and legal decisions, regulations, population, weather patterns, agriculture, national parks, education, and health, to name just a few topics. Since the middle 1990s, most government documents have been available through the World Wide Web. The Government Printing Office (GPO) maintains a *Catalog of U.S. Government Publications* online at <http://www.gpoaccess.gov/index.html>. The GPO site has a searchable database. Information about legislation is also available at the Web site THOMAS, a service of the Library of Congress, which you can access at <http://thomas.loc.gov/>. A directory of all federal government sites that provide statistical information is at <http://www.fedstats.gov>.

The LexisNexis database service provides access to a huge number of other governmental reports and documents. For example, it includes the *Congressional Information Service (CIS),* which indexes all papers produced by U.S. congressional panels and committees. These documents include the texts of hearings (for example, testimony about homelessness) and reports (for example, a comparative study of temporary shelters for homeless people).

32i What is field research?

Field research is primary research in that it involves going into real-life situations to observe, survey, interview, or be part of some activity firsthand. A field researcher might, for example, go to a factory, a lecture, a day care center, or a mall—anywhere that people are engaged in their everyday activities. A field researcher might also conduct interviews of experts and other identified individuals. Because field research yields original data, you can consider it a PRIMARY SOURCE.

Conducting field research takes advance planning. Be sure to allow time to gather the data you want, ANALYZE it, and then SYNTHESIZE it with other sources and with your own knowledge and experience. In general, the activity of field research makes selective notetaking difficult. Therefore, go over your notes right after your research session, while your memory is fresh, and highlight major categories of information. Also, fill in any details you might not have written down. What doesn't seem useful one day might become important later.

Field research many times involves events that can't be revisited. Therefore, record as much information as possible during your research and decide afterward what information you can use. If conditions make taking notes impossible (for example, a dark performance hall), the instant you have an opportunity, find a quiet place and write down notes as fully as you can.

DOCUMENTATION is as important for field research as it is for all other research. Interviews and some performances involve another person's words, concepts, and insights. To document correctly, use the guidelines in Chapter 33 for documenting quotations, paraphrases, and summaries. If you include your own work (creating an original questionnaire, for example), say that it's yours in your paper and list it, as you would any source, in the WORKS CITED (MLA style) or REFERENCES (APA style) at the end of your paper.

Observing and surveying

To observe effectively, you must avoid injecting yourself into the situation. You should try to remain objective so that you can see things clearly. A report from someone with a bias in one direction or another makes the material useless. For observations of behavior (for example, the audience at a sporting event or elementary school children at play during recess), you can take notes during the activity. Permission to videotape instead of taking notes is hard to get because of privacy concerns.

If you intend to go to an event such as a concert or a play, buy your tickets immediately and be ready with alternative dates if you can't get your first choice. Similarly, if you intend to visit a museum, go as soon as possible so that you can go back again as needed.

If you want to survey a group of people on an issue, allow time to write, reflect on, and revise a questionnaire. Provide time to test the questionnaire on a few people and revise ineffective or ambiguous questions. For detailed information on the mechanics of creating a questionnaire, see Box 173 in 41a.

Interviewing an expert

An expert can offer valuable information, a new point of view, and firsthand facts, statistics, and examples. Probably the best place to start is with the faculty at your college. Your teachers are also scholars and researchers who have expertise in many areas. They may suggest good print and online sources, as well as other experts to contact. Indeed, your family and friends might qualify as experts, if they have been involved in any way with an issue you are researching.

Make every attempt to conduct interviews in person so that you can observe body language and facial expressions as you talk. However, if distance is a problem, you can conduct interviews over the phone or online.

BACKGROUND
In "Copyrights and Conversations: Intellectual Property in the Classroom" (*Computers & Compositions* 15(2): 243–251), Janice R. Walker claims that writing instructors can help students arrive at an enhanced understanding of the nature of scholarship in the digital age by focusing on copyright issues when approaching rules of citation and prohibitions against plagiarism.

BACKGROUND
Current technology is capable of reading student texts for both stylistic elements and content, and educators and administrators are beginning to test software that grades papers. In their essay "What Happens When Machines Read Our Students' Writing?" (*College English,* March 2001: 480–499), Anne Herrington and Charles Moran survey the history of this type of technology and evaluate two grading programs, WritePlacer Plus and Intelligent Essay Assessor. Their conclusions are highly critical: "We have serious concerns about the potential effects of machine reading of student writing on our teaching, on our students' learning, and therefore on the profession of English" (495).

To interview someone in a large corporation or an institution (an insurance company or a hospital, for example), your best approach is to contact the public relations office or customer service department. Professional organizations, such as the American Bar Association (a lawyer group), often have special staff to respond to researchers. Also, public officials are sometimes available for interviews, and many federal and state government offices have full-time representatives to provide information to the public.

Perhaps even more than for other kinds of field research, you definitely need to plan far ahead for interviews. It takes time to set up an appointment so that you can fit your research needs into other people's schedules. Part of planning is having a solid knowledge of your topic—you don't want to waste others' time or try their patience by asking for information you should have gathered before the interview. Don't expect your interview to replace your doing research yourself.

Although you might not always be granted the interviews you seek, you can assume that many people remember their own experiences doing academic research, and they're open to trying to help. Box 139 provides specific suggestions for interviewing an expert.

BOX 139   CHECKLIST

 Taking notes during interviews

- Rehearse how to ask your questions without reading them (perhaps highlight the key word in red). Looking your interviewee in the eye as you ask questions is invaluable for establishing ease and trust. If you are interviewing on the telephone, be organized and precise.

- Create a shortcut symbol or letter for key terms you expect to hear during the interview. This cuts down on your time needed to look away from your interviewee.

- Take careful notes, listening especially for key names, books, or other print or online sources.

- Avoid using a tiny notebook or small sheets of paper. Standard 8½-by-11-inch paper allows you sufficient room to write without having to turn pages often.

- Bring extra pens (in case one runs out of ink) or pencils (in case one breaks).

- Never depend on tape recording an interview. People have become very reluctant to permit anyone to record them. If you want to ask permission in advance when you schedule the interview, or if you want to ask in person when you arrive for the interview, never imply

→

Taking notes during interviews (*continued*)

that recording is essential to you or the research. (Indeed, increasingly reports have reached instructors that when tape recording is mentioned, the interviewee cancels the appointment on the spot.)

■ If conditions make notetaking impossible, write detailed notes as soon afterward as you possibly can. In all cases, go over and fill in your notes while your memory is fresh so you can highlight major categories of information.

32j **How do I evaluate sources?**

Finding a source is only part of your effort. Your next step is to evaluate the quality of each source you find. First, decide whether the information in the source relates to your topic in more than a vague, general sense. Ask how a source might help you answer your research question (31c). Finally, using the criteria in Box 140, evaluate each source with a cold, critical eye.

The unregulated nature of the Web creates special responsibilities for online researchers. You need to evaluate Web sources particularly carefully for two reasons. First, since anyone can post anything on the

BACKGROUND
Many library Web sites contain suggestions for evaluating sources. You can find them by entering a search phrase like "evaluating sources" (or "resources") in a search engine. Examples of such suggestions are available at the following Web sites, active at the time this handbook went to press:

● *Thinking Critically About World Wide Web Resources*
  http://www.library.ucla.edu/libraries/college/help/critical/index.htm

● *Thinking Critically About Discipline-Based World Wide Web Resources*
  http://www.library.ucla.edu/libraries/college/help/critical/discipline.htm

● *Evaluating Web Resources*
  http://www2.widener.edu/Wolfgram-Memorial-Library/webevaluation/webeval.htm

---

BOX 140   SUMMARY

 Evaluating sources

1. **Is the source authoritative?** Generally, encyclopedias, textbooks, and academic journals (*The American Scholar, Journal of Counseling and Development*) are authoritative. Books published by university presses (Northwestern University Press) and by publishers that specialize in scholarly books are also trustworthy. Material published in newspapers, in general-readership magazines (*Newsweek, U.S. News and World Report*), and by large commercial publishers (Prentice Hall) may be reliable, but you want to apply the other criteria in this list with special care, cross-checking names and facts whenever possible. If the same information appears in different sources, it is likely reliable. Web sites maintained by professional organizations, such as the National Council of Teachers of English at <http://www.ncte.org>, are authoritative.

→

QUOTATION: ON RESEARCH
While place might determine what research methods are *possible,* the research question determines what research methods are *necessary.*

—Cindy Johanek

> ## Evaluating sources (*continued*)
>
> 2. **Is the author an expert?** Biographical material in the article or book may tell you if the author is an expert on the topic. Look up the author's expertise in a reputable, up-to-date biographical dictionary in your college library. Alternatively, enter the author's name in an Internet search engine. Look to see if the author has a degree in this field and whether he or she is affiliated with a reliable institution. Also, if an author is often cited by professionals in the field and published in journals, he or she is probably considered an expert.
>
> 3. **Is the source current?** Check the publication date. Research is ongoing in most fields, and information is often modified or replaced by new findings. Check databases and online subject directories to see if newer sources are available.
>
> 4. **Does the source support its information sufficiently?** Are its assertions or claims supported with sufficient evidence? If the author expresses a point of view but offers little evidence to back up that position or resorts to logical fallacies, reject the source. Use wise judgment, and don't take chances.
>
> 5. **Is the author's tone balanced?** Use your critical thinking skills when you evaluate a source (see Chapter 5). If the TONE is unbiased and the reasoning is logical, the source is probably useful.

Web, some sources you find may very well be plagiarized. Second, many sources on the Web have been written by individuals posing as experts and giving false or misleading information.

You are always accountable for the sources you choose. To evaluate a source, use the list in Box 140. These criteria can help you separate the sources you want to look at more closely from those not likely to be reputable. Most sites also contain material that will help you assess their credibility, such as a bibliography, links to the author or editor, or a description of the sponsoring organization. You want to discard sites that do not contain such verifying information, however useful they may seem. To err on the side of caution is far better than to use a corrupt source.

An important question to ask about any Web site is why the information exists and why it was put on the Internet. Be sure to question the motives of the site's author, especially if you are being asked to take a specific action. Box 141 summarizes the questions to ask about online sites.

Judging the reliability of an online site

Reliable sites are

- **From educational, not-for-profit, or government organizations.** One sign is an Internet address ending in *.edu, .org, .gov,* or a country abbreviation such as *.us* or *.uk.* However, if any of these organizations fail to list their sources, don't use them. After all, many colleges and universities now host student Web sites, which also end in *.edu.*

- **From expert authors.** Experts have degrees or credentials in their field that you can check. See if their names appear in other reliable sources, in bibliographies on your topic, or in reference books in your college's library. Check whether the site's author gives an e-mail address for questions or comments.

- **From reliable print sources.** Online versions of the *New York Times, Time* magazine, and other publications that are produced by the publisher are just as reliable as the print versions.

- **Well supported with evidence and presented in a balanced, unbiased fashion.**

- **Current or recently updated.**

Questionable sites are

- **From commercial organizations advertising to sell a product (*.com*); Web sites that are advertisements or personal pages; junk mail.** These sites may or may not list sources. If they fail to, don't use them. If they do, check that the sources are legitimate, not a front for some commercial enterprise.

- **From anonymous authors or authors without identifiable credentials.** Chat rooms, Usenet, discussion groups, bulletin boards, and similar networks are questionable because they don't give credentials or other qualifying information.

- **Second-hand excerpts and quotations.** Materials that appear on a site that is not the official site of the publisher (such as a quotation taken from the *New York Times*) may be edited in a biased or inaccurate manner. Such sources may be incomplete and inaccurate.

- **Unsupported or biased.** These sites carry declarations and assertions that have little or no supporting evidence.

- **Old** or from a Web site that hasn't been updated in a year or more.

QUOTATION: ON RESEARCH
I have come to believe that a scholar can be scholarly and still be ethically and pathetically connected to the subject.
—Jacqueline Jones Royster

QUOTATION: ON READING
You know, children, I don't read such small stuff as letters, I read men and nations.
—Sojourner Truth

Most sites also contain material that will help you assess their credibility, such as a bibliography or links to the author or editor. Sites that do not contain such verifying information should be discarded, however useful they may seem. It is far better to err on the side of caution than to use a plagiarized source. Box 142 gives you details on applying these general guidelines to individual online sources.

BOX 142   SUMMARY

 Evaluating each online source

Evaluating Authority

1. Is an author named? Are credentials listed for the author? (Look for an academic degree, an e-mail address at an academic or other institution, a credentials page, a list of publications. The last part of an e-mail address can be informative: *.edu* is an address at an educational site; *.gov* is an address at a government site; and *.com* is an address at a commercial or business site.) Be careful: Many colleges and universities now host student Web sites. These sites often end with *.edu,* as do regular academic sites.

2. Is the author recognized as an authority in reputable print sources? Is the author cited in any bibliographies found in print sources?

3. Do you recognize the author as an authority from other research on your topic? Is the site cross-referenced to other credible and authoritative sites?

Evaluating Reliability

4. Do you detect from the language or layout of information either bias or an unbalanced presentation?

5. Ask, Why does the information exist? Who gains from it? Why was it written? Why was it put on the Internet?

6. Are you asked to take action of any kind? If yes, don't use the source unless you're sure the site isn't trying to manipulate you toward its bias. For example, the World Wildlife Fund can ask for contributions and still maintain a Web site that contains reliable information. Conversely, a hate group can't be trusted to be objective.

7. Is the material outdated? Is the date recent, or was the last update recent?

8. Does the author give an e-mail address for questions or comments?

→

Evaluating each online source (*continued*)

Evaluating Value

9. Is the information well supported with evidence? Or do the authors express points of view without backing up their position with solid evidence?

10. Remember to read online sources using reflective reading (5c and 5d) and reasoning (5a and 5b). Is the TONE unbiased (5c.2 and 21g) and the reasoning logical (5i and 5j)?

Chapter 33

Using Sources and Avoiding Plagiarism

33a How do I use sources well?

Now's the time to turn from researching to writing your research paper. When you use SOURCES well, your chances of writing a successful research paper increase greatly. In your work so far, you've built a solid foundation by choosing a research-suitable TOPIC, one that's neither too general nor too narrow (31b); formulating a RESEARCH QUESTION (31c); establishing a search strategy for finding sources to answer that question (32b); locating sources that apply to your particular treatment of the topic (32c–32h); writing a WORKING BIBLIOGRAPHY of what you've found (31i); evaluating each source carefully to make sure it's reliable and trustworthy (32j); and taking CONTENT NOTES on the sources that have passed your careful evaluation (31j).

Now you're ready to use CRITICAL THINKING to pull together a SYNTHESIS of your sources combined with your own thinking about the topic. To synthesize well, you think through the information gathered from your sources by

- Mastering the information from each source
- Finding relationships among the sources' information
- Adding your own thinking to the mix

Your written synthesis is your research paper. To write effectively, you organize your paper around a logical sequence based on the main points in your synthesis. Further, you want to support each main point and important subpoint with specific ideas or words drawn from your sources to show that your claims originate with authorities on your topic.

As you marshal your support, keep the RENNS formula, discussed in 4f, in mind: Be specific by using **R**easons, **E**xamples, **N**ames, **N**umbers, and the five **S**enses. Also, if your PURPOSE is persuasive rather than informative, remember to present opposing viewpoints evenhandedly and then refute them reasonably (6k).

A successful research paper relies on your drawing from your sources. You integrate suitable material into your paper by using QUOTATIONS (33h), PARAPHRASES (33i), and SUMMARIES (33j), while always being sure to avoid PLAGIARISM. Your SOURCE-BASED WRITING needs to be

- Accurate
- Effective
- Honest (the only way to avoid plagiarism)

The final step in using sources well is to use correct documentation (Chapters 34–36). **Documentation** means making two types of entries in your research paper each time you draw upon a source for support:

1. Writing a parenthetical citation for each quotation, paraphrase, and summary you take from sources (for examples in MLA STYLE, see section 34c).
2. Composing a WORKS CITED list, MLA's name for a BIBLIOGRAPHY for the end of your paper. This list needs to include full bibliographic information on each source from which you have quoted, paraphrased, and summarized in your paper (for examples in MLA style, see 34d).

Today's bibliographies differ from those of the past. The root word *biblio-* means "book," so traditionally, the bibliographic information referred to a book's title, author, publisher, and place and year of publication. Now that the age of the Internet, CD-ROMs, and other technologies is here, researchers include in their bibliographies all the sources they've used not only in print but also from the various technologies.

A **documentation style** refers to a specific system for providing information on sources used in a research paper. Documentation styles vary among the disciplines. This handbook presents five documentation styles in Chapters 34–36, as shown in Box 143.

BOX 143　SUMMARY

Where to find the MLA, APA, CM, CSE, and COS information you need

MLA Style: Red Tab, Chapter 34

- MLA parenthetical citations: 34b–34c
- Guidelines for compiling an MLA-style Works Cited list (Box 151): 34d
- Directory of MLA Works Cited list models: 34d.1
- Content or other notes with MLA parenthetical documentation: 34d.2

→

TEACHING TIP
In the belief that most students who plagiarize from their sources do so because they don't know how to avoid the problem, Kathleen Mouton has devised a technique that can be demonstrated in class to help students avoid taking notes that are too close to the words of the source. She suggests that instructors ask students to read a short, informative passage of material and then put it away and make notes from memory. Students can check afterward to make sure that facts (such as dates and names) are correct. With larger amounts of material, students can stop frequently to make their notes, still being careful not to look at the source while recording each note.

BACKGROUND
In "The Long and Short of It," Robert F. Hogan, the late former executive director of the National Council of Teachers of English, gives the etymology of the word *plagiarism.* Hogan writes, "The word stems from *plaga,* the Latin word for hunting net. One particular use for such a net was *plagium*—the snaring and capturing of another's slave or child." In the sixteenth century, the meaning evolved in English "to include stealing another person's words or ideas."

In 2003, the National Council of Writing Program Administrators (WPA) adopted a position paper, "Defining and Avoiding Plagiarism: The WPA Statement on Best Practices." The document is available at <http://wpacouncil.org>. Authored by a blue-ribbon panel, it defines plagiarism in instructional contexts as occurring "when a writer deliberately uses someone else's language, ideas, or other original (not common-knowledge) material without acknowledging its source." WPA advises faculty not to label as plagiarizers the student "who attempts (even if clumsily) to identify and credit his or her source, but who misuses a specific citation format or incorrectly uses quotation marks or other forms of identifying materials taken from other sources." Certainly, such a student has produced writing that doesn't follow proper conventions, and in the same way that writing →

Background (continued)

with excessive grammatical errors would warrant a lower grade, so too would poor citation practices.

The WPA Statement notes that students plagiarize for a number of reasons. Students often fear failure and risk-taking in a culture that emphasizes grades; they often have poor time-management skills and therefore rush writing projects; some may view the assignment or the consequences of cheating as unimportant; some may come from cultural backgrounds where students incorporate other writers' language very differently, and so on.

The WPA Statement offers ways for educators to prevent plagiarism. In addition to having a clear policy that students understand and can follow, and in addition to providing students with ample opportunities to learn about citation practices, this document suggests that instructors not use "recycled or formulaic assignments that may invite stock or plagiarized responses." Asking that students generate process assignments toward the final paper, including early drafts, peer responses, and analyses of their own work, will also help students write documents that are difficult to plagiarize.

**TEACHING TIP: STOPPING
PLAGIARISM BEFORE IT HAPPENS**
Techniques for plagiarism-proofing assignments are plentiful: requiring submission, in the student's own handwriting, of working bibliographies, note cards, outlines, and rough drafts; assigning unusual topics and changing them every semester; replacing the semester-long research project with several shorter ones to prevent students from having time to contact research-paper mills; limiting research to the use of a particular casebook. All of these efforts work to some degree, but at the price of turning us into thought police, ever on the alert for the student who might find a way around our system. We take on extra stress and extra paperwork—and students continue to think of us as fussy creatures who demand they follow rituals

➜

Where to find the MLA, APA, CM, CSE, and COS information you need *(continued)*

APA Style: Blue Tab, Chapter 35
- APA in-text citations: 35b–35c
- Guidelines for compiling an APA-style References list (Box 152): 35f
- Directory of APA References list models: 35f
- Abstracts and content notes: 35d–35e

CM Style: Green Tab, Chapter 36
- Guidelines for compiling CM-style bibliographic notes (Box 153): 36a
- Directory of CM-style bibliographic note models: 36b

CSE Style: Purple Tab, Chapter 36
- Guidelines for compiling a CSE-style Cited References list (Box 154): 36c
- Directory of CSE-style list of references models: 36d

COS: Yellow Tab, Chapter 36
- COS parenthetical citations: 36e
- Differences between print and online publication in COS bibliographic notes: 36e
- Guidelines for compiling a COS Works Cited list (Box 155): 36f

33b What is plagiarism?

To **plagiarize** is to present another person's words or ideas as if they were your own. Plagiarism, like stealing, is a form of academic dishonesty or cheating. Because it's a serious offense, plagiarism can be grounds for a failing grade or expulsion from college.

33c How do I avoid plagiarism?

Here's how to avoid plagiarism. First, understand that researchers use sources carefully by honestly and suitably QUOTING (33h), PARAPHRASING (33i), and SUMMARIZING (33j) their ideas and words—a popular memory device for this is **Use QPS.** Second, become comfortable with the concept of DOCUMENTATION, which you need to use each time you quote, paraphrase, and summarize your sources. Box 144 describes the main strategies you can use to avoid plagiarism.

BOX 144   SUMMARY

 Strategies for avoiding plagiarism

- Use DOCUMENTATION to acknowledge your use of the ideas or phrasings of others, taken from the sources you've compiled on your topic.

- Become thoroughly familiar with the documentation style that your instructor tells you to use for your research paper (Chapters 34–36). To work efficiently, make a master list of the information required to document all sources that you quote, paraphrase, or summarize according to your required documentation style.

- Write down absolutely all the documentation facts that you'll need for your paper, keeping careful records as you search for sources. Otherwise, you'll waste much time trying to retrace your steps to get a documentation detail you missed.

- Use a consistent system for taking CONTENT NOTES. Perhaps use different colors of ink or another coding system to keep these three uses of sources separate:

  1. Quotations from a source (require documentation)
  2. Material paraphrased or summarized from a source (requires documentation)
  3. Thoughts of your own triggered by what you've read or experienced in life (no documentation required), making sure to maintain the distinction between your own thinking and the ideas that come directly from a source

- Write clear, perhaps oversize, quotation marks when you're directly quoting a passage. Make them so distinct that you can't miss seeing them later.

- Consult with your instructor if you're unsure about any phase of the documentation process.

Box 145 on the next page lists major types of plagiarism, all of which you can avoid by following the advice in Box 144.

Never assume that your instructor can't detect plagiarism. Instructors have keen eyes for writing styles different from the ones students

Teaching Tip: Stopping Plagiarism Before It Happens (continued)
peculiar to English classes. If we are to stop wasting energy tracking down plagiarized passages in the library stacks, we need to take steps to counter the mixed signals about plagiarism that our students have received over the years—and continue to receive.

In a survey of fourteen first-year composition classes at Brigham Young University, Doris R. Dant found that 17 percent of the students reported being advised by their high school teachers to copy "the information word for word from other sources." Dant also found that there was a correlation between the number of teachers who taught when to document sources and the students' avoidance of plagiarism. Students who reported that *all* their teachers explained how to credit sources were far more likely to understand the concept of plagiarism and to avoid copying reports than those students who received such instruction from just a few of their teachers.

Only 47 percent of the students questioned understood, when they were seniors in high school, how to write an unplagiarized report. Among the untrained students, some felt that putting ideas into their own words and providing a bibliography (no parenthetical references or footnotes) was sufficient. Others felt that copying was fine, provided that they supplied footnotes, parenthetical references, or a bibliography (no quotation marks). Almost 6 percent had no idea what the word *plagiarism* meant. Not surprisingly, over 60 percent of the students in these groups reported having copied high school reports.

Some students, however, consciously plagiarize to receive higher grades, and you may want to devote class time to a discussion of the ethics of plagiarism. To start the discussion, you might report that in a survey of 150 first-year Indiana University students, Barry M. Kroll found that most respondents regarded plagiarism as a violation of one's responsibility to do one's own work, as a failure to give authors just credit for their work, or as →

Teaching Tip: Stopping Plagiarism
Before It Happens (continued)
theft of someone's ideas. Few students identified deliberate plagiarism as lying, fraud, or a
betrayal of trust, which are issues, Kroll believes, that students need to consider in a
class discussion.

TEACHING TIP

In "Beyond 'Gotcha!': Situating Plagiarism in
Policy and Pedagogy" (*CCC*, September
2002: 85–115), Margaret Price examines current scholarship about this academic issue
and calls for a contextual approach to plagiarism. Price includes practices she uses to
help her students understand plagiarism as a
"context-specific phenomena."

TEACHING TIP

To give your students practice in notetaking
before they are assigned research paper topics, you might distribute copies of a newspaper or magazine article on a popular subject
and ask your students to take notes in support
of a particular thesis.

Once they (and you) are sure of their
skills, the students can move on to more complex issues with confidence, but at first they
should keep to popular subjects that interest
them.

Encourage students to paraphrase, summarize, and quote as they feel necessary and
to take as many (or as few) notes as they feel
would be useful in supporting a thesis. Then,
collect their notes and distribute copies of all
or some sets of notes. As a class (or in
groups), discuss the notes one set at a time.

1. Do all the notes support the thesis?

2. Are paraphrases accurate?

3. Are summaries accurate?

4. Are quotations appropriate and accurate?

5. Are quoted words within paraphrases and
summaries placed in quotation marks?

6. Would any material be better presented in
a different kind of note?

BOX 145   **SUMMARY**

 Types of plagiarism

You're plagiarizing if you do any of the following:

- Buy a paper from an Internet site, another student or writer, or any other source

- Turn in any paper that someone else has written, whether it was given to you, you downloaded it from the Internet, or you copied it from any other source

- Change selected parts of an existing paper, and claim the paper as your own

- Combine the ideas from many sources and claim that they're your own thoughts

- Use general or specific ideas from a source without using full and correct documentation telling where you got the ideas

- Copy or paste into your paper any KEY TERMS, PHRASES, sentences, or longer passages from another source without using documentation to tell precisely where the material came from

- Neglect to put quotation marks around words that you quote directly from a source, even if you document the source

---

generally produce and from your own style in particular. In addition, instructors can access Web sites that electronically check your submitted
work against all material available online. Further, Internet sites such as
<http://www.turnitin.com> allow instructors to check your writing
against hundreds of thousands of papers for free or for sale on the World
Wide Web and the Internet. (Also, that site adds your paper to its huge
database of student papers so that no one can plagiarize your work.)
Moreover, when instructors receive papers that they suspect contain
plagiarized passages, they can check with other professors to see whether
a student paper looks familiar.

Another important way to avoid plagiarism is to dive willingly into
any interim tasks your instructors build into their research assignments.
These tasks can help you enormously as you conduct your research and
write your paper. For example, many instructors today set interim deadlines such as a date for handing in a WORKING BIBLIOGRAPHY (31i), a list
of all documentation details for sources you've located in your search
but haven't yet evaluated for their value and reliability. Another possible
assignment is to prepare an **annotated bibliography,** which includes
all documentation information and a brief summary or commentary on

each source that you've evaluated (32j) as trustworthy and useful for your research paper. Further, some instructors want to read and coach you about how to improve one or more of your research paper drafts. In some cases, they might want to look over your research log (31e), content notes (31j), and/or photocopies of your sources.

33d How do I work with the Internet to avoid plagiarism?

The Internet can both greatly help researchers and create potential new problems. One problem is that the Internet allows anyone to say anything, so many Internet sources lack reliability and aren't legitimate for research purposes (32j). The second problem is that students might plagiarize more readily from Internet sources.

For example, you might be tempted to download a completed research paper from the Internet. *Don't.* That's intellectual dishonesty, which can get you into real trouble not only with your instructor but also with the college. Or you might be tempted to borrow wording from what you wrongly consider an "obscure" Internet source. *Don't.* Not only is this intellectual dishonesty, but instructors will easily detect it (33c). Box 146 provides guidelines for avoiding plagiarism of Internet sources.

BOX 146   SUMMARY

Guidelines for avoiding plagiarizing from the Internet

- Never cut and paste directly into your paper from online sources. You can too easily lose track of what language is your own and what material came from a source. You'll need to document each item.

- Keep downloaded or printed Internet sources in computer files that are separate from your draft, whether you intend to draw upon the sources as quotations, summaries, or paraphrases. Be extremely careful about how you manage those copies. Whenever you know the exact place where you think an item would fit in your paper, record that location very clearly (use another color or a much larger font), but never paste it in.

- Make sure that you write every detail of information that identifies the source and is called for in the documentation style you need to use.

→

EXTRA EXERCISE A

Which of the following statements should be documented, and which need not be documented?

1. The Declaration of Independence was issued in 1776.

2. The sediments on the ocean floor are the accumulation of silt carried by rivers to the sea, volcanic dust, coastal sands, and discarded shells of living creatures.

3. Levi Strauss, the inventor of blue jeans, came to the United States from Germany in 1848.

4. Coca-Cola is a popular soft drink all around the world.

5. According to Germaine Greer, the reason few women artists have achieved greatness is that they have historically internalized their oppression, thereby draining the energy required for creative work.

6. The United States is a substantially less secure society today than it was forty years ago.

7. The Olympic Games are held every four years.

8. The initials GDP stand for the term *gross domestic product.*

9. As a society, we should read poetry because it makes us live more fully and live more deeply.

10. Henry David Thoreau lived at Walden Pond for two years.

Guidelines for avoiding plagiarizing from the Internet (*continued*)

- If you're taking CONTENT NOTES (31j) in a computer file, copy or paste material onto a blank page if you intend to use it as a direct quotation from a printed or downloaded source. Make certain to place quotation marks around the quoted material and to include proper documentation. Do this at the moment you copy or paste the quotation. If you put off documenting until later, you may forget to do it or get it wrong. Also, in a different font or color, type your reason for thinking the quotation might be useful.

- SUMMARIZE or PARAPHRASE materials *before* you include them in your paper. If for the sake of convenience you've printed or downloaded Internet sources into separate files, never copy directly from those files into your paper. On the spot, summarize or paraphrase the sources.

- QUOTE carefully if you decide you must quote a passage directly from a source. Make sure to use quotation marks; perhaps signal with a different font or color that you have quoted.

- Keep all documentation information together as you work with each source. Then, at the very moment you put a quote, paraphrase, or summary in your paper, enter all documentation information in a parenthetical citation and in your bibliography. Never put this off until later, because the details might slip your mind, you might forget to do the documentation entirely, or you might get it wrong as you try to reconstruct your thinking.

- If you think that you may have plagiarized by mistake, check your work against papers and files on the Internet. Try typing one or two sentences—always putting them in quotation marks—into the search window at google.com. You might also submit your work to one of the for-profit plagiarism-detection services. These for-profit services charge you money for their work, and they also keep a copy of your paper in their databases.

33e   What don't I have to document?

You don't have to document common knowledge or your own thinking. **Common knowledge** is information that most educated people know, although they may need to remind themselves of certain facts by looking up information in a reference book. For example, here are a few facts of common knowledge that you don't need to document.

- Bill Clinton was the U.S. president before George W. Bush.
- Mercury is the planet closest to the sun.
- Normal human body temperature is 98.6°F.
- All the oceans on our planet contain salt water.

Sometimes, of course, a research paper doesn't contain common knowledge. For example, Chandra Johnson, whose research paper appears in Chapter 34, had only very general common knowledge about the broad topic of artificial intelligence. She had even less knowledge of her narrowed topic, "emotions and artificial intelligence." Johnson's research paper consists of some of her common knowledge. For example, she had seen the movie *A.I. Artificial Intelligence* and knew its plot, and she also knew about the *Star Trek* television series and the character of Mr. Spock. However, most of her paper consists of ideas and information that she quotes, paraphrases, and summarizes from sources.

A very important component of a research paper that doesn't need documentation is **your own thinking,** which is based on what you've learned as you built on what you already knew about your topic. It consists of your ANALYSIS, SYNTHESIS, and interpretation of new material as you read or observe it. You don't have to document your own thinking. Your own thinking helps you formulate a THESIS STATEMENT and organize your research paper by composing TOPIC SENTENCES that carry along your presentation of information. For example, suppose that you're drawing on an article about the connections between emotions and logic in people. While reading the article, you come to a personal conclusion that computers can't have emotions. This idea is not stated anywhere in the article you are reading or in any other source you use. Obviously, you need to cite the ideas from the article that led to your conclusion, but you don't need to cite your own thinking. On the other hand, if you find a source that states this very idea, you must cite it.

33f What must I document?

You must document everything that you learn from a source. This includes ideas as well as specific language. Expressing the ideas of others in your own words doesn't release you from the obligation to tell exactly where you got those ideas—you need to use complete, correct documentation. Here's an example in action:

SOURCE

Searle, John R. "I Married a Computer." Rev. of *The Age of Spiritual Machines,* by Ray Kurzweil. *New York Review of Books* 8 Apr. 1999: 34+. [This source information is arranged in MLA documentation style.]

ORIGINAL (SEARLE'S EXACT WORDS)

We are now in the midst of a technological revolution that is full of surprises. No one thirty years ago was aware that one day household computers would become as common as dishwashers. And those of us who used the old Arpanet of twenty years ago had no idea that it would evolve into the Internet. [This appears on page 37 of the source.]

PLAGIARISM EXAMPLE (UNDERLINED WORDS ARE PLAGIARIZED)

The current technological revolution is surprising. Thirty years ago, no one expected computers to be as common today as air conditioners. What once was the Arpanet has evolved into the Internet, and no one expected that.

Even though the student changed some wording in the example above, the ideas aren't original to that student. To avoid plagiarism, the student is required to document the source.

CORRECT EXAMPLE (USING QUOTATION, PARAPHRASE, AND DOCUMENTATION)

John Searle states that we live in a technologically amazing time of change in which computers have "become as common as dishwashers" (37). Twenty years ago, no one could have predicted the Arpanet would become the Internet (37). [This citation is arranged in MLA documentation style.]

The writer of the example above has used Searle's ideas properly through a combination of quotation and paraphrase and documentation. She correctly quotes the phrase "become as common as dishwashers." She paraphrases the statement "We are now in the midst of a technological revolution that is full of surprises," rephrasing it as "we live in a technologically amazing time of change." She also paraphrases the sentence "And those of us who used the old Arpanet of twenty years ago had no idea that it would evolve into the Internet" as "Twenty years ago, no one could have predicted the Arpanet would become the Internet." Finally, she gives the author's name in the sentence and twice includes parenthetical citations, which would lead the reader to find the source on the WORKS CITED page. Sections 33g through 33j explain exactly how to use sources effectively and document correctly.

33g How can I effectively integrate sources into my writing?

Integrating sources means blending information and ideas from others with your own writing. Before trying to integrate sources into your writing, you need to have ANALYZED and then SYNTHESIZED the material. Analysis requires you to break ideas down into their component parts so that you can think them through separately. The best time to do this is while you're reading your sources and taking CONTENT NOTES. Synthesis requires you to make connections among different ideas, seeking relationships and connections that tie them together.

33h How can I use quotations effectively?

A **quotation** is the exact words of a source enclosed in quotation marks. You face conflicting demands when you use quotations in your writing. Although quotations provide support, you can lose coherence in your paper if you use too many quotations. If more than a quarter of your paper consists of quotations, you've probably written what some people call a "cut and paste special"—merely stringing together a bunch of quotations. Doing so gives your readers—including instructors—the impression that you've not bothered to develop your own thinking, and you're letting other people do your talking.

In addition to avoiding too many quotations, you also want to avoid using quotations that are too long. Readers tend to skip over long quotations and lose the drift of the paper. Also, your instructor might assume that you just didn't take the time required to PARAPHRASE or SUMMARIZE the material. Generally, summaries and paraphrases are more effective for reconstructing someone else's argument. If you do need to quote a long passage, make absolutely sure every word in the quotation counts. Edit out irrelevant parts, using ellipsis points to indicate deleted material (29d and 33h.1). Box 147 provides guidelines for using quotations. Sections 33h.1 and 33h.2 give examples of acceptable and unacceptable quotations.

QUOTATION: ON WRITING
I often quote myself. It adds spice to my conversation.

—George Bernard Shaw

BOX 147   SUMMARY

 Guidelines for using quotations

1. Use quotations from authorities on your subject to support or refute what you write in your paper.
2. Never use a quotation to present your THESIS STATEMENT or TOPIC SENTENCES.
3. Select quotations that fit your message. Choose a quotation only in these cases:
   - Its language is particularly appropriate or distinctive.
   - Its idea is particularly hard to paraphrase accurately.
   - The authority of the source is especially important to support your thesis or main point.
   - The source's words are open to interpretation.

→

Guidelines for using quotations (*continued*)

4. Never use quotations in more than a quarter of your paper. Instead, rely on paraphrase (33i) and summary (33j).
5. Quote accurately. Always check each quotation against the original source—and then recheck it.
6. Integrate quotations smoothly into your writing.
7. Avoid PLAGIARISM (33b–d).
8. Enter all DOCUMENTATION precisely and carefully.

33h.1 Making quotations fit smoothly with your sentences

When you use quotations, the greatest risk you take is that you'll end up with incoherent, choppy sentences. You can avoid this problem within each sentence, when the words you quote fit smoothly with three aspects of the rest of your sentence: grammar, style, and logic. Based on the source material that follows, examine these examples.

SOURCE
Goleman, Daniel. *Emotional Intelligence.* New York: Bantam, 1995. 9.
[This source information is arranged in MLA documentation style.]

ORIGINAL (GOLEMAN'S EXACT WORDS)
These two minds, the emotional and the rational, operate in tight harmony for the most part, intertwining their very different ways of knowing to guide us through the world.

INCOHERENT GRAMMAR PROBLEM
Goleman explains how the emotional and rational <u>minds "intertwining</u> their very different ways of knowing to guide us through the world" (9). [Corrected: Goleman explains the process of emotional and rational minds "intertwine their very different ways of knowing to guide us through the world" (9).]

INCOHERENT STYLE PROBLEM
Goleman explains how the <u>emotional minds based on reason</u> work together by "intertwining their very different ways of knowing to guide us through the world" (9). [Corrected: Goleman explains how the emotional and rational minds work together by "intertwining their very different ways of knowing to guide us through the world" (9).]

INCOHERENT LOGIC PROBLEM

Goleman explains how the emotional and rational minds <u>work together by</u> "their very different ways of knowing to guide us through the world" (9). [Corrected: Coleman explains how the emotional and rational minds work together by combining "their very different ways of knowing to guide us through the world" (9).]

CORRECT USE OF THE QUOTATION

Goleman explains how the emotional and rational minds work together by "intertwining their very different ways of knowing to guide us through the world" (9). [This citation is arranged in MLA documentation style.]

After writing sentences that contain quotations, read the material aloud and listen to whether the language flows smoothly and gracefully. Perhaps you need to add a word or two placed in brackets (29c) within the quotation so that its wording works grammatically and effortlessly with the rest of your sentence. Of course, make sure your bracketed additions don't distort the meaning of the quotation. For example, the following quotation comes from the same page of the source quoted above. The bracketed material explains what *these minds* refer to in the original quotation—this helps the reader understand what was clear in the context of the original source but isn't clear when quoted in isolation.

ORIGINAL (GOLEMAN'S EXACT WORDS)

In many or most moments, these minds are exquisitely coordinated; feelings are essential to thought, thought to feeling.

QUOTATION WITH EXPLANATORY BRACKETS

"In many or most moments, these minds [emotional and rational] are exquisitely coordinated; feelings are essential to thought, thought to feeling" (Goleman 9). [This citation is arranged in MLA documentation style.]

Another way to create a smooth integration of a quotation in your sentence is to delete some words, always using an ellipsis where the deletion occurs. You also might delete any part of the quotation that interferes with conciseness and the focus you intend in your sentence. When you use an ellipsis, make sure that the remaining words accurately reflect the source's meaning and that your sentence structure still flows smoothly. The original of the following quotation appears on page 548.

QUOTATION WITH ELLIPSIS

Goleman contends that, generally, "these two minds, the emotional and the rational, operate in tight harmony . . . to guide us through the world" (9). [This citation is arranged in MLA documentation style.]

QUOTATION: ON WRITING

You could compile the worst book in the world entirely out of selected passages from the best writers in the world.

—G. K. Chesterton

In the example above, the words "for the most part, intertwining their very different ways of knowing" have been deleted from the original material so that the quotation is more concise and focused.

33h.2 Using quotations to enhance meaning

Perhaps the biggest complaint instructors have about student research papers is that sometimes quotations are simply stuck in, for no apparent reason. Whenever you place words between quotation marks, they take on special significance for your message as well as your language. Without context-setting information in the paper, the reader can't know exactly what logic leads the writer to use a particular quotation.

Furthermore, always make sure your readers know who said each group of quoted words. Otherwise, you've used a *disembodied quotation* (some instructors call them "ghost quotations"). Although quotation marks set off someone else's words, they need explanation and context, or they'll tell the reader nothing about who is being quoted and why. This reflects poorly on the clarity of your writing.

SOURCE

Wright, Karen. "Times of Our Lives." *Scientific American* Sept. 2002: 58–66. [This source information is arranged in MLA documentation style.]

ORIGINAL (WRIGHT'S EXACT WORDS)

In human bodies, biological clocks keep track of seconds, minutes, days, months and years.

INCORRECT (DISEMBODIED QUOTATION)

The human body has many subconscious processes. People don't have to make their hearts beat or remind themselves to breathe. "In human bodies, biological clocks keep track of seconds, minutes, days, months and years" (Wright 66).

CORRECT

The human body has many subconscious processes. People don't have to make their hearts beat or remind themselves to breathe. However, other processes are less obvious and perhaps more surprising. Karen Wright observes, for example, "In human bodies, biological clocks keep track of seconds, minutes, days, months and years" (66).

Rarely can a quotation begin a paragraph effectively. Start your paragraph by relying on your TOPIC SENTENCE, based on your own thinking. Then, you can fit in a relevant quotation somewhere in the paragraph, if it supports or extends what you have said.

Another strategy for working quotations smoothly into your paper is to integrate the name(s) of the author(s), the source title, or other information into your paper. You can prepare your reader for a quotation using one of these methods:

- Mention in your sentence directly before or after the quotation the name(s) of the author(s) you're quoting.
- Mention in your sentence the title of the work you're quoting from.
- Give additional authority to your material. If the author of a source is a noteworthy figure, you gain credibility when you refer to his or her credentials.
- Mention the name(s) of the author(s), with or without the name of the source and any author credentials, along with your personal introductory lead-in to the material.

Here are examples of the methods listed above. They use author names and source titles effectively.

SOURCE

Gardner, Howard. *The Disciplined Mind: What All Students Should Understand.* New York: Simon & Schuster, 1999. 72. [This source information is arranged in MLA documentation style.]

ORIGINAL (GARDNER'S EXACT WORDS)

While we all possess all of the intelligences, perhaps no two persons—not even identical twins—exhibit them in the same combination of strengths.

INTEGRATING AUTHOR'S NAME WITH QUOTATION

Howard Gardner explains, "While we all possess all of the intelligences, perhaps no two persons—not even identical twins—exhibit them in the same combination of strengths" (72). [This citation is arranged in MLA documentation style.]

INTEGRATING AUTHOR'S NAME AND SOURCE TITLE

Howard Gardner explains in *The Disciplined Mind: What All Students Should Understand:* "While we all possess all of the intelligences, perhaps no two persons—not even identical twins—exhibit them in the same combination of strengths" (72). [This citation is arranged in MLA documentation style.]

INTEGRATING AUTHOR'S NAME, CREDENTIALS, AND SOURCE TITLE

Howard Gardner, a psychologist and the author of fifteen books on the human mind, states in *The Disciplined Mind: What All Students Should*

QUOTATION: ON WRITING

I quote others only the better to express myself.

—Montaigne

ANSWERS: EXERCISE 33-1

1. *Analysis:* Quotation does not relate clearly to the sentence it follows. A traditional introduction to the quotation is needed. *Acceptable version* (answers will vary): Scientists are learning more about how people learn languages, which is an ability unique among all the animal kingdom. For example, "human beings differ from chimpanzees in having complex, grammatical language" (Ridley 60).

2. *Analysis:* Quotation omits several words but does not indicate where material has been deleted. *Acceptable version* (answers will vary): People might assume that individuals can acquire speaking abilities through hard individual work, "but language . . . must be learned from other language-speaking human beings" (Ridley 60).

3. *Analysis:* Sentence is grammatically incorrect. The quotation does not fit with the rest of the sentence. The first part of the sentence should be revised so that the information flows smoothly. *Acceptable version* (answers will vary): The language learning process is enabled "by genes that open and close a critical window during which language takes place" (Ridley 60).

4. *Analysis:* Tense of the verb in the quotation is incorrect. Brackets can be used to change the tense of the verb in the quotation so that it is grammatically correct, or the quotation might begin later. *Acceptable version* (answers will vary): In 2002, one gene important for language development was "discovered on human chromosome 7 by Anthony Monaco and his colleagues" (Ridley 60).

5. *Analysis:* Quotation is inaccurate. The writer substitutes "children" and "they" for "a child" and "he or she." *Acceptable version* (answers will vary): Parents should continually read to and speak with young children, because "if the child is not exposed to a lot of spoken language during the critical learning period, he or she will always struggle with speech" (Ridley 60).

Understand, "While we all possess all of the intelligences, perhaps no two persons—not even identical twins—exhibit them in the same combination of strengths" (72). [This citation is arranged in MLA documentation style.]

INTEGRATING AUTHOR'S NAME WITH YOUR OWN THINKING AS INTRODUCTORY ANALYSIS

The psychologist Howard Gardner claims that humans possess eight intelligences, but he notes: "While we all possess all of the intelligences, perhaps no two persons—not even identical twins—exhibit them in the same combination of strengths" (72). [This citation is arranged in MLA documentation style.]

You can also integrate a quotation into your own writing by interrupting the quotation with your own words. If you insert your own words *within* the quotation, you are required to put those words between brackets, as with the word "eight" in the following example:

"While we all possess all of the [eight] intelligences," Howard Gardner explains, "perhaps no two persons—not even identical twins—exhibit them in the same combination of strengths" (72). [This citation is arranged in MLA documentation style.]

◉ **ALERT:** After using an author's full name in the first reference, you can decide to use only the author's last name in subsequent references. This holds unless another source has that same last name. ◉

EXERCISE 33-1

Working individually or with your peer-response group, read the following original material, from "What Makes You Who You Are" by Matt Ridley in *Time* (2 June 2003): 60. Then, read items 1 through 5 on the facing page and explain why each is an incorrect use of a quotation. Next, revise each numbered sentence so that it correctly uses a quotation. End each quotation with this MLA-style parenthetical reference: (Ridley 60).

ORIGINAL (RIDLEY'S EXACT WORDS)

Human beings differ from chimpanzees in having complex, grammatical language. But language does not spring fully formed from the brain; it must be learned from other language-speaking human beings. This capacity to learn is written into the human brain by genes that open and close a critical window during which learning takes place. One of those genes, FoxP2, has recently been discovered on human chromosome 7 by Anthony Monaco and his colleagues at the Wellcome Trust Centre for Human Genetics in Oxford. Just having the FoxP2 gene, though, is not enough. If a child is not exposed to a lot of spoken language during the critical learning period, he or she will always struggle with speech.

UNACCEPTABLE USES OF QUOTATIONS

1. Scientists are learning more about how people learn languages. "Human beings differ from chimpanzees in having complex, grammatical language" (Ridley 60).

2. People might assume that individuals can acquire speaking abilities through hard individual work, "but language must be learned from other language-speaking human beings" (Ridley 60).

3. Helping the language learning process "by genes that open and close a critical window during which learning takes place" (Ridley 60).

4. In 2002, one gene important for language development "has recently been discovered on human chromosome 7 by Anthony Monaco and his colleagues" (Ridley 60).

5. Parents should continually read to and speak with young children, because "if children are not exposed to a lot of spoken language during the critical learning period of childhood, they will always struggle with speech" (Ridley 60).

EXERCISE 33-2

Working individually or with your peer-response group, do the following:

1. For a paper that argues how a person should choose a spouse, write a two- to three-sentence passage that includes your own words and a quotation from the paragraph below, from "What's Love Got to Do with It?" by Anjula Razdan in *Utne* (May-June 2003): 69–72. After the quoted words, use this parenthetical reference: (Razdan 70).

ORIGINAL (RAZDAN'S EXACT WORDS)

Fast forward a couple hundred years to a 21st-century America, and you see a modern, progressive society where people are free to choose their mates, for the most part, based on love instead of social or economic gain. But for many people, a quiet voice from within wonders: Are we really better off? Who hasn't at some point in their life—at the end of an ill-fated relationship or midway through dinner with the third "date-from-hell" this month—longed for a matchmaker to find the right partner? No hassles. No effort. No personal ads or blind dates.

2. For a paper arguing that biologists need more funding to speed up our understanding of the earth's living creatures before many more of them become extinct, quote from the Wilson material in Exercise 33-6 (section 33j). Be sure to include at least one numerical statistic in your quotation. (For documentation purposes, keep in mind that Wilson's article appears on pages 29–30 in the original source.)

ANSWERS: EXERCISE 33-2

1. Answers will vary; here is one possibility:

> Several generations ago, parents or matchmakers arranged most marriages, and the practice still continues in many cultures. However, in America today, people choose their own spouses, usually on the basis of "love instead of social or economic gain" (Razdan 70).

2. Answers will vary; here is one possibility:

> Biologists are a long way from classifying all of the earth's living creatures. In fact, "biologists estimate that as few as 10% of the different kinds of insects, nematode worms, and fungi have been discovered" (Wilson 29–30).

3. Answers will vary because students write on the topics of their research papers.

BACKGROUND
In "A Dramatistic Approach to Understanding and Teaching the Paraphrase," Phillip Arrington describes how he teaches paraphrasing. He begins his strategy by "playing with variations" of an original writing, such as Karl Marx's *The Communist Manifesto*. It then "moves to playing with Marx's language within a specific situation," such as paraphrasing Marx "for your [the student's] political science professor."

EXTRA EXERCISE C
Working in small groups or in pairs, students can learn good techniques of paraphrasing by trying to find acceptable synonyms for key words in a passage. The italicized words and phrases in the following excerpts can be used for the exercise.

1. It is clear that between what a man calls (a) *me* and what he simply calls (b) *"mine,"* the line is difficult to draw. We (c) *feel and act about* certain things that are ours very much as we (d) *feel and act about* ourselves.... In its widest possible sense, a man's Self is the sum total of all that he can call his, not only his (e) *body* and his (f) *psychic powers,* but his (g) *clothes* and his (h) *house,* his (i) *wife and his children,* his (j) *ancestors* and his (k) *friends,* his (l) *reputation* and his (m) *works,* his (n) *land and horses and yacht and bank account.* If they (o) *wax and prosper,* he feels triumphant, if they (p) *dwindle and die away,* he feels (q) *cast down*—not necessarily in the same degree for each thing, but in much the same way for all.

—William James,
Principles of Psychology

2. Subject to (a) *infinite variables* of winds and currents, of (b) *supply and demand,* of crops and markets, trade has a way of (c) *carving its own paths* not always obedient to (d) *the mercantilist faith.* The faith was (e) *embodied* in Britain's Navigation Act, enacted under Oliver Cromwell in 1651 in the interests of the (f) *rising middle class* and the industrial towns and major trading ports—the so-called Cinque Ports, so long (g) *influential* in British history. Aimed specifically at

→ 554

3. Write a two- to three-sentence passage that includes your own words and a quotation from a source you're currently using for a paper assigned in one of your courses. If you have no such assignment, choose any material suitable for a college-level research paper. Your instructor might request a photocopy of the material from which you're quoting, so make a copy to have on hand.

33i   How can I write good paraphrases?

A **paraphrase** precisely restates in your own words and your own writing style the written or spoken words of someone else. Select for paraphrase only the passages that carry ideas you need to reproduce in detail. Because paraphrasing calls for a very close approximation of a source, avoid trying to paraphrase a whole chapter—or even a whole page; use SUMMARY instead. Expect to write a number of drafts of your paraphrases, each time getting closer to effectively rewording and revising the writing style so that you avoid PLAGIARISM. Box 148 provides guidelines for writing paraphrases.

BOX 148   **SUMMARY**

 ### Guidelines for writing paraphrases

1. Decide to paraphrase authorities on your subject to support or counter what you write in your paper.
2. Never use a paraphrase to present your thesis statement or topic sentences.
3. Say what the source says, but no more.
4. Reproduce the source's sequence of ideas and emphases.
5. Use your own words and writing style to restate the material. If some technical words in the original have no or awkward synonyms, you may quote the original's words—but do so very sparingly. For example, you can use the term *human chromosome 7* if you're paraphrasing the original source by Matt Ridley in Exercise 33-1.
6. Never distort the source's meaning as you reword and change the writing style.
7. Expect your material to be as long as, and often longer than, the original.
8. Integrate your paraphrases smoothly into your writing.
9. Avoid plagiarism (33b–d).
10. Enter all DOCUMENTATION precisely and carefully.

Here's an example of an unacceptable paraphrase and an acceptable one.

SOURCE

Goleman, Daniel. *Emotional Intelligence.* New York: Bantam, 1995. 9.
[This source information is arranged in MLA documentation style.]

ORIGINAL (GOLEMAN'S EXACT WORDS)

These two minds, the emotional and the rational, operate in tight harmony for the most part, intertwining their very different ways of knowing to guide us through the world. Ordinarily there is a balance between emotional and rational minds, with emotion feeding into and informing the operations of the rational mind, and the rational mind refining and sometimes vetoing the inputs of the emotions. Still, the emotional and rational minds are semi-independent faculties, each, as we shall see, reflecting the operation of distinct, but interconnected circuitry of the brain.

In many or most moments, these minds are exquisitely coordinated; feelings are essential to thought, thought to feeling. But when passions surge, the balance tips: it is the emotional mind that captures the upper hand, swamping the rational mind.

UNACCEPTABLE PARAPHRASE (UNDERLINED WORDS ARE PLAGIARIZED)

The emotional and the rational parts of our mind operate in tight harmony for the most part as they help us make our way through our lives. Usually the two minds are balanced, with emotion feeding into and informing the operations of the rational mind, and the rational mind refining and sometimes overruling what the emotions desire. Still, the emotional and rational minds are semi-independent faculties, for as research shows, although they function separately, they are linked in the brain.

Most of the time our two minds work together, with feelings necessary for thinking and thinking necessary for feeling. Nevertheless, if strong emotions develop, it is the emotional mind that captures the upper hand, swamping the rational mind (Goleman 9).

ACCEPTABLE PARAPHRASE

According to Goleman, the emotional and rational parts of our mind work together to help us make our way through our lives. Usually, the two minds have equal input. The emotional mind provides information to the logical mind, and the logical mind processes the data and sometimes overrules emotional desires. Nevertheless, while the two minds show a biological connection in the brain, each can assert some independence.

TEACHING TIP
Sometimes students fall into the habit of using summaries to take notes, forgetting that they can also be used in developing the thesis of a paper. You may find it helpful to remind students that when they want to introduce ideas from sources but have no need to use direct quotation, summaries are a useful strategy to employ. In them, the writer can provide unusual facts, background information, and even other points of view on the subject. When summaries are used in this way, however, it is important to make sure that they fit smoothly and easily into the text. A series of unconnected summaries will not make an effective piece of writing.

ANSWERS: EXERCISE 33-3
Analysis: Paraphrase is unacceptable because it uses many words and phrases from the original. *Acceptable paraphrase* (answers will vary): Paul Fussell explains that people used to shrink new pairs of Levis to fit their own bodies by putting them on wet and wearing them until they dried. This created the important illusion for young Americans that each pair of jeans was unique to them (49).

ANSWERS: EXERCISE 33-4

1. Answers will vary; here is one acceptable paraphrase:

> Years ago, only generals and leaders practiced censorship, and then in a random fashion. World War I witnessed the first organized censorship, when German and French commanders restricted battle photography to a few individuals. Television and photographic coverage of the Vietnam War was fairly unrestricted, and the images, which implicitly criticized the war, shocked the public. The mainstream media had not previously served to upset citizens, let alone convey antiwar sentiments.

2. Answers will vary.

Most of the time our two minds work together, with feelings necessary for thinking and thinking necessary for feeling. Still, if strong emotions develop, passions overrule logical thinking (9). [This citation is arranged in MLA documentation style.]

The first attempt to paraphrase is not acceptable. The writer simply changed a few words. What remains is plagiarized because the passage keeps most of the original's language, has the same sentence structure as the original, and uses no quotation marks. The documentation is correct, but its accuracy doesn't make up for the unacceptable paraphrasing. The second paraphrase is acceptable. It captures the meaning of the original in the student's own words.

EXERCISE 33-3

Working individually or with your peer-response group, read the original material, a paragraph from *Uniforms: Why We Are What We Wear,* by Paul Fussell (Boston: Houghton, 2002): 49. Then, read the unacceptable paraphrase, and point out each example of plagiarism. Finally, write your own paraphrase, starting it with a phrase naming Fussell and ending it with this parenthetical reference: (49).

ORIGINAL (FUSSELL'S EXACT WORDS)

Until around 1963, part of the routine for Levi's wearers was shrinking the trousers to fit, and the best way to do that was to put them on wet and let them dry on your body. This gave the wearer the impression that he or she was actually creating the garment, or at least emphasizing one's precious individuality, and that conviction did nothing to oppose the illusion of uniqueness precious to all American young people.

UNACCEPTABLE PARAPHRASE

Paul Fussell says that until around 1963 Levi's wearers used to shrink new trousers to fit. The best way to do that was to put them on wet and let them dry while wearing them. Doing this created the impression that wearers were actually creating the garment or emphasizing their precious individuality. It reinforced the illusion of uniqueness precious to all American teens (49).

EXERCISE 33-4

Working individually or with your peer-response group, do the following:

1. For a paper on the place of censorship in the coverage of military conflicts, paraphrase the following paragraph from *Regarding the*

Pain of Others by Susan Sontag (New York: Farrar, 2003): 65. Start with words mentioning Sontag, and end with this parenthetical reference: (65).

ORIGINAL (SONTAG'S EXACT WORDS)

There had always been censorship, but for a long time it remained desultory, at the pleasure of generals and heads of state. The first organized ban on press photography at the front came during the First World War; both the German and French high commands allowed only a few selected military photographers near the fighting. (Censorship of the press by the British General Staff was less inflexible.) And it took another fifty years, and the relaxation of censorship with the first televised war coverage, to understand what impact shocking photographs could have on the domestic public. During the Vietnam era, war photography became, normatively, a criticism of war. This was bound to have consequences: Mainstream media are not in the business of making people feel queasy about the struggles for which they are being mobilized, much less of disseminating propaganda against waging war.

2. In one of your sources for a current research assignment, locate a paragraph that is at least 150 words in length and write a paraphrase of it. If you have no such assignment, choose any material suitable for a college-level paper. Your instructor may request that you submit a photocopy of the original material, so make a copy to have on hand.

33j How can I write good summaries?

A **summary** differs from a PARAPHRASE (33i) in one important way: A paraphrase restates the original material completely, but a summary provides only the main point of the original source. A summary is much shorter than a paraphrase. Summarizing is the technique you will probably use most frequently in writing your research paper, both for taking notes and for integrating what you have learned from sources into your own writing.

As you summarize, you trace a line of thought. This involves deleting less central ideas and sometimes transposing certain points into an order more suited to summary. In summarizing a longer original—say, ten pages or more—you may find it helpful first to divide the original into subsections and summarize each. Then, group your subsection summaries and use them as the basis for further condensing the material into a final summary. You will likely have to revise a summary more than once. Always make sure that a summary accurately reflects the source and its emphases.

Answers to Extra Exercise D
Here are possible summaries.

1. An "insightful judge of character," a clever and sometimes deceitful politician, and an independent and purposeful ruler, Elizabeth I, queen of England from 1558 to 1603, continually triumphed over her enemies and weathered political crises to help make England into one of the most powerful countries of Europe.

2. Although people occasionally identify Georgia O'Keeffe as photographer Alfred Stieglitz's model and wife or as a hermit artist from New Mexico, people will recall her finally for her paintings. Whatever their opinions of her art, all find it original, personal, forceful, and unforgettable.

When you're summarizing a source in your CONTENT NOTES, take care not to be tempted to include your personal interpretation along with something the author says. Similarly, never include in your summary your own judgment about the point made in the source. Your own opinions and ideas, although they have value, don't belong in a summary. Instead, jot them down immediately when they come to mind, but separate them clearly from your summary. Write your notes so that when you go back to them you can be sure to distinguish your opinions or ideas from your summary. Highlight your personal writing with a screen of yellow or some other color, or use an entirely different font for it. Box 149 provides guidelines for writing good summaries.

BOX 149   SUMMARY

 ## Guidelines for writing summaries

1. Use summaries from authorities on your subject to support or refute what you write in your paper.
2. Identify the main points your want to summarize and condense them using your own words without losing the meaning of the original source.
3. Never use a summary to present your THESIS STATEMENT or TOPIC SENTENCES.
4. Keep your summary short.
5. Integrate your summaries smoothly into your writing.
6. Avoid PLAGIARISM (33b–d).
7. Enter all DOCUMENTATION precisely and carefully.

Here's an example of an unacceptable summary and an acceptable one.

SOURCE

Tanenbaum, Leora. *Catfight: Women and Competition.* New York: Seven Stories P, 2002. 117–18. [This source information is arranged in MLA documentation style.]

ORIGINAL (TANENBAUM'S EXACT WORDS)

Until recently, most Americans disapproved of cosmetic surgery, but today the stigma is disappearing. Average Americans are lining up for procedures—two-thirds of patients report family incomes of less than $50,000 a year—and many of them return for more. Younger women undergo "maintenance" surgeries in a futile attempt to halt time. The latest fad is Botox, a purified and diluted form of botulinum toxin that is injected between the eyebrows to eliminate frown lines. Although the procedure costs between $300 and $1000 and must be repeated every few months, roughly 850,000 patients have had it performed on them. That number will undoubtedly shoot up now that the FDA has approved Botox for cosmetic use. Even teenagers are making appointments with plastic surgeons. More than 14,000 adolescents had plastic surgery in 1996, and many of them are choosing controversial procedures such as breast implants, liposuction, and tummy tucks, rather than the rhinoplasties of previous generations.

UNACCEPTABLE SUMMARY (UNDERLINED WORDS ARE PLAGIARIZED)

Average Americans are lining up for surgical procedures. The latest fad is Botox, a toxin injected to eliminate frown lines. This is an insanely foolish waste of money. Even teenagers are making appointments with plastic surgeons, many of them for controversial procedures such as breast implants, liposuction, and tummy tucks (Tanenbaum 117-18).

ACCEPTABLE SUMMARY

Tanenbaum explains that plastic surgery is becoming widely acceptable, even for Americans with modest incomes and for younger women. Most popular is injecting the toxin Botox to smooth wrinkles. She notes that thousands of adolescents are even requesting controversial surgeries (117-18). [This citation is arranged in MLA documentation style.]

The unacceptable summary above has several major problems: It doesn't isolate the main point. It plagiarizes by taking much of its language directly from the source. Examples of plagiarized language include all the underlined phrases. Finally, the unacceptable summary includes the writer's interpretation ("This is an insanely foolish waste of money") rather than objectively representing the original. The acceptable summary concisely isolates the main point, puts the source into the writer's own words, calls attention to the author by including her name in the summary, and remains objective throughout.

EXERCISE 33-5

Working individually or with your peer-response group, read the original material from *Diversity: The Invention of a Concept* by Peter Wood (San Francisco: Encounter, 2003): 23–24. Then, read the unacceptable summary. Point out each example of plagiarism. Finally, write your own summary, starting it with a phrase mentioning Wood and ending it with this parenthetical reference: (23–24).

ANSWERS: EXERCISE 33-6

1. Answers will vary; here is one possible summary:

> According to Wilson, biologists have only classified a small percentage of earth's living creatures. Biologists are constantly discovering new kinds of life, from microorganisms to large mammals, on our planet (29–30).

2. Answers will vary; here is one possible summary:

> Sontag observes that military leaders first consistently censored photography in World War I. The relaxation of censorship during the Vietnam War resulted in images that shocked the public and served to criticize the war, something the media previously had not intended (65).

3. Answers will vary.

ORIGINAL (WOOD'S EXACT WORDS)

Among the many meanings of diversity, let's for the moment distinguish two: the actual racial and ethnic condition of America, which I will call *diversity I,* and the diversiphile ideal of how American society should recognize and respond to its racial and ethnic composition, which I will call *diversity II.* In principle, it ought to be easy to distinguish between these two meanings. One refers to the facts, the other to hopes or wishes. *Diversity I* is the sort of thing that we might expect could be counted, or at least approximated, with wide agreement. We know with reasonable certainty, for example, that about 13 percent of the U.S. population considers itself of African descent. We can and do argue with one another over the significance of this fact, but the fact itself is not seriously in dispute.

Diversity II, by contrast, is an ideal. It expresses a vision of society in which people divide themselves into separate groups, each with profound traditions of its own, but held together by mutual esteem, respect and tolerance. It would be futile, however, to look for general agreement about the exact details of this ideal.

UNACCEPTABLE, PLAGIARIZED SUMMARY

Peter Wood distinguishes between *diversity 1,* the actual racial and ethnic condition of America, and *diversity 2,* the diversiphile ideal of how American society should recognize and respond to its racial and ethnic composition. *Diversity 1* could be counted or approximated with wide agreement. *Diversity 2* is an ideal vision of society, but there can be no general agreement about the exact nature of this ideal (23–24).

EXERCISE 33-6

Working individually or with your peer-response group, do the following:

1. Summarize the following paragraph from "Vanishing Before Our Eyes" by Edward O. Wilson in *Time* (24 Apr. 2000): 29–30. Start your summary with a phrase mentioning the author, and end with this parenthetical reference: (29–30).

ORIGINAL (WILSON'S EXACT WORDS)

By repeated sampling, biologists estimate that as few as 10% of the different kinds of insects, nematode worms, and fungi have been discovered. For bacteria and other microorganisms, the number could be well below 1%. Even the largest and most intensively studied organisms are incompletely cataloged. Four species of mammals, for example, have recently been discovered in the remote Annamite Mountains along the Vietnam-Laos border. One of them, the saola or spindlehorn, is a large cowlike animal distinct enough to be classified in a genus of its own. Earth, as far as life is concerned, is still a little-known planet.

2. Write a summary of your paraphrase of the Sontag material in Exercise 33-4. Use the parenthetical reference given there.

3. Write a summary of a passage from a source you're currently using for a paper assigned in one of your courses. If you have no such assignment, choose any material suitable for a college-level research paper. Your instructor might request a photocopy of the material you're summarizing, so make a copy to have on hand.

33k Which verbs can help me weave source material into my sentences?

The verbs listed in Box 150 can help you work quotations, paraphrases, and summaries smoothly into your writing. Some of these verbs imply your position toward the source material (for example, *argue, complain, concede, deny, grant, insist,* and *reveal*). Other verbs imply a more neutral stance (for example, *comment, describe, explain, note, say,* and *write*). For many examples of effective use of such verbs, see the student research papers presented in sections 34e.2, 35h.2, and 40g.3.

BOX 150   SUMMARY

Verbs useful for integrating quotations, paraphrases, and summaries

acknowledges	confirms	endeavors to
agrees	connects	establishes
analyzes	considers	estimates
argues	contends	explains
asks	contradicts	expresses
asserts	contrasts	finds
balances	declares	focuses on
begins	demonstrates	grants
believes	denies	illuminates
claims	describes	illustrates
comments	develops	implies
compares	discusses	indicates
complains	distinguishes	informs
concedes	between/among	insists
concludes	emphasizes	introduces

→

TEACHING TIP
Many activities in other courses require students to write about readings and employ paraphrasing and summarizing. Students are asked to synthesize, analyze, respond to, and critique readings in exams and for papers and other assignments. They may compose book reviews, interpret literature, analyze arguments, and relate textbook material to experiments in lab reports. Paraphrasing and summarizing are also effective study techniques that can be applied to any reading assignment. They are particularly helpful to students trying to identify the main points of a piece of writing and relate them to each other. Students often disagree in identifying the main points of a text. For that reason, students generally find it informative to compare their paraphrases and summaries, discussing why they made certain choices.

QUOTATION: ON WRITING

[Plagiarism is] like lip-synching to someone else's voice and accepting the applause and rewards for yourself.

—<http://owl.english.purdue.edu/workshops/hypertext/ResearchW/plag.html>

Verbs useful for integrating quotations, paraphrases, and summaries (*continued*)

maintains	proves	shows
means	questions	signals
negates	recognizes	specifies
notes	recommends	speculates
notices	refutes	states
observes	rejects	suggests
offers	remarks	supports
organizes	reports	supposes
points out	reveals	thinks
prepares	says	wishes
promises	sees	writes

Chapter 34

MLA Documentation with Case Study

BACKGROUND
The Bibliographical Society of America was organized at the American Library Association's St. Louis Conference in 1904. It succeeded the Bibliographical Society of Chicago, founded five years earlier. The object of the society is "to promote bibliographical research and to issue bibliographical publications." Its membership is made up of professors, librarians, instructors, rare book dealers, collectors, and other bibliophiles. It is responsible for many publications dealing with published American writing.

34a What is MLA style?

The Modern Language Association (MLA) sponsors the **MLA style,** a DOCUMENTATION system widely used in English courses and many of the humanities. MLA style involves two equally important features that need to appear in research papers.

First, MLA style calls for you to acknowledge your SOURCES within the text of your research papers by using **parenthetical documentation.** Section 34b explains how parenthetical documentation works, and section 34c shows nineteen models of parenthetical documentation, each of which shows you a different type of source.

Second, MLA style calls for you to list complete bibliographic information about each source that you've mentioned in your parenthetical references. This bibliographic list, titled **Works Cited,** needs to appear on a separate page at the end of your research paper. It includes only the sources you've actually used in your research paper, not any you've consulted but haven't used. Section 34d gives instructions for composing your Works Cited pages, followed by seventy-one models, each based on a different kind of source (book, article, Web site, etc.) that you might use in your research papers.

For examples of research papers that use MLA-style parenthetical documentation and Works Cited lists, see sections 34e.2 and 40g.3. As you read these papers, notice how the two requirements for crediting sources work together so that readers can learn the precise origin of the material that is QUOTED, PARAPHRASED, and SUMMARIZED. If you need more information than I cover in this chapter, consult the sixth edition of the *MLA Handbook for Writers of Research Papers* (2003) by Joseph Gibaldi.

563

TEACHING TIP
Because documentation can be tedious, working in groups can alleviate some of the frustration that students feel. Initially, a class can work as a whole, with one or two people recording choices on the chalkboard. Later, small groups can work on documentation exercises in parenthetical references, footnoting, or the preparation of lists of Works Cited or References.

34b What is MLA parenthetical documentation?

MLA-style **parenthetical documentation,** also called either *parenthetical references* or *in-text citations*, is the method required to place SOURCE information in parentheses within the sentences of your research papers. This information, given each time that you QUOTE, SUMMARIZE, or PARAPHRASE specific parts of sources in your paper, signals readers that your material draws on scholarship about your TOPIC.

In parenthetical references, an author's name (or, if none, a shortened title of the work) identifies the source, and the exact page number tells where readers can locate the original material. For readability and good writing technique, always try to introduce names of authors and titles of sources in your own sentences. Then, you need only put into parentheses the page number where you found the material. When possible, position a parenthetical reference at the end of the quote, summary, or paraphrase it refers to—preferably at the end of a sentence, unless that would place it too far from the source's material. When you place the parenthetical reference at the end of a sentence, put it before the sentence-ending period. The one exception to this rule concerns quotations that you set off block style (MLA requires that quotations longer than four typed lines be handled this way), where you put the parenthetical reference after the period.

34c What are MLA guidelines for parenthetical documentation?

This section shows examples of how to handle parenthetical documentation in the body of your research papers. The following directory corresponds to the numbered examples that follow it. Remember, try to integrate authors' names and titles of SOURCES into your sentences whenever possible (34b).

Directory—MLA Parenthetical Citations

1. Paraphrased or Summarized Source—MLA
2. Source of a Short Quotation—MLA
3. Source of a Long Quotation—MLA
4. One Author—MLA
5. Two or Three Authors—MLA
6. More Than Three Authors—MLA
7. More Than One Source by an Author—MLA

1. Citing a Paraphrased or Summarized Source—MLA

According to Brent Staples, IQ tests give scientists little insight into intelligence (293). [Author name cited in text; page number cited in parentheses.]

In "The IQ Cult," the journalist Brent Staples states that IQ tests give scientists little insight into intelligence (293). [Title of source, author name, and author credentials cited in text; page number cited in parentheses.]

IQ tests give scientists little insight into intelligence (Staples 293). [Author name and page number cited in parentheses.]

2. Citing the Source of a Short Quotation—MLA

Given that "thoughts, emotions, imagination and predispositions occur concurrently . . . [and] interact with other brain processes" (Caine and Caine 66), it is easy to understand why "whatever [intelligence] might be, paper and pencil tests aren't the tenth of it" (Staples 293).

Coles asks, "What binds together a Mormon banker in Utah with his brother, or other coreligionists in Illinois or Massachusetts?" (2).

3. Citing the Source of a Long Quotation—MLA

A long quotation in MLA style consists of more than four typed lines. It is set off block style, indented one inch or ten spaces from the left margin. Never put quotation marks around a set-off quotation because the indentation and block style communicate that the material is quoted. At the end of an indented quotation, place the parenthetical reference after the end punctuation mark.

MLA

EXTRA EXERCISE A

Devise parenthetical references for the following quotation and paraphrase. The source is provided at the end of each selection.

1. "If indeed we note in [Thomas Carlyle's] writings those passages in which the words and rhythms are most resonant, and the accent falls with the strongest emphasis, we shall find they are the expression of the cosmic wonder and terror which formed the darkly flaming background of all his thoughts." (Logan Pearsall Smith, "Thomas Carlyle: The Rembrandt of English Prose," *Reperusals and Re-Collections,* Harcourt, 1936, 115.)

2. Ethologists study the traits that distinguish a group—a group of people or a group of animals. They try to discover how the group usually acts by observing its members in their natural surroundings, and to understand their behavior by testing it, when possible, in the laboratory. (Sally Carrighar, "Ethology," from *Wild Heritage,* Houghton, 1965, 174–175.)

Answers to Extra Exercise A

1. (Smith 115).

2. (Carrighar 174-75).

Gray and Viens explain how, by tapping into a student's highly developed spatial-mechanical intelligence, one teacher can bolster a student's poor writing skills:

> The teacher asked that during "journal time" Jacob create a tool dictionary to be used as a resource in the mechanical learning center. After several entries in which he drew and described tools and other materials, Jacob confidently moved on to writing about other things of import to him, such as his brothers and a recent birthday party. Rather than shy away from all things linguistic--he previously had refused any task requiring a pencil--Jacob became invested in journal writing. (23-24)

4. Citing One Author—MLA

Give an author's name as it appears on the source: for a book, on the title page; for an article, directly below the title or at the end of the article. Many nonprint sources also name an author; for CDs, tapes, and software, for example, check the printed sleeve or cover. For an online source, identify the author exactly as identified online.

> One test asks four-year-olds to choose between one marshmallow now or two marshmallows later (Gibbs 60).

5. Citing Two or Three Authors—MLA

Give the names in the same order as in the source. Spell out *and.* For three authors, use commas to separate the authors' names.

> As children get older, they begin to express several different kinds of intelligence (Todd and Taylor 23).

> Another measure of emotional intelligence is the success of inter- and intrapersonal relationships (Voigt, Dees, and Prigoff 14).

6. Citing More Than Three Authors—MLA

If your source has more than three authors, you can name them all or use the first author's name only, followed by *et al.,* either in a parenthetical reference or in your sentence. In MLA citations, do not underline or italicize *et al.* No period follows *et,* but do use a period after *al.*

> Emotional security varies depending on the circumstances of the social interaction (Carter et al. 158).

👁 **ALERT:** The abbreviation *et al.* stands for "and others"; when an author's name followed by *et al.* is a subject, use a plural verb.

> Carter et al. have found that emotional security varies depending on the circumstances of the social interaction (158). 👁

7. Citing More Than One Source by an Author—MLA

When you use two or more sources by an author, include the relevant title in each citation. In parenthetical citations, use a shortened version of the title. For example, in a paper using two of Howard Gardner's works, *Frames of Mind: The Theory of Multiple Intelligences* and "Reflections on Multiple Intelligences: Myths and Messages," use *Frames* and "Reflections." Shorten the titles as much as possible, keeping them unambiguous to readers and starting them with the word by which you alphabetize each work in WORKS CITED. Separate the author's name and the title with a comma, but do not use punctuation between the title and the page number. When you incorporate the title into your own sentences, you can omit a subtitle, but never shorten the main title.

> Although it seems straightforward to think of multiple intelligences as multiple approaches to learning (Gardner, Frames 60-61), an intelligence is not a learning style (Gardner, "Reflections" 202-03).

8. Citing Two or More Authors with the Same Last Name—MLA

Use each author's first initial and full last name in each parenthetical citation. This is the only instance in MLA style where you use an initial in a parenthetical reference. If both authors have the same first initial, use the full name in all instances.

> According to Anne Cates, psychologists can predict how empathetic an adult will be from his or her behavior at age two (41), but other researchers disagree (T. Cates 171).

9. Citing a Work with a Group or Corporate Author—MLA

When a corporation or other group is named as the author of a source you want to cite, use the corporate name just as you would an individual's name.

> In a five-year study, the Boston Women's Health Collective reported that these tests are usually unreliable (11).

> A five-year study shows that these tests are usually unreliable (Boston Women's Health Collective 11).

MLA

MLA

10. Citing a Work Listed by Title—MLA

If no author is named, use the title in citations. In your own sentences, use the full main title and omit a subtitle, if any. For parenthetical citations, shorten the title as much as possible (making sure that the shortened version refers unambiguously to the correct source), and always make the first word the one by which you alphabetize it. "Are You a Day or Night Person?" is the full title of the article in the following citation.

> The "morning lark" and "night owl" connotations are typically used to categorize the human extremes ("Are You" 11).

11. Citing a Multivolume Work—MLA

When you cite more than one volume of a multivolume work, include the relevant volume number in each citation. (In the Works Cited, list the multivolume work once and give the total number of volumes; see item 9 in the Works Cited examples in 34d.1.) Give the volume number first, followed by a colon and one space, followed by the page number(s).

> By 1900, the Amazon forest dwellers had been exposed to these viruses (Rand 3: 202).

> Rand believes that forest dwellers in Borneo escaped illness from retroviruses until the 1960s (4: 518–19).

12. Citing Material from a Novel, Play, or Poem—MLA

When you cite material from literary works, providing the part, chapter, act, scene, canto, stanza, or line numbers usually helps readers locate what you are referring to more than do page numbers alone, especially because literary works frequently appear in different editions. Unless your instructor tells you not to, use arabic numerals for these references, even if the literary work uses roman numerals.

For novels that use them, give part and/or chapter numbers after page numbers. Use a semicolon after the page number but a comma to separate a part from a chapter.

> Flannery O'Connor describes one character in The Violent Bear It Away as "divided in two--a violent and a rational self" (139; pt. 2, ch. 6).

For plays that use them, give act, scene, and line numbers. Use periods between these numbers.

> In Hamlet, we find the most quoted of Shakespeare's lines, Hamlet's soliloquy beginning "To be, or not to be: that is the question" (3.1.56).

For poems and plays that use them, give canto, stanza, and line numbers. Use periods between these numbers. Because the typed or typeset abbreviation for *line (l.,* plural *ll.)* can be misread as the numeral 1, the *MLA Handbook* advises beginning your first reference to lines with the word *line* (or *lines*). After the first citation, omit the word and give only the numbers.

> In "To Autumn," Keats's most melancholy image occurs in the lines "Then
> in a wailful choir the small gnats mourn / Among the river swallows"
> (3.27-28).

13. Citing a Work in an Anthology or Other Collection—MLA

You may want to cite a work you have read in a book that contains many works by various authors and that was compiled or edited by someone other than the person you are citing. For example, suppose you want to cite "Several Things" by Martha Collins, which you have read in a literature text edited by Pamela Annas and Robert Rosen. Use Martha Collins's name and the title of her work in the sentence and the page numbers in a parenthetical citation.

> In "Several Things," Martha Collins enumerates what could take place in
> the lines of her poem: "Plums could appear, on a pewter plate / A dead red
> hare, hung by one foot. / A vase of flowers. Three shallots" (2-4).

14. Citing an Indirect Source—MLA

When you want to quote words that you found quoted in someone else's work, put the name of the person whose words you are quoting into your own sentence. Give the work where you found the quotation either in your sentence or in a parenthetical citation beginning with *qtd. in.*

> Martin Scorsese acknowledges the link between himself and his films: "I
> realize that all my life, I've been an outsider. I splatter bits of myself all
> over the screen" (qtd. in Giannetti and Eyman 397).

> Giannetti and Eyman quote Martin Scorsese as acknowledging the link
> between himself and his films: "I realize that all my life, I've been an
> outsider. I splatter bits of myself all over the screen" (397).

15. Citing Two or More Sources in One Reference—MLA

If more than one source has contributed to an idea, opinion, or fact in your paper, acknowledge all of them. In a parenthetical citation, separate each block of information with a semicolon followed by one space.

> Once researchers agreed that multiple intelligences existed, their next
> step was to try to measure or define them (West 17; Arturi 477; Gibbs 68).

Because long parenthetical citations can disturb the flow of your paper, you might want to use an endnote or footnote for citing multiple sources; see 34d.2.

16. Citing an Entire Work—MLA

References to an entire work usually fit best into your own sentences.

> In Frames of Mind, Gardner proposes a revolutionary expansion of our understanding of human intelligence.

17. Citing an Electronic Source with a Name or Title and Page Numbers—MLA

The principles that govern parenthetical references for electronic sources are exactly the same as the ones that apply to books, articles, letters, interviews, or any other source you get information from on paper or in person.

When an electronically accessed source identifies its author, use the author's name for parenthetical references. If an electronic source does not name the author, use its title for parenthetical references and for the first block of information in that source's Works Cited entry. (See item 10 in this section for an example of a work cited by its title.) When an electronic source has page numbers, use them exactly as you would the page numbers of a print source.

18. Citing an Electronic Source with Paragraph or Screen Numbers—MLA

When an electronic source has numbered paragraphs or screens (instead of page numbers), use them for parenthetical references, with two differences: (1) Use a comma followed by one space after the name (or title); and (2) use the abbreviation *par.* for a reference to one paragraph or *pars.* for a reference to more than one paragraph, followed by the number(s) of the paragraph(s) you are citing.

> Artists seem to be haunted by the fear that psychoanalysis might destroy creativity while it reconstructs personality (Francis, pars. 22-25).

19. Citing an Electronic Source Without Page or Paragraph Numbers—MLA

Many online sources do not number pages or paragraphs. Simply refer to those works in their entirety. Here are two examples referring to "What Is Artificial Intelligence?" by John McCarthy, a Web site without page numbers or paragraph numbers. While either citation is acceptable, try to include the name of the author in your sentence.

> The science of artificial intelligence includes efforts beyond trying to simulate human intelligence (McCarthy).

John McCarthy notes that the science of artificial intelligence includes efforts beyond trying to simulate human intelligence.

34d How do I compile an MLA-style Works Cited list?

In MLA style, **Works Cited** pages give complete bibliographic information for each source used in research papers. This Works Cited list includes only the sources from which you QUOTE or PARAPHRASE or SUMMARIZE. Never include sources that you have consulted but do not refer to in the paper. Box 151 gives general information about a Works Cited list, and the rest of this chapter provides models of specific kinds of Works Cited entries.

BOX 151   SUMMARY

 ## Guidelines for an MLA-style Works Cited list

■ **TITLE**

Works Cited

■ **PLACEMENT OF LIST**

Start a new page numbered sequentially with the rest of the paper, after Notes pages, if any.

■ **CONTENTS AND FORMAT**

Include all sources quoted from, paraphrased, or summarized in your paper. Start each entry on a new line and at the regular left margin. If the entry uses more than one line, indent all lines—beginning with the second—one-half inch or five spaces from the left margin. Double-space all lines.

■ **SPACING AFTER PUNCTUATION**

The *MLA Handbook* explains that computer type fonts have influenced many users of MLA style to leave one space rather than two spaces after punctuation at the ends of sentences. The *MLA Handbook* uses one space but says that it is perfectly acceptable to use two unless your instructor asks you to do otherwise. Always put only one space after a comma or a colon.

■ **ARRANGEMENT OF ENTRIES**

Alphabetize by author's last name. If no author is named, alphabetize by the title's first significant word (not *A*, *An*, or *The*).

→

MLA

MLA

QUOTATION: ON WRITING

My writing is a process of rewriting, of going back and changing and filling in. In the rewriting process you discover what's going on, and you go back and bring it up to that point.

—Joan Didion

QUOTATION: ON WRITING

Writer's block is a natural affliction. Writers who have never experienced it have something wrong with them. It means there isn't enough friction—that they aren't making enough of an effort to reconcile the contradictions of life. All you get is a sweet monotonous flow. Writer's block is nothing to commit suicide over. It simply indicates some imbalance between your experience and your art, and I think that's constructive.

—Stanley Kunitz

Guidelines for an MLA-style Works Cited list (*continued*)

- **AUTHORS' NAMES**

  Use first names and middle names or middle initials, if any, as given in the source. Do not reduce to initials any name that is given in full. For one author or the first-named author in multiauthor works, give the last name first. Use the word *and* with two or more authors. List multiple authors in the order given in the source. Use a comma between the first author's last and first names and after each complete author name except the last. After the last author's name, use a period: Fein, Ethel Andrea, Bert Griggs, and Delaware Rogash.

  Include *Jr., Sr., II, III,* but do not include other titles and degrees before or after a name. For example, an entry for a work by Edward Meep III, M.D., and Sir Feeney Bolton would start like this: Meep, Edward III, and Feeney Bolton.

- **CAPITALIZATION OF TITLES**

  Capitalize all major words and the first and last words of all titles and subtitles.

- **SPECIAL TREATMENT OF TITLES**

  Use quotation marks around titles of shorter works (poems, short stories, essays, articles). Underline titles of longer works (books, names of newspapers or journals containing cited articles).

  For underlining, use an unbroken line like this (unless you use software that underlines only with a broken line like this). The MLA Web site states that although computers can create italic type, underlined roman type may be more exact in student papers. Check which style your instructor prefers.

  When a book title includes the title of another work that is usually underlined (as with a novel, play, or long poem), the preferred MLA style is not to underline the incorporated title: Decoding Jane Eyre. For a second style MLA accepts, see item 20 in 34d.1.

  If the incorporated title is usually enclosed in quotation marks (as with a short story or short poem), keep the quotation marks and underline the complete title of the book, including the final punctuation. This is the only case in which final punctuation is underlined in MLA style: Theme and Form in "I Shall Laugh Purely."

  Drop *A, An,* or *The* as the first word of a periodical title.

- **PLACE OF PUBLICATION**

  If several cities are listed for the place of publication, give only the first. If a U.S. or Canadian city name alone would be ambiguous, also

  →

Guidelines for an MLA-style Works Cited list (*continued*)

give the state's or province's two-letter postal abbreviation (see Box 122 in 30k). For an unfamiliar city outside the United States and Canada, include an abbreviated country name.

- **PUBLISHER**

  Use shortened names as long as they are clear: *Prentice* for *Prentice Hall*, *Simon* for *Simon & Schuster*. For university presses, use the capital letters *U* and *P* (without periods): Oxford UP; U of Chicago P

- **PUBLICATION MONTH ABBREVIATIONS**

  Abbreviate all publication months except *May, June,* and *July.* Use the first few letters followed by a period (*Sept., Dec.*). See Box 121 in 30j.

- **PARAGRAPH AND SCREEN NUMBERS IN ELECTRONIC SOURCES**

  Some electronic sources number paragraphs or screens instead of pages, although most electronic sources include no such information. If paragraphs are numbered, at the end of the publication information give the total number of paragraphs followed by the abbreviation *pars.*: 77 pars. If screens are numbered, give the total number of screens as the final information in the entry. If the source does not number paragraphs or screens, include whatever identifiable information is provided.

- **PAGE RANGES**

  Give the page range—the starting page number and the ending page number, connected by a hyphen—of any paginated electronic source and any paginated print source that is part of a longer work (for example, a chapter in a book, an article in a journal). A range indicates that the cited work is on those pages and all pages in between. If that is not the case, use the style shown next for discontinuous pages. In either case, use numerals only, without the word *page* or *pages* or the abbreviation *p.* or *pp.*

  Use the full second number through 99. Above that, use only the last two digits for the second number unless it would be unclear: *113–14* is clear, but *567–602* requires full numbers.

- **DISCONTINUOUS PAGES**

  Use the starting page number followed by a plus sign (1): 32+.

- **WORKS CITED ENTRIES: BOOKS**

  Citations for books have three main parts: author, title, and publication information (place of publication, publisher, and date of publication).

  →

QUOTATION: ON WRITING
A lot of young writers wait for inspiration.
The inspiration only hits you at the desk.
— Robert Anderson

QUOTATION: ON WRITING
I don't care to talk about a novel I'm doing
because if I communicate the magic spell,
even in an abbreviated form, it loses its force
for me. Once you have talked, the act of communication has been made.
— Angus Wilson

Guidelines for an MLA-style Works Cited list (*continued*)

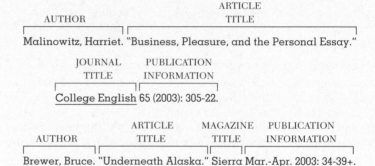

| | BOOK | PUBLICATION |
| AUTHOR | TITLE | INFORMATION |

Didion, Joan. Salvador. New York: Simon, 1983.

■ WORKS CITED ENTRIES: PRINT ARTICLES

Citations for periodical articles contain three major parts: author, title
of article, and publication information (usually periodical title, volume
number, year of publication, and page range).

| | ARTICLE |
| AUTHOR | TITLE |

Malinowitz, Harriet. "Business, Pleasure, and the Personal Essay."

| JOURNAL | PUBLICATION |
| TITLE | INFORMATION |

College English 65 (2003): 305-22.

| | ARTICLE | MAGAZINE | PUBLICATION |
| AUTHOR | TITLE | TITLE | INFORMATION |

Brewer, Bruce. "Underneath Alaska." Sierra Mar.-Apr. 2003: 34-39+.

■ WORKS CITED ENTRIES: PORTABLE ELECTRONIC SOURCES

Publications on CD-ROM, diskettes, tape, and so on should include as
much of the following as is available: author, title of publication, original
print version (if relevant), editor or compiler (if relevant), publication
medium, place of publication, name of publisher, date of publication.
Here is an entry for an article from a CD-ROM encyclopedia:

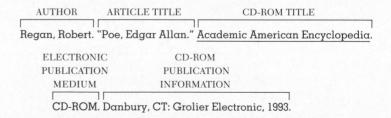

| AUTHOR | ARTICLE TITLE | CD-ROM TITLE |

Regan, Robert. "Poe, Edgar Allan." Academic American Encyclopedia.

ELECTRONIC	CD-ROM
PUBLICATION	PUBLICATION
MEDIUM	INFORMATION

CD-ROM. Danbury, CT: Grolier Electronic, 1993.

■ WORKS CITED ENTRIES: SOURCES FROM THE INTERNET

To document sources reached by entering a URL or Internet address
(including World Wide Web, FTP, and Gopher sites), list as much
of the following information as you can find: author, title, publication

→

Guidelines for an MLA-style Works Cited list (*continued*)

information about a print version (if there is one), publication information about the online source, the date you accessed the material, and the URL (electronic address). For these sources, the URL is required in the Works Cited entry, enclosed in angle brackets <like these>, after the access date and before the period at the end of the entry. Here is an entry for an article in a scientific news magazine that appears on the Web:

AUTHOR ⌐ ⌐ ARTICLE TITLE

Lewis, Ricki. "Chronobiology Researchers Say Their Field's Time

PUBLICATION PUBLICATION ACCESS
TITLE INFORMATION DATE

Has Come." Scientist   11 Dec. 1995:14. 30 Dec. 2003

URL

<http://www.the-scientist.com/yr1995/dec/chrono_951211.html>.

■ **WORKS CITED ENTRIES: SOURCES ACCESSED THROUGH A LIBRARY OR PERSONAL SUBSCRIPTION SERVICE**

Library systems typically subscribe to online services such as EBSCO, InfoTrac, FirstSearch, and so on, and you may access information from them. Individuals may personally subscribe to online services such as America Online. Citations for electronic sources from either type of service generally contain at least six or seven major parts: author, title of work, information about print version (if any), name of database (underlined), name of vendor or computer service, name of library (if accessed through a library service), access date, and URL if it's available and not too long to include. Here is an entry for a journal article accessed through a library service; it also has a print version.

PUBLICATION
AUTHOR ARTICLE TITLE TITLE

Brumfiel, Geoff. "Magnetic Effect Sends Physicists into a Spin." Nature

PRINT SUBSCRIPTION
INFORMATION DATABASE SERVICE LIBRARY

426.6963: 110. Academic Search Elite. EBSCO. Milner Lib., Illinois

ACCESS ACCESS
DATE URL PATH

State U. 27 Dec. 2003 <http://weblink3.epnet.com> Path: Magnets.

QUOTATION: ON WRITING
I don't think that writer's block exists really. I think that when you're trying to do something prematurely, it just won't come. Certain subjects just need time, as I've learned over and over again. You've got to wait before you write about them.

—Joyce Carol Oates

EXTRA EXERCISE B

Using the following information, compile a Works Cited list in MLA style.

1. *Abraham Lincoln: The Man Behind the Myths,* by Stephen B. Oates. Harper & Row, Publishers, New York, Cambridge, Philadelphia, San Francisco, London, Mexico City, São Paulo, and Sydney, 1984.

2. Barbara W. Tuchman. *Practicing History.* Alfred A. Knopf, Inc. Copyright 1936, 1959, 1966, 1974, 1981. New York.

3. *Time's Arrow, Time's Cycle: Myth and Metaphor in the Discovery of Geological Time.* Stephen Jay Gould. Harvard University Press, Cambridge, Massachusetts. 1987.

4. T. C. Smout. *A Century of the Scottish People, 1830–1950.* New Haven and London, 1986, Yale University Press.

5. Thomas J. Peters and Robert H. Waterman Jr. *In Search of Excellence.* Harper & Row, Publishers, New York, 1982.

6. *The Man Who Mistook His Wife for a Hat, and Other Clinical Tales.* Oliver Sacks. New York. Summit Books. "The Autist Artist." No year of publication listed. Pages 204 through 223.

7. *The Rise and Fall of the House of Medici.* 1974. Penguin Books. New York. By Christopher Hibbert.

8. *Capote: A Biography.* 1988. Simon & Schuster. New York. Gerald Clarke.

34d.1 Following MLA guidelines for specific sources in a Works Cited list

The directory below corresponds to the numbered examples that follow it. Not every possible documentation model is shown here. You may find that you have to combine features of models to document a particular source.

Directory—MLA Style

PRINT SOURCES

1. Book by One Author—MLA
2. Book by Two or Three Authors—MLA
3. Book by More Than Three Authors—MLA
4. Two or More Works by the Same Author(s)—MLA
5. Book by Group or Corporate Author—MLA
6. Book with No Author Named—MLA
7. Book with an Author and an Editor—MLA
8. Translation—MLA
9. Work in Several Volumes or Parts—MLA
10. One Selection from an Anthology or an Edited Book—MLA
11. More Than One Selection from the Same Anthology or Edited Book—MLA
12. Signed Article in a Reference Book—MLA
13. Unsigned Article in a Reference Book—MLA
14. Second or Later Edition—MLA
15. Anthology or Edited Book—MLA
16. Introduction, Preface, Foreword, or Afterword—MLA
17. Unpublished Dissertation or Essay—MLA
18. Reprint of an Older Book—MLA
19. Book in a Series—MLA
20. Book with a Title Within a Title—MLA
21. Government Publication—MLA
22. Published Proceedings of a Conference—MLA
23. Signed Article from a Daily Newspaper—MLA
24. Editorial, Letter to the Editor, or Review—MLA
25. Unsigned Article from a Daily Newspaper—MLA
26. Signed Article from a Weekly or Biweekly Periodical—MLA
27. Signed Article from a Monthly or Bimonthly Periodical—MLA
28. Unsigned Article from a Weekly or Monthly Periodical—MLA
29. Article from a Collection of Reprinted Articles—MLA
30. Article from a Looseleaf Collection of Reprinted Articles—MLA

Answers to Extra Exercise B

Works Cited

Clarke, Gerald. *Capote: A Biography.* New York: Simon, 1988.

Gould, Stephen Jay. *Time's Arrow, Time's Cycle: Myth and Metaphor in the Discovery of Geological Time.* Cambridge: Harvard UP, 1987.

Hibbert, Christopher. *The Rise and Fall of the House of Medici.* New York: Penguin, 1974.

Oates, Stephen B. *Abraham Lincoln: The Man Behind the Myths.* New York: Harper, 1984.

Peters, Thomas J., and Robert H. Waterman Jr. *In Search of Excellence.* New York: Harper, 1982.

Sacks, Oliver. "The Autist Artist." *The Man Who Mistook His Wife for a Hat, and Other Clinical Tales.* New York: Summit, n.d. 204-23.

Smout, T. C. *A Century of the Scottish People, 1830-1950.* New Haven: Yale UP, 1986.

Tuchman, Barbara W. *Practicing History.* New York: Knopf, 1981.

PORTFOLIOS DEFINED

Portfolios offer an effective, interactive learning strategy and assessment tool that raises students' abilities and motivation to assume responsibility for learning. Portfolios require that students go beyond merely keeping a writing folder as a work bin that does little more than house a number of grades to be averaged. Instead, portfolios should become a collection of work that profiles a student's commitment and achievement. To create such a profile appropriately, the student must be included in the selection of content, the basis for the selection, and the guidelines for evaluation, and must engage in ongoing self-reflection. This process is properly identified as authentic or performance assessment because it relies on what the student actually produces in a given situation. The power of the process lies in students' ability to see patterns of behaviors in their work, set independent goals, and monitor their own growth.

Portfolios will and should be as varied and diverse as the teachers and students creating them because they arise directly out of the needs of the class or program and the instruction delivered. This flexibility is a major strength of portfolio assessment; however, there are characteristics or guidelines that make the process distinctive. All portfolios should include work created over time, work selected by the instructor, work selected by the student, and an in-depth explanation or analysis in which the student justifies how and why the included work represents effort, progress, and achievement.

THREE-PHASE PROGRAM: DIAGNOSTIC, WORKING, AND DISPLAY PORTFOLIOS

Although the individuality and flexibility of portfolios are their chief benefits, sometimes the process of managing the paperwork seems overwhelming. To avoid the helter-skelter stress associated with portfolios, a three-phase portfolio template should allow for sensible implementation and yet maintain the diversity of instructional and learning needs. This is just one approach that has proved workable; feel free to design your own program.

62. URL Access: Poem—MLA
63. URL Access: Work of Art—MLA
64. URL Access: Interview—MLA
65. URL Access: Film or Film Clip—MLA
66. URL Access: Cartoon—MLA
67. URL Access: TV or Radio Program—MLA
68. URL Access: Academic Department Home Page—MLA

OTHER ONLINE SOURCES

69. Online Posting—MLA
70. Synchronous Communication—MLA
71. E-Mail Message—MLA

PRINT SOURCES

1. Book by One Author—MLA

Welty, Eudora. One Writer's Beginnings. Cambridge: Harvard UP, 1984.

2. Book by Two or Three Authors—MLA

Gordon, Edward E., and Elaine H. Gordon. Literacy in America: Historic Journey and Contemporary Solutions. Westport, CT: Praeger, 2003.

Kelly, Alfred H., Winfred A. Harbison, and Herman Belz. The American Constitution: Its Origins and Development. New York: Norton, 1983.

3. Book by More Than Three Authors—MLA

Moore, Mark H., et al. Dangerous Offenders: The Elusive Target of Justice. Cambridge: Harvard UP, 1984.

Give only the first author's name, followed by a comma and the phrase *et al.* ("and others"). Otherwise, you must list all authors.

4. Two or More Works by the Same Author(s)—MLA

Gardner, Howard. Intelligence Reframed: Multiple Intelligences for the 21st Century. New York: Basic, 1999.

---. Multiple Intelligences: The Theory in Practice. New York: Basic, 1993.

Give author name(s) in the first entry only. In the second and subsequent entries, use three hyphens and a period to stand for exactly the same name(s). If the person served as editor or translator, put a comma and the appropriate abbreviation (*ed.* or *trans.*) following the three hyphens. Arrange the works in alphabetical (not chronological) order according to book title, ignoring labels such as *ed.* or *trans.*

5. Book by Group or Corporate Author—MLA

American Psychological Association. <u>Publication Manual of the American Psychological Association</u>. 5th ed. Washington: APA, 2001.

Boston Women's Health Collective. <u>Our Bodies, Ourselves for the New Century</u>. New York: Simon, 1998.

Cite the full name of the corporate author first, omitting a beginning A, An, or The. When a corporate author is also the publisher, use a shortened form of the corporate name at the publisher position.

6. Book with No Author Named—MLA

<u>The Chicago Manual of Style</u>. 15th ed. Chicago: U of Chicago P, 2003.

If there is no author's name on the title page, begin the citation with the title. Alphabetize the entry according to the first significant word of the title (*Chicago,* not *The*).

7. Book with an Author and an Editor—MLA

If your paper refers to the work of the book's author, put the author's name first; if your paper refers to the work of the editor, put the editor's name first.

Brontë, Emily. <u>Wuthering Heights</u>. Ed. Richard J. Dunn. New York: Norton, 2002.

Dunn, Richard J. ed. <u>Wuthering Heights</u>. By Emily Brontë. New York: Norton, 2002.

8. Translation—MLA

Kundera, Milan. <u>The Unbearable Lightness of Being</u>. Trans. Michael Henry Heim. New York: HarperPerennial, 1999.

9. Work in Several Volumes or Parts—MLA

Chrisley, Ronald, ed. <u>Artificial Intelligence: Critical Concepts</u>. Vol. 1. London: Routledge, 2000. 4 vols.

If you are citing only one volume, put the volume number before the publication information. If you wish, you can give the total number of volumes at the end of the entry. MLA recommends using arabic numerals, even if the source uses roman numerals (*Vol. 6* for Vol. VI).

10. One Selection from an Anthology or an Edited Book—MLA

Galarza, Ernest. "The Roots of Migration." <u>Aztlan: An Anthology of Mexican American Literature</u>. Ed. Luis Valdez and Stan Steiner. New York: Knopf, 1972. 127-32.

Portfolios (continued)

Diagnostic Portfolio (Weeks 1–4)

This portfolio is created during the early weeks of the term through the assembly of all early work, which could include everything from in-class and formal writing assignments to journal entries to text and class notes. The whole point of this phase is to provide a clear, written record of the student's current abilities and commitment. This means that students must reflect (in a cover essay) on the implications of their work by analyzing their grades and teachers' comments; self-analysis allows students to set individual goals to be fulfilled throughout the remainder of the semester. This process is a modified application of the scientific method (see section 41e).

Working Portfolio (Weeks 5–13)

This portfolio contains all the work produced during the semester (except, of course, for the work already housed in the Diagnostic Portfolio): all formal and informal writing assignments, all prewriting and drafts, and any independent work on individual needs identified in the Diagnostic Portfolio, such as grammar remediation. The Working Portfolio could also contain all work associated with the research project, such as bibliography and note cards and photocopies of articles. The purpose of this phase in the portfolio process is to document progress and commitment and the relationship between the two. This does, indeed, profile time on task. In fact, this is the phase that clearly illustrates the relationship between quantity and quality of work.

Display Portfolio (Weeks 14–16)

This portfolio contains best works only. Therefore, the only pieces in this phase will be clean, polished drafts of writing produced and chronicled in the previous portfolio phases. The only new work in this section will be the final reflection essay that discusses in depth the student's achievement and establishes the evidence of the grade desired by the student. This discussion should include references to the work contained in both of the other portfolios.

→

579

Portfolios (continued)
**SHARPENING THE
LISTENING–READING–
WRITING CONNECTION**
Portfolios offer a structured, systematic "reading in the content course" approach. Indeed, the success of portfolio assessment rests in the comforting roots of its pedagogy, the synergistic relationship among listening, reading, and writing. Understanding this fundamental connection, as used in portfolio assessment, will make for effective and exciting results. Foster students' critical reading skills by asking them to pay attention to the purpose of each assignment, your feedback, and the textbook's information. For example, the Diagnostic Portfolio not only establishes pre-existing abilities and becomes a measuring tool for future growth and reflection but also quickly establishes the ongoing connection among listening, reading, and writing.

Using a variety of early-semester learning activities—such as in-class and take-home writing assignments, teacher feedback and scores, interest and behavior inventories, a diagnostic grammar test, and class notes—ask students to discuss their strengths and needs by providing a set of reflective questions. Once the student has identified an individual list of needs, require a textbook reconnaissance for the solutions for each problem, and have the student create a study plan based on the pages required to study, projected amount of time needed to study, and ways to measure mastery of each skill need. Notice that the student has had to actually read teacher comments, survey the textbook, establish prior knowledge, and use inference, prediction, and time-management skills. ➡

Give the author and title of the selection first and then the full title of the anthology. Information about the editor starts with *Ed.* (for "Edited by"), so do not use *Eds.* when there is more than one editor. Give the name(s) of the editor(s) in normal first name, second name order rather than reversing first and last names. The sample papers in section 40g provide further examples of documenting selections from anthologies.

11. More Than One Selection from the Same Anthology or Edited Book—MLA

Gilbert, Sandra M., and Susan Gubar, eds. <u>The Norton Anthology of Literature by Women</u>. New York: Norton, 1985.

Kingston, Maxine Hong. "No Name Woman." Gilbert and Gubar 2337-47.

Welty, Eudora. "The Petrified Man." Gilbert and Gubar 2322-32.

If you cite more than one selection from the same anthology, you can list the anthology as a separate entry with all the publication information. Also, list each selection from the anthology by author and title of the selection, but give only the name(s) of the editor(s) of the anthology and the page number(s) for each selection. Here, *ed.* stands for "editor," so it is correct to use *eds.* when more than one editor is named. List selections separately in alphabetical order by author's last name.

12. Signed Article in a Reference Book—MLA

Burnbam, John C. "Freud, Sigmund." <u>The Encyclopedia of Psychiatry, Psychology, and Psychoanalysis</u>. Ed. Benjamin B. Wolman. New York: Holt, 1996.

If the articles in the book are alphabetically arranged, omit volume and page numbers. If the reference book is frequently revised, give only the edition and year of publication.

13. Unsigned Article in a Reference Book—MLA

"Ireland." <u>The New Encyclopaedia Britannica: Macropaedia</u>. 15th ed. 2002.

If you are citing a widely used reference work, do not give full publication information. Instead, give only the edition and year of publication.

14. Second or Later Edition—MLA

Gibaldi, Joseph. <u>MLA Handbook for Writers of Research Papers</u>. 6th ed. New York: MLA, 2003.

If a book is not a first edition, the edition number appears on the title page. Place the abbreviated information (*2nd ed., 3rd ed.*, etc.) between the title and the publication information. Give only the latest copyright date for the edition you are using.

15 Anthology or Edited Book—MLA

Purdy, John L., and James Ruppert, eds. <u>Nothing But the Truth: An Anthology of</u>
<u>Native American Literature</u>. Upper Saddle River, NJ: Prentice, 2001.

Here, *ed.* stands for "editor," so use *eds.* when more than one editor is
named; also see items 10 and 11 in 34d.1.

16. Introduction, Preface, Foreword, or Afterword—MLA

Angeli, Primo. Foreword. <u>Shopping Bag Design 2: Creative Promotional</u>
<u>Graphics</u>. By Judi Radice. New York: Lib. of Applied Design-PBC
International, 1991. 8.

Give first the name of the writer of the part you are citing, then the
name of the cited part, capitalized but not underlined or in quotation
marks. After the book title, write *By* and the book author's full name, if
different from the writer of the cited material. If the writer of the cited
material is the same as the book author, include only the last name after
By. Following the publication information, give inclusive page numbers
for the cited part, using roman or arabic numerals as the source does.
When the introduction, preface, foreword, or afterword has a title (as
below), include it in the citation before the section name.

Fox-Genovese, Elizabeth. "Mothers and Daughters: The Ties That Bind."
Foreword. <u>Southern Mothers</u>. Ed. Nagueyalti Warren and Sally Wolff.
Baton Rouge: Louisiana State UP, 1999. iv-xviii.

17. Unpublished Dissertation or Essay—MLA

Byers, Michele. " 'Buffy the Vampire Slayer': The Insurgence of Television as a
Performance Text." Diss. U of Toronto, 2000.

State the author's name first, then the title in quotation marks (not underlined), then a descriptive label (such as *Diss.* or *Unpublished essay*),
followed by the degree-granting institution (for dissertations), and, finally, the date.

18. Reprint of an Older Book—MLA

Hurston, Zora Neale. <u>Their Eyes Were Watching God</u>. 1937. Urbana:
U of Illinois P, 1978.

Republishing information can be found on the copyright page. Give the
date of the original version before the publication information for the
version you are citing.

Portfolios (continued)
**INSTRUCTOR FEEDBACK IN THE
USE OF PORTFOLIO ASSESSMENT**
Too often, teachers hold on to information
that students really need. Portfolio assessment can be a tool to communicate this very
information in a nonthreatening and motiva-
tional manner. Instructor feedback is a valuable communication opportunity. Generally
speaking, feedback comes to the student in
one of two ways: grades and teacher comments. Students very often ignore the comments and are angered or discouraged by the
grades. The portfolio process can help students make insightful connections between
the two.

INDIVIDUAL ASSIGNMENTS
First, be sure that feedback never corrects
the mistake but only identifies it. Use correction symbols (see "Response Symbols" at the
back of this book) to identify the error; then
ask students to look up the rule, pull the
faulty sentence out of context for a grammar
exercise, and explain why the rule applies and
how to fix the error. In this way, feedback becomes an opportunity for a reflective journal
entry.
  If the paper is holistically scored, the
score itself becomes the feedback, and students should be provided with a rubric or
definition of what that score represents. The
student is then required to analyze, in a reflective journal entry, the reasons the paper
received the score it did, in addition to the
ways in which the paper could be rewritten to
improve it. Both holistic and trait scoring
should then allow the student to read the audience by responding to the implications of
the feedback.
→

Portfolios (continued)
PORTFOLIO FEEDBACK

Regardless of the kind of portfolio you implement, the scoring process can be a valuable opportunity to further the dialogue between student and instructor, and it can be accomplished rather quickly with a score sheet. Simply identify beforehand (this is an excellent occasion to include the class's participation) the traits and characteristics you expect to observe at each grade level; then, create a checklist for each of those characteristics. Be sure to leave room for a section marked "Comments" for individual explanations of your score, as needed. In this way, the scoring of portfolios can be a quick, holistic approach that provides meaningful feedback to the student.

PORTFOLIO SCORES

If you decide to use the three-phase portfolio, you have available three separate but distinct scores reflecting specific skills, strategies, and achievement that can be translated into percentages. Some instructors prefer to weight specific assignments within each portfolio. This weighted value can be included in the assessment score sheet. Again, the purpose of portfolios is to showcase the process as well as the product, so you want to create a scoring system that clearly and efficiently communicates your values.

STUDENT REFLECTION

The most crucial step in portfolio assessment is training students to think about their own work and the instructor's response to that work. This training occurs through the use of teacher-generated reflective questions about individual assignments as well as collections of assignments, as in a portfolio. That means that these questions can be used to introduce or review concepts, track progress, and justify ➜

19. Book in a Series—MLA

Goldman, Dorothy J. <u>Women Writers and World War I</u>. Literature and Society
    Ser. New York: Macmillan, 1995.

Mukherjee, Meenakshi. <u>Jane Austen</u>. Women Writers Ser. New York:
    St. Martin's, 1991.

20. Book with a Title Within a Title—MLA

The MLA recognizes two distinct styles for handling normally independent titles when they appear within an underlined title. In the MLA's preferred style, the embedded title should not be underlined or set within quotation marks.

Lumiansky, Robert M., and Herschel Baker, eds. <u>Critical Approaches to Six</u>
    <u>Major English Works</u>: Beowulf <u>Through</u> Paradise Lost. Philadelphia: U of
    Pennsylvania P, 1968.

However, the MLA now accepts a second style for handling such embedded titles. In the alternative form, the normally independent titles should be set within quotation marks, and they should be underlined.

Lumiansky, Robert M., and Herschel Baker, eds. <u>Critical Approaches to Six</u>
    <u>Major English Works</u>: "Beowulf" <u>Through</u> "Paradise Lost." Philadelphia:
    U of Pennsylvania P, 1968.

Use whichever style your instructor prefers.

21. Government Publication—MLA

United States. Cong. House. Committee on Resources. <u>Coastal Heritage Trail</u>
    <u>Route in New Jersey</u>. 106th Cong., 1st sess. H. Rept. 16. Washington:
    GPO, 1999.

---. ---. Senate. <u>Bill to Reauthorize the Congressional Award Act</u>. 106th Cong.,
    1st sess. S 380. Washington: GPO, 1999.

For government publications that name no author, start with the name of the government or government body. Then, name the government agency. *GPO* is a standard abbreviation for Government Printing Office, the publisher of most U.S. government publications.

22. Published Proceedings of a Conference—MLA

Harris, Diana, and Laurie Nelson-Heern, eds. <u>Proceedings of the National</u>
    <u>Education Computing Conference, June 17-19, 1981</u>. Iowa City: Weeg
    Computing Center, U of Iowa, 1981.

23. Signed Article from a Daily Newspaper—MLA

Killborn, Peter T. "A Health Threat Baffling for Its Lack of a Pattern." New York
    Times 22 June 2003, natl. ed.: A14.

Omit *A* or *The* as the first word in a newspaper title. Give the day,
month, and year of the issue (and the edition, if applicable). If sections
are designated, give the section letter as well as the page number. If an
article runs on nonconsecutive pages, give the starting page number followed by a plus sign (for example, 23+ for an article that starts on page
23 and continues on page 42).

24. Editorial, Letter to the Editor, or Review—MLA

"Downtown's Architectural Promise." Editorial. New York Times 4 Aug. 2003: A12.

Hansen, Roger P. Letter. Sierra Jan.-Feb. 2003: 8.

Shenk, David. "Toolmaker, Brain Builder." Rev. of Beyond Big Blue: Building
    the Computer That Defeated the World Chess Champion by Feng-Hsi-
    ung Hsu. American Scholar 72 (Spring 2003): 150-52.

25. Unsigned Article from a Daily Newspaper—MLA

"A Crusade to Revitalize the City Opera." New York Times 25 Jan. 2001,
    late ed.: B6.

"Fire Delays School Election." Patriot Ledger [Quincy, MA] 14 June 1994: A1.

If the city of publication is not part of the title, put it in square brackets
after the title, not underlined.

26. Signed Article from a Weekly or Biweekly Periodical—MLA

Fonda, Daren. "Plucky Little Competitors." Time 21 Oct. 2002: 60-62.

27. Signed Article from a Monthly or Bimonthly Periodical—MLA

Langewiesch, William. "Anarchy at Sea." Atlantic Monthly Sept. 2003: 50-80.

28. Unsigned Article from a Weekly or Monthly Periodical—MLA

"The Price Is Wrong." Economist 2 Aug. 2003: 58-59.

29. Article from a Collection of Reprinted Articles—MLA

Brumberg, Abraham. "Russia After Perestroika." New York Review of Books
    27 June 1991: 53-62. Rpt. in Russian and Soviet History. Ed. Alexander
    Dallin. Vol. 14 of The Gorbachev Era. New York: Garland, 1992. 300-20.

Portfolios (continued)

achievement. The following questions serve
as models that can be adapted to fit the individual needs of a group, program, or student; actual questions should come from the
teacher's observation of obstacles to achievement. Therefore, any of the Boxes featured
throughout this handbook can be turned into
reflective journal entries to focus the student
on an immediate and apparent need, yet the
best source for reflective questions is the behavior of the student in both cognitive and affective domains.

**Reflective Questions for Diagnostic
Portfolios**

Describe your current writing process.

    Has your writing process changed in any
    way?

    How long do you spend writing an essay?

    In what ways do you use your textbook?

    What information learned in class has
    helped you the most so far?

    What do you like or dislike about writing?

    Which is your strongest piece of writing
    (in-class or take-home work) and why?

    What is the relationship between your
    performance on the grammar test and
    your writing scores?

    Based on the grammar test and teacher
    feedback, what do you need to study?

    How many pages in the handbook do
    these skills cover?

    How long do you think you need to study
    each skill?

    How will you measure your mastery of
    these skills?

    What is your plan of study?

    How will you use your textbooks?

    What is your greatest strength as a writer? →

Portfolios (continued)
Reflective Questions for Working and Display Portfolios
Describe your current writing process and the ways in which it has changed from the beginning of the semester.

In what ways did your Diagnostic Portfolio indicate your needed improvement?

How did you ensure mastery of these skills and concepts?

How does the Display Portfolio reflect the goals set in the Diagnostic Portfolio?

How does the Display Portfolio reflect the effort that was exhibited in the Working Portfolio?

Why did you choose these pieces for your Display Portfolio?

How do they represent growth?

Summarize your learning—just what have you learned, and how do your portfolios reflect this learning?

What do you still need to learn?

If you did not achieve certain diagnostic goals, explain how you will ensure mastery of these needs in the next level of study.

What grade do these portfolios indicate you have earned? Explain your judgment.

For cover letters and journal entries, reflection will be an ongoing informal process, much as for a journal entry; however, formal self-assessment is the cornerstone of the portfolio. In the three-phase portfolio approach, there are two cover letters: one included in the Diagnostic Portfolio and one included in the Display Portfolio. These are formal and should be polished, best works. This is an excellent opportunity to incorporate business writing skills.

PORTFOLIO HINTS
To ensure the maximum benefit of portfolio assessment, use the following guidelines.

What Students Should Do

• Date and label everything. Dating and labeling will show when and where success occurred.

30. Article from a Looseleaf Collection of Reprinted Articles—MLA
Hayden, Thomas. "The Age of Robots." US News and World Report 23 Apr. 2001, 44+. Applied Science 2002. Ed. Eleanor Goldstein. Boca Raton, FL: SIRS, 2002. Art. 66.

Give the citation for the original publication first, followed by the citation for the collection.

31. Article in a Journal with Continuous Pagination—MLA
Tyson, Phyllis. "The Psychology of Women." Journal of the American Psychoanalytic Association 46 (1998): 361-64.

If the first issue of a journal with continuous pagination ends on page 228, the second issue starts with page 229. Give only the volume number before the year. Use arabic numerals for all numbers.

32. Article in a Journal That Pages Each Issue Separately—MLA
Adler-Kassner, Linda, and Heidi Estrem. "Rethinking Research Writing: Public Litaracy in the Composition Classroom." WPA: Writing Program Administration 26.3 (2003): 119-31.

When each issue begins with page 1, give both the volume number (26) and the issue number (3), separated by a period.

33. Abstract from a Collection of Abstracts—MLA
To cite an abstract, first give information for the full work: the author's name, the title of the article, and publication information about the full article. If a reader could not know that the cited material is an abstract, write the word *Abstract,* not underlined, followed by a period. Give publication information about the collection of abstracts. For abstracts identified by item numbers rather than page numbers, use the word *item* before the item number.

Marcus, Hazel R., and Shinobu Kitayamo. "Culture and the Self: Implications for Cognition, Emotion, and Motivation." Psychological Review 88 (1991): 224-53. Psychological Abstracts 78 (1991): item 23878.

34. Published and Unpublished Letters—MLA
Brown, Theodore. Letter to the author. 7 Dec. 2002.

Williams, William Carlos. Letter to his son. 13 Mar. 1935. Letters of the Century: America 1900-1999. Ed. Lisa Grunwald and Stephen J. Adler. New York: Dial, 1999: 225-26.

35. Microfiche Collection of Articles—MLA

Wenzell, Ron. "Businesses Prepare for a More Diverse Work Force." St. Louis Post
 Dispatch 3 Feb. 1990: 17. NewsBank: Employment 27 (1990): fiche 2, grid D12.

NONPRINT SOURCES

36. Interview—MLA

Friedman, Randi. Telephone interview. 30 June 2003.

For a face-to-face interview, use *Personal interview* in place of *Telephone interview*. For a published interview, give the name of the interviewed person first, identify the source as an interview, and then give details as for any published source: title; author, preceded by the word *By;* and publication details. For a URL-accessed interview, see item 64 of this section.

37. Lecture, Speech, or Address—MLA

Kennedy, John Fitzgerald. Address. Greater Houston Ministerial Assn.
 Houston. 12 Sept. 1960.

38. Film, Videotape, or DVD—MLA

It Happened One Night. Screenplay by Robert Riskin. Dir. and Prod. Frank
 Capra. Perf. Clark Gable and Claudette Colbert. 1934. Videocassette.
 Columbia, 1999.

Shakespeare in Love. Screenplay by Marc Norman and Tom Stoppard. Dir.
 John Madden. Prod. David Parfitt, Donna Gigliotti, Harvey Weinstein,
 Edward Zwick, and Marc Norman. Perf. Gwyneth Paltrow, Joseph
 Fiennes, and Judi Dench. DVD. Miramax, 2003.

Give the title first, and include the director, the distributor, and the year. For older films subsequently released on videocassette, DVD, or laser disc, provide the original release date of the movie before the type of medium. Other information (writer, producer, major actors) is optional but helpful. Put first names first.

39. Recording—MLA

Smetana, Bedrich. My Country. Cond. Karel Anserl. Czech Philharmonic Orch.
 LP. Vanguard, 1975.

Springsteen, Bruce. "Lonesome Day." The Rising. Sony, 2002.

Put first the name most relevant to what you discuss in your paper (performer, conductor, the work performed, etc.). Include the recording's

Portfolios (continued)

- Reflect frequently. Students have to learn how to think, so they need frequent practice in written reflection. Also, individual reflections become the prewrites for the cover letters.

- Revise and resubmit work frequently. Students need to see that work does improve with effort. To minimize your workload, encourage peer editing of drafts, and use holistic scoring and rubrics whenever possible.

What Instructors Might Need to Do

- Encourage cross-curriculum connections. Students too often don't understand that writing is a tool for success in other courses. If possible, allow students to submit work required in other classes along with reflections discussing the impact of their writing instruction in other academic situations.

- Publish rubrics for the portfolio itself. Students need to understand the criteria, so short paragraphs describing an A, B, C, D, or F portfolio should enhance success. These standards may include criteria about work habits (timeliness, neatness, etc.) as well as about the work product.

- Require a specified length for the cover letters to ensure in-depth details.

- Clarify the relationship between the cover essays and the portfolios. For the process offered here, there are two cover letters: one placed in the Diagnostic Portfolio and one placed in the Display Portfolio (which actually discusses the work in all three portfolio phases).

- Confer frequently with the student and examine the student's portfolio. These conferences don't have to take much time because of the evidence of the student's work. Be sure to have the student take notes of any advice given during the conference as a portfolio entry.

- Place the workload on the student whenever possible. The more work students do, the more they learn.

RESEARCH: PORTFOLIO APPROACHES AND ACTIVITIES
The research project offers a sound opportunity for a task-oriented, self-contained portfolio or a rich selection for a program or class portfolio. Obviously, the research process requires the student to synthesize multiple correlated skills and concepts. By carefully dating, labeling, and reflecting on this sophisticated reading and writing task, students can see, refine, and deepen learning before, during, and after various strategic stages of the process. The pivotal components of portfolio assessment that delineate it from traditional assessments are student reflection and input. Students must assume the responsibility of creating and defending the meaning and quality of the learning taking place.

Reading-Writing Connection
Place the responsibility for learning on the student by reiterating the reading-writing connection. The technical aspects of the research format and the density of the instructional material strain the functional and textual reading abilities of many students. Well-guided reflection can activate reading strategies such as previewing, skimming, and questioning and provide dated portfolio entries.

Provide five to ten minutes of class time for the students to skim the entire chapter and to record impressionistic responses to the following prompts: Record your first reaction to this material. What seems clear to you? What confuses you? Which sections seem most important and why? Write out five questions, and rank them from "dumb" to "important." How much time do you need to study this chapter to understand the material and why? When will you do this studying?

Using the Reporter's Questions in Reflecting and Researching
Keep the instructional responsibility on the student by using the material summarized in the special Boxes throughout this handbook as the basis of reflective informal journals.

→

title, the medium for any recording other than a CD (e.g., *LP*, *Audiocassette*), name of the issuer (e.g., *Vanguard*), and the year.

40. Live Performance—MLA
Via Dolorosa. By David Hare. Dir. Steven Daldry. Perf. David Hare. Lincoln Center Theater, New York. 11 Apr. 1999.

41. Work of Art, Photograph, or Musical Composition—MLA
Cassatt, Mary. La Toilette. Art Institute of Chicago.

Mydans, Carl. General Douglas MacArthur Landing at Luzon, 1945. Soho Triad Fine Art Gallery, New York. 21 Oct.-28 Nov. 1999.

Schubert, Franz. Symphony no. 8 in B minor.

Schubert, Franz. Unfinished Symphony.

Do not underline or put in quotation marks music identified only by form, number, and key, but do underline any work that has a title, such as an opera or ballet or a named symphony.

42. Radio or Television Program—MLA
"Episode One." The Forsyte Saga. By John Galsworthy. Adapt. Stephen Mallatratt and Jan McVerry. Prod. Sita Williams. Masterpiece Theatre. PBS. WGBH, Boston. 6 Oct. 2002.

Not for Ourselves Alone: The Story of Elizabeth Cady Stanton and Susan B. Anthony. Writ. Ken Burns. Perf. Julie Harris, Ronnie Gilbert, and Sally Kellerman. Prod. Paul Barnes and Ken Burns. PBS. WNET, New York. 8 Nov. 1999.

Include at least the title of the program (underlined), the network, the local station and its city, and the date(s) of the broadcast. For a series, also supply the title of the specific episode (in quotation marks) before the title of the program (underlined) and the title of the series (neither underlined nor in quotation marks), as in the first example above.

43. Map or Chart—MLA
The Caribbean and South America. Map. Falls Church, VA: AAA, 1992.

44. Advertisement—MLA
American Airlines. Advertisement. ABC. 24 Aug. 2003.

Canon Digital Cameras. Advertisement. Time 2 June 2003: 77.

PORTABLE ELECTRONIC SOURCES

45. CD-ROM Database: Abstract with a Print Version—MLA

Marcus, Hazel R., and Shinobu Kitayamo. "Culture and the Self: Implications

for Cognition, Emotion, and Motivation." Psychological Abstracts 78

(1991): item 23878. PsycLIT. CD-ROM. SilverPlatter. Sept. 1991.

All the information through *item 23878* is for the print version of this source. The volume number is 78, and the abstract's number is 23878. All the information from *PsycLIT* to the end of the entry is for the electronic version of the source. *PsycLIT* is the name of the CD-ROM database, and *SilverPlatter* is the name of the producer of the CD-ROM. The CD-ROM was issued in September 1991.

46. CD-ROM: Article from a Periodical with a Print Version—MLA

"The Price Is Right." Time 20 Jan. 1992: 38. Time Man of the Year. CD-ROM.

Compact. 1993.

Information for the print version ends with the article's page number, 38. The title of the CD-ROM is *Time Man of the Year*, its producer is the publisher Compact, and its copyright year is 1993. Both the title of the print publication and the title of the CD-ROM are underlined.

47. CD-ROM: Selection from a Book with a Print Version—MLA

"Prehistoric Humans: Earliest Homo sapiens." The Guinness Book of Records

1994. London: Guinness, 1994. The Guinness Multimedia Disk of Records.

CD-ROM. Version 2.0. Danbury, CT: Grolier Electronic, 1994.

Version 2.0 signals that this CD-ROM is updated periodically; the producer changes version numbers rather than give update dates.

48. CD-ROM: Material with No Print Version—MLA

"Artificial Intelligence." Encarta 2003. CD-ROM. Redmond, WA: Microsoft, 2003.

Encarta 2003 is a CD-ROM encyclopedia with no print version. "Artificial Intelligence" is the title of an article in *Encarta 2003*.

49. Work in More Than One Publication Medium—MLA

Clarke, David James. Novell's CNE Study Guide. Book. Network Support

Encyclopedia. CD-ROM. Alameda, CA: Sybex, 1994.

This book and CD-ROM come together. Each has its own title, but the publication information—*Alameda, CA: Sybex, 1994*—applies to both.

Research: Portfolios (continued)

For example, certain items in Box 128, "Sample schedule for a research project," in section 31d, combined with the exemplified research log in section 31e, provide excellent roots for reflective questions and answers.

Item 2, "Choose a topic suitable for research," could be presented as a two- to three-minute class opener to establish prior knowledge and preview the lesson in the following manner: What would be a suitable topic for research and why? What topics would you like to learn and read about? Does this topic have two sides? Which side do you presently support and why?

Item 10, "Locate and evaluate sources," could yield a subsequent set of questions: Where would information on this topic likely be found? Who would be best qualified to offer an opinion and why? How many different types of sources might be available? Where and how could you locate these sources?

This procedural model yields as many questions for lively class discussion and quiet written reflection as you have time for in your curriculum. Choose your own focus and create questions that help students connect the function, form, and processes of learning activities to knowledge.

Research Portfolio: Task-Oriented, Self-Contained Profile of a Student Researcher

The following information can be quickly and easily translated into an overview handout for a research portfolio. Such a handout provides the student with a reference document throughout the learning and assessment process. However, many of the question, reflection, and writing activities may be assigned in an ongoing fashion through daily, informal journals that can, by design, preview, reinforce, or review specific steps in the research process. To reinforce the relationship among reading, listening, speaking, and writing, try scheduling some time for small group and whole class discussion as

Research: Portfolios (continued)
talk-aloud reflections. Sponsor a "hallway bull session" in class; just remind students to record their questions and understandings.

Before research begins, establish prior knowledge and stimulate learning readiness by asking students to record reflections in any or all of the following ways: Briefly describe your research history—how many times have you researched? How will information already learned in this class help in the research process? What are the purposes of research? What was the required documentation style? Describe your success with the process. Describe your struggles with the process. Describe your preferred method of research.

As research proceeds, encourage students to track and document every minute spent on research by dating and recording reflections on any or all of the following topics (you may want to reword these prompts in language appropriate for your student audience):

- Concepts: What is the value of your topic—who cares or needs to know about it? What is its value to the audience? What are the inherent biases for or against the topic? What propaganda techniques are used by opposing sides of this topic, if any, and how are they employed? Record and describe new understandings or changed views as you research. What action, if any, do you want from your reader?

- Procedures: Date and record questions that occur to you as you listen to instruction and lectures, hunt for proper formats in the textbook, create bibliography and note cards, and then apply the style rules to your paper. Date, record, and label answers to your questions as you learn them. Using the model in Box 128 in section 31d, present your own step-by-step research process. Discuss why you might implement your own adaptations of textbook- or lecture-given procedures. This method can be quickly refined into an additional five minutes of quickly written reflections that create a daily record of the attention you are giving to your studies.

SOURCES FROM LIBRARY OR PERSONAL SUBSCRIPTION SERVICES

Online sources fall into two categories: (1) those you access through a library online service, such as EBSCO or FirstSearch, or a personal service, such as America Online; and (2) those you access by browsing the Internet or entering a specific URL. For source material reached through an online service, give the name of the service, and if you used a keyword (for your search), give it after the access date.

50. Library Subscription Service: Abstract with a Print Version—MLA

Marcus, Hazel R., and Shinobu Kitayamo. "Culture and the Self: Implications for Cognition, Emotion, and Motivation." Psychological Abstracts 78 (1991). PsycINFO. Ovid. Milner Lib., Illinois State U. 10 Apr. 2003 <http://gateway1.ovid.com/ovidweb.cgi>.

This entry is for the same abstract from *Psychological Abstracts* shown in item 45, but here it is accessed from an online database (*PsycINFO*) by means of an online service (*Ovid*). This entry notes *PsycINFO*, the name of the online database, whereas item 45 notes *PsycLIT*, the name of the CD-ROM database; and it notes *Ovid*, the service through which *PsycINFO* was accessed, whereas item 45 notes the CD-ROM producer, *SilverPlatter.* The name of the library shows where the source was accessed and *10 Apr. 2003* is the date that the abstract was accessed. The entry ends with the specific URL used.

51. Personal Subscription Service: Material with No Print Version—MLA

"Microsoft Licenses OSM Technology from Henter-Joyce." WinNews Electronic Newsletter 1 May 1995. CompuServe. 15 May 1995.

Many personal subscription services do not provide a separate URL for individual materials they offer.

52. Personal Subscription Service, Access with a Keyword: Article from a Periodical with a Print Version—MLA

Wynne, Clive D. L. "'Willy' Didn't Yearn to Be Free." New York Times. 27 Dec. 2003: Op-ed page. New York Times Online. America Online. 29 Dec. 2003. Keyword: nytimes.

Information applying to the print version of this article in the *New York Times* ends with *Op-ed page,* and information about the online version starts with the title of the database, *New York Times Online. America Online* is the service through which the database was accessed, and *29 Dec. 2003* is the access date. The keyword *nytimes* was used to access *New York Times Online,* as noted after the access date.

53. Personal Subscription Service Showing a Path—MLA

When you access a source by choosing a series of keywords, menus, or topics, end the entry with the "path" of words you used. Use semicolons between items in the path, and put a period at the end.

Futrelle, David. "A Smashing Success." Money.com 23 Dec. 1999. America

Online. 26 Dec. 1999. Path: Personal Finance; Business News; Business

Publications; Money.com.

54. Library Subscription Service: Article—MLA

For an article accessed through a library's online service, first give information about the source. Then, list the name of the online database, the name of the online service through which it was accessed, the name of the library, and the access date. Give the URL of the online service's home page, if you know it, after the access date. Enclose the URL in angle brackets and put a period after the closing bracket.

Dutton, Gail. "Greener Pigs." Popular Science Nov. 1999: 38-39. ProQuest

Periodical Abstracts Plus Text. ProQuest Direct. Public Lib., Teaneck, NJ.

7 Dec. 1999 <http://proquest.umi.com>.

VandeHei, Jim. "Two Years After White House Exit, Clinton Shaping

Democratic Party." Washington Post, final ed. 21 June 2003: A1.

Academic Universe. LexisNexis. Bobst Lib., New York U. 12 Nov. 2003

<http://web.lexis-nexis.com/>.

SOURCES FROM INTERNET SITES

This section shows models for online sources accessed through an Internet browser, such as Web sites; FTP and Gopher sites; listservs; discussion groups; and other online sources. For such sources, provide as much of the following information as you can.

1. The author's name, if given.
2. In quotation marks, the title of a short work (Web page, brief document, essay, article, message, and so on); or underlined, the title of a book.
3. Publication information for any print version, if it exists.
4. The name of an editor, translator, or compiler, if any, with an abbreviation such as *Ed.*, *Trans.*, or *Comp.* before the name.
5. The underlined title of the Internet site (scholarly project, database, online periodical, professional or personal Web site). If the site has no title, describe it: for example, *Home page.*
6. The date of electronic publication (including a version number, if any), or posting, or the most recent update.

Research: Portfolios (continued)

- Technology. Date, record, and label the ways in which technology enhances or complicates your work. Do you have access to a computer or word processor? How often and in what ways do you use the library's or learning center's computerized databases? How often and in what ways do you use the Internet? Discuss the ease or frustration of your experiences. What are the greatest benefits of computers in the research-writing process?

Once research concludes, ask students to determine the value of their work by assigning themselves a grade and then defending that grade through a formal reflective summary and synthesis of learning activities, growth, and mastery. Remember, the following questions only serve as models; experiment and create your own questions that mirror your instructional emphasis.

- Concepts: Readdress relevant questions asked before research began with the intent to demonstrate dynamic understanding. Also, include a discussion about things you still need to learn, as evidenced in the portfolio: In what ways would you improve your use of the research process? This paper? What still confuses you? Based on feedback and grades, what do you still need to learn? How would you do so, if given the chance? Record and reflect on the connections between research and writing strategies learned earlier in the term. For example, discuss the way in which the use of verbs helped you integrate source material into your prose (see 33g and 33k).

- Procedures: Discuss the effectiveness of bibliography and note cards (see 31i and 31j). In what way does your portfolio reflect the use and value of your various sources (32j)? Describe your search strategy and its success (32b). Discuss why you implemented your own adaptations of textbook- or lecture-given procedures. How have research skills developed study skills? How are these skills relevant to other courses, life, or career? →

MLA

Research: Portfolios (continued)
- Technology: What new technological knowledge or skills did you gain from the research process? What are the pitfalls or limitations of technology?

Creating a Research Process Profile

This approach allows students to showcase their growing understanding and mastery of the research process. Encourage students to chronicle the research process through a show-and-tell technical report that demonstrates skills and applications and discusses procedural decisions and the impact of those decisions. Consider, for example, the following series of steps and journal reflections:

1. Create a registry that logs and tracks sources (31e).

2. Create and catalog bibliography cards (31i).

3. Provide sample photocopies or printouts of sources.

4. Use these to identify and highlight possible ideas for note cards.

5. Create and label note cards (31j).

6. Reclassify cards into outline order (31l).

7. Write a draft from the note cards rearranged into outline order (31m).

8. Complete the writing process.

9. Write an informal research summary reflection. It should describe your individual adaptations or variations from the expected procedures; describe the relationship between steps in the procedure; discuss challenges, understandings, and rewards met through this process; and discuss any specific, new knowledge and fact versus opinion, authoritative sources, notetaking, and synthesis skills. In what way does this profile prove your mastery and the grade you seek? (See Box 132 in section 31m for points that can be adapted. A sample sentence may read, "This researcher worked with her notes in front of her.")

10. Write a formal draft of the research reflection.

→

7. The name of a sponsoring organization, if any.

8. The date you accessed the material.

9. The URL in angle brackets (< >), with a period after the closing bracket. If the URL is too long or complicated, simply use the URL of the site's search page or of a subscription service, followed by *Keyword* or *Path*, and the links you followed. In MLA style, turn a URL, do so only after a slash.

55. Online Book—MLA

Chopin, Kate. The Awakening. 1899. PBS Electronic Library. 10 Dec. 1998. PBS. 12 Dec. 2003 <http://www.pbs.org/katechopin/library/awakening>.

56. Online Book in a Scholarly Project—MLA

Herodotus. The History of Herodotus. Trans. George Rawlinson. Internet Classics Archive. Ed. Daniel C. Stevenson. 11 Jan. 1998. Massachusetts Institute of Technology. 15 May 2003 <http://classics.mit.edu/Herodotus/history.html>.

57. Online Government-Published Books—MLA

United States. Cong. Research Service. Space Stations. By Marcia S. Smith. 12 Dec. 1996. 4 Dec. 2003 <http://fas.org/spp/civil/crs/93-017.htm>.

United States. Dept. of Justice. Natl. Inst. of Justice. Comparing the Criminal Behavior of Youth Gangs and At-Risk Youths. By C. Ronald Hoff. Oct. 1998. 4 Dec. 2003 <http://www.ncjrs.org/txtfiles/172852.txt>.

For government publications that name no author, start with the name of the government or government body, and then name the government agency. For a government text, the title is followed by the writer of the publication, if available.

58. Articles in Online Periodicals—MLA

Didion, Joan. "The Day Was Hot and Still. . . ." Rev. of Dutch: A Memoir of Ronald Reagan, by Edmund Morris. New York Review of Books 4 Nov. 1999. 6 June 2002 <http://www.nybooks.com/nyrev/www.archdisplay.cgi?19991104004R>.

Gold, David. "Ulysses: A Case Study in the Problems of Hypertextualization of Complex Documents." Computers, Writing, Rhetoric and Literature 3.1 (1997): 37 pars. 4 Dec. 1999 <http://www.cwrl.utexas.edu/~cwrl/v3nl/dgold/title.htm>.

Keegan, Paul. "Culture Quake." Mother Jones Nov.-Dec. 1999. 6 Feb. 2003
    <http://www.mojones.com/mother_jones/ND99/ quake.html>.

Lewis, Ricki. "Chronobiology Researchers Say Their Field's Time Has Come."
    Scientist 11 Dec. 1995: 14. 30 Dec. 2003 <http://www.the-scientist.com/
    yr1995/dec/chrono_951211.html>.

Rimer, Sarah. "Retired Doctors Head Back to Work." New York Times on the
    Web 4 Dec. 1999. 4 Dec. 1999 <http:/nytimes.com/yr/mo/day/news/
    national/retired-doctors.html>.

59. URL Access: Professional Home Page—MLA

American Association for Artificial Intelligence. 17 Mar. 2003 <http://
    www.aaai.org>.

60. URL Access: Personal Home Page—MLA

Hesse, Doug. Home page. 15 Nov. 2003. 22 Dec. 2003 <http://www.ilstu.edu/
    ~ddhesse>.

For home pages, include as much of the following information as you
can find:

1. If available, the name of the person who created or set up the home
   page. If first and last names are given, reverse the order of the first
   author's name.
2. The title, underlined. If there is no title, add the description *Home
   page,* not underlined, followed by a period.
3. For a professional home page, the name of the professional (not
   commercial) sponsoring organization.
4. The date you accessed the material.
5. The URL in angle brackets (< >), with a period after the closing
   bracket.

61. URL Access: Government or Institutional Web Site—MLA

Home Education and Privacy Tutoring. Home page. Pennsylvania Department
    of Education. 17 Oct. 2002 <http://www.pde.state.pa.us/home_education/
    site/default.asp>.

62. URL Access: Poem—MLA

Browning, Elizabeth Barrett. "Past and Future." The Women's Studies Database
    Reading Room. U of Maryland. 9 June 2003. 17 Oct. 2003 <http://
    www.mith2.umd.edu/WomensStudies/ReadingRoom/Poetry/>.

591

Research: Portfolios (continued)
Creating a Research Skill Profile
This variation of the show-and-tell technical
approach allows students to showcase and illustrate the relationship between building individual skills and creating the final product.
Encourage students to target independent and
individual needs and demonstrate goal setting,
time on task, growing understanding, and, ultimately, mastery. Once the need is targeted,
chronicle growth by creating a series of reflections based on the following steps:

1. Create a self-monitoring log or registry
for daily work.

2. Survey instruction and feedback (scores
and comments), and write a list of things you
need to know to earn the desired grade
(needs will run the gamut from time management to grammar to computer skills).

3. Locate print resources that address each
item on the need-to-know list (take note of
textbooks, libraries, learning centers), and set
up a study system.

4. Locate nonprint resources that address
each need-to-know item (take note of computer software, tutors, peers, teacher conferences, etc.).

5. Set up a study schedule timeline.

6. Create and organize print copies of each
study session.

7. Label each study session with date, time
spent on task, and purpose of task.

8. After each study session (or periodically),
write an application reflection discussing how
the information studied will improve research
writing. Remember, voluminous practice produces skill, so reflect and write often.

9. As mastery of an individual skill is
achieved, make a significant registry entry as
proof or evidence of growth and reward.

10. Upon completion of the research project, write a final informal self-assessment defending the value of your studies and the
worth of your new information. Assign yourself a grade, and give evidence to support the
worth of that judgment.

11. Write a final, formal draft to submit with
the registry.

→

Research: Portfolios (continued)

Portfolio Assessment as Action Research

Portfolios are wonderful research resources in themselves. Based on a shared curriculum and the sound pedagogy of self-monitoring for comprehension, the portfolio can be designed to explore specific contextual learning issues. For example, the ESL student or any special student population may be able to articulate successful study strategies that might be of benefit to other students. Sometimes, the complex issues surrounding testing and assessment clash with the instructional program or student needs; portfolios may offer a method of tracing and assessing these complex issues.

- Portfolio research empowers teachers. Remember that this reflective learning strategy will empower you, the instructor; quick, holistic reads and scores will provide a valuable and authentic tracking record of comprehension. The implications in research are numerous. For example, you may wish to document your own program's effectiveness by tracking the characteristics of the students' reflections, portfolio products, and grades to traditional or objective measurements, such as GPA or standardized test scores. Or if you want to track your teaching effectiveness in strategic lessons to ensure mastery, student reflections offer sound primary documents on which to base such assessments. Also, students reflect teacher values; if you ask meaningful questions that interest you, students will respond in kind.

- Portfolio research empowers students. The foundation skill of self-monitoring by creating a series of responses to teacher prompts allows students the opportunity to teach themselves to see and solve problems. Sometimes, the very act of talking or writing through a problem provides insight or solution. Therefore, this ongoing self-assessment is of particular benefit to students who come to the college writing class with unrealistic expectations or scant preparation. Students eagerly accept the

→

63. URL Access: Work of Art—MLA

Van Gogh, Vincent. The Starry Night, 1889. Museum of Modern Art, New York.
5 Dec. 2003 <http://www.moma.org./>. Keyword: Starry Night.

64. URL Access: Interview—MLA

Pope, Carl. Interview. Salon. 29 Apr. 2002. 27 Dec. 2003 <http://archive.salon.com/
people/interview/2002/04/29/carlpope/index_np.html>.

65. URL Access: Film or Film Clip—MLA

Columbus, Chris, dir. Harry Potter and the Sorcerer's Stone. Trailer. Warner
Brothers, 2001. 5 Dec. 2003 <http://www.hollywood.com/>.

66. URL Access: Cartoon—MLA

Harris, Sidney. "We have lots of information technology." Cartoon. New Yorker.
27 May 2002. 26 Aug. 2003 <http://www.cartoonbank.com>.

67. URL Access: TV or Radio Program—MLA

Chayes, Sarah. "Concorde." All Things Considered. Natl. Public Radio. 26 July
2000. 7 Dec. 2001 <http://www.npr.org/programs/atc/archives>.

68. URL Access: Academic Department Home Page—MLA

English. Dept. home page. Rutgers U, New Brunswick. 26 Feb. 2003. <http://
english.rutgers.edu>.

OTHER ONLINE SOURCES

69. Online Posting—MLA

Woodbury, Chuck. "Free RV Campgrounds." Online posting. 4 Dec. 1999. The
RV Home Page Bulletin Board. 21 Dec. 1999 <http://www.rvhome.com/
wwwboard/messages/4598.html>.

Be cautious about using online postings as sources. Some postings contain cutting-edge information from experts, but some contain trash. Unfortunately, you have no way to know whether people online are who they claim to be. To cite an online message, give the author name (if any), the title of the message in quotation marks, and then *Online posting.* Give the date of the posting and the name of the bulletin board, if any. Then, give the access date and, in angle brackets, the URL.

70. Synchronous Communication—MLA

Bleck, Bradley. Online discussion of "Virtual First Year Composition: Distance
Education, the Internet, and the World Wide Web." 8 June 1997. DaMOO.
27 Feb. 1999 <http://DaMOO.csun.edu/CW/brad.html>.

Give the name of the speaker, a title for the event ("Virtual First Year Composition: Distance Education, the Internet, and the World Wide Web"), the forum (DaMOO), event or posting date, access date, and URL.

71. E-Mail Message—MLA

Thompson, Jim. "Bob Martin's Opinions." E-mail to June Cain. 11 Nov. 2003.

Start with the name of the person who wrote the e-mail message. Give the title or subject line in quotation marks. Then, describe the source (*E-mail*) and identify the recipient. End with the date.

34d.2 Using content or bibliographic notes in MLA style

In MLA style, footnotes or endnotes serve two specific purposes: (1) You can use them for content (ideas and information) that does not fit into your paper but is still worth relating; and (2) you can use them for bibliographic information that would intrude if you were to include it in your text. Place a note number at the end of a sentence, if possible. Put it after any punctuation mark except the dash. Do not put any space before a note number, and put one space after it. Raise the note number a little above the line of words, as shown in the following examples.

TEXT OF PAPER

Eudora Welty's literary biography, <u>One Writer's Beginnings</u>, shows us how both the inner world of self and the outer world of family and place form a writer's imagination.[1]

CONTENT NOTE—MLA

[1] Welty, who valued her privacy, always resisted investigation of her life. However, at the age of seventy-four, she chose to present her own autobiographical reflections in a series of lectures at Harvard University.

TEXT OF PAPER

Barbara Randolph believes that enthusiasm is contagious (65).[1] Many psychologists have found that panic, fear, and rage spread more quickly in crowds than positive emotions do, however.

BIBLIOGRAPHIC NOTE—MLA

[1] Others who agree with Randolph include Thurman 21, 84, 155; Kelley 421–25; and Brookes 65–76.

Research: Portfolios (continued)

challenge to prove themselves by justifying the impact of mistakes or immaturity, then demonstrating the outcomes of changed behavior based on reflection and goal setting. In this sense, students will be studying themselves by observing, documenting, and explaining their behavior, your instruction, and feedback. However, the talented, gifted student also benefits through this process. Again and again, talented students exceed expectations and offer creative, stimulating models for peers.

Portfolio Hint

The student is the key. The student is the very center of instruction and, therefore, must demonstrate a strong work ethic to substantiate learning. Too many teachers fear giving numerous writing assignments because of the volume of scoring. We all know that students do not do much work if the assignment is not to be graded. However, four components of portfolios fuel their success: clearly communicated standards, holistic scoring, organized independent work (homework), and student reflection. Student success courses warn students that for every hour spent in class, students must also spend three hours out of class working independently. Portfolios give that out-of-class work a framework that helps illuminate the relationship between work and knowledge. So devote some class time early in the term to training students in reflection and journal writing, and then encourage them to assume full responsibility; expect them to do this, and they will.

34e A student's MLA-style research paper

34e.1 Researching and writing the paper

Case Study

Chandra Johnson was given this assignment for a research paper: Write a research paper on the general subject of technology. The paper should be 1,800 to 2,000 words long and should be based on a variety of sources. The final paper is due in six weeks. Interim deadlines for parts of the work will be announced. To complete this assignment, you need to engage in three interrelated processes: conducting research, understanding the results of that research, and writing a paper based on the first two processes. Consult the *Simon & Schuster Handbook for Writers*, especially Chapters 31–33, which give practical, step-by-step guidance on what this assignment entails.

Chandra Johnson was eager to plan her research schedule so that she could budget her time and not end up in a panic of time pressure. She knew from experience that she would likely have the most trouble in the first stages of her research process as she narrowed her topic and began to look for useful sources. She resolved to face the challenge calmly and patiently.

The general topic assigned was "technology." Johnson realized that she had to take many steps to narrow it to a TOPIC suitable for a research paper (31b). Collecting possible subject headings and topic key words was her first step. Because she was working in her room and had a connection to the Internet, she first connected to the google.com subject directory. While she didn't find a heading there for "technology," she did find ones for "computers" and "science." Clicking on the "science" category, Johnson found a link to "technology." When she looked at the headings under "technology," the topic "artificial intelligence" caught her attention. Ever since she had seen the movie *A.I. Artificial Intelligence*, she had been fascinated by the possibility that people might someday be able to make machines that acted like humans. She browsed several links under "artificial intelligence" and jotted ideas in her research log. However, she soon became confused by all of the options that were available. It was time, Johnson decided, to proceed more systematically through library resources.

When she was next on campus, she went to the library to check its online catalog. Johnson decided that finding some general books on the subject of artificial intelligence would help her get a sense of this complicated topic. She entered the phrase as a keyword search and learned it was a Library of Congress Subject Heading, which meant she was on a helpful track. Furthermore, her library owned several recent books on the topic. She chose a few that looked promising. Johnson copied information about them, including their call numbers, onto some note cards she'd brought for her working bibliography, then e-mailed the full citations to herself as a backup. She noticed that the call numbers were mostly around Q335 but that others began with BD or BF. She found that the latter call numbers were from the philosophy and psychology sections of the library.

To limit her search—and because she knew this field was changing rapidly—she decided to focus on books written in the past ten years. Although the most promising volume was checked out, another current book, *Arguing A.I.: The Battle for Twenty-First-Century Science,* was almost as promising. From the book's cover, Johnson saw that its author, Sam Williams, was a freelance writer and not an expert, so she knew she'd have to check his ideas. However, because the book discussed several important figures in artificial intelligence, including John McCarthy and Ray Kurzweil, it pointed to some expert sources that she later consulted for her paper, including a "Website Resources Directory."

At this point, Johnson was still feeling overwhelmed. Clearly, there was a vast amount of information available on artificial intelligence, and she would need to narrow her search. One breakthrough came as she explored ideas in her research log. As a broad draft RESEARCH QUESTION, she asked, "What is artificial intelligence?" only to realize that there was an even more basic question: "What is intelligence?"

Johnson looked up "intelligence" in the *Columbia Encyclopedia,* a general reference book she was familiar with from high school. A concept developed by Howard Gardner of Harvard University captured her interest. Gardner states that human intelligence actually consists of eight different kinds of intelligence and not just IQ (for "intelligence quotient"). She wrote down Gardner's name as a possible authority (see Box 131 in 31i) and was delighted to find several books by him in her library's catalog. One of them, *Frames of Mind,* became a source on her topic. Further reading in the area of multiple intelligences stirred her interest in emotional intelligence. Books by Daniel Goleman and Antonio Damasio seemed particularly valuable, and after checking the authors' credentials, she added the book titles to her bibliography cards (31i). Eventually her reading led her to narrow her topic and develop her research question, "Do computers need emotions for scientists to consider them intelligent?" The flowchart illustrates Johnson's process of narrowing her topic.

To find out if there were more current resources focusing specifically on the role of emotions in creating artificial intelligence, Johnson checked online databases available through her library. Her college library uses EBSCO, FirstSearch, and IBIS online services, each with

QUOTATION: ON WRITING
Of making many books there is no end; and much study is a weariness of the flesh.
—Ecclesiastes 12:12

QUOTATION: ON WRITING
The wastepaper basket is the writer's best friend.
—Isaac Bashevis Singer

QUOTATION: ON WRITING
You must learn to write rather than be a writer. Write as well as you can. Don't think of what is wanted, what is popular, what will sell. Write what you want, and write as well as you can.
—Margery Sharp

BACKGROUND
In "Making a Place for Music in Basic Writing" (*Journal of Basic Writing,* Fall 1995: 31–37), Sarah Coprich Johnson offers a specific application to enhance learning of one of Howard Gardner's eight multiple intelligences.

Flowchart of Chandra Johnson's narrowing process

links to scholarly full-text databases and online journals. In addition, because Johnson was still trying to learn the issues, she consulted *Readers' Guide Abstracts,* which led her to several popular articles. Through EBSCO, she clicked on "Academic Search Elite" and discovered several sources by combining "artificial intelligence" and "emotions" as her search terms. However, she wanted to make certain she was finding the best sources. From her experience with finding books, she knew that artificial intelligence sources existed in both computer sciences and psychology, so she asked a reference librarian what databases she should search. He recommended ComputerDatabase and PsycInfo.

The search of these databases resulted in the articles by Allen, Bates, Kurzweil, and many others that Johnson ultimately used. She also identified more than two dozen citations that she ultimately did not include in the paper. Many of these did not focus specifically enough on the role of emotions in artificial intelligence, some repeated sources she already had, some were too basic, and some were written at such a high technical level that she knew she didn't have the time or expertise to figure them out.

Finally, Johnson decided to see if there were important current sources available on the World Wide Web. She typed "artificial intelligence" into the Google search engine and was delighted (and a little lucky) that the first match that appeared was the home page of the American Association for Artificial Intelligence <http://www.aaai.org>. She also found an online searchable "Bibliography for Artificial Intelligence." This last source led her to John McCarthy's Web site. As she knew from the book by Williams, McCarthy was a computer science professor at Stanford University and one of the founders of the field of artificial intelligence, which confirmed that his Web site would be credible.

As Johnson conducted her research, she didn't know where to stand on the issue. Many scientists believed that emotions were an important part of artificial intelligence, and many others did not. Of the scientists who believed that emotions were important, some of them thought it impossible to program a computer or robot to experience them, while others considered emotions within reach. Johnson herself was skeptical. However, she intentionally sought sources that took different sides on the debate. She took content notes on her computer, opening a new file for each source and taking care to distinguish direct quotations from her own summaries, paraphrases, and interpretations.

After taking notes, Johnson was ready to DRAFT her research paper. Thinking about her PURPOSE, she first concluded that she should persuade her readers to take a specific position about the role of emotions in artificial intelligence. However, as she completed her outline and first and second drafts, she realized that the topic was too complicated for her to argue for a specific position. Johnson altered her purpose to informing readers about the various issues surrounding emotions and artificial intelligence. Her goal was to make readers see her paper as a thoughtful attempt to explain the issues. As Johnson wrote, she used her note cards carefully to make sure she always knew when she was quoting a source and when she was summarizing. She made sure to put in the correct PARENTHETICAL DOCUMENTATION (34c) for each source. She also kept a WORKING BIBLIOGRAPHY (31i) so that she would be ready to list each one of the sources in her WORKS CITED list (34d.1) at the end of her paper. By the time Johnson came to the final draft of her research paper, she decided to drop a few sources because they repeated what others, whom she considered better authorities, had said.

Johnson struggled with her concluding paragraph. She had to synthesize complicated material in a fairly limited space. Here's an early draft of her concluding paragraph, which you can compare to the one in her final draft in 34e.2.

The importance of emotions in creating artificial intelligence may

be a matter of definition. For some, like the American Association for

Artificial Intelligence, artificial intelligence already surrounds us in

QUOTATION: ON WRITING
Writing represents a unique mode of learning—not merely valuable, not merely special, but unique. . . . Writing serves learning uniquely because writing as process-and-product possesses a cluster of attributes that correspond uniquely to certain powerful learning strategies.

—Janet Emig

QUOTATION: ON WRITING
Sometimes writer's block is no more than a signal that you have not done enough research.

—Sophy Burnham

cars, in computers, in something as simple as postal machines that can sort handwritten postcards. We just fail to recognize it. For others, the true measure of artificial intelligence is consciousness. John Searle argues that just because a computer can *simulate* consciousness does not mean that it *has* consciousness (37). According to this reasoning, a machine that accurately detects and produces emotions may be smarter than a machine that cannot. However, we cannot say it is conscious, and so we cannot say it is intelligent in the same ways that humans are intelligent.

34e.2 Analyzing the research paper

MLA style doesn't call for a title page for research papers. Many instructors, however, require a title page. Inquire as to your instructor's preference. If you're asked to use a title page, follow the format on the facing page.

Title page of Chandra Johnson's research paper

1/3 DOWN

The Role of Emotions
in Artificial Intelligence

TITLE: DOUBLE-SPACE IF MORE THAN ONE LINE

by
Chandra Johnson

BY ON SEPARATE LINE; DOUBLE-SPACE TO NAME

INSTRUCTOR	Professor Gregor
COURSE, SECTION	English 101, Section C5
DATE SUBMITTED	24 November 2003

1 "

QUOTATION: ON WRITING
A title page is like a tray of hors d'oeuvres; it suggests what is to come.
—Susie R. Rambo

BACKGROUND
A direct title tells exactly what the essay will be about. An indirect title hints at the essay's topic. In either case, it stands alone, not as part of the body of the essay. (See section 3c.3.)

If you follow MLA style by not using a title page, use the headings shown on the first page of the sample research paper (see pages 600 and 602). Follow precisely the format instructions shown.

If you use a title page, never assign it a page number. Use the arabic numeral 1, without *page* or *p.*, for the first page of the actual paper. Put your last name followed by a space and the page number in the upper right corner, one-half inch below the top edge of the page. (Many writers take advantage of the word processing function that inserts page numbers and last name as a header, updating automatically.) Then, type the paper's title, centering it on the page, one-half inch below the name-number heading. Continue numbering sequentially through to the last page of your WORKS CITED list. Use one-inch margins on all sides of the sheet of paper.

BACKGROUND
In "Scoring Peers' Papers: Teaching Audience Awareness and Generating Enthusiasm" (*Teaching English in the Two-Year College,* December 1993: 300–305), Sharon Albert and Kathryn Ring explain a teaching process that asks students from two classes to grade each others' papers. While the identities of individual graders and writers remain anonymous, students develop the sense of writing to a real audience rather than simply to their instructor.

First page of a paper without a title page

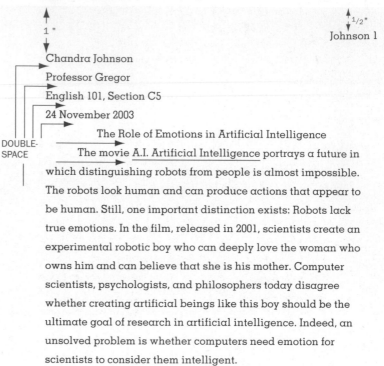

1 "

1/2"
Johnson 1

Chandra Johnson

Professor Gregor

English 101, Section C5

24 November 2003

DOUBLE-SPACE

The Role of Emotions in Artificial Intelligence

The movie <u>A.I. Artificial Intelligence</u> portrays a future in which distinguishing robots from people is almost impossible. The robots look human and can produce actions that appear to be human. Still, one important distinction exists: Robots lack true emotions. In the film, released in 2001, scientists create an experimental robotic boy who can deeply love the woman who owns him and can believe that she is his mother. Computer scientists, psychologists, and philosophers today disagree whether creating artificial beings like this boy should be the ultimate goal of research in artificial intelligence. Indeed, an unsolved problem is whether computers need emotion for scientists to consider them intelligent.

In MLA style, including an outline of your final draft is optional, according to your instructor's requirements. When you include an outline, ask your instructor where to place it: before the actual paper, at the end of the paper, or as a separate document. Number all outline pages in lowercase roman numerals starting with *i*, without *page* or *p.* Type your last name and the needed lowercase roman numeral in the upper right corner, one-half inch down from the top of the sheet of paper. Then, one-inch from the top, center the word *Outline.* As shown in the accompanying sample outline, place your thesis statement one double space below *Outline,* and use underlining for only the words *Thesis statement.* Switch to arabic numerals for numbering the pages of the paper itself.

Johnson's instructor required that an outline be submitted with the final draft of her research paper. Johnson chose to use a topic outline, not a sentence outline (see 2r). Either type is acceptable in MLA style, though many instructors prefer a sentence outline because it communicates more information than a topic outline does. Follow the format of the outline shown here: Even if your instructor doesn't require you to submit an outline, you might find that developing one helps clarify your thoughts and ensure that you've covered your TOPIC fully. Examining a paper's "skeleton" helps you focus on the overall shape and organization of your research paper—and it may reveal gaps in your paper's development that you need to fill in.

Outline for Chandra Johnson's research paper

Outline

I. Introduction

   A. Example from the movie <u>A.I.</u>

   B. <u>Thesis statement</u>: An unsolved problem is whether computers need emotions for scientists to consider them intelligent.

II. Definitions of intelligence

   A. General definitions

   B. Artificial intelligence (AI)

     1. Qualities of AI

     2. Scientists' opinions of how close we are to AI

     3. Turing test

     4. Chess room argument

III. Types of intelligence

   A. Gardner's eight intelligences

   B. Emotional intelligence

     1. Goleman's research

     2. Damasio's research

IV. Emotions and artificial intelligence

   A. Believers' and doubters' positions on emotions

   B. The role of recognizing and conveying emotions

     1. Children's learning

     2. Applying Disney's techniques to robots

V. Conclusion

   A. The remaining controversy

   B. No emotions in computers any time soon

BACKGROUND

A formal outline (see section 2r) follows conventions concerning content and format that ensure that relationships among ideas are clear and that the content is orderly. In a topic outline, each item is only a word or a phrase. In a sentence outline, each item is a complete sentence.

QUOTATION: ON WRITING

The desire to write grows with writing.

—Erasmus

MLA

Use ½-inch top margin, 1-inch bottom and side margins; double-space throughout.

Johnson 1

Put identifying information in upper left corner; double-space.

Chandra Johnson

Professor Gregor

English 101, Section C5

24 November 2003

Center title one double space below identifying information.

The Role of Emotions in Artificial Intelligence

Start first line of paper one double space below title.

The movie <u>A.I. Artificial Intelligence</u> portrays a future in which distinguishing robots from people is almost impossible. The robots look human and can produce actions that appear to be human. Still, one important distinction exists: Robots lack true emotions. In the film, released in 2001, scientists create an experimental robotic boy who can deeply love the woman who owns him and can believe that she is his mother. Computer scientists, psychologists, and philosophers today disagree whether creating artificial beings like this boy should be the ultimate goal of research in artificial intelligence. Indeed, an unsolved problem is whether computers need emotion for scientists to consider them intelligent.

Defining human intelligence is a major focus of cognitive

In MLA style, put author and page number in parentheses when author is not named in the sentence.

science, a broad field that studies the mind (Pfeifer and Scheier 5). Members of this field include psychologists, linguists, and computer scientists, among others. Cognitive scientists agree that human intelligence includes several broad abilities. These consist of the abilities to think abstractly, to learn, to adapt to new situations in life, and to profit from experience (7). Intelligence calls for more than the ability to recall information or perform set routines. It involves using past knowledge, intuition, creativity, and experience in new, unfamiliar situations, and learning from them. It also requires using

⟶

(Proportions shown in this paper are adjusted to fit space limitations of this book. Follow actual dimensions discussed in this book and your instructor's directions.)

Commentary

1. **Computer tip.** Following MLA style, Johnson used her name and the page number as a running header throughout the paper. She used the "header" command in her word processing program to insert the proper information on each page automatically.

2. **Introductory strategy.** Johnson attracts the reader's interest by referring to a recent popular movie. From that specific example, she moves to introducing the topic more broadly. Because the movie *A.I.* gave her the idea for her paper topic, the introduction came fairly easily to her.

3. **Thesis.** The last sentence of Johnson's introductory paragraph is her THESIS STATEMENT. In it she tries to prepare readers for the main message of the paper.

4. **PROCESS NOTE:** Paragraph 2 begins to define intelligence. In an early draft, Johnson started writing about scientists' attempts to create artificial intelligence in robots. Later she decided that it made more sense to talk generally about intelligence in humans and then discuss computers and robots.

5. **Summarizing a source.** For much of her initial definition of intelligence, Johnson drew on a scholarly book. She decided to summarize concepts from that book rather than paraphrase or quote them. Note that she took care to include page citations.

6. **PROCESS NOTE:** Johnson revised the sentences from "These consist" through "It also requires" many times. In her first draft, she put all the characteristics of intelligence into one long sentence. She saw immediately that she needed to break the characteristics into small chunks. She set about figuring out which characteristics would go together logically. She then wrote several versions of her shorter sentences, trying to vary lengths and use a variety of words to make the writing more interesting. After she turned in her first draft, however, she discovered that she had repeated "intuition" and "creativity" (see beginning of page 2 of the paper). She wished she had seen that slip earlier.

QUOTATION: ON WRITING
Had I known the answer to any of these questions, I would never have needed to write.

—Joan Didion

QUOTATION: ON WRITING
Each paragraph almost discovers the paragraph it precedes. When I end one paragraph I know it must lead to another.
—Roger Rosenblatt

In MLA style, header has student's last name and page number.

Johnson 2

intuition and creativity (Pfeifer and Scheier 10). For example, when college student Joshua Vrana, who worked part time in a store, was asked to develop a Web site for the store, he created it from his knowledge of Web design, the store, and its customers. In so doing, he drew creatively upon his knowledge and experience, thereby using all aspects of human intelligence.

7

Cognitive scientists disagree on a definition of artificial intelligence. At one extreme are those who regard it as the ability of a machine to perform every intelligent act that a human can perform. Table 1 lists some of those acts. This is a very high standard. At the other extreme, scientists define artificial intelligence as the ability to perform even a small act that requires human intelligence. For example, the American Association for Artificial Intelligence believes that artificial intelligence already exists in machines as simple as postal machines that can sort handwritten postcards. This is a very low standard.

8

9

10

Table number, title, and format appear in MLA style.

Table 1

Some Qualities of Artificial Intelligence

11

Category	Examples
Problem solving	Using informed search methods to solve problems; game playing
Logical behavior	Planning for practical action; acting appropriately for a given situation
Knowledge and reasoning	Using memory; dealing with uncertainty; reasoning using probability; making simple and complex decisions

(continued)

→

Commentary

7. **Example from experience.** Johnson decided that the point about intuition and creativity would be clearer if she gave an example. She remembered a conversation with her friend Joshua Vrana about a project he had completed at his job, and she realized it would illustrate the point effectively.

8. **Elaborating a key issue from the thesis.** Johnson's topic sentence in this paragraph signals the reader that she is about to explain the disagreement between scientists over the proper measure of artificial intelligence. By starting one sentence with "At one extreme" and another sentence with "At the other extreme," she hoped to contrast and clarify the two positions. She had to write several drafts to state the distinctions clearly and concisely.

9. **Reference to a table.** Although she did not want to interrupt her paragraph, Johnson felt her readers would benefit from a reference to Table 1, which would soon follow.

10. **Example.** To provide support for her claim, Johnson included the example from the American Association for Artificial Intelligence.

11. **Table.** Johnson faced a length restriction in this paper, but she needed to present a good deal of information. She decided the most effective way to summarize much of that information would be to include a table. Developing the table also helped her to clarify the ideas it contained.

    As she formatted her paper's final draft, Johnson discovered that the table would not fit on one page. She had two choices: (1) put the table (and any other tables she might create) into an appendix to be placed before her Works Cited list; (2) divide the table between two pages so that it would fall exactly where she wanted her readers to see it. She chose the second option after checking with her instructor.

QUOTATION: ON WRITING
He that will write well in any tongue must follow this counsel of Aristotle: to speak as the common people do, to think as wise men do.

—Roger Ascham

MLA

BACKGROUND

Ellipsis indicates the omission of words from a quotation. Three spaced dots, known as *ellipsis points,* are used to show that some of the original writer's words have been left out. If an omission occurs at the beginning of a quotation, ellipsis points are not needed to show the omission. They are also unnecessary at the end of a quotation as long as the sentence in which it occurs is complete. (See section 29d.)

Johnson 3

Table 1   *(continued)*

Some Qualities of Artificial Intelligence

Category	Examples
Learning	Learning from observations and experience
Communicating, perceiving, and acting	Using language with people; becoming aware of surroundings through the senses; interacting with the environment

Table source note appears in MLA style.

Source: Adapted from Rolf Pfeifer and Christian Scheier, "Topics in Classical AI," in Understanding Intelligence (Cambridge, MA: MIT P, 2000) 46.

While the dream of creating robots with human intelligence has existed almost a century, scientists disagree on how close we have come to realizing that dream. Perhaps the most famous example occurred when computer engineers developed IBM's Deep Blue computer, which beat chess grandmaster Garry Kasparov in 1997 (Hayden 46). However, Murray Campbell, one of Deep Blue's creators, has conceded that the computer "did not exhibit human qualities and therefore was not 'intelligent' " (qtd. in Stix). Some computer scientists take a much different position. For example, Hans Moravec believes that "robot computers [will] achieve human intelligence . . . around 2040" (qtd. in Minerd 9). Ray Kurzweil is even more optimistic in that he believes that Moravec's prediction will come true as early as 2029 and that by the end of the twenty-first century, machine-based intelligences will rightfully claim to be human (21).

In MLA style, put author and page number in parentheses when author is not named in text.

No page number is cited when a document is only one page.

Square brackets show words added or changed to make a quotation flow.

12

13

14

15

→

606

Commentary

12. **PROCESS NOTE:** Johnson revised this paragraph several times because it covers several different opinions (note the number of sources cited in a relatively short space). The example of Deep Blue illustrates efforts to create intelligent computers. The quotation from one of Deep Blue's creators was particularly effective because he takes a position opposite the one we might expect.

13. **Key transition within a paragraph.** Because she was summarizing two very different positions in this paragraph, Johnson needed a strong sentence to signal a contrast between scientists who doubt the possibility of artificial intelligence and those who think we are close to achieving it. In an early draft she had divided this material into two paragraphs, but she later decided it would work better as a single paragraph.

14. **Modified quotation.** To make the quotation from Moravec fit the flow of the sentence, Johnson had to add the word *will*. She enclosed the word in brackets to signal that it was not part of the original quotation. (The original source was written in the hypothetical future and simply said that "computers achieve human intelligence.") Johnson also omitted some words from the source, indicating the omission with an ellipsis.

15. **PROCESS NOTE:** Johnson encountered several references to the work of Ray Kurzweil. Because many of his claims seemed extreme, she was skeptical about whether he was a credible source. However, she found that other respected authors frequently cited him, even if it was only to criticize his ideas. She concluded that Kurzweil offered a perspective that she should represent in her paper.

MLA

TEACHING TIP
Students sometimes think they are the only readers who skip over long quotations. You may want to assure them that they are not alone. The implication for students as writers, of course, is that when they feel they must include a lengthy quotation, in order to present a complicated idea in detail, for example, it is helpful to prepare the reader by explaining its importance. To make it as brief as possible, all irrelevant material should be deleted so that every word counts.

Johnson 4

The Turing test, developed in 1950 by the British mathematician Alan Turing, is one commonly accepted measure of artificial intelligence (McCarthy). A researcher sits in one room, another person in a second room, and a computer in a third room. The researcher does not know whether a person or a computer is in each room. Communicating only through a keyboard and screen, the researcher asks the same questions of both the person and the machine. If the computer answers and the researcher cannot tell whether the response comes from a machine, the computer passes the test.

16

World Wide Web source has no page numbers.

However, some people dispute the Turing test. The prominent philosopher John Searle argues that the appearance of proper answers does not prove the existence of intelligence. He offers "the chess room argument."

> Imagine that a man who does not know how to play chess is locked inside a room, and there he is given a set of, to him, meaningless symbols. Unknown to him, these represent positions on a chessboard. He looks up in a book what he is supposed to do, and he passes back more meaningless symbols. We can suppose that if the rule book . . . is skillfully written, he will win chess games. People outside the room will say, "This man understands chess, and in fact he is a good chess player because he wins." They will be totally mistaken. The man understands nothing of chess, he is just a computer. (qtd. in Allen 30)

17

18

Use block-indent of 1-inch (or ten spaces) for a quotation longer than four typed lines.

The ellipsis indicates words omitted from a quotation.

In MLA style, parenthetical information follows the period in a block quotation.

The disagreements about defining artificial intelligence result partly from how complicated the idea of human

→

Commentary

16. **Example of summary.** Johnson compressed a lengthy description of the Turing test into a brief summary. **PROCESS NOTE:** The first time that Johnson wrote about the Turing test, she needed three full paragraphs to present all the information. She was determined to revise and condense it. She deleted sentences, which she kept in a separate document, in case she wanted to reinstate some information. She ended up with a "nutshell" version in her final draft.

17. **Block-indented quotation.** Johnson was unable to produce a satisfactory summary or paraphrase of Searle's "chess room argument." She decided instead to quote the entire passage. Because the passage was longer than four typed lines, Johnson needed to indent it. She reviewed the MLA guidelines for the format of block quotations and the exact position of the parenthetical citation.

18. **PROCESS NOTE:** Johnson found that Searle's "chess room argument" is actually a variation on his more famous "Chinese room argument," in which the man in the room is simply passing back Chinese symbols without knowing what they mean. She read several essays about Searle's work in John Preston and Mark Bishop, eds., *Views into the Chinese Room: New Essays on Searle and Artificial Intelligence* (Oxford: Oxford UP, 2002). She took several notes and wrote summaries. However, Johnson eventually realized that this material was taking her away from the thesis of her paper. Although she had invested many hours, she dropped this work from her paper.

QUOTATION: ON WRITING

I'm not alone when I'm writing—the language itself, like a kind of trampoline, is there helping me.

—William Stafford

MLA

Johnson 5

intelligence has become. Between 1980 and 1996, the well-respected Howard Gardner, a researcher in psychology at Harvard University, defined seven distinctive categories of human intelligence. Those categories are linguistic, mathematical, spatial, kinesthetic, musical, interpersonal, and intrapersonal intelligence (Goleman 38). In 1996, Gardner   19 added an eighth intelligence: naturalistic. He calls this eight-item list of abilities "multiple intelligences." Gardner believes that every person is born possessing a combination of all eight intelligences (qtd. in Hoerr).   20

Daniel Goleman, another highly regarded researcher in psychology, groups the concepts of intrapersonal and interpersonal intelligence under the label "emotional   21 intelligence." Goleman says that emotional intelligence involves more than having traditional feelings of anger, sadness, fear, enjoyment, love, surprise, disgust, or shame (289-90). It determines how well people do in life (28). A study of high school valedictorians, for example, shows that they frequently have less successful careers than classmates who   22 excel at interpersonal or emotional skills (35). Goleman assigns five aspects to emotional intelligence: "knowing one's emotions," "managing emotions," "motivating oneself," "handling relationships," and "recognizing emotions in others" (43). The last of these is crucial in the context of artificial intelligence because it determines how people respond to other people and, in turn, how the other people respond back.

The neurologist Antonio Damasio explains that scientists   23 and philosophers historically dismissed the significance of

In MLA style, put only page number in parentheses when author is named in text.

Quotation marks around phrases show they appeared separately in the source.

Commentary

19. **PROCESS NOTE!** In her first draft, Johnson wrote two or three sentences about each of the eight types of human intelligence. Later she decided that writing so much about the topic would draw attention away from the main topic of her paper, artificial intelligence. In a second draft she simply listed the eight types of intelligence, leaving extra space for emotional intelligence, the most important type for the purpose of her paper. Although she was frustrated at having to omit so much of her work from the final draft, she realized her paper was stronger as a result.

20. **Expert source.** When Johnson first began reading about intelligence, she came across the name of Howard Gardner in several sources. When she realized that Gardner is a leading expert on multiple intelligences, she knew she could depend on the quality of his work.

21. **Elaborating a key point.** Since emotion is a key concept in her paper, Johnson discusses it at some length in this paragraph. Early in her search process, she had used the keywords "emotions" and "intelligence" to search her library's book catalog. Goleman's book came up through that search; so did the book by Pfeifer and Scheier, which refers extensively to Goleman's work.

22. **Example.** To illustrate the point that success in life does not depend only on verbal and quantitative intelligence, the kinds of intelligence typically associated with schools, Johnson gave the example of some high school valedictorians.

23. **Introduction to paraphrase.** Johnson includes the information that Damasio is a neurologist when she paraphrases his work. Because she was drawing on the work of experts from so many fields, she thought this identifying information would help her readers.

QUOTATION: ON WRITING

I put a piece of paper under my pillow, and when I could not sleep I wrote in the dark.
—Henry David Thoreau

MLA

QUOTATION: ON WRITING

Vigorous writing is concise. A sentence should contain no unnecessary words, a paragraph no unnecessary sentences, for the same reason that a drawing should have no unnecessary lines and a machine no unnecessary parts. This requires not that the writer make all his sentences short, or that he avoid all detail and treat his subjects only in outline, but that every word tell.

—William Strunk

Johnson 6

emotions (38). Traditionally, they associated logic and reason with intelligence. Early scientists and philosophers believed emotion belonged to the body, not the mind (39).

The character of Mr. Spock in the original Star Trek television series represents this belief. Incapable of emotion, Spock is flawlessly logical. Certainly, everyone would agree that he is intelligent.   24

However, Damasio would be unconvinced by the claim that Spock is intelligent--and not just because Spock is a Vulcan. Damasio conducted numerous experiments with people who lost various emotions through brain injuries.   25 These people otherwise seemed to possess all their reasoning and logical abilities, but they had trouble making logical

Introductory phrase smoothly leads into direct quotation.

decisions. The experiments led Damasio to conclude that "emotion is integral to the process of reasoning and decision making" (41). He tells of a patient, David, who suffered a disease that destroyed parts of his brain and left him unable to learn any new fact, to recognize any new person, or to remember recent events or people he had just met. Damasio and his colleagues performed an experiment in which one person   26 treated David rudely and another person treated him well for a

Paragraph summarizes several pages of source material, as parenthetical citation shows.

period of five days. Although David could not remember details of how these people treated him, he behaved differently in the presence of the two people. Clearly, he had learned on an emotional level, which made him respond sensibly (43-47).

The strongest believers in artificial intelligence mostly   27 downplay the role of emotions, maintaining that only logic and reason define intelligence. Others give a qualified yes to "the provocative question whether robots will in fact need to have

→

Commentary

24. **Example from popular culture.** Johnson hesitated to give Mr. Spock as an example of intelligence without emotion. The original *Star Trek* series is nearly four decades old, and she worried the reference might be dated. However, she decided that Mr. Spock was enough a part of popular culture that even people who weren't directly familiar with the show would understand the reference. She checked with several friends just to be sure.

25. **Evaluating a source.** The central issue of Johnson's paper is whether emotion is a necessary part of intelligence. In two sources she found early in her research, she had seen references to Antonio Damasio's work, and she wondered if it would help her to make connections between emotions and reasoning. It did, so she drew heavily on Damasio's book in this section. First, however, she checked his credentials. When she discovered that he was an award-winning researcher and head of the neurological sciences department at a major medical school, she was satisfied that he was a reliable source.

26. **PROCESS NOTE:** Without the story of Damasio's patient David, Johnson knew that the paragraph was extremely thin. However, the story took five pages in the original source. To write a summary of those pages, Johnson kept drafting and cutting until she achieved the length she wanted. She then asked a student friend to read her summary and then the five original pages to make sure she had summarized the story fairly and accurately.

27. **PROCESS NOTE:** In the course of her research, Johnson encountered many different opinions, both on the achievability of artificial intelligence and on the role of emotions in intelligence. She found it very difficult to synthesize all this material in a manner that read smoothly. Finally, she recognized that believers and doubters of the possibility of artificial intelligence differed in terms of the importance they assigned to emotions. This discovery gave her a way to organize this paragraph.

QUOTATION: ON WRITING

Writing is an odd thing to do. You turn your back on the real world and favor an invisible world you invent. You have to search deep in your inner life. I hear things in a kinesthetic way. I tap into a rhythm of language to portray what I feel.

—Mary Gordon

MLA

QUOTATION: ON WRITING

It's as hard to get from almost finished to finished as to get from beginning to almost done.

—Elinor Fuchs

Johnson 7

emotions, similar to the way humans have emotions" (Pfeifer and Scheier 642). Doubters, however, point to emotions, feelings, and intuition as the main barriers to artificial intelligence. The ability to write fiction, for example, depends on feelings that computers can never experience. One skeptic even asserts that computers have "inner lives on a par with rocks" (Bringsjord 33).   28 Programmers design computer programs to be efficient and to sort problems into separate steps, ignoring everything that is not part of those steps. In contrast, part of being human is getting bored, angry, or off the subject. John Searle believes that cognitive   29 scientists make a terrible mistake when they imagine that the brain works the same way that computers do (qtd. in Allen 30).

Recognizing that the brain does not function through logic alone, some researchers are now studying how humans learn and are trying to incorporate their discoveries into computers. For example, children learn mainly by interacting in social situations with others. Emotions play a large role in those situations

Cite part of title when source lists no author.

("Sociable" 1). As an illustration, a baby learns that smiling   30 causes adults to pay more attention to her, so she smiles a lot. In contrast, a two-year-old learns to recognize when someone is angry and to avoid that person. A child's growth in emotional intelligence would be hard to build into a computer. Nonetheless, Donald Norman and his colleagues believe that understanding how emotions combine with cognition in humans is vital to developing computer systems that can function by themselves (38). In fact, scientists at Vanderbilt University have built robots that recognize some basic human emotions (Johnson).

Programming robots so that they can express as well as   31 sense emotions is important, because people's abilities to convey

→

Commentary

28. **Colorful quotation.** Bringsjord's statement that computers have "inner lives on a par with rocks" is not a particularly important or well-reasoned assertion. However, Johnson thought it added color to her paper and helped to make her point, so she included it here.

29. **PROCESS NOTE:** At one point in her second draft, Johnson had included all of the observations from Searle in one place (see page 4 of the research paper). However, she decided that using the reference here to close off the paragraph about emotions was a powerful strategy, so she moved this material when she wrote her final draft.

30. **Popular-press source.** Here Johnson's information comes from a popular source, the magazine *USA Today.* She realized that in comparison to the many scholarly sources cited in her paper, this one might seem insignificant. However, other things she had read convinced her that the position given in the article was accurate. Because she planned to include the example of Kismet, a robot described in the article, later in her paper, she decided to keep the reference to *USA Today* here. Note that no author was listed for the article, so Johnson referred instead to the first word of the title in her parenthetical citation.

31. **PROCESS NOTE:** Johnson's research made clear that there are two main challenges in creating emotional intelligence in computers: getting computers to recognize emotions and getting them to convey emotions. She revised this topic sentence more than any other in her paper so that it would effectively signal those challenges.

QUOTATION: ON WRITING

There mark what ills the scholar's life assail:
Toil, envy, want, the patron, and the goal.
—Samuel Johnson

MLA

MLA

QUOTATION: ON WRITING

Sometimes I organize a piece so carefully that I will not only know the general thought I want to end with, I will write the last sentence before having written anything else. This sentence will contain all of the feeling of a piece unwritten, but I know it will be there and almost always I'm right.

—Roger Rosenblatt

Johnson 8

emotions affect the responses that they get from others. To try to learn how inanimate objects suggest emotions, scientists have studied some unlikely sources. One group of researchers

Put quotation marks around even short phrases or key terms taken directly from a source and give source at end of sentence.

analyzed how Disney animators created "the illusion of life" by seeming to give cartoon characters emotions (Bates 122). Using Disney techniques, scientists created computer "creatures" that seemed to display emotions in response to simple situations (123). Further work led to robots that appeared more humanlike. For example, scientists gave a robot named Kismet appealing, childlike features. Kismet's "features, behavior, and 'emotions' " seem to allow the robot to "interact with humans in an intuitive natural way" ("Sociable" 1). Nevertheless, creating the appearance of emotions is much different from creating the existence of emotions.   32

Concluding paragraph summarizes paper.

Do computers need emotions for scientists to consider them intelligent? This question remains unanswered and controversial. As Sam Williams notes, "The current tension over artificial intelligence is a reflection of our own society's tension over the future and what it holds" (xvi). Computers can indeed do some things that resemble a few kinds of intelligence that humans possess, and that is enough to satisfy some scientists. However, Gardner, Goleman, Damasio, Pfeifer and Scheier, and others regard emotions as a crucial part of human intelligence. At present, computers lack anything like the kinds of emotions found in human beings, and scholars like John Searle doubt that computers will ever have them. Clearly, robots like the little boy in A.I. exist only in movies. The possibility of creating real robots similar to him remains only in the very distant future, if at all.   33 34 35 36

→

Commentary

32. **Using a technical source.** The article by Bates, from a scientific journal, was fairly difficult to understand. Johnson focused on the theories, findings, and implications of the article rather than on the methodologies, which were harder to follow. This was the oldest source that Johnson consulted for her paper. However, as the reference to the robot Kismet (later in the paragraph) makes clear, the Bates study is still pertinent to current research.

33. **Research question.** Johnson's research question appears at the start of her last paragraph. Often, the research question doesn't directly appear at all in a paper, but Johnson thought it would be a good way to signal her conclusion.

34. **PROCESS NOTE:** Johnson liked the quotation from Sam Williams and tried several places to fit it in her paper. In the first draft, for example, she put it in the opening paragraph. Eventually she decided it helped summarize the deep controversy in her topic, so she moved it instead to the concluding paragraph.

35. **Summary of positions.** Johnson summarizes both positions on the question to show that she has weighed her evidence. By choosing to summarize Searle's argument last, she shows that she agrees more with his position, that emotions are an important part of artificial intelligence, than with the position of the others.

36. **Forceful conclusion.** In her last two sentences, Johnson returned to the movie example she used at the beginning of her paper. She thought this put a pleasing frame around the paper and made it seem complete.

QUOTATION: ON WRITING

In every real sense, the writer writes in order to teach himself, to understand himself, to satisfy himself; the publishing of the ideas is a curious anticlimax.

—Alfred Kazin

MLA

QUOTATION: ON WRITING

Whatever machine you use, however sophisticated your technology, it's ideas that count. In the beginning was the idea. No machine will give you the ability to spot an opening, take a new idea, and see it through to profitable fruition.

—Tom Crabtree

Johnson 9

In MLA style, the list of sources, called Works Cited, begins a new page. Double-space throughout.

List sources in alphabetical order.

Divide a URL only after a slash.

Works Cited

Allen, Frederick E. "The Myth of Artificial Intelligence."

American Heritage Feb.-Mar. 2001: 28-30.

American Association for Artificial Intelligence. "The AI Effect."

13 Sept. 2003 <http://www.aaai.org>.

Bates, Joseph. "The Role of Emotion in Believable Agents."

Communications of the ACM 37.7 (1994): 122-25.

Bringsjord, Selmer. "Just Imagine: What Computers Can't Do."

Education Digest 66.6 (2001): 31-33.

Damasio, Antonio. The Feeling of What Happens: Body and

Emotion in the Making of Consciousness. New York:

Harcourt, 1999.

Gardner, Howard. Frames of Mind: The Theory of Multiple

Intelligences. New York: Basic, 1994.

Goleman, Daniel. Emotional Intelligence. New York: Bantam,

1995.

Hayden, Thomas. "The Age of Robots." US News and World

Report 23 Apr. 2001: 44-50.

Hoerr, Thomas. "The Naturalistic Intelligence." Building

Tool Room. 20 Sept. 2003 <http://www.newhorizons.org/

strategies/mi/hoerr1.htm>.

Johnson, R. Colin. "Robots Taught to Be Sensitive to Human

Emotions." Electronic Engineering Times 13 Jan. 2003: 43.

Kurzweil, Ray. "Spiritual Machines: The Merging of Man and

Machine." Futurist Nov. 1999: 16-21.

McCarthy, John. "What Is Artificial Intelligence?" 29 Mar. 2003.

16 Sept. 2003 <http://www-formal.stanford.edu/jmc/

whatisai.html>.

37

38

39

→

Commentary

37. **Search strategy.** Johnson developed a working bibliography that was nearly three times as long as the list of sources she finally used. Initially, she went online to see what sources she could find on the Internet. However, she was overwhelmed by the number of references to "artificial intelligence." After some effort, she identified a few key sources. Library resources were more useful. The library's book catalog revealed many useful volumes, and the databases she searched turned up both scholarly and popular sources. *PsycINFO* and *ComputerDatabase* were the two most useful databases.

38. **Credible Internet source.** Johnson checked that this professional organization of scientists and professors would be a reliable source of information.

39. **Computer tip.** Including a long and complicated URL in a Works Cited page is often tricky. Copying the URL from the browser window and pasting it directly into the Works Cited page reduces the chance of error. Be sure to divide a URL only after a slash, the rule in MLA style.

QUOTATION: ON WRITING

The ink of the scholar is more sacred than the blood of the martyr.

—Muhammad

Johnson 10

Minerd, Jeff. "Robots: Our Evolutionary Heirs?" Futurist

    Feb. 1999: 8-9.

Norman, Donald A., Andrew Ortony, and Daniel M. Russell.

    "Affect and Machine Design: Lessons for the Development

    of Autonomous Machines." IBM Systems Journal 42.2 (2003):

    38-45. ComputerDatabase. InfoTrac. Bergen County

    Cooperative Lib. System, NJ. 14 Sept. 2003 <http://

    www.infotrac.galegroup.com>.

Pfeifer, Rolf, and Christian Scheier. Understanding Intelligence.

    Cambridge, MA: MIT P 2000.

"'Sociable Machine' Interacts with Humans," USA Today June

    2001: 1-2. General Reference Center. InfoTrac. Bergen

    County Cooperative Lib. System, NJ. 14 Sept. 2003. <http://

    www.infotrac.galegroup.com>.

Stix, Gary. "2001: A Scorecard." Scientific American Jan. 2001: 36.

Williams, Sam. Arguing A.I. The Battle for Twenty-First-Century

    Science. New York: AtRandom.com Books, 2002.

Single quotation marks inside double quotation marks indicate words that were in quotation marks in the source.

40

41

Commentary

40. **Full text online.** Although this source initially appeared in an issue of *USA Today* magazine and old issues were not stocked at her college library, Johnson found a complete copy of the article online, through a database in the library. Because she used the online version, she cited its source.

41. **Proofreading the Works Cited page.** In proofreading her paper, Johnson made sure this list contained all the works she cited in her paper—and only those works.

QUOTATION: ON WRITING

My task which I am trying to achieve is by the power of the written word to make you hear, to make you feel. It is, before all, to make you see.

—Joseph Conrad

MLA

BACKGROUND

The term *bibliography* is derived from two Greek roots. The first root is *biblia,* the plural form of the word meaning "book" or "papyrus," so named after the Phoenician city *Byblos* (now Jubayl), from which papyrus was exported. *Biblia* has been responsible for many words in the English language dealing with books. For example, a *biblioclast* is a destroyer of books, and a *bibliognost* is someone who is knowledgeable about books. A *bibliolater* is a lover of books. A *bibliopegist* is a bookbinder.

The second Greek root is *graphos,* meaning "to write." At one time, *bibliography* meant "the writing of books," but in the seventeenth century the term came to mean "writing about books." At the same time, *bibliography* began to receive wide usage in Latin and began to replace such words as *catalogus* and *bibliotheca* in the titles of bibliographies, the making of which became increasingly important as bibliographers struggled to devise some type of organization for keeping track of the flood of publications that resulted from the invention of printing. Nevertheless, the term *bibliography* was not included in Samuel Johnson's dictionary of 1755 and was not found in the *Encyclopaedia Britannica* until its third edition in 1797. According to the *Oxford English Dictionary,* not until the early nineteenth century was the word *bibliography* first used to refer to "the systematic description and history of books, their authorship, printing, publication, editions, etc." or to a book about such matters.

Chapter 35

APA Documentation with Case Study

35a What is APA style?

The American Psychological Association (APA) sponsors the **APA style,** a DOCUMENTATION system widely used in the social sciences. APA style involves two equally important features that need to appear in research papers.

First, APA style calls for you to acknowledge your SOURCES within the text of your research papers by using **in-text citations** in parentheses. Section 35b explains how APA in-text citations work, and section 35c shows sixteen models of such parenthetical reference citations, each of which gives you an example of a different type of source.

Second, APA style calls for you to list complete bibliographic information about each source that you've mentioned in your parenthetical references. This bibliographic list, titled **References,** needs to appear on a separate page at the end of your research papers. It includes only the sources you've actually used in your research paper, not any you've consulted but haven't used. Section 35f gives instructions for composing your References pages, followed by forty-six models, each based on a different kind of source (book, article, Web site, etc.) that you might use in your research papers.

For an example of a research paper that uses APA-style in-text citations in parentheses and a References list, see section 35h. As you read the paper, notice how the two requirements for crediting sources work together so that readers can learn the precise origin of the material that is quoted, paraphrased, and summarized.

35b What are APA parenthetical in-text citations?

The APA-STYLE DOCUMENTATION guidelines here follow the recommendations of the *Publication Manual of the American Psychological Association,* Fifth Edition (2001), which is the most current print edition. The URL for APA's general Web site is <http://www.apa.org>; it answers some basic style questions and mostly refers you to the *Publication Manual.* However, APA has set up a special free Web site devoted exclusively to **electronic sources** (APA term for *online sources,* CD-ROMs, etc.). APA provides this because electronic sources are still evolving rapidly and therefore tend to change. Anyone with Internet access can use the site at <http://www.apastyle.org/elecgeneral.html>. It offers links to selected specific examples of citations of electronic sources, some of which aren't covered in the APA *Publication Manual;* unusually direct, practical FAQs; and other useful material. For example, as this book goes to press, this APA special Web site gives examples of Internet articles based on a print source; articles in an Internet-only journal; articles in an Internet-only newsletter; stand-alone document, no author identified, no date given; document available on university program or department Web site; electronic copy of a journal article, three-to-five authors, retrieved from a database. Best of all, you can sign up for free update notices sent to your e-mail address whenever APA posts an update to this site.

APA style requires parenthetical IN-TEXT CITATIONS that identify a SOURCE by the author's name (if no author, use a shortened version of the title) and the copyright year. For readability and a good writing style, you can often incorporate the name, and sometimes the year, into your sentence. Otherwise, place this information in parentheses, located as close as possible to the material you QUOTE, PARAPHRASE, or SUMMARIZE. Your goal is to tell readers precisely where they can find the original material.

The *Publication Manual of the American Psychological Association,* Fifth Edition (2001), recommends that if you refer to a work more than once in a paragraph, you give the author's name and the date at the first mention and then give only the name after that. An exception is when you're citing two or more works by the same author, or when two or more of your sources have the same name. In such cases, each separate citation must include the date to identify which work you're citing.

APA style requires page numbers for direct quotations and recommends them for paraphrases and summaries. However, some instructors expect you to give page references for paraphrases and summaries, so find out your instructor's preference to avoid any problems in properly crediting your sources.

TEACHING TIP

Students often wonder why they need to be scrupulous in their documentation of information, sometimes thinking of the process as just another pointless but difficult exercise devised by the teacher. It may help them understand the demands of documentation if you point out the reasons behind it. You will probably think of additional reasons, but here are some that you might find useful to mention.

1. Using someone else's ideas or words is like using anything that belongs to another person: The borrower has an ethical obligation to the owner not to claim the article as his or her own. Thus, the writer must acknowledge that the ideas or words of someone else belong to another person. In the case of long quotations—the reprinting of an entire work or a substantial portion of it—the writer must request and receive permission from the original author or publisher to use it.

2. Other researchers of the same subject may be intrigued by a reference to a particular work or author, prompting them to look for the original so that they can read the entire piece. Citation of complete publication information will greatly simplify finding the original work and even the original passage.

3. Careful documentation protects the researcher from any charge of plagiarism. When all sources are acknowledged, there can be no doubt about what the researcher has gleaned from others and what is original.

4. References to sources inform the reader that the researcher has been thorough. A study that does not indicate that standard work in the field has been considered will be taken less seriously than one that shows that the researcher is aware of what has already been written about the topic.

5. Particularly in science, the test of research findings is the replication of experiments by other researchers. Researchers can repeat such work only if the steps of the process have been clearly documented, with careful reference to the work of others in the field.

APA

BACKGROUND

As commonly used, the term *bibliography* sometimes refers to a science, sometimes to an art, and sometimes to the product of the art. As a science, it is an organized body of knowledge dealing with all aspects of books, both as physical objects and as the expression of ideas. Bibliography as an art consists of the techniques for finding, organizing, and presenting information about books. The bibliography that is produced by that art is a systematic listing of books that share common characteristics.

The objective of a bibliography may be analytical or systematic. Analytical bibliography tries to discover information about authorship, publication, and derivation of a text. Systematic bibliography produces systematic lists of books. The result is many different kinds of bibliographies. For example, bibliographies may be critical (critically appraising the books they list), current or retrospective, comprehensive or selective, annotated or not, enumerative (presenting an inventory) or subject-oriented (presenting content). In all their varied forms, they provide the modern researcher with valuable assistance in finding out where to look to learn what is already known about a subject.

Put page numbers in parentheses, using the abbreviation *p.* before a single page number and *pp.* when the material you're citing falls on more than one page. For a direct quotation from an electronic source that numbers paragraphs, give the paragraph number (or numbers). Handle paragraph numbers as you do page numbers, but use *para.* or ¶ (the symbol for paragraph) rather than *p.* or *pp.* If no paragraph numbers appear in the source, look for other ways to identify the location, such as sections introduced by main headings.

35c What are APA guidelines for in-text citations?

The directory below corresponds to the numbered examples that follow it. The examples show how to cite various kinds of sources in the body of your research paper. Remember, though, that you often can introduce source names, including titles when necessary, and sometimes even years, in your own sentences rather than in the parenthetical IN-TEXT CITATIONS.

Directory—APA In-text Citations

1. Paraphrased or Summarized Source—APA

People from the Mediterranean prefer an elbow-to-shoulder distance from each other (Morris, 1977). [Author name and date cited in parentheses.]

Desmond Morris (1977) notes that people from the Mediterranean prefer an elbow-to-shoulder distance from each other. [Author name cited in text; date cited in parentheses.]

2. Source of a Short Quotation—APA

A recent report of reductions in SAD-related "depression in 87 percent of patients" (Binkley, 1990, p. 203) reverses the findings of earlier studies. [Author name, date, and page reference in parentheses immediately following the quotation.]

Binkley (1990) reports reductions in SAD-related "depression in 87 percent of patients" (p. 203). [Author name followed by the date in parentheses incorporated into the words introducing the quotation; page number in parentheses immediately following the quotation.]

3. Source of a Long Quotation (and Format of Quotation)—APA

Incorporate a direct quotation of fewer than forty words into your own sentence and enclose it in quotation marks. Place the parenthetical in-text citation after the closing quotation mark and, if the quotation falls at the end of the sentence, before the sentence-ending punctuation. When you use a quotation longer than forty words, set it off in block style indented one-half inch or five to seven spaces from the left margin. Never enclose a set-off quotation in quotation marks because the placement in block style carries the message that the material is quoted. Place the parenthetical reference citation one space after the end punctuation of the last sentence.

DISPLAYED QUOTATION (FORTY OR MORE WORDS)

Jet lag, with its characteristic fatigue and irregular sleep patterns, is a common problem among those who travel great distances by jet airplane to different time zones:

> Jet lag syndrome is the inability of the internal body rhythm to rapidly resynchronize after sudden shifts in the timing. For a variety of reasons, the system attempts to maintain stability and resist temporal change. Consequently, complete adjustment can often be delayed for several days—sometimes for a week—after arrival at one's destination. (Bonner, 1991, p. 72)

TEACHING TIP
Asking students to make up a title and citation for their imaginary autobiography, perhaps published this year by Simon & Schuster, may inject a little fun into learning to cite a book. Similarly, they might enjoy making up article titles and citations for the imaginary Journal of Fanciful Ideas.

APA

4. One Author—APA

One of his questions is, "What binds together a Mormon banker in Utah with his brother, or other coreligionists in Illinois or Massachusetts?" (Coles, 1993, p. 2).

In a parenthetical reference in APA style, a comma and a space separate a name from a year and a year from a page reference. (Examples 1 through 3 above show citations of works by one author.)

5. Two Authors—APA

If a work has two authors, give both names in each citation.

One report describes 2,123 occurrences (Krait & Cooper, 1994).

The results that Krait and Cooper (1994) report would not support the conclusions Davis and Sherman (1992) draw in their review of the literature.

When you write a parenthetical in-text citation naming two (or more) authors, use an ampersand (&) between the final two names, but write out the word *and* for any reference in your own sentence.

6. Three, Four, or Five Authors—APA

For three, four, or five authors, use all the authors' last names in the first reference. In all subsequent references, use only the first author's last name followed by *et al.* (meaning "and others").

FIRST REFERENCE

In one anthology, 35% of the selections had not been anthologized before (Elliott, Kerber, Litz, & Martin, 1992).

SUBSEQUENT REFERENCE

Elliott et al. (1992) include 17 authors whose work has never been anthologized.

7. Six or More Authors—APA

For six or more authors, name the first author followed by *et al.* in all in-text references, including the first. (See section 35f, model 3, for the correct References format.)

8. Author(s) with Two or More Works in the Same Year—APA

If you use more than one source written in the same year by the same author(s), alphabetize the works by their titles for the References list, and assign letters in alphabetical order to the years—(1996a), (1996b), (1996c). Use the year-letter combination in parenthetical references.

Note that a citation of two or more such works lists the years in alphabetical order.

> Most recently, Jones (1996c) draws new conclusions from the results of
> 17 sets of experiments (Jones, 1996a, 1996b).

9. Two or More Authors with the Same Last Name—APA

Include first initials for every in-text citation of authors who share a last name. Use the initials appearing in the References list. (In the second example, a parenthetical citation, the name order is alphabetical, as explained in item 12.)

> R. A. Smith (1997) and C. Smith (1989) both confirm these results.

> These results have been confirmed independently (C. Smith, 1989;
> R. A. Smith, 1997).

10. Work with a Group or Corporate Author—APA

If you use a source in which the "author" is a corporation, agency, or group, an in-text reference gives that name as author. Use the full name in each citation, unless an abbreviated version of the name is likely to be familiar to your audience. In that case, use the full name and give its abbreviation at the first citation; then, use the abbreviation for subsequent citations.

> This exploration will continue into the 21st century (National Aeronautics
> and Space Administration [NASA], 1996). [In subsequent citations, use the
> abbreviated form, NASA, alone.]

11. Work Listed by Title—APA

If no author is named, use a shortened form of the title for in-text citations. Ignoring *A, An,* or *The,* make the first word the one by which you alphabetize the title in your References. The following example refers to an article fully titled "Are You a Day or Night Person?"

> Scientists group people as "larks" or "owls" on the basis of whether
> individuals are more efficient in the morning or at night ("Are You," 1989).

12. Reference to More Than One Source—APA

If more than one source has contributed to an idea or opinion in your paper, cite the sources alphabetically by author in one set of parentheses; separate each block of information with a semicolon, as in the example on the next page.

BACKGROUND

Until the middle of the fifteenth century, the only books available to Europeans were handwritten manuscripts, which were costly and often inaccurate. The development of printing made books available to the common people for the first time.

The major breakthrough in the history of printing was the invention of movable type, the making of a stamp for each letter on a separate base so that the letters could be assembled to form a page. Although this system was already known in China and Korea (where it was little used because of the large number of Chinese characters and the lack of suitable ink), its discovery in Europe was made independently. Credit for the European development has been given to Johannes Gutenberg (c. 1400–1468), though scholars increasingly acknowledge other contributors to his work. The so-called Gutenberg Bible, printed c. 1455, was not his first printed work, but it is his most famous one.

Today, it is often remarked that the world is going through another printing revolution. With the availability of copying machines, memory typewriters, word processing computer programs, and a variety of desktop printers, methods of producing printed material have undergone another major shift. Whereas only a few years ago having a document printed meant handing it over to a professional printer, today it is likely to be produced on equipment readily available in most offices and many homes.

APA

BACKGROUND
The site <http://owl.english.purdue.edu/internet/index.html> offers a large collection of online resources.

APA

Conceptions of personal space vary among cultures (Morris, 1977; Worchel & Cooper, 1983).

13. Personal Communication, Including E-Mail and Other Nonretrievable Sources—APA

Telephone calls, personal letters, interviews, and e-mail messages are "personal communications" that your readers cannot access or retrieve. Acknowledge personal communications in parenthetical references, but never include them in your References list at the end of your research paper.

> Recalling his first summer at camp, one person said, "The proximity of 12 other kids made me—an only child with older, quiet parents—frantic for eight weeks" (A. Weiss, personal communication, January 12, 1996).

14. Reference to an Entire Online Source—APA

If an online source does not provide page numbers, use the paragraph number preceded by the abbreviation *para.* If you cannot decipher the page number or the paragraph, cite the heading and the number of the paragraph following it.

> (Anderson, 2003, para. 14)

> (Migueis, 2002, Introduction, para. 1)

15. Other References to Retrievable Online Sources—APA

When you quote, paraphrase, or summarize an online source that is available to others, cite the author (if any) or title and the date as you would for a print source, and include the work in your References list.

16. Source Lines for Graphics and Table Data—APA

If you use a graphic from another source or create a table using data from another source, give a note in the text at the bottom of the table or graphic, crediting the original author and the copyright holder. Here are examples of two source lines, one for a graphic from an article, the other for a graphic from a book.

GRAPHIC FROM AN ARTICLE—APA

Note. The data in columns 1 and 2 are from "Bridge over Troubled Waters? Connecting Research and Pedagogy in Composition and Business/Technical Communication," by J. Allen, 1992, *Technical Communication Quarterly, 1* (4), p. 9. Copyright 1992 by the Association of Teachers of Technical Writing. Adapted with permission of the author.

GRAPHIC FROM A BOOK—APA

Note. From *How to Lower Your Fat Thermostat: The No-Diet Reprogramming Plan for Lifelong Weight Control* (p. 74), by D. Remington, A. G. Fisher, and E. Parent, 1983, Provo: Vitality House International. Copyright 1983 by Vitality House International. Reprinted with permission.

35d What are APA guidelines for writing an abstract?

As the APA *Publication Manual* explains, "an abstract is a brief, comprehensive summary" (p. 12) of a longer piece of writing. APA estimates that an abstract should be limited in length to about 120 words or less. Your instructor may require that you include an abstract at the start of a paper; if you're not sure, ask. Make the abstract accurate, objective, and exact. Actually, when studying the social sciences, you may have become familiar with effective abstracts, for many disciplines have online abstracts of longer sources. See 35g for guidelines on formatting an Abstract page. Here is an abstract prepared for the research paper on biological clocks that appears in 35h.2.

> Circadian rhythms, which greatly affect human lives, often suffer disruptions in technological societies, resulting in such disorders as jet lag syndrome and seasonal affective disorder (SAD). With growing scientific awareness of both natural circadian cycles and the effects of disturbances of these cycles, individuals are learning to control some negative effects.

35e What are APA guidelines for content notes?

Content notes in APA-style papers add relevant information that cannot be worked effectively into a text discussion. Use consecutive arabic numerals for note numbers, both within your paper and on any separate page following the last text page of your paper. See 35g for instructions on formatting the Footnotes page.

35f What are APA guidelines for a References list?

The REFERENCES list at the end of your research paper provides complete bibliographic information for readers who may want to access the sources you draw upon for your paper.

Include in a References list all the sources you QUOTE, PARAPHRASE, or SUMMARIZE in your paper so that readers can find the same sources with reasonable effort. Never include in your References list any source that's not generally available to others (see item 13 in 35c).

General format guidelines are presented in Box 152. The directory that follows the box corresponds to the numbered examples in this section. Not all documentation models are shown here. You may have to combine features of models to document a particular source.

BOX 152   SUMMARY

 Guidelines for an APA-style References list

■ **TITLE**

References

■ **PLACEMENT OF LIST**

Start a new page numbered sequentially with the rest of the paper, before Notes pages, if any.

■ **CONTENTS AND FORMAT**

Include all quoted, paraphrased, or summarized sources in your paper that are not personal communications, unless your instructor tells you to include all the references you have consulted, not just those you have to credit. Start each entry on a new line, and double-space all lines. In the 2001 edition of the *Publication Manual* (section 5.18), the APA recommends that student papers follow journal formatting by using a *hanging indent* style: The first line of each entry begins flush left at the margin and all other lines are indented. The hanging indent makes source names and dates prominent. Type the first line of each entry full width, and indent subsequent lines one-half inch. The easiest way to do this is through the word processor's ruler bar.

Shuter, R. (1977). A field study of nonverbal communication in Germany,
   Italy, and the United States. *Communication Monographs, 44,*
   298–305.

■ **SPACING AFTER PUNCTUATION**

The 2001 APA manual calls for one space after punctuation marks, including within displayed quotations (see 35c, item 3).

■ **ARRANGEMENT OF ENTRIES**

Alphabetize by the author's last name. If no author is named, alphabetize by the first significant word (not *A, An,* or *The*) in the title of the work.   →

Guidelines for an APA-style References list (*continued*)

- **AUTHORS' NAMES**

  Use last names, first initials, and middle initials, if any. Reverse the order for all authors' names, and use an ampersand (&) between the second-to-last and last authors: Mills, J. F., & Holahan, R. H.

  Give names in the order in which they appear on the work (on the title page of a book; usually under the title of an article or other printed work). Use a comma between the first author's last name and first initial and after each complete name except the last. Use a period after the last author's name.

- **DATES**

  Date information follows the name information and is enclosed in parentheses. Place a period followed by one space after the closing parenthesis.

  For books, articles in journals that have volume numbers, and many other print and nonprint sources, the year of publication or production is the date to use. For articles from most magazines and newspapers, use the year followed by a comma and then the exact date that appears on the issue. Individual entries in 35f show how much information to give for various sources.

- **CAPITALIZATION OF TITLES**

  For book, article, and chapter titles, capitalize the first word, the first word after a colon between a title and subtitle, and any proper nouns. For names of journals and proceedings of meetings, capitalize the first word, all nouns and adjectives, and any other words four or more letters long.

- **SPECIAL TREATMENT OF TITLES**

  Use no special treatment for titles of shorter works (poems, short stories, essays, articles). Italicize titles of longer works (books, names of newspapers or journals). Underlining can be used in place of italic type if italic typeface is unavailable. Draw an unbroken line that includes end punctuation.

  Do not drop *A*, *An*, or *The* from the titles of periodicals (such as newspapers, magazines, and journals).

- **PUBLISHERS**

  Use a shortened version of the publisher's name except for an association, corporation, or university press. Drop *Co., Inc., Publishers*, and the like, but retain *Books* or *Press*.

  →

EXTRA EXERCISE A

Using the same sources that appeared in Extra Exercise B in Chapter 34, compile a References list, following APA style.

Answers to Extra Exercise A

References

Clarke, G. (1988). *Capote: A biography.* New York: Simon & Schuster.

Gould, S. J. (1987). *Time's arrow, time's cycle: Myth and metaphor in the discovery of geological time.* Cambridge, MA: Harvard University Press.

Hibbert, C. (1974). *The rise and fall of the House of Medici.* New York: Penguin Books.

Oates, S. B. (1984). *Abraham Lincoln: The man behind the myths.* New York: Harper & Row.

Peters, T. J., & Waterman, R. H., Jr. (1982). *In search of excellence.* New York: Harper & Row.

Sacks, O. (n.d.). The autist artist. In *The man who mistook his wife for a hat, and other clinical tales* (pp. 204-223). New York: Summit Books.

Smout, T. C. (1986). *A century of the Scottish people, 1830-1950.* New Haven, CT: Yale University Press.

Tuchman, B. W. (1981). *Practicing history.* New York: Knopf.

APA

Guidelines for an APA-style References list (*continued*)

■ **PLACE OF PUBLICATION**

For U.S. publishers, give the city and add the state (use the two-letter postal abbreviations listed in most dictionaries and in Box 122 in 30k) for all U.S. cities except Baltimore, Boston, Chicago, Los Angeles, New York, Philadelphia, and San Francisco. For publishers in other countries, give city and country spelled out; no country name is needed with Amsterdam, Jerusalem, London, Milan, Moscow, Paris, Rome, Stockholm, Tokyo, and Vienna. However, if the state or country is part of the publisher's name, omit it after the name of the city.

■ **PUBLICATION MONTH ABBREVIATIONS**

Do not abbreviate publication months.

■ **PAGE NUMBERS**

Use all digits, omitting none. *Only* for references to parts of books or material in newspapers, use *p.* and *pp.* before page numbers. List all discontinuous pages, with numbers separated by commas: pp. 32, 44-45, 47-49, 53.

■ **REFERENCES ENTRIES: BOOKS**

Citations for books have four main parts: author, date, title, and publication information (place of publication and publisher).

AUTHOR DATE   TITLE

Wood, P. (2003). *Diversity: The invention of a concept.*

PUBLICATION INFORMATION

San Francisco: Encounter Books.

■ **REFERENCES ENTRIES: ARTICLES**

Citations for periodical articles contain four major parts: author, date, title of article, and publication information (usually, the periodical title, volume number, and page numbers).

AUTHOR   DATE   ARTICLE TITLE

Herxheimer, A., & Waterhouse, J. (2003). The prevention and treatment

                 VOLUME   PAGE
PERIODICAL TITLE   NUMBER   NUMBER

of jet lag. *BMG: British Medical Journal, 326,*   296-297.

→

QUOTATION: ON WRITING
Good writing is full of surprises and novelties, moving in a direction you don't expect.
—Iris Murdoch

Guidelines for an APA-style References list (*continued*)

■ **REFERENCES ENTRIES: ELECTRONIC AND ONLINE SOURCES**

Styles for documenting electronic and online sources continue to evolve. The 2001 APA *Publication Manual* (pp. 268–281) and the APA Web page <http://www.apastyle.org/elecref.html> are the best sources for up-to-date advice on these formats. Here are two examples of entries. The first is for an abstract on CD-ROM, a searchable "aggregated database" (i.e., a compilation of resources grouped for directed or simplified access). You are not required to document how you accessed the database—via portable CD-ROM, on a library server, or via a supplier Web site—but a "retrieval statement" that accurately names the source (in this case, the database) and lists the date of retrieval is required. (If you include an item or accession number, place it in parentheses.)

        AUTHOR   DATE   ARTICLE TITLE
Marcus, H. F., & Kitayamo, S. (1991). Culture and the self:

    Implications for cognition, emotion, and motivation.

    JOURNAL TITLE AND
    PUBLICATION INFORMATION   RETRIEVAL INFORMATION
    Psychological Abstracts, 78. Retrieved October 2, 2003, from

    PsycINFO database (Item 1991-23978-001).

The second example is for an article in a newspaper on the World Wide Web. The retrieval statement gives the access date and the URL, which "names" the source.

AUTHOR   DATE   ARTICLE TITLE
Markel, H. (2003, September 2). Lack of sleep takes its toll on

               ONLINE   RETRIEVAL
           NEWSPAPER TITLE   INFORMATION
    student psyches. *The New York Times*. Retrieved December 27, 2003,

    from http://www.nytimes.com

Notice that the only punctuation in the URL is part of the address. Do not add a period after a URL.

BACKGROUND: ON WRITING
In "The Use and Overuse of Electronic Research in Freshman Composition Research Papers: Problems in Traditional and Online Universities" (Abstract, ERIC ED459461, 2002), Suzanne Abram finds that instructors teaching purely online writing courses have to take special steps to insure that their students use a range of sources.

Directory—APA Style

PRINT SOURCES

1. Book by One Author—APA
2. Book by Two Authors—APA
3. Book by Three or More Authors—APA
4. Two or More Books by the Same Author(s)—APA
5. Book by a Group or Corporate Author—APA
6. Book with No Author Named—APA
7. Book with an Author and an Editor—APA
8. Translation—APA
9. Work in Several Volumes or Parts—APA
10. One Selection from an Anthology or an Edited Book—APA
11. Selection from a Work Already Listed in References—APA
12. Signed Article in a Reference Book—APA
13. Unsigned Article in a Reference Book—APA
14. Second or Subsequent Edition—APA
15. Anthology or Edited Book—APA
16. Introduction, Preface, Foreword, or Afterword—APA
17. Unpublished Dissertation or Essay—APA
18. Reprint of an Older Book—APA
19. Book in a Series—APA
20. Book with a Title Within a Title—APA
21. Government Publication—APA
22. Published Proceedings of a Conference—APA
23. Signed Article from a Daily Newspaper—APA
24. Editorial, Letter to the Editor, or Review—APA
25. Unsigned Article from a Daily Newspaper—APA
26. Signed Article from a Weekly or Biweekly Periodical—APA
27. Signed Article from a Monthly or Bimonthly Periodical—APA
28. Unsigned Article from a Weekly or Monthly Periodical—APA
29. Article from a Looseleaf Collection of Reprinted Articles—APA
30. Article in a Journal with Continuous Pagination—APA
31. Article in a Journal That Pages Each Issue Separately—APA
32. Published and Unpublished Letters—APA
33. Map or Chart—APA

NONPRINT SOURCES

34. Interview—APA
35. Lecture, Speech, or Address—APA
36. Motion Picture—APA
37. Music Recording—APA
38. Live Performance—APA
39. Work of Art, Photograph, or Musical Composition—APA

40. Radio or Television Broadcast—APA
41. Information Services—APA

ELECTRONIC AND ONLINE SOURCES
42. Article from an Encyclopedia on CD-ROM—APA
43. Computer Software—APA
44. Books Retrieved from Databases on the Web—APA
45. Article from a Periodical on the Web—APA
46. Electronic Copy of a Journal Article Retrieved from a Database—APA
47. Personal or Professional Site on the Web—APA
48. File Transfer Protocol (FTP), Telnet, or Gopher site—APA
49. Synchronous Communications (MOO, MUD, IRC)—APA
50. Web Discussion Forum—APA
51. Listserv (Electronic Mailing List)—APA
52. Newsgroup—APA

PRINT SOURCES
1. Book by One Author—APA

Welty, E. (1984). *One writer's beginnings*. Cambridge, MA: Harvard University
Press.

Use the hanging indent style: the first line of an entry is flush to the left margin and all other lines are indented one-half inch.

2. Book by Two Authors—APA

Gordon, E. E., & Gordon, E. H. (2003). *Literacy in America: Historic journey and
contemporary solutions*. Westport, CT: Praeger.

3. Book by Three or More Authors—APA

Moore, M. H., Estrich, S., McGillis, D., & Spelman, W. (1984). *Dangerous
offenders: The elusive target of justice*. Cambridge, MA: Harvard
University Press.

For a book by three to six authors, include all the authors' names. For a book by more than six authors, use only the first six names followed by *et al*.

4. Two or More Books by the Same Author(s)—APA

Gardner, H. (1993). *Multiple intelligences: The theory in practice*. New York:
Basic Books.

Gardner, H. (1999). *Intelligence reframed: Multiple intelligences for the 21st
century*. New York: Basic Books.

References by the same author are arranged chronologically, with the earlier date of publication listed first.

5. Book by a Group or Corporate Author—APA

American Psychological Association. (2001). *Publication manual of the American Psychological Association* (5th ed.). Washington, DC: Author.

Boston Women's Health Collective. (1998). *Our bodies, ourselves for the new century.* New York: Simon & Schuster.

Cite the full name of the corporate author first. If the author is also the publisher, use the word *Author* as the name of the publisher.

6. Book with No Author Named—APA

The Chicago manual of style (15th ed.). (2003). Chicago: University of Chicago Press.

7. Book with an Author and an Editor—APA

Brontë, E. (2002). *Wuthering Heights* (R. J. Dunn, Ed.). New York: Norton.

8. Translation—APA

Kundera, M. (1999). *The unbearable lightness of being* (M. H. Heim, Trans.). New York: HarperPerennial. (Original work published 1984)

9. Work in Several Volumes or Parts—APA

Chrisley, R. (Ed.). (2000). *Artificial intelligence: Critical concepts* (Vols. 1-4). London: Routledge.

10. One Selection from an Anthology or an Edited Book—APA

Galarza, E. (1972). The roots of migration. In L. Valdez & S. Steiner (Eds.), *Aztlan: An anthology of Mexican American literature* (pp. 127-132). New York: Knopf.

Give the author of the selection first. The word *In* introduces the larger work from which the selection is taken.

11. Selection from a Work Already Listed in References—APA

Gilbert, S., & Gubar, S. (Eds.). (1985). *The Norton anthology of literature by women.* New York: Norton.

Kingston, M. H. (1985). No name woman. In S. Gilbert & S. Gubar (Eds.), *The Norton anthology of literature by women* (pp. 2337-2347). New York: Norton.

Provide full information for the already-cited anthology (first example), along with information about the individual selection. Put entries in alphabetical order.

12. Signed Article in a Reference Book—APA

Burnbam, J. C. (1996). Freud, Sigmund. In B. B. Wolman (Ed.), *The encyclopedia of psychiatry, psychology, and psychoanalysis* (p. 220). New York: Holt.

Use *In* to introduce the larger work from which the selection is taken.

13. Unsigned Article in a Reference Book—APA

Ireland. (2002). In *The new encyclopaedia Britannica: Macropaedia* (Vol. 21, pp. 997-1018). Chicago: Encyclopaedia Britannica.

14. Second or Subsequent Edition—APA

Gibaldi, J. (2003). *MLA handbook for writers of research papers* (6th ed.). New York: Modern Language Association.

A book doesn't state if it's a first edition. However, after the first edition, the edition number appears on the title page. In your entry, place the year of the edition after the title and in parentheses.

15. Anthology or Edited Book—APA

Purdy, J. L., & Ruppert, J. (Eds.). (2001). *Nothing but the truth: An anthology of Native American literature.* Upper Saddle River, NJ: Prentice Hall.

16. Introduction, Preface, Foreword, or Afterword—APA

Fox-Genovese, E. (1999). Foreword. In N. Warren & S. Wolff (Eds.), *Southern mothers.* Baton Rouge: Louisiana State University Press.

If you're citing an introduction, preface, foreword, or afterword, give its author's name first. After the year, give the name of the part cited. If the writer of the material you are citing is not the author of the book, use the word *In* and the author's name before the title of the book.

17. Unpublished Dissertation or Essay—APA

Byers, M. (2000). *Buffy the Vampire Slayer: The insurgence of television as a performance text.* Unpublished doctoral dissertation, University of Toronto, Ontario, Canada.

18. Reprint of an Older Book—APA

Hurston, Z. N. (1978). *Their eyes were watching God.* Urbana: University of Illinois Press. (Original work published 1937)

Republishing information appears on the copyright page.

19. Book in a Series—APA

Give the title of the book, but not of the whole series.

Goldman, D. J. (1995). *Women writers and World War I.* New York: Macmillan.

APA

20. Book with a Title Within a Title—APA

Lumiansky, R. M., & Baker, H. (Eds.). (1968). *Critical approaches to six major English works:* Beowulf *through* Paradise Lost. Philadelphia: University of Pennsylvania Press.

Never italicize a title within a title, even though it would appear in italic typeface if it were by itself.

21. Government Publication—APA

U.S. Congress. House Subcommittee on Health and Environment of the Committee on Commerce. (1999). *The nursing home resident protection amendments of 1999.* Washington, DC: U.S. Government Printing Office.

U.S. Congressional Subcommittee on Technology of the Committee on Science. (1998). *Y2K: What every consumer should know to prepare for the year 2000 program.* Washington, DC: U.S. Government Printing Office.

U.S. Senate Special Committee on Aging. (1998). *The risk of malnutrition in nursing homes.* Washington, DC: U.S. Government Printing Office.

U.S. Senate Special Committee on the Year 2K Technical Problem. (1999). *Y2K and H_2O: Safeguarding our most vital resources.* Washington, DC: U.S. Government Printing Office.

Use the complete name of a government agency as author when no specific person is named.

22. Published Proceedings of a Conference—APA

Harris, D., & Nelson-Heern, L. (Eds.). (1981, June). *Proceedings of the National Education Computing Conference.* Iowa City: University of Iowa, Weeg Computing Center.

23. Signed Article from a Daily Newspaper—APA

Killborn, P. T. (2003, June 22). A health threat baffling for its lack of a pattern. *The New York Times*, p. A14.

24. Editorial, Letter to the Editor, or Review—APA

Downtown's architectural promise. (2003, August 4). [Editorial]. *The New York Times*, p. A12.

Hansen, R. P. (2003, January/February). [Letter to the editor]. *Sierra*, 8.

Shenk, D. (2003, Spring). Toolmaker, brain builder. [Review of the book *Beyond big blue: Building the computer that defeated the world chess champion*]. *The American Scholar, 72*, 150-152.

25. Unsigned Article from a Daily Newspaper—APA

Changes sought in medical services for veterans. (2003, August 5). *The New York Times*, p. A10.

26. Signed Article from a Weekly or Biweekly Periodical—APA

Fonda, D. (2002, October 21). Plucky little competitors. *Time*, 60–62.

Use the abbreviation *p*. (or *pp*. for more than one page) for newspapers. Do not use this abbreviation for magazines or journals. Give year, month, and day-date for a periodical published every week or every two weeks.

27. Signed Article from a Monthly or Bimonthly Periodical—APA

Langewiesche, W. (2003, September). Anarchy at sea. *The Atlantic Monthly*, 292(2), 50-80.

Give the year and month(s) for a periodical published every month or every other month.

28. Unsigned Article from a Weekly or Monthly Periodical—APA

The price is wrong. (2003, August 2). *The Economist*, 58-59.

29. Article from a Looseleaf Collection of Reprinted Articles—APA

Hayden, T. (2002). The age of robots. In E. Goldstein (Ed.), *Applied Science 2002. SIRS 2002*, Article 66. (Reprinted from *U.S. News & World Report*, pp. 44+, 2001, April 23).

30. Article in a Journal with Continuous Pagination—APA

Tyson, P. (1998). The psychology of women. *Journal of the American Psychoanalytic Association, 46*, 361-364.

Give only the volume number after the journal title, and italicize the volume number.

31. Article in a Journal That Pages Each Issue Separately—APA

Adler-Kassner, L., & Estrem, H. (2003). Rethinking research writing: Public literacy in the composition classroom. *WPA: Writing Program Administration, 26*(3), 119-131.

Give the volume number, italicized with the journal title. Give the issue number in parentheses; do not italicize it.

32. Published and Unpublished Letters—APA

Williams, W. C. (1935). Letter to his son. In L. Grunwald & S. J. Adler (Eds.), *Letters of the century: America 1900-1999*. New York: Dial.

In the APA system, unpublished letters are considered personal communication inaccessible to general readers, so they do not appear in the

APA

References list. Personal communications do not provide recoverable data and so are cited only in the body of the paper (see model 34).

33. Map or Chart—APA

The Caribbean and South America [Map]. (1992). Falls Church, VA: American
　　Automobile Association.

NONPRINT SOURCES
34. Interview—APA

In APA style, a personal interview is considered personal correspondence and is not included in the References list. Cite the interview in the text with a parenthetical notation saying that it is a personal communication.

Randi Friedman (personal communication, June 30, 2003) endorses this view.

35. Lecture, Speech, or Address—APA

Kennedy, J. F. (1960, September 12). Address. Speech presented to the Greater
　　Houston Ministerial Association, Houston, TX.

36. Motion Picture—APA

Capra, F. (Director/Producer). (1934). *It happened one night* [Motion picture].
　　United States: Columbia Pictures.

Capra, F. (Director/Producer). (1999). *It happened one night*
　　[Videocassette]. (Original movie released 1934)

Madden, J. (Director), Parfitt, D., Gigliotti, D., Weinstein, H., Zwick, E.,
　　& Norman, M. (Producers). (2003). *Shakespeare in love* [DVD]. (Original
　　movie released 1998)

37. Music Recording—APA

Smetana, B. (1975). *My country* [With K. Anserl conducting the Czech
　　Philharmonic Orchestra]. [Record]. London: Vanguard Records.

Springsteen, B. (2002). Lonesome day. On *The rising* [CD]. New York: Sony.

38. Live Performance—APA

Hare, D. (Author), Daldry, S. (Director), & Hare, D. (Performer). (1999, April 11).
　　Via dolorosa [Live performance]. New York: Lincoln Center Theater.

39. Work of Art, Photograph, or Musical Composition—APA

Cassatt, M. *La toilette* [Artwork]. Chicago: Art Institute of Chicago.

Mydans, C. (1999, October 21-November 28). *General Douglas MacArthur landing at Luzon, 1945* [Photograph]. New York: Soho Triad Fine Art Gallery.

Schubert, Franz. *Unfinished symphony* [Musical composition].

40. Radio or Television Broadcast—APA

Burns, K. (1999, November 8). In Barnes, P., & Burns, K. (Producers), *Not for ourselves alone: The story of Elizabeth Cady Stanton and Susan B. Anthony* [Television broadcast]. New York and Washington, DC: Public Broadcasting Service.

If you're citing a television series produced by and seen on one station, cite its call letters.

41. Information Services—APA

Chiang, L. H. (1993). *Beyond the language: Native Americans' nonverbal communication.* (ERIC Document Reproduction Service No. ED 368 540).

ELECTRONIC AND ONLINE SOURCES

Information from online sources that your readers cannot readily retrieve for themselves—many e-mail messages and discussion list communications, for example—should be treated as personal communication (see model 34). Never include them in your References list. If you have a scholarly reason to cite a message from a newsgroup, forum, or electronic mailing list that is available in an electronic archive, then document an author name; the exact date of the posting; the subject line or "thread" (do not italicize it) followed by an identifier in square brackets—[Msg 23]; and a "Message posted to" statement that lists the URL of the message or of the archive. Following is an example:

Hesse, D. (2003, August 1). Research on large class size [Msg 192]. Message posted to http://lists.asu.edu/archives/wpa-l.html

The APA system for documenting electronic and online sources in a References list has been evolving. At the time of this writing, the guidelines in the APA *Publication Manual,* fifth edition (2001), remain most current. In general, APA recommends giving author, title, and publication information as for a print source. This information is followed by a "retrieval statement" that leads the reader as directly as possible to your source.

APA

BACKGROUND: ON WRITING
In "Writing in a Psychology Classroom: Learning and Adopting the APA Epistemology" (Diss., University of North Dakota, 2000), SuEllen Shaw studies how students learn to use APA style, which includes learning the values and habits of thinking associated with that style.

In contrast to MLA style, APA style doesn't require you to use angle brackets around URLs in retrieval statements. Also, APA allows you to break a URL either after a slash or before a period.

42. Article from an Encyclopedia on CD-ROM—APA

Artificial intelligence. (2003). *Encarta 2003*. Retrieved December 10, 2003, from
     Encarta database.

The retrieval statement gives the retrieval date in full and the name of the database. The entry ends with a period.

43. Computer Software—APA

Transparent Language Presentation Program (Version 2.0 for Windows)
     [Computer software]. (1994). Hollis, NH: Transparent Language.

Provide an author name, if available. Standard software and program languages do not need to be listed in References. Provide the name and, in parentheses, the version number in the text.

44. Books Retrieved from Databases on the Web—APA

Adams, H. (1918). *The education of Henry Adams*. New York: Houghton Mifflin.
     Retrieved December 4, 1999, from Project Bartleby database: http://
     www.columbia.edu/acis/bartleby/159/index/html

The first information is for the printed version of *The Education of Henry Adams*. The retrieval statement gives the access date, the name of the database, and the URL of the specific work.

Chopin, K. (1899). *The awakening*. Retrieved December 12, 2003, from PBS
     database: http://www.pbs.org/katechopin/library/awakening

45. Article from a Periodical on the Web—APA

Parrott, Andy C. (1999). Does cigarette smoking cause stress? *American
     Psychologist, 54*, 817-820. Retrieved December 7, 2003, from
     http://www.apa.org/journals/amp/amp5410817.html

46. Electronic Copy of a Journal Article Retrieved from a Database—APA

Wright, K. (2002, September). Times of our lives. *Scientific American, 287*, 58–64.
     Retrieved July 2, 2003, from Academic Search Elite database.

47. Personal or Professional Site on the Web—APA

Hesse, D. (2003, November). Home page. Retrieved December 22, 2003, from
     http://www.ilstu.edu/~ddhesse

Williams, R. W. (2002, November). Neurogenetics at UT Health Science Center.
     Retrieved November 11, 2002, from http://nervenet.org

48. File Transfer Protocol (FTP), Telnet, or Gopher Site—APA

Taine, H. A. (2001, April). *The French Revolution Volume II*. Retrieved
    October 21, 2002, from ftp://ibiblio.org/pub/docs/books/gutenberg

After the retrieval data, supply the FTP, telnet, or gopher search path.

49. Synchronous Communications (MOO, MUD, IRC)—APA

Give the name of the speaker, a title for the event, the date of the event
or posting, the access date, and the URL.

Bleck, B. (1997, June 8). Online discussion of virtual first year composition:
    Distance education, the Internet and the World Wide Web. Retrieved
    February 27, 1999, from http://lrc.csun.edu/DaMOO/cw/brad.html

50. Web Discussion Forum—APA

Higa, S. (2002, June 26). A potential bookmark [Msg. 483]. Message posted to
    http://groups.yahoo.com/group/Modern_Era/messages/483

51. Listserv (Electronic Mailing List)—APA

Caruso, T. (2002, June 30). CFP: Flannery O'Connor and feminism. Message
    posted to Calls for Papers electronic mailing list, archived at
    http://www.english.upenn.edu/CFP/archive/American/0421.html

52. Newsgroup—APA

Boyle, F. (2002, October 11). Psyche: Cemi field theory: The hard problem made
    easy [Msg 1]. Message posted to news://sci.psychology.consciousness

35g What are APA format guidelines for research papers?

Ask whether your instructor has instructions for preparing a final draft.
If not, you can use the APA guidelines here.

General instructions—APA

Use 8½-by-11-inch white bond paper. The APA *Publication Manual* recommends double-spacing for a final manuscript of a student research
paper. Set at least a one-inch margin on the left (slightly more if you
submit your paper in a binder) and leave no less than one inch on the
right and at the bottom.

    Leave one-half inch from the top edge of the paper to the title-and-
page-number line, described on the next page. Leave another one-half
inch (or one inch from the top edge of the paper) before the next line on

TEACHING TIP
Computers have taken much of the old tedium out of formatting research papers. You
may want to explain to students such now-
quaint practices of having to measure pages
to leave room for footnotes, creating templates to put behind papers in a typewriter, or
hiring typists to produce the final draft. However, as ubiquitous as computers and word
processing are, a surprising number of students still do not know how to use such labor-
saving features as the ruler line to set
margins, paragraph indentations, block quotations, and hanging indents or the header
feature to set running titles and page numbers. Spending a few minutes demonstrating
these features in a classroom, lab, or your office can make students very appreciative.

the page, whether that is a heading (such as "Abstract" or "Notes") or a line of your paper.

👁 **ALERT:** Most word processing programs set the top and bottom margins at one inch as their default. Also, they generally set the "header" function at a default of one-half inch. Therefore, formatting the margins for your paper is probably less troublesome than it might seem. You simply need to check the default settings. 👁

Use indents of one-half inch for the first line of all paragraphs, except in an abstract, the first line of which is not indented. Do not justify the right margin. Indent footnotes one-half inch.

Order of parts—APA

Number all pages consecutively. Use this order for the parts of your paper:

1. Title page
2. Abstract (if required)
3. Body of the paper
4. References
5. Appendixes, if any
6. Footnotes, if any
7. Attachments, if any (questionnaires, data sheets, or other material your instructor asks you to include)

Title-and-page-number line for all pages—APA

Use a title-and-page-number line on all pages of your paper. Leaving a margin of one-half inch from the top edge of the paper, type the title (use a shortened version if necessary), leave a five-character space, and then type the page number. End the title-and-page-number line one inch from the right edge of the paper. Ask whether your instructor wants you to include your last name in this title-and-page-number line. The "header" tool on a word processing program will help you create the title-and-page-number line easily.

Title page—APA

Use a separate title page. On it, begin with the title-and-page-number line described above, using the numeral 1 for this first page. Then, center the complete title vertically and horizontally on the page. Use two or more double-spaced lines if the title is long. Do not italicize (or underline) the title or enclose it in quotation marks. On the next line, center your name, and below that center the course title and section, your professor's name, and the date.

👁 **ALERTS:** (1) Use the guidelines here for capitalizing the title of your own paper and for capitalizing titles you mention in the body of your paper. (*Note:* See "Special treatment of titles," in Box 152, on the capitalization of titles in a References list, since different rules apply.)
(2) Use a capital letter for the first word of your title and for the first word of a subtitle, if any. Start every noun, pronoun, verb, adverb, and adjective with a capital letter. Capitalize each main word in a hyphenated compound word (two or more words used together to express one idea): *Father-in-Law, Self-Consciousness.* Capitalize the word after a colon or a dash.
(3) Do not capitalize articles (*a, an, the*) unless it starts a title or one of the preceding capitalization rules applies to it. Do not capitalize prepositions and conjunctions unless they are five or more letters long. Do not capitalize the word *to* used in an infinitive. 👁

Abstract—APA

See 35d for advice about what to include in an abstract of your paper. Type the abstract on a separate page, using the numeral 2 in the title-and-page-number line. Center the word *Abstract* one inch from the top of the paper. Do not italicize (or underline) it or enclose it in quotation marks. Double-space below this title, and then start your abstract, double-spacing it. Do not indent the first line.

Set-off quotations—APA

Set off (display in block form) quotations of forty words or more. Double-space to start a new line for the quoted words, indenting each line of the (double-spaced) quotation one-half inch or five to seven spaces from the left margin. Do not enclose the quoted words in quotation marks.

If you are quoting part of a paragraph or one complete paragraph, do not indent the first line more than one-half inch. But if you quote two or more paragraphs, indent the first line of the second and subsequent paragraphs one inch.

When the quotation is finished, leave one space after the sentence-ending punctuation, and then give the parenthetical citation. Begin a new line to resume your own words.

References list—APA

Start a new page for your References list immediately after the end of the body of your paper. Use a title-and-page-number line. Drop down one inch from the top of the paper and center the word *References.* Do not italicize (or underline) it or put it in quotation marks. Double-space below it. Start the first line of each entry at the left margin, and indent any subsequent lines one-half inch from the left margin. Use this "hanging indent" style unless your instructor prefers a different one. Double-space within each entry and between entries.

APA

APA

TEACHING TIP
You might want to explain that formats are of major importance in many disciplines other than English composition. The formats constitute "genres" that readers expect. The formats ease communication because readers know where to look for specific information: background, data, conclusions. You might invite colleagues from a few other disciplines to serve as guest experts for part of a class period and explain how they conduct and write research. Alternatively, you may have students interview some professors to learn about their writing practices, then write up an account for the class.

Notes—APA

Whenever you use a content note in your paper (35e), try to arrange your sentence so that the note number falls at the end. The ideal place for a note number is after the sentence-ending punctuation. Use a numeral raised slightly above the line of words and immediately after the final punctuation mark.

Put your notes on a separate page after the last page of your References list. Use a title-and-page-number line. Then, center the word *Footnotes* one inch from the top of the paper. Do not italicize (or underline) it or put it in quotation marks.

On the next line, indent one-half inch and begin the note. Raise the note number slightly, and then start the words of your note leaving no space. If the note is more than one typed line, do not indent any line after the first. Double-space throughout.

35h   A student's APA-style research paper

The final section of this chapter presents a student research paper prepared to conform to the style of the American Psychological Association (APA). I discuss the researching, planning, drafting, and revising processes of the student, Carlos Velez, and show the final draft of the paper, including its abstract.

Case Study

Carlos Velez was given this assignment for a research paper in a course called Introduction to Psychology: Write a research paper of 1,800 to 2,000 words about an unconscious process in humans. For guidance, refer to the *Simon & Schuster Handbook for Writers,* Chapters 31 through 33. Use the documentation style of the American Psychological Association (APA) explained in Chapter 35. Your topic and working bibliography are due in two weeks. An early draft of your paper is due two weeks later (try to get it close to what you hope will be your last draft, so that comments from me and your peers can concretely help you write an excellent final draft). Your final draft is due one week after your early draft with comments is returned to you.

35h.1   Researching and writing the paper

After Carlos Velez read his assignment, he started PLANNING by listing various unconscious processes in humans so that he could pick one most interesting to him. Referring to his class notes and the textbook from his psychology course, he found these topics: "sleep," "dreams," "insomnia," "biological clocks," "daydreams," "hypnosis," and meditation. He favored the topic "biological clocks" because of his experiences with jet lag whenever he traveled between his home in California (in the Pacific Time Zone) and his grandparents' home in Puerto Rico (in the Atlantic Time Zone, where it is four hours later).

Velez then checked to see whether he could find enough sources useful for research on "biological clocks." From his home computer, he went to his college's Web site and found the college library home page. He was pleased to find that the online book catalog listed several appropriate books that had not been checked out. The online databases provided the entire text of hundreds of journal, magazine, and newspaper articles. Using the Yahoo search engine, he found even more sources. During his search, he tried a variety of terms, like "biological clocks" and "jet lag," which he thought of himself, and "circadian rhythms" and "chronobiology," which he found in articles. Skimming through the online articles, he printed those he thought he could use. Then, he went to his college library to check out several books and to review some other materials that were available only in the library.

So that he could compile a WORKING BIBLIOGRAPHY, Velez began to read and take content notes. The working bibliography that he submitted consisted of twenty-six SOURCES, though he had reviewed and rejected about twelve others (he knew that this represented real progress for him). Velez did not intend to use all twenty-six sources in his paper, but he wanted them available as he wrote his early drafts. Not surprisingly, his instructor urged him to reduce the list once DRAFTING began; otherwise, Velez would risk writing too little about too much. He redoubled his efforts to read even more critically to evaluate his sources (see 5c.3, 5d, and 32j) and weed out material. He narrowed his list to nineteen sources, took detailed notes on each, and began to group his material into emerging subtopics.

Velez had entire books about biological clocks, so he realized that he would need to narrow the TOPIC sufficiently to shape a THESIS STATEMENT. The narrowing process worried him because he had been told in other college courses that his topics for research papers were too broad. He was determined this time to avoid that same problem.

To start drafting his paper, Velez spread his note cards around him for easy reference, but he felt somewhat overwhelmed by the amount of information at hand, and he wrote only a few sentences. To break through, he decided to type a DISCOVERY DRAFT to see what he had absorbed from his reading and notetaking. That very rough draft became his vehicle for many things, including creating an effective thesis statement, inserting source information according to APA documentation style, and checking the logical arrangement of his material.

Revising for Velez started with his thesis statement, a process that helped him further narrow his focus. He started with "Biological clocks

QUOTATION: ON WRITING
As late as 1806 I was waiting for genius to descend upon me so that I might write. . . . If I had spoken around 1795 of my plan to write, some sensible man would have told me "to write every day for an hour or two." Genius or no genius. That advice would have made me use ten years of my life that I spent stupidly waiting for genius.

—Stendhal

APA

are fascinating," which expressed his feelings but said nothing of substance. His next version served him well, as he revised his discovery draft into a true first draft: "Biological clocks, our unconscious timekeepers, affect our lives in many ways, including compatibility in marriage, family life, jet travel, work schedules, illnesses, medical treatments, and the space program." That version proved to Velez that he was covering too much for an 1,800- to 2,000-word research paper, and he wanted to drop some material. He decided first to inform his readers about the phenomenon of biological clocks and then to discuss the effects of those clocks on people's alertness in the morning and later in the day, on travelers on jet airplanes, and on workers' performance. For his final draft, Velez used this more focused thesis statement: "Biological clocks, also known as circadian cycles, are a significant feature of human design that greatly affects people personally and professionally."

Velez used a word processing program that has a template for an APA-style document. Although this provided the overall format, he had to attend very closely to the details of correct parenthetical IN-TEXT CITATIONS (see 35b and 35c) within his paper and a correct REFERENCES list (see 35f and 35g) at the end. Because Velez had used MLA DOCUMENTATION STYLE in other courses, he made sure not to confuse the two styles. For example, he saw that APA-style parenthetical citations include the year of publication (whereas MLA-style citations do not). For format and style details of the References list at the end of his paper, he found Box 152 in section 35f especially helpful.

As Velez checked the logical arrangement of his material, he realized that because he had dropped some aspects of biological clocks when he finally narrowed his topic sufficiently, he needed a little more depth about the aspects that he was retaining. A few hours at the computer led him to what he needed, including examples about baseball players and emergency room physicians. Velez learned from his research experiences the difference between researching a topic too broadly (and therefore gathering too many sources for the assignment) and researching a few aspects of a topic in depth by focusing on selected sources. His final draft, which appears on the following pages, draws on nineteen sources, a number that is down considerably from the twenty-six with which he started.

Velez's title page and abstract page are shown here. For guidelines on writing an abstract, see 35d and 35g.

35h.2 Analyzing the research paper

In APA style, position the title-and-page-number line $1/2$″ from top of paper.

$1/2$″

Biological Clocks   1

← 1″→

In APA style, center the following information in the middle of the page: title, your name, course title and section, the professor's name, and the date; use double-spacing.

Biological Clocks:

The Body's Internal Timepieces

Carlos Velez

Introduction to Psychology 115, Section P1

Professor Robert Schmitt

November 17, 2003

APA-style title page

1″

$1/2$″

Biological Clocks   2 ← 1″→

Abstract

Circadian rhythms, which greatly affect human lives, often suffer

DOUBLE-SPACE

disruptions in technological societies, resulting in such disorders

as jet lag syndrome and seasonal affective disorder (SAD). With

APA style requires that an abstract be placed on a separate page.

growing scientific awareness of both natural circadian cycles

← 1″→ and the effects of disturbances of these cycles, people are

learning to control some negative effects.

APA-style abstract page

QUOTATION: ON WRITING

I have the words already. What I am seeking is the perfect order of words in the sentence. You can see for yourself how many different ways they might be arranged.

—James Joyce

APA STYLE:
1″ margins;
double-space
throughout

Biological Clocks   3

Biological Clocks:

The Body's Internal Timepieces

INTRODUCTION:
Gets reader's
attention

Life in modern technological societies is built around timepieces. People set clocks on radios, microwave ovens, VCRs, and much more. Students respond to bells that start and end the school day in kindergarten through twelfth grades. While carefully managing the minutes and hours each day, individuals are often forced by styles of family and work life to

THESIS
STATEMENT:
Gives paper's
focus

violate another kind of time: their body's time. Biological clocks, also known as circadian cycles, are a significant feature of human design that greatly affects people personally and professionally.

FIRST HEADING *The Body's Natural Cycles*

PARAGRAPH 2:
First body
paragraph
gives
background
information

The term *circadian*, which is Latin for "about a day," describes the rhythms of people's internal biological clocks. Circadian cycles are in tune with external time cycles such as the 24-hour period of the earth's daily rotation as signaled by the rising and setting of the sun. In fact, according to William Schwartz, professor of neurobiology and a researcher in the

Statement by
Schwartz is in
article by Lewis

field of chronobiology (the study of circadian rhythm), "All such biological clocks are adaptations to life on a rotating world" (as cited in Lewis, 1995, p. 14). Usually, humans set their biological clocks by seeing these cycles of daylight and darkness. Studies conducted in caves or similar environments that allow

Author name(s)
and year in
parentheses
when not
included
in text

researchers to control light and darkness have shown that most people not exposed to natural cycles of day and night create cycles slightly over 24 hours (Czeisler et al., 1999). Human perception of the external day-night cycle affects the production

→

(Proportions shown in this paper are adjusted to fit space limitations of this book. Follow actual dimensions discussed in this book and your instructor's directions.)

Biological Clocks 4

and release of a brain hormone, melatonin, which is important

in initiating and regulating the sleep-wake cycle, as Alfred

Lewy and other scientists at the National Institutes of Health

in Bethesda, Maryland, have found (Winfree, 1987).

Each individual's lifestyle reflects that person's own

circadian cycle. Scientists group people as "larks" or "owls"

on the basis of whether individuals are more efficient in the

morning or at night. The idea behind the labels is that "in

nature certain animals are diurnal, active during the light

period; others are nocturnal, active at night. The 'morning lark'

and the 'night owl' connotations typically are used to categorize

the human extremes" ("Are You," 1989, p. 11).

Disruptions of Natural Cycles

"Owls" who must stay up late at night and "larks" who

must awaken early in the morning experience mild versions of

"jet lag," the disturbance from which time-zone travelers often

suffer. Jet lag, which is characterized by fatigue and irregular

sleep patterns, results from disruption of circadian rhythms

in most people who fly in jets to different time zones:

> Jet lag syndrome is the inability of the internal body
>
> rhythm to rapidly resynchronize after sudden shifts in
>
> the timing. For a variety of reasons, the system attempts
>
> to maintain stability and resist temporal change.
>
> Consequently, complete adjustment can often be
>
> delayed for several days--sometimes for a week--after
>
> arrival at one's destination. (Bonner, 1991, p. 72)

According to Richard Coleman (1986), "the number, rate,

and direction of time-zone changes are the critical factors in

determining the extent and degree of jet lag symptoms" (p. 67).

Margin notes:

In APA style, header has shortened title and page number

No page numbers for paraphrases and summaries

PARAGRAPH 3: Defines larks and owls

Partial title used because source does not give an author

SECOND HEADING

PARAGRAPH 4: Applies terms to jet lag

In APA style, block-indented paragraph for quotations over 40 words indents ½" or five to seven spaces

Quotations require page number with *p.* or *pp.* for more than one page

→

QUOTATION: ON WRITING
Until you understand a writer's ignorance, presume yourself ignorant of his understanding.
—Samuel Taylor Coleridge

APA

QUOTATION: ON WRITING

If you would not be forgotten,
As soon as you are dead and rotten,
Either write things worthy reading,
Or do things worth the writing.

—Benjamin Franklin

APA

Biological Clocks   5

In general, eastbound travelers find it harder than westbound travelers to adjust.

PARAGRAPH 5:
Additional specific support for previous paragraph

Proof of this theory can be found in the national pastime, baseball. Three researchers analyzed win-loss records to discover whether jet lag affected baseball players' performance (Recht, Lew, & Schwartz, 1995). The study focused on the records of teams in the eastern and western United States over a period of 3 years. If a visiting team did not have to travel through any time zones, it lost 54% of the time. If the visiting team had traveled from west to east, it lost 56.2% of the time. But if they had traveled from east to west, the visitors lost only 37.1% of the time.

Statistics illustrate example

PARAGRAPH 6:
New example describes problem as it affects another group, shift workers

Another group that suffers greatly from biological-clock disruptions consists of people whose livelihoods depend on erratic schedules. This situation affects 20 to 30 million U.S. workers whose work schedules differ from the usual morning starting time and afternoon or early evening ending time (Weiss, 1989). Sue Binkley (1990) reports that Charles Czeisler, director of the Center for Circadian and Sleep Disorders at Brigham and Women's Hospital in Boston, found that 27% of the U.S. workforce does shift work. Shift work can mean, for example, working from 7:00 a.m. to 3:00 p.m. for six weeks, from 3:00 p.m. to 11:00 p.m. for six weeks, and from 11:00 p.m. to 7:00 a.m. for six weeks. Shift workers are at greater risk for heart disease, stomach disorders, insomnia, mood disorders, and infertility (Latta & Van Cauter, 2003). In a 1989 report to the American Association for the Advancement of Science, Czeisler states that "police officers, [medical] interns, and

Specific details to illustrate example

→

many others who work nights perform poorly and are involved in more on-the-job accidents than their daytime counterparts" (as cited in Binkley, 1990, p. 26).

Other researchers confirm that safety is at risk during late-shift hours. In a study of 28 medical interns observed during late-night shifts over a 1-year period, 25% admitted to falling asleep while talking on the phone, and 34% had had at least one accident or near-accident during that period (Weiss, 1989, p. 37). Investigations into the *Challenger* space shuttle explosion and the nuclear-reactor disasters at Three Mile Island and Chernobyl reveal critical errors made by people undergoing the combined stresses of lack of sleep and unusual work schedules (Toufexis, 1989).

PARAGRAPH 7: Additional specific support

Emergency room physicians experience these two stresses all the time. Their professional group, the American College of Emergency Physicians (ACEP), after investigating circadian rhythms and shift work, drafted a formal policy statement, approved by ACEP's board of directors in 1994. The policy calls for "shifts . . . consistent with circadian principles" to prevent burnout and keep emergency physicians from changing their medical specialty. Also, such a policy would provide the best care for patients (Thomas, 1996).

PARAGRAPH 8: One group's response to information on biological clocks

Ellipsis indicates words have been omitted within a direct quotation

If jet lag and circadian disruptions caused by shift work are obvious ways to upset a biological clock, a less obvious disruption is increasingly recognized as a medical problem: the disorder known as seasonal affective disorder (SAD). Table 1 lists some of the major symptoms of SAD.

PARAGRAPH 9: Applies problem to a medical condition

→

QUOTATION: ON READING
The readers and the hearers like my
   books,
But yet some writers cannot them digest;
But what care I? For when I make a feast
I would my guests should praise it, not the
   cooks.
　　　　　　　　　　—Sir John Harington

APA

QUOTATION: ON WRITING

[The writing process] is sort of like when you've got no electricity and you've gotten up in the middle of the night to find the bathroom, feeling your way along in the dark. I can't hardly tell you what I do because I really don't know.

—Carolyn Chute

Biological Clocks   7

Table 1

Table title   Common Symptoms of Seasonal Affective Disorder (SAD)

Table lists items efficiently, making them easy to find

Sadness	Later waking
Anxiety	Increased sleep time
Decreased physical activity	Interrupted, unrefreshing sleep
Irritability	Daytime drowsiness
Increased appetite	Decreased sexual drive
Craving for carbohydrates	Menstrual problems
Weight gain	Work problems
Earlier onset of sleep	Interpersonal problems

Note below table provides source

Note. From *The Clockwork Sparrow* (p. 204), by S. Binkley, 1990, Englewood Cliffs, NJ: Prentice Hall. Copyright 1990 by Prentice Hall. Reprinted with permission.*

THIRD HEADING

Ways to Help People Affected by Cycle Disruptions

PARAGRAPH 10: Solution to problem

SAD appears to be related to the short daylight (photoperiod) of winter in the temperate zones of the northern and southern hemispheres. Michael Terman, a clinical psychologist at Columbia Presbyterian Medical Center's New York State Psychiatric Institute, has studied SAD patients for many years. He has observed their inability to function at home or at work from fall to spring (Caldwell, 1999). Research by Kelly Rohan, Sandra Sigmon, and Diana Dorhofer (2003) suggests that negative thought patterns and reduced activity enjoyment also correlate with SAD. The phenomenon of SAD not only illustrates the important role of circadian rhythms but also dramatically proves that an understanding of circadian principles can help scientists improve the lives of people who experience disruptions of their biological clocks. Binkley (1990) claims

→

*For professional publications APA recommends that tables appear on separate pages at the end of your paper. Determine your instructor's preference.

that exposure to bright light for periods of up to two hours

a day during the short-photoperiod days of winter reduces

SAD-related "depression in 87 percent of patients . . . within

Specific method for reducing SAD

a few days; relapses followed" when light treatment ended

(pp. 203-204). The treatment works because specific cells in the

retina of the eye transmit information to "two clusters of 10,000

nerve cells in the hypothalamus of the brain" that control the

body's biological clock (Wright, 2002, p. 60).

Lengthening a person's exposure to bright light can also

help combat the effects of jet lag and shift work. Specific

suggestions for using light to help reset a jet traveler's

PARAGRAPH 11: Applies solution in previous paragraph

biological clock include trying to sleep when it gets dark at your

destination and "being outdoors as much as possible during the

afternoon" (Herxheimer & Waterhouse, 2003, p. 297). Night-shift

workers should stay in the dark during the day and can benefit

from strong bright light exposure at work (Boivin & James, 2002).

More substantial changes may be required to help some

people affected by disruptions of their biological clocks. Susan

Black (2000) summarizes research that shows most adolescents'

PARAGRAPH 12: Continues solution

biological clocks are set so that they cannot fall asleep until

after 10:30. Since they need a little more than 9 hours of sleep

per night, the customary school starting time of 7:30-8:30 a.m.

comes too early. Adolescents may be able to reset their

circadian clocks by going to sleep 15 minutes earlier--

including on weekends--over a gradual period of several

weeks. Conversely, schools may need to consider later

starting times.

Establishing work schedules more sensitive to biological

PARAGRAPH 13: Specific system to reduce time-shift problems

clocks can increase a sense of well-being and reduce certain

→

QUOTATION: ON WRITING
I have long since decided if you wait for the perfect time to write, you'll never write. There is no time that isn't flawed somehow.
—Margaret Atwood

APA

QUOTATION: ON WRITING

No tears in the writer, no tears in the reader. No surprise for the writer, no surprise for the reader.

—Robert Frost

Biological Clocks   9

In APA style, summary of two sources separated by semicolon for in-text citations

safety hazards. A group of police officers in Philadelphia were studied while on modified shift schedules (Locitzer, 1989; Toufexis, 1989). The officers were changed between day shifts and night shifts less frequently than they had been on former shift schedules. Also, they rotated forward rather than backward in time; and they worked four rather than six consecutive days. The officers reported 40% fewer patrol car accidents and decreased use of drugs or alcohol to get to sleep. Overall, the police officers preferred the modified shift schedules. Charles Czeisler, who conducted the study, summarizes the importance of these results: "When schedules are introduced that take into account the properties of the human circadian system, subjective estimates of work schedule satisfaction and health improve, personnel turnover decreases, and work productivity increases" (as cited in Locitzer, 1989, p. 66).

Conclusion

CONCLUSION: Points to future

Scientists like Charles Czeisler are guiding individuals to live harmoniously with their biological clocks. The growing awareness of the negative effects of shift work and travel across time zones has led to significant advances in reducing problems caused by disruptions of people's natural cycles. The use of light to manipulate the body's sense of time has also helped. As more of us realize how circadian rhythms can affect our lifestyles, we might learn to control our biological clocks instead of our biological clocks controlling us.

→

Biological Clocks   10

References

Are you a day or night person? (1989, March 4). *USA Today*, p.11.

Binkley, S. (1990). *The clockwork sparrow*. Englewood Cliffs, NJ: Prentice Hall.

Black, S. (2000, December). A wake-up call on high-school starting times. *Education Digest*, 6, 33-38. Retrieved September 7, 2003, from Academic Search Elite database.

Boivin, D. B., & James, F. O. (2002). Circadian adjustment to night-shift work by judicious light and darkness exposure. *Journal of Biological Rhythms*, 17, 556-567.

Bonner, P. (1991, July). Travel rhythms. *Sky Magazine*, 72-73, 76-77.

Caldwell, M. (1999, July). Mind over time. *Discover*, 20, 52. Retrieved September 8, 2003, from General Reference Gold database (Article A55030836).

Coleman, R. (1986). *Wide awake at 3:00 a.m.: By choice or by chance?* New York: Freeman.

Czeisler, C., Duffy, J. F., Shanahan, T. L., Brown, E. N., Mitchell, J. F., Rimmer, D. W., et al. (1999, June 25). Stability, precision, and near-24-hour period of the human circadian pacemaker. *Science*, 284, 2177-2181.

Herxheimer, A., & Waterhouse, J. (2003). The prevention and treatment of jet lag. *BMJ: British Medical Journal*, 326, 296-297.

Latta, F., & Van Cauter, E. (2003). Sleep and biological clocks. In M. Gallagher and R. J. Nelson (Eds.), *Handbook of Psychology* (Vol. 3, pp. 355-375). New York: Wiley.

Lewis, R. (1995, December 24). Chronobiology researchers say their field's time has came. *The Scientist*, 9, 14. Retrieved September 6, 2003, from http://www.the-scientist.com/yr1995/dec/chrono_951211.html

→

Begin References on new page

Double-space throughout

List References in alphabetical order

See page 628 for advice about formatting an APA-style References list using a "hanging indent" style

QUOTATION: ON READING
A book is like a garden carried in the pocket.
　　　　　　　　—Chinese proverb

QUOTATION: ON WRITING
Writing comes more easily if you have something to say.

—Sholem Asch

Biological Clocks   11

Locitzer, K. (1989, July/August). Are you out of sync with each other? *Psychology Today, 23,* 66.

Recht, L., Lew, R., & Schwartz, W. (1995, October 19). Baseball teams beaten by jet lag [Letter]. *Nature, 377,* 583.

Rohan, K. J., Sigmon, S. T., & Dorhofer, D. M. (2003). Cognitive-behavioral factors in seasonal affective disorder. *Journal of Consulting and Clinical Psychology, 71,* 22-30.

Thomas, H. A. (1996). Circadian rhythms and shift work. ACEP Online. Retrieved August 28, 2003, from http://www.acep.org/ 1,509,0.html

Toufexis, A. (1989, June 5). The times of your life. *Time, 133,* 66-67.

Weiss, R. (1989, January 21). Safety gets short shrift on long night shift. *Science News, 135,* 37.

Winfree, A. (1987). *The timing of biological clocks.* New York: Freeman.

Wright, K. (2002, September). Times of our lives. *Scientific American, 287,* 58-64. Retrieved September 12, 2003, from Academic Search Elite database.

Source is a letter appearing in *Nature* publication

Chapter 36

CM, CSE, COS Documentation

BACKGROUND
In 2003, the University of Chicago Press published a new edition of *The Chicago Manual of Style: The Essential Guide for Writers, Editors, and Publishers*. Its Preface begins: "In preparing this fifteenth edition of *The Chicago Manual of Style,* we have sought to address the increasing proportion of our users who work with . . . electronic publications, Web sites, and other nonbook or nonprint documents" (xi).

This chapter presents three more systems of documentation (in addition to MLA STYLE in Chapter 34 and APA STYLE in Chapter 35). The first two are the styles of the University of Chicago Press (CM) and the Council of Science Editors (CSE). Additionally, some instructors require Columbia Online Style (COS) to document electronic sources, although with the very recent publication of updated-for-electronic-sources manuals (for all but CSE style), COS is often no longer necessary as a separate style.

CM-STYLE DOCUMENTATION

The University of Chicago Press endorses two styles of documentation. One is an author-date style similar to the APA style of IN-TEXT CITATIONS and a list of sources usually called WORKS CITED or REFERENCES.

The other CM style uses a bibliographic note system that consists of footnotes or endnotes and a Bibliography that lists all sources used in a research paper. I present this style here because it's often used in such humanities courses as art, music, history, philosophy, and sometimes English.

36a How does the bibliographic note system work in CM style?

The *Chicago Manual* (CM) **bibliographic note system** gives information about each source in two places: in a **footnote** or an **endnote** and, if required, in a **Bibliography** that begins on a separate page at the end of a research paper.

When using footnotes or endnotes, the first time a source is named, you can choose either to give full bibliographic information or—but only if you have a Bibliography at the end of your research paper—to use shortened information that includes the last name(s) of the author(s) and the key words in the work's title. When a source is named again, you can give less information in the later endnote or footnote.

659

BACKGROUND
Colorado State University maintains a number of excellent resources for writing teachers, including "teaching guides" on a variety of topics at <http://writing.colostate.edu/teaching_guides.cfm>. Also, the Academic Writing site at <http://wac.colostate.edu/aw/> includes an online journal about teaching writing. The WAC Clearinghouse at <http://wac.colostate.edu/> is a national center for sources about writing across the curriculum.

In CM style, place your notes either before the Bibliography at the end of a paper (endnotes) or at the foot of the page on which you refer to a source (footnotes). Microsoft Word and most other word processing programs offer built-in ways to use footnotes and endnotes. In Word, for example, the "Insert" menu contains a command for footnotes; selecting the footnotes command also provides an option for endnotes. For more detailed explanations, use the "Help" menu in your software. Following is an example of how text and footnotes work together in CM style. Below that is a sample from a research paper showing text and full bibliographic endnotes.

TEXT

Ulrich points out that both Europeans and Native Americans told war stories, but with different details and different emphases.[3]

FOOTNOTE (ON SAME PAGE)

3. Laurel Thatcher Ulrich, *The Age of Homespun: Objects and Stories in the Creation of an American Myth* (New York: Knopf, 2001), 269.

TEXT

Perhaps the most famous attempt to create artificial intelligence occurred when computer engineers developed IBM's Deep Blue computer, which beat chess grandmaster Garry Kasparov in 1997.[11] However, Murray Campbell, one of Deep Blue's creators, has conceded that the computer "did not exhibit human qualities and therefore was not 'intelligent'."[12] Some computer scientists take a much different position. For example, Hans Moravec believes that "robot computers [will] achieve human intelligence . . . around 2040."[13]

Endnotes (before bibliography at end of paper)

11. Thomas Hayden, "The Age of Robots," *U.S. News and World Report,* April 23, 2001, 46.

12. Gary Stix, "2001: A Scorecard," *Scientific American,* January 2001, 36.

13. Jeff Minerd, "Robots: Our Evolutionary Heirs?" *Futurist,* February 1999, 9.

CM-style text and bibliographic notes (as endnotes)

CM style requires a separate Bibliography only if abbreviated footnotes or endnotes are used. The alphabetical Bibliography list (similar to the "Works Cited" in MLA style or "References" in APA style) is sequenced by authors' last names, and it belongs on a separate page at the end of a research paper. A perfect match between the information in endnotes or footnotes and the Bibliography is required.

Box 153 provides guidelines for compiling CM-style bibliographic notes. The directory and examples in 36b show how to prepare notes according to CM style.

BOX 153   SUMMARY

 ## Guidelines for compiling CM-style bibliographic notes

■ **TITLE AND PLACEMENT**

- Use Notes if you're using endnotes. Place them on a separate page, before your bibliography. If you're using footnotes, place them at the bottom of the page on which the source needs to be credited. Never use a label, such as *Footnotes,* above the footnote(s) at the bottom of the page. Also, never use a line to divide off the footnote(s).

- Use Bibliography for your list of sources on a separate page at the end of your research paper.

■ **FORMAT FOR ENDNOTES AND FOOTNOTES**

- Include an endnote or a footnote every time you use a source.

- Number notes sequentially throughout your paper whether you're using endnotes or footnotes.

- Use superscript (raised) arabic numerals for the footnote or endnote numbers in your paper. Position note numbers after any punctuation mark except the dash, preferably at the end of a sentence if the note number is no more than several words from the source material.

- Never use raised numbers in the endnote or footnote itself. Place the number followed by a period on the same line as the content of the note. (Some word processing programs override this same-line rule in CM style, so you might need to adapt to those demands. If this happens, use a consistent style throughout your paper—and be sure to get your instructor's

→

TEACHING TIP
Many college libraries and writing centers maintain Web pages that compare different documentation styles, generally including MLA, APA, CSE, COS, and others. Because these Web addresses change so frequently, I don't include them here. However, a search for "style guide" or "citation style" or "documentation style" will turn up plenty of links. Alternatively, use the search engine's directory to find links. At the time of my writing this item, for example, the path "Reference, Style Guides" on Google.com led to a list of resources at <http://directory.google.com/Top/Arts/Writers_Resources/Style_Guides/>.

One possible assignment for students, working individually or in groups, is to browse the Internet to select "the top ten sites for providing help with documentation." Students might then write an annotation for each site, identifying what's there and telling why the site is useful for student writers. The whole collection could be published as a resource, either in paper or online. An addition to this assignment could ask students to identify some sources that are less helpful (perhaps because they are outdated or incomplete, have poor examples, or are incorrect) and explain why these Web sites are inferior to the others.

BACKGROUND

The University of Chicago Press maintains a Web site for *The Chicago Manual of Style.* Connect to the press's main address at <http://www.press.uchicago.edu/> and follow the link to the CMS. The Web site maintains answers to a long list of frequently asked questions and includes a space for users to query the editors of the manual.

Guidelines for compiling CM-style bibliographic notes (*continued*)

permission to deviate from standard CM style before you hand in the final draft of a research paper.)

- Place footnotes at the bottom of the page on which you've used the material that calls for crediting your source.

- Place endnotes at the end of your paper, before the Bibliography, on a separate page titled Notes. Center the word *Notes*, neither underlined nor in quotation marks, about an inch from the top of the page, and double-space after it. For the notes themselves, single-space both within each note and between notes. Indent each note's first line three-tenths of an inch (0.3″ tab), which equals about three characters, but place subsequent lines flush left at the margin.

■ **SPACING AFTER PUNCTUATION**

A single space, not two spaces, follows all punctuation, including the period.

■ **AUTHORS' NAMES**

- In endnotes and footnotes, give the name in standard (first name first) order, with names and initials as given in the original source. Use the word *and* before the last author's name if your source has two or three authors. If your source has more than three authors, follow the guidelines for model 3 in 36b.

- In the Bibliography, invert the name (last name, first name) that comes first in a list of two or three authors. If your source has four to ten authors, give all the authors' names. If your source has eleven or more authors, list only the first seven and use *et al.* for the rest.

■ **CAPITALIZATION OF SOURCE TITLES**

Capitalize the first word and all major words.

■ **SPECIAL TREATMENT OF TITLES**

- Use italics for titles of long works, and use quotation marks around the titles of shorter works. However, if italics aren't available in your word processing program, you can use underlining.

- Omit *A*, *An*, and *The* from the titles of newspapers and periodicals. For an unfamiliar newspaper title, list the city

→

Guidelines for compiling CM-style bibliographic notes (*continued*)

(and state, in parentheses, if the city is not well known): *Newark (NJ) Star-Ledger,* for example. You can use postal abbreviations for states, though some instructors might prefer the older abbreviated forms of states (e.g., Ala. for Alabama; Fla. for Florida; Pa. for Pennsylvania).

■ PUBLICATION INFORMATION

Enclose publication information in parentheses. Use a colon and one space after the city of publication. Give complete publishers' names or abbreviate them according to standard abbreviations in *Books in Print,* available in the reference section of most libraries. Omit *Co., Inc.,* and the like. Spell out *University* (never use *U* alone) and *Press* (never use *P* alone). Do not abbreviate publication months.

■ PAGE NUMBERS

- For inclusive page numbers, give the full second number for 2 through 99. For 100 and beyond, give the full second number only if a shortened version would be ambiguous: *243–47, 202–6, 300–304.*
- List all discontinuous page numbers; see the model at "First Endnote or Footnote: Book," toward the end of this box.
- Use a comma to separate parenthetical publication information from the page numbers that follow it. Use the abbreviations *p.* and *pp.* with page numbers only for material from newspapers, for material from journals that do not use volume numbers, and to avoid ambiguity.

■ CONTENT NOTES

Try to avoid using content notes. If you must use them, use footnotes, not endnotes, with symbols rather than numbers: an asterisk (*) for the first note on that page and a dagger (†) for a second note on that page.

■ FIRST ENDNOTE OR FOOTNOTE: BOOK

For books, include the author, title, publication information, and page numbers when applicable.

1. Eudora Welty, *One Writer's Beginnings* (Cambridge: Harvard University Press, 1984), 25-26, 30, 43-51, 208.

→

Guidelines for compiling CM-style bibliographic notes (*continued*)

■ **FIRST ENDNOTE OR FOOTNOTE: ARTICLE**

For articles, include the author, article title, journal title, volume number, year, and page numbers.

> 1. D. D. Cochran, W. Daniel Hale, and Christine P. Hissam, "Personal Space Requirements in Indoor versus Outdoor Locations," *Journal of Psychology* 117 (1984): 132-33.

■ **SECOND MENTION IN ENDNOTES OR FOOTNOTES**

If you give full, or shortened, bibliographic information in your first endnote or footnote, subsequent citations of the same source can be brief. Include the author name(s), the title of the work, and a page reference. For example, a second citation of the Welty book in the example above might be:

> 14. Welty, *One Writer's Beginnings*, 46.

If the title has more than four words, give a shortened version that contains the key words. See model 4 in 36b for additional guidelines.

36b What are CM-style guidelines for bibliographic notes?

The directory below corresponds to the sample bibliographic note forms that follow it. In a few cases, I give sample Bibliography forms as well. If you need a model that is not here, consult *The Chicago Manual of Style*, Fifteenth Edition (Chicago University Press, 2003), which gives footnote, endnote, and Bibliography forms for a multitude of sources.

Directory—CM Style for Footnotes and Endnotes

1. Book by One Author—CM
2. Book by Two or Three Authors—CM
3. Book by More Than Three Authors—CM
4. Multiple Citations of a Single Source—CM
5. Book by a Group or Corporate Author—CM
6. Book with No Author Named—CM
7. Book with an Author and an Editor—CM
8. Translation—CM

9. Work in Several Volumes or Parts—CM
10. One Selection from an Anthology or an Edited Book—CM
11. More than One Selection from an Anthology or an Edited Book—CM
12. Signed Article in a Reference Book—CM
13. Unsigned Article in a Reference Book—CM
14. Second or Subsequent Edition—CM
15. Anthology or Edited Book—CM
16. Introduction, Preface, Foreword, or Afterword—CM
17. Unpublished Dissertation or Essay—CM
18. Reprint of an Older Book—CM
19. Book in a Series—CM
20. Book with a Title Within a Title—CM
21. Government Publication—CM
22. Published Proceedings of a Conference—CM
23. Signed Article from a Daily Newspaper—CM
24. Editorial, Letter to the Editor, or Review—CM
25. Unsigned Article from a Daily Newspaper—CM
26. Signed Article from a Weekly or Biweekly Magazine or Newspaper—CM
27. Signed Article from a Monthly or Bimonthly Periodical—CM
28. Unsigned Article from a Weekly or Monthly Periodical—CM
29. Article from a Collection of Reprinted Articles—CM
30. Article in a Journal with Continuous Pagination—CM
31. Article in a Journal That Pages Each Issue Separately—CM
32. Personal Interview—CM
33. Published and Unpublished Letters—CM
34. Film, Videotape, or DVD—CM
35. Recording—CM
36. Computer Software—CM
37. ERIC Information Service—CM
38. Secondary Source—CM

ELECTRONIC SOURCES

39. Source from a CD-ROM—CM
40. Online Book—CM
41. Article from a Periodical Available Only Online—CM
42. Article Accessed Through a Database—CM
43. Source from an Internet Site—CM
44. Electronic Mailing List—CM
45. E-Mail Message—CM

1. Book by One Author—CM

Footnote or Endnote

1. Eudora Welty, *One Writer's Beginnings* (Cambridge: Harvard University Press, 1984).

Bibliography

Welty, Eudora. *One Writer's Beginnings*. Cambridge: Harvard University Press, 1984.

The format is the reverse of the note above, in which first lines indent. In bibliographic form, the first line is placed flush left to the margin and the second and other lines are indented three-tenths inch (0.3″ tab). Notice also where periods replace commas.

2. Book by Two or Three Authors—CM

Footnote or Endnote

1. Edward E. Gordon and Elaine H. Gordon, *Literacy in America: Historic Journey and Contemporary Solutions* (Westport, CT: Praeger, 2003).

2. Alfred H. Kelly, Winfred A. Harbison, and Herman Belz, *The American Constitution: Its Origins and Development* (New York: Norton, 1983).

Bibliography

Kelly, Alfred H., Winfred A. Harbison, and Herman Belz. *The American Constitution: Its Origins and Development*. New York: Norton, 1983.

In a Bibliography entry, invert only the name of the first author listed.

3. Book by More Than Three Authors—CM

1. Mark H. Moore et al., *Dangerous Offenders: The Elusive Target of Justice* (Cambridge: Harvard University Press, 1984).

Give the name of the author listed first on the title page, and then put either *et al.* or *and others*, using no punctuation after the author's name.

4. Multiple Citations of a Single Source—CM

For subsequent references to a work you've already named, give the last name of the author, the title of the work, and the page number, all separated by commas. Shorten the title if it is longer than four words. This example shows the form for a subsequent reference to the work fully described in model 1.

1. Welty, *One Writer's Beginnings*, 25.

If you cite two or more authors with the same last name, include first names or initials in each note.

2. Eudora Welty, *One Writer's Beginnings*, 25.

3. Paul Welty, *Human Expression*, 129.

If you cite the same source as the source immediately preceding, you may use *Ibid.*, followed by a comma and the page number, instead of repeating the author's name and the title.

4. Ibid., 152.

5. Book by a Group or Corporate Author—CM

1. American Psychological Association, *Publication Manual of the American Psychological Association*, 5th ed. (Washington, DC: American Psychological Association, 2001).

2. Boston Women's Health Collective, *Our Bodies, Ourselves for the New Century* (New York: Simon & Schuster, 1998).

If a work issued by an organization has no author listed on the title page, give the name of the organization as the author of the work. The organization may also be the publisher of the work.

6. Book with No Author Named—CM

1. *The Chicago Manual of Style*, 15th ed. (Chicago: University of Chicago Press, 2003).

Begin the citation with the name of the book.

7. Book with an Author and an Editor—CM

1. Emily Brontë, *Wuthering Heights*, ed. Richard J. Dunn (New York: Norton, 2002).

In this position, the abbreviation *ed.* stands for "edited by," not "editor." Therefore, *ed.* is correct whether a work has one or more than one editor. (Also see models 10 and 16.)

8. Translation—CM

1. Milan Kundera, *The Unbearable Lightness of Being*, trans. Michael Henry Heim (New York: HarperPerennial Library, 1999).

The abbreviation *trans.* stands for "translated by," not "translator."

9. Work in Several Volumes or Parts—CM

The two notes below show ways to give bibliographic information for a specific place in one volume of a multivolume work. Use whichever you

CM

prefer, staying consistent throughout a paper. If you are writing about the volume as a whole (as opposed to citing specific pages), end the note with the publication information.

1. Ernest Jones, *The Last Phase*, vol. 3 of *The Life and Work of Sigmund Freud* (New York: Basic Books, 1957), 97.

1. Ernest Jones, *The Life and Work of Sigmund Freud*, vol. 3, *The Last Phase* (New York: Basic Books, 1957), 97.

If you're citing an entire work in two or more volumes, use the form shown below.

2. John Herman Randall, Jr., *The Career of Philosophy*, 2 vols. (New York: Columbia University Press, 1962).

10. One Selection from an Anthology or an Edited Book—CM

1. Ernest Galarza, "The Roots of Migration," in *Aztlan: An Anthology of Mexican American Literature*, ed. Luis Valdez and Stan Steiner (New York: Knopf, 1972), 127-32.

Give page numbers for the cited selection.

11. More Than One Selection from an Anthology or an Edited Book—CM

If you cite more than one selection from the same anthology or edited book, give complete bibliographical information in each citation.

12. Signed Article in a Reference Book—CM

1. John C. Burnbam, "Freud, Sigmund," in *The Encyclopedia of Psychiatry, Psychology, and Psychoanalysis*, ed. Benjamin B. Wolman (New York: Henry Holt, 1996), 220.

13. Unsigned Article in a Reference Book—CM

1. *Encyclopaedia Britannica*, 15th ed., s.v. "Ireland."

The abbreviation *s.v.* stands for *sub verbo,* meaning "under the word." Capitalize the heading of the entry only if it is a proper noun. Omit publication information except for the edition number.

14. Second or Subsequent Edition—CM

1. Anthony F. Janson, *History of Art*, 6th ed. (New York: Abrams, 2001).

Here the abbreviation *ed.* stands for "edition." Give the copyright date for the edition you are citing.

15. Anthology or Edited Book—CM

1. Eduardo del Rio, ed. *The Prentice Hall Anthology of Latino Literature* (Upper Saddle River, NJ: Prentice Hall, 2002).

Here the abbreviation *ed.* stands for "editor." For a source with two or more editors, use the plural *eds.*

16. Introduction, Preface, Foreword, or Afterword—CM

1. Elizabeth Fox-Genovese, foreword to *Southern Mothers*, ed. Nagueyalti Warren and Sally Wolff (Baton Rouge: Louisiana State University Press, 1999).

If the author of the book is different from the author of the cited part, give the name of the book's author after the title of the book.

17. Unpublished Dissertation or Essay—CM

1. Michele Byers, " 'Buffy the Vampire Slayer': The Insurgence of Television as a Performance Text" (PhD diss. University of Toronto, 2000), 23-24.

List the author's name first, then the title in quotation marks (not italicized), a descriptive label (such as *PhD diss.* or *master's thesis)*, the degree-granting institution, the date, and finally the page numbers you are citing.

1. Claire J. Kramsch, "Context and Culture Online" (paper presented at the annual meeting of the Modern Language Association, New Orleans, December 2001).

To cite a paper read at a meeting, give the name of the meeting in parentheses, along with the location and the date.

18. Reprint of an Older Book—CM

1. Zora Neale Hurston, *Their Eyes Were Watching God* (1937; repr., Urbana: University of Illinois Press, 1978).

Republishing information is located on the copyright page. List the original date of publication first, followed by the publication information for the reprint.

19. Book in a Series—CM

1. Dorothy J. Goldman, *Women Writers and World War I*, Literature and Society Series (New York: Macmillan, 1995).

If the series numbers its volumes and the volume number is not part of the title, you would include the volume number after the series title. Separate the volume number from the series title with a comma.

20. Book with a Title Within a Title—CM

1. Aljean Harmetz, *The Making of "The Wizard of Oz"* (New York: Hyperion, 1998).

QUOTATION: ON WRITING
The actual process of writing . . . demands complete, noiseless privacy, without even music; a baby howling two blocks away will drive me nuts.

—William Styron

CM

If the name of a work that is usually italicized appears in a title, add quotation marks around it. If the name of a work that is usually in quotation marks appears in a title, keep it in quotation marks and italicize it.

21. Government Publication—CM

1. House Committee on Resources. *Coastal Heritage Trail Route in New Jersey,* 106th Cong., 1st sess., 1999, H. Rept. 16.

If a government department, bureau, agency, or committee produces a document, cite that group as the author. In a Bibliography entry, the author is often identified as *U.S. Congress,* followed by either "House" or "Senate" and the committee or subcommittee, if any, before the title of the document.

22. Published Proceedings of a Conference—CM

1. Arnold Eskin, "Some Properties of the System Controlling the Circadian Activity Rhythm of Sparrows," in *Biochronometry,* ed. Michael Menaker (Washington, DC: National Academy of Sciences, 1971), 55-80.

Treat published conference proceedings as you would a chapter in a book.

23. Signed Article from a Daily Newspaper—CM

1. Peter T. Kilborn, "A Health Threat Baffling for Its Lack of a Pattern," *New York Times,* sec. A, June 22, 2003, national edition.

Because many newspapers print more than one edition a day and reposition the same articles on different pages, CM style recommends that you omit page numbers from note entries. When applicable, identify the specific edition (such as *Southeastern edition* or *final edition*); make this the last information in the entry, preceded by a comma. For a paper that specifies sections, use *sec.* before the section's letter or number or use *section* before a section's name (such as *Weekend section*). If a paper gives column titles, you may use the title (not italicized or in quotation marks) in addition to or in place of the article title. Separate all items with commas.

24. Editorial, Letter to the Editor, or Review—CM

1. "Downtown's architectural promise," editorial, *New York Times,* sec. A, August 4, 2003.

2. Roger P. Hanson, letter to the editor, *Sierra,* January/February 2003, 8.

3. Joan Didion, "The Day Was Hot and Still . . . ," review of *Dutch: A Memoir of Ronald Reagan,* by Edmund Morris, *New York Review of Books,* November 4, 1999, 4-6.

Before page numbers, use a comma for popular magazines and a colon for journals.

25. Unsigned Article from a Daily Newspaper—CM

1. "Changes Sought in Medical Services for Veterans," *New York Times*, sec. A, August 5, 2003.

26. Signed Article from a Weekly or Biweekly Magazine or Newspaper—CM

1. Daren Fonda, "Plucky Little Competitors," *Time*, October 21, 2002, 60-62.

For general-readership weekly and biweekly magazines and newspapers, give the month, day, and year of publication. Separate page numbers from the year with a comma.

27. Signed Article from a Monthly or Bimonthly Periodical—CM

1. Tom Bissell, "A Comet's Tale: On the Science of Apocalypse," *Harper's*, February 2003, 33.

For general-readership monthly and bimonthly magazines, give the month and year of publication. Separate page numbers from the year with a comma.

28. Unsigned Article from a Weekly or Monthly Periodical—CM

1. "The Price Is Wrong," *Economist*, August 2, 2003, 58-59.

29. Article from a Collection of Reprinted Articles—CM

1. Thomas Hayden, "The Age of Robots," *Applied Science*, Social Issues Resources Series (Boca Raton, FL: Social Issues Resources, 2002).

Cite only the publication actually consulted, not the original source. If you use a Bibliography, cite its location in both the reprinted publication you consulted and the publication where the article first appeared.

30. Article in a Journal with Continuous Pagination—CM

1. Phyllis Tyson, "The Psychology of Women," *Journal of the American Psychoanalytic Association* 46 (1997): 361-64.

31. Article in a Journal That Pages Each Issue Separately—CM

1. Linda Adler-Kassner and Heidi Estrem, "Rethinking Research Writing: Public Literacy in the Composition Classroom," WPA: Writing Program Administration 26, no. 3 (2003): 119-31.

The issue number of a journal is required only if each issue of the journal starts with page 1. In this example, the volume number is 26 and the issue number, abbreviated as *no.*, is 3.

CM

32. Personal Interview—CM

1. Randi Friedman, interview by author, September 30, 2003, Ames, Iowa.

For an unpublished interview, give the name of the interviewee and the interviewer, the date of the interview, and the location of the interview.

33. Published and Unpublished Letters—CM

1. William Carlos Williams to his son, 13 March 1935, in *Letters of the Century: America 1900-1999*, ed. Lisa Grunwald and Stephen J. Adler (New York: Dial, 1999), 225-26.

2. Theodore Brown, letter to author, December 7, 2002.

For an unpublished letter, give the name of the author, the name of the recipient, and the date the letter was written.

34. Film, Videotape, or DVD—CM

1. Marc Norman and Tom Stoppard, *Shakespeare in Love*, DVD (1998; New York: Miramax Films/Universal Pictures, 2003).

2. Robert Riskin, *It Happened One Night*, VHS (1934; Hollywood: Columbia Pictures, 1999).

In note 1, the first information gives the authors of the screenplay. If the point of the note was about the director or the producers, then the title would appear first and the abbreviations *dir.* and/or *prod.* ("directed by," "produced by") would follow a comma after the title along with the relevant names.

35. Recording—CM

1. Bedrich Smetana, *My Country*, Czech Philharmonic, Karel Anserl, Vanguard SV-9/10.

Bedrich Smetana is the composer and Karel Anserl is the conductor.

2. Bruce Springsteen, "Lonesome Day," on *The Rising*, Sony CD B000069 HKH.

36. Computer Software—CM

1. Dreamweaver Ver. MX, Macromedia, San Francisco, CA.

Place the version or release number, abbreviated *Ver.* or *Rel.*, directly after the name of the software. Then, list the company that owns the rights to the software, followed by that company's location.

37. ERIC Information Service—CM

1. Hunter M. Breland, *Assessing Writing Skills* (New York: College Entrance Examination Board, 1987), ERIC, ED 286920.

ERIC stands for *Educational Resources Information Center.*

38. Secondary Source—CM

1. Mary Wollstonecraft, *A Vindication of the Rights of Woman* (1792), 90, quoted in Caroline Shrodes, Harry Finestone, and Michael Shugrue, *The Conscious Reader*, 4th ed. (New York: Macmillan, 1988), 282.

When you quote one person's words, having found them in another person's work, give information as fully as you can about both sources. Note 1 shows the form you use when the point of your citation is Mary Wollstonecraft's words. If your point is what Shrodes, Finestone, and Shugrue have to say about Wollstonecraft's words, handle the information as in note 2.

2. Caroline Shrodes, Harry Finestone, and Michael Shugrue, *The Conscious Reader*, 4th ed. (New York: Macmillan, 1988), 282, quoting Mary Wollstonecraft, *A Vindication of the Rights of Woman* (1792), 90.

ELECTRONIC SOURCES

If there is a print version of the source (as in model 42), provide information about that source. Also include information about how to find the electronic version. Unlike some other documentation styles (such as MLA), CM style does not generally recommend including "access dates," nor does it include angle brackets around URLs. Following are examples in CM style of a few common types of electronic sources. For additional types, consult *The Chicago Manual of Style*.

39. Source from a CD-ROM—CM

If you're citing a portion of a CD-ROM, include the author (if named) and title of that portion, then the title of the CD-ROM, the publisher, and the date. The following example omits the author's name.

1. "Artificial Intelligence," *Encarta 2003*, CD-ROM. Microsoft, 2003.

40. Online Book—CM

Include the author's name, the title, and access information—in this case, the name of the organization that sponsors the site, and the URL.

1. Kate Chopin, *The Awakening* (PBS, 1998), http://www.pbs.org/katechopin/library/awakening.

41. Article from a Periodical Available Only Online—CM

Include the author, title of the article, title of the publication, volume and issue number (if given), publication date, and URL.

1. Veronica Austen, "Writing Spaces: Performances of the Word," *Kairos* 8, no. 1 (2003), http://english.ttu.edu/kairos/8.1/binder2.html?coverweb/austen/austen.html.

BACKGROUND
Technological developments have made reproducing written work as easy as pushing a button on a photocopier or hitting the "Send," "Print," or "Download" keys on a computer. If copyright laws sometimes seem too demanding to instructors or researchers, for whom seeking permission to copy something can take time and energy, the effort is nonetheless required by law. In "Copyright: It's for the Public Good" (*Chronicle of Higher Education*, May 9, 2003: B35), Peter Givler discusses how copyright benefits teachers and scholars. He notes that "Shakespeare . . . furnishes an instructive example of the perils of authorship before copyright. Under the laws of his day, once his company had performed one of his plays, Shakespeare lost the legal ability to prevent further performance by anyone else. All he could do to control performance rights, as it were, was to keep the acting script, or prompt book, under lock and key."

42. Article Accessed Through a Database—CM

Include the author, title of the article, title of the publication, volume and issue number (if given) of the original publication, the original publication date, and the URL of the database through which you accessed the article. CM style recommends that you include an access date when citing information retrieved through a database. Insert the access date in parentheses after the URL, followed by a period.

> 1. Gail Dutton, "Greener Pigs," *Popular Science* 255, no. 5 (November 1999): 38-39, http://proquest.umi.com (accessed September 2, 2003).

43. Source from an Internet Site—CM

Provide the author's name, the title of the Web page, the title or owner of the site, and the URL. When no specific author is listed, you may use the owner of the site as the author, as in the following example. Include an access date if your source is likely to be updated frequently, as is often the case with Internet sites.

> 1. American Association for Artificial Intelligence, "AI Overview," American Association for Artificial Intelligence, http://www.aaai.org/AITopics/html/overview.html (accessed December 22, 2003).

44. Electronic Mailing List—CM

> 1. T. Caruso, e-mail to Calls for Papers mailing list, June 30, 2002, http://www.english.upenn.edu/CFP/archive/American/0421.html.

45. E-Mail Message—CM

> 1. Jim Thompson, e-mail message to author, November 11, 2003.

USING AND CITING GRAPHICS—CM

Place the credit line for a table or illustration from another source next to the reproduced material. (If you intend to publish your paper, you must receive permission to reprint copyrighted material from a source.) Spell out the terms *map, plate,* and *table,* but abbreviate *figure* as *fig.*

REPRINT OF A FIGURE—CM

> Reprinted by permission from Dennis Remington, A. Garth Fisher, and Edward Parent, *How to Lower Your Fat Thermostat: The No-Diet Reprogramming Plan for Lifelong Weight Control* (Provo, Utah: Vitality House International, 1983), 74, fig. A2-1.

CSE-STYLE DOCUMENTATION

In its style manual, *Scientific Style and Format* (1994), the Council of Science Editors (CSE) endorses two documentation systems widely used in mathematics and the physical and life sciences. (Note that before 2000, the organization was called the Council of Biology Editors; that earlier name appears on the group's 1994 style manual.) At the time of this writing, CSE is preparing a revised seventh edition of *Scientific Style and Format*. For up-to-date information, see <http://councilscienceeditors.org>.

36c What should I know about CSE-style documentation?

The first system endorsed by CSE uses name-year parenthetical references in the text of a paper, together with an alphabetically arranged Cited References (or References) list that gives full bibliographic information for each source. This kind of IN-TEXT CITATION system tied to a required BIBLIOGRAPHY is similar to both MLA style (Chapter 34) and APA style (Chapter 35).

The second CSE system marks citations in the text of a paper with numbers that correlate with a numerically arranged Cited References list. This chapter covers the numbered reference system, sometimes referred to as a *citation-sequence system*. Here's the way it works:

1. The first time you cite each source in your paper, assign it an arabic number in sequence, starting with 1.
2. Mark each subsequent reference to that source with the assigned number.
3. Use superscript (raised) numbers for source citations in your sentences, although numbers in parentheses are also acceptable.
4. Don't use footnotes or endnotes to credit your sources. Use only a Cited References list, and number each entry in the order of its appearance in your paper, starting with 1. Place the number, followed by a period, on the same line as the content of the citation. Never list sources alphabetically. Never underline or use italics for titles of works.

Here's an example of a sentence that includes in-text citations and the corresponding cited references.

IN-TEXT CITATIONS

Sybesma[1] insists that this behavior occurs periodically, but Crowder[2] claims never to have observed it.

CITED REFERENCES

1. Sybesma C. An introduction to biophysics. New York: Academic Pr; 1977. 648 p.

2. Crowder W. Seashore life between the tides. New York: Dodd, Mead; 1931. New York: Dover Reprint; 1975. 372 p.

CSE

Thereafter, throughout your paper, follow each citation of Sybesma's *An Introduction to Biophysics* by a superscript 1 and each citation of Crowder's *Seashore Life* by a superscript 2.

When you're citing more than one reference—for example, a new source and the previous three sources as well as a source from your first page—list each source number, followed by a comma with no space. Use a hyphen to show the range of numbers in a continuous sequence, and put all in superscript: $^{2,5-7,8}$

Box 154 gives guidelines for compiling a Cited References list.

BOX 154   SUMMARY

Guidelines for compiling a CSE-style Cited References list

■ **TITLE**

Cited References or References

■ **PLACEMENT OF LIST**

Begin the list on a separate page at the end of the research paper. Number the page sequentially with the rest of the paper.

■ **CONTENT AND FORMAT OF CITED REFERENCES**

Include all sources that you QUOTE, PARAPHRASE, or SUMMARIZE in your paper. Center the title about one inch from the top of the page. Start each entry on a new line. Put the number, followed by a period and a space, at the regular left margin. If an entry takes more than one line, indent the second and all other lines under the first word, not the number. Single-space each entry and double-space between entries.

■ **SPACING AFTER PUNCTUATION**

CSE style specifies no space after date, issue number, or volume number of a periodical, as shown in the models in section 36d.

■ **ARRANGEMENT OF ENTRIES**

Sequence and number the entries in the precise order you first used them in the body of your paper.

■ **AUTHORS' NAMES**

Reverse the order of each author's name, giving the last name first. For book citations, you can give first names or use only the initials of first and (when available) middle names; for journal citations, use

→

Guidelines for compiling a CSE-style Cited References list (*continued*)

only initials. Don't use a period or a space between first and middle initials. Use a comma to separate the names of multiple authors identified by initials; however, if you use full first names, use a semicolon. Don't use *and* or *&* with authors' names. Place a period after the last author's name.

- **TREATMENT OF TITLES**
  - Never underline titles or enclose them in quotation marks.
  - Capitalize a title's first word and any proper nouns. Don't capitalize the first word of a subtitle unless it's a proper noun.
  - Capitalize the titles of academic journals. If the title of a periodical is one word, give it in full; otherwise, abbreviate the title according to recommendations established by the *American National Standard for Abbreviations of Titles of Periodicals*.
  - Capitalize a newspaper title's major words, giving the full title but omitting a beginning *A, An,* or *The*.

- **PLACE OF PUBLICATION**
  Use a colon after the city of publication. If the city name could be unfamiliar to readers, add in parentheses the U.S. state or Canadian province postal abbreviation (see Box 122 in section 30k): Springfield (VA). If the location of a non-U.S. city will likely be unfamiliar to readers, add in parentheses the country name, abbreviating it according to International Organization for Standarization (ISO) standards. For example, Nijmegen (NLD) refers to a city in the Netherlands. ISO abbreviations can be accessed at <http://www.emeatrade.com/arabic/Visitors/Country_Abbreviations.htm>.

- **PUBLISHER**
  Give the name of the publisher, without periods after initials, and use a semicolon after the publisher's name. Omit any beginning *The* or ending term such as *Co., Inc., Ltd.,* or *Press*. However, for a university press, abbreviate *University* and *Press* as *Univ* and *Pr* without periods.

- **PUBLICATION MONTH ABBREVIATIONS**
  Abbreviate all month names longer than three letters to their first three letters, but do not add a period.

→

CSE

BACKGROUND
The best-established online journal devoted to the developments in writing, rhetoric, technology, and pedagogy is *Kairos,* available at <http://english.ttu.edu/kairos/>.

Guidelines for compiling a CSE-style Cited References list (*continued*)

■ **INCLUSIVE PAGE NUMBERS**

Shorten the second number as much as possible, making sure that the number isn't ambiguous. For example, use 233–4 for 233 to 234; 233–44 for 233 to 244; but 233–304, not 233–04.

■ **DISCONTINUOUS PAGE NUMBERS**

Give the numbers of all discontinuous pages, separating successive numbers or ranges with a comma: *54–7, 60–6.*

■ **TOTAL PAGE NUMBERS**

When citing an entire book, the last information unit gives the total number of book pages, followed by the abbreviation *p* and a period.

■ **FORMAT FOR CITED REFERENCES ENTRIES: BOOKS**

Citations for books usually list author(s), title, publication information, and pages (either total pages when citing an entire work or inclusive pages when citing part of a book). Each unit of information ends with a period.

1. Stacy RW, Williams DT, Worden RE, McMorris RO. Essentials of biological and medical sciences. New York: McGraw-Hill; 1955. 727 p.

■ **FORMAT FOR CITED REFERENCES ENTRIES: ARTICLES**

Citations for articles usually list author(s), article title, and journal name and publication information, each section followed by a period. Abbreviate a journal's name only if it's standard in your scientific discipline. For example, *Exp Neurol* is the abbreviated form of *Experimental Neurology.* In the example below, the volume number is 184, and the issue number, in parentheses, is 1. Notice the lack of space after the semicolon, before the parentheses, and after the colon.

1. Ginis I, Rao MS. Toward cell replacement therapy: promises and caveats. Exp Neurol 2003;184(1):61-77.

36d What are CSE guidelines for specific sources in a list of references?

The directory below corresponds to the sample references that follow it. If you need a model not included in this book, consult *Scientific Style and Format,* Sixth Edition (1994). If you're looking for examples for citing electronic and online sources, consult a recent issue of a journal in the discipline in which you are writing.

Directory—CSE Style

1. Book by One Author—CSE

1. Hawking SW. Black holes and baby universes and other essays. New York: Bantam Books; 1993. 320 p.

Use one space but no punctuation between an author's last name and the initial of the first name. Do not put punctuation or a space between first and middle initials (*Hawking SW*). Do, however, use the hyphen in a hyphenated first and middle name (*Gille J-C* represents Jean-Claude Gille in model 2 below).

CSE

2. Book by More Than One Author—CSE

1. Wegzyn S, Gille J-C, Vidal P. Developmental systems: at the crossroads of system theory, computer science, and genetic engineering. New York: Springer-Verlag; 1990. 595 p.

3. Book by a Group or Corporate Author—CSE

1. Chemical Rubber Company. Handbook of laboratory safety. 3rd ed. Boca Raton (FL): CRC; 1990. 1352 p.

4. Anthology or Edited Book—CSE

1. Heerman B, Hummel S, editors. Ancient DNA: recovery and analysis of genetic material from paleontological, archeological, museum, medical, and forensic specimens. New York: Springer-Verlag; 1994. 1020 p.

5. One Selection or Chapter from an Anthology or Edited Book—CSE

1. Basov NG, Feoktistov LP, Senatsky YV. Laser driver for inertial confinement fusion. In: Bureckner KA, editor. Research trends in physics: inertial confinement fusion. New York: American Institute of Physics; 1992. p 24-37.

6. Translation—CSE

1. Magris C. A different sea. Spurr MS, translator. London: Harvill; 1993. 194 p. Translation of: Un mare differente.

7. Reprint of an Older Book—CSE

1. Carson R. The sea around us. New York: Oxford Univ; 1951. New York: Limited Editions Club Reprint; 1980. 220 p.

8. All Volumes of a Multivolume Work—CSE

1. Crane FL, Moore DJ, Low HE, editors. Oxidoreduction at the plasma membrane: relation to growth and transport. Boca Raton (FL): Chemical Rubber Company; 1991. 2 vol.

9. Unpublished Dissertation or Thesis—CSE

1. Baykul MC. Using ballistic electron emission microscopy to investigate the metal-vacuum interface [dissertation]. Orem (UT): Polytechnic Univ; 1993. 111 p. Available from: UMI Dissertation Express, http://tls.il.proquest.com/hp/Products/DisExpress.html, Document 9332714.

10. Published Article from Conference Proceedings—CSE

1. Tsang CP, Bellgard MI. Sequence generation using a network of Boltzmann machines. In: Tsang CP, editor. Proceedings of the 4th Australian Joint

Conference on Artificial Intelligence; 1990 Nov 8-11; Perth, AUS.
Singapore: World Scientific; 1990. p 224-33.

11. Signed Newspaper Article—CSE

1. Kilborn PT. A health threat baffling for its lack of a pattern. New York Times 22 June 2003;Sect A:14.

Sect stands for Section. Note that there is no space between the date and the section.

12. Unsigned Newspaper Article—CSE

1. [Anonymous]. Supercomputing center to lead security effort. Pantagraph 2003 July 4;Sect A:7.

13. Article in a Journal with Continuous Pagination—CSE

1. Aldhous P. More heat than light. Nature 2003;420:730.

Give only the volume number (420), not an issue number, before the page numbers. Note that there is no space between the year and the volume or the volume and the page.

14. Article in a Journal That Pages Each Issue Separately—CSE

1. Ginis I, Rao MS. Toward cell replacement therapy: promises and caveats. Exp Neurol 2003;184(1):61-77.

Give both the volume number and the issue number (here, 184 is the volume number and 1 is the issue number).

15. Journal Article on Discontinuous Pages—CSE

1. Richards FM. The protein folding problem. Sci Am 1991;246(1):54-7, 60-6.

16. Article with Author Affiliation—CSE

1. DeMoll E, Auffenberg T (Department of Microbiology, University of Kentucky). Purine metabolism in *Methanococcus vannielii*. J Bacteriol 1993;175:5754-61.

17. Entire Issue of a Journal—CSE

1. Whales in a modern world: a symposium held in London, November 1988. Mamm Rev 1990 Jan;20(9).

The date of the symposium, November 1988, is part of the title of this issue.

18. Article with No Identifiable Author—CSE

1. [Anonymous]. Cruelty to animals linked to murders of humans. AWI Q 1993 Aug;42(3):16.

CSE

19. Map—CSE

1. Russia and post-Soviet republics [political map]. Moscow: Mapping Production Association; 1992. Conical equidistant projection; 40 × 48 in.; color, scale 1:8,000,000.

20. Unpublished Letter—CSE

1. Darwin C. [Letter to Mr. Clerke, 1861]. Located at: University of Iowa Library, Iowa City, IA.

21. Videorecording—CSE

1. The discovery of the pulsar: the ultimate ignorance [videocassette]. London: BBC; 1983. 1 cassette: 48 min, sound, color.

22. Slide Set—CSE

1. Human parasitology [slides]. Chicago: American Society of Clinical Pathologists; 1990. Color. Accompanied by: 1 guide.

23. Electronic Sources—CSE

Because the CSE style book was published in 1994, its instructions for citing electronic sources are minimal. In 2003, the CSE Web site noted that forthcoming revised guidelines would follow the *National Library of Medicine Recommended Formats for Bibliographic Citation* and referred users to this Web site: <http://www.nlm.nih.gov/pubs/formats/internet.pdf>

In general, the CSE style book advises that you cite electronic sources by starting with a statement of the type of document, and then provide the information you would give for a print version. Next, supply specific information that can help a reader locate the electronic source. End with your access date for online sources or the date of the update that you used for a CD-ROM database.

COS DOCUMENTATION

The development of electronic and Internet sources in the 1990s created a gap in existing documentation systems. *The Columbia Guide to Online Style* (COS) by Janice R. Walker and Todd Taylor (Columbia UP, 1998) filled that gap, and some instructors continue to recommend COS. Since the late 1990s, however, MLA, APA, and other systems have incorporated considerably more detailed information about electronic documentation styles. Now that COS tends to be used less frequently, this chapter outlines only the basic elements of the COS system. If your instructor requires you to use COS, consult the companion Web site for more specific guidelines.

36e How do I cite sources in the body of a paper using COS?

COS uses many of the same citation elements that are present in predominantly print documentation styles such as MLA and APA. However, COS includes new format elements unique to electronic publications. COS for the humanities is similar to MLA style, while COS for the sciences shares elements of APA style. Be sure to find out from your instructor which style to use.

For print publications, in-text or PARENTHETICAL REFERENCES include elements such as the author's last name and the page number of the reference. Many electronic sources lack such elements, and COS allows for these differences. If an author's name is unknown, refer to the material by its title. Since most electronic sources are not numbered, page references may be irrelevant. Commonly, COS parenthetical citations use only the author's name for humanities style and the author's name and date of publication for scientific style.

👁 **ALERT:** If page numbers, sections, or other navigational aids are available, separate them with a comma and include them in the parenthetical citation as well. 👁

Here are examples of in-text citations using COS guidelines for the humanities and for the sciences.

Humanities style

According to the survey, over 80% of the students waited until the night before an exam to begin studying (Jani).

When the author's name is included in the sentence, the in-text citation is unnecessary. If there is more than one work by the author, use the work's title.

Scientific style

The research proved conclusively that individuals deprived of sleep were as dangerous as those driving under the influence of drugs or alcohol (Rezik, 2000).

If the publication date is unavailable, use the date of access (in day-month-year format).

BACKGROUND
The site <http://www.columbia.edu/cu/cup/cgos/idx_basic.html> provides advice to students about using Columbia Online Style.

36f How do I create COS bibliographic citations?

Box 155 on the facing page gives guidelines for a COS Works Cited list. The labeled screen below identifies elements mentioned in Box 155. For more specific COS guidelines for sources in a Works Cited list, consult the companion Web site.

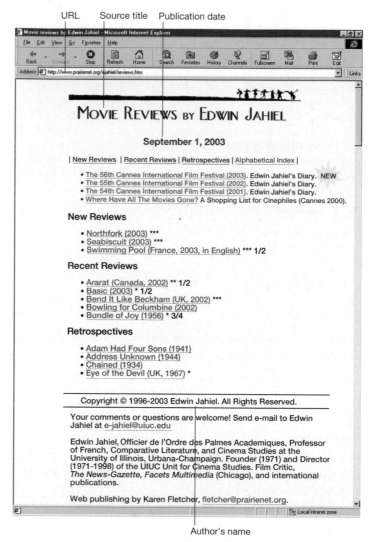

Web page showing elements to be included in COS bibliographic citations

QUOTATION: ON WRITING
Writing is the supreme solace.
                    —W. Somerset Maugham

BOX 155   SUMMARY

 Guidelines for a COS Works Cited list

■ **TITLE**
Works Cited

■ **PLACEMENT OF LIST**
- If you are producing a print document, begin the Works Cited on a new page, numbered sequentially with the rest of the paper. *Works Cited* should be centered, one inch below the top of the page, in upper- and lowercase letters. The title should not be enclosed in quotation marks or boldfaced, italicized, or underlined.
- If your document is a hypertext publication, you may use a separate file and a link to this page in the table of contents.

■ **CONTENT AND FORMAT**
See MLA guidelines in Box 151 in 34d.

■ **ARRANGEMENT OF ENTRIES**
See MLA guidelines in Box 151 in 34d.

■ **AUTHORS' NAMES**
Finding the author of a source may not be simple. Often, online writers use an alias. List your source by these alternative names when they are the only ones you find. If an author cannot be identified, cite the source by its title.

   In humanities style, give the author's full last name and first and middle names (if available). In scientific style, give the author's full last name and first and middle initials (if applicable). List any additional authors by first name (humanities) or first initial (scientific), followed by the full last name.

■ **CAPITALIZATION AND SPECIAL TREATMENT OF TITLES**
Use italics rather than underlining for the titles of complete works. Since hypertext links are underlined online, an underlined title may confuse your readers.

   In humanities style, enclose titles of articles and excerpts from longer works in quotation marks, and capitalize all major words. In scientific style, do not distinguish titles of articles and excerpts of longer works in any way, and capitalize only the first word of the title and proper nouns. (If a title is unavailable, use the file name.)

→

COS

Guidelines for a COS Works Cited list (*continued*)

■ **PLACE OF PUBLICATION, PUBLISHER, AND ELECTRONIC ADDRESS**

When citing electronic sources available in fixed formats, such as software and certain electronic publications, a publisher and city are usually listed and should be cited.

In online publishing, the city of publication and publisher are often not relevant to Web sites and other open-format electronic sources. In those cases, provide the URL (uniform resource locator), which is a source's entire electronic address. For long addresses that exceed a line, follow MLA style: Break only after slashes and do not hyphenate.

■ **VERSION OR FILE NUMBER**

When applicable, provide the specific file number or version of a program for your reference.

■ **DOCUMENT PUBLICATION OR LAST REVISION DATE**

Include a page's publication date or the date of its last revision, unless it is identical to the access date. For humanities style, abbreviate all names of months longer than three letters to their first three letters, followed by a period. Give the date in a year-month-day format with a comma after the year. Enclose the date in parentheses, followed by a period. For scientific style, do not abbreviate names of months. Give the date in a day-month-year format, and do not enclose it in parentheses.

■ **DATE OF ACCESS**

With the constant updates of online material, readers may have a difficult time finding the same content in a source you cite. Always provide the date of access for an online source because it specifies the version of the page you have cited. For humanities and scientific styles, abbreviate names of months to three letters, followed by a period. Give the date in a day-month-year format enclosed in parentheses, followed by a period.

■ **NAVIGATION POINTS**

On the World Wide Web, a given site usually occupies one page, regardless of its length. When available, list any helpful navigational aids, such as page references, paragraph numbers, sections, or parts, in your citation. Keep in mind that often these aids are not available.

→

Guidelines for a COS Works Cited list *(continued)*

- **BIBLIOGRAPHIC CITATION: HUMANITIES**

  Follow this form as closely as possible in your citations:

  Author's Last Name, First Name. "Title of Document." *Title of Complete Work* [if applicable]. Version or File Number [if applicable]. Document date or date of last revision [if known and if different from access date]. Protocol and address, access path or directories (date of access).

- **BIBLIOGRAPHIC CITATION: SCIENCES**

  Follow this form as closely as possible in your citations:

  Author's Last Name, Initial(s). (Date of document [if known and if different from date accessed]). Title of document. *Title of complete work* [if applicable]. Version or File number [if applicable]. (Edition or revision [if applicable]). Protocol and address, access path or directories (date of access or visit; or date of message).

COS

BACKGROUND

The Non-Designer's Design Book, Second Edition, by Robin Williams (Berkeley, CA: Peachpit Press, 2003) is an excellent introduction to design principles. Williams suggests that document design can be reduced to four basic principles: proximity, alignment, repetition, and contrast. This work takes readers through each principle, suggesting guidelines for each and providing examples from brochures, pamphlets, newsletters, posters, and flyers that use or abuse these principles.

Chapter 37

Effective Print Document Design

37a What is document design?

Document design refers to the visual appearance of a print document (how it looks), as opposed to the content of the document (what it says). Of course, design and content are closely related. For example, you need your document to look clean and accessible so that readers can easily find the information they seek. The process of document design includes everything from setting margins and headings to choosing and placing graphics to determining the use of color.

Document design is important for several reasons, not least because first impressions count. As soon as readers see your document, they form an opinion about you and your project. A well-designed document shows that you respect your readers and have spent time formatting your work so that it's attractive and readable. Making a good first impression influences readers to respond positively to your message.

Some document design is standardized and therefore gives you few options. As explained in Chapters 34, 35, and 36, the formatting of discipline-related styles such as those of the Modern Language Association (MLA), the American Psychological Association (APA), and *The Chicago Manual of Style* (CM) needs to conform to the guidelines that these professional organizations require, especially for formatting research papers. In addition, you need to format letters, memos, and e-mail messages according to customary patterns (42a–42e). Most word processing programs have templates and "wizards" that provide many standard formats for such documents.

Other documents allow more leeway for your design creativity. Flyers, brochures, manuals, and certain kinds of reports give you considerable room for originality. In addition, some instructors encourage including design elements, such as pictures, in course papers. However, always check with your instructor before spending time and effort incorporating extensive design elements into your paper because some instructors don't want visuals in papers. Overall, the best design is always the one appropriate to the assignment or situation at hand.

You don't have to be a design expert to produce well-designed documents. Professional designers will produce work well beyond the abilities of most students and instructors, yet with modest tools and knowledge, you can produce simple yet effective documents. Box 156 lists types of software that you can use for document design.

BOX 156 SUMMARY

Computer programs used in designing documents

Word Processing Software

Most word processing programs, such as Microsoft Word and Corel WordPerfect, have features that allow you to vary the format of your document and create charts, graphs, and tables. Word processing programs are sufficient for formatting most basic documents in ACADEMIC WRITING, BUSINESS WRITING, and public writing. In fact, such programs can do things once possible only with more complicated page layout software.

Page Layout Software

Page layout software—for example, Adobe PageMaker and Microsoft Publisher—makes precise control of the elements of your document, such as text and graphic placement, possible. Though these programs take time to learn, they help you produce effective advanced documents such as newsletters, brochures, and other formats you might use in writing for the public (Chapter 42).

Graphic Design Software

Graphic design software—for example, Macromedia FreeHand and Adobe Photoshop—allows you to create and edit graphics, pictures, and other forms of art. You can then save these files in formats that are compatible with word processing and page layout software to insert into your written document.

37b What are basic principles of design?

The basic principles of design—whether for a chair, a car, a painting, or a written document—are *unity, variety, balance,* and *emphasis.* Box 157 on page 691 describes these principles for effectively communicating your message in a document. The Web site for this book, <www.prenhall.com/troyka>, contains regularly updated links to several of the best sources for tips on design from professional document designers.

The sample flyer for the Nature Club reflects the four design principles of Box 157. *Unity* results from similar parts of the flyer sharing the same features. All of the headings (except the title) use the same font

BACKGROUND

In *The Computer and the Page: The Theory, History, and Pedagogy of Publishing, Technology, and the Classroom* (Norwood, NJ: Ablex, 1996), James Kalmbach provides an overview of how technological advances have altered writing classrooms. *Reading Images: The Grammar of Visual Design,* by Gunther R. Kress and Theo Van Leeuwen (London: Routledge, 1996) explains how visual elements have specific effects on readers that writers should recognize and use to their advantage. Kress's later work, *Literacy in the New Media Age (Literacies)* (London: Routledge, 2003), takes his thinking a step further, as Kress contends that the screen and the image have replaced the book and writing as the dominant medium of communication.

The Nature Club

Welcome!
The Nature Club is open to all members of the campus community. Our purpose is to share our common enjoyment of nature and to address environmental concerns. We meet the first Wednesday of each month, 7:00 p.m., in 114 Mercer Hall.

Spring Speakers
James Franklin
Biology
"Prairie Wildlife"
    January 15

Sarah Minkowski
Political Science
"Alaskan Refuges
and Energy Policy"
    February 12

Ceasar Sanchez
The Nature Conservancy
"The Last Best Places"
    March 12

Sherita Jones
State House of Representatives
"Pending Environmental
Legislation"
    April 9

Upcoming Special Events
- Fund-raising Dance for
  The Nature Conservancy
    February 19

- Salt River Canoeing
    April 18

- Camping and Hiking in
  Grand Teton National Park
    June 3–10

For more information, contact

Jesse Langland, President
The Nature Club
jk14@0000.edu

Flyer for The Nature Club

BOX 157   SUMMARY

Principles of document design

- **Unity** results from repetition and consistency. Ask: Do all elements in my document work together visually?
- **Variety** comes from a logical, appropriate break from unity that adds interest. Ask: Have I introduced design elements, where appropriate, that break up monotony—such as inserting headings in academic papers that add to clarity or on-the-topic illustrations that add to content?
- **Balance** refers to a sense of harmony or equilibrium. Ask: Are the parts of my document in proportion to each other?
- **Emphasis** directs the eye to what is most important. Ask: Does my document design draw attention to what is most important?

BACKGROUND
Karen A. Schriver's *Dynamics in Document Design* (New York: Wiley, 1997) offers practical approaches to teaching design in the classroom. Her fourth chapter, for example, examines the ways in which poor document design may cause readers to lose confidence in their own intelligence rather than lose faith in the document's designer. Schriver's sixth chapter examines the integration of verbal and visual features in texts.

and color, and all of the body text uses a separate font. In addition, dates for the speakers and events are displayed in a matching indented format. Unity also emerges from the colors of the headings and the picture: The green headings of "The Nature Club" and "For more information, contact," along with the color of the bullets, picks up the green colors of the grasses in the picture, while the blue headings reflect the blue of the sky.

Variety in the flyer comes from the use of a photograph to complement the text. Headings colors and sizes are different from the main text. Variety also creates *emphasis*. For example, the title of the organization is the largest text on the page. Headings signal different types of information, and the ample use of white space allows information to stand out clearly. Green bullets in one of the lists call attention to the three special events. The contact information is in a type font different from the preceding text, and its position at the lower right makes it stand out.

Finally, the page demonstrates *balance* in many ways. Each side of the flyer contains three groups of material, with space between them: on the one side are the title, welcome, and speakers' names; on the other, picture, events, and information. The information about "Spring Speakers" and "Special Events" is similar in format. The portions of the page also demonstrate the principle of balance. Consider the top half of the flyer and notice how the green text of "The Nature Club" diagonally balances the green of the field grasses and how the blue text of "Welcome!" diagonally balances the deep blue portion of the sky.

EXERCISE 37-1

Following are two alternative versions of the flyer for The Nature Club. Each of the two has problems with unity, variety, balance, or emphasis—or a combination of all four. Working alone or in groups, identify the problems in each design.

ANSWERS: EXERCISE 37-1

1. The first version of the flyer violates principles of unity, emphasis, and balance. The writer uses a distracting variety of typefaces and colors, and he fails to use bulleted lists correctly or white space effectively, even splitting the "special events" between two columns. The title of the organization is too small to attract attention, and the clip art included in the right column doesn't match the content of the flyer; it appears to have been thrown in gratuitously.

2. The second version of the flyer primarily violates the principles of variety and emphasis. Because everything is centered, there is no excitement to the page. Furthermore, all the body text is the same typeface and size; there are no headings to draw interest. Except for the photograph, there are no colors, highlights, or graphical elements.

The Nature Club

Welcome!

The Nature Club is open to all members of the campus community. Our purpose is to share our common enjoyment of nature and to address environmental concerns. We meet the first Wednesday of each month, 7:00 p.m., in 114 Mercer Hall.

Spring Speakers

James Franklin, Biology
"Urban Wildlife"
  January 15

Sarah Minkowski, Political Science
"Alaskan Refuges and Energy Policy"

Ceasar Sanchez, The Nature
Conservancy
"The Last Best Places"
  March 12

Sherita Jones, State House
of Representatives
"Pending Environmental
Legislation"
  April 9

Upcoming Special Events
• Fund-raising Dance for
  • The Nature Conservancy
    • February 19

• Salt River Canoeing
• April 18

• Camping and Hiking in
• Grand Teton National Park
• June 3–10

For more information, contact

Jesse Langland, President
The Nature Club
jk14@0000.edu

Two alternative versions of The Nature Club flyer

The Nature Club

The Nature Club is open to all members of the campus community. Our purpose is to share our common enjoyment of nature and to address environmental concerns. We meet the first Wednesday of each month, 7:00 p.m., in 114 Mercer Hall.

Our spring speakers will be: James Franklin, Biology; "Urban Wildlife"; January 15; Sarah Minkowski, Political Science; "Alaskan Refuges and Energy Policy"; February 12; Ceasar Sanchez, The Nature Conservancy; "The Last Best Places"; March 12; Sherita Jones, State House of Representatives; "Pending Environmental Legislation"; April 9.

We have several upcoming special events, including: Fund-raising Dance for The Nature Conservancy; February 19; Salt River Canoeing; April 18; Camping and Hiking in Grand Teton National Park; June 3–10.

For more information, contact
Jesse Langland, President
The Nature Club
jk14@0000.edu

BACKGROUND
A comprehensive list of document design resources, indexed by topic, is available online at <http://www.wcdd.com/index.html>. Some of the topics include links to sites dealing with graphics, type, desktop publishing, journals, books, and organizations associated with document design

BACKGROUND
Students whose documents utilize symbols or icons should consider the guidelines offered by Stuart Mealing and Masoud Yazdani in "A Computer-based Iconic Language," found at <http://www.intellectbooks.com/iconic/com_base/icon-2.htm>. Mealing and Yazdani suggest that icons should be "graphically clear; semantically unambiguous; without cultural, racial or linguistic bias; adaptable (open to modification to express nuance); and simple."

37c What is page layout?

Layout is the arrangement of text and visuals on a page, which makes the document a kind of spatial composition. You use layout to reinforce the organizational plan of your writing. For example, when you begin a new paragraph of an essay, you start a new line and indent from the left margin. When using block style for a business letter, you add a space between paragraphs. In each case, your layout decision indicates that you are moving to a new idea. The Web site available with this book <www.prenhall.com/troyka> contains regularly updated links to several of the best Web sites that provide help with page layout.

37c.1 Positioning text and visuals

If you're using both text and visuals in a document, arrange them so that they balance and complement each other. Unless the style you're using dictates otherwise, don't put all text or all visuals on one page. Experiment with ideas for layout by creating mock-up pages on a computer or by sketching possibilities by hand. Group related items together. If you're writing a survey questionnaire, for example, you might number and name each category, and then use a lettered or bulleted list for the questions. You also might indent the lettered lists. Such a visual grouping of like items makes the information more immediately understandable to your reader. Box 158 gives tips on page layout and positioning text and visuals.

BOX 158   SUMMARY

 Page layout: Positioning text and visuals

- Consider the size of visuals in placing them so that they don't cluster at the top or the bottom of a page. That is, avoid creating a page that's top-heavy or bottom-heavy.

- Avoid splitting a chart or table between one page and the next. If possible, the entire chart or table should fit on a single page.

- Try working with layout by dividing a sheet of paper into sections. Divide it in half (either horizontally or vertically), then divide it into fourths or eighths (depending on the amount of text and the size of your visuals).

- Use the "Table" feature of your word processing program to position text and visuals exactly where you want them. Turn off the grid lines when you are done so that the printed copy shows only the text and visuals.

→

BACKGROUND
A Web site hosted by Pennsylvania State University suggests that a "well-designed poster is eye-catching, attractive, and communicates information effectively and economically." Guidelines for constructing effective posters are offered at <http://www.pop.psu.edu/info-core/library/posters.htm>.

Page layout: Positioning text and visuals (*continued*)

- Use the "Print Preview" feature to show you what the printed version will look like. This helps you revise before completing your final document.
- Print out hard copies of various layouts and look at them from different distances. Ask others to look at your layouts and tell you what they like best and least about them.
- Consider grouping all the visuals in an appendix if putting your graphics exactly where you want them is too difficult to work out. (Such a case is an exception to the rule that tells you to avoid placing either all visuals or all text on one page.)

37c.2 Using white space

White space, the part of your document that is blank, is as important as all other elements of design. White space allows readers to read your document more easily and to absorb information in chunks rather than in one big block. White space also indicates breaks between ideas and thereby focuses attention on the key features of your document.

Traditionally, ACADEMIC WRITING includes relatively little white space, except occasionally between sections of a document. For academic writing, you need to use double spacing. It gives instructors and peers space to write comments in response to your writing. BUSINESS WRITING usually calls for single-spaced lines, with an added line of white space between paragraphs. Flyers, brochures, posters, reports and other documents tend to make extensive and varied use of white space because they rely more heavily on graphical elements such as illustrations, different fonts and colors, bulleted lists, and so on.

37c.3 Justifying and indenting

When you make your text lines either even in length or even in relation to the left or right margin, you're **justifying** them. There are four kinds of justification, or ways to line up text lines on margins: left, right, centered, and full, as shown below and on the next page.

Left justified text (text aligns on the left)

Right justified text (text aligns on the right)

TEACHING TIP
Several students will be familiar with *zines,* alternative or underground magazines with origins in fanzines and published in print or online. Having groups of students produce a zine on a particular topic or subject matter offers a good opportunity for them to try design strategies. Owing to their spirit and origins, zines typically use counterculture or retro formats, even relying on pasted and taped photocopied documents in a raw pastiche. However, some zines are becoming more polished in their design, and the freewheeling nature of these publications, designed for local or insider distribution, provides a kind of free experimentation area that more staid genres do not. A clearinghouse of information on zine publishing is available from *The Book of Zines: Readings from the Fringe,* edited by Chip Rowe (New York: Henry Holt, 1997). The online site for the clearinghouse can be found at <http://www.zinebook.com/>. Dagmar Corrigan and Chidsey Dickson published an article on electronic zines in the classroom in the online journal *Kairos* (Summer 2002). The article, can be found at <http://english.ttu.edu/kairos/7.2/binder.html?sectiontwo/corrigan/description.html>, contains links to specific assignments and directions to students.

> **Center justified** text (text aligns in the center)

> **Full justified** text (both left and right justified to full length, or measure, of the line of type)

Most documents are left justified, including those for ACADEMIC WRITING and BUSINESS WRITING. This means that the right ends of the lines are unjustified, or *ragged.* Such a setup helps avoid end-of-line hyphens for broken words (see 29g), which are correct but distracting to the reader. (Most lines in textbooks are full justified, so you'll see many hyphens.)

Use center, right, and full justification in designing announcements, advertising, and similar public writing, because they can attract attention (see Chapter 42). Such documents also often include features such as wrapping text around boxes, pictures, or objects. Below is an example of text wrapped around a picture.

Rain forests are a special category of forests. They are found only in tropical regions of the world, usually close to the equator. Rainfall averages eighty inches a year, which explains why the forests are identified as *rain* forests. The rain combined with the warm tropical temperatures creates dense, lush vegetation. One major value of rain forests is biomedical. The plants and animals of the rain forests are the source of many compounds used in today's medications. A drug that helps treat Parkinson's disease is manufactured from a plant that grows only in South American rain forests.

Text wrapped around a picture

When you move text toward the right margin, you are *indenting.* College essays and research papers usually call for indenting the first line in paragraphs. The standard indentation is one-half inch. (See the indenting formats of student research papers in MLA style in 34e and in APA style in 35h.) Business writing requires paragraphs in block style, which calls for no indent of first lines and single spacing within paragraphs, with double spacing reserved only for between paragraphs. Never mix these two styles of indenting. Box 159 lists helpful tips on using justification and indentation.

BOX 159   SUMMARY

Tips on justifying and indenting

■ Use the ruler line in your word processing program to control the indentation of text instead of using the space bar or tab keys. The top arrow of the bar sets the paragraph indentation, while the bottom arrow sets the indentation for everything else in the paragraph.

   Alternatively, use the "Increase Indent" and "Decrease Indent" functions on your computer to control the indentation of text. This ensures that the indents stay constant in relation to the rest of the document, even if you change the type size or font (37d.2) of the text.

■ Use indents to indicate subsections of a document except in academic writing. For example, in a brochure, you might left justify headings and then indent the subsequent text.

■ Indent bulleted and numbered lists (37d.3) to make them stand out.

37c.4 Setting margins and borders

Margins are the boundaries of a page, which means the white space or blank areas at the top, bottom, and sides of a paper or screen. College essays and research papers call for one inch of space on all sides. Margins in BUSINESS WRITING are also usually one inch on all sides.

BOX 160   SUMMARY

Tips for using margins and borders

■ **Narrow margins** allow you to fit more information on a page but also decrease the amount of white space available. This can make a page appear cluttered, dense, and difficult to read.

■ **Wide margins** let you fit less information on a page. For ACADEMIC WRITING, margins greater than one inch make your document look thin because there's less content on a page.

■ **Borders** can be made of thin lines of repeated small graphic elements (such as asterisks). Simplicity is the key: Getting too fancy can be distracting.

■ **Color** should be used sparingly. Stick to darker colors (blue or black or red) and avoid heavy (thick) rules that distract from the content.

BACKGROUND
In "Design for Reading," a site at <http://www.worsleypress.com/media/simple.txt>, Gordon Woolf recommends that document designers study successful documents, like newspapers, to determine what principles govern these publications. For example, he addresses issues of establishing effective picture placement and breaking up long blocks of text with drop quotes and sidebars.

Borders around text serve to set off information, as in a table or chart. A sales brochure, for example, might "box in"—enclose in four borders, or *rules*—testimonials from satisfied customers, or a newsletter might set off upcoming events in a special box. A single rule (a simple straight line, horizontal or vertical) can emphasize breaks between major sections of a long report. Box 160 on page 697 contains a list of guidelines for how to use margins and borders effectively.

37d   How do I format text?

Text in writing consists of words and letters. To format text, you need to decide which typeface you'll use. A **typeface** is a particular style of type, such as Verdana or Century. A **font** is a specific kind of typeface, such as Verdana italics or Century bold. You also have to decide how you'll present headings and how you'll highlight important material.

37d.1   Writing headings

Think of headings as headlines in your document. Headings clarify your organization and tell your readers what to expect in each section. Longer documents, including this handbook, use headings to break content into chunks that are easier to digest and understand. Keep your headings brief and informative so that your readers can use them as cues. Also, write in PARALLEL structure and use consistent capital letters. Box 161 presents common types of headings, with examples showing parallel structure. Box 162 offers additional help on writing and formatting headings.

BOX 161   SUMMARY

 Common types of headings

- **NOUN PHRASES can cover a variety of topics.**
  Executive Branch of Government
  Legislative Branch of Government
  Judicial Branch of Government
- **Questions can evoke reader interest.**
  When and How Does the President Use the Veto Power?
  How Does the Legislative Branch Make Laws?
  How Does the Supreme Court Decide Whether to Consider a Case?

→

Common types of headings (*continued*)

- **GERUNDS and *-ing* phrases can explain instructions or solve problems.**
  Submitting the Congressional Budget
  Updating the Congressional Budget
  Approving the Congressional Budget
- **Imperative sentences can give advice or directions.**
  Identify a Problem
  Poll Constituents
  Draft the Bill

BACKGROUND
Susan Hilligoss's *Visual Communication* (Boston: Longman, 2001) includes a discussion of the rhetoric of visual information. This textbook offers chapters that detail tips for planning effective documents: brochures, newsletters, Web sites, and others.

BOX 162   SUMMARY

 Guidelines for writing and formatting headings

- **Create headings in larger type than the type size in the body of your text.** You can use the same or a contrasting typeface, as long as it coordinates visually and is easy to read.
- **Use parallel structure in writing headings.** Always start your listed items with the same part of speech. For example, the items in this box all start with VERBS. In longer documents, you can vary the form of the heading at different levels. For example, you might make all first-level heads questions and all second-level heads noun phrases. Any combination is acceptable, as long as you are consistent throughout your document.
- **Change the format for headings of different levels.** Changing the format for different levels of headings creates a clear outline for the reader. You can do this in various ways: You can center heads or left justify them; you can vary the typeface by using boldface, italics, or underlining; or you can use various combinations of capitals and lowercase letters (37d.2 and 37d.3). Always be consistent in the style you use within each document.

  Level one heading (most important)   **First-Level Head**
  Level two heading   <u>Second-Level Head</u>
  Level three heading   *Third-level head*

37d.2   Choosing type fonts and sizes

Fonts are different typefaces. Most computer programs come with a variety of fonts, and you can download more from the Internet. Be sure to consult your instructor or a style manual for your discipline before you format your paper. Fonts are divided into two major categories: *serif* and *sans serif.* Serif fonts have little "feet" or finishing lines at the top and bottom of each letter, and sans serif fonts do not (*sans* means "without"). Generally, readers of print more easily read serif fonts for extended periods of time, while sans serif fonts are effective when reserved for shorter documents or for headings.

SERIF FONTS	**SANS SERIF FONTS**
Times New Roman 12 pt	Arial 12 pt
Bookman Old Style 12 pt	Helvetica Neue 12 pt
Garamond 12 pt	Verdana 12 pt
Palatino Linotype 12 pt	Optima 12 pt

Examples of serif and sans serif fonts

Display fonts are excellent for special effects, so use them sparingly and reserve them for appropriate occasions such as invitations, announcements, printed programs, and so on.

Bauhaus 93	Braggadocio
Old English Text MT	CASTELLAR
Broadway	Monotype Corsiva

Examples of display fonts

Fonts come in different sizes (heights) that are measured in "points" (units smaller than .02 inch). Most word processing programs have font sizes ranging from 6 points, which is tiny, to 72 points, which is close to an inch. See example on the opposite page.

8 point

12 point

16 point

24 point

For most ACADEMIC WRITING, select fonts that range from 10 to 12 points for body text and from 14 to 18 points for headings. Since different font faces and sizes take up different amounts of room on a line and on a page, some instructors specify a specific typeface and size to ensure that students produce a certain amount of text per page. See Box 163 for guidelines to follow in using fonts.

BOX 163   SUMMARY

 Guidelines for using type fonts

- **Choose readable fonts.** Serif fonts are more comfortable to read for long periods of time. Therefore, body text is usually in a serif font. For body text in college work, a serif font such as Times New Roman is appropriate. Sans serif fonts are easier to read from a distance and are good choices for headings and posters.
- **Pick different font sizes for headings.** Varying sizes helps distinguish headings from body text. It also helps readers see different levels of headings; see Box 162 on page 699.
- **Avoid fancy typefaces for essays and research papers.** Many instructors consider elaborate fonts too distracting for college work.
- **Notice the difference between how a font appears on a screen and on a printed document.** If you're designing a document to appear on a computer screen, choose fonts that are screen-friendly. If you're making a print document, choose a print-friendly font.

37d.3 Highlighting

Highlighting draws attention to key words or elements of a document. You can highlight in various ways, but the one guideline that applies in all cases is this: *Use moderation.* For example, putting headings in bold is a good way to set them off, but emphasis is lost if too many words are in bold. Using different fonts and type sizes is one way of highlighting. This section looks at three other ways: (1) boldface, italics, and underlining; (2) bulleted and numbered lists; and (3) color.

Boldface, italics, and underlining

Italics and underlining—they mean the same thing—have special functions in writing (for example, to indicate titles of certain works; see 30f), but they're also useful for emphasis and for headings. **Boldface** is reserved for heavy emphasis.

Bulleted and numbered lists

You can use bulleted and numbered lists when you discuss a series of items or steps in a complicated process or when you want to summarize key points or guidelines. A bulleted list identifies items with small dots or squares. Lists provide your reader with a way to think of the whole idea you are communicating. For this reason, they work particularly well as summaries. In ACADEMIC WRITING, use such lists sparingly, if at all. Complete sentences and explanations are better.

Color

Adding color to a document can change it dramatically. A colorful flyer announcing a campus event, for example, can be as attention-getting as a magazine advertisement, as The Nature Club flyer illustrates. Take time, however, to think about your reasons for adding color to a specific project. How does color suit the genre of your document? How will it help you accomplish your purpose? What expectations does your audience have about the use of color? Academic writing rarely calls for color. On the other hand, brochures, advertising materials, posters, mass-mail sales letters, and letters soliciting donations all rely on color and varying fonts to add appeal to their message. Use color for variety and emphasis, but never overuse it.

37e How should I incorporate visuals?

Visuals, also called *graphics,* can enhance document design when used appropriately. A visual can condense, compare, and display information more effectively than words, but only if its content is suitable. A graph showing how sales increased over a period of time, for example, makes the point more quickly and clearly than an explanation. A photo or drawing can illustrate or reinforce a point you want to make.

Most word processing programs offer help for formatting and placing visuals. When produced on a color printer, charts, diagrams, and other graphics can look quite dramatic. However, resist any temptation to use visuals simply for the sake of using visuals. They should enhance your writing, not replace it. The Web site for this book contains links to Web sites on using visuals.

37e.1 Using charts and graphs

Business and scientific reports rely heavily on charts and graphs, and so do some research papers. They are compact ways to present large amounts of information.

Bar graphs compare values, such as the number of different majors at a college, as shown in the graph below.

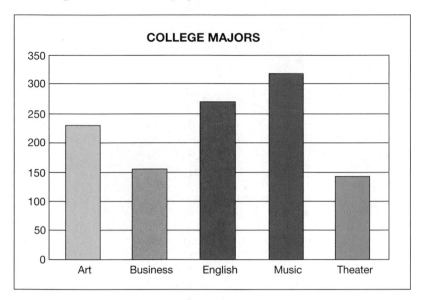

Line graphs indicate changes over time. For example, advertising revenue is shown over an eight-month period in the graph below.

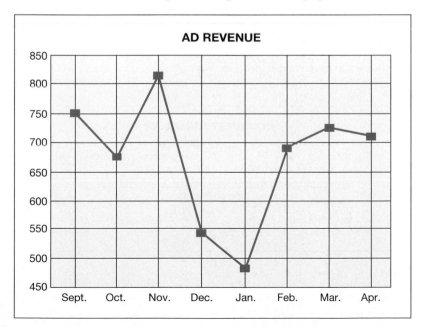

QUOTATION: ON DESIGN
If a major project is truly innovative, you cannot possibly know its exact cost and its exact schedule at the beginning. And if in fact you do know the exact cost and the exact schedule, chances are that the technology is obsolete.

—Joseph G. Gavin Jr.

Pie charts show the relationship of each part to a whole, such as a typical budget for a college student, as shown in the chart below.

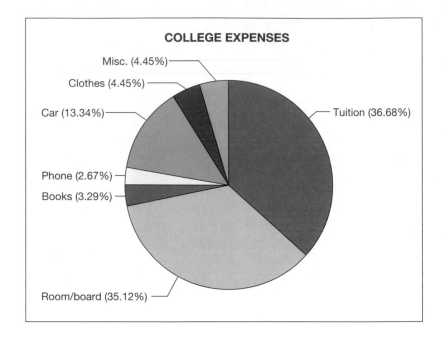

COLLEGE EXPENSES

Misc. (4.45%)
Clothes (4.45%)
Car (13.34%)
Phone (2.67%)
Books (3.29%)
Tuition (36.68%)
Room/board (35.12%)

37e.2 Using other types of visuals

Time lines display events over time, such as the progress of historical events or a manufacturing process.

CONQUESTS TIME LINE

Sicily, 241 BC
Carthage, Macedonia, Greece, 146 BC
Judea, 63 BC
Egypt, 31 BC

509 BC   Roman Republic   **27 BC**

Punic Wars, 264—146 BC
Sardinia, Corsica, 238 BC
Pergamum, 133 BC
Gaul, 58—50 BC

Diagrams show the parts of a whole, as in the diagram of the human brain on the next page.

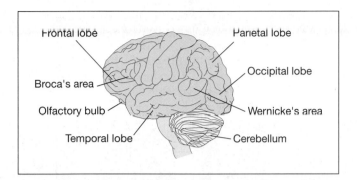

Tables present data in list form, as shown in the MLA-style research paper in 34e, the APA-style research paper in 35h, and below.

Table 1 Total Number of Computer Lab Users by Semester		
Semester	Number of Users	Percentage (%) of Student Population
Spring 2004	2321	25.8
Summer 2004	592	6.6
Fall 2004	3425	38.1

Clip art refers to pictures, sketches, and other graphics available on some word processing programs. It can also be downloaded from the Internet. Though clip art is rarely, if ever, appropriate in ACADEMIC WRITING and BUSINESS WRITING, it can add interest to flyers, posters, newsletters, and brochures designed for certain audiences. The Web site for this book, <www.prenhall.com/troyka>, contains regularly updated links to several of the best clip art sources. Here are samples of clip art.

Photographs can be downloaded from a digital camera or scanned from printed photos, books, and articles into a computer. Web sites exist that contain thousands of photographs available free or for a minimal charge. (See the Web site for this book for examples.) Once a photograph

QUOTATION: ON DESIGN
Less is more.
     —Ludwig Mies van der Rohe

is in your computer, you can place it in your document, usually with an "Insert" or "Import" command. A modest software program like Microsoft Photo Editor or a powerful program like Adobe Photoshop can help you adjust a photograph by cropping it (trimming the top, bottom, or sides), rotating it, or even modifying colors. Cropping can have a powerful effect on the meaning an image conveys to your audience, as the photos below show.

Original version and cropped version of one photograph

When you use a photograph, always be sure to give credit to the SOURCE so you don't PLAGIARIZE the material. You may even need to secure written permission from the source to use the photo, so check the copyright information that accompanies the picture.

Box 164 offers guidelines and additional help in using visuals in your documents.

BOX 164   SUMMARY

Guidelines for using visuals

■ **Design all visuals to be simple and uncluttered.** They should be clearly labeled, as needed, and easy to read.

■ **Never use unnecessary visuals.** Putting cute clip art on the pages of your writing won't make your reader think your work is well done. However, including a chart that summarizes your findings might.

■ **Number figures and tables, if more than one, and number them sequentially.** If possible, choose only one term in a relatively short piece of writing: *Table 1, Table 2;* or *Figure 1, Figure 2,* and so forth).

→

Guidelines for using visuals (*continued*)

- **Never overwhelm your text with visual elements.** If the visuals you want to use are much larger than the text, consider putting them on separate pages or in an appendix.
- **Credit your source if a visual isn't your own.** Always avoid plagiarism by crediting your source using DOCUMENTATION. If your source includes a statement or symbol that says it's copyrighted, you need written permission to use any part of it in your work. Check for this information in a print source by looking for a copyright notice (often at the beginning or end of the document) or a credits list. For a Web page, look at the top or bottom of the document.)

QUOTATION: ON WRITING
[My stories] run up and bite me on the leg—I respond by writing down everything that goes on during the bite. When I finish, the idea lets go and runs off.

—Ray Bradbury

Chapter 38

Effective Web Writing and Design

38a What should I know about writing for the Web?

The WORLD WIDE WEB, known popularly as *the Web,* consists of millions of locations on the Internet. These locations, called *Web sites,* are made up of one or a series of **Web pages.** Web pages can inform, entertain, and persuade through text, images, color, and often sound and video. If you want to create your own Web page, or a class assignment or group project requires one, this chapter will help you get started. (If you are interested in creating a Blog, or Web log, see 42h.)

Print documents communicate in a *linear* fashion: You begin at page one and proceed to the last page, moving in a straight line. A Web document, on the other hand, is *nonlinear:* Web pages are created in ways that allow readers to jump from page to page (or to other linked material, such as movies or sound) in whatever order they wish. Web documents, as a result, provide readers with exceptional flexibility. This affects how you design a Web page because you need to consider not only how each page looks but also how each page relates to the other pages you've created on your Web site.

Almost all Web sites have a *home page*, a page that introduces the site and provides links to the other pages that the site contains. The home page functions like a table of contents in print or, perhaps better, the entryway to a public building. You want the people who visit your home page to find it appealing, with clear directions for how they can navigate your site, or move from page to page. Most guidelines and principles that contribute to good design in printed documents apply equally to Web design. Basic design questions apply: Why create a Web page? Who will view your Web page? What features will you include on your Web page to appeal to those readers? As you make these decisions, you want to rely on the basic design principles of unity, variety, balance, and emphasis discussed in 37b.

Early in your planning process, look at some Web sites that seem similar to what you have in mind. For example, if you're creating a site for a club or organization, look at Web sites for clubs or organizations you know of or have heard about. If you're creating a personal home page—a page that contains information about yourself, your interests, and your accomplishments—look at several other personal home pages.

Shown below is the home page of The Nature Club's Web site (the club whose flyer I discussed in 37b). Most of the information is similar to the information on the flyer shown there. However, notice how several of the headings from that flyer have now become links to other pages within the site. Links appear prominently, right under the name of the club. Visitors to this home page can tell in a glance what kinds of information the Web site contains and go directly to the pages that interest them.

QUOTATION: ON DESIGN

My own creed as a playwright is fairly close to that expressed by the painter in Shaw's play *The Doctor's Dilemma,* "I believe in Michelangelo, Velásquez and Rembrandt; in the might of design, the mystery of color, the redemption of all things by beauty everlasting and the message of art that has made these hands blessed. Amen."

—Tennessee Williams

QUOTATION: ON DESIGN

Designing a website that takes into account the human element requires both an understanding of our nature as well as our physiological limitations. Usable websites incorporate human tendencies and limitation into its overall design.

—Michael L. Bernard

The Nature Club's home page

BACKGROUND

Focusing on the reception rather than the technical production of Web pages, Darrell Sano's book recommends that Web communicators focus on the organization of information before they address any design issues. Sano's text, *Designed Large-Scale Web Sites: A Visual Design Methodology* (1996), also analyzes poorly designed Web pages, providing readers with cautionary tales of miscommunication and misdirection.

BACKGROUND

In "Ezines and Freshman Composition" Dagmar Stuehrk Corrigan and Chidsey Dickson provide an assignment sequence and rationale for asking students to write and publish electronic zines (underground magazines). Their essay is published in *Kairos* (Summer 2002) at <http://english.ttu.edu/kairos/7.2/binder.html?sectiontwo/corrigan/description.html>.

38b How do I plan a Web site?

Planning a Web site involves two main decisions: (1) What will be the different pages within the site, and how will users navigate between them? (2) What will be the design of each page within the site? (See 38.c.) Creating a Web site is a process very much like writing a paper. You generate ideas and plan; draft and revise; edit and proofread.

Begin by determining all the pages your site might contain and whether pages should be grouped into *categories:* groups of pages all on the same topic. For example, if you wanted to include a page for each event that a club has sponsored, you could use the category "Special Events." People using the club's home page might click on a "Special Events" link that then directs them to pages for individual events.

To generate a list of categories, you might use the planning techniques of BRAINSTORMING, FREEWRITING, and CLUSTERING discussed in Chapter 2. Once you have a complete list, decide whether you can group any of the pages together; too many links from your home page can be overwhelming, but too few can make for overly long or complicated pages in your Web site. Then draft a map of your Web site to show how all the pages fit together. Below is the map of The Nature Club Web site.

Map of The Nature Club's Web site

Web design is similar to print design, but users look at your document on a computer screen instead of on separate sheets of paper. This means that your Web site should load quickly on viewers' screens, be easy to read and navigate, and provide the right amount of information for your intended audience. Research shows that people viewing a Web page tend to expect a single screen full of information at a time and don't like to scroll down to read a lengthy document. One main exception is when they're reading a full-text article online that they've located through a database.

The distinction between a Web *site* and a Web *page* is important. The site is the larger category. A site may consist of a single page or of many connected pages. As a rule, if your site is to contain a good deal of information, you will need to create several different pages.

Once you've drafted a map of your Web site, you begin designing and creating your individual Web pages. Generally, all the pages within a site need to have the same basic design and similar navigation features. That way your Web site will look unified, and users will have an easier and more pleasant experience.

38c How do I create a Web page?

Create a Web page, first, by planning its general appearance. Make decisions about the placement of texts and graphics, the use of color and white space, and what you want to emphasize. Here's some general advice about designing Web pages.

1. **Choose an appropriate title.** Make sure your page has a title that tells readers exactly what they'll find there.
2. **Keep backgrounds and texts simple.** Dark text on a plain light background is easiest to read, with white being the preferred background, even by expert Web designers. Sans serif fonts (37d.2) tend to be easier to read on computer screens than serif fonts, in contrast to print documents. Multiple typefaces, sizes, and colors, multiple images and graphics, and busy backgrounds are difficult to bring together effectively if you lack design training. Professional Web designers tend these days to strive for a clean, uncluttered look.
3. **Use images to attract attention to important elements of your page and to please the reader.** Readers will tend to look first at pictures and graphics on a page, so make sure to choose—and position—them to reinforce your page's content.
4. **Unify the pages in your site.** If your Web site has multiple pages, make each of them share some features, perhaps the same basic layout, font, color scheme, and header or navigation bar. A navigation bar is a set of links that appears on every page within a site and that allows users to get back to the site's home page and to major parts of the site.

Generally, the bottom of the home page includes the date the page is updated, or added to, along with the name of the page's creator or a contact person who can answer questions, perhaps including an e-mail address for that person. See Box 165 on the next page for questions to ask yourself about the special aspects of planning Web site layout.

BACKGROUND: WRITING ONLINE VERSUS PRINT
According to Jakob Nielsen, P. J. Schemenaur, and Jonathan Fox, writing for publication on the Web differs from writing for print in the following ways: "79% of users scan the page instead of reading word-for-word; reading from computer screens is 25% slower than from paper; and web content should have 50% of the word count of its paper equivalent." A complete list of the differences between writing for these media is available on the Sun Microsystems' Web page, <http://www.sun.com/980713/webwriting/>.

BACKGROUND
The Web site *Desktop Publishing* with Jacci Howard Bear offers several useful tutorials at <http://desktoppub.about.com/>.

TEACHING TIP
Students may be more familiar with word processing software than with Web page software, so novice designers may wish to begin their designs in Microsoft Word. Jeffrey Branzburg addresses how to "Create a Web Page with Your Word Processor" in his *Technology and Learning* article (January 2003).

BOX 165   SUMMARY

 Questions for designing a Web page

Navigation

How do I want my readers to move through the content on the page? How do I arrange information so that it's clear and easy to read? How will my readers navigate between different pages on my site? Do I provide my readers with links back to my home page and to the other content?

Grouping Content

How do I arrange content on my page? How will I group related elements? How can I use headings and subheadings to help group content? Are blocks of text short? Should I arrange some elements in lists?

Emphasizing Content

How can I make the title of my page stand out? How will I draw attention to the most important material? Can I use color, sound, or animation to enhance, not detract from, the text?

Placement of Images

Where will I put images on my page? How will I arrange images so that they don't distract from the other content on the page?

Choosing Backgrounds

What background will support my content most effectively? Can my text be read easily against the background? Would a single color or a pattern be better?

Establishing Links

Are my links obvious to a reader, or are they buried in text? Will my site provide links to the other pages in my site? What other reputable sites might interest my readers?

38c.1 Using HTML editors

Web sites are written in a computer program language. The original language format is called **HTML,** for **H**yper**T**ext **M**arkup **L**anguage. Originally, people designing Web pages had to know several HTML commands and type each of them into the Web page they were creating. For example, here is what The Nature Club page looks like in HTML code.

The Nature Club home page in HTML code

Producing Web pages became much easier with the development of programs called *HTML editors.* HTML editors generate "tags," or codes, for you much in the same way that word processing programs generate boldface type or other formatting. The three most common HTML editors are Netscape Composer, which is often distributed free with versions of Netscape; Microsoft FrontPage, which comes with many versions of Microsoft Internet Explorer; and Macromedia Dreamweaver. Your college's computer lab may have these programs or others. Also, you can purchase an HTML editor or download one from the Internet.

HTML editor programs employ *WYSIWYG* (What You See Is What You Get, pronounced "whizzy-wig") coding. The advantage of WYSIWYG programming is that as you work, you "see" the page you are creating rather than just the words and codes you type. You create your page by typing in text and inserting images and other content, and then the WYSIWYG editor generates the needed codes for you.

BACKGROUND
The Web site *Design & Publishing*, located at <http://www.graphic-design.com/>, offers several resources, including tips on designing Web sites, using Adobe Photoshop for improving digital photographs, selecting fonts, and so on.

The most important codes are those for links. In most programs you create a link by first highlighting the words you want to serve as the link and then by providing the URL, or Web address, of the page you want users to see when they click on the link. The illustration below shows a link being created to the page describing the Salt River canoeing event.

Dialog box used to insert a link

Creating a link

Space limitations prevent me from including detailed directions for using various HTML editors. Fortunately, numerous tutorial and advice Web sites exist on the Web. For links to places where you can get help, connect to the Web site for this handbook, <www.prenhall.com/troyka>.

38c.2 Using images

Web pages that you create can include many different kinds of graphics. For example, small icons such as colored balls can be used to mark off a list of items (the way bullets are used in print documents, as shown in many places in this book). You can also use photographs imported from a digital camera or inserted using a scanner. Graphic design programs allow you to create your own graphics. Some WYSIWYG editors come with clip art and images. You can also download photographic images and other graphics from the Internet. The Web site for this handbook, <www.prenhall.com/troyka>, contains regularly updated links to several useful sites.

As in print documents, images on Web pages are effective only if they help communicate the message you want to deliver. Simply dropping in an image in a random spot is more distracting than helpful. Try to find graphics that provide a consistent look. Also, consider whether the images you're using are appropriate for your audience.

Keep in mind that graphics, especially photographs, require lots of digital storage space, which means they can take a long time (up to several minutes) to download, especially through a phone modem. Therefore, use only the images that enhance your page. You also want to optimize images for the Web, which means using a feature in programs like Adobe Photoshop or Macromedia Fireworks to reduce the size of an image file to allow it to load faster. Images in a Web page exist as separate files, which means that even when you cut and paste an image into a Web page, the HTML editor is including a link to the separate file that contains the image. The designer of The Nature Club Web site, for example, used Dreamweaver software. In Dreamweaver, one way to insert an image is to "Copy" the image from its source, open the Web page you're building, place your cursor in the spot you want the image to go, and use "Paste" to insert the image. When you save the page you've made, Dreamweaver will ask if you want to save the image file along with the Web page, usually in the same folder. If you don't save the image file with the Web page and put both on the server, your readers won't be able to see it.

The two Web pages on the next two pages make excellent use of images. The Guthrie Theater page prominently features a costumed actor, her arms opened as if to welcome users to the Web site. The page designer has made the background actors in the image less visible so that the image isn't too cluttered or distracting. The image balances the main categories on the page, cleverly labeled "Act I," "Act II," and "Act III." The word "Magic" is in the largest type on the page, so it stands out beneath the image.

The Jet Propulsion Laboratory home page features four images. Most prominent is the large central photograph of an exploding star, over the caption "Celestial Fireworks." Immediately, visitors to this site perceive that the site contains dramatic information to engage even nonscientists. The second most prominent image is the complex graphic that forms the backdrop to the site sponsor's name, Jet Propulsion Laboratory. Including images of planets, stars, and galaxies, with spacecraft passing by them, the graphic dramatically conveys the purpose of the laboratory. It also calls attention to the navigation links on the page. Finally, two smaller graphics draw users' attention to featured links, "More News" and "Multimedia."

QUOTATION: ON DESIGN
Architecture starts when you carefully put two bricks together. There it begins.
—Ludwig Mies van der Rohe

BACKGROUND
The informative Web site *3D Cafe*, found at <http://www.3dcafe.com/asp/default.asp>, offers free material for Web designers, including tutorials, three-dimensional models, Web tools, and more.

BACKGROUND
Try <http://www.andyart.com> to download free images, animated gifs, and templates, among other things. ScreamDesign sponsors the site.

QUOTATION: ON DESIGN
To me, a building—if it's beautiful—is the love of one man, he's made it out of his love for space, materials, things like that.
—Martha Graham

BACKGROUND
The United States Copyright Office sponsors a site, at <http://www.copyright.gov>, that provides comprehensive information on copyrights.

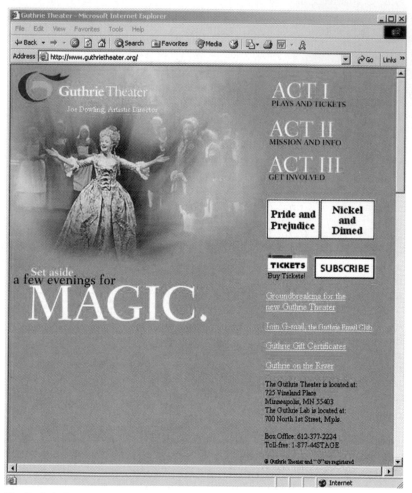

The Guthrie Theater home page

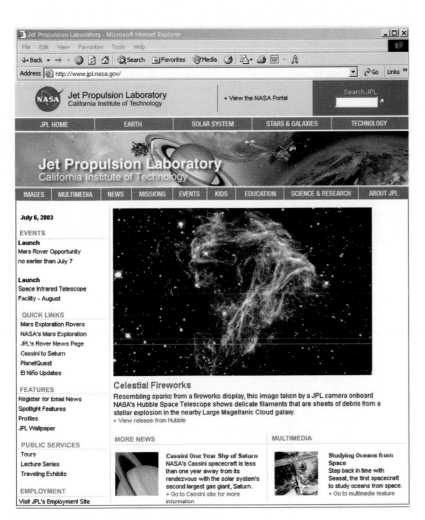

The Jet Propulsion Laboratory home page

BACKGROUND: DESIGN
While the Web supports many Web-writing style guides, one of the most comprehensive may be found at <http://www.w3.org/Provider/Style/>. This site covers some of the most basic considerations of style, including readability, document size, organization, and titles. In addition, novice designers may wish to read Georgia Tech's *Online Guide to Good Web Design* at <http://www.lcc.gatech.edu/gallery/dzine/>. Finally, Michael Bernard's "Criteria for Optimal Web Design (Designing for Usability)" includes a list of questions relating to usability that Web designers should answer prior to finalizing and publishing their works. These questions address both the physical differences among users and a browser's capabilities and how these affect the reception of the text. Bernard's Web site, *Optimal Web Design*, hosted by Wichita State University, is available at <http://psychology.wichita.edu/optimalweb/visual.htm>. A related newsletter associated with this site can be found at <http://www.usabilitynews.org>.

BACKGROUND

At <http://www.bellsnwhistles.com/>, a Web site created by Charles H. Tupper, students will find the claim "Everything you need to build your Website—for free!" At this URL, students can find software, Web tools, HTML codes, and other helpful resources.

QUOTATION: ON WRITING

Good writing comes from having something to say and saying it well. This simple fact is equally true in any medium. It was true in the time of the ancients and was true in the time of the medieval monks. It remained true through the invention of the printing press, the typewriter and the word processor. It is truer than ever in the age of on-line publishing and hypertext.

—Christopher B. Daly

38c.3 Using tables and frames

Tables and frames are devices that allow you to use HTML editors to place text and images accurately. The word *table* here differs from the display visual discussed in 37e.1. Unlike designing with pen and paper or with computer drawing software, HTML editors don't allow you to position materials immediately at different points on the screen. First, you have to define specific areas, and the easiest way to do this is with tables. A table divides the screen into a grid of spaces. You can then change the size of different rows, columns, or cells in the table in order to place blocks of text, images, links, and so on exactly where you want them. As with print documents, you can use the table feature to arrange text and images (see Box 158 on pages 694–695). The illustration below shows the basic table design underlying The Nature Club Web site.

Tables used to create The Nature Club home page

Optionally, you may choose to create frames on your Web site. A frame is a part of a Web page that functions independently of the other parts of the page. A common use of frames is for menus of links. When a user clicks on a link, its contents appear in a new frame or box on the page, while the original frame remains unchanged. For example, in the Jet Propulsion Laboratory's home page (38c.2), the column of links at the far left may be designed as a frame; while new content appears in a larger frame on the right of the page, the left frame remains unchanged. Using frames appears to be diminishing in popularity, as many sites instead use navigation bars—a line of links, often with a graphic, that occurs at the top or bottom of every page. Your HTML editor will provide advice for using tables and frames, as do various Web sites.

38d How do I display my Web page?

Having created a Web page, you're ready to display it on the World Wide Web. To do this, you need two things: First, you need space on a Web server, a centralized computer that is always online and that is primarily dedicated to storing and making available Web pages. Second, you need the ability to load all of your files to that server, including the page(s) you have made and any associated graphics that you have included.

Finding space on the Web

You can create HTML files (using a WYSIWYG or not) either online or offline, but you'll need to upload them to a Web server for the files to be visible on the Web. In other words, you need a host. If you have a commercial Internet Service Provider (ISP), such as America Online or Earthlink, you may be able to use it to post your Web page. Your college may offer Web space to its students, so check with your computing service office. If your college doesn't offer space, some services on the Internet offer free Web space as well as help in building Web pages. Try Yahoo! GeoCities at <http://geocities.yahoo.com/home/>. Note that if you use "free" Web space, the provider may insert advertising on your page.

You will also need some kind of File Transfer Protocol (FTP) program to upload the HTML files to your Web server. The host of your space should be able to advise you on the best way to upload files and which FTP program to use.

Using nontext files

If you've used graphics, pictures, icons, or sound on your Web page, you'll also need to upload those files to the Web server where your page is now located. Otherwise, they can't be accessed by Web browsers, the programs viewers use to access your site.

BACKGROUND: DISABILITY CONSIDERATIONS
The World Wide Web Consortium (W3C) has a comprehensive site devoted to exploring how people with disabilities use and experience the Web at <http://www.w3.org/WAI/>, then click on "Accessibility," for example. This site includes guidelines for constructing sites that are "universally" usable.

BACKGROUND
A database of thousands of digital texts (poetry, drama, fiction, and nonfiction) is maintained by the Electronic Literature Directory. Works that make extensive use of electronic techniques are linked from this page at <http://www.eliterature.org/dir/>.

Be careful to save the files with the correct extensions. Picture files normally have *.jpg* or *.gif* extensions, and sound files normally have *.wave, .au,* or *.midi* extensions. If your files don't have the correct extensions, the Web browser will not be able to process them.

Editing your page

Before you publish your Web page (that is, before you upload it to a server), edit and proofread it as carefully as you would a print document. Some WYSIWYG editors allow you to preview a Web page in a Web browser, but most likely you'll have to upload your site to the Web server where it will be hosted. The key difference between editing a Web page and a print document is that you also need to check that all the parts of your page are working properly. Use the checklist in Box 166.

BOX 166   SUMMARY

Editing checklist for a Web site

- **Are any images broken?** Broken images show up as small gray icons instead of the pictures you want. The usual cause of broken images is mistyping the file name or failing to upload the image to the server along with the your Web page.
- **Do all the links work?** For each link to a page on your own site, be sure a file with that exact name exists on the server. For example, if you're linked to a page called *essay.html* from your home page, make sure there's a file called *essay.html* on the server. Mistyped or mislabeled files can cause broken links.
- **Does your site work on different browsers and computers?** Your site needs to look the same on different browsers and different computers. If it doesn't, you may want to revise your HTML. Using default settings for font, text size, and color ensures that your page is compatible with most browsers.
- **Is the Web site highly readable?** As with print documents, the most important part of designing your Web page is making it easy to read. Ask friends and other students to give you feedback about your page before you publish it.

Publishing your page

Posting a Web page is a form of publishing. Like all original writings, your Web site is automatically copyrighted. If you want to make this clear to users (to discourage plagiarism, for example) include a copyright notice by typing the word *copyright*, the copyright symbol ©, the year of publication, and your name. If you want feedback, include your e-mail address. If you use material from SOURCES, credit them completely by using DOCUMENTATION. Always ask for permission to use someone else's work on your Web site. Plagiarism is plagiarism (Chapter 33), whether the medium is print or electronic.

38e How do I maintain my Web site?

Be sure to maintain your Web site by checking and updating it at least weekly. The Internet is always changing, and if your page contains links to other sites, you need to make sure your links still work. You may also want to add new information; new links; features such as ways of searching the site; calendars of upcoming events (if appropriate); or pages for user comments. One of the best things about a Web page is that you can change it as often as you like, and readers only have to visit the page again to see the changes. Always put a date at the bottom of your page to let visitors know when you last updated the site. Keep in mind that viewers tend to be wary of pages that haven't been updated recently. They perceive that the information may be old or unreliable or that the author doesn't care.

There's a wealth of information about document design on the Internet. The Web site for this book, <www.prenhall.com/troyka>, contains regularly updated links to several of the best sources for advice on document design.

QUOTATION: ON WRITING

The translation from paper to an electronic medium has a number of advantages. First and foremost, students are engaged by designing Web documents in a way they are not by a traditional print report. . . . Second, the demands of designing for the Web are high. . . . Designing good documents for the Web forces students not only to address significant technical issues but also to hone their skills in communication in order to entice the fickle Web user. Finally, the fact that the projects are accessible to friends and family in distant places, as well as to prospective employers, definitely encourages more thoughtful and polished work than that found in text reports. Just by virtue of being "published," even if they are never looked at by anyone outside of class, these documents become more significant in the eyes of their authors.

—Carole Meyer

QUOTATION: ON WRITING

Because our students are often well-armed with technological proficiency—occasionally more so than educators—and because they primarily have experience with *reading* electronic or online text, we, as teachers, may find it useful to tap into these "private literacies," those acquired in and through popular culture, as we push our students to think critically about *writing* (text production) and issues of audience and readership (text consumption).

—Joe Wilferth

Part Six

Writing Across the Curriculum—
and Beyond

BACKGROUND
One of the most important developments within composition studies in the past twenty years has been the recognition that academic disciplines vary considerably in terms of what constitutes "good writing." Different disciplines have different discourse conventions, tacitly held strategies ranging all the way from what constitutes appropriate evidence to what organizational method is expected to what constitutes a good style. To cite a small example, the passive voice, anathema to most instructors in the humanities, is often preferred in the natural sciences. Students need to analyze and adjust to the kinds of writing expected in different disciplines, especially as they encounter such varied genres as essays, lab reports, position papers, reviews of the literature, personal responses, research proposals, and so on. Perhaps the classic early article documenting the different advice students receive when working through the curriculum is Lucille Parkinson McCarthy's "A Stranger in Strange Lands: A College Student Writing Across the Curriculum" (*Research in the Teaching of English,* October 1987: 233–265).

Chapter 39

Comparing the Disciplines

39a How do the disciplines compare?

The humanities, the social sciences, and the natural sciences all have their own perspectives on the world. Each of the disciplines also has its own customary primary sources, analytic strategies, and writing styles. To understand some of the differences among the disciplines, consider these three quite different paragraphs about a mountain.

HUMANITIES

The mountain stands above all that surrounds it. Giant timbers—part of a collage of evergreen and deciduous trees—conceal the expansive mountain's slope, where cattle once grazed. At the base of the mountain, a cool stream flows over rocks of all sizes, colors, and shapes. Next to the outer bank of the stream stands a shingled farmhouse, desolate, yet suggesting its active past. Unfortunately, the peaceful scene is interrupted by billboards and chairlifts, landmarks of a modern, fast-paced life.

SOCIAL SCIENCES

Among the favorite pastimes of North American city dwellers is the "return to nature." Many outdoor enthusiasts hope to enjoy a scenic trip to the mountains, only to be disappointed. They know they have arrived at the mountain that they have traveled hundreds of miles to see because huge billboards are directing them to its base. As they look up the mountain, dozens of people are riding over the treetops in a chairlift, littering the slope with paper cups and food wrappers. At the base of the mountain stands the inevitable refreshment stand, found at virtually all American tourist attractions. Land developers consider such commercialization a way to preserve and utilize natural resources, but environmentalists are appalled.

NATURAL SCIENCES

The mountain rises approximately 5,600 feet above sea level. The underlying rock is igneous, of volcanic origin, composed primarily of granites and feldspars. Three distinct biological communities are present on the mountain. The community at the top of the mountain is alpine, dominated by very short grasses and forbs. At middle altitudes, the community is a typical northern boreal coniferous forest community, and at the base and lower altitudes, deciduous forest is the dominant community. This community has, however, been highly affected by agricultural development along the river at its base and by recreational development.

These examples illustrate that each discipline has its own perspective and emphasis. The paragraph written for the humanities describes the mountain from the individual perspective of the writer—a perspective both personal and yet representative of a general human response. The paragraph written for the social sciences focuses on the behavior of people as a group. The paragraph written for the natural sciences reports observations of natural phenomena.

As you study and write in each of the academic disciplines, you experience alternative ways of thinking. As you come to know the habits of mind that characterize each discipline, you develop specialized vocabularies to participate in its conversations. As the range of your perspectives grows, you gain lifelong access to the major benefits of a college education: the abilities to think through alternative points of view, to make connections among different sources and types of knowledge, and to make fully informed decisions. Indeed, you discover that no matter what differences exist among the academic disciplines, all subject areas interconnect and overlap. Box 167 describes the similarities and

BACKGROUND

In *Electronic Communication Across the Curriculum* (Urbana, IL: National Council of Teachers of English, 1998), Donna Reiss, Dickie Selfe, and Art Young present twenty-four essays that investigate what happens when proponents of Writing Across the Curriculum (WAC) incorporate computer-mediated tools and techniques, such as e-mail, asynchronous learning networks, MOOs (text-based virtual reality environments), and the World Wide Web, into their pedagogies.

BACKGROUND

In "Clearing the Air: WAC Myths and Realities" (*College English*, May 2000: 573–583), Susan McLeod and Elaine Maimon, two pioneers in WAC theory and practice, refute common WAC myths in a "full scale corrective." They offer a comprehensive definition of WAC and refer readers to models worthy of emulation.

BOX 167   SUMMARY

Comparing the disciplines

Humanities (history, languages, literature, philosophy, art, music, theater, and so on)

Types of assignments: reviews, essays, response statements, analyses; original works such as stories, poems, autobiographies, creative nonfiction

Primary sources: literary works, manuscripts, paintings and sculptures, historical documents, films, plays

Secondary sources: reviews, journal articles, research papers, books

Usual documentation styles: MLA, CM

→

TEACHING TIP

The humanities example paragraph offered here reflects one type of writing: a personal response. For other types of writing in the humanities, students frequently encounter assignments in which they have to interpret, or respond to, an existing literary or artistic work. An example of this type is the following paragraph about Robert Frost's poem "The Mountain."

> At one level, Robert Frost's poem "The Mountain" is about faith and the way people take for granted powerful and somewhat mysterious things in their daily lives. The narrator of the poem encounters an ancient man walking slowly at the base of a mountain, behind an ox cart. The man tells of "a curious thing," a brook that starts on the top of the mountain that is "cold in summer, warm in winter" when it steams "like an ox's breath." However, the narrator discovers that the old man has never been to the top of the mountain even though he has lived beneath it his whole life. He simply has faith that the brook is there and hasn't seen the need to climb to see for himself.

**PORTFOLIO APPROACHES
AND ACTIVITIES FOR WRITING
ACROSS THE CURRICULUM**

Literacy is ultimately the student's responsibility. The instructional cycle is complete only to the degree that students can translate information into a skill or tool. Portfolios allow students to transfer what they have learned in a writing course to other courses. By identifying, organizing, and reflecting on the various writing and reading activities necessary to master a course, students learn connections between curricula that exceed what can be taught.

The American Association for Higher Education (AAHE) provides extensive advice for using student portfolios across the curriculum, including the 2001 volume *Electronic Portfolios: Emerging Practices in Student, Faculty, and Institutional Change,* edited by Barbara Cambridge, Susan Kahn, Daniel P. Tompkins, and Kathleen Blake Yancey. For

➡

Comparing the disciplines (*continued*)

Social sciences (psychology, sociology, anthropology, education, and so on)

Types of assignments: research reports, case studies, reviews of the literature, and analyses

Primary sources: surveys, interviews, direct observations, tests and measures

Secondary sources: journal articles, scholarly books, literature reviews

Usual documentation style: APA

Natural sciences (biology, chemistry, physics, mathematics, and so on)

Types of Assignments: lab reports, research proposals and reports, science reviews

Primary sources: experiments, field notes and direct observations, measurements

Secondary sources: journal articles, research papers, books

Usual documentation styles: Vary by discipline, but often CSE

---

differences among the academic disciplines. Box 168 summarizes the strategies that are important in all academic writing situations, regardless of the discipline.

BOX 168   **SUMMARY**

 Strategies important in all academic writing situations

1. Consider your PURPOSE,* AUDIENCE, and TONE (Chapter 1).
2. Use the WRITING PROCESS to PLAN, SHAPE, DRAFT, REVISE, EDIT, and PROOFREAD (Chapters 2–3).
3. Develop a thesis (Chapters 2–3).
4. Arrange and organize your ideas (Chapter 2).
5. Use supporting EVIDENCE (Chapters 2–4).

*Find the definition of all words in small capital letters (such as PURPOSE) in the Terms Glossary at the back of this book directly before the Index.

➡

Strategies important in all academic writing situations (*continued*)

6. Develop paragraphs thoroughly (Chapter 4).
7. Critically read, think, synthesize, and write (Chapter 5).
8. Avoid confusing SUMMARY with SYNTHESIS (Chapter 5).
9. Reason well; use good logic (Chapter 5).
10. Write effective sentences (Chapters 16–19).
11. Argue well (Chapter 6).
12. Choose words well (Chapters 19–21).
13. Use correct grammar (Chapters 7–15).
14. Spell correctly (Chapter 22).
15. Use correct punctuation and mechanics (Chapters 23–30).

Consider the following examples of how various different disciplines can interconnect.

- In a humanities class, you might read *Lives of a Cell*, a collection of essays about science and nature written by the noted physician and author Lewis Thomas. As you consider the literary style of the writer, you also think deeply about biology and other sciences.

- In a philosophy class exploring the concept of infinity, you might read selections from *A Brief History of Time* by the astronomer Stephen Hawking.

- In an art history class discussing the Italian Renaissance, you might read social and political histories to understand how artists at the time earned a living and how that influenced their choice of subject matter.

- In an education course, you might read court decisions and laws to understand how and why schools must meet the needs of people with disabilities.

39b What are primary research and secondary research in the disciplines?

PRIMARY SOURCES offer you firsthand exposure to information, providing the exciting experience of discovering material on your own. But research methods differ among the disciplines when primary sources are used.

In the humanities, existing documents are primary sources; the task of the researcher is to analyze and interpret these primary sources.

Portfolio Approaches and Activities (continued)

additional resources, see the AAHE Web site, at <http://www.aahe.org/publications.htm>, and follow the links to publications.

Scoring Issues

Scoring a content portfolio (an application of Writing Across the Curriculum) can be as simple as assigning a percentage as if it were an independent project. Even 10 percent of a final college grade will provide an incentive to make the process work. However, truthfully, the more the process is valued and weighted, the more the student pays attention to the process. Holistic scoring, accompanied with published rubrics and eventually even sample student portfolios, makes the process surprisingly manageable. However, checklists and point systems for individual entries work just as well. In fact, the great strength of portfolio assessment is that the instructor is free to choose weights and values. A portfolio is a means to an end, a framework to house learning, a way to connect learning to assessment.

Reading-Writing-Listening Connection

Understanding the interdependence of lecture, reading, notetaking, test taking, and essay writing marks a mature student. Portfolios can become a system of tracking and communicating that connection, thereby nurturing this maturity. Ideally, success will demonstrate itself in measurable ways, such as in quiz and test scores, reading speed, and organizational and time management skills.

Students need to develop inferential, interpretive reading skills. These critical thinking skills, the cornerstone of portfolios, are recorded by careful student notetaking.

Notetaking

Notetaking is a key portfolio activity if teachers take time to recommend notetaking strategies. Provide visual models for students. Present an outline of the daily lesson in an overhead as you present a lecture, or divide the board into vertical sections with headings such as "Questions," "Answers," and "Applications" to guide small-group work. Reward ➡

Portfolio Approaches and Activities (continued)

good notetakers with warm-up, open-note quizzes as a bridge between lessons (an excellent portfolio entry or series of entries).

Creating a Content Portfolio

1. Establish prior knowledge and current needs: Use informal journal writing.

Preview the course: Read syllabus; mark calendar for important due dates.

Review prior experience: Identify barriers (consider everything from time management and reading and writing skills to the specialized vocabulary or jargon of the course).

Recognize your audience: Consider the instructor; record instructor's opinions and preferences.

Identify resources: library, learning centers, tutors, instructor office hours.

2. Set temporary goals and activities for study sessions: Use a formal essay.

Keep written records of all activities in and out of class (31e); use a notetaking system for academic research (31i and 31j) and for self-study and class notes (Chapter 5).

Reflect frequently: What did I learn? How will this help? What is its relevance? Its importance?

Label and organize everything: date, type, and purpose of assignment. Set up sections as needed: class notes, reading log, research project, test previews, reviews and repairs, and so on.

3. Adjust goals as necessary and continue reflective study process. Comment on successes and growth as they occur.

4. Reflect on your progress in final piece of formal writing. Prove you deserve the grade you want.

Typical primary source material for humanities research could be a poem by Dylan Thomas, the floor plans of Egyptian pyramids, or the early drafts of musical scores. A humanities class assignment might invite you to create primary sources yourself. For example, in a studio art class, you paint, draw, or sculpt. In a music composition class, you create pieces of music.

In the social and natural sciences, primary research entails either designing and undertaking experiments that measure the effect of some specific action or making careful direct observations of natural or social phenomena. The task of the researcher in the social and natural sciences is to conduct experiments or observations or to read the firsthand reports of experiments and studies by the people who conducted them. The researcher then has to analyze and explain what those reports and studies mean or why they're significant.

SECONDARY SOURCES—articles and books that draw on primary sources—are important but are not firsthand reports. In the humanities, secondary sources offer analysis and interpretation in that the author of a secondary source steps between you and the primary source. In the social and natural sciences, secondary sources SUMMARIZE, then SYNTHESIZE findings, and draw parallels that offer new insights.

39c How do I use documentation in the disciplines?

Writers use DOCUMENTATION to give credit to the sources they have used. A writer who neglects to credit a source is guilty of PLAGIARISM, a serious offense that can lead to negative academic consequences (33b). DOCUMENTATION STYLES differ among the disciplines.

In the humanities, most fields use the documentation style of the Modern Language Association (MLA), as explained and illustrated in Chapter 34. The student research paper in Chapter 34 and the student literary analysis in Chapter 40 use MLA documentation style. CM (Chicago Manual) style is sometimes used in the humanities, as explained and illustrated in Chapter 36. In the social sciences, most fields use the documentation style of the American Psychological Association (APA), as explained and illustrated in Chapter 35. The student research paper in Chapter 35 uses APA documentation style. (Research writing in the social sciences is also discussed in the first half of Chapter 41.) In the natural sciences, documentation styles vary widely, although the Council of Science Editors (CSE) style is frequently used (see Chapter 36). Ask each of your science and technology instructors about the particular documentation style required for his or her assignments.

Chapter 40

Writing About Literature and the Humanities

40a What are the humanities?

The humanities consist of a set of disciplines that seek to represent and understand human experience, art, thought, and values. These disciplines include literature, languages, philosophy, and history, although at some colleges history is grouped with the social sciences. Also, many colleges consider the fine arts (music, art, dance, theater, and creative writing) part of the humanities, while other colleges group them separately.

40b What forms of inquiry do I use to write about the humanities?

Inquiry calls for thinking beyond the obvious by intelligently questioning, investigating, and examining a subject. Because the humanities cover an impressively broad range of knowledge, writing in the various disciplines involves several forms of intellectual inquiry. These include responses, narratives, interpretations, critiques, and analysis of works or objects or ideas. In practice, many writing assignments in the humanities require you to combine these activities, but I present each of them individually here for ease of reference.

SYNTHESIS plays a major role in the habits of mind involved in inquiry. Synthesis relates several texts, ideas, or pieces of information to one another. For example, you might read several accounts of the events leading up to the Civil War and then write a synthesis that explains what caused that war. Or you might read several philosophers' definitions of morality and then write a synthesis of the components of a moral life. Unsynthesized ideas and information are like separate spools of thread, neatly lined up, possibly coordinated but not integrated. Synthesized ideas and information are threads woven into a tapestry—a new whole that shows relationships.

TEACHING AND RESOURCE TIP
Arguably, the single most comprehensive Internet site for humanities research is Voice of the Shuttle (VoS) at <http://vos.ucsb.edu/>, which has won numerous awards. Originated by Alan Liu at the University of California, Santa Barbara, by 2003 the contents of this site included pages on General Humanities Resources, Anthropology, Archaeology, Architecture, Area & Regional Studies, Art & Art History, Classical Studies, Cultural Studies, Cyberculture, Gender Studies, History, Legal Studies, Literature (in English), Literatures (Other Than English), Literary Theory, Media Studies, Minority Studies, Music & Dance, Philosophy, Photography, Politics & Government, Postindustrial Business Theory, Religious Studies, Science, Technology & Culture, and Technology of Writing. Each page leads to numerous specific resources.

Responses in the humanities

In a response, you give your personal reaction to a work, supported by explanations of your reasoning. For example, do you like *Hamlet?* What is your reaction to America's dealings with Hitler in the 1930s? Do you agree with Peter Singer's philosophical arguments against using animals in scientific experiments? Some instructors want you to justify your response with references to a text, while other instructors do not. Clarify what your instructor wants before you begin.

Narrative in the humanities

When you write a NARRATIVE, you construct a coherent story out of separate facts or events. Historians, for example, assemble public records, diaries and journals, news events, laws, incidents, and related materials to create a chronological version of what happened. Similarly, biographers take isolated events in people's pasts, interviews with the people themselves if possible, interviews of those who know or knew the people, letters written to or from the people, and related SOURCES to form a coherent story of their subjects' lives.

Interpretation in the humanities

An interpretation explains the meaning or significance of a particular text, event, or work of art. For example, what does Plato's *Republic* suggest about the nature of a good society? What message does Picasso's painting *Guernica* convey about the nature of war? What was the significance of President Richard Nixon's visit to China in the early 1970s? What does it suggest when language authorities in some countries try to ban new words that originated in other languages (such as the French trying to exclude English terms like *skateboard*)? Your reply isn't right or wrong; rather, you present your point of view and explain your reasoning.

Critique in the humanities

In a critique (also called a CRITICAL RESPONSE or a review), you present judgments about a particular work, supported by your underlying reasoning. For example, movie, book, music, and art reviews present a writer's carefully reasoned, well-supported opinion of a work. Critical responses and reviews may focus on the literary form, or genre, of a work (for example, "How does this poem satisfy the conventions of a sonnet?" or "Is this painting an example of Expressionism or Impressionism?"). Responses or reviews may focus on a work's accuracy, logic, or conclusions ("Is this history of the development of rap music complete and accurate?"). Finally, responses or reviews may analyze a work's relations to other works ("Is the Broadway version of *The Producers* better or worse than the earlier film version?") or a work's similarities to and differences from the "real" world ("To what extent does *Everybody Loves Raymond* accurately portray middle-class family life?").

Analysis in the humanities

When you engage in analysis, you examine material by breaking it into its component parts and discovering how the parts interrelate. You examine and explain texts, events, objects, or documents by identifying and discussing important elements in them. These elements can include formal matters (how the work is put together) or the ideas, assumptions, and evidence they include. The humanities use a number of *analytic frameworks,* or systematic ways of investigating a work. Box 169 summarizes some common analytic frameworks used most notably in literary analysis. Nearly all writing in the humanities depends on analysis to some extent.

WHAT ELSE?

Strategies and Resources is a free 400-page book written especially for instructors who adopt this handbook. It offers a "primer for students" on reading and writing about literature and includes definitions, samples of student writing, and the complete text of "The Necklace" by Guy de Maupassant. Also, it offers specific, practical ways to "stimulate students to carry out deeper and more methodical explorations of literary works."

BOX 169   **SUMMARY**

 ## Selected analytic frameworks used in the humanities

Cultural/New Historical

Explores how social, economic, and other cultural forces influence the development of ideas, texts, art, laws, customs, and so on. Also explores how individual texts or events provide broader understandings of the times in which they were written or occurred or in today's world.

Deconstructionist

Assumes that the meaning of any given text is not stable or "in" the work. Rather, that meaning always depends on contexts and the interests of those in power. The goal of deconstruction is to produce multiple possible meanings of a work, usually in order to undermine traditional interpretations.

Feminist

Focuses on how women are presented and treated, concentrating especially on power relations between men and women.

Formalist

Centers on matters of structure, form, and traditional literary devices (plot, rhythm, images, symbolism, DICTION; see Box 171, pp. 734–735).

Marxist

Proceeds from the assumption that the most important forces in human experience are economic and material ones. Focuses on power differences between economic classes of people and the effects of those differences.

Reader-Response

Emphasizes how the individual reader determines meaning. The reader's personal history, values, experiences, relationships, and prior reading life all contribute to how he or she interprets a particular work or event.

BACKGROUND
In "Critical Analysis of Literature: Making the Connection between Reading and Writing" (*English Journal,* March 2000: 85–88), Michael A. Gunther describes a reading-writing course design that encourages students to actively read, think, debate, and write about literature.

40c   What is literature?

Literature includes fiction (novels and short stories); drama (plays, scripts, and some films); poetry (poems and lyrics); as well as nonfiction with artistic qualities (memoirs, personal essays, and the like). Since ancient times, literature has represented human experiences, entertained, and enlarged readers' perspectives about themselves, others, diverse cultures, and different ways of living.

By writing about literature, you shape and refine the insights that result from your reading. Writing about reading, more than reading without writing, helps you move to a deeper understanding of other people and of ideas, times, and places. Writing about literature facilitates your investigations of how authors use language to stir the imaginations, emotions, and intellects of their readers. And, of course, writing allows you to share your own reading experiences and insights with other readers.

40d   What reading skills help me interpret literature?

In academic work, although you may initially read a work for sheer enjoyment, during further readings you need to attend more closely to various elements in the text. Interestingly, many readers are surprised to discover that CRITICAL READING actually enhances their enjoyment of the text.

Critical reading means reading systematically, closely, and actively (5d). Above all, it means asking questions: What does the work mean? Why has the author made particular choices in plot, characterizations, and word choice? What other works influenced the author's choices? How do readers react to the work?

Sometimes instructors ask students to answer questions that deal with material on a literal level: that is, to tell exactly what is said on the page. If a question asks what happens in the plot or what a passage is saying, you need to answer with a SUMMARY or PARAPHRASE of the work. If a question asks about the historical context of a work, or asks for biographical or situational information about the author, you likely need to do some research and then report exactly what you find.

More often, assignments call for making INFERENCES, which I discuss in detail in section 5c. Making inferences means reading "between" the lines to figure out what is implied but not stated. This reading skill is especially crucial for reading literature because it tends to "show" rather than to "tell." It depicts events, characters, conversations, and settings, but the author doesn't say precisely what the work means. For example, your instructor might ask you to discuss why a character does something for which the author provides no explicit reason; to explain the effect of images in a poem; to investigate how a work depicts the roles of women, men, and/or children; or to explore the author's stance on a social issue. In such papers you're not only analyzing the literary text but also examining your own experiences and beliefs.

To read a literary work closely, and then to write about it, you look for details or passages that relate to each other. In so doing, you can form a TOPIC or THESIS STATEMENT for writing about the text. As you read, mark up the text by selectively underlining or highlighting passages, by writing notes, comments, or questions in the margin, or by taking notes separately on paper or on a computer. If you use the third method, be sure to note exactly what part of the text you're referring to so that you don't lose track of what applies to what.

BACKGROUND
Jeff Passe uses educational research and theory to promote student participation in curricular development in *When Students Choose Content: A Guide to Increasing Motivation, Autonomy, and Achievement* (Thousand Oaks, CA: Corwin Press, 1996).

40e What forms of inquiry do I use to write about literature?

Several different types of inquiry are used for writing about literature. They include all types discussed in 40b, with the following adaptations.

Personal response to literature

In a personal response you explain your reaction to a work of literature or some aspect of it. As with all effective papers about literature, you explain your response through discussions of specific passages or elements from the text. You might write about whether you enjoyed reading the work—and why. You might discuss whether situations in the work are similar to your personal experience, and why such observations are worth the reader's consideration. You might explain whether you agree with the author's point of view (Box 171, pp. 734–735)—and why. You might answer a question or explore a problem that the work raised for you—for example, how you reacted when a likeable character broke the law.

Interpretation of literature

Most works of literature are open to more than one interpretation. Your task, then, is not to discover the single right answer. Instead, you determine a possible interpretation and provide an argument that supports it. The questions in Box 170 on the next page can help you write an effective interpretation paper.

Formal analysis of literature

A formal analysis explains how elements of a literary work function to create meaning or effect. The term "formal analysis" refers to analysis of *formal elements* that make up a work of literature, such as the plot structure

BACKGROUND
In "A Student-Written Syllabus for Second-Semester English Composition" (*Teaching English in the Two-Year College,* February 1994: 27–32), Amber Dahlin explains that her sophomore composition students in Alaska designed their class reading list in a literature anthology, and as the semester progressed, so did the students' skills in critical reading and general metacognitive analysis.

BOX 170   SUMMARY

Questions for a literary interpretation paper

1. What is the central theme of the work?
2. How do particular parts of the work relate to the central theme of the work?
3. What do patterns, if they exist in various elements of the work, mean?
4. What meaning does the author create through the elements listed in Box 171?
5. Why does the work end as it does?

of a novel or the rhythm of a poem. Box 171 describes many of these formal elements. Your instructor may ask you to concentrate on just one formal element (for example, "How does the point of view in the story affect its meaning?") or to discuss how a writer develops a theme through several elements (for example, "How do setting, imagery, and symbolism reveal the author's viewpoint?").

To prepare to write your formal analysis, read the work thoroughly, looking for patterns and repetitions. Write notes as you read to help you form insights about these patterns and repetitions. For example, if you need to analyze a character, you want to pay attention to everything that character says or does, everything that other characters say about him or her, and any descriptions of the character.

BOX 171   SUMMARY

Major elements of formal analysis in literary works

PLOT	Events and their sequence
THEME	Central idea or message
STRUCTURE	Organization and relationship of parts to each other and to the whole
CHARACTERIZATION	Traits, thoughts, and actions of the people in the plot
SETTING	Time and place of the action
POINT OF VIEW	Perspective or position from which the material is presented—by a narrator, a main character, or another person either in the plot or observing the plot

→

Major elements of formal analysis in literary works (*continued*)

STYLE	Words and sentence structures chosen to present the material
IMAGERY	Pictures created by the words according to other aspects (simile, figurative language, etc.) discussed in this box
TONE	Author's attitude toward the subject of the work—and sometimes toward the reader—expressed through choice of words, imagery, and point of view
FIGURE OF SPEECH	Unusual use or combination of words, as in metaphor and simile, for enhanced vividness or effect
SYMBOLISM	Meaning beneath the surface of the words and images
RHYTHM	Beat, meter
RHYME	Repetition of similar sounds for their auditory effect

Cultural Analysis of literature

A cultural analysis relates the literary work to broader historical, social, cultural, and political situations. Instructors might ask you to explain how events or prevailing attitudes influence the writing of a work or the way readers understand it. For example, "How did Maxine Hong Kingston's experience as a Chinese American affect the way she tells her story in *The Woman Warrior*?" or "How do differences between the institution of marriage in the early nineteenth century and today affect readers' interpretations of *Pride and Prejudice*?" Box 172 lists some common focuses for cultural analysis.

BOX 172   SUMMARY

 Major topics for cultural analysis

GENDER	How does a work portray women or men and define—or challenge—their respective roles in society?
CLASS	How does a work portray relationships among the upper, middle, and lower economic classes? How

→

BACKGROUND
Susan G. LeJuene describes, in "Writing for the Ignorant Reader" (*Teaching English in the Two-Year College,* December 1998: 163–167), a pedagogical approach she used in her composition and literature course. She argues that students must address literary texts in a relaxed manner; they should target their papers to the "ignorant reader" rather than assume a false academic stance and a knowledgeable audience.

Major topics for cultural analysis (*continued*)

	do characters' actions or perspectives result from their wealth and power—or the lack thereof?
RACE AND ETHNICITY	How does a work portray the influences of race and ethnicity on the characters' actions, status, and values?
HISTORY	How does a work reflect—or challenge—past events and values in a society?
AUTOBIOGRAPHY	How might the writer's experiences have influenced this particular work? Similarly, how might the times in which the writer lives or lived have affected his or her work?
GENRE	How is the work similar to, or different from, other works of its type, often—but not always—those written at the same general time? Literature's genres include fiction and memoirs, plays, and poems.

40f What special rules apply to writing about literature?

When you write about literature, certain special elements come into play.

40f.1 Using first and third person appropriately

Many instructors require students to use the FIRST PERSON (*I, we, our*) only when writing about their personal point of view in evaluations; they want students to use the THIRD PERSON (*he, she, it, they*) for all other content. These rules are becoming less rigid, but be sure to ask about your instructor's requirements.

40f.2 Using present and past tense correctly

Always use the PRESENT TENSE when you describe or discuss a literary work or any of its elements: *George Henderson* [a character] ***takes*** *control of the action and **tells** the other characters when they may speak.* The present tense is also correct for discussing what the author has done in a specific work: *Because Susan Glaspell* [the author] ***excludes*** *Minnie and John Wright from the stage as speaking characters, she **forces** her audience to learn about them through the words of others.*

Use a PAST-TENSE VERB to discuss historical events or biographical information: *Susan Glaspell **was** a social activist who **was** strongly **influenced** by the chaotic events of the early twentieth century.*

40f.3 Using primary and secondary sources

Some assignments call for only your own ideas about the literary work that is the subject of your essay. In such cases, you are dealing only with a PRIMARY SOURCE. In writing about literature, a primary source is the original creative work (a poem, play, story, novel, memoir, diary). Other assignments require you additionally to use SECONDARY SOURCES, which consist of interpretations of literary works. As with all source-based writing, you need to DOCUMENT primary sources and secondary sources because you want to ensure that readers never mistake someone else's ideas as yours. Otherwise, you're PLAGIARIZING, which is a serious academic offense (for a complete discussion, see Chapter 33).

Most literature instructors require students to use the DOCUMEN-TATION STYLE of the Modern Language Association (MLA), described in Chapter 34. However, some instructors prefer APA style (Chapter 35) or CM or CSE style (Chapter 36), so check with your instructor before you begin to conduct your research.

Secondary sources include books, articles, and Web sites in which experts discuss some aspect of the literary text or other material related to your topic. You might use secondary sources to support your own ideas, perhaps by drawing upon the ideas of a scholar who agrees with you or debating the ideas of a scholar who disagrees with you. Or, if you think that you have a new or different interpretation, you might summarize, analyze, or critique what others have written, in order to provide a framework for your own analysis. You can locate secondary sources by using the research process discussed in Chapters 31 and 32. A particularly important resource for research about literature is the *MLA International Bibliography,* which is the most comprehensive index to literary scholarship (Box 138 in section 32e).

40g Sample student essays

This section includes three student essays of literary analysis. Two do not use SECONDARY SOURCES (40g.1 and 40g.2) and one does use them (40g.3). All three essays use MLA STYLE DOCUMENTATION.

40g.1 Student essay interpreting a plot element in a short story

The student essay in this section interprets a plot element in Edgar Allan Poe's story "The Tell-Tale Heart."

Edgar Allan Poe was an important American journalist, poet, and fiction writer born in 1809. In his short, dramatic life, Poe gambled, drank, lived in terrible poverty, saw his young wife die of tuberculosis, and died himself under mysterious circumstances at age forty. He also

TEACHING TIP
In "Grading with an Attitude" (*Pedagogy*, Fall 2002: 416–419), Mark Gellis describes a strategy whereby he returns literature papers to students only in conferences. Using what he calls "just in time grading," he writes comments that function as notes for oral comments in face-to-face exchanges. Gellis writes:

> My advice about how to conference is simple. First, tell your students what they did well before you explain what they did badly. It boosts their morale and makes them more willing to listen to the "bad news." Second, offer constructive criticism. Focus on solving problems. Discussing problems for their own sake is a dead end. Third, focus on only a few things. Know before you meet with a student . . . [what will most benefit that student]. I sometimes tell students that one aspect of good writing is to do one thing well instead of ten things badly. The same is true for conferences. If you tell students about every single error in their papers, most of them will be overwhelmed; they will shut down and stop listening to you.

created the detective story and wrote brilliant, often bizarre short stories that still stimulate readers' imaginations.

When the student Valerie Cuneo read Poe's "The Tell-Tale Heart," first published in 1843, she was fascinated by one of the plot elements: the sound of a beating heart that compels the narrator of the story to commit a murder and then to confess it to the police. In her paper shown below, Cuneo discusses her interpretation of the source of the heartbeat.

Cuneo 1

Valerie Cuneo

Professor Aaron

English 10B

2 February 2004

The Sound of a Murderous Heart

In Edgar Allan Poe's short story "The Tell-Tale Heart," several interpretations are possible concerning the source of the beating heart that causes the narrator-murderer to reveal himself to the police. The noise could simply be a product of the narrator's obviously deranged mind. Or perhaps the murder victim's spirit lingers, heart beating, to exact revenge upon the narrator. Although either of these interpretations is possible, most of the evidence in the story suggests that the inescapable beating heart that haunts the narrator is his own.

The interpretation that the heartbeat stems from some kind of auditory hallucination is flawed. The narrator is clearly insane--his killing a kind old man because of an "Evil Eye" demonstrates this--and his psychotic behavior is more than sufficient cause for readers to question his truthfulness. Even so, nowhere else in the story does the narrator imagine things that do not exist. Nor is it likely that he would intentionally attempt to mislead us since the narrative is a confessional monologue through which he tries to explain and justify his actions. He himself describes his "disease" as a heightening of his senses, not of his imagination. Moreover, his highly detailed account of the events surrounding the murder seems to support

→

this claim. Near the end of the story, he refutes the notion that he is inventing the sound in his mind when he says, "I found that the noise was not within my ears" (792). Although the narrator's reliability is questionable, there seems to be no reason to doubt this particular observation.

Interpreting the heartbeat as the victim's ghostly retaliation against the narrator also presents difficulties. Perhaps most important, when the narrator first hears the heart, the old man is still alive. The structure of the story also argues against the retaliation interpretation. Poe uses the first-person point of view to give readers immediate access to the narrator's strange thought processes, a choice that suggests the story is a form of psychological study. If "The Tell-Tale Heart" were truly a ghost story, it would probably be told in the third person, and it would more fully develop the character of the old man and explore his relationship with the narrator. If the heartbeat that torments the narrator is his own, however, these inconsistencies are avoided.

The strongest evidence that the tell-tale heart is really the narrator's is the timing of the heartbeat. Although it is the driving force behind the entire story, the narrator hears the beating heart only twice. In both of these instances, he is under immense physical and psychological stress--times when his own heart would be pounding. The narrator first hears the heartbeat with the shock of realizing that he has accidentally awakened his intended victim:

> Meantime the hellish tattoo of the heart increased. It grew quicker and quicker, and louder every instant. The old man's terror must have been extreme! It grew louder, I say, louder every moment!--do you mark me well? I have told you that I am nervous: so I am. And now at the dead hour of the night, amid the dreadful silence of that old house, so strange a noise as this excited me to uncontrollable terror. (791)

→

QUOTATION: ON READING
Language is the soul of intellect, and reading is the essential process by which that intellect is cultivated beyond the commonplace experiences of everyday life.
—Charles Scribner Jr.

Cuneo 3

As the narrator's anxiety increases, so does the volume and frequency of the sound, an event easily explained if the heartbeat is his own. Also, the sound of the heart persists even after the old man is dead, fading slowly into the background, as the murderer's own heartbeat would after his short, violent struggle with the old man. This reasoning can also explain why the narrator did not hear the heart on any of the seven previous nights when he looked into the old man's bedchamber. Because the old man slept and the "Evil Eye" was closed, no action was necessary (according to the narrator-murderer's twisted logic), and, therefore, he did not experience the rush of adrenaline that set his heart pounding on the fatal eighth visit.

The heart also follows a predictable pattern at the end of the story when the police officers come to investigate a neighbor's report of the dying old man's scream. In this encounter, the narrator's initial calm slowly gives way to irritation and fear. As he becomes increasingly agitated, he begins to hear the heart again. The narrator clearly identifies it as the same sound he heard previously, as shown by the almost word-for-word repetition of the language he uses to describe it, calling it "a low, dull, quick sound—much such a sound as a watch makes when enveloped in cotton" [Poe's emphasis] (792). As the narrator-murderer focuses his attention on the sound, which ultimately overrides all else, his panic escalates until, ironically, he is betrayed by the very senses that he boasted about at the start of the story.

Cuneo 4

Work Cited

Poe, Edgar Allan. "The Tell-Tale Heart." Anthology of American
Literature. Vol. 1. Ed. George McMichael, Frederick
Crewes, J. C. Levenson, Leo Marx, and David E. Smith.
Upper Saddle River: Prentice, 1997. 767-70.

40g.2 Student essay analyzing the characters in a drama

The following student essay analyzes the actions and interactions of the male and female characters in *Trifles*, a one-act play by Susan Glaspell (1882–1948). Glaspell was a feminist and a social activist who wrote many plays for the Provincetown Players, a theater company she co-founded on Cape Cod, Massachusetts. She wrote *Trifles* in 1916, four years before women were allowed to vote in the United States. In 1917, Glaspell rewrote *Trifles* as the short story "A Jury of Her Peers." In both versions of the work, two married couples and the county attorney gather at a farmhouse where a taciturn farmer has been murdered, apparently by his wife. The five characters try to discover a motive for the murder. In doing so, they reveal much about gender roles in marriage and in the larger society.

After reading *Trifles*, Peter Wong said to his instructor, "No male today could get away with saying some of the things the men in that play say." The instructor encouraged Wong to analyze that reaction.

Wong 1

Peter Wong
Professor Minoc
Drama 250
12 April 2004

Gender Loyalties: A Theme in Trifles

Susan Glaspell's play Trifles is a study of character even
though the two characters most central to the drama never

→

741

QUOTATION: ON WRITING
I spent 15 years wandering about, weighed horribly with masses of paper and little else. Yet for this vocation of writing I was and am willing to die, and I consider very few other things of the slightest importance.
—Katherine Anne Porter

Wong 2

appear on stage. By excluding Minnie and John Wright from the stage as speaking characters, Glaspell forces us to learn about them through the observations and recollections of the group visiting the farmhouse where the murders of Minnie Wright's canary and of John Wright took place. By indirectly rounding out her main characters, Glaspell invites us to view them not merely as individuals but also as representatives in a conflict between the sexes. This conflict grows throughout the play as characters' emotions and sympathies become increasingly polarized and oriented in favor of their own gender. From this perspective, each of the male characters can be seen to stand for the larger political, legal, and domestic power structures that drive Minnie Wright to kill her husband.

That George Henderson speaks the first line of the play is no accident. Although his power stems from his position as county attorney, Henderson represents the political, more than the legal, sphere. With a job similar to a district attorney's today, he is quite powerful even though he is the youngest person present. He takes control of the action, telling the other characters when to speak and when not to and directing the men in their search for evidence that will establish a motive for the murder. As the person in charge of the investigation, George Henderson orders the other characters about. Mrs. Peters acknowledges his skill at oratory when she predicts that Minnie Wright will be convicted in the wake of his "sarcastic" cross-examination (speech 63).

Glaspell reveals much of the conflict in the play through the heated (but civil) exchanges between George Henderson and Mrs. Hale. His behavior (according to the stage directions, that of a gallant young politician) does not mask his belittling of Minnie Wright and of women in general:

> COUNTY ATTORNEY. I guess before we're through she
> may have something more serious than preserves
> to worry about.

→

Wong 3

HALE. Well, women are used to worrying over trifles.

[The two women move a little closer together.]

COUNTY ATTORNEY. [With the gallantry of a young
politician.] And yet, for all their worries, what
would we do without the ladies? [The women do
not unbend. He goes to the sink, takes a dipperful
of water from the pail, and pouring it into a basin,
washes his hands. Starts to wipe them on the
roller-towel, turns it for a cleaner place.] Dirty
towels! [Kicks his foot against the pans under
the sink.] Not much of a housekeeper, would you
say, ladies? (speeches 29-31)

As this excerpt shows, George Henderson seems to hold
that a woman's place is in the kitchen, even when she is locked
up miles away in the county jail. He shows so much emotion at
the discovery of dirty towels in the kitchen that it is almost as
if he has found a real piece of evidence that he can use to
convict Minnie Wright, instead of an irrelevant strip of cloth.
It is apparent that his own sense of self-importance and
prejudicial views of women are distracting him from his real
business at the farmhouse.

Sheriff Henry Peters, as his title suggests, represents the
legal power structure. Like the county attorney, Henry Peters is
also quick to dismiss the "trifles" that his wife and Mrs. Hale
spend their time discussing while the men conduct a physical
search of the premises. His response to the attorney's asking
whether he is absolutely certain that the downstairs contains no
relevant clues to the motive for the murder is a curt "Nothing
here but kitchen things" (speech 25). Ironically, the women are
able to reconstruct the entire murder, including the motive, by
beginning their inquiries with these same "kitchen things."
Sheriff Peters and the other men all completely miss the
unfinished quilt, the bird cage, and the dead bird's body.
When the sheriff overhears the women talking about the

→

QUOTATION: ON WRITING
Form in literature is an arousing and fulfill-
ment of desires. A work has form insofar as
one part of it leads a reader to anticipate another part, to be gratified by the sequence.
—Kenneth Burke

Wong 4

quilt, his instinctive reaction is to ridicule them, saying, "They
wonder if she was going to quilt it or just knot it!" (speech 73). Of
course, the fact that Minnie Wright was going to knot the quilt
is probably the single most important piece of evidence that
the group could uncover, since John Wright was strangled with
what we deduce is a quilting knot. Although he understands the
law, the sheriff seems to know very little about people, and this
prevents him from ever cracking this case. His blindness is
made clear when he chuckles his assent to the county attorney's
observation that Mrs. Peters is literally "married to the law"
(speech 145) and therefore beyond suspicion of trying to hinder
the case against Minnie Wright. This assumption is completely
wrong, for Mrs. Peters joins Mrs. Hale in suppressing the
evidence and lying to the men.

 Rounding out the male characters is Lewis Hale, a
husband and farmer who represents the domestic sphere.
Although Lewis Hale may not be an ideal individual, he
provides a strong foil for John Wright's character. We might
expect Lewis Hale, as Mrs. Hale's spouse, to be a good (or at
least a tolerable) person, and, on the whole, he is. Although he,
too, misses the significance of the "trifles" in the kitchen and
mocks the activities of his wife and Mrs. Peters, he seems less
eager than the other men to punish Minnie Wright--possibly
because he knew John Wright better than they did. Lewis Hale
is clearly reluctant to provide evidence against Minnie Wright
when he speaks of her behavior after he discovers the body:

> HALE. She moved from that chair to this one over here
> [Pointing to a small chair in the corner.] and just
> sat there with her hands held together and looking
> down. I got a feeling that I ought to make some
> conversation, so I said I had come in to see if
> John wanted to put in a telephone, and at that
> she started to laugh, and then she stopped and
> looked at me—scared. [The county attorney, who

→

has had his notebook out, makes a note.] I dunno,

maybe it wasn't scared. I wouldn't like to say it

was. . . . (speech 23)

Lewis Hale is the only man who tries to bring up the incompatibility in the Wrights' marriage, citing John Wright's dislike for conversation and adding, "I didn't know if what his wife wanted made much difference to John--" (speech 9), but George Henderson cuts him off before he can pursue this any further. Lewis Hale is a personable and talkative man--not at all like John Wright, whom Mrs. Hale likens to "a raw wind that gets to the bone" (speech 103). Lewis Hale is a social being who wants to communicate with the people around him, as his desire for a telephone party line indicates. The Hales' functional marriage shows that gender differences need not be insurmountable, but it also serves to highlight the truly devastating effect that a completely incompatible union can have on two people's lives. Mrs. Hale reminds us that even a marriage that "works" can be dehumanizing:

MRS. HALE. I might have known she needed help! I

know how things can be--for women.

I tell you it's queer, Mrs. Peters. We live close

together and we live far apart. We all go through

the same things--it's all just a different kind of the

same thing. (speech 136)

The great irony of the drama is that the women are able to accomplish what the men cannot: They establish the motive for the murder. They find evidence suggesting that John Wright viciously killed his wife's canary--her sole companion through long days of work around the house. More important, they recognize the damaging nature of a marriage based on the unequal status of the participants. Mrs. Hale and Mrs. Peters decide not to help the case against Minnie Wright, not because her husband killed a bird, but because he isolated her, made her life miserable for years, and cruelly destroyed her one

→

Wong 6

source of comfort. Without hope of help from the various misogynistic, paternalistic, and uncomprehending political, legal, and domestic power structures surrounding her, Minnie Wright took the law into her own hands. As the characters of George Henderson, Henry Peters, and Lewis Hale demonstrate, she clearly could not expect understanding from the men of her community.

→

Wong 7

Work Cited

Glaspell, Susan. <u>Trifles.</u> <u>The Prentice Hall Anthology of</u> <u>Women's Literature.</u> Ed. Deborah H. Holdstein. Upper Saddle River: Prentice, 2000. 301-11, 1038-48.

40g.3 Student MLA-style research paper analyzing two poems

The student essay that follows is a literary analysis of two poems by Claude McKay that draws on SECONDARY SOURCES.

Born in 1889 on the Caribbean island of Jamaica, Claude McKay moved to the United States in 1910 and became a highly respected poet. Paule Cheek, a student in a class devoted to writing about literature, chose to write about Claude McKay's nontraditional use of a very traditional poetic form, the sonnet. A sonnet has fourteen lines in a patterned rhyme and develops one idea. In secondary sources, Cheek found information about McKay's life that she felt gave her further insights into both the structure and the meaning of McKay's sonnets "In Bondage" and "The White City." For your reference, both poems appear below.

In Bondage

I would be wandering in distant fields
Where man, and bird, and beast, lives leisurely,
And the old earth is kind, and ever yields
Her goodly gifts to all her children free;
Where life is fairer, lighter, less demanding,
And boys and girls have time and space for play
Before they come to years of understanding—
Somewhere I would be singing, far away.
For life is greater than the thousand wars
Men wage for it in their insatiate lust,
And will remain like the eternal stars,
When all that shines to-day is drift and dust.
But I am bound with you in your mean graves,
O black men, simple slaves of ruthless slaves.

The White City

I will not toy with it nor bend an inch.
Deep in the secret chambers of my heart
I muse my life-long hate, and without flinch
I bear it nobly as I live my part.
My being would be skeleton, a shell,
If this dark Passion that fills my every mood,
And makes my heaven in the white world's hell,
Did not forever feed me vital blood.
I see the mighty city through a mist—
The strident trains that speed the goaded mass,
The poles and spires and towers vapor-kissed,
The fortressed port through which the great ships pass,
The tides, the wharves, the dens I contemplate,
Are sweet like wanton loves because I hate.

BACKGROUND
In "Using Reader-Response in a College Literature Class" (*Teaching English in the Two-Year College*, May 1995: 136–140), Derek Soles presents specific techniques to help students enjoy poetry in literature classes.

Cheek 1

Paule Cheek

Professor Bartlestone

English 112, Section 03

14 March 2004

Words in Bondage: Claude McKay's

Use of the Sonnet Form in Two Poems

The sonnet has remained one of the central poetic forms of the Western tradition for centuries. This fourteen-line form is easy for poets to learn but difficult to master. With its fixed rhyme schemes, number of lines, and meter, the sonnet form forces writers to be doubly creative while working within it. Many poets over the years have modified or varied the sonnet form, playing upon its conventions to keep it vibrant and original. One such writer was Jamaican-born Claude McKay (1889-1948).

The Jamaica of McKay's childhood was very different from turn-of-the-century America. Slavery had ended there in the 1830s, and McKay was able to grow up "in a society whose population was overwhelmingly black and largely free of the overt white oppression which constricted the lives of black Americans in the United States during this same period" (Cooper, Passion 5-6). This background could not have prepared McKay for what he encountered when he moved to America in his twenties. Lynchings, still common at that time, were on the rise, and during the Red Scare of 1919 there were dozens of racially motivated riots in major cities throughout the country. Thousands of homes were destroyed in these riots, and several black men were tortured and burned at the stake (Cooper, Claude McKay 97). McKay responded to these atrocities by raising an outraged cry of protest in his poems. In two of his sonnets from this period, "The White City" and "In Bondage," we can see McKay's mastery of the form and his skillful use of irony in the call for social change.

McKay's choice of the sonnet form as the vehicle for his protest poetry at first seems strange. Since his message was a

→

radical one, we might expect that the form of his poetry would
be revolutionary. Instead, McKay gives us sonnets--a poetic
form that dates back to the early sixteenth century and was
originally intended to be used exclusively for love poems. The
critic James R. Giles notes that this choice

> is not really surprising, since McKay's Jamaican
> education and reading had been based firmly upon the
> major British poets. From the point quite early in his life
> when he began to think of himself as a poet, his models
> were such major English writers as William Shakespeare,
> John Milton, William Wordsworth. He thus was committed
> from the beginning to the poetry which he had initially
> been taught to admire. (44)

McKay published both "The White City" and "In Bondage"
in 1922, and they are similar in many ways. Like most sonnets,
each has fourteen lines and is in iambic pentameter. The
diction is extremely elevated. For example, this quatrain from
"In Bondage" is almost Elizabethan in its word choice and order:

> For life is greater than the thousand wars
> Men wage for it in their insatiate lust,
> And will remain like the eternal stars,
> When all that shines to-day is drift and dust.
> (lines 8-12)

If this level of diction is reminiscent of Shakespeare, it
is no accident. Both poems employ the English sonnet rhyme
scheme (a b a b c d c d e f e f g g) and division into three
quatrains and a closing couplet. McKay introduces a touch of
his own, however. Although the English sonnet form calls for
the "thematic turn" to fall at the closing couplet, McKay defies
convention. He incorporates two turns into each sonnet instead
of one. This allows him to use the first "mini-turn" to further
develop the initial theme set forth in the first eight lines
while dramatically bringing the poem to a conclusion with
a forcefully ironic turn in the closing couplet. Specifically, in

→

QUOTATION: ON WRITING

To begin with, our perception of the world is deformed, incomplete. Then, our memory is selective. Finally, writing transforms.

—Claude Simon

Cheek 3

"The White City," McKay uses the additional turn to interrupt his description of his "Passion" with a vision of "the mighty city through a mist" (l. 9). In "In Bondage," he uses the additional turn to justify his desire to escape the violent existence that society has imposed on his people.

McKay also demonstrates his poetic ability through his choice of words within his customized sonnets. Consider the opening of "In Bondage":

> I would be wandering in distant fields
> Where man, and bird, and beast, lives leisurely,
> And the old earth is kind, and ever yields
> Her goodly gifts to all her children free;
> Where life is fairer, lighter, less demanding,
> And boys and girls have time and space for play
> Before they come to years of understanding—
> Somewhere I would be singing, far away. (ll. 1-8)

The conditional power of would in the first line, coupled with the alliterative wandering, subtly charms us into a relaxed, almost dreamlike state in which the poet can lead us gently through the rest of the poem. The commas in the second line force us to check our progress to a "leisurely" crawl, mirroring the people and animals that the line describes. By the time we reach the eighth line, we are probably ready to join the poet in this land of "somewhere . . . far away."

Then this optimistic bubble is violently burst by the closing couplet:

> But I am bound with you in your mean graves,
> O black men, simple slaves of ruthless slaves.
> (ll. 13-14)

In "The White City" McKay again surprises us. This time, he does so by turning the traditional love sonnet upside down; instead of depicting a life made endurable through an overpowering love, McKay shows us a life made bearable through a sustaining hate:

→

750

> I will not toy with it nor bend an inch.
> Deep in the secret chambers of my heart
> I muse my life-long hate, and without flinch
> I bear it nobly as I live my part.
> My being would be a skeleton, a shell,
> If this dark Passion that fills my every mood,
> And makes my heaven in the white world's hell,
> Did not forever feed me vital blood. (ll. 1-8)

If it were not for the presence of "life-long hate" in the third line, this opening would easily pass as part of a conventional love sonnet. However, as the critic William Maxwell notes in "On White City," the first quatrain is "designed to ambush those anticipating another rehearsal of love's powers." The emotion comes from "deep in the secret chambers" of the speaker's heart (l. 2), it allows him to transcend "the white world's hell" (l. 7), and it is a defining "Passion." Once again, however, McKay uses the couplet to defy our expectations by making it plain that he has used the form of the love sonnet only for ironic effect: "The tides, the wharves, the dens I contemplate, / Are sweet like wanton loves because I hate" (ll. 13-14).

McKay's impressive poetic ability made him a master of the sonnet form. His language could at times rival even Shakespeare's, and his creativity allowed him to adapt the sonnet to his own ends. His ironic genius is revealed in his use of one of Western society's most elevated poetic forms in order to critique that same society. He held that critique so strongly that shortly after publishing these poems, McKay spent six months in the Soviet Union, where he met with Communist leaders (Hathaway 282). McKay once described himself as "a man who was bitter because he loved, who was both right and wrong because he hated the things that destroyed love, who tried to give back to others a little of what he had got from them. . ." (qtd. in Barksdale and Kinnamon 491). As these two sonnets show, McKay gave back very much indeed.

→

QUOTATION: ON WRITING
We are nauseated by the sight of trivial personalities decomposing in the eternity of print.

—Virginia Woolf

Cheek 5

Works Cited

Barksdale, Richard, and Kenneth Kinnamon, eds. Black Writers of America: A Comprehensive Anthology. New York: Macmillan, 1972.

Cooper, Wayne F. Claude McKay: Rebel Sojourner in the Harlem Renaissance. Baton Rouge: Louisiana State UP, 1987.

---, ed. The Passion of Claude McKay. New York: Schocken, 1973.

Giles, James R. Claude McKay. Boston: Twayne, 1976.

Hathaway, Heather. "Claude McKay." The Concise Oxford Companion to African American Literature. Ed. William L. Andrews, Frances Smith Foster, and Trudier Harris. New York: Oxford UP, 2001. 282-83.

Maxwell, William. "On 'The White City.'" New Negro, Old Left: African American Writing and Communism between the Wars. New York: Columbia UP, 1999. Modern American Poetry. 5 Mar. 2004 <http://www.english.uiuc.edu/maps/poets/m_r/mckay/whitecity.htm>.

McKay, Claude. "In Bondage." Literature: An Introduction to Reading and Writing. 4th ed. Ed. Edgar V. Roberts and Henry E. Jacobs. Englewood Cliffs: Prentice, 1995. 772-73.

---. "The White City." Literature: An Introduction to Reading and Writing. 4th ed. Ed. Edgar V. Roberts and Henry E. Jacobs. Englewood Cliffs: Prentice, 1995. 967.

Chapter 41

Writing in the Social Sciences and Natural Sciences

BACKGROUND
The site <http://wac.colostate.edu> contains advice about teaching writing in various disciplines. One section of this Web site, the Teacher Exchange, shares assignments, syllabi, classroom activities, and so forth.

SOCIAL SCIENCES

41a How do I gather information in the social sciences?

The social sciences focus on the behavior of people as individuals and in groups. The social science field includes disciplines such as economics, education, geography, political science, psychology, and sociology. At some colleges, history is included in the social sciences; at others, it's part of the humanities.

The social sciences use several methods of inquiry. They include observations, interviews, questionnaires, and experiments. Some of these methods lead to *quantitative research,* which analyzes statistics and other numerical data, and other methods lead to *qualitative research,* which relies on careful descriptions and interpretations.

Observation is a common method for inquiry in the social sciences. To make observations, use whatever tools or equipment you might need: a laptop or notebook, sketching materials, tape recorders, cameras. As you observe, take complete and accurate notes. In a report of your observations, tell what tools or equipment you used, because your method might have influenced what you saw (for example, your taking photographs may make people act differently than they would otherwise).

Interviews are useful for gathering people's opinions and impressions of events. If you interview, remember that interviews are not always a completely reliable way to gather factual information, because people's memories are not precise and people's first impulse is to present themselves in the best light. If your only source of factors is interviews, try to interview as many people as possible so that you can cross-check the information. See Box 139, in section 32i, on taking notes during interviews.

TEACHING TIP

Faculty development efforts over the past twenty years have encouraged instructors in all disciplines to use a range of assignments. Some colleges require students to take a given number of "writing intensive" courses in disciplines other than English. Among them are "writing-to-learn" exercises, tasks in which the goal is to have students learn course material and develop insights, in contrast to their demonstrating specific discourse conventions or genres. Writing-to-learn assignments are often briefer and less formal than the kinds of case studies or research reports students prepare in the social and natural sciences. For these assignments, students might keep course journals or observation logs, or they might do practice interviews with classmates. Faculty might interrupt lectures to ask students to write for five minutes on a focused question based on the lecture or a concept in the textbook chapter assigned for that day. Or, faculty might give students narrowly framed problems that can be solved in one page of writing. Another strategy is to hand each student a 5-by-9-inch card on which they write—on one side only—their current knowledge of a definition or concept, and at the end of a lecture or discussion they use the other side of the card to write their new or amended knowledge.

In contrast with writing-to-learn, students needing to become fully fledged members of a discipline have to master that discipline's writing style. A powerful tool is systematic analysis and reflection. Students might write summaries of articles in professional journals. They might compare an article in a professional science journal with an article on the same topic in a more popular magazine such as *Discover* or *Scientific American.* You can also guide them to pay close attention to the use (or lack) of citations, the voice of the writing, the organizational method, the use (or lack) of narrative techniques, and so on.

The following questions can serve as models for student reflection. Students can apply them to studies they have read as well as to their own work. They can ask themselves these questions—and write down their

👁 **ALERTS:** (1) If you use abbreviations to speed your notetaking, be sure to write down what they stand for so that you'll be able to understand them later when you write up your observations. (2) Before you interview anyone, master any equipment you might need to use so that mechanical problems do not intrude on the interview process (32i). 👁

Questionnaires systematically gather information from a number of individuals using a pen-and-paper or Internet-based survey. To write questions for a questionnaire, use the guidelines in Box 173. When you administer a questionnaire, be sure to survey enough people so that you do not reach conclusions based on too small a sample of responses.

BOX 173   **SUMMARY**

 Guidelines for writing questions for a questionnaire

1. Define what you want to find out and then write questions that will elicit the information you seek.
2. Phrase questions so that they are easy to understand.
3. Use appropriate language (21b) and avoid artificial language (21h–21m).
4. Be aware that how you phrase your questions will determine whether the answers that you get truly reflect what people are thinking. Make sure that your choice of words does not imply what you want to hear.
5. Avoid questions that invite one-word answers about complex matters that call for a range of responses.
6. Test a draft of the questionnaire on a small group of people. If any question is misinterpreted or hard to understand, revise and retest it.

Experiments are also sometimes used in the social sciences. For example, if you want to learn how people react in a particular situation, you can set up that situation artificially and bring individuals into it to observe their behavior. People who take part in such experiments are usually called "subjects."

With all methods of inquiry in the social sciences, you need to be *ethical.* This means that you're required to treat subjects fairly and honestly. In addition, you aren't allowed to treat them in ways that could

→

cause them harm in body, mind, or reputation. In fact, it is standard now for professional social scientists to seek explicit written permission from their subjects, and panels of authority often review research proposals to make sure the studies are ethical.

41b How can I understand writing purposes and practices in the social sciences?

The purpose of much writing in the social sciences is explanatory. Writers try to explain both what a behavior is and why it happens. SUMMARY and SYNTHESIS (5e) are important fundamental strategies for explanatory writing in the social sciences.

ANALYSIS (4i and 5b) helps social scientists write about problems and their solutions. For example, an economist writing about financial troubles in a major automobile company might start by breaking the situation into parts: analyzing employee salaries and benefits, the selling prices of cars, and the costs of doing business. Next, the economist might show how these parts relate to the financial health of the whole company. Finally, the economist might suggest how specific changes would help solve the company's financial problems.

Social scientists often also use ANALOGY (4i) to make unfamiliar ideas clear. When an unfamiliar idea is compared to one that is more familiar, the unfamiliar idea becomes easier to understand. For example, sociologists may talk of the "culture shock" that some people feel when they enter a new society. The sociologists might compare this shock to the reaction of someone suddenly being moved hundreds of years into the future or the past.

Social scientists are particularly careful to define their KEY TERMS when they write, especially when they discuss complex social issues. For example, if you are writing a paper on substance abuse in the medical profession, you must first define what you mean by the terms *substance abuse* and *medical profession*. Does *substance* mean alcohol and drugs or only drugs? What defines *abuse*, and how do you measure it? By *medical profession*, do you mean nurses and doctors or only doctors? Without defining such terms, you confuse readers or lead them to wrong conclusions.

In college courses in the social sciences, your goal is usually to be a neutral observer, so most of the time you need to use the THIRD PERSON (*he, she, it, one, they*). Using the FIRST PERSON (*I, we, our*) is acceptable only when you write about your own reactions and experiences. Some writing in the social sciences overuses the PASSIVE VOICE (8o and 8p). Style manuals for the social sciences, however, recommend using the ACTIVE VOICE whenever possible.

Teaching Tip (continued)

answers—before, during, or after they write their papers.

- What is the purpose of this study?
- What might/did you expect to learn or prove?
- What barriers or obstacles might/did you encounter?
- How might/did you overcome them?
- What kinds of unexpected understandings might/did you encounter?
- What types of writing did you read?
- What type of paper did you choose to write, and why?

An additional strategy is to have students apply the scientific method and the parts of a science report to a formal, final reflective essay in a portfolio (see Portfolio Approaches and Activities for Writing Across the Curriculum in the annotations for instructors in Chapter 39). Instead of the scientific method's being the basis for the formal, final reflective essay, you might direct students (according to what your course covers) to reflect upon how they combined objective and subjective observations; dealt with the differences between primary and secondary sources; learned to read in the discipline for both literal and inferential thinking; employed both creative and critical thinking; and so on. This can truly be a bridge between reflecting, writing, and content courses.

41c How can I use documentation style in the social sciences?

If you use SOURCES when writing about the social sciences, you must credit these sources by using DOCUMENTATION. The most commonly used DOCUMENTATION STYLE in the social sciences is that of the American Psychological Association (APA). APA documentation style uses PARENTHETICAL REFERENCES in the body of a paper and a REFERENCES list at the end of a paper. APA documentation style is described in detail in Chapter 35. You can also find a sample student research paper using APA documentation style in section 35h.

Chicago Manual (CM) documentation style is sometimes used in the social sciences. The CM BIBLIOGRAPHIC NOTE style is described in detail in Chapter 36.

41d How can I write different types of papers in the social sciences?

Case studies and research papers are the two major types of papers written in the social sciences.

41d.1 Writing case studies in the social sciences

A case study is an intensive study of one group or individual. If you write a case study, describe situations as a *neutral observer.* Refrain from interpreting them unless your assignment says that you can add your interpretation after your report. Also, always differentiate between fact and opinion (5c.2). For example, you may observe nursing home patients lying on their sides in bed, facing the door. Describe exactly what you see: If you interpret or read into this observation that patients are lonely and watching the door for visitors, you could be wrong. Perhaps because medicines are injected in the right hip, patients are more comfortable lying on their left side, which just happens to put them in a position facing the door. Such work requires FIELD RESEARCH (32i).

A case study is usually presented in a relatively fixed format, but the specific parts and their order vary. Most case studies contain the following components: (1) basic identifying information about the individual or group; (2) a history of the individual or group; (3) observations of the individual's or group's behavior; and (4) conclusions and, perhaps, recommendations as a result of the observations.

41d.2 Writing research papers in the social sciences

RESEARCH WRITING in the social sciences can be based on your FIELD RESEARCH (41d.1 on case studies; 41a on interviews, questionnaires, or data analysis). Papers that primarily explain your own original research based on primary sources are sometimes called *research reports*. More often for students, social science research requires you to consult SEC-ONDARY SOURCES (see Chapters 31 and 32, especially 32e on using periodicals and 32f on using specialized reference works). These sources are usually articles and books that report, summarize, and otherwise discuss the findings of other people's research. You can find a sample of a student research paper using secondary sources, written for an introductory psychology course, in Chapter 35.

NATURAL SCIENCES

41e How do I gather information in the natural sciences?

The natural sciences include disciplines such as astronomy, biology, chemistry, geology, and physics. The sciences focus on natural phenomena. Scientists form and test hypotheses, which are assumptions made in order to prove their logical soundness and consequences in the real world. They do this to explain CAUSE AND EFFECT (5h) as systematically and objectively as possible.

The scientific method, commonly used in the sciences to make discoveries, is a procedure for gathering information related to a specific hypothesis. The scientific method is the cornerstone of all inquiry in the sciences. Box 174 gives guidelines for using the scientific method.

BOX 174 **SUMMARY**

 Guidelines for using the scientific method

1. Formulate a tentative explanation—known as a *hypothesis*—for a scientific phenomenon. Be as specific as possible.
2. Read and summarize previously published information related to your hypothesis.
3. Plan and outline a method of investigation to uncover the information needed to test your hypothesis.
4. Experiment, following exactly the investigative procedures you have outlined.
5. Observe closely the results of the experiment, and write notes carefully.
6. Analyze the results. If they prove the hypothesis to be false, rework the investigation and begin again. If the results confirm the hypothesis, say so.
7. Write a report of your research. At the end, you can suggest additional hypotheses that might be investigated.

41f What are writing purposes and practices in the natural sciences?

Because scientists usually write to inform their AUDIENCE about factual information, SUMMARY and SYNTHESIS are important fundamental writing techniques (5e).

Exactness is extremely important in scientific writing. Readers expect precise descriptions of procedures and findings, free of personal biases. Scientists expect to be able to *replicate*—repeat step by step—the experiment or process the researcher carried out and obtain the same outcome.

Completeness is as important as exactness in scientific writing. Without complete information, a reader can misunderstand the writer's message and reach a wrong conclusion. For example, a researcher investigating how plants grow in different types of soil needs to report these facts: an analysis of each soil type, the amount of daylight exposure for each plant, the soil's moisture content, the type and amount of fertilizer used, and all other related facts. By including all this information, the researcher tells the reader how the conclusion in the written report was founded in the experiment or analysis. Specifically, in the soil example just described, plant growth turns out to depend on a combination of soil type, fertilizer, and watering.

Because science writing depends largely on objective observation rather than subjective comments, scientists generally avoid using the FIRST PERSON (*I, we, our*) in their writing. Another reason to avoid the first person is that the sciences generally focus on the experiment rather than on the person doing the experimenting.

When writing for the sciences, you are often expected to follow fixed formats, which are designed to summarize a project and present its results efficiently. In your report, organize the information to achieve clarity and precision. Writers in the sciences sometimes use charts, graphs, tables, diagrams, and other illustrations to present material. In fact, illustrations in many cases can explain complex material more clearly than words can.

41g How do I use documentation style in the natural sciences?

If you use SECONDARY SOURCES when you write about the sciences, you are required to credit your sources by using DOCUMENTATION. DOCUMENTATION STYLES in the various sciences differ somewhat. Ask your instructor which style to use.

The Council of Science Editors (CSE) has compiled style and documentation guidelines for the life sciences, the physical sciences, and mathematics. CSE documentation guidelines are described in sections 36c and 36d.

41h   How do I write different types of papers in the natural sciences?

Two major types of papers in the sciences are *reports* and *reviews.*

41h.1   Writing science reports

Science reports tell about observations and experiments; such reports are sometimes called laboratory reports when they describe laboratory experiments. Formal reports feature the eight elements identified in Box 175. Less formal reports, which are sometimes assigned in introductory

---

BOX 175   **SUMMARY**

Parts of a science report

1. **Title.** This is a precise description of what your report is about. Your instructor may require a *title page* that lists the title, your name, the course name and section, your instructor's name, and the date. If so, there is no recommended format in CSE style; generally, students use APA format (35g) or their instructor's.

2. **Abstract.** This is a short overview of the report. Readers may review this to decide whether or not your research is of interest to them.

3. **Introduction.** This section states the purpose behind your research and presents the hypothesis. Any needed background information and a review of the literature appear here.

4. **Methods and Materials.** This section describes the equipment, material, and procedures used.

5. **Results.** This section provides the information obtained from your efforts. Charts, graphs, and photographs help present the data in a way that is easy for readers to grasp.

6. **Discussion.** This section presents your interpretation and evaluation of the results. Did your efforts support your hypothesis? If not, can you suggest why not? Use concrete evidence in discussing your results.

7. **Conclusion.** This section lists conclusions about the hypothesis and the outcomes of your efforts, with particular attention given to any theoretical implications that can be drawn from your work. Be specific in suggesting further research.

8. **Cited References.** This list presents references cited in the review of the literature, if any. Its format conforms to the requirements of the documentation style in the particular science that is your subject.

college courses, might not include an abstract or a review of the literature. Ask your instructor which sections to include in your report.

Sample student science report

The sample science report here is by a student in an intermediate course in biology. Like the sample below, your typed report would likely follow APA format for margins, page numbering, and title page. The text and references would follow CSE-style recommendations.

Effectiveness 1

Adam Furman

Biology 201, Lab

Professor Joshua Mann

November 13, 2003

Title of report ⟶ The Effectiveness of Common Antibiotics

Title of sub-section ⟶ Introduction ⟵ Abstract omitted on this sample

The purpose of this experiment was to test the effectiveness of antibiotics against two common bacteria.

Antibiotics are substances that inhibit life processes of bacteria. There are two types of antibiotics. One interferes with cell wall synthesis, causing death. The other disrupts protein synthesis, thus preventing replication.

Escherichia coli is a gram-negative bacterium. It is found in the colon of many mammals, including humans. Commonly, it contaminates beef and chicken products. Staphylococcus epidermidis is a gram-positive bacterium found naturally on the skin. This bacterium is often the cause of infected burns and cuts. Both bacteria were used in this experiment.

It is hypothesized that five chemical antibiotics will be effective against both bacteria. Also hypothesized is that two natural antimicrobials, Echinacea and garlic, would not work very well.

Methods and Materials

Using aseptic techniques, two petri dishes were inoculated. Staphylococcus epidermidis was used on one dish and Escherichia coli on a second dish. A sterile paper disc was saturated with Streptomycin. The disc was placed on one of the

⟶

Effectiveness 2

dishes. The process was repeated for the other dish. Both dishes were marked with identification and location of the paper discs. Each of the following was also saturated on paper discs and placed into its own zone on both dishes: sterile water (control), Ampicillin, Erythromycin, Chloramphenicol, Tetracycline, Gentamycin, Echinacea, and garlic.

The dishes were incubated overnight at room temperature. The zone of inhibition of growth in centimeters was measured and recorded.

Results

Streptomycin, a protein synthesis disrupter, worked effectively to prevent growth of the S. epidermidis and the E. coli. Tetracycline inhibited the reproduction of the S. epidermidis and the E. coli. Ampicillin, a common bactericide, worked better on the S. epidermidis than the E. coli, because the S. epidermidis is gram positive and the E. coli is gram negative. Gentamycin effectively prevented the growth of E. coli. Erythromycin and Chloramphenicol behaved similarly to the Ampicillin.

The antibiotics behaved as expected in regard to effectiveness against gram-positive and gram-negative bacteria. As hypothesized, the Echinacea inhibited growth only slightly, indicating that it probably would not function as an antibiotic. The garlic had a zone of inhibition greater than expected for a non-antibiotic. Zero centimeters of inhibition from the sterile water control demonstrates that there was no contamination of the experiment.

Discussion section omitted in this sample ———▶

Conclusion

The results imply that the Ampicillin would be an effective treatment against S. epidermidis infection and Gentamycin would prove effective in treating an infection of E. coli.

As with any experiment, it would be wise to repeat the tests again to check for accuracy. Other antibiotics could be tested against a larger range of bacteria for broader results.

No Cited References needed in this type of science report ———▶

41h.2 Writing science reviews

A science review is a paper discussing published information on a scientific topic or issue. The purpose of the review is SUMMARY: to assemble for readers all the current knowledge about the topic or issue. Sometimes, the purpose of a science review is SYNTHESIS: to suggest a new interpretation of the old material. Reinterpretation combines the older views with new and more complete or more compelling information. In such reviews, the writer must present evidence to persuade readers that the new interpretation is valid.

If you're required to write a science review, you want to (1) choose a very limited scientific issue currently being researched; (2) use information that is current—the more recently published the articles, books, and journals you consult, the better; (3) accurately PARAPHRASE (33i) and SUMMARIZE (33j) material; and (4) DOCUMENT your sources (Chapters 34–36). If your review runs longer than two or three pages, you might want to use headings to help your reader understand the organization and idea progression of your paper. See Chapters 32–33 for advice on finding and using sources.

Chapter 42

Business and Public Writing

QUOTATION: ON WRITING
If the first novel has been successful, the writer buys a serious, writerly object that bespeaks investment and confidence—a word processor, a new bookshelf, reams of white paper. . . . In any case, a new and bigger wastebasket.

—Jayne Anne Phillips

Business and public writing start where writing in all other disciplines does, with thinking about your PURPOSE and your AUDIENCE. This chapter explains how to write typical business correspondence—letters, memos, resumes, job application letters, and e-mail messages. The second part of this chapter discusses types of public writing, writing intended for members of your community, for readers in general, or for public officials. Box 176 gives you general guidelines for business and public writing.

BOX 176 SUMMARY

 Guidelines for business and public writing

- Consider your audience's needs and expectations.
- Have a clear purpose.
- Put essential information first.
- Make your points concisely, clearly, and directly.
- Use conventional business formats.

BUSINESS WRITING

42a How do I write and format a business letter?

Business letters give information, build goodwill, or establish a foundation for discussions or transactions. Experts in business and government agree that the letters likely to get results are short, simple, direct, and human. Following is the most useful advice for writing business letters:

WHAT ELSE?
Strategies and Resources is a free 400-page book written especially for instructors who adopt this handbook. It discusses in detail the teaching of workplace and business writing and includes many examples of business letters and memos, resumes, and proposals and reports.

- Address the person by name.
- Tell what your letter is about in the first paragraph.
- Be honest, clear, and specific.
- Use correct EDITED AMERICAN ENGLISH.
- Be positive and natural.
- Edit ruthlessly.

Keep the following points in mind when writing a business letter:

- **Format:** Select block style (in which all lines begin at the left margin) or modified block style (lines for inside address and body begin at left margin; heading, closing, and signature begin about halfway across the page).
- **Paper:** Use only 8 1/2-by-11-inch paper. The most professional colors are white or very light beige. (Business letters from other countries are often on other sizes of paper. Still, write back on U.S. and Canadian standard size.)
- **Letterhead:** When writing from a company, use its official letterhead. If you're writing on your own behalf, use or create your own letterhead on your computer. Center your full name, address, and phone number at the top of the page. Use a larger size font than for the content of the letter. Avoid any font that's fancy or loud. After all, your letter carries a serious business message.
- **Name of recipient:** Be as specific as possible. An exact name (or at least a specific category of people) tells readers you have taken the time to do some research. If you use a category, place the key word first: For example, use "Billing Department," not "Department of Billing." Avoid using "To Whom It May Concern," which implies you didn't do the necessary research and expect the person who receives the letter to do the work of figuring out the specific recipient. Such letters are often ignored.
- **Spacing:** Use single spacing within paragraphs and double spacing between paragraphs.
- **Content:** Write using CONCISE and clear language. Open by explaining immediately your purpose for writing. Check that your information is accurate and includes all relevant facts. Never repeat yourself. Use as even-handed a TONE as possible. Indeed, you can express disappointment or make a complaint without resorting to inflammatory language. A reasonable approach always gets the best results.
- **Tone:** Use a medium LEVEL OF FORMALITY in word choice and style.
- **Final copy:** Proofread carefully. Your neat, error-free letter reflects well on you and your company or organization. Also, your reader is more likely to read it because you took the time to show the importance of your message and your respect for your reader.

In a business letter, always use GENDER-NEUTRAL LANGUAGE in the salutation (the opening "To" or "Dear"). If you don't know the specific person to whom you need to address your letter, take the steps listed in Box 177; see also 21g.

BOX 177   SUMMARY

 ## Writing a gender-neutral salutation

1. Telephone the company to which you are sending the letter. State your reason for sending the letter, and ask for the name of the person you want to receive it.

2. Never address the person by first name. For a man, use Mr. or another appropriate title. For a woman, use Ms. or another appropriate title, unless you are specifically told to use Miss or Mrs. or another title such as Dr.

3. If you use a title alone instead of a name, keep the title generic and gender-neutral.

   NO Dear Sir: [obviously sexist]

   Dear Sir or Madam: [*Madam* is an out-of-date term, and few women like its connotation]

   YES Dear Human Resources Officer:

   Dear IBM Sales Manager:

The sample envelope below and sample business letter on the next page are models of typical formats you can use.

Jan Dubitz
742 Lincoln Hall
Northeast College
2038 Washington Blvd.
Chicago, IL 60312

ENVELOPE: Fold letter in thirds horizontally and insert in an appropriate-size envelope. Place your return address in the upper left corner and the mailing address in the middle of the envelope.

Ms. Yolanda Harper
Abco Rental Company
1249 Logan Rd.
Chicago, IL 60312

Sample envelope

TEACHING TIP

Combine business writing formats such as business letters and resumes (42a–42c) with literature or content course topics. For example, you might ask students to create a resume based on the biography of a significant author, inventor, or leader. Or perhaps reward students for creating and sending real-life documents, such as letters to the editor of a newspaper or periodical or to a federal, state, or local politician. These documents, along with any reciprocal communication, become substantial portfolio entries that show commitment and mastery, if you use portfolios in your writing class (see the annotations for instructors in Chapter 39).

Jan Dubitz
742 Lincoln Hall Northeast College
2038 Washington Blvd.
Chicago, IL 60312
(210) 555-3723

September 14, 2003

▲
4 spaces
▼

Ms. Yolanda Harper
Abco Rental Company
1249 Logan Rd.
Chicago, IL 60312

Dear Ms. Harper:

▲
2 spaces
▼

SALUTATION: Use an appropriate title (*Mr., Ms., Dr., Professor*) and the person's name. If you do not know the name, use a title (*Dean of Students, Human Resources Coordinator*). Add a colon at the end of the salutation.

I rented a refrigerator from your company on August 27. After only two weeks, the freezer compartment no longer keeps food frozen. Per the rental agreement, this is my written request for a replacement refrigerator. The agreement states that you will replace the refrigerator within five business days from the receipt of my letter.

I will call you next week to arrange the exchange. Thank you for your prompt attention.

Sincerely,
━━━━━ **CLOSING:** Capitalize only the first word (*Yours truly, Sincerely yours*) and follow with a comma.

4 spaces   *Jan Dubitz* ━━━━━ **SIGNATURE:** If you have a title, type it underneath your name. Sign letter in space above your name.
Jan Dubitz

Enc: Copy of rental agreement ━━━━━ **OTHER:** Use *Enc:* or *Enclosure:* if you include material *with* your letter. Use *cc:* to indicate that you have sent any courtesy copies.

Sample business letter

42b How do I write a memo?

Many business memos are sent through e-mail, although some are printed and circulated on paper. Be specific, not general, in your "subject" line. Prefer "Results of Evaluation" over "Update." Readers need to determine quickly the importance of a memo by reading the headings, especially the "subject" line. A memo from a supervisor asking for sales figures will receive prompt attention, whereas a memo from the office manager about new forms for ordering supplies will probably not receive a careful reading until the time comes to order more supplies.

The AUDIENCE for a memo, sent through e-mail or on paper, is usually "local." For example, in the workplace, local audiences can be senior management, other levels of supervisors or managers, people at your level, all employees, or customers. Non-local audiences can be people who share interests (religious, political, or leisure-time groups) or causes (environment, education, health care). Be as specific as possible in naming your memo's audience on the "to" line.

The PURPOSE of memos, whether sent through e-mail or on paper, is to give new information; to SUMMARIZE, clarify, or SYNTHESIZE known information; to put information officially on the record; to make a request or suggestion; or to record recent activities and outcomes. Most word processing software provides formats for paper memos. All e-mail services provide an on-screen format for entering headings. For example, in versions of Microsoft Word™, you can click FILE>NEW>MEMO. Select the style you want—"Professional" is a good choice for workplace use. A memo has the following parts:

- **Headings**

TO:	[Your audience, named as specifically as possible]
FROM:	[Your name]
DATE:	[Month, day, and year you're writing]
SUBJECT:	[Memo's topic, specifically and concisely stated]

- **Contents**

  Introductory paragraph: State the memo's purpose and give needed background information.

  Body paragraph(s): State the point of the memo and why it's worth the recipient's time to read it. Or, as the sample memo in this chapter shows, give the data required.

  Conclusion: End with a one- or two-sentence summary or, when appropriate, with a specific recommendation. If the memo is short, like the sample memo, end either with a sentence of instructions or a thank-you message.

BACKGROUND
In *Moving Beyond Academic Discourse: Composition Studies and the Public Sphere* (Carbondale: Southern Illinois University Press, 2002), Christian Weisser builds a case for having students do increased amounts of writing for readers beyond the academy.

BACKGROUND
The site <http://jobstar.org/tools/resume/index.cfm>, which is sponsored by JobStar, offers helpful definitions on various types of resumes as well as suggestions for creating a customized resume.

Before sending your memo, proofread it to eliminate grammar and spelling errors, to check the accuracy of the content, and to make sure it's clearly and concisely stated. Perhaps ask others to review it before you send it out.

One or at most two pages is the expected length of a memo. If you need more pages, you're writing a report (see 42f and sample on opposite page).

42c   How do I create a resume?

A **resume** details your employment experience, education, and other accomplishments for a potential employer. Because your resume will be compared to those of numerous other applicants, take time to make a favorable impression. Format your resume so that it's easy to read, and include only information relevant to the position available. A worksheet to help you think through what to say, and not say, in a resume appears on pages 771–72.

Use the guidelines below for writing a resume; also, examine the sample on page 770. A helpful Web site for writing resumes is <http://www1.umn.edu/ohr/ecep/resume/>.

- Use the Resume Worksheet to draft your resume.
- Adjust the emphasis in your resume to fit your purpose: For a job as a computer programmer, you need to emphasize different facts about yourself than what you'd offer when applying to be a retail salesperson.
- Fit all information on one page (or two at the most—but one-pagers usually appeal to employers more) by stressing what will interest your potential employer. If you must use a second page, put the most important information on the first page.
- Put the most recent item first in each category.
- Use clear headings to separate blocks of information.
- Write telegram-style under the headings. Start with verb phrases, not with the word *I*, and omit *a, an, the*. Write, for example, "Created new computer program to organize company's spreadsheets," not "*I* created *a* new computer program to organize *the* company's spreadsheets."
- Don't pad entries with irrelevant information or wordy writing.
- *Never* lie.
- Include references or state that you can provide them "upon request" (and have them ready to go).
- Print your resume on high-quality, white or very light beige paper.
- *Multilingual writers:* For a job in the United States or Canada, never include personal information that may be expected in other countries. For example, don't state your age, marital status, or religion.

TO: English Teaching Assistants

FROM: Professor Thomas Nevers, Director,

         First-Year Composition

DATE: December 1, 2003

SUBJECT: New Computer Programs

Several new writing programs will be installed in the English computer labs. Training sessions are scheduled during the week before classes begin next semester.

Tuesday, January 6	9:00-11:00 a.m.
Wednesday, January 7	1:00-3:00 p.m.
Thursday, January 8	8:30-10:30 a.m.
Friday, January 9	1:30-3:30 p.m.

Please stop by my office by December 12 to sign up for one of the two-hour workshops.

Sample memo

BACKGROUND

Service learning projects combine classroom learning with volunteer work in a community setting, usually a not-for-profit agency. They can be exceptional ways for students both to learn real-world business writing skills and to contribute to the lives of others. See Robin J. Crews, *Higher Education Service-Learning Sourcebook* (Westport, CT: Oryx/Greenwood, 2001).

Margaret Lorentino
1338 Sunflower Lane
Rochelle, IL 61068
(815) 555-3756

OBJECTIVE: Seeking a full/part-time position as a medical transcriptionist to utilize my medical, computer, and office skills

EDUCATION: Certificate of Completion, Medical Transcription
                 Kishwaukee College, Malta, IL, December 2003
                 Bachelor of Science, Marketing
                 Northern Illinois University, DeKalb, IL, May 2003
                 Associate in Arts; Studied Nursing and Business
                 Harper Junior College, Palatine, IL, December 1990

EMPLOYMENT: Kishwaukee College, Malta, IL, January 2000–Present
                 Lab Assistant and Computer Skills Teacher
                 RTD Real Estate, Muncie, IN, August 1994–August 1995
                 Receptionist, Accounting Assistant
                 Northwestern Mutual Life, Schaumburg, IL,
                 May 1991–July 1992
                 Sales Assistant
                 Reliable Personnel, Park Ridge, IL, May 1990–May 1991
                 Temporary Employment Manager

SKILLS: Computer
                 • Experienced with Microsoft Office 2003
                 • Type 60 wpm
                 • Have experience with Lotus, Excel, and Access
                 • Teach basic computer skills in first-year
                   college English classes

                 Organizational
                 • Girl Scout leader, soccer coach, Sunday school
                   teacher
                 • Trained employees in data entry and accounting
                   principles
                 • Managed a temporary workforce of 20–30 employees

REFERENCES: Available upon request

Sample resume

RESUME WORKSHEET

Photocopy and fill in this resume worksheet to help you create
your own resume.

(Name) _____

(Address) _____

(City, State, Zip) _____

(Home Telephone) _____

(Work Telephone) _____

(Fax Number, if one) _____

(E-mail Address) _____

Position Desired or Career Objective _____
_____
_____

[Include below only if relevant and meaningful; add more lines in a category,
as necessary.]

Education (most recent education first)

1. (Degree or Certificate) _____ (Dates) _____
   (Institution) _____
   (Major or Area of Concentration) _____

2. (Degree or Certificate) _____ (Dates) _____
   (Institution) _____
   (Major or Area of Concentration) _____

Experience (most recent experience first)

1. (Job Title) _____ (Dates) _____
   (Employer) _____
   (Responsibilities and Accomplishments) _____
   _____
   _____

2. (Job Title) _____ (Dates) _____
   (Employer) _____
   (Responsibilities and Accomplishments) _____
   _____
   _____

→

BACKGROUND

EmoticonUniverse.com, found at <http://emoticonuniverse.com/>, is a useful resource that features popular e-mail acronyms, symbols, and figures. Of course, for business writing, you want to warn students away from using them, but telling students about the site is fun and allows you to emphasize when emoticons are appropriate.

License or Certification, if any (nursing, accounting, massage therapy, etc.)

1. (License) _____ (Dates) _____
   (Issuing Agency) _____

2. (License) _____ (Dates) _____
   (Issuing Agency) _____

Related Experience

(Description) _____ (Dates) _____
(Organization or Company) _____
(Duties/Accomplishments) _____

Honors/Awards, if any

_____
_____
_____

Publications/Presentations, if any

_____ (Dates) _____
_____ (Dates) _____

Activities/Interests (clubs, organizations, volunteer work)

_____
_____
_____

Special Abilities, Skills, Knowledge (languages, computer, travel)

_____
_____
_____

References (personal, professional)

_____
_____
_____

42d How do I compose a job application letter?

A job application letter always needs to accompany your resume. Avoid simply repeating what is already in the resume. Instead, acquaint yourself with available descriptions of the position and its responsibilities, and connect the company's expectations to your experience. Stress how your background has prepared you for this position. Follow the guidelines below for writing your letter; also, examine the sample job application letter.

- Use one page only.
- Use the same name, content, and format guidelines you use for a business letter (42a).
- Open by identifying the position you want to apply for.
- Address the letter to a specific person. If you can't find out a name, use a title (such as "Human Resources Coordinator"). Avoid using "To Whom It May Concern" (42a) because it tells employers you've made only a minimal effort.
- Think of your letter as a polite sales pitch about you. Don't be shy, but don't exaggerate what you can do for the company if you get the job.
- Explain how your background will meet the requirements of the job at this workplace in particular.
- Stress your qualifications for the specific position for which you're applying.
- If the job will be your first, give your key attributes—keeping them relevant and true—such as that you're punctual, self-disciplined, a "team player," eager to learn, and ready to work hard for the company.
- State when you're available for an interview and also how you can be reached easily by mail and telephone (and cellphone, if you have one).
- Edit and proofread carefully. Even one misspelled word can hurt your chances.

The sample letter on the next page is by Margaret Lorentino, a mother with young children, who seeks a position that would allow her to work at home. She is responding to a newspaper ad for a medical transcription position. The format is modified block style.

WHAT ELSE?

Strategies and Resources, a 400-page book provided free to faculty who use this handbook, offers specific, practical ways to apply this statement: "Writing skills that have previously been only marginally palatable take on the allure of real life when they are taught using documents from the world of business."

Margaret Lorentino
1338 Sunflower Lane
Rochelle, IL 61068

December 1, 2003

Ms. Arlene Chang
Employment Coordinator
Rockford Medical Center
820 N. Main St.
Rockford, IL 61103

Dear Ms. Chang:

I had a chance to talk with you last spring about your company at the Kishwaukee College Job Fair. I am very interested in the medical transcription position that I noticed in the <u>Rockford Register Star</u> on November 29.

I will be completing my Medical Transcription Certificate at the end of December. I have taken courses in medical transcription, medical office procedures, and keyboarding, as well as numerous computer courses. I have a bachelor's degree in marketing from Northern Illinois University and also studied nursing for almost a year at Harper Junior College. I believe that this background would help me in this position.

The enclosed resume will give you the details of my experience and qualifications. I think that my experience and education make a great combination for this position. I am available for an interview at your convenience. My home phone number is (815) 555-3756.

Sincerely yours,

Margaret Lorentino

Margaret Lorentino

Sample job application letter

42e **What are guidelines for writing e-mail?**

Today, a great deal of business and other communication is conducted by e-mail. Business and professional e-mails differ from casual, everyday e-mails and instant messages that you send to friends and family. An e-mail resembles a business memo, but it is relayed in electronic form. Follow the guidelines below for writing a business e-mail.

- Write a specific, not general, topic in the Subject box. Unless you do this, you won't capture your reader's attention. After all, attention spans when reading e-mail can be quite short, especially for business people who get dozens of e-mails a day and therefore tend to skim the screen.

- Use block style by single-spacing within paragraphs and double-spacing between paragraphs.

- Never write in all capital letters or all lowercase letters. Not only are they hard (and annoying) to read, but all capital letters are considered "flaming," the written equivalent of shouting. This is poor, even insulting, "netiquette," the word for etiquette online.

- Use bulleted or numbered lists when itemizing.

- Keep your message brief and your paragraphs short. Reading a screen is harder on the eyes than is reading a print document, which means that business people tend to skim e-mail.

- Be cautious about what you say in a business e-mail. After all, the recipient can forward to others without your permission, even though this practice is considered unethical and rude. And, of course, never give personal information to strangers, and never give credit information on a nonsecure site.

- Forward an e-mail message *only* if you have asked the original sender for permission.

- Check your e-mail and any attachments to make sure your message is clear, your TONE is appropriate, and your spelling, grammar, and punctuation are correct.

- Use emoticons only if you are sure the reader appreciates them. :-) Some people do not. :-(

- Never make personal attacks on others, share jokes that would offend some groups of people, or gossip in a business e-mail.

- Never "spam" (send unsolicited, or "junk," mail).

When you want to include in your e-mail a separate document, such as a business report, a proposal, or the like, compose it in a word processing program, and then attach the document to an e-mail message using the "Attachments" function of your e-mail service. Attached documents, rather than copied and pasted documents, look better because

BACKGROUND: ON "PUBLIC WRITING" AND "CIVIC DISCOURSE"

Writing teachers and scholars have long been vexed by what to call the huge variety of writings produced for nonexpert readers who are reading not in academic or vocational settings but, rather, as members of a diffuse and varied public. A common term, which we generally adopt here, is "public writing." Indeed, over twenty-five years ago, Janice Lauer, Gene Montague, Andrea Lunsford, and Janet Emig distinguished between "four worlds of writing: the academic, the vocational, the personal, and the public" (*The Four Worlds of Writing*, New York: Harper and Row, 1981). However, "public" has always been something of a fuzzy term. Defined as the opposite of "private," for example, "public" writings could include nearly anything intended for other readers. The conventional limiting distinction, then, has been between audiences that are defined by some specialized knowledge or affiliation (including different academic, professional, and vocational discourse communities, such as literary scholars, lawyers, and restaurant operators) and audiences either with no specific identities or, at most, some broader affiliation (for example, residents of a certain town or locality, people of specific genders or political beliefs, or even people who share hobbies).

Complicating definitions even further are the various reasons that people write for these public audiences. Both newspaper editorials and comic strips are public writings. So are brochures and manifestos—but also poems and memoirs and novels. A published letter to the editor is public writing, but what about a letter to a legislator? In that last instance, no one beyond the legislator and his or her staff is likely to read it. But surely the letter is not academic, personal, or vocational discourse.

In light of this situation, several rhetoricians have adopted a more precise name for the kinds of public writing most common in undergraduate composition courses: "civic discourse." The word *civic* invokes the rhetorical situations that are part and parcel of functioning as an active citizen in a democratic

⟶

they maintain the original formatting (margins, spacing, italics). One word of caution: If an attached file is large, alert your recipient to its size so that the person can decide whether to download it—and ask whether they'd prefer to receive the document by fax or in the mail.

In the sample e-mail below, a reporter is writing to MP3 users on a listserv (Internet discussion group) for the first time.

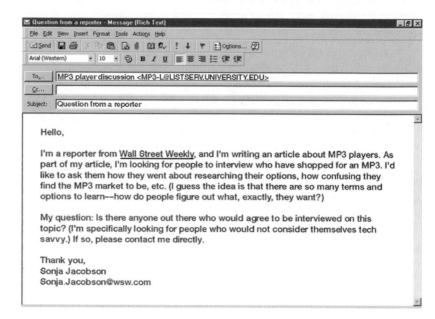

E-Mail to listserv of MP3 users

PUBLIC WRITING

In addition to ACADEMIC WRITING and BUSINESS WRITING, you may also find occasion to do *public writing*—writing addressed either to members of your community, the community as a whole, or public officials. Some public writing is also known as *civic writing* because you're communicating as a citizen in order to affect actions or beliefs in a democratic society.

Examples of writing for the public include letters to the editor of a newspaper or magazine, to your congressional representative, and to a group you either belong to or want to address. You might write a newspaper article to publicize a local theater group, a brochure to draw new members into a service organization, a proposal to your town government for building a park at the site of a burned-down warehouse, or an e-mail to your state representative urging her to vote for a certain bill.

Writing for the Internet is perhaps the broadest form of public writing, in the sense that anything you post there is available for anyone to read—anyone, that is, with access to the Internet. On the Internet, you might post book reviews on a bookseller's Web site or a message about an upcoming concert to a newsgroup. You might create a Web site for an organization, a social cause, or a special interest group and share information and ideas through your site. You might keep a Web log, or Blog (see 42h). Although the Internet provides easy access to broad publics, access does not guarantee attention. The best Web site in the world has little impact if no one visits it.

In all of these examples—and you can add many more of your own—you are generally writing for an AUDIENCE that you do not know personally. You are also discussing subjects that you think affect others, not just you alone. For these reasons, public writing requires that you take special care in analyzing your audience, being honest, and establishing your credibility.

"Establishing credibility" means convincing your readers that they need or want to listen to you. You do this by being accurate and honest and by explaining your connection with the reader(s). What do you have in common with your readers? How does your experience make you a reputable source—or, have you done research to become a knowledgeable source? Can you name other authorities who agree with your perspective? Readers can discern fake information quite quickly.

For example, if you are writing a letter to the editor of your local newspaper, you will gain credibility if you begin, "As a resident of Green County for twelve years," and then go on to give your opinion. By establishing yourself first as a member of your audience's community, you convey that you have a sincere and long-standing interest in the welfare of that community. Or suppose you are writing to ask one of your state senators to support a bill for a new wildlife refuge. You might present your argument on the basis of your research into the benefits and drawbacks of setting aside the land. In this way, you make yourself credible by demonstrating that you understand the complexities of the issue.

Sections 42f, 42g, and 42h describe three common types of public writing for civic purposes: reports, letters to the editor or political representatives, and other types.

42f   How do I write reports for the public?

Reports for the public vary in length, format, and content. An "action brief" from a political organization might consist of a few pages detailing recent developments on an issue of concern. A "technology update" from a local association of people with a shared, specialized hobby might contain news of technological advances, along with critical reviews and, perhaps, information on where to purchase each item. An "impact

Background on "Public Writing" and "Civic Discourse" (continued)
society. Writing in such situations aims to affect law, policy, practices, knowledge, and beliefs. It tends to have a persuasive emphasis at its core, even if that emphasis is muted. To promote the term *civic discourse* is to remind teachers and students of the roots of composition studies in ancient Greek and Roman rhetoric.

While civic discourse is generally also public writing, not all public writing is necessarily civic discourse. Plenty of nonfiction is published for personal or artistic expression and for entertainment or contemplation—not necessarily to compel fellow citizens toward a certain action or stance.

study" may explain the effect that a proposed development will have on the local environment or economy.

Write your material in an evenhanded TONE so that your credibility is supported by your fairness. If you want to criticize something, be sure your argument is well reasoned and supported—and that it lacks BIAS or malice toward any person(s) or specific idea(s). This doesn't means that your writing needs to be limp. Indeed, you can choose writing that's spirited, enthusiastic, and even stirring.

To write a public report, follow the guidelines in Box 178.

BOX 178   **SUMMARY**

Writing a public report

- Decide how far to go in your report. Will you only inform, or will you also analyze the information you present? Or—going one step further—will you make a recommendation based on the information and your analysis?

- State your findings in an objective tone. Though you may later bring in your opinion by interpreting the data or recommending a course of action, your credibility depends on your first reporting accurately.

- A formal report usually follows the organization listed below. Depending on the purpose of your report, however, you might combine or expand any of the sections.
  - **Introduction:** Explains the purpose of the report, describes the problem studied, and often describes or outlines the organization of the entire report.
  - **Methods:** Describes how the data were gathered.
  - **Results:** Presents the findings of the report.
  - **Discussion:** States the implications of your findings.
  - **Conclusion:** Makes recommendations or simply summarizes the findings.

The following two pages show the cover and the executive summary to a report on climate changes in the Great Lakes region. An executive summary is a brief overview sometimes included before a lengthy report. The report was produced by The Union of Concerned Scientists and The Ecological Society of America. The entire work, which contains the elements described in Box 178, was published online and as a 105-page booklet.

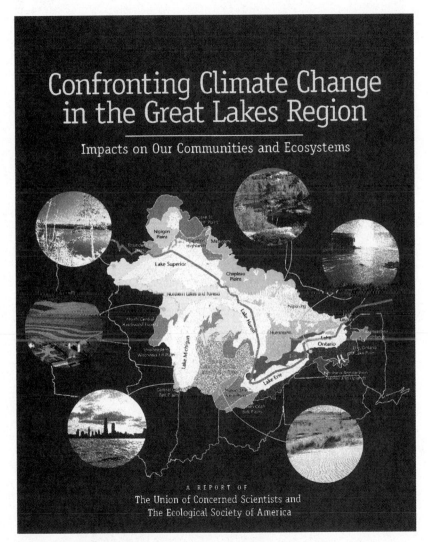

Confronting Climate Change in the Great Lakes Region

Impacts on Our Communities and Ecosystems

A REPORT OF
The Union of Concerned Scientists and
The Ecological Society of America

Cover of a public report

QUOTATION: ON WRITING
I for one appreciate a good form letter, having worked on Capitol Hill and learned several dozen cordial ways to say nothing.
—Carrie Johnson

Executive Summary

The Great Lakes region of the United States and Canada is a land of striking glacial legacies: spectacular lakes, vast wetlands, fertile southern soils, and rugged northern terrain forested in spruce and fir. It is also home to 60 million people whose actions can profoundly affect the region's ecological bounty and the life-sustaining benefits it provides. Now that the world is entering a period of unusually rapid climate change, driven largely by human activities that release heat-trapping greenhouse gases into the atmosphere, the responsibility for safeguarding our natural heritage is becoming urgent.

Growing evidence suggests that the climate of the Great Lakes is already changing:
- Winters are getting shorter.
- Annual average temperatures are growing warmer.
- The duration of lake ice cover is decreasing as air and water temperatures rise.
- Heavy rainstorms are becoming more common.

This report examines these trends in detail and discusses the likelihood that they will continue into the future. The consequences of these climatic changes will magnify the impacts of ongoing human disturbances that fragment or transform landscapes, pollute air and water, and disrupt natural ecosystems and the vital goods and services they provide. *Confronting Climate Change in the Great Lakes Region* explores the potential consequences of climate change, good and bad, for the character, economy, and environment of the Great Lakes region during the coming century. It also examines actions that can be take now to help forestall many of the most severe consequences of climate change for North America's heartland.

CONFRONTING CLIMATE CHANGE IN THE GREAT LAKES REGION
Union of Concerned Scientists • The Ecological Society of America

Executive Summary of a public report

42g How do I write letters to my community or its representatives?

Letters to your community include letters to the editors of newspapers and magazines, statements of position for a local or national newsletter, and material you self-publish (38d). Such letters allow you to participate in a discussion with a community of peers. When writing in response to a particular piece of writing in the same publication, always begin by referring precisely to what you are responding to, using title, section, and date, if possible.

In the following example, a citizen argues for preserving a city park in its present form.

To the Editor:

Re "Parking Plan Threatens Green Space" (news article, May. 14):

For well over a century, Lincoln Park has provided a welcome oasis in downtown Springfield. Office workers eat lunches there, school children play there on the way home, and evening concerts and other events unite the community.

It is very shortsighted, then, that the City Council now considers converting a third of the park into additional parking.

I acknowledge that parking downtown has gotten difficult. As the manager of a small shop, I know that our customers sometimes have trouble finding a parking place. However, the park itself is one of the reasons our downtown has become more popular in the past decade. Ironically, destroying the park's attractive green space will reduce the need for more parking, which will hurt business.

A better solution is for the city to purchase the vacant property at the corner of Main and Jefferson and build a multistory garage. No doubt this option is more expensive than using the park. However, I'm sure most citizens would prefer to leave future generations a legacy of trees, grass, and inviting benches rather than a debt of sterile concrete.

John C. Bradway
Springfield, May 17, 2003

Many letters to the editor propose solutions to a community problem. These letters aim to persuade other readers that a problem exists and that a particular solution is not only feasible but also the most advantageous of all the possible alternatives. Keep the following guidelines in mind when writing to propose a solution:

- Explain briefly the specific problem you are attempting to solve.
- Tell how your solution will solve all elements of the problem.
- Address briefly the possible objections or alternatives to your proposed solution.
- State why your solution offers the most advantages of all the alternatives.

Letters to your civic and political leaders can influence their opinions and actions. You might write in reaction to a proposed law or course of action, to object to an existing law or situation, or to thank or compliment the person for action taken. State your purpose at the outset; be concise; and end by clearly stating what action you request so that a response, if given, can be to the point.

42h   What other types of public writing exist?

In addition to the writing that they do for business, civic, or academic purposes, many people write simply to express themselves or to entertain others. The most obvious examples are fiction, poetry, plays, film scripts, and, at another level, instant messages or postings to an Internet discussion group. In addition, many people write for or produce newsletters or Web sites related to their hobbies or special interests. The Internet has made publication to very broad publics not only instantaneous but also cost free, giving writers the capability of sharing words, graphic designs, and images.

One form of public writing that has exploded in popularity in recent years is the Web log, or *Blog* (the last letter of W*eb* plus *log*). Blogs are online journals that writers update on a fairly regular basis, usually daily. Some writers focus their Blogs on a single topic or a narrow range of topics. Others record the events of their lives, as in a diary—that is, a diary open for all the world to see and read.

Special software allows Bloggers (as the authors are known) to create Blogs. As with a Web site, writers need access to a server to publish their work. Many Internet providers (such as Yahoo! and AOL) support Blogs. Additionally, there are Web sites such as *Blogger*, <http://new.blogger.com>, that not only maintain your Blog but also allow you to read the Blogs of thousands of other people.

Shown on the opposite page is a section of a Blog written by John Lovas, a professor of writing at a California community college. Notice how Lovas's Blog combines references to his professional and personal life and includes pictures as well as words.

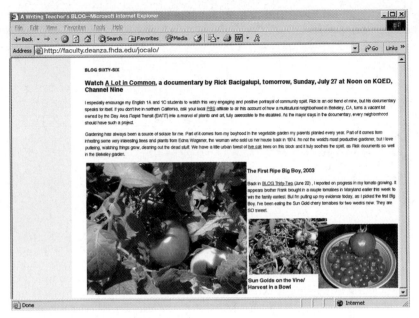

A Blog page

One complaint frequently lodged against pressure writing situations such as exams is that they little resemble "normal" writing situations that allow revision. Without debating the merits of this complaint, we note pragmatically that exams aren't likely to disappear soon from colleges. What teachers can do is to extend the learning associated with exams by encouraging students to reflect on the experiences before, during, and after the testing scenario.

The more involved students are in evaluating their progress, the more significant their progress seems to be. The reflective nature of portfolios encourages students to explore why they performed as they did, how they might change, and the impact of that change once it occurs and is tracked.

Objective tests are a necessity in many content courses. These tests are often seen as separate and unrelated to writing skills. Yet the connection, though underlying, is potent. Objective testing is an assessment of reading and listening comprehension. The strain is now placed on inferential and contextual reading. Essay tests bear down on whole language skills and create a literacy pressure cooker. Tests assess testing skills as well as content knowledge. A portfolio approach allows students to study themselves; writing becomes a reflective study tool in every curriculum, even math.

Following are some strategies instructors might pass along to students to foster reflection on the exam process. Instructors might begin the process by reminding students to use a good notetaking system (review Chapter 5).

1. *Before the test:* Write a summary of how you prepared for the test and how well prepared you feel. Predict test questions and score. Prepare your test-taking strategy (43d).

2. *During the test:* Read instructions carefully. Immediately record any information you fear you may forget. Manage your time. Relax. Note questions that gave you trouble for review.

Chapter 43

Writing Under Pressure

The demands of writing under pressure can sometimes seem overwhelming, but if you break the challenge into small, sequential steps and then focus on each step in turn, you can succeed. When you write under the pressure of time constraints, you are expected to write as completely and clearly as possible. If you tend to freeze under pressure, force yourself to take slow, deep breaths or to use a relaxation technique such as counting backward from ten. When you turn to the task, remember to break the whole into parts so that the process is easier to work through.

Writing answers for essay tests is one of the most important writing tasks that you face in college. Common in all disciplines, including the natural sciences, essay tests demand that you recall information and also put assorted pieces of that information into contexts that lead to GENERALIZATIONS you can support. Essay tests give you the chance to SYNTHESIZE and apply your knowledge, helping your instructor determine what you've learned.

43a How do I prepare for essay exams?

Begin preparing for exams well before the day of the test itself. Attend class diligently and take good notes. Just as important, be an active reader, annotating your textbook and putting concepts into your own words. Reading and writing are closely connected, but there is no substitute for actually doing some writing yourself.

Perhaps the best preparation comes from writing practice exams. Doing this will give you experience in writing under pressure about course material. Your instructors may offer questions they used in previous years, or they may provide a number of questions to guide your studying. Alternatively, you and your classmates may generate your own exam questions. Use cue words and key words drawn from your course material to help develop potential questions. Finally, ask each instructor if books or notes are allowed in the exam. Some exams are "open book," meaning that you can use your books or notes; most, however, are closed book.

43b What are cue words and key words?

Most essay questions contain a *cue word,* a word of direction that tells what the content of your answer is expected to emphasize. Knowing the major cue words and their meanings can increase your ability to plan efficiently and write effectively. Be guided by the list of cue words and sample essay test questions in Box 179.

BOX 179 **SUMMARY**

 Cue words found in questions for essay tests

■ *Analyze:* **to separate something into parts and then discuss the parts and their meanings**
  Analyze Socrates' discussion of "good life" and "good death."

■ *Clarify:* **to make clear, often by giving a definition of a key term and by using examples to illustrate it**
  Clarify T. S. Eliot's idea of tradition.

■ *Classify:* **to arrange into groups on the basis of shared characteristics**
  Classify the different types of antipredator adaptations.

■ *Compare and contrast:* **to show similarities and differences**
  Compare and contrast the reproductive cycles of a moss and a flowering plant.

■ *Criticize:* **to give your opinion concerning the good points and bad points of something**
  Criticize the architectural function of modern football stadiums.

■ *Define:* **to state precisely what something is and thereby to differentiate it from similar things**
  Define the term *yellow press.*

■ *Describe:* **to explain features in order to make clear an object, procedure, or event**
  Describe the chain of events that constitutes the movement of a sensory impulse along a nerve fiber.

■ *Discuss:* **to consider as many elements as possible concerning an issue or event**
  Discuss the effects of television viewing on modern attitudes toward violence.

→

Background: Teaching Self-Monitoring (continued)

3. *Immediately after the test:* Write a summary of how well you did, what you think you might have missed and why, and a prediction of your score. Try to remember and record key phrases and verbs from test items. Analyze the questions to determine the instructor's emphasis, biases, or preferences (43a and 43b).

4. *When you receive your scored test:* Review missed questions and search for correct answers. Write why you answered incorrectly and justify the correct answer. Then, write a study plan for the next exam.

BACKGROUND
In "Writing into Silence: Losing Voice with Writing Assessment Technology" (*Teaching English in the Two-Year College,* May 1999: 380–87), Joanne Drechsel analyzes assessment methods that value both the writer and the reader, arguing for assessment tools grounded in theory over computerized assessment and objective testing.

BACKGROUND
In "The Popularity of Formulaic Writing (and Why We Need to Resist)" (*English Journal,* September 2000: 61–67), Mark Wiley outlines Jane Schaffer's approach to teaching writing and defends formulaic writing, particularly in light of essay test taking as a primary focus of recent assessment issues.

BACKGROUND
In "An Apologia for the Timed Impromptu Essay Test" (*College Composition and Communication*, February 1995: 30–45), Edward M. White discusses the value of essay tests, with all their disadvantages, over other forms of language testing.

Cue words found in questions for essay tests (*continued*)

- *Evaluate:* **to give your opinion about the importance of something**

  Evaluate Margaret Mead's contribution to anthropology.

- *Explain:* **to make clear or intelligible something that needs to be understood or interpreted**

  Explain how the amount of carbon dioxide in the blood regulates rates of heartbeat and breathing.

- *Illustrate:* **to give examples of something**

  Illustrate the use of symbolism in Richard Wright's novel *Native Son*.

- *Interpret:* **to explain the meaning of something**

  Give your interpretation of Maxine Kumin's poem "Beans."

- *Justify:* **to show or prove that something is valid or correct**

  Justify the existence of labor unions in today's economy.

- *Prove:* **to present evidence that cannot be refuted logically or with other evidence**

  Prove that smoking is a major cause of lung cancer.

- *Relate:* **to show the connections between two or more things**

  Relate increases in specific crimes in the period 1932–1933 to the prevailing economic conditions.

- *Review:* **to evaluate or summarize something critically**

  Review the structural arrangements in proteins to explain the meaning of the term *polypeptide*.

- *Show:* **to point out or demonstrate something**

  Show what effects pesticides have on the production of wheat.

- *Summarize:* **to identify the major points of something**

  Summarize the major benefits of compulsory education.

- *Support:* **to argue in favor of something**

  Support the position that the destruction of rain forests is endangering the planet.

Each essay question also has one or more *key words* that tell you the information, topics, and ideas you are to write about (compare to KEYWORD). For example, in the question "Criticize the architectural function of the modern football stadium," the cue word is *criticize* and the key words are *architectural function* and *football stadium*. To answer the question successfully, you need first to define the term *architectural function,* then to describe the typical modern football stadium (mentioning major variations when important), and then to discuss how well the typical modern football stadium fits your definition of architectural function.

43c How do I write effective responses to essay test questions?

An effective response to an essay test question is complete and logically organized. Here are two answers to the question "Classify the different types of antipredator adaptations." The first one is successful; the second is not. The sentences are numbered for your reference, and they are explained in the text.

ANSWER 1— YES

(1) Although many antipredator adaptations have evolved in the animal kingdom, all can be classified into four major categories according to the prey's response to the predator. (2) The first category is hiding techniques. (3) These techniques include cryptic coloration and behavior in which the prey assumes characteristics of an inanimate object or part of a plant. (4) The second category is early enemy detection. (5) The prey responds to alarm signals from like prey or other kinds of prey before the enemy can get too close. (6) Evasion of the pursuing predator is the third category. (7) Prey that move erratically or in a compact group are displaying this technique. (8) The fourth category is active repulsion of the predator. (9) The prey kills, injures, or sickens the predator, establishing that it represents danger to the predator.

ANSWER 2—NO

(1) Antipredator adaptations are the development of the capabilities to reduce the risk of attack from a predator without too much change in the life-supporting activities of the prey. (2) There are many different types of antipredator adaptations. (3) One type is camouflage, hiding from the predator by cryptic coloration or imitation of plant parts. (4) An example of this type of antipredator adaptation is the praying mantis. (5) A second type is the defense used by monarch butterflies, a chemical protection that makes some birds ill after eating the butterfly. (6) This protection may injure the bird by causing it to vomit, and it can educate the bird against eating other butterflies. (7) Detection and evasion are also antipredator adaptations.

On the next page, an explanation is given of what happens, sentence by sentence, in the two answers to the question about antipredator adaptations.

BACKGROUND

In "Toward a New Theory of Writing Assessment" (*College Composition and Communication,* December 1996: 549–66), Brian Huot explores a theory of writing assessment "based on our understandings about the nature of language, written communication, and its teaching."

BACKGROUND

Namok Choi investigates the relationship between test type and students' attitudes about testing in "The Effects of Test Format and Locus of Control on Test Anxiety" (*Journal of College Student Development,* November–December 1998: 16–20).

BACKGROUND
A study of over 240 students, who each wrote three to five essays holistically scored by expert raters, showed that student performances on those essays varied widely. The study, "Does Holistic Assessment Predict Writing Performance? Estimating the Consistency of Student Performance on Holistically Scored Writing Assignments," was conducted by John R. Hayes, Jill A. Hatch, and Christine M. Silk and reported in *Written Communication* (January 2000): 3–26.

SENTENCE	ANSWER 1: YES	ANSWER 2: NO
1	Sets up classification system and gives number of categories based on key word	Defines key word
2	Names first category	Throwaway sentence—accomplishes nothing
3	Defines first category	Names and defines first category
4	Names second category	Gives an example for first category
5	Defines second category	Gives an example for second (unnamed) category
6	Names third category	Continues to explain example
7	Defines third category	Names two categories
8	Names fourth category	
9	Defines fourth category	

Answer 1 sets about immediately answering the question by introducing a classification system, as called for by the cue word *classify*. Answer 2, by contrast, defines the key word, a waste of time on a test that will be read by an audience of specialists. Answer 1 is tightly organized, easy to follow, and to the point. Answer 2 rambles, never names the four categories, and says more around the subject than on it.

43d What strategies can I use when writing under pressure?

If you use specific *strategies* when writing under pressure, you can be more comfortable and your writing will likely be more effective. As you use the strategies listed in Box 180 on the facing page, remember that your purpose in answering questions is to show what you know in a clear, direct, and well-organized way. When you're studying for an essay exam, write out one-sentence summaries of major areas of information. This technique helps fix the ideas in your mind, and a summary sentence may become a thesis sentence for an essay answer.

The more you use the strategies in the box and adapt them to your personal needs, the better you'll use them to your advantage. Practice them by making up questions that might be on your test and timing yourself as you write the answers. Doing this offers you another benefit: If you study by anticipating possible questions and writing out the answers, you'll be very well prepared if one or two of them show up on the test.

> BOX 180   **SUMMARY**
>
> ## Strategies for writing essay tests
>
> 1. Do not start writing immediately.
> 2. If the test has two or more questions, read them all at the start. Determine whether you're supposed to answer all the questions. Doing this gives you a sense of how to budget your time, either by dividing it equally or by allotting more time for some questions than for others. If you have a choice of questions, select those about which you know the most and can write about most completely with in the time limit.
> 3. Analyze each question that you answer by underlining the *cue words* and *key words* (see 43b) to determine exactly what the question asks.
> 4. Use the writing process as much as possible within the constraints of the time limit. Try to allot time to plan and revise. For a one-hour test on one question, take about ten minutes to jot down preliminary ideas about content and organization, and save ten minutes to reread, revise, and edit your answer. If you're pressed suddenly for time—but try to avoid this—consider skipping a question that you can't answer well or a question that counts less toward your total score. If you feel blocked, try FREEWRITING (2g) to get your hand and your thoughts moving.
> 5. Support any GENERALIZATIONS with specifics (see 4f about using the RENNS TEST for being specific).
> 6. Beware of going off the topic. Respond to the cue words and key words in the question, and do not try to reshape the question to conform to what you might prefer to write about. Remember, your reader expects a clear line of presentation and reasoning that answers the stated question.

EXERCISE 43-1

Look back at an essay that you have written under time pressure. Read it over and decide whether you would change the content of your answer or the strategies you used as you were writing under pressure. List these specific strategies, and if you think they were useful, add them to Box 180.

BACKGROUND

Kathleen Blake Yancey offers a historical account of three "waves" of writing assessment—objective tests, holistic scoring, and portfolios—in "Looking Back as We Look Forward: Historicizing Writing" (*College Composition and Communication,* February 1999: 483–503).

ANSWERS: EXERCISE 43-1
Answers will vary.

Chapter 44

Oral Presentations

Preparing an oral presentation and writing an essay involve some of the same processes. In each, you determine your PURPOSE, analyze your AUDIENCE, and work to deliver a clear, controlling idea. This chapter will help you move from written to oral delivery and show you how to use what you know about writing to prepare effective oral presentations. You will also learn about the special considerations that apply to speaking, instead of writing, your thoughts.

PREPARING AN ORAL PRESENTATION

44a How do I determine my purpose and topic?

Just as writing purposes change from one situation to the next, so do speaking purposes. You might address students living in your dorm to *inform* them about a film club you are starting on Monday nights. You might try to *persuade* the history department or the registrar to transfer credits from a class you took overseas. The toast you give at a friend's wedding is meant, in part, to *entertain* the wedding guests.

In the academic setting, to inform and to persuade are the most common purposes: To *inform* is to help your audience understand something; to *persuade* is to influence the attitudes and behaviors of your audience.

With a general purpose in mind, you are ready to think about your TOPIC. Sometimes your topic will be assigned, but if not, follow these guidelines: Select a topic that you care about and that your audience will care about also. Choose one that you either already know about or that you can learn about in the time you have to prepare. Be sure you can do justice to your topic within the time constraints of the presentation itself.

Now, narrow your topic to the one main point you want to make, and state the specific purpose of your speech. Write your specific purpose as an INFINITIVE PHRASE: *to inform about . . . , to convince that . . . , to show how . . . , to explain why . . . .* Use specific terms and precise language.

44b How do I adapt my speech's message to my audience?

To determine how best to approach your TOPIC, consider your AUDIENCE and adapt your message accordingly. Begin by asking yourself these questions: How much does my audience already know about this topic? What terms and concepts will they not know? What information must I provide as a foundation for my message? Does my audience have a particular bias toward my topic that I need to consider?

Based on your responses to these questions, you will probably find that your audience falls into one of three categories: *uninformed, informed,* or *mixed.* Box 181 offers help in adapting your message to each type of audience.

BOX 181 SUMMARY

Adapting oral presentations to the audience

Uninformed Audience

Limit the number of new ideas you present. Use visual aids to establish the basics, avoiding technical terms as much as possible. Define new terms and concepts. Repeat key ideas and use vivid examples.

Informed Audience

Don't waste their time with the basics, but introduce new ideas and concepts. From the beginning, reassure them that you will be covering new ground.

Mixed Audience

Start with simple concepts and move toward more complex ones. In the introduction, acknowledge the presence of the more informed members of the audience and explain that you are only reviewing the basics so that everyone can build from the same knowledge base.

Adapting your presentation to the general needs and expectations of your audience does not mean catering to their views and saying only

BACKGROUND

The Web page at <http://www.siu.edu/~tw0a/orallec.htm>, sponsored by Southern Illinois University, offers a list of questions to help students plan and present their oral presentations.

what they might want to hear. It means rather that you need to consider their knowledge of your topic and their interest in it. You can then make your message understandable and relevant by using appropriate language and examples.

44c How do I formulate my speech's working thesis?

As with the THESIS STATEMENT of an essay, the working thesis for an oral presentation makes clear the main idea and the speaker's PURPOSE. It also reflects the speaker's AUDIENCE analysis in its content (neither too sophisticated nor too simple) and its language (the word choice is at the right level). In addition, a working thesis is a practical preparation step because it helps you stay on your topic, and it introduces and connects the key concepts of your presentation.

Box 182 demonstrates how a student speaking on infertility worked from a general purpose and topic to arrive at a specific purpose and working thesis.

BOX 182   SUMMARY

 Formulating a working thesis for a speech

GENERAL PURPOSE   To inform

TOPIC   "Infertility"

SPECIFIC PURPOSE   To explain medical advancements in the treatment of infertility

WORKING THESIS   The sorrow of infertility is becoming a thing of the past for many couples thanks to medical procedures such as donor insemination, in vitro fertilization, and egg harvesting.

44d How do I organize my oral presentation?

When you have compiled the information you will use in your oral presentation, develop an organizational outline. An organizational outline shows the three-part structure of an oral presentation—introduction, body, conclusion—and lists major points (as lettered headings) with two to three supporting points (as numbered subheadings). Use sentences for your main points to sharpen your thinking as you DRAFT. Box 183 presents a typical organizational outline.

BOX 183   SUMMARY

Organizational outline for an oral presentation

Title

General purpose:
Topic:
Specific purpose:
Thesis statement:

Introduction

A. _____

B. _____

(transition)

Supporting material

A. _____

   1. _____

   2. _____

(transition)

B. _____

   1. _____

   2. _____

(transition)

C. _____

   1. _____

   2. _____

(transition)

Conclusion

A. _____

B. _____

C. _____

QUOTATION: ON SPEAKING
Have common sense and . . . stick to the point.

—W. Somerset Maugham

Introduction

The members of an audience waiting to hear a speaker have three questions in mind: Who are you? What are you going to talk about? Why should I listen? They are good questions, and you want to respond to them in the introduction to your talk. Here are some suggestions:

- Grab your audience's attention with a question, a quotation, a fascinating statistic or fact, an anecdote, background information, or a compliment. Whether someone introduces you or not, tell your audience what qualifies you to speak on your particular subject.

- Explain briefly the organization of your talk. This gives your audience a road map so that they know where you are starting, where you are going, and what they can look forward to as you speak.

Supporting material

Though much of the advice given for oral presentations applies to written communication as well, audiences for oral presentations generally need some special help from the speaker. When you are reading an article and lose sight of the main point, you can turn back a few paragraphs and reread. But when you are listening to a speech and your mind wanders, you cannot ask the speaker to go back and repeat.

As a speaker, you can employ strategies to keep listeners interested and aware of your purpose and where you are. Below are some suggestions.

- Give signals to show where you are on the road map. Use *first, second,* and *third* appropriately. Show CAUSE AND EFFECT with words such as *subsequently, therefore,* and *furthermore.* If you are telling a story, use signpost terms such as *before, then,* and *next.*

- Define unfamiliar terms and give vivid examples to help the audience understand new ideas and concepts.

- Comment on your own material. Tell the audience what is significant, memorable, or relevant—and why.

- Repeat key ideas. If you do so sparingly, you can emphasize the importance of the idea and help the audience remember it.

- Provide internal summaries. Every so often, take a moment to recap what you have covered as reassurance for both yourself and your audience.

Conclusion

In the conclusion of a speech, an audience looks for a sense of closure. Here are some ways to conclude your presentation.

- Signal the end with verbal ("In conclusion") and nonverbal (facial expressions, gestures) cues.

- Offer a fresh restatement of your main message—but do not introduce new ideas.

- Use a dramatic clincher statement, cite a memorable quotation, or issue a challenge.
- When you say "Finally," make sure you mean it. In other words, do not conclude more than once.

44d.1 Researching my speech

Doing research for an oral presentation requires the same kind of planning as doing research for written documents. To keep yourself calm and focused, divide the preparation into manageable tasks, according to a realistic time line (31d). Set small goals and stick to your calendar in order to give yourself enough time to research, organize, and practice your presentation (44i). Review Chapters 31–33 for help on finding and evaluating sources, taking notes, planning a research strategy, and documenting sources. An oral presentation won't have a WORKS CITED or REFERENCES page to be read out, but your instructor might ask you to turn in such a typed list before or after you give your presentation.

44d.2 Drafting my speech

Most of the preparation involved in an oral presentation is written work. Writing helps you take four important steps in your preparation: (1) to organize your thoughts; (2) to distance yourself from the ideas and remain objective; (3) to pay attention to words and language; and (4) to polish for clarity and impact.

When drafting your speech, it may help you to review Chapters 20–22 on usage and the impact and correct form of words. In particular, see section 21b for a discussion of a medium LEVEL OF FORMALITY in language, which is an appropriate level for most public speaking. Careful DICTION (21e) will make your speech both easy to listen to and memorable. Box 184 presents some tips on language that apply specifically to oral presentations.

QUOTATION: ON READING
Lists of books we reread and books we can't finish tell more about us than about the relative worth of the books themselves.
—Russell Banks

BOX 184   SUMMARY

Using language effectively in oral presentations

- **Recognize the power of precise words.**

  "Never in the field of human conflict was so much owed by so many to so few."

  —Winston Churchill

  Substitute "history" for *the field of human conflict* and note the diminished effect.

→

Using language effectively in oral presentations (*continued*)

■ **Take care not to offend.** If you see the slightest chance that a word, phrase, or example could offend your audience, don't use it. Such material distracts your listeners and detracts from your message. It also suggests that you're insensitive to the impact of SLANTED LANGUAGE (21h). Avoid SEXIST PRONOUNS and NOUNS (10s and 21g).

■ **Use guide phrases.** Words such as *now, first, my next point,* and so on help listeners follow your organization.

■ **Use the active voice.** The ACTIVE VOICE is generally desirable in writing (8o), but it is crucial in oral presentations. Listeners can more easily grasp your point if you state the subject at the beginning of a sentence. Consider the following two sentences:

Gun control is an issue that must be considered by all citizens. [passive]

All citizens must consider the issue of gun control. [active]

44e How do I present a speech collaboratively?

At some point, you might be asked to present an oral report as part of a group. As with collaborative projects of any sort, special considerations apply.

■ Make sure, when choosing a topic, that most members of the group are familiar with the subject. All members of the group are required to be able to contribute in some way.

■ Find out whether all members of the group are required to speak for an equal amount of time. If so, agree on firm time limits for each person, so that everyone can participate in the delivery. If there is no such requirement, students who enjoy public speaking can take more responsibility for delivery, while others do more of the preparatory work or contribute in other ways.

■ Lay out clearly what each member's responsibilities are in preparing the presentation. Try to define roles that complement one another; otherwise, you may end up with overlap in one area and no coverage in another.

■ Allow enough time for practice. Though each member can practice on his or her own part alone, schedule practice sessions for the entire presentation as a group. This will help you (a) work on transitions, (b) make sure the order of presenters is effective, and (c) time the length of the presentation.

DELIVERING AN ORAL PRESENTATION

When you write a document to be read, you not only consider the information you present, you also think about DOCUMENT DESIGN—the "how" of presentation for written documents (Chapter 37). When preparing an oral presentation, you also must consider how—not just what—you present. In oral presentations, the "how" is called *delivery*.

44f How do I choose an oral presentation style?

Presentation style is the way you deliver your speech: You may memorize it, read it, or speak *extemporaneously*—that is, without a text. (An extemporaneous speech can be spur of the moment or carefully prepared, but it is delivered free of text, possibly using notes but never reading from them word by word.)

Memorized speeches often sound unnatural, and there is no safety net if you forget a word or sentence. Fortunately, memorization is not necessary in most academic and professional speaking situations.

Reading as a presentation style is often boring for listeners, and it can create an uncomfortable barrier between you and your audience. If you must read your speech, remember to make frequent eye contact with the audience, vary your tone of voice, and use appropriate gestures.

Presenting extemporaneously is usually your best choice. You are well prepared, and you have an outline or index cards to keep you focused. A presentation outline, which isn't the same as an organizational outline (44d), lists the major points you want to make, but the language you use to develop these points is "of the moment." The outline or index cards will need to include the names of any sources so that you can correctly cite their contributions to your speech. Box 185 gives specific help in preparing the two main types of presentation aids. Choose whichever feels more comfortable to you.

BOX 185　SUMMARY

Preparing oral presentation aids

For a presentation outline, follow the same style as the organizational outline (Box 183 in 44d) with these changes:

Using Sheets of Paper

- Type the outline in a large font so that you can glance at it easily without holding the pages close to your face.

→

Churchill wrote his own speeches. When a leader does that, he becomes emotionally invested with his utterances. . . . If Churchill had had a speech writer in 1940, Britain would be speaking German today.

　　　　　　　—James C. Humes

TEACHING TIP
The History Channel maintains a large Web site of famous speeches from the fields of politics, entertainment, science and technology, and war and diplomacy; go to <http://www.historychannel.com/speeches/>. Another good resource is the *Online Speech Bank,* at Web site <http://www.americanrhetoric.com/speechbank.htm>. Over five thousand speeches are available.

Preparing oral presentation aids (*continued*)

- Number or label in large handwriting the sequence of your pages so that you don't lose your place.
- Clearly label or separate the introduction, supporting material, and conclusion. Perhaps use different fonts or colors for each section.
- Try to enter only key words and phrases as cues to what you want to say. Otherwise, you can end up keying in a word-for-word script of your presentation.
- Highlight key points you cannot afford to skip—small sticky notes can help as long as they don't cover your words.
- Write in visual cues to remind you to pause, use a visual, emphasize a point by gesture and/or voice, and so on.
- Use only one side of each sheet of paper so that you avoid flipping pages over, which can look like you're aimlessly shuffling paper.

Using Index Cards

- Follow the advice above for using separate sheets of paper.
- Choose a suitable size of index card. Often, 3-by-5-inch cards are too small.
- Use only one side of each card.
- Use only one index card per major point. For minor points, use another card that you number in relation to the card with the main point.
- Use various colors of pen on white cards or different card colors to separate the introduction, supporting material, and conclusion of your speech.

44g How do I vary my voice and use nonverbal communication in my speech?

Your voice is the focus of the presentation, so be aware of it and project. If you are unsure of your volume, it is fine to ask the audience if they can hear you. Articulate—speak slowly and deliberately—but not so slowly that there is no rhythm or pace to the speech. Change the tone of your voice for emphasis and clarity. Insert planned pauses. In general, try to sound like yourself, but in an intensified version. Remember that if you are using a microphone, you do not need to raise your voice.

Eye contact is the most important nonverbal communication tool. Try to make eye contact with your audience immediately. If you have to walk up to a podium, do not begin speaking before you are standing squarely behind the podium, looking directly at the audience. Eye contact communicates confidence.

Your body language can either add to or detract from your overall message. Use appropriate facial expressions to mirror the emotions of your message. Gestures, if not overdone, contribute to your message by adding emphasis. The best gestures appear natural rather than forced or timed. If you are unsure of where to place your hands, rest them on the podium—and try not to fidget. Body movements need to be kept to a minimum and used in pace with the speech. Step forward or backward to indicate transitions, but avoid rocking from side to side. And, of course, dress appropriately for your audience and the type of event.

44h How do I incorporate multimedia into my oral presentation?

Multimedia elements such as visual aids, sound, and video can make ideas clear, understandable, and engaging, but they can never take the place of a well-prepared speech. They add interest to an already interesting topic. They reinforce key ideas by providing illustrations or concrete images for the audience, and if done well, they can make long explanations unnecessary and add to your credibility. Following are the various types of visual aids and their uses.

44h.1 Using traditional visual aids

For all the suggestions in this list, remember one overriding principle: Always make text or graphics large enough to be easily read.

- **Posters.** Posters can be very effective because they can dramatize a point, often with color or images. Make sure the poster is large enough for everyone in your audience to see it.

- **Dry-erase boards.** These boards are preferable to chalkboards because their colors are visually appealing. Use them to emphasize an occasional technical word or to do a rough sketch when illustrating a process.

- **Transparencies.** Transparencies used with an overhead projector combine the advantages of posters and dry-erase boards. You can prepare it in advance and then write on the transparency for emphasis.

- **Handouts.** Handouts are preferable to other visual aids when the topic calls for a longer text or when you want to give your audience something to take home. Short and simple handouts work best during a presentation; save longer and more detailed ones for the end, if possible. If you distribute handouts during the speech, wait until everyone has one before you begin speaking, and do not distribute the handout until you are

TEACHING TIP
An enjoyable and effective teaching strategy frequently is to have students generate "negative examples." Asking students intentionally to create a bad poster or PowerPoint slide, for example, can dramatize for them the qualities of good work. You might even have them "judge" one another's work, with prizes going to the worst example and to the "best worst" example.

BACKGROUND
In a much-cited article in the *Chicago Tribune Magazine* ("Is PowerPoint the Devil?" January 5, 2003), Julia Keller quotes several professionals, including some writing instructors, who have reservations about this software. She includes an entertaining example of Lincoln's Gettysburg Address done as a PowerPoint.

ready to discuss it. Always include DOCUMENTATION information for your SOURCE on the handout, if it's other than your own writing or graphic (see Chapters 34–36 for specific guidelines for using various DOCUMENTATION STYLES). Using handouts has the advantage of your not having to rely on other technologies, which might be missing or broken.

■ **Slides.** The development of digital technologies such as PowerPoint makes photographic slides less common. However, if you use them, make sure before your speech that the slides are in the proper order and correctly placed (upright) in the machine.

44h.2 Using electronic media for my speech

Computer technologies have opened a new range of possibilities for supplementing oral presentations. Generally, ask your instructor if it's permissible to use electronic media, and make sure you have the needed equipment. However, never rely too much on these aids, and make sure that they enhance your presentation rather than detract from it. Especially problematic is your spending so much time developing multimedia materials that you don't concentrate on actually writing your presentation.

PowerPoint slides

PowerPoint, the most widely used presentation software, is a computer program that can create and project digital slides. (Some other presentation software are Aldus Persuasion, Compel, and WordPerfect Presentations.) PowerPoint slides consist of words, images, or combinations of both, and they can sometimes include sound or movies. To create and project digital slides you need a computer with a PowerPoint program or similar software; an LCD projector connected to your computer; and a screen.

The principles of document and Web page design apply to PowerPoint and other presentation software. You want each slide to have unity, variety, balance, and emphasis (37b). Most important, you don't want to present so much information on each slide that your audience pays more attention to reading it than to listening to you or, worse, feels insulted that you are going over material they can clearly figure out for themselves. The major complaint people make about PowerPoint presentations concerns speakers who simply read large amounts of text from slides. If you do that, your audience will quickly—and rightfully—become bored.

Shown on the next page is an example of an effective PowerPoint slide. A student prepared it for a presentation to The Nature Club, whose materials you saw in Chapters 37 and 38. Notice that the slide is clearly titled, well-balanced, and has an attractive picture to capture attention. Most important, it presents the speaker's four points concisely, and everything on the slide is large and clear enough for an audience to see it easily.

Preventing altitude sickness

- Acclimate slowly

- Drink plenty of fluids

- Rest at first sign of difficulty

- Get to lower altitude if breathing worsens

PowerPoint slide

Sound and video clips

A brief sound file (for example, a poet's reading or a politician's speech) or a video clip (an excerpt from a news story or footage you have shot) can occasionally help you illustrate a point during your presentation. These clips can be as simple as a CD or a DVD or as complicated as Wave or Quicktime files on a computer. However, if you use any of them, be sure to follow three important principles. First, keep sound and video clips brief. Second, make sure they're vital to your presentation. Third, be absolutely sure the clips are almost indispensable or greatly enhance your presentation. Otherwise, they can diminish the impact of your message by causing the audience to wonder why, except for the show of it, you've used the clips. Media should enhance your presentation, not substitute for it. Omit anything that doesn't directly relate to your thesis and purpose.

44h.3 Planning for multimedia in my speech

Nothing is more frustrating to you or annoying to your audience than serious technical problems. You need to make sure all of your visual aids and multimedia will work well—and you need a backup plan. Rehearse

801

carefully and often with the technology you need so that your use of the clips is seamless during your presentation.

If you are making a PowerPoint presentation, you need to double-check the in-place computer system before you begin. Hooking your computer up to an LCD projector can be tricky, so make sure you practice with the actual equipment before your presentation. If possible, bring your own laptop in case the software or a specific computer is not compatible with the disk that contains your slides. Presentation software can be very impressive, but you should consider it only an enhancement. Your information—spoken with clarity and authority—is the main attraction.

Arrive early to double-check that any technology you're planning to use is available and working, even if you've practiced with it beforehand. Learn how to turn on computers, video players, and projectors. Learn how to raise or lower the screen, if you're using one, and how to dim the lights. Box 186 offers tips on using visuals.

BOX 186   SUMMARY

 Tips for using visuals in oral presentations

- Make visuals large enough for the entire audience to see.
- Use simple layouts or drawings, nothing cluttered or overly complicated.
- Practice with the visuals you plan to use.
- Keep your focus on the audience, not the visual aid.
- Let the visuals enhance your speech, not distract your audience from your message.
- Never overwhelm your audience and your message by using too many visuals.
- Proofread your written visuals as carefully as you would the final draft of an essay or research paper.
- Whenever possible, arrive early to check the equipment.

44i   What can I do to practice for my oral presentation?

Good delivery requires practice. In preparing to speak, figure in enough time for at least four complete run-throughs of your entire presentation, using visuals if you have them. When you practice, keep the following in mind:

- Practice conveying ideas rather than particular words so that your tone does not become stilted.
- Time yourself and cut or expand material accordingly.
- Practice in front of a mirror or videotape yourself. As you watch yourself, notice your gestures. Do you look natural? Do you make nervous movements that you were not aware of as you spoke?
- Practice in front of a friend. Ask for constructive feedback by posing these questions: What was my main point? Did the points flow? Did any information seem to come from out of nowhere or not fit in with the information around it? Did I sound natural? Did I look natural? How did the visuals add to my message?

If you suffer from stage fright—as almost everyone does—remember that the better prepared and rehearsed you are, the less frightened you will be. Keep in mind that your aim is to communicate, not perform. Box 187 suggests ways to overcome physical signs of anxiety.

BOX 187   SUMMARY

 ## Overcoming anxiety in an oral presentation

- **Pounding heart.** Don't worry. No one else can hear it.
- **Trembling hands.** Rest them on the podium. If there is no podium, hold them behind your back or at your sides.
- **Shaky knees.** Stand behind a table, desk, or podium. If there is no desk, step forward to emphasize a point. Walking slowly from one place to another can also help you get rid of nervous energy. Never, however, rock from side to side.
- **Dry throat and mouth.** Keep water at the podium and take an occasional sip.
- **Quivering voice.** Speak louder until this disappears on its own.
- **Flushed face.** It is not as noticeable as it feels, and it will fade as you continue speaking.

When you're in place and ready to begin, pause for a moment before speaking. Count to five. Take a deep breath. Look at the audience, and then begin. Stop thinking that the audience is there to critique you. Instead, concentrate on delivering your message so that you appear sincere and confident.

PREFACE FOR ESL STUDENTS

If you ever worry about your English writing, you have much in common with me and with many U.S. college students. The good news is that errors you make demonstrate the reliable truth that you are moving normally through the unavoidable, necessary stages of second-language development. Unfortunately, there are no shortcuts. The process is like learning to play a musical instrument. Few people learn to play fluently without making lots of errors.

What can you do to progress as quickly as possible from one writing stage to another? I recommend that you start by bringing to mind what school writing is like in your first language. Specifically, recall how ideas are presented in your written native language, especially when information is explained or a topic requires a logical argument.

Most college writing in the United States is very direct in tone and straightforward in structure. In a typical essay or research paper, the reader expects to find a THESIS STATEMENT that clearly states the central message of the entire piece of writing. Usually, the thesis statement falls in the first paragraph, or in a longer piece, perhaps in the second paragraph. Then, each paragraph that follows relates in content directly to the essay's thesis statement. Also, each paragraph begins with a TOPIC SENTENCE that contains the main point of the paragraph, and the rest of the paragraph supports the point made in the topic sentence. This support consists of RENNS (4f) that provide specific details. The final paragraph brings the piece of writing to a logical conclusion.

Writing structures typical of your native language most likely differ from those in the United States. Always honor your culture's writing traditions and structures, for they reflect the richness of your heritage. At the same time, try to adapt to and practice the academic writing style characteristic of the United States. Later, some college instructors might encourage you to practice other, more subtle English writing styles that allow greater liberty in organization and expression.

Distinctive variations in school writing styles among people of different cultures and language groups have interested researchers for the past thirty years. Such research is ongoing, so scholars hesitate to generalize. Even so, interesting differences have been observed. Many Spanish-speaking students feel that U.S. school writing lacks grace because writers do not include any wide-ranging background material: in fact, U.S. writing teachers usually say such broad introductory material is wordy or not really relevant to the central message. Japanese school writing customarily begins with references to nature. In some African nations, a ceremonial, formal opening is expected to start school writing as an expression of respect for the reader. As a person, I greatly enjoy discovering the rich variations in the writing traditions of the many cultures of the world. As a college teacher, however, my responsibility is to explain the expectations in the United States.

If you were in my class, I would say "Welcome!" and then ask you to teach me about writing in your native language. Using that knowledge, I would respectfully teach you the U.S. approach to writing so that I could do my best to help you succeed in a U.S. college.

Lynn Quitman Troyka

Part Seven

Writing When English Is a Second Language

WHAT ELSE?

Strategies and Resources, a 400-page book provided free to faculty who use this handbook, offers specific, practical ways to help students whose first language is not English. This auxiliary text first examines cultural issues that make studying in the United States a challenging situation for many international students and suggests ways in which a composition teacher can integrate international students into the classroom. It also discusses some of the general concerns in crosscultural education and provides insights into the differing perspectives of international students. The second section describes some of the difficulties new international students may have in speaking and listening. It discusses classroom activities that have proved useful in helping ESL students improve their listening comprehension and speaking abilities. The third section looks more specifically at writing pedagogy for the ESL student, covering such issues as understanding differences in rhetorical expectations of native and nonnative students, handling errors in ESL students' writing, and adapting pedagogical techniques such as peer review and collaborative writing to a class that includes nonnative students (189).

Chapter 45

Singulars and Plurals

45a What are count and noncount nouns?

Count nouns name items that can be counted: *a radio* or *radios, a street* or *streets, an idea* or *ideas, a fingernail* or *fingernails.* Count nouns can be SINGULAR or PLURAL.

Noncount nouns name things that are thought of as a whole and not split into separate, countable parts: *rice, knowledge, traffic.* There are two important rules to remember about noncount nouns: (1) They're never preceded by *a* or *an,* and (2) they are never plural. Box 188 lists eleven categories of uncountable items, giving examples in each category.

BOX 188   SUMMARY

 Uncountable items

GROUPS OF SIMILAR ITEMS	clothing, equipment, furniture, jewelry, junk, luggage, mail, money, stuff, traffic, vocabulary
ABSTRACTIONS	advice, equality, fun, health, ignorance, information, knowledge, news, peace, pollution, respect
LIQUIDS	blood, coffee, gasoline, water
GASES	air, helium, oxygen, smog, smoke, steam
MATERIALS	aluminum, cloth, cotton, ice, wood
FOOD	beef, bread, butter, macaroni, meat, pork
PARTICLES OR GRAINS	dirt, dust, hair, rice, salt, wheat
SPORTS, GAMES, ACTIVITIES	chess, homework, housework, reading, sailing, soccer

→

> ## Uncountable items (*continued*)
>
> | | |
> |---|---|
> | **LANGUAGES** | Arabic, Chinese, Japanese, Spanish |
> | **FIELDS OF STUDY** | biology, computer science, history, literature, math |
> | **EVENTS IN NATURE** | electricity, heat, humidity, moonlight, rain, snow, sunshine, thunder, weather |

Some nouns can be countable or uncountable, depending on their meaning in a sentence. Most of these nouns name things that can be meant either individually or as "wholes" made up of individual parts.

COUNT	You have **a hair** on your sleeve. [In this sentence, *hair* is meant as an individual, countable item.]
NONCOUNT	Kioko has black **hair.** [In this sentence, all the strands of *hair* are referred to as a whole.]
COUNT	**The rains** were late last year. [In this sentence, *rains* is meant as individual, countable occurrences of rain.]
NONCOUNT	**The rain** is soaking the garden. [In this sentence, all the particles of *rain* are referred to as a whole.]

When you are editing your writing (see Chapter 3), be sure that you have not added a plural -*s* to any noncount nouns, for they are always singular in form.

👁 **ALERT:** Be sure to use a singular verb with any noncount noun that functions as a SUBJECT in a CLAUSE. 👁

To check whether a noun is count or noncount, look it up in a dictionary such as the *Dictionary of American English* (Heinle & Heinle). In this dictionary, count nouns are indicated by [C], and noncount nouns are indicated by [U] (for "uncountable"). Nouns that have both count and noncount meanings are marked [C;U].

45b How do I use determiners with singular and plural nouns?

Determiners, also called *expressions of quantity,* are used to tell how much or how many with reference to NOUNS. Other names for determiners include *limiting adjectives, noun markers,* and ARTICLES. (For information about articles—the words *a, an,* and *the*—see Chapter 46.)

BACKGROUND
The Web site <http://www.edunet.com/english/grammar/toc.cfm> by Digital Education Network offers information on plural count and noncount nouns.

Choosing the right determiner with a noun can depend on whether the noun is NONCOUNT or COUNT (see 45a). For count nouns, you must also decide whether the noun is singular or plural. Box 189 lists many determiners and the kinds of nouns that they can accompany.

BOX 189   SUMMARY

Determiners to use with count and noncount nouns

Group 1: Determiners for Singular Count Nouns

With every **singular count noun,** always use one of the determiners listed in Group 1.

a, an, the	**a house**	**an egg**	**the car**
one, any, some, every, each, either, neither, another, the other	**any house**	**each egg**	**another car**
my, our, your, his, her, its, their, nouns with 's or s'	**your house**	**its egg**	**Connie's car**
this, that	**this house**	**that egg**	**this car**
one, no, the first, the second, etc.	**one house**	**no egg**	**the fifth car**

Group 2: Determiners for Plural Count Nouns

All the determiners listed in Group 2 can be used with **plural count nouns.** Plural count nouns can also be used without determiners, as discussed in section 46b.

the	**the bicycles**	**the rooms**	**the idea**
some, any, both, many, more, most, few, fewer, the fewest, a lot of, a number of, other, several, all, all the	**some bicycles**	**many rooms**	**all ideas**
my, our, your, his, her, its, their, nouns with 's or s'	**our bicycles**	**her rooms**	**student's ideas**

→

Determiners to use with count and noncount nouns (*continued*)

these, those	**these bicycles**	**those rooms**	**these ideas**
no, two, three, etc.; *the first, the second, the third,* etc.	**no bicycles**	**four rooms**	**the first ideas**

Group 3: Determiners for Noncount Nouns

All the determiners listed in Group 3 can be used with **noncount nouns** (always singular). Noncount nouns can also be used without determiners, as discussed in section 46b.

the	**the rice**	**the rain**	**the pride**
some, any, much, more, most, other, the other, little, less, the least, enough, all, all the, a lot of	**enough rice**	**a lot of rain**	**more pride**
my, our, your, his, her, its, their, nouns with *'s* or *s'*	**their rice**	**India's rain**	**your pride**
this, that	**this rice**	**that rain**	**this pride**
no, the first, the second, the third, etc.	**no rice**	**the first rain**	**no pride**

👁 **ALERT:** The phrases *a few* and *a little* convey the meaning "some": *I have **a few** rare books* means "I have *some* rare books." *They are worth **a little** money* means "They are worth *some* money."

Without the word *a,* the words *few* and *little* convey the meaning "almost none": *I have **few*** [or *very few*] *books* means "I have *almost no* books." *They are worth **little** money* means "They are worth *almost no* money." 👁

45c How do I use *one of,* nouns as adjectives, and *states* in names or titles?

One of constructions

One of constructions include *one of the* and a NOUN or *one of* followed by an ADJECTIVE-noun combination (*one of my hats, one of those ideas*). Always use a plural noun as the OBJECT when you use *one of the* with a noun or *one of* with an adjective-noun combination.

NO	*One of the **reason** to live here is the beach.*
YES	*One of the **reasons** to live here is the beach.*

NO	*One of her best **friend** has moved away.*
YES	*One of her best **friends** has moved away.*

The VERB in these constructions is always singular because it agrees with the singular *one,* not with the plural noun: ***One** of the most important inventions of the twentieth century **is** [not are] television.*

For advice about verb forms that go with *one of the . . . who* constructions, see section 10l.

Nouns used as adjectives

ADJECTIVES in English do not have plural forms. When you use an adjective with a PLURAL NOUN, make the noun plural but not the adjective: *the **green** [not greens] leaves.* Be especially careful when you use a word as a MODIFIER that can also function as a noun.

> The bird's wingspan is ten inches. [*Inches* is functioning as a noun.]
> The bird has a ten-inch wingspan. [*Inch* is functioning as a modifier.]

Do not add *-s* (or *-es*) to the adjective even when it is modifying a plural noun or pronoun.

NO	Many **Americans** students are basketball fans.
YES	Many **American** students are basketball fans.

Names or titles that include the word states

States is a plural word. However, names such as *United States* or *Organization of American States* refer to singular things—one country and one organization, even though made up of many states. When *states* is part of a name or title referring to one thing, the name is a SINGULAR NOUN and therefore requires a SINGULAR VERB.

NO	The **United States have** a large entertainment industry.
NO	The **United State has** a large entertainment industry.
YES	The **United States has** a large entertainment industry.

45d How do I use nouns with irregular plurals?

Some English nouns have irregularly spelled plurals. In addition to those discussed in section 22c, here are others that often cause difficulties.

Plurals of foreign nouns and other irregular nouns

Whenever you are unsure whether a noun is plural, look it up in a dictionary. If no plural is given for a singular noun, add *-s* to form the plural.

Many nouns from other languages that are used unchanged in English have only one plural. If two plurals are listed in the dictionary, look carefully for differences in meaning. Some words, for example, keep the plural form from the original language for scientific usage and have another, English-form plural for nonscientific contexts: *formula, formulae, formulas; appendix, appendices, appendixes; index, indices, indexes; medium, media, mediums; cactus, cacti, cactuses; fungus, fungi, funguses.*

Words from Latin that end in *-is* in their singular form become plural by substituting *-es: parenthesis, parentheses; thesis, theses; oasis, oases.*

Other words

Medical terms for diseases involving an inflammation end in *-itis: tonsillitis, appendicitis.* They are always singular.

The word *news*, although it ends in *s*, is always singular: *The **news is** encouraging.* The words *people, police,* and *clergy* are always plural even though they do not end in *s: The **police are** prepared.*

EXERCISE 45-1

Consulting all sections of this chapter, select the correct choice from the words in parentheses and write it in the blank.

EXAMPLE   At the beginning of every school year, all (student, students) students can expect (homework, homeworks) homework that teaches them about the toll-free No Bully hot line.

1. One of the main (reason, reasons) _____ for such a hot line is the change in tempers and violent capacities of (American, Americans) _____ students.

2. Because students are often bullied by a fellow classmate when outside the classroom, it is important that they receive (information, informations) _____ about how to react when confronted by such a threat.

3. Many a child in the (United State, United States) _____ is in danger not only of being teased and taunted by others but also of being the victim of a crime in which (blood, bloods) _____ is spilled, such as assault or robbery.

4. Because (many, much) _____ classrooms are unsupervised after school hours, this (time, times) _____ becomes especially dangerous.

5. In a moment of danger, (ignorance, ignorances) _____ can be deadly, so the No Bully hot line was set up to give students (advice, advices) _____ on how to handle bullying and other threatening situations.

ANSWERS AND COVERAGE: EXERCISE 45-1

1. reasons [45c, plural object with *one of*]; American [45c, singular for noun used as adjective]

2. information [45a, singular for noncount nouns]

3. United States [45c, *States* plural in *United States*]; blood [45a, singular for noncount nouns]

4. many [45b, *many* the correct determiner with the plural count noun *classrooms*]; time [45b, singular for count noun after the determiner *this*]

5. ignorance [45a, singular for noncount nouns]; advice [45a, singular for noncount nouns]

ANSWERS AND COVERAGE: EXERCISE 45-2

1. animals [45c, plural object with *one of*]; rattlesnake [45b, singular for count noun used after the determiner *a*]

2. six-foot [45c, singular for noun used as adjective]

3. dirt [45a, singular for noncount nouns]; leaves [45a, plural for count nouns]

4. many [45b, *many* the correct determiner with the plural count noun *yards*]

5. courage [45a, singular for noncount nouns]; friends [45c, plural object with *one of*]

EXERCISE 45-2

Consulting all sections of this chapter, select the correct choice from the words in parentheses and write it in the blank.

EXAMPLE   Because of their innate (intelligence, intelligences) <u>intelligence</u>, many (pet, pets) <u>pets</u> can often be very protective of the humans they love.

1. One of the most frightening (animal, animals) _____ is a poisonous (rattlesnake, rattlesnakes) _____, but not to a twelve-year-old retriever, Partner.

2. Longtime friends Nick and Ross, both eight years old, were chopping down a tree for a campfire when a (six-foot, six-feet) _____ rattlesnake fell from a branch.

3. Partner leaped over (dirt, dirts) _____ and (leave, leaves) _____ to get to the poisonous snake, which he attacked.

4. Verle, Nick's father and Partner's owner, was (many, much) _____ yards away when he heard the racket, and he rushed over just in time to see the rattler sink its fangs into Partner's nose.

5. Within minutes, the rattler was killed by a bystander; and Partner, who showed a lot of (courage, courages) _____ and has now recovered, has become one of the best (friend, friends) _____ Nick and Ross have ever had.

Chapter 46

Articles

BACKGROUND
The Web site <http://www.ruthvilmi.net/hut/help/grammar_help/> sponsored by the Helsinki University of Technology features various quizzes and activities geared to ESL students.

46a How do I use *a, an,* or *the* with singular count nouns?

The words *a* and *an* are called **indefinite articles.** The word *the* is called the **definite article.** Articles are one type of DETERMINER. (For more on determiners, see section 7f; for other determiners, see Box 189 in section 45b.) Articles signal that a NOUN will follow and that any MODIFIERS between the article and the noun refer to that noun.

a chair	**the** computer
a brown chair	**the** teacher's computer
a cold, metal chair	**the** lightning-fast computer

Every time you use a singular count noun, a COMMON NOUN that names one countable item, the noun requires some kind of determiner; see Group 1 in Box 189 (in 45b) for a list. To choose between *a* or *an* and *the*, you need to determine whether the noun is **specific** or **nonspecific.** A noun is considered specific when anyone who reads your writing can understand exactly and specifically to what item the noun is referring. If the noun refers to any of a number of identical items, it is nonspecific.

For nonspecific singular count nouns, use *a* (or *an*). When the singular noun is specific, use *the* or some other determiner. Box 190 on the next page can help you decide when a singular count noun is specific and therefore requires *the*.

👁 **ALERT:** Use *an* before words that begin with a vowel sound. Use *a* before words that begin with a consonant sound. Go by the sound, not the spelling. For example, words that begin with *h* or *u* can have either a

813

BACKGROUND
The site <http://www.edunet.com/english/practice/test-ces.html> by Digital Education Network provides a comprehensive test that helps ESL students assess their English skills.

vowel or a consonant sound. Make the choice based on the sound of the first word after the article, even if that word is not the noun.

an idea	**a g**ood idea
an umbrella	**a u**seless umbrella
an honor	**a h**istory book

One common exception affects Rule 3 in Box 190. A noun may still require *a* (or *an*) after the first use if more information is added between the article and the noun: *I bought **a sweater** today. It was **a** (not the)*

BOX 190   SUMMARY

When a singular count noun is specific and requires *the*

- **Rule 1: A noun is specific and requires *the* when it names something unique or generally and unambiguously known.**

   The sun has risen above **the horizon.** [Because there is only one *sun* and only one *horizon*, these nouns are specific in the context of this sentence.]

- **Rule 2: A noun is specific and requires *the* when it names something used in a representative or abstract sense.**

   Benjamin Franklin favored **the turkey** as **the national bird** of the United States. [Because *turkey* and *national bird* are representative references rather than references to a particular turkey or bird, they are specific nouns in the context of this sentence.]

- **Rule 3: A noun is specific and requires *the* when it names something defined elsewhere in the same sentence or in an earlier sentence.**

   The ship *Savannah* was the first steam vessel to cross the Atlantic Ocean. [*Savannah* names a specific ship.]

   The carpet in my bedroom is new. [*In my bedroom* defines exactly which carpet is meant, so *carpet* is a specific noun in this context.]

   I have **a computer** in my office. **The computer** is often broken. [*Computer* is not specific in the first sentence, so it uses *a*. In the second sentence, *computer* has been made specific by the first sentence, so it uses *the*.]

- **Rule 4: A noun is specific and requires *the* when it names something that can be inferred from the context.**

   Monday, I had to call **the technician** to fix my computer again. [*A technician* would be any of a number of individuals; *the technician* implies the same person has been called before, and so it is specific in this context.]

red sweater. (Your audience has been introduced to *a sweater* but not *a red sweater*, so *red sweater* is not yet specific in this context and cannot take *the*.) Other information may make the noun specific so that *the* is correct. For example, *It was **the red sweater that I saw in the store yesterday*** uses *the* because the *that* CLAUSE makes specific which red sweater is meant.

BACKGROUND
Created by BYU-Hawaii Language Center and sponsored by CNN, the Web site <http://lc.byuh.edu/CNN_N/CNN-N.html> provides ESL students with grammar and vocabulary exercises based on current events.

46b How do I use articles with plural nouns and with noncount nouns?

With plural nouns and NONCOUNT NOUNS, you must decide whether to use *the* or to use no article at all. (For guidelines about using DETERMINERS other than articles with nouns, see Box 189 in 45b.) What you learned in 46a about NONSPECIFIC and SPECIFIC NOUNS can help you choose between using *the* or using no article. Box 190 in 46a explains when a singular count noun's meaning is specific and calls for *the*. Plural nouns and noncount nouns with specific meanings usually use *the* in the same circumstances. However, a plural noun or a noncount noun with a general or nonspecific meaning usually does not use *the*.

> Geraldo grows **flowers** but not **vegetables** in his garden. He is thinking about planting **corn** sometime. [three nonspecific nouns]

Plural nouns

A plural noun's meaning may be specific because it is widely known.

> **The oceans** are being damaged by pollution. [Because there is only one possible meaning for *oceans*—the oceans on the earth—it is correct to use *the*. This example is related to Rule 1 in Box 190.]

A plural noun's meaning may also be made specific by a word, PHRASE, or CLAUSE in the same sentence.

> Geraldo sold **the daisies from last year's garden** to the florist. [Because the phrase *from last year's garden* makes *daisies* specific, *the* is correct. This example is related to Rule 3 in Box 190.]

A plural noun's meaning usually becomes specific by its use in an earlier sentence.

> Geraldo planted **tulips** this year. **The tulips** will bloom in April. [*Tulips* is used in a general sense in the first sentence, without *the*. Because the first sentence makes *tulips* specific, *the tulips* is correct in the second sentence. This example is related to Rule 3 in Box 190.]

A plural noun's meaning may be made specific by the context.

> Geraldo fertilized **the bulbs** when he planted them last October. [In the context of the sentences about tulips, *bulbs* is understood as a synonym for

tulips, which makes it specific and calls for *the*. This example is related to Rule 4 in Box 190.]

Noncount nouns

Noncount nouns are always singular in form (see 45a). Like plural nouns, noncount nouns use either *the* or no article. When a noncount noun's meaning is specific, use *the* before it. If its meaning is general or nonspecific, do not use *the*.

> Kalinda served us **rice.** She flavored **the rice** with curry. [*Rice* is a noncount noun. By the second sentence, *rice* has become specific, so *the* is used. This example is related to Rule 3 in Box 190.]
>
> Kalinda served us **the rice that she had flavored with curry.** [*Rice* is a noncount noun. *Rice* is made specific by the clause *that she had flavored with curry*, so *the* is used. This example is related to Rule 3 in Box 190.]

Generalizations with plural or noncount nouns

Rule 2 in Box 190 tells you to use *the* with singular count nouns that carry general meaning. With GENERALIZATIONS using plural or noncount nouns, omit *the*.

> **NO**   **The tulips** are **the flowers** that grow from **the bulbs.**
> **YES**   **Tulips** are **flowers** that grow from **bulbs.**
>
> **NO**   **The dogs** require more care than **the cats** do.
> **YES**   **Dogs** require more care than **cats** do.

46c   How do I use *the* with proper nouns and with gerunds?

Proper nouns

PROPER NOUNS name specific people, places, or things (see 7b). Most proper nouns do not require ARTICLES: *We visited* **Lake Mead** *with* **Asha** *and* **Larry.** As shown in Box 191, however, certain types of proper nouns do require *the*.

BOX 191   SUMMARY

Proper nouns that use *the*

- **Nouns with the pattern** *the* . . . *of* . . .
  the United States **of** America   **the** Fourth **of** July
  the Republic **of** Mexico   **the** University **of** Paris

→

Proper nouns that use *the* (*continued*)

- **Plural proper nouns**
  the United Arab Emirates
  the Johnsons
  the Rocky Mountains [*but* Mount Fuji]
  the Chicago Bulls
  the Falkland Islands [*but* Long Island]
  the Great Lakes [*but* Lake Superior]
- **Collective proper nouns (nouns that name a group)**
  the Modern Language Association
  the Society of Friends
- **Some (but not all) geographical features**
  the Amazon   **the** Gobi Desert   **the** Indian Ocean
- **Three countries**
  the Congo   **the** Sudan   **the** Netherlands

Gerunds

GERUNDS are PRESENT PARTICIPLES (the *-ing* form of VERBS) used as nouns: ***Skating** is challenging.* Gerunds are usually not preceded by *the*.

NO	**The constructing** new bridges is necessary to improve traffic flow.
YES	**Constructing** new bridges is necessary to improve traffic flow.

Use *the* before a gerund when two conditions are met: (1) The gerund is used in a specific sense (see 46a), and (2) the gerund does not have a DIRECT OBJECT.

NO	**The designing fabric** is a fine art. [*Fabric* is a direct object of *designing*, so *the* should not be used.]
YES	**Designing** fabric is a fine art. [*Designing* is a gerund, so *the* is not used.]
YES	**The designing of** fabric is a fine art. [*The* is used because *fabric* is the object of the preposition *of* and *designing* is meant in a specific sense.]

817

ANSWERS AND COVERAGE: EXERCISE 46-1

1. *the* dawn of *the* twenty-first century [Rule 1, widely understood meaning of singular count nouns]; *an* invention [46a, nonspecific use of singular count noun]; *the* United States of America [46c, proper noun that uses *the*]

2. *The* digital camera [Rule 2, representative use of singular count noun]; *a* computer monitor [46a, nonspecific use of singular count noun]

3. *a* result [46a, nonspecific use of singular count noun]; *a* bad photo [46a, nonspecific use of singular count noun]; *the* screen [Rule 2, representative use of singular count noun]; *the* poor photo [Rule 3, singular count noun defined elsewhere in same sentence]; *a* new one [46a, nonspecific use of singular count noun]

4. *an* aunt, *a* Web page [46a, nonspecific uses of singular count nouns, *a* or *an* depending on sound]

5. *the* appearance [Rule 2, representative use of singular count noun]; *the* chief disadvantage [Rule 1, widely understood meaning of singular count noun]; *the* digital camera [Rule 2, representative use of singular count noun]

ANSWERS AND COVERAGE: EXERCISE 46-2

1. *a* good idea, *an* antibacterial property [46a, nonspecific uses of singular count nouns, *a* or *an* depending on sound]

2. to treat burns [46b, omit article with generalization about the plural *burns*]; *the* skin [Rule 2, representative use of singular count noun]; *the* healing process [Rule 1, widely understood meaning of singular count noun]

3. *the* pain [Rules 1 and 4, wide comprehension of noun's meaning and the context make use specific]

4. *a* person [42a, nonspecific use of singular count noun]; *the* least painful . . . burn [Rule 3, singular count noun made specific by the words *least painful or scarred*]

5. *the* burn [Rule 2, representative use of singular count noun]; *the* first person [Rule 3, singular count noun made specific by the word *first*]

EXERCISE 46-1

Consulting all sections of this chapter, select the correct article from the words in parentheses and write it in the blank.

EXAMPLE   Be forewarned: (A, An, The) <u>The</u> camera as we know it may soon be obsolete.

1. At (a, an, the) _____ dawn of (a, an, the) _____ twenty-first century comes (a, an, the) _____ invention so advanced that it may rid (a, an, the) _____ United States of America of every camera that has come before it.

2. (A, An, The) _____ digital camera, which allows photos to appear on (a, an, the) _____ computer monitor, takes up virtual space, not physical space.

3. As (a, an, the) _____ result, if you see (a, an, the) _____ bad photo on (a, an, the) _____ screen, you can simply erase (a, an, the) _____ poor photo to make room for (a, an, the) _____ new one.

4. With this new technology, (a, an, the) _____ aunt can even e-mail photos to her niece or nephew, or she can post photos to (a, an, the) _____ Web page.

5. Digital cameras allow people to alter (a, an, the) _____ appearance of people or things, which, according to many critics, is (a, an, the) _____ chief disadvantage of (a, an, the) _____ digital camera.

EXERCISE 46-2

Consulting all sections of this chapter, decide which of the words in parentheses is correct and write it in the blank. If no article is needed, leave the blank empty.

EXAMPLE   For (a, an, the) _____ years, people have worked under (a, an, the) <u>the</u> assumption that (a, an, the) <u>the</u> best remedy for (a, an, the) <u>a</u> burn is butter.

1. This kind of treatment seems to be (a, an, the) _____ good idea because butter looks and feels like ointment, but butter doesn't contain (a, an, the) _____ antibacterial property like ointment does.

2. In using butter to treat (a, an, the) _____ burns, you are coating (a, an, the) _____ skin with debris that must be removed later to keep it from interfering with (a, a, the) _____ healing process.

3. In actuality, cold water without ice will not only ease (a, an, the) _____ pain but also prevent scarring and further damage.

4. In fact, (a, an, the) _____ person who keeps the finger submerged for at least several minutes and as long as half an hour will have (a, an, the) _____ least painful or scarred burn, according to doctors.

5. However, if (a, an, the) _____ burn is serious, (a, an, the) _____ first person to be consulted should be a doctor.

Chapter 47

Word Order

TEACHING TIP
At the Web site <http://www.eslhouse.com/teacher_lounge/guest.taf>, you can find several supplemental articles, stories, and ideas for teaching English as a second language, and also communicate with ESL teachers from around the world.

47a How do I understand standard and inverted word order in sentences?

In **standard word order,** the most common pattern for DECLARATIVE SENTENCES in English, the SUBJECT comes before the VERB. (To understand these concepts more fully, review sections 7l through 7p.)

SUBJECT VERB

That book was heavy.

With **inverted word order,** the MAIN VERB or an AUXILIARY VERB comes before the subject. The most common use of inverted word order in English is in forming DIRECT QUESTIONS. Questions that can be answered with a yes or no begin with a form of *be* used as a main verb, with an auxiliary verb (*be, do, have*), or with a MODAL AUXILIARY (*can, should, will,* and others; see Chapter 50).

Questions that can be answered with a yes or no

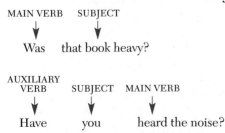

MAIN VERB SUBJECT

Was that book heavy?

AUXILIARY VERB SUBJECT MAIN VERB

Have you heard the noise?

To form a yes-or-no question with a verb other than *be* as the main verb and when there is no auxiliary or modal as part of a VERB PHRASE, use the appropriate form of the auxiliary verb *do*.

A question that begins with a question-forming word like *why, when, where,* or *how* cannot be answered with a yes or no: **Why** *did the book fall?* Some kind of information must be provided to answer such a question; the answer cannot be simply yes or no because the question is not "*Did* the book fall?" Information on *why* it fell is needed: for example, *It was too heavy for me.*

Information questions: Inverted order

Most information questions follow the same rules of inverted word order as yes-or-no questions.

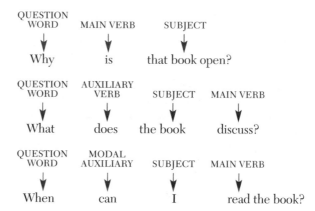

Information questions: Standard order

When *who* or *what* functions as the subject in a question, use standard word order.

BACKGROUND
For an interactive quiz on word order (from *The Internet TESL Journal*), visit <http://www.aitech.ac.jp/~iteslj/quizzes/js/>.

QUESTION WORD: SUBJECT — What

MAIN VERB — was the problem?

ALERT: When a question has more than one auxiliary verb, put the subject after the first auxiliary verb.

FIRST AUXILIARY — Would

SUBJECT — you

SECOND AUXILIARY — have

MAIN VERB — replaced the book?

The same rules apply to emphatic exclamations: ***Was*** *that book heavy!* ***Did*** *she enjoy that book!*

Negatives

When you use negatives such *as never, hardly ever, seldom, rarely, not only,* or *nor* to start a CLAUSE, use inverted order. These sentence pairs show the differences, first in standard order and then in inverted order.

I have never seen a more exciting movie. [standard order]
Never have I seen a more exciting movie. [inverted order]

She is not only a talented artist **but also** an excellent musician.
Not only is she a talented artist, **but she is also** an excellent musician.

I didn't like the book, and **my husband didn't either.**
I didn't like the book, and **neither did my husband.**

ALERTS: (1) With INDIRECT QUESTIONS, use standard word order.

| NO | She asked **how did I drop** the book. |
| YES | She asked **how I dropped** the book. |

(2) Word order deliberately inverted can be effective, when used sparingly, to create emphasis in a sentence that is neither a question nor an exclamation (also see 19e).

47b How can I understand the placement of adjectives?

ADJECTIVES modify—describe or limit—NOUNS, PRONOUNS, and word groups that function as nouns (see 7f). In English, an adjective comes directly before the noun it describes. However, when more than one adjective describes the same noun, several sequences may be possible. Box 192 shows the most common order for positioning several adjectives.

BOX 192   SUMMARY

 Word order for more than one adjective

1. **Determiners, if any:** *a, an, the, my, your, this, that, these, those,* and so on

2. **Expressions of order, including ordinal numbers, if any:** *first, second, third, next, last, final,* and so on

3. **Expressions of quantity, including cardinal (counting) numbers, if any:** *one, two, few, each, every, some,* and so on

4. **Adjectives of judgment or opinion, if any:** *pretty, happy, ugly, sad, interesting, boring,* and so on

5. **Adjectives of size or shape, if any:** *big, small, short, round, square,* and so on

6. **Adjectives of age or condition, if any:** *new, young, broken, dirty, shiny,* and so on

7. **Adjectives of color, if any:** *red, green, blue,* and so on

8. **Adjectives that can also be used as nouns, if any:** *French, Protestant, metal, cotton,* and so on

9. **The noun**

1	2	3	4	5	6	7	8	9
a		few		tiny		red		ants
the	last	six					Thai	carvings
my			fine		old		oak	table

47c How can I understand the placement of adverbs?

ADVERBS modify—describe or limit—VERBS, ADJECTIVES, other adverbs, or entire sentences (see 7g). Adverbs may be positioned first, in the middle, or last in CLAUSES. Box 193 on the facing page summarizes adverb types, what they tell about the words they modify, and where each type can be placed.

👁 **ALERT:** Do not let an adverb separate a verb from its DIRECT OBJECT or INDIRECT OBJECT. 👁

BOX 193   SUMMARY

Types of adverbs and where to position them

ADVERBS OF MANNER	▪ describe *how* something is done	Nick **carefully** groomed the dog.
	▪ are usually in middle or last position	Nick groomed the dog **carefully.**
ADVERBS OF TIME	▪ describe *when* or *how long* about an event	**First,** he shampooed the dog.
	▪ are usually in first or last position	He shampooed the dog **first.**
	▪ include *just, still, already,* and similar adverbs, which are usually in middle position	He had **already** brushed the dog's coat.
ADVERBS OF FREQUENCY	▪ describe *how often* an event takes place	Nick has **never** been bitten by a dog.
	▪ are usually in middle position	
	▪ are in first position when they modify an entire sentence (see "Sentence adverbs" below)	**Occasionally,** he is scratched while shampooing a cat.
ADVERBS OF DEGREE OR EMPHASIS	▪ describe *how much* or *to what extent* about other modifiers	Nick is **extremely** calm around animals. [*Extremely* modifies *calm.*]
	▪ are directly before the word they modify	
	▪ include *only,* which is easy to misplace (see 14a)	
SENTENCE ADVERBS	▪ modify the entire sentence rather than just one word or a few words	**Incredibly,** he was once asked to groom a rat.
	▪ include transitional words and expressions (see 4g.1), as well as such expressions as *maybe, probably, possibly, fortunately, unfortunately,* and *incredibly*	
	▪ are in first position	

QUOTATION: ON WRITING
I regard the writing of humor as a supreme artistic challenge.
—Herman Wouk

ANSWERS AND COVERAGE: EXERCISE 47-1

1. For almost two hundred years [47c, adverb of degree is positioned before the words it modifies, *two hundred years*]

2. Why are they returning [47a, inverted word order for questions, form of *be* precedes subject]

3. are extremely precise [47c, adverb of degree or emphasis is positioned before the word it modifies, *precise*]

4. The first whales [47b, expression of order follows determiner *the* but precedes all other modifiers (if any) and the noun]

5. The last humpbacks; by late December or early January [47b, expressions of order precede the words they modify]

ANSWERS AND COVERAGE: EXERCISE 47-2

1. A few beautiful flowers [47b, expressions of quantity precede adjectives of opinion]

2. Did you grow [47a, inverted word order for questions, form of *do* precedes subject]

3. my husband's favorite [47b, *husband's* as adjective that can also be a noun is positioned before the word it modifies, *favorite*]

4. was extremely impressed [47c, adverb of degree is positioned before the word it modifies, *impressed*]

5. her happily planting seeds [47c, adverb of manner is positioned before the word it modifies, *planting*]

EXERCISE 47-1

Consulting all sections of this chapter, find and correct any errors in word order.

1. For two hundred years almost, the North Pacific humpback whales have returned to the tropic waters of Hawaii.
2. Why they are returning to these particular waters year after year?
3. The humpbacks do not accidentally arrive in Hawaiian waters; they are precise extremely in searching for this specific location, where they gather to complete their breeding rituals.
4. The whales first to arrive are sighted sometime in late November, after completing a 3,000-mile journey.
5. The humpbacks last to migrate to Hawaii arrive by December late or January early.

EXERCISE 47-2

Consulting all sections of this chapter, find and correct any errors in word order.

1. A beautiful few flowers began to bloom in my garden this week.
2. A neighbor asked me, "You did grow all these yourself?"
3. "Yes," I replied, "the roses are my favorite husband's, but the tulips are my favorite."
4. My neighbor, who extremely was impressed with my gardening efforts, decided to grow some flowers of her own.
5. Weeks later, as I strolled by her house, I saw her planting happily seeds from her favorite type of plant—petunias.

Chapter 48

Prepositions

QUOTATION: ON WRITING
If the writing is honest it cannot be separated
from the man who wrote it.
—Tennessee Williams

Prepositions function with other words in PREPOSITIONAL PHRASES (7o). Prepositional phrases usually indicate *where* (direction or location), *how* (by what means or in what way), or *when* (at what time or how long) about the words they modify.

This chapter can help you with several uses of prepositions, which function in combination with other words in ways that are often idiomatic—that is, peculiar to the language. The meaning of an IDIOM differs from the literal meaning of each individual word. For example, the word *break* usually refers to shattering, but the sentence *Yao-Ming **broke into** a smile* means that a smile appeared on Yao-Ming's face. Knowing which preposition to use in a specific context takes much experience in reading, listening to, and speaking the language. A dictionary like the *Dictionary of American English* (Heinle and Heinle) can be especially helpful when you need to find the correct preposition to use in cases not covered by this chapter. Section 48a lists many common prepositions. Section 48b discusses prepositions with some expressions of time and place. Section 48c discusses combinations of verbs and prepositions called PHRASAL VERBS. Section 48d discusses prepositions with PAST PARTICIPLES. Section 48e discusses common expressions using prepositions.

48a How can I recognize prepositions?

Box 194 lists many common prepositions.

BOX 194   SUMMARY

Common prepositions

about	according to	after	along	among
above	across	against	along with	apart from

→

BACKGROUND
The Web site <http://www.english-zone.com/
grammar/1preps.html> offers quizzes of varying levels on prepositions.

Common prepositions (*continued*)

around	by	in back of	on	till
as	by means of	in case of	onto	to
as for	concerning	in front of	on top of	toward
at	despite	in place of	out	under
because of	down	inside	out of	underneath
before	during	in spite of	outside	unlike
behind	except	instead of	over	until
below	except for	into	past	up
beneath	excepting	like	regarding	upon
beside	for	near	round	up to
between	from	next	since	with
beyond	in	of	through	within
but	in addition to	off	throughout	without

48b How do I use prepositions with expressions of time and place?

Box 195 shows how to use the prepositions *in*, *at*, and *on* to deliver some common kinds of information about time and place. The box, however, does not cover every preposition that indicates time or place, nor does it cover all uses of *in*, *at*, and *on*. Also, the box does not include expressions that operate outside the general rules. (Both these sentences are correct: *You ride **in** the car* and *You ride **on** the bus.*)

BOX 195   SUMMARY

Using *in*, *at*, and *on* to show time and place

Time

- ***in* a year or a month** (*during* is also correct but less common)
  in 1995   **in** May
- ***in* a period of time**
  in a few months (seconds, days, years)

→

Using *in*, *at*, and *on* to show time and place (*continued*)

- ***in* a period of the day**
  in the morning (afternoon, evening)
  in the daytime (morning, evening) *but* **at** night

- ***at* a specific time or period of time**
  at noon   **at** 2:00   **at** dawn   **at** nightfall
  at takeoff (the time a plane leaves)
  at breakfast (the time a specific meal takes place)

- ***on* a specific day**
  on Friday   **on** my birthday

Place

- ***in* a location surrounded by something else**
  in the province of Alberta   **in** the kitchen
  in Utah   **in** the apartment
  in downtown Bombay   **in** the bathtub

- ***at* a specific location**
  at your house   **at** the bank
  at the corner of Third Avenue and Main Street

- ***on* a surface**
  on page 20
  on the second floor *but* **in** the attic *or* **in** the basement
  on Washington Street
  on the mezzanine
  on the highway

BACKGROUND
At the Web site <http://www.wordskills.com/reception.shtml>, students can find a different phrasal verb posted each day, along with its definition.

48c How do I use prepositions in phrasal verbs?

Phrasal verbs, also called *two-word verbs* and *three-word verbs,* are VERBS that combine with PREPOSITIONS to deliver their meaning. In some phrasal verbs, the verb and the preposition should not be separated by other words: ***Look at*** *the moon* [not ***Look*** *the moon* ***at***]. In **separable phrasal verbs,** other words in the sentence can separate the verb and the preposition without interfering with meaning: *I **threw away** my homework* is as correct as *I **threw** my homework **away.***

Here is a list of some common phrasal verbs. The ones that cannot be separated are marked with an asterisk (*).

SELECTED PHRASAL VERBS

ask out	get along with*	look into
break down	get back	look out for*
bring about	get off	look over
call back	go over*	make up
drop off	hand in	run across*
figure out	keep up with*	speak to*
fill out	leave out	speak with*
fill up	look after*	throw away
find out	look around	throw out

Position a PRONOUN OBJECT between the words of a separable phrasal verb: *I threw **it** away.* Also, you can position an object PHRASE of several words between the parts of a separable phrasal verb: *I threw **my research paper** away.* However, when the object is a CLAUSE, do not let it separate the parts of the phrasal verb: *I threw away **all the papers that I wrote last year.***

Many phrasal verbs are informal and are used more in speaking than in writing. For ACADEMIC WRITING, a more formal verb is usually more appropriate than a phrasal verb. In a research paper, for example, *propose* or *suggest* might be a better choice than *come up with*. For academic writing, acceptable phrasal verbs include *believe in, benefit from, concentrate on, consist of, depend on, dream of* (or *dream about*), *insist on, participate in, prepare for,* and *stare at.* None of these phrasal verbs can be separated.

EXERCISE 48-1

Consulting the preceding sections of this chapter and using the list of phrasal verbs in 48c, write a one- or two-paragraph description of a typical day at work or school in which you use at least five phrasal verbs. After checking a dictionary, revise your writing, substituting for the phrasal verbs any more formal verbs that might be more appropriate for academic writing.

48d **How do I use prepositions with past participles?**

PAST PARTICIPLES are verb forms that function as ADJECTIVES (49f). Past participles end in either *-ed* or *-d,* or in an equivalent irregular form (8d). When past participles follow the LINKING VERB *be,* it is easy to confuse them with PASSIVE verbs (8n), which have the same endings. Passive verbs describe actions. Past participles, because they act as adjectives, modify NOUNS and PRONOUNS and often describe situations and conditions. Passive verbs follow the pattern *be* + past participle + *by: The child **was frightened by** a snake.* An expression containing a past participle, however, can use either *be* or another linking verb, and it can be followed by either *by* or a different preposition.

- The child **seemed frightened by** snakes.
- The child **is frightened of** all snakes.

Here is a list of expressions containing past participles and the prepositions that often follow them. Look in a dictionary for others. (See 49b on using GERUNDS after some of these expressions.)

SELECTED PAST PARTICIPLE PHRASES + PREPOSITIONS

be accustomed to	be interested in
be acquainted with	be known for
be composed of	be located in
be concerned/worried about	be made of (*or* from)
be disappointed with (*or* in someone)	be married to
be discriminated against	be pleased/satisfied with
be divorced from	be prepared for
be excited about	be tired of (*or* from)
be finished/done with	

48e How do I use prepositions in expressions?

In many common expressions, different PREPOSITIONS convey great differences in meaning. For example, four prepositions can be used with the verb *agree* to create five different meanings.

agree to means "to give consent": *I cannot **agree to** my buying you a new car.*

agree about means "to arrive at a satisfactory understanding": *We certainly **agree about** your needing a car.*

agree on means "to concur": *You and the seller must **agree on** a price for the car.*

agree with means "to have the same opinion": *I **agree with** you that you need a car.*

agree with means "to be suitable or healthful": *The idea of having such a major expense does not **agree with** me.*

829

You can find entire books filled with English expressions that include prepositions. The following list shows a few that you're likely to use often.

SELECTED EXPRESSIONS WITH PREPOSITIONS

ability in	different from	involved with [*someone*]
access to	faith in	knowledge of
accustomed to	familiar with	made of
afraid of	famous for	married to
angry with *or* at	frightened by	opposed to
authority on	happy with	patient with
aware of	in charge of	proud of
based on	independent of	reason for
capable of	in favor of	related to
certain of	influence on *or* over	suspicious of
confidence in	interested in	time for
dependent on	involved in [*something*]	tired of

Chapter 49

Gerunds, Infinitives, and Participles

QUOTATION: ON WRITING
If it sounds like writing, I rewrite it.
—Elmore Leonard

PARTICIPLES are verb forms (see 8b). A verb's *-ing* form is its PRESENT PARTICIPLE. The *-ed* form of a regular verb is its PAST PARTICIPLE; IRREGULAR VERBS form their past participles in various ways (for example, *bend, bent; eat, eaten; think, thought*—for a complete list, see Box 60 in section 8d). Participles can function as ADJECTIVES (a **smiling** *face, a* **closed** *book*).

A verb's *-ing* form can also function as a NOUN (**Sneezing** *spreads colds*), which is called a GERUND. Another verb form, the INFINITIVE, can also function as a noun. An infinitive is a verb's SIMPLE or base FORM, usually preceded by the word *to* (*We want everyone* **to smile**). Verb forms—participles, gerunds, and infinitives—functioning as nouns or MODIFIERS are called VERBALS, as explained in section 7e.

This chapter can help you make the right choices among verbals. Section 49a discusses gerunds and infinitives used as subjects. Section 49b discusses verbs that are followed by gerunds, not infinitives. Section 49c discusses verbs that are followed by infinitives, not gerunds. Section 49d discusses meaning changes that depend on whether certain verbs are followed by a gerund or by an infinitive. Section 49e explains that meaning does not change for certain sense verbs no matter whether they are followed by a gerund or an infinitive. Section 49f discusses differences in meaning between the present participle form and the past participle form of some modifiers.

49a How can I use gerunds and infinitives as subjects?

Gerunds are used more commonly than infinitives as subjects. Sometimes, however, either is acceptable.

Choosing the right health club is important.
To choose the right health club is important.

831

BACKGROUND
The site <http://www.bbc.co.uk/worldservice/learningenglish/quizzes/index.shtml>, hosted by the BBC, offers numerous quizzes for ESL students interested in practicing their English.

👁 **ALERT:** When a gerund or an infinitive is used alone as a subject, it is SINGULAR and requires a singular verb. When two or more gerunds or infinitives create a COMPOUND SUBJECT, they require a plural verb. (See 7l and 10e.) 👁

49b When do I use a gerund, not an infinitive, as an object?

Some VERBS must be followed by GERUNDS used as DIRECT OBJECTS. Other verbs must be followed by INFINITIVES. Still other verbs can be followed by either a gerund or an infinitive. (A few verbs can change meaning depending on whether they are followed by a gerund or an infinitive; see 49d.) Box 196 lists common verbs that must be followed by gerunds, not infinitives.

> Yuri **considered** *calling* [not *to call*] the mayor.
> He **was having trouble** *getting* [not *to get*] a work permit.
> Yuri's boss **recommended** *taking* [not *to take*] an interpreter to the permit agency.

BOX 196   SUMMARY

🌀 Verbs and expressions that must be followed by gerunds

acknowledge	detest	mind
admit	discuss	object to
advise	dislike	postpone
anticipate	dream about	practice
appreciate	enjoy	put off
avoid	escape	quit
cannot bear	evade	recall
cannot help	favor	recommend
cannot resist	finish	regret
complain about	give up	resent
consider	have trouble	resist
consist of	imagine	risk
contemplate	include	suggest
defer from	insist on	talk about
delay	keep (on)	tolerate
deny	mention	understand

Gerund after go

The word *go* is usually followed by an infinitive: *We can* **go to see** [not *go seeing*] *a movie tonight*. Sometimes, however, *go* is followed by a gerund in phrases such as *go swimming*, *go fishing*, *go shopping*, and *go driving*: *I will* **go shopping** [not *go to shop*] *after work*.

Gerund after be + complement + preposition

Many common expressions use a form of the verb *be* plus a COMPLEMENT plus a PREPOSITION. In such expressions, use a gerund, not an infinitive, after the preposition. Here is a list of some of the most frequently used expressions in this pattern.

SELECTED EXPRESSIONS USING *BE* **+ COMPLEMENT + PREPOSITION**

be (get) accustomed to	be interested in
be angry about	be prepared for
be bored with	be responsible for
be capable of	be tired of
be committed to	be (get) used to
be excited about	be worried about

We **are excited about** *voting* [not *to vote*] in the next presidential election.
Who **will be responsible for** *locating* [not *to locate*] our polling place?

👁 **ALERT:** Always use a gerund, not an infinitive, as the object of a preposition. Be especially careful when the word *to* is functioning as a preposition in a PHRASAL VERB (see 48c): *We are committed* **to changing** [not *to change*] *the rules.* 👁

49c When do I use an infinitive, not a gerund, as an object?

Box 197 on the next page lists selected common verbs and expressions that must be followed by INFINITIVES, not GERUNDS, as OBJECTS.

She **wanted** *to go* [not *wanted going*] to the lecture.
Only three people **decided** *to question* [not *decided questioning*] the speaker.

Infinitive after be + complement

Gerunds are common in constructions that use a form of the verb *be* plus a COMPLEMENT and a PREPOSITION (see 49b). However, use an

BACKGROUND
A great resource for both ESL teachers and teachers with ESL students is *Dave's ESL Cafe*, found at <http://www.pacificnet.net/~sperling/eslcafe.html>. This Web site offers quizzes, links, quotations, and discussion forums among its various resources.

BOX 197	SUMMARY

Verbs and expressions that must be followed by infinitives

afford	consent	intend	promise
agree	decide	know how	refuse
aim	decline	learn	require
appear	demand	like	seem
arrange	deserve	manage	struggle
ask	do not care	mean	tend
attempt	expect	need	threaten
be left	fail	offer	volunteer
beg	force	plan	vote
cannot afford	give permission	prefer	wait
care	hesitate	prepare	want
claim	hope	pretend	would like

infinitive, not a gerund, when *be* plus a complement is not followed by a preposition.

> We **are eager *to go*** [not *going*] camping.
> I **am ready *to sleep*** [not *sleeping*] in a tent.

Infinitive to indicate purpose

Use an infinitive in expressions that indicate purpose: *I read a book **to learn** more about Mayan culture.* This sentence means "I read a book for the purpose of learning more about Mayan culture." *To learn* delivers the idea of purpose more concisely (see Chapter 16) than expressions such as *so that I can* or *in order to.*

Infinitive with the first, the last, the one

Use an infinitive after the expressions *the first, the last,* and *the one: Nina is the first **to arrive*** [not *arriving*] *and the last **to leave*** [not *leaving*] *every day. She's always the one **to do** the most.*

Unmarked infinitives

Infinitives used without the word *to* are called **unmarked infinitives,** or sometimes *bare infinitives.* An unmarked infinitive may be hard to recognize because it is not preceded by *to.* Some common verbs followed by unmarked infinitives are *feel, have, hear, let, listen to, look at, make* (meaning "compel"), *notice, see,* and *watch.*

Please let me **take** [not *to take*] you to lunch. [unmarked infinitive]
I want **to take** you to lunch. [marked infinitive]

I can have Kara **drive** [not *to drive*] us. [unmarked infinitive]
I will ask Kara **to drive** us. [marked infinitive]

The verb *help* can be followed by a marked or an unmarked infinitive. Either is correct: *Help me* **put** [or **to put**] *this box in the car.*

👁 **ALERT:** Be careful to use parallel structure (see Chapter 18) correctly when you use two or more gerunds or infinitives after verbs. If two or more verbal objects follow one verb, put the verbals into the same form.

> NO　We went **sailing** and **to scuba dive.**
> YES　We went **sailing** and **scuba diving.**
>
> NO　We heard the wind **blow** and the waves **crashing.**
> YES　We heard the wind **blow** and the waves **crash.**
> YES　We heard the wind **blowing** and the waves **crashing.**

Conversely, if you are using verbal objects with COMPOUND PREDICATES, be sure to use the kind of verbal that each verb requires.

> NO　We enjoyed **scuba diving** but do not plan **sailing** again.
> 　　[*Enjoyed* requires a gerund object, and *plan* requires an infinitive
> 　　object; see Boxes 196 and 197 in this chapter.]
>
> YES　We enjoyed **scuba diving** but do not plan **to sail** again.　👁

49d　How does meaning change when certain verbs are followed by a gerund or an infinitive?

With stop

The VERB *stop* followed by a GERUND means "finish, quit." *Stop* followed by an INFINITIVE means "interrupt one activity to begin another."

> We **stopped** *eating.* [We finished our meal.]
> We **stopped** *to eat.* [We stopped another activity, such as driving, in order to eat.]

With remember *and* forget

The verb *remember* followed by an infinitive means "not to forget to do something": *I must* **remember to talk** *with Isa. Remember* followed by a gerund means "recall a memory": *I* **remember talking** *in my sleep last night.*

QUOTATION: ON WRITING
The act of writing requires a constant plunging back into the shadow of the past where time hovers ghostlike.

　　　　　　　　—Ralph Ellison

ANSWERS AND COVERAGE:
EXERCISE 49-1

1. riding [49b, gerund after preposition *about*]

2. take [49c, unmarked infinitive with *let*]

3. to bring [49c, infinitive following *force*]

4. to walk [49c, infinitive following *need*]

5. Stepping [49a, gerund as subject]

6. losing [49b, gerund after *be* + complement *angry* + preposition *about*]

7. reunite *or* to reunite [49c, marked or unmarked infinitive with *help*]

8. to call [49c, infinitive following *tend*]

9. leaving [49b, gerund following *acknowledge*]

10. answering, identifying [49b, gerund after preposition *by*]

The verb *forget* followed by an infinitive means "fail to do something": *If you **forget to put** a stamp on that letter, it will be returned. Forget* followed by a gerund means "do something and not recall it": *I **forget having put** the stamps in the refrigerator.*

With try

The verb *try* followed by an infinitive means "make an effort": *I **tried to find** your jacket.* Followed by a gerund, *try* means "experiment with": *I **tried jogging** but found it too difficult.*

49e Why is the meaning unchanged whether a gerund or an infinitive follows sense verbs?

Sense VERBS include words such as *see, notice, hear, observe, watch, feel, listen to,* and *look at.* The meaning of these verbs is usually not affected by whether a GERUND or an INFINITIVE follows as the OBJECT. *I **saw** the water **rise*** and *I **saw** the water **rising*** both have the same meaning in American English.

EXERCISE 49-1

Write the correct form of the verbal object (either a gerund or an infinitive) for each verb in parentheses. For help, consult 49b through 49e.

EXAMPLE   People like (think) <u>to think</u> that they have a good memory, but everybody shows signs of forgetfulness from time to time.

1. Think about (ride) _____ the railroad to work on a rainy Monday morning.
2. The comfortable reclining seats let passengers (take) _____ a relaxing nap on the way to work.
3. Because of the rain, commuters are forced (bring) _____ an umbrella and a raincoat, along with their usual traveling items.
4. Once they reach their destination, passengers forget that they need their umbrellas and raincoats (walk) _____ the few blocks to work.
5. (Step) _____ out into the rain makes the passengers suddenly realize that they've left their umbrellas and raincoats on the train, which has already left the station.
6. However, they need not be angry about (lose) _____ the forgotten item.
7. Many railroads have lost-and-found offices that help (reunite) _____ the rightful owners with their lost possessions.

8. After losing a possession, passengers tend (call) _____ the lost-and-found office in search of the missing article.

9. Some commuters even acknowledge (leave) _____ gifts, false teeth, wooden legs, and bicycles aboard the train.

10. Most times, people can claim their possessions either by (answer) _____ a few questions to ensure proper ownership or by (identify) _____ the lost item.

QUOTATION: ON WRITING
The profession of book writing makes horse racing seem like a solid, stable business.
—John Steinbeck

49f How do I choose between -*ing* and -*ed* forms for adjectives?

Deciding whether to use the -*ing* form (PRESENT PARTICIPLE) or the -*ed* form (PAST PARTICIPLE of a regular VERB) as an ADJECTIVE in a specific sentence can be difficult. For example, *I am amused* and *I am amusing* are both correct in English, but their meanings are very different. To make the right choice, decide whether the modified NOUN or PRONOUN is causing or experiencing what the participle describes.

Use a present participle (-*ing*) to modify a noun or pronoun that is the agent or the cause of the action.

> Micah described your **interesting** plan. [The noun *plan* causes what its modifier describes—interest; so *interesting* is correct.]
>
> I find your plan **exciting.** [The noun *plan* causes what its modifier describes—excitement; so *exciting* is correct.]

Use a past participle (-*ed* in regular verbs) to modify a noun or pronoun that experiences or receives whatever the modifier describes.

> An **interested** committee wants to hear your plan. [The noun *committee* experiences what its modifier describes—interest; so *interested* is correct.]
>
> **Excited** by your plan, they called a board meeting. [The pronoun *they* experiences what its modifier describes—excitement; so *excited* is correct.]

Here are frequently used participles that convey very different meanings, depending on whether the -*ed* or the -*ing* form is used.

amused, amusing	frightened, frightening
annoyed, annoying	insulted, insulting
appalled, appalling	offended, offending
bored, boring	overwhelmed, overwhelming
confused, confusing	pleased, pleasing
depressed, depressing	reassured, reassuring
disgusted, disgusting	satisfied, satisfying
fascinated, fascinating	shocked, shocking

ANSWERS AND COVERAGE: EXERCISE 49-2

1. interesting [*life* conveys rather than experiences interest]

2. horrified [*observers* experience rather than convey horror]; injured [*Kahlo* experiences rather than causes injury]

3. disappointed [*Kahlo* experiences rather than causes disappointment]

4. disturbing [*images* cause rather than experience disturbance]

5. fascinating [*works of art* cause rather than experience fascination]; overwhelming [*paintings* overwhelm rather than experience being overwhelmed—*overwhelming* modifies the pronoun *them*, for which the referent is *paintings*]

ANSWERS AND COVERAGE: EXERCISE 49-3

1. fascinating [*history* conveys rather than experiences fascination]

2. Raised [*Carrey* experienced what the modifier describes]

3. surprising [*news* conveys rather than experiences surprise]

4. disappointed [*Carrey* experiences rather than causes disappointment]; canceled [the *TV series* experiences rather than causes the cancellation]

5. amusing [*appearances* cause rather than experience amusement]

EXERCISE 49-2

Choose the correct participle from each pair in parentheses. For help, consult 49f.

EXAMPLE   It can be a (satisfied, satisfying) <u>satisfying</u> experience to learn about the lives of artists.

1. The artist Frida Kahlo led an (interested, interesting) _____ life.
2. When Kahlo was eighteen, (horrified, horrifying) _____ observers saw her (injured, injuring) _____ in a streetcar accident.
3. A (disappointed, disappointing) _____ Kahlo had to abandon her plan to study medicine.
4. Instead, she began to create paintings filled with (disturbed, disturbing) _____ images.
5. Some art critics consider Kahlo's paintings to be (fascinated, fascinating) _____ works of art, though many people find them (overwhelmed, overwhelming) _____.

EXERCISE 49-3

Choose the correct participle from each pair in parentheses. For help, consult 49f.

EXAMPLE   Learning about the career of a favorite actor or actress is always an (interested, interesting) <u>interesting</u> exercise.

1. Canadian Jim Carrey is an actor-comedian with a very (fascinated, fascinating) _____ history.
2. (Raised, Raising) _____ by his parents in southern Ontario, Carrey grew up in one of the most media-rich areas in North America.
3. Biographies reveal the (surprised, surprising) _____ news that this bright and talented student dropped out of school during the tenth grade.
4. After relocating to Los Angeles in the 1980s, the (disappointed, disappointing) _____ Carrey discovered the difficulties of acting after his first (canceled, canceling) _____ TV series left him briefly out of work.
5. Carrey's career skyrocketed with his (amused, amusing) _____ appearances on *In Living Color,* a TV show that led to a string of box-office hits: *The Mask; The Truman Show; Liar, Liar;* and *Bruce Almighty.*

EXERCISE 49-4

Choose the correct participle from each pair in parentheses. For help, consult 49f.

EXAMPLE   Studying popular myths that turn out to be false can be a (fascinated, <u>fascinating</u>) fascinating experience.

1. While doing research for a paper about birds, I discovered some (interested, interesting) _____ information about ostriches.
2. I encountered an (unsettled, unsettling) _____ passage in a book, which said that ostriches do not, in fact, stick their heads into the sand for protection when they feel fear.
3. This myth about (frightened, frightening) _____ ostriches began among the ancient Arabs and has since been passed on by many reputable writers.
4. In reality, an ostrich does not have to do something as useless as bury its head in the sand when a predator approaches, because a (hunted, hunting) _____ ostrich can reach speeds of nearly 35 mph and can thus outrun most other animals.
5. A (threatened, threatening) _____ ostrich can also kick its way out of many dangerous situations with its powerful legs, and with its 8-foot-tall frame, it presents itself as a (frightened, frightening) _____ opponent.

Chapter 50

Modal Auxiliary Verbs

AUXILIARY VERBS are known as *helping verbs* because adding an auxiliary verb to a MAIN VERB helps the main verb convey additional information (see 8e). For example, the auxiliary verb *do* is important in turning sentences into questions. *You have to sleep* becomes a question when *do* is added: *Do you have to sleep?* The most common auxiliary verbs are forms of *be, have*, and *do*. Boxes 62 and 63 in section 8e list the forms of these three verbs.

MODAL AUXILIARY VERBS are one type of auxiliary verb. They include *can, could, may, might, should, had better, must, will, would*, and others discussed in this chapter. Modals differ from *be, have*, and *do* used as auxiliary verbs in the specific ways discussed in Box 198.

This chapter can help you use modals to convey shades of meaning. Section 50a discusses using modals to convey ability, necessity, advisability, possibility, and probability. Section 50b discusses using modals to convey preferences, plans or obligations, and past habits. Section 50c introduces modals in the PASSIVE VOICE.

BOX 198   SUMMARY

 Modals and their differences from other auxiliary verbs

- Modals in the present future are always followed by the SIMPLE FORM of a main verb: *I **might go** tomorrow.*
- One-word modals have no *-s* ending in the THIRD-PERSON SINGULAR: *She **could** go with me; he **could** go with me; they **could** go with me.* (The two-word modal *have to* changes form to agree with its subject: *I **have to** leave; she **has to** leave.*) Auxiliary verbs other than modals usually change form for third-person singular: *I **do** want to go; he **does** want to go.*

→

Modals and their differences from other auxiliary verbs (*continued*)

- Some modals change form in the past. Others (*should, would, must,* which convey probability, and *ought to*) use *have* + a PAST PARTICIPLE. *I **can do*** it becomes *I **could do*** it in PAST-TENSE CLAUSES about ability. *I **could do*** it becomes *I **could have done*** it in clauses about possibility.
- Modals convey meaning about ability, necessity, advisability, possibility, and other conditions: For example, *I can go* means "I am able to go." Modals do not describe actual occurrences.

BACKGROUND
At the Web site <http://isu.indstate.edu/writing/esl/esl.html#modals>, the Indiana State University OWL (Online Writing Lab) offers several quizzes on modal usage.

50a How do I convey ability, necessity, advisability, possibility, and probability with modals?

Conveying ability

The modal *can* conveys ability now (in the present), and *could* conveys ability before (in the past). These words deliver the meaning "able to." For the future, use *will be able to.*

> We **can** work late tonight. [*Can* conveys present ability.]
> I **could** work late last night, too. [*Could* conveys past ability.]
> I **will be able to** work late next Monday. [*Will be able* is the future tense; *will* here is not a modal.]

Adding *not* between a modal and the MAIN VERB makes the CLAUSE negative: *We **cannot** work late tonight; I **could not** work late last night; I **will not be able to** work late next Monday.*

👁 **ALERT:** You will often see negative forms of modals turned into CONTRACTIONS: *can't, couldn't, won't, wouldn't,* and others. Because contractions are considered informal usage by some instructors, you will never be wrong if you avoid them in ACADEMIC WRITING, except when you are reproducing spoken words. 👁

Conveying necessity

The modals *must* and *have to* convey a need to do something. Both *must* and *have to* are followed by the simple form of the main verb. In the present tense, *have to* changes form to agree with its subject.

> You **must** leave before midnight.
> She **has to** leave when I leave.

In the past tense, *must* is never used to express necessity. Instead, use *had to*.

PRESENT TENSE	We **must** study today. We **have to** study today.
PAST TENSE	We **had to** [not *must*] take a test yesterday.

The negative forms of *must* and *have to* also have different meanings. *Must not* conveys that something is forbidden; *do not have to* conveys that something is not necessary.

> You **must not** sit there. [Sitting there is forbidden.]
> You **do not have to** sit there. [Sitting there is not necessary.]

Conveying advisability or the notion of a good idea

The modals *should* and *ought to* express the idea that doing the action of the main verb is advisable or is a good idea.

> You **should** go to class tomorrow morning.

In the past tense, *should* and *ought to* convey regret or knowing something through hindsight. They mean that good advice was not taken.

> You **should have** gone to class yesterday.
> I **ought to have** called my sister yesterday.

The modal *had better* delivers the meaning of good advice or warning or threat. It does not change form for tense.

> You **had better** see the doctor before your cough gets worse.

Need to is often used to express strong advice, too. Its past-tense form is *needed to*.

> You **need to** take better care of yourself. You **needed to** listen.

Conveying possibility

The modals *may, might,* and *could* can be used to convey an idea of possibility or likelihood.

> We **may** become hungry before long.
> We **could** eat lunch at the diner next door.

For the past-tense form, use *may, might,* and *could,* followed by *have* and the past participle of the main verb.

> I **could have studied** French in high school, but I studied Spanish instead.

Conveying probability

In addition to conveying the idea of necessity, the modal *must* can also convey probability or likelihood. It means that a well-informed guess is being made.

> Marisa **must** be a talented actress. She has been chosen to play the lead role in the school play.

When *must* conveys probability, the past tense is *must have* plus the past participle of the main verb.

> I did not see Boris at the party; he **must have left** early.

EXERCISE 50-1

Fill in each blank with the past-tense modal auxiliary that expresses the meaning given in parentheses. For help, consult 50a.

EXAMPLE I (advisability) <u>should have</u> gone straight to the doctor the instant I felt a cold coming on.

1. Since I (necessity, no choice) _____ work late this past Monday, I could not get to the doctor's office before it closed.
2. I (advisability) _____ fallen asleep after dinner, but I stayed awake for a while instead.
3. Even after I finally got into bed, I (ability) _____ not relax.
4. I (making a guess) _____ not _____ heard the alarm the next morning, because I overslept nearly two hours.
5. When I finally arrived at work, my boss came into my office and said, "Julie, you (necessity) _____ stayed home and rested if you are sick."

EXERCISE 50-2

Fill in each blank with the past-tense modal auxiliary that expresses the meaning given in parentheses. For help, consult 50a.

EXAMPLE I (advisability) <u>should have</u> waited for a rainy afternoon to visit the Empire State Building.

1. Since I (necessity, no choice) _____ work all week, Sunday was my only free day to visit the Empire State Building.
2. I (advisability) _____ known that because it was such a clear, beautiful day, everyone else would want to visit this New York City landmark, too.
3. The lines for the elevator were terribly long, and even though I am physically fit, I (ability) _____ not possibly climb the eighty-six flights of stairs to the observation deck near the top of the building.

ANSWERS AND COVERAGE: EXERCISE 50 1

1. had to *or* needed to [either past-tense form of modal auxiliary is acceptable]

2. should have *or* ought to have [either past-tense form of modal auxiliary is acceptable]

3. could [past-tense form of modal auxiliary]

4. must/could/might/may; have [any of the past-tense forms for conveying possibility and making a guess is acceptable]

5. should have *or* ought to have [either past-tense form of modal auxiliary is acceptable]

**ANSWERS AND COVERAGE:
EXERCISE 50-2**

1. had to *or* needed to [either past-tense form of modal auxiliary is acceptable]

2. should have *or* ought to have [either past-tense form of modal auxiliary is acceptable]

3. could [past-tense form of modal auxiliary]

4. must/could/might/may have [any of the past-tense forms for conveying possibility and making a guess is acceptable]

5. should have *or* ought to have [either past-tense form of modal auxiliary is acceptable]

4. The other visitors to the Empire State Building (probability) _____ noticed how impatient I was becoming by the look on my face.

5. Then I heard the security guard say to the woman in line ahead of me, "You (advice, good idea) _____ come yesterday. Because of the light drizzle, hardly anyone was here."

50b How do I convey preferences, plans, and past habits with modals?

Conveying preferences

The modal *would rather* expresses a preference. *Would rather,* the PRESENT TENSE, is used with the SIMPLE FORM of the MAIN VERB, and *would rather have,* the PAST TENSE, is used with the PAST PARTICIPLE of the main verb.

> We **would rather see** a comedy than a mystery.
> Carlos **would rather have stayed** home last night.

Conveying plan or obligation

A form of *be* followed by *supposed to* and the simple form of a main verb delivers a meaning of something planned or of an obligation.

> I **was supposed to meet** them at the bus stop.

Conveying past habit

The modals *used to* and *would* express the idea that something happened repeatedly in the past.

> I **used to** hate going to the dentist.
> I **would** dread every single visit.

👁 **ALERT:** Both *used to* and *would* can be used to express repeated actions in the past, but *would* cannot be used for a situation that lasted for a period of time in the past.

> **NO**   I **would** live in Arizona.
> **YES**   I **used to** live in Arizona. 👁

50c How can I recognize modals in the passive voice?

Modals use the ACTIVE VOICE, as shown in sections 50a and 50b. In the active voice, the subject does the action expressed in the MAIN VERB (see 8n and 8o).

Modals can also use the PASSIVE VOICE (8p). In the passive voice, the doer of the main verb's action is either unexpressed or is expressed as an OBJECT in a PREPOSITIONAL PHRASE starting with the word *by*.

PASSIVE	The waterfront **can be seen** from my window.
ACTIVE	**I can see** the waterfront from my window.
PASSIVE	The tax form **must be signed** by the person who fills it out.
ACTIVE	The person who fills out the tax form **must sign** it.

EXERCISE 50-3

Select the correct choice from the words in parentheses and write it in the blank. For help, consult 50a through 50c.

EXAMPLE   When I was younger, I (would, used to) <u>used to</u> love to go bicycle riding.

1. You (ought to have, ought have) _____ called yesterday as you had promised you would.
2. Judging by the size of the puddles in the street outside, it (must be rained, must have rained) _____ all night long.
3. Ingrid (must not have, might not have been) _____ as early for the interview as she claims she was.
4. After all the studying he did, Pedro (should have, should have been) _____ less frightened by the exam.
5. I have to go home early today, although I really (cannot, should not) _____ leave before the end of the day because of all the work I have to do.

EXERCISE 50-4

Select the correct choice from the words in parentheses and write it in the blank. For help, consult 50a through 5c.

EXAMPLE   We (must have, must) <u>must</u> study this afternoon.

1. Unfortunately, I (should not, cannot) _____ go to the movies with you because I have to take care of my brother tonight.
2. Juan (would have, would have been) _____ nominated class valedictorian if he had not moved to another city.
3. You (ought not have, ought not to have) _____ arrived while the meeting was still in progress.
4. Louise (must be, must have been) _____ sick to miss the party last week.
5. Had you not called in advance, you (may not have, may not have been) _____ aware of the traffic on the expressway.

ANSWERS AND COVERAGE: EXERCISE 50-3

1. ought to have [50a, correct form for modal auxiliary expressing advisability]

2. must have rained [50a, correct form for past-tense modal auxiliary expressing likelihood]

3. might not have been [50a, correct form for past-tense modal auxiliary expressing possibility or likelihood]

4. should have been [50c, passive modal auxiliary with *Pedro* receiving the action of the verb]

5. should not [50a, correct form for modal auxiliary expressing negative advisability rather than negative ability]

ANSWERS AND COVERAGE: EXERCISE 50-4

1. cannot [50a, correct form for modal auxiliary expressing negative ability rather than negative advisability]

2. would have been [50c, passive modal auxiliary with *Juan* receiving the action of the verb]

3. ought not to have [50a, correct form for past-tense modal auxiliary expressing advisability]

4. must have been [50a, correct form for past-tense modal auxiliary expressing possibility or likelihood]

5. may not have been [50a, correct form for past-tense modal auxiliary expressing possibility or likelihood]

Terms Glossary

This glossary defines important terms used in this handbook, including the ones that are printed in small capital letters. Many of these glossary entries end with parenthetical references to the handbook section(s) or chapter(s) where the specific term is fully discussed.

absolute phrase A phrase containing a subject and a participle that modifies an entire sentence. (7o)

- **The semester** [subject] **being** [present participle of *be*] **over,** the campus looks deserted.

abstract noun A noun that names something not knowable through the five senses: *idea, respect.* (7b)

academic writing Writing you do for college classes, usually intended to inform or to persuade. (1d)

action verbs Strong verbs that increase the impact of your language and reduce wordiness. *Weak verbs,* such as *be* or *have,* increase wordiness. (16e)

active voice An attribute of verbs showing that the action or condition expressed in the verb is done by the subject, in contrast with the *passive voice,* which conveys that the action or condition of the verb is done to the subject. (8n, 8o)

adjective A word that describes or limits (modifies) a noun, a pronoun, or a word group functioning as a noun: *silly, three.* (7f, Chapter 11)

adjective clause A dependent clause, also known as a *relative clause.* An adjective clause modifies a preceding noun or pronoun and begins with a relative word (such as *who, which, that,* or *where*) that relates the clause to the noun or pronoun it modifies. Also see *clause.* (7p)

adverb A word that describes or limits (modifies) verbs, adjectives, other adverbs, phrases, or clauses: *loudly, very, nevertheless, there.* (7g, Chapter 11)

adverb clause A dependent clause beginning with a subordinating conjunction that establishes the relationship in meaning between the adverb clause and its independent clause. An adverb clause modifies the independent clause's verb or the entire independent clause. Also see *clause, conjunction.* (7p)

agreement The required match of number and person between a subject and verb or a pronoun and antecedent. A pronoun that expresses gender must match its antecedent in gender also. (Chapter 10)

analogy An explanation of the unfamiliar in terms of the familiar. Like a simile, an analogy compares things not normally associated with each other; but unlike a simile, an analogy does not use *like* or *as* in making the comparison. Analogy is also a rhetorical strategy for developing paragraphs. (4i, 21d, 41b)

analysis A process of critical thinking that divides a whole into its component parts in order to understand how the parts interrelate. Sometimes called *division,* analysis is also a rhetorical strategy for developing paragraphs. (4i, 5b, 40e, 41b)

antecedent The noun or pronoun to which a pronoun refers. (9l–9s, 10o–10t)

APA style See *documentation style.*

appeals to reason Tools a writer uses to convince the reader that the reasoning in an argument is sound and effective; there are three types— logical, emotional, and ethical appeals. (6i)

appositive A word or group of words that renames a preceding noun or noun phrase: *my favorite month,* **October.** (7n)

argument A rhetorical attempt to convince others to agree with a position about a topic open to debate. (1b, Chapter 6)

articles Also called *determiners* or *noun markers,* articles are the words *a, an,* and *the. A* and *an* are indefinite articles, and *the* is a definite article; also see *determiner.* (7f, Chapter 46)

assertion A statement. In a thesis statement, an assertion expresses a point of view about a topic; in an argument, an assertion states the position you want to argue. (2q, 6c)

audience The readers to whom a piece of writing is directed; the three types include *general audience, peer audience,* and *specialist audience.* (1d)

auxiliary verb Also known as a *helping verb,* an auxiliary verb is a form of *be, do, have, can, may, will,* or certain other verbs, that combines with a main verb to help it express tense, mood, and voice. Also see *modal auxiliary verb.* (8e)

balanced sentence A sentence composed of two parallel structures, usually two independent clauses, that present contrasting content. (18b)

base form See *simple form.*

bias In writing, a distortion or inaccuracy caused by a dislike or hatred of individuals, groups of people, or ideas. (5c2)

bibliographic notes In a note system of documentation, a *footnote* or *endnote* gives the bibliographic information the first time a source is cited. (33f, 34d.2, Chapter 36)

bibliography A list of sources used or consulted for research writing. (Chapters 34, 35, and 36)

body paragraphs Paragraphs that provide the substance of your message in a sequence that makes sense. (4c)

Boolean expressions In a search engine, symbols or words such as And, Or, Not, and Near that let you create keyword combinations that narrow and refine your search. (2l, 32c.4)

brainstorming Listing all ideas that come to mind on a topic and then grouping the ideas by patterns that emerge. (2h)

bureaucratic language Sometimes called *bureaucratese;* language that is overblown or overly complex. (21m)

business writing Writing designed for business, including letters, memos, resumes, job application letters, and e-mail messages. (1e, 4a, Chapter 42)

case The form of a noun or pronoun in a specific context that shows whether it is functioning as a subject, an object, or a possessive. In modern English, nouns change form in the possessive case only (city = form for subjective and objective cases; city's = possessive-case form). Also see *pronoun case.* (9a–9k)

cause and effect The relationship between outcomes (effects) and the reasons for them (causes). Cause-and-effect analysis is a rhetorical strategy for developing paragraphs. (4i, 5h–5j)

chronological order Also called *time order,* an arrangement of information according to time sequence; an organizing strategy for sentences, paragraphs, and longer pieces of writing. (4h)

citation Information that identifies a source quoted, paraphrased, summarized, or referred to in a piece of writing; *in-text citations* appear within sentences or as *parenthetical references.* Also see *documentation.* (Chapters 33 and 34)

classical argument An argument with a six-part structure consisting of introduction, thesis statement, background, evidence and reasoning, response to opposing views, and conclusion. (6f)

classification A rhetorical strategy for paragraph development that organizes information by grouping items according to underlying shared characteristics. (4i)

clause A group of words containing a subject and a predicate. A clause that delivers full meaning is called an *independent* (or *main*) *clause.* A clause that lacks full meaning by itself is called a *dependent* (or *subordinate*) *clause.* Also see *adjective clause, adverb clause, nonrestrictive element, noun clause, restrictive element.* (7p)

cliché An overused, worn-out phrase that has lost its capacity to communicate effectively: *flat as Kansas, ripe old age.* (21h, 21j)

climactic order Sometimes called *emphatic order,* an arrangement of ideas or other kinds of information from least important to most important. (4h, 6f)

clustering See *mapping.*

coherence The clear progression from one idea to another using transitional expressions, pronouns, selective repetition, or parallelism to make connections between ideas. (3c.4, 4g)

collaborative writing Students working together to write a paper. (1d, 3f)

collective noun A noun that names a group of people or things: *family, committee.* Also see *noncount noun.* (7b, 10j, 10t)

colloquial language Casual or conversational language. Also see *slang.* (21h)

comma fault See *comma splice.*

comma splice The error that occurs when only a comma connects two independent clauses; also called a *comma fault.* (Chapter 13)

common noun A noun that names a general group, place, person, or thing: *dog, house.* (7b)

comparative form The form of a descriptive adjective or adverb that shows a different degree of intensity between two things: *bluer, less blue; more easily, less easily.* Also see *positive form, superlative form.* (11e)

comparison and contrast A rhetorical strategy for organizing and developing paragraphs by discussing similarities (*comparison*) and differences (*contrast*). It has two patterns: *point-by-point* and *block organization.* (4i)

complement An element after a verb that completes the predicate, such as a direct object after an action verb or a noun or adjective after a linking verb. Also see *object complement, predicate adjective, predicate nominative, subject complement.* (7n)

complete predicate See *predicate.*

complete subject See *subject.*

complex sentence See *sentence types.*

compound-complex sentence See *sentence types.*

compound construction A group of nouns or pronouns connected with a coordinating conjunction. (9d)

compound noun See *subject.*

compound predicate See *predicate.*

compound sentence See *coordinate sentence, sentence types.*

compound subject See *subject.* (7l, 10e)

compound word Two or more words placed together to express one concept. (22g)

conciseness An attribute of writing that is direct and to the point. (Chapter 16)

concrete noun A noun naming something that can be seen, touched, heard, smelled, or tasted: *smoke, sidewalk.* (7b)

conjunction A word that connects or otherwise establishes a relationship between two or more words, phrases, or clauses. Also see *coordinating conjunction, correlative conjunction, subordinating conjunction.* (7i)

conjunctive adverb An adverb, such as *therefore* or *meanwhile*, that communicates a logical connection in meaning. (7g)

connotation An idea implied by a word, involving associations and emotional overtones that go beyond the word's dictionary definition. (21e.2)

contraction A word where an apostrophe takes the place of one or more omitted letters. (27d)

coordinate adjectives Two or more adjectives of equal weight that modify a noun. (24e)

coordinate sentence Two or more independent clauses joined by either a semicolon or a comma with coordinating conjunction showing their relationship; also called a *compound sentence.* Also see *coordination.* (17b)

coordinating conjunction A conjunction that joins two or more grammatically equivalent structures: *and, or, for, nor, but, so, yet.* (7i, 13c.3, 17b, 17c)

coordination The use of grammatically equivalent forms to show a balance or sequence of ideas. (17a–17d, 17i)

correlative conjunction A pair of words that joins equivalent grammatical structures, including *both . . . and, either . . . or, neither . . . nor, not only . . . but* (or *but also*). (7i)

count noun A noun that names an item or items that can be counted: *radio, streets, idea, fingernails.* (7b, 45a, 45b, 46a, 46b)

critical reading A parallel process to critical thinking where you think about what you're reading while you're reading it. (5d, 40d)

critical response Formally, an essay summarizing a source's central point or main idea. It includes a *transitional statement* that bridges this summary and the writer's synthesized reactions in response. (5f)

critical thinking A form of thinking where you take control of your conscious thought processes. (5a, 5b, 31b, 32j)

cumulative adjectives Adjectives that build meaning from word to word: *distinctive musical style.* (24e)

cumulative sentence The most common structure for a sentence, with the subject and verb first, followed by modifiers adding details; also called a *loose sentence.* (19e)

dangling modifier A modifier that attaches its meaning illogically, either because it is closer to another noun or pronoun than to its true subject or because its true subject is not expressed in the sentence. (14d)

declarative sentence A sentence that makes a statement: *Sky diving is exciting.* Also see *exclamatory sentence, imperative sentence, interrogative sentence.* (7k)

deduction, deductive reasoning The process of reasoning from general claims to a specific instance. (5i)

definite article See *articles.*

definition A rhetorical strategy in which you define or give the meaning of words or ideas. Includes *extended definition.* (4i)

demonstrative pronoun A pronoun that points out the antecedent: *this, these; that, those.* (7c, 7f)

denotation The dictionary definition of a word. (21e.1)

dependent clause A clause that cannot stand alone as an independent grammatical unit. Also see *adjective clause, adverb clause, noun clause.* (7p, 12b)

description A rhetorical strategy that appeals to a reader's senses—sight, sound, smell, taste, and touch. (4i)

descriptive adjective An adjective that names the condition or properties of the noun it modifies and (except for a very few, such as *dead* and *unique*) has comparative and superlative forms: *flat, flatter, flattest.*

descriptive adverb An adverb that names the condition or properties of whatever it modifies and that has comparative and superlative forms: *happily, more happily, most happily.* (7g)

determiner A word or word group, traditionally identified as an adjective, that limits a noun by telling how much or how many about it. Also called *expression of quantity, limiting adjective,* or *noun marker.* (7f, 45b, Chapter 46)

diction Word choice. (21e)

direct address Words naming a person or group being spoken to. Written words of direct address are set off by commas. (24g)

- The answer, **my friends,** lies with you. Go with them, **Gene.**

direct discourse In writing, words that repeat speech or conversation exactly and so are enclosed in quotation marks. (15e, 24g, 28b)

direct object A noun or pronoun or group of words functioning as a noun that receives the action (completes the meaning) of a transitive verb. (7m)

direct question A sentence that asks a question and ends with a question mark: *Are you going?* (23a, 23c)

direct quotation See *quotation.*

direct title A title that tells exactly what the essay will be about. (3c.3)

discovery draft A first draft developed from focused freewriting. (2g, 3a)

documentation The acknowledgment of someone else's words and ideas used in any piece of writing by giving full and accurate information about the person whose words were used and where those words were found. For example, for a print source, documentation usually includes names of all authors, title of the source, place and date of publication, and related information. (33e–33k, Chapters 34–36)

documentation style A system for providing information about the source of words, information, and ideas quoted, paraphrased, or summarized from some source other than the writer. Documentation styles discussed in this handbook are MLA, APA, CM, CSE, and COS. (33f, Chapters 34–36)

document design A term for the placement of tables, graphs, and other illustrations on printed and online material. (Chapter 37)

double negative A nonstandard negation using two negative modifiers rather than one. (11c)

drafting A part of the writing process in which writers compose ideas in sentences and paragraphs. *Drafts* are versions—*first* or *rough, revised,* and *final*—of one piece of writing. (3a)

edited American English English language usage that conforms to established rules of grammar, sentence structure, punctuation, and spelling; also called *standard American English.* (21c)

editing A part of the writing process in which writers check the technical correctness of grammar, spelling, punctuation, and mechanics. (3d)

elliptical construction The deliberate omission of one or more words in order to achieve conciseness in a sentence. (7p, 15h, 16d.3)

essential element See *restrictive element.*

euphemism Language that attempts to blunt certain realities by speaking of them in "nice" or "tactful" words. (21e)

evaluate A step in the critical thinking process where you judge the quality of the material you are assessing. (5b, 5c.3, 5g)

evidence Facts, data, examples, and opinions of others used to support assertions and conclusions. Also see *sources.* (5g)

exclamatory sentence A sentence beginning with *What* or *How* that expresses strong feeling: *What a ridiculous statement!* (7k)

expletive The phrase *there is (are), there was (were), it is,* or *it was* at the beginning of a clause, changing structure and postponing the subject:

■ **It is** Mars that we hope to reach. [Compare: *We hope to reach Mars*]. (9n, 16c)

expository writing See *informative writing*.

expressive writing Writing that reflects your personal thoughts and feelings. (1c.1)

faulty parallelism Grammatically incorrect writing that results from non-matching grammatical forms linked with coordinating conjunctions. (18e)

faulty predication A grammatically illogical combination of subject and predicate. (15g)

field research Primary research that involves going into real-life situations to observe, survey, interview, or be part of some activity. (32i, 41d.1)

figurative language Words that make connections and comparisons and draw on one image to explain another and enhance meaning. (21d)

finite verb A verb form that shows tense, mood, voice, person, and number while expressing an action, occurrence, or state of being.

first person See *person*.

focused freewriting A technique that may start with a set topic or may build on one sentence taken from earlier freewriting. (2g)

freewriting Writing nonstop for a period of time to generate ideas by free association of thoughts. Also see *discovery draft*. (2g)

fused sentence See *run-on sentence*.

future perfect progressive tense The form of the future perfect tense that describes an action or condition ongoing until some specific future time: *I will have been talking*. (8j)

future perfect tense The tense indicating that an action will have been completed or a condition will have ended by a specified point in the future: *I will have talked*. (8i)

future progressive tense The form of the future tense showing that a future action will continue for some time: *I will be talking*. (8j)

future tense The form of a verb, made with the simple form and either *shall* or *will*, expressing an action yet to be taken or a condition not yet experienced: *I will talk*. (8g)

gender The classification of words as masculine, feminine, or neutral. (10s, 21g)

gender-free language See *gender-neutral language*.

gender-neutral language Also called *gender-free language* or *nonsexist language*, it uses terms that do not unnecessarily say whether a person is male or female, as with *police officer* instead of *policeman*. (10s, 21g)

generalization A broad statement without details. (1c.3, 1d)

gerund A present participle functioning as a noun: **Walking** *is good exercise.* Also see *verbal.* (7e, 46c, Chapter 49)

helping verb See *auxiliary verb.*

homonyms Words spelled differently that sound alike: *to, too, two.* (22f)

hyperbole See *overstatement.*

idiom A word, phrase, or other construction that has a different meaning from its literal meaning:

- He lost his head. She hit the ceiling. (Chapter 48)

illogical predication See *faulty predication.*

imperative mood The mood that expresses commands and direct requests, using the simple form of the verb and often implying but not expressing the subject, you: *Go.* (8l)

imperative sentence A sentence that gives a command: *Go to the corner to buy me a newspaper.* (7k, 12b.3)

incubation The prewriting technique of giving ideas time to develop and clarify. (2m)

indefinite article See *articles, determiner.*

indefinite pronoun A pronoun, such as *all, anyone, each,* and *others,* that refers to a nonspecific person or thing. (7c, 7f, 10i)

independent clause A clause that can stand alone as an independent grammatical unit. (7p)

indicative mood The mood of verbs used for statements about real things or highly likely ones:

- I think Grace is arriving today. (8l, 15d)

indirect discourse Reported speech or conversation that does not use the exact structure of the original and so is not enclosed in quotation marks. (15e, 24h)

indirect object A noun or pronoun or group of words functioning as a noun that tells to whom or for whom the action expressed by a transitive verb was done. (7m)

indirect question A sentence that reports a question and ends with a period:

- I asked if you are leaving. (23a, 23c, 47a)

indirect quotation See *quotation.*

induction The reasoning process of arriving at general principles from particular facts or instances. (5i)

inductive reasoning A form of reasoning that moves from particular facts or instances to general principles. (5i)

inference What a reader or listener understands to be implied but not stated. (5c.2)

infinitive A verbal made of the simple form of a verb and usually, but not always, *to* that functions as a noun, adjective, or adverb. Infinitives without the word *to* are called *unmarked* (or *bare*) *infinitives*. (7e, 8k, Chapter 49)

infinitive phrase An infinitive, with its modifiers and object, that functions as a noun, adjective, or adverb. Also see *verbal phrase*. (7e)

informal language Word choice that creates a tone appropriate for casual writing or speaking. (1e, 21h)

informative writing Writing that gives information and, when necessary, explains it; also known as *expository writing*. (1c.2)

intensive pronoun A pronoun that ends in *-self* and that emphasizes its antecedent. Also called *reflexive pronoun:*

■ Vida **himself** argued against it. (7c)

interjection An emotion-conveying word that is treated as a sentence, starting with a capital letter and ending with an exclamation point or a period: *Oh! Ouch!* (7j, 24j)

interrogative pronoun A pronoun, such as *whose* or *what,* that implies a question:

■ **Who** called? (7c, 12b.1)

interrogative sentence A sentence that asks a direct question:

■ Did you see that? (7k)

in-text citation Source information placed in parentheses within the body of a research paper. Also see *citation, parenthetical reference*. (34b, 35b)

intransitive verb A verb that does not take a direct object. (8f)

invention techniques Ways of gathering ideas for writing. Also see *planning*. (2g–2m)

inverted word order In contrast to standard order, the main verb or an auxiliary verb comes before the subject in inverted word order. Most questions and some exclamations use inverted word order. (10h, 19e, Chapter 47)

irony Words used to imply the opposite of their usual meaning. (21d)

irregular verb A verb that forms the past tense and past participle in some way other than by adding *-ed* or *-d*. (8d)

jargon A particular field's or group's specialized vocabulary that a general reader is unlikely to understand. (21k)

key terms In an essay, the words central to its topic and its message. (6e)

keywords The main words in a source's title or the words that the author or editor has identified as central to that source. Use keywords in searching for sources online or in library databases. (32c.4)

levels of formality Word choices and sentence structures reflecting various degrees of formality of language. A formal level is used for ceremonial and other occasions when stylistic flourishes are appropriate. A medium level, neither too formal nor too casual, is acceptable for most academic writing. (21b)

levels of generality Degrees of generality used to group or organize information or ideas as you write, as when moving from the most general to the most specific. Conversely, *levels of specificity* move from the most specific to the most general. (2o)

limiting adjective See *determiner.*

linking verb A main verb that links a subject with a subject complement that renames or describes the subject. Linking verbs, sometimes called *copulative verbs,* convey a state of being, relate to the senses, or indicate a condition. (8a, 8c)

logical fallacies Flaws in reasoning that lead to illogical statements. (5j)

main clause See *independent clause.*

main verb A verb that expresses action, occurrence, or state of being and that shows mood, tense, voice, number, and person. (8b)

mapping An invention technique based on thinking about a topic and its increasingly specific subdivisions; also known as *clustering* or *webbing.* (2j)

mechanics Conventions governing matters such as the use of capital letters, italics, abbreviations, and numbers. (Chapter 30)

metaphor A comparison implying similarity between two things. A metaphor does not use words such as *like* or *as,* which are used in a simile and which make a comparison explicit: *a mop of hair* (compare the simile *hair like a mop*). (21d)

misplaced modifier Describing or limiting words that are wrongly positioned in a sentence so that their message is either illogical or relates to the wrong word or words. Also see *squinting modifier.* (14a)

mixed construction A sentence that unintentionally changes from one grammatical structure to another, incompatible one, so that the meaning is garbled. (15f)

mixed metaphors Incongruously combined images. (21d)

MLA style See *documentation style, parenthetical reference.*

modal auxiliary verb One of a group of nine auxiliary verbs that add information such as a sense of needing, wanting, or having to do something or a sense of possibility, likelihood, obligation, permission, or ability. (8e, Chapter 50)

modifier, modify A word or group of words functioning as an adjective or adverb to describe or limit another word or word group. Also see *misplaced modifier.* (7n, Chapter 11, 19d)

mood The attribute of verbs showing a speaker's or writer's attitude toward the action by the way verbs are used. English has three moods: imperative, indicative, and subjunctive. Also see *imperative mood, indicative mood, subjunctive mood.* (8l, 8m)

narrative A rhetorical strategy that tells a story; a narrative deals with what is or what has happened. (4i)

noncount noun A noun that names a thing that cannot be counted: *water, time.* Also see *collective noun.* (7b, Chapters 45 and 46)

nonessential element See *nonrestrictive element.*

nonrestrictive clause See *nonrestrictive element.*

nonrestrictive element A descriptive word, phrase, or dependent clause that provides information not essential to understanding the basic message of the element it modifies and so is set off by commas. Also see *restrictive element.* (24f)

nonsexist language See *gender-neutral language.*

nonspecific noun A noun that refers to any of a number of identical items; it takes the indefinite articles *a, an.* (46a)

nonstandard English Language usage other than what is called *edited American English.* (21c)

noun A word that names a person, place, thing, or idea. Nouns function as subjects, objects, or complements. (7b)

noun clause A dependent clause that functions as a subject, object, or complement. (7p)

noun complement See *complement.*

noun determiner See *determiner.*

noun phrase A noun and its modifiers functioning as a subject, object, or complement. (7o)

number The attribute of some words indicating whether they refer to one (*singular*) or more than one (*plural*). (8a, 10b, 15b, Chapter 45)

object A noun, pronoun, or group of words functioning as a noun or pronoun that receives the action of a verb (*direct object*); tells to whom or for whom something is done (*indirect object*); or completes the meaning of a preposition (*object of a preposition*). (7m)

object complement A noun or adjective renaming or describing a direct object after verbs such as *call, consider, name, elect,* and *think:*

■ I call some joggers **fanatics.** (7n)

objective case The case of a noun or pronoun functioning as a direct or indirect object or the object of a preposition or of a verbal. A few pronouns change form to show case (*him, her, whom*). Also see *case.* (Chapter 9)

outline Technique for laying out ideas for writing. An outline can be formal or informal. (2r, 3ll)

overstatement Deliberate exaggeration for emphasis; also called *hyperbole.* (21d)

paragraph A group of sentences that work together to develop a unit of thought. They are the structured elements of an essay, which is composed of an *introductory paragraph, body paragraphs,* and a *concluding paragraph.* Also see *shaping.* (2n, Chapter 4)

paragraph arrangement Ordering sentences by specific techniques to communicate a paragraph's message. (4h)

paragraph development Using specific, concrete details (RENNS) to support a generalization in a paragraph; rhetorical strategies or patterns for organizing ideas in paragraphs. (4f, 4i)

parallelism The use of equivalent grammatical forms or matching sentence structures to express equivalent ideas and develop coherence. (4g.4, Chapter 18)

paraphrase A restatement of someone else's ideas in language and sentence structure different from those of the original. (33i)

parenthetical reference Information enclosed in parentheses following quoted, paraphrased, or summarized material from a source to alert readers to the use of material from a specific source. Parenthetical references, also called *in-text citations,* function together with a list of bibliographic information about each source used in a paper to document the writer's use of sources. Also see *citation.* (34b)

participial phrase A phrase that contains a present participle or a past participle and any modifiers and that functions as an adjective. Also see *verbal phrase.* (7o)

passive construction See *passive voice.*

passive voice The form of a verb in which the subject is acted on; if the subject is mentioned in the sentence, it usually appears as the object of the preposition *by:*

- **I was frightened by** the thunder. [Compare the active voice: The thunder **frightened me.**]

The passive voice emphasizes the action, in contrast to the *active voice,* which emphasizes the doer of the action. (8n–8p)

past participle The third principal part of a verb, formed in regular verbs, like the past tense, by adding *-d* or *-ed* to the simple form. In irregular verbs, it often differs from the simple form and the past tense: *break, broke, broken.* (7e, 8b, 49f)

past perfect progressive tense The past perfect tense form that describes an ongoing condition in the past that has been ended by something stated in the sentence: *I had been talking.* (8j)

past perfect tense The tense that describes a condition or action that started in the past, continued for a while, and then ended in the past: *I had talked.* (8g, 8i)

past progressive tense The tense that shows the continuing nature of a past action: *I was talking.* (8j)

past subjunctive The simple past tense in the subjunctive mood. (8m)

past tense The tense that tells of an action completed or a condition ended. (8g)

past-tense form The second principal part of a verb, in regular verbs formed by adding *-d* or *-ed* to the simple form. In irregular verbs, the past tense may change in several ways from the simple form. (8b, 8d)

peer-response group A group of students formed to give each other feedback on writing. (1d.1)

perfect infinitive Also called *present perfect participle*, a tense used to describe an action that occurs before the action in the main verb. (8k)

perfect tenses The three tenses—the present perfect (*I have talked*), the past perfect (*I had talked*), and the future perfect (*I will have talked*)—that help show complex time relationships between two clauses. (8g, 8i)

periodic sentence A sentence that begins with modifiers and ends with the independent clause, thus postponing the main idea—and the emphasis—for the end; also called a *climactic sentence.* (19e)

person The attribute of nouns and pronouns showing who or what acts or experiences an action. *First person* is the one speaking (*I, we*); *second person* is the one being spoken to (*you, you*); and *third person* is the person or thing being spoken about (*he, she, it, they*). All nouns are third person. (8a, 10b, 40f.1)

personal pronoun A pronoun that refers to people or things, such as *I, you, them, it.* (7c, 9n)

persuasive writing Writing that seeks to convince the reader about a matter of opinion. It is also known as *argumentative writing.* (1c.3, Chapter 6)

phrasal verb A verb that combines with one or more prepositions to deliver its meaning: *ask out, look into.* (48c)

phrase A group of related words that does not contain both a subject and a predicate and thus cannot stand alone as an independent grammatical unit. A phrase functions as a noun, verb, or modifier. (7o)

plagiarism A writer's presenting another person's words or ideas without giving credit to that person. Documentation systems allow writers to give proper credit to sources in ways recognized by scholarly communities. Plagiarism is a serious offense, a form of intellectual dishonesty that can lead to course failure or expulsion. (1f, 33b, 33c)

planning An early part of the writing process in which writers gather ideas. Along with shaping, planning is sometimes called *prewriting.* (Chapter 2)

plural See *number.*

positive form The form of an adjective or adverb when no comparison is being expressed: *blue, easily.* Also see *comparative form, superlative form.* (11e)

possessive case The case of a noun or pronoun that shows ownership or possession: *my, your, their,* and so on. Also see *case, pronoun case.* (Chapter 9, 27a–27c)

predicate The part of a sentence that contains the verb and tells what the subject is doing or experiencing or what is being done to the subject. A *simple predicate* contains only the main verb and any auxiliary verbs. A *complete predicate* contains the verb, its modifiers, objects, and other related words. A *compound predicate* contains two or more verbs and their objects and modifiers, if any. (7l)

predicate adjective An adjective used as a subject complement:

■ That tree is **leafy.** (7n)

predicate nominative A noun or pronoun used as a subject complement:

■ That tree is a **maple.** (7n)

prediction A major activity of the *reading process,* in which the reader guesses what comes next. (5c)

premises In a deductive argument expressed as a syllogism, statements presenting the conditions of the argument from which the conclusion must follow. (5i)

preposition A word that conveys a relationship, often of space or time, between the noun or pronoun following it and other words in the sentence. The noun or pronoun following a preposition is called its *object.* (7h, Chapter 48)

prepositional phrase A preposition and the word it modifies. Also see *phrase, preposition*. (7h, 7o)

present infinitive Names or describes an activity or occurrence coming together either at the same time or after the time expressed in the main verb. (8k)

present participle A verb's *-ing* form. Used with auxiliary verbs, present participles function as main verbs. Used without auxiliary verbs, present participles function as nouns or adjectives. (8b, 7e, 49f)

present perfect participle See *perfect infinitive*.

present perfect progressive tense The present perfect tense form that describes something ongoing in the past that is likely to continue into the future: *I have been talking*. (8j)

present perfect tense The tense indicating that an action or its effects, begun or perhaps completed in the past, continue into the present: *I had talked*. (8g, 8i)

present progressive tense The present-tense form of the verb that indicates something taking place at the time it is written or spoken about: *I am talking*. (8j)

present subjunctive The simple form of the verb for all persons and numbers in the subjunctive mood. (8m)

present tense The tense that describes what is happening, what is true at the moment, and what is consistently true. It uses the simple form (*I talk*) and the *-s* form in the third-person singular (*he, she, it talks*). (8g, 8h)

prewriting All activities in the writing process before drafting. Also see *planning, shaping*. (2e–2m)

primary sources Firsthand work: write-ups of experiments and observations by the researchers who conducted them; taped accounts, interviews, and newspaper accounts by direct observers; autobiographies, diaries, and journals; expressive works (poems, plays, fiction, essays). Also known as *primary evidence*. Also see *secondary source*. (5g.2, 32a, 32i)

process A rhetorical strategy in writing that reports a sequence of actions by which something is done or made. (4i)

progressive forms Verb forms made in all tenses with the present participle and forms of the verb *be* as an auxiliary. Progressive forms show that an action, occurrence, or state of being is ongoing. (8g, 8j)

pronoun A word that takes the place of a noun and functions in the same ways that nouns do. Types of pronouns are *demonstrative, indefinite, intensive, interrogative, personal, reciprocal, reflexive*, and *relative*. The word (or words) a pronoun replaces is called its *antecedent*. (7c, Chapter 9)

pronoun-antecedent agreement The match in expressing number and person—and for personal pronouns, gender as well—required between a pronoun and its antecedent. (10o–10t)

pronoun case The way a pronoun changes form to reflect its use as the agent of action (*subjective case*), the thing being acted upon (*objective case*), or the thing showing ownership (*possessive case*). (9a–9k)

pronoun reference The relationship between a pronoun and its antecedent. (9l–9s)

proofreading Reading a final draft to find and correct any spelling or mechanics mistakes, typing errors, or handwriting illegibility; the final step of the writing process. (3e)

proper adjective An adjective formed from a proper noun: *Victorian, American.* (30e)

proper noun A noun that names specific people, places, or things and is always capitalized: *Dave Matthews, Buick.* (7b, 30e, 46c)

purpose The goal or aim of a piece of writing: to express oneself, to provide information, to persuade, or to create a literary work. (1b, 1c)

quotation Repeating or reporting another person's words. *Direct quotation* repeats another's words exactly and encloses them in quotation marks. *Indirect quotation* reports another's words without quotation marks except around any words repeated exactly from the source. Both *direct* and *indirect quotation* require *documentation* of the *source* to avoid *plagiarism.* Also see *direct discourse, indirect discourse.* (Chapter 28, 33h)

readers Readers are the audiences for writing; readers process material they read on the literal, inferential, and evaluative levels. (1b, 5c)

reading process Critical reading that requires the reader to read for *literal meaning,* to draw *inferences,* and to *evaluate.* (5c)

reciprocal pronoun The pronouns *each other* and *one another* referring to individual parts of a plural antecedent:

■ We respect **each other.** (7c)

References In many documentation styles, including APA, the title of a list of sources cited in a research paper or other written work. (31h, 31i, 32c, 35f)

reflexive pronoun A pronoun that ends in *-self* and that refers back to its antecedent:

■ They claim to support **themselves.** (7c)

regular verb A verb that forms its past tense and past participle by adding *-ed* or *-d* to the simple form. Most English verbs are regular. (8b, 8d)

relative adverb An adverb that introduces an adjective clause:

■ The lot **where** I usually park my car was full. (7g)

relative clause See *adjective clause.*

relative pronoun A pronoun, such as *who, which, that, whom,* or *whoever,* that introduces an adjective clause or sometimes a noun clause. (7c)

RENNS Test See *paragraph development.* (4f)

research question The controlling question that drives research. (31c)

research writing Also called *source-based writing,* a process in three steps: conducting research, understanding and evaluating the results of the research, and writing the research paper with accurate documentation. (Chapter 31)

restrictive clause See *restrictive element.*

restrictive element A word, phrase, or dependent clause that contains information that is essential for a sentence to deliver its message. Do not set off with commas. (24f)

revising, revision A part of the writing process in which writers evaluate their rough drafts and, based on their assessments, rewrite by adding, cutting, replacing, moving, and often totally recasting material. (3c)

rhetoric The area of discourse that focuses on the arrangement of ideas and choice of words as a reflection of both the writer's purpose and the writer's sense of audience. (Chapter 1)

rhetorical strategies In writing, various techniques for presenting ideas to deliver a writer's intended message with clarity and impact. Reflecting typical patterns of human thought, rhetorical strategies include arrangements such as chronological and climactic order; stylistic techniques such as parallelism and planned repetition; and patterns for organizing and developing writing such as description and definition. (4i)

Rogerian argument An argument technique adapted from the principles of communication developed by the psychologist Carl Rogers. (6h)

run-on sentence The error of running independent clauses into each other without the required punctuation that marks them as complete units; also called a *fused sentence* or *run-together sentence.* (Chapter 13)

search engine An Internet-specific software program that can look through all files at Internet sites. (32b, 32c.3)

secondary source A source that reports, analyzes, discusses, reviews, or otherwise deals with the work of someone else, as opposed to a primary source, which is someone's original work or firsthand report. A reliable secondary source should be the work of a person with appropriate credentials, should appear in a respected publication or other medium, should be current, and should be well reasoned. (5g.2, 32a, 32i, 39b, 40b)

second person See *person.*

sentence See *sentence types.*

sentence fragment A portion of a sentence that is punctuated as though it were a complete sentence. (Chapter 12)

sentence types A grammatical classification of sentences by the kinds of clauses they contain. A *simple sentence* consists of one independent clause. A *complex sentence* contains one independent clause and one or more dependent clauses. A *compound-complex sentence* contains at least two independent clauses and one or more dependent clauses. A *compound* or *coordinate sentence* contains two or more independent clauses joined by a coordinating conjunction. Sentences are also classified by their grammatical function; see *declarative sentence, exclamatory sentence, imperative sentence, interrogative sentence.* (7k, 7q, 17b)

sentence variety Writing sentences of various lengths and structures; see *coordinate sentence, cumulative sentence, periodic sentence, sentence types.* (19a)

sexist language Language that unnecessarily communicates that a person is male or female. For example, *fireman* is a sexist term that says only males fight fires, while *fire fighter* includes males and females. (10s, 21g)

shaping An early part of the writing process in which writers consider ways to organize their material. Along with planning, shaping is sometimes called *prewriting.* (2n–2r)

shift Within a sentence, an unnecessary abrupt change in *person, number, subject, voice, tense, mood,* or *direct* or *indirect discourse.* (15a–15c)

simile A comparison, using *like* or *as,* of otherwise dissimilar things. (21d)

simple form The form of the verb that shows action, occurrence, or state of being taking place in the present. It is used in the singular for first and second person and in the plural for first, second, and third person. It is also the first principal part of a verb. The simple form is also known as the *dictionary form* or *base form.* (8b)

simple predicate See *predicate.*

simple sentence See *sentence types.*

simple subject See *subject.*

simple tenses The present, past, and future tenses, which divide time into present, past, and future. (8g, 8h)

singular See *number.*

slang A kind of colloquial language, it is coined words and new meanings for existing words, which quickly pass in and out of use; not appropriate for most academic writing. (21a)

slanted language Language that tries to manipulate the reader with distorted facts. (21h)

source-based writing See *research writing*.

sources Books, articles, print or Internet documents, other works, and persons providing credible information. In *research writing*, often called *outside sources*. (1f, Chapters 32 and 33)

spatial order An arrangement of information according to location in space; an organizing strategy for sentences, paragraphs, and longer pieces of writing. (4h)

specific noun A noun understood to be exactly and specifically referred to; uses the definite article *the*. (46a)

split infinitive One or more words coming between the two words of an infinitive. (14b)

squinting modifier A modifier that is considered misplaced because it is not clear whether it describes the word that comes before it or the word that follows it. (14a)

standard American English See *edited American English*.

standard word order The most common order for words in English sentences: The subject comes before the predicate. Also see *inverted word order*. (19e, Chapter 47)

stereotype A kind of hasty generalization (a *logical fallacy*) in which a sweeping claim is made about all members of a particular ethnic, racial, religious, gender, age, or political group. (5j)

subject The word or group of words in a sentence that acts, is acted upon, or is described by the verb. A *simple subject* includes only the noun or pronoun. A *complete subject* includes the noun or pronoun and all its modifiers. A *compound subject* includes two or more nouns or pronouns and their modifiers. (7l)

subject complement A noun or adjective that follows a linking verb, renaming or describing the subject of the sentence; also called a *predicate nominative*. (7n)

subjective case The case of the noun or pronoun functioning as a subject. Also see *case, pronoun case*. (Chapter 9)

subject-verb agreement The required match between a subject and a verb in expressing number and person. (10b–10n)

subjunctive mood A verb mood that expresses wishes, recommendations, indirect requests, speculations, and conditional statements.

■ I wish you **were** here. (8l, 8m)

subordinate clause See *dependent clause*.

subordinating conjunction A conjunction that introduces an adverb clause and expresses a relationship between the idea in it and the idea in the independent clause. (7i, 13c.4, 17f, 17g)

subordination The use of grammatical structures to reflect the relative importance of ideas. A sentence with logically subordinated information expresses the most important information in the independent clause and less important information in dependent clauses or phrases. (17e–17i)

summary A brief version of the main message or central point of a passage or other discourse; a critical thinking activity preceding synthesis. (5e, 33j)

superlative form The form of an adjective or adverb that expresses comparison among three or more things: *bluest, least blue; most easily, least easily.* (11e)

syllogism The structure of a deductive argument expressed in two *premises* and a *conclusion.* The first premise is a generalized assumption or statement of fact. The second premise is a different assumption or statement of fact based on evidence. The conclusion is also a specific instance that follows logically from the premises. (5i)

synonym A word that is very close in meaning to another word: *cold* and *icy.* (21e)

synthesis A component of critical thinking in which material that has been summarized, analyzed, and interpreted is connected to what is already known (one's prior knowledge) or to what has been learned from other authorities. (5b, 5e)

tag question An inverted verb-pronoun combination added to the end of a sentence, creating a question that asks the audience to agree with the assertion in the first part of the sentence. A tag question is set off from the rest of the sentence with a comma:

- You know what a tag question is, **don't you?** (24g)

tense The time at which the action of the verb occurs: the present, the past, or the future. Also see *perfect tenses, simple tenses.* (8g–8k)

tense sequence In sentences that have more than one clause, the accurate matching of verbs to reflect logical time relationships. (8k)

thesis statement A statement of an essay's central theme that makes clear the main idea, the writer's purpose, the focus of the topic, and perhaps the organizational pattern. (2q)

third person See *person.*

title The part of an essay that clarifies the overall point of the piece of writing. It can be *direct* or *indirect.* (3c.3)

tone The writer's attitude toward his or her material and reader, especially as reflected by word choice. (1e, 5c.2, 6i)

topic The subject of discourse. (2d)

topic sentence The sentence that expresses the main idea of a paragraph. A topic sentence may be implied, not stated. (4e)

Toulmin model A model that defines the essential parts of an argument as the *claim* (or *main point*), the *support* (or *evidence*), and the *warrants* (or *assumptions behind the main point*). (6g)

transition The connection of one idea to another in discourse. Useful strategies within a paragraph for creating transitions include transitional expressions, parallelism, and the planned repetition of key terms and phrases. In a long piece of writing, a *transitional paragraph* is the bridge between discussion of two separate topics. Also see *critical response*. (4g.1, 4j)

transitional expressions Words and phrases that signal connections among ideas and create coherence. (4g.1)

transitive verb A verb that must be followed by a direct object. (8f)

understatement Figurative language in which the writer uses deliberate restraint for emphasis. (21d)

unity The clear and logical relationship between the main idea of a paragraph and the evidence supporting the main idea. (3c.4, 4d, 4e)

unstated assumptions Premises that are implied but not stated. (5i)

usage A customary way of using language. (Chapter 20)

valid Correctly and rationally derived; applied to a deductive argument whose conclusion follows logically from the premises. Validity applies to the structure of an argument, not its truth. (5i)

verb Any word that shows action or occurrence or describes a state of being. Verbs change form to convey time (*tense*), attitude (*mood*), and role of the subject (*voice*, either *active* or *passive*). Verbs occur in the predicate of a clause and can be in verb phrases, which may consist of a main verb, auxiliary verbs, and modifiers. Verbs can be described as *transitive* or *intransitive*, depending on whether they take a direct object. Also see *voice*. (Chapters 8 and 44)

verbal A verb part functioning as a noun, adjective, or adverb. Verbals include *infinitives*, *present participles* (functioning as adjectives), *gerunds* (present participles functioning as nouns), and *past participles*. (7e, Chapter 49)

verbal phrase A group of words that contains a verbal (an infinitive, participle, or gerund) and its modifiers. (7o)

verb phrase A main verb, any auxiliary verbs, and any modifiers. (7o)

verb tense Verbs show tense (time) by changing form. English has six verb tenses. (8g)

voice An attribute of verbs showing whether the subject acts (*active voice*) or is acted on (*passive voice*). Verbs are sometimes referred to as *strong* or *action verbs* or *weak verbs*. (8n–8p)

warrants One of three key terms in the *Toulmin model* for argument; refers to implied or inferred assumptions. They are based on *authority, substance,* and *motivation.* (6g)

Web See *World Wide Web.*

webbing See *mapping.*

Web page On the Internet, a file of information. Such a file is not related in length to a printed page, as it may be a paragraph or many screens long. (38c)

wordiness An attribute of writing that is full of empty words and phrases that do not contribute to meaning. The opposite of *conciseness.* (16a)

World Wide Web The *Web,* a user-friendly computer network allowing access to information in the form of text, graphics, and sound on the Internet. (Chapter 38)

working bibliography A preliminary list of useful sources in research writing. (31i)

Works Cited In MLA documentation style, the title of a list of all sources cited in a research paper or other written work. (34a)

writer's block The desire to start writing, but not doing so. (3b)

writing process Stages of writing in which a writer gathers and shapes ideas, organizes material, expresses those ideas in a rough draft, evaluates the draft and revises it, edits the writing for technical errors, and proofreads it for typographical accuracy and legibility. The stages often overlap; see *planning, shaping, drafting, revising, editing, proofreading.* (Chapters 1, 2, and 3)

writing situation The beginning of the writing process for each writing assignment as defined by four elements: topic, purpose, audience, special requirement. (2c)

Index

List of Boxes by Content

List of Boxes by Content (*continued*)

List of Boxes by Content (*continued*)

HOW TO FIND INFORMATION IN THIS HANDBOOK

You can use your *Simon & Schuster Handbook for Writers* as a reference book, just as you use a dictionary or an encyclopedia. At each step, use one or more suggestions to find the information you want.

Step 1: Use lists to decide where to go.

- Scan the Overview of Contents (on inside front cover).
- Scan the Index at the back of the book for a detailed alphabetical list of all major and minor topics.
- Scan the Part Openers.

Step 2: Locate the number that leads to the information you seek.

- Find a chapter number.
- Find a number-letter combination for a section in a chapter and the question it asks.
- Find a box number.
- Find a page number.

Step 3: Check elements on each page, to confirm where you are in the book.

- Look at the top of each page for the color bar that identifies the part.
- Look for the shortened title at the top of each page (left page for chapter title and right page for section title).
- Look for a section's number-letter combination in white inside a blue rectangle.
- Look for a box title and number.
- Look for a page number at the bottom of the page.

Step 4: Locate and read the information you need. Use special features, illustrated on the opposite page, to help you.

- Use cross-references to related key concepts.
- Find the definition for any word printed in small capital letters in the Terms Glossary starting on page 846
- Use ◉ **ALERTS** ◉ and ⊕ **ESL NOTES** ⊕ for pointers about related matters of usage, grammar, punctuation, and writing.